The Great Interwar Crisis and the Collapse of Globalization

Also by Robert Boyce

BRITISH CAPITALISM AT THE CROSSROADS, 1919–1932: A Study in Politics, Economics, and International Relations

FRENCH FOREIGN AND DEFENCE POLICY, 1918–1940: The Decline and Fall of a Great Power

THE COMMUNICATIONS REVOLUTION AT WORK: Studies on the British and Canadian Experience (Editor)

THE ORIGINS OF WORLD WAR TWO: The Debate Continues (Co-edited with Joe Maiolo)

PATHS TO WAR: New Essays on the Origins of the Second World War (Co-edited with E. M. Robertson)

The Great Interwar Crisis and the Collapse of Globalization

Robert Boyce

First published 2009 by
PALGRAVE MACMILLAN

Palgrave Macmillan in the UK is an imprint of Macmillan Publishers Limited, registered in England, company number 785998, of Houndmills, Basingstoke, Hampshire RG21 6XS.

Palgrave Macmillan in the US is a division of St Martin's Press LLC, 175 Fifth Avenue, New York, NY 10010.

Palgrave Macmillan is the global academic imprint of the above companies and has companies and representatives throughout the world.

Palgrave® and Macmillan® are registered trademarks in the United States, the United Kingdom, Europe and other countries.

ISBN-13: 978–0–230–57478–6 hardback
ISBN-10: 0–230–57478–5 hardback

This book is printed on paper suitable for recycling and made from fully managed and sustained forest sources. Logging, pulping and manufacturing processes are expected to conform to the environmental regulations of the country of origin.

A catalogue record for this book is available from the British Library.

A catalog record for this book is available from the Library of Congress.

10 9 8 7 6 5 4 3 2 1
18 17 16 15 14 13 12 11 10 09

Printed and bound in Great Britain by
CPI Antony Rowe, Chippenham and Eastbourne

Contents

Tables

Preface

This book is the result of a long engagement with the history of the interwar period. This is easily the most heavily trodden field in history, and no rational scholar would deliberately set out to replace the accepted version of events that led from one world war to the next. Yet, over many years of teaching, research and reflection, I have become increasingly aware that the whole does not equal the sum of the separate parts. Academic historians, aiming to produce research based upon all the available evidence, usually become specialists in one or another aspect of their field. Such is the abundance of evidence on the interwar years that more than one historian has devoted his or her career to an aspect as precise as the Paris peace conference of 1919, war debts and reparations, central bank cooperation in the context of the revived gold standard, Italian fascism or Japanese militarism, the crisis of French foreign policy or the plight of Jews in pre-war Germany. The result has been a dazzling abundance of outstanding theses, research essays, monographs and biographies. But because the underlying source of interest is the Second World War and the catastrophes that accompanied it, all the paths traced by historians lead towards this end which therefore appears hugely over-determined. As a result, little attention has been paid to how the different strands fit together and as yet there is nothing that could be regarded as a persuasive synthesis. Even after nearly seventy years, historians have still not produced a plausible explanation of why in barely more than a single generation a second world war followed the first.

But there has been another failing in the historiography which in its way is equally remarkable. Diplomatic historians acknowledge that interwar international relations broke down amidst the chaotic conditions created by the world economic depression; in other words that the collapse of the international political system was due in part to the collapse of the international economic system. Yet there seems to be no satisfactory explanation of the economic depression itself. Economic historians, to be sure, have devoted a great deal of time and effort to explaining the *origins* of the depression that began in 1929, and produced studies of the highest quality on certain components of the depression. Yet they have made little attempt to explain why *this* depression became the deepest, most prolonged and catastrophic the world has ever witnessed. Once again, the price of specialization seems to have been an absence of a satisfactory general explanation. This led me to surmise that the chronic failure to devise persuasive answers to two of the largest questions of twentieth-century history owed to the fact that diplomatic and economic historians persist in treating them as essentially discrete issues. Since, as seems likely, it was not a coincidence that the international political and economic systems collapsed at practically the same time, it followed that the answer to the one question is bound up intimately with the answer to the other. Put differently, neither question could be answered except by treating the economics, politics and diplomacy of the period as dimensions of a single dynamic whole.

This seemed to be a plausible hypothesis, but of course it aggravated the problem of evidence, analysis and expertise. I have nevertheless persisted with the challenge, with the results set out in the following chapters. Doubtless, other students of the period will find much to criticise in it, since the work spans the office of four British prime ministers (three of them in office at least twice), five American presidents and twenty French *présidents du conseil*, and seeks to integrate political, diplomatic, financial, monetary and commercial history as well as the influence of political ideas and beliefs, the history of the peace-making and the history of European reconstruction and integration. The result is a new history of interwar Britain, the United States and France, the international relations of the 1914–39 period, the world economic depression and the place of globalization in the twentieth century. It is on the cogency of the broad thesis that the account deserves to stand or fall. But I hope readers will find it at the least thought-provoking and thus an aid to understanding both the interwar period as well as our own time.

I wish to thank Special Collections, Library Services, University of Birmingham for permission to quote from the Neville Chamberlain papers; the Baker Library, Harvard Business School, for permission to quote from the Thomas W. Lamont Collection; the British Library for permission to quote from the Earl Balfour, Lord Robert Cecil and Lord Curzon papers; the British Library of the Political and Economic Science for permission to quote from the Dalton diary; the Syndics of Cambridge University Library for permission to quote from the Baldwin Papers; the Bank of England for permission to quote from the Norman, Niemeyer and other papers at the Bank; the Federal Reserve Bank of New York for permission to quote from Harrison, Strong and other papers in the Bank's archive; the Master, Fellow and Scholars of Churchill College, Cambridge, for permission to quote from the Hankey papers at the Churchill Archives Centre; the Yale University Library, for permission to quote from the Henry Lewis Stimson Papers; the Guardian and the Times, London, for permission to quote from their newspapers; the University of Newcastle for permission to quote from the Runciman papers; and Her Majesty Queen Elizabeth II for permission to quote from material in the Royal Archives, Windsor.

Since historical research could scarcely be advanced without the professional contribution of archivists and librarians, I am very grateful for the assistance I have received at the Hoover Presidential Library, the Federal Reserve Bank of New York, the Bibliothèque Nationale de France, the Archives Nationales, the archives of the Ministère des Affaires Etrangères, the Ministère de l'Économie, des Finances et de l'Industrie and the Banque de France, the Bank of England, the National Archives at Kew, the House of Lords Record Office, the British Library, the Churchill Archives Centre, the LSE's British Library of Political and Economic Science and many other institutions in Britain and abroad.

In preparing this book, I have received help and encouragement from many people. At an early stage, I enjoyed the hospitality of Anne-Marie and Jean-Louis

Perol, which enabled me to spend several summers in comfort in Paris. Later, my work in that wonderful city was sustained by the kindness of Claude and Veronique Sauzay and Evelyn and Jean-Marie Courchinoux. My friends and former students, Ninon Vinsonneau and Clarisse Berthezene, with their husbands, have also provided the warm welcome and hospitality that has sustained my research. In England, I have been sustained by lively discussions with my friends and colleagues, Alan Marin, Ray Richardson, Alan Sked and Robert Wade, while drawing upon the acute contributions of Stephen Schuker, Robert Young and other scholars.

I have tried out many of my arguments in preliminary and piecemeal form at conferences. While the papers were probably less than wholly persuasive, each occasion was invariably a stimulus to thought and analysis which has been indispensable in the preparation of the present work. Accordingly, my thanks for invitations go to Olivier Feiertag and Michel Margairaz to participate in the bicentenary conference of the Bank of France, to Jacques Bariéty and colleagues in the Association of Contemporary European History to speak at conferences on Aristide Briand, the League of Nations and Europe, to Ranald Michie and Philip Williamson to participate in the conference on the British Government and the City of London in the twentieth century, to Albert Kechichian and Nicolas Roussellier to contribute to their colloque on the economic education of French political leaders in the Third and Fourth Republics, to Laurence Badel, Stanislas Jeannesson and N. Piers Ludlow to speak at the conference on national administrations and European integration, and to Antoine Capet of the Université de Rouen to present papers at no less than four international conferences on British history and society. I am similarly grateful to my friends and colleagues, Georges-Henri Soutou of the Université de Paris IV-Sorbonne and to Maurice Vaisse, Pierre Melandri and Jean-Pierre Azéma of the Institut d'Etudes Politiques, Paris, for inviting me to spend time at their institutions and providing the stimulus of their company.

My chief debt however goes to my wife, Dr Gudrún Sveinbjarnardottir, who has found time in her own busy career to take an interest in my work and share the strains that years of research and writing inevitably produce.

Introduction

M. Seydoux is chasing a mirage of longstanding, viz. that economics in the case of France and Germany will overcome race antagonism.

Sir William Tyrrell, permanent under-secretary of state at the Foreign Office, 20 March 1928[1]

I believe that that civilisation which he speaks of can only be saved by the co-operation of Anglo-Saxons; we cannot count on the other races.

President Hoover's message to Ramsay MacDonald, British prime minister, 27 January 1932[2]

I have rather come to the conclusion that the average Englishman – whilst full of common-sense as regards internal affairs – is often muddleheaded, sloppy and gullible when he considers foreign affairs. One often hears such phrases as 'the Germans are so like us'. Nothing is more untrue.

Sir Horace Rumbold, ambassador to Germany, to Geoffrey Dawson, editor of the *Times*, 13 June 1936[3]

If the history of the interwar period now seems familiar territory, this is hardly surprising since the narrative has remained essentially unchanged for nearly seventy years. Summarized in seven sentences, it runs as follows. In 1918, when Germany sued for peace, the Entente and Associated powers imposed the Versailles settlement in which, largely at French insistence, Germany suffered substantial losses of territory and population as well as onerous demands for reparations and the ignominy of blame for the war. Meanwhile in the East, Poland re-emerged along with several new states that further encroached upon German land and influence, while the Bolshevik seizure of Russia created an additional source of instability in Europe and beyond. In the following ten years, the English-speaking powers assisted the recovery of Germany, Austria and other countries in Central Europe and sought to reduce the bitter legacy of the Versailles settlement. Their efforts were disrupted when the Wall Street crash triggered the onset of the world economic slump. The collapse of trade and soaring unemployment created the conditions for Hitler to take power in Germany and tempted Japan and Italy to embark upon aggressive imperialist adventures. Attempting to avoid a breakdown of the existing order, the conservative powers Britain and France, with the encouragement of the United States, appeased the aggressor powers. When appeasement failed, the conservative powers turned to policies of deterrence and accelerated their rearmament while drawing closer together in anticipation of the coming conflict.[4]

This largely unchanging narrative has given rise to two questions which underlie practically all the output of Western historians since the interwar period itself. First, did some means exist to forestall the rise of the aggressor powers? Second, after they did arise, why did the conservative powers not immediately recognize the danger they posed or act more effectively to resist them? Focus upon these questions has led historians to examine and re-examine the peace negotiations of 1919, the Ruhr crisis of 1923–4 and the struggle to end reparations, the events surrounding Mussolini's and Hitler's rise to power, the Manchurian crisis, the failure of the League of Nations and the Abyssinian, Rhineland and Czech crises. It has also yielded a generally sympathetic picture of Britain and the United States, since historians have found little to criticize in their policies unless it was for pursuing appeasement beyond the point when it ceased to be appropriate and turning too belatedly towards deterrence.

Yet remarkably, despite almost constant refinement of the conventional narrative and the excellent treatment of many individual elements of the story, key issues and events remain a puzzle. Thus, for instance, no satisfactory explanation exists for the breakdown of the coalition of victor powers almost before the Armistice was declared in 1918, nor why British political leaders, 'realist' as well as 'idealist', firmly closed their ears to the insistent warnings of their military advisers about Germany's probable course of action and the basis for a suitable framework of security: this after Britain had incurred enormous casualties in a close-fought war with Germany. The conventional narrative treats the hollowing out of the Versailles settlement as a contribution to peace, although it encouraged German revisionism and insecurity elsewhere, and it overlooks all the evidence from modern history that the security of Western Europe cannot be purchased at the expense of insecurity in Eastern Europe. Finally, it fails properly to integrate or shed light on the terrible world economic slump of 1929–33, which is introduced merely as a sort of *deux ex machina* to explain the breakdown of international relations and which, left to economists and economic historians to analyse, has itself never been fully explained.

The purpose of the present account is to point towards a new way of understanding the course of events in this crucial period. It offers a different narrative which traces a different contour over the events, assigns different roles to the leading powers and yields different conclusions as to why the peace established after the First World War broke down within barely more than twenty years, as well as presenting a new explanation of the world depression and suggesting radically different connections with the world situation today. It is not a comprehensive account of interwar history. Indeed, for reasons that will become clear, most of the familiar landmarks listed above are touched on only briefly. Starting at the peace settlement of 1919, with a brief backward glance at the origins of the First World War, the centrepiece of the study is the pattern of events that led to and through the global economic and political crisis that occurred midway between the world wars. Though mentioned in other studies, this crisis remains the most thoroughly misunderstood episode of the interwar years. Yet, as will be explained, it provides the key to understanding the course of interwar history and a unique perspective on the present crisis of our globalized world.

The contours of twentieth-century history were decisively shaped by the two world wars. The scale of the wars, their human cost and their long-term consequences can scarcely be exaggerated. Yet, while constituting a radical breakdown of the international political system, their impact upon global economic activity was less straightforward. The First World War disrupted international trade and destroyed human and physical capital on a huge scale.[5] Nonetheless, the belligerent powers in both the warring coalitions successfully intervened at the domestic and international levels of economic relations. By controlling imports, rationing access to scarce resources and mobilizing manpower, all the major powers excepting Russia managed to contain inflation and sustain economic activity at a high level until practically the end of the war. Similarly, the Second World War fractured the international trade and payments system, yet the leading powers of the contending alliances introduced parallel systems of regulated trade and payments that served their interests reasonably well. None of the powers succumbed to economic breakdown or radically altered course on account of economic constraints. In fact, both world wars stimulated the expansion of agricultural and industrial production, and in the economic as well as the political sphere the wars produced winners as well as losers. In each case, the breakdown of the international political system was thus accompanied by the radical transformation of the international economic system, but not its collapse. The conjuncture of events that occurred midway through the interwar years was different.

Shortly after the First World War, economic and political dislocation resulted in a brief but severe world economic slump when international trade plummeted and unemployment soared. This, however, scarcely discouraged the leading capitalist countries from returning to the liberal policies of prewar times. On the domestic front, governments swiftly reduced taxes and spending, balanced or sought to balance their budgets and removed controls on production, prices and labour. Public sector employment, although higher than before the war, declined to levels far below those reached after the Second World War.[6] Meanwhile, the victor powers rapidly restored the global trade and payments system. Within a few years they removed most of the quantitative trade controls that had been introduced as emergency measures during or just after the war. They also stabilized currencies or where necessary created new ones, fostered the expansion of international credit and capital lending, restored the international gold standard and followed this by tackling the rise in tariff barriers. The second great era of globalization begun in 1815 and interrupted in 1914 thus resumed, and by the second half of the 1920s, international trade and capital movements were again growing faster than physical output.[7] As early as 1924, world trade exceeded the value reached in 1913; by 1929, it was 40 per cent greater.[8] But already by 1927, signs appeared of declining commitment to economic liberalization, and in 1929 the process halted with the onset of another slump, which rapidly intensified to become an economic depression of unparalleled severity.[9]

Between 1929 and 1933 world industrial production declined by perhaps 37 per cent,[10] world trade declined in constant prices by at least 27 per cent and in current prices by 68 per cent[11] and world agricultural prices declined by 75 per cent from levels reached in 1923–5.[12] Many countries retreated into autarky, foreign investment practically ceased, and by June 1933, the international monetary system was reduced to chaos. At its worst, industrial unemployment reached 22 per cent in Britain, 37.6 per cent in the United States and 44.3 per cent in Germany.[13] In Germany, wholesale trade declined below 1914 levels, foreign exports declined from over 1,250 billion RM a month to merely 374 million RM, and steel production declined by nearly 75 per cent to levels not seen since the turn of the century.[14] In Japan, farmers dependent upon raw silk exports for purchases of essential market goods faced a decline of 44 per cent in silk prices between 1925 and 1929, and a further 55 per cent decline between 1929 and 1931.[15] France initially appeared to be unaffected by the slump, with registered unemployment reaching only 276,000 in 1933. But many more were reduced to part-time employment, women and older workers withdrew from the workforce and some of the 2.4 million foreign workers who had found employment in the country during the 1920s quietly returned home to Spain, Portugal and especially Italy.[16] Faced with a serious budget deficit and an overvalued exchange rate, which led to fiscal, monetary and trade restrictions, unemployment in France continued to rise until 1936, when it reached 850,000 or 7 per cent of the registered workforce. To this should be added the destruction of perhaps 1.3 million jobs in the same period and widespread hidden unemployment. French unemployment thus probably rose above 18 per cent and moreover did not substantially decline until 1938.[17] In the United States, where the slump was particularly acute, 34 million of its 123 million people, according to one estimate, had no income at all.[18] Collapsing prices and unsustainable farming methods drove thousands of sharecroppers and homesteaders westward thousands of miles in the hope of new lives in California. Canada, more dependent upon raw materials production, was even worse affected. For the first and only time in the twentieth century, emigration exceeded immigration as destitute settlers abandoned the New World and returned to their countries of origin.[19] Peasants in rural Hungary, Roumania, India and China with nowhere to go faced starvation.

The slump also coincided with an extraordinary political crisis. Mussolini, leader of the first and as yet the only fascist state, did little to rock the international boat before 1930. But in May that year, his speeches became more aggressive, and by 1932 he was not only siding with Germany on treaty revision but also had begun to consider armed aggression overseas and sent agents to look over Abyssinia.[20] In Germany, Hitler made his political breakthrough in the Reichstag elections of September 1930 when the Nazi party won 107 seats compared with a mere 12 in the previous election two years earlier. Thereafter, with unemployment soaring and the Nazis gaining support, German governments intensified their pressure for treaty revision, throwing Europe into turmoil with the revelation of secret plans for an economic *Anschluss* with Austria in March 1931, their refusal to stop rearming and their declaration of a unilateral halt to further reparation payments in January 1932. One year later, with economic recovery barely under way, President Hindenburg invited Hitler to form a government.

Meanwhile in Japan extremists harassed, attacked and in several cases assassinated liberal political leaders for their alleged failure to defend national interests at home or abroad. In September 1931, military units forced the hand of the civilian government in Tokyo by staging an incident that justified the conquest of Manchuria. That same month, Britain abandoned the gold standard and turned to a National government dominated by Conservatives who were committed to ending 90 years of free trade in favour of a policy of imperial protectionism. Having stared into the abyss of financial collapse, Britain delayed rearmament until 1936, and instead of seizing the proffered hand of France it intensified efforts to minimize its European commitments.[21] France in turn delayed its rearmament for financial reasons; indeed for several years it actually *reduced* defence spending. Confronted with the emerging Nazi challenge, France was obliged to seek Britain's interested friendship even if this meant pursuing an unwelcome policy of appeasement.

Thus, in contrast to the two world wars, midway through the interwar period the international economic system *and* the international political system simultaneously broke down. It was a unique moment and comparable in importance to the world wars themselves.[22] But was it a single crisis or two separate crises – one economic, the other political – that simply coincided? If it was two separate crises, then diplomatic historians need not concern themselves with the economic crisis, which has its own discrete causes and separate trajectory. Coincidences happen in history, and to judge by the existing historical literature this is how one should see the period, since the output of diplomatic and economic historians remains almost wholly unintegrated. Their focus is different, their chronology is different and the stories they tell are almost wholly separate from one another.

Economists and economic historians, seeking to explain the extreme unevenness of economic activity between the wars, generally restrict themselves to economic factors. The author of a recent study of French interwar monetary policy refers to 'the new orthodoxy in the historical literature, attributing the contractionary force causing depression to monetary policy and gold standard orthodoxy.'[23] In fact, ever since Milton Friedman and Anna Schwartz published *A Monetary History of the United States* in 1961, economists have relied mainly on a monetary explanation of the slump and indeed mainly on *American* monetary decisions to explain the course of world events.[24] Most economic historians remain sceptical of the economists' emphasis upon monetary policy. While acknowledging the role of policy errors by American central bankers, the absence of an international lender of last resort and the deflationary bias of the gold standard which locked countries into a downward spiral of prices, wages and employment, they also point to developments such as the rapid increase in commodity production and the mounting dollar shortage in Europe in the 1920s, along with the rigidities created by trade unions, fixed debt, unemployment insurance and other factors, which made it hard for developed countries to adjust to declining price levels while holding to fixed exchange rates. A standard British/Australian text on modern economic history somewhat lamely concludes, 'There is enough evidence to suggest that both long-run and short-run factors were operating to bring about the depression of the 1930s, but as yet we have little understanding of how this complex of forces interacted to produce a world-wide depression.'[25] But while differing from the economists in their analytical breadth, economic historians similarly treat the economic crisis separately from the political crisis.

Diplomatic historians, seeking to define the path from the First World War to the Second, go further than economists or economic historians in accepting a partial link between the economic and political crises. They generally agree that the world economic slump created conditions that favoured the ascendancy of Nazism in Germany, militarism in Japan and a more reckless aspect of fascism in Italy, while at the same time causing the democratic powers to become more cautious, hold back from rearming and turn inwards to address problems of public finance and mass unemployment or look towards overseas possessions or spheres of influence for alternative trade outlets. Diplomatic historians thus also assume two separate crises, while accepting a connection between them, with the direction of the causal relationship running from the economic crisis to the political crisis.[26] This seems plausible enough, especially as the claim of a single crisis produced by the interaction of economic and political factors requires it to be shown that the causal connection ran in *both* directions, and that the economic slump was at least partly the *result* as well as a *cause* of the international political crisis. On the face of it, this seems thoroughly implausible, since the slump was preceded neither by war or threat of war nor by any other major political upheaval. The connection, however, can be grasped by bearing in mind two simple but crucial observations.

First, with the exception of Soviet Russia, *all* the major powers in the 1920s, including Italy, Germany and Japan, broadly shared the principles of economic liberalism and remained integrally linked through capitalist market relations. This enabled them to share in the benefits of the return to globalization which accelerated their postwar economic recovery, but it also reduced their autonomy and increased their vulnerability to events elsewhere in the world. Despite their different political regimes, therefore, global contagion was a serious risk.

Second, markets can function only within a framework of rules, restraints and institutions capable of ensuring social and political as well as economic stability. It may be commonplace to speak of free markets or laissez-faire capitalism and to suggest that an efficient capitalist system must be free from political interference. But all economic activity is embedded within a legal, social and cultural framework sustained by a political system without which no market could function. At the national level, this framework consists of laws governing contracts, rules on accounting and regulatory agencies such as the central bank, treasury, law courts and police, as well as informal institutions which provide the basis of trust on which most transactions rely. Under capitalism, the search for profits prompts entrepreneurs to shrug off restraints or press for reductions in regulation. In good times, politicians often yield to their imprecations to remove 'red tape', relax banking and accounting rules, redraw labour and consumer laws in favour of capital and reduce taxes and public spending towards the minimum for civil order and national defence. The result is usually a period of excess, followed by a slump and the exposure of unacceptable business practices, when the pendulum swings the other way towards greater regulation and public intervention in support of workers, consumers, savers and small investors. Capitalist market relations create scope for expanding employment and great wealth accumulation. But they also potentially lead to a rapacious consumption of resources, dangerously large externalities such as industrial injuries and environmental degradation and periods of large-scale unemployment, social distress and political upheaval. Most governments are wise enough to recognize both the benefits and the dangers of capitalist market relations, and the need to intervene to mitigate the worst consequences. The framework of rules and institutions is thus periodically loosened or tightened, but it is never done away with, since to do so would lead eventually to a breakdown of the capitalist system itself.[27]

The same principle applies to capitalism at the international level. Here, too, investment and trade can function only within a framework of rules, restraints and institutions. Internationally, this includes the exchange of enforceable commercial treaties, trustworthy information about markets, access to insurance, the coordinated intervention of central banks and in recent times the operation of international institutions such as the Bank for International Settlements (BIS), the International Monetary Fund (IMF), the World Bank and the World Trade Organization (WTO), to ensure that currencies remain convertible and markets remain open. It also includes an effective security system, although this is seldom recognized to be an essential underpinning for the economic system. In modern times, international security has been provided by one or more great powers, willing and able to uphold the states system of the developed world while projecting their power further abroad to limit banditry and piracy on commercial routes, protect global marketplaces and safeguard large-scale overseas investments from arbitrary appropriation, political upheaval or revolution. Until the Great War, Britain provided the key institutions for the global economy, including the Bank of England, Lloyds of London, the Baltic Exchange and other institutions of the City of London, as well as the security provided by the far-ranging squadrons of the Royal Navy. After the onset of the Cold War, the United States undertook many of the same functions for the non-Communist world. The interwar years were quite another matter.[28]

In the aftermath of the Great War, Britain, supported by the international merchants and bankers of the City of London and New York, led the way in restoring the international trade and payments system. But this involved it in removing national obstacles to its global project, reintegrating Germany into the global system and systematically stripping away the framework of European security created at the Paris peace conference. First, it turned its back on the

Anglo-American guarantee to France. Then, over the next ten years, it sought to reduce the reparations burden upon Germany, end military inspections of Germany, accelerate the withdrawal of Allied troops from the Rhineland and hasten the return of the Saar to German political control. All the while it pressed France to disarm and abandon its alliances with countries in Eastern Europe, while indicating sympathy for Germany's revisionist ambitions in the East. Something similar occurred in the Far East. There the United States discouraged Britain from renewing the Anglo-Japanese alliance in 1922, and instead to adopt the three treaties of the Washington conference, which lacked any enforcement mechanism and thus scarcely deserved to be called a security framework. Already by 1927, therefore, the global security framework had become remarkably flimsy. This played into the hands of nationalists and imperialists in both hemispheres, encouraging them to demand stronger defences or further revision of the international order. The result was a climate of insecurity which deterred states from wholeheartedly supporting international monetary, financial and commercial reform and led them instead to subordinate their economic policies to national security. Between 1927 and 1929, global economic relations as well as global political relations became increasingly precarious, with nearly all postwar trade treaties far shorter in duration than before the war, gold hoarding on the rise and the international monetary system increasingly short of liquidity and lacking the means of forestalling minor crises from turning into major crises.

The capitalist system, always prone to fluctuations, was bound to experience a downturn sooner or later, and so far as can be judged the slump in 1929 was scarcely exceptional. But in both hemispheres the slump triggered a rapid deterioration in international relations, which further damaged business confidence and support for liberal economic solutions. Thus a vicious circle was set in motion, with national *in*security turning an ordinary economic downturn into a deep and prolonged economic depression, while the deterioration in economic conditions undermined the basis of peace. This therefore was not merely the coincidence of two discrete crises, one economic, the other political, but a single crisis in which economic and political events reacted upon one another in a dynamic, if indeterminate, fashion to create the conditions for a radical breakdown, then to bring it about.

Historians almost invariably claim the primacy of either the economic or the political-diplomatic-security factors in this crisis, depending upon their area of competence or the starting-point of their analysis. But by resisting arbitrary choices and assembling the picture with care, it can be shown that the collapse of the world economic system and the collapse of the world political system between the wars were intimately bound up together. Accounts that present the two crises as discrete events are therefore unsatisfactory. Similarly, accounts that claim the direction of the causal relationship ran from economic crisis to political crisis are unsatisfactory, as are those that would claim the reverse, since the causal relationship ran in both directions. The great interwar crisis, which included the slump and led to the Second World War, was thus a *dual* crisis, and one of the most important, if also thoroughly misunderstood, events of modern history.[29]

A comprehensive survey of interwar history would treat the Middle East and Asia as well as the West, and devote extensive space to all seven major powers: Britain, France, Germany, Italy, Japan, Soviet Russia and the United States. But notwithstanding important developments elsewhere, the fact remains that Europe was still the cockpit of the interwar world. At least six European countries – Austria, Bulgaria, Germany, Hungary, Italy and Soviet Russia – sought to revise the peace settlement of 1919, and renewed conflict in Europe threatened to draw in all of the world's powers. In the event, some of the powers were more destructive of world order than others. The Russian Bolshevik regime from 1917 and Mussolini's Fascist regime in Italy from 1922 constituted potential threats to the world order. But neither they nor for that matter Japan or China contributed substantially to the origins of the great interwar crisis. Not until it was fully under way, with economic conditions severely depressed and the global security framework shattered, did they contribute importantly to the downward spiral of events.

The case of Germany is different. It was mainly to contain Germany that France agitated for a new security framework at the Paris peace conference, and with good reason, for thereafter Germany posed a continual challenge to the international system. In November 1918, Germany set aside its imperial regime in favour of a republic with a highly democratic constitution. But despite the formal transformation, Germany's political culture remained little changed. Its civil and military élites continued to favour a hierarchical, authoritarian state. Its people generally believed that Germany had been undefeated on the battlefield, deceived by President Wilson's offer of the Fourteen Points into accepting the Armistice, and forced to accept grossly unfair terms at Versailles. Their support for the republic was therefore conditional upon its commitment to revise the peace settlement. After the Ruhr crisis in 1923 and the nightmare of hyperinflation, their support became doubly conditional upon the republic's ability to safeguard them against renewed inflation and currency chaos. With individual savings wiped out by the hyperinflation, however, Germany became highly dependent upon foreign bank lending and vulnerable to the shifting winds of international finance. Once foreign loans and credits began to dry up in 1927, declining economic fortunes confronted the government with the dilemma of declining revenues and increasing expenditure, the latter due to rearmament as well as a new scheme of insurance for the unemployed whose numbers rapidly grew. The government, a centre-left coalition, attempted to meet the crisis by modestly increasing revenue and decreasing expenditure. When the spectre of renewed inflation drove the German middle classes into the arms of extreme nationalist parties, republican politicians saw little alternative but to adopt a more aggressively nationalist stance of their own.

The uncertainty over Germany's future and the speed with which it was overwhelmed by economic and political troubles from the later months of 1927 constitute a vital component of the great interwar crisis. But since it is the best understood component and likely to be familiar to readers, it is treated only summarily in the following account.[30] Instead, the focus is upon the three great democratic powers, Britain, France and the United States. In the 1920s, they constituted roughly 25 per cent of the world's economic activity and produced nearly 60 per cent of the world's manufactured goods.[31] Together they controlled 33 per cent of world trade,[32] and supplied no less than 70 per cent of manufactured exports.[33] In 1924–8, they provided over 85 per cent of the world's capital lending and investment.[34] In 1929, they possessed nearly 60 per cent of the world's monetary gold reserves.[35] They thus dominated the world economy. Moreover, as the main victors in the Great War, they also dominated the world's political system. They therefore had the opportunity to construct a robust framework of international security as well as a stable international payments system, and after the crisis began they possessed the means to alleviate it or forestall its worst consequences. Since the world's fate rested largely in their hands, they deserve to be the central focus of the history of the great interwar crisis.

Like Germany, interwar Britain, France and the United States have all been the subject of intensive historical examination, but they appear in a new light in this account. To take the United States first, something close to a consensus now exists among historians on America's role in world affairs after the First World War. Summarized briefly, historians affirm that political leaders in Washington were aware of the nation's continuing reluctance to become involved in foreign conflicts. Yet they were also alive to America's global interests which required them to engage in international affairs, and they recognized the huge influence America was able to wield on account of its now unrivalled financial and commercial strength. They therefore established an informal alliance with the international bankers and financiers of Wall Street, who shared their interest in the pacification and reconstruction of Europe and the liberalization of world trade. Woodrow Wilson, who occupied the White House from 1913 to 1921, chose to participate directly in the negotiation of the peace settlement in 1918–19 and sought a leading role for the United States in the League of Nations. His Republican successors rejected direct participation in international relations. But they too were internationalists who displayed a clear-sighted view of great power relations and exercised a leading, albeit indirect, role in world affairs. Largely through their informal alliance with Wall Street, they systematically reshaped the world to suit American interests.[36]

As the present account explains, scarcely a single element of this interpretation of American history bears scrutiny. Despite the current practice of treating America's rise to world power as an ineluctable process stretching back to the founding of the 13 colonies, it is quite impossible to transform the postwar Republican administrations of Harding, Coolidge and Hoover into 'independent internationalists' without grave injustice to the evidence.[37] Nor is it satisfactory to remove Wilson from his time by transforming him into a champion of American corporate interests. This is scarcely an improvement upon the older view of him as the naïve or idealistic champion of global governance, to which he was allegedly prepared to subordinate American independence.[38] The origins of the current misrepresentation of America's world role go back more than half a century to efforts by radical historians to present the United States as a country driven from its earliest beginnings by an ideological preference for individual salvation rather than collective action. Accepting this version of the past, if not the radical politics that originally inspired it, most American historians have set aside the concept of isolationism, treating it as an irrelevance by the 1920s if not long before. The extraordinary historiographical shifts in the treatment of American foreign relations deserve a book of its own. Suffice it to say here that isolationism remains crucial to an understanding of American history, although like all such terms it requires careful definition based upon actual historical usage. Thus understood, isolationism re-emerges as the key not only to inter-war American foreign relations but also to crucial aspects of American domestic politics.

The point so frequently overlooked is that in the American context isolationism always meant the avoidance of political-diplomatic entanglements with 'old Europe', and in particular the imperial powers Britain, Spain and France, but it emphatically did not mean the avoidance of commercial and financial links with Europe. Isolationist attitudes did nonetheless have an economic dimension, for such was the suspicion of European entanglements that many Americans looked with fear and loathing upon New York as the chief conduit for capital imports from Europe and especially the City of London as well as the main reception centre for European immigration. This remained the case even after America became a net capital exporter. Indeed, at no time was the political gulf between New York and the rest of the country greater than in the period described in the present account.[39] The claim that political leaders in Washington during the 1920s worked closely, if informally, with New York's bankers to shape world affairs is thus not only unfounded, but also reflects a deeper misunderstanding of American foreign policy-making and American history itself. More important for our purposes, it obscures the actual role that the United States played in the origins, course and outcome of the great interwar crisis.

As the present account shows, the United States exercised a manifold influence upon the course of international events after the Great War. With an economy as large as that of Britain, Germany, Japan and France combined, a dominant position in nearly all the 'sunrise' industries of the day,[40] producer of nearly half the world's industrial output, the world's greatest exporter and the largest foreign lender, it could scarcely fail to influence the world economy and the behaviour of other countries.[41] Its influence was nonetheless inconsistent and frequently destructive of international stability, largely because Washington, its political capital, and New York, its financial capital, would not or could not work together. Through sins of omission as well as commission, the United States bears a heavy responsibility for the great interwar crisis.

In Britain, where economic history exists as a separate academic discipline, some excellent work has been carried out on institutions such as the Bank of England, the Treasury and the prime minister's Economic Advisory Council, as well as certain commercial banks, manufacturing firms and shipping lines, which helps inform British foreign economic policy in the interwar period. Few of these studies, however, shed much light upon the dynamic relationship between economic decision-making, politics and foreign relations. Britain, even more than the United States, was divided by its two main sources of wealth: manufacturing and extractive industries on the one hand, mercantile-financial activity on the other. Each of them imposed its stamp upon the social, the cultural and even the physical landscape of the country, creating by the twentieth century two overlapping but distinct communities. In the half century before the Great War, the dominant business interests of the two communities were able to agree upon liberal economic policies, including free trade, the gold standard, unrestricted capital movements or 'free trade in capital', a balanced budget and fiscal restraint. But the war obliged the state to extend its control over the economy and spurred businessmen to organize themselves more effectively to influence as well as respond to state decisions. The Federation of British Industries and the National Union of Manufacturers emerged, and the Accepting Houses Committee, the Clearing Bankers Association and the Bank of England itself took on increased importance. Following the Armistice, business leaders in both communities agreed in principle on the desirability of returning to prewar policies, but their priorities sharply diverged. Industrialists objected to the deflationary action favoured by City merchants and bankers to hasten the return of sterling to the gold standard, and leaned increasingly towards trade protection. After sterling was restored to gold in 1925 and interest rates remained at historically high levels, British industry found itself struggling to compete in world markets and displayed open frustration with the merchants' and bankers' dogmatic liberalism. The growing division between the two communities unsettled the Conservative government, which sought to represent both of them in Parliament, and left it practically immobilized.[42]

In a thoughtful analysis of the world slump, Charles Kindleberger identifies the main cause as the absence of leadership of the international economic system:

> The 1929 depression was so wide, so deep and so long because the international economic system was rendered unstable by British inability and United States unwillingness to assume responsibility for stabilizing it in three particulars: (a) maintaining a relatively open market for distress goods; (b) providing counter-cyclical long-term lending; and (c) discounting in crisis. … The world economic system was unstable unless some country stabilized it, as Britain had done in the nineteenth century and up to 1913. In 1929, the British couldn't and the United States wouldn't.[43]

Kindleberger's argument is in a sense self-evidently true, because had there been a hegemon, then order would undoubtedly have been maintained. Two important caveats must however be entered.

In the first place, the distinction between inability and unwillingness is more difficult to establish than Kindleberger allows. Britain, for instance, *was* able to contribute to the rebuilding of international economic relations after the First World War. In fact, of all the victor powers, Britain contributed most to the reconstruction of the global economic system. However, the division between British industry and finance over economic priorities was aggravated by the restoration of sterling to the gold standard at the prewar rate of exchange, which intensified industry's problems and increased its opposition to further unilateral domestic price-level adjustment. Britain's international economic leadership therefore declined after 1925, but this was as much a consequence of inappropriate policy choices as unavoidable weakness.

The second caveat is that the necessity for leadership applies as much to the maintenance of international security as to the functioning of the international economic system. In the sphere of international security between the wars, Britain remained in a position to make a decisive contribution, indeed *the* decisive contribution, had it chosen to participate in a coherent European security framework. The fact that it did not, had consequences that are hard to exaggerate for the stability of the international economic system as well as the international political system.

As for modern British diplomatic history, the field has long been dominated by historians who emphasize, even celebrate, the realist character of the country's external policy and the statesmen who made and applied it.[44] Most of this historical output is however remarkably narrow in focus. Policy-making is represented as the preserve of experts operating largely free of external pressures, whose sole concern was the defence of national or imperial interests. Almost no attempt is made to link foreign policy to the political economy of the country or specific interests, or to investigate the links between foreign economic and diplomatic policies. One generally looks in vain for any reference in this literature to international monetary, commercial or financial policy: this of the great power that depended more than any other upon overseas commerce and finance for its prosperity, indeed its very survival.

Just as noteworthy are two other omissions. One is the political dimension of foreign policy. It is no doubt wrong to present British foreign policy as simply another field for party political manoeuvring. But it is scarcely more satisfactory to present foreign policy-making as a matter above politics, uninfluenced by doctrinal differences between the parties, the expedient purposes of their leaders or the preferences of powerful sectional interests. As described in the present account, Britain's renewed commitment to globalization after the Great War and determination to remove obstacles to trade and investment created by the Versailles settlement were driven by the ambitions of the most internationalist element of the City of London, in face of strong reservations expressed by the most dynamic sectors of manufacturing industry. Similarly, Britain's retreat from political as well as economic internationalism in the later 1920s cannot be understood without proper regard for the struggle between the industrial and mercantile-financial communities over the direction of economic policy. Ultimately, nothing affected British diplomacy more than the undermining of the country's leadership of the international economic system and its retreat into imperial protectionism. Discussion of foreign policy independently of economic policy and the political context thus obscures key influences upon the decision-making process.[45]

The second omission is that of ideological or pre-political influences upon foreign policy. Practically all modern statesmen no doubt prefer to regard themselves as dispassionate, practical individuals, capable of resisting arbitrariness, 'group think' and small-minded prejudice. Foreign policy-making in modern times is however almost uniquely susceptible to such tendencies, given the insistence of politicians upon controlling foreign affairs, their domestic preoccupations and their generally parochial ignorance of other nations in the international states system. Historians of interwar Britain almost invariably present British states-men as rational actors. Yet the same historians frequently acknowledge a puzzling lack of coherence, consistency or rationality in British foreign policy. Thus David Marquand observes of Ramsay MacDonald, who occupied 10 Downing Street four times between the wars: his 'suspicions of the French seem perverse forty years later, [but] there can be no doubt that most of his countrymen shared them.'[46] Paul Kennedy refers to 'a curious blindness' among the British public and its leaders towards the ambitions of the fascist powers, and describes Neville Chamberlain in particular as 'a touch naïve' in his attitude towards Germany.[47] N. H. Gibbs acknowledges that 'until the spring of 1939, British planners, civil and military alike, [who] counted on the alliance with France without sufficiently examining its practical implications...were guilty of the most elementary mistake of both wanting their cake and eating it.'[48] Brian Bond claims that British statesmen engaged in a deliberate act of forgetting after the Armistice in 1918, behaving as if the war had been 'abnormal' and a ghastly mistake. 'In retrospect it seems astonishing that virtually no official attempt was made to garner the experience of the First World War while it was still fresh.' And he adds, 'British Governments in the middle and later 1930s allowed wishful thinking to blind them to strategic reality'; even the military high command failed to face up to 'geographical and political realities'.[49] More recently, two historians offer a rational explanation of British postwar policy only to concede that there were 'many...paradoxes at the heart of British decision-making', 'obvious, yet confusing, contradictions', more than one 'tragic misreading of reality' and a 'failing to look far into the future', and they conclude that 'British policy was based too much on aspirations, wishful thinking and...hope'.[50] Two other historians, one English, one French, conclude,

> The failure of appeasement was not only a failure of British diplomacy, but also of British understanding of Europe – in a sense, of British understanding of human nature.... [T]he supposedly practical and empirical British – veering crazily between fear of French power and disdain for French weakness – had been governed by utopianism and wishful thinking.[51]

The issue underlying the statesmen's puzzling behaviour was in each case their refusal squarely to confront the need for a Continental commitment alongside France and its Eastern allies to contain the recrudescence of aggressive German nationalism. At the end of the previous world war in 1815 a combination of insular influences and the pull of overseas interests had also led Britain to retreat from a Continental commitment. Nevertheless, its statesmen safeguarded their victory by joining the Quadruple Alliance and instigating fundamental and practically irreversible changes in the European balance of power. France was reduced to its 1790 frontiers, a new buffer state was created by the amalgamation of the territories making up present-day Netherlands, Belgium and Luxembourg, Austria was compensated by the acquisition of Venice and other Italian lands, and most importantly Prussia was extended westwards by placing the Rhineland under its control. But after victory in 1918, the behaviour of British statesmen was strangely different. They sought to profit from the outcome by seizing the German navy and acquiring much of Germany's merchant marine and overseas possessions and demanding to be paid reparations. Yet they seemed deaf to all warnings that the European balance of power remained dangerously unstable and required a substantial Continental commitment. After the bloody battles of the Great War it was not surprising that the British public should be reluctant to confront the risk of another Continental conflict. But as the historians of interwar Britain acknowledge, it was also Britain's political leaders and their expert advisers who displayed irrational behaviour.

The third of the major capitalist powers examined in this study is France. Throughout the interwar period, British and American statesmen regarded France with impatience and disdain that bordered on loathing. Even today, English-language historians commonly represent French external policy in the 1920s and 1930s as a study in misjudgement, incompetence and moral failure. Some have highlighted France's excessive demands at the Paris peace conference in 1919 and its support for Poland's acquisition of Upper Silesia and a broad corridor to the sea, or its heavy-handed attempts to secure reparations from an impoverished Germany through the military occupation of the Ruhr in 1923–4 and its withholding of support from Austria and Germany during the great financial crisis of 1931. Others have dwelt upon its equivocation over sanctions against Italy for invading Abyssinia in 1935, its inaction when Germany reoccupied the Rhineland in March 1936 and absorbed Austria in March 1938, its appeasement of Germany at Munich in September 1938 and its failure adequately to rearm before May 1940. But whatever the focus, their work encourages the impression that France frequently had the capacity to shape the course of interwar affairs and all too often acted unwisely or incompetently.[52]

In fact, the Great War greatly weakened France while strengthening Germany, not least by removing Russia from the European states system and leaving France to rely upon a fringe of weak, politically unstable and economically vulnerable countries in Eastern Europe. French statesmen were already aware of their country's weakness when the Ruhr occupation confirmed that, supported only by Belgium, they could not halt Germany's revision of the Versailles settlement. Without the support of Britain and if possible the United States, the postwar international security framework was doomed. Indeed, its prospects were thoroughly blighted because these same powers actively encouraged German revisionism while isolating France on account of its supposed intransigence and militarism. Most English-language accounts accept contemporary claims that France's preoccupation with security was the source of revisionism when in fact it was the other way around. This has diverted attention from Britain's and America's share of responsibility for the postwar security framework, their role in subverting it through pressure on France to disarm, disinterest itself from Eastern Europe and abandon constraints on Germany, and their opposition to regional economic arrangements that might have contributed to European stability. These are not minor errors. They leave the impression of French incompetence in foreign and defence policies, indeed a sort of political decadence, when something closer to the opposite is true.[53]

Of the three main victor powers in 1918, France alone squarely confronted the threat posed by the undiminished strength of nationalist and imperialist ideology within Germany's civil service, education system, business community and military establishment. It was also the only power to recognize that from the standpoint of politics, economics and above all security, Eastern and Western Europe constituted two halves of a single whole. As French strategists appreciated, to ignore Eastern Europe was to lose sight of the probable dynamics of any future Continental conflict. Germany, lying at the intersection of the two halves, would seek to exploit the Western powers' remoteness from Eastern Europe to extend its dominance over the region. Then, freed from any threat from the East and drawing upon its essential resources, Germany could expand westwards with such force that the Western powers would be unable to halt it unless perhaps by holding firm to the Rhine frontier. This, in the event, was precisely what happened. Not only did Britain, with American encouragement, dissociate itself from Eastern Europe, thus lending encouragement to German imperialism; but it also sought to isolate France by, among other things, holding out promises of security on condition that it abandoned its interest in Eastern Europe as well as the bridgeheads on the Rhine. In turn, Germany, having regained its independence, first moved eastwards, then strengthened by Czech tanks and Russian commodities it proved practically unstoppable in 1940 when it moved against the West.

French leaders sought to maintain allies in the East through a variety of means, including the exchange of defence commitments, arms sales, access to the French capital market, help with currency stabilization and favourable treatment for their exports. But their ability to assist was limited. Historians commonly exaggerate France's power by assuming that in peacetime it was a strong state, capable of harnessing national resources in the coordinated pursuit of national security objectives. In fact, having assumed the direction of the economy during the war, the state swiftly withdrew from its managerial role, returned to liberal principles and sought to 'live within its means'. From huge deficits in 1918, governments were soon spending less on infrastructure and other economic and social functions than before the war, and for five years between 1926 and 1930 the national budget ended in surplus.[54] As a result, the diplomatic service became seriously under-funded,[55] while defence spending remained below national requirements. This was due partly to the constraints of debt servicing, which now constituted the largest claim on tax revenues. But significantly French governments did little to coordinate commercial banking and industry with diplomacy in the furtherance of national interests.[56] Without coercion by the state, French bankers and businessmen were not prepared to subordinate their operations to strategic goals, since their first obligation was to their depositors and shareholders. Even the

Bank of France, whose governor was appointed by the minister of finance, zealously held to its role as the guardian of the national credit and stability of the franc, and discouraged France's client states from spending on rearmament or other security measures when this conflicted with the rules of sound finance.[57] The complaint against France should thus have been that it was too weak, not too strong, and perhaps too liberal as well.

With some justice, French statesmen regarded their country as the leading defender of the international order after the First World War. Besides upholding the Versailles settlement, they sought to maintain the *Entente* with Britain, extend security guarantees to the vulnerable countries of Eastern Europe and contain the revisionist forces of Europe by promoting closer economic and cultural ties with Germany as well as broader regional arrangements. Economic liberals, they also supported efforts to reconstruct the international trade and payments system. Their efforts to maintain the postwar European order were however consistently opposed by the other victor powers whose revisionism encouraged Germany to challenge the *status quo* and shun French proposals for cooperation.

France's predicament had contradictory consequences. Its early efforts to uphold the postwar settlement delayed the economic recovery of Europe and restoration of the franc to the international gold standard. Subsequently, its preoccupation with national security further damaged international economic relations, when it supported a *franc fort*, which involved the Bank of France in accumulating large, arguably excessive, gold reserves. The same concern for national security also left France suspicious of international disarmament initiatives and American foreign direct investment in Europe, which appeared to threaten France's independence. French statesmen and bankers, who regarded themselves as liberals, were almost desperate for good relations with the other leading liberal powers, Britain and the United States. Yet they acted in ways that made them seem illiberal and antagonized their former allies. Inadvertently, therefore, they contributed to the fragility of international political and economic relations, which betrayed signs of crisis from as early as 1927.

The present account also casts a new light on the role of political ideas in interwar affairs. The conventional narrative of interwar history associates the breakdown of the postwar settlement with the rise of extreme political doctrines, including militarism, aggressive imperialism, Communism, anarchism, anti-Semitism and above all fascism and its German variant Nazism. The shelves of academic libraries groan under the weight of learned tomes on these doctrines, and it is true that they made most of the running in the 1930s. But this was not the case in the 1920s or at least until the great crisis began. On the contrary, the dominant political doctrine in this period was liberalism and its economic expression, market capitalism. The three main victor powers were all liberal powers. Though led by parties whose names in some cases suggested otherwise, they hewed to liberal policies of individual freedom, democracy, private property, severely limited intervention in the economy and multilateral trade. True, trade protection temporarily increased in the aftermath of the First World War, but much of it was due to the exceptional weakness of national currencies and international accounts. The almost complete removal of quantitative trade controls, return to the principle of unconditional most-favoured-nation treatment, restoration of the international gold standard and removal of constraints on capital exports confirm that in the 1920s the victor powers still firmly adhered to liberal economic principles. Indeed, *all* the major powers of the world, excepting Soviet Russia, broadly adhered to economic liberalism until 1931, when the crisis was well under way.

Adherence to liberalism and the onset of the crisis were not merely coincidental. British statesmen and their American associates were pursuing liberal ideals when they pressed for the return to globalization after the Great War, including the rapid reintroduction of the international gold standard, which not only contributed to the explosive growth in foreign investment in the later 1920s but also made the world vulnerable to hot money movements and rapidly shifting capital flows. They were also pursuing liberal ideals when they promoted the restoration of German national sovereignty, the reduction of reparations and armaments and the dismantling of the security system erected at the Paris peace conference in 1919. Thus it was liberalism, a political doctrine almost completely overlooked by historians of the period, which shaped the events leading to the breakdown of the international political and economic systems in the great interwar crisis. The ascendancy of extreme doctrines of Left and Right was largely the *consequence* of the crisis. While originating years before, they did little more than expand to occupy the space left by the failure of liberalism. The role of liberalism in shaping the interwar period was thus far greater and far more problematical than is generally appreciated. It deserves to be retrieved from the margins of interwar history to which constant emphasis upon other, ostensibly more extreme, destructive and 'interesting' doctrines has consigned it.

A second component of interwar political ideas is treated only cursorily in the present account, but is important enough to deserve mention here. This is the influence of racism upon the events that led to the interwar crisis. It is now commonly assumed that racism substantially influenced the behaviour only of the aggressor powers, and that insofar as it existed in the liberal democratic powers it appeared only in the form of mild anti-Semitism or colour prejudice. In light of the appalling consequences of the racial policies of the aggressor powers and in particular Nazi Germany's responsibility for the Holocaust, the term racism now possesses an ineradicably sinister connotation. Yet, our unceasing preoccupation with Nazism and the Holocaust has obscured the ubiquitous place of racism in interwar history. For, as will be seen, publicists, academics, politicians and statesmen in the democratic powers also frequently employed racial categories in their discourse and allowed them to influence their thinking on international affairs. Those who did so, one might imagine, were conservatives or reactionaries: individuals who in the 1930s sympathized with Nazi Germany on account of its authoritarian, anti-Communist and anti-Semitic policies. In fact, they were more likely to be *liberals*, whose sympathy for Germany existed *in spite of* its authoritarian, anti-Semitic regime.

As they had done before the Great War, so in the interwar period members of the English educated classes casually and unselfconsciously employed racist language, using the terms race, nation and people in a loose, interchangeable and frequently inconsistent way. Historians who equate racism with extremism or who define it in narrowly biological or genetic terms generally treat this usage as of little account. Yet it is clear that many if not most people in British public life engaged in racial stereotyping, and that whatever the biological or genetic assumptions they made, they accepted that racial groups possessed distinct and largely immutable characteristics which defined their suitability as friends or allies. Moreover, they assumed that the whole of humankind was comprised of distinct races, which they took to be a more basic and enduring order than that of religion or nation-states. Thus when they looked across the English Channel they saw a continent comprised not only of Protestants, Catholics and Jews or of Frenchmen, Germans, Italians, Poles and so forth, but also of a constellation of racial groups. Though they differed in the terms they used to describe them and recognized the existence of numerous minorities, they commonly assumed that Europe comprised three dominant racial groups, the Latins, the Slavs and the Germanic, Teutonic or Anglo-Saxon peoples. Britain, they generally assumed, belonged to the third group.[58]

While Britain had absorbed people of diverse origins, its educated classes generally believed that their traditions, leading institutions and spirit of liberty all derived from the country's Anglo-Saxon heritage. Despite the Great War, which had found them on the side of the leading Latin and Slav powers against their Teutonic cousins, many continued to feel an affinity with Germans as well as Americans and their kith and kin in the British Empire. At the turn of the century, the imperialist, Joseph Chamberlain, had confidently predicted that 'If the union between England and America is a powerful factor in the cause of peace, a new Triple Alliance between the Teutonic race and the two great branches of the Anglo-Saxon race will be a still more potent influence in the future of the world'.[59] The Great War reduced but by no means eliminated interest in an alliance of this sort.[60] Such was the enduring appeal of racial categories that even after four and a half years of war with Britain's Teutonic cousins, the notion of an underlying solidarity remained.

Similar thinking also informed the outlook of American middle classes and contributed to a deeply ambiguous attitude towards Britain and the countries of Continental Europe.[61] Since the war of independence, Americans remained suspicious of 'old Europe'. Yet, as school textbooks affirmed, America was an Anglo-Saxon country, and its founding fathers, explorers, business leaders and statesmen commonly regarded themselves as part of the 'Anglo-Saxon race', whose blood alone bore the genius of America's institutions and its unquenchable thirst for liberty.[62] The Civil War had renewed antagonism with Britain, but towards the end of the nineteenth century, as the United States expanded its influence abroad and Social Darwinism became popular, Americans reaffirmed their Anglo-Saxon roots and cousinhood with Britain. As they did so, they assigned a hierarchy of value to other peoples of the world on closely similar lines to their British contemporaries.[63] Most, it seems, regarded Germans as their kith and kin. Meanwhile, the huge influx of immigrants from Eastern and Southern Europe that began in the 1880s aroused intense anxiety among older residents, who talked of 'hybrid-ization' and the decline of the superior White Anglo-Saxon Protestant (WASP) stock.[64] Anti-Semitism and colour prejudice were for the time being secondary issues. More pressing was the imagined threat posed by 'inferior' *white* stock, which gave rise to federal legislation intended to control their numbers before the First World War and more draconian measures in the 1920s.[65] So evident was this preoccupation and so influential was it upon the course of international affairs that the present account employs the term Anglo-Saxon powers to reflect the racial basis of national self-definition in both Britain and the United States between the world wars.[66]

France, it is commonly assumed, was exceptionally afflicted by one form of racism, namely anti-Semitism, which erupted at the time of the Dreyfus affair in the 1890s and again between the wars when Léon Blum, a secular Jew, led the Popular Front to electoral victory in 1936. But while anti-Semitism was viru-lent in right-wing circles, the historical preoccupation with the subject creates a misleading impression. For it obscures the fact that the French public, like their counterparts elsewhere in the developed world, commonly assumed that *all* humankind was comprised of races and that racial characteristics shaped the behaviour of all powers in the international system.[67] In the years before and after the Great War they were chiefly preoccupied by the economic ascendancy of Britain and the United States and the military threat posed by Germany. They equated British and American economic success with a *'capitalisme sauvage'*, which they took to be synonymous with the more aggressive and unruly *'races anglo-saxonnes'*.[68] They also regarded Germans as a race apart, a belief reinforced by the Great War. While some French publicists defined the Prussians as the aggressive and brutal element in Germany, many more presented Germans generally as bar-barians with inherently dangerous proclivities.[69]

Since Ernest Renan's onslaught in the 1880s, surprisingly few French intellec-tuals or academics accorded race a central place in explaining human behaviour or equated race with nation.[70] This was true even of Charles Maurras, royalist agitator, author and darling of the Right. While encouraging anti-Semitism by denouncing all those who would not, in his opinion, assimilate within the nation, he explicitly rejected a biological basis for national character and scorned the Germans for doing so.[71] In the interwar period few books appeared in France on race or with racist assumptions.[72] Yet the wider public accorded race a more prominent place. Together with large-scale immigration from Italy, Poland and Russia after 1918, hostility to the German or 'Boche' sustained the appeal of Maurras's warning against being swamped by aliens.[73] So common and so casually did the language of race inform public discourse that a committee of the French Senate in 1927 rejected votes for women because 'the woman of Latin race does not feel nor evolve in the same way as the woman of Anglo-Saxon or Germanic race.'[74] That same year a new and rela-tively liberal nationality law employed the term *race française*.[75]

What British, American or French writers meant when they referred to race is often unclear, and the extent of racial categorization in the liberal democratic powers cannot be precisely measured (though French statesmen left less evidence of racial stereotyping in their diplomatic record than their British counterparts). What can be said with confidence is that so far from being the preserve of the aggressor powers, racism influenced the behaviour of *all* the powers in the interwar years. Indeed, implausible as this must now seem, it arguably had a greater effect upon the course of world affairs by its influence within the liberal democratic powers in the period leading to the great interwar crisis than by its influence within the authoritarian, aggressor powers in the 1930s.

The great interwar crisis did not lead inevitably to the Second World War any more than the First World War led inevitably to the interwar crisis itself. It did nonetheless create the conditions that enabled Hitler to take power in Germany and drove Mussolini in Italy and militarists in Japan towards aggressive expansion overseas. It also diverted Britain from economic internationalism and onto the path of imperial protectionism, intensified American isolationism, deterred France and Britain from rearmament until the fascist and militarist powers had gained a large and intimidating lead, and increased support for the political left which deterred statesmen from allying with the Soviet Union. Since these were vital elements in the origins of the Second World War, the interwar crisis can properly be regarded as the main antecedent of the war. This being the case, the present study points to a radically new interpretation of not only the world economic depression but also the origins of the Second World War. Blame, a moral judgement that lies outside the proper functions of the historian, can no doubt remain with the régimes that chose to embark upon military aggression. But responsibility for the war, a much broader concept, must be shared by the great liberal powers which, through their action or inaction, contributed importantly to the breakdown of the international political and economic systems between the wars, that is to say the great interwar crisis, and therefore to the war.

The significance of the great interwar crisis does not end there. In the short run, the crisis intensified empire building, but it almost certainly accelerated the downfall of empires as well. During the crisis, Britain, France and the lesser imperial powers sought to compensate for declining trade, employment and prestige by organizing their empires into coherent blocs. With the United States and Soviet Russia, empires in themselves, acting similarly, Japan, Italy and Germany, the so-called have-not powers, followed suit. Increased imperialist rivalry and colonial exploitation in turn heightened national self-consciousness among the subject peoples of the empires.[76] The Second World War merely accelerated the trends set in motion by the interwar crisis, and once the war ended nationalist movements gained sway in most of the colonial territories. But it was not just the colonial peoples who reacted to the crisis. Within the metropolitan countries themselves, the interwar crisis generated support for a more rational approach to national economic affairs. After the war, economic experts in the British Treasury, the French planning office and elsewhere deprecated captive markets and the inefficiencies that accompanied them. And once the nationalist movements increased the cost of retaining the empire, they too opposed the imperial project.[77]

Following the First World War, the leading capitalist powers engaged in a concerted *retour en avant* to the globalized world of 1914. Following the

Second World War, all the capitalist countries, excepting only the United States, maintained interventionist policies owing to their awareness of the link between economic distress and political unrest. The political class had long been aware of this linkage, but after the devastating experience of the interwar crisis when liberalism threatened to give way almost everywhere to forms of political extremism, they were prepared to do far more to avoid mass unemployment and deprivation, even if that meant setting aside some of their liberal principles. At the international level the interwar crisis led the capitalist powers to adopt the Breton Woods agreement and establish the International Monetary Fund (IMF), the International Bank for Reconstruction and Development (IBRD), the central component of what was to become the World Bank, and the General Agreement on Tariffs and Trade (GATT), forerunner of the WTO, which have regulated economic relations within the 'free world' for the past 60 years.

After 1945, the absence of any event remotely comparable to the slump of 1929–33 encouraged the impression that these institutions were sufficient to maintain international stability, and that appropriate lessons from the interwar crisis had been drawn. Yet arguably this is not the case. For just as scholars have consistently failed to grasp the dual nature of the interwar crisis, so experts and authorities almost invariably continue to apply a bifurcated approach to current international affairs, treating questions of international economic and political security as largely discrete issues. Until recently, with the United States acting as a hegemon and extending its security umbrella over the 'free world', this has not greatly mattered. Nonetheless, as explained in the concluding section, grounds exist for thinking that it may now matter greatly to all of us. Only one instance exists of the collapse of globalization in the industrial or post-industrial age. In face of the revolutionary changes in the international balance of power brought on by the past 60 years of globalization, understanding the great interwar crisis may be essential if we are to forestall the present crisis from ending in a calamity of comparable magnitude.

1
The Liberal Powers, Peace-Making and International Security, 1914–19

1.1 Introduction

Despite the heavy rain, huge crowds gathered to welcome Marshal Ferdinand Foch, the Allied supreme commander, and Georges Clemenceau, the French premier,[1] when they arrived at London's Victoria Station on Saturday, 30 November 1918. The procession, with King George V and Foch in the first carriage and David Lloyd George, the British prime minister, and Clemenceau in the second, set off for Trafalgar Square where the carriages separated, the first going to Buckingham Palace, and the second to the French embassy in Knightsbridge. Lloyd George later commented on the size and enthusiasm of the crowds, claiming that no previous visitors to England had ever received such a welcome. It was, he added, much greater than the crowd that turned out for Woodrow Wilson, the American president, when he arrived at Charing Cross Station on Boxing day, four weeks later.[2] The visit afforded the first occasion to celebrate Allied solidarity in the victory over the Central powers after a struggle lasting nearly four and a half years, and for the leaders of the great democratic powers to begin the task of constructing a durable peace. This was a remarkable opportunity, given their near monopoly of global power, one that would recur only once 70 years later when the Communist bloc collapsed in 1991, leaving the Western powers again in unchallenged control of international affairs. In public, spokesmen for the powers in 1918 encouraged hope that, having won the war together, they would now work together to create a new world order. But the conversations between French and British leaders which began in Downing Street on the evening of 30 November revealed that Allied solidarity was already a thing of the past.

The great interwar crisis that began in 1927 did not follow inevitably from the breakdown in relations between the victorious powers in 1918 and their failure to construct a stable world order: too many opportunities arose in the intervening decade to improve upon their peace-making efforts for such a claim to bear scrutiny. It was nevertheless a remarkable opportunity to place postwar political and economic relations on a solid footing. Their failure to do so aggravated the problems of global stability in the postwar period. This contributed to the great interwar crisis, and made it harder to contain it once it began.

1.2   Britain and the deceptions of war

In the early years of the twentieth century, British statesmen set aside 'splendid isolation' – a phrase coined not long before, just as its relevance was coming into question – by promoting a *rapprochement* with the United States and entering into an alliance with Japan in 1902, the *Entente cordiale* with France in 1904 and a similar arrangement with Russia in 1907.[3] The decision for the *Entente* with France, Britain's oldest rival, reflected the coincidence of a number of developments, including the increased burden of Britain's expanded empire, the spectre of conflict with Russia with whom France was allied, and the rapid rise of Germany, now Europe's industrial giant and its most restless power. Since the Kaiser's accession to the imperial throne in 1890, practically every step Germany took on the international stage seemed calculated to raise suspicions as to its ambitions: its 'meddling' in South Africa, its decision in 1898 to construct a high seas fleet capable of rivalling the Royal Navy, its confrontation with France over Morocco in 1905 and again in 1911. When the Committee of Imperial Defence first assessed the risk of foreign invasion shortly after its creation in 1903, the putative enemy was France. When it repeated the exercise in 1908, the putative enemy had become Germany. Many in Britain, including Lloyd George, rising star of the Liberal party, still doubted the wisdom of the *Entente*, but leading soldiers and statesmen were persuaded of the need to go beyond its merely negative terms and convert it into a defensive alliance.[4] As Sir Eyre Crowe, assistant secretary in the Foreign Office, warned ministers in January 1907, Germany now possessed the power to threaten British security and had repeatedly spurned its gestures of good will. Closer relations with France had therefore become a necessity.[5]

The General Staff in July 1909 explained the uniquely dangerous situation. For centuries, the cardinal principle of British defence policy had been to oppose any foreign power that sought to dominate the Continent and occupy the North Sea and Channel ports, since this would expose Britain to the disruption of its trade and the threat of invasion, and thus undermine its independence. In earlier times, Britain had been able to rely upon its naval power to blockade a Continental challenger, while preparing forces for a counter-attack at a time and place of its own choosing. But with Germany building a large naval fleet and modern technology increasing the speed and range of military operations, Britain no longer enjoyed the luxury of being able to wait on events and respond in its own time. If Germany attacked in the West, naval intervention would come too late to affect the outcome. France would face 'overwhelming force', and its defeat would leave Britain without a Continental ally and dangerously exposed to invasion. The General Staff therefore recommended a 'military *entente*', later redefined as a military alliance, to which both powers committed their naval and military strength, and the creation of a British expeditionary force comprising five infantry divisions and one of cavalry, totalling some 110,000 men, to be available for immediate despatch to the Continent.[6] The Liberal government baulked at the idea of a formal military commitment to France. Nevertheless, by 1914, it had created an expeditionary force of six divisions and entered into a secret agreement with

France whereby, in the event of German aggression in the West, the Royal Navy would take responsibility for the North Sea and Atlantic coast while the French navy would concentrate its forces in the Mediterranean.[7]

On 4 August 1914, German armies invaded Belgium, smashed through Liège and swept across the frontier into France. The expectations of British soldiers and statesmen had been confirmed, and the expeditionary force proved its value when it was inadvertently thrust into the path of the westernmost German army, which was briefly thrown off stride by the encounter.[8] Shortly afterwards, the British force joined the French in a counter-attack at the Marne that halted the German offensive and allowed time for Britain's contribution to be augmented. Four years later, when the second battle of the Marne took place, the British army on the Western front numbered 60 divisions. This was an unprecedented commitment to the Continent. Yet even then the coalition of 103 French divisions, 60 British, 18 American, 12 Belgian and 2 Italian, or 195 divisions in all, was 11 fewer than the German total and only just sufficient to stop the German forces from making a decisive breakthrough.[9]

Despite the pattern of events that had led to this situation, British politicians consistently refused to acknowledge the need for a Continental commitment. This was due in part to the 'liberal conscience', to use Michael Howard's phrase, which was shared by Liberal and Labour party leaders and found strong expression within the Cabinet itself. By 1914, most liberals regarded war as the work of dynastic regimes or capitalists, evidence of human failure and acceptable only in the most extreme circumstances.[10] But the politicians themselves had encouraged opposition to a Continental commitment by presenting Britain not as a European power with overseas interests but as a world power which derived its strength chiefly from its possessions in Asia and settler colonies in the temperate zones of the eastern and western hemispheres, for whom Europe was more a distraction than a vital interest. One reason for turning away from Europe was the unwelcome economic and social costs of a Continental commitment. Britain had become a great power in the sixteenth century by seeing off challenges from major Continental powers, notably Spain and France, and thereafter as an island it had been able to limit the fiscal burden of defence and concentrate upon overseas trade and commerce. This had facilitated the rise of merchants and bankers to a central place in the national political-economy: economic groups who favoured liberal economic policies and a foreign policy that minimized the risk of war.[11] And after such a long period when isolationism – that is to say, isolation from Continental Europe – had apparently served the country's interests so well, it was politically unpalatable to have to acknowledge that Britain was after all part of Europe, its fate inescapably bound up with the Continent. It was equally difficult to accept that Britain must ally with France, its 'hereditary enemy', since both had declined demographically and economically relative to Germany. The politicians did not want to admit it or the electorate to hear it. Accordingly, Sir Edward Grey, the foreign secretary, with the approval of Herbert Asquith, the prime minister, had entered into understandings with France on naval and military dispositions without acknowledging them to the public or, until the outbreak of war, even to the full Cabinet where opposition to a Continental commitment remained strong.[12]

Liberal traditions, economic costs and historical conflict with France do not however fully explain the depth of unease about going to war in 1914. Almost certainly as important was the dismay among Britain's educated classes at the predicament created by this particular war. For a century the country's leading historians had taught that Britain was an Anglo-Saxon country. Other peoples had migrated to the British Isles, but it was the Germanic tribes whose courage, love of liberty and tradition of voluntary association that had shaped British society. Magna Carta, the independent Church of England, parliamentary government: all were fruits of their genius.

This was the view of Henry Lytton Bulwer, the Liberal politician, author and diplomat, who affirmed in 1832 that England's liberty derived from its Germanic ancestry.

> With that land, and the people of that land, the people of this country must be ever connected. It was in the free forests of Germany that the infant genius of our liberty was nursed. It was from the free altars of Germany that the light of our purer religion first arose.

Charles Kingsley, professor of modern history at Cambridge in the 1860s, wrote that the English were Teutons who had settled in Britain, 'to till the ground in comparative peace, keeping unbroken the old Teutonic laws, unstained the old Teutonic faith and virtue'. Their mission, he added, was universal, for 'the welfare of the Teutonic race is the welfare of the world.' Sir Charles Dilke's *Greater Britain: A Record of Travel* (1869) anticipated a racial struggle, ending with the triumph of the Anglo-Saxons and 'the gradual extinction of the inferior races [which] is not only a law of nature, but a blessing to mankind.' William Stubbs, Regius professor of modern history at Oxford from 1866 to 1881, similarly affirmed that the English 'are a people of German descent in the main constituents of blood, character and language, but most especially ... in the possession of the elements of primitive German civilisation and the common germs of German institutions.' Lord Macaulay, Thomas Carlyle, Goldwyn Smith, Lord Acton, Edward Freeman, James Froude, J. R. Seeley and J. R. Green, all in their turn contributed to the myth of Anglo-Saxonism.[13]

Reinforced by studies in philology, ethnology and the pseudo-sciences of phrenology and eugenics, the myth went beyond mere academic theorizing and became part of conventional wisdom for several generations of educated Englishmen before the Great War. Germany's behaviour since 1890 had aroused deep suspicion among Britain's diplomats, outbursts of public anger and popular speculation that German forces might mount a surprise attack on Britain.[14] Nevertheless, the English middle classes found it difficult to believe they could actually find themselves fighting their Teuton cousins: a sentiment widely shared by their counterparts in Germany.[15] When suddenly war became imminent in the summer of 1914, they betrayed deep dismay at the prospect of Britain aligning itself with France and Russia, the leading Latin and Slav powers, against Germany.

Thus on 1 August, the principals of Manchester and Mansfield Colleges, Oxford, the Cavendish professor of experimental physics at Cambridge and six other leading academics issued 'An Appeal to Scholars', which affirmed that 'War upon [Germany] in the interest of Servia and Russia will be a sin against civilisation', and protested against 'being drawn into the struggle with a nation so near akin to our own, and with whom we have so much in common'.[16] Other academics endorsed the appeal,[17] and on 3 August some sixty members of Cambridge University, including the historians J. H. Clapham, J. Holland Rose and C. K. Webster, the mathematician E. W. Hobson, the scientists J. E. McTaggart, G. H. F. Nuttall and G. Sims Woodhead, and the philosophers Bertrand Russell and James Ward signed an open letter urging neutrality. Leading liberals including the Lord Mayor of Manchester, the Lord Provost of Glasgow and the Bishops of Lincoln and Hereford issued a manifesto calling for resistance to the jingoists and warning that Britain must not side with 'only partly civilised' Soviet Russia against Germany, which they described as 'highly civilised ... with a culture that has contributed enormously in the past to Western civilisation, racially allied to ourselves and with moral ideals largely resembling our own'. A similar appeal was issued by the journalist and author J. A. Hobson, the historians J. L. Hammond and G. M. Trevelyan, the sociologist Graham Wallas, the Oxford classicist Gilbert Murray, the Labour politician James Ramsay MacDonald, and seven others.[18] A few weeks later, T. B. Strong, the vice-chancellor of Oxford, expressed regret that Britain should find itself at war against Germany, 'the one power in Europe with which we have the closest affinity'.[19]

John Maynard Keynes, the Cambridge-trained economist, evidently shared their racial assumptions and their horror at the implications of the war. Probably for this reason, he declared himself a conscientious objector, despite being excused from military service on account of his work at the Treasury.[20] William Beveridge, the administrator and social reformer, was equally disturbed. On 3 August 1914 he wrote to his mother,

> The whole thing is an incredible nightmare come true. I can't of course ... help feeling relieved that apparently we are to join in (because it seems necessary and in a sense our duty) but it's all against the grain with me to go in against the Germans with the French and Russians.[21]

Beatrice Webb, the waspish chronicler of English political society, shared the gloom. Today they were being told the war was necessary to defend France, Belgium and Holland, she noted in her diary. 'To the Englishman of tomorrow it may seem a mistaken backing-up of the Slav against the Teuton.' Perhaps, she reflected, it would be better if no one won.[22]

Most Britons of all classes accepted that German aggression had brought on the war, and anger erupted in different parts of the country after reports of German air raids, the sinking of ships or alleged war crimes in Belgium. The same prejudice, stirred up by elements of the press, led to the victimization of individuals with German names or connections, and prompted the Royal family to change its name from Saxe-Cobourg-Gotha to Windsor. But such was the anxiety among the middle classes that the government supported the rapid publication of *Why We Are at War* by a group of Oxford historians.[23] Even so, Oxford University continued the German Rhodes scholarship scheme until forced by an Act of Parliament to suspend it in March 1916.[24] To maintain morale among the troops, the Army's propaganda depicted the enemy as an Asiatic 'Hun', and in the heat of battle soldiers expressed unreasoning hatred while engaging in extreme brutality. Yet, in spite of the mounting level of casualties, officers, drawn largely from the middle classes, seldom displayed anything but regret at the need to fight the Germans.[25] In many cases the carnage seems to have had the effect of increasing their hostility towards the French rather than the Germans. This displacement was equally evident among some upper-class officers, including Field-Marshal Haig, commander of the British forces, whose diary is replete with hostile references to the French. Historians usually put this down to the frustrations of coordinating operations with their French allies and competition for scarce resources. But it was frequently evident among officers who had little if any dealings with their French counterparts. Many, it seems, suspected that the clever, self-interested, 'materialistic' French had drawn phlegmatic and trusting Britain into a war of their own making and were now leaving the British to do all the fighting. The British middle classes had no quarrel with ordinary Germans. They reserved their criticism for the Kaiser and the High Command, whom they defined as Prussian rather than German and held chiefly responsible for the war.

Grey, the foreign secretary, drew this distinction, describing Prussians as brutes and aggressors and fundamentally different from ordinary Germans. As he wrote to a colleague in October 1914, 'it is the Prussian Junkers alone, I believe, who have created all this [conflict], and the rest of the Germans are people more akin to ourselves than any other race.'[26] Asquith, in his first statement on war aims, affirmed that they must fight on 'until the military domination of Prussia is wholly and finally destroyed.'[27] The popular novelist, H. G. Wells, repeatedly drew a similar distinction between the German people – 'the greatest people in Europe' – and those who had led them to war.[28] Sir Nevile Henderson, later to be British ambassador to Germany, elaborated on the racial explanation of the war. '[I]t was the Prussians rather than the Germans whom we regarded as our real enemies and…not the Germans as a race.' He personally had nothing but respect for 'the great qualities of order and efficiency, probity and kindness of the purer German of Northwest, West, and South Germany, with whom an Englishman on his travels abroad finds himself in such natural sympathy.' The trouble arose from the Prussians, whose character was corrupted by a 'considerable admixture of Slav blood', and who dominated the country through the Kaiser and military high command. '[T]he Prussians, of whom even Goethe spoke as barbarians, are a distinctive European type, which has imposed itself and its characteristics upon the rest of Germany.'[29] It followed that once the Prussians were removed from power, there would be no basis for further Anglo-German enmity.

Despite anger at the whole of Germany in some quarters, the 'two Germany' thesis remained a commonplace among the British middle classes.[30] The Oxford historians who argued the case for war in 1914 presented it as a struggle between Prussianism and Anglo-Saxonism.[31] Lloyd George, who succeeded Asquith as prime minister in 1916, subscribed to the same thesis.[32] So too did Lord Haldane, the minister largely responsible for preparing the British Expeditionary Force before the war,[33] Sir Cecil Spring Rice, ambassador in Washington, and Winston Churchill, first lord of the Admiralty. Churchill, addressing his remarks to the American public shortly after the outbreak of the war, affirmed that Britain was fighting 'Prussian militarism', which bore no relation to 'the quiet, sober, commercial elements in Germany, nor of the common people of Germany, with all their virtues'.[34] Towards the end of the war, Spring Rice spoke of 'gentle, kind, sympathetic' Germans and the Prussian brutes who had seized political control and 'put the soul of the German people in chains.'[35] Leo Maxse, editor of the *National Review*, had constantly drawn this distinction before the war, despite agitating on behalf of the National Service League.[36] J. L. Garvin, a fellow Conservative and editor of the *Observer*, made it the constant theme of his weekly editorials as the war closed. Only 'rabid vengeance confounds the whole German people with its former militarist-political system and with the crimes of that system', he warned readers, while making weekly appeals for generosity to the 'German race'. Significantly, he never mentioned the plight of other 'races' whose fate was being settled at the conference.[37]

The dilemma confronting Asquith, Grey and the inner circle of policy-makers in August 1914 was resolved in timely fashion when Germany launched its Western offensive by invading Belgium on the way to France. This enabled them to point to Britain's commitment to defend Belgian neutrality as their justification for going to war. As they well knew, Britain's security requirements demanded intervention to forestall Germany's hegemony on the Continent and occupation of the North Sea and Channel ports, regardless of Britain's legal obligations to Belgium or any other country. But it was politically more convenient to present the decision as the fulfilment of a moral obligation to defend 'little Belgium', deriving from a promise made in 1839, than candidly to admit the hollowness of prewar myths of invulnerability and indifference to the fate of Europe.[38] Henry Wickham Steed, foreign editor of the *Times*, affirmed this point in an address at King's College London in 1916, when he asked rhetorically if Britain should have remained neutral had Germany respected Belgian neutrality in its drive to the West. His answer was 'Certainly not – though in that case the nation might have been less unanimous, thanks to the ignorance in which our responsible statesmen had left it as to the fundamental conditions of our national safety.'[39]

Thrice during the war, German armies came perilously close to smashing through the Allies' lines, eliminating France and exposing Britain to the threat of invasion. After the launch of the final German offensive in March 1918, British leaders in desperation agreed to place their forces under the supreme command of Marshal Foch. Eight months later when the Armistice halted the fighting, Britain had lost 573,000 men, 511,000 of them on the Western front in north-western France and Belgium.[40] Yet, even this searing experience was not enough to prompt a frank acknowledgement that Britain was a part of Europe and must participate in a European security framework after the war. If anything, it seems to have strengthened the temptation to escape from this unwelcome prospect.

True, Britain's status as a great power during the war, indeed its very survival, had depended upon its ability to draw resources from its overseas Empire and the United States. Support for Britain had also increased demands from Dominions leaders for a voice in future Imperial policy-making, which meant in practice opposition to a postwar Continental commitment. Added to this was the astounding scale of casualties, which increased reluctance within Britain to contemplate involvement in another Continental war. But powerful as these influences were, they did not alter by one iota the reality of Britain's situation. Put simply, access to the vast resources of the Empire and Americas, albeit vital to Britain in the recent war, had become necessary only because of the breakdown of order in Europe. Moreover, a special relationship with the United States and close relations with Britain's Empire partners could be no guarantee against the need to fight another major European war. It scarcely reflected well on the quality of Britain's political leaders or their professional advisers that even after the Armistice they should have persisted in claiming that Britain had fought the war for Belgium's or France's sake and that Britain could disinterest itself from Europe's fate if the postwar settlement was not to its liking. At the peace conference in Paris, Lloyd George affirmed that 'Great Britain declared war on Germany in 1914 in order to honour its signature to a treaty that guaranteed the neutrality of Belgium.' Britain also deserved credit for its 'generosity towards France. We did our best to support her. Hundreds of thousands of our young men died on French soil.' He had apparently persuaded himself that this was why Britain fought, but it remained a pernicious myth all the same.[41]

At the time of the Armistice and for the foreseeable future, Europe was bound to remain an extremely unstable place. Everywhere the sacrifices and pent-up frustrations of the war placed huge demands on governments to share out the national wealth more equitably. In Central and Eastern Europe, nationalism and revolution aggravated the turmoil. The victor powers broadly agreed on recognizing a resurrected Poland, 'the redemption of the oppressed races in Austria and Hungary ... the completion of Italian unity', and other measures to address national frustrations. The war had also stimulated much talk of reimposing international law upon interstate relations through a league of nations. But laws were of scant value without the means of enforcing them, and Europe would never be stable so long as Austria, Bulgaria, Hungary, Soviet Russia and above all Germany remained determined to overturn the territorial changes in the East. Since practically no one in Germany believed their country was responsible for the war, they opposed a peace settlement that recognized the national aspirations of the Lithuanians, Czechs and Poles. As Wickham Steed put it, the fundamental challenge facing the peacemakers was therefore 'the position of the German people as a solid block of some 70,000,000 in the centre of Europe'.

> As long as the German people are animated by the feelings and aspirations which led them to make war, and remain obedient instruments of Prussian dynastic policy, so long will they continue to be a peril to the peace of mankind. The Allies cannot and do not want to destroy the German people. But they can, and are morally bound to, build up against the weight of the German block a system of political and economic counterpoise that shall again create a true balance of power, military, political, and economic, and with it a guarantee of freedom in Europe.[42]

This in a nutshell was 'the German problem', which had preoccupied British statesmen in the decade before the war and would preoccupy Western statesmen for much of the twentieth century. In the age of nationalism it was highly problematic to attempt to break up Germany (though the superpowers belatedly accepted this solution after the Second World War), nor was it realistic simply to trust Germany to be content with its postwar frontiers, given that it had not been content with its much greater prewar frontiers and was bound to be even less content with its post-1918 frontiers after they were reduced to meet the claims of France, Belgium, Denmark and especially the Slav countries to the East. Arguably, therefore, Steed offered the only realistic approach to the problem. Yet after the Armistice British statesmen were not prepared to acknowledge the problem and Britain's essential role in maintaining European stability. Now that the Prussians were presumed to be gone, leaving Germany for the Germans, they resisted pressure to join in 'a system of political and economic counterpoise that shall again create a true balance of power ... and with it a guarantee of freedom in Europe': in short, an effective postwar international security framework.

In November 1918, British policy-making was firmly in the hands of David Lloyd George, despite his somewhat precarious position as prime minister of a coalition government. A Liberal, he had appointed the Conservative Arthur Balfour to the Foreign Office in place of the Liberal Grey on entering 10 Downing Street in December 1916, and made further concessions to the Conservatives after the general election in December 1918, when they gained over 50 per cent of the parliamentary seats. Nevertheless, their preponderance in the Commons and the Cabinet had only a modest influence on Lloyd George's handling of the peace negotiations. Although Balfour and Lord Curzon went to Paris as part of the British delegation, he consulted them only occasionally and was prepared to leave them in the dark on some of the most momentous decisions.[43] Similarly with public opinion: although the British people initially favoured punitive measures against Germany and the other enemy powers, Lloyd George was scarcely a prisoner of their demands. In the latter stages of the 1918 general election, he risked stirring up public opinion by promising to make Germany pay heavily for the war. But he was a master of manipulating public opinion, and having encouraged hopes of revenge, he was also quick to exercise a moderating influence on the country. Mentally agile, self-confident and frequently charming, he displayed rhetorical and tactical skills that left his political opponents in awe and somewhat afraid of him. There may never have been a more brilliant, recklessly energetic occupant of 10 Downing Street. But while master of the British parliamentary scene, he had seldom travelled abroad and possessed only superficial knowledge of European and international affairs. On domestic affairs he was a radical and capable of important innovation; on foreign affairs his outlook was thoroughly conventional and largely shaped by pride in Britain's imperial greatness and the usual suspicions of Europe. A skilful negotiator, he enjoyed outmanoeuvring opponents, but often the short-term political gains seemed more important to him than the longer-term interests of his country.

With the exception of General Sir Henry Wilson, chief of the imperial general staff, nearly everyone in the prime minister's circle owed their reputations to imperial connections. This included Viscount Milner, the South African proconsul; Philip Kerr, Lloyd George's private secretary and a former member of Milner's 'kindergarten'; Sir Maurice Hankey, the Cabinet secretary and former marine officer; and General Smuts, the South African minister of defence and sole Dominions statesman in the Imperial War Cabinet, who exercised the greatest influence on Lloyd George during the conference.[44] Lloyd George was somewhat better qualified to address economic issues, having had four years of hands-on experience as chancellor of the exchequer. Yet here too he appears to have relied little upon experts, deferring to them only when it suited him to do so and otherwise proceeding on the basis of his own calculations of political or national advantage. He eventually admitted deep disappointment with the outcome of the peace negotiations. But, as will be seen, it was probably for the wrong reasons, for Britain under his leadership signally failed to construct either a robust security framework or solid foundations for international economic stability.

1.3   France: Between realism and hope

France had entered the war in 1914 in a mood of resignation, its leaders aware of their country's weakness, and emerged four years later relieved to be on the winning side but aware that the country remained essentially as weak if not weaker than before. The German armies had been hurled back beyond France's northern frontier – but at what cost! Some 1,394,000 men had been killed and a similar number seriously injured. In relation to population this was a heavier casualty toll than any other belligerent country aside from Serbia, and in view of France's uniquely low birth rate it seemed certain to affect its military strength for much longer than its potential allies and enemies. Along the Belgian frontier from Dunkirk to Metz, ten departments, hitherto the most industrialized in the country, lay devastated with scarcely a building intact. The cost of reconstruction would be enormous, as would be the cost of supporting the 700,000 invalids, 600,000 widows and 1,100,000 orphans left by the war. The state, moreover, was already burdened by the massive internal and external debt accumulated during the war.[45] One bright spot was the resourcefulness demonstrated by French engineers and technocrats during the war. Despite the relatively low status of technical education and the modest scale of French industry before 1914, they had succeeded in relocating industrial production outside the war zone and greatly expanding the output of weapons and munitions. By the autumn of 1918, France was able to supply not only its own three-million-man army but also much of the requirements of the two million American troops who had disembarked in France with little more than the uniforms on their backs.[46] This was encouraging, and with the addition of the resources of Alsace-Lorraine and perhaps other territory along the Franco-German frontier, France could hope to reduce Germany's relative industrial strength. But even then the postwar industrial balance was bound to leave Germany in a preponderant position, while the strategic balance seemed certain to favour Germany even more.

During the first three years of the war, France's survival had depended upon its alliance with Russia. By the time Russia withdrew from the war in the autumn of 1917, its loss had been offset by the presence of Britain and the United States at France's side. But the two Anglo-Saxon powers were as reluctant to remain engaged in Europe after the war as they had been to enter the lists against Germany. Russia's absence was therefore bound to have a massive impact upon the European balance of power. An expanded Roumania and the new states of Poland, Czechoslovakia and the Kingdom of Serbs, Croats and Slovenes could be expected to line up with France in the new balance. But even then, Germany would stand like a colossus in central Europe, constrained only by small, divided and ill-defended states.

In several respects, French leadership in 1918 resembled that of Britain. In each case, one man dominated the scene. Georges Clemenceau, like Lloyd George, had made his reputation in parliament and consolidated it in the final phase of the war when as premier he led his country to victory. They were both intimidating figures, in Clemenceau's case owing to a personality marked not by charm but brutality of language and an intense commitment to causes that seldom allowed for compromise. Like Lloyd George, Clemenceau was a radical liberal, interested in modest social reform and almost totally indifferent to economic issues. Like Lloyd George, he was also thoroughly uninhibited and frequently indulged in vulgar wit and sexual innuendo, and at the peace conference he found it almost unbearable to endure the earnest President Wilson with his folksy homilies and moralistic appeals for universal justice and peace.[47] The French press treated Clemenceau with respect, although the majority of leading journals stood politically either to the left or the right of him. He had demanded that the Chamber of Deputies accord him the right to negotiate the peace-making as he saw fit and received an overwhelming vote of confidence. Potential opposition existed from political rivals frustrated at his high-handed exercise of power, and from the military high command, which now enjoyed enormous prestige and sought to ensure that the victory it had secured was not thrown away in the peace-making. Raymond Poincaré, the president of the Republic, was deeply envious of Clemenceau for occupying centre-stage and frustrated at his own lack of influence.[48] Aristide Briand, a rival in republican circles, was reputedly impatient to step in should Clemenceau lose credibility or become incapacitated. Marshal Foch, the Allied supreme commander, was equally disgruntled at being excluded from the French delegation and disturbed that Clemenceau did not rely more heavily upon his advice. But despite his 77 years, Clemenceau was inured to struggle and still remarkably vigorous. Like Lloyd George, he deferred to no man and entered the negotiations in a position of authority, confident that he spoke for his country.

There, however, the similarities ended. Although Clemenceau had played little part in the direction of foreign affairs before the war, he largely made up for this by foreign travel. As a young man just out of university, he had spent nearly four years working and travelling in the United States. He had been to England many times and made an extensive visit to South America just before the war. For many years he had also taken an annual cure at Carlsbad, then in Austria, now the Czech Republic, and made a point of passing through Germany to reach it. From Carlsbad he had occasionally visited his sister-in-law who lived in Vienna, and travelled to Galicia and other parts of Europe. He thus had first-hand knowledge of the Anglo-Saxon, the Germanic and the Slavic worlds. With good reason he was known as an Anglophile.[49] While a student in Paris in the 1860s, his interest in politics had drawn him towards English liberalism. With the intensity that characterized his life, he translated John Stuart Mill's study of Auguste Comte, which was published, as well as the first volume of Mill's *Logic*. After the turn of the century he became a strong partisan of the *Entente cordiale* with Britain, and on becoming premier in October 1906 he had sought to transform it into a formal alliance. He was aware of the militarist dimension of German culture and from his frequent travels to Central Europe the potentially destabilizing influence of Austria-Hungary. Indeed, in 1914 he anticipated by several months its role in provoking the events that would lead to a general war.

Clemenceau's confrontational manner and brutal invective had made him many enemies during his career as journalist, editor and later politician. He had probably fought more duels in defence of his honour than any German political contemporary. As war leader from November 1917 onwards he pursued victory with almost fanatical intensity, mobilizing the country's resources as never before and hounding opponents suspected of favouring a compromise peace. Yet Keynes's thumbnail portrait of him in *The Economic Consequences of the Peace* as a sort of French Bismarck, cold-bloodedly bent upon revenge against Germany, reveals more about Keynes's chronic Francophobia than it does of Clemenceau's character or intentions.[50] A product of the severely rationalist Paris faculty of medicine, he placed a high value on plain speaking and decisive leadership, but his cause was the defence of republican values, including universal civil rights and equality before the law. He was not only a Dreyfusard and an atheist but also an anti-militarist and anti-imperialist. As premier before the war he had worked consistently for *détente* with Germany, and in his travels he deliberately avoided setting foot in any of France's colonies or protectorates. He was also a nationalist, aware that nations had become practically the sole legitimate basis for sovereign states and hence the key determinant of international relations. This left him deeply sceptical of talk of a new world order governed by a League of Nations. Once Russia under the Bolsheviks abandoned the Alliance, he offered to support independent Polish and Czechoslovak states in the hope that they might eventually contribute to the European balance of power. But he worried that nationalism in Eastern Europe was not sufficiently developed to withstand the subversive efforts of Lenin's Bolsheviks.

Clemenceau was also resigned to the prospect that, whatever the decisions taken at the peace conference, France would be left confronting a larger, faster growing German nation hard up against its eastern frontier. Twice in his lifetime German armies had invaded France, and he had known men who witnessed an earlier invasion in 1815. Although Germany had cast aside its imperial régime just before the Armistice and instituted a republican state, he did not believe that a change of régime necessarily meant a change in political and cultural values or the end of imperialist ambitions. This might eventually occur, but the presence of men at the head of the new government who had devoutly supported the Kaiser and the war left him sceptical. He, like many contemporaries in France as well as Britain, shared the notion of two Germanys: the Prussians and the rest. The Prussians were the evil geniuses of the country: aggressive, brutal and inherently ill-intentioned.[51] But whereas his British contemporaries chose to believe that the Prussian element had been swept away with the end of the *Kaiserreich*, he and his French colleagues held that the Prussian influence had thoroughly infected Germany's institutions and remained dangerously virulent. Indeed, French preoccupation with Prussianism, which continued long after the rise of Nazism, betrayed a racial view of Germany inherently predisposed to aggression.[52] This left Clemenceau no choice but to concentrate upon constructing a postwar framework of security. He accepted that in the short run security could be obtained by punishing the Germans who were responsible for the latest aggression and enforcing disarmament. But in the longer run he could see no practicable solution unless Britain joined France in deterring German revisionism. He was cautiously hopeful that British leaders had drawn the appropriate lessons from the war. If the United States also agreed to enter the lists on the side of European stability, so much the better, but he had few illusions about its continued aloofness from the affairs of the 'old world'.[53]

1.4   The United States: Returning from the crusade

With the benefit of hindsight it is possible to see a pattern in American history wherein the United States continuously expanded from 13 modest colonies on the eastern seaboard westwards across the Appalachians to the Pacific, south to the Rio Grande, north to Alaska, west to Hawaii and the Philippines, informally outwards to the Caribbean basin and Central and South America, and eventually to its present status as the world's only super-power. But subjective reality and objective reality are seldom the same. Ever since independence, the strongest impulse behind American foreign policy has been the popular tendency to regard the world beyond America's shores as a dangerous place and to insulate the country from foreign threats, which until recently came chiefly from Europe. George Washington gave expression to this view in his farewell address to the nation in 1797, when he warned his fellow citizens to avoid entanglement with the European powers. 'Europe has a set of primary interests, which to us have none or very remote relation.'[54] Thomas Jefferson, the third president, issued a similar injunction in his inaugural address in 1801: 'Peace, commerce, and honest friendship with all nations; entangling alliances with none.'[55] Several years later, referring to the struggle for independence then taking place in Latin America, he made clear that it was Europe he had in mind.

> [Whatever form the new states take], they will be American governments, no longer to be involved in the never-ceasing broils of Europe. The European nations constitute a separate division of the globe; their localities make them a part of a distinct system; they have a set of interests of their own in which it is our business never to engage ourselves. America is a hemisphere to itself. It must have its separate system of interests; which must not be subordinated to those of Europe...[56]

James Monroe, the fifth president, warned the European powers in December 1823 against attempting to reverse the trend towards independence in Latin America and went further by indicating that the United States now regarded the Americas as its exclusive sphere of influence. He did not suggest, however, that the United States should cut its commercial or cultural ties with Europe; it would not have occurred to him to do so. In fact, he specifically affirmed that these ties were desirable and should be developed:

> Of events in [Europe], with which we have so much intercourse and from which we derive our origin, we have always been anxious and interested spectators. The citizens of the United States cherish sentiments the most friendly in favour of the liberty and happiness of their fellow-men on that side of the Atlantic. In the wars of the European powers in matters relating to themselves we have never taken any part, nor does it comport with our policy so to do. It is only when our rights are invaded or seriously menaced that we resent injuries or make preparation for our defense.[57]

The Monroe doctrine, as it subsequently became known, summed up American foreign policy for over a century. The United States ensconced within its informal American empire wished simply to be left alone by the European powers, so it could pursue its domestic affairs and foreign commerce unhindered and reach out beyond the Americas to the countries across the Pacific. The term isolationism applied exclusively to Europe and specifically to political and strategic relations. Already in Washington's time the United States was Britain's largest customer, and in the following decades it grew to become Europe's largest supplier of primary products and manufactured goods as well as its largest borrower of capital. Nevertheless, isolationism still informed American foreign policy at the end of the nineteenth century and well beyond.[58]

The outbreak of war in 1914 brought Europe's quarrels dangerously close to America's shores. By and large, Americans sympathized with the plight of their fellow Anglo-Saxons in Britain. But with their criticism of German aggression mitigated by the 'two Germany' thesis, they hewed to the isolationist policy of trading with both sides while avoiding any political involvement. After an initial slump in trade, American order books were soon swollen by Allied demand for foodstuffs, raw materials and munitions, while American banks engaged in huge loan operations to facilitate the business. William Jennings Bryan, the secretary of state, warned President Wilson that a policy of 'business as usual' would draw the United States into the conflict, and when Wilson disregarded his warnings, he resigned. Despite the country's increasing commerce with the Entente powers, Wilson won re-election in November 1916 with the slogan, 'He kept us out of war'. He still had popular backing when he severed relations with Germany on 3 February 1917, after its announcement of unrestricted U-boat warfare against shipping in the Atlantic. The release of the Zimmermann telegram a few weeks later, confirming that Germany was prepared to extend its operations to the Americas by inciting Mexico to aggression, sent a shock wave through the country. The sense of outrage at European interference in America prompted Congress overwhelmingly to endorse the President's request for war powers.[59] Yet the isolationist impulse remained strong not just in the mid-West, but also in Washington itself.[60]

Although Americans were now at war with Germany, they still harboured suspicions of Britain and indeed of Europe as a whole. Reflecting these suspicions, Wilson declared the United States to be an 'associated' power rather than an ally of Britain and France. The 1916 legislation authorizing a major expansion of the navy to keep America's enemies at bay was supplemented in 1918 by a bill to create a navy 'second to none', that is to say one as large as if not larger than the Royal Navy. Wilson's decision to set out his principles of peace in the Fourteen Points on 8 January 1918 was a unilateral act intended as a warning to the Allies as much as an assurance to Germany and the Central powers that the United States remained opposed to European imperialism.[61] Germany, facing total defeat in September 1918, approached Washington to arrange an Armistice on the assumption that the United States would act independently and offer more generous terms than its European allies. As anticipated, Wilson agreed to bilateral negotiations, allowing the Allies a say in the terms of the Armistice only after the negotiations were well advanced. On board the SS Washington at Hoboken, New Jersey, just before sailing to Europe in December, Wilson betrayed suspicions of Britain in answer to a question from journalists about plans to enlarge the US navy. The United States would build up its forces if Britain did not recognize America's right to complete naval security:

> the United States would show her how to build a navy. We would be in a position to meet any program England or any other power might set forth. ... We have now greater navy yards, thousands more shipbuilders than we ever had

before, and an abundance of raw materials such as would make it possible for us to have the greatest navy in the world.[62]

In several respects Wilson was well qualified to lead the United States delegation to the peace conference. A former academic and president of Princeton University, he had, to quote his biographer, a 'thorough grounding in international law, modern history, and comparative systems of government; and he had taught all these subjects with increasing effectiveness and some distinction after 1885.'[63] As a Southerner, he also shared the region's interest in overseas markets and its preference for low tariffs. This has prompted one widely cited account to portray him at the peace conference as the managing director of USA plc, pursuing a world order that would serve the interests of American corporate enterprise.[64] But this is a caricatural study which overlooks the powerful influence of other American traditions upon his negotiating posture. During his time at Princeton and as governor of the state of New Jersey he had displayed a strong affinity with the Progressive movement. His record of reforms as governor, when he sought to check the irresponsibility of large corporations and reduce the corruption that threatened to undermine popular democracy, made him a Progressive in all but name. This in turn can be seen as a development from his deep-seated Southern suspicion of big business and banking.

In his campaign for the presidency in 1912 he had singled out Wall Street's 'money trust' as the greatest threat to the nation.[65] One of his first actions as president was banking reform. He seized upon a proposal for a federal reserve system with branches located around the country to ensure that control over the money supply and credit would not be monopolized by Wall Street. To reinforce the point, he also insisted that the governing board must be located in Washington, the political capital, rather than New York, the financial capital, and comprised mainly of regional bankers and political appointees. William McAdoo, his first secretary of the Treasury, wrote of the Administration's struggle to overmaster the 'powerful, centralized and ruthless engine of high finance' by creating a reserve banking system that would secure 'its freedom from Wall Street control'.[66] Jacob Schiff, senior partner at Kuhn, Loeb & Company, warned Paul Warburg, a young partner involved in preliminary discussions on establishing an American central bank, that provincial critics regarded central control of money and credit as contrary to American tradition and feared the extension of Wall Street influence, which they associated with globalism, cosmopolitanism – and Europe. Warburg must therefore avoid any reference to European practice, since this would arouse certain opposition. With Wilson and McAdoo sharing this anti-New York, anti-European prejudice, the Federal Reserve System was the nearest the United States could come to a recognizable central bank. In its original form it was ill-equipped and remote from the markets it was meant to regulate.[67] Wilson and McAdoo in fact had New York banking friends, and when America entered the Great War they relied upon Wall Street for finance. But by no stretch of the imagination could they be regarded as the agents of corporate America.

For similar reasons Wilson shared the Progressives' visceral suspicion of Britain. Until the First World War, the United States had been a large net exporter of commodities and importer of capital to finance the development of its infrastructure and industry. Most of this capital came from London and most of it passed through New York. By the early years of the twentieth century, New York seemed to many Americans a suspiciously cosmopolitan city because it was the gateway for the recent wave of non-English speaking immigrants from Southern and Eastern Europe. These suspicions were intensified by New York's intimate links with foreign, and especially British, commercial and financial interests, and its role as the channel through which the City of London's loans and investments flowed into the heartland of America.[68] Wilson, the author of several studies of the American constitution and government, was deeply imbued with the outlook of the founding fathers. Along with most of his contemporaries, he held Britain in healthy respect. But he exaggerated its influence and viewed it as an imperial power with competing interests to America and a parliamentary system of government which reflected the interests of its upper classes. France he knew little about and tended to equate with Germany as a militarist, imperialist – and typically European – power.

President since March 1913, Wilson could claim major accomplishments in banking, tariff reform, transport and other sectors. But he remained a solitary man who found it hard to delegate responsibility. This was particularly so in the field of foreign affairs, largely, one suspects, because of his intense suspicion of the European powers. Thus he arrogated to himself the most sensitive work of his secretaries of state, and went so far as to type his own letters at critical moments of the war.[69] Suspicious that his Republican opponents did not appreciate the national interests at stake, he called on voters to support the Democrats before the November 1918 congressional elections, which infuriated opponents who had set aside party rivalry on account of the war and contributed to the Democrats' loss of control of both houses of Congress. Even then, he did not include any prominent Republicans in his delegation when he set off in December 1918 for the peace conference in Paris.[70] On board ship, he referred to the European statesmen with whom he would be dealing as élites, remote from and ill-qualified to speak for the ordinary peace-loving people of their respective countries. Besides a strong hint of populism and even demagoguery, his observations revealed a profoundly cynical view of old world politics.[71] In fact, it was not the European leaders who lacked a popular mandate, but Wilson himself, now that Congress was in Republican hands. But this became an issue only after the completion of the peace negotiations, which he played a key part in shaping.

1.5   Clemenceau, Foch and French postwar security

Clemenceau, speaking in the Chamber of Deputies just after news was received of Austria-Hungary's abandonment of the war, affirmed his belief that France's postwar security depended upon the maintenance of the Franco-British alliance.

'We have made friends of our old secular enemies, the English, and we love them well. We see the enormous contribution they have made on the field of battle.' Moreover, 'the wartime alliance must be followed by an indissoluble peacetime alliance.'[72] The great postwar challenge, he hinted, was no longer to put Germany in its place but to persuade Britain to remain involved in Europe. He was cautiously hopeful of succeeding, and from all the evidence his decision to make the *Entente* the centrepiece of French policy had strong support in parliament and throughout the country. In London on 1 December, he allowed Marshal Foch to set out his views on postwar security for Lloyd George and a small group of colleagues. Foch had been impressed by Britain's forthrightness in seizing Germany's colonies, its navy and a large part of its merchant fleet, and he therefore set out France's security requirements in similarly matter-of-fact terms.[73] France, he explained, could not tolerate a reversion to its prewar predicament, where it faced a vastly more powerful Germany camped right on its eastern frontier. Though Germany was temporarily defeated, the European balance of power had been gravely damaged by the Bolshevik seizure of Russia. The only way to restore the balance was to hold the Rhine and allow the Rhineland to contribute to the West's defence. Even then, by his reckoning, Germany, including German-speaking territories in Central Europe, would have a postwar population of 65–75 million, while France including Alsace-Lorraine, together with Belgium, Luxembourg and the Rhineland would amount to less than 55 million. He therefore asserted that in addition to the Rhineland frontier, France absolutely needed Britain's continued support if the European balance were to remain stable.

Lloyd George and Andrew Bonar Law, the leader of the House and chancellor of the exchequer, heard Foch out, but betrayed deep scepticism in their questioning. How, they asked, could it be reconciled with President Wilson's Fourteen Points, which stressed the need to respect the 'territorial integrity [of] great and small states alike'? What if the Rhinelanders wished to be reunited with Germany? Would their alienation not cause just the sort of friction that had been created in 1871 when Germany insisted upon absorbing Alsace-Lorraine? Foch rejected the comparison, since France was not proposing to absorb the Rhineland. On the contrary, it sought a tripartite Franco-British-Belgian condominium for the region, the creation of one or more autonomous states within it, and the granting of economic advantages to induce the people to remain content with their new status; the details could be settled by the Allies.[74] Nothing he could say reduced in the slightest British opposition or allayed their suspicion of French imperialism. Lloyd George nevertheless recognized the opportunity created by Foch's appeal, and in subsequent conversation he allegedly persuaded Clemenceau to abandon France's claim on Palestine and the oil-rich region of Mosul in return for the promise of British support for French policy towards the Rhineland. But this was never recorded and Lloyd George denied that any such agreement had been made.[75] He later credited Clemenceau with his own brand of cleverness by claiming that the French premier had absented himself while Foch, the Allied supreme commander, spoke, to win the British audience around to the French plan.[76]

Some historians have questioned Clemenceau's commitment to Foch's plan, suggesting that he allowed Foch to advance it simply as a bargaining tool or perhaps to bring home to Foch himself the strength of British opposition to it.[77] In his retirement, Clemenceau muddied the waters by accusing Foch (and Poincaré) of Bismarckian ambitions. But in fact their disagreement was limited to the postwar status of the 5.5 million Rhinelanders: while Foch was prepared to see the Rhineland contribute soldiers to a French-led alliance, Clemenceau held that it should be left independent of both Germany and France.[78] Not only was Lloyd George's suggestion of an intention to deceive at variance with Clemenceau's personality, but all the evidence also points to the conclusion that Clemenceau supported Foch's plan, albeit remaining unsure of Allied support. Foch, with his government's knowledge and approval, had already called in Paul Tirard, a senior assistant of General Lyautey in Morocco, to form the *Contrôle général de l'administration des territoires rhénans occupés*, and Engineer General Maugas to head an economic committee for the purpose of integrating the economy of the occupied territory with those of Belgium, Luxembourg and France.[79] A few weeks later Clemenceau requested his closest collaborator, André Tardieu, to reformulate the plan so as to address British and American objections.[80] At the time of his visit to London, Lloyd George and other ministers were in the midst of electioneering and promising tough measures against the '*Boche*'. Clemenceau, while disappointed by their failure to agree on policy, continued to assume that Britain, too, would wish to see Germany hobbled once and for all.[81] Thus he remained cautiously hopeful of securing approval for the Foch plan or something similar. He could not know at this stage how far Britain had already turned away from questions of European security.

Since the Armistice, Germany had abruptly ceased to preoccupy or even seriously to worry British statesmen. One reason was that Germany had been driven out of its overseas possessions, and thus no longer posed a threat to Britain's imperial interests. Having been captured during the war, the German colonies were in the process of being handed over to one or another British dominion or in a few cases France, while German interests in China were transferred largely to Japan. The fifth of Wilson's Fourteen Points, which the British government had endorsed, called for 'a free, open-minded, and absolutely impartial adjustment of all territorial claims, based upon a strict observance of the principle that in determining all such questions of sovereignty the interests of the populations concerned must have equal weight with the equitable claims of the government whose title is to be determined.' This was simply finessed by applying Wilson's concept of League mandates to the German colonies, while modifying its application to ensure that the colonies would remain indefinitely under the control of the mandate powers.[82]

Another reason for British indifference was that Germany's high seas fleet had been interned at Scapa Flow and no longer posed a threat to British sea lanes or imperial interests. Added to this was the preoccupation of British statesmen with problems closer to home. Some ten thousand troops awaiting repatriation from northern France mutinied in early January 1919 and five thousand more at the end of the month, while those who returned to civilian life flocked to join trade unions and threatened strike action when wages failed to keep up with inflation. In February the 'triple alliance' of miners, railwaymen and dockers was resurrected, raising the spectre of a national strike. At almost the same moment ministers suddenly realized that expenditure was threatening to exceed revenue by an even greater margin than in previous years, sending national finances out of control.[83] Meanwhile employers, facing accelerating inflation and growing labour unrest, demanded an end to wartime restrictions and a return to 'normal' tax levels.[84] If that were not enough, there was trouble in Ireland, India, Egypt and other parts of the empire.

Yet another reason was the terrible bloodletting of the recent war, which strengthened hopes that it was indeed the war to end all wars. But public opinion everywhere hoped for peace and Britain was by no means the worst affected by the war. In any case this does not explain why British military and diplomatic advisors – men selected for their ability to think clearly about national security and not be distracted by short-term problems or swayed by emotional or irrational influences – as well as leading politicians and commentators displayed such indifference towards Germany. The decisive reason, it seems, was the confidence they placed in the 'two Germany' thesis.

To some of those who had taken to calling Germans barbarians or a primitive orientalized 'Hun', the abdication of the Kaiser on 9 November and dissolution of the German High Command was of little or no consequence. 'Do not let us deceive ourselves,' the *Morning Post* warned. 'We are fighting not against Autocracy or Democracy but against Germany, and although the Germans, like PROTEUS, take new shapes when they are hard pressed, they remain Germans.'[85] But to most British observers, this was an event of signal importance since, in the words of the *Daily Telegraph*, 'It is the Kaiser and the HOHENZOLLERNS who have made Germany what it is, and who are responsible for those sins against ethical and religious principles which have so revolted the conscience of mankind.'[86] Thus, Evelyn Wrench wrote on hearing news of the Kaiser's flight to Holland,

> The great event we had been living for had come at last, for to us the Kaiser was the symbol of Prussian might, Prussian efficiency and Prussian war-spirit. Once the influence of the Kaiser and of the military clique was eradicated, we believed that...Germany would adopt a democratic form of Government and settle down as a happy member of the European family.[87]

Lloyd George as well as Asquith and Arthur Balfour, both former prime ministers, were equally confident of this outcome. Speaking at the Lord Mayor's Banquet at the Guildhall two days later, Balfour affirmed:

> What ever may happen in the future, this at all events is certain in the present, that that nightmare of slavery that hung over mankind so long as German militarism remained undefeated has gone forever – (cheers) – and all the

difficulties we may have to meet sink into insignificance compared with that great and unspeakable blessing.[88]

In the words of a leading liberal daily, 'the fall of the Kaiser...will stand in history, far more than the formal acceptance of any Armistice terms, for the ultimate symbol and guarantee of victory.'[89] Despite more than four years of war, the 'two Germany' thesis thus emerged in Britain more strongly than ever. The Labour party leadership evidently subscribed to it.[90] So too did much of the Conservative party: Austen Chamberlain, the chancellor of the exchequer, who remained sceptical of Germany's transformation, found it unpopular to express his doubts.[91] Most crucially, Lloyd George and his inner circle subscribed to it. As Lord Riddell, Lloyd George's closest companion, was to write

> The official point of view is that the German nation were not responsible for the war, that the Junkers have been ejected, that the German Government should be supported, that German industries should be revived and that, generally, the Germans should not be regarded with suspicion.[92]

This was wishful thinking. More cautious French observers remained aware that Germany, despite its conversion to a republic, was governed by men who had doggedly supported the war, its civil administration, law courts and universities were dominated by men of a similar outlook, and its defeated military leaders continued to enjoy great prestige.[93] But British statesmen seemed impatient to draw a line under recent history and assume that another war with Germany was out of the question. As a result, even before the peace conference began they were prepared to appease Germany. They refused to examine the potential threat that Germany posed to the European balance of power or the crucially important role of Eastern Europe within the overall balance. Instead, they took out their frustration on France for constantly raising these awkward questions.

1.6   The preliminary peace conference and the League of Nations

Once the Armistice was signed on 11 November 1918, the victorious powers had intended to hold a brief preliminary conference among themselves to establish a common position, then to convene a conference attended by all the belligerent powers where the peace settlement would be negotiated. In the event, the latter conference never took place. The preliminary conference was delayed several weeks to allow President Wilson to reach Paris, and when it convened on 8 January 1919 so many contentious issues emerged that it proved impossible to make rapid headway. The preparation of a draft treaty lasted until 8 May, by which time delegates had hardened their positions on the main components of the peace, and were no longer willing to undertake full-scale negotiations with Germany. Instead, German delegates were summoned to Paris to receive the draft treaty and allowed only a few weeks to comment on its terms. The Allied delegates briefly considered their objections, then summoned them again to Paris for a signing ceremony that lasted no more than ten minutes. Later, observers raised many criticisms at the way the business of the preliminary conference was handled, not least the insistence of the 'big three' leaders on taking direct control of practically every issue and their reluctance to delegate more responsibility to their professional advisers. There is something in this, although in the democratic age politicians have seldom been able to resist the temptation to engage in summit diplomacy. If there was an avoidable error, it was to underestimate the magnitude of the challenge brought on by the collapse of four great land empires of Russia, Austria-Hungary, Germany and the Ottoman Empire, and the insistence of another continental empire, the United States, that valuable time should be devoted to establishing a new international forum for dispute resolution.

To Woodrow Wilson, the League of Nations was the keystone of the edifice to be constructed at Paris, and he saw to it that it should be the first substantive item on the preliminary conference agenda. Lloyd George and Clemenceau were both sceptical that the proposed League would serve any important purpose, but were prepared to put on a show of interest for Wilson's sake.[94] In Lloyd George's case the popularity of the League idea among British Liberal voters encouraged him to endorse it, but he did so mainly as part of his negotiating strategy. Several senior colleagues and advisers continued to regard the proposed League as a snare and a delusion, but the Imperial War Cabinet reluctantly came around to the view that on balance it would serve Britain's interest to have an international deliberative body after the war, particularly as it would provide a means of working with the United States and sustaining its interest in Europe.[95] In December 1918, Wilson had allowed a bill to go before Congress for a massive increase in the American navy. The implications of the bill deeply disturbed ministers in London and strengthened their view that in the event Britain was forced to choose between France and the United States at the peace conference, it must choose the United States. Lloyd George, who strongly shared this view, pointed out to colleagues that as the League of Nations was the one thing Wilson keenly wanted from the settlement, Britain would be wise to support it. Wilson would then be more likely to side with Britain on other issues, and if he was obliged to return to Washington before the conference ended, he could claim that he had secured his main objective.[96] But as Lloyd George told Sir Henry Wilson in March, 'he was only in favour of a League of Nations when it was reduced in its activities to absolutely insignificant and innocuous proportions.'[97]

Clemenceau's position was similar, if not the same. Writing some years later of Wilson's proposal, he dismissed it as 'a parliament of parliaments, without any instrument of authority, that was the talisman we were offered.'[98] Like Lloyd George, he may have been modestly influenced by public opinion, since a movement in support of the League had also arisen in France. But like his British counterpart it was chiefly to retain Wilson's goodwill, for strategic reasons, that he was prepared to support the League proposal. Unlike Lloyd George, however, he was determined to expose the limits of the League's effectiveness to underline the need for other security provisions.[99]

Lloyd George was content to delegate the task of negotiating the League of Nations constitution or 'covenant' to Lord Robert Cecil and General Smuts, both of them enthusiasts; Clemenceau called on Senator Léon Bourgeois, a leading French proponent of the League and author of an influential proposal for an international organization in 1910.[100] Wilson, in contrast, demonstrated his zeal for the League proposal by insisting upon chairing the conference's commission on the League and attending every one of its lengthy sessions. The importance he attached to the League and the campaign he undertook to secure American participation, which led to the breakdown in his health, contributed to the view that his aim was to abandon America's traditional isolationism and play a leading role in world affairs. Historians therefore commonly portray him as an idealist confronted by realist opponents at the peace conference and in the Senate, or more generously as an internationalist opposed by narrow nationalists. On occasion, the language he employed to describe America's future world role did indeed point towards a radical break with the past. In his second inaugural address in March 1917, for instance, he declared

> The greatest things that remain to be done must be done with the world for a stage and in cooperation with the wide and universal forces of mankind.... We are provincials no longer. The tragical events of the thirty months of vital turmoil through which we have just passed have made us citizens of the world.[101]

Nonetheless, the crude dichotomies used to define his posture obscure the basic assumptions informing his initiative, which place him squarely within the American diplomatic tradition.

In the first place, if Wilson's support for US membership of a League of Nations was new, the spirit that informed his policy was by no means so. As George Kennan has written, long before Wilson took office and until at least the Second World War, American foreign policy was dominated by a 'legalistic-moralistic approach to international problems'. This derived from America's own success in resolving differences among its 13 founding colonies through the adoption of common institutions and laws, and from the hugely optimistic assumption that the Anglo-Saxon concept of civil law could be applied with equal effectiveness to global interstate relations. Just such an assumption informed Wilson's enthusiasm for the League.[102] In the second place, Wilson envisaged the League not as a form of world government, but rather as an agency for containing and pacifying Europe. In early March 1919, he received word of a 'round robin' resolution signed by 37 US senators against American participation in the League in its current form. This was a disturbing development, since the signatories comprised over a third of the Senate, more than enough to block ratification of the scheme. Wilson's colleagues advised him to appease critics by insisting upon a reference to the Monroe doctrine in the covenant, thereby excluding the Americas from the League's writ. He hesitated only from fear that such a request would prompt demands for exclusion clauses from other countries, which would undermine the project altogether. But he saw no objection in principle, and to reassure Americans he soon demanded a reference to the Monroe doctrine.[103] For him the League's role lay not in the Americas but elsewhere, in Europe and perhaps beyond. Back briefly in Washington, he went further and described the League as a means of extending the Monroe doctrine to the whole world.[104] This was to become a favourite theme in his campaign for ratification of the peace treaty.[105] While he never clearly spelled it out, the implication was that the League would effectively halt all further imperialist activities by the European powers, in Europe as well as overseas.[106]

Within the Senate and elsewhere in the United States, the main objection to the League was that it would draw America into ceaseless conflicts in Europe and elsewhere. In fact, Wilson sought to create the League precisely to contain Europe's tendency to disturb the international order and force a response from America. In theory, membership of the League would require the United States to intervene against international law-breakers everywhere in the world. Article 10 of the covenant seemed clear on this:

> The Members of the League undertake to respect and preserve as against external aggression the territorial integrity and existing independence of all Members of the League. In case of any such aggression or in case of any threat or danger of such aggression the Council shall advise upon the means by which this obligation shall be fulfilled.

However, Wilson assumed that in practice, by uniting other powers against a would-be aggressor, the League would minimize the need for America's direct involvement. Those closest to the source of trouble would be the first to be called upon, and he assumed that the threat of diplomatic censure and economic isolation would usually suffice. In those rare cases where the United States' involvement was required, Congress could be expected to recognize the need, as had been the case in 1917. But even then he intended no automatic commitment of American forces.[107] This became abundantly clear at the commission hearings in Paris on 11 February, when Senator Bourgeois exposed Wilson's assumptions by setting out the French attitude to the League proposal.

Observing that it was Wilson himself who had called for the creation of 'a force so superior to that of all nations or to that of all alliances, that no nation or combination of nations can challenge or resist it', Bourgeois proposed two amendments to the draft covenant.[108] The first would augment the League executive by creating a military agency to coordinate armed forces of its own or contingents earmarked by member states for its use. The second would accord the League the right to verify each nation's force levels and to set limits on them in light of the risks to which the nation was exposed on account of its respective geographical position and the nature of its frontiers. France, he observed, was prepared to accept the limitations on its sovereignty that these amendments implied. Wilson, however, immediately ruled them out. The American constitution, he said, would not allow US forces to be placed under international control. In any case, he did not want to see the League become an armed power in its own right. '[I]f we organise ... an international army, it would appear that we were substituting international militarism for national militarism.' Bourgeois called on his colleague Larnaud to explain the case for a League with definite enforcement powers:

> Several nations which have taken part in this war are afraid of having made sacrifices in vain. The protection which results from the existence of a League of Nations will perhaps become a guarantee of safety, but within what period of time? Perhaps within a hundred years. By that time the militarist spirit will no doubt have disappeared, but at the present moment we are emerging from a terrible war. Can it be thought that we shall pass immediately from the state of intensive militarism in which we live to a state of practical disarmament? ... The idea of an international force is bound up with the very idea of the League of Nations, unless one is content that the League should be a screen of false security.[109]

Wilson, however, wanted nothing to do with a League that possessed international, let alone supranational, power. The only means of making it an effective agency for peace, he insisted, 'lies in our having confidence in the good faith of the nations who belong to the League'. The United States would not commit itself in advance to provide armed forces for League operations.

> All that we can promise, and we do promise it, is to maintain our military forces in such a condition that the world will feel itself in safety. When danger comes, we too will come, and we will help you. But you must trust us. We must all depend on our mutual good faith.[110]

Eventually members of the commission agreed to take up the French proposals, but Wilson's remarks confirmed that a League with the assured capacity to identify aggressors and intervene with military force was out of the question. The council of the League, comprised partly of permanent members representing the great powers, and partly of temporary members chosen from the lesser powers, would have the authority only to report to and advise the assembly. It was for the assembly to decide on sanctions against an aggressor. Initially 40 states would be represented in the assembly, each one with a single vote and, as decisions required unanimous approval, the power of veto over collective action. It was naïve to think that a body of this sort could substitute for traditional alliance relations, but Wilson's refusal to support a more robust institution should be seen as a reflection of his unwillingness to contemplate a substantial increase in America's commitment to postwar international security. By his lights, it was not the United States but Europe that must change, by accepting the rule of law and ending the anarchy that endangered world peace. The United States sought the League not to engage with Europe but to contain Europe and safeguard America's freedom. It was, in short, a means of imposing American principles upon Europe in place of its supposed imperialist, militarist traditions, to contain the threat that Presidents Washington, Jefferson and Monroe had warned against. Notwithstanding the institutional innovation, it thus reflected an isolationist approach to the postwar world order.[111]

The United States was not the only isolationist power. During the lengthy deliberations on Bourgeois's amendments, Lord Robert Cecil said little and allowed Wilson to veto them. At one point he indicated that Britain might go part of the way with France by agreeing to 'a permanent Commission ... to advise the League of Nations on naval and military questions.'[112] But he left no room for doubt that Britain wanted only a deliberative body, not an armed league for the enforcement of peace terms on Germany, and in the corridors he warned a French representative not to press his demands further. The French should understand, he said, that 'the League of Nations was their only means of getting the assistance of America and England, and if they destroyed it they would be left without an ally in the world.'[113] The following day, after another lengthy meeting of the commission, Cecil repeated his warning. France, he said, should be grateful for America's willingness to join a league, since it could easily disinterest itself from Europe. The same was also true of Britain, which had a greater interest in Europe, 'yet to a certain extent could stand apart.' France must therefore avoid antagonizing them, or they might wash their hands of Europe and join in an Anglo-American alliance.[114]

While the reasoning was deeply flawed, there was no doubt that Cecil spoke for the British delegation. Bourgeois, whose wartime league proposal had set out the enforcement function in detail, was no doubt disappointed. But Clemenceau, who had almost certainly anticipated this outcome, was now in a position to argue that as the Anglo-Saxon powers were not prepared to enforce the peace through the League, another means of enforcing it must be found.

1.7 Security in the East

Although statesmen in Paris were chiefly concerned with the settlement of Germany's relations in the West, they appreciated that there could be no enduring stability unless a *modus vivendi* of some sort was established between Germany and its eastern neighbours. By the time the conference began, debate had ended on whether to recognize the six secession states, Estonia, Latvia, Lithuania, Poland, Czechoslovakia and the Kingdom of Serbs, Croats and Slovenes, soon to be known as Yugoslavia. Albeit reluctantly, Britain joined the other victor powers in recognizing them all. Nevertheless, wide disagreement remained over their frontiers, particularly that of Poland, as well as territorial changes affecting Czechoslovakia, Hungary and Roumania, and the appropriate response to the challenge posed by the revolutionary Bolshevik régime in Moscow. Even before the first plenary meeting of the conference on 18 January, leading delegates meeting as the Council of Ten devoted several long sessions to the Bolshevik question. Clemenceau took the lead in calling for decisive military action against the Bolsheviks. Already, he claimed, they had the upper hand in the Baltic provinces, Poland and Hungary, and their influence was apparent in Vienna, Italy and even among workers in France. Unless decisive action was soon taken, he feared they would gain sway throughout Central Europe.

Baron Sonnino, the Italian foreign minister, strongly endorsed his call, but neither Lloyd George nor Wilson could be persuaded to act. While acknowledging that the Bolsheviks posed a threat to the international order, they constantly emphasized the practical obstacles to intervention. As Lloyd George pointed out, the Germans had felt compelled to leave a million troops in the East even in March 1918, when the Bolsheviks at their weakest had signed the Brest-Litovsk treaty. De Scavenius, the Allied emissary, reported that an additional 150,000 troops were required just to keep the anti-Bolshevik forces from collapsing; and since Bolshevik forces numbered 300,000, they would have to arm at least 400,000 Russians if they hoped to defeat them. Britain and France already had troops with the anti-Bolshevik forces, but they were reluctant to stay on and fight. And since none of the Western powers was prepared to supply more than a small fraction of the forces required for a major operation, Lloyd George ruled out a military solution. He proposed instead that the warring Russian parties, including the Bolsheviks, should be invited to Paris to negotiate a compromise settlement.[115] Clemenceau strongly protested at inviting Bolshevik representatives to Paris and declared that he would resign before agreeing to this. Prinkipo, an island in the Sea of Marmora, was therefore selected as the meeting place.[116]

Back in London, Lloyd George chaired two meetings of the Cabinet on 13 February devoted to the Bolshevik question. Winston Churchill, the recently appointed minister of war and air, vigorously argued for large-scale support of the White forces in Russia. But Lloyd George along with most of his colleagues remained cautious, and General Sir Henry Wilson, who attended at the prime minister's request, was non-committal about the chances of a successful intervention.[117] Churchill nevertheless set off for Paris where he put the case for intervention to the Council of Ten on 14 and 15 February. At the first meeting he got nowhere in face of President Wilson's opposition.[118] But the following day, with Lloyd George in London, President Wilson on his way back to Washington and Orlando off to Rome, Clemenceau was the only senior statesman present when Churchill, more forcefully than before, pressed for an ultimatum to the Bolsheviks and preparations for large-scale military intervention. That very day the Prinkipo conference was to have taken place, but as Churchill observed, since none of the White forces was prepared to meet the Bolsheviks, negotiations were out of the question.

Churchill obtained Clemenceau's and Sonnino's backing for military intervention, but Sir Arthur Balfour and Colonel Edward House, standing in for President Wilson, entered reservations.[119] Meanwhile Lloyd George, informed of developments in Paris, privately upbraided Churchill for his unauthorized initiative while letting it be known that he would countenance no action before he returned on the 28th.[120] Churchill, deeply frustrated at the Allies' appeasement of the Bolsheviks, appealed to Lloyd George to reconsider his decision,[121] and was present on 27 February when Clemenceau again put the case for military intervention. This time Churchill said little, leaving Clemenceau to confront a reluctant House. Despite his blunt request that the United States should stand aside and allow Europe to act, the Council merely referred the issue back to military advisers for further study.[122] Three weeks later it came up again in a different form when Marshal Foch presented plans to transform the Polish and Roumanian armies into effective instruments for containing the Bolshevik advance. But Lloyd George, who was now present, impatiently dismissed the plans. Foch, he said, was seeking 'the perpetuation of a great mischief'.[123]

Two days later, Jules Cambon, the French diplomat who chaired the conference's commission on Polish affairs, presented its report on the future Polish-German frontier to the Council. Despite the fact that the commission, including the British representative, James Headlam-Morley, had unanimously agreed to the report, Lloyd George vigorously rejected this as well. Referring to the proposed inclusion of Danzig and Marienwerder in Poland, he warned that far too many Germans would fall under Polish jurisdiction. Not only would this violate the Fourteen Points, he claimed, but also that Germany was unlikely to sign a treaty that caused it such offence. Even if it were forced to do so, the result would be to store up trouble for the future: the equivalent of the prewar Alsace-Lorraine issue in the East.[124] The commission reconvened, and on 22 March Cambon appeared before the Council to present its slightly modified report. Once again, the British representative on the commission had endorsed the report, and once again Lloyd George refused to budge. The proposed corridor, giving Poland access to the sea, was bound to antagonize Germany, he warned. 'To add this corridor to Poland is simply to create another Alsace Lorraine.'[125] Clemenceau raised the Bolshevik issue again on 27 March, when he called on Marshal Foch to present the Council of Four with a modified plan for military assistance to Poland and Roumania. With Bolsheviks installed in Budapest and support for them increasing in Vienna, Slovenia and elsewhere, Foch urged the erection of a military barrier behind which Bolshevik influence could be suppressed. By now, however, President Wilson was back from America, and with Lloyd George's support he firmly rejected Foch's plan. The most they would agree to was limited assistance to Poland alone.[126]

The opposition that Wilson and Lloyd George put up to further military intervention against the Bolsheviks should be seen in the context of their attitude towards Eastern Europe as a whole. Differences between them were apparent, notably over Poland, for which Wilson displayed markedly greater sympathy than did Lloyd George. But neither man regarded Eastern Europe as an essential component of the international order. For Lloyd George and, it seems, Wilson and most of their colleagues, the Slavic region formed the lowest branch of the European racial tree. They recognized that there were talented Slav artists, musicians and scientists, but they nevertheless regarded them as a race driven by its emotions which made it prone to excesses and incapable of governing itself let alone others. They therefore sympathized with Germans who abhorred the thought of their countrymen being forced to live under the Polish flag. As a Foreign Office official warned in

March 1919 with regards to Danzig, placing Germans under Polish government 'would be like handing over a Scottish town to its Irish population.'[127]

The pervasiveness of this prejudice led one independent British expert to protest to London. British colleagues, he wrote, should not be so ready to assume that Germany was the sole bearer of civilization in Eastern Europe or to ignore the cultural accomplishments of the Slavic people.[128] His complaint was ignored. Lloyd George observed, 'The Poles are a hopeless set of people: very like the Irish .... They have quarrelled with every one of their neighbours...and they are going to be beaten.'[129] Cecil made the same comparison and similarly suggested that Poles understood only force: 'Slavs', he wrote, referring to the Poles, 'have always seemed to me to be a kind of orientalised Irish. They demand more than they expect to get and they rather respect a man or a country which declines to yield to their unreasonable demands.'[130] General Smuts, intensely pro-German and anti-Slav, drew on his South African experience to assert with equal condescension that the Poles were 'kaffirs'.[131] This led them to conclude that it was pure folly to allow Poles control over their Germanic neighbours, and appropriate for Germany to extend its influence eastwards so long as this could be done without war.[132] Foch all too presciently warned against this British view. 'They do not understand. ... It is serious. If Poland falls, Germany and Russia will combine. You will have a worse position than in 1914'.[133] But Hankey, the most influential of British administrators, encouraged Lloyd George to share his 'dislike and contempt' for the Poles, and to 'orientate our policy so as to make Germany and not Poland the barrier between eastern and western civilisation.'[134]

As for Russia, the Slavic great power, British and American statesmen believed it had never enjoyed effective government except with the discipline provided by Germans or Jews. In keeping with this view, they regarded the Bolshevik revolution as a sort of Jewish-led revolt of the masses.[135] During negotiations at the peace conference, they used the spectre of Bolshevism overtaking Germany, Europe or the whole of the West as a means of dissuading France from persisting with sanctions against Germany. Lloyd George eventually warned of a Bolshevik onslaught organized and led by officers of a disaffected Germany, in his attempt to bring the French to heel.[136] But neither he nor President Wilson was able to grasp Lenin's doctrine or ambitions. They found it impossible to think of Bolshevism as anything more than an uprising against Tsarist absolutism, which would lose its revolutionary impetus once Russia established representative institutions. On one occasion Wilson drew a parallel between the Bolsheviks and the independence movement in colonial Virginia.[137] Several times Lloyd George equated the Bolshevik revolution with the great French revolution of 1789, not only in its excesses but also in its virtual inevitability and progressive impulse.[138] He associated those most anxious to crush it with the reactionary Right, and assumed that the only countries in serious danger of contagion were those still dominated by an *ancien régime*. Thus he minimized the significance of Bolshevik control of Hungary with the comment that 'there are few countries so much in need of revolution.'[139]

Appearing before the Council of Ten in January, Joseph Noulens, the former French ambassador to Petrograd, presented an acutely accurate report on Bolshevik leadership, its ambitions for world revolution and its attitude towards the bourgeois powers of the West:

> It meant to conquer the world, and to make peace with no Governments save Governments representing only the labouring classes. It stated openly that the only legitimate war was civil war. It would respect no League of Nations. Should we even be weak enough to undertake any agreements with such a Government, they would, on the very next day, send among us propagandists, money, and explosives. According to their open professions, they intended to spread revolution by every means.[140]

Lloyd George dismissed this as scaremongering. Disliking the message, he attacked the messenger, claiming that Noulens was a mouthpiece for reactionary opinion in Russia and France who had spent too long among the Whites. He was 'a shallow and unintelligent partisan rather than a witness. He repeated the gossip and hearsay of the Parisian journals of the extreme Right about the horrors of Bolshevism.'[141] French policy, Lloyd George believed, was driven by the frustrations of small investors whose Russian bonds had become worthless.[142] And on more than one occasion he deprecated Allied military intervention in Eastern Europe on the grounds that countries requiring foreign intervention to be saved from Bolshevism scarcely deserved saving.[143] Like Wilson, he strongly suspected the French of raising the spectre of Bolshevism simply to justify arming the Poles and enabling them to expand their territory at the expense of Soviet Russia and Germany. The most urgent need, in his and Wilson's opinion, was the demarcation of Germany's frontiers, which would appease opinion in Germany and discourage it from turning to Bolshevism. They therefore became steadily more annoyed with France for its policy of siding with Poland over the fate of Danzig, West Prussia, the Polish Corridor and Upper Silesia.

No doubt France was seeking to build up Poland at Germany's expense, and no doubt this would sow dragon's teeth for future harvest. But for his part Lloyd George grossly exaggerated the injustice done to Germany. The territorial settlement left twice as many Poles under German jurisdiction as it placed Germans under Polish jurisdiction.[144] Besides, by any reasonable calculation Germany stood to lose nothing like 13 per cent of its territory and 10–13 per cent of its population that the Germans claimed and English language accounts henceforth uncritically accepted. As illustrated by the statistics cited in Table 1.1, actual losses were barely 9.5 per cent of the territory and less than 2 per cent of the German population.[145] Nor did Lloyd George or Wilson address the question that Clemenceau and Foch insistently put, namely how to maintain stability in postwar Europe if Germany, with nearly all the war-making potential of 1914, remained determined to re-draw the national borders of Europe and enjoyed the immense additional advantage of being able to dominate weak states on its eastern frontier unhindered by a powerful Soviet Russia. To Balfour's suggestion that Britain should be content to

Table 1.1 Germany's territorial and population losses (in Europe) as the result of the peace settlement, 1919

In 1914, Germany comprised 540,857.5 square kilometres, and at the last prewar census (1 December 1910) a population of 64,925,993. Most of its losses due to the settlement can be calculated in a crude way from the 1910 census and the 8 October 1919 census.[a] They include

Territory transferred from Germany post First World War	Territory in square kilometres	Population transferred
1. Eupen-Malmédy and the district of Moresnet transferred to Belgium	989.1	60,924
2. Most of West Prussia and Posen, transferred to Poland	46,791.6	3,491,967
3. Elsass-Lothringen (Alsace-Lorraine), transferred to France	14,528.5	1,874,014
4. Northern Schleswig transferred to Denmark	3,983.4	166,895[b]
5. Memel, transferred from East Prussia to Lithuania	13.7	141,000
6. Upper Silesia transferred to Poland and the Hultschin district transferred to Czechoslovakia[c]	3,227.5	857,761[d]
Total	**69,533.9 (13.0%)**	**6,591,561 (10.2%)**

On this basis, the total losses arising from the Peace Settlement are 69,533.9 square kilometres of land and 6,591,561 inhabitants, or 13 per cent of the land and 10.2 per cent of the people.

Practically all accounts of the Peace Settlement present statistics of this order. Nonetheless, they greatly overstate Germany's losses, not least because much of the land and people in question had been acquired in the previous half century by conquest and were not historically or ethnically German. The Nazis themselves made little protest against the loss of Elsass-Lothringen or northern Schleswig. Instead, with the exception of Eupen-Malmédy, they concentrated their anger upon losses in the East.[e] Thus, even on the most generous basis, Germany's 'undeserved' losses comprised:

Territory transferred from Germany post First World War	Territory in square kilometres	Population transferred[f]
1. Eupen-Malmédy and the district of Moresnet transferred to Belgium	989.1	60,924
2. Most of West Prussia and Posen, transferred to Poland	46,791.6	3,491,967

Continued

Table 1.1 Continued

Territory transferred from Germany post First World War	Territory in square kilometres	Population transferred[f]
3. Upper Silesia transferred to Poland	3,227.55	857,761
4. Memel, transferred to Lithuania	13.7	141,000
Total	51,022.0 (9.4%)	4,550,652 (7.0%)

On this basis, Germany's losses arising from the Peace Settlement are 51,022.0 square kilometres of land and 4,550,652 inhabitants, or 9.4 per cent of the land and 7 per cent of the people.

However, even this overstates Germany's losses for three reasons. First, a large fraction of the people transferred from German sovereignty in the East were non-Germans. Second, when territory was transferred some of the ethnic Germans refused to be transferred with it and instead moved elsewhere in Germany. This is indicated by the fact that the population of regions of Prussia not directly affected by the settlement grew only slightly faster than the rest of Germany between 1905 and 1910, but much faster than the rest of Germany (7 per cent versus 4.6 per cent) between 1910 and 1925. Third, the official German statistics on which practically all historians rely, may substantially overstate the German losses. In the words of Britain's leading authority in 1919, 'The figures of the 1910 census are demonstrably falsified, and even if they were accurate they would describe a state of things artificially created by the policy of ruthlessly suppressing the Polish language and of substituting German for Polish peasants on the land by the expenditure of public money to which the Poles as taxpayers are compelled to contribute, and this on top of 'the more or less natural advantages of the dominant people...especially the presence of large numbers of German officials (railway porters and post office clerks, &c.) and their families'.[8] But even if we leave aside the population 'gains' from the transferred regions, take into account only the non-Germans involved in the territorial changes, and accept the official German figures, the 'undeserved' losses become:

Territory transferred from Germany post First World War	Territory in square kilometres	Population transferred
1. Eupen-Malmédy and the district of Moresnet transferred to Belgium	989.1	60,924
2. Most of West Prussia and Posen, transferred to Poland	46,791.6	743,000
3. Upper Silesia, transferred to Poland	3,227.55	310,000
4. Memel, transferred to Lithuania	13.7	71,200
Total	51,022.0 (9.4%)	1,185,124 (1.8%)

Continued

Table 1.1 Continued

On this basis, Germany's losses amounted to 51,022.0 square kilometres of land and 1,185,124 inhabitants, or 9.4 per cent of its land and 1.8 per cent of its (prewar) population: a far cry from the 13 and 10–13 per cent invariably claimed elsewhere.

Notes:
a) Statisches Jahrbuch für das Deutsches Reich, 1920, tables pp. 1, 2; ibid., 1925, tables pp. 1, 2.
b) On the population of Memel, see Dawson, Germany under the Treaty, p. 244.
c) The Hultchin district of Prussia that went to Czechoslovakia comprised approximately 61 square kilometres and 70,000 people in 1919: Dawson, Germany under the Treaty, pp. 230–1.
d) (911,542 inhabitants adjusted downwards by 5.9 per cent, being the average population growth of German territory not directly affected by the Peace Settlement in the 1919–25 period): Statisches Jahrbuch für das Deutsches Reich, 1933, tables p. 5.
e) See for instance, Berber (ed.), Das Diktat von Versailles, pp. 684, 685f. and passim.
f) Statistics from Temperley (ed.), A History of the Peace Conference of Paris, ii, pp. 175, 190–1, 205–6, 214–5 tables i, ii, iii; Donald, The Polish Corridor and the Consequences, pp. 22–3 and passim; Morrow with Sieveking, The Peace Settlement in the German-Polish Borderlands, pp. 108 table, 183 table, 237 table xvi, 255.
g) BDFA, Pt. II, ser. 1, vol. 8, no. 83, H.J. Paton memorandum, 27 Feb. 1919. h) See f. 150.

see an imperialist Germany expanding eastwards, where resistance was likely to be weaker than in 1914, Lloyd George made no comment.[146]

Lloyd George and Wilson were scarcely alone in refusing to address this issue. It would take until 1939 for British statesmen to recognize the importance of Eastern Europe in the international balance of power, and American statesmen even longer. This, however, was only part of the Anglo-Saxon powers' broader failure to support the construction and maintenance of a European security framework.

1.8 Stability in the West

Woodrow Wilson, addressing the French Senate on 20 January 1919, described France as serving humanity's cause in the recent war from its stand on the Rhine, 'the frontier of freedom'.[147] Senators in the *Palais du Luxembourg* were delighted with his words, since they described precisely how they viewed themselves, and they encouraged Clemenceau to hope that Wilson as well as British leaders would support his proposals to establish a security frontier on the Rhine. Marshal Foch meanwhile had drafted the paper on the future of the Rhineland he had promised in London,[148] and Clemenceau circulated it to other delegates, although, old Dreyfusard that he was, he refused the Catholic Foch permission to present it to the conference.[149] Debate on the Rhineland only began on 25 February, with the circulation of a second paper drafted by André Tardieu at Clemenceau's request.[150] Since this constituted the clearest statement of French thinking on postwar security, it deserves careful examination.

Foch, in his 10 January memorandum, emphatically disavowed any interest on France's part in annexing the Rhineland; his earlier proposal that troops might be raised in the region for the defence of France and its allies did not appear in this document. But he also made clear that, with Russia lost from the balance of power, France would not under any circumstances allow the Rhineland to be returned to Germany.[151] Tardieu, alive to the obligations created by the Fourteen Points, affirmed that no change in sovereignty would take place without the express approval of the Rhineland's inhabitants. Tardieu also stressed the Allies' common interest in a different régime in the Rhineland. The region had on several occasions become a staging-ground for invasions, most recently in 1870 and 1914. On the last occasion France had paid an immense price to repel the invaders, but the German armies had come perilously close in 1914 to seizing the North Sea and Channel ports, which would have made it practically impossible for Britain and the overseas powers to contribute to stemming German aggression. They therefore had a common interest in ensuring that the Rhineland and the bridgeheads on the right bank of the river were removed from German hands.

> [I]t is not a question of strengthening one Ally or another; rather it is a question of removing Germany's capacity to create damage by imposing conditions that are essential to the common security of the Western democracies and their overseas Allies and Associates, at the same time as safeguarding the very existence of France. It is not a question of annexing a single grain of German soil; it is a question of removing Germany's offensive capacity.[152]

Tardieu then reviewed the three solutions favoured by Britain and the United States. The first, demilitarization of the Rhineland, was simply inadequate. The elaborate railway network on the right bank would enable Germany swiftly to concentrate forces at the bridgeheads and retake the left bank before the Allies could react. Besides the left bank, the Allies must also retain control of the bridgeheads, and especially if they were to be able to assist Poland, Czechoslovakia or Yugoslavia in the event of German aggression. The second alternative, German disarmament, was fine in theory, but would in practice require greater inspection and control than Germany or any other great power would tolerate for more than a few years. Thereafter Germany could surreptitiously manufacture large quantities of arms in hundreds of locations, and in addition to its several million war veterans, it could soon train several million more. The third alternative, reliance upon the League of Nations, was equally unrealistic since Wilson had rejected French proposals to equip the League with a military capability, and collective security through the League could scarcely be arranged in time to deter a sudden act of aggression. The United States could respond to a foreign threat only at the end of a process starting with a decision by the executive committee of the League, followed by the convening of Congress, if not already in session, the introduction of a resolution and debate, and finally the mobilization and transport of troops: a process likely to take weeks if not months. The same was true for a British response. Had such an elaborate procedure been required in 1914, the British Expeditionary Force could not possibly have been despatched in time to make a difference. In that case the French army would have been outflanked at Charleroi on 24 August and the war lost.[153]

Tardieu posed the question whether a change in the status of the Rhineland would destabilize international relations by creating a source of frustration akin to Alsace-Lorraine before the war. His own answer was firmly negative. On the contrary, by reducing Germany's war-making capacity, it would conduce to stability and peace, and was thus fully compatible with the principles of the new League of Nations. In the postwar period, Germany without 'Posen', Schleswig and Alsace-Lorraine, but with the support of 7 million German Austrians, would have a population of 68 million, compared with only 42 million for France, Belgium and Luxembourg. And even this understated the imbalance, for France had lost its great eastern ally Russia to the Bolsheviks, and the fractious secession states could never be expected to provide a similar counterweight. In the meantime Germany would have twice the number of militarily trained men and each year its growing population would provide three times the number of young men of military age as France. This would be a permanent source of instability, if something was not done to right the balance. By removing the Rhineland from German control, the ratio would still be 62 million to 42 million.

Finally, Tardieu addressed the question of the Rhinelanders themselves and their willingness to accept separation from Germany. In a few sentences he reviewed their origins as a Celtic people *'latinisés par Rome'*, and their reluctant acceptance of Prussian rule since 1815. He accepted that they were German by language and memory. But he asserted that their present reluctance to return to Prussian-dominated rule or face socialist domination created a suitable climate for independence. The Allies could foster it by promising an end to military service, relief from war debts, enhanced trade relations and the prospect of self-government under the protection of the League of Nations.

With the benefit of hindsight it is clear that the French Rhineland proposal stood no chance of finding its way into the peace treaty. Members of the American delegation had responded with outrage to early reports of French policy, betraying sympathy for Germany and loathing of France that made any meeting of minds on security unlikely. General Tasker Bliss, Wilson's chief military adviser, was convinced that the French sought the 'complete and lasting ruin' of Germany, a policy he described in January 1919 as 'little less than ... insanity.'[154] Charles Seymore, a Yale historian and expert adviser to the American delegation, betrayed a similarly caricatural notion of France. Days after arriving in Paris, he wrote home that 'French politicians and functionaries as a class are absolutely selfish in their national aims and unscrupulous in their methods; and the influence of finance and business in politics, while concealed, is enormous and at times disgusting.'[155] Herbert Hoover, the American food administrator and recently appointed director-general of relief in Europe, betrayed equal hostility towards the French when they insisted upon maintaining the blockade on Germany, a prejudice he still harboured ten years later when he entered the White House.[156] Wilson in private displayed a similar prejudice, which grew into a near obsession as the conference dragged on. On 21 January 1919, just a day after his address to the French Senate, he described the French public to the British journalist A. G. Gardiner as 'hysterical' about Germany, which, in his opinion, posed no further threat to France, and put it down to the 'militarism' that still dominated French society.[157] Returning from the meeting of the Supreme War Council on 8 February, he described Clemenceau as 'unreliable – tricky – not trustworthy or truthful.'[158] In a private conversation with Wilson few days later, William Rappard, the Swiss statesman, was startled to hear him pour out his hatred of the French, who were 'stupid, petty, insane'.[159]

Similar prejudice was equally common in post-Armistice Britain.[160] Four and a half years as Allies had done little if anything to alter British assumptions that France was racially different and morally inferior, a rival for empire and a potential enemy. True, some Frenchmen were highly intelligent and even very likeable, but as one nation to another Britain and France remained far apart.[161] General Sir Henry Wilson, who spoke fluent French and sided with Marshal Foch on most security issues, was a rare exception.[162] Field-Marshal Douglas Haig occupied the opposite Francophobic extreme, which had become so marked by the end of the war that he refused even to attend the reception for Foch when he visited London. He had frequently complained of French cowardice and mendacity during the war: 'What Allies to fight with!'[163] The British army had won the war, he recorded in his diary, and he would not take part 'in any triumphal ride with Foch, or with any pack of foreigners, through the streets of London, mainly in order to add to Lloyd George's importance'.[164]

Lloyd George himself candidly acknowledged to Clemenceau after the peace conference that France and Britain would always remain enemies.[165] Smuts, who advised Lloyd George at the peace conference, displayed a similar prejudice against the French and an equally strong sympathy towards the Germans.[166] Sir George Graham, the chargé d'affaires at the Paris embassy, confidently predicted that the French, by occupying the Rhineland, would 'have Germany at their mercy for all time; and then, as sure as winter follows summer, they, feeling themselves absolute masters of the Continent, will turn round on us.'[167] Even reputed Francophiles such as Sir Eyre Crowe, the assistant under-secretary at the Foreign Office, and Lord Hardinge, the permanent under-secretary and from November 1920 ambassador to France, betrayed a deep-seated prejudice against France. Crowe had been the most consistent advocate of closer Franco-British relations before the war, and was to remain so afterwards. Nevertheless, he shared the view that innate flaws in the French character made cooperation with them very difficult. 'It arises partly from the traditions of French diplomacy', he wrote in a paper circulated to the Cabinet after the war,

> but still more from the mentality of the French race, and it represents a difference both of outlook and methods, as compared with the British, which is fundamental. Perhaps the difference can be best defined as a contrast between the British habit of endeavouring to deal with the current problems of diplomacy, as they arise, on the merits of the particular case, and the French practice of subordinating even the most trivial issues to general considerations of expediency, based on far-reaching plans for the relentless promotion of French prestige and the gratification of private, generally monetary and often sordid, interests

or ambitions, only too frequently pursued with a disregard of ordinary rules of straightforward and loyal dealing which is repugnant and offensive to normal British instincts. It is this divergence of national character and conduct flowing from them which has made consistent co-operation between British and French Governments and agents always difficult, and sometimes impossible . . . . [I]t cannot honestly be said that there is a good prospect of the French changing their ways in this respect, however sincere their friendship for this country. They are not really conscious of the extent of their shortcomings and therefore not amenable to argument or capable of responding to remonstrance.[168]

Lord Hardinge also spoke of the French as an arrogant, chauvinist, imperialist race, who were incapable of showing gratitude to Britain for coming to their help in 1914.[169] As he commented to Curzon after the war, the French were a Latin race, and '[w]ith Latin races it is essential to stand up to them, the only thing that really matters being the question of form.'[170] He, Crowe and some colleagues in the Foreign Office were prepared to overlook this in the interests of the Franco-British *Entente*. But for other British contemporaries the same attitude was part of a loose, circular argument, which assumed that the French should be grateful to Britain for saving them from defeat in the recent war, and concluded that their absence of gratitude demonstrated their unworthiness and justified Britain in withdrawing from any further Continental commitment.[171] The assumption was manifestly false, since Britain had entered the war not as an act of generosity to anyone, but in fulfilment of its own strategic imperatives, which remained unchanged by the war. But evidently the temptation to ignore these realities was almost irresistible, not only for politicians but also more surprisingly for many of their senior advisers. It then provided justification for lining up with President Wilson against the French policy of containing Germany and in favour of appeasement.[172]

Wilson was still in the United States, leaving Colonel House to stand in for him in Paris when Tardieu's memorandum on the Rhineland was circulated. House had earlier opposed France's Rhineland policy, but he knew and liked Tardieu since the latter's time as French high commissioner in Washington in the latter part of the war, and almost uniquely in the American camp he was well-disposed towards France.[173] When Tardieu persuaded him that the French Rhineland scheme could be squared with the Fourteen Points, he agreed to support the creation of a separate Rhineland republic.[174] This put Lloyd George on the spot. He continued to hold out against the French proposal, but Clemenceau on 12 March angrily demanded to know what alternative he was prepared to accept.[175] Afraid that the United States was on the verge of giving way and at loggerheads with the French over reparations, he turned to the idea of granting France a security guarantee, first proposed by the *Times* a few weeks earlier.[176] Wilson, who disembarked at Brest on 13 March, got wind of developments and ordered an immediate halt to negotiations. The following day, Lloyd George called on Wilson and soon persuaded him to join Britain in offering Clemenceau a guarantee against unprovoked aggression as an alternative to his Rhineland scheme. They then met Clemenceau at the Hôtel Crillon where they made their offer. As an added inducement, Lloyd George also volunteered to build a Channel tunnel, to overcome the bottleneck that had slowed the movement of British arms and men to the Continent during the recent war.[177]

Clemenceau took three days to consult his closest colleagues, Paul Pichon, the foreign minister, Louis Loucheur and Tardieu, before responding.[178] While pleased with the proposed guarantees, he insisted upon additional safeguards against German aggression. As he pointed out, the guarantees ensured France's ultimate survival in the event of another war. But since it would take months, if not years, for Britain and the United States actually to send forces, France must secure its frontiers against invasion. This led to another fortnight of exceptionally intense negotiations during which Clemenceau requested sovereignty over the Saar and the permanent occupation of the Rhineland as well as pleading for an economically and militarily viable Poland. The claim to the Saar infuriated Wilson, who regarded as spurious the French historical and economic justifications, and got up merely to justify its crude imperialism. Lloyd George, while expressing some appreciation of the economic case, sided with Wilson.[179]

On 31 March, Clemenceau secured another audience for Foch who repeated his arguments for the Rhineland, to no avail.[180] Utterly out of patience with French security demands and exhausted by the negotiations, Wilson signalled his readiness to abandon the conference on 6 April by calling for the USS Washington to proceed to Brest.[181] Thereupon Clemenceau, seeing no hope of gaining sovereignty over the Saar, agreed to League administration of the territory and a referendum after 15 years to decide on its future. In the event that the Saarlanders voted to rejoin Germany, France would dispose of its ownership of the Saar's mines on terms defined by an arbitral committee.[182]

The fate of the Rhineland involved another week of bitter wrangling before a compromise was reached. Lloyd George wanted the military occupation to last only two years; Clemenceau held out for an indefinite occupation – until, as Foch said, the Germans had a 'change of heart'.[183] Lloyd George appealed to Clemenceau to rely upon the Anglo-American guarantees and not encroach upon German sovereignty. If Germany had known that Britain and the United States had guaranteed Belgium and France in 1914, he insisted, it would never have gone to war. Foch at Clemenceau's request explained that, on the contrary, Germany might have been tempted into sudden aggression, so as to destroy France before the Anglo-Saxon powers could intervene. This prompted Lloyd George and Wilson to ask how Germany could possibly raise the large army this would require without alerting the other powers. Clemenceau and Foch replied that Germany was a large country and could quite well disguise its preparations until they were already advanced, especially as the Anglo-Saxon powers opposed the inspections necessary to monitor secret rearmament.[184]

Clemenceau held out until 15 April, when Wilson acquiesced in a compromise that went some way to satisfy French demands. The Rhineland and a 50 km strip along the right bank of the Rhine would be permanently demilitarized, and the region would be occupied by Allied forces and evacuated in stages over 15 years, with the proviso that the occupation might be prolonged if Germany failed to meet its reparation commitments.[185] Eventually Clemenceau also secured agreement on, among other things, a reduction in the German peacetime army from 140,000 to 100,000 long-serving troops, the elimination of the high command, heavy weapons and half the munitions initially proposed, and the creation of Allied military, naval and air control commissions to monitor German disarmament. But he was uneasily aware that they lacked the certainty of permanently removing the Rhineland from German sovereignty. Unfortunately for him, the British and American guarantees were even less substantial than he imagined.

To Clemenceau it seemed almost self-evident that Britain and France shared a common interest in containing Germany, and that Britain would not wish to repeat the tragic mistake of 1914 when it had left this unclear until the German offensive was already underway. He had sought but failed to secure British and American agreement on the precise operation of the guarantees, including what would be considered a *casus belli* or 'unprovoked aggression', and whether this would include a breach of the disarmament terms or the demilitarized zones on either side of the Rhine.[186] Nevertheless, he appears to have regarded the guarantees as important symbols of support: confirmation that Britain and the United States recognized their common security interests.[187] From all the evidence, however, Lloyd George proffered the British guarantee to France merely as a bargaining ploy and nothing more. He did not even mention his intention to offer the guarantee to Hardinge, the permanent under-secretary of the Foreign Office, Balfour, the foreign secretary, or other members of the Imperial War Cabinet.[188] Nor did he consult on the additional inducement of the Channel tunnel, which Churchill had casually suggested a fortnight before.[189] Initially he said nothing about making the British guarantee conditional upon an American commitment, and it was not until the final drafting session that he slipped in the word 'only', which enabled Britain to back out of its commitment when the United States Senate failed to ratify the Treaty.[190] But this was at most a form of reinsurance against liability, for he had kept the wording of the guarantee sufficiently imprecise to ensure that future British governments would remain free to decide how to apply it. Meanwhile he could use the guarantee to secure a variety of French concessions in the remaining weeks of the conference. Indeed, with his offer of the guarantee he initiated a routine that was to become a feature of Franco-British relations throughout the interwar years, when Britain's promise of support was repeatedly proffered as a means of inducing France to acquiesce in appeasing Germany. Curzon acknowledged the stratagem when he observed to Lord Grey that a British guarantee might be even better without a parallel American commitment.

> France...would then be exclusively dependent on our own. You know the immense importance in which [France] holds this guarantee Treaty, and the unceasing terror in which she lives concerning her eastern border.... [I]t might be a great advantage to us to have this lever in our possession, and to be able to

use it to obtain an equitable solution of some of the problems [in the Near and Middle East] with which we are confronted.[191]

President Wilson appears to have offered the American guarantee for essentially similar reasons. Like Lloyd George, he was impatient with France's Rhineland proposal which appeared to him unreasonable and provocative. The guarantee was intended to persuade Clemenceau to abandon it without adding to America's liabilities. Wilson, too, had refused Clemenceau's request to define precisely the terms of the guarantee,[192] while acknowledging to Lloyd George that it 'amounted to very little more than Article 10 of the Covenant.'[193] Indeed, he added the rider that the guarantee would come into operation only after a decision by the League, and furiously protested when Senator Bourgeois sought to reopen the question of equipping the League with a military coordinating agency.[194] Clemenceau thus emerged from the deliberations with a number of minor safeguards against German aggression. But his great hope of securing an informal, if not formal, alliance with Britain and if possible the United States went unrealized. He was anxious to believe that the guarantees bore at least a symbolic importance for France. But the circumstances in which they were offered left no room for doubt that they were valueless.

1.9   Reparations, war debts and financial reconstruction

In light of the importance that reparations and war debts assumed in the 1920s, it is remarkable that the financial terms of the peace settlement were taken up only in the latter stages of the conference. Typically of statesmen at this time, Lloyd George, Clemenceau and Wilson were preoccupied with politics and security, and showed scant interest in financial or economic issues. But it is also true that the financial problems that were to dog the European countries after the war were not immediately apparent. When President Wilson publicly affirmed in his Fourteen Points that there would be 'no annexations, no contributions, no punitive damages', neither Lloyd George nor Clemenceau signalled their disagreement.[195] It was only at the last minute that they persuaded Wilson to include an addendum to the section of the Armistice that referred to the restoration of all Belgian and French territories, which stated: 'By it they understand that compensation will be made by Germany for all damage done to the civil population of their Allies and their property by the aggression of Germany by land, by sea, and from the air.'[196] After the Armistice they began to encourage hopes that Germany could be made to pay massive compensation to the Allies. Campaigning in the British general election, Lloyd George claimed that Germany would bear 'the full cost of the war', and used phrases such as paying 'to the limit of her capacity', 'obtaining the fruits of victory' and 'the loser pays'.[197] Just before polling day, his colleague, Sir Eric Geddes, memorably declared, 'The Germans, if this Government is returned, are going to pay every penny; they are going to be squeezed as a lemon is squeezed – until the pips squeak. My only doubt is not whether we can squeeze hard enough, but whether there is enough juice.'[198]

Similar claims were made in France. As *Le Matin*, the country's largest circulation paper, put it on the morrow of the Armistice, the Germans 'must learn by the sweat of their brow that one does not violate justice with impunity.'[199] *'Le Boche paiera'*. Yet as late as January 1919, Lloyd George contemplated omitting the chancellor of the exchequer from his re-formed Cabinet, such was the apparent unimportance of finance in political decision-making.[200] It was only in the following weeks, when the United States stopped further credits to the Allied powers, inflation accelerated and pressure mounted for tax reductions along with demands that the government honour its wartime promises of better peacetime conditions, that Lloyd George became seriously exercised about reparations.

When on 21 February deliberations got under way in the conference reparations commission, attention focused on two questions: how much Germany could be expected to pay and what the payments should cover. The British Board of Trade and the Treasury had proposed a total reparation bill of £3 billion and £2 billion respectively. But early in 1919, Lloyd George handed the reparations issue over to Lord Sumner, a law lord, and Lord Cunliffe, the recently retired governor of the Bank of England. The two, who acquired notoriety at the conference as the 'heavenly twins', were already known to favour enormous reparations and now recommended the extraordinary sum of £25 billion.[201] This was intended to cover not only the physical damage directly caused by the war but also separation allowances, pensions for widows, orphans and the severely wounded, and the cost of fighting the war. The French strategy, devised at this time, was to seek payment for direct damages, but not the total cost of the war, since this would reduce France's share of the payments.[202] The British proposal to include pensions and other survivors' benefits nearly doubled the total liability and raised protests from President Wilson and American experts, who constantly warned against over-burdening Germany.

Briefly on 15 March it seemed that a workable solution might emerge when a new committee comprising leading authorities from Britain, France and the United States dismissed the reparations total proposed by the heavenly twins as unrealistic, and advocated a nominal bill of £6 billion.[203] This, they believed, was the maximum that could reasonably be demanded on the basis of the Armistice terms, and the maximum that Germany could or would tolerate paying over 30 years. In fact, the total was considerably smaller than it appeared because the report included the provision that half the bill should be paid in depreciated German currency, and at least £1 billion should be credited to Germany in the first two to three years for the loss of its merchant marine and overseas territories. This would leave the reparations bill only modestly higher than the early recommendations of the Board of Trade and Treasury experts. Wilson, who had consistently advocated moderation, accepted the report. More surprisingly, so too did Lloyd George and Clemenceau. But three days later Lloyd George turned his back on it, recalled Sumner and Cunliffe, and proposed a total that in practice would be three times as much as proposed in the report.[204] Although a new *ad hoc* three-man committee was formed, it did not even suggest a new total when it reported on 25 March, but instead merely set down the three powers' recommendations: for the United States a minimum of £5 billion and a maximum of £7 billion, for France a minimum of £6.2 billion and a maximum £9.4 billion, and for Britain a single figure of £11 billion.[205]

Despite the fact that Britain was now demanding by far the largest reparations total, Lloyd George skilfully turned the tables on the French when the Council of Four resumed deliberations on 23 March. While claiming to be embarrassed by the 'absurd figures' advanced by Sumner and Cunliffe, he argued that the only solution was to leave the final decision on Germany's liability to an expert commission meeting after the conference, when reason might again prevail.[206] Then, when the French prolonged deliberations, he accused them of driving Germany into the arms of the Bolsheviks by their excessive demands, while Wilson, more than ever biased against the French, applauded his appeal for moderation.[207] Immediately, Lloyd George called upon General Smuts, whom Wilson held in high regard, to make the case for including separation allowances and pensions within the reparations bill.[208] Wilson's acceptance of Smuts' argument, which Wilson's biographer describes as 'his most important concession at the conference', shocked his advisers who had expected him to hold out against a large reparations bill.[209] Wilson later explained that he did so simply because America, seeking no reparations for itself, could not properly stand in the Allies' way.[210]

A part of the explanation is almost certainly that Wilson's health had given way under the strain of attempting single-handedly to manage American foreign relations, and he was no longer able to stay the pace set by Lloyd George and Clemenceau.[211] It seems he still assumed that Germany would only pay reparations for a single generation, in which case how they were used could make little difference to Germany's burden. If so, it was an error of the first order to allow Lloyd George to slip in an amendment that removed the time limit on German payments.[212] This was clever of Lloyd George, but it scarcely contributed to resolving the problem. In fact, three crucial questions remained unanswered: what the total reparations bill for Germany would be, how Germany would – or could – pay such a sum, and how the Allies would divide up the payments among themselves, What was more, the question of war debt repayment had not even been formally raised at the conference, let alone answered.[213] The most that could be said is that the three democratic powers had postponed the crisis that was bound to come when it became fully apparent that covering the huge costs of the war through reparations could not be squared with the goal of rapid postwar economic recovery.

The Supreme Economic Council, kept in being after the Armistice, was pulled in different directions by the three leading powers once the conference began. The French delegates sought to convert it into a league of victor powers by maintaining the wartime controls over commodity procurement, to favour their economic recovery while containing German ambitions.[214] The Americans and British initially supported the French proposal, and they soon reached agreement on clauses in the peace treaty that required Germany to grant most-favoured-nation treatment to the Allies while authorizing them to withhold the same treatment from Germany for a five-year period.[215] But in the United States and Britain, opposition soon emerged to controls on foreign trade, and with France rapidly dismantling its own controls, effective constraints upon Germany became impossible.[216] American financial experts, scornful of French and British greed on reparations, had kept quiet on war debts and were now content to concentrate on short-term relief schemes for the Allies and newly created countries.[217] Mounting evidence that Europe's virtual bankruptcy could not be overcome by hand-outs led British experts in early April to propose a thorough assessment of the Continent's reconstruction needs.[218] This was welcomed by the French but flatly turned down by the American delegation's financial advisers.[219] Increasingly worried, British advisers had Lloyd George submit to Wilson a proposal drafted by J. M. Keynes, bearing the longwinded title, 'Scheme for the Rehabilitation of European Credit and for Financing Relief and Reconstruction'.

The Keynes plan, as it became known, was a simple arrangement whereby ex-enemy as well as secession states would issue up to £1.4 billion in bonds. These would be guaranteed by the Allied and Associated powers along with Europe's neutral states, and the majority of funds thus raised would be paid over to the Allied powers as reparations, with the balance – a total of £75 million in the case of Austria, Hungary and Bulgaria, and £200 million in the case of Germany – retained for the purchase of food and raw materials.[220]

Wilson's financial advisers swiftly persuaded him to reject the scheme. They accepted that Europe faced an acute crisis and that in an economically inter-dependent world the United States could not escape the consequences of a European collapse. Nevertheless, they recognized that the American public was deeply ignorant of Europe's plight and becoming rapidly more impatient to see an end to all foreign loans and credits. As Russell Leffingwell, assistant secretary of the Treasury, reminded his colleagues in Paris,

> The American people have lived an existence of provincial isolation for one hundred years; foreign trade has never been an important factor in our commercial or industrial life; we think of ourselves as having performed heroic deeds and borne great sacrifices to save France and Italy and hence England from annihilation by the Hun; and now we are inclined to feel that there is a disposition on Europe's part to exploit our generosity and to take advantage of us in financial matters. Unfortunately though it be, these are...[the]views of the average American.[221]

The Keynes plan had two other strikes against it. One was that Wilson opposed large-scale reparations, and despite its title the plan was a none-too-subtle means of getting the United States to subsidize substantial German reparation payments to the Allied powers. The second was that it offered a public solution to Europe's plight, involving state guarantees, whereas the Americans favoured private or commercial solutions. Thomas Lamont and Bernard Baruch, Wilson's two leading advisers, were from Wall Street, which had profited enormously from war finance operations.

They persuaded themselves that the United States possessed everything needed to contribute to European recovery without being drawn into arrangements that involved governments and would be seen to favour Britain and France more than the United States. American manufacturers were geared up to produce the required exports, the Treasury had just secured Congressional approval for the War Finance Corporation to extend another $1 billion in export guarantees, and Wall Street could supplement this with commercial loans. All that remained was for European governments to restore investor confidence through policies of sound finance, open their markets to international trade and forgo spending their foreign credits on arms or public works (aside from transport facilities).[222]

Unfortunately it was not as simple as this. The European crisis was much more acute than the Americans' liberal market-based solution allowed for, and the same nationalism that made Americans so suspicious of collaborating with Britain and France was equally prominent in Europe. Nations had made huge sacrifices to defend or gain their independence, in some cases failing disastrously. In the absence of a credible international security framework, national defence was bound to take priority over balanced budgets and private investment. The American plan, leaving European reconstruction to capital market solutions, was therefore no more practicable than the Keynes plan. In the event, aside from the provision of further relief supplies, nothing was agreed before the conference ended.

1.10   The beginning of appeasement

The compilation of the draft treaty on 5 May sent a *frisson* through the British delegation, who now saw just how many unwelcome demands the victor powers would impose upon Germany.[223] At a special meeting of the Imperial War Cabinet on 1 June, Smuts denounced the treaty and threatened to leave the conference rather than sign it in its present form. Thereafter he pressured Lloyd George to demand radical revision.[224] Lloyd George defended the treaty, pointing out that it was the product of lengthy, multilateral negotiations and could not be set aside at this stage simply because of British dissatisfaction. Nonetheless, he shared his colleagues' frustration and agreed that a special effort should be made to improve Germany's frontier settlement with Poland.[225] But the actual start of appeasement can be dated somewhat earlier, to the weekend of 21–3 March, when Lloyd George, frustrated by French policy, gathered seven advisers for two days of reflection at Fontainebleau, the grand palace built by Charles V 20 km south-east of Paris. The resulting memorandum, drafted by Philip Kerr and circulated to the French and Americans, has won praise from subsequent generations of historians as an exemplary statement of enlightened internationalism.[226] This was just how Lloyd George and his colleagues regarded it, and it is difficult to quarrel with the principles he professed to apply:

> From every point of view ... it seems to me that we ought to endeavour to draw up a peace settlement as if we were impartial arbiters, forgetful of the passions of war. The settlement ought to have three ends in view. First of all it

must do justice to the Allies, by taking into account Germany's responsibility for the origin of the war, and for the way in which it was fought. Secondly, it must be a settlement which a responsible German Government can sign in the belief that it can fulfil the obligations it incurs. Thirdly, it must be a settlement which will contain in itself no provocations for future wars, and which will constitute an alternative to Bolshevism, because it will commend itself to all reasonable opinion as a fair settlement of the European problem.[227]

In retrospect, it can be said that parts of the Fontainebleau memorandum, in particular its references to the danger of territorial arrangements that placed large numbers of Germans and Magyars under foreign rule, seem almost prescient. Thus it warned that leaving 2.1 million Germans behind the Polish frontier, as proposed by the conference's commission on Polish affairs, must lead sooner or later to war in the East. But what the memorandum failed to acknowledge was that no territorial settlement acceptable to Germany was likely to be acceptable to Poland or Czechoslovakia; and no settlement was likely to last without a security framework that safeguarded Eastern Europe against renewed German aggression, since East and West were two halves of a single whole. The memorandum invited the Continental countries to rely for their security upon the League of Nations and by disarming along with Germany. But as Clemenceau was to point out, this was ingenuous, coming from Britain which insisted upon safeguarding its own independence by maintaining the largest navy in the world. He was equally put out by Lloyd George's warning that France was playing with fire by making excessive demands on Germany. As he observed, Lloyd George's warning would carry more conviction were he prepared to modify Britain's own extensive demands on Germany: its navy, its merchant marine, its colonies, its leased territory in China, its coaling and telegraph stations and other overseas interests. Lloyd George ignored these penalties when he warned:

> The greatest danger that I see in the present situation is that Germany may throw in her lot with Bolshevism and place her resources, her brains, her vast organising power at the disposal of the revolutionary fanatics whose dream is to conquer the world for Bolshevism by force of arms.... [W]ithin a year we may witness the spectacle of nearly three hundred million people organized into a vast red army under German instructors and German generals equipped with German cannon and German machine guns and prepared for a renewal of the attack on Western Europe. This is a prospect which no one can face with equanimity. Yet the news which came from Hungary yesterday shows only too clearly that this danger is no fantasy.[228]

Surprisingly, Clemenceau passed over Lloyd George's reference to Alsace-Lorraine, used to illustrate the consequences of an oppressive peace settlement, which was no less revealing. According to the Fontainebleau memorandum, Prussia-Germany's seizure of these French provinces in 1870 should have made Germany stronger and France weaker, but in fact it had done just the opposite because it led France to create alliances and eventually force the return of the lost provinces:

> France itself has demonstrated that those who say you can make Germany so feeble that she will never be able to hit back are utterly wrong. Year by year France became numerically weaker in comparison with her victorious neighbour, but in reality she became ever more powerful. She kept watch on Europe; she made alliance with those whom Germany had wronged or menaced; she never ceased to warn the world of its danger and ultimately she was able to secure the overthrow of the far mightier power which had trampled so brutally upon her. You may strip Germany of her colonies, reduce her armaments [armies] to a mere police force and her navy to that of a fifth rate power; all the same in the end if she feels that she has been unjustly treated in the peace of 1919 she will find means of exacting retribution from her conquerors.[229]

The last sentence was perhaps fair comment, but the history itself was remarkably self-serving. The assertion that France had grown stronger after 1870 and eventually prevailed over Germany ignored the fact that France had made no effort to regain Alsace-Lorraine for 40 years, and had only done so in a war brought on largely by Germany itself. Put differently, France might never have regained its lost provinces had Germany not made the mistake of going to war in 1914. In fact, Lloyd George was baldly suggesting that the Great War had been a war of revenge instigated by France. It is tempting to treat this as merely an unfortunate use of language, and to assume he meant simply that ill-feeling over the disposition of territories in 1870–1 contributed to the tense atmosphere of the prewar period. But Lloyd George was to repeat the claim many times in the next few years without correction from colleagues that French revanchism over Alsace-Lorraine – not German aggression – caused the war.[230] Placed in context, there are compelling grounds for thinking he believed it.

Summarized briefly, Lloyd George and most of his countrymen had entered the war with great reluctance. The French were their *Entente* partners and deserved some support, but they remained French, Britain's 'hereditary enemy', a race apart, whereas the Germans, notwithstanding the foolishness of the Kaiser and his Prussian high command, were Britain's cousins. Four years after the outbreak of a war which had cost a million casualties, therefore, Britain's educated classes betrayed a scarcely veiled loathing of the French. Being Latins, they were clever, witty, sophisticated, but also self-regarding, mercurial, 'materialistic' and amoral. Had they not employed these qualities to draw Britain into the war in furtherance of their own national interests? In short, had it not been a French war, in which the British, trusting and phlegmatic, had been deceived into fighting their own cousins, to serve French imperialism?[231]

Viewed in this light, Lloyd George's statement was not inappropriately phrased at all. On the contrary, it was fully consistent with much that followed. Among other things, it helps explain the bitterness with which most British statesmen regarded France. It also explains their opposition to severe sanctions against

Germany, despite the million Britons injured or killed fighting the Germans and their allies, their reluctance to believe that Britain and Germany could ever again go to war with one another, and their determination to discourage France from repeating its allegedly aggressive behaviour in Europe. In the words of the Fontainebleau memorandum, the Germans were 'one of the most vigorous and powerful races of the world'. The Latins and Slavs in contrast were represented essentially as troublemakers who could hope for security only once German 'rights' were satisfied.

The Fontainebleau memorandum was revealing in other ways as well. The suggestion that France was now playing a dangerous game in its oppression of Germany hardly squared with the evidence adduced to support it. In the first place, Germany's territorial and population losses in Europe, now blamed on France, were actually much smaller than Britain claimed. In any case, they were largely unavoidable if Wilson's Fourteen Points were to be implemented and the nations surrounding Germany were granted their independence. Second, it was Britain, rather than France, that had insisted upon stripping Germany of its colonies and merchant marine and reducing its navy to that of a fifth-rate power, and Britain that was chiefly responsible for inflating reparation demands. If the Fontainebleau memorandum revealed anything, it was the tendency of British observers to view the recent war as a quarrel among the Continental powers, and to regard Britain as the arbiter, holding the ring rather than bearing its share of responsibility as one of the competitors for empire and markets.

In the final weeks of the conference, Lloyd George strove almost frantically for concessions to Germany and emerged with some success. At his insistence, Clemenceau and Wilson agreed to withhold Upper Silesia and Danzig from Poland, leaving the fate of the former to be decided by a plebiscite and placing the latter under League of Nations control.[232] He also secured their agreement to a reduction in charges for the Allied armies of occupation in the Rhineland, Germany's early admission to the League and several other lesser concessions. This was the start of a process of appeasement that continued throughout the 1920s and 1930s and ended only in June 1940.[233]

1.11 Security unravelled

On 28 June 1919, the German treaty was signed in a brief ceremony in the Hall of Mirrors at the Palais de Versailles where in another ceremony 48 years earlier France's provinces of Alsace and Lorraine were formally annexed by the new Second Reich. In July 1919, the British Parliament approved the treaty as well as the guarantee to France after a brief, almost perfunctory debate.[234] In Paris ratification took only somewhat longer. Within the specially constituted peace treaties commission of the Chamber of Deputies, conservative critics sided with Marshal Foch in denouncing the security provisions of the treaty as gravely deficient. Louis Barthou, the *rapporteur-général*, left no doubt that he shared this view during his blunt interrogation of Clemenceau on 17 July. Louis Marin, another conservative nationalist, proposed that ratification should be set aside until the

US Senate confirmed the Anglo-American guarantee and the terms of the other peace treaties were known. By now the Socialists had also decided to oppose the treaty because it was too repressive. But most parliamentarians took the view that there was nothing to be gained from delay, and despite angry criticism from right and left, the Chamber and the Senate endorsed the treaty in early October.[235]

In the United States it was a different story. By the time Wilson submitted the treaty to Congress for ratification it was already clear that his decision to incorporate the League covenant within it would be a major stumbling block. Since March, Henry Cabot Lodge, the Republican chairman of the Senate committee on foreign relations, had campaigned against participation in the League, claiming that it constituted a dangerous encroachment upon American sovereignty. Lodge made no secret of his personal dislike of Wilson and his intention to turn this issue to advantage against his Democratic opponent. Wilson reciprocated Lodge's enmity, but being absent in Paris until late June and chronically unable to delegate responsibility he found little time to enter into the game of persuasion on Capitol Hill which the occasion demanded.

In fact, the differences between the two men were less than they appeared. Lodge the New Englander and Wilson the Southerner were both keenly interested in the expansion of overseas trade and sought a peace favourable to American commerce.[236] Wilson was no more prepared than Lodge to see the League encroach upon American sovereignty or draw the country into foreign conflicts against its will. No doubt Wilson looked forward to the United States providing moral leadership for the world through the new organization. But he was satisfied that his reservation reaffirming the validity of the Monroe doctrine effectively safeguarded American interests in the Western hemisphere. As for Article X of the covenant, which called upon member states to 'undertake to respect and preserve as against external aggression the territorial integrity and existing political independence of all Members of the League', this constituted in his eyes only a moral commitment, the practical significance of which remained for Washington to determine whenever the occasion arose. As he explained to senators, the United States would decide when and how it applied.[237] The problem nevertheless was the look of the thing, as Lodge appreciated. If the proposed League impressed the Europeans, it was bound to disturb Americans, who feared being further entangled in Europe's wars.

During 1919, Lodge reminded American audiences of the founding fathers' warnings against being drawn into Europe's imperialist conflicts. In a major speech to the Senate in August he returned repeatedly to this theme:

> I think it is just as undesirable to have Europe interfere in American affairs as Mr. Monroe thought it was in 1823, and equally undesirable that we should be compelled to involve ourselves in all the wars and brawls of Europe. ... We shall be of far more value to the world and its peace ... by adhering to the policy of Washington and Hamilton, of Jefferson and Monroe, under which we have risen to our present greatness and prosperity. ... We have interests of our own in Asia and in the Pacific which we must guard upon our own account, but the less we undertake to play the part of umpire and thrust ourselves into European

conflicts the better for the United States and the world. ... The United States is the world's best hope, but if you fetter her in the interests and quarrels of other nations, if you tangle her in the intrigues of Europe, you will destroy her power for good and endanger her very existence.[238]

Lodge's warnings seemed all too salutary in the present climate of opinion, for the spectre of Bolshevism was spreading through the country like a contagion, feeding the suspicions of those who longed to break with Europe. Ironically, A. Mitchell Palmer, Wilson's own attorney general and a supporter of the League proposal, encouraged the Red scare after his own home was bombed in June 1919. With special funds from Congress, he created a General Intelligence (or Radical) Division under a young law-school graduate, J. Edgar Hoover, and in November 1919 he launched spectacular raids on the homes of alleged subversives in New York, casting his net ever wider until January 1920. Amidst almost unprecedented labour unrest and widespread hysteria, over six thousand 'alien radicals', many of them recent arrivals from Europe, were arrested and some six hundred were deported without trial.[239] The resulting clamour obstructed Wilson's efforts to persuade the largely Republican Senate that his League would actually protect the United States from further European troubles. Convinced that he could bring the people around to his project, he embarked on 3 September on an ambitious speaking trip, starting in Minneapolis and continuing through the Republican heartland of the West and South-West, in the hope of impressing his Senatorial opponents with a groundswell of popular support. In the event, he received a decidedly mixed reception, and the strain of 40 speaking engagements in 22 days in the Western heat proved too much. On 25 September at Pueblo, Colorado, he collapsed and shortly afterwards suffered a stroke that left him partially paralysed.[240]

Senators, invited to vote on unconditional approval of the treaty on 19 November, came down decisively against it. Democratic colleagues appealed to Wilson to accept reservations of some sort. But the President so badly misjudged the situation that, in threatening to turn it into a partisan issue in the forthcoming Congressional and Presidential elections, he ensured overwhelming opposition to the covenant and treaty.[241] On 19 March 1920, the Senate voted for a second time on the treaty, this time accompanied by Lodge's strongly worded reservations, but failed to secure the necessary two-thirds majority required for ratification. The outcome confirmed the enduring strength of the isolationist tradition in America, which Lodge had skilfully exploited. Yet it is unlikely that a different result would have made much difference to the subsequent course of events. While the presence of an American on the League Council might have provided some reassurance to other countries, his veto powers would have been governed by the same isolationist tradition that had been the hallmark of American foreign policy since independence.[242] Already disillusionment with the peace-making process was apparent throughout the country. By the time of the second Senate vote in March 1920, interest in the outcome had largely subsided.

Disillusionment was also increasing in Britain. Negative reports of the peace-making process had already begun to circulate when Keynes's *Economic Consequences of the Peace* was published in December 1919 and quickly became an international best seller. Combining acute economic analysis and witty pen portraits, Keynes presented Lloyd George as too clever by half and Wilson as a sanctimonious plodder, out of his depth in negotiations with his more worldly European colleagues. But his most vivid portrait was of Clemenceau, whom he presented as a bloodless zealot, bent upon destroying Germany regardless of the consequences for the rest of the world. Profoundly sympathetic to Germany and scornful of Slavic Poland, Keynes's account helped to convince British observers that France was chiefly responsible for the adoption of an oppressive, unfair and unsustainable treaty.[243]

Robert Graves, the poet and novelist, encountered the strength of feeling among the English educated classes shortly after the war. Having put off university in 1914 and spending much of the war as a junior officer on the Western front, he went up to Oxford after being demobilized in 1919. There he found

> anti-French feeling among most ex-soldiers amounted almost to an obsession. [His contemporary and fellow officer and poet] Edmund [Blunden], shaking with nerves, used to say at this time: 'No more wars for me at any price! Except against the French. If there's ever a war with them, I'll go like a shot.' Pro-German feeling had been increasing. With the war over and the German armies beaten, we could give the German soldier credit for being the most efficient fighting-man in Europe. ... Some undergraduates even insisted that we had been fighting on the wrong side: our natural enemies were the French.[244]

Graves's account of his war experience takes considerable liberties with the truth, but there is no reason to doubt his reference to postwar Oxford and Blunden's reaction to the conflict.[245] G. E. R. Gedye, an officer on the political intelligence staff of the British Army of the Rhine, wrote of the sudden resurgence of 'racial kinship' between Briton and German in the spring of 1919 and a corresponding anger at French mistreatment of their defeated enemy.[246] Numerous accounts confirm that British ex-servicemen's organizations became very anti-French between the wars.[247] The same attitude was reflected in February 1920 when the Oxford University Union supported the motion, 'that the Peace Treaty is an economic disaster for Europe', and another motion in May of that year that 'condemns the vacillating policy of this Government towards Germany, and recommends the immediate re-establishment of cordial relations.'[248] In October 1920, a letter signed by 57 eminent Oxford academics expressed regret at the disruption of relations with their German and Austrian counterparts during the war and appealed to them to help restore 'a wider sympathy and better understanding between our kindred nations.'[249] Despite the controversy stirred up by the letter, students of the Cambridge Union soon adopted the motion 'that this House desires to associate itself with the sentiments expressed in the Oxford letter to the German professors.'[250] Early the following year the Cambridge Union defeated a motion favouring a Franco-British alliance, while not to be outdone the Oxford Union defeated a motion endorsing 'the continuance of an Anglo-French Entente as a guiding principle in British foreign policy.'[251]

The pattern continued in March 1923 when the Oxford Union adopted the motion 'that...the crushing defeat of Germany was a blow both for Europe and for Great Britain'. Several weeks later Union members adopted by 128 to 71 the motion that 'the selfishness of French policy since 1918 has condemned humanity to another World War', and in June, with the prime minister speaking in opposition, they narrowly defeated the motion that 'the Treaty of Versailles is devoid of the principles of wisdom and justice'.[252] Ten years later they voted 275 to 153 that 'this House will in no circumstances fight for its King and Country.'[253] Historians, overlooking the earlier motions, commonly treat this one as evidence of pacifism, which is probably not an accurate and certainly not a complete explanation of the students' motives.[254] As for Edmund Blunden, even while fighting the Germans on the Western Front he believed that 'the War was a great crime'.[255] Siegfried Sassoon, another poet and officer who came to regard the war as a form of madness, confirms that Blunden reacted to it by becoming apologetic towards Germany and that until the very eve of the Second World War he remained 'strongly imbued with the German point of view, and seems unable to realise the meaning of Nazi aims and methods.'[256]

Nor was he alone. The Great War, so far from reducing Anglo-Saxonism and racial conceptions of Europe among the English educated classes had almost certainly increased them.[257] Ernest Barker, professor of politics and principal of King's College London, acknowledged as much in 1925 when he spoke of his unease at the burgeoning of racial theorizing, which was 'greatly in vogue today'.[258] Yet Barker himself accepted that race was the bedrock of politics and international affairs. It was, he wrote, 'of practical importance, and a matter of civic duty to understand the racial basis of national life...and...it may also be no less important, and no less a matter of duty, to control that composition by deliberate policy'.[259] Like other members of England's liberal intelligentsia, he evidently feared that Britain had weakened the Anglo-Saxon bloodstock by allowing itself to be drawn into war alongside the great Latin and Slav powers. Suspicion of France and sympathy for Germany were now commonplace in Britain's liberal circles, even more than among conservatives.

Some of this feeling was evident in the Cabinet committee charged with considering the Channel tunnel proposal, promised by Lloyd George at the peace conference. In light of the experience of the recent war, when congestion in the Channel ports had seriously delayed the movement of men and goods and tied up large amounts of shipping acutely needed elsewhere, expert advice was initially more favourable to a tunnel than it had ever been before. Having opposed a tunnel many times before the war, the army and the navy now supported the proposal, along with City merchants and bankers and a majority of members of the House of Commons.[260] But Hankey, the ubiquitous secretary to the Cabinet and Committee of Imperial Defence (CID) and chairman of the Home Ports Defence Committee, frantically discouraged ministers from supporting the project by warning that it would so expose Britain to Continental threats as to require peacetime conscription and result in 'an enormous increase' in the number of foreigners reaching England's shores.[261] Balfour, chairman of the CID and former prime minister, also warned colleagues against it. Always anxious to present himself as the embodiment of reasonableness, he acknowledged that a tunnel must seem advantageous. But he advanced the seemingly common-sense objection that Britain might become dangerously dependent upon a tunnel and hence vulnerable to the sabotage of this lifeline. To this, he added in cryptic, Rumsfeld-like words:

> The dangers I have adverted to are known, and in a certain sense are calculable, but I am even more afraid of the dangers which are not known and which are not calculable. All that has happened in the last five years in the way of military and naval development – submarines, aircraft and long-range guns – have tended without exception to render the Channel Tunnel a more dangerous experiment. These have all made it more difficult for us to be sure that it will be open when we want it to be open, and closed when we want it to be closed.[262]

Lord Curzon, speaking for the Foreign Office, warned more pointedly of the dangers emanating from France. The British and French were two different races who would never fully understand one another or bury their differences. While for the time being their relations were good, this could not be expected to last, since the French were an inherently self-interested, short-sighted, aggressive people.

> It must be remembered that until a century ago France was England's historic and natural enemy, and that real friendship between the inhabitants of the two countries has always been difficult owing to differences of language, mentality and national character. These differences are not likely to decrease. The slightest incident may arouse the resentment or jealousy of the French and fan the latent embers of suspicion into a flame. ... It is almost certain that we shall have conflicts with France in the future as we have had in the past. ... The Foreign Office conclusion is that our relations with France never have been, are not, and probably never will be, sufficiently stable and friendly to justify the construction of a Channel tunnel, and the loss of the security which our insular position ... continues to bestow.[263]

Lord Hardinge, who appeared before the committee, opposed the tunnel for similar reasons. Queried by a minister who suggested that in the age of aerial flight his fear of invasion through a Channel tunnel was anachronistic or exaggerated, Hardinge replied that air travel was precisely what made it so grave a threat. With aircraft, an enemy could swiftly land troops, seize the British end of the tunnel and open the gates to sudden invasion. Such a claim begged at least two large questions: how an enemy power could without detection concentrate a large military force near the Continental entrance to the tunnel before charging through it? And whether such a threat could plausibly arise except as the culmination of a major crisis, when security precautions would naturally be taken? Clearly the enemy he had in mind was France, since only France could concentrate an invasion force across the Channel without alerting British observers. Indeed, he made no secret of his belief that France remained Britain's 'natural' enemy and a permanent threat to its security.[264] But the very idea that France threatened Britain then or at any time in the foreseeable future beggared belief. Hardinge, as head of the Foreign Office, should have known better than anyone that scarcely a Frenchman in a position of authority was not fixated by the menace of a resurgent Germany just across the Rhine and looked to Britain for help.

Winston Churchill, the minister of war, continued to favour the construction of a Channel tunnel.[265] But Austen Chamberlain, A. C. Geddes, Christopher Addison and most other Cabinet ministers swiftly cooled to the idea on hearing that it would mean a substantial Continental commitment.[266] Though their deliberations were framed almost exclusively in terms of defence, security and economic advantage, they betrayed a deep-seated fear of involvement with their European neighbours. As the author of a recent history of the Channel tunnel observes, their dispassionate language occasionally gave way to a deeper, irrational hostility to a land link to the Continent, which 'revealed the arguments they put forward in their official capacities for the superstructure, the façade, the screens, that they really were.'[267] Colonel Repington, the former military correspondent for the *Times*, now with the *Morning Post*, probably expressed the dominant view of British officialdom when he warned,

> We shall have, as it is, a considerable infusion of Latin blood owing to the large number of marriages contracted by our men in France...The Anglo-Saxon stock is perhaps brightened up, and its womenfolk, at all events, improved in looks, by a Latin alliance once in every half-dozen centuries or so, but enough is as good as a feast, and we can have too much Latin. The Latin races have great qualities of their own, but they are different from ours, and things which alter the character of a stock usually cause it to deteriorate. Our insularity is a heaven-sent benefit, and although when the Tunnels are opened, there will be feasting and speech-making galore and indescribable enthusiasm, many then living will feel it is a very bad day and that we shall have rashly sacrificed our precious insularity for dubious commercial gain.[268]

With the majority of ministers sceptical if not deeply opposed, the Cabinet set aside the tunnel project without a formal decision being taken. Keeping a distance from Europe was now a central strand of both British and American foreign policy.

Thus ended a most remarkably unsuccessful peace-making process. Germany had been punished, yet left potentially stronger than before in a Europe of shattered empires. Meanwhile the Anglo-Saxon powers departed in righteous indignation at France for obstructing what they regarded as their own moderate and enlightened recommendations. What they had not done was to devise a security framework that France, which had suffered invasion, found in the least credible. Indeed, having drafted and signed a treaty, they had proceeded to walk away from it, leaving France alone to uphold it. This was bound to place an acute strain on their mutual relations. It also encouraged German nationalists to exploit divisions within the victors' camp in their pursuit of revision. In turn, it prompted French nationalists to hold the line more rigidly than ever. This left Europe unstable and vulnerable to renewed conflict. It remained to be seen whether the world economic system could function within a security framework as fragile as this.

2
The Emasculation of International Security after the Great War

2.1 Introduction

At 10.30 a.m. on 4 March 1921, a procession of four motor cars set off from the White House along Pennsylvania Avenue to the open space at the eastern end of the Capitol Building where dignitaries were already taking their places in the stands erected for the inaugural ceremonies. The day was bright and cold, and the crowds were as large as on previous occasions. But instead of the usual marching bands, banners and bright uniforms, the event was marked by an absence of colour except for the thousands of national flags carried or draped from buildings. The contrast was also apparent when Warren G. Harding, the president-elect, and Woodrow Wilson, the outgoing president, emerged from the first car, the former vigorous and upright, the latter bent, enfeebled and barely able, even with help, to reach the Senate office where he was to sign the final batch of legislation. Having taken the oath of office, Harding read out his prepared speech, a microphone for the first time enabling it to be heard down the Avenue.[1]

The speech, couched in the inflated language of the hustings and frequently woolly to the point of incoherence, alternated oddly in its assertive and defensive claims. The recent war, Harding asserted, had demonstrated America's readiness to fight for justice and liberty. But it had also reconfirmed the wisdom of the Founding Fathers in opposing political entanglements with Europe. As he put it

> The recorded progress of our Republic, materially and spiritually, in itself proves the wisdom of the inherited policy of non-involvement in Old World affairs. Confident of our ability to work out our own destiny, and jealously guarding our right to do so, we seek no part in directing the destinies of the Old World. We do not mean to be entangled. ... America, our America, the America builded on the foundation laid by the inspired fathers, can be a party to no permanent military alliance. It can enter into no political commitments nor assume any economic obligations which will subject our decisions to any other than our own authority.

The war, along with advancing technology, had brought peoples into closer contact and brought a universal call for solidarity in face of the threat of renewed conflict. America recognized 'the new order in the world, with the closer contacts which progress has wrought.' It was 'ready to encourage, eager to initiate, anxious to participate in any seemly programme likely to lessen the probability of war and promote that brotherhood of mankind which must be God's highest conception of human relationship.' But it had no intention of joining the European powers in maintaining the new order, nor of revisiting the question of joining the League of Nations. Referring to the presidential election, which he had won more decisively than any candidate before him, Harding spoke of 'a referendum' in which the 'popular will of America' had voted decisively against a change in national policy 'where internationality was to supersede nationality.' But this, he averred, 'is not selfishness, it is sanctity. It is not aloofness, it is security. It is not suspicion of others, it is patriotic adherence to the things which made us what we are.' Similarly with external trade, experience had shown that America could not maintain its high standard of living if it allowed the free import of goods. He therefore proposed to raise the tariff at the first opportunity. But in like manner he insisted that this was not a rejection of international solidarity, since of course, 'ties of trade bind nations in the closest intimacy, and none may receive except as he gives.'[2]

2.2   The persistence of isolationism in postwar United States

The 1920 Census, which reported the rise in America's population from 91.6 million to 105.3 million over the previous decade, also affirmed that the country was now predominantly urban, with over 50 per cent of the population living in towns and cities.[3] This along with certain technological and social developments has led historians to stress the differences between prewar and postwar America.[4] Certainly from a demographic and economic standpoint remarkable changes had occurred since the turn of the century. The large corporation, which made its appearance before 1900, now occupied a central place in most sectors of industry and dominated many of them. This was the heyday of mass production industry, where huge economies of scale were obtained by mechanizing manufacturing processes and standardizing products. It was also the moment when the second industrial revolution became most evident: the revolution based upon electrical power, heavy chemicals, the internal combustion engine and new retail distribution techniques; and in practically every one of the new sectors America had captured a lead over its foreign rivals. Between 1911–15 and 1921–5, US exports more than doubled, with the largest increase in manufactured goods.[5] The United States was about to overtake Britain not only as the world's leading exporter of manufactures but also as the greatest trading nation (imports and exports combined). Besides, American manufacturers were no longer content simply to export from the domestic market. In 1914 American direct investment abroad amounted to perhaps $2.6 billion, most of it in the extractive industries or infrastructure development. By 1919, the total had shot up to $3.9 billion, with a large fraction of it now concentrated in manufacturing plant, equipment and distribution networks.[6] In contrast, foreign direct investment in the United States, largely controlled from the City of London, had declined slightly from approximately $1.2 billion in 1914, on account of the financial demands of the war.[7]

With the shift into semi- and fully-manufactured goods, American industry became not only stronger than its rivals but also more visible internationally, with many of its products – Singer sewing machines, Proctor & Gamble detergents, Hoover vacuum cleaners, Remington Rand typewriters, Ford cars, Firestone tires, Texaco and Esso petrol stations – becoming familiar names throughout the world. Cinema dramatically increased awareness of the 'American way of life' and the consumer goods that went with it. The war had constrained the film industry in the European belligerent countries which had largely pioneered it, while in America the industry rapidly expanded. With popular genres identified and the star system established, the 1920s became the first great age of Hollywood. Its films were not only a highly profitable export but also vivid proof to the rest of the world of America's economic ascendancy.

Developments in the financial sector were equally startling. Although American investment banks had grown in size along with industrial corporations in the decades before the war, it was only in the 1920s that concentration within the banking sector yielded the modern corporate structure centred on Wall Street, which characterizes it today. During the country's three years of neutrality, the New York banks rapidly expanded their role in international finance by arranging loans for Britain and its Continental allies. Then with the United States at war they also undertook to market the government's Liberty bonds, volunteering to do so free of commission in a gesture of patriotism. Hitherto only a few New York banks had engaged in retail securities business, and they were sceptical that more than 350,000 people would be prepared to purchase the bonds. However, the bonds were issued in small denominations – usually $100 – and by 1919 over 11 million Americans subscribed to one or more of the series.[8] The practical effect was to create a taste for investments among a vastly wider public, which the banks and brokerage houses lost no time in exploiting. In 1913, securities dealers in the whole of the United States numbered 250. By 1929, the number had risen over twenty-five times to 6500.[9] Before the decade was out, employment in the financial sector had grown to at least 400,000, and it paid out more in salaries than farming and mining combined.[10]

As a result of these developments, American economic relations with the rest of the world radically changed. For many years before the war the United States had enjoyed a comfortable current account surplus, but had offset this by large foreign borrowings and debt service payments. Since then, exports had risen faster than imports, foreign borrowing had ceased, and the resulting current account surplus allowed a huge build-up in monetary gold reserves and a startling increase in foreign lending and investment. In 1914, America's foreign commercial debts exceeded its foreign claims by an estimated $3.7 billion; by 1919 the position was almost precisely reversed, with foreign claims exceeding debts by $3.7 billion – to which should be added $7.32 billion in government

war debt claims on 12 European countries.[11] The change in fortunes continued after the Armistice. In the ten years before the war, the United States had
earned a surplus on goods and services averaging $257 million a year. In the ten
years after the war, the surplus rose to an annual average of over $1800 million,
a seven-fold increase.[12] Much of this increase came from trade with Europe.
America's surplus in merchandise trade with Europe had averaged $530 million
between 1904 and 1913. In the ten years after the war the comparable figure was
$1722 million.[13] Some of the surplus was retained in gold or foreign exchange
or re-loaned abroad on short-term. But much of it was exported as long-term
direct or portfolio investment, which rose from $21.4 million (net) per annum
in the ten years before the war to $502 million per annum in the ten years after-
wards, an increase of over 23 times.[14] Between 1919 and 1929 American banks
floated foreign loans totalling $7.5 billion in new capital, which exceeded the
total foreign lending of Britain, France, the Netherlands and all other creditor
countries combined.[15] Indeed, with Britain and France economically weakened
and deeply indebted by the war, the United States was the only country able to
respond on a large scale to the world shortage of capital for reconstruction and
development.

In the circumstances, it is tempting to present the United States in 1920 as a great
power, even the world's leading power.[16] But the ability of a state to project power
or influence abroad requires not only adequate physical or financial resources
but also appropriate institutions and the will to act, and the United States at this
time lacked both. The Census of that year suggested why this was so. America, it
claimed, was now mainly an urban society. This received wide notice, but not its
definition of urban areas as communities as small as 2500 inhabitants. Given that
most communities even ten times this size possessed modest social and cultural
institutions and existed mainly to serve their surrounding regions, the appropriate inference from the Census statistics is that the great majority of Americans
still lived in small towns or rural areas; and of course those who had recently
migrated from rural areas or small towns to larger towns commonly imported
their values with them. Even on the modest definition of urbanization in the
1920 Census, no less than 74 of 96 US senators represented predominantly rural
states.[17] Notwithstanding the ascendancy of the large corporation in many sectors of business, small and medium-size firms were still far more numerous and
exercised a decisive influence upon Congress.[18]

It is true that rural radicalism diminished as a force in national politics in the
1920s. Only in the 1924 presidential election did the Progressives mount an
organized challenge to the two main political parties, and shortly thereafter both
the Progressive party and its leader, Robert LaFollette, passed from the scene.
The increased use of motor cars and the telephone, the spread of rural electrifica-
tion, the introduction of radio broadcasting, film distribution and other technical innovations, all features of the 1920s, tended to reduce rural and regional
isolation and with it suspicions of cosmopolitanism. Nevertheless, in voting for
Harding in 1920, with his promise to return to 'normalcy', Americans were signalling their desire for smaller government, the defence of family values and, in

the words of Michael Parrish, 'ethnic relations...predicated on the domination of white Protestants and the subordination of people of color.' Their governing assumption seemed to be that 'the values of their grandparents' era – hard work, thrift, self-restraint – would remain infallible guides to personal conduct; the farm and the small town would continue to be the centre of the nation's moral universe.'[19] So far from embracing the changes affecting the country – the growth of trade unions, the migration of African Americans from the South to fill industrial jobs in the North, the arrival of non-WASP immigrants from Southern and Eastern Europe – many Americans regarded them as threats to their familiar world. As Richard Hofstader observed, the result was an intensified conflict between metropolis and small town:

> The 1920's proved to be the focal decade in the *Kulturkampf* of American Protestantism. Advertising, radio, the mass magazines, the direct advance of popular education, threw the old mentality into a direct and unavoidable conflict with the new. The older, rural, and small-town America, now fully embattled against the encroachments of modern life, made its most determined stand against cosmopolitanism, Romanism, and the skepticism and the moral experimentalism of the intelligentsia.[20]

Small-town America continued to display suspicion of urban culture associated with the East Coast. New York especially remained a target because in addition to being the main gateway for non-WASP immigrants, it was now the undisputed financial capital of the country. Before the war, Wall Street had been the conduit through which most foreign capital – mostly from London – flowed, prompting suspicions of cosmopolitanism or, equally untoward, Anglophilia. The banks, bond dealers and stockbrokers clustered around Wall Street had set the terms by which manufacturers, merchants and farmers elsewhere in the country could borrow money. The financiers controlled most of the railways and other services on which they depended. Wall Street thus became known in provincial America as the locus of the 'Money Power', 'Gold Power' or 'Money Trust', which allegedly exercised parasitic control over productive industry through a web of interlocking directorates and its control of the price of money and access to financial markets.[21] In 1896, William Jennings Bryan, a former congressman from Nebraska, had won the Democratic nomination for the presidency with a speech denouncing the Republicans, the British and the financiers of Wall Street as enemies of the American way of life: 'You shall not press down upon the brow of labor this crown of thorns. You shall not crucify mankind upon a cross of gold.'[22] Bryan and his followers accused Wall Street of being the Trojan Horse of British capital and colluding in its exploitation of farmers and workers. Attacks on 'Eastern finance' frequently betrayed an element of anti-Semitism, with claims of a secret alliance of 'Jewish bankers and British gold'.[23] Wartime developments did little to moderate these suspicions. With the concentration of financial power in a handful of giant New York banks, provincial suspicions of Wall Street remained intense. And as will be seen, these suspicions informed American foreign policy-making for much of the interwar period.[24]

This outlook would have constrained Harding and his vice-president, Calvin Coolidge, were it not for the fact that they largely shared it themselves. Harding, whose education went no further than a provincial normal school in Ohio, had been publisher and editor of the *Marion Daily Star* since the age of 19 and entered national politics only in November 1914. Anti-immigrant, anti-union, anti-socialist, anti-intellectual and pro-WASP, he had frequently railed against the urban, industrial trends that were undermining the older America. As he put it on one occasion,

> Immigration has become a sewer that empties onto American soil the pauper, the heathen, the contract laborer, the Mosts and Fieldings [Chicago anarchists]. This daily arrival is numbered by the thousands and they are infesting the American social body with sores that no civilization and education, as a physician, can cure.[25]

He aggressively championed the Monroe doctrine, applauded America's confrontation with Britain over Venezuela in 1896 and with Spain over Cuba in 1898, and called for the annexation of Canada and 'civilizing' of Mexico by sending in the US cavalry in 1913.[26] He also supported protective tariffs as an essential safeguard for manufacturers and workers. Election to the Senate may have widened his perspective somewhat. But even in 1915 he affirmed that 'We can live without Europe quite as well as Europe can live without us.' At the Republican state convention in Columbus in August 1918, he attacked Wilson for including trade liberalization in his Fourteen Points, declaring it to be internationalism and therefore socialism.[27] In March 1919 he signed Senator Lodge's 'round robin' against US membership of the League of Nations.[28] During the presidential election of 1920 he reaffirmed his support for the Monroe doctrine, declaring that he 'would rather make Mexico safe and set it aglow with the light of new-world righteousness, than menace the health of the republic in old-world contagion.'[29] And he continued to advocate restrictions on non-WASP immigration as well as heightened protection against foreign imports. As he explained to a Labor Day audience,

> I believe in the protective policy which prospers America first and exalts American standards of wage and American standards of high living above the Old World. ... If we buy abroad, we will slacken production at home, and slackened production means diminished employment, and growing idleness and all attending disappointments.[30]

President Wilson had begun his first term by reducing import protection with the Underwood Tariff. On the last day of his second term he vetoed the emergency tariff bill adopted by the Republican-dominated Congress. In his words,

> If we wish Europe to settle her debts, governmental or commercial, we must be prepared to buy from her, and if we wish to assist Europe and ourselves

by the export of either food, raw materials, or financial products, we must be prepared to welcome commodities which we need and which Europe will be prepared, with no little pain, to send us. Clearly, this is no time for the erection of high trade barriers.[31]

No sooner had Harding entered the White House than he launched what he called his 'America first' strategy. He immediately signalled his readiness to implement an emergency tariff, and in May 1921 he signed into law an act that sharply increased duties notably on farm staples. He followed this by appointing two well-known protectionists to the US Tariff Commission. He also approved an Emergency Agricultural Credit Act which subsidized the dumping of American agricultural products abroad. The Fordney-McCumber Tariff, introduced in April 1922, included across-the-board increases in import duties. Taken together, postwar Republican Administrations raised the average level of protection over 60 per cent, above where it was when Wilson took office in 1913.[32]

In April 1921, Harding approved a separate peace with Germany, thus confirming America's dissociation from the Treaty of Versailles and desire to draw a line under the recent conflict.[33] In May he signed the Emergency Quota Act, known as the 'Three Per Cent Law', which limited immigration from Europe to an annual quota equal to 3 per cent of each 'nation' resident in the United States in 1910. The following May he approved the re-enactment of these provisions, and in May 1924 his successor, Calvin Coolidge, signed a new Immigrant Quota Act, the 'Two Per Cent Law', which used the census of 1890 as the basis of a 2 per cent quota. On each occasion the aim was to halt large-scale immigration from Southern and Eastern Europe as well as East Asia, while favouring the Anglo-Saxon and Germanic sources of old stock America.[34]

On trade and immigration, Harding displayed strongly nationalist credentials. Historians nonetheless have seized upon other features of his administration to portray him as an enlightened president who, while avoiding direct involvement in European affairs, worked closely with Wall Street in efforts to reconstruct Europe and re-establish global markets so as to serve American business.[35] Harding's secretary of commerce, Herbert Hoover, a successful mining engineer and promoter, swiftly transformed his department into a champion of US business abroad. In June 1921, the president invited representatives of J.P. Morgan and other leading Wall Street investment banks to a conference at the White House to discuss the large volume of loans currently being issued to European borrowers. One leading historian therefore describes Harding as an 'independent internationalist' rather than an isolationist.[36]

The notion of a partnership between Washington and New York, however, scarcely bears scrutiny. Harding shared the fears that had led William Jennings Bryan in 1915 to resign as secretary of state in Woodrow Wilson's government: that the bankers would draw the United States into European entanglements by their loans and credits. His difficulty was that he did not want to impede legitimate business, nor to become liable for compensating lenders if their loans were not repaid. He therefore sought a purely informal agreement whereby the bankers would notify the Administration of any prospective loans to foreign governments so that the Administration could advise if it was desirable for them to proceed. The bankers accepted this arrangement, but when certain banks subsequently disregarded it the State Department published the Administration's request for notification, now indicating that it was interested in all foreign loans rather than only those to foreign governments.[37] The apparent widening of the arrangement was probably inadvertent, the result of a lack of coordination within the Administration. But in any case, far from demonstrating collaboration between New York and Washington, the arrangement reflected the Administration's frustration with Wall Street and fear of its cosmopolitan activities. Harding and his colleagues hoped that by limiting loans for arms purchases they could contain militarism and imperialism in Europe, and perhaps also force European countries to pay their war debts to America. But far from seeking to manipulate European powers into accepting American reforms, they were chiefly concerned to stop European powers from manipulating America. By overseeing the issue of loans to Europe, they sought to limit, if not decrease, America's economic integration with the 'Old World'. In the event, Wall Street bankers largely avoided Europe while it remained in turmoil, and concentrated their foreign lending activity instead upon Canada and Latin America. In turn, Washington restricted its influence over foreign lending almost exclusively to instances where foreign governments had yet to settle their war debts with the US Treasury.[38]

As a senator, Harding had twice travelled to Europe as well as visited the Philippines and several other overseas destinations. Coolidge, his vice-presidential running mate, could not claim even this worldliness. The son of a village shopkeeper in Plymouth Notch, Vermont, who until mid-career had been a lawyer of undistinguished reputation, Coolidge attracted national attention in September 1919 when, as governor of Massachusetts, he denounced a policemen's strike in Boston just as the nation-wide 'Red scare' reached a paroxysm of hysteria. Until then, he had never held national office. Indeed, he had visited Washington only once and had never been west of the Alleghenies let alone further abroad.[39] Harding betrayed his small-town suspicions of Wall Street by looking first to Charles Dawes, a banker from Chicago, and then to Andrew Mellon, a banker from Pittsburgh, to fill the post of secretary of the Treasury, while shunning candidates from New York.[40] Coolidge, a New Englander, did not display the same prejudices when he became president after Harding's sudden death in August 1923. On the contrary, he regularly included bankers and industrialists in his dinners at the White House, and far more than Harding he relied upon Mellon, one of America's richest men, for practical advice. Yet he shared most of Harding's outlook, including suspicion of centralized government and the need to maintain the Monroe doctrine, stiff tariff protection and a navy strong enough to keep potential enemies from America's shores.

Historians nevertheless abjure the term isolationism since Harding and his Republican successors aggressively promoted American business abroad, actively supported international disarmament and defended the Open Door in China. This ignores the traditional meaning of isolationism in the United States and obscures their intention, which was to remain faithful to the injunctions of the Founding Fathers to avoid political entanglements with the European powers while enjoying their freedom to expand American commerce abroad.[41] It also constitutes a gross anachronism by ignoring the semi-rural character of America in the era that shaped their outlook. Above all, it obscures a key feature of international relations in the 1920s. The United States now possessed the most dynamic economy and the largest lending resources in the world. It rapidly increased its foreign trade, loans and investments, which deeply implicated it in the welfare and stability of the rest of the world. Yet its leaders were not prepared to engage in serious dialogue with leaders of the other major powers or to recognize that it was in America's own interest to share the burdens of international payments adjustment. They refused to face up to the fact that global markets, like national markets, cannot long function without a framework of agreed rules, institutions and security, and hence that in the profoundly unstable conditions of the 1920s it was no longer appropriate for the United States simply to revert to its traditional posture of claiming political and economic rights without accepting the corresponding responsibilities.

2.3 Postwar Britain: Internationalism and isolationism

In 1914 Britain had found itself ill-prepared for the long and exhausting struggle that lay ahead. The shock of discovering that the country had come to rely upon Germany for essential items such as dyestuffs (which include the same chemicals used in making explosives), precision instruments, timing devices and airplane engines, that domestic industry could not supply the arms and munitions necessary to prosecute the war, and that its dependence upon imported foodstuffs made it vulnerable to the German submarine campaign, prompted the government to take urgent action. By the Armistice in November 1918 the struggle for survival had led to a wholesale abandonment of liberal policies, including free trade, the gold standard, low taxes and limited government provision of social services and regulation of the labour market, which had been in place for over half a century. Lord Milner, Leo Amery and others on the imperialist wing of the Conservative party drew the lesson that Britain must not run the same risks again by returning to economic liberalism. Instead it should exploit the solidarity shown by the Dominions, India and the colonies to forge the Empire into a coherent economic bloc. The country now faced a host of problems, including a vastly inflated national debt, the loss of earnings from the disposal of foreign assets, the costly reconversion of industry to peacetime production and the challenge of regaining overseas markets as well as a large pent-up demand for housing and consumer goods, which fuelled wage and price inflation. Yet with the return of peace it soon became clear that there would be no fundamental change in Britain's economic policy.

One reason was the reluctance of the Conservative party to reopen old wounds after its failure to carry the country on a policy of Tariff Reform in 1905. Another was the almost universal tendency to look upon the Edwardian era as a golden age when under *laissez-faire* Britain had enjoyed expanding overseas trade, growing prosperity and social stability. A third was the lesson drawn by most leading Conservatives and nearly all Liberal and Labour leaders, that Britain's wartime survival was due to access to the resources not only of the Empire but also of the United States and the rest of the world. Eventually during the 1920s, the industrial community showed signs of supporting an Empire-first policy. The far more influential mercantile-financial community ensured that these signs were not heeded.[42]

By the twentieth century, Britain's physical landscape had been profoundly altered by the development of intensive farming, mining and manufacturing. These sectors of the economy provided the majority of employment nationally and shaped the culture of the Midlands and the North as well as much of Scotland and Wales. Yet it was commerce and finance, centred on the City of London, that generated greater wealth and exercised greater influence over the economic policies of the country. The banks, investment houses, commodity brokers, bullion merchants, insurance and shipping companies and commercial law firms clustered around the Bank of England, the Stock Exchange, Lloyds of London and the Baltic Exchange in the square mile of the City constituted the most important collection of markets and market makers in the world; and to a greater extent than its rivals New York and Paris, London looked outwards for its business rather than towards the domestic economy. From the 1880s the City invariably returned Conservatives to Parliament. Nonetheless, few City notables were drawn to Chamberlain's Tariff Reform movement after the turn of the century, and at the end of the Great War the City overwhelmingly favoured the return to economic internationalism, including the restoration of sterling to the gold standard at the earliest possible opportunity.

The ability of the City to ensure that Britain adhered to this posture was due partly to its large, probably preponderant, role in financing the Tory party. But the City had other advantages as well. Physically it was adjacent to the seat of government in Westminster, and home to most of the national press which was concentrated on Fleet Street. Socially it enjoyed the prestige that derived from the integration of wealthy City families with landed society, which had been a feature of the nineteenth century. Their sons also attended the same public schools and Oxbridge colleges that produced the administrators and soldiers of the Empire and the mandarins of Whitehall. Recruits to industry needed education in science and technology; not so the bankers, merchants, administrators and soldiers, for whom a classical education or the challenge of pure mathematics offered suitable mental training. Through their common culture and education, they formed a community that dominated London and the Home Counties. Their interest in maintaining a vast overseas Empire without jeopardizing access to other markets, and their relative indifference to the fate of domestic industry, made them enthusiastic exponents of the liberal ideology that underpinned the country's commitment to individual liberty, limited government and *laissez-faire* economic policies.[43]

The exigencies of the Great War prompted industrialists to establish organizations, notably the Federation of British Industries (FBI) and the National Union of Manufacturers (NUM), to represent their views to government and coordinate the implementation of policy. The merchants and financiers had no such 'peak' organization, yet they remained much better placed to influence public policy. Industrial opinion differed between the mine-owners, shipbuilders, engineers and textile manufactures who relied heavily upon overseas markets and therefore tended to side with finance on liberal economic policies; the farmers and small manufacturers who relied almost wholly upon the home market and leaned towards protection; and industrialists in new sectors such as chemicals, electricity and the internal combustion engine who needed large but also prosperous and stable markets such as might be provided by the British Dominions within a united Empire. In contrast to the men of industry, City merchants and financiers scarcely differed over the need for unrestricted global markets.[44] The City's advice dovetailed nicely with the Treasury's preoccupation with limiting public spending and balancing the Budget. It also complemented the Foreign Office's interest in liberal trade and financial policies as a means of minimizing international friction and increasing the interested friendship of foreign countries. Beyond the City-Whitehall nexus, this posture was reinforced by the League of Nations Union, the leading expression of postwar hopes that liberal principles would henceforth govern international relations.

The chief agency for the City's internationalist strategy was the Bank of England. For nearly a hundred years the strength of Britain's balance of payments had enabled the Bank to maintain the gold standard with relative ease. This enhanced the Bank's prestige, but it also meant that there was remarkably little discussion of monetary or financial issues outside the boardrooms of the City. Amidst the uncertainty of the postwar period, the press and government bodies therefore relied heavily upon the Bank's governor and court of directors for advice on these issues. Since the Bank was a private company and by tradition all its directors were drawn from the merchant banks, shipping companies and other trading firms of the City, their advice was predictable: abandon exchange, lending and trade controls and return to the gold standard, and rely upon the recovery of international commerce and finance to underpin Britain's postwar prosperity.[45]

The City's influence was exemplified by the working of the Committee on Currency and Foreign Exchanges after the War, instituted by the government in the last year of the war. The Committee, chaired by Lord Cunliffe, governor of the Bank of England, and composed overwhelmingly of City financiers, heard several dozen like-minded City men and economists advocate the early return to the gold standard at the prewar parity of £1 = $4.86.[46] The sole expression of industrial opinion came from the FBI, which, nervous about addressing such an abstruse subject, delegated an expert to appear before the committee to defend its submission. While favouring the gold standard in principle, the FBI had grave misgivings about restoring sterling to gold while industry, burdened with heavy taxes and reconstruction costs, faced the challenge of regaining overseas markets, and it urged the government to rely upon the recovery of trade rather than monetary expedients to float sterling back to its prewar parity.[47] The FBI's advice was ignored. Reporting in August 1918, the Committee recommended an early return to the gold standard, which, it claimed, was the view of all the witnesses who appeared before it. The gold standard was 'the only effective remedy for an adverse balance of trade and an undue growth of credit'. This was precisely what the FBI warned against. Nevertheless, the Committee suggested that this was what industry wanted and needed. 'We are glad to find that there was no difference of opinion among the witnesses who appeared before us as to the vital importance of these matters.'[48]

The government was unable to implement the Committee's recommendations immediately. Indeed, in the first year after the war demobilization, industrial unrest and Imperial sentiment forced a temporary change of course. In February 1919, ministers agreed to maintain restrictions upon manufactures from outside the Empire to assist the reabsorption of labour into British industry.[49] In March they agreed to delay the balancing of the Budget and maintain public spending as if the war had continued until the summer. They also relaxed controls on domestic investment while maintaining the embargo on capital exports, and removed the peg on the sterling-dollar exchange, allowing the pound to depreciate.[50] On 31 March they agreed formally to suspend the gold standard – suspended *de facto* since August 1914 – until 31 December 1925.[51]

Industrialists and financiers meanwhile raised an outcry against the continuation of wartime control on business and high levels of public spending, which allegedly obstructed recovery and fuelled an inflationary wage-price spiral. The chancellor of the exchequer, Austen Chamberlain, sought to address this problem in his first postwar Budget, which included a reduction of £919 million, or fully 36 per cent, in public spending. In the autumn, a bonfire of red tape began.[52] Meanwhile Chamberlain faced constant pressure from the governor of the Bank of England and officials in the Treasury to accept the Cunliffe committee's recommendations, and in December 1919 he announced his support. Already the Bank had begun to tighten credit and ratchet up interest rates. In March 1920, Bank rate reached the almost unheard of level of 7 per cent, where it was held for a record 12 months.[53] Chamberlain's second postwar Budget in April 1920 included another massive reduction in spending: almost 30 per cent, from £1666 million to £1177 million, leaving a 12 per cent surplus (£164 million) to be used for debt reduction.[54] Despite the onset of a severe slump that spring and repeated protests from the FBI, the deflationary internationalist policy favoured by the Bank, the City and the Treasury remained in place for the next five years.[55] Meanwhile the wartime commitment to promote Imperial economic unity faded, and the government withdrew the guarantee of a minimum price for wheat given to British arable farmers at the end of the war. Aside from motor manufacturing, only dyestuffs and a few minor industries of strategic importance secured protection from foreign competition.

This did not halt the British economy from growing in the 1920s. But considering the whole period from the Armistice to 1930, Britain's *industrial* growth was slower than that of every other developed country excepting only Soviet Russia.[56] The staple export industries, such as shipbuilding, heavy engineering and cotton and wool textiles, which confronted the formidable combination of tight and dear money, an over-valued exchange rate, a secular decline in world demand and increased competition, fared particularly badly. As a result, while the Midlands and South-East prospered, much of the North and the Celtic fringe experienced slow or negative growth and abnormally high unemployment.[57] Nationally, registered unemployment – a conservative measure – rose above 16 per cent in 1922. Subsequently it declined somewhat, but even in 1929, the last of the 'boom' years, it remained over 12 per cent. Since unemployment and external trade were the main criteria by which contemporaries judged national economic performance, observers commonly described Britain as depressed and liberal commentators looked for recovery through the removal of inter-governmental debts and other obstacles to international trade. Criticism from industry of Britain's policy mix was generally played down in the national press.

From 1920, Britain's posture towards the world economy diverged sharply from that of the United States. Recent events had done nothing to close the gap between New York and Washington or reduce Washington's opposition to involvement in collective schemes for European reconstruction. In Britain, no such gap existed: the City sought to regain its place at the centre of the international trade and payments system, while the government assisted by promoting international peace. The British economy, weakened by the war, was no longer capable of generating substantial balances to finance European reconstruction or underwrite currency stabilization.[58] But with Americans noticeably absent, it was British statesmen and British financiers, working together through the League of Nations and at a succession of conferences, who led the way in restoring the international trade and payments system. The same British leaders occasionally betrayed disdain and even hostility towards the United States. By their lights, America behaved with remarkable immaturity in demanding an 'Open Door' to world markets without contributing to Europe's reconstruction. America also made their task harder by its protectionist trade policy, its rigid insistence upon full repayment of the capital value of war debts, and its tendency, evident at the Washington conference of 1921–2 and in its opposition to renewal of the Anglo-Japanese Alliance, to regard Britain as an imperialist opponent rather than a partner in global affairs. Too much can be made of this, however, for British leaders did not allow their attitudes to America to deflect them from the task of restoring a globalized economy. Rather more surprising was their attitude towards continental Europe and the question of European security.

The terrible ordeal of Ypres, Loos, the Somme and Passchendaele had demonstrated as never before the cost of participating in a Continental land war, and once the Central Powers were defeated Britain seemed to close its mind to involvement in any future Continental conflict. On 15 August 1919, the Cabinet adopted the Ten-Year Rule as the basis of defence spending. Henceforth,

> It should be assumed for framing revised Estimates, that the British Empire will not be engaged in any great war during the next ten years, and that no Expeditionary Force is required for this purpose.[59]

The Ten-Year Rule, annually renewed, was to remain the basis of British defence planning until 1932, and for most of the 1920s its assumption of no major war for ten years seemed reasonable enough. But as N. H. Gibbs points out, its introduction was to say the least hasty, since in August 1919 Britain was still technically at war with Germany, the Bolsheviks threatened Central Europe, and the Near East was in turmoil.[60] The Cabinet had acted after Lloyd George warned them of the danger of civil unrest and even revolution among British workers, and called upon them to support policies of domestic appeasement even if this meant taking some risks with external security.[61] But the implicit assumption, seldom acknowledged but frequently alluded to by ministers, was that with the Kaiser gone, the high command dissolved, the high seas fleet scuttled and Germany forbidden by the peace treaty from constructing another, Britain had no further reason to fear Germany. This overlooked the fact that the threat that had obliged Britain to enter the war in 1914 came not from the German navy but the German army, which had nearly secured Continental hegemony and control of the Channel ports. Equally revealing was the ambiguous clause in the Ten-Year Rule that referred to the dispensing of further need for an expeditionary force. Did this mean that such a force would not be required for ten years or not ever? In either case, it pointed towards rejection of a Continental commitment: a kind of Euroscepticism *avant la lettre*, which was to find its sharpest expression during the 1920s and 1930s in Britain's strained relations with France.

Within six months of the Armistice, Britain had largely demobilized its army, yet France still retained 850,000 men under the colours two years after the war.[62] The size of the French army and its use for intervention in Germany, Poland, Morocco and elsewhere led to British denunciations of French 'imperialism' and 'militarism'. But it was the 54 French submarines and 47 French air squadrons that most exercised British leaders. Britain's vulnerability to French aerial invasion led to the setting up of a special enquiry by the Committee of Imperial Defence (CID) in November 1921 and the decision in August 1922 to create a 23-squadron air force.[63] At the Washington naval disarmament conference that year, British delegates expressed fear of another war and, pointedly alluding to France, called for limits on land armies and a total ban on submarines. But they seemed scarcely to believe their own rhetoric. The £2 million for the Air Ministry scheme was approved on the assumption that it come from within existing Service estimates. Meanwhile no steps were taken to set aside the Ten-Year Rule. As the War Office acknowledged, France, facing a still powerful Germany across the Rhine, was really no threat to Britain at all. British annoyance at France probably owed more to the embarrassing demands it made upon Britain to remain committed to Continental Europe. As the Great War had demonstrated and the Second World War would demonstrate again, Britain could devote itself to its Empire and maintain liberal economic policies only if conditions in Continental Europe allowed it to do so. British politicians and statesmen preferred not to acknowledge this, since it would require fundamental changes in their economic and defence policies. Instead, they made France out to be unreasonable and aggressive, and then used this to justify their aloofness from the Continent. Harold Nicolson, the historian and former diplomat, described this illogic in his biography of

Lord Curzon, the foreign secretary:

[Curzon] was a bad European. His attitude towards continental affairs was governed by those prejudices and egoisms which affected the average Englishman of the upper middle classes towards the close of the nineteenth century. His ideal world would have been one in which England never intervened in Europe and Europe never intervened in Africa or Asia. America, as a distant, even if rebellious, plantation, was in either case not expected to intervene at all. His conceptions of the European problem were thus egoistic, traditional and limited. Let England have peace upon the continent and therefore an expanding market. Let England have the balance of power on the continent, and thereby security at other people's expense.... [He also betrayed a] deficient sense of proportion. He should have realised that French security was the basis of the whole European system. It was a basis in regard to which we ourselves were in a false position. Realising that falsity, Curzon winced away from the basis. It was owing to his disinclination, or inability, to face this central reality that other, wholly secondary, differences acquired such disproportionate value.[64]

Paul Cambon, the French ambassador to the Court of St James's from 1898, observed to his successor, the Comte de Saint-Aulaire, in 1921, 'The trouble is that the British still don't understand that Napoleon is dead.' Saint-Aulaire soon found this to be all too true. Lord Curzon himself was fascinated by Napoleon, read every account of Napoleon he could lay his hands upon and made several pilgrimages to his last residence on the remote island of St Helena.[65]

2.4 Postwar France: Liberty, normality, insecurity

France, no less than Britain and the United States, demonstrated a strong desire to return to the normality of prewar times. The war had forced the relocation of industry from the border regions of the north to Paris, the Rhône, the Atlantic ports and elsewhere.[66] Engineering and management techniques were improved, and several industries including airframe and motor manufacturing developed rapidly under the stimulus of war.[67] Socially, the national community emerged more integrated, if not more united, than before, with conscription drawing millions of peasants out of their regions for the first time, and the provinces of Alsace and Lorraine restored to French sovereignty. With demobilization came a massive rise in trade union membership and a substantial increase in support for the Socialist Party, still known as the *Section Française de l'Internationale Ouvrière (SFIO)*.[68] But the country's essential conservatism was strikingly reconfirmed in the legislative elections of 16 and 30 November 1919. The four centre-right parties making up the *Bloc national* gained 417 of the 616 seats in the Chamber of Deputies, the Radicals 86 seats and the Socialists only 68, with the remainder going to the monarchist and bonapartist remnant. Most of the Radicals (57 of 86) had refused an electoral pact with the *Bloc national*. They distinguished themselves by their dogmatic secularism, support for social reform and endorsement of the League of Nations as the cornerstone of French security.[69] But if they were collectivists in international relations, they remained stubbornly anti-collectivist when it came to the economy. Like their *Bloc national* opponents, they favoured liberal policies of low taxes, limited government and defence of private property rights, which were thus the preferred policies of fully five-sixths of the new Parliament. For the time being, however, a complete return to prewar economic policies was out of the question.

In 1914, reluctance to levy taxes had left governments to pay for the war mainly through borrowing and the acquisition and disposal of French foreign investments. By the Armistice, French portfolio investments abroad had been reduced from perhaps 40 billion francs (£1.6 billion) in 1913 to 18.5 billion francs (£740 million).[70] Meanwhile, the state owed 19 billion francs (£760 million) in advances from the Bank of France, over 35 billion francs (£1.4 billion) in short-term *bons de la défense nationale*, £390 million in short-term borrowings from Britain, and over $2.35 billion (£485 million) in short-term borrowings from the United States. Total public debt thus increased over six times between 1913 and 1919, from 34 billion francs (£1.36 billion), to 212.6 billion francs (£8.5 billion): more than ten times the annual expenditure of the state before the war. While in theory the total was smaller after deduction of the 7.5 billion francs (£300 million) that France had loaned to Russia and other allies, in fact practically none of these loans was recoverable.[71] In addition to the interest and amortization charges on the public debt, the country faced heavy outlays for other purposes as well. One major charge was the cost of restoring the region devastated by the war. For four-and-a-half years the fighting had swung back and forth across ten northern departments, leaving in its wake the destruction of 594,000 dwellings and 20,000 factories as well as nearly 5000 bridges, 53,000 km of roads, 5000 km of railways, 8 million acres of land, and over half the coal mines in the country.[72] A second charge was compensation for the victims of the war. To 700,000 widows and 750,000 orphans of the 1,310,000 soldiers killed in the war, and 200,000 soldiers who survived with serious permanent injuries (*les grands mutilés*), pensions or allowances had to be paid.[73] Governments also faced the cost of maintaining almost a million men in arms, financing their operations in the Levant, Morocco, Poland, the Crimea, on the Rhine and elsewhere, and assisting new allies in Eastern Europe. Military spending remained at or above 1 billion francs for most of the 1920s, considerably more than before the war.[74]

The financial predicament that confronted France at the Armistice threatened the liberal foundations of its political economy, indeed threatened to produce runaway inflation, bankruptcy and social upheaval. The government slashed public spending and cut back on its military forces so far as it thought prudent. But unlike the British government, it did not seek to reduce the public deficit through higher taxes. Instead, it looked to Britain and the United States for relief on its war debts, and to Germany for large-scale reparation payments. In the meantime it allowed the franc to depreciate. Officially this was still the *franc Germinal*, with a gold parity equivalent of 25 francs = £1 since Napoleonic times. But with inflation soaring, it declined to 42 francs = £1 by the end of 1919, and to 65 francs = £1 in 1920, before recovering to 48 francs = £1 in April 1921 when the world slump temporarily halted the wage-price spiral. Postwar British and French economic policies differed so much as to make it difficult to compare their economic and social consequences. Britain managed to restore the pound sterling to the gold standard at its prewar exchange rate and swiftly regained an important role in international finance. But its deflationary policies slowed domestic economic growth to a crawl, aggravated the plight of the staple export industries and at one point provoked workers into a general strike. In contrast, the French authorities eventually restored the franc to the gold standard, but only at one-fifth its prewar exchange rate and not before accelerating depreciation had pushed elements of the middle classes into virtual insurrection. Nonetheless the French combination of government deficits, a competitive exchange rate and the reduction of public and private debt through the effects of inflation sustained a rapid growth of the real economy, which regained prewar levels of output by early 1924, at least two years before Britain, and continued to grow rapidly until the end of the decade. Whereas in Britain registered unemployment remained at or above a million, or at least 10 per cent of the industrial workforce, in France the economic boom produced full employment and drew in a million foreign workers.[75]

However, if there is room for dispute over the domestic effects of their policies, there can be little doubt as to the effect of their differences upon international relations. Among French leaders the central challenge in the postwar years was to construct a security framework capable of containing Germany, once it regained its capacity to dominate Europe. They worried about the new threat from Bolshevik Russia, not least because of its appeal to elements of the French working class. But in view of Soviet Russia's industrial backwardness and political divisions they regarded it as wholly secondary to the threat posed by Germany, with its large and fast-growing population, military traditions, extraordinary industrial and war-making capacity, and profound restlessness. French leaders recognized that Germans of every stripe believed they had been duped into accepting the Treaty of Versailles and were determined to revise the peace settlement. At present, a majority of Germans supported the Weimar republic and favoured peaceful Treaty revision. Nonetheless, those who hankered for a return to authoritarianism, militarism and aggression continued to occupy key positions in the judiciary, the civil service, the military and the boards of heavy industry, and the risk remained that they might regain political power. French leaders regretted the loss of the Anglo-American guarantee and sought to persuade Britain to renew its commitment. But they also hoped that Britain would recognize its own interest in a European-wide security framework. Germany was particularly frustrated by the territorial changes that accompanied the creation of the secession states, and if permitted it would pursue an expansionist policy in the East, possibly linking up with Bolshevik Russia. French leaders were determined to forestall this, for once Germany bestrode the whole of Central and Eastern Europe it would be too powerful for the Western powers to face down. Hence a European security system worthy of the name could not be limited to a guarantee of the Rhineland, but must comprehend the whole of the Continent. As Marshal Foch repeatedly warned,

> [Germany] would burst asunder all the provisions of the Treaty of Versailles one after the other. First, the Polish corridor would disappear, and then Czechoslovakia and Austria would rapidly follow, and instead of an already sufficiently powerful Germany of some 65 million inhabitants, we should be faced with a Germany of well over 100 millions, and then it would be too late for us to endeavour to check her ever-growing land-hunger or power.[76]

This remained a common theme of French diplomacy in the postwar years. Yet British leaders merely toyed with the idea of renewing the guarantee and firmly refused to discuss strategic issues with Foch or other French experts. Meanwhile, differences over reparations and war debts aggravated relations, with British leaders increasingly insistent upon suppressing inter-governmental debts and normalizing relations with Germany to hasten the revival of trade, and their French counterparts equally determined to obtain reparations sufficient to cover the yawning gap in their national budget and constrain German industry by the tax burden placed upon it. British leaders held that France, while legally entitled to reparations, was foolish to insist upon them since Germany could pay only by earning foreign exchange through aggressive exporting or by printing marks, which in either case would aggravate Europe's crisis. French leaders regarded their reparation claims as both legally justified and fully within Germany's capacity to pay (at least so long as some were paid in kind). They believed that reducing reparation demands would only encourage the nationalists in Germany, who were certain to gain credibility among their frustrated and disoriented compatriots with every concession the Allies made.

Who was right? It is impossible to do more than speculate on how much Germany might have been made to pay, since the validity of the economic calculations must depend upon a host of wholly untestable assumptions about the effect of Allied demands upon German society and politics. What is clear is that differences over reparations strained Franco-British relations to the breaking point. The British working classes, sympathetic to France at the time of the Armistice, soon became as hostile as their middle- and upper-class compatriots, once the postwar slump triggered high unemployment. This hollowed out support for the *Entente*, which became an empty shell even before French and Belgian troops occupied the Ruhr in January 1923. Diplomatic exchanges on European security continued during the Ruhr crisis and eventually culminated in the Locarno agreements of October 1925. But long before this it was clear that Britain and France, the only powers capable of forging an effective security framework for Europe, would fail to do so.

2.5 The breakdown of the Franco-British Entente

On 10 January 1920, the Treaty of Versailles came into force. Six days later Clemenceau was defeated in the election for president of the Republic, and on

18 January he resigned as premier. For the next ten years French politics was dominated by four men, Alexandre Millerand, Raymond Poincaré, Aristide Briand and Edouard Herriot. Despite markedly different personalities and political style, they had much in common, including a commitment to parliamentary democracy and liberal economics, and the conviction that Germany remained unreconciled to its place in postwar Europe and that France must therefore restore the *Entente* as the cornerstone of its foreign and security policy. But whereas Briand and Herriot accepted the need to tailor foreign policy to fit the exigencies of the *Entente*, Millerand and Poincaré presented themselves as advocates of firmness and sought to make the *Entente* fit their own policy objectives. Millerand, who formed the government after Clemenceau resigned, occupied the premier's office and the foreign ministry until September 1920 when he became president of the Republic, a post he held until May 1924. He is widely regarded as more committed to containing Germany than the other leaders. But here too it is easy to confuse style with substance.

Immediately upon taking office, Millerand confronted reports of Germany's failure to meet the timetable for disarmament and deliveries of coal. On 10 January, the paramilitary *Einwohnerwehr* and the political police were to have been disbanded; they were not. On 10 March all surplus arms and munitions were to be handed over to the Inter-Allied Control Commission; they were not. On 31 March the *Reichswehr* was to be reduced to 200,000 men; it was not. Meanwhile Allied military inspectors in Germany were obstructed in their efforts and two French officers were assassinated.[77] And on 12 March the *Reichswehr* stood by while troops, taking orders from Wolfgang Kapp and a group of officers, seized Berlin in a short-lived *coup d'état*. When this was followed by Communist-led disturbances in the industrial towns of the Ruhr, the German government urgently requested Allied permission to send troops into the demilitarized zone to restore order. Millerand, who had been agitating for military sanctions against Germany since February, strenuously opposed this departure from the terms of the peace treaty, but Lloyd George temporized and secured Millerand's assurance that he would do nothing without Allied agreement. However, when the German government on 31 March ordered troops to enter the Ruhr, Millerand insisted that Germany must allow French troops to occupy five towns, Frankfurt, Darmstadt, Hamburg, Hanau and Dieburg. Curzon responded furiously, declaring that France had broken its word and indicating that this meant the end of the *Entente*.[78] Cambon, the French ambassador, who had sought to discourage Millerand from military action,[79] endured what he described as the 'most painful and serious' dressing down in his 40-year career.[80] Aware that the Germans were taking a great interest in Franco-British divisions, since reports from the German embassy were being secretly monitored, Cambon warned Millerand of the dangers he was running.[81] Millerand was in no mood to back down, however, and threatened to stay away from the next Allied conference at San Remo.[82] Hankey, the influential Cabinet secretary, wrote of 'the danger of being dragged at the heels of the French, who are a very provocative people, into a new war', and agitated for an end to 'this horrible continental entanglement'.[83]

French dissatisfaction with the slow pace of German disarmament was intensified by failure to obtain reparations and in particular coal. The deliberate flood-
ing or blowing up of the majority of French mines during the final retreat of
German forces in 1918 had left the country desperately short of coal, a problem
compounded by the reincorporation of the province of Lorraine with its steel-
making plants, which potentially doubled French steel output but also increased
its need for coal. Acquisition of the Saar mines, with their annual production
of 8 million tons, provided some relief, but the key to French recovery was the
27 million tons that Germany was required to deliver annually under the terms
of the peace treaty. German deliveries, however, were not due to start until
April 1920, and in the event only 801,000 tons were shipped in April and
1,094,000 tons in May, barely half the amount specified in the treaty. France
was obliged to fall back on British supplies for nearly 40 per cent of its requirements. But whereas Germany's coal was to be credited to its reparations account at
German domestic prices, British coal was sold at world prices, which in this period
of shortages were several times higher.[84] To add to French frustration, British coal
supplies, never adequate, were halted completely when French troops began their
occupation of the German towns and later resumed at a much lower volume. Such
vulnerability and Britain's willingness to exploit it for financial and political gain
caused intense annoyance in Paris, where the conservative press accused Britain
of great unfairness.[85] Curzon, humourless, hypersensitive to imagined slights and
certain that the French press invariably danced to the government's tune, took
great umbrage at the press criticism. 'Nothing', he advised Cabinet colleagues in
May, 'could well be more provocative or hostile than the French press, always – as
we know – in the closest relations with the French Foreign Office and with French
statesmen'. 'Nothing', he added, 'can alter the fundamental fact that we are not
liked in France, and never will be, except for the advantages which the French
people may be able to extract from us.'[86]

Briefly, relations improved when Allied leaders met informally first at Lympne,
near Hythe, in May, then across the Channel at Boulogne in June. The withdrawal
of German forces from the Ruhr had ended the Franco-German confrontation.
Meanwhile Lloyd George had become impatient to encourage Greek ambitions in
Anatolia while Turkey was still on its knees, and sought French support for this
adventure. Millerand, though doubtful of the wisdom of antagonizing Turkish
nationalists, was prepared to go along with it in return for Lloyd George's support of French reparation demands. He therefore endorsed the Treaty of Sèvres,
which favoured Greece at Turkey's expense. He also indicated his willingness to
accept the British proposal of a reparations *forfait*: a single payment made possible by a large international bond issue on the security of German reparation
obligations, which, it was hoped, would end controversy over their future.[87] But
when Poincaré resigned in protest as president of the Reparations Commission
and criticism mounted in Parliament, Millerand retreated from this proposal.[88]

Franco-British relations held up the following month when the leaders met
again at Spa, where for the first time they invited a German delegation to attend.
Lloyd George was taken aback at the appearance of two German generals in

uniform and annoyed at the uncooperative manner adopted by Walter Simons, the foreign minister, who headed the German delegation. Lloyd George was heard to say of Simons, 'I had the feeling that for the first time I had met a real Hun!'[89] He agreed to threaten Allied military sanctions to secure Germany's promise of regular coal deliveries. Millerand in turn agreed to substantial concessions, including a 10 per cent reduction in the amount of coal delivered and a change in its valuation from the German domestic price to the much higher world market price, as well as a slowdown in the application of German disarmament obligations.[90] But it remained to be seen if Britain would follow up its threat of military sanctions in the likely event of further German non-cooperation. Meanwhile, Franco-British differences over Soviet Russia, Poland and the Near East became steadily more acute.

Since 1919, Lloyd George had been impatient to end support for the White forces in Russia and come to terms with the 'Reds'. In his words, 'the Soviet Government appeared to include some very intelligent men', who would probably accept a *modus vivendi* with the West if not constantly threatened, and he made no secret of his view that Poland's 'imperialist and annexationist policy' was an obstacle to the appeasement of both Soviet Russia and Germany.[91] French leaders, while unable to provide substantial aid to the Whites after the mutiny of sailors forced the recall of their Black Sea squadron in March 1919, held to a diametrically different policy. Not only did they reject the British thesis that the Bolsheviks would abandon their revolutionary ambitions in return for normalized relations with the West; but they also regarded Poland as a bulwark against German imperialism and the spread of the Bolshevik virus into Central Europe. German nationalists welcomed and even supported the rapid westward advance of the Red Army, hoping it would bring the destruction of Poland and lead to a German-Russian alliance against the West. This, as French leaders appreciated, would mean not only the end of independent Poland but also the Versailles settlement and quite probably result in German hegemony in Europe.[92] At Spa, however, Millerand preferred to secure British agreement on German disarmament and reparations rather than insisting upon greater support for Poland.

Since Marshal Foch accepted that France could not send troops, Millerand agreed to Lloyd Georges's proposal of an Anglo-French military mission to Warsaw.[93] The British component was modest compared to the French, which included General Weygand, Foch's deputy.[94] Hankey, designated by Lloyd George as secretary to the mission, betrayed deep prejudice against the Poles. Woefully ignorant of the situation and spending only two days in the country, he dismissed the Poles as displaying 'not the smallest sign of capacity or efficiency', and discouraged the prime minister from placing any confidence in them.[95] This was precisely what Lloyd George wished to hear.[96] Since May, a high-level Bolshevik delegation had been in London to negotiate the resumption of commercial relations. French officials were disturbed to find that even in August, with the Red Army practically at the gates of Warsaw, the British government made no move to break off the negotiations.[97] They were even more annoyed when Lloyd George, without consulting them, advised the Poles to accept the Bolsheviks' terms.[98] To add to their frustration, Sir Ronald Tower, the League of

Nations High Commissioner in Danzig, opposed the landing of French military supplies for Poland on the grounds that it would violate the relevant clauses of the Treaty of Versailles.[99] They would have been further annoyed to hear that in October, Lloyd George discouraged leaders of the Little Entente (Roumania, Czechoslovakia and Yugoslavia) from admitting Poland to their group or having anything to do with it.[100]

Until Harding's Republican administration was installed in Washington in March 1921, French leaders remained hopeful of a substantial American contribution to the settlement of inter-governmental debts. This had been particularly true of Clemenceau and André Tardieu, his wartime assistant who had been French high commissioner in America during the latter part of the war. André François-Poncet, a colleague and business counsellor, found Clemenceau in October 1919 bitterly disappointed at Britain but still remarkably sure of America's goodwill towards France. In the Tiger's own words,

> England is the disillusion of my life! Not a day passes without my receiving a message from one or another of our foreign agents reporting acts of real hostility towards us. I believed that the comradeship in arms, the blood spilt in common, would suppress the old traditional prejudices. Not a bit of it. The sickness is without remedy! As to the United States, that is a different matter! Here, there is still room for hope: we can count on its friendship.[101]

Millerand, whose wife was English, placed greater hopes on Britain. Nevertheless he too looked expectantly for signs of cooperation from Washington.[102]

The same was true of British leaders, their optimism sustained by regular contact with bankers from New York, who encouraged them to believe that Britain and the United States shared the same objectives, including open markets and the removal of inter-governmental debts as an obstacle to the recovery of world commerce. The second Senate vote on the ratification of the Versailles Treaty, held on 19 March 1920, ended any prospect that the United States would accept the Treaty and therefore also some responsibility for reparations. Yet British leaders continued to hope that Washington would recognize its own interest in writing down the debts. They differed among themselves only on how to encourage this outcome. Austen Chamberlain, urged on by his Treasury advisers, favoured a unilateral reduction of Britain's own war debt and reparation demands in the expectation that other European states would do likewise and the United States would follow suit.[103] Curzon at the Foreign Office was prepared to support Chamberlain's approach, but they met opposition from Sir Robert Horne, the president of the Board of Trade, and Winston Churchill, the secretary of state for war, who had the prime minister's ear. Rather than risking unilateral concessions, Churchill recommended that any relief on the French debt should be made contingent upon French concessions on reparations, and that Washington should be informally warned that it must contribute war debt concessions if it did not want to be held responsible for aggravating Europe's crisis. The Cabinet adopted Churchill's proposal, and Lloyd George sought to line up the French behind this policy in

June 1920 at the second Lympne (Hythe) conference.[104] Soon afterwards, London and Paris independently approached Washington and, while denying any wish to apply pressure, invited the American administration to contribute to the reduction of inter-governmental debts.[105]

All the evidence pointed towards a negative response. Benjamin Strong, the new governor of the Federal Reserve Bank of New York, along with leading Wall Street bankers and directors of several large corporations, favoured American participation in a comprehensive debt settlement.[106] Their views were echoed in the *New York Times*, the *New York Herald Tribune*, *New Republic* and a handful of other liberal journals. But outside New York, American opinion was generally opposed to concessions on war debts. A wave of hostility towards France arose in the late spring after the publication of highly coloured reports of atrocities committed by its colonial troops in Germany. The Hearst press, the newspaper chain with the largest circulation in America, constantly prejudiced opinion against France, Britain and further entanglements with Europe.[107] Meanwhile, Wilson's secretary of the Treasury, Carter Glass, and his officials refused to budge from their claim that American war debts had no connection with Allied reparation demands on Germany. In 1919, they had taken the view that the key to Europe's recovery was restored confidence: ratification of the Treaty of Versailles would remove the uncertainties clouding economic prospects, and sufficient commercial credit could then be mobilized to sustain recovery, enabling the American debts to be paid. Despite America's refusal to ratify the Treaty, US Treasury officials continued to claim that the key was restored confidence, which would come when the Allies accepted debt-funding agreements with the United States.[108]

Nothing said or done during the presidential election campaign increased the prospects of an American contribution to a general settlement. Harding, the Republican candidate, who led from the start, made only passing reference to inter-governmental debts, which, he indicated, should be treated just like commercial obligations.[109] Politicians in London and Paris nevertheless remained hopeful that once in office the Republicans would accept the bankers' view of the debt issue, and in spring 1921 France sent René Viviani, the wartime premier and a popular figure in America, personally to request Harding to settle war debts.[110] Only after he returned empty-handed and Congress proceeded to stipulate severely restricted terms of reference for the administration's World War Foreign Debt Funding Commission did the European powers face up to the likelihood that Washington would not contribute to a major writing down of inter-governmental debts. French leaders saw no option but to resume their demands for German reparations. Lloyd George and colleagues remained reluctant to give up on the United States, but by December 1921 they too accepted that there was scant hope of relief from this quarter. As Lloyd George commented to Briand and Louis Loucheur, the French minister of reconstruction,

> the United States would not come in until it had become quite plain to them that an attitude of selfishness blocked the way to the economic peace of the world. At present she neither understood nor realized the position and there was nothing to be done but to go on without her.[111]

British officials contemplated the unilateral cancellation of their own claims on European Allies and the payment of US war debt demands, but decided against it.

In September 1920, Millerand, profiting from his reputation for firmness on reparations, gained election as president of the Republic, and called upon Georges Leygues, a close associate, to form the next government. Sensing the impatience of the press and Parliament to see French reparation demands actually met, Leygues took the first opportunity to visit London in the hope of coordinating policies. Not only did he fail in his quest, but embarrassingly, he also failed to secure an audience with George V who was entertaining the Emir Faisal, the Arab leader whom the French had only recently driven out of the Lebanon and was now Britain's choice as King of Iraq.[112] This effectively sealed Leygues' fate, and when the Chamber of Deputies reconvened in the New Year he was defeated in a vote of confidence by the decisive margin of 463 to 125.

Shortly beforehand, Millerand took the opportunity to name the Comte de Saint-Aulaire as Cambon's successor at the London embassy. This was a surprise choice, for Saint-Aulaire was the youngest ambassador in the French foreign service and had only recently taken up his post in Madrid. The reason was nevertheless clear enough. Frustrated by Lloyd George's manoeuvrings, Millerand sought an envoy who would vigorously assert French interests. At the Elysée palace, Millerand explained to Saint-Aulaire his mission:

> We are counting on you for the maintenance and operation of our necessary alliance with London, but on an equal footing. Anglophilia should not degenerate into Anglomania or Anglo-idolatry. This is what I told the council of ministers in securing your appointment.[113]

Saint-Aulaire proved well suited to the task. Repeatedly, he squared off with Curzon, and on more than one occasion he was left standing when Curzon, unused to assertive opposition from foreigners, collapsed. Saint-Aulaire effectively represented France from February 1921 until December 1924, despite his disdain for Leygues' successor, Aristide Briand, whom he regarded as lazy and opportunistic.[114]

As Saint-Aulaire took over at Albert Gate House, Cambon, the outgoing ambassador, observed to him, 'You will be astonished at the friendliness of the British public and the hostility of the government.'[115] Saint-Aulaire soon found this to be true. Among the British working classes, the terrible carnage of the war had stirred sympathy for their French counterparts. But while Saint-Aulaire was constantly in demand for public functions, at the official level 1921 proved to be an exceptionally difficult year for Franco-British relations. As well as numerous secondary issues, serious differences arose over German disarmament and reparations, Upper Silesia, the Graeco-Turkish conflict and the American initiative on disarmament. That relations did not break down may be largely credited to Briand's vision and diplomatic skills. By 16 January 1921, when he formed his sixth government, Briand had over twenty years of parliamentary experience including 16 months as premier during the most difficult period of the war. He had never been much interested in economic or financial issues, nor until now had he taken direct responsibility for foreign affairs.[116] But in one respect at least this placed him at an advantage, for he could claim that he bore no responsibility for the Treaty of Versailles, which increased his margin of manoeuvre. He was also a popular figure in the Chamber of Deputies: a man of the Right who enjoyed the support of the *Bloc national*, but also an old socialist who, unlike President Millerand, remained on good terms with many Radical and Socialist deputies. Reputedly too lazy to read ministerial papers, he soon demonstrated mastery of his foreign policy brief as well as formidable negotiating skills aided by a razor-sharp wit. Lloyd George, who enjoyed running rings around his French opponents, found himself unable to do so with Briand. Indeed, according to his mistress, Frances Stevenson, he became increasingly frustrated that Briand regularly beat him at his own game.[117]

Briand set out his ministerial plans on 20 January, including his intention to remove the remaining wartime controls on the economy, and the dual basis of foreign policy that he was to pursue consistently for the next ten years. The first element was, as he put it, his republican commitment to 'pacifism'. France had emerged from the recent war as the military and moral victor, but also severely impoverished, while Germany, the aggressor, remained far wealthier. Germany must therefore compensate France. Nonetheless, he was committed to peace or at least the minimum use of force, and sought to work with Germany rather than pursue revenge or retribution. This was more than mere rhetoric. Briand, like most French leaders, recognized that one means of containing Germany was to develop commercial, industrial and financial links, thereby increasing its stake in the post-war settlement. Millerand, who relied for advice upon Jacques Seydoux, the economic expert at the Quai d'Orsay, was drawn towards this solution.[118] Eventually Briand went further down this road than most of his colleagues. In theory, it should have complemented the second element of his policy, namely the re-establishment of an *entente* or *accord* with Britain and if possible America. As he put it

> This accord is the primordial condition for the settlement of all the questions on which the re-establishment of peace depends. We will do everything to maintain and develop it. We have firm confidence that our friend and ally, England, will aid us with all its forces. Nothing can weaken relations between these great powers, which have learned to know one another better and respect one another in the terrible conflict where they spilt their blood together. It is their intimate union that assures the peace of the world. Whether it is the execution of the Treaty of Versailles, the settlement of the Eastern Question, the maintenance of the peace established by the treaties in Central Europe or relations with peoples of Eastern Europe, the close alliance between Great Britain and France is the basis of our external policy.[119]

Briand never abandoned this policy, but under the vigilant eye of conservative critics in Parliament and the Paris press, he had to tread a fine line between collaboration with Britain and firmness towards Germany. Cynicism at the manner in which Britain had undercut French security at the peace conference gave rise to several Paris cabaret acts in which Lloyd George was portrayed as a trickster or conman. So unrestrained were the productions that the French ambassador in London, worried at their potential damage to relations with Britain, demanded the intervention of the police.[120] Notwithstanding the occasionally acerbic commentary of the press and cabaret entertainers, French opinion remained well-disposed to the *Entente*. But with Britain, Germany and France all firmly entrenched in conflicting positions, the prospects of resolving the disarmament and reparations issues were dim.

Within four days of taking office, Briand sparred with Lloyd George for the first time at the Quai d'Orsay over Germany's adherence to the terms of the peace treaty. Foch presented evidence of its duplicitous approach to disarmament. Although the *Reichswehr* had been reduced to 100,000 men, he warned that it was largely composed of long-service officers and non-commissioned officers who, together with the 150,000 state police, 30,000 civilian police and 17,000 gendarmerie constituted the nucleus of a formidable force whose enlisted men could be drawn from the patriotic organizations and the *Einwohnerwehren*. This made it all the more essential for the Allies to insist upon strict fulfilment of other treaty obligations, including the abolition of conscription, which the German states had not so far done, the surrender and destruction of war materials, the disbanding of the paramilitary *Freikorps* and the confiscation of weapons from private hands.[121] Observing that greater progress had occurred since the Spa conference in July 1920 when the Allies had shown a united front, Briand appealed for a new display of unity and the threat of sanctions to secure fulfilment of the terms that Foch had set out.[122] Lloyd George, however, dismissed Briand's appeal. Germany had made 'a sincere effort to meet the Allies in regard to disarmament', he claimed, and 'on no condition' would he support the French threat of sanctions.[123]

Turning to reparations, French and British differences seemed at first equally unbridgeable. Paul Doumer set out French demands for a total reparations bill of approximately 200 billion gold marks (£8 billion), or 12 billion annually over 42 years, with France receiving 52 per cent as agreed at Spa, or approximately 125 billion RM in all.[124] Lloyd George dismissed this as 'not a serious contribution made to serious people', and after further wrangling he announced his intention to return to London.[125] Both sides, however, were posturing. French ministers had anticipated opposition from Britain and other Allies to Doumer's claim. Their chief concern was to ensure that, whatever happened, France would receive some payments to cover the exceptional burden of reconstructing the devastated regions, and in particular that Germany actually made some payment by 1 May, the deadline for its interim instalment of 20 billion gold marks.[126] On the British side, Lord Hardinge, the recently appointed ambassador to France, cautioned Lloyd George against adopting an unyielding position.

A former viceroy of India as well as twice permanent secretary of the Foreign Office, Hardinge was steeped in the prejudices of late Victorian England and regarded France as one of the 'Latin races', who lacked the steadfastness of the Anglo-Saxons and lived for 'form'.[127] Shortly before the Paris conference he recorded in his diary his horror of an alliance with France: 'no sane Englishman could possibly be tempted by the idea of being dragged at the wheels of the Chauvinism and pseudo-Imperialism of France. We would suffer more and have to condone more.'[128] But after Leygues' decisive defeat in Parliament, he became apprehensive of mounting French frustration and advised Lloyd George to accept some of Briand's demands. Otherwise, Hardinge warned, they were likely to see the return of Poincaré, whose recent articles in *Le Temps* and *Revue des Deux Mondes* left little doubt that he would take an unyielding line on reparations and be even harder to deal with than Briand.[129]

Experts were requested to draw up a compromise scheme, and on 29 January the Allies agreed to issue Germany a schedule of reparation payments totalling 226 million gold marks payable in 42 annuities from 1 May 1921, equal to a 12 per cent *ad valorem* tax on German exports, and a set of disarmament demands. They also included a list of military and commercial sanctions for each infraction of their demand, and at Briand's request they added a statement affirming Allied solidarity.[130]

Briand received an overwhelming vote of confidence on 4 February when he presented the results to the Chamber of Deputies.[131] But with the Graeco-Turkish conflict the subject of an international conference in February and the German problem far from solved, Sir Eyre Crowe, the permanent under-secretary of the Foreign Office, reopened the question of a British guarantee to France. With Franco-British relations drifting towards crisis, he advised, the offer of a guarantee would make France more cooperative. At present, no French government could reduce its reparation demands upon Germany even though it knew they were unrealistic, because the French public were fearful of appeasing their larger, more dynamic and potentially aggressive neighbour. A British guarantee would make concessions possible. It might also induce France to 'make concessions to British interests in the East, and perhaps elsewhere'. And, Crowe added, it would be popular with the British public.[132]

Curzon showed little interest and refused to circulate Crowe's paper to the Cabinet.[133] It was nonetheless the first of no less than three occasions that year when British leaders considered extending a guarantee to France, each time in circumstances roughly analogous to those of April 1919 when Lloyd George first made the offer. On each occasion, they became worried about French determination to pursue a punitive policy towards Germany, and hoped that a guarantee might restrain France or make it more amenable to their own appeasement policy. Since the war, they had regularly asserted that Britain's frontier was on the Rhine.[134] The service chiefs agreed and soon advocated a straightforward alliance with France. But the politicians were being ingenuous, for had they actually believed that Britain's frontier was on the Rhine, they would have regarded a guarantee to France as something more than a device for gaining French concessions. They would also have shared France's determination to resist German domination of Eastern Europe, which would tilt the economic, demographic and ultimately the military balance decisively in Germany's favour and against France. But in fact they persisted in believing that Britain had nothing to fear from Germany, now that its Prussian leaders were removed and the Royal Navy dominated the English Channel and North Sea. The guarantee was a favour to be bestowed on France or an inducement to follow Britain's lead, not a necessity for *British* security. The same pattern was repeated in the 1930s, when the offer of staff conversations supplanted that of a guarantee. Only in February 1939 did British leaders accept that the Rhine was indeed Britain's frontier and even later that the Eastern Europe formed an integral component of the European balance of power.

Franco-British relations seemed to be on a better footing after the Allies received a German delegation at Lancaster House in the first week of March 1921. Lloyd George and Briand insisted that Germany could pay substantial reparations if German industrialists were persuaded to cooperate with their government by turning over a part of their foreign earnings. They appeared to disagree only over the means of persuasion, Lloyd George favouring an externally applied tax of 50 per cent on German exports, Briand arguing for military sanctions as agreed at their meeting in Paris. In the event, Briand's case for strong action was strengthened by the combative approach of the German chancellor, Dr Simons, who, anticipating divisions between the Allies, declared that Germany could pay no more than 50 billion gold marks – indeed only 30 billion marks, since Germany had already paid 20 billion RM in the form of ships and other sequestered goods – and then only if it regained Upper Silesia without waiting for the scheduled plebiscite. In private discussions, Lloyd George agreed that the Allies should 'make themselves as disagreeable as possible', to induce Simons to be more forthcoming.[135] He therefore took the lead when the conference resumed the following day, setting out the Allies' dissatisfaction with Germany, their demands and their threatened sanctions. Britain, he pointed out, would have to levy taxes of £500 million that year and for years afterwards just to cover the servicing of its colossal debts along with the pensions and disability allowances arising from the war. France's predicament was even worse. In addition to the debt and pensions burden, the French government must find 12 billion francs (£600 million) annually for several years to reconstruct its devastated northern departments. Nonetheless, under the Paris proposals of January, Germany was required to pay only £120 million that year: one-fourth of Britain's liabilities and one-ninth of France's, and this from a larger country with lower taxes.[136]

Lloyd George's speech, which included details of the war damage suffered by Belgium and France, illustrated by large-scale photographs that Briand helpfully supplied, could well have been written by French leaders, and indeed parts of it almost certainly were. Thus when Simons held his ground, Lloyd George saw little choice but to declare that sanctions would be applied. To his surprise, Foch, who was present, announced that French troops were ready to move the following morning. Almost immediately they occupied Duisburg, Ruhrort and Düsseldorf, three commercial towns in the Ruhr, the 60 by 30 mile region which contained no less than five-sixths of Germany's coal and four-fifths of its steel production. On 13 March customs posts were erected at all the German Rhine crossings, separating the west bank economically from the rest of Germany.

Briefly the sanctions appeared to work when on 23 March the German government paid 1 billion gold marks on account to the Reparations Commission. But already it seemed doubtful that Germany would meet the Commission's demand for 12 billion RM before 1 May. The German government, aware of American frustration at the impact of the reparations dispute on trade, sought to persuade Washington to mediate with the Allies. Washington rejected Berlin's approaches, which threatened to draw it into Europe's political conflicts.[137] London, however, seemed ready to compromise. In the final conversations at the London conference, Lloyd George had openly acknowledged his suspicions that the customs barrier on the Rhine, the sanction most strongly favoured by France, masked a larger imperialist ambition. Repeating his belief that the Great War was the result of French ambitions to regain Alsace-Lorraine, he requested Briand solemnly to promise that he would not repeat history by pursuing similar designs on the Rhineland.

> There was a real horror in this country of creating another Alsace-Lorraine. Alsace-Lorraine had cost Europe so much; we all had had to pay for it. He would like M. Briand to pledge his Government and country here that this customs régime would end the moment Germany had come to a satisfactory arrangement with regard to disarmament, reparations and war criminals.[138]

In March, the German government disputed the Reparations Commission's claim that it still owed 12 billion RM by 1 May, and indicated that it would not meet the Paris demands. This led to Franco-British conversations at the country home of the banker, Sir Philip Sassoon, at Lympne in late April, which came close to breakdown before Lloyd George indicated his readiness to compromise on the demands. With conversations continuing at Downing Street, the Reparations Commission issued its long-awaited statement on the total reparations bill. This amounted to 132 billion gold marks (£6.6 billion), to be paid in three series of bonds. The A and B series, of 12 billion and 38 billion RM respectively, were to be issued before the end of the year and carry an interest rate of 5 per cent. The C series, worth nominally 85 billion gold marks, were also to be delivered to the Reparations Commission, but would only be issued when the Commission was satisfied that Germany had the financial means to service them, and in the meantime they would carry no interest.[139]

British leaders were content with the Commission's recommendations, since the A and B bonds, the only ones they believed likely ever to be paid, totalled only 50 million gold marks (£2.5 billion). The French, however, were also satisfied with them, both on account of the large total demand and because the nominal value of the C bonds roughly equalled Europe's total war debts to the United States. Not only did this point to the link between reparations and war debts, but also by giving priority to the A and B bonds it implicitly established the priority that France constantly sought for the reconstruction of its devastated regions. Briand, indeed, proposed to issue the A and B bonds in the international markets so as to make Germany's general credit-worthiness dependent upon servicing this debt and to secure early reparation payments, while attempting at the same time to establish at least a moral connection between the C bonds and American war debt claims.[140] But Lloyd George seized upon the Commission report as grounds for putting off a showdown with Germany, claiming that Berlin must be allowed time to consider its response. Briand protested against further temporizing, which merely played into Germany's hands, and indicated his determination to apply sanctions. Lloyd George warned that unilateral action would wreck the 'alliance'. A few days later, however, he agreed to new demands accompanied by an ultimatum that the Allies would occupy the Ruhr, if Germany did not accept them by 12 May.[141] This produced a short-lived crisis in Berlin before a majority in the Reichstag approved the terms. But despite the Allies' ostensible unity, Lloyd George's ill-tempered complaints of French intransigence could not have made it clearer that Britain would resist further sanctions if, as seemed likely, Germany defaulted again.

Besides reparations, the crisis in Upper Silesia now also strained Franco-British relations. The plebiscite held on 21 March 1921 had resulted unexpectedly in a substantial majority (707,605 vs 497,359) in favour of restoring German sovereignty rather than transferring the territory to Poland. But the geographic distribution of votes yielded a checkerboard pattern, including the crucially important industrial triangle, Gleiwitz-Beuthen-Kattowitz, where the communes containing the steel mills voted in the majority for German control while the communes containing the coal mines that fuelled the mills voted mainly for Poland.[142] French leaders, mindful of Germany's undiminished military potential and the loss of their own ally Russia, looked to Poland as a vital substitute. Only the previous month, Briand had signed a defensive alliance with Poland. French representatives on the Inter-Allied Control Commission therefore pressed for a division of Silesia that accorded Poland the maximum benefit the plebiscite outcome allowed. Political bias was however apparent on every side. Lloyd George, disregarding the strategic argument for bolstering Poland, signalled to British representatives in the region that he favoured the restoration of the whole region to Germany.[143] He expressed outrage that France should claim part of the region for Poland when the plebiscite itself had been restricted only to part of Silesia and a clear majority even here had signalled their preference for Germany. Neither he nor anyone else pointed to the irony that Britain in this same year applied a closely similar policy in Ireland by restricting its interest to six of the nine counties of Ulster which could be counted on to produce a Protestant majority and thereby justify the retention of most of northern Ireland for the Crown.[144]

With the outcome undecided in Upper Silesia, Germany and Poland built up rival 'volunteer' forces. The increase in incidents led Curzon to protest in his usual haughty manner at French partisanship in Poland's favour and to threaten support for German paramilitary action.[145] This evoked a pained response from Briand, who denied partisanship and urged that Allied warnings should be sent to Berlin as well as Warsaw.[146] That same day Lloyd George seemed deliberately to aggravate the situation by declaring in Parliament that Poland had no legitimate claim to Upper Silesia.[147] Briand did his best to restrain French protests, claiming in the Chamber of Deputies that Lloyd George's speech had been badly translated and reaffirming that France remained loyal to the *Entente*.[148] Lloyd George nevertheless continued to brief journalists against France, while Curzon added his tuppence worth.[149] Yet Curzon protested to the French ambassador at the vituperative criticism of British policy in extreme French right-wing journals, which he persisted in believing were government controlled.[150] He also reacted angrily to Hardinge's report from an unnamed source that the French government would use the entry of German troops into Upper Silesia to justify their occupation of the Ruhr. Action on these lines was openly favoured by right-wing publicists and politicians such as Jacques Bainville, Maurice Barrès and Léon Daudet, but not by Briand, who consistently put the maintenance of the *Entente* before sanctions against Germany. But Hardinge, who so misunderstood the French scene as to believe that Briand was merely the mouthpiece of an Anglophobe Quai d'Orsay,[151] failed to make this clear, and Curzon warned Briand that unilateral French action would 'shake the *Entente* to its foundations'.[152]

A few weeks later, French opinion was inflamed by the news that French troops in Upper Silesia had been fired upon and briefly held prisoner by German 'self-protection' forces. Several other serious incidents followed, culminating on 4 July when a French officer was assassinated.[153] Under intense pressure from Parliament and the press, Briand announced that the military mission in Upper Silesia would be strongly reinforced. Despite the Control Commission's repeated request for military reinforcements,[154] Curzon accused the French of improper and provocative action.[155] When Briand insisted nonetheless on sending a division of troops to safeguard existing personnel, Curzon again berated France for its disloyalty.[156] At an informal Franco-British conference in August, Lloyd George launched repeated salvos against French policy. He charged that the French approach to Silesia would produce 'a fresh Alsace-Lorraine' and possibly another war.[157] The French were supporting the Poles 'for the purpose of crippling Germany. The British purpose, on the other hand, was to treat both sides fairly.'[158] Hardinge was disturbed to hear Lloyd George and Curzon in the corridors, speaking of their readiness for a 'rupture with the French'.[159] A Franco-British compromise was out of the question, but a breakdown was averted when Lloyd George proposed and Briand hastily agreed that the League of Nations should be handed the task of drawing a new German-Polish frontier.[160] The League's decision, unanimously approved by the Council in October and implemented that winter, came close to meeting Polish aspirations while disappointing Germany.[161]

In April 1921 yet another source of Franco-British friction arose when the Greek offensive towards Constantinople stalled and soon threatened to end in a rout. From the outset, Briand had been reluctant to prolong hostilities with the Turks, and on 10 March representatives of France and the new nationalist government in Angora (later Ankara) initialled an agreement settling differences over the frontier between Turkish Cilicia and the French mandate of Syria. But despite Saint-Aulaire's warnings of the need for greater clarity, in view of British sensibilities on Imperial issues, Briand allowed the matter to drift.[162] In May, British officials complained that their small military force at Constantinople was jeopardized by the French refusal to accept a unified command.[163] On 19 June, Briand promised closer cooperation between their forces, but took issue with Curzon on the appropriateness of further threatening the Turks.[164] Meanwhile he sent Henri Franklin-Bouillon, a former minister and currently president of the Chamber of Deputies foreign affairs commission, to reopen negotiations with Angora to resolve their bilateral differences. Queried by Curzon about the nature of the visit, Briand declared that 'M. Franklin-Bouillon had no mission from the French Government, but had gone as a French journalist to report upon the situation.'[165] Curzon, aware that this was stretching the truth, suspected the French of treachery.[166]

On 30 May, in the midst of this controversy and with the future of Franco-British relations being debated in the British and French press, Sir Eyre Crowe renewed his proposal of a unilateral guarantee to France.[167] The following day, Saint-Aulaire, probably aware of Crowe's initiative, took up the issue with him. He feared that the two countries were 'drifting apart and that, in the existing state politics, separation spelt disaster.' Since their interests were complementary rather than conflicting, he hoped they could reach a firm agreement 'based on France giving every assistance she could to Great Britain in the East, while England stood firmly by France on the Rhine.'[168] That same day, Raymond Poincaré, writing in the *Revue des Deux Mondes*, called for a new understanding with Britain and the negotiation of a bilateral alliance.[169] Meanwhile, the French minister of war, Louis Barthou, on a tour of the Rhineland, made a similar appeal to the British high commissioner:

> He and his colleagues were most anxious to see [the] Entente Cordiale trans-
> formed into an alliance. An Entente was an indefinite thing not clear to those
> who took part in it or to those who were opposed to it. France had … continual
> fear of [the] Entente breaking down and finding herself standing alone in face
> of Germany. An alliance with England would give France that sense of security
> which was necessary for her at the present time and would help her return to
> normal conditions.[170]

A week later, Lord Hardinge acknowledged that a guarantee to France was probably advisable. France's confrontational policy towards Germany on the Rhine, in Upper Silesia and over reparations, he wrote to Curzon, derived from its fear that Germany would soon become a formidable threat again. A British guarantee now would 'tend to quell the restless spirit which exists at present in France, and would probably produce more friendly relations between the two countries'. In fact, Hardinge's description of Germany's potential for future aggression – its large and rapidly growing population, its industrial might, the possibility of it reverting to 'a monarchy founded on a military and reactionary basis' – was to prove broadly accurate a decade later.[171] But neither he nor Crowe perceived that such a Germany was a threat to Britain as well as to France. They therefore treated the offer of a British guarantee as a major concession for which France would be expected to pay dearly.[172] Lord Derby, the former ambassador to France, similarly favoured a guarantee or alliance as a gift to be bestowed on France rather than a means of augmenting British security.[173] But others, including Curzon and Lloyd George, opposed even the offer of a unilateral guarantee.

Saint-Aulaire soon warned Briand against pursuing the issue. Contrary to the British view that France should offer substantial concessions for a British guarantee, he reminded Briand that France had already made important concessions for the joint British-American guarantee in 1919, which had never materialized. It was therefore unreasonable to be expected to pay twice over. In any case, a guarantee against unprovoked aggression – the form the British offer invariably took – was dangerously vague and no basis for French security. A bilateral alliance and radically improved Franco-British relations, in his view, would only come when Britain recognized the need for it. Unfortunately, he added, 'British opinion, which was so slow to recognize the German threat [in 1914], will not be less slow in understanding that, if scarcely immediate, this threat has by no means vanished.'[174]

By autumn the Upper Silesia dispute had been largely resolved, but not the crisis in Turkey or the reparations problem, both of which now became more acute. Trouble over Turkey arose in September, when Curzon learned of Franklin-Bouillon's return to Angora. The Quai d'Orsay continued to minimize the significance of his visit, which only added to Curzon's fury when news reached him that Franklin-Bouillon had signed a treaty with Youssef Kemal Bey on 20 October. French officials were able to deny that it amounted to a separate peace, as Curzon suggested, since the treaty only dealt with the disputed territory between Turkey and Syria and other local issues. They felt justified in ending this dispute since, left to confront Germany alone in Europe, France had to reduce its commitments elsewhere; fair play, to work, must be reciprocal.[175] But in London, Curzon and Lloyd George, who had staked their reputations on the outcome of the Turkish crisis, angrily protested at this apparent betrayal. Meanwhile the Paris press publicized the rift, while reminding readers of British efforts to squeeze France out of the Middle East to dominate the region and monopolize its oil.[176]

Since May, Germany's failure to pay reparations and British opposition to further sanctions had led Briand to see if payments could be obtained through direct negotiations with Germany. French leaders remained as sceptical as ever of German goodwill. But as negotiations were supported by both the German government and leading German industrialists, and Britain advocated direct German participation in the reconstruction of the devastated regions, Loucheur and his German counterpart, Walther Rathenau, met on three occasions at Wiesbaden between 12 June and 7 October, when they initialled an agreement.[177] If implemented, France would purchase German finished and semi-finished goods to a value of 1–1.5 billion gold marks, to be ordered through a special agency set up for the purpose; the German government would pay for them, and the amount would be credited to Germany's reparations account. Potentially, the agreement was hugely important. In the first place, it would approximately halve Germany's requirement for gold or foreign exchange to pay reparations, thus greatly alleviating the infamous transfer problem.

Second, Germany's barons of heavy industry would gain a stake in reparation payments, which might remove their opposition. More generally, it promised to reintegrate the French and German economies, thereby underpinning the peace in Europe. From Berlin the British ambassador, Lord D'Abernon, advised Curzon to accept the agreement so long as Germany received full credit for its goods and not the 35–45 per cent that France proposed.[178] But French and British industrialists strongly protested against the agreement, claiming it would exclude them from reconstruction contracts, and the British government objected that it would give France priority on reparations.[179] The French government, ambivalent about becoming so integrated with Germany, set the agreement aside. Meanwhile, news of the League of Nation's decision on Upper Silesia turned the German government decisively away from a constructive settlement with France.[180]

In view of his background as a financier and reputation as a friend of Germany,[181] D'Abernon's encouragement of the Wiesbaden agreement was perhaps predictable. Rather more surprising was his view of reparations in general. It was, he wrote to Curzon, a commonplace to claim that Germany could make reparation payments only through increased exports, which would damage British industry, and that reparation payments were chiefly responsible for the disastrous decline in the exchange value of the German currency. He was satisfied that these claims did not bear scrutiny. German trade competition was due not to reparations but to its much lower cost of production, which in turn was due *inter alia* to better industrial organization, lower wages and lower taxation on industry. True, relief from reparations would enable Germany to become a better customer for British exports and lessen its own need to export. Nevertheless, extracting reparation payments from Germany ultimately increased its cost of production and reduced its competitive advantage. On balance, therefore, abandoning reparations would increase, not decrease, Germany's industrial competitiveness.

> The root fallacy of the German system is to imagine that balance of trade is a cause and not a result. It is said, 'Germany has a debit balance of trade, and therefore she cannot pay this or that'. The truth is that she has a debit balance of trade because she has not been compelled to pay out of income, and has not been compelled to tax. Germany is consuming more than she legitimately could if she met her obligations. Thus, what is in reality the result of non-payment of reparation is put forward as a proof of inability to pay. This is a complete inversion of cause and effect.[182]

D'Abernon readily accepted that the greatest practical obstacle was the German government's unwillingness or inability to remove existing subsidies to industry and levy the necessary taxes. If it did so, instead of simply printing the money it required, reparations would not have the disastrous effect upon the value of the mark so often claimed of them. After all, he observed, using an example he knew from first hand, Britain did not ruin countries before the war when it required them to service the loans they had taken out.

> The fact that Egypt made annually to France and England a payment of inter-
> est equivalent approximately to 50 per cent of her total State revenue had no
> upsetting effect upon Egyptian exchange. In each of these cases the remit-
> tance was made possible by national economy, and was not provided by infla-
> tion. But payment will never be made through national economy while the
> bolt-hole of inflation is available.[183]

German reparation payments, one might claim, were not comparable to repayment of prewar loans to Egypt, since the latter loans, at least in theory, contributed to Egypt's foreign earnings capacity. All the same, D'Abernon's observations
deserved careful reflection (and still do to-day, since historians commonly
ascribe Germany's hyperinflation to its budget deficits, which arose from Allied
reparation demands and the German government's reluctance to pay them).[184] As
D'Abernon explained, a concerted effort by the Allies to collect German foreign
exchange earnings would have met much, if not all, of their reparation demands
and removed the temptation for the German government to create budget deficits
in the first place.

D'Abernon's colleagues, finding his analysis inconvenient, chose to ignore it.
By the time it reached London, Germany had requested another moratorium, and
the Foreign Office, the Treasury, the Bank of England, the City and the Cabinet
itself readily supported it. For all of them it seemed self-evident that Germany
had only two means of making payment. One was by raising an international
loan, which was out of the question so long as Germany was wracked by inflation
and political instability. The other was by earning a large export surplus, which
was theoretically possible but would pose a severe challenge to British manufacturers and merchants. In the meantime, Allied reparation demands discouraged
foreign investment in Germany, generated a flight of capital and set back the
recovery of not only Germany but also Europe as a whole. The near hopelessness of the situation seemed to be demonstrated by the plummeting value of the
mark on the foreign exchanges. From the prewar gold parity of 25 RM = £1, it had
sunk to 240 RM by May 1921, 450 RM by September, 700 RM by October and
1150 RM by the end of November. As the Treasury put it, the mark had already
fallen to a tiny fraction of its prewar value and would 'dwindle towards zero', if
the Allies insisted upon further reparations now. This would be a terrible blow to
City financial houses which had tied up much of their capital financing German
imports of food and raw materials.

> The position may be summed up in this way. The German Government can-
> not make further payments unless the industrial[ist]s will find the necessary
> foreign exchange. The industrial[ist]s will only do that if they can get credits in
> London. They cannot get credits in London unless there is a moratorium, for
> London finance regards the position as hopeless otherwise.[185]

All this seemed borne out in the following months by the mark's accelerating decline, which reached 2400 RM = £1 by July 1922, after the temporary moratorium ended, 20,000 RM = £1 by November and 225,000 RM = £1 after the Franco-Belgian occupation of the Ruhr began in January 1923. What the Treasury official did not point out was that the Reichsmark's weakness was largely due to the practice of German merchants and industrialists of holding their foreign exchange earnings on deposit abroad rather than repatriating them. This was greatly facilitated by the decision of the British government, yielding to pressure from the City which feared that German money was going to Holland and the United States, to abandon its right under the Treaty to locate and seize German commercial balances in City banks.[186] The City thus became a haven for German flight capital and a collaborator in the collapse of the mark. Britain's decision was communicated to Berlin but not Paris, which infuriated French officials when they learned about it from the *Board of Trade Journal*.[186] But the Treasury official, instead of pointing a finger at the City for its self-interested role in the disruption of reparation payments, 22 per cent of which were owed to the British Exchequer, singled out France as the problem. Since France was likely to object to another German moratorium, he advised that Britain should consider using threats or inducements – in particular, financial credits to help cover France's £350 million budget deficit – to secure France's acquiescence.[187]

Amidst the bitterness engendered by these disputes, Arthur Balfour, the former prime minister and current chairman of the CID, signalled his concern at the strength of the French air force, which comprised 47 independent air squadrons as against the RAF's mere 3.[188] This led to the setting up of a CID subcommittee on the 'Continental air menace', as it was called, and the recommendation to create a metropolitan air force with 500 warplanes. With the collapse of Lloyd George's coalition government and formation of a Conservative government under Andrew Bonar Law, a new committee was formed in March 1923 to review the need for strengthening air defences.[189] The impetus for the enquiry no doubt derived partly from interservice competition over scarce resources and the ambitions of Air Marshal Sir Hugh Trenchard to strengthen the RAF. He and other partisans of a larger air force made the most of the fact that France had built a bomber fleet and claims by certain military strategists that the next war could be won by aerial bombardment alone. Yet the suggestion that Britain should make preparations against a possible French air attack verged on the absurd. As the Army General Staff noted, so long as France faced a larger, potentially menacing German threat across the Rhine, it was practically inconceivable that it would attack the one ally capable of ensuring its survival.[190] In any case, it was no secret that France had already savagely reduced spending on aircraft production, making it only a matter of time before its current air force would become obsolete.[191] Lord Derby, now secretary of state for war, explained the improbability to CID colleagues. Balfour nonetheless persisted in arguing the worst-case scenario:

> He was in agreement with Lord Derby that ... the possibility of France attacking this country was decidedly remote, but he was doubtful if we possessed

sufficient confidence in the French nation, who were at present in a somewhat hysterical condition, which would enable us to say, 'We throw down our
weapons; you can stab us in the back if you wish, but we are certain that you
will not.' He did not consider that the country could accept such a position of
defencelessness.[192]

In fact, of course, Britain was far from defenceless. Without a single warplane,
the Royal Navy could retaliate against a French attack by bombarding vulnerable
coastal towns such as Dunkirk, Calais, Dieppe, Le Havre, Brest and Bordeaux. It
made no sense to prepare for every conceivable threat, without regard in each
case to intentions and exposure to counter-attack, since otherwise preparations
would have to be made against even minor powers. Given their common strategic interests, British leaders would have been wiser to regard a strong French air
force as grounds for *reducing* defence spending rather than increasing it. But such
was the Francophobia in political circles that most ministers sided with Balfour,
and, borrowing the principle applied to the Navy of a one-power standard while
allowing for the need for economies, they agreed to a Home Defence Force of
52 squadrons, comprising 'in the first instance' 394 bombers and 204 fighters.
In June 1923 Parliament accepted this without cavil.[193] Sir Eyre Crowe was left to
observe the tendency in Whitehall and Downing Street 'towards the substitution
of an *Entente* with Germany in place of that with France'.[194]

In November 1921, the United States briefly returned to the international scene
when it convened a naval disarmament conference in Washington. Its principal motive was to relieve pressure on the federal budget by securing the agreement of other major naval powers to end their large-scale construction plans
and mutually reduce their naval fleets. As with all such initiatives, the challenge
was to find a formula that left the relative position of the participants largely
unchanged. The Washington conference broadly accomplished this by means of
a five-power treaty, which fixed the total tonnage of British and American capital
ships at 525,000 tonnes each, while allowing Japan 60 per cent and France and
Italy 35 per cent of this total. Washington's other motive for the conference,
albeit never spelt out, was to contain British and Japanese power in East Asia and
the Pacific, so as to safeguard US interests in the region. This was obtained by persuading Britain not to renew the Anglo-Japanese Alliance, and by the adoption of
two other treaties. The four-power treaty required the signatory powers, Britain,
the United States, Japan and France, to respect each other's rights in the region
and consult in the event of potential conflict. The nine-power power treaty called
on the signatories to respect the 'Open Door' in China.

The treaties were typical of the Anglo-Saxon powers' approach to security
in the interwar period, before the experience of a Second World War persuaded them to act differently. This was to give primacy to disarmament whilst
eschewing firm international commitments. The five-power treaty contained a
relatively unambiguous commitment to disarmament, with specific targets for
all the signatories. But in place of the Anglo-Japanese Alliance, with its precise
obligations upon the two signatories, the four-power treaty called merely for

consultation. Similarly the five-power treaty contained no obligations on the signatories in the event that its terms were disregarded by one or another power. As British leaders appreciated, their decision to yield to American pressure and abandon the Anglo-Japanese Alliance was bound to disappoint Japan, for whom the Alliance represented Western acknowledgement of Japan's place among the great powers. To make matters worse, the five-power treaty, while ostensibly reducing the risk of conflict in East Asia and the Western Pacific, actually left Japan the strongest power in the region, which by no means added to international stability.[195] Scarcely less important was the antagonism the conference fuelled against France.

Briand chose to lead the French delegation to Washington in the hope of reviving the wartime Franco-American friendship and even, if the occasion arose, reopening the question of an American guarantee to France. He found himself snubbed at the opening session of the conference where the American organizers had placed him at a side table with delegates from minor powers rather than at the centre table with Britain, Japan and other leading participants.[196] A few days later he was startled to hear Balfour, representing Britain, call for land forces to be taken into consideration and question the legitimacy of France's army. Briand, who had not been informed that Britain would raise the issue of land forces, protested and took the first opportunity to defend French policy. France, he insisted, was no different from the Anglo-Saxon powers in maintaining forces appropriate to its defence requirements. The only difference was that, whereas Britain and the United States enjoyed the protection of the seas, France confronted a neighbour on its very frontier that only recently had attempted to conquer it and remained potentially far more powerful than France could hope to be. No doubt, he added, there were many in Germany who sought to escape from the horrors of war, to consolidate the peace and develop democratic institutions. But there was also 'another Germany', which had learned nothing from the war and continued to agitate for authoritarian government and aggressive policies. The memoirs of General Ludendorff, just published, vividly illustrated the reactionary view, with its proud assertion that for nations as well as individuals conflict was the natural order of things. For evidence that many in Germany still shared this view, Briand pointed to its resistance to reparation payments, disarmament and the punishment of war criminals. He therefore dismissed demands that France should abandon its military forces. But at the same time he reaffirmed France's pacific spirit, observing that since the war its army had been reduced by as much as British and American naval forces in percentage terms, and would soon be reduced further when conscription was shortened from two years to eighteen months.[197]

Briand's speech, a brilliant exposition of the argument for security before disarmament, would be unexceptionable today. The British and American press nevertheless continued to publish furious attacks by George Bernard Shaw, H. G. Wells and others, who made France out to be the greatest danger to world peace. At a press conference on his departure from Washington, Briand betrayed his frustration. Challenged by a correspondent from the Hearst newspaper chain to explain how his commitment to peace could be squared with the presence of French tanks on the Rhine, he observed that the United States was itself constructing a new generation of battleships. To the correspondent's protestation that they were intended only to maintain the peace, he responded, 'Very well, but so far as I know, battleships were not invented for fishing sardines.' The journalist, thus silenced, retaliated in print by misquoting Briand on Franco-Italian parity, which caused outrage in Italy. Meanwhile, in the conference, further criticism was directed at the French submarine fleet.[198]

As Briand sailed from New York on the liner 'Paris' bound for Le Havre, Walther Rathenau, representing the German government, visited London where he informed Curzon that the collapse of the mark made it impossible to pay the 750 million RM in reparations due in early 1922. Curzon assured him that Britain would be content with a much-reduced payment. But since France could be expected to resist concessions, he invited the French minister of industrial reconstruction, Loucheur, for conversations with Sir Robert Horne, the chancellor of the exchequer, and Lloyd George, at Chequers. There, British ministers sought to interest him in a broad scheme wherein reparations as well as war debts would be subordinated to the recovery of European trade: something along the lines of the Wiesbaden agreement but embracing Soviet Russia as well as Germany. Loucheur responded by appealing for British support for fiscal and financial controls on Germany, rather than giving way before its self-inflicted weakness. He also revived Briand's proposal of late April to commercialize the A and B reparation bonds, while offering the C bonds to the United States in payment of war debts. The British ministers rejected financial controls out of hand. As Lloyd George said, they had no intention of treating Germany like Turkey or China. But they immediately consulted the American ambassador on the issue of reparation bonds, only to be told that Washington would not hear of transferring its war debt claims to Germany.[199] The reparations dispute thus threatened to erupt into a new crisis when on 5 December Saint-Aulaire spoke with Curzon 'in a purely private, unofficial and confidential capacity' about the possibility of a 'defensive alliance', one that addressed both direct aggression in the West and indirect aggression such as a German assault on Poland.[200]

Just who initiated the proposal on this occasion remains unclear. Hardinge understood that Saint-Aulaire had spoken without authority from Briand, who seemed surprised by the initiative when queried about it. If this was true, President Millerand may have been responsible, since it is extremely unlikely that Saint-Aulaire would have acted on his own, especially as only six months earlier he had advised Briand against such an initiative.[201] Saint-Aulaire himself claimed that Curzon had raised the subject with him, although Curzon's report of their meeting suggests otherwise.[202] This seems the most likely explanation, since only a few days earlier the British Cabinet had heard deeply worrying reports that a German default would spell disaster for the City and discussed at some length different means of discouraging France from opposing another moratorium or occupying the Ruhr as security.[203] Whatever the origins, Briand promoted an alliance when he travelled to London on 19 December for talks with Lloyd George.

Their meeting began with Lloyd George setting out his grand scheme for European reconstruction. The current economic slump, he explained, had left Britain with two million unemployed. They were costing the government £1 each per week or £100 million a year, which was driving the Exchequer into the red and threatening to cause a deflationary spiral by forcing up taxes and further discouraging trade. Germany meanwhile was being dragged down by reparation demands, and it would never pay until or unless it expanded its foreign trade. Briand agreed and invited Loucheur to explain how they might integrate German trade and industry into the British-West European economy by implementing the Wiesbaden agreement. But Lloyd George was more interested in assisting Germany by reopening trade with Eastern Europe and in particular with Bolshevik Russia. Asserting that drastic action was needed, he proposed the creation of an international trade corporation with a paid-up capital of £20 million to prime the pump. Once trade revived in the East, Germany would become a credible borrower again, and by contracting an international loan Germany could make reparation payments sufficient to rebuild France's devastated region. If they therefore suspended reparations for a year while setting up the machinery required for the scheme, Germany was likely to support the reparations regime. The United States would contribute support through the international loan. And Soviet Russia could be brought in from the cold. A new initiative was essential, for they could no longer rely on the White forces to overthrow the Bolsheviks. Besides, Lenin and Trotsky 'were anti-revolutionary and were fighting their own revolutionary wing. ... If Lenin and Trotsky knew that they had Western Europe behind them, they would defy the extremists.'[204]

Briand indicated agreement in principle with Lloyd George's scheme, perhaps seeing in it a belated recognition that the Western powers could not safely disregard Eastern Europe, in which case Britain might be drawn into a comprehensive security pact. 'He had in mind', he told Lloyd George, 'a very broad Alliance in which the two Powers would guarantee each other's interests in all parts of the world, act closely together in all things and go to each other's assistance whenever these things were threatened.' If they formed an alliance, Britain would soon see France reducing its military establishment. Lloyd George responded that the British people would not accept such a wide-ranging commitment. They were

> not very much interested in what happened on the eastern frontier of Germany; they would not be ready to be involved in quarrels which might arise regarding Poland or Danzig or Upper Silesia. On the contrary, there was a general reluctance to get mixed up in those questions in any way.[205]

However, he was prepared to offer a guarantee to France against unprovoked aggression, and he could secure Parliamentary approval for it.

On the face of it, this was an important concession. But, as Saint-Aulaire explained to Curzon, the sort of guarantee Britain offered was of doubtful value to France. A revanchist Germany was almost certain to address its grievances in the East before attacking in the West. France would then face a dilemma: either to withhold support from Poland or Czechoslovakia and jeopardize containment in the East, or to support them and 'provoke' German aggression against France, thus removing the cover of the British guarantee.

> At the very most a British guarantee would save France, if not from another Charleroi because of the congenital slowness of the British army, then another Sedan, but it would not save it from a Polish Sadowa, which would be Germany's best preparation for another Sedan.[206]

Germany would appreciate the dilemma and be certain to exploit the potential rift between Britain and France.

Briand, alive to this objection, told Lloyd George that the real need was a clear display of Franco-British solidarity, which would deflate the ambitions of Germany's reactionary element and strengthen the credibility of its progressive forces. In order to draw Britain into a European-wide security system, he therefore repeated Saint-Aulaire's proposals for a two-tier arrangement, with a loose security pact along the lines of the five-power treaty for East Asia agreed at the Washington conference, including Germany if possible, but underpinned by a firm bilateral Franco-British alliance.

> Such an arrangement might include three or four Powers but the nucleus of it should be a complete Alliance between Great Britain and France, around which other Nations would gather. He repeated with emphasis that Germany should be a party to the Pact.[207]

Lloyd George remained non-committal, but encouraged Briand to hope for an agreement when they met at Cannes in the New Year.[208]

With French political leaders divided on German policy and Briand prepared to pursue Loucheur's scheme for extensive Franco-German economic collaboration, the potential influence of a British commitment to Continental security was greater than ever. Ironically, however, Britain's willingness to consider a Continental commitment was further reduced by the conjuncture of numerous differences with France, over French insistence upon the right to increase its submarine fleet, the administration of Tangier, Turkey, the Near East and Mesopotamia. None, in fact, arose from French ill-will, but Curzon and Hardinge, both former viceroys of India, tended to see the hoary hand of French imperialism everywhere and to believe that France was now bent upon the destruction of the British Empire. They therefore advised Lloyd George to offer Briand a unilateral guarantee as a means of inducing him to make concessions on the issues that concerned them, but under no circumstances to consider an alliance.[209]

Lloyd George was happy to take their advice, and at Cannes he invited Briand to proceed on the same lines as in 1904, when the *Entente* was established. Britain would be prepared to grant a unilateral guarantee against unprovoked aggression, just as soon as differences between the two countries were cleared away.

In effect, France must agree to support Britain in forcing an appropriate settlement on Turkey, concede British rights in the administration of Tangiers, abandon plans to expand its submarine fleet and support his own proposal for a European economic and financial conference with a virtually unlimited remit, to which all countries would be invited, including Germany and Soviet Russia.

Briand in turn renewed his proposal for a two-tier security arrangement, starting with a bilateral Franco-British alliance, followed by a consultative agreement among all the European powers. If an alliance were first agreed, he assured Lloyd George, they would find it easy to clear up outstanding issues.[210] Thereupon he submitted a draft alliance, produced after consultation with the Quai d'Orsay, which included a military convention, a clause defining violation of the demilitarized Rhineland as direct aggression against France and another clause designed to address the issue of indirect aggression in Eastern Europe.[211] Lloyd George, who insisted upon describing it as an offensive and defensive alliance, indicated again that a commitment of this sort was out of the question, but he promised to consult the Cabinet on a more modest agreement.[212]

Two days later, the Cabinet met to consider their response. Andrew Bonar Law, the lord privy seal, explained the alternatives before them on the basis of Lloyd George and Curzon's wildly distorted reports. On the one hand, the French proposed 'an offensive and defensive alliance', which 'would give France the right to ask us to maintain an Army up to the level desired by her', and practically force Britain 'to send large military forces to the Continent *or wherever they were required by France.*' On the other hand, the prime minister proposed a ten-year guarantee 'to defend the soil of France against unprovoked aggression by Germany', once the 'Eastern Question and other main points at issue between the two governments have been cleared up.' In other words, he proposed to defend France itself, but make no commitment if France insisted upon the demilitarized status of the Rhineland or went to the assistance of its allies in Eastern Europe.[213] Bonar Law continued:

> Under the proposed guarantee... we should not have to make any special military preparations. Our military policy would remain unaffected, and we should only provide the military forces required for the needs of the British Empire. If Germany attacked France, the whole of the resources of the British Empire would be available to support France. Such a guarantee would give confidence in France and would help the thoughtful section of French opinion to fight the Chauvinist party in France.
>
> Such a guarantee would also give us a free hand with regard to Germany. It must be remembered that to many people in this country the idea of giving any assistance to Germany was repellent; but we must realise that Germany is to us the most important country in Europe not only on account of our trade with her, but also because she is the key to the situation in Russia. By helping Germany we might under existing conditions expose ourselves to the charge of deserting France; but if France was our ally no such charge could be made.[214]

The Cabinet endorsed the prime minister's proposal.[215] But before anything more could be done, President Millerand, kept informed of negotiations at Cannes by a sceptical Saint-Aulaire, became convinced that Briand was losing control of the situation. Millerand, Barthou and other Cabinet colleagues as well as much of the Paris press feared that Briand had given way to Lloyd George on the Bolsheviks' repudiation of Russia's debt and on reparations from Germany, and was on the point of accepting the will-o'-the-wisp of a unilateral British guarantee against unprovoked aggression in return for substantive concessions elsewhere. In their view, Britain had already undermined France's security by blocking its establishment of a frontier on the Rhine, reneging on the 1919 guarantee and encouraging German resistance to reparation payments, and was now undermining its efforts to isolate the Bolshevik regime.[216] Publication in French newspapers of a photograph from Cannes, in which Briand appeared to be taking a golf lesson from Lloyd George, seemed to illustrate France's subordinate relationship and loosed a torrent of complaint in the press and Parliament. Briand had no choice but to suspend the conference to defend his actions in Paris.[217] He appeared first before the Cabinet, and then spoke to the Chamber of Deputies. But so strongly was the current running against him, he resigned without waiting for a vote of confidence to be held.[218]

2.6   The Ruhr crisis and international security

Poincaré, who succeeded Briand as premier and foreign minister on 14 January 1922, was regarded in London as the embodiment of French militarism and intransigence. His reputation was due in part to his punctilious and abrasive manner, along with his frequent press articles on foreign affairs which demanded action to force Germany to respect its Treaty commitments and took Britain to task for its appeasement,[219] but also to German subsidized propaganda which presented him as a prime mover in the events of 1914 that had led to Russia's mobilization and the outbreak of war. Appearances aside, however, Poincaré differed little from Briand in politics or policy. His Cabinet comprised much the same personnel as Briand's; and so far from being more intransigent, his *Union sacrée* government would have included Clemenceau's confidant Tardieu as well as several Radicals, had his offers of posts been accepted.[220] He approached sanctions no less cautiously. And like Briand, he regarded closer relations with the Anglo-Saxon powers, and particularly Britain, as of inestimable value to French security. However, he was not prepared to abandon French claims on Germany merely in the hope of a strengthened *Entente*, nor would he be fobbed off with an empty formula of words.

On 14 January, before completing the formation of his Cabinet, Poincaré had the opportunity to review the question of a security pact when Lloyd George passed through Paris on his return from Cannes. Meeting at the British embassy, where Hardinge interpreted, Poincaré accepted that the guarantee Lloyd George had offered might serve as the basis for an agreement. But he insisted that it must be modified in three respects. In the first place, it should be a reciprocal rather than a unilateral obligation. A unilateral guarantee created the impression of a favour bestowed by Britain upon France and encouraged the view that France should offer concessions to obtain it. This would be quite inappropriate, since in his view and that of all his colleagues Germany posed as great a threat to Britain as to France. This had been true in 1914 and was even more so now with the development of mechanized and aerial assault forces. Second, he demanded the inclusion of a military convention, since without it the pact would be empty of real content. As he put it, he would rather have a military convention without a pact than a pact without a convention. Third, he insisted that the pact must involve a much lengthier commitment than the ten years Lloyd George proposed. For the next ten years Germany would pose little military threat, and in any case France would have the security that came from controlling the Rhineland during that time. The threat could be expected to materialize precisely in the ten years that followed. Lloyd George offered to consider the first and last points, but ruled out a military convention, claiming that the British Parliament would never accept it. However, when Poincaré insisted, pointing out that military agreements had been made under the prewar *Entente* in 1911 and 1912, Lloyd George volunteered that Britain might accept informal military contacts over the period of the pact. As Poincaré disliked the publicity surrounding summit diplomacy, they agreed to leave the next stage of negotiations to Curzon and Saint-Aulaire.[221]

Poincaré was confident that he would secure a British commitment on far better terms than the one offered to Briand.[222] But events soon confirmed that little had actually changed. On the train back to London, Lloyd George confided to his friend, Lord Riddell, the newspaper publisher, that Poincaré had lost touch with reality in hoping for a military convention which set out force levels to back up a reciprocal guarantee. 'Poincaré', he repeated, 'is foolish'. He had no intention of going beyond a promise to support France in some undefined way in the event of Germany's 'unprovoked aggression'.[223] Reports from Saint-Aulaire in London alerted Poincaré to the remoteness of a substantive agreement. According to an informed source, Lloyd George, as he had done with Clemenceau in 1919, had offered Briand a guarantee without bothering to consult either the Foreign Office or the War Office, which led Saint-Aulaire to conclude that it was not a serious offer.[224] Corroboration came from General de la Panousse, the French military attaché in London, who found General Sir P. Chetwode, deputy-chief of the Imperial General Staff, deeply disturbed by the savage retrenchment being carried out under the so-called Geddes axe, which in eight to ten years time would leave the British army with fewer divisions available for a Continental expedition than in 1914 and fewer Territorial divisions to back them up.[225]

Saint-Aulaire submitted a new draft agreement to Curzon on 23 January 1922. This was a bilateral alliance in all but name and followed closely the draft that Briand produced earlier in the month.[226] Curzon offered no hope that his colleagues would accept it. He himself thought France was unreasonable to demand more now than it had been offered and accepted in 1919, and would support no agreement until France cooperated on the four issues that Lloyd George had set out for Briand.[227] Poincaré remained optimistic that Lloyd George would support an agreement on account of the importance he attached to the success of his forthcoming economic conference at Genoa. Since Britain would need France's cooperation there, he urged Saint-Aulaire to persist with conversations.[228] But, as Saint-Aulaire became aware, the rift between Lloyd George and Curzon had widened almost to breaking point. Curzon regarded the Genoa conference as a monumental folly and an example of Lloyd George's political opportunism which he had no intention of supporting. As for Lloyd George, Saint-Aulaire believed he would simply string France along with the offer of a pact to obtain its support at Genoa. Saint-Aulaire repeatedly sought to raise the pact in conversations with Curzon and Foreign Office officials, but could not expedite its adoption.[229]

At the opening of a two-day conference with Lloyd George at Boulogne on 1 March, Poincaré again raised the security pact. Lloyd George agreed to discuss it but insisted that they must first reach agreement on the Genoa conference. Then, adopting his most aggressive manner and claiming that Britain was staggering under the weight of two million unemployed, he warned that France must support his efforts at the conference to revive European trade or he would have no hesitation in 'isolating' France. Poincaré, setting aside his opposition to contact with the Bolshevik régime, confirmed France's willingness to attend the conference on certain conditions. These were discussed at length, and it was only towards the end of the second day that Lloyd George reverted to the security pact. Since, however, Poincaré was obliged to return to Paris, the issue was held over.[230]

French observers speculated on Poincaré's decision to pass up the chance to discuss a security pact, while British observers took this as proof of his disdain for British friendship.[231] In fact, so keen was he to obtain a pact that he soon accepted modifications to his draft agreement of 23 January. André Maginot, the minister of war, supported by Jules Laroche of the Quai d'Orsay, advised him not to insist upon formal staff talks if this proved a sticking point with the British, since in any case they would eventually recognize the practical need for them.[232] Shortly afterwards, Poincaré received word – almost certainly from Lord Cavan, the new Chief of the Imperial General Staff – that if he dropped this condition, he could count on France's friends in the British army to make up for the omission.[233] Presently he indicated he would accept a pact without reference to staff talks and a term of only 20 years instead of the 30 years he had originally requested.[234] It made no difference. Following the Genoa conference, Saint-Aulaire's repeated requests for Britain's response to the French proposal were simply brushed aside.[235]

Meanwhile reports from London confirmed that the British public, working classes as well as middle classes, had become thoroughly disaffected with France. In January, the Cambridge Student Union debated the motion 'that this house deplores the present attitude of France in international affairs'. Speakers for the motion, who claimed that France sought to crush Germany, which was fatal to British trade and employment, handily won the debate by 149 to 80.[236] In February, the National Executive of the Labour Party and the Trades Union Congress (TUC) declared their opposition to a Franco-British pact.[237] In March, Jacques Bardoux, the eminent foreign correspondent of *Le Temps* and frequent visitor to England, privately warned Poincaré that hostility towards France among British liberals had become worryingly strong. The immediate reason was the remarkably bad press France had received over its policy at the Washington conference. British opinion was always sensitive about naval issues and had been greatly disturbed by hostile reporting on France's ambitions to expand its submarine and cruiser fleet. But the more fundamental reason was the severe economic slump, which had generated large-scale unemployment, disillusionment with the peace settlement and extreme impatience with France for apparently obstructing the recovery of international trade.[238]

What could be done? Bardoux feared that the difference in outlook was too profound to be altered by a propaganda campaign; nor was the British press amenable to this approach. France, he believed, would do better to encourage understanding through institutions such as the Institut Français, the Fondation Rothschild and the university extension programme. Among other things, he suggested that the Institut might organize a series of lectures in England on aspects of contemporary France; perhaps an 'Entente Cordiale cup' could be introduced for rugby, association football and hockey. Diplomatic activity was important, but sports were probably more so. As the recent French victory at Twickenham illustrated, the British public commonly equated athletic prowess with noble qualities. But regaining the interested friendship of moderate liberal opinion would take time, and he warned that negotiations for an alliance must be completed before the next general election. The victory of a 'radical-worker coalition', he warned, would rule out any such agreement for the foreseeable future and leave France vulnerable.[239]

Lloyd George, always alert to the popular mood in Britain, sought to exploit it in his effort to ensure that the Genoa conference was a success. Passing through Paris on his way to Genoa on 8 April, he met Poincaré and Louis Barthou, the minister of justice, who would represent France at the conference. He pointed out how unpopular France had become among 'the lower classes in England', and warned them not to obstruct measures for opening up pan-European trade: 'if he and Barthou returned with empty hands it might mean the end of the *Entente*.' Hardinge, who was present, claimed that 'Poincaré was fightened, changed his tone and promised to make no more difficulties'.[240] But in fact Poincaré was not cowed by such warnings. Once again, he feared that French interests including its reparations from Germany and its frozen investments in Soviet Russia were to be sacrificed on the altar of British commerce. Acting like Millerand towards Briand at Cannes, he constantly bombarded Barthou at Genoa with warning telegrams, advising him to break off negotiations and keeping him on a tight leash to the end.[241] This had a bearing on the slow pace of the conference proceedings, which dragged on for six weeks. But it had little bearing on the *rapprochement* of Germany and Soviet Russia at Rapallo, which occurred within a week of the conference opening, while negotiations on Russian debt relief were still wide open, and which virtually destroyed any chances of the conference succeeding. British and French observers, however, drew different lessons from Rapallo. To the former it confirmed their view that reparations must be reduced if not set aside altogether to keep Germany within the Western camp. To the latter it offered further proof of Germany's unwillingness to accept the peace settlement and the need for vigilance, firmness and a Franco-British alliance.

Poincaré, writing to Saint-Aulaire in early May, suggested that surely now the British would see why France sought more than a unilateral guarantee of its Rhineland frontier. A guarantee was necessary, but it should be obvious that Germany would first turn East and swallow up Poland before turning West.[242] Saint-Aulaire warned that British interest in a mutual pact had waned.[243] Poincaré's speech at Bar-le-Duc on 23 April, a ringing affirmation that France would not yield an inch in its claims to reparations and if necessary would act alone to protect its interests, had been badly received in London.[244] Elements of the British press blamed France for the failure of the Genoa conference. At the Foreign Office, Curzon, referring to France as well as Germany and Soviet Russia, complained that the European powers were 'relapsing … into the deepest slime of prewar treachery and intrigue'.[245] Curzon's advisers agreed. In a private exchange, Sir Sydney Waterlow urged the French diplomat, Jacques Seydoux, for the sake of 'civilisation,' to abandon the 'chimera' of reparations and 'the policy of Louis XIV in Europe'; in which case Britain would be prepared to guarantee France against aggression and provide financial assistance.[246] Seydoux bridled at the reference to Louis XIV. France, he pointed out, had entered the recent war with a debt of 30 billion francs. It emerged with a debt of 300 billion francs, its monetary system shattered, its labour force sadly diminished and an enemy across the Rhine that was prepared to destroy its own currency rather than pay reparations, all the while remaining rich by any standard. Would Louis XIV merely have discussed this situation for two years?

> Germany has disarmed neither materially nor morally; it is engaged in an economic war against you as well as us, and merely biding its time before preparing for another war; and you are disarmed against German aviation as well as German chemical warfare as we learned at Washington.
>
> And here, permit me to remind you of the past. Under your excellent monarch [Edward VII] you became aware that German expansion threatened the very foundations of your Empire, and entered a *rapprochement* with us. … I was in Berlin when the [Entente] was concluded. I immediately felt from that day Germany had decided upon war. We did everything to convince you; recall the press campaign by Tardieu. You only opened your eyes at the last minute; perhaps had you opened them earlier, many things would have been different.
>
> We were right then; why do you imagine that we are wrong today? … At this solemn moment, our governments are seeking a common approach. I believe it is possible, if we return to the attitudes we adopted in 1904.
>
> … My professor at the Ecole des Sciences Politiques, Albert Sorel, the eminent historian and philosopher, liked to repeat: 'England is an island' – we don't forget and we ask you never to forget this other maxim: 'France is in Europe'.[247]

The gap in thinking ruled out a Franco-British pact. Indeed, on 29 May Balfour circulated a note to colleagues advising them that 'the unthinkable must be faced', of a French aerial attack on London. They must therefore give the RAF the means to bomb Paris in retaliation.[248]

In June 1922, the British government decided to settle its war debt to the United States, now that Washington had set up the World War Foreign Debt Funding Commission and issued requests for negotiations to begin.[249] With some hesitation, ministers also agreed to notify Britain's debtors that it would expect them to begin repayments, although only as much as Britain was required to pay the United States after deducting its reparation receipts.[250] The note, drafted by Balfour, was singularly ill-judged. In the United States it aroused deep resentment for suggesting that America was responsible for the continuing war debt-reparations tangle, while representing Britain as morally superior for seeking foreign cover 'only' for the whole of its external liabilities.[251] It was also badly received in France, which faced the prospect of increased British war debt demands to the extent that Germany escaped reparation payments.[252] As could have been expected, it therefore hardened French determination to obtain reparations and contributed to the collapse of a conference in London in early August, when Poincaré, over Lloyd George's protests, insisted upon physical guarantees if Germany was to be conceded a further moratorium.[253] Advised that France's budget deficit was reaching unsustainable levels, pressured by conservative nationalists to stand firm on reparations, and aware that he could suffer the same fate as Leygues and Briand when Parliament reconvened in October if he yielded, Poincaré dug in his heels. Speaking on 21 August at Bar-le-Duc at the dedication of the memorial to the *Voie sacrée*, the road that had kept Verdun supplied and the whole of France from collapsing in 1916, he announced, 'we want payment and we will be paid.'[254] Days later, the situation in the Near East abruptly deteriorated.

In March 1922, an opportunity had arisen to end the confrontation with Turkey when nationalist officials signalled their readiness for an armistice in their conflict with the Greeks and a negotiated settlement. The French government favoured acceptance of the Turks' condition that the Greeks must evacuate Smyrna within four months. But when Britain sided with Greece, the conflict continued. The Greek army had hitherto performed well, but it now faced an enemy force that was larger and better equipped than before, being supplied by Bolshevik Russia and, according to British sources, France.[255] On 5 September, the Turks broke through the Greek lines, and on 9 September they sacked Smyrna, massacring hundreds. Turkish units soon threatened the Allied neutral zone below the Dardanelles and Bosphorus. The British chose to stand fast since, as Winston Churchill, the colonial secretary, put it, 'If the Turks take Gallipoli and Constantinople, we should have lost the whole fruits of our victory.'[256] But the French government, having repeatedly advocated a compromise peace and disturbed by the near hopelessness of the military position on the Asian side of the Straits, withdrew its troops on 18 September, prompting the Italians to follow suit and leaving a British force of barely 300 men to defend the towns of Ismid and Chanak.[257] Five days later, a thousand Turkish troops entered the neutral zone, and on 29 September General Harington, the local commander, was ordered to issue an ultimatum for them to withdraw. Wisely he held back, for the following day the Turks indicated their readiness to negotiate. This halted the slide to war, and with the signing of a convention on 11 October the crisis temporarily ended.

By then, however, serious political damage had been done. The British Dominions, especially Canada and Australia, took it amiss that they should receive a call to arms at the eleventh hour, having scarcely been informed of the danger let alone consulted. Henceforth, they would not accept that Britain could merely take their support for granted.[258] Franco-British relations suffered a comparably damaging blow.[259] Curzon, sent to Paris on 20 September to rally French support, tactlessly accused Poincaré of deserting Britain at Chanak, which provoked such an angry response from Poincaré that he broke down in tears.[260] Crowe, generally regarded as one of the strongest Francophiles in Whitehall, furiously blamed France for the débâcle and claimed that its withdrawal of troops from Chanak had 'struck a fatal blow to the Entente.'[261] Austen Chamberlain, lord privy seal and another ostensible Francophile, publicly accused France of badly letting Britain down.[262] Bonar Law, the Conservative party leader, warned France in a letter to the *Times* to support British efforts for a just settlement of the Straits question or Britain would turn its back on Europe.

> We cannot act alone as the policeman of the world. The financial and social condition of this country makes that impossible. It seems to me, therefore, that our duty is to say plainly to our French Allies that the position in Constantinople and the Straits is as essential a part of the Peace settlement as the arrangement with Germany, and that if they are not prepared to support us there, we shall not be able to bear the burden alone, but shall have no alternative except to imitate the Government of the United States and to restrict our attention to the safeguarding of the more immediate interests of the Empire.[263]

Barely a week later, Lloyd George's coalition collapsed, to be replaced by a Conservative government headed by Bonar Law. Saint-Aulaire, who had cited Bonar Law's letter as evidence of his narrowly British outlook and preference for a policy of disengagement from Europe, soon reported signals from Downing Street in favour of the *Entente*.[264] But he was also obliged to add that, notwithstanding the prime minister's goodwill, the new government had no intention of departing from existing British policy on reparations.[265]

On 10 October, Sir John Bradbury, British representative on the Reparations Commission, requested colleagues to work with the German government on a plan for monetary and financial reform. In the absence of radical measures to end the inflationary spiral, he warned, the German economy would collapse, making the country ungovernable. He therefore proposed a four-year moratorium on reparations, in return for which Germany would issue creditors with five-year Treasury bills, to be redeemed after the moratorium. To ensure that financial reforms were carried through, the Allied powers should insist upon controls on the note issuing and credit creating powers of the Reichsbank.[266]

Poincaré acknowledged the seriousness of Germany's financial crisis and was prepared to consider a moratorium when the German government approached the Reparations Commission in November. But he insisted first upon obtaining a physical guarantee of eventual payment, and was prepared to accept nothing less than the occupation of the industrial valley of the Ruhr.[267] British leaders strained every effort to discourage him, holding out various inducements including a common approach to Washington on war debts and support for an international loan on the security of reparation bonds, while hinting that the future of the *Entente* was at stake.[268]

Briefly in mid-November, unease at the implications for the *Entente* of independent action caused Poincaré to hesitate. But frustration at reports of British encouragement of German non-payment, along with pressure from President Millerand and the conservative press led him to persist, prompting the breakdown of an Allied conference at Lausanne where emotions over the Chanak affair spilled over into deliberations on German reparations.[269] Subsequently Poincaré resisted Bonar Law's last-minute efforts to find an alternative solution.[270] The Reparations Commission, by a majority of three to one, with France, Belgium and Italy for and Britain against, declared Germany to be in default in its obligation to deliver supplies first of timber, then coal. And on 11 January 1923, Poincaré ordered a team of engineers guarded by French and Belgian troops to seize control of the mining and industrial assets of the Ruhr.

British and American leaders were convinced that Poincaré sought to exploit Germany's inability to pay as an excuse to disrupt its economy and promote the breakup of the country. Poincaré's officials in the Rhineland had indeed harboured such ambitions for several years, although until the latest crisis Poincaré himself had resisted subversive action. Nevertheless, he shared the view that France had been short-changed at the Peace conference in 1919 when it had been promised, then refused, the Anglo-American guarantee, and he now insisted that France must augment its security vis-à-vis Germany some other way. He also believed it likely that if the Rhineland became autonomous from the rest of Germany, it would trigger a process that would end in a looser, and therefore less dangerous, federation of German states. As he put it shortly before the occupation, 'we have not the least thought of annexation, but it is another thing to have a Rhineland without Prussians; basically it comes down to constituting a zone that is neutral in its sympathies by drawing its people towards us'.[271] Disturbed by the evidence from Rapallo of Germany's incorrigible revisionism and annoyed by Britain's refusal to hold Germany to its Treaty commitments, which merely encouraged its resistance, he therefore approved the occupation of the Ruhr. He was determined to obtain reparation payments, but he also anticipated that his economic demands would result in important political consequences.[272]

The occupation of the Rhineland and Saarland in 1919 and the temporary occupation of the five Ruhr towns in 1921 had passed off almost without incident. This probably led Poincaré to assume that the occupying troops would meet no resistance when they re-entered the Ruhr.[273] But it soon became clear that this occupation would be far more contentious. German miners, railwaymen and steelworkers in the Ruhr almost immediately responded to a call to strike, and the Cuno government in Berlin supported their passive resistance through financial subsidies.

French efforts to maintain coal output and redirect it to France led to confrontations, dozens of casualties, and the expulsion of some 100,000 German officials and others who sought to resist the occupiers. Meanwhile inflation in Germany, already running at an annual rate of several thousand per cent when the occupation began, accelerated into hyperinflation, reducing almost to nothing the value of the mark and severely crippling the national economy. French engineers and Belgian railwaymen, backed by sizeable military units, eventually managed to appropriate a large fraction of the Ruhr coal, but not before the heavy cost of the operation aggravated French inflation, shaking confidence in the franc.

Cuno held out until August, hoping to exploit the gulf that had opened up between Britain and France, but with Germany in crisis and Poincaré showing no sign of giving way, he resigned. In his place, Gustav Stresemann, another conservative with close links to business, became foreign minister and briefly chancellor as well. As early as 3 September, Stresemann informed the French ambassador in Berlin of his wish to negotiate a settlement, and on 25 September he unilaterally ended support for passive resistance. Poincaré's colleagues and advisers urged him to seize the opportunity. With Germany on its knees, they believed he could insist upon a settlement that included extensive French participation in German industry. This would not only ensure payment of reparations but would also give France greater purchase over Germany. They may have been right, although neither Germany nor Britain were likely to have tolerated French participation in German industry for long. What is certain is that Poincaré's prolonged inaction while currency chaos descended upon Germany merely intensified German and Anglo-Saxon animosity towards him. Worse, his last-minute decision to support the radical separatist movement in the Rhineland proved a fiasco. His officials were caught unprepared for the initiative, the separatists had almost no following, and the new chancellor in Berlin, Wilhelm Marx, was himself a Rhinelander and an effective opponent of the breakaway movement. Not only was the movement swiftly and brutally crushed, but the larger movement for Rhineland autonomy was also discredited. Poincaré, in contrast to Briand, was better at dragging his heels in stubborn opposition than adapting to changing circumstances or innovating policy.[274]

In May 1923, Stanley Baldwin had become prime minister when illness forced Bonar Law to retire from politics. Baldwin continued his predecessor's cautious policy, resisting pressure from Curzon to break with France while constantly pressing Poincaré to accept a negotiated settlement. He was thus in a position to exploit Poincaré's embarrassment. The Franco-German confrontation also drew American bankers into the crisis. President Harding had scrupulously avoided political entanglements with Europe, but by the autumn of 1922 he felt impelled to take an interest in the growing dispute over reparations. This was not, as historians have claimed, evidence of America's pursuit of world 'financial supremacy'.[275] Nothing, in fact, was further from Harding's mind. His motive for involvement was not financial or political hegemony, but rather unease at being held responsible for Europe's social turmoil on account of US war debt demands and his impatience to see trade revived and above all agricultural exports, on account of the recent slowdown in the US economy.

Charles Evans Hughes, the secretary of state, and other members of the Administration strenuously denied any connection between US war debt demands and reparations. But the argument was transparently flawed, and the very need to repeat it was indication enough of the pressure they felt themselves to be under from European critics.[276] As for trade, American farmers and other producer groups had done very well during the four years of war when European production was disrupted. But subsequently European production had recovered and production elsewhere expanded, driving down prices and spreading distress in rural America. The revival of prairie radicalism in the early 1920s, after a period of quiescence, made this a matter of particular importance to the Administration. In December 1922, therefore, Hughes, with Harding's approval, invited Europeans to call on the good offices of 'distinguished Americans', by which he meant leading businessmen, if this would forestall the impending occupation of the Ruhr.[277] London and Berlin welcomed US involvement, but Paris showed no sign of modifying its policy. Washington therefore held back, anxious to avoid becoming embroiled in European controversy. On 11 October 1923, however, with the Ruhr crisis still unresolved and Germany sinking into political turmoil, Harding's successor Coolidge, renewed the American offer. He would not contemplate directly involving the American government in a dispute involving reparations. But he appreciated the value that Europeans attached to access to US capital markets and hoped they would listen to the views of independent American businessmen.[278]

Baldwin and Dominions leaders, attending the Imperial conference in London, were delighted to learn of Coolidge's offer.[279] Not only did it chime perfectly with their view that commercial activity should come before reparations but it also raised hopes that at last the United States would acknowledge the link between its war debt demands and German reparation payments; an issue made all the more important since Britain had negotiated a debt funding agreement with the United States earlier that year. Despite British urgings, Poincaré again held back, refusing to introduce American influence into the reparations settlement until he had received assurances that the Reparations Commission would remain in overall control and that an expert enquiry would have no authority to alter Germany's total reparations liability of 132 billion gold marks. But when Britain and the United States yielded on his main demands, two expert committees were formed.[280] The second committee, chaired by Reginald McKenna, chairman of the Midland Bank and former Liberal chancellor of the exchequer, would investigate means of repatriating German flight capital. The more important first committee, chaired by the American banker, General Charles G. Dawes, was called upon to identify suitable means of balancing the German state budget and stabilizing the mark.

Dawes was an excellent choice. As a prominent banker, his imprimatur on a scheme of reforms would provide the necessary reassurance to American investors for the loan required to float Germany off the rocks. As a Chicagoan, he would not arouse the suspicions of an international stitch-up, which might have occurred had he been a director of J.P. Morgan or another Wall Street bank. And as a wartime liaison officer in Paris, he was also one of the few mid-Westerners sympathetic to France and able to exercise some influence on French leaders: a crucial factor since obviously they would be called upon to make the largest concessions. Dawes lacked the technical skills for the difficult task of devising the programme of reforms. But he had as colleagues Owen D. Young, chairman of the General Electric Corporation and RCA and a non-executive director of the Federal Reserve Bank of New York, and Henry M. Robinson, a member of the wartime Supreme Economic Council and another banker. They too reflected the care that Washington put into the selection of the team. Robinson, like Dawes a prominent Republican, came from Los Angeles and hence was 'free of any Wall Street taint'.[281] Young, albeit from New York, was generally known as an industrialist rather than a banker. He was also a Democrat, hence attracting cross-party support, and an exceptionally competent lawyer-businessman. Together with Sir Josiah Stamp, a prominent British businessman, statistician and former civil servant, Young was instrumental in devising the Dawes Plan by which reparations could be resumed without further endangering the stability of the German currency.

Poincaré's decision to support the work of the Dawes committee was consistent with his approach to the crisis. To him, upholding the reparations régime constituted an obligation upon all the signatories of the Treaty of Versailles, including Britain; and morally, if not legally, the United States as well as Britain was dutybound to help France secure justice. Confirmation that the Anglo-Saxon powers were at last prepared to devise a workable reparations scheme therefore seemed to him a major step forward. As a lawyer, statesman and spokesman for the beleaguered French taxpayer, this seemed to be exactly what was needed, and he soon endorsed the Dawes plan when it was circulated in April 1924.[282] In the event, he appears to have underestimated the influence over reparations that the Anglo-Saxon bankers would obtain when their loans and credits became essential to restart the German economy. But the concessions were made by his successors, and in any case their importance can be exaggerated since, after the bruising experience of 1920–4 which nearly destroyed the franc as well as the mark, it was extremely unlikely that France would ever again act alone against a recalcitrant Germany. Far more important, he appears to have overestimated his success in regaining Britain's support for the principles on which the Versailles settlement was based. Bonar Law, Baldwin and his successor in January 1924, James Ramsay MacDonald, leader of the first Labour government, were all prepared to support the revival of reparations, but only because they could see no alternative for the time being. None of them, however, was prepared to fill the gap in the postwar security framework left by the loss of the Anglo-American guarantee to France. They were superficially friendly in their dealings with French leaders, and Bonar Law and Baldwin at least were probably sincere. But MacDonald and Baldwin also followed the now familiar path of holding out hope of improved security arrangements to expedite the settlement of the Franco-German dispute, without any serious intention of accepting a British commitment to Continental security.

In September 1923, the fourth Assembly of the League of Nations endorsed the Draft Treaty of Mutual Assistance, a Franco-British initiative, which called upon member states to support general disarmament in return for stronger collective security against aggression. Under the Draft Treaty, the League Council within four days of the outbreak of a conflict would meet and decide which of the parties was the aggressor. Thereupon military sanctions, authorized under Article 16 of the League Covenant, would become automatic rather than merely optional as before, although signatories would be obliged to assist victims of aggression only within their respective region of the world. The Draft Treaty reflected the French thesis that disarmament, however desirable, must follow rather than precede adequate security provision. By the spring of 1924, 18 countries including France had confirmed their readiness to ratify it. Britain, along with the British Dominions, the Netherlands and the Scandinavian countries, nevertheless opposed it, not least because as a world power its obligation to provide military assistance would not be limited to a single region. MacDonald informed Edouard Herriot, Poincaré's successor, of British opposition when they met for the first time in June 1924. But, he suggested, it was his experts who were opposed, whereas he favoured a security arrangement including Britain, France and Belgium, which he would willingly help to devise once the more pressing issues were cleared away.

> *Mr. MacDonald*: ... We must assure our well-being, but we will work also to resolve the great moral problems of the peace of the world. Let us therefore settle first the question of the Dawes Report; then we will go on to that of inter-Allied debts, then to the problem of security, and we will try to remove from Europe the risks of war which threaten it ...

> *M. Herriot*: I thank Mr. MacDonald warmly for what he has just said. In effect, the most important result of our interview is a sort of moral pact of continuous co-operation between us for the good of our two nations and in the general interests of the whole world. I will do all that is possible and even the impossible to respond to his appeal ...[283]

Herriot was no less anxious than his predecessors to contain Germany, anticipating accurately that in ten years time Germany would again pose a serious threat to France.[284] But unfortunately, as leader of the *Cartel des gauches*, the centre-left coalition that had triumphed in the April 1924 legislative elections, he assumed that the British Labour government shared similar values to the *Cartel* and would join France in a constructive solution to their common reparation and security problems. In fact, MacDonald and his Labour party colleagues were if anything even more opposed to a Continental commitment and more hostile to France than their Liberal or Conservative predecessors. In conversations with Herriot, MacDonald spoke of infusing international relations with a new morality, while promising to address France's need for security, once an agreement was reached on reparations.[285] Skilfully, he suggested that it was the international bankers who demanded concessions on reparations, when it was largely he and Norman of the Bank of England who insisted upon them.[286] Herriot, anxious to make up with Britain, yielded on many aspects of the security and reparations settlement, including who was to determine any future default and define sanctions.[287] This merely earned the scorn of MacDonald and his advisers, who treated Herriot's decision to set aside his brief to demonstrate his commitment to the *Entente* as mere incompetence and personal weakness. It also infuriated Ambassador Saint-Aulaire who encouraged conservative critics in Paris to denounce Herriot for weakness and incompetence, a judgement frequently repeated by historians.[288] But what choice did Herriot have, given the evidence that Poincaré's unilateral approach to reparations had proven intolerably expensive in economic and security terms?[289] Since no one then or later has identified a third alternative, he was almost bound to accept MacDonald's vague assurance that Britain would stand 'shoulder to shoulder' with France in the event of a German default on the Dawes Plan.[290] He welcomed MacDonald's promise to appear with him at the fifth League of Nations Assembly in September, when all the replies on the Draft Treaty of Mutual Assistance had been received. In return, as MacDonald hoped, he promised to work closely with Britain at the forthcoming diplomatic conference in London to ratify the Dawes Plan.

With Herriot as good as his word, MacDonald succeeded at the conference in reducing reparations – from 132 billion gold marks, as originally agreed, to 30 billion of which slightly over 15 billion were for France – and in relaxing France's grip on the rules governing suspension of future reparations and sanctions in the event of another deliberate German default. At the League Assembly shortly afterwards, MacDonald rejected the Draft Treaty, but presented himself as a champion of international order and challenged other countries to join Britain in a new agreement on binding arbitration for international disputes. When Herriot warned that arbitration by itself was not sufficient, MacDonald sat down with him and hammered out a joint Franco-British resolution, which soon evolved into the 'Protocol for the Pacific Settlement of International Disputes', known simply as the Geneva Protocol.[291] By this Protocol, arbitration would be backed by force. Signatory countries would be required to accept the arbitration of disputes by a League committee of arbitrators, and any country that refused to do so or rejected the committee's decision would be declared an aggressor against whom the League would take 'any action that may be deemed wise and effectual to safeguard the peace of nations'. The Protocol would come into force immediately upon the successful conclusion of a general disarmament conference, scheduled to open in June 1925.

On the face of it, this constituted a major British commitment to European security; and indeed a number of MacDonald's fellow ministers regarded it as dangerously binding. But, as MacDonald recognized, an arrangement that left the League Council to decide on arbitration, aggression and the appropriate sanctions scarcely went beyond the commitment that countries made when they joined the League. Britain, with a seat on the Council, could always block unsuitable resolutions. The Protocol was, in his words, a 'harmless drug to soothe nerves'.[292] In any case, the Labour government had no intention of ratifying it, as was evident from the King's speech opening the new session of Parliament in October, which mentioned disarmament and arbitration while referring only vaguely to the Protocol.[293] The government soon escaped the embarrassment of going back on its own proposal when it was defeated in the general election of 29 October.

The new Conservative administration led by Stanley Baldwin had no intention of proceeding with the Protocol either. But there was still ways to go in the settlement of the reparations dispute and pacification of Europe. The immediate problem was that France objected to the first stage of evacuating the Rhineland, scheduled to begin on 10 January 1925, in face of evidence that Germany was still evading the disarmament clauses of the Treaty. Since MacDonald had promised Herriot in July that he would consider the security issue and Herriot had reminded him of his promise in August, experts were surveyed on means of satisfying the French demand, and a subcommittee of the CID was created in December to collate the results.[294]

The Imperial General Staff concluded that something should be done, since it was only a matter of time before Germany once again became a threat to European peace.

> The General Staff hold that it would be the height of unreason to assume that so virile a nation as Germany will rest content indefinitely with the reduced status and forfeitures of territory imposed on her as the result of an unsuccessful war; and that, given the opportunity, renewed aggressive action by Germany is probable, or at least possible, in the present generation.

In their submission they mentioned the possibility of relying upon a strengthened League of Nations, only to dismiss it as 'visionary and remote'. The only practical solution, they decided, was a defensive alliance with France and Belgium. Britain should avoid any commitment to France that specified the number of troops to be deployed or required the withdrawal of forces engaged in Imperial policing in peacetime. Nor should it accept any commitment regarding Germany's eastern frontier. A tripartite alliance was nonetheless essential.

> [T]he General Staff, looking ahead as far as they dare, see the balance of manpower steadily increasing in favour of Germany, but only usable for purposes of aggression if supplemented by adequate armaments. The future security of France and Belgium lies in the denial to Germany of the capacity to provide and maintain armaments on the scale necessary for the prosecution of a great war. This implies a policy based on a firm hold on Lorraine and, for the present, the Saar, and on the firm maintenance of Articles 42 to 44 and 429 of the Treaty. For the implementing of this policy, which is purely defensive and is based on the Treaty of Versailles, France and Belgium require the moral and material support of Great Britain. The anxiety of France in regard to this support can only be allayed by a defensive alliance. There is no doubt in the opinion of the General Staff that such an alliance would make for peace.[295]

The naval staff agreed with this view.

> The point of primary interest is that the Pact would ensure the security of the Channel ports. This was, in this sphere, our main preoccupation in the late war, and in any future war our interest in their security will be even greater on account of the great development of artillery, aircraft and other forms of offensive action.[296]

Hitherto, the air staff had resisted such a commitment, holding that France was as much a threat as Germany, while asserting that if Britain adopted any pact, it should include Belgium and if possible Germany.[297] But by the end of 1924 they too supported a tripartite pact, since they feared Germany's revival as a military power and believed that a pact, together with the demilitarization of the Rhineland, was the most effective means of forestalling German aggression against France and Belgium and ultimately against Britain itself.[298]

The general staff's basic assumptions, broadly shared by all the service chiefs, were set out with remarkable force a few weeks later:

> The question at issue is clearly not well understood by the majority of the British public. For us it is only *incidentally* a question of French security.... The true strategic frontier of Great Britain is the Rhine; her security depends entirely upon the present frontiers of France, Belgium and Holland being maintained and remaining in friendly hands. The great guiding principle of the German General Staff in making plans for a future war will be, as in the last war, to try to defeat her enemies in detail. Any line of policy which permitted Germany (with or without allies) first to swallow up France, and then to deal with Great Britain would be fatal strategically.[299]

The British service chiefs still shied away from a thorough analysis of the European balance of power, passing hastily over Eastern Europe and the near certainty that Germany would seek to 'defeat her enemies in detail' on her eastern frontier before using the additional security and resources thus obtained to launch its western offensive. But they did at least acknowledge that allying with France and Belgium in a common security pact was not an option, to be offered or withheld depending upon the concessions obtained, but a necessity for Britain's own security.

Austen Chamberlain, foreign secretary in the new government, shared the service chiefs' view, and with the backing of his Foreign Office advisers he sought Cabinet approval to offer an alliance to France and Belgium in place of the Protocol.[300] He was aware that British and Dominions support for such an alliance had greatly declined since 1919.[301] But he did not anticipate the extent of opposition among his own colleagues, when for three days in early March they debated the issue. Curzon, Balfour, Birkenhead and Amery opposed any substantive Continental commitment. Churchill, the chancellor of the exchequer, indicated his willingness to consider some general commitment, but rejected the general staff's main argument. Britain, he told colleagues, could 'stand alone'. 'I decline to accept as an axiom that our future is involved with that of France.'[302] Chamberlain nevertheless believed that colleagues would support him in offering a security guarantee to France and Belgium in place of the Protocol, and passing through Paris on 7 March on his way to Geneva he informed Herriot of his intentions.[303] Led by Amery, however, Cabinet colleagues intensified their opposition to a Continental commitment. Chamberlain, fearing he had been put in a false position, sent his resignation to Baldwin.[304] Meanwhile, to save face at Geneva, he proposed to support a German proposal for a Rhineland Pact: a much looser arrangement involving Germany as well as the former wartime Allies. The proposal had actually originated with Lord D'Abernon, the British ambassador, who suggested it to Stresemann as a means of forestalling Britain's adoption of an alliance with France. Stresemann had seized upon it, and for similar reasons Chamberlain's colleagues, including Amery, welcomed it as well.[305] After lengthy negotiations, the Pact was adopted at a conference in Locarno in October.

By the Rhineland Pact, the centrepiece of the Locarno agreements, Britain along with Fascist Italy guaranteed France and Belgium against German aggression, and guaranteed Germany against French and Belgian aggression. By a separate treaty signed at Locarno, Germany agreed to submit to arbitration any disputes that threatened the peace on its Eastern frontier. Independently France entered into mutual guarantees with Poland and Czechoslovakia against external aggression. Chamberlain presented Britain's support for the Rhineland Pact as the realization of its commitment to guarantee France in 1919, which in a literal sense it was. But as he privately assured the CID, the Pact, so far from increasing Britain's foreign commitments, actually diminished them.[306] As a signatory of the League Covenant, Britain had a general obligation to help maintain the peace everywhere. The Rhineland Pact limited its geographical commitment to Western Europe. Moreover, even within this limited region, it did not specify Britain's obligations in the event of aggression.

To the British government, the Pact was just another 'harmless drug to soothe nerves'. But in fact it was far from harmless. In the first place, it discouraged British defence strategists from thinking further about a Continental commitment.[307] Second, it served to warn France that if it wished to obtain British support against German aggression, it should abandon further support to its Eastern allies. French leaders had hesitated before agreeing to the Pact precisely for this reason. In the end they did so in the hope that it might eventually lead to a stronger commitment from Britain. Crowe, the under-secretary of the Foreign Office, had encouraged this hope.[308] But, in fact, the Pact did no such thing. Instead, as the French feared, it simply encouraged Germany to continue on the path of revision in Eastern Europe.[309]

2.7 Conclusion

Since 1918, the United States had hewed rigidly to its isolationist tradition, which indeed was reinforced by the recent crisis in the Ruhr. When at this time

Washington again became involved in Europe, it was minimal and due largely to the plight of American cotton, tobacco, wheat, pork and other producers who were suffering from the decline in overseas demand. The offer to Europe of disinterested advice from American business leaders seemed not only advantageous from an economic point of view but also politically acceptable, since it enabled Washington to remain at arm's length from European politics. On this basis it was pleased to have Charles Dawes, Owen Young and informally the directors of J.P. Morgan contribute to European economic recovery through their role in the Dawes Plan and stabilization of the German currency. Their efforts were successful, indeed almost too successful, for they lent credibility to the view that, with only a little encouragement from Washington, market forces were sufficient to ensure America's access to overseas markets and continued prosperity. The United States could enjoy expanding world trade without contributing to the framework of international law, institutions and security that 'free markets' required. Thus, it seemed, isolationism worked. This was a dangerous delusion, but at least for a few more years it retained some plausibility.

Britain too became involved in Europe through the Rhineland Pact, centre-piece of the Locarno treaties. But this was merely a gesture designed to appease France, Germany and liberal opinion in Britain itself. The test of any security commitment is the evidence of practical provisions for ensuring that in the event of a challenge the commitment will be honoured with force and not merely more words. For the Rhineland Pact, Britain made no such provisions. Despite the military chiefs of staff's advice that they were necessary, the politicians could not bring themselves to act. Even Austen Chamberlain, the sole member of the Cabinet with much enthusiasm for the Pact, had, as one sympathetic historian puts it, 'given little thought to [practical enforcement measures], and had refused to allow military considerations to affect Locarno.'[310]

Among the advice that Chamberlain received on Europe, some at least was realistic and far-sighted. Shortly before the Locarno negotiations, the Foreign Office historian, James Headlam-Morley, drew his attention to the importance of defending the postwar European order:

> We are too timid and modest about our own achievements; there is too much criticism and not enough defence. Cannot we recognize that the settlement of 1919 was an immense advance on any similar settlement made in Europe in the past? In broad outline, it represents a peace of reason and justice, and the whole fabric of the continent depends on its maintenance.[311]

In particular, Headlam-Morley defended the settlement in Central and Eastern Europe, since the region formed an integral part of the European balance of power. Poland's survival was vital to prevent the alliance of the two outcast powers Germany and Bolshevik Russia, and because Germany's reconquest of the eastern marches would make it a more formidable threat when it next turned westwards. But the existing order in the former Austrian lands was scarcely less important:

> Has anyone attempted to realize what would happen if there were to be a new partition of Poland, or if the Czechoslovak State were to be so curtailed and dismembered that in fact it disappeared from the map of Europe? The whole of Europe would at once be in chaos. ... Imagine, for instance, that under some improbable condition, Austria rejoined Germany; that Germany, using the discontented minority in Bohemia, demanded a new frontier far over the mountains, including Carlsbad and Pilsen, and that at the same time, in alliance with Germany, the Hungarians recovered the southern slope of the Carpathians. This would be catastrophic, and, even if we neglected to interfere in time to prevent it, we should afterwards be driven to interfere, probably too late.[312]

In December 1925, just as the Locarno agreements were ratified, Joseph Addison, counsellor at the British embassy in Berlin, warned Chamberlain that German support for them was barely lukewarm. This, he suggested, was scarcely surprising, since Germans firmly believed that they were not responsible for the Great War, that they had lost it only because of treachery on the home front, and that, having accepted a settlement based on Wilson's Fourteen Points, they had been tricked into accepting the Versailles Treaty, which was unique in the scale of its iniquity. It followed that 'a man or woman who builds on these foundations is hardly likely to erect in his or her mind a palace of peace'. For now, the German army had practically ceased to exist. But the German people remained no less militaristic in temperament than before nor less convinced that war was natural, necessary and even beneficial.

> There never was a moment in historical times when the German was not first and foremost a soldier by instinct and was not fighting in all the armies of the world. The only difference is that his energies are now confined within his own borders and his exertions devoted to the military supremacy of his own country, with the result that the nuisance has become evident to the rest of the world. Moreover, he cannot usually be got to see anything morally wrong in modern warfare, and if he thinks about it at all, will tell you, as a perfectly sane man once said to me, that war is *'eine Göttliche Institution'*, designed by Providence to eliminate the weak and very properly exalt the strong.[313]

Despite Germany's recent adoption of democratic government, Addison believed that Herriot, the former French premier, had been correct when he said Germans invariably behaved *'[ou] en maître ou en valet'*. The clear inference of Addison's long and thoughtful report was that Britain should adopt a policy of firmness to deter Germany from returning to its bullying ways. This was especially the case, he warned, since Germany on entering the League of Nations intended to waste no time before raising challenges on such sensitive issues as Danzig, the Polish Corridor, Upper Silesia and *Anschluss* with Austria.[314]

Addison's warning, if cynically phrased, was well-corroborated. In December 1924, the Inter-Allied Military Commission of Control reported that Germany was still in serious breach of the disarmament clauses of the Versailles Treaty. According to Allied inspectors, Germany had not suppressed its High Command but reconstituted it in a new guise; short-term recruits had been taken on and trained; the conversion of munitions factories to civilian production was far from complete; important stocks of arms had been found and the reorganization of the state police had not even begun.[315] Brigadier-General J. H. Morgan of the Inter-Allied Commission of Control publicly warned that Germany, 'the least idealistic nation in the world and the most realist, watches, waits, plans and despite all her dynastic catastrophes and changes of political form, remains after the war more identical with what she was before than any other nation in Europe.'[316]

Similar warnings followed in later years.[317] Yet they had no effect upon British policy. Having agreed to welcome Germany into the League of Nations and award it a seat on the League Council, the British government continued to strip away the security framework established at Versailles. Despite the disturbing evidence presented by Morgan's Control Commission, Chamberlain insisted that it be wound up and Allied forces withdrawn from the most northerly of the three Rhineland occupation zones, centred on Cologne, by February 1926.[318] He also agreed with the German thesis that since Germany had had to disarm, the victor powers were morally obliged to do so as well.[319] And in March 1927, barely two months after Allied military inspections in Germany ended, he joined Stresemann in pressing France to reduce the number of Allied troops in the two remaining occupation zones of the Rhineland. Briand, constrained by the conservative Paris press, the High Command and his own Cabinet colleagues, refused. But Chamberlain kept up the pressure, and in August of that year Briand agreed to a 12 per cent reduction in troops.[320] Meanwhile Governor Norman sided with American bankers in pressing for an early revision of the Dawes plan on reparations payments, so as to relieve Germany of much of its public external debt.[321]

The effect of British policy was deeply insidious. In the first place, it encouraged German statesmen to continue their revisionism rather than acquiesce in the postwar settlement. Second, it encouraged them to maintain good relations with the Anglo-Saxon powers who supported their revisionism, while feeling free to disregard any French initiatives that did not find favour in London or Washington. Third, it created the impression in the Anglo-Saxon world that France and not Germany was standing in the way of peace, thus feeding the already intense Francophobia in political and business circles. So far from building peace, it therefore contributed to the undermining of international relations.

This was an odd outcome, given Chamberlain's openly expressed sympathy for France. But among British diplomats, Addison and Headlam-Morley were in a small minority, and Headlam-Morley himself had only belatedly adopted a favourable view of the postwar order. As a member of the British delegation at the peace negotiations in 1919, he had laboured for a settlement based upon what he called the 'elementary principles of humanity and Christianity', and deplored

French efforts to create a viable Poland, which he called 'a disastrous policy'.[322] Upon circulation of the draft Treaty, he had written to his brother, the Rev. A. C. Headlam, asserting that it was, 'I am sure, quite indefensible and in fact is, I think, quite unworkable.'[323] This, not his later view, was the general view within the Foreign Office where, until well after 1933, most senior officials displayed the same 'moralistic-legalistic approach to international problems' that George Kennan later identified as the feature of contemporary American foreign policy-making.[324] In their view, the 'old diplomacy' of secret treaties, military alliances, financial subsidies and balance of power should give way to a new diplomacy of collective security through the League of Nations, arbitration and disarmament.

Some historians explain this 'idealism' as a reaction to the awful bloodletting of the recent war. On the face of it this seems plausible, for no one who has studied the contemporary British press and private correspondence can fail to be struck by the frequency of moral judgements on international relations and the exaggerated hopes placed on the influence of the League of Nations, even among the well-travelled officials of the Foreign Office. Yet against this must be set the fact that Britain spent at least as much on defence as other major powers in the 1920s, and more than before the war, and was prepared to rearm against France.[325] Other historians place greater importance upon the restraining influence of Britain's overburdened finances, its onerous commitments beyond Europe and its sensitivity to the opinion of the Dominions who demonstrated in the Chanak crisis that Britain could no longer take their support for granted in any future conflict, particularly one in Europe. But this begs the question why ostensibly hard-headed statesmen should have betrayed such woolly thinking on grand strategy: why, given the crucial importance of Europe for British security and the limited means at their disposal, they set the wrong priorities.

Their behaviour reflected a sort of Euroscepticism: abhorrence of commitments in Continental Europe which would reduce Britain's independence and compromise its liberal policies. Britain clearly stood to gain by avoiding a commitment to any single region and especially to Europe, which would require a large standing army and heavy taxes to support it. Yet, as the recent war confirmed and the next war would do so again, Britain's fate was inescapably bound up with that of Europe. The additional influence that subverted rational calculations of national security was the deep river of racialist bias, which sustained opposition to a Continental commitment that aligned Britain with Latin France and its Slavic allies against Teutonic Germany. Now that Germany had shed its Prussian militarism along with the Kaiser, Britain would not be dragged at the heels of 'chauvinistic' France. Even less would it be drawn into conflict by the Slavs, who, in the words of one Cabinet minister, were 'a kind of orientalised Irish'.[326] Its preferred outcome was one where Germany re-established hegemony in its eastern hinterland, leaving Britain to focus upon its overseas Empire – even though this would leave the Continent dangerously unstable and in turn Britain's own economic prosperity vulnerable.

Chamberlain held that Britain had no interest in Eastern Europe: 'the less that is said [about this region] the better it will be'.[327] Notwithstanding Headlam-Morley's warning that the security of Western Europe – including Britain – was inescapably bound up with the fate of Central and Eastern Europe, most senior British diplomats agreed with Chamberlain. Sir William Tyrrell, the permanent under-secretary at the Foreign Office, advised him that with regard to Eastern Europe 'Let sleeping dogs sleep – or if they won't, let us try to make them sleep.'[328] Tyrrell and his colleagues felt confident that Germany was no longer a threat, so long as the Western powers promptly addressed its legitimate grievances against the Versailles settlement. They believed that the greater threat to peace arose from France dragging its heels on revision and obstructing it by maintaining its network of alliances in the East. France, whose narrowly self-interested 'materialism' made it untrustworthy and hence 'feminine', was unreasonably fearful of Germany and driving it into the arms of nationalists.[329] They dismissed the French thesis – accepted by Britain and other great powers after 1945 – that establishing Europe's security must precede, not follow, arbitration and disarmament, professing to see in it the expression of old-style imperialism.

An informal exchange between Miles Lampson at the Foreign Office and Eric Phipps, first secretary at the Paris embassy, captures the mixture of impatience, scorn and racism with which British diplomats regarded their Gallic neighbours. 'Are the French quite mad?' Lampson asked. 'If they delay German entry into the League of Nations, they risk losing Locarno. Do they realize that if they lose Locarno they will have lost *almost certainly for all time* all chance of a guarantee from us?'[330] Phipps responded, 'I do not think the French are really mad, but they are very feminine', though Lampson might think 'the two things are almost identical'.[331] This exchange took place in May 1926, when France had been made almost helpless by the franc crisis. British observers nevertheless persisted in regarding France as dangerously strong. Indeed, with the *de facto* stabilization of the franc in December, the subsequent accumulation of huge foreign exchange and gold reserves, and continuing economic growth, France seemed stronger than ever. French authorities, looking ahead a decade or so when Germany had shrugged off the last restraints from Versailles and rearmed, remained nervously aware of their vulnerability. British observers, focusing narrowly on the present, chose to believe that France's preoccupation with security was mere hysteria: a fixation that was blocking appeasement and driving Germany towards political extremism. In their view, 'the root cause of European instability and unrest was French insecurity.'[332]

The isolationism of the Anglo-Saxon powers placed France in an increasingly acute dilemma. French security policy was based upon the essentially sound assumption that the peace settlement had done all too little to reduce Germany's formidable war-making potential or remove the 'Prussian' elements within Germany: the politicians, industrialists, ministerial officials, judges, professors, soldiers, even trade unionists who hankered for a return to authoritarian government and restoration of a greater Germany. To make matters worse, the Russian empire was now in the hands of a hostile Communist régime. Rather than contributing to the balance of power, the Soviet Union was prepared to destroy it by supporting German revisionism and secret rearmament, all the while hoping to gain control of Germany through the spread of revolution in Central Europe. This made it even more important for France to prop up Poland and the countries of the Little Entente, probable first targets of German aggression. French policy thus sought to contain rather than crush Germany, and through firmness to persuade Germans to abandon their revisionist dreams. Most contemporary British observers (and not a few latter-day historians) nonetheless insisted that France's preoccupation with security was an unreasoning obsession.[333] This was wholly misplaced. Indeed, in light of the threats to European stability from a still largely unreformed Germany as well as a newly Bolshevized Russia, any other posture would have been little short of madness.

Britain's revisionist strategy aroused angry outbursts from French nationalist commentators, and occasionally Poincaré and Saint-Aulaire allowed their frustration to show in exchanges with British officials. But by and large French leaders displayed none of the exaggeration or irrational prejudice in their references to Britain that regularly appeared when their British counterparts discussed French policy or national character.

This was not because racial assumptions informed thinking in France less than in Britain. Like Britain, France possessed a vast empire in which non-Europeans were subjected to officially sanctioned discrimination. Like Britain, official France harboured a mild anti-Semitism, which tolerated Jews in the Ministry of the Interior and the Conseil d'État but not in the Inspection des Finances, the Cour des Comptes or the Quai d'Orsay – just as they were tolerated in the British Home Office and Treasury but not in the Foreign Office.[334] Saint-Aulaire proclaimed at the opening of the French Institute in South Kensington in February 1921 that the defeat of the 'barbarians' and the 'eclipse of Slavism', had 'confer[red] on Latin and Anglo-Saxon genius the moral and intellectual direction of humanity', and he contrasted 'the old polished races like ours, and the hideous mixture of pedantry, platitude, and arrogance, which characterized the [German] *parvenus*, the profiteers of science'.[335] French leaders seemed convinced that Germany was still controlled, directly or indirectly, by Prussians, whose belligerent character and base ethics derived from their nature, their blood. Yet for French leaders and practically the whole of the French political class, national security was too pressing a matter to be based upon prejudice. Since France needed the Anglo-Saxon and Slavic countries as allies, the racial geography of Europe was bound to seem different from the vantage point of Paris.

Poincaré in occupying the Ruhr had sought to demonstrate that France would insist upon its Treaty rights, if possible with Britain, if necessary alone. In the event he made three disastrous miscalculations: first, that Germans would put up little or no resistance to the occupation; second, that by separating the Rhineland economically from the rest of Germany and placing it under French control, he would foster Rhenish autonomy and a radical weakening of the central government in 'Prussian' Berlin; and third, that the Rhenish separatist movement could serve French interests. Belatedly he pursued a solution to the German problem as radical as that of Marshal Foch. Yet this should not obscure the fact that his chief ambition had always been to persuade Britain, and if possible the United States, to accept their share of responsibility for upholding the Versailles settlement. Were they to stand together, Germany could not hope to shrug off the restraints of Versailles in pursuit of territorial revision and Continental hegemony. The nationalists' project would thus become unrealistic, and the Rapallo option of alliance with Soviet Russia would appeal only to the most reactionary of nationalists, isolating them from most of the middle class. Moderate policies would be much more likely to prevail.

However, with Britain encouraging German revision, America aloof and France alone defending Versailles, German nationalists could sustain the myth of an oppressive peace, focus hostility on France and undercut their moderate opponents at home. However skilful or determined French leaders might be, they could not impose a unilateral solution upon Germany or negotiate a bilateral solution: Britain's participation, at least, was essential to an enduring peace. Clemenceau, Millerand, Briand, Herriot and Poincaré all knew this. Their assumptions and aims were remarkably similar. But so too was their record in office, for none of them proved able to unite the Western powers in a coherent security system. Even now, British and American historians frequently place responsibility for the failure of the Versailles settlement at France's door on account of its lack of statesmanship or will.[336] The implicit assumption is that the challenge of containing Germany was essentially France's problem and not equally that of the Anglo-Saxon powers. That this view should still prevail in the English-speaking world is itself a measure of the difficulty faced by France in the interwar years.

The world was therefore more precarious in 1925 than it had been at the time of the Armistice seven years before. In 1918, Japan had been tied into the international security system by the Anglo-Japanese alliance, which provided it with a measure of security and respect and enabled London to exercise some restraint on Tokyo. In the West, France had been prepared to deploy military power to contain Soviet Russia and enforce the peace settlement with Germany. But since then the United States had encouraged the replacement of the Anglo-Japanese alliance with the three treaties of the Washington conference, which did little to underpin stability in East Asia. Meanwhile, the United States and Britain withdrew their guarantees from France, Italy under Fascism engaged in irresponsible, opportunistic meddling whenever the occasion arose, and Germany, encouraged by bankers and statesmen of the Anglo-Saxon powers, constantly agitated for an end to all constraints on its freedom of action. Already France was yielding in its struggle to uphold the terms of the Treaty. The framework of security essential for long-term international stability was thus emasculated, leaving not just Europe but the whole world in a dangerously fragile state.

3
The Limits of Globalization

3.1 Introduction

All through Saturday 21 May 1927, spectators gathered in front of the Opera in Paris to watch the electric screen displaying the progress of Captain Charles Lindbergh, who had set off the previous morning in his monoplane, 'The Spirit of Saint Louis', from Long Island, New York, in the hope of becoming the first man or woman to fly the Atlantic from west to east. Others meanwhile drove to Le Bourget airport to be on hand for his arrival. By late afternoon, when news broke of his sighting off the south-west coast of Ireland, the sea of cars heading for Le Bourget had forced incoming vehicles off the road, mounted the raised tramway tracks that ran along the median, spilled onto the pavements and obliged pedestrians to retreat into shops and cafés before grinding almost to a halt. By 8:30 p.m., as Lindbergh passed over Cherbourg, the vertical lights along the coast and the London-Paris routes had been activated and the route to Le Bourget indicated by two straight rays from the powerful lighthouse on nearby Mont Saint Valérien and flashing red rockets fired from Le Bourget itself. Shortly after 10 p.m., the sound of a motor could be heard in the darkness above the airstrip, and after circling three times Lindbergh set his aircraft down. The crowd, estimated at over 150,000, surged past the 500 special police and soldiers of the 34th Aviation Regiment who had been drafted in to keep order. Lindbergh, dragged feet first from his plane, was nearly killed by the crush of jubilant well-wishers.[1] The welcoming committee, caught up in the crowd, failed to reach him and for a time he vanished. Luckily for Lindbergh, his helmet was knocked or pulled off, the sight of which diverted the crowd enough for two French pilots to spirit him to safety.[2] Eventually Myron Herrick, the American ambassador, found him alone, asleep in an officers' cabin. To Herrick's relief, he turned out to be a polite, well-spoken, handsome Midwesterner who appeared to embody the innocence and energy of the New World, and in the weeks that followed, he proved to be an effective representative of America as he made his highly publicized way around Europe's capitals.[3]

The excitement that Saturday evening was focused upon Lindbergh himself, who had performed one of the greatest acts of individual heroism of the age.

But as many appreciated, his feat was part of a more general process of globalization begun more than a century earlier, interrupted by the war, and now sustained largely by American capital. Technology, one element of the process, was revolutionizing communications. Besides rapid strides in aviation, illustrated by Lindbergh's flight, a new generation of transoceanic cables which more than doubled transmission speeds had recently been laid on the main communications routes. Short-wave radio-telegraph links, introduced commercially in 1924, now also spanned the globe and threatened to make even the new cables obsolete. The telephone line between London and Paris might still be crackling and unreliable,[4] but the first transatlantic telephone service was scheduled to open to the public before the end of 1927, and radio broadcasting was becoming an important source of news and entertainment. Equally influential were films, largely from Hollywood, which portrayed the luxuries and excitement of the new age to audiences throughout the world.

Another element in this latest stage of globalization was the huge expansion in international financial activity, both capital investment and short-term credit operations. 'Hot money' – funds without a permanent home that migrated swiftly from one market to another in search of security – added to the instability of currencies that before the war had seemed solid and enduring. A third element was the expansion of corporate enterprise. Multinational firms, the great majority American, rapidly extended their global reach, dominating newer industries such as electrical manufacturing and distribution, office equipment, chemicals and motor vehicles, as well as oil extraction, refining and distribution, mining and refining essential base metals such as aluminium, copper, nickel, lead and zinc, and production of rubber, gutta percha and their manufactured products.

If such things could be measured, it might be found that the rate of global technological and economic change in the 1920s was little different from earlier or later decades. But it was occurring when states seemed less able to confront the consequences, since the international framework of security was weak and becoming weaker, leaving people in Europe, East Asia and elsewhere fearful of the adverse consequences of globalization. There was nothing surprising in the fact that the cost of Lindbergh's flight was largely assumed by partners of J.P. Morgan & Company, the Wall Street bank that symbolized America's global financial power.[5] Nonetheless, it was almost certainly fortunate for the reception Lindbergh received that this fact remained unknown to his well-wishers in France and elsewhere.

3.2   British economic ambitions and the limits of leadership

In November 1918 Continental Europe emerged from the war in turmoil, its political system shaken by revolution and the collapse of four great empires, its economic system dislocated by war, inflation, the repudiation of sovereign and commercial debt, and the breakup of what had previously been a highly integrated market. In July 1914, Europe had comprised 20 independent countries between which goods moved easily and passports were scarcely required. By the

Armistice, it comprised 27 countries of much smaller average physical and demographic size, and 20,000 km of additional frontiers.[6] These frontiers became barriers to trade because states lacked the means to pay for imports whether through exports, foreign exchange or foreign credit, and faced runaway inflation. Yet remarkably most of Europe regained prewar levels of production by 1925 and for the next four years enjoyed unprecedented prosperity. Some credit was due to the Federal Reserve Bank of New York and its Wall Street allies, who supported Europe's recovery. But their efforts stood in sharp contrast to the isolationist and stiffly protectionist Administrations in Washington, whose nationalist policies ran counter to New York's internationalism. In the absence of official American help, responsibility for Europe's stabilization and recovery fell largely to Britain. While scarcely pro-European and deeply suspicious of French designs, Britain's political and economic élite appreciated that their own prosperity was bound up with world trade, which could scarcely revive so long as the Continent remained in crisis. Since no other country was able or willing to provide a lead, Britain had no alternative but to do so.

As it happened, Britain was well equipped for leadership. Economically, its position was decidedly weaker than before the war. In July 1914, Britain's financial houses managed a portfolio of overseas investments well in excess of £3 billion, perhaps twice that of their nearest rivals in France.[7] By 1919, the portfolio had shrunk to less than half the prewar total, and there was little prospect of it being quickly restored. Britain remained the world's greatest trading nation, taking imports, exports and re-exports together, but it had lost ground in overseas markets. As a result, the surplus available for reinvestment abroad was barely two-thirds the prewar level in money terms and far less in constant values. Between 1907 and 1913 Britain's annual current account surplus had averaged approximately £175 million, and exceeded £200 million in the last full year before the war. After the war, Britain's current account surplus became markedly less predictable and in the ten years between 1920 and 1929 averaged only £115 million or thereabouts.[8] To make matters worse, the country was saddled with £1122 million in war debts, 80 per cent of which were owed to the United States and over nine-tenths of this to the US Treasury. In theory, these debts were offset by claims of over £2000 million upon France, Russia, Italy and other wartime Allies. Indeed, including reparation claims on Germany, Britain's balance sheet from the war showed credits exceeding liabilities by over three times.[9] But after the vast political upheavals that had engulfed Russia and Central Europe, no one seriously imagined that all the war debt and reparation obligations would be fulfilled.

Even so, Britain was still better off than other major European powers. Not only had it emerged from the war with a strong currency, substantial lending resources and scarcely any direct damage, but also having acted as banker to the Allies and coordinated much of their shipping and re-supply, it possessed a wealth of talent for the task of directing European reconstruction. To revive trade, the forest of protectionist barriers recently erected would have to be cut back and the narrow bilateral arrangements replaced by multilateral agreements. But this was out of the question until countries possessed a reliable medium of exchange. The first task therefore was to stabilize currencies or where necessary create new ones. The Treasury backed these efforts, but true to its liberal traditions Britain relied mainly upon private institutions and international organizations to restore global markets.

The Economic, Financial and Transit Section of the League of Nations Secretariat began its work in July 1919 in temporary offices near Westminster. Like the League itself, whose first secretary-general was the British diplomat, Sir Eric Drummond, the Economic Section was headed by a British civil servant. Sir Arthur Salter, knighted for his work as the wartime director of ship requisitioning, became the first director, and when he left to become secretary-general of the Reparations Commission in late 1919, his place was taken by Walter Layton, a former Cambridge economics don whose war work included membership of the Milner mission to Russia in 1917 and the Balfour mission to the United States the same year. When Layton left to become editor of the *Economist*, his successor was Frank Nixon, a Board of Trade official, before Salter took over again in 1922. Initially the Economic Section possessed little means of assisting member states in economic difficulty. This changed when the League created Financial and Economic Committees in October 1920, both of them serviced by the Economic Section.

The Financial Committee made a singularly important contribution to Europe's recovery by overseeing the stabilization of currencies in Central Europe, starting with the Austrian schilling in 1922–3, continuing with the Hungarian pengo in 1923–4 and followed by some eight other European currencies over the next five years. Besides French, Swiss, Dutch, Swedish and Italian nationals, two of the seven members were British: Sir Henry Strakosch, a City financier and authority on money markets and central banking, and Sir Basil Blackett, controller of finance at the Treasury, who in 1922 was succeeded at the Treasury and on the committee by Sir Otto Niemeyer. Salter, who participated in the committee's deliberations, acted as a virtual eighth member. The composition reflected the contemporary prospects of mobilizing capital for international financial reconstruction. Whereas some funds could be obtained in Amsterdam, Paris, Zurich and other markets, the City of London remained the world's greatest clearing-house for capital and credit. Though the British economy no longer generated large surpluses for investing or lending abroad, the City attracted funds from around the world and enjoyed extensive links with the banking community of New York, where the abundance of capital was not matched by knowledge of European conditions. This relationship was assiduously fostered by Montagu Norman, governor of the Bank of England. At the same time, he sought to make the League Financial Committee the agency for setting the rules in the postwar monetary and financial system. Thus he would not agree to London merchant banks lending to foreign countries until or unless the countries had obtained the Financial Committee's approval of their financial reconstruction plans. Norman's informal control over the London capital market and his influence over opinion in New York gave force to his judgement. With some justice, observers regarded the committee as an arm of the Bank of England.

Until 1914 the Bank of England took almost no direct interest in international monetary and financial relations. The governor, elected for a two-year term from among the merchant bankers, financiers and ship-owners comprising the Bank's court of governors, was not expected to sever his private connections during his term of office. By and large his task was limited to overseeing domestic credit conditions and movements in the gold market, which provided the signals for setting Bank rate (or rediscount rate) and other interest rates. Since the gold standard rules were commonly understood, policy was not actively coordinated with other central banks and personal contacts with foreign central bankers were rare.[10] All this, of necessity, changed after the Great War, which left the international monetary system in a shambles. As luck would have it, the Bank also gained a leader in Norman who was prepared to transform its operations to realize his global ambitions.

Norman, the son of a prominent City banker and descendant of governors of the Bank of England on both sides of his family, had already been a member of the Bank's court for seven years when the war began. Thereupon he volunteered to assist the deputy-governor, Sir Brien Cokayne, with his vastly expanded duties, and was well qualified to succeed him in 1918 when the wartime governor, Lord Cunliffe, retired and Cokayne was elected to the top office. A question nevertheless remained over Norman's suitability for the post. Deeply neurotic, he had suffered recurrent bouts of depression, which contributed to his abandonment of studies at Cambridge after one year and left him unable to function for weeks at a time. Despite his highly mannered appearance – including cloak and cane, casually worn wide-brimmed hat and Van Dyke beard – which seemed calculated to attract attention, he was also an extremely private man with intense likes and dislikes who could be captivating but found it difficult to maintain normal relationships with friends or colleagues. This was why he was available for work in the Bank in 1914, for his relations with fellow partners at the merchant bank Brown Shipley and Company had broken down, and after 15 years with the firm he was without a job. Aware of his potential instability, the Bank's court hesitated over his appointment as deputy-governor. The court nonetheless agreed, and two years later he succeeded Cokayne as governor of the Bank on 31 March 1920.[11]

Over the next two decades, Norman demonstrated a great flair for central banking. He strengthened the Bank's authority within the City, thereby ensuring its responsiveness to central bank policy; fostered relations with other central banks by encouraging visits and exchanges of personnel and creating an international department within the Bank to support this development; assisted in the creation of central banks in the British Dominions; lent decisive backing to the League Financial Committee during its critical early years when Central Europe most urgently required international help, and became a mainstay of the Bank for International Settlements when it opened its doors in May 1930. A few of Norman's fellow directors resented his mannered ways, excessive secrecy and increasingly permanent occupancy of the governor's office. But all of them shared his vision and remained broadly satisfied with his direction of the Bank. He was thus re-elected at two-year intervals throughout the interwar years and retired only in 1944.[12] Not only did he keep in tune with City opinion, but for much of the 1920s he also enjoyed the enthusiastic backing of the Treasury, whose officials favoured the restoration of the gold standard at the earliest opportunity for the discipline it imposed upon governments. As will be seen, however, his neurotic extremism of thought and action eventually proved disastrous for the City, Britain and the world.

At the centre of Norman's vision was the gold standard, which he regarded as the sheet anchor of the world's capitalist system and a panacea for Britain's political and economic ills. In his view, the Great War had led the state to encroach dangerously upon the prerogatives of capital, impose confiscatory taxes, ominously expand public debt and spend profligately, which ran down savings and investment and reduced sterling to only a fraction of its prewar value in real terms. To reverse this decline and do justice to sterling holders, he believed Britain must restore the gold standard and to do so at the prewar parity of £1 = \$4.86.[13] The gold standard would remove monetary policy from the political arena by placing control in the hands of the independent Bank of England. It would attract foreign funds to London, since wealth-holders would know that the Bank of England was prepared to exchange sterling for gold at an unchanging rate of 77s 10 1/2d = 1 standard ounce and to defend this rate through Bank rate changes and other means available to it. This in turn would increase the resources available for lending and credit operations, which would facilitate trade and help revive Britain's ailing export industries. It would also restore the City of London to its place at the centre of the global capitalist system. Not only would the gold standard provide the discipline to maintain Britain's international competitiveness, but it would also do so without the need for any external restrictions such as import duties or foreign exchange controls. Norman was prepared to use capital export controls to hasten the return to gold. But once the gold standard was restored, he assumed that all such 'artificial' interference with the capitalist system would quickly vanish.

The zeal with which Norman embraced the principles of the gold standard was evident in his extreme aloofness from political influence. He refused to receive foreign finance ministers at the Bank or visit foreign central banks that he did not regard as independent.[14] He kept his own government at arm's length by insisting that all communications with Westminster and Whitehall should be channelled through the Treasury.[15] Despite the Bank's increasingly important international role, he shunned contact with the Foreign Office, going so far as to discourage his own Bank officials when abroad from notifying British diplomatic missions of their presence.[16] He also refused to account for his actions to the press or the public, since this would imply that he was in some sense responsible to them.[17] On several occasions, he sought to avoid media attention by travelling under the name of his personal secretary, E. H. D. Skinner. The exposure of his deception increased the curiosity of the press, which consciously or unconsciously may have been his intention.[18] Despite his ostentatious disdain for publicity, he carefully cultivated relations with the City editors of the British press. Several, including Arthur Kiddy of the *Morning Post* and the authoritative *Banker's Magazine*, Oscar Hobson of the *Manchester Guardian* and Francis Williams of the *Daily Herald*, were persuaded that they had privileged access to the governor. Courtney Mill, the long-time City editor of the *Times*, frequently allowed himself to become the governor's mouthpiece. Since in the 1920s press comment on monetary and financial policy seldom appeared outside the City pages, their loyalty to Norman allowed him to cast a powerful influence over City and élite opinion throughout Britain.[19]

Thus far, Norman's vision was fairly conventional, albeit pursued to extremes, but his sights were constantly fixed upon a global rather than merely a national goal. In the first instance, this involved the establishment of independent central banks in every major country in the world. Once established, they would become linked to one another through the international gold standard, enabling them to ensure global stability without the need for restrictions on the movement of goods, services or capital. Indeed, a global network of central banks, independent of governments, would radically reduce the capacity of states to interfere with markets. Pierre Quesnay, the young adviser to Emile Moreau, governor of the Bank of France, met Norman for the first time on a visit to London in October 1926. Afterwards he warned Moreau not to underestimate Norman's ambition. Norman's immediate goal was to ensure London's place as 'the great international financial centre'. But beyond that, Quesnay wrote,

> The economic and financial organization of the world appears to him the great objective of the twentieth century. He does not believe that governments have the necessary qualities to do this, which can only be done by central banks independent of both governments and private financiers. If the central bankers work together, they can remove from political control the essential problems facing the development of national prosperity, such as monetary security, the intensification [*sic*] of credit, and the movement of prices. They would thus discourage domestic political conflict from damaging nations and their economic progress.
>
> Norman is a doctrinaire, as are most of the leading men here (Niemeyer, Salter, etc). But it would be a mistake to assume that it is a cover for national ambition: they are determined to realise the aforementioned project.[20]

Perhaps if every power had subscribed to Norman's global vision, it might have produced peace and prosperity. But, as Quesnay indicated, it was utopian and dangerously so. While Norman claimed to be anti-political, in fact his actions had the most serious implications for the security of Europe and the world. For in seeking to eliminate obstacles to the free working of international markets, Norman strenuously opposed French efforts to uphold the Treaty of Versailles, in particular the reparation clauses and the military occupation of the Rhineland, while encouraging Germany to demand revision. He also encouraged the involvement of American banking interests in European and in particular German reconstruction. In this respect, his project nicely complemented the foreign policy of postwar British governments. Doubtless, he believed that appeasing Germany and promoting prosperity would contribute to Europe's stability. But by working for the removal of its framework of security, he was in fact hastening a new era of political and economic instability. Meanwhile he pursued the restoration of the gold standard with single-minded intensity.

In January 1923, Norman travelled to Washington with the chancellor of the exchequer, Stanley Baldwin, in response to an American request to negotiate a war debt funding agreement. The Congressional committee responsible for negotiations agreed to reduce the amortization rate and forgive the accumulated interest, but insisted upon full repayment of the capital sum borrowed. Britain thus faced a debt of £947 million, requiring 62 annual payments of $185 million (£38 million): equivalent to at least a third of its net annual foreign earnings in 1923.[21] Bonar Law, the prime minister, thought the terms excessive and threatened to resign rather than accept them. But Norman regarded a settlement on almost any terms as essential to Britain, since it would remove this element of uncertainty overhanging sterling, and as the world's greatest creditor Britain could scarcely be seen to repudiate its own obligations. He encouraged Baldwin to acquiesce, and when Baldwin publicly endorsed the terms on his return to Britain, Bonar Law gave way rather than provoke a political crisis at home and anger in America.

That same month, Norman's hopes for international stabilization received a severe setback when French and Belgian troops (nominally supported by Italy) occupied the Ruhr. Norman, along with most British observers, condemned France for pursuing reparations which Germany seemed incapable of paying, and welcomed the Dawes plan for the safeguards it provided against further efforts to secure reparations by force. Not only did the plan reduce the destabilizing potential of reparations until a final settlement could be worked out, but it also made possible the creation of a new German currency to replace the one destroyed by hyperinflation and cleared the way for foreign investment in Germany which now flooded in from the United States, Britain and elsewhere. To Norman and his City colleagues, this was all to the good. Contrary to historians' claims that they were engaged in a 'struggle for supremacy' with New York, they appreciated that London could not possibly supply all the credit needs of Europe, the British Empire and the rest of the world. Hence they were pleased that New York banks were now mobilizing American savings for the international market, and looked forward to fruitful collaboration with them.[22] They were however disturbed to see that the dollar was becoming the main currency in international finance while sterling floated, and that South Africa and other countries were prepared to return to the gold standard without waiting for Britain. Sterling, they decided, must not be left behind in the general return to gold.

By December 1924, the prospects of restoring sterling to the gold standard seemed bright. Only a year before, the Labour Party was preparing to take office, the Ruhr occupation threatened chaos in Europe, and sterling was slumping to $4.20, its lowest rate for two years. Now the Conservatives were back in office with a working majority, the Ruhr crisis was practically settled, and the pound had recovered to within a few points of its gold parity ($4.86). Since the legislation suspending the gold standard was due to expire in December 1925 and expectations of a return were growing, the markets would be keenly disappointed if the government sought a further delay. The existing momentum made the decision seem almost inevitable, and according to most accounts it provoked little controversy until sterling was driven off the gold standard six years later. In fact, leading proponents of an early restoration appreciated that it was a very considerable gamble. But in their impatience they minimized some of the risks and overlooked others, while doing their best to limit participation in the debate.[23]

As should have been obvious to everyone, sterling's recent strength owed to a combination of fleeting factors. Sterling had gained from the flight of Dutch and German capital during the Ruhr crisis, and later from French capital fleeing the victory of the *Cartel des Gauches* in May 1924. A further source of strength derived from a reduction in US interest rates and rising inflation in America, which contributed to the extraordinary flow of funds from the United States to Germany, much of it via London, once the adoption of the Dawes plan ended the Ruhr crisis.[24] The influence of speculation on an early return to gold became especially evident in the autumn of 1924. Sterling was normally weaker in the autumn from pressure to fund the disposal of overseas harvests. Despite the windfall benefits of higher coal prices, owing to the temporary disruption of German production, Britain's current account showed no sign of improvement during the third or fourth quarters: rather the contrary. Nevertheless, sterling rose strongly on the foreign exchanges.

Norman visited New York in late December to discuss a possible return to gold with Benjamin Strong of the Federal Reserve Bank of New York and senior partners of J.P. Morgan & Company, the British government's fiscal agent in America. While clearly hoping that Britain would take an early decision to return and ready to assist with a substantial credit, the Americans felt called upon to warn Norman not to expect the benign conditions in the United States to continue much longer. In Strong's words, American foreign lending in 1924 was 'unusual – much the largest ever known'. It was unlikely to continue at present levels and was meanwhile adding to Europe's already heavy burden of external liabilities. As for the favourable influence of American interest rates, he invited Norman to bear in mind that the United States was 'a new country', given to bouts of exuberance, which would eventually require the monetary authorities to intervene, whatever the international situation. Norman should only take the final step back to a fixed exchange rate if he were prepared to defend the rate with robust action. This proved to be salutary advice, but Norman would not be put off.[25] A committed Atlanticist, he persuaded himself that by establishing a 'special relationship' with Strong, the Bank of England could weather any future storm.[26]

Back in London, Norman found nervousness on all sides at the prospect of an immediate return to gold. Several clearing bank chairmen, including Reginald McKenna of the Midland Bank and Sir Christopher Needham of the District Bank in Manchester, with heavy commitments to domestic industry, expressed reservations, while even among the Bank of England's court of governors several colleagues betrayed misgivings.[27] Winston Churchill, the chancellor of the exchequer, confided to Norman his worries about the probable effect of returning to gold upon industry, especially when unemployment was already disturbingly high. Churchill, while no expert on monetary policy, had received warnings from McKenna and the press baron and financier Lord Beaverbrook, along with leading industrialists such as Sir Josiah Stamp, chairman of LMS Railways and a director of Nobel Industries, Sir Alfred Mond, chairman of Mond Chemicals, and directors of the NUM and the FBI.

In January 1925, the long-awaited rise in US interest rates occurred, forcing up the British Bank rate and contributing to a decline in commodity price levels. But Sir Otto Niemeyer, Churchill's chief Treasury adviser, vigorously sided with Norman while doing his best to filter out opposing views. Norman himself discouraged the chancellor from consulting industry, labour or other interests. 'In connection with a golden 1925, the merchant, manufacturer, worker, etc., should be considered (but not consulted any more than about the design of battleships).'[28] Churchill, only half aware of the deep unease in industrial circles, reviewed the pros and cons of early action by convening a gathering of experts comprised exclusively of liberal economists and City bankers. McKenna, one of those present, now accepted the case for action, telling the chancellor, 'There is no escape; you have to go back; but it will be hell.'[29] Within this narrow circle of advisers, the only hold-out was the economist, John Maynard Keynes: a brilliant thinker and frequent contributor to the press, but politically not of the same weight as Niemeyer, Norman or McKenna. Thus isolated, Churchill acquiesced, and in his first budget speech to the House of Commons on 28 April 1925 he announced the immediate restoration of the gold standard.[30]

The decision to return to gold, usually treated by economic historians as at most a miscalculation of perhaps 10 per cent in the equilibrium rate for sterling,[31] reflected an almost frightening disregard for the interests of domestic British industry. Several older sectors such as textiles, shipbuilding and engineering had taken on massive debt immediately after the war to cover the cost of expansion or reconversion, only to face new competitors in overseas markets and a 52 per cent decline in wholesale price levels between the end of the war and 1925.[32] The effort to restore the gold standard involved sharply tighter and dearer money, which added to industry's troubles and left several of the regional banks such as Martins and the District Bank with disturbingly high levels of non-performing debt. Nor was it only the old staple exporting industries that struggled: growth industries such as motor cars were also affected by the deflationary conditions, and even relatively strong firms such as Austin and Wolseley ended in receivership as a result.[33] Industry had already been forced into serious confrontation with labour when Norman received warning from his American banking friends that he could not expect the recent rise in wholesale price levels to continue. Indeed, even before the final decision to return to gold, Niemeyer reported to Churchill that price levels had resumed their decline, which was to continue uninterruptedly for the next seven years.[34] British bankers constantly spoke of the need for industry to restore its international competitiveness, but there was probably *no* equilibrium rate of costs and prices where industry could have thrived.

Churchill soon found that the return to gold was as disastrous as he had feared. Efforts to adjust to the recent rise in the exchange rate and higher Bank rate aggravated industrial relations, especially in the coal industry which faced the resumption of competition from the mines of the Ruhr. Within barely two months of restoring the gold standard, British mine-owners threatened a national lockout when the National Union of Mineworkers (NUM) rejected their demands to accept lower wages and longer working hours. Churchill privately reproved Norman for landing the government in this predicament and pressured him to set aside any idea of a further rise in Bank rate to build up monetary reserves or attract foreign deposits to London.[35] Direct intervention by Baldwin, the prime minister, and a nine-month government subsidy to the mine-owners averted a lockout. In the breathing space thus provided, Norman raised Bank rate and persuaded Churchill to allow him to remove capital controls.[36] Meanwhile, however, coal and other commodity prices continued to slide. When the coal subsidy ended in April 1926 and the employers' demands were renewed, the NUM was joined by other unions in a nine-day general strike. Albeit brief and largely peaceful, this was Britain's first general strike in almost a hundred years and it sent a shock wave through the political establishment.

Spokesmen for the industrial community had already voiced their unease at the decision to return to gold. Their objections multiplied after McKenna of the Midland Bank publicly expressed his dissatisfaction in early 1927.[37] Critics from the newer sectors of industry such as electrical machinery and motor manufacturing, despite their relatively strong economic growth, were particularly outspoken, although angry complaints also came from farm leaders, directors of steel, engineering, cotton and wool textile firms, and the FBI itself, which published a series of articles on the adverse effect of monetary policy upon industrial progress.[38] Sir Alfred Mond, now chairman of Imperial Chemical Industries, the largest industrial firm in Britain, instigated talks between employers and trade union leaders. This encouraged speculation about the formation of a producers' alliance to challenge the liberal economic strategy of the mercantile-financial community.[39]

Although little came of these talks, the evidence of dissatisfaction within industry had important consequences. In the first place, the Conservative government, unnerved by the gulf opening up between Britain's industrial and mercantile-financial communities, became increasingly divided with some ministers pressing for an imperial protectionist policy and others, including the prime minister, holding back. 'Safeguarding' – the current euphemism for tariff protection – was extended to a handful of industries, but rather than a decisive retreat into protection or a renewed commitment to economic internationalism, the result was stalemate and inaction.[40] Second, it put paid to Norman's hopes of liberating himself from political interference and expanding the City's role in international finance. Once back on gold, he had anticipated a virtuous circle, with foreign balances attracted to London by the gold guarantee for sterling, City banks enabled to expand foreign lending, and British industry benefiting from stronger export demand. Instead, under a constant barrage of criticism from

Churchill and industrial leaders, he was unable to give even a half-turn of the wheel. Against his better judgement, he kept Bank rate down to 5.5 per cent.[41] Taking into account the deflationary trend in wholesale price levels, this meant that real interest rates were a swingeing 10–12 per cent: possibly the highest in Britain's peacetime history. But even this was not enough to attract substantially more foreign funds to London. With the Bank's currency reserves barely above the 'Cunliffe minimum' of £150 million, Norman struggled on, occasionally tucking away foreign exchange in various accounts rather than including them in the official reserves, which would have increased pressure for a Bank rate reduction.[42] Meanwhile, to keep sterling at par, he was obliged to reintroduce informal restrictions on capital exports.[43]

The practical result of these developments was to undercut Britain's leadership of the general return to globalization. Britain remained influential in international economic relations for a few years more, since fear that it might retreat into imperial protectionism acted as an inducement to other countries to support liberal reforms. Britain's potential contribution to European security also ensured respect for its views. But Norman and the City aside, Britain's commitment to globalization as well as the means to encourage it were now largely gone. Even Norman's commitment was soon to be tested by America's aggressive corporate expansion. By 1927, therefore, the century of Britain's global economic leadership had to all intents and purposes ended. Indeed, in both the monetary-financial and the commercial spheres, Britain was henceforth more often part of the problem rather than the solution.

3.3 France, economic leadership and security: Monetary and financial relations

Perhaps no feature of the interwar economic experience had greater political significance than Britain's and France's constantly divergent economic experience. Between 1920 and 1922, Britain experienced a severe slump, prompting it to demand revision of the war debt-reparations regime and reintegration of Germany and Soviet Russia into the world economy. The slump scarcely affected France. Between 1922 and 1929, Britain struggled under an over-valued currency and the cost of supporting at least a million registered unemployed. France meanwhile enjoyed the benefits of financial and monetary ease, including full employment, balanced budgets and rapid economic growth. In 1929, another economic slump led Britain to abandon a century-long commitment to economic internationalism in favour of Imperial protectionism. France, having returned to the gold standard in 1928, seemed unaffected by the slump. From the latter part of 1932, Britain enjoyed sustained economic recovery, which ostensibly confirmed the wisdom of turning from unilateral domestic adjustments to unilateral external adjustments. The slump meanwhile affected France seriously in 1932 and did not substantially ease until 1938. Their constantly diverging economic experience led to endless disputes over policy and mutual incomprehension.

British observers, who commonly assumed that Britain was a model of liberal internationalism, looked upon France as incorrigibly *dirigiste* and protectionist, and ascribed its prosperity in the 1920s to aggressive trade and monetary policies. Yet French authorities regarded themselves as defenders of liberal economic and political values, and indeed scarcely an office-holder in Paris between 1918 and 1936 wished to expand the economic role of the state let alone displace private capital as the basis of employment and wealth creation.[44] Like their counterparts in Britain, the United States and elsewhere, they drew their norms and goals from the prewar era when France had enjoyed prolonged stability and growth, stood at the forefront of technical innovation in the motor industry and other sectors, and ranked second only to Britain as a global investor. But, as in Britain and elsewhere, the exigencies of war had obliged them to intervene more in economic affairs, and the débâcle of the Ruhr reminded them that economic policy must be tempered by the exigencies of national security. British observers, while agreeing in principle, drew the opposite conclusion that national security demanded renewed commitment to globalization and appeasement of Germany. Almost inevitably, therefore, France's prosperity in the 1920s aroused envy, resentment and fear in Britain, which drove the powers even further apart.

At the start of the Ruhr crisis in January 1923, the French franc stood at 69.74Ff = £1, down 64 per cent from its prewar gold standard rate of 25.22Ff = £1, which remained the nominal parity.[45] Thereafter, the lengthy stalemate over reparations, controversy over refinancing the state's short-term debt and the introduction of a new currency in Germany in November 1923, which effectively drove the franc out of French-occupied territory in Germany, depressed the franc further. The first serious speculative attack on 15 December 1923 did not seriously worry the French authorities. Since the selling pressure appeared to come from Germany and its sympathizers in Austria and the Netherlands, they assumed the speculators would soon exhaust their resources.[46] Certainly it was not the reason why they agreed to the institution of the Dawes committee, on which British and American experts held sway.[47] This was already on the cards by the autumn of 1923 when hyperinflation wiped out German savings, making it essential for the Western powers to help re-establish Germany's currency and credit before reparation payments could be resumed.[48] In any case, Poincaré, the premier, was ready to make concessions once Germany demonstrated its willingness to honour its Treaty obligations and cooperate with the *Mission interalliée de contrôle des usines et mines* (MICUM) in the delivery of reparations in kind.

French authorities were more disturbed after the second speculative attack on the franc, starting in mid-January 1924, which confirmed a loss of confidence in the franc in France as well as abroad. Poincaré responded swiftly by proposing a 20 per cent increase in taxes to close the budgetary gap and end the state's repeated recourse to the Bank of France for advances. Legislation for the *double décime* languished in Parliament until late March, and the franc slumped further to 129Ff = £1. But once the tax increases were approved, the government secured a credit from J.P. Morgan & Company with which the Banque Lazard frightened speculators into covering their short positions. This *Verdun financier*, as the operation was known, brought a spectacular recovery of the franc to 61Ff = £1 by the end of April.[49] But on 11 May the franc suffered a renewed blow by the victory of the *Cartel des Gauches*, a centre-left alliance, in the parliamentary elections.

The first Cartel government, formed exclusively of Radicals, with Edouard Herriot as premier and Etienne Clémentel as minister of finance, had no intention of altering property rights or undermining savings. Over half (53 per cent) of the Radical Party's executive were drawn from manufacturing, small business and the independent farming sector, and much of the party's electoral support came from small towns and rural regions.[50] Nevertheless its mildly progressive programme, which included the reinstatement of the 20,000 railwaymen who had lost their jobs in 1920 as the result of strike action, extension of the eight-hour day to seamen and railwaymen, unionization of civil servants, a modest increase in income tax and death duties and greater efforts to suppress tax evasion, was treated as semi-revolutionary by conservative opponents. The Radicals' allies in the Socialist Party raised the temperature by demanding a capital levy, which Herriot did not altogether rule out, and Herriot himself antagonized conservatives by his own strident anti-clericalism. The government proposed to eliminate sectarian education in Alsace-Lorraine, legalize divorce and suppress the recently established diplomatic mission to the Vatican, while at the same time permitting Communists to organize legal demonstrations and establishing diplomatic relations with Soviet Russia. Outraged, the French cardinals issued an emotional appeal to merchants, industrialists and bankers to support a campaign of resistance.[51] Herriot's complaint that 'the Christianity of the catacombs' had become 'the Christianity of the bankers' only raised the temperature further.[52]

Herriot might still have been able to shrug off his critics attacks had it not been for the government's intractable financial predicament. By 1925 the problem was no longer mainly a budget deficit, since current expenditure was largely covered by current revenue.[53] Rather it was the vast unconsolidated short-term debt created by earlier governments to pay for the war and reconstruction, which had reached the astounding total of 305 billion francs (£4.7 billion at 65Ff = £1) by May 1924 – up ten times from 1913 – and required constant renewal or consolidation. Unfortunately for Herriot, high levels of public spending sustained by debt had resulted in accelerating inflation which predisposed investors to shun public bonds or notes when the *Cartel des Gauches* took office. Thus between May 1924 and July 1926 the Treasury faced the reimbursement of nearly 22.5 billion francs in short-term debt, while obtaining only 4.9 billion francs in ten-year Treasury bonds, leaving the rest to be covered by a budget surplus or advances from commercial banks or the Bank of France.[54] The government might have raised the ceiling on bank note issue and short-term advances from the Bank. But this would have reduced confidence in the *Cartel* further, and Herriot, an economic liberal, refused. The government had little choice but to turn to the Bank of France, which resulted in confrontation with the Bank's council of regents. Formally the issue was a matter of legal principle, since the Bank's statutes barred it from advancing more than 23.2 billion francs to the government. But the council of regents was largely comprised of members of the *haute banque française*, while the *Cartel* represented 'the people'. Thus when the Bank refused further accommodation and right-wing critics accused the *Cartel* of confiscating wealth through its mismanagement of the economy, the *Cartel* and its support-ers accused the Bank of a deliberate strike of capital: a *mur d'argent* by moneyed interests who chose to transfer their wealth abroad and undermine the franc to block a progressive government.[55]

Since the effect of the franc's slide was to make French exports more com-petitive and sustain a high level of economic activity, a few manufacturers actu-ally welcomed currency depreciation and looked forward to it continuing. But they appear to have been a small minority even among producer groups.[56] By and large, France was a cautious liberal country with a high rate of personal sav-ings. Since 1914 domestic savings had been almost wholly absorbed by national defence bonds, Treasury bills and notes issued for the reconstruction of the liber-ated regions. The decline of the franc, from 61Ff = £1 when the *Cartel* was elected to 91Ff = £1 by January 1925 and to 100Ff = £1 by mid-June 1925, therefore deeply affected a broad swathe of the middle classes, whose savings had already been eroded by inflation.[57]

Herriot's government, defeated in the Senate on 10 April 1925, was followed by no less than six more *Cartel* governments in the next 15 months, each one striving without success to find a formula acceptable to both investors and the *Cartel's* centre-left parliamentary majority. Briand, back in the premier's office on 28 November 1925, sought to regain international confidence in the franc by negotiating war debt funding agreements with Britain and the United States. But in face of strong opposition from Poincaré and right-wing deputies and senators, the agreements remained unratified in the spring of 1926. Briand appealed for cooperation from the Bank of France or at least from the industrialists on the council of regents, but was firmly rebuffed.[58] Joseph Caillaux, his finance minis-ter, similarly failed to secure parliamentary approval for six months of emergency powers, to enable the government to stabilize the franc by pushing through rati-fication of the war debt agreements, new taxes and a forced loan.[59] On 20 July, Herriot formed another government, only to be confronted by a flat refusal of cooperation from the governor of the Bank of France unless his government imme-diately obtained parliamentary approval for a new contract with the central bank. Herriot regarded this as 'a knife to the throat' by the moneyed interests, but never contemplated going beyond the law to resist.[60] Meanwhile, at each stage of the political crisis, the franc fell further: to 128Ff = £1 by January 1926, 172Ff = £1 by 19 May and 238.50Ff = £1 by 21 July, the day Herriot's short-lived second govern-ment fell. By then, *bons de la défense nationale* had lost approximately 90 per cent of their original value and a mood of crisis engulfed the country.

Right-wing political *ligues*, including the *Légion*, the *Jeunesses Patriotes* and the *Faisceau*, modelled on Mussolini's Fascist blackshirts, had made their appearance after the Cartel's election in 1924 and now boasted a combined membership of at least 140,000.[61] The authoritarian nationalist *Ligue des Patriotes*, *Ligue de la Défense Catholique* and *Fédération Nationale Catholique*, all presided over by General Noël de Castelnau, similarly grew by leaps and bounds, with the *Fédération* alone claiming 1,800,000 members by 1926.[62] Their main target was the French politicians who were allegedly mismanaging the economy and confiscating the nation's savings. But that spring, as the franc sank and shopkeepers began to alter prices on goods several times a day, rumours circulated of foreign manipulation.[63] In Paris there was talk of an 'Anglo-Saxon-Bank of England-Morgan combination to enslave France', by driving down the franc until it agreed to pay war debts or make further concessions to Germany.[64] Conspiracy theories of this sort became so widespread that on several occasions American tourists in Paris were abused by passers-by and in a few instances threatened with violence.[65] The women and children of some well-to-do French families went abroad for safety, precious possessions were buried in gardens and rumours circulated of an imminent coup d'état by right-wing conspirators including, it was said, Marshal Pétain.[66] On 19 July 1926, queues formed outside retail banks and branches of the public *Caisses d'Épargne* to withdraw deposits.[67] On the evening of 21 July, as news circulated of Herriot's defeat, excited crowds outside the Palais Bourbon sang the Marseillaise and roughed up *Cartelliste* deputies as they emerged from the building.[68]

The collapse of Herriot's second government marked the end of the *Cartel des Gauches* and the end of the financial crisis. Such was the shock of incipient currency collapse that normal party politics were set aside. Poincaré formed a government of National Union which included no less than five former premiers (Briand, Barthou, Leygues, Herriot and Painlevé), three ministers from Herriot's Cartel government (Briand, Painlevé and Queuille), three prominent centre-right *Alliance républicaine et démocratique* politicians (Barthou, Leygues and Fallières), one independent centre-right member (Tardieu), and one 'pure right' member (Marin, president of the *Fédération républicaine*). With Briand as foreign minister and Poincaré himself in control of finance, the public were assured of continuity on both fronts.[69] The result was the so-called Poincaré miracle when the franc recovered to 208Ff = £1 on Friday, 23 July, the day the government was formed, to 199 francs the following Monday, to 179 francs by 17 August, lower again in September.[70]

Poincaré owed his success largely to the popular belief that he, the wartime president and punctilious defender of the national interest, would not let down the holders of *bons de la défense nationale*. Probably influenced by Baron Edouard de Rothschild, a leading member of the Bank of France's council of regents, Poincaré made it known that he regarded devaluation as a form of fraud upon wealth-holders and looked forward to a progressive rise in the franc's value.[71] But as early as the first week of August, Maurice Bokanowski, the minister of commerce, industry and civil aviation, and Emile Moreau, Poincaré's own appointee as governor of the Bank of France, appealed to him to recognize that after 12 years of high inflation, the restoration of the *franc Germinal* (25.22Ff = £1) would deal a terrible blow to industry and employment.[72] Léon Jouhaux, secretary-general of the *Confédération Générale du Travail* (CGT) and a friend of the premier, similarly warned him that further revaluation threatened to cause mass unemployment.[73] Poincaré hesitated and in September called on Jacques Rueff, a young assistant from the Ministry of Finance, to prepare a study of the limits of revaluation that firms could tolerate without having to force down wages.[74]

By November, with the franc rising above 140Ff = £1, Moreau warned Poincaré more insistently of the dangers of further revaluation. Reports were reaching him of more and more firms facing difficulties, including the motor manufacturers Citroen and Peugeot. Poincaré, as yet unwilling to contemplate devaluation, minimized these reports and instead requested Moreau to intervene in the foreign exchange markets to steady the franc.[75] Moreau refused, insisting that Poincaré first agree to stabilize the franc, ratify the war debt agreements and turn over monetary policy to the Bank.[76] By mid-December the franc had reached 120Ff = £1 and the situation was getting out of control. Charles Rist, the distinguished economist and vice-governor of the Bank of France, more than once threatened to resign, and senior officials at the Ministry of Finance became nearly frantic at the growing demand for francs. Moreau finally agreed to intervene, in his own words, to avoid 'a national catastrophe' involving the closure of numerous industrial and commercial firms and widespread unemployment. On 20 December, the Bank's recently created foreign exchange department entered the market, selling £930,000 of francs and ordering another £100,000 of francs to be sold for the Bank's account in New York, to hold the franc down to 120Ff = £1.[77] Poincaré treated this as merely smoothing out the revaluation process. There were nonetheless compelling reasons, international and domestic, for transforming this *de facto* stabilization rate into a permanent one.

In the aftermath of the war, France's failure to obtain reparations from Germany had left it facing massive budget and current account deficits and almost desperate for financial help from London and New York. Both markets remained firmly closed to France. Commercial bankers were deterred from lending to France by the unsettled conditions in Europe, and from 1922 the British and American governments opposed loans of any kind to France until the French government entered into acceptable war debt funding commitments.[78] French authorities became all the more frustrated when City of London financiers welcomed German flight capital and supplied credit to Germany while refusing funds to Poland and other targets of German territorial revision. French authorities associated the franc's weakness with the failure of the Ruhr occupation and Germany's revival, assisted by the Anglo-Saxon powers. But until Poincaré's return in July 1926, they could do nothing but watch and wait.

American aloofness was a source of occasional unease. Despite its vast wealth, the United States seemed interested only in obtaining repayment of its war debts and profiting from German recovery, regardless of the consequences for Europe's security. Coolidge's election in November 1924 and the nomination of William Borah, an outspoken isolationist from the western state of Idaho, as chairman of the Senate Foreign Relations Committee were soon followed by reports that Washington would insist upon taking responsibility for the disarmament conference now being prepared by the League of Nations and holding it in the United States.[79] French authorities found it worrying that the United States seemed prepared to use its financial muscle to promote disarmament while refusing to contribute to international security or even to give it serious consideration, and were determined to resist the transfer of the conference to America.[80] In April 1925, Coolidge affirmed Washington's keen interest in the disarmament conference and, without naming France, warned that foreign powers that failed to cooperate would not be allowed to borrow in American markets for 'militarist' purposes.[81] A few weeks later, he raised the possibility of using American war debt claims to influence French defence policy.[82] For now, France did not require foreign financial assistance to rearm. But this was a grim reminder that it could not count on the Anglo-Saxon financial markets for loans to bolster national defence, and that it must rely upon its own resources for rearmament. This was a strong argument for stabilizing the franc at a defensible exchange rate.[83]

More than American isolationism, however, French authorities worried constantly about British action, and in particular about the troubling role that Norman of the Bank of England was playing in Europe. They did not oppose Norman's efforts to assist Austria, Hungary and other former enemy states.[84] Indeed, the Bank of France had encouraged French commercial banks to participate in the July 1923 loan to Austria, and the Ministry of Finance similarly pressed the Bank of France as well as commercial banks to take a tranche of the Dawes loan to Germany.[85] It disturbed them nonetheless to see Norman using his influence over the London market and the League Financial Committee to draw European countries under his sway. Apprehension about Austria's interest in merging (*Anschluss*) with Germany had led French authorities to propose a committee of *Entente* representatives to oversee financial aid to Austria in 1923. Norman refused to allow political oversight and insisted that the League Financial Committee should alone be responsible.[86] Hungary in turn escaped political supervision owing to Norman's influence.[87] Norman's undisguised opposition to France during the Ruhr crisis and sympathy for Germany drove officials at the Quai d'Orsay, the *rue de Rivoli* and the *rue de la Vrillière* into a quiet fury. It particularly disturbed them that he was so enthusiastic about Hjalmar Schacht, the new governor of the Reichsbank, who made no secret of his determination to see the Versailles settlement overturned.[88] Norman seemed ready to destroy Britain's industrial base for the sake of the City of London and the gold standard. Worse, he seemed prepared to equip Germany with a stable currency, reduce its war debts and, with its domestic debt practically eliminated by hyperinflation, enable German industry to gain an insurmountable lead over British and French competition. In Paris, Norman's behaviour seemed not just extraordinarily short-sighted but downright dangerous.[89]

In 1924 French authorities accepted the Dawes plan, including the loss of control over the Reparations Commission, which henceforth required a unanimous vote before Germany could again be declared in default on reparations, thus giving Britain a veto over the Commission's decisions. In 1925, they acquiesced in the withdrawal of Allied troops from the northernmost Rhineland zone centred on Cologne, despite evidence that Germany was in flagrant breach of its disarmament commitments. In spring 1926, they negotiated war debt funding agreements with the United States and Britain in an effort to restore international confidence in the franc and regain access to the Anglo-Saxon financial markets. The agreements, albeit as yet unratified, committed France to repay debts of no less than £2062 million over 62 years or an average of £33.3 million a year. In fact, payments during the first ten years (1926–36) would average only £19.85 million a year.[90] But even this represented a heavy charge on France's current account, which had fluctuated wildly since the war. Despite the buoyant conditions of 1927–9, its surplus, including reparation receipts, averaged only £87 million a year in the 1920s. Thus even at the lower initial repayment rate, war debts absorbed nearly a quarter of France's net external earnings. Despite French efforts, moreover, the agreements included only very limited suspension or revision rights in case of future adversity.[91] The need for a substantial current account surplus was therefore another reason for stabilizing the franc at a substantially devalued rate.

The lessons French authorities drew from their recent experience also had a direct bearing upon exchange rate policy. Moreau and Ministry of Finance officials were determined to avoid Norman's mistake in 1925 of overreaching himself by an excessive revaluation of the currency, which damaged the British economy even while it exposed the Bank of England to constant pressure.[92] To some extent this reflected the different sources of Norman's and Moreau's authority and their different perceptions of the role of their respective institutions. Both the Bank of England and the Bank of France were private, shareholder-owned institutions. But Norman, elected by the court of governors of the Bank of England and thus by the most international elements of the City, took for granted that what was good for Britain's mercantile-financial interests was good for the country as a whole. Moreau, a former civil servant, received shares in the Bank of France when he became governor, which made him a rich man and one of the *deux cent familles* who allegedly controlled France through their voting rights in the Bank. He was nonetheless appointed by the president of the Republic on the nomination of the minister of finance, and he remained clear that the Bank of France must act as the 'arbiter of the economic interests of the nation'. For this reason he was more sensitive to the burden of adjustment that exchange rate changes imposed upon domestic industry.[93] He and Poincaré were also determined to reassert French financial influence over Continental Europe for reasons of national security.[94] This too militated in favour of holding the franc at a level which the Bank of France could defend independently of the Anglo-Saxon powers.

Since 1925, Norman had encouraged central bankers in the smaller countries of Europe to adopt the gold exchange standard. Instead of holding their currency reserves in gold bullion, they would hold sterling, dollars or other currencies backed by gold. To enable them to stabilize their currencies, he offered them a sterling credit and saw to it that a substantial sterling or sterling-dollar loan was arranged in London under the auspices of the League Financial Committee, once the Committee approved their reconstruction plans. Several of the smaller central banks, seeing no alternative, proceeded on this basis. The City of London benefited twice over, from the commissions for arranging the stabilization loans and from the central bank deposits. But to French observers, Norman's gold exchange standard arrangements seemed deeply unwise, not to say reckless, since the Bank of England's gold reserves thus became the underpinning not only for sterling but also for numerous other currencies. This amounted to a pyramiding of credit upon a dangerously slender base. While in the short term it accelerated the stabilization of currencies, it stored up certain trouble for the future. Moreover, it enabled Norman to extend his control over Europe's smaller central banks, requiring each of them to accept an adviser from London in return for their stabilization or reconstruction loan.

French observers deplored these arrangements. Jacques Seydoux, assistant director of the political and economic section of the Quai d'Orsay, wrote to Aimé de Fleuriau, Saint-Aulaire's successor in London, in May 1926 of the 'triumph of the Norman system'.[95] Moreau, who met Norman for the first time in July 1926, came away convinced that he was a British imperialist: pro-German and no friend of France.[96] So long as the franc was in free fall, French authorities could only watch while Norman made his next moves in the direction of Poland and France's other allies. As Seydoux complained to Roland de Margerie, ambassador in Berlin,

> For the time being and for the foreseeable future, France as well as Germany will be under the financial heel of England and America. We can do nothing and we have no choice but to do the bidding of the bankers of Wall Street and the City.[97]

The effect, nonetheless, was to make them more impatient to restore the franc to gold to regain the financial influence that France had enjoyed in prewar times.

Separate yet linked to the quest for international influence was their determination to restore respect for the Bank of France itself. For 12 years the Bank, a private institution, had been forced to open its coffers to the state, set aside orthodox rules of banking and expand the note issue to the point where the credibility of the currency and the state were both nearly destroyed. Moreau, albeit a political appointee, insisted no less emphatically than the private bankers and industrialists on the council of regents that the Bank must regain its independence from the government for the sake of the economic, political and social stability of the country. No less than Norman in London, Moreau held that only an independent central bank could impose the necessary discipline upon the politicians, whose proclivity to bribe the electorate with its own money posed a constant threat of inflation. Since the restoration of the *franc Germinal* could only be a distant aspiration, he had no hesitation in advocating a sharp devaluation to get back to gold without further delay.[98] Unfortunately for him, with parliamentary elections less than two years away, Poincaré refused to acknowledge publicly that the franc must be substantially devalued. This encouraged those who had earlier fled the franc to repatriate their funds while others speculated on the franc's revaluation, obliging the Bank of France to contain the upward pressure by selling francs while accumulating sterling and other foreign exchange. At the start of 1927 the Bank's sterling balances stood at barely £5 million. By 4 February they had risen to £21 million, by 28 March to £45 million, by 21 April to £72 million and by 3 May to £82 million.[99]

The recovery of confidence in the franc encouraged the French authorities to adopt more aggressive action. Having long felt aggrieved at the British authorities' refusal to help when France needed support, they now decided to right old wrongs. In 1916 they had transferred £42 million gold to the British Treasury as a contribution to a sterling loan of £72 million, and although subsequently they had reduced the loan to £33 million, the British authorities had returned less than half of the gold. Now that the Bank of France was holding down the franc at 124Ff = £1 and sterling balances were piling up in its accounts, Poincaré requested the renegotiation of the 1916 loan. More forthrightly, Moreau, who regarded the British loan terms as 'quite intolerable', proposed the more radical course of requesting the immediate and complete repayment of the loan and restitution of the remaining £18.375 million in gold, which the French believed morally if not legally still belonged to them.[100] News of the request prompted rumours in Paris that the Bank of England, having absorbed the French gold into its general reserves, would be unable to return it without grave embarrassment. Because French commentators wrongly believed the gold had merely been a deposit rather than sold to the British Treasury, which had paid no interest on it, their reports were strongly tinged with *Schadenfreude*.[101]

In the event, Norman met the French request to settle the debt and return the gold with little difficulty, and on 21 April he appeased the growing army of critics at home by reducing his Bank rate from 5 to 4.5 per cent.[102] Barely three weeks later, however, Moreau posed a new challenge by requesting Norman to convert up to £20 million sterling into gold for shipment to Paris.[103] Moreau was pleased to demonstrate that Britain could no longer push France around. As he wrote in his diary of the recent debt settlement, 'Norman is troubled by my offer, but he cannot get away from it. Thanks to the strong financial situation that we have regained, the roles are reversed. It is he who is the supplicant now.'[104] His new demand for gold was intended chiefly to discourage speculation on a revaluation of the franc, thus enabling him to hold the exchange rate steady until Poincaré agreed to the formal stabilization of the franc. Until now he had supplied francs on demand, while placing the sterling he acquired on deposit in London. But since this seemed only to fuel the speculation, he decided to sell sterling for gold to force up interest rates in London. He accepted that much of the speculation through London originated from other centres: as evidence, Berlin alone had lost almost 1 billion gold marks (about £50 million) in recent months. But in view of the fact that German interest rates remained unchanged, he suspected that Schacht might actually welcome this outflow, perhaps intending to use the mark's weakness as an excuse to demand revision of the Dawes plan. Moreau decided to lance the boil by converting his sterling balances into gold. Once sterling came under the pressure, Norman would be forced to raise his interest rates. This would increase the cost of credit to Germany and other centres of speculative operations, and remove upward pressure on the franc.[105]

Bankers in the City of London soon grew agitated at French gold purchases.[106] Norman was furious at Moreau's deliberate pressure on his market rates. As he complained to Governor Strong of the New York Fed, Moreau was 'playing havoc in London' and 'menacing the gold standard'.[107] Chamberlain, the foreign secretary, called in de Fleuriau, the French ambassador, to warn of serious consequences for Franco-British relations if interest rates had to rise.[108] Meanwhile, on 27 May Norman travelled to Paris to persuade Moreau to desist.

As Norman pointed out, speculation in the franc took place largely from London because it was the sole financial centre in Europe with a free gold market and the capacity for large-scale foreign exchange operations. It was the fulcrum of the international gold standard, and Moreau threatened to upset the delicate mechanism of the London markets in his crude effort to force up interest rates by draining London of gold. So long as the French authorities did not rule out an eventual revaluation of the franc – and some of the Bank of France's own regents were known to favour the full restoration of the *franc Germinal*, a five-fold increase in value – the speculation was bound to continue. The only sure means of ending it was for the French authorities formally to stabilize the franc. If this was politically impossible, they should at least announce categorically that they would not allow speculation to affect the present exchange rate. They should also take steps to reduce the demand for francs by action within their own market. Rather than forcing up interest rates in London, they should lower rates in Paris, since it must be obvious that a deposit rate of 6.5 per cent made holding francs exceptionally attractive even without the prospect of speculative gains. They should also open their capital market by lifting the embargo on foreign loans and permitting more foreign securities to be listed on the Bourse. Norman urged Moreau to recognize that pressuring the Bank of England offered no answer to his predicament. Speculators, who were mostly foreign, stood to gain far too much by buying francs to be deterred even by a substantial increase in the cost of borrowing. Besides, since the British clearing banks were loaned up to the hilt to domestic industry and highly illiquid, French pressure on the pound would do little to affect the supply of credit. It would merely increase its cost to Britain's already beleaguered industrial sector. Barely a month earlier, Norman explained, he had appeased industrial opinion by reducing Bank rate. If he now had to reverse this decision, it would 'cause a riot'. Moreau must see that if he persisted in his sales of sterling, he would force Britain off the gold standard.[109]

Moreau remained convinced of the reasonableness of his operations. Norman's protests seemed merely to prove the fragility of the gold exchange standard and confirm that his imperialist reach had dangerously exceeded his grasp. But Moreau accepted that he neither could nor should push his advantage too far. That evening, when Pierre Quesnay, his assistant, raised the possibility of the Bank of France disposing of all its £70 million sterling balances, Harry Siepmann, Norman's adviser on central bank relations, warned that in this case Britain would demand immediate repayment of the £600 million war loans to France, which were still unconsolidated.[110] This was tough talk, but as Rist observed, France could hardly contemplate driving Britain off the gold standard. Poincaré had already warned Moreau to avoid a showdown with Norman, and Strong in

New York issued similar appeals.[111] Moreau acquiesced. While deriving some satisfaction from cutting Norman down to size, his objective was not chiefly to embarrass Norman but to hold the franc at its current rate to restore it to the gold standard at a suitable parity. He therefore withdrew his demand for gold in return for Norman's promise of future cooperation.[112]

Over the next 18 months, the French authorities went some way to realize their ambitions. Moreau took a small participation in the $25 million central bank credit for the stabilization of the Belgian franc in October 1926, and a similar share of the stabilization credit for Italy in December 1927. In each case, Norman and Strong dominated the operation. But when it came to the Polish stabilization in the autumn of 1927, Moreau insisted upon a central role. Norman, he believed with some justice, hoped to get control of Poland to force it to make territorial concessions to Germany.[113] He therefore joined with Strong in organizing the central bank credit, effectively replacing Norman as director of the European side of the operation.[114] Towards the end of the year, when France's other allies, Roumania and Yugoslavia, sought assistance to stabilize their currencies, he went further and insisted that Norman must allow the Bank of France to lead. Britain could take charge of Bulgaria and Greece, but France was determined to support the countries within its alliance system and not allow them to become financially dependent upon London. Nor would Moreau tolerate any role for the League Financial Committee on account of Norman's influence over it; instead France would nominate the expert advisers to accompany the stabilization loans and credits. On 21 February 1928, he travelled to London 'to offer Norman peace or war'.[115]

Norman, outraged at Moreau's demands, sought to dissuade American central bankers from supporting French initiatives. But as Moreau noted with pleasure, Strong had grown uneasy at being associated with Norman's manoeuvres in Continental Europe and out of sympathy with the gold exchange standard. Since Strong now sided with Moreau on the need for the greater discipline of a gold bullion standard, he felt confident of realizing his goal of sharing the leadership of the international monetary system and exercising a special role in Eastern Europe. He therefore requested Norman to call on him in Paris where he set out his demands.[116] Norman, bereft of American support had no choice but to retreat, and with ill grace he acquiesced in an informal spheres-of-influence agreement with Moreau. In the event, the Roumanian stabilization was carried through in February 1929, while the Yugoslav stabilization was only effected in May 1931, on the eve of the European-wide financial crisis.[117]

Meanwhile, Moreau prepared plans for the revival of the Paris market, the *place de Paris,* as an international financial centre. While scarcely expecting to replace the City of London or New York, he anticipated that with the franc back on gold and sterling stripped of its artificial advantages, Paris could regain the place it had occupied before the war.[118] Meanwhile diplomats undertook a careful survey of French financial interests in Austria, Bulgaria, Hungary, Poland, Czechoslovakia, Yugoslavia and other countries of importance to national security. French financial influence had declined while British, American and German influence had increased, and officials were determined to see the stronger franc used to right the balance.[119]

In January 1928 the French government partially lifted the embargo on capital exports, in place since April 1918.[120] As expected, the parliamentary elections in May favoured the Centre Right, enabling Poincaré to form a new government. By now, however, his reputation rested so firmly on his defence of the franc that he still refused to acknowledge that the currency must be radically devalued.[121] Poincaré threatened more than once to resign before agreeing to fix the franc on the gold standard at the *de facto* rate of 125Ff = £1, where Moreau had held it since December 1926. This constituted an 80 per cent devaluation of the prewar *franc Germinal*, and some of the Bank's regents were reluctant to accept the loss.[122] Moreau, however, justified action on the grounds that a currency solidly backed by gold was essential 'to reinforce in international relations the prestige and independence of the country.'[123] Poincaré alluded to the same function when he told the Chamber of Deputies, 'Unlike other stabilisations…we did not stabilize on another currency, whether the dollar or sterling; and we did not rely upon foreign credits. We stabilized with our own means, and on gold.'[124] As both Moreau and Poincaré confirmed, the gold franc was not only an essential discipline on the national economy and element in the recovery of French commerce; it was also the essential underpinning of France's independence and national security.

Henceforth, on both sides of the Channel, the Bank of France's huge gold reserves appeared to be a powerful political weapon. Yet in the event they proved singularly difficult to wield. One constraint was France's continuing need for good relations with Britain and to a lesser extent the United States. The other derived from the simple but hugely important fact that France was a liberal capitalist country. Foreign observers generally assumed that the centralized French state was capable of issuing marching orders to French merchants, bankers and industrialists in the furtherance of national political or strategic ends. This was far from the case, for the bankers and businessmen had a fiduciary duty to safeguard their shareholders' or investors' interests. This was equally true of the Bank of France itself, which as a shareholder-owned institution was expected to make a profit as well as maintaining the stability of the franc. Just as private interests limited the government's ability to assist France's allies or punish its enemies through commercial and financial policy, so the Bank's shareholders and monetary goals constituted an effective constraint upon using the franc as a political weapon.[125]

France's decision to rejoin the United States and Britain on the gold standard in 1928 ostensibly strengthened the global system. But since the decision was informed as much by nationalism as liberalism, it scarcely augured well for global cooperation. And despite the increased need for agreed rules to address currency and payments problems, no such rules existed.

3.4   France, economic leadership and security: Commercial relations

During the latter years of the 1920s, crises occurred in the Balkans, Morocco, Egypt, Iraq, China and elsewhere. The key to world stability nevertheless remained the containment of Germany within the Europe states system. Crises elsewhere could annoy or discomfit the great capitalist powers, but only the German problem was, properly speaking, vital, since only a German crisis was likely to draw in all the world's powers. By now, however, no security system existed for maintaining order: merely the remnants of the Versailles Treaty created by the three principal victor powers, to which only France remained committed. Britain continued to promote Treaty revision in favour of Germany. The United States remained deeply isolationist, demanding that the European powers should join it in disarmament while stubbornly refusing to consider their security needs or even nominally to support the League's procedures for addressing threats of aggression. It pressed Britain to reduce its naval forces at a conference in Geneva in June 1927, and expressed outrage when British statesmen refused to compromise their global interests by accepting the American formula.[126] It also condemned Britain and France in 1928 when they agreed upon a *quid pro quo* on sea and land forces rather than facilitate the Coolidge administration's efforts to justify further tax reductions by means of disarmament.[127]

The Ruhr débâcle had demonstrated that France could not act alone to uphold the terms of the Peace Treaty, since to do so risked unsustainable financial burdens and international isolation. Poincaré implicitly acknowledged this lesson by keeping on Briand as foreign minister when he again took over the reins of government in July 1926. The two men could scarcely have been more different in temperament and methods of work: Poincaré intense, humourless, assertive and a stickler for details, Briand charming, witty, informal and notoriously reluctant to consign his views to paper. Neither, however, was under any illusion about the threat from Germany. Poincaré was infuriated though not surprised that Stresemann, having just signed the Locarno treaties, should begin large-scale subsidies to Alsace separatist groups.[128] Briand in private called Germans '*des mufles*' [thugs].[129] Both men also accepted that France's predicament – Germany's increasing revisionism, France's isolation – demanded action on several fronts. Their first priority was to remove the vulnerability created by the franc's weakness. This, as we have seen, they accomplished in spectacular fashion by the 'Poincaré miracle' of 1926, which soon resulted in a massive build-up of gold and foreign exchange. But ironically, while freeing France from the threat of financial blackmail and enabling it once more to extend financial help to friendly states, the consequence was further to constrain its Continental defences.

While French defence spending rose temporarily between 1927 and 1931–2, this was largely to cover the exceptional cost of implementing the new conscription law of March 1928, which reduced the call-up period to a single year. In almost every other respect this was a time of decline. Practically all the army's equipment, including tanks and aircraft, were dated from the war and ageing fast. Stocks were steadily run down. Planning for military-industrial cooperation was suspended. The retreat from the Rhineland and the decision to rely largely upon fixed frontier fortifications ineluctably created a cautious, defensive mentality among the High Command. And politically the Army was practically friendless, with Communists, Socialists and most Radicals opposed to existing defence expenditure, and centre-right Republicans more concerned to defend the 'Poincaré miracle' through lowered taxes and balanced budgets than to finance rearmament. The result, as Maurice Vaïsse writes, was *'une armée en trompe-l'oeil'*: a large force, but poorly organized, equipped and led, and incapable of fulfilling its purpose.[130]

On the diplomatic front, French leaders continued to give priority to fostering relations with the Anglo-Saxon powers, which they still hoped to draw into Europe's security system. To this end they participated actively in the League of Nations, including the preparatory committee of the international disarmament conference. Largely for the same reason, they also demonstrated willingness to appease Germany by making concessions on a range of issues. Thus, for instance, they set aside their complaints about German infractions of its disarmament obligations,[131] agreed to wind up the Inter-Allied Military Control Commission without prior commitment to other forms of surveillance, and supported German membership of the League of Nations.[132] Britain, France's most important potential ally, remained their chief concern. But in 1927–8 they also promoted the Kellogg-Briand pact outlawing war as an instrument of policy, in the hope of altering America's image of France as an imperialist and militarist power.[133] Briand arranged a solemn signing ceremony for the pact in the Salle de l'Horloge at the Quai d'Orsay in June 1928. But his efforts went for naught, since the ever-suspicious Coolidge administration turned the pact from a bilateral agreement into a declaration open to all countries to endorse. Representatives of 14 countries attended the Paris ceremony, including Germany, Czechoslovakia, Poland, Britain and the principal British Dominions as well as the United States and France. That same day, Coolidge invited other countries to add their signatures and eventually no less than 57 did so. But since no practical means of enforcement was even discussed, the declaration added nothing to the framework of international security.[134]

Unable to draw the Anglo-Saxon powers into a European framework, French leaders saw no alternative but to engage in direct dealings with Germany in an effort to gain new purchase over their former enemy. This began in 1924, even before the Dawes plan was formally adopted, when they quietly encouraged a revival of cultural exchanges. French intellectuals had defined the war as a clash of civilizations; German *Kultur* being the expression of an inherently brutal, aggressive people, they had rejected links with German academies of arts and science after the Armistice.[135] Yet in 1924, the Berlin Philharmonic Orchestra was invited to perform in Paris. In 1926 a *Comité d'échanges interscolaire franco-allemand* was established with the backing of several prominent Radical politicians, including Edouard Herriot and Ferdinand Buisson, as well as the *Ligue des Droits de L'Homm*e, the *Ligue des femmes pour la paix et la liberté* and *Jeune République*. That same year the French government decided to open a student residence in Berlin and a network of French Institutes in the principal German cities. Implementation was delayed by the financial crisis, but meanwhile the government sought to revive the study of German in schools through the exchange of teachers, and, having hitherto blocked German academies from membership of the International Research Council, it took the lead in lifting the ban.[136] Thomas Mann was invited to speak at the Sorbonne in 1926 and Heinrich Mann in 1927. The following year, the *Office National des Universités* was officially requested to develop inter-university links, and towards the end of the decade the Quai d'Orsay organized an encounter of prominent French Catholics with members of the German Centre Party.[137] It also informed Leopold von Hoesch, the German ambassador in Paris, that the country club of Saint-Cloud would again welcome applications for membership from German colleagues, thus giving them an entrée to perhaps the most exclusive social circle in France.[138] The German government responded to these French initiatives by opening a branch of the German Academic Exchange Service (DAAD) in Paris, but otherwise did little to reciprocate.[139] Despite French efforts to open the door to the International Research Council, German academies maintained a counter-boycott out of resentment at France's alleged mistreatment of Germany.[140]

French officials had greater success developing commercial relations. Having entered the Great War second only to Britain as a world creditor and fourth among trading nations, France emerged from the ordeal with its foreign investments reduced by nearly 60 per cent, huge war debt obligations to Britain and the United States, an enormous swathe of the country devastated by the grinding destruction of the Western front, and its industry ill-prepared for the expected 'war after the war' to regain foreign commercial markets.[141] French statesmen and industrialists, pessimistic about their ability to compete internationally, paid lip-service to British and American calls for open markets while accepting the need for tight controls on imports, at least until the devastated regions were put back on their feet. In April 1918, before the war ended, the government signalled its retreat from liberal trade relations by denouncing all existing commercial treaties. Shortly afterwards, it supplemented the tariff with a battery of import and export prohibitions, and in 1921 and again in 1922 it introduced large across-the-board increases in import duties.[142]

The retreat into autarky was more however apparent than real, for the prohibitions, introduced as an emergency, were practically all removed before the end of 1920. As for the higher duties, they did little more than compensate for the effects of inflation, since French duties were defined in money terms rather than *ad valorem* rates, and in the three years after the Armistice the franc declined by fully a half against the pound sterling and dollar.[143] This was reflected in the performance of France's postwar external commerce. In the ten years after the Armistice, French trade expanded considerably faster than the world average; yet only in one year, 1924, during the interwar period, did visible exports exceed imports.[144] Nevertheless the additional duties *seemed* to be a step backwards, and no doubt they had the effect of dislocating trade and antagonizing France's friends as well as former enemies who regarded them as the commercial counterpart of France's diplomatic efforts to contain Germany.

In 1924, France confronted a daunting situation, first because the Dawes plan made German economic recovery a virtual certainty, and second because Germany was due to regain its tariff autonomy on 10 January 1925, after the relevant clause of the Treaty of Versailles expired. French leaders were acutely aware that Germany was industrially the stronger power, and could use its large demand for foodstuffs and raw materials as a means of extending its influence in Europe. Nonetheless they saw little alternative but to contain Germany by embracing it bilaterally and eventually within a broader European framework.

Under the Dawes plan, France made remarkable concessions to facilitate the import of German reparations in kind. Municipal projects in which at least 20 per cent of the cost went on German reparations in kind received an interest rate subsidy from the French state. Equipment purchased from Germany for the devastated regions benefited from a 40 per cent reduction in import duties, and equipment purchased from Germany for the French armed forces or the *équipement nationale* came in duty free. The *Comité des forges*, representing French heavy industry, had vigorously opposed the expansion of reparations in kind when Herriot contemplated it in 1925. Robert Pinot, the *Comité*'s vice-president, complained that the government seemed more interested in the health of the German economy than the French economy. The government, strongly encouraged by the Quai d'Orsay, nevertheless persisted in devising concessions.[145] During the fourth Dawes year (1927–8), reparations in kind reached a value of 478 million RM or 72 per cent of all German exports to France.[146] Even that figure understated the importance of the concessions, for in many cases the purchase of some German equipment for a project made further purchases of German equipment essential on account of its compatibility.[147]

Germany's recovery of tariff autonomy in 1925 had potentially serious implications for France directly, since at least 8 per cent of its exports went to Germany and an abrupt closing of this market would damage the French economy. Officials also feared a serious backlash in the Saar and Alsace-Lorraine if they found themselves further cut off from adjacent German markets. To continue bilateral trade after January 1925, France agreed to provisional arrangements; bilateral negotiations on a permanent agreement began in August. Stresemann hopefully suggested this would be 'the last tariff Germany would make with France'. If France agreed to end its military occupation of the Rhineland, he would willingly consider a commercial agreement leading to a complete customs union within five years and the reciprocal participation of French and German capital in their respective industries.[148] But accelerating inflation had revived protectionist agitation by French industrial and agricultural lobby groups and their friends in Parliament, and with the Ministry of Finance also demanding action to halt the depreciation of the franc, the government was forced to retreat. In December 1924, it introduced a bill authorizing large increases in duties on a hundred manufactured items. At the first opportunity the Reichstag responded by voting a sizeable increase in German tariff protection. This temporarily halted the commercial negotiations, and the situation was aggravated in 1926 when the French government decreed a 30 per cent increase in import duties on 6 April and a similar increase on 14 August. As before, these measures merely compensated for the effects of currency depreciation without stopping the growth of imports or reversing France's visible trade deficit. Nevertheless they provoked strong protests from Germany and elsewhere.

Franco-German relations were further soured by reports of French obstruction of a comprehensive settlement of their differences. In Geneva on 10 September 1926, Briand welcomed Stresemann as head of the first German delegation to the League of Nations with a rousing speech before the seventh annual Assembly. A week later, reports circulated that Briand and Stresemann had secretly met in the lakeside village of Thoiry.[149] According to Stresemann as well as contemporary press reports, Briand offered a comprehensive settlement of Franco-German differences including the withdrawal of France's remaining troops from the Rhineland, the immediate return of the Saar without a plebiscite, the negotiated recovery of Eupen-Malmédy from Belgium and (at Stresemann's request) a reduction in reparations, in exchange for German financial assistance to France. This would take the form of a large bond issue on the security of its railways, providing reparation payments in advance along with a large financial payment to reacquire the Saar mines from their French owners. Briand, however, overestimated the readiness of his colleagues in Paris to accept concessions to Germany on this scale. He quickly retreated, modified his record of the Thoiry meeting to create the impression that Stresemann had been the *demandeur*, and thus avoided a confrontation with Poincaré and colleagues. Stresemann, annoyed but hopeful of an eventual settlement with Briand, allowed the blame to fall on Poincaré who once again became Germany's *bête noire*.[150] But now that the franc had substantially recovered from its recent slide, France no longer needed German financial help or to make the concessions that Briand had allegedly offered.

Briand, still anxious for Franco-German *rapprochement*, sought to ameliorate relations by promoting industrial integration on a Europe-wide basis. Jacques Seydoux, his economic adviser at the Quai d'Orsay, outlined the strategy in an exchange with Emile Mayrisch, the Luxembourg steel-maker. Mayrisch, who had sided with France during the Ruhr crisis, informed Seydoux of his recent encounters with German industrialists from the Ruhr and elsewhere. Having benefited from the hyperinflation to divest themselves of practically all their debt, the German industrialists now found American bankers eager to supply working capital to facilitate their operations. Mayrisch was struck by the remarkable ability of the Germans to work together in horizontal and vertical combinations, and even more by their ambition to dominate the European market and meet their American competitors head-to-head in world markets. Seydoux, who had the highest regard for Mayrisch, scarcely doubted his analysis. It corroborated his belief that Germany's interest in combining with steel-makers in Belgium, Luxembourg and France was part of a dangerously ambitious dream of world power, and confirmation that present-day Germany had scarcely changed from before the war.

> For the time being the German industrialists want peace, and will make this loudly known to all. But they are bound to frighten their neighbours by the belligerency of their youth, the revelations of secret arms, etc. And if their plans fail, recourse to violence is always open.

Germany can be expected to take advantage of the concessions granted to it in the first four years of the Dawes Plan, to strengthen its economic and financial position. After that, when the Plan fully bites, the Germans will try to escape from it as soon as possible. Remember the recent exchange:

'[Ambassador von] Hoesch: there are no more differences between France and Germany.
Seydoux: There's the execution of the Dawes Plan.
Hoesch: During the next 3 or 4 years you have nothing to worry about.'

As M. Revoil said back in 1911, what we have most to fear is an economic crisis in Germany. German prosperity is the guarantee of peace. But if their plan for hegemony fails, as all such plans do, then Germany will find itself back in the situation of 1914 where it has more to gain from disorder than order. But in the meantime Germany marches towards prosperity and she has an interest in order: its people are tired of war and any new war will be the end of civilization: even in Germany this is acknowledged.[151]

Despite this gloomy but all too accurate evaluation, Briand and Seydoux saw no alternative but to encourage industrial agreements with Germany and other European countries. No more than in 1918 did this signify French interest in an alliance with Germany.[152] Instead, it reflected the cautious hope that through industrial collaboration France might sustain Germany's prosperity and divert it from aggressive ambitions. France, Seydoux observed, would like to see British industry join European ententes as a counter-weight to Germany. Unfortunately, he saw no chance of this, given that British policy favoured finance at the expense of industry, and British financial interests aggressively sought open markets in Europe in competition with Wall Street. Nevertheless, if France coordinated its industrial, commercial and diplomatic strategies, it might yet resist the pressures of German industry and British finance.

Thus, we find ourselves placed between Britain with its financial interests and Germany with its industry, which will eventually merge. Neither will want to see its weaker component crushed by the other. Nor do we. Our interest is to encourage vast economic and financial ententes, which will avoid conflicts. We should therefore play the role of arbiter and conciliator. We need British financial support to escape from our present crisis, because we allowed the Dawes Plan to restore German finances, but not ours. And we need German industry to supply our factories, because we did not profit from the Ruhr operation by finding a solution to the coal issue. Isolation would be fatal. For we will be the first target of a German-British economic entente. We should therefore return to a policy of equilibrium, which served us well earlier, until we were forced to choose between them. By this means, we can obtain financial help, develop our agricultural production and rationalise our industry. It will above all permit us to work for the consolidation of peace in Europe and abroad.[153]

Over the next two years, Seydoux with Briand's encouragement worked assiduously to promote his strategy of industrial ententes. He pressed the reluctant steel-makers in the *Comité des Forges* to agree to conversations with their German counterparts, and in September 1926 they negotiated a European Steel Cartel involving Belgium and Luxembourg. Steel remained the raw material of war *par excellence*. Moreover, with iron ore in Lorraine, the coking coal needed to convert it into steel in the Saar and Ruhr, and the market for steel products largely in Germany, it was a source of potential conflict between France and Germany.[154] Promotion of the Cartel thus constituted an important political act.[155] Several of the leading French and German steel producers were strident nationalists, yet they chose to participate because in several instances they maintained commercial links or investments across the Rhine frontier.[156] Although free to withdraw from the Cartel at short notice, the French hoped the Cartel would become a durable bridge between the two countries.

Behind the scenes, Briand also supported several organizations devoted to European integration, which had sprung into life in the aftermath of the Ruhr crisis. In May 1926, Emile Mayrisch convened a small but select group of French and German industrialists, journalists and public figures. The *Comité franco-allemand d'information et de documentation* remained deliberately small, informal and as its name suggested inconspicuous. Nevertheless it met eight times between May 1926 and May 1930, and appears to have provided an effective forum for the discussion of European industrial cooperation. Comprised of two subcommittees, its members included on the French side Charles Laurent, the former ambassador to Germany, president of the Banque du Nord and of the International Committee of the Suez Canal, who acted as president of their subcommittee; René-Paul Duchemin, president of the *Confédération Générale de la Production Française*; Arthur Fontaine, president of the International Labour Office (ILO); Théodore Laurent, vice-president of the *Comité des Forges*; Étienne Fougère, president of the *Association Nationale d'Expansion Économique*; Henri de Peyerimhoff de Fontenelle, president of the *Comité des Houilliers de France*; Comte Wladimir d'Ormesson, the writer and ambassador; André Siegfried, professor at the *École des Sciences Politiques* and Mgr Jullien, bishop of Arras. On the German side Alfred von Nostitz-Wallwitz, the former minister of the State of Saxony, acted as president, with members including Karl Haniel, president of the *Gute Hoffnungshütte*; Franz von Mendelssohn, president of the Berlin Chamber of Commerce; Abraham Frowein, president of the National Federation of German Industry; Ernst Poensgen, vice-president of the *Vereinigte Stahlwerke* of Düsseldorf; Ernst von Simson, director of I.G. Farben; Emil Georg von Strauss, director of the Deutsche Bank; Thilo von Wilmowski, president of the Saxon Landowners' Society and vice-president of Krupps; Félix Deutsch, president of the *Allgemeine Elektrizitäts Gesellschaft* (AEG); the steel baron Fritz Thyssen; the diplomats Franz von Papen and Prince Hatfeldt and Mgr Christian Schreiber, the protestant bishop of Berlin.[157]

Members of the committee participated in many of the most important European industrial ententes, including potash, iron and steel, steel rails, tubes and strip, heavy chemicals, coal and electrical equipment.[158] Mayrisch himself became president of the European Steel Cartel (EIA), popularly known in France as the *Entente cordiale d'acier*, upon its formation on 30 September 1926. The cartel established quotas on basic steel production for the participating countries through negotiation among representatives of their respective peak organizations, the agreed proportions being Germany 40 per cent, France 32 per cent, Belgium 12.5 per cent, Luxembourg 8.5 per cent and the Saar 6.5 per cent.[159] Mayrisch died in a car accident in March 1928 on his way to a meeting of the cartel in Paris. By this time Seydoux had extended the Quai d'Orsay's support to other organizations promoting European integration.

One such organization was the *Comité d'Action Économique et Douanière* (CAED), established by Jacques Lacour-Gayet, the spokesman for France's department and chain stores in the rapidly expanding retail distribution sector. A former civil servant, Lacour-Gayet was a safe pair of hands so far as the Quai d'Orsay was concerned, and the CAED employed as its director Charles Elbel, the former deputy director of the Ministry of Commerce.[160] Another was the *Union Douanière Européenne* (UDE), established as a follow-up to the *Appel aux Européens*, a manifesto issued on 12 March 1925, affirming that Europe's political peace required economic peace, which in turn required a European customs union. The *Appel* was signed by ten prominent individuals including Professor Charles Gide of the Collège de France, Professor Elemer Hantos of Budapest, Van Gijn, the former Dutch finance minister and Edgar Stern-Rubarth, the former head of Wolff, the German news bureau.[161] Seydoux and his colleagues strongly suspected that the German members who dominated the UDE hoped to use it to promote the *Anschluss* of Austria and Germany and eventually a German-dominated *Mitteleuropa*.[162] The Quai d'Orsay officials nevertheless believed they must use every means available to promote *rapprochement* while there was still time. Hence they encouraged Gide and Yves Le Troquer, a deputy and former minister, to form a French committee of the UDE in January 1927, which thereafter was chaired by Lucien Coquet, director of the *Revue d'Alsace et de Lorraine*, founded in 1918, and *conseiller du commerce extérieur de la France*.[163] The *Revue* itself appears to have been subsidized by the French government.[164]

Similar was the Quai d'Orsay's relationship with the Pan-European Union, the best-known of the pro-European organizations between the wars. The Union was founded in April 1924, but gained prominence with its first congress held in the Vienna *Konzerthaus* between 3 and 6 October 1926. French statesmen regarded the Union as essentially a stalking-horse for the old Pan-German *Mitteleuropa* movement and its founder, Count Richard Coudenhove-Kalergi, as an Austrian adventurer. Louis Loucheur commented that in his dealings with the Union, *'il sentait le boche à plein nez'*.[165] For some time, they had refused Coudenhove's requests to meet Briand. But since Coudenhove enjoyed growing support elsewhere, Briand consented to meet him briefly in January 1926, and in the autumn he sought to take advantage of the first congress of the Pan-European Union in Vienna when it became evident that it would be a success.

The congress attracted a sort of who's who of progressive European opinion, including Edouard Benes, the Czech foreign minister, Joseph Caillaux, a former

French minister of finance, Paul Loebe, a senior SPD deputy, Francesco Nitti, a former Italian premier, Nicola Politis, the Greek prime minister and Ignaz Seipel, the Austrian chancellor, along with Konrad Adenauer, mayor of Cologne, Stresemann, Albert Einstein, Heinrich and Thomas Mann, Count Sforza, Guglielmo Ferrero, Gaetano Salvemini, Giuseppe Saragat, Herriot, Loucheur, Joseph Paul-Boncour, Henry de Jouvenel, Jules Romains, Paul Valéry, Paul Claudel, Ortega y Gasset, Miguel de Unamuno, Salvador de Madariaga, Winston Churchill, Leo Amery, Philip Noel-Baker, Wickham Steed, George Bernard Shaw and Alexander Kerensky.[166] Briand instructed the ambassador to Austria, Henri de Beaumarchais, to attend, and sent a personal message of support. Later he held a reception at the Quai d'Orsay to welcome back the unofficial French delegation. On 2 May 1927, when the council of the Pan-European Union met in Paris, Loucheur at Briand's instigation was elected president of the French section of the Union and Briand accepted an invitation to become its honorary president.[167]

That month another French initiative bore fruit when the first World Economic Conference opened in Geneva. The proposal for the conference originated with Loucheur, while minister of commerce in the Painlevé government, when he spoke at the sixth Assembly of the League of Nations in September 1925. A *Polytechnicien* who had made a fortune before the war in the electrical distribution industry, Loucheur had entered politics in 1916 when Briand called upon him to become minister in charge of economic mobilization. Subsequently he remained almost constantly in government and from the Armistice was closely associated with Briand and proponents of an economic *rapprochement* with Germany. French firms had participated in a number of international cartels or ententes before the war, including those regulating sales of aluminium, steel and potash. Loucheur was keen to revive and expand them after the war. He saw them as a means of promoting a Franco-German *rapprochment* without exposing France to the danger of domination by its more powerful neighbour across the Rhine. But he assumed that German industrialists would also find them attractive as a means of increasing market stability and securing the scale economies necessary to warrant new investment and enable them to confront their American competitors. France and Germany would thus both gain from the collaboration, and by drawing in other European participants, German industry would become enmeshed in a network of agreements that restricted its potential to dominate the Continent. War, Loucheur told the 1925 League Assembly, usually had economic origins. He was a liberal who favoured the elimination of trade barriers. But he believed some government intervention was essential to ensure a 'rational economic system' that would contain the tendency of economic competition to aggravate nationalism, leading to the recrudescence of protectionism and ultimately to aggression.[168] All League members were invited to attend the World Economic Conference. But since Loucheur anticipated that only the European states would actively participate, he assumed it would serve as a forum for promoting European economic integration. Alive to the challenge posed by American economic expansion, he now spoke of creating a 'United States of Europe' or a European customs union.[169]

Once the League Council approved Loucheur's conference proposal in December 1925, the Economic Section created a preparatory committee which began its work in April 1926. Reports from Germany encouraged Loucheur to hope that the Conference would succeed by promoting industrial ententes, which he believed to be the only practical means of stabilizing markets and reducing tariffs.[170] French diplomats affirmed that German businessmen were enthusiastic about the conference proposal and that the German government might have proposed an international conference had France not done so.[171] Ernst Trendelenberg, political director of the German Foreign Ministry and its chief commercial negotiator, assured Loucheur that Germany was prepared to work with France at the conference.[172] But other countries were at best cool towards the French approach. Reports from Italy indicated that it would claim the right to speak for countries without colonies and demand greater opportunities for emigration and enhanced access to raw materials.[173] Reports from Britain indicated indifference towards industrial ententes and keen interest in suppressing non-tariff barriers, reducing tariffs and securing universal acceptance of the most-favoured-nation principle in its unconditional form. For a country like Britain, which had no general tariff and hence almost no means of bargaining for access to foreign markets, trade discrimination represented the great threat, greater even than protectionism. Hence, British officials strongly opposed the conditional form of most-favoured-nation treatment, where such treatment was conceded only through bilateral negotiations. France and Spain were now the only European countries that still held to the conditional form. They had extended most-favoured-treatment to Britain on account of its free-trade policy, but nevertheless British officials were determined to see the unconditional form formally endorsed. They were also increasingly impatient to see further reductions in European trade barriers, not least because opposition to free trade was growing within Britain itself.

Salter, head of the League Economic Section, saw to it that the preparatory committee included a strong contingent of pro-free trade experts, including Walter Layton, editor of the *Economist* and stalwart of the British Liberal party. He also called on the committee to consult the Rome-based International Institute of Agriculture (IIA) and the International Chamber of Commerce (ICC), the latter dominated by British and American mercantile-financial interests.[174] In October 1926, 'A Plea for the Removal of Restrictions on European Trade' appeared in newspapers across Europe, bearing the signatures of 180 prominent 'businessmen'. This turned out to be the work of a small group of City men, and most of the signatories were merchants or bankers rather than industrialists.[175] The French feared they might lose control of the conference agenda, and deliberated at length on issues to be excluded, such as immigration, war debts and reparations. Unsure of the direction it might take, they were content to see the conference remain an unofficial affair with delegates nominated by national governments but attending as individuals.[176]

The conference, which opened on 4 May and lasted for three weeks, was attended by over four hundred delegates and experts from 50 countries including the United States and Soviet Russia, as well as organizations such as the IIA,

ICC and the ILO. Loucheur, elected honorary vice-president at an early plenary session, set out the case for industrial ententes in his acceptance speech. 'Old Europe', he warned, could not compete with America unless it adopted the model of American industry. While ruling out a political 'United States of Europe', he called for economic unity through sectoral ententes as the only way of overcoming Europe's trade barriers and implementing the scale economies required to meet American competition.[177] But his advice received a cool reception from several quarters, and British delegates soon weighed in with appeals to concentrate on trade liberalization through tariff reductions. Sir Max Muspratt, a recent past president of the FBI, Sir Norman Hill, a shipowner and Layton urged an end to all discrimination by universal adherence to the most-favoured-nation principle, adoption of common customs nomenclature, simplification of tariff schedules and above all reduction of import duties. Britain, they warned, was suffering from heavy unemployment on account of economic nationalism elsewhere. Unless the Conference set in train a process of trade liberalization, public opinion would soon demand that Britain abandon free trade and retreat into imperial protectionism.[178]

French delegates continued to argue for industrial ententes and the conditional form of the most-favoured-nation clause, which they believed to be a more effective means of tackling trade protection. They were nonetheless alive to the risk of driving Britain into a change of policy. Britain, for all its troubles, was still the world's greatest trading nation and France's most important trading partner. Moreover, France, like most other European countries, enjoyed a sizeable surplus on bilateral trade with Britain, which would be jeopardized if Britain adopted a general tariff and granted large preferences to Empire produce. If these were not sufficient grounds for giving way, France also had a compelling strategic argument. With Briand at the Quai d'Orsay, France remained determined to draw Britain into European affairs rather than driving it away. French delegates therefore retreated on all fronts, and by the close of the Conference they agreed to a series of recommendations that closely reflected the British agenda.

Industrial ententes were mentioned in the Conference report but neither endorsed nor condemned, although their potential damage to consumers was noted. Instead, trade liberalization by reducing external protection dominated the recommendations. Governments were urged to abandon all non-tariff barriers to trade such as export subsidies, discrimination in transport rates and administrative devices including the unfair use of health regulations and veterinary and phytopathological restrictions on trade in animals, animal products and food crops. In particular they were called upon to endorse the convention outlawing prohibitions, as quantitative trade controls including quotas and import-licensing arrangements were known. They were also urged to reduce tariff barriers. Tariff schedules had become vastly more detailed in recent years, with many of them containing thousands of items rather than the hundreds that were common before the war, a development that reflected efforts to limit the scope of trade concessions or to favour one trading partner over others.[179] Governments were called upon to simplify their tariff schedules and support League efforts to devise a standard nomenclature. They were also invited to reduce tariff levels by every means available: unilateral action, bilateral negotiation and multilateral action under the auspices of the League of Nations. To ensure that trade liberalization benefited the largest number of countries, they were requested to adopt the most-favoured-nation clause in its widest and most unconditional form. Finally they were invited to create an Economic Consultative Committee, which would report to the League Council on the implementation of the World Economic Conference's recommendations. Thus the Conference, initiated by France in hope of promoting European industrial integration, ended by promoting freer, if not free, trade.[180]

To most economists, merchants, bankers and political observers in the Anglo-Saxon world, the World Economic Conference marked a victory for their liberal approach to international economic relations and a defeat for what they regarded as the over-regulated, 'statist' French approach.[181] Briefly the Conference helped sustain the momentum for further globalization. Thirty new commercial treaties were negotiated within 12 months of the conference and another 42 the following year, nearly all of which committed the parties to the most-favoured-nation principle in its unconditional form.[182] France contributed by entering into its first postwar commercial treaty with Germany on 17 August 1927. Remarkably generous to Germany, France not only exchanged most-favoured-nation treatment, but also reduced duties on a wide range of items of special importance to Germany and – going against the world trend – fixed approximately half the duties in its tariff schedule for the duration of the treaty.[183] This was a surprising development since only six months earlier France had introduced, then withdrawn, a tariff bill with much higher duties, and was the last major hold-out on the most-favoured-nation principle.[184] Widely known as the 'economic Locarno', the Franco-German treaty was hailed by one authority as 'the greatest single contribution to liberal trading policies and to the cause of international co-operation in the twenty-five years since 1914.'[185]

The League Economic Committee meanwhile launched a concerted onslaught against non-tariff barriers to trade. It encouraged League members to sign conventions on the standardization of customs nomenclature and simplification of customs procedures, the elimination of veterinary and phytological restrictions as a disguised form of agricultural protectionism, new rules on the protection of intellectual property and the use of bills of exchange and acceptance of arbitration in commercial disputes.[186] It also scheduled an international 'prohibitions' conference in October 1927 to remove the remaining quantitative trade controls introduced after the war. The Economic Consultative Committee's first report to the League Council in May 1928 sounded a cautiously optimistic note. Numerous non-tariff barriers had been removed since the World Economic Conference, and while some tariffs had risen, 'on balance there appears to have been some improvement during the year.'[187]

Nevertheless global economic relations remained ominously precarious. Whereas before the war bilateral commercial treaties were commonly concluded for 10 to 12 years, practically all treaties negotiated after the war were terminable within a year or less.[188] The Economic Consultative Committee reported in the spring of 1929 that this had become especially evident in 1928, when all but 5 of 42 new treaties were concluded for no more than a year. It also noted anxiously that fewer treaties had consolidated or contractualized specific duties, and in contrast to 1927 numerous agreements had been negotiated with the explicit purpose of deconsolidating duties. Several countries, including Italy, Lithuania, Switzerland and the United States, had also increased duties, and a number of others – Brazil, Egypt, Finland, Mexico, Portugal, Roumania, Turkey – were preparing new tariffs which would probably include higher duties.[189] The world economy continued to expand and the Wall Street crash was still six months away, but already by 1928 signs were multiplying that the era of globalization was nearing its end.

3.5   The impact of American economic expansion

It is one of the many ironies of interwar history that Europe, having emerged from the Ruhr crisis with the help of American commercial lending, should then have faced destabilization from American economic expansion. US banks had largely shunned Europe while it remained in turmoil, preferring instead to meet the large pent-up demand for credit in Canada and Latin America. But once the Franco-German confrontation ended, US lending to Europe dramatically increased. By the end of the decade, Germany, the main recipient, held at least $755 million in American short-term loans and $1.5 billion in long-term loans.[190] The counterpart to Europe's demand for dollars, however, was a chronic deficit on current account, due to the huge imbalance in visible trade. To borrow the jargon of economic history, Europe was undergoing 'a prolonged structural transformation crisis',[191] and it is probably true that in the 1920s America's competitive advantage in manufacturing was too great to be overcome by anything governments might or might not do.[192] Political decisions nevertheless aggravated Europe's plight. In the first place, despite its current account deficit Britain was required to pay the United States almost $950 million in war debts between 1923 and 1929, and Europe as a whole paid over almost $1100 million before 1930.[193] Second, the United States government sharply increased trade barriers against imports from Europe, most of which were manufactured goods and many of them defined as 'luxuries' and hence more heavily taxed. The Republicans' Fordney-McCumber of 1922 increased average duties on imports from 26 per cent, where they had been since 1913 under the Democrats, to 33 per cent, an increase of 27 per cent. This was a large increase by any standard, but especially at a time when the American current account was already strongly positive.[194] All the while Hoover, the secretary of commerce, aggressively promoted American exports. Between 1918 and 1924, the United States exported $18,639 million in goods to Europe and imported only $5988 million, leaving a surplus of $12,651 million. Even in the more normal conditions of 1925–9, the United States earned $11,944 million from exports to Europe, nearly twice the $6365 million that it imported.[195]

Among European consumers the demand for US goods continued to grow. But increasingly they attracted widespread comment in the press and official circles, much of it hostile. One reason for the heightened interest was no doubt because in contrast to earlier times when America's exports were chiefly commodities such as cotton, tobacco, wheat and timber, after the war a large and growing fraction of its exports were finished manufactures and thus identifiably American in origin. During the five years 1925–9, total US exports rose in value by less than 7 per cent, but exports of non-food consumer goods and motor vehicles and components rose by over 45 per cent.[196] A second reason was that the fastest growing US exports were products of the most dynamic sectors of industry.[197] 'Old Europe', it seemed, was falling hopelessly behind its transatlantic neighbour. This was especially the case in the most visible of all export sectors, namely the motion picture industry. Although Europe had pioneered filmmaking, American firms stole a march on their competitors during the Great War and consolidated their lead in the 1920s. This was the decade in which Hollywood perfected the star system, established a global distribution network and captivated audiences throughout the world with films that frequently depicted American progress and prosperity. The remarkable success of American film companies, facilitated by the 1918 Webb-Pomerene act which allowed them to participate in cartels overseas so long as they did not restrict competition inside the United States, became wholly one-sided. For every dollar European films earned in America, American films earned $1500 in Europe.[198] This was disturbing enough, but since they popularized styles and shaped consumer demand, many believed that trade now followed the film more than the flag. During the 1920s, therefore, Britain, France, Germany and other European countries introduced quotas on cinema screen time in their attempt to limit American domination of the market.[199]

American economic expansion took several forms, including manufactured exports, bank lending and portfolio investments. But the most controversial form by the late 1920s was American direct investment in foreign manufacturing through the construction of branch plants or the acquisition of existing foreign firms. Postwar Republican Administrations in their isolationism disliked the idea of American businessmen acquiring or setting up operations in Europe, preferring instead to see them concentrate their activities in the Americas, the Caribbean Basin or East Asia. Hoover, whose isolationism was intensified by a neo-mercantilist approach to economics, disliked *all* direct foreign investment, since in his view it meant transferring American capital and technology abroad and paying foreign workers to compete with Americans.[200] In the event, most US foreign direct investment after the First World War went to regions outside Europe. But the scale of activity everywhere was extraordinary. Between 1919 and 1929 total US foreign direct investment nearly doubled from $3880 million to $7553 million.[201] Moreover, most of the foreign direct investment in Europe occurred after the Reichsmark and other major currencies were stabilized, that is to say in the five years between 1924 and 1929. In dollar terms, American corporations expanded abroad almost as much in this brief period as they had done in the previous half century or more. Europeans could scarcely be indifferent to this extraordinary expansion, whether it took place in Europe itself or in overseas markets where their firms hoped to compete. To add to the threat, American direct investment was concentrated in the most dynamic sectors of economic activity. By 1928 it began to appear that all of Europe's most profitable industry must eventually end up under American control.

Telecommunications was one sector where American investment created serious friction on both sides of the Atlantic during the 1920s. Washington had taken almost no interest in international communications until the outbreak of war in 1914. But on the day war broke out, the Royal Navy cut the submarine cable linking Germany to the United States via the Azores,[202] and in 1916 the western section was diverted to England to enable the British government to claim ownership of it as a prize of war.[203] The result was that all high-speed communications from the United States to Europe had to be sent by cables controlled by Britain or France or by radio which could be intercepted by anyone. Alive to the strategic importance of communications, the Wilson administration set about to end the country's dependence upon foreign systems. The Federal government introduced licences for the operation of transmitters in the United States. It also prevailed upon the General Electric Company to acquire the British controlling interest in the American Marconi Company, and on the strength of these assets to create the Radio Corporation of America (RCA) in 1919.[204] That year, American statesmen at the Paris peace conference demanded the restitution of the German Atlantic cable, claiming that the law of war did not allow the sequestration of commercial assets and angrily objecting when the British refused to give way.[205] Meanwhile another dispute arose between the Americans and the Japanese over the island of Yap, a former German possession in the Western Pacific. Japan had been granted control of all German territories in this region, but the United States insisted upon making an exception for Yap because of its potential value as a relay station for a future American-owned cable to East Asia. In December 1921 the Americans finally prevailed, obtaining unhindered rights to land and operate cables on the island.[206]

Convinced that Britain systematically read all foreign communications sent on British-controlled cables for its own commercial or diplomatic advantage, the Wilson Administration also sought to weaken the British hold on international communications. It therefore refused the British-owned Anglo-American Telegraph Company permission to land a cable at Miami because it would connect to cables owned by Anglo-American's subsidiary, the Western Telegraph Company, which possessed monopoly rights in several countries on the East coast of South America. When the British cable ship neared the Florida coast in August 1920, US Navy warships began a stand-off that lasted several months.[207] Two months later the Administration insisted upon convening an electric communications conference in Washington to pressure the British, French and Japanese into concessions. From his sick bed, President Wilson issued threats that all hope of American membership of the League of Nations would be lost if Britain and France did not yield, and that the United States might recognize an independent Ireland in the absence of British concessions.[208] British authorities responded to US obstruction of their cable interests by pressuring the Portuguese government to refuse landing rights on the Azores to American cable companies.

Eventually in 1922 the Western Telegraph Company agreed in principle to renounce its monopoly rights in South America, and ten months later, when the monopolies were actually abandoned, Washington finally granted permission to Anglo-American to land its cable in Miami.[209] British authorities, annoyed at US action, retaliated by siding with Western Telegraph in defence of its preferential position in the Azores, where an American firm sought permission to land a new cable.[210] The acrimonious dispute over American access to the Azores dragged on until November 1923.[211]

The effect of these disputes was to impress American authorities with Britain's imperial reach, which appeared to them global in scope and aggressively hostile to American interests.[212] But from the British and Continental perspective the balance of forces appeared fundamentally different. The North Atlantic cable route, successfully spanned in 1867, had been the work of an Anglo-American consortium, and for the next 40 years the British-owned Eastern Telegraph Company dominated this and other international routes. However, the situation changed abruptly early in the twentieth century when the American firms that owned the domestic telegraph network in the United States turned their attention outwards to the international market.

Britain was a signatory to the revised International Telegraph Convention of 1875, which obliged the Post Office, operator of Britain's inland telegraph system, to gather and deliver telegraphs on a non-discriminatory basis. American telegraph companies enjoyed the benefit of this Convention when transmitting messages to and from Britain and beyond. But as the United States was not a signatory to the Convention, the same firms were free to discriminate against foreign-owned cables when they collected or received messages in the United States. Exploiting this advantage, they switched traffic to American cables and swiftly drove British firms out of the North Atlantic route. As late as 1910, British firms owned or controlled 5 of the 13 commercial transatlantic cables. By 1911 American firms owned or leased all 13; only the 4 state-owned French and German cables, which were not operated on commercial principles, remained out of their grasp.[213] It was against this background that the British authorities appropriated the German Atlantic cable in 1914, and reopening it in July 1917 declared it – perhaps unfortunately – part of the All-Red system.[214] While American vulnerability in international communications in 1919 could scarcely be gainsaid, Britain's action reflected its own vulnerability not only to German military aggression but also to the unregulated expansion of American corporate power.

American telegraph operators never missed an opportunity to draw an unfavourable comparison between Europe's state monopolies and their own free market in communications.[215] That the practical result of their free market was the elimination of competition, however, was evident not only on the Atlantic route but also in the United States itself where two firms, Western Union and the McKay System, dominated the domestic network. Monopoly was also a feature of American operations elsewhere. The All-American Telegraph Company, which provided the sole communication link down the west coast of Latin America, enjoyed monopoly landing rights in several of the countries along the route. Only after the confrontation at Miami over British monopolies on the east coast of Latin America did Washington call upon All-American to renounce its monopolies on the west coast.[216] But this by no means ended the practice of forming American monopolies. RCA, in its bid to establish a global radio-telegraph network, acquired monopoly rights in Poland with the knowledge and approval of the Federal government.[217] And when in the 1920s RCA found opportunities more attractive in the United States and reduced its new investment in global communications, International Telegraph and Telephone (ITT) took up where RCA had left off. ITT had only come into being in 1920 with the merger of two telegraph companies in Cuba and Puerto Rico, but under its ambitious founder, Sosthenes Behn, and backed by J.P. Morgan & Company, it embarked upon a course of expansion that by 1929 made it the largest American employer overseas and one of the largest companies in the world.[218]

In 1924, ITT obtained the contract to operate the whole of the Spanish telephone and telegraph system, and in 1926 the contract to modernize Italy's long-distance telephone system. To gain maximum profit from the modernization of the Spanish system, it purchased the International Western Electric Company, an equipment manufacturer with factories in London, Antwerp, Milan, Paris, Barcelona and elsewhere.[219] ITT rapidly expanded its manufacturing facilities, chiefly in Europe where it employed over 30,000 workers by 1929, and 95,000 worldwide.[220] Using its monopoly control over the collection and delivery of messages in Spain, it also gained control of a vast network of submarine cables in the South Atlantic. In 1927 it acquired All-American Cables Inc., and in 1928 the Commercial Cable Company. Together they operated 25,000 nautical miles of cables between Spain and Latin America.[221]

The world slump swiftly altered ITT's fortunes, but until then there seemed to be no limit to its expansion. Thus in the winter of 1927–8, when the advent of short-wave radio swiftly made the vast network of British-owned cables unprofitable, their owners threatened to sell out to ITT if the British government did not come to their assistance. In view of the technical revolution taking place, it was not at all certain that ITT or any other American firm would have been a buyer. But the threat was credible enough to oblige the government to act, since Britain's defence and security required continued control over a global network of secure lines. The Baldwin government therefore created Cable & Wireless, a private company under public regulation, which acquired the worldwide assets of the Eastern and Associated Telegraph Companies, the Pacific Cable Company, which was jointly owned by the Australian, New Zealand, Canadian and British governments, the British Marconi Company, and the highly successful British Post Office short-wave 'beam' radio system, which was made to subsidize the non-viable cables. Cynical American observers saw this as a further instance of British imperialism: a deliberate attempt to exclude American firms from imperial and European markets and the antithesis of the Open Door. To British statesmen, however, it was a purely defensive measure, undertaken in near desperation to safeguard essential overseas communications, which otherwise might cease to operate or fall into foreign hands.[222]

A second sector where large-scale US foreign direct investment attracted increasing public attention in Europe was resource extraction and in particular petroleum, natural rubber and base metals. In 1919, British and Continental European commercial interests still dominated the production of rubber, tin and nitrates and owned a large stake in the production of many other commodities. But, in the aftermath of the Great War, European foreign direct investment stalled and even declined in face of capital shortages and capital export controls instituted to prop up national currencies. Meanwhile, US investment powered ahead, particularly in raw materials extraction and production in Canada, Latin America and the Caribbean Basin. Despite their rapid ascendancy over foreign rivals, American businessmen nevertheless continued to represent themselves as the underdog, largely on account of their experience with oil and rubber.

In the case of oil, two giant British-controlled firms, Royal Dutch Shell and Anglo-Persian Oil, continued to hold the lion's share of concessions in Persia, only yielding a minority interest to France after the war.[223] Standard Oil of New Jersey, known as Jersey Standard, complained of their efforts to exclude it from this region. But in the meantime it took the lead among US oil companies in developing overseas distribution networks, their investment in this sector rising by 77 per cent between 1919 and 1929, of which 45 per cent was concentrated in Europe.[224] At the same time they invested $854 million in foreign oil-producing properties, of which $500 million or 58.5 per cent was concentrated in Latin America and the Caribbean Basin.[225] On 31 July 1928, eight months after oil was discovered at Kirkuk in Iraq, Walter Teagle, chairman of Jersey Standard entered into an agreement with Royal Dutch Shell, Anglo-Persian and the Compagnie Française des Petroles to create the Turkish Petroleum Company, taking 23.75 per cent of the shares of this vehicle for exploring the resources of the region. In September 1928, Teagle met Sir John Cadman of Anglo-Persian and Sir Henry Deterding of Royal Dutch Shell at the latter's baronial castle at Achnacarry in Scotland, where they signed an agreement ending their global competition. The Achnacarry agreement remained well hidden from the public. But the increasingly ubiquitous presence of Jersey Standard's ESSO petrol stations along Europe's highways attracted public attention and increasingly adverse comment.[226]

Controversy over rubber began in 1922 when the British authorities introduced the Stevenson scheme to prevent the collapse of production in Malaya and Burma. In light of the importance of rubber in the recent war, they felt compelled to intervene in face of the temporary decline in demand, to keep the plantations in operation. New York bankers expressed sympathy for the scheme, which seemed to them a reasonable means of safeguarding an investment that required years before it could produce a return.[227] But as at least 70 per cent of natural rubber was consumed in the United States and American tire manufacturing firms had few alternative sources of raw materials, they complained loudly of exploitation, and Hoover seized the opportunity to demonstrate his support for American commercial interests.[228] In December 1923, Harvey Firestone, chairman of the eponymous American firm, took the first step towards a major venture in production in Liberia, which finally got off the ground in 1928. In 1926,

Henry Ford sought to fulfil his ambition to produce his own tires by embarking upon a comparably ambitious venture in Brazil, and in 1928 the Goodyear Tire & Rubber Company turned to Sumatra and the Philippines to establish plantations. That year the British government wound up the Stevenson rubber scheme, which had served its purpose.[229] By then, however, it had helped to convince a new generation of Americans of the predatory character of British imperialism.[230]

The irony was that just as Britain abandoned controls over rubber production, American corporations extended their monopoly control over a range of other commercially and strategically vital raw materials. Among the most important, albeit little appreciated by the general public, were the mineral ores used in the production of specialty steels required for machine tools and military purposes. These largely passed into American hands in the 1920s. American Smelting and Refining Company, which controlled about a third of the world's production of lead, copper and silver, held a large stake in Bolivia's tungsten deposits, one of the few known sources of this invaluable mineral, since before the war. It added to its holdings in the 1920s.[231] In the case of manganese, US commercial interests in 1917 invested in Brazilian production, which supplied 80 per cent of current American requirements.[232] Further expansion came in 1923 when the Union Carbide and Carbon Corporation acquired an important property in the British colony of the Gold Coast; and shortly afterwards the American entrepreneur, Averell Harriman, obtained a concession to develop manganese production in Soviet Russia.[233] Chrome was another steel alloy that attracted large-scale US investment in the 1920s. Until the end of the war, the only production under American control abroad was that of the Mutual Chemical Company in Quebec.[234] However, in 1926 Mutual Chemical and the Vanadium Corporation of America acquired a modest stake in Southern Rhodesia, and in 1928 Union Carbide became the major shareholder in African Chrome Mines Limited, which owned properties in Southern Rhodesia and South Africa. Union Carbide now owned the largest manganese and chrome mines in Africa. But to minimize political objections in Britain, it obscured its investments behind ostensibly British-owned firms.[235]

American control of nickel, another 'twentieth-century metal', followed a similar pattern.[236] Already before the war, the New York-based International Nickel Company (Inco) owned the world's largest nickel mine at Sudbury, Ontario. In 1916 the firm yielded to local pressure when claims that its output was ending up in German munitions used against Canadian soldiers led it to construct a refinery at Sudbury, allowing Canadians to control exports. In 1928 the firm again sought to allay public disquiet, this time in Britain, by transferring its registered office from New Jersey to Toronto. Shortly afterwards, it announced the acquisition of the British-owned Mond Nickel Company. The transaction was presented as a merger of American and British interests, with the two companies equally represented on the new board. But the name remained Inco, and it eventually returned its registration to New Jersey. With over 90 per cent of the world's output, it dominated the nickel market.[237]

Two other strategically important mineral resources that came under American control at this time were nitrates and copper. As late as 1919, nitrate production in

Chile, the source of nearly all the world's needs, was dominated by British firms, with only 3 per cent in American hands. But in 1924 the Guggenheim brothers of New York purchased the Anglo-Chilean Nitrate and Railway Company. Five years later, in the spring of 1929, control shifted decisively towards the United States when the Guggenheims acquired control of the Lautaro Nitrate Company from British investors. Lautaro, the giant of the industry, had a share value six times its nearest rival. Its acquisition allowed the Guggenheims to name the president of the Chilean Nitrate Producers' Association and thus exercise control over this essential ingredient of chemical fertilizers and explosives.[238]

A similar development occurred in copper mining and smelting. From 1916, when Anaconda Copper Company and the Guggenheims' Kennecott Copper Company began mining operations, American commercial interests controlled an important share of Chilean as well as Canadian, Peruvian and Mexican production. Control of Chilean production became almost total in 1929, when Anaconda acquired the British stake in the Chile Copper Company, which owned the largest mine in the country. By this time American interests had extended further abroad when in 1925 the American Metal Company made its first investment in Northern Rhodesia and South Africa. In 1928 the same firm joined forces with Ernest Oppenheimer's Anglo-American Corporation to take control of the Roan Selection Trust. The Guggenheim brothers suffered a setback in January 1929 when Oppenheimer and the British mining magnate, Sir Edmund Davis, outbid them for N'Changa Copper Mines, another major Northern Rhodesian property. But by this time Americans controlled upwards of 90 per cent of world copper production.[239]

Taking advantage of the Webb-Pomerene Act, leading American producers along with a few foreign firms in October 1926 set up Copper Exporters' Inc. in Brussels to fix wholesale prices.[240] British and other European electrical manufacturers soon began to complain that the higher cost of copper made it impossible for them to compete with American manufacturers who were thus able to dominate this sector of industry.[241] This was not the only instance where the United States government tolerated cartels so long as they affected only foreign interests. International General Electric belonged to the European-based incandescent lamp cartel, and other US firms belonged to the pipe and casing cartel formed early in 1928, the cork trust and various petroleum market sharing agreements. Yet in January 1929, the US Department of Justice took action against the potash cartel formed by the *Deutscheskalisyndikat* and the French *Société Commerciale des Potasses* because its pricing arrangements affected American consumers. The irony was not lost on European observers.[242]

Discriminatory copper prices were in fact only one of several handicaps facing European electrical manufacturers in their struggle with American competitors in the latter half of the 1920s. Another was the higher borrowing costs and restricted bank lending in Britain, Germany and elsewhere, and a third was the remarkable ease with which American firms could raise new capital on the booming stock markets of New York. This facilitated their takeover of numerous foreign electrical distributors and other utility companies from European investors, which in turn increased the market for American electrical manufacturing exports. So comprehensive did this takeover activity become that British diplomats in Latin America, fearing the eclipse of British influence in the region, urgently appealed for action to shore up British investments.[243]

American takeovers of electrical utility firms within Britain led the Cabinet in March 1928 to instigate an internal enquiry into the practical implications for the country.[244] The experts reassured ministers that as yet they need not fear the consequences.[245] But by the winter of 1928 a new burst of US takeover activity stirred widespread comment in the national press and Parliament. Having purchased control of much of the Latin American electrical market,[246] the American and Foreign Power Company, a former subsidiary of General Electric and backed by J.P. Morgan & Company, now acquired the assets of the Shanghai Municipal Council, including the largest power station in China, and also several important utilities in India. By the end of the year it employed 47,000 workers in its overseas operations.[247] In France, the US-based International Power Securities acquired control of the *Union d'Électricité*, which supplied electricity to Paris.[248] In Britain, Utilities Power & Light Corporation of Chicago purchased the Greater London and Counties Trust Company, Britain's largest electrical distribution company, along with numerous other smaller distributors, and announced a $50 million investment program over the next five years.[249]

The electrical manufacturing industry had gone the same way since 1923, when the New York-based International General Electric Company (IGEC) began a massive buying spree, which left it dominant over practically the whole of Europe before the end of the decade. In Germany, three firms dominated the sector after the war: *Siemens & Halske A. G.*, *Allgemeine Elektrizitäts Gesellschaft* (AEG) and the *Verkaufgemeinschaft*, along with *Osram Kommerziale Gesellschaft*, formed by the big three in 1920 to control the incandescent lamp market. By 1929, IGEC had acquired a large stake in AEG and Osram, installing O. D. Young and several other directors on their boards, while Westinghouse entered into patent sharing agreements with Siemens. By the end of the year, American influence extended to every substantial German electrical manufacturing firm.[250] It was the same in France where seven firms dominated the sector, but only the smallest one remained free of American influence or control by 1929.[251]

In Britain the industry was dominated by five firms, of which IGEC controlled only one, British Thomson-Houston, before 1928. By January 1929, however, IGEC had extended its control to three other firms, Metropolitan-Vickers, Edison Swan and Ferguson Pailin, which were merged with Thomson-Houston into a holding company, Associated Electrical Industries. Increased stock market activity in the shares of the British General Electric Company, the one firm not yet in American hands, indicated that it too would soon pass into IGEC's control. To fend off a takeover, the chairman of British GE, Sir Hugo Hirst, announced a new share offering open only to existing British shareholders. This sparked an uproar among American financial institutions, who condemned Hirst's discriminatory offering as 'financial Bolshevism' and threatened to retaliate against British investors.[252] The *Economist* and other Fleet Street journals sagely pointed out that Britain enjoyed large earnings from its own foreign investments, and that 'America is [only] doing now what Britain did last century.' Since Britain stood to lose a great deal by encouraging discrimination against its own vast portfolio of overseas investments, they sided with the Americans in denouncing the GE share offer.[253] Hirst was deeply embarrassed by the furore. In public he had encouraged the impression of being a robust British imperialist. Privately, he consulted O. D. Young of IGEC and accepted his formula that would surreptitiously extend American control over Hirst's firm through shareholdings by Associated Electrical Industries.[254] Meanwhile the London Stock Exchange raised objections to the proposed GE share offer, which was abandoned in favour of a new offering that did not discriminate against American investors.[255]

Other sectors of European industry in which American foreign direct investment became rapidly more prominent in the second half of the decade included aluminium, where the Aluminum Company of America (Alcoa) became a major participant at this time, cosmetics and soap where Hudnut Perfumery, Pond's Cream, Elizabeth Arden, Helena Rubinstein and Colgate-Palmolive-Peet began producing locally, retail distribution where the 800 stores of Boots the chemist became American-owned in 1928, sewing machines where Singer expanded its European operations, shoemaking, farm equipment, elevators and cameras where United Shoe Machinery, International Harvester, Otis and Eastman Kodak became the respective market leaders, and office machinery where National Cash Register Company and Boroughs Adding Machine Company expanded their prewar operations and were joined by IBM and Remington-Rand, both of which had manufacturing facilities in Germany, France and Britain before the end of the decade. But if there was one industry in which American foreign direct investment had a greater impact than any other it was motor vehicle manufacturing. This was not only because the industry occupied an increasingly important place in all the major economies of Europe and already provided large-scale employment. But it was also largely because the motor car itself had become the supreme aspirational consumer good, the symbol of both personal and national success.

European vehicle manufacturers had expanded during the war, some of them incorporating mass production techniques in their operations. But most remained too small to benefit from potential economies of scale and none of them managed to keep up with the major American firms, notably Ford, whose operations were vastly larger. Whereas Citroën, Europe's leading manufacturer, reached an output of barely 103,000 units in 1928, its peak year, Ford had already exceeded one million units in 1919.[256] That same year (1919), Ford began construction of its gigantic new River Rouge plant at Dearborn, near Detroit, which became the embodiment of America's second industrial revolution. As yet, Ford had only one major manufacturing operation overseas: a factory at Trafford Park, Manchester, which underwent expansion in 1920 to enable output to reach 25,000 units. Construction of a tractor plant at Cork, begun in 1917, was held up by the Troubles until 1922. Elsewhere Ford initially met postwar demand by exporting fully assembled units. But to economize on shipping costs, it soon began to invest in assembly plants abroad. During the early 1920s, Canada and Latin America were the chief targets of its expansion. However, once the Ruhr crisis ended in 1924 it ventured further afield, erecting assembly plants in Copenhagen and Antwerp in 1924, Bordeaux and Berlin-Plotzensee in 1926, and by 1929 in Spain, Turkey, South Africa, India, Ceylon, Malaya and Japan.

Among Ford's major American competitors, Chrysler expanded abroad more cautiously, limiting its activity largely to the purchase of Dodge Brothers, which manufactured trucks in Britain and cars in Canada, and the construction of an assembly plant in Germany.[257] The General Motors Corporation (GM), however, rapidly expanded overseas from 1924, when it announced plans for an assembly plant in London. The following year it purchased the small but well-regarded Vauxhall Company of Luton, with the intention of transforming it into a major manufacturing operation.[258] In 1927 it set up a large assembly plant in Osaka, Japan, and early in 1929 it challenged French car makers by starting production of a new six-cylinder Chevrolet at its plant in Anvers.[259] In March 1929 it acquired Adam Opel AG, which produced 50 per cent of Germany's cars and motorcycles, and announced its intention to double its capacity; in October 1929 it accepted an offer from Cologne's *Burgomeister*, Konrad Adenauer, to establish a production plant in the city.[260] With Ford dominating the Latin American market, GM the Australasian market, and the two together the Canadian market, British and Continental manufacturers saw their share of overseas markets dwindle to little more than 27 per cent of the total.[261] And as exports declined and American competitors reached inside their home markets, British car production ceased to expand in 1928 while Continental firms expanded more slowly.[262]

By 1929 rumours abounded that GM, which had chosen to expand abroad largely through the acquisition of foreign firms, was about to acquire one or another flagship national manufacturer such as Renault, Citroën, Fiat, BMW and Daimler-Benz.[263] Ford added to the apprehension by announcing in November 1928 its decision to build a factory at Dagenham capable of producing 200,000 units.[264] This was twice Citroën's total output, four times Fiat's and eight times Opel's, thus potentially dwarfing Europe's largest independent producers. Through Europe the belief spread that Washington was actively supporting this strategy because the domestic American market was now 'saturated', and therefore profits and markets must be found abroad. According to a report circulated by the British Foreign Office,

> The invasion by the North American motor car industry ... forms part of a preconcerted [sic] plan between the principal producing companies, Ford, General Motors and Chrysler as well as the firms carrying on the subsidiary industries, and in agreement with the United States Government, with the object of securing an outlet to the overproduction of the North American ... industries ... which the Government must maintain at all costs under penalty of seeing unemployment grow and so cause the fall in salaries which would give rise to a general labour conflagration and social disturbances of a very serious character.[265]

Hitherto, Europe's more ambitious producers had hoped to compete with the Americans on their own terms.[266] But news of Ford's expansion plan prompted renewed talk of a common front of European manufacturers against 'the American invasion'.[267] So strong was the disquiet that before the end of the decade American motor vehicles became the target of boycott or vandalism in several countries of Europe.[268]

3.6 The search for a 'third way' in international economic relations

Until 1928, the expansion of American economic activity overseas had almost no direct effect upon the policies pursued by other countries. European banks and municipalities were glad of the chance to borrow in the United States, European investors acquired steadily larger holdings of American stocks and shares, and Europe's growing tourist receipts went far to offset its payments deficit with America.[269] Europeans, however, grew uneasy at the prospect of becoming merely a living museum or pleasure ground for well-heeled American tourists. Whereas European capital never came close to controlling a decisive portion of American business, the spectre of American economic domination created acute unease in Britain and Continental Europe. Since, as will be seen in the next chapter, the reaction in 1929 contributed substantially to the dual crisis, it is worth devoting a few pages to a survey of attitudes as they evolved in the principal countries concerned.

To illustrate the impact of the American challenge upon Britain in the years leading up to the crisis, it is instructive to follow the trajectory of the industrialist and politician, Sir Alfred Mond. In 1925 he was managing-director of Brunner Mond Chemicals Limited, a highly successful firm started by his German-born father, and chairman of Amalgamated Anthracite, the largest coal syndicate in South Wales. He was also a Liberal front-bench spokesman on economic affairs and leading authority on free trade. Speaking as an industrialist, nonetheless, he marked his distance from most British economic liberals by forthrightly criticizing the decision to return to the gold standard in April 1925 on account of its adverse effect upon mining and other industries that had to compete in world markets. Within the heavy chemicals sector, Brunner Mond already faced serious competition from the vastly larger *I. G. Farbenindustrie A.G.* of Germany and the three large firms that dominated the American market, Union Carbide and Carbon Corporation, Allied Chemical and Dye Corporation and E. I. Du Pont de Nemours. To salvage the domestic market, he took the lead in arranging the merger of Brunner Mond, Nobel Industries and other manufacturers into Imperial Chemical Industries (ICI). On its creation in October 1926, ICI immediately became the largest industrial firm in Britain. Mond, chairman of the new enterprise, was now able to negotiate a market sharing agreement with *I. G. Farben* and Du Pont. But it signalled his repudiation of economic and political liberalism. He crossed the floor of the House of Commons to join the Conservatives, and turned his back on free trade in favour of an aggressive strategy of imperial protectionism.[270]

On 3 May 1927, the day before the World Economic Conference opened in Geneva, Mond addressed Unionist MPs at Westminster on his new vision of 'the

British Empire as an Economic Unit'. The United States, he observed, demonstrated the enormous advantages for modern industry of a large and relatively homogeneous market. There, 48 states were united into a single unit, such that 'an advertisement issued in New York will reach the Pacific, and will sell the same pair of boots in Milwaukee as it can on the East Coast and the West Coast.'[271] The United States, in fact, had created a virtuous circle whereby the scale economies of mass production enabled American manufacturers to pay wages far above levels elsewhere, turning workers into consumers of their own production, thus hugely increasing demand, output and the consequent efficiency gains. Those who had visited America recently to witness at first hand this development and others who observed it from overseas accepted they were witnessing a new industrial revolution, which could be ignored only at their peril. Was it not evident that the future lay with large economic units or blocs on a scale comparable to the United States?

> There can be no denial that there is, in modern economic tendencies, a growth, both in private industry and in public and economic thought, of the idea of the creation of greater economic units, both industrially and internationally, and I would add imperially.[272]

On his recent tour of Continental capitals, Mond claimed, nearly everyone he had spoken to agreed that Europe must unite economically 'to enable Europe to go on existing against the continent of North America'. Britain could remain strong and independent only by applying the same lesson and forging the British Empire into a similar economic bloc or unit. But it must act fast. Otherwise,

> its constituent parts will be forced economically into unions with other countries and complexes, whether wishful [sic] or not; sentiment will not be able to stay for ever the course of the flood-tide of economic pressure. That would be one of the greatest disasters to the British-speaking people, and one of the greatest disasters to civilisation.[273]

So convinced was Mond of this outcome that for the next two years he devoted much of his time to promoting a radical change in the course of Britain's international policy. Among the platforms he used were the Empire Industries Association, the British Empire Producers' Organisation, the National Union of Manufacturers and eventually the Empire Economic Union, which was created specifically to mobilize conservative opinion in support of an Empire economic bloc. Another was the Mond-Turner conference, created with members of the TUC, in which Mond sought, with limited success, to persuade industrial workers to collaborate with their employers on the American basis of higher wages and higher production.[274]

Mond was by no means alone in urging that Britain emulate America by transforming the Empire into an economic unit of comparable size. From the autumn of 1925 he was joined by the pioneer engine manufacturer, Sir Ernest

Petter, the director of the Iron and Steel Trades Confederation, Sir William Larke, the long-time director of the Society of Motor Manufacturers and Traders, Alfred Hacking, the chairman of British General Electric, Sir Hugo Hirst, the former chancellor of the exchequer, Sir Robert Horne, and spokesmen for the Empire Industries Association, the National Federation of Iron and Steel Manufacturers, the National Union of Manufacturers, and other bodies representing industry.[275] Support for their campaign increased when delegations sponsored by the Federation of British Industries, the *Daily Mail*, the Master Printers and the British government itself toured the United States to witness at first hand its industrial organization. In practically every instance, their main destination was Henry Ford's vast integrated car manufacturing plant in Detroit, and on their return their enthusiastic reports received wide publicity.[276] Meanwhile a flood of books, pamphlets and press reports appeared on America's industrial transformation, including Bertram Austin and W. Francis Lloyd's *The Secret of High Wages: The New Industrial Gospel*,[277] J. Ellis Barker's *America's Secret: The Causes of her Economic Success*,[278] André Siegfried's *America Comes of Age*, Hugh Vowles' 'Dynamic Detroit: A Glimpse of Americanism',[279] and the Hon. George Peel's *The Economic Impact of America*.[280]

Most susceptible to this literature were conservatives who deplored the allegedly divisive impact of liberalism upon British society and Imperial unity. The popular campaign was led by Lord Beaverbrook, publisher of the *Daily Express*, at this time billed as the largest circulation newspaper in the world. A Canadian who had made his first fortune financing industry, Beaverbrook sided with industry in the increasingly open conflict with the City that arose in the aftermath of the 1926 General Strike. At his insistence, his papers frequently carried leading articles on 'Our Real Fight with America' and 'The Devouring Republic'.[281] From time to time he also directed his attack against Norman of the Bank of England for pinioning British industry to an over-valued exchange rate and exposing it to the vagaries of the international financial markets. So compelling was the case for emulating America's economic success, however, that advocates also appeared within the liberal camp. From 1926, the *Round Table*, a mainstay of liberal imperialism, repeated the argument that 'the economic tendency of the age is unquestionably in the direction of larger and larger units', and that Europe therefore must unite economically if it was not to suffer the fate of the Greek city states in face of the Roman Empire.[282] On the eve of the World Economic Conference, Walter Layton, editor of the *Economist*, warned that Britain was approaching a crossroads, where US economic domination of the Americas and the transformation of Europe into another large economic unit would leave Britain no choice but to organize the Empire into a similar economic bloc.[283]

Inside the Cabinet and in public, Leo Amery, the colonial secretary, vigorously argued the case for abandoning free trade in favour of an ambitious policy of imperial protectionism. Convinced that in the age of large-scale mass production industry, nations could survive only within large blocs, he was one of the few Britons to participate in the movement for European integration. In 1927, he toured the Empire to rally support for Imperial economic unity.[284] In 1928, he warned colleagues of the threat of US economic expansion to the Empire,[285] adding that in the absence of a bold Imperial policy to address the unemployment problem, they faced defeat at the next general election.[286] At the previous election the government had promised deserving industries 'safeguarding', but because of the stringent conditions laid down, only a few secondary industries had been successful in their applications. Cunliffe-Lister, president of the Board of Trade, and Neville Chamberlain, minister responsible for local government, cautiously sided with Amery, and the Cabinet conceded protection in penny packets.[287] Since November 1924 it had introduced protection for silk and rayon, a quota on cinema films, a merchandise marks act, an Empire Marketing Board, an export credit scheme, increased imperial preferences on 'breakfast table' duties such as tea, coffee, wine, spirits and dried fruit, as well as renewing protection for the motor and machine tool industries, and resisting the League of Nations' call to remove import quotas on chemical dyestuffs.[288] On a comparison of duties levied per £100 of imports, Britain thus became substantially more protective than Belgium, Germany or France.[289] In September 1928, Amery optimistically noted among his colleagues 'a very healthy atmosphere of breaking away from Geneva and internationalism generally.'[290] But the Cabinet baulked at granting 'safeguarding' to major industries such as steel and wool textiles.[291] Despite Amery's energetic campaigning and repeated threats to resign from the Cabinet, his colleagues refused to support a fundamental change of policy.[292] Baldwin, the prime minister, insisted that more radical action must wait until after the forthcoming election.[293]

The reasons for the government's immobility are not hard to find. Still fresh in many minds was the general election fiasco in December 1923 when the Conservatives, without preparing the ground, had gone to the country on a protectionist platform. As a result, the Labour party gained office for the first time. It was rumoured plausibly that Baldwin had put Churchill, a free trader, in 11 Downing Street when they regained office in 1924 precisely to stop protectionists such as Amery from repeating this mistake.

A second reason was that the growing divide between the industrial and the mercantile-financial communities in Britain also divided the Conservative party. If much of its electoral support derived from the managers and skilled workers of industry, most of its finances probably came from the City. And while industry was not yet united in favour of a retreat into protectionism, finance remained firmly opposed. In any case, Britain's economic situation still presented a mixed picture. Relying mainly on the statistics for unemployment and overseas trade, nearly everyone spoke of Britain's economic situation in the 1920s as one of depression and decline. But despite the heavy unemployment in the older export industries, economic output and exports were expanding, albeit from the depressed levels of 1919–21 and more slowly than practically every other developed country. The situation had not yet reached the point where Conservative leaders were prepared to risk all by abandoning global ambitions in pursuit of the decidedly uncertain goal of a united Empire bloc. As most informed British observers were uncomfortably aware, the time had passed when India and the self-governing

Dominions could be persuaded to subordinate their national ambitions in favour of Imperial economic unity. Despite periodic displays of Imperial solidarity, they were determined to defend and nurture their own manufacturing industry and would not contemplate giving British firms free access to their markets. Indeed, British observers were mainly worried that in the absence of greater inducements from Britain, the centrifugal tendencies of the world economy would soon pull the Empire apart.

A third reason for resisting a more aggressive Empire policy was fear that it would antagonize the United States. British relations with the United States in the latter half of the 1920s were soured by a number of developments, not least by the sorry mishandling of the Geneva disarmament conference in July 1927. The British delegation, ill-prepared for the Americans' aggressive demands for equality in ancillary warships of the cruiser class, had dug in their heels rather than give way on this challenge to their global interests. Sir Maurice Hankey, the Cabinet secretary and the most influential official in Whitehall, urged Lord Balfour, the *éminence grise* of the Cabinet, to hold fast against the American challenge:

> Time after time we have been told that, if we made this concessions or that concession, we should secure goodwill in America. We gave up the Anglo-Japanese Alliance. We agreed to pay our debts, and we have again and again made concessions on this ground. I have never seen any permanent result follow from a policy of concession. I believe we are less popular and more abused in America than ever before, because they think us weak. The only thing that has really done us any good has been the Balfour Note on international debts, where we stood up to them firmly. I would refuse either to be blackmailed or browbeaten and stand absolutely to our pre-concerted plan.[294]

The failure of the conference led to angry recriminations on both sides, and in the autumn of 1928 reports of a semi-secret Franco-British agreement on avoiding controversial disarmament issues so aggravated Anglo-American relations that the British press talked of a possible war between the two Anglo-Saxon powers. But within British governing circles there was little dispute that Britain needed the interested friendship of the United States, especially now that its imperial and international interests were greater than ever.[295] Not for one moment were British statesmen prepared to see the relationship break down. Indeed, Baldwin took steps to restore friendly relations before leaving office in June 1929.[296]

But if the government was not prepared to retreat into Imperial protectionism, neither was it willing to resume its role as leader of the globalization movement. This became evident when Stresemann called on fellow League Council members in June 1927 to support the recommendations of the World Economic Conference. Belgium, Czechoslovakia and Germany had already endorsed them, but Austen Chamberlain, in the chair that day, would only say that his government had not had time to consider them and therefore could not add its support.[297] The government belatedly approved the resolutions, but further signs that Britain was abandoning economic internationalism appeared when the League-sponsored prohibitions conference opened in Geneva in October.

By the latter half of the 1920s most countries had removed the quantitative trade controls they introduced to contain balance of payments problems in the aftermath of the war. A few restrictions nonetheless remained in place, notably a French quota on scrap iron exports, a German quota on coal imports and a British quota on dyestuffs imports, and in view of their political sensitivity none of the countries concerned was prepared to act without the assurance that the others would follow suit. The prohibitions conference thus gave the British government a remarkable opportunity to consolidate progress in the removal of non-tariff barriers by taking the lead. Despite appeals from the Board of Trade, however, the government held back.[298] Not only did it insist upon retaining the dyestuffs quota, but it also introduced an exception within the draft convention for veterinary and phytopathological restrictions on agricultural imports into Britain. During the 1920s, allegations that 'sanitary' restrictions were used as disguised forms of trade protection had been a commonplace in Europe. To eliminate suspicions and the ill-will thus caused, the draft prohibitions convention called upon signatory countries to accept rules drawn up by the International Institute of Agriculture governing their use. But the British Ministry of Agriculture warned that Britain, being an island, had much more to lose than other countries in signing away its control over sanitary restrictions, and the Cabinet was not prepared to antagonize farmers by overriding the Ministry's opposition. The opt-out therefore remained.[299] The prohibitions conference eventually adopted a convention, but since most of the signatory countries made their ratification conditional upon the ratification of other countries, it remained in suspension until the world slump swept it away.

Meanwhile in London the combination of persistently high unemployment, industrialists' and farmers' complaints about the deflationary impact of the gold standard and American economic expansion created increasing turmoil. British diplomats warned that the relentless US takeover of British firms was sanctioned by Washington because of the 'saturation' of the domestic American market, which shook Chamberlain, Cunliffe-Lister and other members of the government, who shared a Malthusian view of economics.[300] News that Hoover planned to tour Latin America before he took up the presidency in the spring of 1929 led them to fear an accelerated American takeover of the market there. To counter his influence, they immediately mounted a British trade mission to the region.[301]

Publicly, Norman of the Bank of England sided with the liberal internationalists of the City in opposing protectionist measures such as the discriminatory British General Electric share offering.[302] In March 1929, he joined the Treasury in batting away a Foreign Office proposal to make foreign loans conditional upon export commitments, since this would tie the City's hands and amount to a subsidy to industry.[303] But he could not ignore the fact that continued US takeovers of British industry were intensifying the backlash against internationalism, which threatened his capacity to defend the gold standard and sterling, and he became increasingly worried that Britain would lose control of firms on which it depended for much of its overseas earnings. In the midst of the General Electric controversy he thoroughly frightened Baldwin, the prime minister, at the spectre of American domination. 'The American money power is trying to get hold of some of the natural resources of the Empire. They are working like beavers', Baldwin warned Ramsay MacDonald, the Labour leader. Tom Jones, the assistant secretary of the Cabinet, who recorded this exchange, warned Baldwin of the dangers of associating with Hirst and advocates of radical action against American capital. 'The PM was inclined to agree', Jones noted, 'but dreaded American control. He has been talking to the Governor of the Bank of England.'[304]

In private, Norman also advised General Sir Herbert Lawrence, chairman of the Anglo-International Bank, to safeguard his bank against American takeover.[305] He also attempted to interest London banks in forming a consortium to purchase a controlling interest in British overseas banks and other firms in danger of falling into American hands. Nothing came of this because the London banks were already heavily loaned, and declining commodity prices made some of the overseas investments unattractive at present prices. Besides, American competitors had almost unlimited financial resources while the bull market in New York continued.[306] Norman however persisted. He appealed to the Treasury for advice, and in May he chaired a meeting at the Bank with Treasury officials and leading City bankers to address the crisis.[307] Economic liberals to a man, they agreed that in principle markets should be left to operate as freely as possible. But they accepted that certain key or strategic industries should be protected from foreign takeover: 'South American Railways or other like companies providing large orders for British industry. Shipping Companies, such as Royal Mail, Cunard, P&O. Overseas Banks, such as South American and Eastern Banks. Armament Firms, such as Vickers-Armstrongs. Bank of England and other large British Banks.'[308] Presently a number of defence-related British companies such as Fairey Aviation, Imperial Airways, Rolls Royce and Marconi International Marine as well as numerous British overseas firms including the Burmah Corporation, the Rubber Plantations Investment Trust and the Buenos Aires and Pacific Railway altered their articles of association to ensure continued British ownership.[309]

After the Conservative party's defeat in the May 1929 general election, debate immediately erupted among party supporters over Britain's future strategy. Beaverbrook, encouraged by Mond (now first Baron Melchett) and Amery, embarked upon an 'Empire crusade' and threatened to create a separate party if Baldwin did not abandon economic internationalism in favour of imperial protectionism.[310] With Britain, hitherto the champion of globalization, in active retreat, a turning point had been reached in the interwar period. This, it should be noted, came before the Wall Street crash and the start of the world economic slump.

A similar pattern emerged in Germany. Since Versailles, German statesmen had remained distinctly lukewarm about the European movement not only because of the chastening effect of the wartime blockade which had underlined their dependence upon overseas resources, but also on account of their confidence that, given the opportunity, Germany could compete successfully in global markets, and their interested friendship with Britain and the United States, on whom they counted to restrain France and support their efforts at Treaty revision.[311] Stresemann, the dominant influence on German external policy from September 1924 to October 1929, was especially impatient to see a final settlement of reparations and an early end to the Allied occupation of the Rhineland.[312] But the gathering pace of American economic expansion and the destructive impact of the Wall Street boom, which had practically halted inward credits in 1928 and brought on a recession in Germany, shook the political and economic establishment.[313] Some German firms, like their British counterparts, changed their articles of association to defend against takeover.[314] Others formed cartels as a means of defence and began to look more seriously at European integration.[315] Much of Germany's raw materials and over two-thirds of its capital borrowings came from overseas, but Europe absorbed almost 75 per cent of its exports, a percentage little changed from before the war.[316] Stresemann, while not prepared to abandon world markets, acknowledged that Germany must look to Europe as its base for competing with the United States in the new age of industrial concentration. He first set out his thesis to the *Übersee Klub* of Hamburg in 1925:

> In face of the concentration of the world's financial and economic forces in one State, which forms almost a continent in itself, stands a Europe where the majority of great powers have been replaced by an infinity of small states.... Economic life tends towards concentration: unproductive intermediaries are eliminated; the production of primary materials is integrated with the production of finished goods in a single gigantic organism. And at this very moment, in this impoverished and war-torn Europe, you see an accumulation of tariff barriers, of passport problems, of obstacles to the freedom of individual re-location and similar features that recall the lamentable epoch when Germany was divided into tiny states.... In face of the balkanisation of Europe, it seems to me essential for the development of German production that a large free trade zone should be created.... If the countries of Europe maintain their customs barriers and seek unrealistically to preserve their economic autarky, they will not withstand the capitalism, the gold reserves and the technological superiority of the United States; they simply will not compete with a continent blessed with an extraordinary abundance of man-power.[317]

His second public affirmation of the necessity for European economic integration came in his speech at Oslo University on 29 June 1927, after receiving the Nobel Peace Prize.[318] His interest in 'Europe' appeared to grow in 1928, and in June 1929, when they met during a session of the League Council, he encouraged Briand to think that he supported European integration.[319]

Another German who expressed interest in 'Europe' was Hjalmar Schacht, president of the Reichsbank and a powerful influence in German business circles. In 1926 he visited the United States and returned convinced that Europe must emulate the American economic model:

> the American system of amalgamation, of massed production, and of adjustment of production to consuming power over a vast area must be adopted

by Europe if Europe is to survive against American competition. ... The old system of innumerable small firms competing with one another and producing goods which are not required by the market has got to be modified.[320]

This conviction was to affect his political decisions in the following years. Until the late 1920s, he hoped that the City of London would provide the finance Europe needed for its industrial transformation and assist in organizing Europe economically. But in 1929, he turned to the Nazis since they supported the anti-liberal action needed to strengthen Germany's industrial defences.[321]

Meanwhile the link between developments in global capitalism and the need for European economic integration became the themes of innumerable books and pamphlets, including Julius Hirsch's *Das amerikanische Wirtschaftswunder*, Oskar Sommer's *Amerika will die Zeit festbinden*, J. Walcher's *Ford oder Marx: Die praktische Lösung der sozialen Frage*, Gustav Meyer's *Die Amerikanisierung Europas* and Eugen Diesel's *Der Weg durch das Wirrsaal*. Some authors argued for emulation of America, while others, reflecting the romantic anti-capitalism of the Right, warned of increasing Americanization and the stifling effects of mass production and mass consumption on German culture.[322] Liberal or anti-liberal, however, in almost every case the underlying theme was that a second industrial revolution was under way, transforming the optimal scale of production and creating the need for large, relatively homogeneous markets. Besides the United States, some observers accepted that the Soviet Union was also making great strides under the New Economic Plan to realize Russia's enormous economic potential. Thus, they warned, the world would soon become dominated by five or six large blocs, including an American bloc that embraced North and South America, the British Empire, the Soviet Union, and an economically federated Europe.[323] The prewar German preoccupation with geopolitics thus revived in a vigorous if slightly modified form.[324] While German industrialists and trade union leaders turned increasingly towards the movement for European integration, behind the scenes the *Auswärtiges Amt* played on current anxieties by quietly encouraging interest in a German-dominated *Mitteleuropa*.[325]

Not all Germans, of course, drew the same conclusions. In his untitled second book, written in the spring of 1928, Adolf Hitler insisted that Germany's incipient crisis could have been predicted since the war when Weimar's leaders adopted a liberal 'bourgeois national policy' of recovery through the expansion of German foreign trade. Since he believed that overseas markets were limited and would eventually shrink when the branch plants established abroad increased their production, it seemed to him only a matter of time before the developed countries entered into a suicidal struggle to dispose of their industrial surpluses to pay for necessary raw materials and foodstuffs. Germany's hopes of surviving in these circumstances were limited by Britain's control over large parts of the developing world and even more by the rapid growth and expansion of American industry. As he explained

the American union is now the stiffest competitor in many areas. The size and wealth of its internal market permits production levels and thus production facilities that decrease the cost of the product to such a degree that, despite the enormous wages, underselling no longer seems at all possible. The development of the automotive industry can serve as a cautionary example here. It is not only that we Germans, for example, despite our ludicrous wages, are not in a position to export successfully against the American competition even to a small degree; [at the same time] we must watch how American vehicles are proliferating even in our own country. This is only possible because the size of the internal American market and its wealth of buying power and also, again, raw materials guarantee the American automobile industry internal sales figures that alone permit production methods that would simply be impossible in Europe due to the lack of internal sales opportunities. The result of that is the enormous export capacity of the American automobile industry. At issue is the general motorization of the world – a matter of immeasurable future significance. Because the replacement of human and animal power with the engine is just at the beginning of its development; the end cannot be yet assessed at all today. For the American union, in any case, today's automobile industry leads all other industries.[326]

Hitler observed that many of his compatriots, alive to the need for expanded markets, had chosen to join the European integration movement. While this reflected awareness of Germany's predicament, he was certain their approach could not provide the solution because of the irreconcilable national differences among the countries of the Continent. Europe, he told his followers, must urgently unite to avoid succumbing to American hegemony.[327] Britain could concentrate upon organizing its Empire; the 'American union' could absorb the other overseas markets. Germany's mission was to organize Continental Europe into a comparable political-economic bloc, which could only be accomplished through force.[328]

While Hitler's Malthusian economics may seem merely risible today, they did not appear absurd at the time, not least because of Germany's staggering economy and its failure to make headway in the crucial world market for cars and components. Significantly, when invited to address leading German industrialists at Düsseldorf in January 1932, Hitler made almost no change to his earlier analysis, except to inflate the challenge of the Soviet Union as a potential economic competitor.[329] Leaders of German big business, being the most thoroughly integrated into the global capitalist system, were sceptical of his autarkic Continental strategy and, with few exceptions, refrained from supporting the Nazi party. But they constituted only a small fraction of the German business community. Among directors of Germany's vastly more numerous medium and small firms, for which overseas markets meant little or nothing, it was a different story. From all the evidence, they found much to agree with in Hitler's analysis. The Nazi party concentrated its efforts on wooing them rather than directors of the larger, more globalized sector and succeeded all too well when the world economic slump intensified their anxieties about the decline of the national market and the growth of Communism among the working classes.[330]

Until July 1926 when Poincaré returned to reassure the markets, France's chronic inflation and currency depreciation made it appear the sick man of Europe. Yet in physical output the French economy performed much better than the British or German economies, and once the franc was stabilized *de facto* in December 1926 France was able and willing to share leadership of the world economy. The Bank of France, with the encouragement of the Ministry of Finance, sought to work with other central banks in the management of the international gold standard. It also assisted friendly states to return to gold, and sought to restore the *Place de Paris* as an international credit and capital market. The Ministry of Commerce in turn promoted trade expansion through industrial 'ententes' and reciprocal tariff bargaining, and from August 1927 it generalized concessions offered in bilateral treaties through the application of the unconditional most-favoured-nation principle. But, as we have seen, French and British central bankers remained at odds in their approach to the gold standard, and differences over trade also divided France and the Anglo-Saxon powers.

The Franco-German commercial treaty of August 1927 spurred angry protests from both Britain and the United States. Britain, already in dispute with France over new restrictions on coal imports, complained that French concessions to Germany disadvantaged British trade. The United States objected to the discrimination implicit in granting Germany but not America most-favoured-nation treatment, and threatened an all-out trade war if this was not remedied.[331]

British authorities still regarded their own country as free trade and hence morally superior to protectionist France and the rest of Continental Europe. But the accumulation of the excise, McKenna, Safeguarding, and silk duties over the previous ten years weakened claims of being free trade. Moreover, practically every one of these new duties fell with particular weight upon French trade. Indeed, by now French exports to Britain were subject to greater taxes than British exports to France.[332] The duty on silk and artificial silk (or rayon), introduced in April 1925, struck with particular force Lyon, capital of French silk production, whose mayor, Edouard Herriot, happened to be the current premier. But the French were even more annoyed that Britain should maintain the pretence that its excise duties were not protective when in fact they applied almost exclusively to imported goods such as dried fruit, tea, coffee, wines and spirits, and moreover they included a substantial preference that favoured Imperial producers. They therefore responded to British complaints about the new Franco-German commercial treaty by offering only minor concessions while renewing their invitation to renegotiate the 1882 Anglo-French treaty. The British ambassador professed to be disappointed with this response. But Cunliffe-Lister was aware that British trade enjoyed relatively favourable treatment in France. He therefore declined the offer of negotiations and abandoned his protest.[333]

The American protest against the Franco-German commercial treaty presented a more formidable challenge. French authorities regarded American talk of the 'Open Door' with the same cynicism as British claims of free trade.[334] The introduction of the Eighteenth Constitutional amendment in 1920 prohibiting the consumption of alcoholic beverages could not have been better designed to discriminate against French trade. Under the Republicans the American tariff constituted a formidable barrier to imports from all foreign countries but especially France because of the exceptionally high duties levied on 'luxury' goods. Nevertheless the French government was anxious to avoid a break with the United States as much for political as for economic reasons. In November 1927, therefore, the Ministry of Commerce offered enough concessions to end the confrontation.[335]

But while France demonstrated its interest in maintaining good relations with the Anglo-Saxon powers, neither Britain nor the United States displayed a comparable interest in good relations with France. As a result, these disputes antagonized French opinion and encouraged the government to maintain a defensive posture. This was reinforced by the appearance of a flood of pamphlets and essays on the American challenge towards the end of the decade. Combined with nervousness about resurgent German nationalism and France's loss of purchase over Germany, the effect was to shake French confidence in economic internationalism.

Among the many French publications on American economic ascendancy, some dwelt upon the subversive effects of materialism and in a few cases bordered on the hysterical. These included Charles Pomaret's *L'Amérique à la conquête de l'Europe*, J. L. Chastanet's *L'Oncle Shylock ou l'impérialisme américain à la conquête du monde*, Kadmi Cohen's *L'abomination américaine*, Georges Duhamel's *Scènes de la vie future* and in 1931 Robert Aron and Arnaud Dandieu's *Le cancer américain*, to which may be added the journal *Esprit*, established in 1932 by the Catholic intellectual Emmanuel Mounier to advance the concept of 'personalism' in face of the levelling effects of the American-dominated machine age. But like popular journalism elsewhere, these publications received a mixed reception, and notwithstanding provocative titles the majority of French reportage attempted a dispassionate evaluation of the implications of America's economic expansion. Among the latter were Jean Bonnefon-Craponne's *La pénétration économique et financière des capitaux américains en Europe*, Pierre Laurent's *L'impérialisme économique américain*, Francis Delaisi's *Les Deux Europes*, Lucien Romier's *Qui sera maître: l'Europe ou les Etats-Unis?* and André Siegfried's *Les Etats Unis d'aujourd'hui*, first published in 1927 and reprinted ten times by 1931.[336] By and large the insights they provided were similar to those in British and German publications. Where they differed – and this was also true of French policy-makers – was less in their perception of the challenge than in the connection they drew between Europe's economic future, national security and European economic integration. Confronted with a deeply dissatisfied and increasingly unconstrained Germany, French observers looked to the Anglo-Saxon powers for support, but found them indifferent to the instability their economic behaviour was causing on the Continent. The logic of their predicament fostered ideas of pan-European action to embrace Germany and sustain French influence in Europe.

As early as January 1922, Briand had observed privately to diplomatic colleagues, 'We will soon find ourselves trapped between two collossi, Russia and the United States. This is why we shall have to create a United States of Europe, at least in the economic sphere.'[337] Four years later he repeated his prediction at a private meeting of the Foreign Affairs Commission of the Chamber of Deputies:

> The time is coming when Europe will no longer be prepared to remain in its present divided state. It will become, like America, a federal state. This will be essential to regulate its anarchic production; otherwise it will face social catastrophe. Eventually we will see a coalescing of economic interests, though necessarily dominated by a coalescing of political interests. A formula for a European federal union must be found. France must direct its efforts towards this goal.[338]

Herriot was the first French political leader publicly to affirm his country's interest in a 'United States of Europe', during the debate on foreign policy in the Chamber of Deputies on 28 January 1925.[339] The occasion left in no doubt the primacy of security in national calculations. Events leading to the recent Dawes plan had highlighted France's vulnerability to economic pressure from the Anglo-Saxon powers to compromise with Germany. In the meantime, French statesmen sought to fend off challenges to national sovereignty from Anglo-Saxon capital.

During the peace negotiations, vulnerability to British and American oil interests had led France to demand a share of the German concession in Turkey, later to become the Iraq Petroleum Company. This was followed by a series of initiatives intended to address the domination of the great Anglo-American oil companies: creation of the Petroleum Department in the Ministry of Commerce in 1922, and the state-controlled *Compagnie Française des Pétroles* in 1924, legislation in 1928 to regulate the import and distribution of oil within France and creation of the *Compagnie Française de Raffinage* in 1929 after the discovery of oil in Iraq.[340] Anxiety over accelerating American influence within the French economy itself led to a change in tax laws intended to discourage foreign ownership of French firms. The decision provoked a strong protest from Washington and the threat of sanctions.[341] Eventually legal action obliged Paris to retreat, but in the summer of 1928 a new conflict began when Washington protested at the French government's decision to introduce a quota on foreign films shown in French cinemas.[342]

Meanwhile the unresolved war debt issue strained Franco-American relations. Whereas most Americans regarded the repayment of war debts as a legitimate demand and believed they had already made generous concessions on accumulated interest and amortization rates, practically all French observers regarded Washington's demands as profoundly unjust in view of the vastly greater human and physical sacrifices their country had made in the common cause. Under pressure, the Briand government on 29 April 1926 had signed a war debt funding agreement specifying payments of $6847 million spread over 62 years. Three months later another government led by Briand signed a similar funding agreement with Britain, calling for the payment of £653 million ($3174 million) over the same period.[343] However, as the French Parliament was not prepared to accept war debt obligations before the adoption of a definitive reparations agreement, the agreements went unratified for the next three years. The deadline for ratification of the American debt agreement was 31 July 1929, when further delay would trigger a demand for the immediate repayment of $400 million for war stocks sold to France at the end of the war.[343] And, as the deadline approached, frustration in France mounted, adding to resentment against the United States. In Parliament and the press, critics likened America to Shylock and complained that it used war debt receipts to buy up French firms, thereby reducing France to the status of a semi-colony.[344]

While these protests contained a good deal of hyperbole, the speed of American economic expansion, including recurrent rumours of an American takeover of one of France's leading auto manufacturers, together with the widespread sense of injustice and awareness that French security was intimately bound up with national economic strength, intensified interest in European integration. No one in Paris imagined that European integration could be realized quickly or extend beyond economic relations for the foreseeable future. Nonetheless by August 1928 Poincaré had become sufficiently disturbed by the influence of American business in France to raise it in agitated terms during his first meeting with Stresemann.[345] Despite profound differences of temperament with Briand, Poincaré agreed that Europe was being dangerously squeezed from two directions, by the Soviet political threat from the East and the American economic threat from the West, and that France should exploit the spreading apprehension elsewhere in Europe to promote economic integration.[346]

3.7   Conclusion

In the ten years after the Great War, as the world economy expanded, international trade as well as capital flows far exceeded prewar levels. The great Victorian era of globalization was thus restored. Yet the United States, one of the three main victor powers in the recent war and the principal beneficiary of globalization contributed remarkably little in the way of leadership. The international bankers of New York who supplied the bulk of the capital and credit necessary for the return to globalization were treated almost as heroes in Europe, where the supply of dollars enabled countries to escape the postwar financial chaos. But by themselves the bankers could not hope to clear away all the obstacles to trade and payments or re-establish the framework of trust, regulatory institutions and security needed to sustain the global system when difficulties arose. Britain in contrast made a critically important contribution, officially and unofficially, to economic liberalization after the war. But this was not matched by contributions on the security front, and by 1927 official British support for economic reform had ominously ceased. In view of Britain's uniquely important place in the global economy, indications that it might retreat behind an imperial protectionist barrier, favouring the British self-governing Dominions and colonies while discriminating against foreign countries, contributed to nervousness about the prospects for international commerce. By 1928, American contributions to economic reform were also negative, with Washington's concessions on war debts and the New York Fed's assistance to foreign central banks more than offset by the Republicans' mercantilist approach to foreign commerce and their open indifference to France's efforts to maintain a security framework in Europe. The great globalization project, lacking Anglo-Saxon leadership, was seriously jeopardized.

France, the third victor power and creditor power, sought to contribute leadership as best it could. But its contributions on the security front were systematically opposed by Britain and the United States, while its contributions on the commercial, financial and monetary fronts from 1924 onwards illustrated the manifold ways in which international economic relations were bound up with security considerations. The decision to return to the gold standard at the sharply devalued rate of 124 Ff = £1, which Anglo-Saxon critics later singled out as a major cause of the economic crisis of 1929–32, is a particular case in point. The decision reflected France's determination to safeguard domestic industry from the difficulties British industry faced from an over-valued exchange rate, assist its Eastern European allies and avoid further vulnerability to external political pressures. But the influence of politics was not all on the French side. Norman imagined that his efforts to restore the gold standard placed monetary and financial policy above politics. Yet his goal of empowering central bankers was a political one. Moreover, his pursuit of globalization and his efforts to promote liberal reforms in Europe with German and American central bankers, while excluding the French, nicely complemented the aims of postwar British governments. French politicians and bankers quite properly regarded France as a liberal country. But only in the Anglo-Saxon countries was the illusion maintained that economics and politics could be treated as discrete issues.

Of statesmen in the three powers, only the French recognized the vital importance of Eastern Europe to international security. They were also among the first to appreciate that modern industrial capitalism as exemplified by the United States demanded larger units particularly in Europe where the recent war had thrown up additional commercial barriers. Experts in the League Economic Section devised commercial reforms that would allow Europe to move towards regional arrangements under League auspices.[347] Their proposal was due to be circulated in 1929. By now a majority on the League Economic Committee favoured modification of the most-favoured-nation principle to allow for open-ended, trade-creating free trade areas.[348] But the League proposal required individual countries to agree to a European exception in their most-favoured-nation agreements, permitting European countries to discriminate against non-European countries, and Britain and the United States had already indicated their firm opposition to preferential arrangements of this sort. Given their commitment to globalization, or to use the contemporary American phrase the 'Open Door', this was not surprising. It was nonetheless extremely unfortunate, for it was evident to any unblinkered observer that Europe's economic recovery was very fragile and that the Continent remained the world's powder-keg.

What was needed was not more liberalism nor more foreign lending or investment. Rather it was a general recognition that the process of globalization had imposed strains and exposed vulnerabilities, not least among the larger powers of

Europe, which brought on a widespread reaction. World production and trade continued to increase until the latter half of 1929. Already by 1928, however, progress on trade liberalization had not only ceased but was slipping into reverse on account of declining commodity price levels, Europe's worsening payments problems, the virtual absence of effective institutions or international leadership and the crumbling framework of security. Europe and the world thus entered a period of instability in conditions of extraordinary, perhaps unique, vulnerability.

4
The Crisis Begins, 1927–9

4.1 Introduction

On the morning of Thursday, 19 December 1929, the lord mayor of the City of London accompanied by sheriffs, mace-bearer and sword-bearer stood on the dais of the Guildhall before a large and distinguished audience to welcome their two special guests. The first, escorted by the master of the Honourable Company of Bakers, was the Labour prime minister, James Ramsay MacDonald, a handsome, square-shouldered man of 63 years. The second, slight, lame and two years older, was the chancellor of the exchequer, Philip Snowden, who came forward on crutches from the rear of the platform. Those unfamiliar with the British scene might have found it surprising that leaders of a socialist party committed to the 'common ownership of the means of production, distribution and exchange' should be offered the freedom of the City, unofficial headquarters of the capitalist world. But their reception confirmed that the City regarded them as reliable moderates who could be counted upon to restrain the radical elements in the Labour movement. The two men in turn were openly delighted at being received by the City. Snowden spoke for them both when he affirmed that it was

> one of the greatest honours which could come to any man in recognition of public work. ...The association of the City with our struggles for national liberty, with the growth of our civic institutions, with the development of our trade and commerce, and with the building up of our world Empire, had given it a unique place in British history, and to be a Freeman of the City ... made one feel a part of that great City and gave one a more definite share in its traditions and its glories. (Cheers)[1]

Each man, the lord mayor explained, had earned the City's special gratitude in his own way. The prime minister had done so by signally improving Anglo-American relations since he took office in June 1929. Relations had become increasingly strained after the breakdown of the Geneva naval conference in 1927 and reached a low point in the autumn of 1928, when news of a separate Franco-British arms agreement caused an uproar in Washington and threats of a naval arms race. MacDonald, a devoted Atlanticist, had seized the first opportunity to visit Washington for talks with President Hoover. Now, speaking to the Guildhall audience, he reaffirmed his belief that with America's friendship Britain had no credible enemies and could proceed confidently with plans for a new naval disarmament conference early the next year. The lord mayor indicated the City's overwhelming support for this view. The chancellor's contribution was to stand up to the French as well as the Belgians and Italians at the recent conference at The Hague on reparations, and to threaten to walk out unless Britain was conceded a larger piece of the reparations cake. As he explained to the Guildhall audience, 'I had long felt that in the many negotiations which had taken place since the War...the other nations had not...sufficiently recognized the generosity of Great Britain and the sacrifices that we had made for the sake of peace and European reconstruction.' But in fighting Britain's corner he wished it to be understood that he was upholding, 'not...merely national interests but...general interests, for good relations between nations, and the peace of the world.'[2] Not only had he secured justice on reparations, but he had also secured a commitment from France that the last remaining Allied forces would be withdrawn from the Rhineland in the new year.

So strong was Britain's Atlanticism and its antagonism towards France that the spectacle of a Labour prime minister and chancellor being fêted by the City attracted little comment.[3] Yet their actual accomplishments should have given enthusiasts pause for reflection. Snowden had attended the Hague conference knowing that if he could obtain an increase in the 'standard' rate of reparation receipts, the British press would present it as a national victory. Like Mrs Thatcher a half-century later, he also appreciated that it was politically popular to present Britain as righteous victim of the clever, materialistic French and other European powers. But in fact his aggressive negotiating tactics may well have had the effect of *reducing* Britain's reparation receipts, because the formula he accepted involved lower payments in the early years of the Young plan in return for higher payments later when reparations might well be abandoned.[4] In any case, the larger purpose of the Hague conference had been to underpin the peace by securing a reparations settlement that was acceptable to Germany and removed the need for continued military occupation of the Rhineland. Yet in demanding Britain's 'rightful share' of reparations, Snowden helped to ensure that Germany obtained disappointingly little relief on payments. Moreover the conference was followed almost immediately by the death of Gustav Stresemann, Germany's leading advocate of international dialogue, and an upsurge in militant German nationalism. MacDonald's decision to make improved relations with the United States the priority for British foreign policy proved scarcely more propitious. While Anglo-American differences were reduced, Washington remained aloof from global affairs. Indeed, if anything, it was becoming *more* isolationist than before, for reasons that MacDonald's City hosts could well appreciate.

On 3 September, shortly before MacDonald had sailed for America, the New York Stock Exchange reached its postwar peak. By the morning of 24 October, 'Black Thursday', the market had already drifted sharply lower, and by 19 December,

Table 4.1   Twelve bell-weather stocks on the NYSE (closing prices)

Stock	3 Sept. 1929 market peak	24 Oct. 1929 'Black Thursday'	19 Dec. 1929 post-crash trough	22 Apr. 1930 post-crash peak	9 Jul. 1932 depression trough
American Telegraph & Telephone	302	268	217¾	254½	71
Atchison Topeka & Santa Fe Railroad	293	261	223	232½	19½
Chrysler Corp	71⅝	45¾	34¾	39⅝	5¾
DuPont Chemicals	214½	167½	112	135	22⅞
General Electric	390¼	307	228	90⅞	9⅝
General Motors	71¾	53½	40	50⅞	7⅞
RCA	98	58	42½	67¾	3⅝
Remington Rand	50⅛	47⅜	27⅛	42¾	1⅜
Sears Roebuck	171	128½	97	91¼	10½
Standard Oil of New Jersey	292	251	215¼	232¾	28
Union Pacific Railroad	257⅝	205½	167½	192	21¾

Note: On 9 July 1932 the NYSE reached its nadir in the interwar period, when only 200,000 shares were traded, the lowest volume since 13 Sept. 1924: *Times*, 11 Jul. 1932, p. 19.

the day of the Guildhall ceremony, leading shares had slumped by over a third from their September peaks (see Table 4.1). This was a massive decline but not necessarily disastrous, since major stock markets have always tended to over-shoot or undershoot realistic values by a considerable margin, and indeed by the end of the year shares recovered a quarter of their losses. But the Crash had come at a time when global financial movements were threatening the newly re-established gold-standard-based monetary system, a general retreat from trade liberalization and economic slump, and, equally important, international rela-tions were marked by acute nervousness and suspicion. The Crash thus added to existing uncertainties, and in the absence of agreed rules of economic behaviour, international institutions for dealing with global imbalances and a framework of security, countries large and small were aggravating the economic slump by retreating into nationalism or imperialism.

4.2   Bankers and the crisis

While neither the stock market crash in 1929 nor the world economic slump in 1929–33 could have been predicted, it is too often forgotten that the inter-national financial crisis which formed the backdrop to them was long antici-pated by leading international bankers. As early as August 1925, Norman of the Bank of England privately acknowledged that the Dawes plan on reparations was unsustainable and feared a repeat of the Ruhr crisis unless more was done to restrain France. He therefore became impatient for the introduction of the Locarno agreements and German enrolment in the League of Nations so as to contain the political reactions to a new debt crisis.[5] In the event, reparations continued for another six years, but almost immediately the international monetary and financial system came under strain from other directions. As Norman wrote to Schacht of the Reichsbank in December 1926, he had hoped that the restoration of the gold standard in Europe and elsewhere would be accompanied by effective coordination among the central banks, enabling them to maintain exchange stability without the need for large gold reserves. For this reason he had promoted the temporary expedient of the gold exchange standard whereby secondary central banks relied mainly upon deposits at the Bank of England and the Federal Reserve Bank of New York rather than actual gold for the reserve assets underpinning their currencies. Unfortunately coordination was proving impossible. Practically half the world's monetary gold remained in the vaults of the American Federal Reserve System where it was 'sterilized' rather than allowed to expand the money supply. To all intents and purposes, Norman wrote, 'the Americans are on a different gold standard…and no matter how much gold Europe may send to New York no results are thereby produced on their market conditions.' To make matters worse, European countries returning to the gold standard generally found it cheaper to purchase gold in the London bullion market than in New York on account of the lower shipping and insurance charges. This put sterling under constant pressure, and since industrialists loudly complained of high interest rates and advocates of a managed currency such as Keynes and McKenna had the ear of the chancellor, Norman was constrained from raising Bank rate, as called for by the markets. Instead, he had been obliged to fall back on informal capital export controls, which disappointed colleagues in the City. As Norman put it, the 'international machine is greatly out of gear'.[6] Schacht acknowledged that his own position was scarcely more favourable. Since the end of the Ruhr crisis, American bankers had been constantly pressing German firms and public authorities to take up dollar loans. Despite his best efforts, he was unable to contain this expansion of debt and had lost control of his market.[7]

Pressure on sterling increased early in 1927 when the Bank of France attempted to hold the franc at 120Ff = £1, while speculators, operating largely out of London, sold sterling to purchase francs in the expectation of a revaluation. It further increased in May when Governor Moreau set about deliberately to tighten market rates in London by presenting sterling balances for gold at the Bank of England. Norman did what he could to dissuade Moreau from this tactic, warning him that much more pressure would drive sterling off the gold standard.[8] Briefly the two central banks remained in conflict. However, Moreau recognized the unwisdom of driving sterling to the wall, and in late May he accepted a *modus vivendi* whereby he would purchase only new gold offered on the London bullion market. Governor Strong in New York helped out by offering Moreau to take an initial £1.5 million sterling off his hands and eventually acquired £12.35 million in exchange for the equivalent in gold held for him on earmark in London.[9]

In June, Moreau took the further step of promising an early reduction of interest rates in Paris. He also instructed his exchange dealers to offer a better price for dollars, florins, Swiss francs and other currencies, so as to induce speculators to cease their operations in sterling.[10] Presently Norman and Moreau agreed to an informal spheres-of-influence agreement. Neither Moreau nor Poincaré felt much sympathy towards Britain and were determined to see France fully regain its monetary and financial independence now that it had the resources to do so.[11] But so long as Britain acknowledged France's legitimate interests in regions strategically important to it, they would not push sterling to the brink. Once the *modus vivendi* was agreed, angry talk in the City and Westminster of 'deliberate [French] sabotage' died away.

The Bank of England's position nevertheless remained precarious. French sterling balances, having risen from almost nothing in January 1927 to £80 million by May, reached nearly £180 million before the franc was formally stabilized in June 1928, and the French authorities were clearly impatient to dispose of them for gold.[12] Even the £30 million sterling for which Norman offered to find buyers in the summer of 1927 exceeded the free gold at the Bank of England after cover for the note issue was deducted from the reserves. Without reform of the international monetary system, the Bank could scarcely operate as regulator of the pivotal London gold, capital and credit markets, let alone act as lender of last resort to other central banks. In fact, in the two years since Britain returned to the gold standard, sterling and the international monetary system itself had become distinctly more precarious than before.

In the first week of July 1927, Governor Strong convened an informal conference of central bankers, out of the glare of publicity at the Long Island home of Edgar Whitney, a partner at J.P. Morgan. With Norman, Schacht and Charles Rist of the Bank of France as well as Strong and several Morgan partners present, the conference provided a unique opportunity to discuss the problems affecting the international money and payments system. Rist, standing in for Moreau, found the American bankers worried by the Bank of France's recent build-up of sterling balances and openly impatient to see the franc stabilized on gold. He refused to be drawn on the timing of France's return to the gold standard. As to the Bank's sales of sterling, he insisted that under the gold standard rules it should be free to buy or sell currencies for gold.[13] But Russell Leffingwell, the former assistant secretary of the Treasury and one of the most influential of the Morgan partners, admonished him to bear in mind the peculiar circumstances in which they lived. Europe's rapid reconstitution of gold reserves was aggravating price deflation and would, in his opinion, have the same nefarious effect as the elimination of bimetallism between 1871 and 1895.

> The effect of such a depression, in his eyes, would be particularly dangerous for the industrialised countries. While considering it inevitable, while refusing to envisage any system of 'managed money', while desiring that we should return as soon as possible to the automatic operation of the gold standard, he could not envisage without apprehension a rapid slump in world prices.[14]

Rist was also aware of the downward trend in price levels and of the shortage of gold available for monetary purposes, which aggravated the deflationary trend.[15] But since France had suffered 12 years of almost uninterrupted inflation, he took a more sanguine view of deflation than his Anglo-Saxon colleagues. For him, the greater danger was their pursuit of 'artificial' measures to escape the need for downward price-level adjustment.[16]

The second problem the central bankers discussed was Europe's chronic payments deficit with the United States. Schacht and the Anglo-Saxon bankers put this down to the heavy burden of inter-governmental debt. Their view was that governments must radically reduce reparations, and to do it before they caused Germany a renewed crisis. But since Rist insisted that inter-governmental debts lay outside their remit, they moved on to technical market issues. The central problem, as Norman put it, was that while the United States possessed vastly greater monetary gold stocks than Britain, central banks in need of gold almost invariably drew from London rather than New York because the combined cost of shipping and insurance was only 1 per cent from London and 3 per cent from New York. As a result, the Bank of England frequently faced pressure to sell gold, despite its slender metallic reserves. Strong pointed out that he was bound to face criticism if he sold gold below parity to Europeans. But he was prepared to consider the purchase of British commercial bills or, if some means could be found, of lowering the cost of transferring gold to and from Europe so as to reduce the pressure on the London bullion market. Meanwhile he would leave US gold purchases on deposit in Europe for re-lending to other central banks at below market rates. He would also help Europe out by reducing his discount rate. He appreciated that this would probably fuel the stock market boom in America, but compared with the importance of forestalling a rise in interest rates in London and Berlin and sustaining Europe's commercial and industrial activity, it seemed a small price to pay. As he put it,

> I'm prepared to go even further and accept a small amount of inflation. It will be necessary not only to lower my discount rate, but also to lower the call money rate which chiefly affects the Stock Exchange. The only risk is that it will encourage share speculation. But I attach no importance to this and am ready to run the risk.[17]

Since a rate reduction would also facilitate the movement of crops in the United States, he believed Americans would not object.

The Long Island conference seemed an auspicious event, when the world's leading central bankers came together to address common problems, with American bankers assuming the leadership of the international monetary system. But in fact it did little more than expose the vulnerability of the central bankers themselves. Since the Armistice, leading spokesmen for the City of London, Wall Street and other financial centres had encouraged politicians to cast off wartime regulations, return to globalization and rely upon the discipline of the gold standard to ensure stability and prosperity. Through a combination of persistent effort and the support of liberal or conservative governments, they had persuaded most countries to accept fixed exchange rates linked to gold. But since the winter of 1924 a new era of price deflation had begun, with wholesale commodity prices declining fully 15 per cent by the time of the Long Island conference. In public, Norman or his mouthpieces brushed aside price deflation as of no account. Had not Britain and the rest of the world prospered during the 25 years of deflation in the late nineteenth century?[18] Behind closed doors on Long Island, however, Norman admitted deep anxiety at the downward trend of price levels. As Rist recorded,

> Would the central banks not be accused of deliberately provoking the decline by a policy of dear money? Norman was already facing strong criticism from British industry, who are facing a prolonged period of falling prices. Nothing seems to him more threatening to the future of 'European industry' than a prolonged period of [price-level] decline. He was hence very depressed.[19]

Central bankers on both sides of the Atlantic were now obliged constantly to look over their shoulders at domestic opposition to the gold standard system. Since 1925, Norman on his biweekly visits to the Treasury had to endure tirades from Churchill who regularly reminded him of the failure of the gold standard to alleviate Britain's unemployment or industrial problems.[20] Norman had conceded one reduction in Bank rate at Churchill's urging in October 1925, but subsequently he refused any further reduction, leaving the real rate of interest at a swingeing 9 or 10 per cent, confident that Churchill would not risk a crisis by publicly challenging his policy. Nonetheless public criticism of the Bank increased after the General Strike and the lengthy coal stoppage in 1926, and when McKenna, chairman of the Midland Bank, called for an enquiry into the monetary system in February 1927, criticism from industrialists, trade unionists, farmers and others had made Norman's management of the sterling exchanges almost impossible.[21]

Strong's position was, if anything, more difficult. Although the American economy as a whole had performed well since the war, rural areas of the country had enjoyed little prosperity on account of the decline in world commodity prices. Dissatisfaction had found expression in a resurgence of prairie radicalism, which led to a third party candidate in the 1924 presidential election. When this brought no result, attention turned increasingly to monetary reform. The Stable Money League, established in the 1921 slump by the Yale economist, Irving Fisher, was soon dominated by Midwestern economists and publicists such as Professor John Commons, W. F. Gephart and the publisher Henry Wallace. Re-established as the Stable Money Association in 1925, it attracted wider support nationally, while forming several branches overseas including Britain where Keynes, McKenna and Sir Josiah Stamp became members.[22] While its membership remained small, its potential influence in the United States was large, first because its objective of price stability appealed to the politically important rural regions, and second because its campaign threatened to reawaken suspicions of the plutocratic, cosmopolitan bankers of Wall Street.

Reflecting the groundswell of support for monetary reform, Congressman James Strong of Kansas in 1926 introduced a bill requiring the Federal Reserve System to use all its powers to stabilize the purchasing power of the dollar. For three weeks the House Banking and Currency Committee heard the evidence of politicians and experts, and eventually gathered 600 pages of testimony. Although the bill was subsequently withdrawn, that was not the end of the matter, for in 1927 Representative Strong in collaboration with economists of the Stable Money Association prepared a new bill for presentation to Congress.[23] Governor Strong of the New York Fed was acutely aware of the threat the Association posed to his autonomy and indeed to the gold standard itself. As he privately admitted, he shared the fears expressed by Leffingwell, Norman and other bankers that the deflationary trend in prices would damage the world economy and that they would be blamed for it.

> My feeling has been that further price declines will make the issue one of vital importance to banks of issue and I am anxious that we in this country should have a good alibi. The only alibi is a low discount rate by the reserve banks, and if our friends in Washington are willing to ignore the stock market as an influence upon our policies, we may be able in the near future to establish the alibi.[24]

Thus by August 1927 Strong accepted that the international monetary system was in a state of incipient crisis, which seemed destined to become worse. Since neither he nor the other central bankers could halt the crisis, he became increasingly concerned to deflect criticism from themselves and the institutions they represented.

Strong's efforts came too late for Schacht, who was obliged to raise interest rates on 10 June 1927 and again in October.[25] Norman was more fortunate. On 3 August the sterling exchanges were strong enough for the Bank of England to buy £429,000 in new gold. This was the first time in months it had increased its reserves, and the City welcomed the news. Norman not only got through the next 12 months without raising interest rates, but also managed to build gold reserves to a postwar peak on 12 September 1928 of £173.9 million, well above the 'Cunliffe minimum' of £150 million.[26] Yet, as he and his fellow central bankers appreciated, none of the fundamental problems identified at Long Island had been resolved. Commodity price levels continued their downward trend. Monetary gold stocks failed to meet demand. Germany's economy ceased to expand just about the time of the Long Island conference, and by 1928 was heading into recession.[27] And Europe's current account deficit with the United States continued to grow. For the time being it was covered by a massive outflow of US foreign lending, but this merely put off the day of reckoning while adding to Europe's liabilities. Meanwhile, the stock market speculation that Strong had downplayed increasingly preoccupied the American banking community and discouraged further lending to Europe.

Norman rested his hopes upon strengthened central bank relations, based upon two bedrock principles: first that issuing banks must be wholly free from political control, and second, those requiring international support must secure approval for their request from the League of Nations Financial Committee. Independence, he believed, was essential, if the banks were to be able to impose appropriate interest rates and credit restraint upon their domestic financial markets. The League Financial Committee would ensure that issuing banks operated on a common set of rules, including efficient means of employing available gold stocks. In theory, the Bank of England could undertake this role, but he appreciated that in an age of nationalism advice would be far more acceptable if it came from an agency of the League.[28] Sir Arthur Salter, head of the Economic Section of the League secretariat, sought to strengthen the Committee by co-opting an American national who enjoyed the confidence of the New York financial markets, and he called on Norman to see what could be done.[29] Norman in turn approached J. P. Morgan, and was delighted when Jeremiah Smith, a Boston lawyer and associate of investment bankers Brown Brothers Harriman, the American affiliate of his old firm, agreed to serve.[30] Unlike Salter, Norman was not so sanguine to imagine that American banks would allow the League Financial Committee to regulate their foreign loans. He hoped nonetheless that Smith's appointment would diminish American suspicions of the Committee and increase its regulatory role.

Despite Norman's best efforts, the Financial Committee's influence declined. Once Sir Otto Niemeyer resigned from the Treasury in 1927 to join the Bank of England, France became the only country officially represented on the Committee, the other members being bankers or economists of varying distinction.[31] Meanwhile Governor Moreau made no attempt to hide his hostility towards the Committee and sought direct charge of stabilization operations for countries that formed part of France's security system. This led to angry confrontations between Norman and Moreau over Poland in 1927 and Roumania and Yugoslavia in 1928, from which Moreau emerged the winner while Norman was left embarrassed and humiliated.[32] Not only did Norman fail to secure a role for the Financial Committee in their stabilization operations. Worse, his attempt to line up New York against France only served to alienate Strong, who feared an American backlash from reports that he was supporting the Bank of England's dictatorship over the League Committee.[33]

The more fundamental problem was that few if any of the countries on the gold standard were prepared to trust in the operating rules that Norman promoted. The lesson French authorities drew from Norman's troubles with sterling was that the franc should be restored to convertibility only when the Bank of France possessed gold reserves sufficiently large to cope with any challenge.[34] Other European countries were equally impatient to build up their gold reserves, almost certainly out of regard for national security as much as in reaction to their recent experience of currency depreciation. Norman hoped they would be content for the time being to hold their reserves in sterling, which unlike gold would earn them interest if kept on deposit in London. To his intense frustration he found that neither international solidarity nor the promise of financial gain would induce them to cooperate.[35] Evidently it was not that they did not trust sterling. Rather, they were simply not prepared to trust anyone with their reserves, as the gold exchange standard required, and not even the probability that competition for available monetary gold would further deflate price levels deterred them from disposing their sterling balances for gold.

> To Continental nations the choice was not between gold economy and social convulsion but between the independence of their reserves and a problematical advantage to be gained by slightly diminishing the rapidity of the price decline. In fact, the Gold Exchange Standard might be quite suitable to certain of the smaller countries but to the rest, even if it were desirable in the general interest, it would certainly be distasteful and, on a calculation of advantage, not worth the sacrifice of independence.[36]

As a result, demand for gold constantly outran supply from 1925 onwards (see Table 4.2), and with foreign exchange shunned and gold in effect 'sterilized' whenever banks of issue were able to do so, monetary reserves failed to expand as Norman had hoped. This contributed to the exceptionally high interest rates in Britain, Germany and elsewhere, and aggravated the downward trend of commodity price levels. It also increased the precariousness of the global economic system, with practically all the countries of Europe predisposed to reintroduce commercial or financial controls rather than raising interest rates or tolerating the loss of gold to address a current account deficit. Disentangling political from economic influences here is probably a fruitless exercise, since they played upon each other in a circular way. Nevertheless the chronic malfunctioning of the international monetary system after 1925 cannot be understood without due regard for the influence of nationalism and national insecurity on both sides of the Atlantic.

One banker who refused to duck the problem was Sir Henry Strakosch, chairman and managing-director of the Union Corporation and member of the League Financial Committee since its formation in 1920. For 30 years Strakosch had been involved in the promotion of South African gold mining, which had led him to become an authority on the monetary uses of gold and author of the South African Currency and Bank Act (1920). A proponent of the gold standard, he had nonetheless become convinced that the deflationary trend in world price levels was chiefly due to the inappropriate use of the world's limited stocks of monetary gold

Table 4.2   Gold holdings of central banks and treasuries (in £ millions)

	End 1925	End 1926 change	End 1927 change	End 1928 change	End 1929 change	Change (4 years)
USA	819	838+19	818−20	770−48	802+32	−17
France	164	175+11	202+27	258+56	336+78	+172
Britain	145	151+6	152+1	153+1	146−7	+1
World	1881	1951+70	2001+50	2083+82	2143+60	+262

Source: Strakosch, 'Gold and the Price Level', Annex B.

(see Table 4.3), and that the problem was bound to become rapidly worse unless the leading central banks agreed upon common rules of action. In his words

> The conclusion is irresistible that, if we are to be saved the complex reactions, the economic jolts and setbacks, and the social and political friction which frequent and violent changes in the distribution of national wealth and income through fluctuations in the purchasing power of gold produce – if, in a word, economic progress is not to be seriously impeded, concerted action by the gold standard countries is imperative. If it is impossible to control the supply of monetary gold – and it is manifest that it cannot be controlled – then it is clear that the problem can only be attacked from the side of monetary policy.[37]

Unwilling simply to watch the crisis worsen, Strakosch turned first to Salter in June 1927 and soon convinced him to use his considerable influence at Geneva to promote an enquiry into the gold question. A fortnight later he turned to Norman, impressing upon him the urgency of confronting the price-level issue.[38] Norman was impressed. Through Courtney Mill, City editor of the *Times*, and other conservative journalists, he had hitherto discouraged support for the views of economists such as Ralph Hawtrey of the Treasury and J. M. Keynes who were advancing similar arguments.[39] Yet he was aware of the serious implications of a gold shortage and declining price levels for British industry and for his own stewardship of the Bank of England. Besides, Strakosch was no academic theorist but a City man who had made a fortune in exchange dealing and corporate finance while finding time to publish several tracts on gold and money, to represent South Africa at the Genoa conference of 1922, the Imperial conference of 1923 and at Geneva and occasionally to advise Norman himself on banking issues. Sir Otto Niemeyer, who joined the Bank of England from the Treasury at this time, appears to have been even more convinced by Strakosch's thesis.[40] What followed was a remarkable struggle between supporters and opponents of Strakosch's proposal of a League enquiry into the gold problem, which left Norman acutely embarrassed. On the face of

Table 4.3 Sir Henry Strakosch's estimates of world monetary gold shortfalls (in £ millions)

Year end	New gold available for monetary purposes	Gold sterilized (–) Gold released (+)	Net change to monetary reserves	Additional 3% required for world economic growth	Total shortfalls	*Economist* wholesale price index
1924	+74	−47	+27	62	35 (56.5%)	+6.2
1925	−4	+22	+18	63	45 (72.6%)	−11.2
1926	+70	−19	+51	64	13 (20.3%)	−5.2
1927	+50	+4	+54	65	11 (17.0%)	−2.2
1928	+82	−24	+58	67	9 (13.4%)	−3.8
1929	+60	−74	−14	68	82 (121.0%)	−7.0

Source: Strakosch, 'Gold and the Price Level', Annex C.

it, the dispute was one of principle: whether under the gold standard it was the proper role of central banks to pursue price stability as well as exchange stability. In fact, the differences arose over the practical question whether the international monetary system could be reformed sufficiently to meet the impending crisis. Strakosch was convinced that the central bankers must try, if they were to avoid a backlash from industrialists, workers, farmers and other victims of deflation, which would undercut all the bankers' accomplishments since the war. Strakosch's opponents were equally convinced that the practical obstacles in their way made it extremely unwise to accept responsibility for a goal they could not attain.

In November 1927, Siepmann returned from a tour of European capitals to warn his colleagues at the Bank of England that Continental central bankers were planning to abandon the gold exchange standard just so soon as they could obtain gold to replace their foreign exchange reserves. The French, the Belgians, the Swiss and even it transpired the Hungarians and the Austrians whose currencies had been the first to be stabilized under the auspices of the League Financial Committee were signalling their intention to raise minimum reserve requirements and rely solely upon gold.[41] Niemeyer expressed astonishment at their short-sightedness, observing that the scramble for gold was bound to accelerate the deflationary price trend to everyone's cost.[42] Towards the end of the month, when Strakosch again pressed Norman for action,[43] Norman wrote to Strong, suggesting that Strakosch should join them when they holidayed together at Algeciras in January.

> This is a very abstruse and complicated problem which personally I do not pretend to understand. ... But I rely for information from the outside about such a subject as this not, as you might suppose, on McKenna or Keynes, but on Sir Henry Strakosch. I am not sure if you know him: Austrian origin; many years in Johannesburg ... full of public spirit, genial and helpful ... and so forth. I have probably told you that if I had been a Dictator he would have been a director here years ago. This is a problem to which Strakosch has given much study and it alarms him. He would say that none of us are giving [it] sufficient attention.[44]

Without waiting, Strakosch called on Strong in New York in December to set out his diagnosis of the deflationary problem and means of addressing it. Strong received him politely but coldly.[45] Six months earlier he had accepted the need to halt the continued decline in world price levels. This had led him to reduce interest rates in New York and persuade the eleven other Federal Reserve Banks to follow his lead. Briefly the results had been encouraging, but then everything that could go wrong seemed to do so. Speculation on the revaluation of the franc led to the sale of dollars and loss of American gold reserves, which amounted to $141 million (£29 million) net in the last four months of 1927 and reached a total of $530 million (£109 million) by the end of 1928. As Strong's 1928 annual report acknowledged, this constituted 'the largest gold outflow from the United States that has ever occurred, and reduced the gold stock of this country by about

10 per cent.'[46] Meanwhile the stock market boom continued unabated. To make matters worse, Congressional demands for radical monetary reform were growing louder.

Strong, like Norman, was openly scornful of economic theorists, but like him he was acutely aware of his own vulnerability on account of the deflationary price trend and its acute effect on American farmers and other primary producers. At virtually the same time that Strakosch called upon him, he was holding secret meetings with Representative Strong and John Commons of the Stable Money Association. Since Representative Strong intended to submit a revised bill to Congress on monetary reform and support for it was hard to predict, Governor Strong decided he must try to make it as unobjectionable as possible.[47] But the outflow of gold from the United States together with the stock market bubble had also convinced him that he needed a free hand to raise interest rates and tighten credit, which would antagonize the monetary radicals. In the circumstances, the last thing he wished to encourage was an international enquiry into the purchasing power of gold. Not only would it play into the hands of his domestic critics who believed that central banks could and should keep price levels stable; but it would also associate him more closely with Europe and undermine his authority in the United States.

On 11 January 1928 the Federal Reserve Board, meeting in Washington, reviewed the country's economic and financial situation and decided that it did not warrant an increase in interest rates. Strong, however, had concluded that something must be done to check the growth of credit and stock market speculation, and had already seen to it that the Fed's Open Market Investment Committee, which was operated by the Federal Reserve Banks rather than the Board, should begin selling government securities to reduce liquidity in the banking system.[48] Historians have generally credited support for this action to Strong's strength of character.[49] But probably more important was the peculiar dynamic that existed between New York and the regional bankers. Several of the regional bankers took a narrow view of their remit, holding that their sole function was to ensure a steady supply of credit to business, and that they should have no regard for speculation in stocks and shares. But so suspicious were they of the tentacular influence of Wall Street that they were easily persuaded of the need for rigorous action to stop stock market speculation from draining credit from 'legitimate' business. In fact, the bulk of financing for brokers' loans was actually coming not from banks in the Federal Reserve System, but from the short-term balances of large corporations, investment trusts, private individuals and foreign sources.[50] Such were the regional bankers' suspicions of Wall Street, however, that they agreed to a massive and sustained restriction of credit to the national banking system. Between January and August 1928, the Federal Reserve sold $400 million of government securities and reduced holdings of acceptances by over $200 million. Meanwhile the Reserve Banks raised their discount rates from 3.5 to 4.5 per cent and in most cases to 5 per cent, while correspondingly raising subsidiary rates.[51]

The results were not at all what they expected. Average share prices, having risen 14 per cent in the second half of 1927, stabilized briefly in early 1928 then soared higher. In the 18 months from early March 1928 to September 1929, average share prices rose in percentage terms as much as they had during the whole of the bull market since 1923.[52] Instead of checking securities speculation, the Fed's monetary restriction hit the domestic economy, which became evident in the spring of 1929 when new investment in construction and manufacturing halted, then sharply declined.[53] This was to contribute importantly to the slump in America. But long before this the booming securities markets had drastically curtailed US foreign lending which seriously worsened overseas monetary and credit conditions. Between 1924 and the first half of 1928, US foreign lending had risen rapidly, reaching a total of $983 million in 1928. But in the summer of 1928, when short-term interest rates rose above long-term rates, the trend was abruptly reversed. Not only did US foreign lending sharply decline – in 1929 it was down more than two-thirds from the previous year – but also with the US stock markets soaring and interest payments on short-term call loans in New York spiking up to 6, 8 and 12 per cent, overseas funds actually began to flow into the United States.[54] Having exported nearly $500 million gold in the first half of 1928, the United States imported the same amount in the second half of the year. The result was to place severe pressure on sterling, the mark and other foreign currencies.[55]

Norman, on learning of Strong's hostile reaction to Strakosch's initiative, was prepared to fall back on informal central bank cooperation. Accordingly, in December 1927 he despatched Niemeyer to New York to persuade Strong to back his efforts to encourage cooperation behind the closed doors of the League Financial Committee.[56] Strakosch, however, appreciated that central bank cooperation by itself was wholly inadequate to address the looming crisis and that only international agreement on a major expansion of liquidity would get the world through it. In the spring of 1928 he headed a consortium that purchased the *Economist magazine*, which he soon conscripted into his campaign for monetary reform.[57] His memorandum 'Monetary Stability and the Gold Standard' appeared as a special supplement of the journal in November; a second supplement would follow in 1930. Meanwhile, at his urging, Salter placed his proposal for a gold enquiry on the agenda of the League Economic Consultative Committee, instituted to follow up the resolutions of the 1927 World Economic Conference.[58] From there the proposal went to the League Council, which in June 1928 called on the League Financial Committee to decide how to proceed.[59] Speaking to Strong in Paris shortly before the Council meeting, Salter assured him that the proposed enquiry was aimed not at stabilizing price levels but merely 'the dangers of undue fluctuations' in price levels, and that it would reassure the public that something was actually being done to determine if a gold shortage existed. Strong cautiously agreed to a purely factual enquiry, so long as it was handled by 'practical-minded central banking men' and not 'mere theorists'.[60] By 25 June, however, Salter found that Strong and Moreau had been discussing the proposed enquiry and were now firmly opposed to it.[61]

That day France had finally stabilized the franc on gold close to the current exchange rate. The Bank of France held over £213 million of foreign exchange, largely sterling, which it hoped eventually to convert into gold reserves.[62] Yet even now French authorities betrayed a lack of confidence in their financial position. A few months earlier, Pierre Quesnay, Moreau's assistant, admitted to Siepmann that he was 'terrified' of the prospect of continuing price deflation, but believed there was no way of halting it. Indeed, he expected that within a few years of stabilization the overvaluation of the franc would become as troublesome to France as the overvaluation of sterling had been to Britain. But since he and his French colleagues believed that declining price levels were driven by global overproduction of commodities, they concluded that central banks could do no more than impose the monetary restraints necessary to keep their national economies competitive.[63] Once the franc was back on gold, conservative elements of the French press and the Chamber of Deputies insistently demanded that the Bank of France's reserves should be increased beyond the legal minimum proportion of 35 per cent of currency in circulation.[64] With Strong mortally ill, Moreau therefore assumed the task of mobilizing central bank opposition to Strakosch's gold enquiry.[65] Yet on 9 December the League Financial Committee agreed *nem con* to institute an enquiry into the causes of 'undue fluctuations in the purchasing power of gold', with Henry de Chalendar, the French chairman, and the American, Jeremiah Smith, voting in favour.[66]

This was a remarkable achievement, obtained it seems by Salter's and Strakosch's reiterated assurances of a neutral fact-finding approach that would eschew any *a priori* view of price-level stabilization.[67] But even now opponents of a gold enquiry did not abandon their opposition. Before the end of the year, Moreau complained to Norman of Salter's manoeuvres and predicted gloomily that an enquiry would play right into the hands of politicians who sought to interfere with central bank policy.[68] Where, he demanded to know, did Norman stand?[69] Moreau evidently suspected that Norman was secretly backing Salter's efforts, to revive support for the gold exchange standard and avoid the need for monetary restraint. Norman's reply probably did little to allay his suspicions, for on the one hand he deprecated a gold enquiry as untimely and regrettable, but on the other he suggested that it was probably too late to stop it.[70] Other evidence, however, leaves no doubt that Norman was scarcely less hostile to a gold enquiry than Moreau, and for the same reason: fear of arousing public opinion against the central banks, which would make it impossible for them to operate the gold standard. In his view, they had entered a period of troubled waters requiring them to take drastic action on interest rates and credit to maintain exchange stability. This was not the time to encourage the view that they had any choice in the matter.[71] As he wrote to Schacht, the situation was 'strange and disturbing'.

> In New York, as it seems to me, the Central Bank has ceased to function owing to the extent of speculation on the Stock Exchange.... I am continually being forced to support the sterling-dollar exchange lest New York should withdraw gold from here; and really it is surprising that she has not tended to do so more persistently when we remember how great a magnet is a 10% rate of interest.[72]

He had already told Vissering of the Dutch National Bank that he would have nothing to do with the gold enquiry,[73] and in a private note he indirectly warned Sir Basil Blackett, the former director of finance at the Treasury, that he was supporting Blackett's candidacy for membership of the Court of governors of the Bank of England on the assumption that Blackett would steer clear of the enquiry.[74] Norman was hardly more 'neutral' towards the enquiry than Moreau who sought to persuade their central banking colleagues to boycott it. In face of their opposition, Salter failed to meet his target of March 1929 for launching the Gold Delegation, as the enquiry was now called. It held its first preliminary meeting only on 26 August, by which time the world financial crisis was fully under way.[75]

The central bankers who met in Long Island in July 1927, had been chiefly concerned by the impact of Poincaré's *franc fort* policy. For years, uncertainty over the franc had caused French capital to flee the country. But after Poincaré formed a new government in July 1926, flight capital immediately began to return to Paris, and once the franc was formally stabilized in June 1928, the remaining capital, largely held in London, returned home. Ominously, this left the Bank of France with huge sterling and dollar balances, which it clearly hoped to convert into gold as soon as possible. Selling dollars had little adverse effect, and went some way to reduce Europe's payments deficit with the United States, but disposing of sterling was another matter. The Bank of France's decision to reduce its sterling balances from £293 million to £206 million in the 12 months following stabilization was extremely unwelcome to Norman and colleagues in the City of London.[76] The drain on London was aggravated by the fact that the use of cheques for payment in France was still uncommon, and with the economy booming, French commercial banks could only meet the increased demand for credit by exchanging gold for francs at the Bank of France. Since most of the gold was drawn from the London bullion market, the one free gold market in Europe, this intensified pressure on sterling.[77]

French central bank and commercial operations were, however, only one source of pressure on sterling. Another was the primary producing countries in the outer sterling area, especially Australia and New Zealand, whose current accounts were weakened by the continuing slump in commodity prices.[78] But by far the greatest source of pressure was the American stock market boom and the impact it had upon international capital flows. Although only the German, Swedish, French and Dutch national banks were obliged to raise their discount rates before the autumn of 1928, others had reacted in less obvious ways, and it seemed only a matter of time before all of them would have to impose dearer and tighter money to defend their currencies.[79] Even then, with US short-term borrowing rates at crisis levels, foreign lending practically halted, and almost all of Europe in current account deficit with America, it was far from clear that they possessed the means to keep exchange rates above gold export point.

Norman's predicament was exceptionally acute. He had risked unpopularity by holding Bank rate for two years at a relatively high 4.5 per cent – a real rate of interest of nearly 10 per cent – to build up gold reserves, which reached an all-time peak of £173.9 million in early September 1928.[80] But to avoid the reserves being run down again, he would soon have to raise Bank rate further. And in view of the certain protests from labour, industry and the chancellor of the exchequer himself, he could only do so when the need to act became manifestly obvious. He therefore had to fold his arms and allow an outflow of gold to the United States.[81] He vented his frustration on George Harrison, deputy governor of the New York Federal Reserve Bank and soon to be Strong's successor: 'You will realize that our proposals are like spitting against the wind if your Call Money continues round 8%.'[82]

Early in February 1929, Norman warned his European central bank colleagues of an impending rise in Bank rate, and requested them to coordinate their action with London.[83] The announcement came on 7 February, when Bank rate was increased a full point to 5.5 per cent, and as expected it provoked a storm of objections.[84] Churchill, by now thoroughly out of patience with Norman and facing the prospect of a general election in the next six months, added to his embarrassment during Parliamentary questions by refusing to confirm if he approved or disapproved of the Bank's decision.[85] But Norman had already set off on 24 January for America in a desperate attempt to persuade bankers there to prick the speculative bubble.[86] He called on the new governor, Harrison, the ostensible purpose of his visit, but found that his hands were tied.[87] Harrison, like Strong before him, had appealed to the Federal Reserve Board in Washington for a sharp rise in interest rates too. But the Board, dominated by bankers from the Midwest, South and West, were unsympathetic to New York's troubles and tended to blame the problem on Strong for having reduced interest rates in 1927 out of a misplaced sympathy for Europe.[88] Norman therefore travelled down to Washington in the hope of persuading the Board to halt the stock market frenzy by immediately raising interest rates or risk driving Europe off the gold standard. The visit, in the words of Leffingwell of J.P. Morgan, 'proved a fiasco'.[89] The Board had never received a foreigner before, particularly an Englishman with a cape, cane and Van Dyke beard, and they listened suspiciously to their exotic visitor. They had no intention of altering their policy for the sake of Europe. If anything, his appearance only hardened them against any change.[90] The likelihood of any response from Washington diminished further when news of the visit reached the press, and isolationists in Congress angrily demanded to know precisely what had transpired at Norman's meeting with the Board.[91]

At least ten times the Federal Reserve Bank of New York sought to raise its discount rate to 6 per cent, only to face a veto from the Federal Reserve Board in Washington. From a practical standpoint, the Board may have been justified in their opposition, since the funds fuelling the Wall Street boom came largely from outside the Federal Reserve System. Possibly nonetheless a sharp rate rise might have served as a timely warning to investors and speculators, and thus end the boom which, in reversing the flow of funds from the United States to Europe and the rest of the world, was threatening to shatter the international monetary and payments system. Norman, back in London, resumed his appeals to Harrison and New York banking allies to end the 'chaos in America'.[92] When this produced no response, he travelled to Paris to appeal to J.P. Morgan and his partner

Thomas Lamont, who were participating in the expert enquiry into reparations. His warnings of an imminent breakdown of the gold standard shook Morgan, who telegraphed partners in New York: 'I cannot...too greatly emphasize the importance with which I regard this matter', and he urged them to speak to Harrison or if necessary the secretary of the Treasury, Mellon.[93]

With call money rates on Wall Street reaching as high as 20 per cent, the outflow of funds from Europe to America rose to dangerous levels. By March, Norman estimated that $2 billion (£412 million) had gone to fuel the speculation. A queue formed on Threadneedle Street of central bankers from Germany, Hungary, Greece, Denmark and Italy, all seeking accommodation from the Bank of England.[94] But there was little that Norman could do to help, since borrowers would immediately use their credits to purchase dollars, thus transmitting the pressure back onto sterling. As it was, the Bank of England's gold reserves, having risen slightly after the Bank rate rise in February, declined from £163.2 million on 12 June to £159.1 million on 26 June, to £149.5 million on 24 July and to £140.2 million on 7 August.[95] This was well below the 'Cunliffe minimum' reserve level of £150 million, and several times that summer Norman warned the Bank's Committee of Treasury that they were in sight of abandoning the gold standard.[96] Unable to devise a solution of their own, the international bankers placed their hopes on a radical writing down of reparations and war debts, to alleviate pressure on the European exchanges. Inter-governmental debts were of course a political matter and intimately bound up with European security. But since the alternative appeared to be the collapse of the international monetary system, the bankers had no hesitation in demanding that the governments should act.

4.3   The contest over reparations

The Dawes plan, the interim reparations settlement adopted in August 1924, had been accepted by Britain and Germany only to end the Ruhr occupation. For the next few years, however, nothing was done to place reparations on a permanent footing. One reason was that Germany seemed well able to pay the Dawes annuity, which rose in stages from a modest 1 billion RM (£50 million) in 1924–5 to 2.5 billion RM (£122 million) in 1928–9, the first 'standard annuity year'. Another was the recognition that nothing could be done until after the French parliamentary elections, the German Reichstag elections and the US presidential election, all of which were scheduled to take place between April and November 1928. In Britain, Treasury officials, who were responsible for reparation policy, as well as Governor Norman looked forward to the complete suppression of inter-governmental claims, which they regarded as the *fons et origo* of global financial instability. But they remained convinced that nothing could or should be done until Germany's payment problems made further Dawes payments demonstrably impossible and Washington faced up to the need for a radical write-down of war debts.

The onset of the financial crisis in 1927 accelerated the timetable. Norman and Hjalmar Schacht, the Reichsbank President, attempted unsuccessfully to raise the reparations issue at the Long Island conference of central bankers in July of that year. Eventually they agreed that nothing should be done for 18 months.[97] But before the end of July, Governor Strong in New York, made known his anxiety about the precarious state of Germany's international payments to Parker Gilbert, the Agent-General for Reparations.[98] Gilbert, a former US Treasury official and prospective partner at J.P. Morgan & Company, heeded Strong's warning. In October 1927 he called on the German government to restrain public spending and borrowing.[99] Two months later, without consulting the Reparations Commission, he used his annual report to warn interested governments of approaching difficulties for German external payments and the need for a final reparation settlement to remove the element of uncertainty surrounding the Dawes plan.[100]

While the British Treasury continued to deprecate action on reparations until the United States agreed to concessions on war debts, the Foreign Office sided with the bankers. Austen Chamberlain had been pressing Briand for two years to advance the date for evacuating Allied troops from the two remaining occupation zones of the Rhineland.[101] He renewed his appeal after the Reichstag election in May 1928, won by a coalition of Socialist, Catholic Centre and Liberal parties over the extremists of left and right, and the French parliamentary election the same month, which strengthened the position of Poincaré, Briand and the moderate centre-right. The Allied powers, he advised Briand, should reward the forces of democracy in Germany. Since France would not move on the evacuation of the Rhineland without some guarantee of continued reparation payments, he pressed for reparations and evacuation to be dealt with together.[102]

The superficial goodwill created by the Locarno agreements was now visibly threadbare. Germans made no secret that they had begun rearmament and intended in due course to pursue *Anschluss* with Austria and further territorial revision.[103] Stresemann, encouraged by Chamberlain's intervention, impatiently sought a settlement in the West to concentrate upon Germany's more radical revisionist demands in the East.[104] This made the French government all the more anxious over reparations. With tax burdens far above the 'normal' level of prewar times, French politicians regarded reparations as an essential source of revenue if taxation was ever to be reduced. They also looked to reparations as a means of constraining German industry, which enjoyed substantially lighter tax burdens than French industry on account of the recent hyperinflation and the absence of huge reconstruction charges, and would become still more competitive if reparations were reduced or cancelled. Additionally they attached a moral significance to reparations, payment of which symbolized Germany's guilt for the wrong done to France. So strongly did they hold this view that Parliament had made German reparation payments a condition of war debt payments to Britain and the United States. Nevertheless they recognized the benefits to be derived from replacing the Dawes plan with a definitive settlement. Ratification of the war debt funding agreements with the United States and Britain had been postponed since 1926 in the absence of a definitive reparation settlement with Germany, but time was running out. The American funding agreement would have to be ratified by July 1929, if France were to avoid a charge of $400 million for its acquisition of surplus war material after the Armistice. And if it ratified the American agreement, it would have to proceed with the British agreement or face angry charges of discrimination.

As for the occupation of the Rhineland, the French had until now regarded it as a strategic necessity and a guarantee of reparation payments. But British pressure to normalize relations with Germany had taken its toll. Briand, always flexible as to means, was prepared to acquiesce in some territorial revision between Germany and Poland in the East, if this would pacify Germany. With the second occupation zone due to be evacuated in 1930 and the third and last zone in 1935 (so long as Germany had not repudiated reparations before then), Briand as well as Poincaré and their ministerial colleagues accepted that their hold on the Rhineland was a diminishing asset which should be used soon to secure a favourable repara- tion settlement. They hoped therefore to exchange the immediate evacuation of the Rhineland for a firm German commitment to pay reparations, on the basis of which they could issue international bonds. The funds raised would be used to cover France's war debt obligations, with a modest surplus left to amortise the debt incurred in reconstructing its devastated regions. Germany, which depended upon foreign credit, would find its international credit-worthiness tied to continued reparation payments, and France would no longer need to occupy the Rhineland as a physical guarantee of payment. Officers of the General Staff remained uneasy about abandoning control of Rhineland bridgeheads. But they were now divided on the feasibility of controlling the large and populous hinter- land in the event of a crisis and increasingly worried at the prospect of an aerial attack.[105] Appeasing them with the proposal for a new inspection commission for the Rhineland, Briand pressed ahead, and on 16 September he joined the British and other interested delegates to the ninth League Assembly in calling for a new expert committee to produce a definitive reparation settlement concurrently with negotiations on the early evacuation of the Rhineland.[106]

On 11 February 1929 an expert committee comprising delegates from the coun- tries interested in reparations convened at the Hotel Georges V in Paris. Schacht led the German delegation, Moreau the French delegation and Sir Josiah Stamp assisted by Lord Revelstoke, senior partner of merchant bank Baring Brothers, the British delegation. As in 1924, the American administration had agreed to the participation of US citizens, so long as it was clearly understood that they had no official standing and no right to discuss war debts. And as on the previous occa- sion, the Europeans invited the chief American delegate, the Wall Street lawyer and company director, Owen D. Young, to chair the committee, hoping thereby to highlight for Americans their interest in the issue and bring closer the day when a comprehensive reparation-war debt settlement became possible.

The Young committee, as it was henceforth known, soon faced a crisis when Schacht offered to pay only 800 million RM (£39.6 million) unconditionally per annum: less than a third of the standard Dawes annuity. Moreau flatly rejected this offer and spoke ominously of keeping the French army indefinitely in the Rhineland. For nearly ten weeks the wrangling continued, with the British supporting Schacht's view that reparations must be sharply reduced, and the

Americans, relying upon Parker Gilbert's opinion that a definitive settlement was more important than a sharp reduction, leaning towards the French position. But when Schacht added to the tension by claiming that Germany could only pay more if it imported less and therefore proposed Treaty revision, including the return of German colonies, the Polish Corridor and Upper Silesia, negotiations ground to a halt.[107]

By this time the mark had become distinctly weak and the Reichsbank began to lose gold cover. The weakness was due primarily to the tug of Wall Street where the stock market boom drove interest rates skywards, and also to Germany's current account weakness, but it was aggravated by Schacht's provocative comments and his refusal to raise his discount rate, which encouraged Germans to flee their currency. Schacht nonetheless accused the French of deliberately bearing the mark.[108] This seemed plausible enough to British and American observers, and Norman, always suspecting the worst from France, offered rediscounting facilities to the Reichsbank. But, in fact, so far from attacking the mark, the French government sought to avoid giving Germany the excuse to suspend reparation payments, and French commercial banks by and large maintained their balances in Germany.[109] Behind the scenes, Briand worked for a settlement.[110]

Schacht soon found himself under pressure from several quarters. The German commercial banks, dependent for at least 40 per cent of their working capital upon foreign short-term balances, broke with him and appealed to Young for a settlement. The German government also sought an end to the crisis. With Young, supported by Morgan and Governor Harrison, warning both Schacht and Moreau that the New York market would be closed to them until a reparation settlement was reached, Schacht gave way.[111] By now, not only the German authorities but also the British, French, Italian and especially the American bankers had become extremely nervous about the impact of a breakdown of negotiations upon the international payments system. Stamp found himself under almost as much pressure as Schacht to accept higher reparation payments. He resisted instructions from London, going so far as to threaten to resign from the committee. But as he acknowledged to Young, the British government's final word was 'whatever he did he must not break with the Americans.'[112] Once Schacht backed down, Stamp therefore did so as well. Young then turned to Stamp to draft the plan, observing that Stamp knew his views and could express them rather better than him. 'Yes, Josiah, you have got to write it', added J. P. Morgan. 'All right, Mr. Morgan', Stamp replied, 'I will write it if you will underwrite it.'[113]

The Young plan, largely the handiwork of the master statistician Stamp, constituted a remarkable synthesis of virtually incompatible objectives, which deserved more respect than it received then or later.[114] In fixing a standard annuity of 2.05 billion RM (£100 million), it promised sufficient payments to cover all of Europe's war debt obligations while leaving a modest *solde* for France. The division of reparations into a conditional tranche, which remained a fixed obligation but could be paid into a closed account if the mark exchanges were too fragile for large-scale transfers into foreign currencies, and a much larger unconditional tranche, made it possible to reconcile French and British aims.

France was allocated the largest part of the unconditional tranche. Not only was it scheduled to be paid within a shorter period of time than the conditional tranche, but, being unconditional, it also opened the possibility of being 'commercialized' through an international bond issue. Britain, accorded 22.8 per cent of reparations in the Spa agreement of 1921, accepted a 19.4 per cent share of the payments under the Young plan. This appeared to be a major concession. But by a subtle manipulation of the schedules, Stamp had seen to it that Britain obtained a relatively greater share of payments in the early years of the new scheme, what he called 'the period of reality, viz. the next ten years.' Assuming an interest rate of 5.5 per cent, Britain stood to lose £2,020,000 per annum over the whole 37 years of the plan, but in the first 10 years the losses would be marginal and even in the first 20 years it stood to lose only £580,000 per annum, a sacrifice of barely 3 per cent of its reparation receipts.[115] Since, as Stamp observed, no one in Britain seriously expected reparations to continue more than ten years longer, the chances were that it would do fairly well out of the Young plan, despite the appearance of sacrifice.[116]

Stamp could also report two other welcome innovations. Under the Dawes plan, France, Italy and Belgium had received a large fraction of their reparation payments in the form of deliveries in kind. During the fourth Dawes year (1927–8) alone, deliveries in kind to France amounted to no less than 478 million RM: nearly 37 per cent of French reparation receipts and fully 72 per cent of total French imports from Germany.[117] British merchants and industrialists strongly objected to deliveries in kind, claiming that they constituted a disguised preference and distorted international trade.[118] German deliveries in kind to Italy were equally contentious. South Wales colliery owners, having supplied the Italian state railways' annual requirements of 3 million tons before the war, had lost the whole of this market to German reparation coal and angrily demanded their suppression.[119] As it happened, the French authorities themselves were of two minds about deliveries in kind. Access to German industrial equipment had accelerated the reconstruction of war-damaged regions and drew the two countries closer together. But French industrialists had also strongly protested against deliveries in kind, and French politicians, liberals all, regretted the continued need for large-scale public projects with which to absorb the German goods rather than taking reparations in cash which could be used to reduce taxes.[120] Stamp was therefore able to secure agreement that under the Young plan deliveries in kind would be halved immediately and eliminated altogether in ten years.

More controversially, Stamp had seen to it that the schedule of unconditional payments corresponded exactly with the European powers' schedule of war debt payments to the United States, and moreover that a provision was included whereby any war debt reduction would automatically trigger a corresponding reduction in reparations.[121] Ever since the Armistice, the European powers had sought to establish an identity between reparations and war debts in the hope of persuading Washington to recognize the connection between them and join in a collective settlement. The American authorities had vigorously denied any such connection, claiming that reparations were a political charge imposed by the Allied powers upon Germany whereas war debts were freely contracted obligations and hence wholly different in origin and legitimacy. On hearing that the experts in Paris planned to align reparations and war debts, Henry Stimson, secretary of state in the new Hoover administration, and Andrew Mellon, the secretary of the Treasury, fired off angry protests to Young.[122] Like most New York-based businessmen, Young and his deputy, the banker J. P. Morgan, were not unsympathetic to the Europeans' stratagem. Indeed, according to Stamp, Morgan had muttered, ' "Damn Washington" and seems rather to glory in the prospect of a row.'[123] Young, however, was deeply offended at the charge that he had betrayed American interests and angrily replied that he was in no position to tell the Europeans how much they could demand from Germany. Since Washington had insisted upon his total independence from government, it could hardly complain now of his work.[124] This brought a grudging acknowledgement from Stimson, and Stamp got his way on the alignment of reparations and war debts. The embarrassment displayed by Washington arguably demonstrated the importance of his achievement. But it also confirmed that however compelling the evidence of a link between the obligations, Europe could expect no relief from Washington for the foreseeable future.

This as it happened was only one reason why the Young plan, albeit skilfully devised, came nowhere near to meeting the urgent requirements of the time. In August 1929 a diplomatic conference gathered at The Hague with the dual remit of approving the plan and settling the terms for the early evacuation of the Rhineland. The French arrived hopeful that their concession of evacuation would ensure an early agreement. But as reparations were to be discussed, the United States stayed away. And Britain was represented by Philip Snowden, the chancellor of the exchequer, who clearly did not grasp Stamp's accomplishment and, unthinkingly Francophobe, exploited the occasion to demonstrate his readiness to battle for exclusively British interests. By his own lights, he succeeded magnificently. Instead of winding down deliveries in kind over ten years, as called for in the Young plan, he secured agreement on their rapid and complete suppression. He also pressured the French, Italians and Belgians into restoring 80 per cent of the concession Stamp had made by accepting a reduction in Britain's Spa percentage of reparations. This meant a nominal gain for Britain of £1.9 million annually or £30 million over the life of the plan.[125] The British press presented this as a huge victory. As Beatrice Webb wrote in her diary,

> Snowden's amazing press – 'God be thanked for Snowden' is the refrain – is a revelation of the deep-down and ever-growing resentment against the gross and cynical and self-seeking of France, accentuated by envy at her continued prosperity.[126]

However, despite the cheering in London, the agreements reached at The Hague failed woefully to meet the urgent needs of the international crisis. In the first place, the new reparations settlement did little to alleviate the increasing global imbalances. The standard Dawes annuity from 1929 would have required Germany to pay annually 2.5 billion RM (£122 million); the average Young annuity required payments of 2.05 billion RM (£100 million), a reduction of 20 percent, and in the first five years (August 1929–August 1934) the relief would be closer to 30 per cent. But this still left Germany with a potentially serious current account problem.[127] The new plan also reduced the element of flexibility in the payments scheme. The Dawes plan contained a transfer safeguard clause that allowed Germany to suspend foreign payments in the event of exchange difficulties. Under the Young plan, Germany was obliged to transfer one-third of the payments 'unconditionally', whatever the state of its foreign exchanges.

More importantly, the concession of a moderate reduction in reparations, the early withdrawal of the last remaining troops from the Rhineland, and the failure even to discuss a new inspection commission for the region served merely to incite German demands for further Treaty revision. Alfred Hugenberg, a wealthy newspaper publisher, had taken control of the conservative National People's Party (DNVP) after its dismal showing in the May 1928 Reichstag election had left it practically bankrupt. Shortly after publication of the Young plan, he exploited Schacht's increasingly shrill condemnation of the plan to revive the claim that Germany was being enslaved by the Allies' financial demands and called for German politicians who accepted it to be charged with treason. He also invited Hitler to share the DNVP platform, thus enabling the Nazi leader to emerge from obscurity and gain access to a large, 'respectable' audience for the first time in his career. With the German economy in decline since the previous November and unemployment ominously rising, Hugenberg's Nationalists and Hitler's Nazis demanded a referendum on reparations, which they made a convenient tool for explaining the soaring unemployment and embarrassing the democratic parties of government.[128] Delegates at the Hague conference agreed on completing the evacuation of the Rhineland by the spring of 1930. A year earlier, German statesmen might have hailed this as a major achievement. But it had been anticipated since the Young plan negotiations began, and amidst the controversy over future reparation charges the Allied powers gained little credit for acceding to it.

The one major innovation to emerge from the negotiations was the decision to create a new international institution, the Bank for International Settlements (BIS). The proposal for the bank was first made on 21 February 1929 by the Belgian delegate to the expert committee, the financier Emile Francqui, who envisaged an institution devoted to the collection, transfer and distribution of reparations, the financing of deliveries in kind, and the commercialization of reparations through bond issues, and serving so far as possible to remove the element of politics from the reparation regime.[129] Schacht, probably hearing of Francqui's proposal, had immediately come forward with a far more ambitious scheme whereby the bank would transform the promise of reparation payments into collateral for large loans intended to stimulate international trade.[130] Members of the American delegation were shocked at the audacity of Schacht's proposal, but naively imagined that it might remove reparations from politics and proceeded to outline a more modest scheme wherein the bank would replace the Reparation Commission and Transfer Committee while undertaking limited lending functions.[131]

Stamp leaned to Schacht's side on the bank proposal and against the relative complacency of the Americans. A leading member of the Stable Money Association, Stamp had become increasingly anxious about the relentless decline in world price levels. If something were not done soon to reverse the trend, he believed, the deflationary pressure would severely damage the world economy and ultimately bring down the gold standard itself.[132] Upon taking responsibility for the draft BIS plan on 11 March, therefore, he sought to ensure that the bank would have the capacity to play an important role within the international monetary and payments system.[133] By acting as a clearing-house for both reparations and war debts, it would reduce the volume of international payments and the consequent risk of exchange instability. By managing the transfer of reparation payments, it would go some way to compensate for the greater rigidity of the new reparation arrangements. By holding balances in marks and reinvesting a portion of them in the German economy, it would 'forestall … circumstances which might of themselves lead to a transfer postponement.' Eventually, he hoped, it would go beyond this and contribute to the stability of the international monetary system by providing a clearing-house for central bank gold transfers, creating liquidity and serving as the central bankers' lender of last resort.

> The use of the Bank's credit by central banks within moderate limits and over short periods may in time become a normal function scarcely different in its exercise from the use of central bank credit by banks and bankers. All central banks, for ordinary exchange operations or for other purposes, would frequently find it advantageous to make use of the facility.[134]

This unfortunately was wishful thinking. Effective central bank cooperation and the use of BIS assets to augment world liquidity required the participation of the US Federal Reserve authorities. But Hoover had already decided that the proposed bank was a 'menace' to the United States,[135] and Stimson made brutally clear to the American experts in Paris that Washington would tolerate no connection whatsoever between the Fed and an international bank engaged in reparation transfers.[136] Young and Morgan appealed to the eminent Republican, Elihu Root, in an effort to counter Washington's opposition. To no avail. Washington flatly opposed the Fed's involvement and acquiesced with ill grace when a consortium of commercial banks led by J.P. Morgan eventually agreed to represent American interests on the board of the BIS.[137] But without the involvement of the Fed, the new bank could scarcely moderate or reverse world deflation by supplementing central bank reserve assets. Nor could it hope to supplement the commercial banking system through credit raised on the basis of reparations, since the national treasuries of the recipient countries were not prepared to forgo reparation receipts or leave their transfer to the discretion of an independent institution.

This was as true of the British Treasury as its counterparts elsewhere.[138] The chancellor, Snowden, ignorant of the potential importance of the BIS proposal, was concerned only that it might become a competitor to the City of London. He therefore passed on the task of representing British interest in the bank proposal largely to Norman.[139] Norman had initially been enthusiastic about the BIS proposal, seeing in it a potential solution to the looming financial crisis. But he allowed his attitude to be prejudiced by Schacht, who turned against the proposed bank upon joining the Nationalists in their campaign against the Young plan. Norman therefore devoted his energies to blocking French control of the proposed bank and ensuring some American participation, for which he was prepared to jettison the more ambitious elements in Stamp's proposal.[140]

The BIS, which formally opened its doors on 17 May 1930, marked a small step towards central bank cooperation. In June 1931 it acted as lender of last resort to the Reichsbank when it mobilized short-term credits provided by other member central banks.[141] But with capital of under $100 million (£20.5 million), of which only $21 million (£4.3 million) was paid up – less than one-tenth the capital of the Chase National Bank of New York – it was scarcely up to the task of addressing the global financial crisis then under way. Essentially it was no more than a central bankers' club: exclusive of course, but also marginal to the terrible challenge then facing the international monetary and payments system.[142]

The Hague conference in August 1929 brought Franco-German relations to a crossroads. France, pressured by Germany and Britain, conceded an early end to the military occupation of the Rhineland. Military control of the bridgeheads, so insistently demanded by Marshal Foch, was forsaken without even the *quid pro quo* of monitoring, periodic inspections or other guarantees, which Briand and Poincaré had initially insisted upon. France's hope that reparation payments might be 'commercialized' through an international loan and Germany forced to continue payments to maintain its international credit-worthiness had also been passed over. Here too British and American cooperation was essential, since a loan on the scale envisaged required the active participation of their financial markets. But the Anglo-Saxon powers, while very possibly prepared to underwrite a loan to Germany, would certainly not do so if its main purpose was to facilitate reparation payments to France. The prospect for continued reparation payments was therefore sharply reduced, now that France had abandoned any direct influence over Germany and German opposition to further payments was rapidly mounting. The Locarno era was thus approaching its end, and in the absence of an adequate security framework it threatened to give way to an international political crisis comparable to the economic crisis already threatening the world.[143]

4.4   Herbert Hoover: Aggressive isolationist

Hoover, who became the thirty-first president of the United States in March 1929, seemed in many ways uniquely qualified for leadership of the greatest capitalist power in the world. Born in the Quaker settlement of West Branch, Iowa, orphaned as a boy and brought up in modest circumstances in California, he was the personification of the American rags to riches story. Having obtained a geology degree at Stanford University, he had travelled widely, living for a time in Australia, South Africa, China and England, and by 1914 he had acquired a fortune as a mining engineer, developer and speculator. Soon after the outbreak of war, he took charge of food relief to Belgium, and in 1917 he successfully lobbied for the post of United States Food Administrator. His reputation as successful businessman, humanitarian and administrative genius thus established, he joined the Harding administration as secretary of commerce in 1921. Serious, sober and something of a workaholic, he soon transformed the department from an administrative backwater into a large, well-managed agency for the promotion of domestic and foreign trade.

American historians, revisiting his career, have sympathetically portrayed him as a 'forgotten progressive' and 'independent internationalist' whose approach to foreign policy was characterized by 'balance and perspecuity [*sic*]'.[144] Yet in fundamental respects his outlook scarcely differed from that of his Republican predecessors. The first president from west of the Mississippi, he shared the westerners' tendency to regard Europe as the antithesis of America. His stay in prewar London seems to have impressed him only with Britain's imperial power, and his time as the wartime director of food relief in Belgium, Russia and Eastern Europe left him convinced of Europe's singular propensity for aggression, brutality and ideological extremism.[145] Europe, he warned an audience of American engineers in 1920, was a dangerous place: 'Every wind that blows carries to our shores an infection of social disease from this great ferment; every convulsion there has an economic reaction upon our own people.'[146] His seven years at the Commerce Department revealed a man at once able and energetic, but also ambitious, self-advertising and aggressively isolationist.

Within months of becoming commerce secretary, Hoover called for curbs on American lending to Europe. Albeit opposed to government interference in business as a general rule, when it came to Wall Street bankers and Europe he favoured government controls. His proposals to restrict lending to force a reparation settlement upon Germany, war debt settlements upon the allied powers and disarmament upon France, and his threat to denounce J.P. Morgan & Company's excessive involvement in Europe went well beyond the policy favoured by his Cabinet colleagues.[147] Before the issue was settled, he embarked upon a speaking tour of the mid-West, where he repeatedly thundered against any concessions on war debts.[148] Economists and New York bankers pointed out that the Administration could not have it both ways, raising the tariff against foreign goods while insisting upon full payment of its foreign claims.[149] Hoover shrugged off their criticism and basked in the support he received from the rest of the country. As the *Chicago Daily Tribune* gleefully put it, 'Hoover talks American'.[150] Hoover summed up his view in reply to an admiring correspondent:

> many thanks indeed for your letter on my Toledo speech. If we can get away from the continental propaganda and bunk that this debt cannot be paid, or if

it is paid it will have to be paid in goods which will be an injury to us, we will be in a position to talk sense over it all.[151]

In the mid-1920s he launched a campaign against the British Stevenson plan to regulate rubber prices and other foreign price-stabilization schemes for commodities such as coffee and potash. J.P. Morgan and other investment bankers were broadly sympathetic to these schemes, recognizing that the long-term investment required to bring the plantations or production facilities to fruition might not be forthcoming without the assurance of a reasonable return. But Hoover knew his audience, particularly the tyre manufacturers of Ohio. He therefore railed against the European monopolists as well as the East Coast bankers who supported them, while passing over in silence the price-fixing arrangements for copper, tin, bauxite and other commodities that American firms had organized offshore under the Webb-Pomerene Act.[152] Hoover's aggressive action attracted a good deal of adverse comment in Britain and elsewhere in Europe. In the United States, his narrow nationalism and visceral hostility to Wall Street prompted J.P. Morgan to lead an attempt to block his nomination as the Republican party's presidential candidate in 1928.[153] But Hoover would not be deterred, and the moment Coolidge indicated that he might not run again, he seized the opportunity to thrust himself forward.

On the face of it, the 1928 presidential election campaign was exclusively a domestic affair, with the outcome decided by the personalities of the two candidates. Historians have generally agreed that specific policy issues played a minor part in the contest and foreign affairs even less.[154] At a visceral level, nonetheless, international relations were centrally involved, since the two candidates represented a radical alternatives in the United States' relationship to the rest of the world. The Democratic candidate, Al Smith, was a controversial choice. Governor of New York and a Catholic who favoured repeal of the eighteenth Constitutional amendment prohibiting the production or sale of alcoholic drink, Smith had been associated with the political machine at Tammany Hall and drew on support from tycoons such as fellow Catholic John J. Rascob of General Motors. Most commentators singled out his Catholicism and his views on drink as his chief liabilities, and no doubt they were a disadvantage in the mid-West and South. But Walter Lippmann was probably correct in pointing instead to his connection to New York: the most 'European' of American cities, with the largest number of recent non-English speaking immigrants from Eastern and Southern Europe, and the financial capital of the country.[155] Certainly it was this combination that made him the embodiment of everything that small-town American feared and loathed.

Hoover, the Republican candidate, seemed the very opposite, with his prairie origins and California home, his Quaker faith and support for prohibition, his flat, unemphatic manner of speaking and his repeated claim that he sought to defend the American way of life. While he personally refused to encourage bigotry during the campaign, his campaign manager saw to it that the press reprinted earlier statements by him affirming that Catholicism was alien to American values. Meanwhile leading members of the Republican campaign team assiduously promoted fears of 'rum and Romanism' to mobilize a 'Christian coalition' against Smith.[156] The two men thus appeared to offer voters the choice between a return to Wilsonian internationalism or the continuation of tried and true isolationism.

Hoover devoted only one of his seven full-scale campaign speeches to foreign affairs when on 6 October he spoke at Elizabethton, Tennessee, a small town in the Appalachian hills strategically located for radio broadcasting, which figured for the first time in a presidential election. The theme of his speech was the Kellogg-Briand peace pact on the outlawry of war, an affirmation of good intentions which the United States and some forty other countries had signed the previous year. Hoover reaffirmed his commitment to peace. Yet this Quaker advocate of European disarmament insisted upon armed forces for the United States great enough to protect it 'from even the fear' of foreign invasion, and affirmed his support for the current Navy bill authorizing the construction of an additional fifteen 10,000 ton cruisers and one aircraft carrier.[157]

Meanwhile, Hoover's Republican allies insistently thrust the tariff issue to the forefront of the campaign. A victory for Smith, they warned rural voters, would mean a return to the Underwood Tariff of 1913, exposing American producers to the destructive forces of foreign competition.[158] Smith, thrown onto the defensive, affirmed his support for the present tariff,[159] and threatened to make inroads on Republican support in the mid-West when George Norris, the Republican senator for Nebraska, chose to back Smith after he endorsed the McNary-Haugen bill for stabilizing agricultural prices. Hoover, however, upped the ante and, reversing his earlier position, promised a special session of Congress on farm relief if nothing was agreed before the end of the present session of Congress in March 1929.[160] Desperate, the Democrats revived an old rumour that Hoover had become a British citizen when living in London before the war, circulating photocopies of an electoral roll from Kensington that allegedly bore his name. Nothing could have discredited Hoover more than proof of a British connection. As Willmott Lewis of the *Times* noted,

> There is, for all who know him, an almost comic inaccuracy in the ascription to Mr. Hoover of 'pro-British' tendencies, but in a country the nationalism of which grows more assertive year by year, it is so good a stick to beat him with that it will not lightly be laid aside.[161]

Smith, however, chose not to pursue the charge, which anyway came too late to affect the outcome of the campaign.

Hoover's final speeches, to a packed house at Madison Square Gardens in New York and in a broadcast address from St Louis, Missouri, dwelt upon 'the constructive side of government', which, treated in isolation, could almost be taken for an endorsement of the progressive tradition of public regulation in the interests of democracy and social justice. But once again Hoover reaffirmed his belief in the superiority of purely voluntary regulation, and represented himself as the defender of American free-market capitalism against his opponent's alien alternative. Thus, he suggested, voters faced a stark choice between 'the American system of rugged individualism and a European philosophy of diametrically opposed doctrines – doctrines of paternalism and state socialism', which would 'destroy the very foundations of freedom and progress upon which the American system is builded [*sic*].'[162]

Four days later, Hoover gained a startling victory, the largest in American history, winning 40 of 48 states, including 6 in the hitherto solidly Democratic south along with New York where upstate Republican support exceeded urban Democratic majorities.[163] With increased Republican majorities in both houses of Congress, Hoover was in a strong position to govern as he wished. Yet the size of his majority owed much to Protestant nativist voters, who would expect their rewards. And despite his occasional affirmations of America's membership in the international community, the campaign had confirmed his deep-seated isolationism. As Lewis of the *Times* warned readers,

> The next President, it would be well to remember, is as completely and unmistakably an American as Coolidge, and with a dash of the aggressive in his patriotism which is lacking in the present occupant of the White House. His is a conception of America romanticized by long residence abroad. For him the American way, whether it be political, social, or religious, is better than any other way, and in its essence different and superior. To call him, as some of his stupid opponents have called him, an 'internationalist' is to misunderstand him completely, unless the word is distorted to mean a belief that the universe could with advantage be remade after the American model. The American standard and manner of living must be jealously[*sic*] and fiercely preserved and nurtured behind barriers, until the distant day when all the world has been won to them or has accepted them.[164]

In the next six months, Hoover took two steps that added to foreign unease at his election. The first was a six-week tour of Latin America, during the long wait for the inauguration in March 1929. In speeches at San Salvador, Managua, Lima, Santiago, Buenos Aires and elsewhere, he affirmed his commitment to a new relationship based upon equality and mutual respect between the United States and its Latin neighbours, and repudiated any claim based upon the Monroe doctrine to interfere in their affairs. The United States, he said, rejected imperialism. Latin American audiences welcomed his assurances,[165] but in Europe and elsewhere his tour added to speculation that, in the words of Pierre-Etienne Flandin, vice-president of the French Chamber of Deputies, the United States was embarking upon a 'huge imperialistic expansion'.[166] Since, as it seemed to many observers, Hoover was first and foremost the steward of America's capitalist system, and its surge in postwar exports seemed proof enough that its domestic market was practically 'saturated', the logical inference seemed to be that Washington was now turning as a priority to Latin America as an outlet for its surplus production. In Britain, continental Europe, Japan and elsewhere, speculation was already widespread of a world carved into economic blocs: an Imperial British, a European, a Soviet, an Asian led perhaps by Japan or Russia and an American bloc. Having fuelled this speculation by his South American tour, Hoover proceeded to add urgency to it three days after his inauguration by calling a special session of Congress to review America's tariff and measures for assisting farmers and manufacturers.[167]

No act in modern times was fraught with greater danger – or more thoroughly misconstrued – than Hoover's decision to reconvene Congress on 15 April 1929. American historians, accepting Hoover's version of the story, almost invariably represent him as taking the decision reluctantly, regretting the Congressional call for sharply increased protectionism, but eventually acquiescing it in June 1930, after the world depression was already underway and many other countries had raised their tariff barriers against American goods.[168] In fact, however, Hoover was aware of what was in store long before the process began. As Willmott Lewis wrote from Washington in December 1928,

> He knows, because his friends have informed him during his absence in Latin America, that the special Session, nominally to be devoted to farm relief, would soon proceed to a general upward revision of the tariff, for most of 'the boys,' as they are called, are 'running hog-wild' on this subject, and the 'lobbyists' are already here in battalions.[169]

Economists, international bankers and other liberal critics, largely in New York, warned of dire consequences if the Administration enacted the Congressional bill.[170] Irving Fisher, the Yale economist, wrote to Hoover pointing out that the United States had a trade surplus of about $700 million when Wilson reduced the tariff 15 years earlier. With a surplus now of over $1 billion, this was no time to be raising the tariff:

> The policy of paying one debt by creating another debt can not go on forever. More and more our industries are going into large-scale production. The economies of this method can be maintained only by selling our standardised goods in increasing quantities to nations that are willing, and permitted, to exchange for them their own specialized products. As McKinley said, we cannot forever sell everything and buy little or nothing.[171]

However, despite hopes in liberal circles that Hoover would restrain Congress from going beyond farm relief, he merely stood aside. As a result, the bill reported out of the House of Representatives on 31 May 1929 contained proposals for a massive across-the-board increase in the tariff schedule.

This was an extraordinary, even perverse, outcome. American farmers, whose plight had prompted action in the first place, had little to gain from the bill, since foreign exporters were likely to absorb the duties to enter the American market, while American agricultural exporters would face even lower prices abroad. In any case, what small advantage they gained from protection was likely to be more than offset by higher costs of machinery and supplies. Nor were American manufacturers suitable candidates for increased protection. Not only did they dominate their domestic market, but they were also making rapid inroads into overseas markets. In fact, maintaining, let alone raising, the American tariff was inappropriate, in light of the country's large and growing current account surplus and the already acute dollar shortage elsewhere in the world. Already by 1928, as we have seen, the trend towards globalization had been halted and a number of countries had raised their tariffs or planned to do so. Perhaps if Hoover had displayed opposition to Congressional tariff plans, something might have been done to halt the trend. But the Congressional demands were no more than the culmination of a process that had begun when the Republicans regained office in 1921 and chimed with Hoover's reputation for aggressive nationalism. Foreign countries therefore chose not to wait for the bill to be enacted before reacting diplomatically or in kind.

In the summer of 1929, every important trading nation in the world, with the sole exception of Britain, formally protested to Washington against the threat of the Congressional bill.[172] The Canadian minister of commerce and finance called for an Empire-wide trade agreement among the British countries as a retaliatory measure, and received support from nearly every chamber of commerce and business association in Australia, New Zealand, South Africa, Canada, India and the West Indies.[173] Congressional demands for draconian increases in duties on 'luxury' imports such as silk, lace, couturier clothing and accessories could scarcely have been better calculated to prejudice the export trade of particular countries such as Japan, Switzerland and France.[174] Predictably, prominent French politicians and businessmen urged immediate action to defend Europe against American hyper-protectionism. In several countries, including Spain, Italy and Switzerland, popular demonstrations or boycotts were mounted against American commercial products. American motor cars, the most visible symbol of the American 'invasion', became targets of physical attack.[175]

The bill was briefly stalled in Congress by an alliance of liberal Republicans and Southern Democrats, and Hoover did not finally sign it into law until 17 June 1930. But as early as January 1930 no fewer than 14 of 27 countries in Europe had raised their tariffs, and of the remaining 13, 7 were planning to do so. The same trend was evident outside Europe: Australia, Canada, India, Egypt and Turkey among other countries had also prepared or implemented substantial tariff increases.[176]

The Smoot-Hawley Tariff has always had its defenders in America. Hoover himself justified it by pointing to the 'flexible provision', introduced in the Fordney-McCumber Tariff, which permitted the president or the Tariff Commission to adjust duties to changing conditions. In fact, however, this provision had generally been used to *increase* protection since 1922, and there was no reason to think it would serve the opposite purpose in Hoover's hands.[177] More recently, one prominent economist has argued that the tariff encouraged import substitution and by implication was an appropriate short-term response to the slump.[178] But this puts the cart before the horse, since the tariff was initiated in a time of prosperity and helped bring on the slump rather than being a response to it. Two other economists argue that at most it could have had only a marginal impact on the American economy, since merely 8 per cent of domestic output was exported.[179] Another economist goes further and argues that the Smoot-Hawley tariff increased the percentage of goods entering America free of duties and provoked practically no foreign retaliation. Hence, 'one can...make a plausible argument that Smoot-Hawley struck a blow for trade liberalization and freer trade.'[180] In fact, however, the increase in duty-free goods was marginal: 66.6 per cent in 1931, the first full year of the Smoot-Hawley tariff, versus an average of 63.8 per cent under the Fordney-McCumber tariff (1922–3) and 66.3 per cent under the Democrats' Underwood tariff (1913–22). At the same time the ratio of all duties to total dutiable imports rose sharply: from 27 per cent under the Underwood tariff, to 38.5 per cent under the Fordney-McCumber tariff and 53.2 per cent under the Smoot-Hawley tariff in 1931; and the ratio of all duties to free and dutiable imports combined rose practically as much: from 9.1 per cent under the Underwood tariff, to 14 per cent under Fordney-McCumber and 17.8 per cent under Smoot-Hawley in 1931.[181] This was a massive rise, with calamitous results.

Since 1924, world economic growth had been sustained largely by the expansion in international trade, which increased at twice the rate of aggregate output. The Smoot-Hawley tariff, or more precisely the threat of the Smoot-Hawley tariff, which coincided with the crisis over global imbalances, severely damaged international trade which in turn accelerated the decline in commodity price levels. Foreign producers, lacking alternative markets, were generally prepared to pay the extra duties to sell their goods in the United States. But few countries would, or in some cases could, tolerate the additional burden on their external payments. While scarcely any of them were prepared to retaliate by openly discriminating against American exports, they joined a general flight into protectionism, which began immediately after Congress adopted the preliminary tariff bill on 30 May 1929. Although the United States was less dependent upon foreign trade than any other developed country, it could not escape the disastrous combination of collapsing world trade and intensifying world price deflation. With protectionism on the increase almost everywhere, the era of globalization was over.

4.5 The Wall Street Crash of October 1929

The Crash of 1929 has become identified so completely with the onset of the world slump that to suggest it was neither the first nor the most important factor in the making of the great interwar crisis must seem at first glance implausible. There are grounds for claiming that this is nonetheless the case. As we have seen, in the spring of 1928 the Federal Reserve Banks had sought to halt the diversion of credit from productive enterprise into stock market speculation by collectively tightening the money supply and raising interest rates. Their actions, however, failed to have the desired effect because the funds fuelling the stock market boom no longer came mainly from Federal Reserve member banks. Member banks had reduced securities loans as a fraction of their total lending from 1927, to service important business customers. The funds for financial speculation came instead from American corporations such as US Steel, General Motors, AT&T and Standard Oil of New Jersey, which switched their large cash balances out of time deposits to take advantage of the much higher interest rates offered on call loans, and from overseas banks and corporations which were similarly drawn to the 7 per cent or more available on ostensibly low-risk, short-term call loans. Corporate time deposits increased from $1.9 billion in 1919 to a peak of $6.9 billion in June 1928. At this time, interest rates on call loans rose above 7 per cent. Thereafter corporate time deposits with banks declined, while corporate lending to brokerage houses sharply increased to at least $5 billion in September 1929, funding over 60 per cent of the call loan market.[182] Brokers thus continued to encourage speculation by allowing their clients to purchase shares on a mere 10 per cent margin and financing the balance by short-term borrowing in the call money market. On the eve of the Crash, brokers' loans and bank loans made directly to investors reached perhaps $15.7 billion or 18 per cent of the value of all listed stocks on the New York Stock Exchange.[183] Compared with the brokers, the commercial banks showed restraint on the loan front. But the banks nevertheless contributed importantly to the boom by switching their underwriting activity from productive enterprise towards new investment trusts. In the later 1920s, new trusts appeared on an almost daily basis. They were promoted as a contribution to industrial finance and as suitable vehicles for the cautious investor who could spread his risk over a wide portfolio of blue-chip shares. In fact, since they raised no new money for industry or commerce, they contributed nothing to the real economy, while their proliferation stimulated demand for existing shares, whose prices were driven skywards.[184]

The New York stock markets, already well up since April 1928, surged ahead on news of Hoover's election victory in November. US Steel, jewel in the crown of J. P. Morgan's industrial-financial empire, had traded at $85 only five years earlier; it now reached $179.5. General Motors shares, which had traded as low as $51 in 1923, rose above $600, adjusted for stock splits and dividends. RCA, or 'Radio', the most glamorous share on the market, rose in the same period from $26 to over $400.[185] The Dow Jones Industrial Index, a weighted average of the most important stocks on the New York Stock Exchange, reached a year-end high of 300, up 50 per cent from a year earlier and almost five times higher than in August 1921.[186] During the first five months of 1929 the markets fluctuated uncertainly. The Federal Reserve System's policy of tighter and dearer money had adversely affected American manufacturers and farmers, who directed their frustration at Wall Street. Antagonism increased in late March when the stock market abruptly declined and call money rose to 20 per cent. Charles Mitchell, chairman of the City Bank of New York, with the tacit encouragement of the New York Fed, signalled his willingness to accommodate brokers embarrassed by the sudden drying up of the call loan market.[187] Mitchell's intervention forestalled the need for brokers to issue their clients with new margin demands and the possibility that distress selling would drive the market into an uncontrollable tailspin. But it provoked intense criticism in Washington and small-town America. From their vantage point, it seemed to fly in the face of the Fed's objective of discouraging stock market speculation. Worse, City Bank was the largest of the Wall Street banks and the world's largest distributor of securities, and Mitchell himself was an outspoken defender of banking interests.[188] Hoover became all the more anxious to keep his distance from Wall Street. His secretary, hearing that Governor Harrison of the New York Fed wished to see the president, advised that this would be unwelcome. 'The President has not even seen members of the Federal Reserve Board down here for fear of the effect on the general situation in New York. I am very certain that it will be far better for him not to see Governor Harrison at this particularly critical juncture.'[189]

Summer was usually a quiet time for the stock markets. Not so in 1929. With brokers encouraging clients to increase their shareholdings and the banks underwriting still more investment trusts, trading volumes on the markets remained remarkably high. The brokers' bullish newsletters were however belied by their demands for greater margin cover, which rose from 10 per cent in mid-summer to 25 and even 50 per cent before the Crash.[190] It was probably these demands that brought the bull market to a halt in early autumn. On 3 September the peak was reached, with the main index, the Dow Jones Industrial Average, at 381. Even now, shares were probably not generally overpriced in view of the strength of the American economy and the earnings and asset value of the firms concerned.[191] But compared with where they stood even two years earlier, their market prices seemed to have reached extraordinary levels. As indicated in Table 4.4, some of the growth stocks, the dotcoms of their day, had indeed soared to dizzying heights: General Motors now stood at $1075 and Radio at $574, Columbia Gramophone, another glamour stock, traded at 165 times earnings and 50 times book value, and even the staid National City Bank of New York traded at 120 times earnings and 13 times book value.[192] While these were unrepresentative of industrial or manufacturing shares, they inevitably attracted public attention and skewed the market indices.

Thereafter the Dow Jones fell back, recovered ground, drifted sideways, then broke sharply on Wednesday 23 October, with the index closing nearly 7 per cent down on the day. The following morning, 'Black Thursday', trading increased ominously and the index slumped another 33 points or nearly 11 per cent. At noon, directors of five leading commercial banks met at J.P. Morgan & Company at 23 Wall Street where they pledged $240 million to support share prices.[193] Their dramatic intervention briefly reassured the market, which closed the day only 6 points down at 299.[194] But with brokers issuing new margin demands and investors obliged to review their positions over a long weekend, the market opened on Monday amidst a blizzard of sell orders. The panic mounted on Tuesday. With the index at one time down 48 points to 212, the *New York Times* spoke of 'the most demoralized conditions of trading in the history of the Stock Exchange and the Curb [Market]'. Share prices continued to fluctuate wildly until Thursday, 14 November, when the Crash ended three weeks after it began. The previous day, the index had fallen to 198, down 35 per cent since Black Thursday and 48 per cent since the market peaked on 3 September. But over the next few

Table 4.4 Total market value of all stocks listed
on the NYSE

Date	Total market value $ million
Jan. 1925	27,072
Jan. 1926	34,489
Jan. 1927	38,376
Jan. 1928	49,736
Jan. 1929	67,478
Jun. 1929	70,921
Jul. 1929	77,264
Aug. 1929	81,569
Sep. 1929	89,668
Oct. 1929	87,074
Nov. 1929	71,759
Dec. 1929	63,589
Jan. 1930	64,708
Feb. 1930	69,009
Mar. 1930	70,807
Apr. 1930	76,075
May 1930	75,305
Jun. 1930	75,019
Jan. 1931	49,020
Jan. 1932	26,694

Source: *New York Stock Exchange Bulletin*, vol. I, no. 3,
Jun. 1930, p. 6; *ibid.*, vol. III, no. 2, Feb. 1932, p. 4.

weeks it recovered strongly, reaching 248 at year end, 25 per cent above the lows
reached in November.[195]

All major stock markets tend to behave violently, and it is tempting to say that
the only remarkable thing about the 1929 Crash was the exceptional violence of
share price movements. Just as share prices in the boom period had not exceeded
the long-run historical average price/earnings ratio, so the Crash did no more
than wipe out gains made in the last phase of the bull market since April 1928.
Moreover, American markets frequently pause or decline in the first half of a
President's four-year term, before recovering strongly in the second half.[196] The
1929 Crash occurred in Hoover's first year in office and by January 1930 left the
stock price index down 33.1 per cent from its peak. But the last stage of the boom
had been extreme, and over the calendar year 1 January 1929 to 1 January 1930
the Dow Jones Industrial Average fell by only 8 per cent, reducing the total market
value of shares on the New York Stock Exchange by just 4.1 per cent (see Table
4.5). It remains the case that, measured from the September peak to the short-run
trough in November 1929, the loss of wealth in the United States alone amounted
to some $30 billion (£6.2 billion), a colossal sum equivalent to twice the total
of US private gross savings in 1929, over a third of national income, and twice
the country's gross foreign investment portfolio.[197] The wealth effect impacted
upon the roughly two million who had invested directly in the stock market or

Table 4.5 Dow Jones quarterly averages, 1921–33

Year	First quarter	Second quarter	Third quarter	Fourth quarter
1921	75.2	74.3	68.3	75.6
1922	83.8	–	–	97.5
1923	101.0	96.2	–	91.0
1924	97.4	91.9	101.9	108.2
1925	120.8	124.7	138.4	153.0
1926	152.9	143.0	160.5	155.3
1927	157.6	167.2	184.8	192.6
1928	199.9	213.4	225.8	267.0
1929	308.4	312.0	354.3	255.6
1930	267.1	265.1	227.9	184.0
1931	176.3	146.2	134.5	94.8
1932	79.5	54.2	61.0	62.1
1933	58.2	–	–	–

Source: Sobel, *The Big Board*, table 11.13, p. 228, table 13.4, p. 280.

indirectly through the proliferating investment trusts. It also impacted upon the firms from which they drew their savings to speculate. This was bound to have a severely deflationary effect upon the American economy. Contemporaries nonetheless had reason to anticipate that the Crash would also favour a resumption of economic activity in America and abroad.[198] The American banking system emerged almost unscathed from the crisis. Not a single important New York bank or brokerage firm failed, and in the liquidation of brokers' loans from roughly $8.5 billion to $4 billion in two months, not a single lender lost money.[199] With short-term funds no longer being drawn into the stock markets, the American Federal Reserve Banks swiftly reduced their discount rates, which enabled foreign central banks to do so as well. The stage thus seemed set for a period of renewed growth, with funds available at cheap rates for investment directly into the real economy rather than into securities speculation.[200] That this did not happen was due to factors largely unrelated to the Crash.

One factor was Washington's isolationism, which had been starkly exposed during the Crash by the ineffectualness of American financial and monetary regulatory mechanisms. When panic dislocated the markets, the New York commercial banks were left to improvise a solution. The New York Fed intervened within days of 'Black Thursday', discounting freely for member banks to allow them to increase their brokers' loans, and assisting New York banks to expand their reserves by open market purchases of bankers acceptances and US government bonds.[201] On 31 October it also reduced its discount rate from 6 to 5 per cent, in coordination with the Bank of England which simultaneously reduced Bank rate from 6.5 to 6 per cent; and between November 1929 and June 1930 the New York Fed reduced its discount rate no less than six times, from 6 per cent to 2.5 per cent.[202] Meanwhile, the Federal Reserve Board did practically nothing. Located in Washington to keep it from Wall Street's control, it was remote from the financial markets and depended for its information upon the New York Fed and the commercial banks, which had little time for consultation while the markets remained in turmoil. The Board dithered, indicated its readiness to cut interest rates on 24 October, then drew back.[203]

Nor did the Administration provide leadership. On Tuesday, 12 November, nearly three weeks after the Crash occurred, Harrison met Mellon, the secretary of the Treasury, to discuss the declining stock markets. Reports circulated of federal action, but no announcement was made that day and the markets slumped further. Mellon preferred to let market forces run their course. In his words, 'It will purge the rottenness out of the system. People will work harder, live a more moral life.'[204] Only after the market closed sharply down again the following day did he announce plans for a 1 per cent reduction in corporate and individual taxes. By mid-December, Democrat and Republican Congressmen joined in approving the legislation. But as existing tax rates were already low, the practical effect was modest to say the least.[205]

Hoover meanwhile took it upon himself to exhort businessmen to maintain wages and spending plans. On 21 November he held the first of several well-publicized meetings of business leaders, including the chairmen of General Motors, General Electric, Standard Oil of New Jersey and DuPont. J. K. Galbraith dismisses them as 'no-business meetings', which is perhaps unfair since moral suasion may have had a place in steadying economic relations.[206] But they did point up two features of Hoover's actions throughout the crisis: his aversion to direct intervention in domestic market relations and to any contact with New York's bankers. To him, as to many Americans, the New York banks – 'Wall Street' – remained too powerful and too heavily engaged in foreign, and particularly European, business. The impact of the stock market boom and subsequent Crash vividly illustrated the extent to which economic relations had again become globalized by the late 1920s. But rather than drawing the lesson that the crisis required an international solution, Hoover became increasingly drawn to unilateral measures. Thus in June 1930, when Congress reported out the dangerously protectionist Smoot-Hawley tariff bill, Hoover did not hesitate to sign it into law.

Two other factors bringing on the world slump were the relentless decline in wholesale commodity prices and the slowdown in nearly all Western economies, which was evident by the spring or summer of 1929.[207] With the important exception of Germany, developed countries experienced economic growth until the fourth quarter of 1929. But the effects of price deflation and monetary and credit restraint had already slowed their economic growth well before then. This added to their dissatisfaction with existing trade relations and readiness to retreat behind national, imperial or regional protectionist barriers, which brought a collapse of international trade and accelerated the decline of price levels and economic activity. It was almost certainly these developments rather than the 1929 Crash that were responsible for the renewed slide in share prices in 1930.

The New York stock markets, having halted their decline in mid-November 1929, recovered nearly 50 per cent of their losses by April 1930, when a new break

Table 4.6 NYSE share price movements, 1923–32

Stocks	1923 low	1929 high (adjusted for stock splits & dividends)	1932 low
Allied Chemical & Die	59	355	42
Anaconda Copper	32	175	3
Atcheson, Topeca & Santa Fe Railroad	94	299	35
DuPont Chemicals	106	1,617	154
General Electric	168	1,612	136
General Motors	51	1,075	40
New York Central Railroad	90	257	9
RCA	26	574	12
Union Carbide	51	420	46
US Steel	85	366	30

Source: Sobel, *The Big Board*, table 13.8, p. 283.

occurred.[208] By the end of 1930 the Dow Jones Industrial Average had collapsed to 158, down nearly 40 per cent from a year before and nearly 60 per cent from the market peak in September 1929.

A third sell-off began in February 1931 and continued almost without interruption until August 1932 when the index reached 41, down nearly 90 per cent from its postwar peak (see Table 4.6). This level had not been seen since 1903 and proved to be the market's low point.[209] By then, share values on the New York Stock Exchange had declined approximately $72 billion (£14.8 billion). This was 1.7 times current US national income or more than the total of all deposits in American banks – and did not include the losses incurred on other exchanges in New York and elsewhere in the country.[210] So severe was the loss in asset values and confidence in equities that even in 1950, 5 years after the Second World War and 21 years after the Crash, the market was still 38 per cent below its 1929 high. Long before then the effect was to weaken New York's standing as America's bastion of internationalism, while further intensifying isolationism in Washington and the rest of the country.

4.6   Conclusion

The Wall Street Crash and the onset of the world slump in October 1929 created the lasting impression that the international economic crisis preceded the political crisis and indeed occurred in conditions of peace and relative optimism. Yet, as we have seen, leading international bankers privately acknowledged as early as July 1927 that the international payments system was severely dislocated. The yawning dollar gap between the United States and the rest of the world was bridged for another year by unprecedented levels of American foreign lending. But in 1928 the French authorities restored the franc to a gold bullion standard and began to dispose of their huge foreign exchange balances, and other European central banks similarly sold foreign exchange balances for gold. Simultaneously, the American stock market boom brought a sharp decline in American foreign lending and a reverse flow of foreign funds into the United States. Germany and other Central European countries, whose recently reconstructed banking systems depended critically upon short-term US deposits as the basis of their commercial lending, felt the impact immediately. The decision of the Federal Reserve System in 1928 to tighten the US money supply through open market operations further aggravated the situation. This decision is cited by Friedman and other economists as the crucial factor in the origins of the global depression, and it did indeed precede the decline in American foreign lending by six months. But it caused neither the decline in lending nor the liquidity crisis in Europe nor the growing retreat from globalization, all of which began in 1927 or the first half of 1928. Its effect became evident only in the spring of 1929 when construction and other sectors of the American economy began to decline, by which time signs of a global crisis were already apparent.

The malfunctioning of the international monetary and financial system contributed to the onset of the world economic slump, and the gold standard bound currencies into a common fate which ensured that deflationary pressure in one country was transmitted to others. Yet economic events were shaped by politics and vice versa. The decision to restore the gold standard in every country concerned was political and the reasons for its malfunctioning were also largely political. The appeal of the gold standard was that it constrained governments from spending beyond their means, safeguarded private wealth and increased the mobility of capital by guaranteeing currency convertibility, as well as facilitating trade and potentially enabling national economies to remain internationally competitive without recourse to more direct forms of intervention such as controls on international trade and payments. Put differently, under the gold standard countries were expected to rely exclusively upon unilateral domestic adjustments to remain competitive rather than resorting to unilateral external adjustments. Bankers, businessmen and wealth holders naturally favoured the gold standard, but so too for their own reasons did politicians throughout the developed world. It was their support that enabled British, American and French central bankers to re-establish gold standard system throughout the developed world.

Yet paradoxically from 1927 the governors of all three central banks found themselves severely constrained in their efforts to operate the gold standard. Norman, having allied with the British Treasury in a skilful campaign to restore sterling to gold at fully 100 per cent of its prewar gold exchange rate, thereafter faced crippling pressure from industry, labour and an angry chancellor, which left him limping along with minimal reserves, scarcely able to assist other central banks that looked to the Bank of England for help and obliged to reintroduce informal curbs on British capital exports. Strong in New York faced similar pressure from regions of the country that were adversely affected by declining commodity prices. Having hitherto encouraged other central banks to return to the gold standard, he reacted by dissociating himself from initiatives for reforming the gold standard's operation and addressing its deflationary bias. In France, Moreau was restrained from restoring the franc to gold until the struggle over which sections of society should pay for the war resulted in the erosion of four-fifths of private savings and public debt. He then secured government agreement to a new gold parity appropriate for domestic industry and national security. Countries with currencies locked together through the gold standard were subsequently dragged into the slump together. But it would be wrong to place sole responsibility for the slump upon the gold standard, when the three central banks jointly responsible for managing its operation were constrained by national pressures from even discussing means of modifying its operation in the interests of price stability.

Nor was it only the gold standard thus affected by the retreat from globalization. While considerable progress was made after the Armistice to liberalize international trade, concessions were reluctantly conceded and nervously monitored. British merchants, bankers and officials initially led in promoting the reopening of markets, and officially Britain remained committed to free trade until September 1931. But already by 1925, Britain had begun its retreat from free trade in the name of national security. And from 1926 growing frustration in industrial circles unsettled the Conservative government and led Britain to forsake its leading role in trade liberalization. With Britain becalmed, France took the lead in the hope that liberalizing trade in Europe would appeal to Germany, facilitate European integration and enable it to regain some purchase over its former enemy. But just as concern over national security prompted France to take the lead in Europe, so for nationalist reasons Germany also drew back. Impatient to revise the financial and territorial provisions of the Treaty of Versailles, German governments looked to the Anglo-Saxon powers for support and therefore eschewed any alignment with France that was likely to strengthen France's hand or antagonize the Anglo-Saxon powers. One can only speculate as to what might have happened had the victor powers remained united behind the postwar settlement. But there is no doubt that Germany was almost bound to exploit their divisions, even though it meant prolonging the economic 'balkanization' of Europe. Meanwhile the United States remained stubbornly isolated from the international arena, with Washington from time to time encouraging individual businessmen to participate in negotiations where American interests might be affected, but refusing to participate in multilateral economic initiatives or to contribute to international security, and meanwhile undermining global stability by intensifying its tariff protectionism. Economic justifications were offered each time the tariff was raised, but the strength of the dollar and the American trade balance point to an underlying political motive, namely fear of foreign entanglements.

Practically all countries enjoyed increasing prosperity in the ten years to 1929. Yet well before 1929 the more vulnerable among them betrayed nervousness about the effect of globalization upon their national sovereignty and the absence of a coherent security framework in Europe or the rest of the world. This was evident in their retreat from the gold exchange standard in 1927 and decline in support for trade liberalization in 1928. It was precisely this nervousness that explains why – despite their relative prosperity – they reacted so quickly to the new challenge from the United States in the summer of 1929. Without even waiting for Congress to approve the new tariff, numerous countries introduced protectionist measures of their own. The most important exception was Britain, where the newly elected minority Labour government supported by Liberals reaffirmed its commitment to economic internationalism and refused to join other countries in protesting against American tariff plans. Despite the government's position, nevertheless, pressure rapidly mounted in British business and political circles for a radical change in economic policy. Before the world economic slump got under way and well before the Wall Street Crash, therefore, all the signs pointed to a general retreat from globalization. At this point the crucial question became whether this would result in the general adoption of beggar-your-neighbour policies and autarky, that is to say a world of isolated national economies, or alternatively a world of regional or imperial trade blocs. Most accounts of the 1930s claim it was the former that emerged. As will be seen, security as well as economic considerations militated in favour of the latter outcome.

5
The Crisis, September 1929–April 1931

5.1   Introduction

On Sunday, 18 May 1930, the *Kaiserhof* in Berlin was busier than usual, for that day the great hotel on the *Wilhelmplatz* opposite the imperial chancellery, later to become the headquarters for Adolf Hitler and Josef Goebbels,[1] was the venue for the second congress of the Pan-European Union, attended by two thousand delegates or guests. Joseph Wirth, the former chancellor and practically the last remaining representative of the left wing of the Catholic Centre Party, officially welcomed the visitors in his capacity as minister of the interior in Heinrich Bruening's government. While carefully avoiding any commitment to the congress's goal, he reaffirmed Germany's desire to live in peace and collaborate with other nations.

Count Richard Coudenhove-Kalergi, the mysterious figure who had founded the Union eight years earlier in Vienna, directed the congress proceedings. Slim, clean-shaven and still barely thirty-five, Coudenhove had persuaded an impressive number of prominent liberal and moderate conservative statesmen and businessmen as well as many eminent scientists, academics and writers from Eastern and Western Europe to attend.[2] The novelist, Thomas Mann, then at the height of his reputation, addressed the gathering on 'Europe as a cultural system [*Kulturgemeinschaft*]'. Louis Loucheur, Briand's adviser on industrial and economic issues, who led the French delegation, spoke on the second day, followed by his German counterpart, Robert Bosch, the Stuttgart industrialist who had financed Coudenhove's organizing work in Germany since 1928.[3] Leo Amery led the diminutive British delegation. A history fellow of All Souls and colonial secretary in Baldwin's second Conservative government (1924–9), Amery deserved to be regarded as Joseph Chamberlain's successor for his unceasing proselytizing for the Empire. Speaking alternately in German and French, he affirmed that Europe must surmount its national divisions if it were ever to realize its economic and political potential, and endorsed the work of the congress. But, he added, Britain's own destiny was to forge an ever-closer union with its own Empire partners, so it could only applaud from the sidelines. Loucheur could scarcely suppress his disappointment at Amery's remarks, but others present acknowledged that Britain was never likely to join Europe.[4]

The congress coincided with several other important 'European' events. In Bâle the previous day, a German representative had called at the new Bank for International Settlements (BIS) to confirm his country's commitment to reparation payments on the basis of the Young plan and its receipt of the Young Loan. At this point the Reparation Commission and the German War Burdens Commission (the *Kriegslastenkommission*) formally ceased to exist. In Paris, André Tardieu, the premier, announced that now Germany was committed to a final reparation settlement, France would withdraw the last of its troops from the Kehl bridgehead by 30 June, thus ending its occupation of the Rhineland.[5] The very next day, 17 May, Briand circulated his 'Memorandum on the Organization of a Regime of Federal Union in Europe' to the 26 other European members of the League of Nations.[6] Meanwhile the business-political elite who comprised the Mayrisch committee gathered at Heidelberg, where they agreed to form a subcommittee to consider the implications of Briand's project for France and Germany.

Not all signs were encouraging, however. The Mayrisch committee had chosen to meet in Heidelberg because nationalist violence had made Berlin and other large German cities too dangerous.[7] In Florence, a large crowd gathered in the *Piazza della Signoria* on 17 May to hear Benito Mussolini's final speech in a week-long tour of Tuscany. Having announced a parade of Italy's military might for the following day, *il Duce* launched into a tirade against the London naval disarmament conference and all those who would attempt to tie Italy's hands:

> To-morrow you will see an armed review of impressive character. It is I who desired it, because, although words are beautiful things, rifles, machine-guns, ships, aeroplanes and cannon are still more beautiful things; because, O Blackshirts, right unless accompanied by force is a vain word, and your own great Niccolo Machiavelli has warned us that prophets who have disarmed will perish.[8]

As these events illustrate, the spring of 1930 was a time of bewildering contrasts. All countries reacted to the world economic slump, but they did so in divergent and far from decisive or effective ways. Several constraints were at work. In the first place, while all countries entered the slump at roughly the same time, its seriousness was not at first evident to everyone.[9] Germany, the most vulnerable, was the first to reach crisis point in January 1930. Britain and Japan reached crisis point some eighteen months later, the United States in the winter of 1932 and France a full year after that. As a result, the need for action became imperative at different times, making cooperation difficult.[10]

The second constraint derived from the fact that Western statesmen possessed only a rudimentary grasp of economics and scarcely comprehended all the economic options available to them. This was as true of Hoover and his Administration in Washington as it was of MacDonald and Snowden who dominated policy-making in London until August 1931, and of Flandin, Briand, Tardieu and Laval who shared the direction of French policy until May 1932. They all accepted the need for a balanced budget and severe constraints on public spending so as not to crowd out private investment or trigger inflation and loss of confidence in the national currency. They all accepted the gold standard as the essential basis for domestic and international exchange and a vital safeguard against the inflationary proclivities of the supposed wild men on the Left. Notwithstanding that Hoover was a protectionist and French statesmen supported some restrictions on the movement of capital and goods, they did not think to challenge the premises of liberal economics. In this respect they were scarcely different from other political and business leaders in the West. Even the most exigent broadsheets including the *New York Times*, the *Times* and *Le Temps*, normally relegated economic issues to the financial pages where they were treated in orthodox fashion.

However, there was a third reason, which was scarcely less decisive than the others. This was the tendency of states to approach economic relations as a matter of importance not only for welfare but also for national security. In the 60 years since the onset of the Cold War in 1947, when Western states accepted the protection of the United States, they have generally found it possible to treat international security and economic issues as discrete fields of decision-making and chosen their economic options chiefly on their technical merits. This was far from the case in the world slump. Not only did decision-making occur in a world possessed of only a fragmentary security framework. But, as the mounting violence in Germany and Mussolini's outburst signalled, the international order also faced new challenges that would destroy what remained of the framework. Deteriorating economic conditions and diminishing international security thus inter-acted to produce an unprecedented crisis.

5.2   French reactions to the dual crisis, September 1929–May 1930

Even today, no issue is more obscure than the course of French external policy in the early stages of the interwar crisis. Ever since the Great War when France survived with the support of allies, French leaders including Millerand, Poincaré and Briand accepted that the only enduring solution to the Franco-German problem was a multilateral one in which the core countries of Europe recognized and fostered their mutual interdependence. A Franco-British *entente* and Franco-German *rapprochement* were both essential, but to contain Germany permanently it must be embedded within a broader European framework. This seemed all the more necessary because of the emergence of the Soviet Union and the United States as potential threats to Europe's political and economic independence. They therefore actively supported European initiatives including the Locarno treaties, the 1927 World Economic Conference, which had been a largely European affair, and the work of the Mayrisch committee and other organizations dedicated to European unity. None of these initiatives, however, had produced substantial results by the spring of 1929 when the need for action became pressing.

The previous autumn, the Poincaré government had agreed to reopen the reparations question and to end military occupation of the Rhineland, if Germany would accept a final and definitive schedule of payments. This held out the promise of advance reparation payment by means of a large international loan raised on the strength of Germany's commitment to pay, and enabled the French government to persuade Parliament to ratify the long-suspended war debt funding agreements with Britain and the United States. But in settling reparations and ending the Rhineland occupation, it also meant that France would lose any direct means of constraining Germany. Briand, with Poincaré's agreement, therefore wasted no time. In June 1929, two months before the reparations conference, he spoke to Stresemann of the need to organize Europe economically as well as politically when they met privately in Madrid where they were attending a session of the League Council. Briand once more stressed the challenge of American commercial expansion, which had destroyed Europe's film industry for want of regional cooperation, and encouraged Stresemann to hope that once the reparations question was resolved he would address the Saar and other issues dividing their two countries. He felt sure that if France and Germany were prepared to work for European unity, other countries including even Italy and Britain would participate.[11] Presently Poincaré spoke on similar lines to a German diplomat in Paris: the differences between Germany and France were nothing to the threat posed by the Soviet Union and the United States to the very future of Europe, so they must work together.[12]

Stresemann was gratified to hear these appeals, since it meant he could hope for an acceleration of Treaty revision.[13] He was apprehensive about Germany's financial dependence upon the United States and appreciated that the tangle of European trade barriers obstructed Germany's growth. But for economic as well as political reasons he would not contemplate supporting a European initiative that could be construed as anti-American. Carl von Schubert, the state secretary, saw in Briand's European idea merely a device for *slowing down* Treaty revision.[14] Bernhard von Bülow, soon to be von Schubert's successor, saw it even more negatively as a device for maintaining French hegemony in Europe, and enumerated a long list of reasons why Germany could not possibly support it.[15]

In view of these attitudes, French hopes of containing Germany by means of European integration, perhaps seems naïve. But by their lights it was a matter of *faute de mieux*. With the last effective constraints on Germany soon to be lifted, only the common threat of economic crisis might draw Europe together and enable France to constrain Germany within a broader European framework. France therefore embarked upon an offensive to promote support. At the International Conference of the European Cinema in Paris in June, French delegates called on European producers and distributors to unite in resistance to American domination of the world market.[16] At the fifth biennial congress of the International Chamber of Commerce in Amsterdam in July, Etienne Clémentel, the minister of commerce, introduced a resolution to favour regional tariff arrangements, while in the corridors French delegates promoted an alliance of European car manufacturers to confront American competition.[17] Meanwhile at the League's Economic Consultative Committee in Geneva, Loucheur, now minister of labour, renewed his call for industrial ententes as a means of organizing Europe. In August, Daniel Serruys, chief trade negotiator at the Ministry of Commerce and president of the League

Economic Committee, arranged meetings with leading German bankers and industrialists to discuss the creation of a European customs union.[18] The association of
French Chambers of Commerce, which had close links to the government, urgently
demanded collective action to safeguard the European market. Several personalities
including Jacques Bardoux, the eminent correspondent of *Le Temps*, and Edouard
Herriot, the former premier, similarly declared in favour of 'Europe'.[19]

Confirmation of the new direction of policy came in July 1929, when Briand, who
had succeeded Poincaré as premier while remaining foreign minister, revealed to
several journalists that he intended to speak at the League Assembly in September
on European federation. It was time, he explained, to build upon the framework
of peace established by the Locarno treaties, apply the lessons of the United States'
economic success and equip Europe to face the consequences of American tariff
policy.[20] His speech in Geneva on 5 September was one of the finest of his career.
By now 67 years old and betraying the ravages of his 60-cigarette-a-day habit, he
began slowly but soon regained his old form.[21] There was, he noted, widespread
anxiety at the possibility of international economic conflict and recognition of
the need for 'economic disarmament' as well as 'political disarmament'. The time
had come for 'a general solution', not a mere technical fix. For some years, he
acknowledged, he had been associated with the idea of European unity. Hitherto
this had been the preserve of philosophers and poets, and he appreciated that
even now many regarded it as a utopian dream. But he was prepared to place his
reputation on the line by promoting it, since 'in all the wisest and most important
acts of man there was always an element of madness or recklessness.' The League
should promote the *rapprochement* of peoples and regional unions, including one
that embraced the League's European members.

> I think that among peoples who are geographically associated, such as the
> people of Europe, there should be a sort of federal bond (*lien fédéral*). These
> people should have the means of entering into contract, discussing their com-
> mon interests and adopting common solutions. They should, in a word, estab-
> lish a bond of solidarity that would permit them, at a given moment, to con-
> front together any grave circumstances that may arise. It is this bond...that I
> would seek to create.[22]

But, he added, the most urgent need for solidarity was on the economic front:

> Evidently the association will act chiefly in the economic domain, since that
> is the most pressing need....I therefore call on colleagues representing other
> European countries to give unofficial consideration to my proposal during this
> Assembly, and to invite their governments to study it, so that we may consider
> later, perhaps at the next Assembly, the possibilities of its realisation, which I
> believe to exist.[23]

Briand's speech marked the first occasion that a major power had formally
endorsed European integration by voluntary means, and it attracted wide

attention. Briand gave no indication of how he proposed to address the economic issue, but there seemed reason to think that he had in mind regional trade preferences. In 1927, the World Economic Conference had endorsed the principle of plurilateral (multilateral) conventions as a means of liberalizing trade, without explaining how this could be reconciled with the most-favoured-nation principle. The League Economic Committee had therefore requested Walter Stucki, the Swiss minister of economics, to investigate the options, and in April 1929, after wide consultation, he presented his long-awaited report. Stucki proposed that states should agree to an exception to the most-favoured-nation clause for plurilateral conventions, so long as they met three conditions: that they contributed to the reduction of tariff barriers, had the approval of the League of Nations, and were open to all countries to join on a similar basis.[24] With British and American members opposed to any departure from the most-favoured-nation principle, the Economic Committee took no decision on Stucki's proposal.[25] The French government, however, not only endorsed the report, but also starting in July 1929 it introduced an exception for plurilateral conventions when bilateral commercial treaties came up for renegotiation. Switzerland, Belgium and the Netherlands did the same.[26]

Jacques Rueff, the young *Inspecteur des Finances* seconded to the French mission in Geneva, subsequently discussed opportunities for European economic integration with Alexis Léger, Briand's chief adviser at the Quai d'Orsay. Rueff saw no hope of progress until Europe confronted the obstacle posed by the most-favoured-nation principle. European countries were simply not going to open their markets to neighbouring countries, if they had to pass on tariff reductions to the United States without receiving reciprocal concessions. He therefore proposed that Briand should urge the introduction of a 'European exception' to the most-favoured-nation principle in all commercial treaties. Already numerous exceptions existed, permitting preferential trade between countries with strong historical or geographical links. A Nordic clause allowed preferential trade among Norway, Sweden and Denmark, an Iberian clause permitted preferences between Spain and Portugal, and a Baltic clause, an Ottoman clause, colonial clauses and British Imperial preference had also gained international acceptance. To make a European exception acceptable to non-participating countries, he believed it would be sufficient to limit it to 'advantages or favours exchanged between European states, by means of multilateral agreements tending to tighten the links of solidarity which exist between the European States.'[27]

Besides Briand's European federation proposal, the League Assembly in September 1929 also debated a proposal for initiating concerted economic action by means of an international tariff truce. The idea originated with Belgian leaders who had become worried that Britain, their largest trading partner, might soon abandon free trade and retreat behind a protective Empire-wide barrier.[28] William Graham, president of the Board of Trade in the Labour government and a strong free trader, had seized upon the Belgian proposal as a means of restraining the international backlash against American protectionism, while offering what he believed to be a more realistic liberal, non-discriminatory alternative to Briand's dangerously narrow regional initiative. As he warned the Assembly,

> Such a policy might, from the economic standpoint, generate that friction which would manufacture war between the nations – war which it is our express purpose in this League to make certain will never recur. Do not let the note of discrimination enter this controversy.[29]

On the face of it, the French decision to support both Briand's proposal and the Anglo-Belgian tariff truce proposal seems odd, indeed contradictory, since the former favoured Europe while potentially discriminating against the rest of the world whereas the latter was universal and non-discriminatory.[30] The explanation lies in the fact that since the spring of 1929 French statesmen shared the fears of Belgian and British statesmen of a recrudescence of protectionism.[31] But they were also confident that European states would not keep their markets open if it meant having to make concessions to the United States and other countries that refused to grant reciprocal concessions, and indeed that only European states would participate in the tariff truce initiative. As René Massigli, head of the French mission in Geneva, put it, without ruling out any countries from the truce, only the European countries were prepared to rule themselves in. 'It is thus possible to envisage, without being excessively optimistic, a collective agreement among the majority of European states, which would be the first step towards a closer association.'[32] Massigli welcomed Stucki's contribution to the League's Second Committee deliberations on the tariff truce proposal. Stucki, he observed, had 'touched on the essential point in demonstrating the importance of limiting the unconditional application of the most-favoured-nation clause, if one wanted to obtain the demobilization of tariffs by means of collective agreements of wide application.'[33] French statesmen thus regarded both Briand's European federation proposal and the Anglo-Belgian tariff truce proposal as *liberal* initiatives, and for the time being were confident that they would complement one another.[34] As Serruys advised Pierre-Etienne Flandin, his minister, the truce promised to be 'the first element [*ébauche*] of a European entente in the economic sphere.'[35]

As early as November 1929, French officials clashed with their British counterparts over the approach to the tariff truce. Speaking at the quarterly meeting of the League Economic Committee, Serruys observed that the League Assembly had expressed no view as to whether the tariff truce should be extended to non-participating countries. Hence the way was open for the establishment of a 'discriminatory régime'. The American and British members of the Committee strongly objected to this suggestion, but Serruys held his ground:

> The stabilization of tariffs should be the first stage in the larger project of preparing the ground for organising production in Europe. It should not be conceived – as the British wanted – as a stage merely towards the reduction of tariffs.[36]

The French government further demonstrated its commitment to European economic integration in the closing weeks of the year when it sought to persuade its Eastern allies to endorse the League-sponsored Prohibitions convention outlawing the use of quantitative trade controls to restrict imports. Here too the only signatories turned out to be European states, and French officials leaned heavily upon Poland and Czechoslovakia to sign up in the hope that this would lower tensions in Central Europe and conduce to greater European cooperation.[37]

For several months more France seemed committed to European economic integration. In February 1930, Flandin travelled to Geneva to attend the opening of the tariff truce conference. As he explained to officials beforehand,

> The essential goal that the French Delegation should pursue...was to create a group of six or seven states, which applied similar commercial principles, to proceed to an agreed reduction of tariffs among themselves, thus forming the core of a European economic unit.[38]

On 17 February, the day the conference opened, Flandin had the German and Belgian delegates to dinner, where he affirmed that France was interested in 'concluding a constructive agreement, strengthening the position of Europe within the League of Nations.'[39] But a political crisis in Paris that day forced Flandin to quit the conference, and when he returned on 7 March he no longer spoke of adopting a plurilateral convention or organizing an inner core of countries for European economic integration.[40] Moreover, France, having sponsored the tariff truce, now appeared strongly opposed to it. The shift in policy became still more evident when Briand, on 17 May, circulated his memorandum on European federation. At the Tenth League Assembly, Briand had spoken of promoting European unity through the integration of markets, and the onset of the world slump had sharply increased the appeal of European economic integration. Yet in what was now being called the Briand plan, economic integration ceased to be the first priority. What had caused him to forsake this ostensibly golden opportunity to exploit Europe's economic frustrations in pursuit of his federation plan? Briand was notoriously reluctant to commit his thoughts to paper and nowhere is the shift explained, but it seems evident that at least three influences were at work.

In the first place, French statesmen recognized that other European countries were reluctant to follow their lead on European economic integration. At the biennial congress of the International Chamber of Commerce in Amsterdam, the League of Nations in Geneva and gatherings elsewhere they had promoted collective economic action, but even friendly states such as Belgium and Poland had held back. While Stresemann was alive, the French had hoped for German cooperation. Indeed, shortly after meeting Briand in Paris in June 1929, Stresemann had captured the headlines by speaking in the Reichstag of the threat posed by American economic imperialism and the need for Europe to unite if it was not to decline into an American colony.[41] But he was already a very sick man, and on 3 October he died. On hearing the news, Briand is alleged to have said, 'Order a coffin for two.'[42] This was perhaps apocryphal, but he recognized Stresemann's unique ability to persuade Germans to accept a liberal-progressive foreign policy and the likelihood that after him Franco-German cooperation would become much more problematic. In fact, his successor as foreign minister, Julins Curtius, and Schubert's successor Bülow as head of the *Auswartiges Amt,* displayed a scarcely concealed coolness towards France. Confronted with Hugenberg's and Hitler's noisy campaign against the Young plan, the German government reacted with nationalist measures of its own, including plans for higher tariffs. The Quai d'Orsay, surveying opinion in Europe in November, found that Italy's recent tariff increase and the threat of Germany following suit were discouraging other countries from joining in a tariff truce.[43]

A second influence upon French policy was the growing opposition of French farmers and industrialists to tariff concessions of any sort. Flandin, the minister of commerce, was acutely sensitive to the clamour manufacturers, and on 14 October 1929 Jean Hennessy, the minister of agriculture, warned Briand that if he persisted with the tariff truce proposal, he must allow a broad exception for agricultural imports in case of emergency.[44] The following week Briand was defeated in a vote of confidence, and only after several weeks of political turmoil was Tardieu able to form a government. Briand once again occupied the Quai d'Orsay. But Tardieu, while not opposed to Briand's federation plan, was more interested in safeguarding French economic interests and developing trade with France's colonies.[45] Already protests against the tariff truce were coming in thick and fast from the *Comité d'action économique et douanière*, regional chambers of agriculture, the federation of machinery manufacturers, the *Comité des forges* and other organizations representing domestic producers.[46] Officials urged ministers to resist demands for protection, warning that it would dangerously diminish France's influence in Europe.[47] But in January 1930, ministers approved a sharp rise in the duty on imported wheat, followed by increased barriers against motor cars and other imports.[48] By February the commerce and the tariff commissions of both houses of Parliament had resolved that the government must enter no agreement that constrained France's sovereignty in tariff matters.[49] The government privately acknowledged that this practically ruled out an effective tariff truce, let alone tariff concessions to other European countries.[50]

A third reason for drawing back was the growing apprehension among French statesmen that by weakening the most-favoured-nation principle they would play into the hands of Germany and undermine their own national security. With agreement in principle to the evacuation of Allied forces from the Rhineland and negotiations under way on the future of the Saar, they became uneasily aware that Germans were already talking openly of a German-Austrian *Anschluss* and a German-dominated *Mitteleuropa* as the next items on their Treaty revision agenda. Eduard Benes, the Czech foreign minister, in a show of support for European integration, had recently appeared on the same platform as the Austrian Coudenhove-Kalergi and delivered part of his speech in German, a language he had not spoken in public for years.[51] But he also warned

Paris to proceed cautiously and avoid giving Germany the excuse to grant preferences to Austria and countries in Eastern Europe.[52] As he appreciated, Germany potentially held far more attraction than France as a market for exports from Central and Eastern Europe. France was practically self-sufficient in forest and farm products, whereas Germany was capable of absorbing all the output of this region in return for markets for its manufactures. Thus, if it offered preferential access to its market, Germany could draw Austria, Roumania, Yugoslavia and ultimately all the other countries of the region into a dependent relationship. Once French statesmen began to reflect on this, they drew back from the preferential idea.

The final straw for them was the opposition of the Anglo-Saxon powers. Paul Claudel, the ambassador in Washington, encouraged Paris to hope that the United States would look kindly upon a European federation. But he warned repeatedly that if this involved any trade discrimination, Washington would certainly raise objections.[53] Massigli in Geneva similarly warned against promoting a European bloc that might separate France from its Eastern allies or antagonize Britain.[54] Arthur Henderson, the British foreign secretary, underlined the point when he called on Briand in early May 1930 to discuss his federation plan. While professing keen interest in it, Henderson sternly warned Briand to do nothing to weaken the League of Nations and abjure any action that might be construed as anti-American. Briand reassured him on both points.[55] Like every French statesman of the interwar period, he hoped eventually to see the United States return to world affairs, but he appreciated that this was still a distant prospect. In the meantime, Britain remained the only major power capable of entering the scales against a resurgent Germany. Partly for this reason, no doubt, Léger, who was responsible for preparing Briand's memorandum, omitted regional economic preferences from successive drafts.[56]

The memorandum that Briand circulated to interested governments on 17 May reaffirmed the pressing need to address the economic crisis engulfing Europe. It called for the integration of the European market, which was carved up by 27 national frontiers and an additional 20,000 km of customs barriers since the war. It also envisaged a common economic policy through industrial ententes and other means, improvements in the infrastructure through coordinated public works projects and cooperation on transport, communications, the provision of credit, labour and migration, and health, intellectual cooperation and inter-parliamentary relations. But instead of calling for immediate economic action, it insisted that the first step must be a political agreement wherein states accepted the principle of European union and agreed to examine together all questions of importance to 'the community of European peoples'. Drawing on the model of the League of Nations, it called for the creation of three institutions: a 'European conference' or assembly representing all the member states, a permanent political executive and a secretariat to service the conference and executive. It stressed the compatibility of the plan with the League Covenant, Article 21 of which envisaged regional pacts. It also denied that the union would in the least compromise the independence and national sovereignty of member states. Finally, it demanded the 'subordination of the economic problem to the political problem'.

> All possibility of progress towards economic union being rigidly determined by the question of security and this question itself being intimately bound up with progress towards political union, the construction of Europe must initially be concentrated upon the political plan. It is this plan moreover that will form the basis of subsequent efforts to elaborate the broad lines of a European economy policy as well as the tariff policy of each individual member state.
>
> Proceeding in the reverse order would not only be impracticable, it would also leave the weakest nations feeling exposed, without guarantees or compensation, to the risk of political domination, *resulting in the industrial domination of the most strongly organised states.*
>
> It is thus logical and normal that the economic sacrifices required by the union can be justified only through a political process capable of creating confidence between peoples and substantially pacifying existing fears.[57]

Briand's decision to subordinate economic action to agreement on security disappointed many European countries and probably doomed his project. Yet in general terms his approach reflected the difficulties facing the whole of Europe. Just as France was not prepared to jeopardize its national security by promoting tariff preferences in Europe, so the other European states were not prepared to compromise their national independence or aspirations in the absence of clear economic benefits. What was needed were substantial inducements to cooperate, which France was in no position to offer. The only country able to do so was Britain, whose economic and political influence was such that its active participation in the union would reassure practically all countries of Europe as to their own future. For the next few weeks, therefore, attention was focused on Britain and its reply to Briand's memorandum.

Meanwhile, Briand suffered a serious blow to his reputation when the last French troops and officials withdrew from the Rhineland. No sooner had they left than members of the paramilitary *Stahlhelm* stormed the bridgehead, desecrated the French flag and noisily confirmed that the Rhineland was again in German hands. The following day the nationalist *Deutsche Allgemeine Zeitung* wrote that 'Germans respond with silence and contempt to those who claim to see the evacuation as a display of generosity.' From Berlin, President Hindenburg and Bruening issued a joint statement demanding the restoration of the Saarland's people to Germany and ending *'Deutschland, Deutschland über alles'*.[58] Clashes between Germans and Poles on the Eastern frontier now also grew more frequent.[59] Privately Bruening assured his Cabinet that he could not possibly accept Briand's plan, since it would rule out Germany's regaining its *'Lebensraum'*.[60] In August, Gottfried Treviranus, minister for the occupied territories, further inflamed the situation by publicly confirming that revision of the Eastern frontier was next on Germany's agenda.[61] The upsurge in German nationalism practically doomed Briand's European federation plan, though other obstacles also arose.

5.3   Britain's initial response to the dual crisis, June 1929 to July 1930

Britain's fourth postwar general election took place on 31 May 1929, four months before the onset of the world economic slump. Since February, Bank rate stood at a swinging 5.5 per cent. This uncommonly high rate had become necessary on account of Sterling's weakness, due to the pull of speculative activity on Wall Street and Britains own trade deficit. If maintained there for long it was bound to stifle economic activity. But for the time being the economy was still expanding, and unemployment, albeit disturbingly high, had fallen from the official 1.3 million total at the start of the year. Except among international bankers in the City, therefore, there was little sense of imminent crisis. This soon changed, however, when Bank rate was raised on 27 September to 6.5 per cent, unemployment sharply increased and trade protection rose ominously throughout the world. Thereafter, the government remained almost wholly preoccupied with declining trade and soaring unemployment.

Perhaps the most remarkable thing about the government's approach to the economic problem was its self-limiting character. Like the first Labour government in 1924, it depended for its majority in Parliament on Liberal votes. But the constraints upon the government were largely of its own making. Notwithstanding Labour's collectivist rhetoric and the recent interest of economists associated with the Lloyd George wing of the Liberal party in employment creation through public works projects financed by borrowing, the two parties scarcely differed on domestic or external policies. To their leaders and most of their economic advisers, borrowing for large-scale public works could not be squared with fiscal and financial orthodoxy. Not only could they not justify such apparently irresponsible action, but also neither could senior Treasury officials nor scarcely anyone in the business community or the financial press. Since deficit spending would therefore have destroyed confidence in the economy, it could scarcely have succeeded even had the government sought to undertake it.

A second form of unilateral domestic action seemed more promising, namely the 'rationalization' of sectors of British industry. Most of the country's unemployment was concentrated in older sectors of industry such as iron and steel-making, shipbuilding and textiles where firms generally operated with outdated machinery and techniques. It seemed possible to restore their international competitiveness and demand for labour by 'rationalizing' production through a process of merging weaker firms into better managed and better capitalized firms. Norman of the Bank of England had been horrified at the victory of the Labour party, which he still imagined to be bent upon imposing socialism in Britain. But he found himself courted by Labour ministers who sought his help with industrial reorganization, and when J. H. Thomas, the lord privy seal who chaired the Cabinet's unemployment committee, approached him in January 1930, he seized the opportunity. Having already formed the Bankers Industrial Development Company as a subsidiary of the Bank to mobilize private capital for rationalization purposes, he invited Thomas to rely upon him.[62] Thomas, a hard-drinking trade unionist with no ideas of his own, readily agreed, not least because several younger members of his committee, including Sir Oswald Mosley, were agitating for more radical proposals that he neither understood nor supported. Unfortunately for Thomas, rationalization on a commercial basis had little chance of success. Not only were the most beleaguered sectors of industry heavily dependent upon exports and world markets were declining, but many of the individual firms were also heavily burdened with debt since the aftermath of the Great War and in no position to take on more, even if the banks were prepared to offer it. Rationalization, when it occurred through the Bank's initiative, was therefore likely to take the form of mergers that reduced excess capacity. In this case, the outcome, in the short run at least, would be more unemployment, not less.[63]

Under pressure to do something the government turned contiously towards financial or monetary reform. The rise in Bank rate in late September 1929 had provoked unprecedented criticism of monetary policy and the Bank of England itself. Industrialists and Tory critics such as Leo Maxse and Lord Beaverbrook demanded action to insulate the British economy from the vagaries of short-term capital movements. The annual conference of the Trades Union Congress called for a Royal Commission on monetary policy, and the Labour Party executive yielded to grassroots pressure for a special debate on the subject at its annual conference at the end of the month.[64] Norman however warned Snowden, the chancellor of the exchequer, to discourage Party members from hoping they could 'treat the depression as soluble by monetary expedients'.[65] Orthodox to a fault and in awe of Norman, Snowden did as requested. Speaking at the conference, he pointed an accusing finger at the Wall Street boom, then announced plans for a wide-ranging enquiry into the relationship between finance and industry in Britain.[66] As he appreciated, a large, heterogeneous committee with a conservative chairman and wide remit could be expected to take months, if not years, to report, and would be unlikely to recommend radical action. This is indeed what happened. The Macmillan Committee, known after its chairman, H. P. Macmillan, a Scottish law lord, deliberated for over a year before producing a lengthy report that did little more than describe Britain's predicament.

Meanwhile, another option, namely external restrictions on trade, dominated debate within the Cabinet and the country as a whole.[67] During the general election in May 1929 the Conservative party, still divided over trade policy, failed to offer a decisive lead. But after its defeat, the press baron Lord Beaverbrook, seized the initiative by launching a campaign for Empire Free Trade. Baldwin, the party leader, and Neville Chamberlain, its leading economic expert, refused to endorse the campaign. But as the slump intensified, even the stoutest defenders of free trade in Manchester and the City of London acknowledged the need for some change of policy. And with the Dominions pressing Britain for a lead, it seemed only a matter of time before the Tories turned to Imperial protectionism. The Labour government seemed more firmly wedded to free trade, which nicely complemented its internationalist aspirations. But by the spring of 1930 divisions appeared within the TUC and the government itself. Thomas, having become the Dominions secretary, openly agitated for a change of direction, and

Graham, the president of the Board of Trade and hitherto a convinced free trader, acknowledged that the magnitude of the slump demanded exceptional action. MacDonald, the prime minister, having no strong views on economic policy, was prepared to acquiesce. But when Snowden threatened to resign rather than accept protectionism, MacDonald dropped the issue rather than face him down.

The government remained preoccupied with the slump, but having practically ruled out unilateral domestic or external action, the only alternative was to pursue collective international action on trade, finance or monetary reform. Here the government was in an enviably strong position, since it enjoyed the interested friendship of a great many countries of the world. The United States had recently surpassed Britain as the world's largest exporter, but Britain was still the world's largest trading nation, taking imports and exports together. Equally important, it possessed far and away the largest visible trade deficit in the world, in 1929 importing a staggering 67 per cent more than it exported.[68] Contemporaries generally regarded the deficit as a sign of Britain's economic weakness. Yet, as indicated in Table 5.1, it constituted an important source of political strength, for it meant that many countries depended critically upon access to the British market to keep their own accounts in balance. Britain also had the attraction of the

Table 5.1 Britain's importance as an import market for selected countries in 1929

Country	Britain's rank as import market	Percentage of exports going to Britain	Value of exports (minus re-exports) going to Britain (£ millions)	Surplus on visible trade with Britain (£ millions)
Germany	1st	9.7	55.8	29.3
France	1st	15.1	52.8	21.2
Belgium	1st	18.2	43.2	23.8
Switzerland	2nd	13.7	12.6	6.2
Italy	3rd	9.9	15.7	−0.3
Czechoslovakia	4th	7.6	6.3	4.2
Denmark	1st	59.6	55.8	45.1
Netherlands	2nd	20.5	41.5	19.7
Finland	1st	38.0	14.8	11.4
Norway	1st	26.8	13.6	3.7
Sweden	1st	25.2	25.3	14.8
Poland	4th	10.3	6.8	2.3
Greece	4th	11.8	2.4	−2.5
Spain	2nd	18.9	18.3	6.2
Portugal	1st	23.4	3.8	0.2
United States	1st	17.0	184.0	138.4
Russia/USSR	1st	29.0	23.1	19.4
Egypt	1st	43.0	21.5	12.6
China	1st	18.2	9.7	−4.4
Japan	1st	19.0	8.2	−5.3

Source: UK *PP*, 1932, Cmd. 3991, 'Statistical Abstract for the United Kingdom', tables 231, 232, pp. 322–3, 326–7; Liepmann, *Tariff Levels and the Economic Unity of Europe*, pp. 206, 245 and passim; LN, *Monthly Bulletin of Statistics*, vol. XIV, no. 1 (Jan. 1933), table V, pp. 14–17.

City of London, which was still the largest international financial market in the world and practically the sole source of monetary gold for other countries. Third, Britain was one of the greatest 'have' powers, with a navy second to none and the capacity to project its power to Continental Europe and much of the rest of the world. Had the government been prepared to exploit these advantages in a vigorous, coordinated way, it might well have been able to carry most countries with it in measures to alleviate the slump if not to overcome it altogether. But it seemed to have learned nothing from recent history.

In the first place, most contemporary observers agreed that dismay at the pace of American economic expansion and its pending tariff increase had been the trigger for the global wave of protectionist action that began in the summer of 1929. The British government nevertheless demanded that the rest of the world should do nothing to annoy the United States, and rigidly defended the most-favoured-nation principle in its most unconditional form. This practically ruled out a reversal of the protectionist trend until or unless the United States agreed to join in, which self-evidently was not about to happen. Second, progress on trade liberalization in the 1920s had been slow, in large part because many countries remained nervous of the implications for national security of opening their markets too far. The Labour government nevertheless approached international economic reform and international security as wholly discrete issues. As might have been predicted, this made progress on either front practically impossible.

MacDonald's handling of Anglo-American relations and naval disarmament vividly illustrated the shortcomings of this piecemeal approach. Under the previous Tory government, apprehension at the spectre of American world financial and economic domination had led to a serious deterioration in Anglo-American relations. In 1927, ill-prepared negotiations to extend the Washington Five-Power Treaty to cruisers, submarines and other auxiliary ships had left each power suspecting the other of aggressive ambitions. Relations worsened the following year upon news of a Franco-British *modus vivendi* on disarmament, which intensified American suspicions of British deceit, and by the autumn of 1928 even conservative broadsheets such as the *Times* spoke of the possibility of conflict between the two powers.[69] MacDonald, on taking office in June 1929, made it his top priority to re-establish close relations with the United States by resolving the naval disarmament issue. At the Washington conference in 1922, Britain had conceded parity to the United States in capital ships, the agreed tonnage ratios being 5 for Britain and the United States, 3 for Japan, and 1.5 for France and Italy. MacDonald now agreed that parity should also apply to cruisers, the auxiliary class now at the top of the agenda. This left unresolved the question of individual ship displacement and weaponry, and for the balance of the summer differences between British and American naval experts threatened to block a settlement. MacDonald, however, continued to yield ground, and with the American Administration predisposed to compromise, the gap narrowed to the point where he volunteered to travel to Washington to reach a settlement. President Hoover, suspicious of Europeans, was far from keen to entertain a British prime minister, but could see no way to refuse.[70] MacDonald therefore boarded the *Berengaria* at Southampton on 28 September, reached New York on 4 October where he was accorded a 19-gun salute and a ticker tape parade, then travelled by train to Washington. Two days of informal conversations with Hoover at his rustic retreat on the Rapidan River in western Virginia produced little result. Both men, however, were pleased to be hailed by the press as crusaders for peace, and agreed that MacDonald should convene a five-power conference in the New Year, to sustain the momentum for naval disarmament.[71]

Preoccupied with maintaining Imperial communications and the sea-lanes of international commerce, British statesmen made their primary objective a settlement acceptable to the United States, the one power capable of mounting an overwhelming challenge to Britain's Imperial and world role. The same preoccupations obliged them to bear in mind Japanese ambitions in the Pacific and ensure that mutual Anglo-American reductions did not result in increasing Japanese naval predominance in the East. MacDonald, who personally led the British delegation at the London naval conference, which opened in the Royal Gallery of the House of Lords on 21 January 1930, therefore concentrated his efforts upon a three-power agreement, and was elated when on 2 April Tokyo finally accepted an Anglo-American formula granting Japan 70 per cent of British and American auxiliary tonnage.[72] Until the conference began, he had assumed that once the three great naval powers reached agreement, France and Italy would fall into line and accept the same ratio for auxiliary ships they had accepted in the 1922 Five-Power Treaty. Dino Grandi, the Italian foreign minister, assured him of his country's willingness to do so, whatever the sacrifices this required. But to British anger and frustration, the French delegation led by Tardieu and Briand refused the terms offered to them of auxiliary tonnage merely 30 per cent of the British or American total and the same as Italy's, which to France with its extra coastline to defend and extensive Imperial commitments meant grave inferiority in the Mediterranean.

MacDonald and British officials should not have been surprised at French obstruction. During the previous autumn, the French had signalled their dissatisfaction with the British decision to push ahead with naval disarmament without regard for its relationship to military disarmament and security. They also made utterly clear their unwillingness to cooperate in any such British initiative unless their sacrifice of naval strength was compensated by British support for a Mediterranean mutual assistance pact as well as some more general security commitment.[73] British statesmen, however, had ignored these warnings in their impatience to settle with the Americans. Indeed, unlike their Tory predecessors, they neither consulted the French nor even allowed them to know what they were discussing with Washington.[74]

The crisis began on 12 February 1930, when the French delegation presented its requirements for auxiliary ship tonnage, which actually exceeded the levels accepted by Britain and the United States. This was partly for bargaining purposes, but it was also because French authorities had chosen to rely mainly upon cruisers and submarines rather than capital ships to meet their particular naval requirements. They had two separate coasts to defend and Imperial interests almost as far-flung as Britain's. They also had an increasingly unstable neighbour in Italy, which if conceded naval parity would be capable of threatening France's communication lines with Algeria, its most important overseas possession. Briand, who led the French delegation to the conference, was as charming and nimble as ever, eschewing confrontation and indicating his readiness to consider any reasonable offer on security. Stimson initially ruled out any American contribution to a settlement with France.[75] Briand, however, skilfully drew him into the negotiations by candidly explaining his predicament. By 23 March, Stimson reversed his position so far as to advise Hoover that the United States should be prepared at least to participate in a consultative security pact.[76] Hoover flatly rejected the suggestion.[77] But the French had never hoped for anything substantial from the United States: it was British support their cooperation depended upon. In Stimson's words, 'what they desired and must have, if they were to reduce their program, was a treaty of mutual assistance with Britain or at least some amplification or clarification of Britain's existing obligations under the League of Nations Covenant.'[78]

Within the British camp, Henderson and senior Foreign Office officials favoured some concession to the French.[79] MacDonald, however, would have none of it, and fell back on racial stereotyping to explain and condemn French obstruction. On 12 February he wrote in his diary, 'France becomes the peace problem of Europe. Mentality is purely militarist. Problem is, will France allow Europe to disarm?' Two days later he returned to the French mind: 'It thinks in guns & bayonets.'[80] To MacDonald, it seemed reasonable for Britain and its Anglo-Saxon cousin across the Atlantic to have navies substantially larger than any other navies in the world, but wholly unreasonable for France to seek a margin of security in face of an increasingly uncontrollable Germany and a menacingly unpredictable Italy. France, after all, was a militaristic nation whose treachery had been demonstrated before the War when Grey was drawn into offering informal military and naval commitments and France had taken advantage of them to provoke a war with the Central Powers.[81] MacDonald supplemented this critique by a general condemnation of the old diplomacy of alliances and balance of power as a recipe for war. But there was no gainsaying his Francophobia or his belief that Britain could remain outside any future European conflict. This was vividly illustrated by his account of his private dinner with Briand on 18 March, as recorded by Stimson:

> He [MacDonald] said France wants to be the biggest military power in Europe and wishes to be able to fight any two nations in Europe successfully and rather expects to fight Italy and Germany. Furthermore, France has now planned to be the economic center of Europe, shaping her development for that purpose. He said he had told Briand that the attitude of France at the Conference meant war and that they were headed straight for it and that Briand agreed and said he was much worried over it. The Prime Minister said he had also told Briand that Great Britain would give no pact of military assistance, saying that the only pact that Great Britain would give was 'only how to keep the peace and not how to fight other nations after they broke the peace.'[82]

At the close of the conference on 22 April, Britain, the United States and Japan agreed to be bound by a 5:5:3.5 ratio on auxiliary ships from 1931 to December 1936, and all five participating powers endorsed supplementary agreements suspending battleship construction and restricting submarine construction and submarine warfare for the same period. MacDonald was thus able to claim that the conference was at least a partial success, a verdict accepted in Britain by all but Churchill and a handful of conservative critics.[83] The effect of treating disarmament without regard to security, however, was far from beneficial for Britain. The decision practically to halt naval construction seriously handicapped Britain when Japan and Germany expanded shipbuilding in the next few years.[84] The conference also deepened the gulf between Britain and Continental Europe by intensifying British prejudice against France and hence against a Continental commitment. The consequence of this approach only became fully evident towards the end of the decade. But it should be remembered that Briand and his colleagues had done their best before the conference to warn British colleagues of the risks they took. That they failed to penetrate the wall of prejudice was not for want of trying.

In the summer of 1929, almost every large trading nation in the world protested to Washington against Congressional plans to intensify American tariff protection. The only exception was Britain, where ministers resisted pressure to join in the protest on account of MacDonald's initiative to improve Anglo-American relations.[85] Just this once, they treated trade within a broader framework of foreign policy, but in September they reverted to form. That month, Britain was represented for the first time at the League of Nations by an economics minister, when Graham joined the delegation to the Tenth Assembly in Geneva. Graham seized upon the Belgian proposal for a tariff truce and, supported by Belgian and French delegates, he secured its approval by the League Assembly. As a token of his commitment to trade liberalization, he also personally attended the first tariff truce conference when it opened in February 1930. By now, leading Tories and spokesmen for business were loudly demanding trade protection, and Graham faced strong pressure to avoid tying Britain's hands in a tariff truce. He still hoped that foreign delegates would cooperate in the tariff truce and subsequent trade liberalization out of fear that if they did not, Britain might abandon free trade and turn towards its Empire partners.[86] But only the European states sent fully accredited delegates to the conference, and they could not be persuaded to tie their hands as Graham wanted, so long as the Soviet Union, the British Dominions and above all the United States reserved the right to raise their import barriers. Graham therefore had no choice but to accept Flandin's modest formula, enjoining signatories to restrain their tariff revision while maintaining a vague opening for subsequent negotiations on trade liberalization.

This was a far cry from the decisive action Graham originally imagined to be possible. The British delegation itself faced accusations of backsliding, when it requested an exception to the agreement for Britain's so-called revenue duties.[87] As the result of sharply falling tax revenues, Snowden had been obliged to abandon his commitment to eliminate revenue duties, which fell largely on the British breakfast table: taxes on tea, coffee, cocoa, sugar and dried fruit as well as tobacco, wine and spirits, which had yielded fully £117 million to the exchequer in 1929. British delegates in Geneva defended the retention of revenue duties with the old argument that they had no protective function since they were levied on British-produced goods as well as imports. But other delegations regarded this as disingenuous since Britain itself produced almost none of the goods concerned, and three-quarters of the revenue duties (in value) included a substantial preference for imports from the British Empire.[88] Britain's own claim to be contributing to trade liberalization was thus compromised.

Before the hoped-for negotiations on trade liberalization could begin, Britain confronted another European initiative when Briand circulated his memorandum on a European federal union. The plan faced opposition from the self-styled 'have-not' powers such as Germany, Hungary and Italy, and general suspicion of French motives, which appears in retrospect to have doomed it in advance. But it should not be forgotten that throughout Europe in the spring of 1930 there was intense interest in some means of alleviating the economic slump, which was devastating national economies, and that Britain was uniquely placed to influence the European response to Briand's plan.[89] In the event, Britain refused to endorse the plan, which thereafter survived only in token form. But in view of the magnitude of the issues at stake, it is worth pausing to consider the motives of British diplomats and politicians for rejecting the first comprehensive approach to Europe's political and economic crisis.

By May 1930, the idea of European integration, if still remote from the mass of people, had attracted the support of a sizeable fraction of the Continent's business and political elite.[90] Yet remarkably, even at this time the clerks of the Foreign Office and their diplomatic colleagues abroad seemed only half aware of the European movement. One reason for their ignorance derived from the institutional constraints upon the Foreign Office's treatment of economic issues. Since Victorian times, the blue bloods of the Foreign Office had been accused of disdaining the vulgar world of trade. If once true, it was much less so after the turn of the century. Nevertheless the Office had found itself marginalized after the Great War, when a host of new economic issues such as reparations and war debts, international monetary reform, the recrudescence of quantitative trade controls and the need for new trade treaties, prompted the Treasury, the Board of Trade, the Dominions Office (from 1925) and other departments of state to insist upon reserving aspects of external relations for themselves. The Foreign Office sought but failed to secure a coordinating role in external policy-making. As a result, its officials were largely excluded from postwar reconstruction initiatives and severely hampered in their grasp of the economic forces that provided the chief impetus of the European movement.[91] Thus, for instance, they seem to have been unaware of the creation in 1925 of the Mayrisch committee, bringing together leading businessmen from France, Germany, Belgium and Luxembourg. Nor did they make anything of the establishment of the

European Steel Cartel in September 1926 or the adoption of the Franco-German commercial treaty in August 1927, or follow the intense debate over the application of the most-favoured-nation principle in Europe after the 1927 World Economic Conference.[92]

Their ignorance was evident in July 1929 when reports reached London of Briand's intention to speak at Geneva on European federation. Questions were asked in Parliament as to Britain's attitude, and Henderson requested a brief on the subject. After a careful search of the diplomatic correspondence and memoranda, the Foreign Office Library reported that to date no serious proposals for European political or economic integration had been made.

> A number of suggestions of this nature have, it is true, been brought to the notice of the department, but chiefly in the form of pamphlets or from idealistic individuals or 'one man' societies, and have neither official backing nor, apparently, any practical bases.[93]

The only 'European' organization that the Foreign Office knew of was Coudenhove-Kalergi's Pan-Europa Society. The fact that it was 'financed almost entirely by the friends of M. Coudenhove and can barely pay its way', amply summed up the feebleness of the movement as a whole, the Foreign Office concluded.[94] Briand's speech to the League Assembly in September did little to alert the Office to developments. Even in May 1930, neither Sir Horace Rumbold, the British ambassador in Berlin, nor his colleagues in London appeared to know much about Coudenhove-Kalergi and his organization.[95]

The more fundamental reason for the Foreign Office officials' decision to disregard the European movement, however, was that it made no sense within their perception of postwar Europe. As they saw it, Continental Europe was simply too divided and France too powerful and aggressive for integration to become a reality. Sir Robert Vansittart, the permanent under-secretary, made this the theme of his first 'Old Adam' memorandum on 1 May 1930, in which he warned the Cabinet of the recrudescence of aggressive nationalism in Europe. He was confident that Germany, especially since Stresemann took over the direction of its foreign affairs in 1924, was reconciled to its place in Europe and scarcely a problem. Britain too had done its part in promoting the appeasement of Europe through the League of Nations and support for disarmament. But France, driven by its exaggerated claims for security, seemed bent upon stirring up trouble with its provocative military alliances, financial subsidies to foreign powers and inflated demands upon Germany. In Vansittart's words,

> It might have been hoped that the adoption by Germany of the policy of 'fulfilment', especially her recognition of the cession of Alsace-Lorraine as definitive, and the steady progress in the general pacification and stabilization of Europe during the last 10 years, would have convinced France that her fears were exaggerated, and that she was safe enough to throw off this hankering for 'Balance of Power'.[96]

Instead, Vansittart and his colleagues believed that France was persisting in its bid for hegemony. They therefore refused to accept at face value reports of French interest in integrating Europe through peaceful, consensual means.

In March 1928 they had reacted sceptically when Jacques Seydoux, the recently retired diplomat and intimate of Poincaré, appealed in the *Times* for Britain to participate in European affairs. Seydoux pointed out that France had recently taken great risks in integrating its economy with Germany's by means of the new commercial treaty. But, he added, if *rapprochement* between France and Germany were to be carried further, Britain must play its part.

> France and Germany cannot do without Great Britain; but Great Britain needs them both. The peace of Europe and of the world demands that any Franco-German entente on the economic plane should have as its corollary a still closer entente between France and Great Britain; for if France desires to be on good terms with Germany, she desires to be on still better terms – on better terms than ever – with Great Britain.[97]

Foreign Office officials seemed unable to appreciate that the 'liquidation of the war' was making France so insecure as to contemplate active leadership of the European movement. Instead, they assumed that behind French appeals for British participation there must be a hidden motive. As Orme Sargent commented on Seydoux's article, 'Mr. Seydoux tries to make our flesh creep. ... He tries to frighten us with the bogey of isolation, but it may well be that this isolation, if it materializes, will be more dangerous to France than to Germany.'[98] Briand's plan to speak on European federation evoked a similar reaction. Ralph Wigram, the chargé in Paris, suggested that it was a ploy to persuade French socialists to support ratification of the war debt agreements when they came to the vote in Parliament that month.[99] Shortly after Briand spoke at Geneva in September, Sargent again speculated on the hidden motives behind his proposal.

> I should be glad to think that this sudden enthusiasm of the French for the idea of Pan-Europa represents only an attempt to protect Europe against eventual economic pressure. I am not at all sure, however, that in the present circumstances it may not in the eyes of the French have the additional merit of affording a means of impressing on this country its economic, if not political, dependence on the Continent of Europe.[100]

Even in the early months of 1930 the Foreign Office was still urging Lord Tyrrell in Paris to identify the 'real' reason behind Briand's initiative.[99] And in May, when Briand's memorandum arrived with the emphasis shifted from economic to political action, officials felt justified in speculating about 'what lies behind the proposals'.[101]

Briand's speech at Geneva in September 1929 and subsequent reports of Edouard Herriot's speaking tour around Europe on the same theme belatedly stirred Foreign Office officials to consider Britain's interest in the European movement.

The librarian, Sir Stephen Gaselee, doubted that the idea was practicable, but suggested that it might serve as a warning to Washington that Europe would not tolerate becoming steadily more dependent upon American capital and goods.

> I think of Pan-Europa as analogous to Fascism. Fascism is not desirable in itself, but serves as a warning against pushing liberalism to extremes. So Pan-Europa is not to be desired *per se*, but in the event of the United States adopting certain policies, and proceeding to certain extremes, Pan-Europa would be a valuable menace to be held up to Washington *in terrorem*.

It should be seen therefore as essentially a gesture or protest. But in any case Britain, being a non-European power, could stand outside a squabble between Europe and the United States.

> We should be in the happy position of the *tertius gaudens*: we could either associate ourselves (though not too closely) with Pan-Europa, or retire to a British Empire equally remote from Europe and America.[102]

Two officials in the American Department dissented from this view. Aware of the tremendous expansion of American capital and commercial exports, and more keenly alive to America's influence upon the rest of the world, they doubted that Britain could simply retire behind the Empire's walls, if the world coalesced into a handful of large economic blocs. As G. H. Thompson put it,

> I am rather apprehensive that...we should find ourselves between the devil and the deep sea. Canada is certainly not remote from the United States, whose economic power in the Dominion is growing daily, and I cannot see the Canadians cutting themselves off from their dear brother to the South. Progress towards the goal of a European economic union seems to me to hold out some hope of maintaining ourselves against the Colossus of the West.[103]

His colleague, T. M. Snow, agreed:

> The great risk to us in this country would be that, through inability to make up our minds definitely to join the European group, or by aspiring to some such disastrous role as the 'interpreter of America to Europe', we might end by falling between two stools. A system of European cartels, *in which we participated*, is very likely the only alternative to the swallowing up by America, one after the other, of the markets of all the European countries, beginning with our own.[104]

However, this remained a minority view within the Foreign Office. Charles Howard Smith and Alan Leeper of the Western and League of Nations Department were prepared to believe that the American economic challenge would eventually force Europe into forming an economic and even a political bloc. Yet they held that the Empire would always be more important for Britain than a European federation. Since a European federation might close Britain off from Continental trade, the only question was whether Britain should try to block its development now or allow it to continue for the time being.[105]

Upon the arrival of Briand's memorandum, the Foreign Office proposed a friendly albeit non-committal reply, largely for Briand's own sake. Perhaps, as Leeper warned, Britain might eventually have to choose between entering a European federation and remaining at the head of the Empire. But for the foreseeable future this seemed unlikely, since Italy and Germany, 'who are far more directly concerned', could be counted on to block the French initiative. This allowed Britain to be politely non-committal and thereby avoid embarrassment to Briand, 'one of the few good "Europeans" in France.'[106] Several of the government's expert advisors, however, found this far too complaisant. Sir Arthur Salter of the League Economic Section warned Henderson that the League would be damaged beyond repair if Briand's plan were allowed to develop. Salter acknowledged that Europe urgently needed economic integration. 'There is nothing elsewhere comparable to the combination in Europe of advanced industrial development and small tariff units', he wrote. He was prepared to envisage a European committee in the League, along the lines of the Austrian, Hungarian and Greek committees, reporting directly to the Council. But with Europe comprising 'a fifth of the world's population and at least four-fifth's of the League's strength', the creation of independent European institutions would have a doubly deleterious effect upon world stability.

> In the first place, a powerful impetus [would be] given to the organization of the world into a few large groups – Europe, Pan-American, British Empire (with perhaps a Russian Asiatic to follow) – each equipped with an organization absorbing the bulk of the work on practical and current problems.

Second, it would reduce the capacity of the League of Nations to restrain these regional or supranational groups from antagonizing one another.

> There would be a conflict between the regional and central [institutions] in which the latter would constantly tend to be weaker. More and more the League would tend, both in economic problems and in questions involving dangers of war, to come in at a later, and too late a stage. We should have, more remotely but ultimately on a larger scale, the same kind of danger which comes from 'alliances' endangering the League's overriding authority.[107]

Salter's association of voluntary European integration with a return to military alliances and global conflict evidently struck a cord with ministers. A few days later, Philip Noel-Baker, the former LSE professor of international relations, now a junior minister in the Foreign Office, and Lord Robert Cecil, the former Tory minister brought in by Labour as adviser on League of Nations affairs, weighed in with their own warnings against Briand's plan. Noel-Baker affirmed in words similar to Salter's that Britain had 'the greatest possible interest, both material and political, in helping to secure closer co-operation by European countries'. But he agreed that the machinery Briand proposed for Europe constituted a serious threat to the League of Nations.[108] Cecil warned that the danger went further. If Europe were allowed to become organized, he wrote, it would stimulate the development of other large blocs, which would not only be a threat in itself, but would also threaten the destruction of the British Empire. For, in contrast to the territorially coherent blocs that were likely to emerge, the Empire comprised scattered territories which could scarcely resist the pull of regional blocs. Thus, if Briand's plan for Europe got off the ground,

> It would add strength to the Pan-European movement and might increase the Asiatic feeling which already exists. World groups of that kind outside the League would be a menace to peace. They would also cause the greatest difficulties to the British Empire. I know that some people like Mr. Amery have a dream of a British Empire group which could be independent of the rest of the world. I see no prospect of such a result. He and others seem to think that Great Britain could divorce herself from Europe. Why? She has been culturally, economically and politically part of Europe for many centuries and still is. ...
>
> But even if we kept out of a European group could Canada hold aloof from an American or India from an Asiatic group? It seems very doubtful. The British Empire would be part of all these groups geographically and economically and their existence without the coordinating system of the League would be a seriously disintegrating influence on the Empire.[109]

In short, Britain's status as a great power required the maintenance of the Empire, which in turn required it to insist upon liberal internationalism in the political and economic spheres – and opposition to European integration.

Cecil's brief as well as Salter's contained glaring contradictions, which should have been evident to the most casual reader. Salter endorsed the principle of regionalism within the League, along with the acknowledgement that Europe must emulate the United States by forging a single internal market commensurate with the imperatives of modern mass-production industry. Yet he described preferential arrangements within Europe, the essential first step towards such a single market, as a provocation to the other regions and hence to be resisted by the League. Nonetheless, he asserted that regional action through the League remained possible, citing the recent tariff truce conference as an example of what could be done. As he pointed out, the conference had become an exclusively European affair not from any desire on the part of the Europeans for separate action, but simply because only European countries had accepted the invitation to participate. Yet it had produced an agreement on tariff action approved by 23 European countries. Salter, however, could hardly have chosen a more unfortunate illustration, since the agreement reached was notoriously weak *precisely* because the overseas countries had refused to cooperate with Europe while demanding to share in any concessions agreed within Europe on account of their most-favoured-nation rights.

Cecil's brief was marked by a similar contradiction. According to his critique, regional blocs or federations including a united Europe were undesirable because they had the potential to become successful and would threaten the destruction of the ramshackle British Empire, which was evidently a desirable institution but had less potential for success. Henderson nevertheless accepted these warnings and requested his Foreign Office advisers to bear them in mind in preparing a much more severely qualified reply to Briand's memorandum.[111]

The Foreign Office received enquiries from practically every other country in Europe, wishing to know how Britain intended to reply. 'Opinion in most countries realises that the attitude of His Majesty's Government will be decisive', one official commented.[112] Until the government took a decision, British envoys could not express a definite view, but they left little doubt that Britain disliked Briand's plan.[113] In Paris on 24 June, Tardieu, the premier, appealed to Lord Tyrrell for a positive reply. In Tardieu's words, the 'grave economic crisis which the whole of Europe was facing' made close cooperation between Britain, France and Germany essential.[114] Two days later, however, Henderson suggested that Britain might postpone any reply until Briand's proposal could be considered further at the League Assembly in September.[115] Briand frantically appealed for a reply by the 15 July deadline, since he was committed to report Europe's views to the Assembly. '[He] quite understood [Henderson's] difficulties as Great Britain occupied a very peculiar position in the world, and especially with regard to Europe, as she was of Europe and yet outside it.' But at the minimum he needed confirmation of Britain's sympathetic interest. If Henderson would offer this, he promised an exchange of views at Geneva and a commitment 'not to do anything except in agreement with you.'[116]

Tyrrell, exceptionally among senior British diplomats, favoured closer relations with France, and he appealed personally several times to Henderson to heed Tardieu's and Briand's requests.[117] The next item on Germany's list of revisionist aims, he wrote, was the Eastern frontier. France did not underestimate the difficulty of resolving it, but

> So far as French opinion is concerned, it is through a federated Europe alone that its peaceful solution seems even conceivable. To me this is the real importance of the 'scheme', and the chief reason why nothing should be done to discourage it.[118]

It was no use. Henderson put the second, essentially negative, reply to a Cabinet committee on 14 July. Two days later – after the deadline set by Briand for replies – the Cabinet perfunctorily approved Henderson's draft, whereupon it was handed to the French Ambassador.[119]

With all the replies now received, Briand prepared his report for the Eleventh League Assembly. Putting the best face on it, he asserted that as no country had actually rejected his plan, the League should authorize him to continue his work.[120] But this was futile as well as disingenuous. For the time being, Europe would not willingly organize without Britain. And Britain would not allow Europe to organize since it threatened to compromise Britain's Imperial and global role. Economic and security problems would have to worsen substantially before either was prepared to reconsider its position.

5.4   Missed opportunities for international monetary reform, 1929–31

In 1929 high interest rates prompted criticism of the gold standard on an unprecedented scale in Britain and deep unease elsewhere. This had enabled Sir Henry Strakosch to overcome opposition from central bankers to the League Gold Delegation enquiry into undue fluctuations in the purchasing power of gold, which began in August of that year. The Macmillan Committee on Finance and Industry began its deliberations in November, and the following month an informal study group comprising prominent City bankers, Treasury officials, economists and leading City editors held the first of several meetings at Chatham House to consider the working of the international monetary system. Ever since then, economists have singled out the gold standard as a major contributor to the world slump. Yet, up to this time the problem was not so much the monetary mechanism but its management: constraints of an essentially political nature upon cooperation among the major central banks. After the slump began, new opportunities for cooperation arose. But once again political obstacles stood in their way.

In 1929, the United States faced widespread foreign criticism for allowing the Wall Street boom to endanger world economic stability by driving up interest rates and diverting loanable funds into speculative activity. But in Britain mounting criticism was also directed at France for aggravating the weakness of the pound sterling by disposing of its foreign exchange balances to build up the Bank of France's gold reserves. By the winter of 1929, the French authorities had become acutely aware of the criticism.[121] There was little they could do to counter the elaborate conspiracy theories popularized by Paul Einzig of the *Financial News* and *The Banker*, George Glasgow of *The Observer*, Francis Williams of the *Daily Herald* and others, who charged that France had deliberately drained gold from London the previous summer to force the British government to accept an unfavourable reparation settlement.[122] In fact, French authorities had never contemplated attacking sterling, and to an impartial observer it should have been obvious they had not done so, since at the same time as sterling fell below gold export point against the franc it also fell sharply against the Dutch florin, Swiss franc and other currencies. Nonetheless they accepted that simply 'sterilizing' gold at the Bank of France while the rest of the world endured a severe economic slump was bound to seem avaricious and destructive. They therefore sought to use their gold reserves as the basis for expanded short- and long-term foreign lending.

The Bank of France did what it could to facilitate the revival of foreign lending by reducing its discount rate from 3.5 to 3 per cent on 31 January 1930 and to 2.5 per cent on 1 May, and fostering the operations of a fledgling acceptance market.[123] The Ministry of Finance also assisted by removing the discriminatory element in the tax on foreign interest payments (25 per cent versus 18 per cent on domestic interest payments) and reducing the stamp tax on foreign loan issues.[124] Largely as a result of these inducements, French foreign lending in 1930 reached 2133 million francs, more than double the volume of new lending in 1929 and over three times that of 1928. But even then, the portfolio of French foreign loans amounted to little more than 80,000 million francs (£655 million), which adjusted for inflation was a small fraction of the total reached in 1914.[125] French authorities also faced two obstacles they were virtually powerless to overcome. One was the conservatism of French lenders, who had still not recovered from the devastating losses incurred on prewar loans to Soviet Russia and elsewhere in Eastern Europe. The other was the rapid deterioration in the international economic and political climate. With trade dwindling, Latin American republics bankrupt, Mussolini issuing belligerent threats and the Nazis and Communists competing for control of Germany, eligible foreign borrowers were becoming increasingly scarce.

Between September 1929 and the spring of 1930, the continuing gap in interest rates between London and Paris and the decline in money movements to New York after the Wall Street Crash enabled the Bank of England to keep sterling above gold export point and rebuild its metallic reserves. From a perilously low £131.7 million, the Bank's metallic reserves rose to a relatively comfortable £163.6 million by April 1930. But hardly had the directors agreed to reduce Bank rate to 3 per cent on 1 May when sterling again slumped below gold export point on the sterling-franc exchange. Thereafter scarcely a week passed without gold flowing to Paris. In 1929 French gold reserves had increased by £45 million. In 1930 they increased by another £110 million, bringing the total by the end of the year to a massive £450 million, three times those of Britain.[126] City editors loudly complained of hoarding, and several confidently asserted that France was accumulating gold for political ends aimed directly or indirectly against Britain.[127] Once again, nothing could have been further from the truth. Both the Bank of France and successive French governments ardently sought closer cooperation with their British counterparts.[128] This became evident after the German Reichstag election on 14 September 1930.

In the Reichstag election of May 1928, held when the German economy was still relatively strong, the parties of the extreme Left and Right had done poorly: the Communists (KPD) obtained 54 seats, the Nazis (NSDAP) a mere 12, and together they gained only 14 per cent of the popular vote. Now in 1930, with unemployment soaring above 3 million and the budget deficit threatening to undermine currency stability and revive the nightmare of hyperinflation, the two parties received 33 per cent of the vote, with the KPD obtaining 77 seats and the NSDAP 107 seats, making it the second largest party in the Reichstag. The results sent a shock wave through the financial markets, causing a flight of capital from Germany and a general shift into liquid balances. For fully 12 months Hitler and his Nationalist allies had dwelt upon the reparation question, using it to explain the slump and accusing the Bruening government of permitting the Western powers to 'enslave' the German people through the Young plan. Since practically all Germans agreed upon the injustice of the Versailles settlement, Bruening was thrown on the defensive and adopted a similarly hostile attitude towards reparations. Germany, he indicated, would not tolerate the burden indefinitely.

The French authorities did not react. Instead they sought to steady the markets by encouraging French commercial banks to maintain their credits in Germany and even increase them.[129] Tardieu, the premier, personally sought to persuade the banks to participate in the loan to Germany arranged by the New York investment bank, Lee Higginson. Meanwhile they looked to Britain to join France in deterring Germany from unilaterally suspending reparation payments, or if that happened to approach the United States together for a cessation of war debt demands.[130] Despite evidence of France's keen interest in cooperation, the British authorities drew back.

In June 1930, the League of Nations Gold Delegation met briefly for a second time since its establishment the previous summer. Strakosch, having almost single-handedly initiated the enquiry, now pressed for a strongly worded report that advocated coordinated action by the major central banks to halt the decline in world price levels. Several other delegates, notably Sir Reginald Mant of South Africa and Professor Gustav Cassel of Sweden, supported him, but Oliver Sprague, the Harvard economist and presently adviser to Norman at the Bank of England, disputed Strakosch's thesis that the 'sterilization' of gold was chiefly responsible for the accelerating decline in world price levels and economic activity. With several of the Continental delegates also lined up against him, Strakosch agreed to limit the report to an analysis of the prospective supply and demand for gold within the international monetary system. Convinced of the need for action, however, he proceeded to insert the core of his argument into the draft. Among other things, it asserted a clear link between gold supplies and price levels, and directly criticized the United States and France for vastly increasing their gold reserves without correspondingly increasing their money supply or credit. It also proposed several means of economizing the use of monetary gold, such as the elimination of gold coinage, the concentration of gold holdings at the central banks, international agreement on the reduction of legal reserve minima and the extension of the gold exchange standard to countries that had not yet returned to the gold standard.[131]

Strakosch was pleased with the document and hopeful that if vigorously promoted, the central banks might be persuaded to abandon their neutral stance on credit creation and actively expand liquidity. Eventually they might be brought to accept price-level stability as one of their objectives along with exchange rate stability. He expected American and French central bankers to dislike the report, which came close to linking their accumulation of fully two-thirds of the world's monetary gold to the present world slump. What he did not anticipate was hostility from Norman at the Bank of England and Snowden at the Treasury.[132]

Since 1928, Strakosch had found an ally in Sir Otto Niemeyer, the Treasury knight who had left public service the previous year to become adviser to the Bank of England. At the Treasury, Niemeyer had pressed Churchill unrelentingly to accept an early return to the gold standard, sweeping aside all claims that it would aggravate deflationary pressures on the economy. But on joining the Bank he soon acknowledged the acute pressures that the gold shortages and high exchange rate placed upon the Bank and the British economy, by encouraging Strakosch in his efforts at international monetary reform.[133] Niemeyer, however, spent most of 1930 in Australia, advising the National Reserve Bank on monetary and financial reforms, and without his forceful presence at Threadneedle Street, Norman maintained his opposition to Strakosch's work in the Gold Delegation. Thus on 28 August, Strakosch received a dusty reception when he called at the Bank to enlist Norman's support. Sprague had resigned from the Gold Delegation on taking up his temporary post at the Bank of England, and Strakosch urged Norman to request him to rejoin it to enhance its credibility in the United States. Norman pretended there was nothing he could do, claiming that Sprague had taken the decision to resign on his own and that it was up to him to rejoin if he wished. Strakosch then urged Norman to give his full and public backing to the Gold Delegation report, and to promote its recommendations at the BIS where central bankers periodically met. Norman claimed not to have read the report, but added that in any case he must 'merge his views' with the other BIS directors.[134] Strakosch impatiently observed that the French and American central bankers scarcely felt it necessary to merge their views with others. When Norman demurred, Strakosch 'complain[ed] vehemently and...bitterly that [the] Gold Committee had been boycotted by [the] Bank of England and flouted or opposed by Central Banks in general.'[135] Nothing he could say, however, would persuade Norman to support his campaign.

As early as 1927, Norman had privately acknowledged the seriousness of the gold problem. In principle, he favoured the establishment of a gold bullion or even a gold specie standard: practically all central bankers did. But since Britain's return to the gold standard in 1925 he was acutely aware of the political obstacles facing central banks that attempted to restore price competitiveness through high interest rates and credit restrictions. Why then did he oppose Strakosch's efforts? The answer is evidently threefold. In the first place, since 1927 when Strakosch began his campaign, Norman feared the adverse publicity that central banks would face if they encouraged the belief that they could halt the downward trend of commodity price levels through collective action, but chose not to do so.[136] The further slump in price levels since 1929 made this objection all the more pertinent.

The second reason was that Norman, particularly at this time, did not wish to compromise the political function of the gold standard as a means of imposing discipline upon governments and in particular the British government. The great problem of a democratic society, in his view, was that the politicians were constantly tempted to 'bribe the electorate with their own money', by undertaking expensive welfare programmes, paid for by taxes on enterprise. To nearly all bankers, financiers, City editors and academic economists, the gold standard was a vital constraint upon overspending. With the gold standard in place, wealth, enterprise and individual freedom were safeguarded; without it, the pressure of the masses would subvert the currency, erode savings and ultimately destroy civilized society itself. In 1930, the discipline of the gold standard seemed more important than ever. Since their first spell in office five years previously, Norman had maintained superficially friendly relations with Snowden, MacDonald and Thomas: Labour party leaders whom he recognized to be almost as conservative as himself. Nonetheless he shared the City's apprehension at the Socialists' return to office in 1929, and after the slump began he became deeply afraid that Labour leaders would give way to the radical element within their party.[137] He was therefore anxious to retain the unfettered operation of the gold standard, and this in turn made it extremely untimely to advertise its shortcomings, as Strakosch seemed intent upon doing. In view of the mounting opposition to the gold standard among industrialists as well as left-wing critics, this was playing with fire in a dangerously combustible building.

The third reason for Norman's opposition derived from his commitment to the City of London. For practically the whole of his adult life he had worked in the City, entering it before the war when its world supremacy was unchallenged and regarding it still as the financial basis of Britain's world power. But he equated the City's fate with the prestige of the pound and feared that Strakosch's initiative would merely highlight the precariousness of sterling. Like nearly all his City colleagues, he favoured Anglo-American solidarity. He was an Atlanticist or more accurately an Anglo-Saxon supremacist. For while he looked to the United States as a partner in the direction of the international monetary system, he also looked upon Germany as Britain's natural ally in Europe and deeply sympathized with its efforts to escape from reparations and other constraints imposed by the Treaty of Versailles. By the same token, he had become intensely annoyed at the Bank of France's extraordinary build-up of gold, which created the spectre of French hegemony on the Continent. Here was another reason for opposing Strakosch's initiative, since it meant implicitly acknowledging sterling's weakness and the need for cooperation with France. While watching hopefully for signs of American cooperation, he preferred to see Britain adapting to falling price levels by making the unilateral domestic adjustments required to keep its economy competitive. He made no reference to his political motives in his encounter with Strakosch or his interviews with the Macmillan Committee. But they became gradually more evident in the autumn of 1930, when a new opportunity for cooperation with France arose.

On 24 September, ten days after the Reichstag election, Briand warned Flandin, the minister of finance, that the constant drain of gold from London to Paris was antagonizing British opinion and obstructing political cooperation.[138] Ministry of Finance officials had no time for British claims that the accumulation of monetary gold in Paris was proof of the malfunctioning of the gold standard, and that France must expand its domestic money supply and foreign lending to ease the plight of countries losing gold. In their view, France was playing by the rules of the gold standard game: secondary influences apart, gold had moved to Paris because the French economy was internationally competitive and investors were confident the French authorities would do what was necessary to maintain the franc at par. It was not France but Britain that refused to accept the rules, by failing to apply the fiscal and financial restraints needed to restore its international competitiveness, and also by continuing to lend abroad on a scale no longer justified by the country's diminished economic strength.[139] The French authorities therefore sought to address British suspicions through diplomatic channels.[140] When by mid-November this brought no result, Tardieu, the premier, let the Paris correspondent of the *Times* know that he was prepared to find an amicable solution to the problem.[141] The immediate upshot was an informal meeting of Sir Frederick Leith-Ross of the British Treasury and Jacques Rueff, the financial attaché in London, who agreed that parallel discussions should take place between Treasury and central bank officials.[142]

French desire for closer cooperation with Britain became still more evident in the New Year, when British and French officials met to discuss monetary policy. On 2 January 1931, just as the British delegation arrived in Paris for the first round of talks, the Bank of France announced the reduction of its discount rate from 2.5 to 2 per cent. Clément Moret, who had succeeded Moreau as governor of the Bank the previous October, was anxious to halt the continuing gold drain from London to Paris. For two months, on his own initiative, he had been buying sterling as it appeared on the French foreign exchange market, to raise it above gold export point.[143] But the decision to reduce the discount rate went directly against his economic judgement. Only a few weeks earlier he had rejected an appeal from Governor Harrison in New York to reduce interest rates. Indeed, left to his own devices, he would have *raised* his discount rate as a signal to the markets of tougher times ahead.[144] His decision to reduce it came at Briand's request, to improve relations with Britain.[145] As Moret explained to a New York Reserve Bank official, he had acted solely for 'international reasons'.[146]

Several other concessions soon followed. In mid-January the Bank of France agreed to accept gold bars of standard fineness. Since the previous June, the constant demand for gold had left the Bank of England unable to supply bars of the higher standard required by the Bank of France, which resulted in extra cost and delays while bars of standard fineness were further refined after shipment to Paris. This had caused serious embarrassment in November, when French savings banks faced a short-lived run by depositors and found it impossible to withdraw balances in London quickly enough to replenish their cash reserves: an episode that caused them to seek even greater liquidity by shunning London altogether. At that time, the Bank of France had been reluctant to alter its requirements for fear of shaking French confidence in the franc.[147] Moret's decision to do so in January was thus an important gesture of solidarity towards Britain, and not least because it reduced the sterling-franc gold export point from 123.89 to 123.45 francs, which amounted to a small but not insignificant 0.36 per cent franc revaluation.[148]

Since May 1930, British Treasury officials had been urging their French counterparts to reduce their international demand for gold by expanding foreign lending.[149] Ministry of Finance officials assured their British counterparts they were doing everything possible to oblige. They had reduced income tax on foreign loan interest to 18 per cent, about the same level as on domestic loan interest and somewhat lower than in Britain. They had lowered the stamp tax to 1 per cent, half the British rate.[150] They had authorized a relaxation of the rules so that a number of foreign securities – albeit mostly 'kaffirs' or South African gold shares – could be listed on the Paris Bourse.[151] They had opened the French Acceptance Bank. The basic problem was the lack of sound borrowers and investor confidence in France. They were nonetheless twisting arms in the *place de Paris*, trying to persuade French banks to underwrite loans for Roumania, Yugoslavia, Poland and Greece.[152] They had even persuaded French bankers to participate in the recent Lee Higginson credit to the German government, despite the bankers' extreme reluctance to increase their exposure to Germany.[153] France supported the proposal for an International Agricultural Mortgage Corporation to enable the countries of Eastern Europe to avoid distress selling of cereal crops, and it was prepared to consider any other initiative Britain proposed for reviving international lending. The large revenue balances the French state had accumulated at the Treasury and the *Caisse d'Amortissements*, which British officials believed to be a major cause of the recent gold drain to France, were being rapidly run down, thus reducing the gold cover required by the Bank of France. Lastly, they pointed out, France's balance of payments was no longer in surplus; and as it deteriorated, French gold imports were almost bound to decline.[154]

A week later, the French representative on the Gold Delegation dropped his opposition to publication of a second interim report.[155] The recommendations again bore the unmistakable mark of Strakosch's influence. The gold exchange standard was again endorsed, and central banks were called upon to limit their metallic reserves to the minimum required to meet foreign demands rather than as backing for the domestic currency issue. More radically, the report placed the onus for international payments adjustment mainly upon the surplus countries rather than those in deficit, as was now the case. While accepting that countries in payments deficit must be prepared to apply deflationary measures to regain equilibrium, it affirmed that countries in payments surplus had a 'correspondingly greater' obligation to contribute to international stability, by ensuring they maintained capital exports at a level approximating to 'their net active balance on income account.'[156] Managed on these lines, it seems fair to say, the gold standard would have ceased to impose a serious drag on world price levels.

However, while British and French Treasury officials debated the principles of international monetary policy, actual reforms rested with the central banks, and the hoped-for conversations between the Bank of England and Bank of France never took place. On Friday, 5 December, Norman made a courtesy call at *rue de la Vrillière* on his way to the monthly meeting of the BIS board of directors in Bâle, to pay his respects to Moret, the new governor. Moret had been hoping to hear from Norman to discuss means of addressing the crisis.[157] Now that Norman had at last made contact, he suggested a number of ways he might help London: by facilitating the issue of British industrial loans on the Paris market, by rediscounting sterling securities lodged with French banks, perhaps by participation in a major

British government conversion loan.[158] To his surprise, he found Norman polite but strangely reticent.[159]

The absence of central bank conversations stirred rumours of a serious rift between Paris and London. Leopold von Hoesch, the German ambassador in Paris, reported that France had sought to take advantage of sterling's weakness by offering a loan with political conditions, which London had rejected as completely unacceptable.[160] Similar reports reached London, prompting a Foreign Office official to ask the Treasury if the French had 'a potential stranglehold over us'.[161] This was a remarkable suggestion, given the French anxiety for collaboration with Britain, and merely exposed the Foreign Office's remoteness from economic affairs and muddle over the realities of European politics. The Treasury reassured the Foreign Office that France did not intend to exploit its financial power in an aggressive manner.[162]

Norman nevertheless remained cool to central bank conversations for reasons hinted by Sprague, his American adviser, Courtney Mill, the City editor of the *Times* and through other channels. Thus Sprague, on the very day that Norman met Moret in Paris, advised Governor Harrison in New York *not* to purchase more sterling, since this would only mask the reality of Britain's financial problems and foster complacency.

> We must forget the patent medicines of credit and monetary management, and, having participated in the previous inflation, we must do a real job of house cleaning. Central banks can do a lot to check the development of an unsound situation but they can't clean it up when it has developed and a breakdown has occurred. Reduction of costs of production – including salaries and wages – where they have been held up despite drastic declines in commodity prices, is essential.[163]

Shortly afterwards, Sprague indicated to Leith-Ross of the Treasury why Norman did not wish to pursue conversations with Moret. Sprague 'emphasised the desirability of not appearing to ask favours from the French and doubted the wisdom of palliatives which might conceal the true position [in Britain] and delay radical remedies.'[164] Norman himself spoke of 'political objections' to a French loan,[165] but it was Norman who raised the objections. As he told an American banker, the British government had weakened the economy by adopting the 'policy of the trade unions'.[166] A French loan would get the politicians off the hook. He was determined to see that Britain did not accept aid from France and especially not now, when sterling's weakness required the 'socialist' government to swallow a large dose of deflation.

Norman had his way. Snowden, the chancellor, echoed his claim that the Gold Delegation had 'done incalculable harm' to Britain's reputation in France and the United States.[167] In January 1931, Snowden also discouraged the Cabinet from hoping for an international solution to the crisis until Britain had put its own house in order.[168] In February, he responded to pressure from the Opposition parties by establishing a committee comprised mainly of conservative City men to identify means of public retrenchment.[169] This was the May committee, chaired by Sir George May, the retired chairman of the Prudential Insurance Company, whose report setting out in highly coloured terms the scale of the prospective Budget deficit appeared in July 1931, just as the pound faced speculative attack on the foreign exchanges.[170]

As in the years before the slump, central bankers in all three major creditor countries faced powerful political constraints upon their operations. Harrison had been able to reduce interest rates rapidly after the Wall Street Crash and engage in vigorous open market operations intended to induce American commercial banks to shift from short-term to long-term lending.[171] The result was not insignificant. In the first half of 1930, US banks issued $830 million (£170 million) in foreign loans and a much larger volume of domestic loans. While the new burst in foreign lending proved short-lived and practically ceased by the latter half of 1930, domestic lending continued.[172] Harrison had also assisted the Bank of England in a small way since the summer of 1930 by making occasional purchases of sterling when it threatened to fall below gold export point, then disposing of the balances when the exchange rate recovered.[173] But he remained acutely aware of Washington's deep suspicions of Wall Street and its supposed cosmopolitanism. Hoover had been opposed to foreign lending ever since his time as secretary of commerce, and as Harrison observed to Moret, 'This hostility still existed among a great number of politicians.'[174] During the Wall Street boom, foreign banks and investors had built up huge short-term balances in the United States, estimated in March 1930 at $2550 million (£525 million).[175] The recent rundown of these balances and the consequent loss of gold from the dollar's reserves had attracted adverse notice in America. Further losses would completely undermine his efforts to encourage foreign lending. For the same reason, he deplored the publication of the Gold Delegation reports. Such was the isolationism in Washington and the rest of the country that they took the reports as evidence that European central banks were conspiring to appropriate America's gold. In the circumstances he could not be seen to be allied to his European colleagues.[176]

Moret's situation in the winter of 1930, while ostensibly easier than Harrison's, was no less governed by political influences. Compared with other major capitalist countries, France appeared to be almost unaffected by the world slump. With recorded unemployment still almost negligible and flight capital accumulating in Paris, conservative writers portrayed France as an island of prosperity protected by Poincaré's financial reforms and its healthy balance of industry and agriculture. But experts at the Ministry of Finance and Bank of France had been aware for some time that France was not immune from the slump's effects. The collapse in October 1930 of the Banque Adam, one of the country's oldest banks, dragged down by the failure of the Banque Oustric, a newer issuing house, had shaken investor confidence.[177] The budgetary surplus had become 'increasingly precarious'.[178] And that winter, for the first time since the *de facto* stabilization of the franc in 1926, French banks reported a loss of deposits and signs of renewed hoarding.[179] In these circumstances the appropriate response for a central bank, Moret believed, was to raise the discount rate and restrict credit. But like Harrison, he too faced political restraints, only in his case they dictated more, not less, international cooperation. Thus against his better judgement he reduced his discount rate to assist the French Treasury officials in their effort to improve Franco-British relations. French ministers were acutely afraid that Bruening would respond to the current surge in popularity of the Communists and Nazis by abandoning the Young plan, and with Britain siding with Germany and the United States indifferent to the crisis, France would be isolated.[180]

Britain thus found itself in a strong position to influence France and might well have persuaded it to support an international monetary conference, the new international lending institution being promoted by the financier Sir Robert Kindersley, or even Strakosch's monetary reforms. British Treasury and Foreign Office officials favoured this linkage of security and economic reform.[181] But Norman, who preferred an Anglo-German condominium in Europe to an *entente* with France, discouraged Snowden from listening to their advice.[182] Despite warnings of worse times ahead for Germany and a probable suspension of reparation payments,[183] he advised the chancellor not to worry. Conditions in Germany had 'considerably improved', he claimed in February 1931.[184] This was true enough, and Snowden once more accepted his judgement. But Germany's restlessness – encouraged by British revisionism – all too soon undercut the stirrings of recovery.

5.5   The Austro-German customs union crisis and the future of Europe

From the end of the Ruhr crisis in 1924 until the spring of 1928, Germany enjoyed a period of relative stability and growth. With the better times, voters abandoned the parties of the extreme Left and Right, as was evident in the May 1928 Reichstag election when, as Thomas Childers has put it, the NSDAP was reduced to 'a marginal splinter party'.[185] Hitler implicitly acknowledged the outcome by playing down the social-revolutionary element of party doctrine and playing up its anti-Marxism, respect for private property and championship of German – as opposed to cosmopolitan – industry. In Childers' words, 'the NSDAP ... had opted for a class, and specifically middle class, strategy.'[186] Hitler's timing was remarkably fortuitous, for barely weeks after the election the German economy began to decline and registered unemployment, which had stood at 1,188,000 or 12.9 per cent in December 1927, rose to 16.7 per cent by December 1928 and to 20.1 per cent by December 1929.[187] Support for the NSDAP was probably already on the increase in Protestant areas of rural Germany on account of the distress caused by the decline in wholesale agricultural prices. But since Germany was largely an urban country, the more important development was the sharp increase in support among the urban middle classes once the slump began.[188] In practically every city, the NSDAP's support was strongest in the electoral districts (*Kreis*) with the highest per capita incomes. This was true of, among others, Hamburg, Essen, Dortmund, Duisburg, Frankfurt, Hanover and only somewhat less so of Stuttgart. It was also true of Berlin, Germany's largest city, where by July 1932 roughly two-thirds of the well-to-do voted for Hitler.[189]

The reason for Hitler's appeal is straightforward enough. The hyperinflation that had rendered the mark worthless in 1923 was a searing experience for everyone, but especially for those on fixed salaries or with savings and investments. While saved from being driven down into the proletariat by their accumulated social capital, which was largely unaffected by the hyperinflation, the spectre of such a terrifying fate left them determined never to repeat the experience. In good times, they were prepared to support moderate liberal or conservative parties. But their support was contingent upon the maintenance of financial stability, and when threatened once more with instability they turned to the Nazi party which promised to safeguard Germany from socialists, Communists, cosmopolitan finance and France's allegedly extortionate reparation demands. To his middle-class supporters, Hitler thus offered a *middle way* between the extremes of liberalism and Communism. They were reassured when Nazi thugs attacked units of the Socialist *Reichsbanner* and the Communist *Rotfront* while Hitler travelled the country denouncing Germany's international blackmailers.

Leaders of the Catholic Centre, the Democrats and the Socialits, the three moderate parties that formed the coalition government after the 1928 election, found themselves in a hopeless dilemma by the winter of 1929. With revenue falling and expenditure rising, they accepted that they must balance the budget to maintain confidence in the currency, but disagreed on how to do it. Centre and Democrat ministers called for substantial reductions in unemployment benefits, since this was the fastest growing form of expenditure. But the SPD had secured the adoption of the unemployment scheme in 1927 after a hard-won battle, and Hermann Müller, the chancellor, and his SPD colleagues were not prepared to see their working-class constituents bear the brunt of the sacrifices. They therefore resigned on 27 March 1930. Perhaps unwisely, Bruening, the Centre Party leader, sought to carry on with only a minority in the Reichstag, relying upon the temporary emergency powers of Article 48 of the constitution to push through his retrenchment plans. This made his government the target of attack from both the Left and the Right. Meanwhile trade slumped further, and registered unemployment rose to over 3 million by September.[190]

The Reichstag election of 14 September, in which Nazi representation in the Reichstag soared, confirmed the soundness of Hitler's strategy. The result damaged international confidence in Germany and intensified the economic slump. Foreign banks withdrew short-term loans, Germans joined in the capital flight and the economy declined further.[191] By December 1930, registered unemployment reached 4.4 million, and by January 1931 to nearly 4.9 million or 34 per cent of the registered workforce.[192]

In view of Germany's central place in the European economy, it might have been expected that concerted efforts would be made to forestall its collapse. Until 1931, however, European statesmen were chiefly concerned not with Germany but with the threat of Britain changing course and the deepening crisis in the agrarian countries of Eastern Europe. Despite the worsening economic slump and the collapse of support for Free Trade even within traditional strongholds such as the Lancashire textile workers and the TUC, Britain's Labour government stoutly resisted change. But by the winter of 1930 it still lacked a coherent policy, and with Keynes publicly campaigning for 'a substantial revenue tariff',[193] and even Norman indicating that he would support emergency import restrictions to shore up sterling,[194] senior Cabinet ministers, including MacDonald, indicated their willingness to introduce emergency trade protection.[195] Practically the only obstacle was the chancellor, Snowden, who seemed prepared to die in the last ditch for Free Trade. MacDonald, who had become alienated from his colleagues and the Labour party itself, refused to challenge Snowden.[196] But to foreign observers it seemed only a matter of time before the slump forced Britain into a change of policy. Reports circulated that sterling was on the ropes,[197] and that British depositors were fleeing the currency.[198] The publication of André Siegfried's best-selling *England's Crisis*, representing Britain as the 'sick man of Europe', heightened fears that Britain would soon be forced to abandon the gold standard or more likely Free Trade.

The spectre of Britain retreating into Imperial protectionism had been the main motive behind the Belgian proposal for a tariff truce in September 1929. After the tariff truce foundered in the autumn of 1930, the Northern countries – Denmark, Sweden, Norway, Luxembourg, Belgium and the Netherlands – adopted the Oslo Convention in 1930 for the same purpose.[199] Although the Convention committed the signatories to little more than prior notification of plans to alter import duties and to bear in mind objections, the Northern countries were strong supporters of economic liberalism, and while individually they were small states, together they accounted for nearly 9 per cent of world trade, more than France and roughly as much as Germany.[200] They also depended crucially upon access to the British market, and since the Reichstag election they had become increasingly worried about a new Franco-German conflict and anxious that Britain should remain involved in European affairs. They therefore approached Britain to join the Convention, hoping it would see this as a liberal alternative to Imperial protectionism. Their efforts brought no result. Britain was not prepared to lend any encouragement to regional European action, even when this did not involve a departure from the most-favoured-nation principle.[201]

The adoption of preferential trade agreements was even more problematic, as became evident in the latter half of 1930 when international efforts were made to address the terrible crisis among the agrarian states of the Danube region. With their largely peasant populations facing destitution as the result of collapsing commodity prices, national representatives met in August 1930 in Warsaw, where they united in calling for tariff concessions from industrialized Western Europe sufficient to absorb their cereal surpluses.[202] They renewed their demand at conferences in Vienna, Bucharest and at the second tariff truce conference held in Geneva in mid-November.[203] French delegates were content to leave it to the Italians, British, Americans and Australians to oppose the preference proposals.[204] Loucheur, while pressing for an 'Economic Federation of Europe', advised Briand against preferences and instead to rely upon industrial 'rationalization' to address Europe's crisis.[205] But by the end of the year French diplomats became convinced that something must be done to save Eastern Europe from the twin threats facing it. One was the menace of Soviet influence, which seemed bound to increase as destitution in the region spread. The other was Germany, which, unlike France, was a major importer of agricultural goods and had recently proposed trade preferences to Roumania and Yugoslavia to secure markets for its manufacturing output. The prospect of Germany drawing the Danube countries into a dependent relationship posed a serious threat to France's security system. Indeed, French statesmen suspected that this was one reason why Germany was attracted to preferential arrangements. But to their intense frustration they could see no practical means of countering the German economic offensive.[206]

Since well before the Reichstag election, Roland de Margerie, the French ambassador in Berlin, had been warning of the strength of German revisionism. As he explained to a government minister passing through Berlin,

> There was too much of a tendency in France to imagine that there exists in Germany a 'republic of the left', favourable to a *rapprochement*, which France should be supporting. In reality, all German parties, whatever their political tendency, are unanimous in favouring a revision of the Treaty of Versailles. The truth is that the German republic, for some years more, will be conservative or it will be nothing. ... In any case, it is certain that the Franco-German *rapprochement* is in decline.[207]

In particular, de Margerie anticipated that Bruening would demand relief from reparations, since pressure for revision was coming from employers' and farmers' organizations, the trade unions, municipalities and from across the political spectrum.[208] But what could France realistically do?

Joseph Avenol, the deputy secretary-general of the League of Nations, expressed deep pessimism in a private letter to Briand in January 1931. Europe, he wrote, urgently needed a psychological lift if it was not to succumb to the neurosis that Germany and Italy were stirring up by their aggressive behaviour:

> Rumours of war, which have passed in waves across Europe, have demoralized public opinion and contributed to the aggravation of the economic crisis. In Holland, the last country to be struck by this wave of pessimism, investors have been seeking to dump all their Central European securities, without distinction, and to concentrate the balances thus created upon a tiny number of investments supposedly sheltered from the general insecurity. [209]

Paradoxically, Germany and Italy needed help more urgently than most other countries, but having wrapped themselves in their nationalist flags, they opposed any initiative associated with France. The only means Avenol could see to hold the line was by re-establishing the Franco-British *entente*. Together they could form the nucleus of a conservative Europe, powerful enough to deter any trouble makers. The obstacle, he believed, was Britain's preoccupation with the fate of sterling, whose weakness British commentators blamed upon France.[210]

Briand sought to take advantage of two conferences due to meet in Paris in February to address the problem of the current cereal surplus in the Danube and disposing of future surpluses. As he observed to Tardieu, France, having initiated the conferences, could not merely fold its arms and allow them to fail, since this would hand the initiative to Germany which was prepared to extend preferences to Poland, Roumania and Yugoslavia. He appreciated that French farmers, millers and other interests were bound to raise objections to almost any initiative they took: that Danube wheat was of poor quality, too expensive, and so on. But the danger of doing nothing was too great to contemplate.

> If we cannot help these countries – if they are to face the competition of over-seas producers and Soviet dumping – they will inevitably try to avoid the social and economic collapse that threatens them by seeking regional ententes, which could only be the first step towards dependence upon the large powers able to help them.[211]

Tardieu remained unenthusiastic. Just four days earlier he had joined Pierre Laval's new government as minister of agriculture. This was an anomalous choice for an urbane former journalist on *Le Temps* and specialist in international rela-tions. The reason, it seems, is that he appreciated the popularity to be gained from a vigorous defence of rural France, which had begun to feel the effects of the slump. Accordingly, he rejected Briand's appeal for limited preferences to the Danube countries. He was only prepared to concede that a few thousand tonnes of cereals might be purchased for the French colonies and League-mandated ter-ritories in view of the prospective shortfall in their harvest, and that the Ministry of Finance might support an international agricultural mortgage scheme.[212] But even these modest concessions met resistance from colleagues who raised objec-tions to the dumping of foreign surpluses in colonial markets.[213]

In the event, the two cereal surplus conferences passed off without incident. André François-Poncet, the secretary of state for the national economy and a rising star in the government who chaired both conferences, chose not to reject prefer-ences when France's allies Roumania and Yugoslavia promoted them on behalf of the whole Danube region. But he insisted that, if approved, they should be subject to the conditions laid down by Stucki's committee on plurilateral conven-tions. He also secured agreement that preferences should be regarded as only one solution and that others including financial credits should be considered.[214] This created a breathing space during which Briand persuaded Algerian and Tunisian authorities as well as the Ministry of War to accept small amounts of Danube wheat and the French millers' association to include a fraction of Danube wheat in their flour.[215] But the issue was temporarily forgotten when news broke that Germany and Austria were secretly negotiating a bilateral customs union.

Perhaps no event better illustrated the destructive dynamic of the interwar crisis than the controversy stirred up by the Austro-German scheme, which erupted on 20 March 1931. By this time the world slump had been under way for 18 months, but it was not yet the Great Depression that was to blight the lives of a whole generation. Not every country had been seriously affected: in France, for instance, the official index of production in the first quarter of 1931 still stood at 104.7 (1928 = 100),[216] and on 14 March 1931 registered unemployment (albeit a gross underestimate) amounted to a mere 47,720.[217] The international monetary system remained intact. And indeed since the New Year numerous signs had appeared that the worst was over. The conclusion of the Franco-British Treasury talks in late February had coincided with a halt to gold movements from London to Paris.[218] Sterling, gilts and share prices in London all moved higher, and wholesale commodity prices ceased falling and actually rose for the first time in 18 months.[219] In the United States, employment, payrolls and production stopped declining.[220] In Britain, registered unemployment had reached 2,643,000 in the first week of January 1931, up 900,000 over the previous nine months. But thereafter it levelled out, and by the third week of March it was 60,000 lower than at the New Year, a development which could not be explained solely by seasonal fluctuations.[221] Germany experienced an even stronger recovery: some capital returned, and in March exports picked up and unemployment declined.[222] In the words of the *Economist*, 'the recent progressive darkening of the skies has, whether temporarily or permanently, ceased.'[223] Rome C. Stephenson, president of the American Bankers' Association, was more confident that the corner had been turned:

> Recovery from the economic slump...is now in sight in the United States. I am confident that the downward course of business has been checked...and that there are no further great unpleasant surprises in store to loose their devastating effects upon the business world.[224]

Had the global economic system operated according to its own discrete rules, the recovery in the first quarter of 1931 might well have continued, notwithstanding the operation of the international gold standard, the wage and price rigidities, and commodity surpluses that economists have singled out as the leading causes of the slump. But as before the framework of security necessary to sustain confidence in global markets remained extremely fragile and suffered a massive blow from the revelation of secret Austro-German negotiations.

Since early 1930, the Bruening government had limped along without a majority in Parliament and relying upon emergency decrees to implement legislation. Lacking a popular mandate and under intense attack from Left and Right, it had turned to foreign policy in the hope of scoring a political success. Curtius, the foreign minister, sought *Anschluss* with Austria, but in the first instance he restricted his aim to a customs union, nominally open to third countries, which he could justify as a contribution to Briand's plan for European confederation. On 3 July 1930, immediately after the last French troops left the Rhineland, he activated plans for a customs union, which the Austrian government cautiously welcomed.[225] He was embarrassed when the secret negotiations were revealed in Vienna in March 1931. But he was pleased to find that in Germany, with the exception of SPD publications, the press welcomed the scheme, treating it with blithe inconsistency as a reassertion of German national interests and as a contribution to European unity.[226] Predictably, however, French reactions to news of the scheme were uniformly hostile.

French observers were certain that the Austro-German scheme breached in spirit if not in law no less than three international treaties, the Versailles Treaty, the Treaty of Saint-Germain and the Protocol of 4 October 1922 adopted at the time of the international Austrian stabilization loan, all of which forbade a German-Austrian merger. To them it was a treacherous blow to the European order which, if tolerated, would lead inevitably to a German-dominated *Mitteleuropa* and bring another war measurably closer.[227] Barely a fortnight earlier, Briand had reassured the Chamber of Deputies that Curtius's recent visit to Vienna did not portend an *Anschluss*. He was acutely embarrassed by news of the customs union scheme, and German and Austrian claims that it was consistent with his own European federation plan only further embarrassed him. He had hoped to become president of France in the forthcoming election, and initially he seemed a shoe-in. He now faced a torrent of criticism from nationalists in the Chamber of Deputies, which gravely diminished his chances.[228] Nevertheless, rather than simply digging in his heels, he sought to turn the crisis into an opportunity to strengthen Central Europe without handing control to Germany.[229]

In Britain, news of the customs union scheme elicited mixed reactions. The British press broadly welcomed the scheme, professing to see in it the first step towards a reversal of protectionism in Europe and warning France not to obstruct it.[230] Governor Norman privately was even more forthright. As he told Stimson, he strongly favoured the scheme and extending it to the whole of Central Europe. The French would of course resist such a development and try to create a competing bloc. But ultimately he believed they would have to give way, since it was natural and inevitable that the Germanic countries should resume their hegemony of the region.[231] From Berlin, Rumbold affirmed that Germany had acted honourably out of economic motives, and warned against action that would humiliate Bruening who was indispensable to the republic.[232] Rumbold's colleagues in London were however more sceptical of German motives and accepted that to support the scheme in face of French and Czechoslovak opposition would serve little purpose. But since they too feared that a purely negative resort to legal objections would damage the moderate governments in Germany and Austria, they cast about for a constructive alternative.[233] Philip Noel-Baker circulated a proposal on 13 April to replace the bilateral customs union scheme with one involving the whole of Continental Europe. The core of the plan was a staged reduction in tariffs, with the benefits limited to participating countries. While accepting that Britain could not possibly join such a scheme, Noel-Baker was sure that participants would concede Britain most-favoured-nation treatment in return for its commitment to remain free trade for, say, three years or simply on account of its existing most-favoured-nation rights. A convinced free trader, he believed the crisis confirmed the desire of Germany, Austria, Czechoslovakia and other countries for trade liberalization. Accordingly, Britain should seize the opportunity to start the process of reducing tariffs.

The advantage to British exporters of a 25% reduction in tariff levels in Europe would in itself be so considerable that an understanding not to impose further tariffs for a fixed period of time would not prove to be a difficult Parliamentary obstacle. In any case the political advantage of securing a settlement of the present European crisis would almost certainly ensure acceptance.[234]

On 17 April, four days after Noel-Baker circulated his proposal, London received a French 'constructive plan'.[235] For a fortnight, French statesmen had been casting about for some means of regaining the initiative from Germany, but as Briand acknowledged in discussions with Benes, their options were limited.[236] Germany had the advantage of large cereal import requirements, which placed it in a strong position to draw the Danube countries into its orbit. France might instead propose that Europe's industrial countries should extend preferences on Danube cereals without demanding reciprocal concessions. This would reveal who was or was not interested in helping the Danube region. If combined with strict limits on the *quantity* of cereal exports involved, French experts believed, it would also forestall opposition from Britain and overseas countries who would surely not object to a mere 5–8 per cent of the European market being reserved for Danube producers.

A second approach open to France was through promoting producer cartels. Cartels had hardly halted the economic slump, but French experts believed they had reduced disorder in the markets where they operated. Since neither the United States nor Britain objected to Europe being organized by means of cartels, and British producers, despite official coolness in London, participated in a number of European cartels, France could promote them in its alternative to the Austro-German scheme. More immediately, however, French officials believed they could block the customs union scheme by discouraging support for it in Austria where the advantages and disadvantages were evenly balanced. Their third approach was therefore through financial inducements to Austria and other countries in the region.

François-Poncet, the minister charged with preparing the French alternative, confidently believed that France's most effective weapon in the struggle to contain Germany was its financial resources. French banks currently had 4–6 billion francs (£32–48 million) in Germany with much more indirectly supporting Germany through Swiss, Dutch and Belgian banks. As yet, the Austro-German scheme had not panicked them, but a word of warning would be enough to persuade them to withdraw their balances, which would shake the German banking system. But since Germany would almost certainly exploit the resulting financial crisis to justify a cessation of reparations, François-Poncet thought it preferable to exploit France's financial strength as an inducement rather than as a weapon, by promising Germany substantially more financial assistance (*'une aide financière infiniment plus efficace'*), if it renounced its customs union scheme in favour of the French alternative. By also offering Austria and the Danube countries extended credit, he believed France could draw them away from Germany.[237]

Could France in fact use cartels or financial resources as either weapons or inducements in its struggle to constrain Germany? Flandin and his advisers at the Ministry of Finance were much less certain than François-Poncet. Cartels had proven to be of limited value in the current crisis: the European Steel Cartel was now moribund, and in any case cartels depended upon private interests to function. They were even more sceptical of the notion that France could effectively deploy its financial power. By their estimate, short-term French balances in Germany were a good deal less than 4 billion francs, and probably no more than 5 per cent of the total foreign balances tied up in Germany. Besides, they anticipated that London would step in if French banks withdrew their balances. As to the suggestion that France could lend still more to Austria and the Danube countries, this overlooked the fact that France's own international payments position was deteriorating and that the recipient countries were scarcely in a condition to take on more debt. Nevertheless, officials on the *rue de Rivoli* as well as their colleagues at the *Quai d'Orsay* believed that France must offer an alternative to the Austro-German scheme rather than simply oppose it. They therefore agreed to include financial support and some mention of cartels.[238] Together with limited unilateral preferences on Polish and Danube cereal exports and Austrian manufactured exports, they formed the basis of the French plan, which was submitted to London on 22 April.[239]

Briand's belief, based on 'good sources', that Britain would acquiesce in European preferences if strictly limited in number and scope, was ill-founded. Board of Trade officials favoured the Austro-German scheme, since they regarded customs unions as legitimate exceptions to free trade. But they strongly objected to Noel-Baker's scheme with its trade preferences, and they were joined by Dominions Office officials who warned of the damage to Imperial relations if Britain allowed the Dominions to face discrimination in European markets. Foreign Office officials turned back to the French plan. They were disappointed that it offered no inducements to Germany, and indeed required Germany to concede unilateral preferences to the Danube countries while withholding them from Soviet Russia despite their most-favoured-nation agreement adopted at Rapallo. But they could not think of a practical alternative.[240]

French statesmen remained convinced of the need for an alternative to the Austro-German scheme. Reports circulated that German and Austrian diplomats were frantically seeking to induce Hungary, Czechoslovakia, Roumania, Yugoslavia, Italy and Switzerland to join the scheme, since they appreciated that if even one of these countries did so the legal case against it would be seriously weakened.[241] De Fleuriau, the ambassador in London, therefore called at the Foreign Office on 4 May with an outline of further proposals,[242] and on 7 May Jacques Rueff, the financial attaché at the embassy, submitted a substantially revised plan. Among the new features were support for an international agriculture mortgage institution to assist Austria and East European countries; acceptance of reciprocal preferences between industrial and agrarian countries and the extension of the scheme to non-European countries which were prepared to participate on an equal basis. Rueff also offered two general assurances: that the European preferences would be created solely by reducing rather than raising tariffs; and that Britain would enjoy all the benefits of the preference scheme simply because of its liberal trade regime.[243]

Henderson raised the Austro-German scheme in Cabinet on 6 May. As he explained to colleagues, he regretted having to oppose it, since Germany needed some basis for hope if it was to avoid 'a revival [*sic*] of Hitlerism'. Fortunately, he observed, the shock caused by the scheme had created the possibility of introducing a European-wide scheme of reciprocal tariff reductions. While Britain could expect to share the benefits, it would mean Europe discriminating against the Dominions, but he hoped colleagues would not oppose the scheme on this account for, as he put it, if Britain were to seize 'this opportunity to co-operate in building up some measure of European economic union, she will be required to make certain sacrifices.' Moreover, if Britain were to refuse its endorsement, 'we shall, rightly or wrongly, be held responsible for making a general system of tariff reduction impossible.' He therefore requested 'a sufficiently free hand to enable His Majesty's Government to contribute to the common work of removing the political danger which had been created by the proposal to set up an Austro-German Customs Union.' This was ambitious talk, but Henderson was merely reading from a Foreign Office script, and he offered no fight when colleagues objected to concessions to Europe. The Cabinet soon agreed that he should adopt 'a non-committal attitude' to alternative schemes when he went to Geneva, and to refer back any 'questions of principle'.[244]

The Foreign Office meanwhile faced intense pressure to support a broad European alternative to the Austro-German scheme. From Berlin, Rumbold repeatedly pointed out the dangers of leaving Bruening empty-handed.[245] Sir Eric Phipps in Vienna warned that the day was fast approaching when Europe as a whole might simply discard the most-favoured-nation principle in the struggle to safeguard markets.[246] Arthur Loveday, Salter's successor at the League Economic Section, and Sir Eric Drummond, the secretary-general of the League, similarly warned of the dangers that Britain ran by dogmatically opposing all derogations from the most-favoured-nation principle.[247] Governor Norman passed on the advice of the Belgian financier, Emile Francqui, that Britain should make a dramatic initiative capable of transforming the situation. If Britain were now to confirm its support for a European free trade area, Francqui was sure that Belgium and other European countries would seize the opportunity with both hands; a view which Norman endorsed.[248] Fernand Vanlangenhove, secretary-general of the Belgian Foreign Ministry, appealed to Britain to join the five low-tariff Oslo convention countries in an open-ended preferential arrangement. He was deeply worried about a Europe divided between Germany and France, which threatened to stifle Belgium's trade and end in conflict. If Britain and the liberal Oslo countries formed a low-tariff area open to all countries willing to share the advantages, through the 'force of attraction' they could draw in much of Europe.[249] All the while, French envoys reaffirmed their hopes for British cooperation.[250]

The Foreign Office did not lose sight of the difficulties that European preferences would pose for the Dominions. As Orme Sargent observed, the Dominions, possibly with the United States, would be sure to object to a European scheme involving preferences.

> For this reason it would be quite impossible for us in any circumstances to take the initiative...but if it were put forward by some other Government and if it

contained all the safeguards [offered in the French plan] ... and if generally it was shown to be advantageous to Europe both politically and economically, then we certainly should hesitate before vetoing the scheme merely because it might be inconvenient to the Dominions Governments.[251]

With Henderson planning to set off for Geneva for the meeting of the Committee of Enquiry for European Union (CEUE) on 15 May and the League of Nations Council on the 18th, time was running out. Sargent therefore drew up a brief for Henderson, advising him to accept the French plan, including the international agricultural mortgage corporation, for which the Treasury had approved a £120,000 contribution to the reserve fund. He then despatched copies of the brief to the Treasury, the Board of Trade and the Dominions Office before telephoning them for their approval. For several days the Foreign Office heard nothing, but on 14 May, Thomas, the Dominions secretary, protested to MacDonald at the recommendation to support the agricultural mortgage corporation. MacDonald, who professed to be unaware of the proposal, demanded a ministerial meeting to review British policy.[252]

Thomas was a desperate man. Eighteen months earlier, as lord privy seal, he had been assigned the task of addressing the problem of chronic unemployment in British industry. Having signally failed in the task, MacDonald had moved him to the Dominions Office. But this too had proven to be a poisoned chalice, when Dominions leaders attending the Imperial conference in October 1930 united in demanding trade concessions from Britain, and Thomas, unable to persuade colleagues to yield, had been obliged to hold out, agreeing only to a further conference devoted to Imperial economic relations, to be held at Ottawa in August 1931. Determined to avoid further embarrassment, he now insisted that Henderson should oppose both the agricultural mortgage scheme and the French plan. As he explained to MacDonald, supporting the agricultural mortgage scheme, which was intended to favour European producers, would be regarded as a slap in the face by British and Dominions farmers who had received no comparable help. Support for the French plan would have even graver consequences:

[the Foreign Office] fails to recognize that, while as an individual State the United Kingdom is a part of Europe, she is also, as a member of the British Commonwealth of Nations, a part of the rest of the world; and its acceptance by us would be a first step in a process which might well end in the United Kingdom having to appear as definitely casting in her lot with Europe as against the rest of the world, including the Dominions.

There is the more immediate consideration that our acquiescence in a scheme of this sort would almost certainly arouse acute criticism overseas, and especially in Canada and Australia. It would inevitably prejudice the Dominions case for insistence on their full most-favoured-nation rights, if indeed it did not lay us open to the charge of having thrown over the Empire in the interests of Europe just at the time when we profess ourselves as anxious to develop a scheme for Imperial economic co-operation.

> By all means, let us find, if we can, an alternative solution to the Austro-German Custom Union proposals [*sic*], but surely our Imperial position will be impossible if we rush into support of proposals which discriminate against the Dominions and in fact force us to choose between Europe and the Empire.[253]

With MacDonald and Graham siding with Thomas, new instructions were cabled to Henderson in Geneva to fall back on a legal challenge to the customs union scheme.[254] Accordingly, at the League Council he proposed that the International Court at The Hague should be asked to rule on the legality of the scheme before any further action was taken. Briand and more reluctantly Curtius agreed.[255] Outside the Council, Johann Schober, the Austrian foreign minister, had already assented to Henderson's request.[256] The Austrian government had always been of two minds about the customs union scheme, and since the recent failure of the Credit Anstalt, the largest bank in the country, it had larger issues to worry about. At meetings of the CEUE over the next few days, Henderson also dissociated Britain from the international agricultural mortgage corporation and the French constructive plan, thus effectively blocking progress on them.[257] This was not the end of efforts to promote European trade preferences: several important initiatives were made in 1932, as will be discussed in Chapter 7. But, for the next year, the financial crisis, which spread from Austria to Germany, then to Britain and eventually to the United States and beyond, dominated relations among the Western powers.

5.6   Conclusion

In 1929, the crisis that had begun two years earlier suddenly became acute when the world slump began. Wage and price rigidities in the leading capitalist countries and adherence to the international gold standard aggravated the deflationary trend already evident in the world economy since 1925. There was however nothing inevitable about the crisis or the depth and length of the slump. Under the gold standard, the world economy began to recover in the first quarter of 1931. Meanwhile, European statesmen proposed numerous reforms, almost any one of which might have moderated the economic downturn and inaugurated an earlier recovery. From February–March 1930, when the United States and the rest of the non-European world refused to participate in the tariff truce conference, it was obvious that multilateral action on the basis of unconditional most-favoured-nation treatment was out of the question. Within Europe, however, support for regional trade liberalization remained strong. Modern trade theory indicates that regional arrangements do not necessarily produce a net increase in trade. But since the practical alternative was a rapid retreat of individual countries into autarky, the case for regional cooperation was strong. The League of Nations committee chaired by Walter Stucki, the Swiss minister of economics, had set out rules for 'plurilateral conventions' in 1929 to ensure that, so far as possible, they led to trade creation rather than trade diversion and involved the widest possible participation. Salter and Pietro Stoppani of the League Economic Section encouraged an initiative on these lines, and Jacques Rueff unofficially sought to interest Drummond, the secretary-general of the League, in a 'European exception' to the most-favoured-nation principle. In 1930, the Danube countries proposed limited European preferences to enable them to dispose of their cereal surpluses. In December, five of Europe's liberal trading nations signed the Oslo convention which at least pointed towards a regional free trade or low-tariff area.

However, until 1931, Britain, with tacit American support, blocked progress on these lines. Britain had long tolerated exceptions to the most-favoured-nation principle for the Northern countries, the Baltic countries, the countries of the Iberian peninsula and of course the British Commonwealth. But despite assurances of most-favoured-nation treatment within regional European schemes, the British Labour government accepted the Board of Trade's objection that the European countries concerned lacked the historical affinity necessary to justify an exception, and the Dominions Office's warning that it would severely damage relations with the Dominions. More generally, Britain and the United States, notwithstanding their own departures from free trade, hewed dogmatically to the liberal principle of unconditional most-favoured-nation treatment. Their opposition to regional schemes deterred Germany from supporting them, since Germany sought the support of the Anglo-Saxon powers in its pursuit of Treaty revision. France, having shunned regional preferences out of fear that Germany might exploit them to its greater advantage in Eastern Europe, was now prepared to support them, but drew back to remain aligned with Britain. The Austro-German customs union crisis thus marked a potential turning point, when, with British encouragement, Germany and France might have joined in constructive regional action within Europe. But Britain continued to oppose European initiatives. And since Britain's endorsement was essential, the moment for constructive action passed.

A similar situation existed with regard to international monetary relations. With some justice, British bankers and economists became disturbed by the maldistribution of the world's monetary gold, two-thirds of which filled the coffers of the American and French reserve banks by 1931. During 1930 alone, US gold stocks rose from £880 million to £944 million, while Bank of France gold reserves rose from £336 million to £431 million: a combined increase of £159 million, equal to the Bank of England's total metallic reserves.[258] But their complaints that France was stifling economic activity by hoarding gold could have no effect in the absence of agreement on new rules for the operation of the gold standard. Strakosch, supported by League officials, secured the Gold Delegation's agreement on a promising formula. French central bankers remained hostile to Strakosch's proposals. Yet, as events in the winter of 1930 confirmed, the Bank of France was susceptible to pressure from the French government. Disturbed by the developments in Germany and Italy, the government persuaded the Bank to make several concessions to Britain, including a reduction in interest rates. Further concessions were by no means out of the question. But they would have required British cooperation on other fronts and notably on security, which the British government was not prepared to offer.

Similarly on the financial front, in January 1931 Norman visited Paris to promote an international credit corporation. The brainchild of Sir Robert Kindersley, chairman of merchant bankers Lazard Brothers, the purpose of the corporation was to revive long-term international lending by spreading the risk among a large body of corporate lenders. In the nervous and depressed markets that winter, any such initiative was worth attempting. Norman and Kindersley placed particular importance on the corporation as a vehicle for mobilizing the credit creating potential of the French and American gold stocks. As Kindersley explained to the Treasury:

> Many authorities are agreed that the maldistribution of Gold has in large measure contributed to the existing world crisis, creating a boom and then a collapse in the United States and restriction elsewhere, and that world recovery will be impeded by the fact that the United States and France, instead of lending back to the World their surplus for a usable balance of payments, have been taking this surplus in the form of Gold.

The corporation would therefore raise funds through bond issues mainly in the United States and France, and perhaps in Switzerland and Holland, but only to a modest extent in Britain.

> This should have the effect
> 1. of diverting the existing flow of gold,
> 2. of re-establishing the credit of the Foreign Governments, Corporations, and so on, to whom the money is lent, to improve the price of their securities in all markets of the World, and the purchasing power of their nationals,
> 3. and of restoring general confidence.[259]

The obvious sticking point was the need for American and French cooperation. Even if called international and domiciled in a neutral country, there was no disguising the fact that the corporation would be essentially British. As Norman admitted to Snowden, 'He very much doubted whether the French and Americans were prepared to put up millions of pounds and let us invest it for them.'[260] Laval, Flandin, Briand and other French leaders were extremely anxious for Britain's friendship, but they would not encourage the *place de Paris* to support the project without assurances as to its purpose. They suspected the City's and in particular Norman's interest in Germany, and had no intention of allowing them to divert French assets to Germany, especially when Germany was exploiting its commercial strength to undermine French influence in Eastern Europe.[261]

Norman presented the Kindersley plan at the March meeting of the BIS board in Bâle. Despite his insistence that all European central bankers should support the plan, he secured only a resolution endorsing it in principle.[262] In early April, he travelled to the United States to canvass support. There he stressed the importance of countering the appeal of the Soviet Union's first five-year plan in the beleaguered countries of Eastern Europe. As he put it, the capitalist powers must unite in combating the Soviet menace, which was 'one of the world's biggest problems.'[263] By now, however, New York bankers were facing attacks from Congressional critics for tying up America's savings in loans to Europe and did not want to hear of a new international lending scheme.[264] President Hoover seemed interested only in the markets of East Asia. His solution was to revalue silver, which he believed would augment the purchasing power of China and India.[265] Neither Norman nor any other authority in London was prepared to entertain this proposal, which they regarded as thoroughly misconceived.[266]

Lamont of J.P. Morgan found Norman 'terribly pessimistic' when they met in London on 8 May. 'England's situation [was] parlous', Norman admitted. He was disturbed by the dire condition of the staple export industries, including steel, shipbuilding, textiles and coal, all of which were being carried by the banks. He was equally disturbed by the government's unwillingness to take its medicine by reducing expenditure in line with its declining revenue. Hostile as ever to France, he had hoped for Anglo-Saxon solidarity and was deeply disappointed by the reception he had received in the United States. His anguish is evident in Lamont's hurried note of their conversation:

> England not master in her own shop [sic], but USA blind & taking no steps to save the world and the gold standard. Should lend to backward countries, but know it to be working in circles. The new credit corporation.[267]

Despite Norman's pessimism, Britain was far from helpless. Its ability to influence the course of events, however, lay not within the markets but within the political framework surrounding the markets where its contribution to security, particularly in Europe, might have opened the way for constructive economic initiatives. The Austro-German customs union crisis belatedly prompted some rethinking of Britain's relationship with Europe inside the Foreign Office. This was evident in the change of message between the first and second of Vansittart's 'Old Adam' papers on the recrudescence of aggressive nationalism or imperialism abroad. The first paper, circulated to the Cabinet in May 1930, was a lengthy, tiresomely over-written, arrogant attack on the Europeans and particularly the French, who were allegedly antagonizing their neighbours and reviving fears of war. The Germans, Vansittart suggested, remained dissatisfied with the peace settlement, but were now wise enough to recognize that they must keep in with Britain. The problem was the French and their nervous, narrow-minded refusal to accommodate revision. While the Continental powers remained mired in the 'old diplomacy' of secret treaties, alliances and balance of power, Britain, along with the Scandinavian countries, was 'the most, indeed…the only, international mind among our contemporaries.' His advice to ministers was to stand aside from Europe's 'hegemonies and combinations', and to build up the League of Nations as a bulwark of peace.[268]

Vansittart's second 'Old Adam' paper, circulated to ministers at the height of the Austro-German customs union crisis, offered rather different advice. Aware that Germany was now gripped by nationalism and within sight of repudiating its Treaty commitments, he suggested that ministers should adopt a 'concrete policy' towards Europe. Britain should actively facilitate Treaty revision while at the same time offering assurances to France. But he gave no hint of what he meant by revision or assurances. Moreover, his advice was again buried in an overlong, overwritten paper, which once more discouraged practical calculations of power and represented Europeans as unworthy of Britain's support. The French, he pointed out, had been promised the incorporation of the Kellogg-Briand pact – outlawing war as an instrument of national policy – into the League of Nations Covenant. They had had the temerity to refuse this chance to abandon their national security in favour of the wholly ineffectual League of Nations.

> Would France be satisfied with this substitute? The answer is doubtful. President Doumergue's speech of the 8th April is, in fact, ominously definite on this point. So long as the League cannot wield 'sanctions' in the form of guns and rifles, so long will France have to keep her own powder dry. If the League is disarmed then must needs France be armed. An unpromising and familiar argument! In every walk of life it is a strong French trait to run great risks by not running small ones; and the course of the last fifteen months of naval negotiation is a fair illustration of the point.

But of course they were Latins and hence short-sighted and self-regarding. They had squabbled with their Italian cousins, and regrettably 'the wrath of Latins is not, as so often hoped, of the *soupe au lait variety*; they not only get cross quickly, they stay there.' They had overreacted to Germany's clumsily handled customs union scheme. 'Thus the whole of Europe, against maybe its better judgment, in any case by a bitter paradox, is being forced to treat what can be represented as the first step towards European federation as an objectionable political manoeuvre destined to wreck the peace of Europe.' Britain could therefore scarcely count on France's help in its lonely task of exorcising the old Adam from Europe.[269] This was hardly the cool, professional assessment of British interests the situation required. Yet when it came before the Cabinet, ministers were content merely to take note of it.[270]

For ten years after the war, Britain and the leading bankers and financiers of America had pressured European countries to reopen their markets and accept the return to globalization whilst at the same time encouraging them to dismantle the postwar framework of security. The result was a fragile world, which began to fall apart in 1927. The headlong retreat behind tariff barriers got underway before the slump began; the upsurge in nationalism and imperialism in Germany, Britain, the British Dominions and elsewhere was also evident before the slump began. Yet once their handiwork began to unravel, the Anglo-Saxon powers merely repeated their calls for non-discriminatory trade, respect for lenders' rights and further disarmament, while signalling their opposition to any departure from their globalizing agenda. The crisis brought on by Austria and Germany created a new opportunity for them to promote a constructive alternative. With the world economy displaying signs of recovery, their support for regional action or a scheme along the lines of Kindersley's lending corporation might have reinforced the upward trend. Instead, they opposed all the proposals put forward or failed to back them with the means at their disposal, leaving France and Germany in bitter confrontation. As a result, confidence declined, the slump resumed for another 18 months and the global economic and political systems were driven to the point of collapse.

6
In the Eye of the Storm, May 1931–February 1932

6.1 Introduction

The twelfth annual Assembly of the League of Nations, which opened on Monday, 7 September 1931, was better attended than any before it. Since the previous year it had been moved from the *Salle de la réformation* to the larger *Bâtiment electoral*, to accommodate the 50 delegations now present. Mexico was admitted to membership while Soviet Russia and the United States sent unofficial observers. For the first time, Americans at home could hear a nightly summary of the Assembly's proceedings through the 35 stations of the National Broadcasting Company. On Saturday, 19 September, reports reached Geneva of an incident near Mukden where Japanese officials accused Chinese troops of destroying a section of the Japanese-owned South Manchuria Railway, and in a suspiciously well-coordinated operation Japanese troops seized control of the city and surrounding region. The League Council was immediately convened alongside the Assembly to address the Manchurian crisis. Historians have described it as the first of several major blows to the League and hopes for collective security. But in the view of most contemporaries, the first major setback had already occurred by the time the League Assembly opened in 1931. This was the League's failure to address the global political-economic crisis, which threatened to overwhelm every one of its member states. M. Titulescu, the Roumanian diplomat and president of the Assembly, warned delegates – two weeks before the Manchurian crisis began – of the awful challenge that faced them:

> The entire world is suffering from a terrible crisis and lack of confidence. The last hopes of the world are now in our hands. We would fail in our duty if, in a spirit of sacrifice, we did not show our solidarity. For that speeches are not sufficient. Our motto should be, 'We must act, and act quickly.'[1]

In the debate that followed, some delegates urged that priority should be given to political action, in particular international disarmament; others pressed for immediate economic action. Most, however, appreciated that the issues were interlinked. Briand, in his final appearance at Geneva, warned that disarmament was out of the question unless or until member states agreed to a viable security framework. Nor could there be 'economic disarmament' unless political confidence was restored, and this was more remote than ever since the economic slump had stirred up Left- and Right-wing extremism everywhere. Curtius, the German foreign minister, in a speech directed mainly to listeners at home, warned that 'the whole foundation of our economic and financial system and, indeed, the whole basis of our civilization, is tottering', before complaining that his country was being martyred by its foreign creditors and provocatively demanding complete equality of arms with its neighbours. At present, he complained, Germany had no heavy artillery, military aircraft, tanks or submarines. If the forthcoming disarmament conference did not result in full equality, Germany would have no choice but to withdraw from the League.[2] Curtius's speech and the angry reaction it stirred in France confirmed the *Times'* observation at the opening of the Assembly that it was 'meeting…in the midst of a moral depression almost as serious as the economic depression which has continued so long and which shows no signs of lifting'.

> Everything this year has conspired to damp the enthusiasm and chill the optimism of the Assembly.…There seems to be no lack of good will among the delegates to the Assembly and among the Governments of which they are both the representatives and, in many cases, the leading members. But on present showing there is a woful [sic] absence of leadership. The prolonged economic crisis seems to have numbed instead of stimulating international statesmanship. Most of the countries from whom useful initiatives might be expected are too much preoccupied with their own internal problems to spare much thought for the more general problems without a solution of which there can be no complete solution for their own.[3]

Briand was clearly a spent force, and Britain offered no effective lead: for the first time since the League's foundation, it did not even send a minister to attend the Assembly. The revelation of plans for an Austro-German customs union in March had triggered an international financial crisis of the first order. Striking first Austria and other vulnerable countries of Central Europe, then Germany, it had reached the very heart of the global capitalist system when it undercut the pound sterling and threatened the dollar. The solution, like the cause, was bound up as much with international security as with economics. But since the Anglo-Saxon powers adamantly refused to address the security issue and generally restricted their economic action to the financial sphere, the solution remained out of reach.

6.2 Financial crisis in Central Europe and the divided creditor powers

Since the end of the Great War, Central Europe remained politically divided, economically weak and acutely dependent upon foreign credit for banking resources and capital investment. France, in no position to lend substantial funds abroad before 1928, had restricted its involvement largely to Czechoslovakia and other allies in the region. British and American commercial lenders provided most of the funds. This had left the region acutely susceptible to changing market conditions in London and New York, and vulnerable to the decline in foreign lending that accompanied the latter stages of the Wall Street boom. Already by the spring of 1929, the Boden Credit-Anstalt was in trouble, and at the instigation of the Austrian government it was taken over by the *Österreichische Credit-Anstalt für Handel und Gewerbe*. But the latter bank, the largest in East-Central Europe, faced the withdrawal of foreign balances in 1930, and the additional uncertainty created by the Austro-German customs union controversy in March 1931 proved the final straw. On 11 May, the press reported that the Credit-Anstalt had been obliged to seek the protection of the state to avoid bankruptcy. Rothschilds had the largest interest in the Credit-Anstalt, but other British banks also had heavy commitments in the affected region, bringing London's stake to perhaps as much as £30 million.[4] To stave off collapse, the Austrian government extended a guarantee to the bank, then in May it turned to a consortium headed by Rothschilds in London and Lazard Frères in New York for a loan to cover the international obligations it had assumed. Meanwhile a flight from the Austrian schilling drove the exchange rate below gold export point. Richard Reisch, president of the Austrian National Bank, therefore approached the BIS for a 100 million schillings (£3 million) credit. This was soon arranged. The BIS itself committed 40 million schillings, while the Bank of England, the Bank of France, the Bank of Italy, the Reichsbank and the Federal Reserve Bank of New York each contributed 10 million schillings, and the remaining 10 million schillings came from five smaller central banks as a gesture of solidarity.[5]

Until now, bankers had shown impressive unity in face of the Austrian crisis. For the first time the BIS acted as a true international central bank by serving as lender of last resort to national issuing banks. Harrison of the New York Fed had been so fearful of American isolationist hostility to Wall Street that he refused to visit the BIS in Bâle or communicate with Gates McGarrah, the BIS president, even though McGarrah was a fellow American.[6] Yet, in face of Austria's threatened collapse, Harrison had not hesitated to join European central bankers in the BIS credit. Governor Moret of the Bank of France had been equally forthcoming. Upon receiving Bâle's request to participate in the international credit, he had immediately sought the Council of regents' approval, 'to demonstrate our solidarity and to further French policy towards Austria'. The regents gave their unanimous consent.[7] Before further action could be taken, however, French bankers and politicians became suspicious of British intentions and withheld cooperation. Austria was a small component of the international trade and payments system, but it occupied an important place in the international security system, and French authorities could scarcely forget the role that Austria had played as Germany's cat's-paw in its imperialist manoeuvres in 1914. While they appreciated the dangers of an Austrian financial crash, they were not prepared to see their resources used in an operation that ultimately favoured Germany's revisionist ambitions in the region.

Two months earlier, MacDonald had invited Bruening to visit him at his official residence of Chequers. The purpose was simply to demonstrate Britain's support for the chancellor in his struggle for political survival within Germany. But already Bruening had encouraged speculation that he would suspend reparations before the end of the year, and after news of the Austro-German customs union scheme the French ambassador requested Britain to postpone Bruening's Chequers visit, since Germans might construe it as encouraging revisionism.[8] Henderson reassured Briand when they met in Geneva that Britain had no intention of reopening the inter-governmental debt settlement until the United States agreed to participate, and would refuse to discuss the issue if Bruening raised it at Chequers.[9] French ministers nevertheless remained uneasy. Central bank governors meeting in Bâle had agreed that as a condition of their help the Credit-Anstalt should accept a controller of their choice. To Moret's horror, Norman proposed Schacht, the former Reichsbank governor who had resigned in protest at the Young plan and was now an ardent supporter of the German National party (DNVP), which openly advocated *Anschluss*. Reacting to France's protest, Norman insisted that he meant only a strong personality like Schacht, to force the Austrians to put their house in order. But this was not the first time that Norman, having caused outrage by his comments, claimed he had been misunderstood. Nor did he please Moret by vetoing his nomination for controller, Charles Rist, the distinguished economist and former deputy-governor of the Bank of France.[10]

In Paris, Baron Edouard de Rothschild, head of the French branch of the Rothschilds bank, appealed directly to Philippe Berthelot, secretary-general of the Quai d'Orsay, to follow London's lead by creating a Paris consortium of Credit-Anstalt creditors. A delay of even 24 hours, he warned, could result in disaster for the whole of Central Europe. Berthelot assured him that ministers wished to help. They did not want to see Austria collapse, since this would almost certainly throw it into the arms of Germany. But they would not be made 'dupes' by allowing France's financial support to be co-opted by the London consortium that Norman had created. Before extending assistance, Austria must issue a public renunciation of the Austro-German customs union scheme, give an assurance there would be no further surprises of this sort and affirm its readiness to pursue good relations in the future.[11]

Four days later, Count Clauzel, the French minister in Vienna, reported that Austria was attempting to escape French influence. Austrian representatives had approached the *Banque de Paris et des Pays Bas* (Paribas) for a 150 million schilling (equivalent) loan on the security of Austrian Treasury bills. But they had then secretly turned to the London bank Morgan Grenfell to see if it would take over the operation. As Clauzel observed, this was both unethical and unwise, since the London banks were in no position to lend more.[12] The extent of the London banks' commitment was now becoming clear. De Fleuriau learned from the Foreign Office that the London Rothschilds had £2 million tied up in the Credit-Anstalt, and the Bank of England itself fully £7 million.[13] This was an extraordinary amount for Britain's reserve bank to commit to a single, second-rate foreign bank. Not surprisingly, Norman was desperate to plug the dyke before the storm in Central Europe destroyed the whole of the City of London.

On Friday, 5 June, Bruening arrived in England to spend the weekend at Chequers. MacDonald seemed surprised that he was preoccupied with economic problems, and resisted his attempts to discuss reparations.[14] On the Saturday, as decrees were issued in Berlin for swingeing budget cuts and tax increases, Bruening declared that Germany could not continue the 'tribute payments' as demanded by the Young plan.[15] MacDonald carried on the visit as if nothing had happened. For Sunday lunch he invited the novelist John Galsworthy and the playwright George Bernard Shaw, who were currently enjoying great popularity in Germany, as well as the poet laureate, John Masefield. Bruening left England empty-handed.[16] French diplomats nonetheless received word that Norman, if not MacDonald, had supported Bruening's demand for revision of the reparations settlement.[17] This made them all the more determined to resist the destruction of their financial and security interests, which brought them into direct confrontation with Britain and presently also the United States.

On 9 June, as Bruening was sailing from Southampton, Austrian representatives began negotiations with the *Banque de Paris et des Pays Bas* (Paribas) for a 150 million schilling (£4.5 million) short-term loan. With each day that passed Austrian banks faced new withdrawals of foreign deposits, and in the single week of 8–12 June, the Austrian National Bank paid out 99 million schillings in foreign exchange. By the end of the week, the loan negotiations in Paris were practically completed. But so bad was the news from Vienna that the Paris bankers refused to proceed with the loan unless London banks shared the liability and the French government guaranteed their tranche of the loan. The Austrian banks warned they must announce an internal moratorium on Monday, 15 June, and only with difficulty did representatives of the London creditors committee persuade them to hold back while Norman personally canvassed support for the loan among City institutions and in New York. British and Austrian representatives appealed to the French government for support.[18] When by Tuesday morning no British or American banks had come forward, the French Cabinet agreed to guarantee the Paris banks' tranche of the loan. Ministers, however, set two crucial conditions. Austria must agree to a League of Nations enquiry into its economic and financial situation, and accept the enquiry's recommendations for reform. It must also give a secret undertaking – which France would be free to publish if it should choose – to take no step, economic or political, that would modify its international status; in other words it should renounce a customs union or *Anschluss* with Germany.[19] The French conditions were delivered to the Austrian representatives at 4 p.m. on Tuesday, 16 June, and a reply was requested by 8 p.m., so the loan arrangements could be completed in time to be announced the following morning, together with the renewal of the BIS credit to the Austrian National Bank.

In view of the importance the French government attached to blocking an *Anschluss*, the conditions it set for the loan guarantee were neither surprising nor particularly objectionable, unless to the Austrians themselves. Having shaken an already nervous Europe by their secret negotiations with Germany for a customs union, Austrian ministers had promised to suspend negotiations until the international court of justice had ruled on its legality. Yet they continued to cause nervousness in Paris by their less than straightforward behaviour. In the circumstances, no French government could have been expected to assist Austria financially without reciprocal concessions. As for the present government, which commanded only a minority of votes in a Parliament already disturbed by recent developments, it could scarcely have survived had it not demonstrated firmness on this issue of vital national interest. Given the British government's recognition that the customs union scheme threatened to divide Europe into armed camps, it might have been expected to sympathize with, and even endorse, the French conditions. Instead, MacDonald, Henderson, Snowden and the whole Labour government reacted with righteous indignation, describing the conditions as an 'ultimatum' and 'blackmail', and registering their 'disgust' at this attempt to gain a political advantage from financial aid. They were therefore pleased to find that Norman had already stepped into the breach.[20]

On 16 June, Sir Robert Kindersley, senior partner in Lazard Brothers and a director of the Bank of England, telephoned Norman from Vienna to warn him that the crisis was getting out of control. If the 150 million schilling loan was not forthcoming, the Austrian banks would have to declare a moratorium the following day. Norman was sure this would mean a 'complete collapse' in Austria, with the contagion spreading throughout Central Europe. The City of London was relatively more implicated in the region than either New York or Paris. Indeed, Norman would have known that several of London's leading banks, including Schroders, Barings, Kindersley's own Lazard Brothers, and possibly Rothschilds, faced bankruptcy if Austria declared a moratorium on external payments. Without waiting for loan negotiations in Paris to be completed, therefore, he hurriedly convened a meeting of directors of the Bank of England and secured their approval to provide the whole 150 million schillings that Austria required, in the form of a one-week loan to the Austrian National Bank.[21]

This, together with the 100 million schilling credit from the BIS consortium, was enough to stave off an immediate moratorium. It also undercut French efforts to secure political concessions from Austria. As MacDonald recorded in his diary on 17 June, 'Governor's loan before France's screwing was known (his own statement to me) smashed their bid, has made France furious & we may expect revenge.'[22] But it did not come in time to save the Austrian government, for Schober had already resigned rather than accept the French conditions.[23] Nor did it resolve the crisis. Having seized the initiative from France, Norman somehow imagined that in the one-week breathing space provided by the loan he could distribute the liability by persuading Paris as well as New York to accept 60 million schillings, with the remaining 25–30 million taken up by British banks. As might have been expected, he found no takers in New York or London. Meanwhile in Paris, Berthelot bluntly reminded Austrian representatives that France's conditions must be met before it extended any further help.[24]

By now, the contagion had spread beyond Austria. As early as 11 May, the day the Credit-Anstalt's failure was announced, the National Bank of Hungary experienced heavy exchange losses. The French government quietly extended 355 million francs (£2.9 million) to the Hungarian treasury.[25] Meanwhile the National Bank of Hungary turned to the BIS for help, and on 18 June, leading central banks under BIS auspices joined in a £2 million credit.[26] In separate operations France also assisted Poland and Yugoslavia.[27] But as in the case of Austria these were merely stopgaps, and ominously cracks now also appeared in the German financial edifice.

6.3   The contagion spreads to Germany

Norman, like many of his British contemporaries, displayed a strong affinity to Germans. This, we may assume, was reinforced by the fact that the German bankers he met were competent, trustworthy, and, with rare exceptions such as Schacht, liberal internationalists. Such was his view of the German character that in April 1931 he told Henry Stimson that German workers were reluctant to take the dole out of respect for the taxpayers.[28] Even in early June he advised MacDonald that Germany was exceptionally resilient: it had weathered economic storms before and would get through this one as well.[29] But already he feared that the Austrian crisis, aggravated by French political meddling, would bring down Germany as well.[30]

Since 21 May, the Reichsbank had lost between 800–900 million RM (£39–44 million) in gold and foreign exchange, with demand running at 60–80 million RM (£3–4 million) a day. But with the threat of a moratorium in Vienna and unconfirmed reports that a major German bank had been obliged to seek government assistance, Norman anticipated trouble when the markets reopened on Monday, 15 June. He therefore telephoned Harrison in New York to appeal for help. It was, he warned, impossible to exaggerate the seriousness of the crisis in Europe. The central banks were attempting to contain the fall-out, but it was 'a world political problem', which could only be resolved through drastic political action. In his view, Washington must work with London to reduce or remove reparation claims which had become an intolerable burden upon Germany, and remove the constraints of the peace treaties which had left Austria economically unviable and Germany permanently nursing its territorial wounds.[31]

The three ministers who shared direction of British government policy, MacDonald, Henderson and Snowden, scarcely disguised their disdain for one another, making it impossible for them to work as a team. Nonetheless they all listened to Norman, and fully shared his sympathy for Germany and loathing for France. When Ray Atherton, chargé d'affaires at the American embassy, asked MacDonald on 6 June if he feared the crisis in Europe would lead to war, MacDonald replied, 'no, revolution'. Then he added,

> An equal danger to Europe was French domination. He asserted that nationalistic considerations dominated French finance and foreign policy, that the

French loans to Czechoslovakia, Roumania, Poland and Yugoslavia were based on French aggrandisement, and that it was idle to expect an international character from French banking or diplomacy.[32]

MacDonald also shared Norman's belief that Britain needed America's help to contain the crisis to Continental Europe. From Friday, 12 June, therefore, he communicated almost daily with Stimson in an effort to hasten American intervention. As Norman anticipated, Germany's exchange position sharply deteriorated on the Saturday morning. That day alone the Reichsbank lost 200 million RM (£9.8 million). Hans Luther, the governor, reacted by raising his discount rate from 5 to 7 per cent, but confidence had been so thoroughly undermined that higher interest rates did little to slow the withdrawal of foreign balances or the German flight from the mark.[33] On Friday, 19 June, with a moratorium threatened the following day, MacDonald appealed to Stimson for immediate action.[34]

MacDonald, like a more recent Labour prime minister, imagined he commanded influence in Washington and had persuaded Hoover to issue his proposal for a general inter-governmental debt moratorium on 20 June.[35] This was hardly the case. As early as January 1931, Stimson had warned Hoover that the scale of American financial exposure in Germany endangered the whole American banking system, and from 6 May Frederick Sackett, the ambassador in Berlin, repeatedly warned that Germany was in serious financial trouble.[36] Hoover denounced angrily 'the Wall Street crowd', for drawing America into Europe's troubles.[37] Ever since the war he had loudly denied any connection between reparations and war debts, and since the Congressional elections the previous autumn he had justified his record by blaming Europe for America's depression.[38] But by 11 May, he was forced to acknowledge that the network of inter-governmental debts was becoming unsustainable, and rather than waiting for individual countries to default on their obligations, he decided to propose a general one-year moratorium.[39] Yet for fully a month he hesitated to act, fearing criticism from his own supporters for weakening America's claim to war debts and bailing out the Wall Street bankers and their European clients.[40] To test opinion, he embarked upon a three-day tour of the Midwest, where he spoke to leading bankers and politicians. To his relief he found the bankers of the interior – as he put it, 'the solid men, not the Wall Street crowd'[41] – favoured a moratorium, not least because in aggregate they had as much money as Wall Street at risk in Germany. Even then he painstakingly sounded Congressional opinion on his return to Washington. Finally on 19 June he called in foreign representatives to inform them of his moratorium proposal. The following day he released it to the press.[42]

British observers were extremely relieved to learn of Hoover's proposal. With Germany freed from annual reparations payments of £90 million, they hoped this would end the panic withdrawals of foreign credits, the German flight from the mark and the threat of a general payments moratorium, and in the breathing space thus provided they could secure lasting improvements in Germany's position. Since the British banking system was thoroughly implicated in the German crisis, this was hugely important. But beyond the immediate value of the moratorium, they took it to be Washington's long-awaited acknowledgement that the United States must share responsibility for international political and economic stability. They therefore assumed that together the Anglo-Saxon powers could force the refractory Europeans to end their destructive rivalries and allow market relations again to flourish. Largely in this expectation, they effusively welcomed what was after all a very modest initiative. The British Treasury spoke of 'this great and wise action'.[43] MacDonald privately mused, 'These things I dreamt of when in the U.S. in 1929 but hardly thought would happen.'[44] In the event, British leaders were soon disappointed, for they thoroughly misunderstood Hoover's motives for intervening.

As events unfolded in the spring, Hoover had received warnings from Eugene Meyer, chairman of the Federal Reserve Board, Harrison of the New York Fed and other authorities that if Germany stopped external payments, European countries would 'gang up' on the United States to abandon war debt demands. Hoover frankly acknowledged to Stimson that his main concern was to avoid being drawn into what he called 'the European mess'.[45] The moratorium seemed to him the best and perhaps the only means of containing European pressure for lasting American concessions.[46] The moratorium thus was an expression of America's enduring isolationism and not, as British observers naïvely assumed, a departure from it. For some time the pros and cons of war debt revision had been debated in the American press. Republicans tended to oppose revision on the grounds that Europe would inevitably use the extra revenue on armaments. Democrats more optimistically favoured war debt concessions, on condition that Europe agreed to disarm. In either case they assumed that Europe remained a source of danger and that its militarism must be curbed by reducing arms expenditure.[47] Hoover fully shared this cynical view of Europe.[48] If he refused to link war debt relief to disarmament, it was only because he feared this would draw the United States further into 'the European mess'.

French ministers believed that Bruening had deliberately provoked the present crisis by his statement in London on 6 June, threatening a unilateral cessation of reparation payments. They were privately furious that Hoover had sprung the moratorium upon them without prior consultation: a surprise only somewhat less unpleasant than the revelation of the Austro-German customs union scheme three months earlier. They were all the more annoyed that Hoover should present himself as the saviour of Germany and the world, when in their opinion he was merely trying to salvage the American banks' huge commercial commitments in Germany, and doing so at France's expense by demanding that it should forgo reparation receipts. They regarded this as a cynical and deeply irresponsible gambit, which jeopardized the hard-won formula contained in the Young plan. For, if Germany were permitted to suspend reparation payments now, what chance was there that it would ever resume them?

Reparation payments had become a matter of economic importance for France, which was beginning to feel the effects of the slump and now faced a substantial deficit in its national budget. But French ministers were more worried that the moratorium meant stepping onto the slippery slope that led to wholesale Treaty revision. Their dilemma was that, with Germany agitating for revision,

France needed the interested friendship of the Anglo-Saxon powers more than ever.[49] They also appreciated that a German crash spelled trouble for everyone.[50] Therefore, while French press and Parliament erupted in anger at the predicament in which Hoover's proposal placed France, French ministers welcomed the moratorium while insisting that in principle at least the unconditional tranche should continue to be paid.[51] Lord Tyrrell sought to explain the French predicament to Henderson, the foreign secretary:

> They are touchy because they think that they have been forced into a position in which they have to choose between appearing as the obstacle to the unanimous adoption of the American offer and giving their consent to the abandonment of a solemn agreement which Germany freely signed and not under duress like the Treaty of Versailles, only 18 months ago. This is the meaning of the excitement and bitterness in the Chambers [of Parliament] and the importance of the reference in Flandin's speech to the sanctity of treaties. You should also realise the widespread nature of the feeling here that once again Germany is deceiving the world. Every intelligent person in Paris realises that Germany is [facing] a serious credit crisis; but nobody believes that she can be really affected by the payment to the Bank for International Settlements of an unconditional annuity which Flandin claimed would represent but six percent of her Budget.[52]

However, if French ministers were annoyed, so too were British and American leaders, and in contrast they made no attempt to hide it. The great fear of British leaders was that Germany would collapse, with incalculable consequences for London, New York and the capitalist system itself. Every day's delay in the adoption of the moratorium brought this spectre closer. They therefore expressed fury at French 'hegemony' on the Continent, which obstructed the Treaty revision with which they hoped to appease Germany. American ministers, including Hoover himself, agreed that Treaty revision was probably necessary. But they were chiefly concerned at the predicament the French placed them in, where to secure adoption of the moratorium they must become more not less involved in European affairs.

On 25 June, MacDonald telephoned Stimson, urging him to resist French efforts to modify the moratorium, 'as yielding would bring the whole proposal to collapse, or would render it pretty useless.' Ten days later his language had become shrill:

> France has been playing its usual small minded & selfish game over the Hoover proposal. Its methods are those of the worst Jews. To do a good thing for its own sake is not in line with French official nature. So Germany cracks while France bargains.

By 11 July he had become almost frantic:

> The behaviour of the French has been inconceivably atrocious. ... [S]uch pettiness & implacability. ... Another war is inevitable if an independent nation in

Europe is to exist. The immediate outlook is black; the more remote one still blacker.[53]

Anger in Washington towards France became equally unrestrained. As Stimson recorded on 25 June, Hoover 'has a pretty strong antipathy against France and is also made a good deal stiffer against France by his fear of our own Congressmen here.'[54] William Castle, the under-secretary of state, who closely shared Hoover's outlook, betrayed total incomprehension of the European situation and put down French behaviour to sheer perversity:

> The French are the most hopeless people in the world. First, they were furious because their pride was injured. Now they are quibbling on methods while the house burns and we have got to waste hours in trying to make them see some sense. An acceptance of the plan would mean instantly good relations with Germany; it would mean the acceptance by this country of the Young Plan; it would mean a cordial atmosphere all round; it would stabilize the gains already made in commodity prices on the French market. And France is willing to risk all of this because French logic sees things in a different way.[55]

The immediate effect of the moratorium proposal had been, as Hoover hoped, to reassure the financial markets that foreign balances could safely be left in Germany. Stock markets everywhere rose sharply on 20 June, with many shares on the Berlin bourse gaining as much as 20 per cent by the close of the day.[56] A rough index of confidence in Germany was the price of the Young plan loan, which had been issued in May 1930 near par, then slumped to 66.75 by 19 June 1931. It recovered to 75 by 22 June before slipping back. The Reichsbank faced renewed pressure on the foreign exchanges on Tuesday, 23 June, and succeeded in holding its currency reserves above the legal minimum of 40 per cent only with the aid of a £1 million overnight deposit from the Bank of England. Norman, alarmed by the situation, requested Harrison's participation in a £20 million standby credit for the Reichsbank. Harrison, however, was loath to take on such a large commitment, and proposed that it should be shared with the Bank of France and the BIS. Despite Norman's expectation that the Bank of France would refuse to cooperate, the £20 million credit was arranged the next day, with the Bank of England, the Federal Reserve Bank of New York, the Bank of France and the BIS taking equal portions.[57] But it did no more than postpone the day of reckoning. By Saturday, 4 July, the credit was exhausted and the Reichsbank's gold and foreign exchange reserves had again fallen below the legal minimum.

The situation was saved on 5 July when the Golddiskont Bank, a subsidiary of the Reichsbank, drew down the whole $50 million (£10 million) of a line of credit negotiated years earlier with the New York-based International Acceptance Corporation. On Tuesday, 7 July, France and the United States finally reached a compromise on the moratorium whereby the unconditional annuity of reparations would continue to be paid into the BIS, but the French tranche would be immediately transferred as a credit to the Reichsbahn and the balance would be returned as a credit to the German government.[58] On Wednesday, the Reichsbank received a 500 million mark (£25 million) guarantee fund from a consortium of leading German industrial firms. On Thursday, Luther made a hurried visit to Paris, London and Bâle to request a large additional credit. He returned empty-handed. Harrison, nervous of a backlash in America, signalled to fellow central bank governors that he would not participate in another credit operation. In any case, he believed Germans themselves were chiefly responsible for the flight from the mark, and looked to Luther to discourage it.[59] Norman, reluctant to act without American involvement, similarly refused to participate.[60] But the spectre of a systemic crisis made him desperate. Earlier in the month he had privately encouraged the Germans to threaten a default on reparations to pressure governments to agree on the Hoover moratorium.[61] Now, at the meeting of central bank governors at BIS headquarters in Bâle on Sunday, 12 July, he shocked Moret by stating that he preferred a crash in Germany to force governments to embark upon Treaty revision. De Fleuriau, who protested to the Foreign Office, reported Norman to say

> He did not wish for further credits for Germany, and that it was much better that there should be complete bankruptcy on the part of Germany as this would raise the whole question of reparations and revision of the Treaty of Versailles, including the Polish Corridor.[62]

The following day, the governors considered Luther's request to renew the £20 million credit arranged the previous month, which was due to be repaid on the 15th. All the governors present agreed to a three-month extension, except for Norman who insisted upon limiting it to 15 days. McGarrah, the BIS president, protested that this was risking calamity. Harrison, who telephoned Norman from New York, similarly warned against this strategy. What, he asked, did Norman think would happen if Germany was pushed to the brink? Norman replied, 'nothing is going to happen – absolutely nothing.' Harrison, keenly aware of Washington's reluctance to become involved in Treaty revision, warned against betting on an immediate political solution. Norman was adamant: the Reichsbank should replace Luther with Schacht who alone could impose the draconian measures now required, and the creditor powers should revise reparations, war debts and so forth. But as the other governors were unwilling to engage in such brinkmanship, Norman joined them in renewing the credit until 4 August.[63]

Luther, who had sent his deputy, Wilhelm Vocke, to the Bâle meeting, remained in Berlin to prepare defences against a run on German banks on the morning of Monday, 13 July. In conjunction with the government, he secured the closure of all stock exchanges on Monday and Tuesday. The *Darmstädter und National* (or *Danat*) *Bank*, fatally weakened by the failure of its client *Nordwolle*, Germany's largest textile firm, closed its doors, reopening later with a state guarantee to enable it to meet its creditors. Other banks remained open, but a government decree obliged them temporarily to suspend cash payments and inter-bank clearances. Another decree concentrated all foreign exchange and foreign payments at the Reichsbank or other institutions designated as its agents. On Wednesday, 15 July, when the markets reopened, the Reichsbank raised its discount rate a full 3 points to 10 per cent and its rate on advances to a swingeing 15 per cent. That same day, the German government duly paid the unconditional reparation annuity to the BIS, and the BIS syndicate renewed its £20 million credit for another three weeks. The combination of exchange controls, record interest rates and central bank cooperation stopped the mark from collapsing. But it meant in practice Germany abandoning the gold standard. This grim fact was reflected in the price of the Young loan, which opened in New York on the Wednesday at 59, a new low.

On 26 June, with France still holding out for special treatment of the unconditional tranche of reparations, Henderson, the British foreign secretary, decided to press Germany for concessions. France, he appreciated, would be readier to accept the moratorium if Germany were to halt construction of the 'Deutschland', the new pocket battleship, and confirm it had abandoned plans for a customs union with Austria.[64] On 30 June, with still no agreement on the moratorium, Washington reluctantly joined London in pressuring Bruening for a gesture of some sort.[65] Yet, paradoxically, the Anglo-Saxon powers remained determined to stop France from obtaining security guarantees from Germany. In early July, British officials learned that Pierre Laval, the French premier, had invited German ministers to Paris to promote a general settlement. With Hoover's encouragement, MacDonald immediately issued invitations for a diplomatic conference in London, so as to enable Germany to avoid having to deal directly with France.[66] MacDonald and Henderson now also took up Bruening's invitation, issued at Chequers, to visit Berlin, to strengthen Germany's resistance to French pressure. When Laval nevertheless persisted in inviting Bruening to Paris, British ministers postponed their visit to Berlin. But determined as ever to counter French pressure on Germany, Henderson seized upon the opening of the French colonial exposition on 15 July as an excuse to visit Paris, where he was joined by Stimson and Andrew Mellon, the secretary of the Treasury, who were separately visiting Europe. With British, American and German ministers in Paris, informal conversations took place over a period of five days.

Briand, Flandin and Laval, the three French ministers who handled the crisis, favoured different means of proceeding. Briand, as before, sought to involve the Anglo-Saxon powers in European security while pursuing *rapprochement* with Germany. However, after being caught out by the Austro-German customs union proposal and humiliated in his recent bid for the French presidency, his health as well as his political standing had declined and he no longer counted for much in the government.[67] Flandin, the finance minister, was not indifferent to the friendship of the Anglo-Saxon powers, but he placed greater emphasis upon constraining Germany. Hoping to exploit Germany's crisis by bringing to bear France's financial resources, he now proposed a £100 million, ten-year loan, jointly guaranteed by the three creditor powers, in return for political concessions.[68]

Laval, the premier, agreed to the loan offer. But rather than using it as a bargaining tool as Flandin sought to do, he was prepared to offer it without conditions as a gesture of friendship to Germany. A lawyer who had begun his political career on the Left but moved steadily Rightwards, he was also an entrepreneur who had acquired a sizeable fortune largely in commercial radio. As yet he had almost no experience of international affairs. He knew that Germany was disregarding its obligation to disarm and in real terms spending two-thirds as much on arms as in 1914.[69] Nonetheless, he believed that France must reach an accommodation with Germany, if it was to survive. In his own words, 'We will always be neighbours of Germany. We face the alternative of reaching agreement with her or of clashing every twenty years on the battlefield.'[70] He was therefore prepared to contemplate radical concessions, including German demands for the return of the Polish Corridor.[71]

A 'realist', Laval was also a materialist who believed that all human relations were governed by the pursuit of economic advantage. This was reflected in his appointment that summer of André François-Poncet as de Margerie's successor at the Berlin embassy. François-Poncet had been the public face of the *Comité des Forges*, the syndicate of French steel-makers, before Poincaré appointed him in 1928 as secretary of state for the national economy, in which capacity he had drafted France's 'constructive' alternative to the Austro-German customs union scheme.[72] Laval followed this up by promoting the establishment of a Franco-German Economic Commission in Berlin to negotiate a 'Franco-German economic and social pact'.[73] But for the time being he sought merely to create the impression of influence over Germany by holding negotiations for a loan in Paris, so he could persuade sceptical French parliamentarians to support it.[74] He and his colleagues considered conditions such as a political truce during the ten-year term of the loan, but in the event they made no specific demands upon Germany: neither renunciation of the Austro-German customs union project nor a halt to the construction of the 'Deutschland', which the Anglo-Saxon powers repeatedly requested. While accepting that a display of firmness was needed to allay public fear, they counted on a face-to-face meeting with German leaders to identify the basis of a *rapprochement*.[75]

French diplomacy divided the British camp. Henderson was prepared to consider the French proposals, but MacDonald treated them as tantamount to aggression and decried Henderson's gullibility. Jealous of his own statesmanship and scornful of nearly all his Labour colleagues, MacDonald persuaded himself that Henderson had personally cancelled their visit to Berlin while encouraging Bruening to visit Paris where he would be bullied by the French. 'The Government has been doing everything it could to prevent the Germans going to Paris & having an ultimatum presented by the French', MacDonald recorded in his diary on 16 July. 'Henderson has thwarted us. F.O. [Foreign Office] here is furious.'[76]

Remarkably similar tensions arose in the American camp. Stimson, like Henderson, was impressed by the moderation of French leaders and recommended their loan proposal for Hoover's consideration. Hoover, however, understood that Germany would not even need a loan if France dropped its reparation demands and the commercial bankers played up by leaving their credits in place. He refused to believe the French could be moderate, and became convinced they had drawn Stimson into their web. He also believed reports that France had withdrawn £40 million from Germany since his announcement of the moratorium proposal.[77] If the French were now proposing a loan, therefore, it was only to 'trick' the Germans into political concessions with which the United States could not be associated.[78] Stimson assured Hoover that the French loan proposal was genuine, and warned him not to be taken in by what New York bankers might be saying or Norman's claims that Germany could be saved without further financial support. But Hoover merely took this as evidence that 'Stimson was completely sold to the French.'[79] Overlooking the six-hour time difference between Washington and Paris, he wore Stimson down with nocturnal telephone calls.[80] The only issue that brought them together was their mutual hostility towards Wall Street and in particular J.P. Morgan, the largest of the international banks.

In mid-July, Pierre Jay, a partner in Morgan's Paris affiliate, Morgan Harjes, informed Moret of the Bank of France that there was no hope of New York participating in another loan to Germany. J.P. Morgan, as France's fiscal agent in the United States, had some obligation to keep Moret informed. But Stimson, on hearing this, was furious. Since the regents of the Bank of France were extremely cool to French participation in a three-country guaranteed loan, Morgan's intervention, he told Jay, was 'folly', since it would only encourage them to dig in their heels, and without the inducement of the loan Franco-German *rapprochement* would be impossible. Explaining this to Hoover, who telephoned him moments later, he was able to tell Jay that the president himself would be speaking to his New York partners about their untimely interference in Washington's diplomatic efforts. 'He turned as white as a sheet when I told him what I thought', Stimson recorded. 'I had one good chance to swat Morgan in the eye and I did it.'[81]

However, aside from their mutual hostility to New York bankers, Stimson and Hoover remained as far apart as ever on the larger issues. Whereas Stimson feared that Morgan's intervention would wreck the chances of a loan and with it the basis for Franco-German *rapprochement*, Hoover feared it would have precisely the opposite effect of driving Germany into the arms of France while entangling the United States in France's imperialism. Already, he complained, the American press was reporting that Stimson had accepted the French terms for the loan, which acutely embarrassed him.[82] Having conceded the moratorium, he now sought to draw a line under political action and turn the problem over to the bankers. Perhaps, he suggested to Stimson, the political representatives in Paris could clear away the 'fringe issues', such as Germany's construction of the 'Deutschland' and its plans for a customs union with Austria. But Stimson should cut short the conversations in Paris since they strengthened France's hand, and resume them in London which was a much safer venue.[83] He believed American bankers would support a purely economic solution to Germany's crisis. As he told Stimson on 18 July, American regional bankers held $300–$400 million in German paper, almost as much as the New York banks. While not prepared to add to their commitments, they would maintain what they had, if foreign bankers did the same. That was as much as the United States could reasonably be asked to do.

> I have talked during the day to the men who will be helpful here and they are not the Morgan crowd. ... [T]he very best men we have (who do not take the Morgan view) believe we will be taking for the present all the burden we can if we try to maintain that total sum. ... Our people have stood up very well and I have the feeling that it is pretty dangerous to try to develop at this particular conference much more than stabilization of the situation.[84]

Despite dissociating themselves from Norman's wild proposals at Bâle, British ministers were impatient to promote radical Treaty revision. William Shone of the British embassy in Washington approached Castle, the acting secretary of state, to propose that the London conference should address 'revision of the Young Plan, extension of the President's proposal for a longer period than a year, and phases [*sic*] of the Versailles Treaty.' Castle warned that the United States would not participate in the conference at all unless the agenda was restricted to measures for dealing with 'the present emergency'.[85] French ministers, deeply suspicious of Britain's revisionist ambitions, issued a similar warning.[86] Once the London conference began, Snowden nevertheless attempted to reopen the reparations question. Stimson flatly refused to discuss it, and Flandin agreed that the subject should be dropped. The politicians turned back to financial options, eventually considering four.

The first option, the French proposal for a government guaranteed loan to Germany, was quickly set aside when British and American representatives refused to support it. Briefly they reviewed the second option: reforms of the Reichsbank's operation by, among other things, reducing its 40 per cent currency reserve requirement to expand its credit creating powers. They soon agreed that in present circumstances such reforms were unlikely to have the desired effect. They then turned to the role of other central banks and whether they could do more by, for instance, rediscounting the Reichsbank's bill portfolio. When Snowden insisted on the need to leave central banks free from government interference, they fell back on their fourth option, Hoover's proposal of a 'standstill' agreement among the commercial banks to keep their German balances in place.

Even now, the size of Germany's total short-term foreign liabilities remained unclear, with estimates ranging from £200 million (Germany)[87] to £288 million (France and the United States).[88] But there was general agreement that perhaps 50 per cent were American and 40 per cent were British, with the balance belonging to lending institutions in other countries. French credits in Germany amounted to at most £16 million, although Bruening confirmed that, contrary to British and American suspicions, French banks had not run down their balances since 20 June when Hoover announced his debt moratorium proposal.[89] MacDonald pressed Flandin to do more by taking over part of London's credits in Germany. Flandin firmly refused, claiming that France was already doing more than Britain or the United States to prop up Germany, since it was largely French balances in London and New York that had made their lending possible.[90] He nevertheless agreed to support a standstill agreement organized by the central banks, which proved to be the sole practical outcome of the conference.

The standstill agreement, introduced provisionally on 29 July and formally on 1 September, succeeded in maintaining some £260 million of foreign short-term funds in Germany. The Reichsbank, forced to raise its discount rate from 10 to 15 per cent on 1 August, was able to reduce it to 8 per cent on 2 September. Neither the Hoover moratorium nor the standstill, however, did more than hold the line. With credit restrictions, penal interest rates and no new foreign lending or investment, Germany desperately needed a large-scale injection of foreign capital, which was out of the question while fears of another war remained.[91] The involvement of the Anglo-Saxon powers was therefore essential. But not only had they refused to extend a commitment to Europe, but had also combined to block French efforts at a new *modus vivendi* with Germany. Indeed, they had pilloried France for attempting to do so. According to MacDonald, France was 'solely responsible for the failure of the Hoover Plan & the present position. ... Again & again be it said: France is the enemy.'[92] With Hoover, Castle and others in the United States and Britain persuaded of this view, the chances of the three creditor powers combining in a constructive approach to the international crisis were remote.

6.4   The sterling crisis

By 1931, the gold standard, which had cost Britain so much to regain six years earlier, had proven to be, in the words of Ralph Hawtrey, the Treasury economist, 'a disastrous failure'.[93] The Bank of England had with difficulty managed to weather the storm created by the General Strike in 1926, the subsequent pressure for monetary reform from domestic agriculture and industry, and the huge dislocation caused by the great bull market on Wall Street in 1928–9. But the onset of the world economic slump in 1929–30 had further weakened the British balance of payments, and as early as mid-1930 doubts surfaced about the underlying stability of sterling.[94]

The Bank of England began to lose gold to France and certain other Continental countries from May 1930.[95] By the autumn, Norman had become acutely nervous. But he was not prepared to press for a multilateral solution and resisted publication of the League of Nations Gold Delegation report, fearing the adverse publicity he and fellow central bankers might receive.[96] Nor was he prepared to seek a bilateral solution through conversations with Moret in Paris. True to the spirit of the gold standard, he chose to fix upon unilateral domestic action. Hence when reports appeared of disorder in the government's finances and a campaign began in business circles and the conservative press for retrenchment, he immediately became involved. Snowden, he found, was already convinced of the need for action.[97] On 14 January 1931, Snowden impressed upon Cabinet colleagues the seriousness of the situation, and secured their agreement to an independent

Committee on National Expenditure to investigate the budget prospects and recommend remedial action.[98] Snowden then appointed several impeccably conservative City men to the committee, and Sir George May, the recently retired director of the Prudential Insurance Company, to chair it. This went some way to satisfy critics, and coincidently the pound recovered and remained strong throughout the spring.

One reason for the stronger pound was the cessation of French demand for monetary gold in late January, owing largely to the rundown of French official balances through a loan conversion operation.[99] A second reason was the seasonal effect, since sterling was normally stronger in the spring before the financing of overseas crops affected the exchange rate. The third and almost certainly the most important reason was the onset of the financial crisis on the Continent, which caused holders of short-term balances to transfer them to the relative safety of London. The Bank of England's gold reserves, having fallen to a dangerously low £140 million in February 1931, soon rose above the 'Cunliffe minimum' of £150 million. On 14 May, the Bank of England reduced Bank rate a half-point to 2.5 per cent. By the second week of July sterling reserves stood at a comfortable £164 million.

Despite the strength of the Bank's reserves, the sterling crisis, which began on 13 July, should have come as no surprise. The staple export industries – coal and steel, shipbuilding, heavy machinery and textiles – had become severely depressed after 1929, with obvious consequences for the balance of payments. Board of Trade estimates in the summer of 1931 put the current account surplus for 1929 at £117 million and for 1930 at £39 million, while anticipating a deficit of at least £56 million for 1931.[100] Seasonal factors now also worked against sterling, as indicated by the fact that the Bank of England had lost gold every summer since the return to the gold standard in 1925. But once again the most important factor was almost certainly the movement of hot money.[101] In other years, the Bank could cover a current account deficit by drawing in short-term balances through higher interest rates. This year the prospect of a standstill on German foreign loan payments and reports that City banks were dangerously overcommitted on the Continent impelled wealth holders to seek a safer home for their balances in New York, Geneva or Paris.

The weakness of sterling against the Dutch florin, the Swiss franc and the American dollar as well as the French franc in the second week of July clearly demonstrated that economic rather than political motives were at work.[102] Yet when it happened, British observers professed surprise and complained that sterling was the victim of a foreign conspiracy. Queried by Harrison on 15 July about the sudden drop in sterling, Norman claimed to be baffled.[103] Others noted the coincidence of sterling's decline, growing disagreement between the Anglo-Saxon powers and France over financial assistance to Germany, and the fact that most of the gold exports from the Bank of England went to Paris, and drew the conclusion that France was using its financial power in an attempt to suborn Britain to its policy of crushing Germany. The City editor of the Labourite *Daily Herald* reported that 'the view is gaining ground that France is deliberately creating a situation to enable her to withdraw gold from London by keeping the exchange rate at a low level. The movement is bound up with developments in Germany'.[104] Harold Cox, City editor of the *Daily Mail* and editor of the prestigious *Banker's Magazine*, concurred. 'The rapidity with which the demand for francs has developed within the brief space of a few days [has] led to a general assumption in markets here that political factors are again at work in the exchange on the eve of the war debt negotiations.'[105]

The *Financial Times*, the *Financial News* and the *Times* were only slightly more circumspect. Under the heading 'Political Factors?', the *Financial Times* observed, 'It is not without significance that whenever an international or Franco-British conference is arranged or contemplated, the Paris rate of exchange definitely develops a strong tendency.'[106] Arthur Wade, City editor of the *Evening Standard*, put it more categorically. 'We know that this movement is due to withdrawal of official funds – that is, funds controlled by the Bank of France and the [French] Treasury.' Coming just before the conference on the Hoover moratorium, 'it looks as if the French authorities regard shipments of gold as moves in the diplomatic game.' The Bank of England, he advised, should not resist the rundown of sterling balances: 'Let the gold go and make London independent of Paris.'[107] George Glasgow in the *Contemporary Review* similarly affirmed that Britain was the victim of financial blackmail. France, he wrote, had induced Britain to fight the Great War on its terms, then to pay for it by extracting reparations from Germany that only British credits had made possible. Having deliberately amassed sterling balances in its pursuit of political influence, '[a]fter 1928 it became a regular element in French diplomacy to use that lever on London.'[108] It is a measure of British suspicions of French power and corruption that Sir Clive Wigram, the King's private secretary, should write, 'Attempts to embarrass us and destroy confidence in our stability as the financial centre of the world, and in the London Bill, were unworthy of a nation whom we pulled out of the fire such a short time ago.'[109]

So general were these suspicions that Lord Tyrrell in Paris took it upon himself to find out if the run on sterling was due to deliberate French selling. He soon reported that the evidence hardly supported the allegations.[110] Another doubter was Tom Johnston, secretary of state for Scotland, who travelled to Paris after Parliament rose for the summer to find out if his colleagues' claims were true. With a member of the British embassy present, he interviewed Laval and Flandin. Both vigorously denied the allegations. Indeed, Flandin suggested that Johnston was looking in the wrong place, for Governor Norman had recently twice asked Moret to buy gold in London 'in order to maintain the pressure on sterling.'[111] Johnston seems not to have taken in Flandin's claim, for he did not press him to elaborate. The interview convinced him nevertheless that the French authorities were anxious to help Britain rather than trying to bring it to its knees.[112] This was fully borne out by subsequent events. Gradually, evidence also emerged that much, probably most, of the hot money fleeing Britain was not French but British. But the Bank of England played this down, and since this was not what its readers wanted to hear, the British press made little of it.[113]

Between Monday, 13 July, when the run on sterling began and the end of July the Bank of England lost over £33 million in gold and £21 million in foreign exchange, driving reserves far below the 'Cunliffe minimum'.[114] The Bank's Committee of Treasury approved a 1 per cent increase in Bank rate at its Thursday meeting on 23 July and a further 1 per cent rise on 30 July, taking Bank rate to 4.5 per cent. But since interest rate action alone seemed incapable of restoring confidence, the Bank on 25 July approached the New York Fed and the Bank of France for a large support credit. The decision to seek assistance from New York was uncontroversial, but the approach to Paris was made with great reluctance. Representatives of the London clearing banks warned that it was 'most undesirable to have recourse to Paris', in view of the political conditions they were sure the French would attach to any credit.[115] In fact, while French commercial banks had reduced their balances in London and the Bank of France had run down its sterling balances from a peak of £166 million in June 1928 to £62 million, the French government had largely maintained its sterling deposits since 1930.[116] Governor Moret, at the instigation of the French government, now intervened in the exchange markets to support sterling.[117] Along with the Ministry of Finance, he also confirmed his willingness to organize a large loan as backing for the pound sterling.[118] Meanwhile, he welcomed the Bank of England's request for a credit and immediately agreed to match New York's contribution by raising £25 million, an enormous amount at this time. But to demonstrate that, contrary to rumours in London, Paris was fully behind the operation, he insisted upon sharing the credit with all the major banks in the *place de Paris*.[119] On Saturday, 1 August, the Bank of England was able to announce the American and French three-month commercial credits. Having simultaneously increased the fiduciary currency issue by £15 million, it now possessed an extra £65 million with which to meet further pressure on sterling.

De Fleuriau, writing to Briand, expressed his hope that the credit operation would reduce British hostility towards France. In his view, the British had made France the scapegoat for the crisis because they were not prepared to admit their own responsibility for allowing sterling to become so vulnerable or to say a word against the United States for its financial recklessness. Echoing Stimson's words,[120] he blamed Norman, 'a thorough-going francophobe', who exercised enormous influence over Labour ministers, the City and the national press, especially the *Times*. But he urged Briand to restrain the French press from responding to British insults, since this would only aggravate British hostility. Ultimately, he was sure, the facts would speak for themselves and charges of French ill-will would be exposed as baseless.[121] Briand probably spoke to members of the Paris press corps, for Tyrrell soon reported that the angry editorials against Britain and Norman in particular were much less evident in July.[122]

Everything, however, seemed to conspire against sterling. The report of the Macmillan Committee on Finance and Industry, instituted in 1929 to justify adherence to the gold standard and deflect criticism from the Bank of England, shook the markets when it appeared on 13 July by setting out for the first time the full scale of Britain's foreign short-term liabilities. The report affirmed that

'Britain's underlying position as a creditor nation remained immensely strong.'[123] But by confirming that Britain's financial institutions had tied up £407 million abroad, much of it in Central Europe, it prompted holders of sterling balances to seek safer havens abroad. Uncertainty continued when the London diplomatic conference ended inconclusively on 24 July, leaving the bankers to organize a *Stillhalt*, or standstill, to halt the panic withdrawal of short-term credits from Germany.

Sterling's plight was further aggravated when the Committee on National Expenditure chaired by Sir George May published its report on 31 July. Warning of a prospective budget deficit of £120 million or nearly 14 per cent of planned expenditure, the committee recommended economies of £97 million, including £81 million from the unemployment insurance scheme and other social services.[124] This was a sensational warning and devastating advice, for in the current budget of £885 million, fully 40 per cent was earmarked for debt servicing or amortization, 12.5 per cent for defence and 9 per cent for administration; only £332.6 million was intended for education, roads, health, housing, police, pensions and unemployment and health insurance. It would thus mean reducing expenditure on welfare and public works by nearly 30 per cent.[125] As Sir Richard Hopkins observed to the chancellor, the report grossly exaggerated the problem since it assumed that even in the midst of an almost unprecedented slump the government should pay down debt at the rate of £52 million per annum and borrow nothing for productive purposes such as the road fund. But as he pointed out, 'the figure of £m.120 will be flashed around the world.' The markets were therefore bound to remain nervous about sterling until the government demonstrated its commitment to sound finance by sharply reducing public expenditure.[126]

Another blow came from an unexpected quarter. On Tuesday, 4 August, when the foreign exchange markets reopened after the Bank holiday, the US and French central bank credits seemed to have their intended effect, for sterling remained above the gold export point throughout the day. But on Wednesday morning the markets panicked when foreign exchange dealers found that sterling was not being supported. Sterling immediately dropped below gold export point, and it was not until the afternoon that the Bank of France's traders intervened to steady the market. By then the Bank of England had lost over £2 million in gold reserves as well as the psychological benefit of the US and French credits.[127]

Most commentators ascribed the break in the market to poor communications between the Bank of England and its Paris agents, with some suggesting that France had again let Britain down.[128] The truth could not have been more different. On 20 July, Norman had suffered another nervous breakdown. Seriously unwell, he sailed for Quebec City where he was to remain for the next two months, leaving the Bank in the hands of Sir Ernest Harvey, the deputy-governor, and Sir Edward Peacock, a partner in Baring Brothers and senior member of the Bank's Committee of Treasury. They, like Norman, were acutely anxious about the state of the financial markets and determined to see that sterling did not go the way of the Austrian schilling or the German mark. They therefore deliberately engineered the break in sterling by ordering the Bank of France to refrain from using the

£25 million credit it had just arranged.[129] They then warned Snowden and leaders of the opposition parties that the situation was black, and that reports from New York and Paris confirmed the Budget must immediately be balanced if sterling was to be saved from collapse.[130] To underline the urgency of the situation, they saw to it that the joint committee of the British Bankers' Association and the Accepting Houses Committee simultaneously issued a similar warning.[131] Thus they hoped the break in the sterling exchanges would jolt the British government into accepting the drastic spending cuts they believed were necessary to restore confidence in sterling.

Three weeks later when the Labour government collapsed, supporters claimed it had been the victim of a 'bankers' ramp'. Political opponents and leader writers ridiculed the claim, and ever since then historians have dismissed it as the ranting of frustrated men. Allegations of an international bankers' ramp are indeed unfounded, and it is also fair to say that the government collapsed largely because of its own incompetence rather than an organized bankers' conspiracy. But the existence of a ramp by bankers – *British* bankers – is amply borne out by the evidence. Norman's refusal to discuss Moret's offer of help in December 1930, his request to New York to cease supporting sterling that month, his repeated requests to Moret in July 1931 to sell sterling for gold when sterling was already facing severe pressure, and his colleagues' decision in August to cause a break in the sterling-franc exchange are all of a piece. As we shall see, Norman made a further attempt to organize a *mur d'argent*, to use the French phrase for a wealth-holders' ramp, while recuperating in Quebec City.

The behaviour of the bankers was not surprising, since they were convinced that without drastic action, sterling, and with it the whole capitalist system, would collapse. City financial institutions, many of them already compromised by the financial crisis in Austria, had just agreed to the standstill in Germany, tying up fully £70 million of their own or their clients' funds. As a result, most of the acceptance houses who dominated the court of governors of the Bank of England were insolvent.[132] This included Lazard Brothers, whose senior partner, Kindersley, had represented the Bank of England in the negotiations for the credit from the Bank of France. Lazards was only kept afloat by a secret £3.5 million lifeline from the Bank of England and assistance from the Treasury.[133] It probably also included Arbuthnot Latham, Goschen & Cunliffe, Helbert Wagg, Huths, Japhets, Kleinworts, Schroeders, Seligmans and Baring Brothers as well as the British Overseas Bank and other financial houses with assets locked up in Central Europe.[134] City bankers had helped to restore sterling to the gold standard, believing that it provided a sheet-anchor against financial chaos. They now believed that sterling must be kept on gold if the chaos were not to overwhelm them. Accordingly, Harvey explained to Harrison, they had decided to engineer a sterling crisis, 'to make the British government understand the seriousness of their position.'[135] Siepmann, the Bank's director of central bank relations, was equally candid with Moret: 'it appeared necessary to them to give a serious warning to the government and to the public.'[136] Besides frightening the government, they also resented the need to accept charity from the French and sought to end their dependence as soon as possible. It suited them that the British press, unaware of the Bank of England's responsibility for the break in sterling, should present it as another French attempt to force Britain's hand on Germany or drive Norman from the Bank of England.

By now, the worst financial crisis in British history had triggered a comparably severe political crisis. This began on the evening of 22 July when Norman called on Snowden to warn him that the Bank's gold reserves were rapidly dwindling. Snowden mentioned that the report of the May Committee would soon be published, revealing a large deficit in the 1932 budget, and he and Norman agreed that urgent fiscal action was necessary to restore confidence in sterling. The following day, Hopkins of the Treasury added his own warning. When Norman met American bankers on 26 July to discuss a long-term loan, Hopkins was sure their first question would be, 'Will steps be first taken about the dole and the budgetary position?'[137]

For two years MacDonald and Snowden, with Norman's encouragement, had fended off 'irresponsible' proposals to deal with the crisis from within the Labour movement. Meanwhile Snowden had dug in his heels against mounting pressure for trade protection, which Cabinet colleagues advanced in a variety of forms. Anxious to demonstrate that a Labour government could act responsibly and unable to see beyond the orthodox assumptions of liberal economics, ministers accepted the need for a balanced budget. Just before the House of Commons rose for the summer, Snowden announced the creation of a Cabinet economy committee, which met for the first time on 12 August. The scale of retrenchment required was daunting. Registered unemployment had risen above 2.5 million or nearly 20 per cent of the registered industrial workforce by the summer of 1931, driving the unemployment insurance scheme – derisively known as the 'dole' – heavily into deficit. Bankers and opposition leaders left no room for doubt that they expected to see the budget balanced largely through the reduction in unemployment benefit.[138] To make matters worse, ministers learned at the first meeting of the committee that the Treasury now predicted the deficit on the 1932 budget would be not £120 million but fully £170 million.[139] Proceeding on the basis of 'equality of sacrifice', ministers prepared a programme of tax increases and economies which was put to the Cabinet on 19 August.

The scale of the financial crisis and the threat, repeated by MacDonald and Snowden as well as the national press, that sterling could go the same way as the German mark in the hyperinflation of 1923, led the Cabinet to accept huge reductions in spending on roads, education, the armed forces, health and other services. They were prepared to approve economies of £57 million and provisionally another £20 million, amounting to no less than 20 per cent of social expenditure.[140] But Treasury and Bank of England officials and opposition party leaders warned that even this fell far short of the economies necessary to restore confidence in sterling. Only a substantial reduction in the dole, they claimed, would reassure foreign bankers of the soundness of the British economy.[141] The Cabinet, which had been meeting almost constantly for the previous three days, reconvened on the morning of Saturday, 22 August. MacDonald and Snowden warned colleagues of the terrible calamity that would befall the country if sterling were driven off the gold standard, and insisted upon a further £20 million in economies, including a 10 per cent reduction in the standard unemployment benefit for insured workers. Ministers, unwilling to cut deeper into social expenditure, drew back from formally approving the economies. But they agreed that MacDonald might see if the larger economies would satisfy the opposition leaders and bankers.[142] What followed soon became obscured by rumour and myth.

According to the account generally accepted in Labour circles, the latest formula for balancing the budget was put to New York bankers, with the request for a loan to save the pound. The bankers, however, refused to accept the formula, and MacDonald and Snowden then jumped ship to join the opposition leaders in a new Conservative-dominated National government. The new government imposed retrenchment on the scale demanded of its predecessor, including savage reductions in unemployment benefit. The Labour government was thus the victim of a 'bankers' ramp' and treachery by MacDonald and Snowden.[143] This account is far from accurate, although what actually happened was scarcely less remarkable.

On the critical weekend, Harvey of the Bank of England had put the government's provisional formula for balancing the budget to Harrison in New York, with the request to see if this would persuade the commercial banks to participate in a large loan for Britain. Harvey was extremely annoyed to be called upon to present the formula as if the government had actually agreed upon it, which was not the case, and Harrison may have detected his reservation.[144] In any event, the New York bankers had been thoroughly chastened by the freezing of loans in Central Europe and were reluctant to commit more funds abroad. Harrison therefore telephoned Norman at the Château Frontenac, the great railway hotel in Quebec City, to seek his advice. Norman bluntly advised Harrison to reject the Labour government's formula for balancing the budget. What was needed, he said, was even more savage retrenchment. If the politicians faced up to their responsibilities and put the British economy on a sound basis, they would not need foreign help. The bankers should therefore not let them off the hook by offering a loan. As Harrison recorded,

> [H]e, Norman, felt that the program was inadequate; that we must not fool ourselves now; that any inadequate program would cause trouble in a year or so and that it was essential that we must force an economic adjustment now and not in a year or so from now; that the programme, in his judgment, must be sufficiently drastic to place the cost of output and wages on a competitive basis with the rest of the world...; that if the Government attacked the situation courageously and did enough by way of drastic readjustment then, in his judgment, they would not need a credit at all.[145]

Harrison was evidently taken aback at Norman's advice. As he knew, the French and American central bank credits to the Bank of England were nearly exhausted and sterling would probably be driven off the gold standard before retrenchment had worked its effect, if the Bank's resources were not replenished. Unwilling to be responsible for the collapse of sterling, he set aside Norman's advice.[146] Instead, he turned back to Harvey and indicated that New York would rely upon his view of the adequacy of the government's budget proposals. Time did not allow the negotiation of a long-term loan. But if the Bank of England and its City allies gave their 'sincere approval' to the budget balancing formula, New York would try to organize a large short-term credit.[147]

Harvey rushed this reply to Downing Street on Sunday evening, where the Cabinet waited.[148] MacDonald appealed to colleagues to agree to the higher level of retrenchment. He acknowledged that it 'represented the negation of everything that the Labour Party stood for'. But he urged them to act 'in the national interest', and warned of 'the calamitous nature of the consequences which would immediately and inevitably follow from a financial panic and a flight from the pound.'

Most of the Cabinet were prepared to agree. But when several ministers still hesitated to accept a reduction in unemployment benefit, MacDonald declared that he was not prepared to carry on.[149] He thereupon wound up the meeting and drove to Buckingham Palace to return the seals of office to the King. For weeks, indeed months, MacDonald had let it be known in the corridors of Westminster that he might be prepared to join a coalition government capable of addressing the economic crisis. The King, doubtless aware of this, urged him to carry on or at least think over his options before resigning. When he returned to Downing Street, Harvey and Peacock also urged him to carry on and hurriedly called in Neville Chamberlain for the Conservatives. Chamberlain, who had welcomed the Labour government's embarrassment over retrenchment, now invited MacDonald to carry on as prime minister of a non-party National government. MacDonald did not immediately agree. But the following morning he went with opposition leaders to the palace where the King gave his approval to a non-party National government with MacDonald once again prime minister.[150]

Members of the new government and their supporters in the country were hopeful that with the 'socialists' out of office, sterling would soon recover. Indeed, over the next fortnight the Bank of England's gold losses declined to an average of £2 million a day. Meanwhile bankers in New York and Paris put up matching £40 million credits for the British government, which were announced on 29 August. On 10 September Snowden, still chancellor of the exchequer, announced in his words 'the most momentous Budget ever introduced to the House of Commons in peacetime.' Besides increases of £82 million in taxes and a £20 million reduction in sinking fund payments – a measure the Treasury had insisted the Labour government must not attempt – Snowden announced economies of £70 million, including a 10 per cent reduction in unemployment benefit.[151]

Confidence in sterling nevertheless did not recover. Indeed, the retrenchment measures seem to have been discounted even before they were announced, for sterling remained stubbornly below gold export point on the exchanges from early September. During the four days 7–10 September, *before* the emergency

Budget was announced, the Bank of England faced average daily losses of £2.4 million in reserves. In the three days of trading *after* the Budget announcement, the Bank's reserve losses increased to a daily average of £2.8 million.[152] Lingering hopes that the run would end were dashed when the reduction in the already meagre pay of sailors announced in the new Budget sparked a mutiny in the Home Fleet at Scapa Flow.[153] News of the mutiny appeared in the press on 15 September. The following day the Bank's reserve losses leapt to £3.9 million and on the 17th to £6.22 million. Before the end of that day, £30 million of the £80 million credits to the government had been exhausted in the effort to hold the pound at par. Harvey, estimating free reserves at barely £55 million, warned that the Bank could carry on for 'ten days at the most'.[154] Bank and Treasury officials hastily considered a range of options: raising Bank rate, mobilizing foreign securities in private hands as collateral for a new foreign loan, attempting to raise additional foreign credits in New York and Paris, emergency import restrictions, a prohibitive duty on luxury imports, exchange controls.[155] None seemed likely to be effective with the speed required. When on Friday, 18 September, the Bank's reserve losses exceeded £17 million, the situation became critical.

In Paris, bankers and political leaders remained ready to help. Governor Moret, on his own responsibility, had been increasing the Bank of France's sterling balances;[156] and Laval called in the chargé d'affaires at the British embassy to promise his personal support for the raising of a loan.[157] But in London neither bankers nor political leaders were prepared to see Britain become more beholden to France. French offers of help were therefore disregarded. Instead, MacDonald turned to America, personally appealing for help to Stimson on Saturday morning. Stimson, at home in suburban Washington, telephoned Hoover who immediately convened his Cabinet.

British ministers would have been gratified by the evidence of Anglo-Saxon solidarity displayed at the White House that day. Hoover and his colleagues seemed genuinely concerned at Britain's fate, and examined various options including an immediate reduction of Britain's war debts. But Congress controlled money bills, and in the time available they could not think of any practical means to help.[158]

That same morning in London the Bank of England lost a further £8.5 million reserves in the half-day of trading, and expected to lose the £6 million that remained from the government credits when the markets opened in New York. Bank and Treasury officials therefore prepared for the suspension of the gold standard on Monday morning.

6.5   Crossing the Rubicon: Britain and the adoption of Imperial protectionism

The suspension of the gold standard on Monday, 21 September 1931, briefly opened a window of opportunity for Britain to resume its leadership of the international monetary and financial system. Keynes, the country's best-known economist, had hitherto been prepared to accept almost any sacrifice to keep sterling on the gold standard. In 1930, as a member of the Macmillan committee, he proposed a 'National Treaty', involving government legislation to reduce fixed costs such

Table 6.1   Rates of exchange on selected dates from 17 Sept. 1931 to 29 Dec. 1932

Date	£/$ par 4.86¾	£/Fr. Franc par 124.21
17 Sep. 1931	4.85³¹⁄₃₂	123.95
24 Sep.	3.88	98½
22 Oct.	3.93¼	99⅞
26 Nov.	3.59⅜	91⅞
31 Dec.	3.38¾	86⅜
30 Jun. 1932	3.60	91⅝
29 Dec.	3.31½	84¹⁵⁄₁₈

as rents, mortgages, wages, pensions and dividends, and thereby restore Britain's international competitiveness.[159] Since this was scarcely practicable, he took up the idea of a 10 per cent revenue tariff, which seemed a simpler means of strengthening the balance of payments and easing pressure on the pound.[160] In the spring of 1931, he travelled to the United States in hope of persuading American bankers to join in coordinated reflationary action.[161] After sterling came under pressure in July, he urged the British government to promote multilateral action by convening a conference of the major economic powers.[162] Britain's abandonment of the gold standard did not shake his commitment to a liberal globalizing agenda. He now repudiated the tariff proposal as no longer necessary or desirable and instead appealed to the government to exploit its freedom from the constraints of the gold standard (see Table 6.1) by easing domestic credit restrictions and promoting international monetary reform. At last, he believed, Britain could resume its international leadership without fear of shaking confidence in the pound.[163] As he wrote to the *Times*,

> May I urge that the immediate question for attention is not a tariff but the currency question? It is the latter which is urgent and important. It is at present a non-party issue on which none of the political parties has taken up a dogmatic attitude. It is suitable, therefore, for non-party handling. It is most certainly unsuitable for a General Election. It offers immense opportunities for leadership by this country. We are probably in a position to carry the whole of the Empire and more than half of the rest of the world with us, and thus rebuild the financial supremacy of London on a firm basis.[164]

Besides Keynes, several other prominent liberal economists and bankers as well as senior Liberal and Labour politicians inside and outside the National government favoured the immediate convening of an international currency conference.[165] Had Britain promoted collective reflation through a combination of floating exchange rates, cheap money and credit expansion while keeping open its huge import market, the suspension of sterling might well have become the turning point of the world slump. But by now Britain intended to address its economic problems not through collective international action but a combination of unilateral external action (protectionism) and imperialism. This was a dangerous, potentially calamitous, strategy, since it threatened to accelerate the trend away from multilateralism and towards economic autarky or competing economic blocs, which would intensify the world depression. It also meant weakening the postwar security framework and encouraging nationalism in Germany and elsewhere, which could only further damage business confidence and trade. Britain might gain some benefit from the depreciation of sterling and import restrictions. It could hardly hope to escape from the broader consequences of retreating into Imperial protectionism.

For more than a month after the suspension of the gold standard, the key institutions of the mercantile-financial community – the Bank of England, the City of London and the Treasury, along with the *Times*, the *Economist*, the *Banker's Magazine* and other leading business journals – refused to accept that the gold standard was finally gone, and rejected Keynes's advice as dangerously radical.[166] Their eyes fixed firmly on the City's invisible earnings, they worried about sterling's loss of prestige and deplored the 'facile optimism' of economists who imagined there was any alternative to the discipline of the gold standard. As the *Banker* put it, while sterling floated it was 'a hundred times more imperative for this country to exercise economy, self-restraint and grim determination to put its affairs in order upon a sound basis.'[167] Bank and Treasury officials pressed the government to announce its intention to restore the gold standard at the earliest possible moment. Perhaps some devaluation was unavoidable, but they were certain that Britain must not seek to gain from this 'sacrifice of prestige and moral standing'. 'If we do not do this at once', Sir Otto Niemeyer of the Bank of England warned, 'we shall be in measurable distance of a knock-out blow.'[168] His colleague, Siepmann, was equally emphatic: 'The public should be told, and the sooner the better, that there is no alternative to the gold standard as an international monetary system', since otherwise they faced German-style hyperinflation.[169] Leith-Ross of the Treasury, fearing the same outcome, wrote to Lord Reading, the foreign secretary, on 5 October, denouncing 'the Cambridge Economists [who] believe we could get along with a managed currency'.

> A policy of this kind might be possible in a self-contained country like Russia, but it is quite impossible for a country like ours whose prosperity and indeed whose livelihood is dependent on the maintenance of international trade. I think therefore that we ought to try and get back to the gold standard as soon as we are able to do so.[170]

By December 1931, Treasury and Bank officials and much of the City had come around to the view that Britain should not return to the gold standard while the world economy remained so unstable. But they were still not prepared to advocate domestic reflation or recommend the formation of an open-ended sterling area, since this would signal a dangerous shift away from the gold standard towards a managed currency. Until 1932, Britain's financial and monetary policies were characterized by extreme caution, reflecting the mercantile-financial community's continuing interest in global markets. Meanwhile, however, the National government turned towards an Imperial bloc.[171]

In August, Liberal and Labour party leaders had joined the Conservatives in a National government to restore confidence in sterling by driving through budget balancing measures. To their consternation, they found that the Conservatives were determined to take advantage of the sterling crisis to secure a mandate for tariff protection. Led by Sir Herbert Samuel, National Liberals protested against an early election, claiming that a three-week election campaign would create the impression of national disunity and undermine confidence in the pound.[172] But with numerous voices in the City, including that of Norman, clamouring for strong government, the Cabinet agreed to dissolve Parliament and set polling day for 27 October.[173]

The general election of 1931 was possibly the most important as well as the most one-sided contest in modern times. It was, in fact, a tariff election which would turn Britain away from a hundred years of economic and political internationalism, although the election campaign itself was dominated by the currency question. The Labour party once again proposed cautious liberal policies, albeit clothed in the language of socialism. National candidates sought to frighten the electorate into voting for them by alleging that their Labour opponents would cause runaway inflation, the collapse of sterling and economic ruin. As the Conservative election manifesto warned, 'We must shrink from no steps to prove the stability of our country and to save our people from the disaster attached to a currency fluctuating and falling through lack of confidence at home and abroad.'[174] In face of these threats, the Labour party's efforts to arouse working-class opposition to tariff protection were of no avail.[175] As Sir Patrick Gower, the Conservatives' chief publicity officer, assured Baldwin, their emphasis upon 'national bankruptcy' would be sure to drown out Labour's cry of 'food taxes'.[176]

Up and down the country, National candidates brandished German bank notes made worthless by hyperinflation and warned that a similar fate would befall sterling if the Labour party were returned to office.[177] MacDonald, opening his campaign with an address to miners at Seaham on 12 October, held up German notes claiming that Labour would produce the same inflationary crisis endured by the Krupps workers in the Ruhr ten years earlier.[178] Snowden, speaking on the BBC on 17 October, presented a similarly doom-laden picture of a Labour victory: 'This is not Socialism. It is Bolshevism run mad [which would] plunge the country into irretrievable ruin.'[179] On 27 October, the morning of the polls, the *Times* sustained the campaign of fear by warning readers, 'Never before has the British democracy [*sic*] been called upon to take a decision which in a single day will preserve or destroy the value of the British currency and the solidity of British credit. ... [T]hat is the only issue.'[180] The message that only a National government could defend the pound and protect Britain from foreign financial attack proved decisive. With 70 per cent of the votes cast for National candidates, 556 were returned against a mere 56 opposition candidates representing the Labour Party, Independent Labour Party or Lloyd George Liberals. Of the successful National candidates, however, only 13 were Labourites, 33 Samuelite Liberals and 35 Simonite Liberals, while fully 475 were Conservatives. Despite the National tag and MacDonald as prime minister, it was essentially a Conservative administration that governed Britain from 28 October.[181]

For Conservative one could almost write Chamberlainite, for one of the most important consequences of the election was the emergence of Neville Chamberlain at the forefront of British politics where he was to remain for the next nine years. Chamberlain had entered politics relatively late and for many years was overshadowed by his more famous father, Joseph, and half-brother, Sir Austen, as well as Curzon, Bonar Law and Baldwin, still the leader of the Conservative party. As a young man, however, he had gained business experience, and as chancellor of the exchequer in the new government he regarded himself as the one minister competent to address the economic crisis facing the country. Intense and insecure, he privately gloated over his ascendancy over colleagues.[182] Yet his policies were those of the typical Englishman who believed that Britain had contributed enough to international stability in the war and subsequently, and now that its efforts had been undone by the narrow nationalism of other countries it should look to its own interests at home and in the Empire. As befitting one who had grown up a Liberal, then Liberal Unionist, before entering the Conservative party, he was content to leave financial and monetary policy in the hands of the Treasury and the Bank of England.[183] Instead, he focused his attention on external commercial policy, convinced that by abandoning free trade Britain could use access to its uniquely large import market to address its current account weakness as well as strengthening the ties of Empire. The goal of a greater British Empire, united by mutual trade preferences, no doubt reflected his wish to fulfil his father's ambition. But he seemed more influenced by the humiliation, fear and anger that he shared with much of the country after sterling was forced off the gold standard, which he blamed largely on the blind selfishness of the United States and France.[184] His policies were thus informed as much by a narrowly English view of the world and a strong sense of national injury as by any simple calculation of economic advantage. This would become obvious in the next few years. But at the outset he had to tread carefully to retain Labour and Liberal ministers in the government, since he believed its National character was essential to carry through his plans for retrenchment and Imperial protectionism.

Chamberlain's first step was to establish a Cabinet committee dominated by protectionists to prepare British policy for the forthcoming Ottawa conference on Imperial economic cooperation.[185] His next step was to assist Walter Runciman, the president of the Board of Trade, who was preparing an anti-dumping bill ostensibly to stop a surge of imports in advance of tariff legislation. Four ministers, including Sir Herbert Samuel, the home secretary, and Philip Snowden, the lord privy seal, continued to oppose a general tariff, but they found it impossible to object to emergency import controls. A bill providing powers to apply duties of up to 100 per cent on 'abnormal' imports, with complete exemption for Imperial imports, was therefore soon adopted.[186] This was followed by a bill restricting 'non-essential foodstuffs', again with exemption for Imperial imports.[187] Before the end of November the Cabinet also agreed in principle to an Empire wheat quota, with preferences for Empire producers to be negotiated at Ottawa.[188]

Meanwhile, Chamberlain concentrated economic policy in his own hands. Disturbed by the presence of Keynes and other liberal internationalists on the prime minister's Economic Advisory Council, he requested MacDonald to restrict its function to providing information and cease further discussion of policy.[189] MacDonald agreed without protest and presently wound up the Council.[190] Chamberlain also discouraged discussion of the Foreign Office paper on an 'all-in' politico-economic approach to the crisis, which was not circulated to ministers in advance of the Cabinet meeting on 15 December and was passed over without discussion.[191]

His next step came on 18 January 1932 when he proposed a general 10 per cent tariff with an Imperial preference to the Cabinet committee on the balance of trade.[192] This amounted to nothing less than the repudiation of the near century-old tradition of free trade, and three National Liberal ministers, Samuel, Sir Archibald Sinclair and Sir Donald Maclean, along with Snowden, MacDonald's sole National Labour colleague, threatened to resign rather than acquiesce in it. The Cabinet crisis dragged on for five days.[193] But having already inserted the thin end of the wedge with the anti-dumping and non-essential foodstuffs bills, Chamberlain was confident of success.[194] In the event, the free traders in the Cabinet agreed merely to abstain when the tariff bill was put to the House of Commons on 4 February.[195]

On Monday, 21 September 1931, the day the gold standard was suspended, sterling declined 14 per cent to $4.20 by the close of trading in New York. The following Saturday it closed the week at 3.84^{1/2}$, down 21 per cent from its gold parity. Thereafter it traded in a narrow range until November, when it declined further to reach a low of $3.23 on 4 December.[196] But it had already recovered to 3.39^{1/2}$ by the year end, and stood at $3.45 on 4 February 1932 when Chamberlain announced the introduction of the tariff. The Bank of England, no doubt correctly assuming that higher interest rates would do little to stem the run on the pound, had kept Bank rate at 4.5 per cent from 30 July to 21 September. It only raised the rate to 6 per cent on 21 September to steady the exchange markets when they reopened on the 23rd. Norman, back at Threadneedle Street, held Bank rate at 6 per cent until January 1932, and would probably have kept it there until sterling returned to its gold parity. But when sterling began to recover he faced a growing clamour from those who feared that it would stifle domestic recovery. He therefore reduced Bank rate to 5 per cent on 18 February, to 4 per cent on 10 March, and in two further stages to 2 per cent on 2 June. Thus began the era of cheap money.[197] This stimulated domestic investment, particularly in the housing market, and eased the government's budget restraints. During the summer, most of the huge 5 per cent War Loan was converted to a 3.5 per cent issue, which reduced debt servicing from nearly 38 per cent of budget expenditure to less than 34 per cent. And with further funding operations in 1934–6 at even lower rates, debt servicing declined by nearly £100 million to less than 25 per cent of government spending.[198]

The economic stimulus of cheap money largely confirmed Liberal predictions and might have formed the basis for collective international action. Now, however, Britain was no longer prepared to provide an international lead. The British economy therefore benefited from sterling's depreciation and cheap money while suffering from the global resort to beggar-your-neighbour policies. The economic consequences of Britain's decision to join the 'world economic suicide club', as the *New Statesman and Nation* described its retreat into protectionism, are almost impossible to estimate.[199] But in any event it is not enough to consider only the economic consequences. The decision contributed to the dual politico-economic crisis, which almost certainly intensified as a result.

6.6 New challenges to the postwar security framework

Until the autumn of 1931, France was still the mainstay of the Western security framework. Albeit frustrated by concessions made to appease its allies, France remained the one great power willing and able to uphold the Versailles settlement. Militarily it was still relatively strong, its Eastern alliances were intact, and it was as yet only modestly affected by the world economic slump. French ministers were nonetheless aware that the slump was fuelling British and American impatience for Treaty revision and increasing political extremism in Germany. Rather than simply await events, therefore, they embarked upon a series of diplomatic initiatives from the spring of 1931. Towards the Anglo-Saxon powers they sought to employ French financial strength to enhance cooperation, while ensuring that efforts to address the economic crisis did not undermine French security. Towards Germany they were prepared to extend economic and financial support in return for assurances of respect for Treaty commitments or at least an end to adventures like the Austro-German customs union scheme. The French ministers' attempt to obtain security in return for financial help was only what leaders of any democratic power in a similar situation could be expected to do. But, as before, they gravely underestimated the depth of race prejudice shaping international relations. The crisis, which went some way to draw the Anglo-Saxon powers closer together, also drove them to adopt a more openly hostile attitude towards France, their Latin rival. As a result, French ministers gained nothing from their increased diplomatic activity. Germany, encouraged by the Anglo-Saxon powers, embarked upon new adventures. Meanwhile, the French economy lost much of its former strength. For France, the six months from September 1931 to February 1932 proved to be even more discouraging than the previous six months.

French diplomatic initiatives continued with an official visit by Laval and Briand to Berlin on 27 September. This was the first time a French premier had visited Germany in over sixty years, and to their relief they were warmly received by large crowds. Germany by now was experiencing an unprecedented economic depression. Although the Hoover moratorium had come into operation in July and the standstill on foreign short-term credits in September, new investment had practically ceased, and registered unemployment reached 35 per cent. Meanwhile the Reichsbank's reserves fell to barely 30 per cent of the note issue, its legal minimum, and continued to decline.[200] French ministers hoped to bargain economic and financial assistance for political concessions from the Bruening government. But Bruening was fighting for his political life against the front formed by the Nationalists and Nazis, who had made reparations – tribute payments, as they called them – the explanation of Germany's economic slump, and continually played up the supposed unfairness of the disarmament clauses of the Versailles Treaty.[201] Bruening could not be seen to compromise with France on these issues, and was encouraged to resist by the growing chorus of support for Treaty revision in the Anglo-Saxon countries. He therefore told his French guests that he had no mandate to discuss any of the substantive issues they sought to raise.[202]

To mark the French visit, Bruening agreed to institute a Franco-German Economic Commission. The brainchild of André François-Poncet, its brief was to improve bilateral economic relations through the promotion of industrial ententes or cartels and other means. The commission soon comprised 40 prominent business and labour leaders from the two countries, organized into four subcommittees. But if there had ever been any chance of transforming Franco-German conflict into constructive engagement through economic initiatives, it had long passed.[203] Karl Ritter, head of the economic department of the German Foreign Ministry and secretary-general of the Commission, asserted that the commission's sole purpose was 'to disguise the absence of any tangible outcome to the French visit'.[204] This was not true for the French, who still hoped to improve relations through economic *rapprochement*. But it accurately reflected attitudes in Germany, where hostility to France was general in official circles. The Germans left the French to prepare subsequent meetings, starting in November in Paris, but they produced little practical result.[205] France, without the backing or endorsement of the other Anglo-Saxon powers, could not hope to contain a determinedly revisionist Germany.

Ten days after the Laval-Briand visit to Berlin, French ministers received Lord Reading, the new British foreign secretary, in Paris. The French were disturbed at the recent upsurge in criticism by British politicians, bankers and journalists, who claimed that France had brought down sterling by disregarding the rules of the gold standard or perhaps by deliberate intent and was now gloating over its victory. This was, in their view, nonsense and pernicious nonsense at that.[206] So far from France being the author of Britain's troubles, they believed they were almost completely of Britain's own making. As they saw it, the Bank of England's efforts in the 1920s to persuade other central banks to adopt the gold exchange standard had resulted in a huge pyramiding of credit upon a modest base of gold reserves. Meanwhile, despite its ambitions to dominate the international monetary system, Britain had not lived within its means, but instead had maintained the 'dole' and lavish public expenditure, which inflated wage levels and made British industry uncompetitive. The result was a chronic current account deficit, which should have triggered credit restraint. Instead, the Bank of England, being the tool of the City of London, permitted massive short-term foreign lending – largely to Germany – leaving it to be covered by equally large-scale foreign short-term borrowing. The British financial system had thus become extremely vulnerable to crisis, making a run on sterling just a matter of time. French ministers did not openly employ the language of the Paris press, which attributed the sterling crisis to '*la décadence anglaise*', or to Britain's unreasoning efforts to marginalize France by building up Germany with its loans.[207] But there is little doubt they shared its viewpoint.[208]

They were all the more annoyed to be charged with misbehaviour, when France had gone so far out of its way to help Britain. In January 1931, government ministers had prevailed upon the Bank of France to refrain from raising its discount rate and instead reduce it to relieve London of further gold movements to Paris. During the sterling crisis in July–September 1931, they had supported the Bank of France's efforts to raise the two large credits in the Paris market, the first for the Bank of England, the second for the British Treasury. As they proudly pointed out, Paris had provided as much support for sterling as the much larger New York market. The French Treasury, as well as the Bank of France, had also maintained its balances in London, despite the risk of an exchange loss. And as late as September they had remained ready to match any loan for Britain raised in New York. On the weekend when British authorities decided to suspend the gold standard, Flandin quit the League Assembly in Geneva to be on hand if Britain required his help. He had not closed the Bourse, as he earlier promised to do, fearing that to do so would cause a panic. But he saw to it that trading was halted in sterling securities and that orders in sterling from British nationals were not executed, thus forestalling a further run on the pound.[209] Subsequently he could report that trading in sterling and sterling-denominated securities had remained orderly throughout the crucial first week of sterling's float.[210]

Flandin and his colleagues suppressed their annoyance at the British attacks because, with Germany in crisis and the French public deeply shaken by recent events, they needed Britain's friendship more than ever.[211] They therefore responded with alacrity when Reading proposed to visit Paris.[212] Britain, they assumed, would seek France's assistance to stabilize the exchanges and prepare for sterling's return to gold. Reading's purpose however was to learn more about Laval's visit to Washington in October, when issues of interest to Britain were likely to be discussed. He was nervous about his Conservative colleagues' agitation for trade protection and hoped to undercut their activities by demonstrating progress in international affairs.

Reading, who spent the whole of 7 October in meetings with Laval, Briand and Flandin, found his French hosts ready to support 'a bold policy', including a reduction in reparations, foreign loans and disarmament. But they would not make unilateral concessions to Germany. As Flandin put it, French banks would not lend five sous to Germany until they received some assurance about its political intentions. But Flandin could promise that French savings would be mobilized for long-term loans to Germany, if it was prepared to offer a 'political truce' committing it to respect the postwar international order for a period of years. Similarly with disarmament, France would be only too pleased to participate, but in Briand's words the United States and other countries must be prepared to 'put teeth into the Kellogg Pact'. France was also prepared to go a long way to remove the reparation problem. It would accept the cancellation of the conditional tranche, if the United States cancelled its war debt demands. France must insist upon Germany's continued payment of the unconditional tranche of the annuity, since otherwise Germany's public debt would be reduced to £8 per capita, compared with France's £56 and Britain's £150, giving German industry an impossible advantage over its competitors.[213] But for the duration of the crisis, Germany could pay over to the BIS in marks the annual £16 million owed to France in inconditional payments, and France would use them to purchase German material for public works or reinvest them in Germany, Austria or elsewhere in Central Europe. The payments would therefore not affect Germany's balance of payments or weaken its domestic economy, and France would also see to it that they did not prejudice British trade. France would emphatically not participate in an international currency conference, which it looked upon as 'little more than an attempt to pilfer the Bank of France.'[214] However, it was ready to assist Britain in stabilizing sterling which, it assumed, Britain wished to undertake immediately after the general election. In return, France expected Britain to compensate the Bank of France for the losses it had incurred on its London balances when sterling left the gold standard.[215]

That same day, Governor Moret raised the question of compensation with the Treasury's Leith-Ross, who had accompanied Reading to Paris. With obvious sincerity, Moret explained how the Bank of France had acted against its better judgement to assist the Bank of England ever since May 1927 when it had heeded Norman's request to refrain from disposing of its sterling balances. Subsequently it had sold sterling only when this could be done without embarrassment to the Bank of England. And during the recent crisis, when on any objective assessment of risk the Bank should have disposed of its remaining sterling balances, it had accepted its moral duty as the Bank of England's agent in Paris by purchasing sterling and supplying credits to the Bank of England and British Treasury. In consequence, the Bank of France had lost 2.7 billion francs (£21.6 million) on its credits and sterling balances of 12.2 billion francs (£100 million).[216] This was nearly seven times its total paid-up capital and published reserves.[217] Technically this bankrupted the Bank, and Moret could not publish its balance sheet until the deficit was covered.[218] He therefore requested an assurance that when Britain stabilized sterling, his sterling balances would be revalued at their full gold value.

Leith-Ross would not hear of it. Neither thanking Moret for his previous support nor apologizing for placing him in his present predicament, he asserted that since several other central banks had also maintained balances in London during the crisis, the Bank of France could hardly claim to have done anything special. Moret, taken aback by his attitude, observed that in view of the Bank's huge losses, his shareholders would probably call for his resignation, and warned that 'if this question could not be satisfactorily solved, it would not be possible for the Bank of France in future to co-operate with the Bank of England.' Leith-Ross challenged him to explain what he meant:

> 'No co-operation' might mean many things; it sounded almost like a declar-ation of war. Did he mean that he must be free to sell his sterling?...Moret said he had not thought of selling his sterling...[but] that if they were to suffer for their loyalty in the past, they could not be expected to extend the same help to London in the future; and the help of Paris and New York would be essential for the re-stabilisation of the pound. I replied that this was not an immediate question. Indeed many people in England were not in favour of our attempting to go back to the gold standard without some better arrangement as to how it should be worked. M. Moret threw up his hands and said that if that view prevailed, it would be the end of London as a financial centre. I replied that it might be that in a few months there were very few countries that would be on the gold standard.[219]

Despite Moret's complaints, French authorities remained determined to cooper-ate with Britain.[220] Laval repeatedly assured Reading: 'if the two countries worked together, everything always went well, but if they split other countries immedi-ately began intriguing and things became difficult.'[221] In due course, the Bank of France agreed to the Bank of England's request to renew the larger part of its credit,[222] and both the French Bank and Treasury retained most of their deposits in London, despite the continuing depreciation of the pound.[223] Reading's visit nevertheless ended in mutual disappointment. British ministers, their eyes fixed on Germany and fearing a Communist takeover, sought to assist the 'moderates' by suppressing reparations and giving way on disarmament.[224] French ministers more realistically feared a Nationalist-Nazi takeover of Germany. But they saw no advantage in assisting Germany, whoever was in power, while it sought to tear down what remained of the international security framework.

Barely a week after Reading returned to London, Laval set off for Washington. Never very promising, the prospects for his trip were dimmed by the eco-nomic crisis in the United States and the frustration generated by it. Reports in September indicated that the federal budget was heading for a deficit of $1 billion (£206 million).[225] To make matters worse, domestic and foreign depositors began a massive run on the dollar, once the collapse of sterling became immi-nent. Between 16 September and 28 October, foreign banks exchanged $712 million (£146.5 million) for gold, while Federal Reserve member banks withdrew $393 million net (£81 million) from the System. The initial stage of the run was dominated by countries determined to remain on the gold standard, including the Netherlands, Belgium and Switzerland as well as France; subsequently dollar sales came mainly from European commercial banks which were facing a decline in their own deposits.[226] During this six-week period the United States experi-enced the most severe money and credit deflation of the whole depression.[227]

The Federal Reserve did what it could to offset its loss of reserve assets.[228] But the 12 regional Federal Reserve Banks had no alternative but to raise their discount rates from 1.5 to 2.5 per cent on 9 October and to 3.5 per cent on 16 October.

Bank failures increased, from 1345 in the whole of 1930 to 1234 in the first nine months of 1931, including 298 in September alone.[229] Since much of the gold exported or earmarked for export was destined for France, American journals accused France of mounting a politically motivated attack on the dollar.[230] The accusations were baseless. The Bank of France had never used its gold reserves for such political purposes and it was certainly not going to use them against the United States now. On the contrary, since Britain had left the gold standard, it was especially keen to cooperate with the New York Fed.[231] The French government, facing pressure from London and Berlin for further Treaty revision, was equally anxious to avoid conflict with the United States.[232] Walter Edge, the American ambassador in Paris, nevertheless reported as fact the existence of a 'thoroughly organized attack on the American dollar which spread through England, France, Switzerland, Germany and Holland.'[233] Hoover, deeply Francophobic and 'fed up with Europe' since the dispute over his moratorium proposal, placed some credence in these accusations.[234] Edge – who had contributed to it – was struck by 'the vicious anti-French propaganda which was sweeping the United States, reaching into the highest circles.'[235] Stimson acknowledged, 'the administration was thoroughly angry with France'.[236] These were hardly propitious conditions for a visit by a French premier.

The most remarkable aspect of Laval's visit was that Hoover should have initi-ated it and Laval agreed to go. Hoover, it seems, remained uncomfortably aware of the scale of American interests at stake in the crisis that threatened to engulf Germany. Accordingly, in mid-September when a member of the New York Council on Foreign Relations floated the proposal for a prominent Frenchman to visit Washington, he casually agreed.[237] Laval hesitated before accepting the invitation, fearing that Hoover might spring another initiative on inter-governmental debts or perhaps disarmament, which he would be obliged to reject. But with legislative elections in France scheduled for May 1932 and the Left gaining popularity, he did not want to appear to be the obstacle to Germany's recovery or international disarmament, or the man who isolated France from the Anglo-Saxon powers. Not speaking English and lacking first-hand knowledge of America, he was reluctant to visit Washington. Paul Doumer, the French president, persuaded him to do so.[238]

In the weeks before Laval travelled to Washington, Hoover received appeals from several quarters to provide leadership in the world crisis. Paul Claudel, in an ostensibly personal act, proposed American participation in a consultative pact to reinforce the Kellogg-Briand pact. He stressed that France fully appreciated the United States' commitment to the principle of 'no foreign entanglements'. But, pointing to America's decision for war in 1917 and Hoover's recent moratorium as examples of pre-emptive action, he advised that if the United States wished to avoid being drawn into further entanglements, it should actively engage in inter-national affairs rather than allowing itself to be overtaken by events. A consulta-tive pact would give France the reassurance needed for constructive negotiations with Germany on reparations and disarmament. These in turn would restore confidence in the international financial system, which was the precondition for overcoming the world slump.[239]

Thomas Lamont of J.P. Morgan, and Shepard Morgan, vice-president of the Chase Manhattan Bank and formerly finance director of the Office of Reparations, separately appealed to Hoover to help surmount the international crisis. Lamont, pointing to French insecurity, advised that a show of American solidarity would provide the psychological boost needed for a settlement in Europe.[240] Morgan offered more precise advice on how America might help solve the crisis. Taking as his starting point American war debt claims, he warned the president that payments were unlikely to resume after the present moratorium while the European powers continued to spend heavily on arms. Yet disarmament was out of the question while German dissatisfaction with the settlement in Eastern Europe left France nervous and encouraged Italy's opportunistic manoeuvring. And so long as the political tensions remained, the economic crisis could only get worse. The United States therefore had an interest in intervening, and should do so in consultation with France. At the appropriate time, it should convene a conference of interested powers and offer to reduce its war debt demands if the other powers made comparable contributions to a general settlement.[241]

Hoover never welcomed advice from Wall Street bankers. Yet shortly before Laval arrived, he received a broadly similar appeal from Hugh Wilson, head of the State Department's Division of Western European affairs, who spoke for several senior diplomats. Like Lamont and Morgan, Wilson stressed the interrelatedness of the elements making up the crisis and the impossibility of the United States escaping it through isolationism. The French, he observed, had long seemed tiresomely dogmatic in linking reparations, security and disarmament. But the fact was they *were* intimately connected, and the Anglo-Saxon preference for dealing with them separately was impracticable.

> In thinking of the four cardinal difficulties of the present time: (1) security, (2) political questions, (3) finance, and (4) disarmament, the Frenchman instinctively interrelates all four problems, and indeed under the present economic conditions of the world, these problems are inescapably intermingled. We are of the opinion, therefore, that we cannot try longer to put these various subjects in compartments; that we must be ready and willing to debate any one of the four and to debate it in relation to the other three.[242]

From the subjects Hoover discussed with Laval in Washington on 20 October, there can be little doubt that he had read the bankers' and diplomats' appeals for action. The first issue Hoover raised was Central Europe, which he described as 'the [most] unstable spot of Europe and the world.' But when Laval adverted to Polish intransigence and the impossibility of reopening the territorial settlement in the East, Hoover turned to reparations and the need to invoke the procedures within the Young plan to address Germany's current payment problems. Subsequently the two men discussed the convening of an international monetary conference before agreeing to rule it out. Laval then took up disarmament, the need to deal with it in conjunction with security, and the desirability of American participation in a consultative pact. In view of the United States' long-standing refusal to be involved in European affairs or reparations, Laval himself was surprised at the direction the conversations took.[243]

That said, Hoover remained chiefly preoccupied by the American economy, which since September was enduring 'the most severe decline in the volume of business ever experienced.'[244] He had found Congressional representatives thoroughly hostile even to an extension of the moratorium on inter-governmental debts, let alone a permanent reduction, when he had met them earlier in the month.[245] He himself remained deeply suspicious of European entanglements, particularly in association with France. Despite raising a range of contentious issues, therefore, he preferred no substantive solutions. The most he would concede was an assurance that if the European powers agreed to reduce inter-governmental debts 'covering the period of business depression', the United States would 'make its necessary contribution'.[246]

Laval left Washington well satisfied with the result,[247] but ironically his trip only made the international crisis more intractable. Speaking to Claudel, he claimed that if the European powers reduced their reparation demands on Germany, he had Hoover's word that the United States would make a corresponding reduction in war debts. This was wishful thinking, for neither Hoover nor Congress was prepared to assist Europe.[248] Meanwhile the prospect of an agreement between France and the United States on inter-governmental debts had led the German government to draw the international bankers onto its side by warning publicly that it would be unable to resume payments on foreign short-term debt when the current standstill ended on 29 February 1932.[249] To make matters worse, William Borah, chairman of the Senate Foreign Relations Committee and a leading isolationist, released the transcript of his meeting with Laval, which indicated that the latter had come to discuss security in Europe and even frontier revision.[250] The suggestion that France sought to entangle the United States in European affairs was certain to intensify isolationist sentiment. Only weeks before, American newspapers had treated reports that Britain would convene an international currency conference as a conspiracy to 'entrap America'.[251] They now suspected Laval of doing the same.

Hoover, preoccupied with domestic economic problems and embarrassed at any association with Europe, was impatient to see the back of his French guest. Forgetting he had invited Laval, he asked an associate, 'What has he come for anyway?'[252] And on the last day of Laval's visit he observed to Stimson,

> France always goes through this cycle. After she is done and begins to recuperate... then she gets rich, militaristic, and cocky; and nobody can get on with her until she has to be thrashed again. And in this matter he saw nothing in the future but a line-up between Germany, Britain, and ourselves against France.[253]

A few weeks later, Hoover requested Congress to reconstitute the World War Foreign Debt Commission, so that America might consider requests from European countries for debt relief on a case-by-case basis. But that was as far as he would go. After taking a swipe at Wall Street, which he accused of contributing to the slump, he concentrated his Message to Congress upon Europe, which he once more blamed for delaying America's economic recovery, and hinted at his willingness to isolate the United States further.

> Although some of the causes of our depression are due to speculation, infla-tion of securities and real estate, unsound investments, and mismanagement of financial institutions, yet our self-contained national economy, with its matchless strength and resources, would have enabled us to recover long since but for the continued dislocations, shocks and setbacks from abroad....I am confident we can make a large measure of recovery independent of the rest of the world. A strong America is the highest contribution to world stability.[254]

Hoover later represented himself as a responsible statesman blocked by an iso-lationist Congress.[255] This was a fanciful construction. Speaking to H. G. Wells at the White House, with the British ambassador present, Hoover observed that America's belief that 'civilisation could be saved' by sending troops to Europe in 1917 had proven ill-founded, since 'after thirteen years, the confusion is worse than ever before'. The only thing for the United States to do was to keep as far away from European entanglements as possible.

> There was...now a large investment of American capital in Europe, but it was small compared to the wealth of our country, and it would be better to write it down to nothing rather than sacrifice the principle of isolation in foreign policy.[256]

In the final months of 1931, French ministers renewed their efforts to improve relations with Britain. When Sir John Simon, Reading's successor as foreign secre-tary, visited Paris in mid-November, Flandin appealed for cooperation on security, promising in return to 'educate' French voters to the need for greater concessions to Germany on reparations.[257] A fortnight later, Flandin visited London where he promised the Bank of France's support for the stabilization of sterling, hoping in return for a common front against Germany. Franco-British cooperation was essential, he affirmed, if Europe's problems were ever to be solved.[258]

However, by now Britain and France had become further estranged than ever. French ministers, while accepting that Germany must suspend reparation pay-ments for the duration of the crisis, continued to insist upon the principle of reparations and the nominal payment of the unconditional tranche. As they appreciated, economics could not be separated from security. Reparations were a component of the peace settlement, and to allow Germany to abandon its commitment to reparations would undermine respect for the whole settlement. Besides, they did not accept that reparations were the insupportable burden that Germany and its Anglo-Saxon friends claimed. Germany still earned a surplus of £100 million on current account, and would not be facing transfer difficulties if it had not accepted the loans and credits that British and American bankers had lavished upon it, or if the Reichsbank had not authorized such remarkably large repayments of commercial credits in recent months: nearly 5 billion RM (£240 million) or almost one-third of Germany's total short-term debt in the 12 months to December 1931.[259] As for their burden on the German budget, reparations amounted to 700 million RM (£34 million) out of a total of 12 billion RM (£580 million) or just under 6 per cent. This was onerous but scarcely oppressive when one considered that Britain had spent over £34 million every five days in the latter stages of the war and French war damages were vastly greater than this.[260] Partly because of these damages, France's own budget was now heading for a deficit of 2.5 billion francs (£20 million).[261] Insofar as sacrifices had to be made, therefore, international bankers with short-term credits in Germany should bear their share. And when the crisis ended, reparation payments should be resumed, since otherwise France would find itself with vastly heavier taxes than Germany and even less able to compete industrially or to defend itself against its larger neighbour.[262]

Chamberlain, his Treasury advisers and most of his Cabinet colleagues refused to listen to the French case. As City bankers frantically reminded them, Britain had at least £100 million tied up in short-term credits to Germany and perhaps half as much again elsewhere in Central Europe. Unless they had clear assurance of repayment, the City, the British economy and perhaps the capitalist system itself might collapse.[263] They therefore believed it was little short of madness for France to persist with reparations, when even a nominal demand for payment increased uncertainty about the mark and deterred bankers from renewing the standstill when it expired on 28 February. The Treasury's advice to the chancellor before his meeting with Flandin illustrated the mood in London:

> The French financial policy has produced an unparalleled crisis which threatens to provoke a collapse of credit and possibly capitalism. ... The only chance of saving the situation is to restore confidence in the future of Germany by arriving at an agreement which will modify the market. This means the abandonment of any prospect of reparations whether cash or kind. ... If the French Government wish us to co-operate with them in the future, they must ... [accept] the absolute necessity of a complete abandonment of reparations and the adoption of a reasonable credit policy in future.[264]

The Treasury insisted that reparations must be cancelled, not simply postponed, and that with the Reichsbank's currency reserves now below the 30 per cent minimum, governments must act immediately. It discouraged Germany from requesting the creation of a special committee, as provided for by the Young plan, to advise on the suspension of reparation payments, since its terms of reference were too narrow.[265] When French opposition left no alternative and a special committee was instituted, Walter Layton, the British representative, pressed Bruening to take a firm stand against further reparation payments and assured him of Britain's support.[266] Meanwhile, the Treasury proposed a clearing office for trade and payments to Germany, hoping that the threat of limiting payments would force France to abandon reparations. Directors of the Bank of England, horrified at the idea of breaking up the international trade and payments system with clearing offices, would not hear of such pressure on Germany.[267] Flandin nevertheless received a cool reception in London. Not only were his British hosts firmly opposed to France's reparation policy, but to his surprise he also found them uninterested in stabilizing the pound and indifferent to his promise of help.[268]

For some months Britain had acted in ways that seemed designed to annoy or disturb French politicians and businessmen. During the summer, Britain had sought help from the Bank of France, then refused to acknowledge any responsibility for the huge losses the Bank incurred upon its sterling loans and deposits. In September, Britain had disrupted the international monetary system by departing from the gold standard and allowing sterling to depreciate 20 per cent, without, as French observers saw it, heeding the rules of the gold standard which called for penal interest rates and credit restrictions. In the 1920s, Britain had been happy to see City bankers lending indiscriminately to Germany; now in the current crisis it was encouraging Germany to halt reparation payments so their commercial credits could be repaid. Britain claimed to be a liberal trading nation, but it had recently intensified restrictions on French agricultural imports on sanitary grounds, which French authorities suspected – correctly – were a form of disguised protection for British farmers.[269] Britain had also introduced temporary duties on 'luxury imports' to save the pound from being driven off the gold standard, but retained them after the gold standard was suspended. These duties struck French trade with particular force, since some 34 billion francs (£274 million) or over 50 per cent of its exports to Britain were defined as luxury goods.[270] Indeed, Britain's emergency and forestalling duties hit France harder than any other country, and combined with the 20 per cent depreciation of sterling they devastated whole sectors of French industry.[271]

Since the sterling crisis began, Britain had also discouraged tourist visits to France. At government request, British banks interrogated individuals as to their reason for purchasing foreign exchange and refused them if their purpose was not 'legitimate'. Some newspapers even refused to take advertisements for winter cruises and publicized the patriotic action of individuals such as the Duke of Connaught, who announced that he was forsaking his annual winter holiday on the Côte d'Azur and going instead to the 'British Riviera' in Cornwall.[272] Such was the intensity of feeling that British tourists setting off for the Channel ports had been spat upon by their own countrymen.[273] Now Britain was about to adopt a general tariff with preferences for the rest of the Empire, which was bound to discriminate against France.[274] French ministers nevertheless expressed only mild protest at these developments, preferring to minimize their differences in the hope of resurrecting the *Entente*.[275] British ministers, the press and public, with no such interest in the *Entente*, gave free rein to their complaints against France.

Leith-Ross, advising Chamberlain on the agenda for Flandin's visit, singled out France as the main source of trouble:

> The French financial policy has produced an unparalleled crisis which threatens to provoke a collapse of credit and possibly capitalism.... We quite

recognise that public opinion in France is difficult, and we have no desire to add to the French Government's difficulties, that is why we accepted the procedure of the Young Plan for the opening of these discussions. But if the French Government wish us to co-operate with them in the future, they must instruct their representative on the Committee to collaborate with his British colleague in framing a report which will convince public opinion both in France and elsewhere of the absolute necessity of a complete abandonment of reparations and the adoption of a reasonable credit policy in future.[276]

Chamberlain agreed. The French were 'illogical...absurd' in their insistence upon reparations in the midst of an unprecedented crisis. Their behaviour was aggravated by Hoover's pusillanimity, since he recognized the need for concessions on war debts but lacked the courage to say so. 'Unless he says so, France doesn't move, and so we are all locked in a suicidal embrace, which will probably drown the lot of us!...Did ever a country exploit her misfortunes more successfully than France?'[277] In November, de Fleuriau warned Paris that recent developments had stirred British prejudices against France to an intensity not seen since the Ruhr crisis.[278] Sir Charles Mendl, the press officer and *eminence grise* of the British embassy in Paris, wrote to a diplomatic colleague of a recent visit to London. 'The feeling in England of intense "gaullophobia" really frightened me. I have never seen anything like it.'[279] Orme Sargent of the Foreign Office similarly warned of 'the burst of Gaullophobia at present raging in this country'. The Treasury's condemnation of the French as malevolent fools, he observed impatiently, reflected its practice of judging everyone through the narrow prism of British finance.[280]

France had entered the slump at practically the same time as other Western countries. But until 1931 the effects had been masked by several factors, including the presence of foreign workers who could be released without appearing in the official unemployment statistics, small firms which resorted to part-time employment, and the extensive agriculture sector which was scarcely affected by unemployment. It was further obscured by the strength of the franc and inflow of flight capital, which encouraged the impression of wealth and solidity. French observers ascribed their country's supposed invulnerability to its healthy balance of industry and agriculture, which contrasted with over-industrialized Germany and the United States, to its fiscal discipline and sound monetary policy.[281] Thus when sterling left the gold standard, they generally treated it as proof of Britain's economic mismanagement and encouraged hope that France would be unaffected since it had not made the same mistakes.[282] Officials in Paris, however, were uncomfortably aware of France's declining economic fortunes as early as 1930.[283] Since then, with remarkable swiftness France had ceased to be an island of prosperity and was becoming a deeply troubled country.

French export trade had fared well in the first half of the 1920s, but much of it comprised 'luxury' goods, and between 1929 and 1932 this component declined in value by 65 per cent, indeed by nearly 30 per cent in the first nine months of 1931 alone.[284] By mid-September 1931, the reappearance of a budget deficit revived the spectre of inflation and currency depreciation, which Poincaré's intervention in 1926 had temporarily exorcized.[285] Britain's abandonment of the gold standard shocked French observers,[286] who were further unnerved by a wave of business and bank failures. With tourism at a standstill, the Compagnie *Générale Transatlantique* became insolvent and survived only with state aid. The Paris department stores *Galeries Lafayette* and *Bon Marché*, symbols of middle-class prosperity, were reported to be bankrupt. The *Banque Nationale de Crédit*, the country's fourth largest joint stock bank with 752 branches, over 10,000 employees and nearly 250,000 depositors, nearly collapsed in late September.[287] The *Banque de l'Union Parisienne*, France's second largest commercial bank, passed its dividend and had to be saved by a consortium led by the Bank of France.[288] Meanwhile, numerous smaller banks faced difficulties including the *Comptoir Lyon-Alemand*, with its head office in Paris and several dozen provincial branches, *Louis Guérin et Fils of Lyon*, the *Banque Champenay of Grenoble*, *the Banque Ramel Tardif of Saint-Étienne* and *the Banque d'Alsace-Lorraine*.[289] By the end of the year, rumours circulated that all French commercial banks except perhaps the Crédit Lyonnais and the Société Générale were in serious trouble.[290]

On 19 November, Flandin confirmed that the government had spent £4 million to prop up the two principal shipping lines, £12 million to assist the railways and £16 million to stop the Banque Nationale de Crédit and the Banque d'Alsace-Lorraine from going under.[291] This was in addition to French loans of 1.1 billion francs (£8.7 million) to assist friendly foreign states,[292] and payment of 2.5 billion francs (£20.2 million) to the Bank of France to cover its sterling losses.[293] Rumours that the reported business failures were just the tip of the iceberg fuelled private hoarding, despite the Bank of France's massive gold reserves.[294] According to a City banker familiar with the French scene, 'lack of confidence has reached such a pitch that there is not a single firm or bank which is not talked about. Consequently all business is brought nearly to a standstill.'[295]

The government, politically conservative and economically liberal, was practically immobilized. Despite mounting pressure from business organizations, it could not raise duties on imports, since most of them had been fixed in bilateral commercial agreements. Nor could it contemplate devaluation of the franc after the financial crisis five years earlier. It therefore introduced a surtax on imports from countries that had recently allowed their currencies to depreciate, and import quotas, thus reversing the trend away from quantitative trade controls since the war. But this merely aggravated relations with France's trading partners while doing nothing to halt the decline in domestic activity. It also held on to reparations and the gold standard, and for security pursued the *Entente* with Britain while seeking improved relations with the United States and Germany. In the event, none of these policies proved effective.

6.7 Conclusion

Until 1931, the British Foreign Office encouraged the view that the 'old diplomacy' of alliances, secret treaties and balance of power should be eschewed and that France must be contained so that Germany could recover its place at the centre of

Europe. Vansittart, the permanent under-secretary, forcefully repeated this view in his second 'old Adam' paper for circulation to the Cabinet in May 1931.[296] But in November 1931, the Foreign Office prepared a paper for the Cabinet that proposed a very different approach to international affairs. The authors were a small group led by Sargent, a future under-secretary, who belatedly recognized the dilemma confronting Europe and the world. As Sargent put it in internal minutes, removing inter-governmental debts was unlikely to promote stability and might undermine it further in the absence of a security framework capable of reassuring the French and persuading 'the Hitlerite element in Germany...that provocation will not work.'[297] The French and their allies in Eastern Europe were bound to fear that suppressing reparations would

> bring nearer the day when Germany, relieved of overhead charges, fully rationalized and re-equipped its industry, and with a growing population, will assume once more her prewar position as the predominant State in Europe, politically and economically. Nor is this fear altogether unfounded, for we should be foolish to suppose that by relieving Germany of her reparations debt we are going to render her a contented and peaceful member of the European community. The removal of reparations is merely one objective in the long-range policy of Germany, which aims at tackling one problem after another. Having first got rid of the Rhineland Occupation and now Reparations, Germany will then be able to concentrate all her energies on her three next objectives:
>
> 1. the political objective of recovering the Polish Corridor and Upper Silesia;
> 2. the economic objective of the commercial penetration of Central Europe (which includes the *Anschluss* with Austria); and
> 3. the military objective of obtaining parity of armaments.
>
> We can hardly assume that in pursuing these objectives Germany will display any degree of tact or prudence, or that she will make any great efforts to consider the susceptibilities of her neighbours; on the contrary, we may expect her truculence to grow in proportion as her prosperity returns. In any case this is undoubtedly how France will envisage the future after the elimination of the reparations problem, and as long as France and her Allies fear such a development there will certainly be no return of political confidence in Europe.[298]

The Foreign Office thus presented the picture of a dual crisis in which the economic and political elements were inextricably bound up together. It advised an 'all-in' diplomatic offensive, putting into play commercial, financial and monetary instruments as well as security and defence.[299] Since France had a well-grounded fear of German ambitions to overturn the postwar settlement, Britain must be prepared to engage fully in bargaining if it was to halt the downward spiral of political-economic relations. Sargent and his colleagues did not underestimate the difficulty of breaking the vicious circle. But they assumed that Britain's dependence upon international trade made it essential to try, and moreover that Britain's departure from the gold standard and drift towards protectionism actually enhanced its capacity to influence the other powers. Britain remained the world's largest import market and the most important source of credit and capital.

Everywhere, but above all in Europe, business and political leaders were almost desperate to know if Britain would stabilize its currency and remain free trade or retreat into imperial protectionism. 'The tariff and the pound are our two trump cards in the game of foreign politics. We have only lately drawn them; and we must consider very carefully when and how they are to be played.'

The acknowledgement that Britain faced a dual crisis, which could be addressed only by recognizing the dynamic of its interrelated politico-economic elements, constituted a major advance in official thinking. Hardly less important was the assertion that Britain must take into account the security of Eastern Europe. Hitherto, the Foreign Office had accepted that the region was too troubled and too remote to warrant Britain's involvement. Indeed, it had pressured France to abandon it, leaving Germany free to pursue its revisionist ambitions. Even now officials hesitated to affirm the integral importance of Eastern Europe to the international balance of power and hence Britain's interest in its fate. But for the sake of French cooperation on a range of vital issues, they accepted that the region could not be ignored. Quoting a recent statement in the *Economist*, they explained:

> A universal sense of insecurity is the evil which is paralysing the economic and financial life of the world; these paralysing fears are political as well as economic; they are predominantly political in France, whose consequent financial policy is the crux of the present international situation; these French fears turn partly upon the insecurity of the East European peace settlement, and anything that can be done by other parties to remove these French fears will, therefore, contribute to producing in France that change of mind which it is of vital importance to produce in the general interest of the world. We may therefore have to ask ourselves: is the danger of being involved in Eastern European commitments really greater for England than the danger of being involved here and now in the world-wide economic and financial breakdown which the present universal sense of insecurity threatens to bring about?

The crisis overtaking Europe and the possibility that Britain would throw away the chance to give an effective lead had thoroughly shaken officials. They therefore warned the Cabinet,

> People in this country seem to be unaware of the extent to which the future of 'civilisation' depends on what happens in Germany in the course of the next six months and of the grave doubt as to whether the upshot will be peace or war, recovery or collapse.... At this crucial moment in our history, it is clear that British foreign policy must be formulated on a very broad basis. This is the first object of the foregoing memorandum, and this must be accepted as axiomatic.... It is fully realised that there are many and serious objections to some of the suggestions contained herein, but they have been formulated after long consideration of the difficulties with which we are faced. If we cannot advance on lines such as these, is there an alternative policy? If there is no alternative, what is in store for Europe? And what is in store for the world?[300]

Sargent and his circle, like some of their counterparts in the US State Department, thus recognized the dual nature of the international crisis and the need for a broad approach to it.[301] This, however, was not at all congenial to leading Cabinet ministers. Sargent's paper had been prepared at the instigation of the Liberal Lord Reading. But Chamberlain and his Conservative colleagues who now dominated the National government were not prepared to forsake their freedom of action on monetary and commercial policy or become entangled with France in European affairs. The Treasury, jealous of its own authority over monetary and financial policy, therefore acted with Chamberlain's agreement to halt the printing of the Foreign Office paper and its circulation to the Cabinet.[302]

Sir Walford Selby, a member of Sargent's circle, warned the new foreign secretary, Sir John Simon, that the public had been misled about the international situation ever since the war. Germany was always being represented as

> the under-dog, to whom more and ever more indulgence must be extended ... [whereas] the armaments of France, her apparent prosperity as compared with the other nations of Europe, are interpreted as justifications for the contention that it is she who is making for the hegemony of Europe.... Could any such conclusion have been reached if all the facts were known as they should be known ... ?[303]

He appealed to Simon to fight his corner when the Cabinet met the next day. Simon managed to have Sargent's paper circulated to the Cabinet, but it appeared along with no less than five other papers on foreign affairs, and since Simon did not share Sargent's vision, he allowed his ministerial colleagues to pass over it.[304] Thereafter, Chamberlain and the Treasury dominated British external policy-making. They addressed the debt issue and disarmament independently while setting aside the question of security in Western and Eastern Europe. Just as the Foreign Office paper warned, the result was that the international security framework became even more fragmented and the economic slump continued to worsen.

7
The Collapse of the Postwar Order, 1932–4

7.1 Introduction

Shortly after 2 p.m. on Saturday, 12 March 1932, the coffin bearing the remains of Aristide Briand was carried from the Ministry of Foreign Affairs on the *Quai d'Orsay*, and placed on the catafalque erected outside. For two days it had lain in state in the *Salle de l'Horloge*, scene of many of Briand's diplomatic triumphs, but now dimmed with black drapery relieved here and there by white stripes, a black carpet covering the floor, and crêpe surrounding the vast gilt and crystal chandelier. During that time, thousands of dignitaries and ordinary citizens had paid their respects, the queue of mourners frequently stretching down the pavement to the Seine, then westwards beyond the *Pont Alexandre III*.[1] Another large crowd gathered on the Champ de Mars adjacent to the Ministry to hear the eulogy of André Tardieu, the premier, before the procession set off for the cemetery at Passy. The coffin, covered with a tricoleur, was guarded by two bareheaded boys in shirtsleeves and shorts, uniform of the Peace Volunteers. This was in keeping with the tributes from around the world which praised Briand's efforts as the 'pilgrim of peace'. Lloyd George spoke of his commitment to 'the cause of appeasement of Europe...international conciliation and good will'. Austen Chamberlain described him as 'the greatest "European" of us all', a man 'passionately devoted to the cause of peace, [who] served it with selfless devotion'. Paul Hymans, the Belgian statesman and current president of the League of Nations Assembly, called him 'the very incarnation of the ideals of peace and friendship among the peoples...who had helped more than almost any other to build up the League of Nations'. Heinrich Bruening, the German chancellor, recalled his efforts to promote a Franco-German rapprochement and described him as 'a sincere and convinced servant of the cause of peace'. Herbert Hoover, president of the United States, with typical awkwardness, praised his 'loyal and unflinching fight for peace both in Europe and this country'.[2]

Tardieu's tribute, delivered from a small platform bristling with microphones and carried live on the BBC's National programme, generously acknowledged Briand's contribution to peace, but also pointed to the realism of his approach. Since January 1921 when he first became foreign minister, and for the past seven years when he occupied the post almost continuously, Briand had pursued a policy of appeasement. But, Tardieu added, he had never reduced or compromised the military guarantees on which France relied until solid alternatives were in place.

> At no time and to no degree, however much they might have facilitated his negotiations, did he ask the Ministries of National Defence for sacrifices. He always declared that they, and they only, must be responsible for the determination of their requirements, and that these requirements must be the limits of his own concessions. Security first was his maxim.[3]

Tardieu's remarks, which passed without comment in the press, deserve recalling.[4] For with Briand's passing, no one emerged with the same capacity to maintain France's objective of peace with security. Peace was now threatened from several directions. While Briand's funeral took place, the League of Nations was meeting in special session to consider Japan's seizure of Manchuria. The very next day, in the first round of the German presidential election, Hitler received 11.3 million votes. This was 7.3 million fewer than the votes for Field-Marshal Paul von Hindenburg, the incumbent. But it was 4.9 million or 77 per cent more than the Nazis obtained in the September 1930 Reichstag election, when they emerged as the second largest party in the country.[5] Across the Alps, Mussolini relentlessly supported German revisionist claims to isolate France. With the political turmoil came worsening economic conditions. World industrial production, having declined over 10 per cent between 1929 and 1930, was down 20 per cent by 1931 and over 30 per cent by 1932.[6] Unemployment rose correspondingly to 2.75 million or 15.6 per cent of the industrial workforce in Britain, 2.8 million or 17 per cent (partly or wholly unemployed) in France, 12 million or 36 per cent in the United States and 6 million or 44.6 per cent in Germany.[7] World trade touched a new low, falling to merely 52.5 per cent of the 1929 level.[8]

Western statesmen, however, did not abandon hope of alleviating the dual crisis. In the year between Briand's death and Hitler's seizure of dictatorial power in March 1933, they came forward with a remarkable number of initiatives. Few of them proved to be politically feasible. Yet a number of opportunities arose that might well have improved the situation, had the leading capitalist powers been willing or able to work together. The point once again is not that any of these initiatives would have been sufficient to end the slump or silence the proponents of extreme nationalism. It is rather that they might have reduced the intensity of the slump and increased hope in multilateral action enough to stave off the collapse of the world economic and political systems.

7.2   Disarmament and the European balance of power, February 1932–April 1934

Early in 1932, two international conferences were scheduled to be held in Switzerland. The first was a gathering of delegates from six countries in Lausanne to address the problem of war reparations, the second a conference attended by delegates from 60 countries at the League of Nations headquarters in Geneva to negotiate a disarmament convention. The reparations conference was convened in haste to consider the report of financial experts who had met in Basle late the previous year. The disarmament conference had been six years in preparation. Formally nothing linked the two events, but French statesmen regarded concessions to Germany on reparations and disarmament as integrally related, since each of them vitally affected French security. Statesmen of the Anglo-Saxon powers also implicitly accepted the connection, since they regarded them both as means of forestalling Germany's collapse into chaos. Accordingly, at both conferences they pressured France to make concessions. Despite the importance they attached to a disarmament agreement and an end to reparations, they nonetheless insisted upon approaching them as discrete issues and refused to address France's legitimate security concerns – with predictably negative results.

The disarmament conference opened on 2 February 1932. But, long before then, Franco-German differences ruled out a successful outcome in the absence of direct intervention by Britain if not also the United States. In April 1931, smarting from criticism of its customs union scheme with Austria, Bruening announced that he would refuse to sign the draft disarmament convention unless all powers signatory to the Treaty of Versailles honoured their commitment to disarm or accord Germany full equality in the sphere of armaments.[9] French statesmen reacted with anger. They had consistently supported disarmament, at least in principle, since failure to do so might lead Germany to claim it was no longer bound by the Treaty and Italy to build up arms for dangerous adventures.[10] Indeed, they had been the instigators of the preparatory committee responsible for the draft disarmament convention and the present conference. In 1921–2 they had found themselves isolated at the Washington naval disarmament conference and pressured by the Anglo-Saxon powers to accept parity with Italy on naval arms. Accordingly, in 1925 when they heard that Coolidge might call a second naval disarmament conference, they requested the League to make preparations for a general disarmament conference, rather than having naval disarmament again treated independently.[11] Now that the conference was about to begin, they viewed Bruening's demand as a provocation and a challenge to the European balance of power.

As Briand pointed out to Arthur Henderson, the British foreign secretary, France had already reduced its military forces to a fraction of prewar levels. Compulsory military service had been cut from three years to two in February 1922, to eighteen months in April 1923 and to one year in March 1928. Trained personnel in France and the Rhineland, numbering 400,000 in 1921, were now down to 229,000 of whom 66,000 were earmarked for overseas duties.[12] France also faced the imminent prospect of a steep decline in the number of men eligible for conscription on account of the lower birth rate during the Great War. Meanwhile, Briand reminded Henderson, Germany had systematically evaded its Treaty obligations on disarmament. French authorities estimated that since 1925 Germany's military budget had nearly doubled.[13] The purpose of the Treaty clauses limiting Germany's postwar military strength had not been to intimidate or punish Germany, but to tip the European balance of power in favour of peace. Despite minor losses of territory after the war, Germany was still far larger than France in population and industrial capacity. To concede equality in arms threatened to turn the clock back to 1914 when Germany militarily dominated the Continent, and force France into massive increases in defence spending. France could contemplate further disarmament only if the Anglo-Saxon powers fully committed themselves to European security.

Briand appealed to Henderson to stand firm against the German demand. He had no doubt that a clear demonstration of Franco-British solidarity would deflect Germany onto a more prudent path. If, however, Britain encouraged Bruening, he would almost certainly persist in his demand, and an aroused German public would make it impossible for him to back down. In Briand's words, 'The common interest is thus to avoid the situation where such an insoluble question is posed, and it is there that the British Government can exercise a decisive influence in Berlin.'[14]

Briand and his colleagues found themselves increasingly beleaguered by contending pressures. British and American statesmen, convinced that Mussolini was committed to peace, repeatedly pressed them to concede naval equality to Italy. They resisted, pointing out that France possessed vastly greater imperial possessions and that the security of metropolitan France depended upon unhindered communications with its North African territories.[15] Meanwhile the Fascist regime in Rome became more restless and antagonistic towards France. While Mussolini spoke of the heroic quality of war, his government seized every opportunity to oppose France on reparations and assistance to the Danube region, and supported Germany's demand for equality in arms.[16] Even more worrying was the British and American pressure on France to concede equality of treatment to Germany, coming as it did amidst evidence of increasing restlessness in Berlin.

France's predicament created deep divisions in public opinion, with the Socialists and Communists arguing for peace through disarmament and their conservative opponents angrily countering with demands for greater arms and security. Frustration erupted on 27 November 1931, during the final session of an International Congress of Disarmament, organized by a coalition of peace groups at the Trocadero in Paris. Outside the hall, right-wing protesters from the semi-fascist *Croix de Feu* in conjunction with the *Jeunesses Patriotes* and *Action Française* demonstrated, while the police, possibly on the advice of government ministers, stood back. When participants from Italy, Germany, Britain and France, including Lord Cecil and the former premiers Paul Painlevé and Edouard Herriot, attempted to speak, they were shouted down by protesters who had infiltrated the gathering and now occupied the stage. Unable to continue, the organizers suspended the Congress.[17]

For years, British statesmen were well aware that German governments had connived in the *Reichswehr's* evasion of the military clauses of the Versailles Treaty. Indeed, since the withdrawal of the Inter-Allied Control Commission in 1927, the *Reichswehr* had made less and less effort to disguise its activities. Just as the

Disarmament Conference opened, the British general staff reported that 'numerous and varied breaches of the great majority of the military clauses have been committed and...their combined effect is considerable.' From various sources they knew that the number of men receiving military training in Germany far exceeded the 100,000 limit fixed by the Treaty; that Germany possessed 'at least the nucleus of an efficient air force camouflaged within the organisation of her powerful civil aviation'; that departments of the Ministry of Defence were developing chemical weapons of mass destruction and that arrangements were well advanced to resume the large-scale manufacture of weapons prohibited by the Treaty.[18] German officials openly refused to accept the *status quo* on their eastern frontier, and rejected the idea of an 'eastern Locarno'.[19] Yet oddly the general staff accepted that German rearmament was 'mainly defensive in character'.[20] Like their political masters, they presented the problem as German fear of French aggression, thus standing reality on its head.

A few weeks before the disarmament conference was due to open, Sir John Simon, the foreign secretary, on the advice of Sir Robert Vansittart, proposed in Cabinet that Britain might offer France a 'Mediterranean Locarno' as an inducement to yield to German demands.[21] Simon's ministerial colleagues opposed any concessions to France. Sharing MacDonald's view that the French were 'an ever active influence for evil in Europe',[22] and the Army general staff's belief that Germany had reason to fear 'destruction' at the hands of France and its allies,[23] they were drawn to Vansittart's alternative proposal that they should threaten to adopt a policy of isolation from Europe.[24] Accordingly, on the eve of the conference they agreed that Britain could not accept any new Continental commitment.[25] In keeping with their isolationist, pro-Imperialist stance, they proceeded to press France to reduce its land defences while approving a new British naval construction programme.[26]

American leaders were reluctant even to participate in disarmament negotiations, since, in the words of Joseph Cotton, the legal expert at the State Department, it would 'plunge us deeply into the European mess.' But having been involved for six years in the preparation of the conference, they were too embarrassed to withdraw at this late stage. As William Castle, the under-secretary, frankly acknowledged, 'we have little to offer, but...our influence may be of some account.' American policy would be that of 'supporting Germany against France...although', he added, 'we should hardly be so stupid as to phrase it in that way.'[27] By the winter of 1931, American statesmen were preoccupied with Japanese aggression in Manchuria, which they regarded as within their sphere of influence. Hoover toyed with the idea of issuing a proposal to the disarmament conference for the reduction of all standing armies to the same level as Germany's. But he was not prepared to contemplate a reduction in the US navy.[28]

Confronted by the scarcely disguised hostility of Germany, Italy, Britain and the United States, and with the future of both Europe and East Asia increasingly obscure, French leaders would have preferred to avoid the disarmament conference as well. But since legislative elections were only three months away and Anglo-Saxon friendship was as important as ever, they felt obliged to participate.

Accordingly, just three days after the conference opened and before the preparatory commission submitted its draft treaty, Tardieu, the minister of war, tabled a French proposal. Predictably it combined disarmament with compulsory arbitration as well as a precise definition of aggression and the organization of an international intervention force under League auspices (including monopoly control of all bombing aircraft and heavy artillery). No one in Paris or Geneva seriously believed the proposal was acceptable. But it enabled France to claim that it supported disarmament, provided of course that it was combined with security.[29]

Tardieu, on becoming premier on 21 February 1932, used his ministerial declaration to the Chamber of Deputies to appeal for a revival of the *Entente*, and urged Britain to refrain from encouraging Germany in its demand for equality in armaments.[30] When Simon visited Paris to attend Briand's funeral, Tardieu proposed that they sit down and resolve their differences, just as their predecessors had done when the *Entente cordiale* was adopted in 1904. This was urgently necessary, in his view, since the most pressing issues – disarmament, reparations, economic policy and assistance to the countries of the Danube – could only be resolved if Britain and France addressed them together. 'Lord Lansdowne and M. Delcassé had found it possible to promote a more general *entente* 28 years ago and the model was worth bearing in mind.'[31] Simon was gratified to hear Tardieu's appeal, since it confirmed that France valued Britain's friendship and might be prepared to pay a high price to obtain it. But he had no intention of lining up Britain with France against German demands. Indeed, despite Tardieu's appeal to avoid encouraging German hopes of obtaining equality in armaments, he did just that. To Rudolf Nadolny, head of the German delegation, Simon observed, 'There were, as he knew, many matters on which British policy approximated much more to the German than to the French point of view', although he must not expect Treaty revision to happen immediately.[32] Norman Davis, head of the American delegation, displayed a similar attitude. After meeting Tardieu at the conference, he observed patronizingly that the French premier seemed 'distinctly more rational than he has been in the past.'

> Not only is he less nationalistic; but he has apparently reached the conclusion that the days of French dictation to Europe are over; that the depression is reaching such proportions that it is a matter of economic life and death to get thoroughly reorganized and to make some savings on the French military budget.[33]

With the conference bogged down in deliberations over qualitative disarmament, involving debate over 'offensive' and 'defensive' weapons, and Bruening under increasing pressure from nationalist opponents in Germany, MacDonald, Stimson and Tardieu travelled to Geneva where they drafted a loose proposal which would have enabled Germany to increase the size of its army. Tardieu, however, pleading an attack of laryngitis, was absent on 29 April when they planned to discuss the proposal further. Bruening, also in Geneva, returned to Berlin empty-handed that evening, and the following day President Hindenburg dismissed him in favour of the nationalist, Franz von Papen. Tardieu's reason for absence was plausible enough, given that he had been campaigning hard in the French legislative elections. But he doubtless disliked the proposal, which merely weakened the military clauses of the Versailles Treaty without offering a concomitant increase in European security.[34] Neither MacDonald nor Stimson was prepared to reconsider a Continental commitment.[35] Yet MacDonald took out his frustration on Tardieu, describing his behaviour as 'crooked and dishonest', and blaming France for bringing down Bruening.[36]

With the American presidential election approaching, Hoover decided to reaffirm his pacifist credentials by launching a disarmament proposal of his own. He had done something similar before the previous presidential election in 1928, and it is difficult to believe that it was not motivated chiefly by the domestic electoral contest. As he acknowledged to advisers, he hoped to exploit the predicament of America's European debtors, about to meet at Lausanne, by affirming that America would concede further relief on their debts after the end of the moratorium year only if they cooperated on disarmament. If they did so, his standing in America would rise. If they did not, he would benefit from American resentment at Europe's apparent preference for arms and armies over debt repayment.[37] His proposal called for a one-third reduction in land forces and the abolition of 'offensive' weapons, including tanks, large mobile guns and heavy artillery, chemical weapons and bombing aircraft. Stimson regarded Hoover's plan as unrealistic – 'a proposition from Alice in Wonderland' – and in its preliminary form which included a one-third reduction in naval forces, one that would merely antagonize Britain and France.[38] By removing reference to naval forces, Washington secured a cautiously favourable response from Britain.[39] But as could have been predicted, the plan embarrassed France while encouraging Germany to become bolder in its demand for equality of treatment.

On 8 May, the second round of voting in the French legislative elections brought a modest leftwards shift, which enabled Edouard Herriot, the Radical party leader, to form a new government.[40] Much to the frustration of Flandin, Tardieu and other conservative opponents, Herriot had managed to persuade voters that he could work more effectively with Britain;[41] and Léon Blum, the Socialist leader, as well as left-wing members of Herriot's own party constantly pressed him to join with Britain on disarmament.[42] Herriot, however, doubted that Germany had abandoned its imperialist ambitions. General Weygand, chief of the army general staff and vice-president of the supreme war council, demanded that he support *rearmament*.[43] And after speaking to Papen at Lausanne in June, he became convinced that another war with Germany was certain.[44] While this made him all the more anxious to cooperate with Britain and the United States, he could not endorse the Hoover plan. France's Eastern allies strongly opposed concessions to Germany, fearing that they would encourage Hungarian and Bulgarian revisionism as well as weakening France itself. The French press, aside from *Le Populaire* and a few other left-wing newspapers, regarded the Hoover plan as a deliberate assault on French security.[45] Since this was also Herriot's view – describing it as *'diplomatie de bombardement'* – and that of his officials, he expressed strong reservations about the plan.[46] Papen seized the opportunity to protest at French obstruction, and with no agreement in sight he walked out of the disarmament conference, bringing it to a temporary halt on 22 July.[47]

This was not the end of the story. Isolated internationally and dismayed by the huge leap in support for the Nazi party in the Reichstag elections on 31 July, Herriot agreed to the reconvening of the conference in September. Then, pressured by Britain and the United States for concessions to induce Germany to return, he endorsed a new French disarmament proposal. The *plan constructif* or Paul-Boncour plan reincorporated key elements of the Tardieu plan and called upon the Continental countries to participate in a mutual assistance pact, leaving Britain and the United States merely to 'consult' in the event of a breach of the agreement.[48] Even this was too much for Britain which urged unilateral appeasement of Germany.[49] In December, with General Schleicher, the *Reichswehr's* representative, occupying the chancellor's office in Berlin and Hitler waiting to take over, Herriot yielded. France agreed to a five-power declaration that constituted the abandonment of the military clauses of the Versailles Treaty and recognized Germany's 'equality of rights in a system which would provide security for all nations'.[50]

This was a major concession by France, and Germany agreed to return to the conference. But it scarcely produced the hoped-for results, because on 30 January 1933, the day before the conference reconvened, Hitler succeeded Schleicher as chancellor. One might imagine that Hitler's seizure of power would have caused Britain to rethink its support for general disarmament. But the 'two Germany' thesis still shaped the outlook of well-placed British observers, who took the violence and anti-Semitism that accompanied Hitler's takeover as reassuring signs that Prussian-dominated Germany was being replaced by a more democratic state. G. P. Gooch, a leading historian of Germany, assured Young Liberals that 'Hitler was not a bad man, though he could be ruthless in pursuing his aims.'[51] A year after Hitler took office, the Berlin correspondent of the *Times* explained in a special report that Germany was engaged in a struggle between the landowners, industrialists and other 'reactionaries', and the popular forces who had put Hitler in power. 'Charming and cultivated as they may be individually, the German Junkers and industrialists as castes are, rightly or wrongly, associated historically with Pan-Germanism, expansionism and war.' The 'new Germany' might appear to be 'impregnated with a spirit of aggressive nationalism and militarism', but all the drumbeating and marching could be expected to die away when Germany regained its self-respect. The best hope of this outcome 'must lie in the further progress of the genuine National Socialist idealists.'[52] Since the outcome of the struggle within Germany remained uncertain, the British government had quietly set aside the Ten-Year rule in 1932 and presently began to make up for underspending on existing defence programmes. But despite warnings of the threat posed by Nazi Germany from several eminent politicians, including Sir Austen Chamberlain, Churchill and Lord Grey, the government preferred to assist the 'progress of the genuine National Socialist idealists'. In particular, it intensified its support for European disarmament.[53]

In March 1933, Britain submitted a plan in MacDonald's name that would remove all restrictions on German army recruitment and weaponry, while merely delaying by a few years the grant of full equality of rights. The French government accepted the MacDonald plan as the basis of deliberations at the conference, while seeking to modify several of its key clauses.[54] Only some of them had been addressed by 29 June when the conference adjourned for the summer, and on 14 October, two days before it was due to reconvene, Hitler announced Germany's withdrawal from the conference as well as the League of Nations. Thereupon the British government pressured French leaders into accepting direct bilateral talks with Germany, which began in January 1934. Hitler brutally rejected France's proposal for a programme of disarmament accompanied by international supervision and the provision for international sanctions. The British government nevertheless persisted in its search for a compromise, sending Anthony Eden, minister of state for League affairs, on a tour of European capitals between 17 February and 1 March. The French government of national concentration, created in the aftermath of civil unrest on 6 February, did not immediately respond. Louis Barthou, the foreign minister, and senior diplomatic advisers preferred that France should go along with Britain to avoid becoming completely isolated. But Gaston Doumergue, the premier, supported by Tardieu, Herriot and the military high command, decided that enough was enough.[55] Accordingly, on 17 April Barthou formally advised the British ambassador that Germany's undisguised rearmament plans made a compromise settlement impossible.[56]

This to all intents and purposes ended the disarmament conference, which adjourned indefinitely on 11 June. Yet if it produced no agreement on disarmament, its importance can scarcely be exaggerated. With the economic slump threatening to destabilize Germany and the whole of the capitalist world, the Anglo-Saxon powers had sought to use disarmament as a means of appeasing Germany. But this merely encouraged German revisionism and played into the hands of extreme nationalists such as Hugenberg and Hitler. When France retreated before British and American pressure, the result was tension with its Eastern allies and turmoil within France itself. And by the time France finally drew the line on further concessions, relations with the Anglo-Saxon powers had also deteriorated almost to breaking point. The disarmament issue thus linked the crises of the international economic and security systems. As will be seen, disputes over financial, monetary, commercial and regional policies, contributed further to the destructive dynamic of the great interwar crisis.

7.3 Reparations and international security, January–July 1932

If the three great liberal powers disagreed on how to implement disarmament, they could at least agree that in principle disarmament was desirable. Reparations found them more fundamentally divided. By January 1932, British statesmen had become convinced that only by eliminating reparations could the world's capitalist system be saved from total collapse. The flight of hot money that had forced Austria, Germany, Britain and most of Europe and the Commonwealth off the gold standard in 1931 had now shifted to the United States, where free gold reserves seemed sufficient to defend the dollar for only a month or so at the current rate of withdrawals. Germany, Austria and other countries of the Danube region were in a particularly bad way. Foreign short-term debt in Germany alone stood at perhaps £600 million, and even in mid-1932 City institutions still had at least £150 million tied up in short-term credits elsewhere in the region.[57] Governments were intervening to suspend payments on foreign debt, and British bankers feared that unless confidence was soon restored, there would be a general crash.[58] Treasury officials, who listened closely to City opinion, were equally worried. As Sir Frederick Leith-Ross put it, 'I do not much like the way in which default is spreading. It is becoming a very fashionable disease and may play havoc with the system of capital and credit before it is finished.'[59] The need for action was especially urgent, since the six-month standstill on German foreign short-term debt would end on 29 February and the international bankers might refuse to renew it if they thought reparations made repayment of commercial debts problematical. Even if they agreed to renew it, the one-year Hoover moratorium on reparations and war debts was due to expire on 1 July, and on 15 July Germany would be obliged to resume reparation payments at the rate of 140 million gold Reichsmarks (£7 million) a month, as specified in the Young plan.[60] Since British statesmen did not believe that Germany would or could meet all of its international financial obligations, they vigorously pressed other creditor governments for the next six months to abandon their reparation claims.

The British analysis was broadly correct. Since the reparation claims overhanging the mark added to the uncertainty of international financial markets, their removal at this time might have had a tonic effect, with important political as well as economic consequences. It might have accelerated Germany's economic recovery, signs of which began to appear in the summer of 1932,[61] and with faster recovery Hitler might have failed in his bid for power through the ballot box. But despite British impatience for action on reparations, the American government refused to abandon its claim to war debts, which increased the French government's reluctance to reopen the reparation settlement. British statesmen saw little prospect of American cooperation in 1932, since this was a presidential election year and the last thing Republican or Democratic party candidates wanted was to be accused of sacrificing American interests for the benefit of Europe. French cooperation was another matter. With Germany increasingly restless, French statesmen missed no opportunity to reaffirm their hopes for closer relations with Britain. But their British counterparts refused to accept that Britain and France had a common interest in maintaining the European *status quo*, and they dismissed proposals to extend a security commitment to France, the key that might have opened the door to a timely and radical settlement of the reparation controversy and much else besides.

The new crisis over reparations began in January 1932. The international bankers who had met at BIS headquarters in Bâle from 7 to 23 December 1931 acknowledged in their report that the slump was far worse than anything anticipated by the authors of the Young plan in 1929; therefore Germany was entitled to request a further suspension of reparation payments when the Hoover moratorium ended on 30 June.[62] But to British bankers and their Treasury associates, an extension of the moratorium would only prolong uncertainty about the future of the mark and delay Germany's recovery. It would also 'leave the French as masters of the situation', which Simon, the foreign secretary, was not prepared to accept. He therefore decided to 'bring the French to reason' by calling in Konstantin Graf von Neurath, the German ambassador, on 6 January, knowing that he was shortly returning to Berlin, and confirmed Britain's commitment to the complete cancellation of reparations.[63] Bruening already knew of Britain's position. Nonetheless, Simon's forthright affirmation encouraged him to act. On 8 January, with Neurath at his side, he informed the press that the uncertainty created by reparation demands was blocking Germany's recovery and aggravating the slump. Germany would therefore make no further payments for the foreseeable future.[64]

The British government denied that any department of state had encouraged Bruening to speak out, which strictly speaking was true.[65] It made no difference. Germany, in the words of the Foreign Office, had 'crossed the Rubicon' on reparations, and the whole of France was furious.[66] The angry reaction was partly due to the parlous state of the French economy. With trade collapsing, the budget deficit soaring, commercial firms and banks failing, and unemployment increasingly evident, France now seemed more vulnerable to external pressures. The other influence at work was the belief shared by practically all French observers that Germany was exploiting a temporary crisis to break free from yet another constraint upon its imperialist ambitions. Reparations were compensation for the damage Germany had inflicted on France in the war; to Paris they were also a necessary constraint upon Germany, saddling its economy with an additional charge. As Laval put it to Walter Edge, 'cancellation of German reparation payments would put Germany in a position where no outside competition could touch her and…he could not understand why Great Britain did not realize it also.'[67] Flandin, the minister of finance, betrayed similar frustration in conversation with Leith-Ross the day after Bruening's declaration: French opinion, he said, was fed up with 'this constant German blackmail', when no sooner had the Allies granted one concession to Germany than it raised some new demand.[68] Aimé de Fleuriau, the ambassador in London, spelled out French fears to Simon. They derived, he said, not so much from the financial losses involved as from the conviction that Germany was seeking to subvert the Versailles Treaty. The Allies must draw a line now or the peace settlement itself would soon be overturned. In this event, another war could only be a matter of time.[69]

The French government demonstrated its fear in several ways. It issued a formal protest to Germany and announced that it would not attend the conference on reparations in February at Lausanne until or unless Germany reaffirmed its treaty obligations. Laval consulted General Weygand, and agreed to recall certain categories of reservists and despatch military units and supplies to the eastern frontier.[70] Flandin followed this by threatening that the Bank of France would withdraw its share of the international credit issued to the Reichsbank the previous June.[71] He also warned a member of the British embassy staff that if Britain sided openly with Germany now, he would face strong pressure from his own Parliament to withdraw French treasury and central bank deposits from London, regardless of the effect on sterling.[72] Within Parliament meanwhile the hostile environment brought new demands for trade protection through bilateral clearing agreements and a general tightening of import quotas.[73]

British statesmen persisted in their efforts to convene an early conference on reparations. Since concessions by the United States on war debts were out of the question for the time being, they sought agreement among creditor countries to settle reparations first before requesting Washington to write off its war debt claims. In particular they attempted to persuade France not to insist upon merely a temporary suspension of claims on Germany or a *solde* (a net benefit after payment of war debts), and instead to accept complete cancellation. Anything less, they warned, would prompt Washington to apply the principle of capacity to pay to its own debtors, since they were treating Germany in similar fashion, and on this basis France would obtain little relief from war debt payments.[74]

British efforts brought no result. Laval, defeated in a Chamber vote on 11 January, managed to form another government the following day. But having failed to secure support from the Radical party, he depended for his survival upon votes from the right of the Chamber where opposition to concessions on reparations was strongest.[75] In fact, the approaching legislative elections made practically all political parties and fractions anxious to demonstrate their firmness on reparations. Despite wishing to cooperate with Britain, Laval thus found himself severely constrained. The most he could do was endorse a declaration affirming that Germany's reparation creditors would attend a conference at Lausanne to find 'a lasting settlement of the question raised in the report of the Basle experts'.[76]

Laval's second government lasted barely six weeks, after which Tardieu took office until the legislative elections in May. Flandin, who remained finance minister, set aside the threat to order the Bank of France to cease supporting the Reichsbank and privately advised Governor Moret to remain aligned with his British and American colleagues.[77] Nor was there any more talk of withdrawing French balances from London. Flandin, however, warned Tyrrell that the government's precarious majority in Parliament obliged it to stand firm on reparations. It would accept a one-year extension of the Hoover moratorium and attend a conference at Lausanne after the French elections. But neither it nor any other French government could survive if it simply abandoned reparations, and especially not without the firm assurance of relief from further war debt demands.[78]

In Britain, the crisis over reparations prompted a renewed outburst of attacks on France. Having largely caused the world depression by its short-sighted policies and forced sterling off the gold standard, critics claimed, France was now driving Germany to the wall by its blind insistence upon reparations in the midst of the world depression. The *Times* observed:

[I]t is perhaps too much to expect the Frenchman-in-the-street to realize that much of his recent prosperity has been built on the ruins of British enterprises;

[and that reparations are] the root of the economic evil. It never occurs to him that French postwar policy may be largely responsible...[79]

The *New Statesman and Nation* accepted that France had inadvertently done Britain a favour by driving it off the gold standard, but it added, 'at the moment she still stands as the leader of the narrow nationalistic spirit in Europe, the chief prop of armaments, the champion of reactionary finance, the implacable creditor'.[80] In the words of Leith-Ross of the Treasury, British sympathies were 'entirely with' Germany in its effort to remove the 'charade' of reparations. From both the economic and political standpoint, he believed France was foolish beyond belief to persist in its reparation demands. The economic effect was to force Germany to become more, not less competitive, to obtain the foreign exchange needed to make the payments, while the political effect was to provide a convenient stick for Hitler to beat his moderate opponents.[81] Sharing this view, the British government intended to distance itself from France and to approach Washington independently, believing that Britain had 'a far stronger moral claim' than France to relief from war debts.[82]

Yet opinion in Britain was more divided than it seemed. Within the mercantile-financial community where the viewpoint of City bankers generally prevailed, the need to cancel German reparations once and for all seemed almost self-evident. But within the industrial community this was very far from the case. Sir Josiah Stamp had compiled statistics showing that, after the German hyperinflation and the massive depreciation of the French franc in the mid-1920s, Britain's tax burdens were much higher than those of Germany or France, and if reparations were cancelled, Germany's tax burdens would be almost incomparably lighter. In this case, Stamp reckoned, the per capita national debt would be £8 per person in Germany compared with £56 in France and £150 in Britain.[83] The Federation of British Industry (FBI), speaking for its members and a wide swathe of public opinion, similarly took issue with City appeals for immediate, complete cancellation. The FBI accepted the necessity of temporary suspension and perhaps some revision of the Young plan, but it was not prepared to see German industry handed a permanent competitive advantage when conditions returned to normal.[84]

A few dissenting voices were also raised at the British embassy in Paris and in the Foreign Office. Sharing French fears of German imperialism, they also shared the French view that Britain's fate was bound up France's and that only Franco-British cooperation could save the existing order in Europe. In the words of Ralph Wigram in Paris, the French firmly believed that if Britain and France could agree on policy, the Germans would acquiesce and there would be peace; but expose divisions between Britain and France and the Germans would seize upon it, making confidence impossible.

I have never yet found anything in the history of what passed between 1870 and 1914 or in that of the last ten years to make me think that the French theory is incorrect or that we shall ever obtain final agreement with the Germans by any other means.[85]

Wigram also shared the view that reparations constrained rather than abetted German imperialism. The Treasury was perhaps correct that reparations forced Germany to earn more foreign exchange. But as Britain's own industrialists pointed out, reparations imposed a charge upon the state that translated into heavier taxes upon the economy and limited Germany's external borrowing. In any case, Wigram observed, reparations were hardly the cause of Germany's imperialism, since it had been aggressively imperialistic through good times and bad.

Selby, Simon's private secretary, strongly agreed. As he pointed out to his chief, British opposition to revival of the *Entente* derived largely from the belief that it had been a major cause of the Great War. This was a popular but pernicious myth. If Britain wanted a stable, liberal Europe, it *must* revive the *Entente*. Franco-British unity would undercut support for Hitler in Germany and strengthen the hand of moderates. It was also the one thing that would lead France to adopt a moderate policy towards Germany. France wanted nothing more than the assurance of British support, but in the absence of the *Entente* it was bound to remain in confrontation with Germany, making cooperation in Europe impossible. 'To sum up, every argument' seems to point in the direction of a direct approach to France.'[86]

British industrial opinion, as ever, received scant attention from the press, and in Whitehall the dissenters were a minority even within the Foreign Service. More common was the view of France offered by Sir Ronald Lindsay, ambassador in Washington and former permanent under-secretary. Lindsay had no doubt that French governments systematically mobilized the Bank of France's resources to suborn Britain and the United States to their imperialist policies in Europe. To escape French domination, he believed, Britain should align itself with the other Anglo-Saxon powers, America and Germany.[87] Vansittart, the current permanent under-secretary, encouraged the Cabinet to share this view, notwithstanding his occasional criticism of German behaviour.[88]

MacDonald, the prime minister, continued his outspoken condemnation of France's 'war mentality'.[89] Vain to the point of self-delusion, he persuaded himself that on returning to office in 1929 he had single-handedly transformed Anglo-American relations from a state of destructive rivalry to one of trust and friendship. He now hoped that mutual hostility towards France might carry the relationship towards a virtual alliance. As he wrote to Stimson, Britain and the United States must work together to save 'civilisation'.[90] Francophobia had reached new heights in the United States in recent months on account of the large-scale withdrawal of French bank deposits, which threatened to drive the dollar off the gold standard. According to Stimson, President Hoover wished MacDonald to know that 'the civilisation of which he speaks can only be saved by the co-operation of the Anglo-Saxons; we cannot count on the other races.' But as Stimson also reported, the slump was intensifying isolationism in the United States.[91] Despite their supposed racial affinity, MacDonald's colleagues accepted that America could be of little help for the time being.

Briefly in late May 1932, Britain seemed about to align itself with France on reparations. Since Germany seemed unlikely to make further payments, especially if President Hindenburg replaced Chancellor Bruening with the conservative nationalist Franz von Papen, Simon accepted that Britain could only bring

France to abandon reparations by joining France in opposition to further war debt payments to the United States. He therefore proposed a three-stage procedure whereby the European powers would first adopt a general resolution on the desirability of cancelling all debts arising from the war; then at the forthcoming Lausanne conference they would abandon reparation and war debt claims among themselves, while postponing ratification of the agreement until after the US presidential election; and finally, with a new Administration in office, they would secure America's agreement to cancel all war debts or, if it refused, unilaterally ceasing further payments.[92] Leith-Ross, who had repeatedly called for an end to the uncertainty of reparations,[93] welcomed Simon's proposal.

> It may of course create regrettable difficulties with America, but we have to choose between that and a complete *débâcle* in Europe. And America is always insisting that it is for Europe to stop quarrelling and to come to some agreement amongst themselves.[94]

Runciman and Chamberlain as well as Simon seemed prepared to support a policy of refusing further payments to the United States.[95] But Chamberlain, possibly after speaking with Governor Norman, betrayed deep unease at the repudiation of Britain's international obligations.[96] As he warned Simon,

> Not only would it cut the ground from under our feet in argument with the Free State [on the Irish Land Annuities issue] and make our lectures to the Balkan States sound like the smuggest hypocrisy, but we should forever have tacked on to us the label 'defaulter' in the U.S.A. where things would be said of us that would make Englishmen blush for generations.[97]

For the time being his difference with Simon seemed limited to negotiating tactics, and he affirmed his readiness to join France in a common approach to the United States after the presidential election in November. He was impatient with the French but annoyed with the Americans, whom he dismissed as 'idiotic Yankees' on one occasion, for placing Britain in this predicament.[98] Yet his horror of debt repudiation, which he called 'Langism and Bolshevism', made it probable that he would break with France if there seemed any other means of settling reparations.[99]

MacDonald, as officials anticipated,[100] took more direct issue with Simon's proposal. He favoured a joint declaration by the European powers that they wished to see an end to all inter-governmental debts, and he supported the renunciation of claims on Germany. But he strongly opposed joining France in a common approach to the United States. Instead he advocated that immediately after the Lausanne conference, Britain should approach Washington to explain its predicament and appeal for cooperation. On Foreign Office advice, Simon warned MacDonald not to expect large concessions from the United States, 'if only we separate ourselves from France as we sometimes have been led to believe'.[101] But MacDonald, against all the evidence, persisted in believing that Washington would grant Britain special treatment on war debts. Nor did he take into consideration that France, treated less generously, would almost certainly maintain its demand for reparations from Germany, thus prolonging the crisis in Europe that British policy sought to address.[102]

MacDonald also persuaded himself that he could draw the United States into a general settlement of economic problems, since President Hoover had recently agreed to participate in an international economic conference. Once the Lausanne conference dealt with reparations, MacDonald thought, they could transfer talks to London where, with Americans present, they could address other issues.[103] Yet, as Stimson had already warned him, Washington would have 'overwhelming difficulty' participating in any follow-up to the Lausanne conference given its connection to reparations or for that matter any conference that dealt with war debts, tariff levels or gold standard reform.[104] Hoover, it seems, had endorsed the conference proposal simply as a means of assuring voters in Nevada, Utah and the other mountain states that something was being done to raise the price of silver.[105] Stimson indeed urged MacDonald to line up *with* France *against* cancellation of reparations, since Washington did not want to face European pressure for the cancellation of war debts.[106]

In May 1932, Herriot returned to office. As in 1926, he cut a modest figure with little of the authority of Briand or Maginot who had both recently passed from the scene. Even Lord Tyrrell, a sympathetic observer, spoke of Herriot's 'weakness of character'.[107] Yet it is hard to exaggerate the difficulties he faced, with Germany determinedly shrugging off the last remaining constraints of the Versailles Treaty and France struggling with a fiscal crisis that aggravated the already deep divisions within Herriot's Radical party as well as the country at large.[108] In fact, Herriot was well suited to lead France at this time. As a young man, he had closely studied Germany and was one of the few Western political leaders who could read and speak German. He admired German accomplishments in philosophy and the arts, but like most Frenchmen he regarded Germans as a flawed race with an inherently aggressive character.[109] A committed liberal, he hoped to reverse France's drift towards autarky and increasing isolation; his chief economic ministers, Henry Germain-Martin, minister of finance, Julien Durand, minister of commerce, Maurice Palmade, minister of the budget, and Georges Bonnet, minister of public works, were all doctrinal liberals.[110] But he shared the general French view that cancellation of reparations would place German industry at a decisive advantage over its competitors and enable Germany to re-enter the capital markets to add to its aggressive potential.[111] And he could scarcely advance a liberal agenda including concessions on reparations without some compensating contribution to national security. The only means he could see was through a revived Franco-British *Entente*. He therefore missed no opportunity to improve relations with London. Tyrrell spoke to him on 6 June, shortly before the Cabinet meeting to settle his ministerial declaration to the Chamber of Deputies.

> He was very emphatic on the necessity for the closest co-operation between Britain and France as the best means of avoiding nations drifting into fascism or Hitlerism. But I do not think that he intends to emphasize this in his public declaration.[112]

On 11 June, British ministers stopped in Paris on their way to the Lausanne conference. Herriot and Germain-Martin received them warmly and agreed in general terms to the three-stage procedure their visitors set out.[113] Four days later at Lausanne, delegates of the six participating countries affirmed their support for 'a final and definitive solution' to the 'problems' facing them, and agreed to make no demand for reparation or war debt payments when the Hoover moratorium expired on 30 June, to facilitate a broader agreement.[114] Despite days of intense argument, however, French delegates remained unwilling to concede a complete and final abandonment of reparations. British ministers, mindful of Tyrrell's advice that French ministers would pay a very high price for a revived *Entente*, privately discussed political concessions they might offer Herriot as an inducement for acquiescence.[115] On 20 June, MacDonald sought to win over Herriot to cancellation:

> He hoped for agreement with France at the same time on other subjects. For instance, a good armaments agreement might be reached at Geneva, which would help everyone both in Europe and America. A little later France and Britain might come to a good trade agreement. He was talking in great confidence that morning, but he wanted M. Herriot to know that he did not like Germany continually coming in and saying, 'We want relief on this particular question.' By these means Germany got the United Kingdom on one side and France on the other. Then, when that particular question was settled, Germany said she had another grievance; and so France never felt secure and Britain never felt secure. Mr. MacDonald said he would like an agreement as to how far France and Britain would listen to pressure on these various questions from Germany. He believed that such an agreement would add greatly to the security of both nations. A list of the points which such an agreement could cover might be elaborated.[116]

Herriot listened eagerly, despite the fact that MacDonald had used this ruse upon him before. But he remained convinced that, in the absence of a robust security framework, reparations were an essential constraint upon Germany, and he appealed for British recognition of their common danger. While accepting that Germany could not pay in the midst of the slump, he believed that when the slump eventually ended Germany could easily pay reparations at the level agreed in the Young plan. This was important for political as well as economic reasons for, as Germain-Martin put it, without the reparations to equalize tax burdens, 'Germany might well triumph over British and Belgian industry; and that would be disastrous.' Germany now had at least 8 billion RM (£400 million) and possibly as much as 11 billion RM (£550 million) in foreign direct investment, and was actively extending its control over foreign firms 'such as the Gnome Motor Works, which made engines for French military aviation.'

> If she was given complete freedom she would become an international danger. In maintaining some means of making her pay in the future the creditor powers would be maintaining suspended over her a sort of counter-weight.[117]

British ministers refused to take this argument seriously. Herriot, they believed, was holding out simply from fear of attacks by his opponents in Paris. But since they could not convince him to accept a 'clean sweep',[118] they abandoned carrots for sticks while pressing Herriot to engage in direct talks with Papen. As Leith-Ross put it, Britain sought 'to set the Germans on them', to bring home the impossibility of obtaining further reparation payments.[119] Runciman admitted to Baldwin that he and his colleagues were

> exceedingly stiff with the French, & were of necessity quite offensive in manner to them, while guarding our actual language, telling them finally the sands were running down & they must go off & confer with the Germans direct & without us.[120]

Papen was happy to oblige and held several private conversations with Herriot and the French delegation in the next fortnight. Among other things, he proposed a consultative pact on issues affecting the European political *status quo*, a Franco-German customs union, a bilateral pact directed against the Soviet Union and an *entente* between the general staffs of the French and German armies, if only France would agree to an immediate and complete end to reparations. Herriot scarcely trusted Papen, but he was impressed by his interest in closer Franco-German relations, not least because that very week he was obliged to slash 1.5 billion francs from defence to balance his budget.[121] Therefore, on returning to Paris, he advised his Cabinet colleagues that a Franco-German rapprochement was to be preferred to further money payments which in any case were likely to be modest.[122] His colleagues agreed, but Papen had meanwhile returned to Berlin where nationalist agitation persuaded him to adopt an unyielding stance. MacDonald and the British delegation also strenuously opposed a Franco-German *entente*, which they took to be a French attempt to constrain Germany and a threat to their influence as the liberal arbiters of Europe. They need not have feared, for when Herriot again spoke to Papen at Lausanne he found him much less forthcoming. No more was heard of a Franco-German *entente*.[123]

When by 28 June the conversations brought no result, British ministers re-entered the fray. They pressed French delegates to accept provisional cancellation along with one further token payment in the form of a deferred bond issue to be deposited with the BIS, and issued only when German credit returned to a 5 per cent basis.[124] Over the next three days, French and German delegates inched towards agreement on the basis of this proposal. Initially the French demanded a bond issue of 6 billion RM (£300 million). The Germans rejected this sum, while refusing to say what they would accept. By 1 July, the French had reduced their demand to 5 billion RM (£250 million) and further agreed that the German bonds would be cancelled if the United States cancelled war debts, thus abandoning claims for a *solde*. By 3 July, the French had come down to 4 billion RM (£200 million), and the Germans affirmed their readiness to issue 2 billion RM (£100 million) in deferred bonds.[125]

British ministers, keen for agreement, once more held out political induce-ments. To the French they offered to communicate all future German propos-als for Treaty revision and to collaborate at the disarmament conference, on preparations for the world economic conference as it was now being called, and on a commercial truce until they could negotiate a new bilateral trade agree-ment following the Ottawa conference. To the Germans they offered to meet their demands for equality in principle on disarmament and removal of Section Eight of the Versailles Treaty which contained Article 231, the so-called war guilt clause. They also proposed a pact among the six participating states to consult on any issue affecting two or more of them.[126]

Herriot had spent 4 July in Paris where divisions in Parliament over fis-cal retrenchment threatened to bring down his government.[127] Returning to Lausanne the next day he exploded in anger on realizing that he was expected to give way not only on reparations but also on disarmament and Treaty revision, and threatened to walk out of the conference.[128] But the British gambled cor-rectly that he would not risk isolation, and by 8 July a compromise was reached. Germany would deposit bonds to a value of 3 billion RM (£150 million) with the BIS as a token of its commitment to reparations. Beyond that the European pow-ers would make no further claim on one another, although in an unfortunately named 'gentlemen's agreement' they acknowledged that this would go unrati-fied until the United States played its part by cancelling war debts. Individual countries would approach Washington to request cancellation immediately after the presidential election.[129] Separately, the British delegation offered France an agreement on mutual consultation, an *accord de confiance*, which they encouraged Herriot to believe would cover both German demands for further Treaty revision and the settlement of war debts with the United States.[130]

British ministers briefly imagined they had finally resolved the reparations problem which had beset the international economy for ten years and, in their view, dragged Germany to the brink of collapse. Runciman congratulated Chamberlain, describing his work at Lausanne as 'a triumph of British policy and statesmanship'.[131] Chamberlain was, as ever, proud of his own handiwork.[132] This was the first time he had represented Britain at an international conference, and hardly had he arrived in Lausanne when he was laid up with gout, which had obliged foreign delegates to call on him at his hotel suite.[133] He was impressed by the respect they showed towards Britain's representative. 'The foreigner', he wrote of the Germans, Italians, French and others, 'is slow to come to grips with substantive issues, so devious, so disbelieving when we bluntly state our object right at the start.'[134] But he was now sure that 'the foreigner' could be managed, if Britain displayed firmness and common sense.

Chamberlain would have done well to be more modest. First reports of agree-ment at Lausanne had been favourably received on America's East coast and attracted little comment elsewhere in the country.[135] But news of a secret pact among the European powers, tying their decision on reparations to America's abandonment of war debt claims, stirred an angry reaction.[136] President Hoover, furious that the Europeans were 'ganging up' against the United States, threatened to denounce their work. Only with the greatest difficulty did Stimson talk him out of it.[137] Hoover did nevertheless send an open letter to Borah, the isolationist chair of the Senate Foreign Relations Committee, warning against pressure by a foreign combination.[138] Meanwhile, from Los Angeles, Randolph Hearst, the newspaper publisher, thundered against the 'gentlemen' of Europe in an address carried nationally by NBC radio.

> How can there be gentlemen whose HONOUR is worthless? … Let us call this secret gang compact by something more descriptive of its true character. Let us call it plainly a crooked conspiracy by European confidence men and their American confederates to rob the American people. It helps to a clearer understanding of a situation to call things by their right names.[139]

Herriot, back in Paris, presented the results of the Lausanne conference to his Cabinet on the morning of 13 July. His colleagues were pleased with the Franco-British *accord de confiance*, which they unanimously endorsed.[140] The Paris press, though sceptical of its precise value, also considered it adequate compensation for ending reparations.[141] But that same morning Ambassador Claudel in Washington warned of an upsurge in American Francophobia: 'the Administration, which was extremely annoyed by the recent gold losses, maintains, despite all assertions to the contrary, a profound resentment against us.'[142] Publication of the gentlemen's agreement only made matters worse, and especially in the West and mid-West the hostility had become *'particulièrement profond'*. To the dismay of ministers, America gave France no credit for its concessions at Lausanne.[143]

Ambassador Lindsay was similarly struck by the hostile reaction to the gentlemen's agreement, especially in Congress.[144] This being an election year, and most of the hostility being directed not at Britain but France, which the American press portrayed as rich, malign and corrupt, he concluded that the reaction was no worse than could be expected.[145] But if there had ever been any question about it, the reactions confirmed that no American contribution to a debt settlement could be expected soon.

In Germany, Papen returned home to attacks from every direction when he acknowledged that reparations were not fully and finally ended. By now, reparations were scarcely a heavy charge on the German economy. The bonds deposited at the BIS would almost certainly never be issued, and in any case they constituted, in Leith-Ross's words, 'a trifling sum': barely one year's payment under the Young plan of 1929. But as Papen knew, Germans had convinced themselves of the deep injustice of reparation demands, and even a modest final payment was bound to provoke opposition, especially with a Reichstag election only a fortnight away. From Berlin, François-Poncet reported to Herriot that the concessions granted to Germany at Lausanne had done nothing to appease the country. If anything, they had merely prompted demands for more concessions. This played into the 'latent civil war' in Germany, and Hitler continued to gain popularity.[146]

The British delegation had received a warmer reception on its return from Lausanne. Only the Franco-British *accord de confiance* aroused controversy in

London when Beaverbrook's *Daily Express* accused the government of lining up with France to confront the United States over war debts.[147] MacDonald and Simon immediately insisted that the agreement involved no substantive commitments of any sort.[148] This satisfied critics, but it underlined the limited achievement at Lausanne. Reparations had not been finally ended and negotiations on a war debt settlement had not even begun.

It is of course impossible to be sure of the consequences had reparations been definitively cancelled in the first half of 1932. Perhaps Hitler and the Nazis now possessed sufficient momentum that nothing would stop their rise to power. Yet, as we know, signs of economic recovery that summer contributed to their decline in the autumn Reichstag election, and a further boost to economic confidence by eliminating reparations might have decisively increased their decline. What we can say is that the opportunity for ending reparations appears to have existed, had the British government been prepared to adopt the 'joined-up' strategy proposed by certain members of the Foreign Office since the previous autumn. As early as 8 January 1932, British ministers recognized that Germany would make no further reparation payments, and indeed they had encouraged this stand. They knew that France would be the chief obstacle to an agreement on cancellation. But they also knew that France would pay a very high price for a revived *Entente* with Britain, to say nothing of an alliance, or for the assurance that Britain would not seek an advantage over France by approaching the United States separately for a war debt settlement. They might therefore have secured France's agreement, had they treated reparations, debts and security together. In choosing not to do so, they passed up the chance of accelerating a European settlement.

7.4   The failure of the regional projects

Throughout the 1920s, observers of international affairs anticipated the division of the world into a handful of large economic blocs. Only the United States with its integrated market of 48 states seemed fully able to realize the potential scale economies of modern mass-production industry. But the Soviet Union, having adopted 'socialism in one country', seemed at last to be developing the vast potential of the Russian empire, and many contemporaries believed that the rest of Europe must soon unite economically, if not politically, if it was to avoid being crushed between these two Leviathans. Briand's attempt to institute a European 'federation' stalled in 1930, but agitation for the economic organization of Europe continued unabated. So too did the campaign for a British Empire economic bloc, and in September 1931, Japan took the first step towards the creation of a unified East Asian bloc by seizing Manchuria and several northern provinces of China.

Foreign observers deplored Japan's military venture. The fact was nonetheless that efforts to liberalize world trade on a non-discriminatory basis had collapsed in 1929. America's intensification of its neo-mercantilism that year had driven other countries to raise their own tariff barriers, and with the worsening of the slump, quantitative trade restrictions, swiftly removed after the Great War, were reintroduced. Those familiar with modern trade theory will appreciate that second-best solutions such as customs unions or common markets, even those limited to a mutual reduction of internal duties, do not necessarily contribute to trade expansion. But with the world heading remorselessly towards autarkic national units, any initiative that revived hopes of a return to multilateralism almost certainly deserved support. Economists at the League of Nations had outlined rules for regional action as early as 1929. First, an agreement should involve the reduction of duties among the signatory countries rather than the raising of duties to non-signatory countries: in other words, it should seek to create trade rather than merely divert trade. Second, it should remain open to all countries to join on a similar basis. Third, it must obtain the imprimatur of the League Economic Committee. Efforts to implement regional trade agreements culminated in 1932, when no less than four important initiatives were taken. Ironically the three progressive initiatives were blocked, whereas the single regressive one, which was also much the largest, was implemented.

7.4.1 The London four-power conference and the French plan for the Danube

For two years, the economic crisis in Eastern Europe had been the subject of investigation by the League of Nations Economic and Financial Committees as well as the Committee of Enquiry for European Union (CEUE), created to follow up Briand's proposal for European federation. The collapse in commodity prices had devastated the agrarian countries, Poland, Hungary, Roumania, Yugoslavia and Bulgaria, and weakened the already precarious economy of Austria as well as driving up unemployment in Czechoslovakia. Conferences were held in the autumn of 1930 and spring of 1931 to identify ways to assist the agrarian countries to dispose of their surplus production and cover their mounting debts. But as late as the winter of 1931 when the CEUE requested proposals, the countries had received only piecemeal bilateral assistance from the major powers of Europe.

Since the start of the slump, France had been the main impetus behind efforts to organize collective help. French statesmen regarded the region as vital to their national security, since the preservation of independent states there barred the way to Germany's domination of the region and ultimately the whole of Europe.[149] They had therefore extended financial support to Austria, Hungary, Poland, Yugoslavia, Roumania and other nearby countries. Indeed, since the war French loans to the five principal countries of the Danube region amounted to 14.54 billion francs (£172 million), while French credits, increased since the start of the slump to help them remain on the gold standard, totalled 1.26 billion francs (£15 million).[150] In 1931, they had also negotiated agreements to import modest amounts of cereals from Hungary (September 1931), Yugoslavia (November 1931) and Roumania (January 1932). But France, as a major cereal producer in its own right, could absorb only a token amount of the region's production. Indeed, since its own farmers were damaged by the slump and clamouring for greater protection, it was not at all certain that Parliament would approve the disguised preferences to the three East-Central European countries.[151] Further financial help was also becoming problematic. French commercial bankers were unwilling to increase their exposure to the region. And with tax revenues declining and the government facing savage retrenchment to balance the national budget, officials doubted that Parliament would approve guarantees for any further foreign loans.[152]

They were still casting about for practical ways of assisting the Danube countries when in January 1932 Hungary declared a moratorium on external loan repayments and the financial crisis threatened to end in a general moratorium throughout the region. The League Financial Committee called on creditor countries to help by guaranteeing international loans. Shortly afterwards, Chancellor Buresch of Austria served notice on Britain, France and Germany that he must have immediate help. Political obstacles, he complained, had blocked every attempt to find outlets for Austrian exports. If no financial help were forthcoming within a month, he would be unable to pay his civil servants and social unrest would follow. Rather than preside over the collapse of his country, he would resign.[153]

The possibility that a breakdown in Austria would revive demands for an economic *Anschluss* with Germany, and that Britain, desperate to protect its investments in the region, would support such a solution on the grounds that no other means existed to save Austria, led French statesmen to intensify their search for an alternative solution.[154] Two options emerged: one from Philippe Berthelot, secretary-general of the *Quai d'Orsay*, for a tripartite scheme of economic integration involving Austria, Hungary and Czechoslovakia, the other from Robert Coulondre, political director of the *Quai d'Orsay*, and René Massigli, France's diplomatic representative at Geneva, for a scheme involving the five principal countries of the Danube.[155] Berthelot's tripartite scheme was simpler and potentially more satisfactory from an economic standpoint. But Benes of Czechoslovakia absolutely refused to participate without his Little Entente partners, Roumania and Yugoslavia.[156] Rather than dividing the Little Entente, Tardieu, now foreign minister as well as premier, opted for Coulondre and Massigli's five-country alternative. The proposal contained two elements: the exchange of preferential duties among the Danube countries, and the grant by Germany, Italy and France of unilateral preferences on certain commodities from the Danube countries. Tardieu circulated a summary to Britain, Germany and Italy on 4 March.[157]

French statesmen did not underestimate the obstacles in the way of a regional solution. Washington, a spokesman warned, would oppose any tariff preferences except as the first step towards a complete customs union in the Danube.[158] The German government, claiming to uphold the most-favoured-nation principle, similarly objected to regional preferences, despite having recently negotiated bilateral trade preferences with Roumania and Hungary.[159] To discourage support for the French proposal, it now offered Austria bilateral preferences as well.[160]

The Fascist government in Italy hesitated before showing its hand, and initially Paris was unsure of its intentions. For ten years Italy had resisted all regional approaches to the economic problem of the Danube.[161] Yet it had lined up with France the previous year to stop Austria falling under German domination through the customs union scheme, and French statesmen were cautiously hopeful that it would do so again in the present crisis.[162] Italy, however, soon betrayed its intention to oppose the French plan which threatened to exclude Italy from economic opportunities and political influence in the region. Like Germany, it sought to draw support away from a regional arrangement by negotiating scarcely disguised bilateral preferences with Austria and Hungary.[163]

Within the Danube region itself opposition existed to the French scheme. Pan-Germanists in Austria's two main political parties, the Christian Social and Socialist Parties, combined within the National Economic Bloc under the slogan 'Nothing against Germany, nothing without Germany' and demanded that Buresch keep clear of any regional scheme.[164] In Hungary, the nationalists opposed cooperation with Czechoslovakia and Roumania until the Treaty of Trianon was radically revised. Even in Czechoslovakia, France's closest collaborator, Benes faced opposition from industrial interests who feared the effect of preferential arrangements with Austria and from agricultural interests who feared the consequences of preferential arrangements with their cereal-producing neighbours.[165]

French statesmen nevertheless received encouragement from two unexpected quarters. One was Austria, where Herr Hornbostel, deputy political director of the Foreign Ministry, approached a member of the French legation with a personal appeal to proceed with the five-country scheme and not to be put off by the opposition in his own country or elsewhere. Austria's pan-German movement shouted louder than other groups, Hornbostel claimed, but the silent majority preferred a 'Western' liberal course of action to absorption in an 'Eastern', authoritarian, German-dominated Europe. Count Clauzel, the minister in Vienna, advised colleagues in Paris to take careful note of this claim. Hornbostel, he observed, was one of the ablest members of the Austrian diplomatic establishment, and he would scarcely have spoken so frankly without the knowledge and approval of Chancellor Buresch. Indeed, the language he used bore a close resemblance to passages in Buresch's recent speeches. Clauzel found it encouraging that Czechoslovakia and Hungary, on bad terms since the war, seemed at last on the point of signing a trade agreement. He could also report that, according to the Czech minister in Vienna, Monsignor Seipel, the Austrian Christian Social leader and advocate of a revived Habsburg monarchy, similarly hoped that France would support 'a Danubian union'.[166]

No less encouraging was Britain's sudden interest in the region. Since the slump began, Britain's concern seemed to have been restricted to the plight of Austria, the one Germanic country in this largely Slavic area, which had enjoyed the bulk of British financial credits outside of Germany itself. Yet in mid-February 1932, Simon volunteered to Benes that the only solution to Austria's plight seemed to be a regional customs union. When Benes observed that a customs union was out of the question and the most they could hope for were preferential tariff arrangements, Simon seemed unphased. The Board of Trade would object, as it did to every initiative that threatened to discriminate against British trade, but he indicated that the government might nevertheless accept preferences on a strictly limited basis. Britain, it seemed, had been driven into the French camp from fear that its huge financial commitments in Central Europe might be lost without a broad recovery plan.[167] Simon appeared to confirm this when he invited German,

Italian and French foreign ministers to London on 6 April to consider economic help for the Danube region.[168]

Tardieu had been looking for just such an opportunity to work with Britain since forming his government on 21 February. Having affirmed the importance of close Franco-British relations in his ministerial declaration, he had instigated an informal approach by Ambassador de Fleuriau to Vansittart of the Foreign Office, and an inspired piece in *Le Temps* on the necessity of the *Entente* for the future of Europe, which attracted notice in London.[169] Despite Simon's encouraging signals, however, the British government remained unprepared to support a constructive plan for the Danube region. For four months it had been preoccupied with the tariff question and plans for the forthcoming Imperial conference at Ottawa. At considerable cost to the unity of the government, Conservative ministers had prevailed upon their Liberal and Labour colleagues to accept a 10 per cent 'revenue' tariff, with preferences to the Dominions to be settled at Ottawa. Ninety years of free trade had thus been set aside to pursue the dream of a united Empire. In Stanley Baldwin's words, it was 'veritably...the parting of the ways', when, they hoped, the Empire would join Britain in an economic bloc of unprecedented scope and potential.[170] Ministers thus had turned away from any possibility of Continental commitments, and their outlook was further influenced by a spate of differences with France. One arose over disarmament, another over the reparations issue. A third was due to the spread of the Colorado beetle in France and Britain's decision to tighten import restrictions in response to it.[171] A fourth derived from increases in French trade restrictions.

Having consolidated 75 per cent of its import duties in various commercial treaties before the slump began, France had few means of addressing its trade deficit, which rapidly worsened after Britain abandoned the gold standard in September 1931. France resorted to quotas, a practice deplored by the Board of Trade, which regarded all quantitative trade controls as inherently arbitrary and open to abuse.[172] More provocatively, France also introduced a 15 per cent surtax on imports from former gold standard countries with depreciated currencies. French ministers claimed this merely levelled the playing field and was not discriminatory since it applied to all countries with recently depreciated currencies. Canada had introduced a similar tax. But the Board of Trade, which had long treated the most-favoured-nation principle as the *sine qua non* of multilateral trade, secured Cabinet approval for retaliation if France did not remove the surtax.[173] Only with difficulty did the Foreign Office stop the dispute from escalating into a trade war.[174]

The result was that British ministers paid little attention to the crisis in the Danube region, which seemed more remote to them than ever. Simon reported to colleagues that France was extremely anxious for British support for their Danube scheme and suggested he should do something to 'humour French susceptibilities'. He did not propose a positive contribution, merely agreement to forgo the most-favoured-nation principle on a very limited number of goods, mostly agricultural, to enable other countries to grant preferences. This would have no practical effect on British producers, and would serve the country's interests since in the long run Britain would benefit more by averting the collapse of the region and facilitating its recovery than by rigidly insisting upon the most-favoured-nation principle. The Cabinet after a brief discussion acquiesced and moved on to other business.[175]

In Paris, ministers and officials carefully reviewed their tactics in anticipation of the London four-power conference. They were hopeful that preferential arrangements would eventually enable the Danube countries to find their feet. But since Roumania, Hungary and Yugoslavia would continue to produce a substantial surplus of cereals, they were certain to turn to Germany, the largest potential market for their surpluses. This created the danger that if Germany were left to extend reciprocal tariff concessions, it would soon dominate the region. France was no longer in a position to guarantee large-scale loans on its own, Flandin, the minister of finance, pointed out. Nor on its own was France likely to persuade Germany to grant unilateral preferences to the Danube countries or permit them to exchange preferences with one another, especially as this would favour Czechoslovakia. Britain's help thus seemed essential, if the region was not to collapse or fall under German domination.[176] Since British banks had huge commitments in the region, Tardieu believed that Britain would be bound to support a constructive plan.[177] He therefore insisted upon visiting London for private conversations with British ministers before the four-power conference began. Joseph Avenol, deputy secretary-general of the League of Nations, warned him that he must persuade the British that the French plan was not directed against Germany or intended to serve merely French interests, but was a contribution to the general pacification of the area.[178] Tyrrell, through an intermediary, advised Tardieu to concentrate on convincing MacDonald. 'Never lose sight of MacDonald's vanity', Tyrrell allegedly said. He might fall in with the French plan, if he could be persuaded that through his efforts the Franco-British *Entente* had spread peace through Europe.[179]

Tardieu, speaking privately with MacDonald on the evening of 3 April, emphasized the essential role of Britain and France in surmounting the crisis in Central Europe and the importance he attached to reviving the *Entente*.[180] Joined by Flandin, he spent the following day in conversations with MacDonald, Chamberlain, Simon and Runciman, setting out the case for joint action in the Danube region. The situation there, he said, was

> in some ways almost as grave as the situation of 20 years ago. Were the countries which were in a position to do so ready to make some sacrifice to prevent a general collapse of Central Europe? It was in that part of Europe where nearly all European troubles originated.[181]

British ministers, however, refused to accept that their national interests were at stake. They were prepared to tolerate trade preferences, so long as they were limited to cereals and had no adverse effect on British producers. But they would grant no preferences of their own.[182] Nor would they consider participation in short-term loans, as Tardieu proposed. Britain, they claimed, had already lent far more to the region than France: £80.5 million as opposed to only £51.4 million by France.[183] Hence, in Chamberlain's words, 'If new financial help was to be given, was it not the turn of somebody else to come forward?' Flandin countered with the claim that since the slump began France had lent in excess of 2.45 billion francs (£29 million) to the countries in the region, which far exceeded loans from other countries.[184]

British ministers were unimpressed. As Chamberlain pointed out, Britain did not guarantee loans even to the Dominions. Indeed, since the sterling crisis in 1931, the London market had been closed to all overseas borrowers, and his colleagues did not intend to create trouble for themselves by reopening it for the Danube countries when they would be negotiating with the Dominions at Ottawa in a few months time.[185] Chamberlain therefore suggested that, rather than throwing good money after bad, the Danube countries should abandon the gold standard and devalue their currencies.[186] French ministers had anticipated this proposal, but decided against it on the grounds that devaluation would do nothing to ease the Danube countries' burden of debt, nearly all of which was external, and would only further undermine confidence in their economic management.[187] Flandin, to appease his British hosts, agreed not to rule it out. But nothing he or Tardieu said could overcome British opposition to joint financial action.

French ministers faced even greater disappointment at the four-power conference. Flandin, who set out the French plan, met immediate objections from Bülow, representing Germany, and Dino Grandi, the Italian foreign minister. The latter pointed out that traditionally 10 per cent of Italian exports and 10–15 per cent of German exports went to the Danube region, and that together Germany and Italy exported at least four times as much to the region as Britain and France: in 1930, roughly £80 million versus £18 million. The French plan would therefore hurt them twice over, by the internal tariff preferences that Czechoslovakia would exploit at their expense, and by the unilateral preferences they were expected to grant to the region. Nor would they listen to Flandin's claim that all the powers would suffer from the collapse of the region and all would benefit from its recovery. So negative were Bülow and Grandi that Chamberlain found himself defending the French proposal for preferences. But as the British policy was essentially one of 'wait-and-see', the conference adjourned after two days of fruitless wrangling.[188]

The following month, a committee of Treasury experts appointed by the four-power conference met to consider the French proposal for a monetary fund to help the Danube countries keep their currencies from collapsing. The British expert held that no further financial help should be extended to the region. If help was required, it should come from the central banks, not governments. But in any case he disagreed with the French expert on the need for fixed exchange rates: the Danube countries should be encouraged to leave the gold standard and allow their currencies to find their equilibrium rate. The German and Italian experts present agreed that help should be left to the central banks.[189]

This was not the end of the matter. At the Lausanne conference the French delegation insisted upon raising the Danube economic crisis and secured a resolution calling upon the Committee of Enquiry for European Union (CEUE) to draft proposals for consideration by the Thirteenth Assembly of the League of Nations in September.[190] The prospects however were dim.

The Treasury, now in charge of British policy, took the view that the problems facing the Danube region were the same ones afflicting the whole world. Until the general problems were addressed, any assistance to the region was simply throwing good money after bad. In any case, British ministers as well as Treasury officials believed that the proposed assistance would almost certainly be counter-productive. Stoppani and colleagues in the League Economic Section were promoting bilateral preferences as the thin end of the wedge for a 'United States of Europe'. Ministers especially disliked this challenge on the eve of the Imperial economic conference at Ottawa. Besides, they believed there was a solution of sorts to the Danube crisis. Since Germany was the region's largest market, it seemed natural and desirable that Germany should increase its economic interest in the region.[191] With Papen in the chancellor's office in Berlin and Hitler waiting in the wings, French statesmen were desperate to forestall this outcome. But to Chamberlain, Runciman and Simon along with their Treasury advisers, the prospect of Germany's domination seemed a matter of almost complete indifference.[192]

7.4.2   The Ouchy Convention

The second of the four major regional initiatives in 1932 began on 20 June when representatives of Belgium, the Netherlands and Luxembourg met at Ouchy, a suburb of Lausanne, and initialled an agreement to form the nucleus of a low-tariff area. The three countries had been among the six that participated in the adoption of the Oslo convention in December 1930, and Fernand Vanlangenhove, head of the Belgian Foreign Ministry who originated the Ouchy convention, had hoped that all six countries would participate in it as well.[193] Ministers of the six met on 3–4 February 1932 in Oslo and again on 14–16 April in Copenhagen. The three Scandinavian representatives, however, were unwilling to join a preferential arrangement at this time. Their economies depended crucially upon foreign trade, and they placed a high value on maintaining the most-favoured-nation principle. But they were mainly concerned to avoid antagonizing Britain, their most important customer, and particularly when the future of British trade policy was about to be decided. The Dutch, Belgians and Luxembourgois were scarcely less mindful of Britain's importance. Their view, however, was that agreement on a low-tariff area before the Ottawa conference convened might encourage Britain to resist demands from the Dominions for preferences based upon higher external protection.[194] On 1 June, they circulated their 'draft agreement for an international convention intended to bring about an increasing reduction in the customs tariffs at present hindering the freedom of trade in Europe'. The plan called upon participating countries:

i. to refrain from introducing new or increased duties on imports from other participating countries or third countries, except in exceptional circumstances;

   ii. to aim to reduce import duties by 10 per cent yearly until they reached 8 per cent of the value of industrial products, 4 per cent of the value of semi-manufactured goods and 0 per cent of the value of raw materials;

  iii. to uphold the most-favoured-nation principle vis-à-vis the other participating countries;

  iv. to unify their customs nomenclature;

   v. to remain committed for an initial 5-year period;

  vi. to invite other states to join on an equal basis and extend the benefits of the agreement to all countries – such as Britain – that were prepared to abide by its provisions without actually joining.[195]

The Norwegian government affirmed its support in principle for the convention, but was not prepared to act in advance of the other two Scandinavian countries. The Benelux countries therefore proceeded on their own to initial it.

News of the Ouchy convention was seized upon by liberals in Britain as a way out of the crisis. For two years Sir Walter Layton, editor of the *Economist* and the *News Chronicle*, and British member of the World Economic Conference preparatory committee, had actively favoured a multilateral trade agreement in Europe.[196] Indeed, Layton's journals along with the *Manchester Guardian* had already begun campaigning for an open-ended low-tariff area on the principles recommended in 1929 by the League of Nations.[197] Along with the *Statist*, they now declared the Ouchy convention 'much the best news for a very long time', and urged the British government to adopt the convention rather than retreat into Imperial protectionism, as it threatened to do.

> By becoming a party to this plan for the gradual elimination of tariff barriers, they will do more than any other one act could possibly do to end the paralysis which, as they admit themselves, is strangling the life out of Europe.[198]

Lloyd George welcomed the Benelux initiative in similar terms.[199] British industry initially seemed largely unaware of the opportunity, but in mid-summer the FBI expressed support for exceptions to most-favoured-nation treatment for regional associations.[200] Speaking for economic liberals more generally, the council of the International Chamber of Commerce in Paris urged all countries to sign up.[201] By now it was clear that, since signatories of the convention and most of its potential members placed an extremely high value upon friendly relations with Britain for both political and economic reasons, its fate rested with the British government.

For three years, Britain, France and other liberal countries had sought some means of overcoming the dilemma created by the United States, which demanded its right to most-favoured-nation treatment whenever one foreign country granted a trade concession to another, while raising its own massive tariff wall ever higher. The Ouchy convention presented a uniquely promising solution. The three Benelux signatories constituted only 4 per cent of world trade (in 1929), but with the participation of the three Scandinavian countries that figure rose to 7.6 per cent, and with Britain's participation to nearly 21 per cent. And if they became involved, many other countries were also sure to join.[202] In fact, Britain needed only endorse the convention without actually signing it, for its authors would almost certainly have extended its benefits to Britain, so long as it maintained a low-tariff regime.

The Ouchy convention in theory threatened to open the floodgates to preferences, and hence discrimination, throughout the world. French authorities feared this eventuality, and also worried about the loss of trade from the expansion of the convention.[203] But the League of Nations had anticipated this danger by proposing that countries introduce an exception to their bilateral most-favoured-nation commitments only for open-ended, liberal trade agreements like the Ouchy convention. If most important trading countries joined it, the risk to the most-favoured-nation principle would be small. Besides, Britain held the whip hand with most countries on account of the fact that it possessed the largest import market in the world and the largest trade deficit. The United States was likely to demand most-favoured-nation rights from the convention signatories while refusing to share in the tariff reductions. But Britain was America's largest export market and bought far more from the United States than it sold. Indeed, for the nine months January–September 1929, just before the slump began, the visible trade balance was four to one in favour of the United States (£140.7 million exports to £34.7 million imports); and in the first nine months of 1931 it was over five to one in favour of the United States (£74 million exports to £13 million imports).[204]

But of course Britain was not prepared to side with Europe if it annoyed the Dominions or the United States. Throughout the spring of 1932, British ministers had their eyes fixed on the Ottawa conference and regarded the Ouchy convention as merely an embarrassment. At the Lausanne conference, the Dutch and Belgian delegations announced they had initialled the convention and requested that it should be regarded as a 'regional' exception to the most-favoured-nation principle, like the special trade relations that were tolerated between the Baltic and the Iberian states. A British representative, ignoring the open-ended character of the Ouchy convention, firmly rejected the request. Geographical propinquity was not sufficient: a 'community of historical or economic interest' must also exist to warrant an exception. Otherwise, an exception could be demanded for trade preferences between France and Germany or France and Spain or Italy; in any case, nothing in their treaties with third countries provided for such an exception.[205]

The Benelux countries proceeded to sign the convention on 18 July.[206] Shortly afterwards at Ottawa the British delegation agreed to substantial preferences for Dominions goods within Britain's new tariff and quotas. After Ottawa, nevertheless, Britain formally condemned the Ouchy convention and warned that if the Netherlands and the Belgium-Luxembourg union chose to proceed with it, Britain must demand all the concessions exchanged without conceding anything in return.[207] For several months the Benelux countries held out, but with their economies in decline and domestic producers demanding greater protection, they abandoned the convention without attempting to implement it.

In December, the broader Oslo group of countries, awaiting developments on the Ouchy convention before deciding how to proceed, set aside plans for a further conference.[208] Britain thus passed up, indeed doomed, the most promising initiative on international trade since the slump began, to pursue a distinctly unpromising and dangerous alternative with the Dominions.

7.4.3 The British Imperial conference at Ottawa

In October 1930, at the Imperial conference in London, the Dominions had pressured British representatives to concede tariff preferences. They got nowhere in face of Philip Snowden and other free traders in the Labour government, who would only agreed to meet again the following year at Ottawa to address the trade question. The conference was postponed until 1932 on account of the financial crisis, and meanwhile the crisis led to a general election in Britain which resulted in the formation of a National government. The Conservatives, who comprised much the largest element in the government's parliamentary ranks, were now firmly committed to protectionism. Nevertheless, they proceeded cautiously to carry the National Liberal and Labour elements with them. Accordingly, as a first step, they secured their approval for emergency trade restrictions. Then, with one foot in the door, they secured agreement to institute a Cabinet enquiry into the balance of payments deficit. This, they anticipated, would force the issue of protection by recommending a modest general tariff.[209]

The long anticipated political crisis began on 18 January 1932, when the Cabinet committee, chaired by Chamberlain, held its final meeting. By a majority of seven to two, with Snowden, now lord privy seal, and Herbert Samuel, the National Liberal home secretary, dissenting, the committee adopted Chamberlain's proposal for a 10 per cent 'revenue' tariff. Snowden and Samuel threatened to resign from the government rather than accept the abandonment of free trade. MacDonald, Baldwin and Chamberlain as well as Walter Runciman, president of the Board of Trade and a leading Liberal, sought to dissuade them by pointing to the many important tasks still facing the government and appealing to their patriotism. With the future of sterling still in the balance, they urged that this was no time to abandon the National government.[210] To sweeten the protectionist pill, they encouraged hope that a modest tariff in Britain would actually serve to liberalize international trade. The government would accompany the tariff with an Import Duties Advisory Council (IDAC) empowered to raise or lower duties. By holding out the possibility of improved access to the British market, the tariff could substantially reduce protectionism abroad, and might even facilitate the establishment of a broad low-tariff area in Europe and beyond. In Chamberlain's words,

> The idea of a flat-rate low level tariff, subject to a number of exceptions, is in line with the policy of those countries on the Continent which are nearest to the Free Trade position. Is there not here an opportunity of beginning an association which, with the aid of a common policy on currency, may presently give the United Kingdom a preponderating influence in directing Europe as a

whole back to sounder methods? [At the same time it would provide a lever for] forcing industry to set its house in order.[211]

Neither Snowden nor Samuel fully believed Chamberlain's claims, but on 23 January, they accepted a compromise whereby they remained in the Cabinet while openly dissenting from the introduction of the tariff. Chamberlain, announcing the government's decision on 4 February to a packed House of Commons, spoke in deliberately moderate language but recalled his father's struggle for tariff reform 30 years earlier.[212] Once Parliamentary approval was obtained, the IDAC was appointed. Without waiting for negotiations on tariff concessions elsewhere, it hastened to fix rates on most manufactured imports at 20 per cent and rates on most other goods between 20 and 33 1/3 per cent. Exception was made for imports from the colonies and dependent territories, which entered Britain free of duties, and temporarily also for imports from the Dominions, pending the outcome of the Ottawa conference in the summer.

For over a hundred years, Britain had been the linchpin of the global trading system. Far and away the world's largest importer, it was still the world's second largest exporter in 1932, after the United States, and its huge deficit on visible trade, covered more or less by invisible earnings from banking, finance, insurance, shipping and other services, enabled the countries that enjoyed trade surpluses with Britain to pay for foreign goods and services. Despite a piecemeal retreat from free trade since the Great War, Britain still enjoyed wide respect for its defence of liberal, non-discriminatory trade. The spectre of Britain erecting a tariff barrier against foreign imports while favouring the Dominions with preferential access to its market thus created acute distress elsewhere. In Britain, too, the departure from free trade gave rise to strong reservations in business as well as political circles.

Leading City bankers and financiers had come out in favour of trade protection in 1930, when it was a matter of saving the pound from collapse. But after Britain had abandoned the gold standard and sterling had depreciated 25 per cent, they saw no further justification for trade protection. Governor Norman privately deprecated plans for 'artificial' Empire trade preferences.[213] Sir William Goodenough, chairman of Barclays Bank, probably spoke for most City bankers when he appealed for the trend towards economic nationalism to be reversed in Britain as well as abroad.[214] As for Ottawa and the introduction of Imperial protectionism, one perceptive City broker reported that 'The comment most frequently heard [in the City] is that it is to be hoped that no trade agreements, entered into with the Dominions, will prevent similar arrangements with other countries.'[215] The City, whose interests were global, did not wish to see Britain retreat into Imperial protectionism.

Outside the City, farmers, landowners, merchants and industrialists continued to favour an active Imperial economic policy. Yet by the spring of 1932, their attention was turning from trade policy to monetary and exchange rate policy. Now that the gold standard was gone, interest rates were coming down and the long downward trend of price levels appeared likely to end, the exchange of trade preferences with the Dominions seemed very small beer indeed. On 13 January 1932, the council of the federation of Chambers of Commerce of the British Empire adopted a motion calling for a uniform Imperial monetary system, with the issuing banks of the Empire coordinating their discount policies, maintaining stable exchange rates among themselves and aiming to reverse the decline in commodity prices.[216] The very next day, the grand council of the FBI issued a statement affirming the need for 'Imperial Monetary Co-operation', directed towards the same end.

> The Government should direct its immediate efforts to building up a British system based primarily on the Empire, on such other countries as desire to come into the system related to sterling...and in due course form the nucleus of a new world financial system.[217]

Sir Basil Blackett, a director of the Bank of England who was working behind the scenes with the FBI,[218] repeated the call shortly afterwards in a public lecture. Britain, he said, needed a global monetary system on account of its global commercial and financial interests. Unfortunately, the gold standard had been 'mismanaged', and would remain unacceptable until the leading creditor powers agreed upon reforms. There was nevertheless a 'half-way house' back to a global system. 'What I have called the sterling area is sufficiently large and diversified to enable it to be to a very large extent self-sufficient.'[219]

Reginald McKenna's long-awaited speech at the annual general meeting of the Midland Bank on 29 January echoed Blackett's advice. What was needed, McKenna affirmed, was active reflation without worrying over-much about the exchanges. 'Deliberate, skilled and resolute monetary management, with or without gold, is a *sine qua non* of steady economic progress.'[220] J. M. Keynes took up the cry, and by the summer authorities such as Sir Robert Horne, the former Conservative chancellor, A. A. Paton, chairman of Martins Bank, Sir William Dampier, Sir Edward Grigg, Leo Amery, Robert Boothby and Sir Josiah Stamp had all affirmed that the Ottawa conference should be used to mobilize Empire support for coordinated monetary reflation, and that the sterling area thus created should become the nucleus of a wider area of exchange stability, investment and economic growth.[221] As the journal of the London Chamber of Commerce observed in May,

> Since our last issue there has been a remarkable awakening in this country to the fact that monetary policy is of the first importance in the present circumstances, and that Ottawa must result in disappointment and disillusionment unless an understanding on this all important question is reached there.[222]

Within the Cabinet, Conservative ministers betrayed increasing unease at the course they had embarked upon. Having succeeded in introducing a general tariff, they talked of the forthcoming Ottawa conference as a unique opportunity for Britain to unite the Empire by means of mutual tariff *reductions*. Yet they could not fail to notice that the Dominions governments were signalling their intention to make large demands for monetary cooperation and renewed access to the London capital market, while favouring British exports only through *increases* in duties against goods from foreign countries.[223] They also became aware that British farmers and landowners were intensely uneasy at the prospect of large-scale preferences for Dominions imports,[224] and that even British industrialists, ostensibly the main beneficiaries of Imperial protectionism, were frightened that Ottawa would close them off from the larger world market outside the Empire.[225]

Chamberlain responded to mounting public pressure by expressing his determination to ensure that Ottawa contributed to commodity price reflation. But he indicated that he expected this to come from the combination of tariff protection, a floating exchange rate and cheap and abundant money rather than more radical means such as the adoption of bimetallism, the creation of an Empire currency, or a deliberately reflationary policy undertaken in coordination with the Dominions.[226] Knowing little about monetary policy, he relied upon advice from Norman and his own Treasury advisers. Predictably they emphasized Britain's global interests and condemned reflation, which they equated with inflation, as 'a deliberate robbery of our creditors'.[227] They preferred a wait-and-see policy, anticipating that sooner or later the principal gold standard countries would agree to a *modus vivendi*. This increased the likelihood of confrontation at Ottawa between the Dominions, impatient for coordinated reflation, and a non-committal Britain.

By now, Conservative leaders doubted that there was any economic benefit to be gained from Ottawa. As Chamberlain admitted, 'I am not looking forward to an enjoyable visit [to Ottawa] for there will be many difficulties and they tell me it will be sweltering hot.'[228] But it was too late to turn back. He and his Conservative colleagues therefore soldiered on, anticipating trouble with the Dominions and sustained largely by fear of failure rather than any rational calculation of national advantage. The spectre before them was that if they did nothing to organize the Empire economically, Canada and eventually the Antipodean Dominions and other territories would drift into the orbit of the United States or another large power. There was thus 'no time to be lost', as Chamberlain put it, especially as agreement with the Dominions would demonstrate that Britain had not declined as a world power.[229]

For ten years Britain had endured heavy unemployment in its staple export industries, which evoked unfavourable comparison with France, the United States and other countries. This had been intensely frustrating to British observers who persuaded themselves that Britain alone had upheld the global system, playing by the rules on trade and monetary policy and supporting disarmament and European pacification while the other powers evaded their responsibilities. Now that the gold standard was gone and sterling had not collapsed, the mood of crisis in Britain had given way to cautious optimism. Meanwhile the countries that had done well in the 1920s were sinking ever deeper into depression. Chamberlain betrayed the sense of wounded pride when he wrote of '[t]hese foreigners ... tumbling over one another to make themselves agreeable to us', now that Britain had armed itself with a general tariff and was preparing to negotiate with the Dominions.[230] Confronting them as head of a more united Empire was another incentive for him to proceed with the Conference.

Tory attitudes towards the United States were more ambivalent. On the one hand they resented Washington's policies on disarmament, war debts and reparations and the crisis in East Asia, which posed serious dilemmas for Britain. On the other hand they were shocked by the depth of the depression in America. For ten years they had looked in vain to Washington for signs of Anglo-Saxon solidarity. Now, in the spring of 1932, Lindsay, the ambassador in Washington, predicted bread riots and perhaps a more general breakdown of civil order.[231] In June, D'Arcy Osborne, the chargé d'affaires at the embassy, described America in a state of systemic crisis:

> The national spirit is moribund, and where it still lives it is inarticulate and helpless. There is a striking absence of social or civic responsibility. The national institutions are in equal disrepute and decadence. ... Justice is a by-word for corruption and the law a common prostitute. Human life and property are less respected and less protected than in any other community of the white race. There are no trusted leaders or counsellors in politics, finance or industry. Banking is discredited and industry paralysed. There are over 10 million unemployed. The buoyancy of the American temperament is submerged in a mood of apathetic despair and paralytic defeatism. The country is not far from spiritual, moral and political defeatism as well as financial bankruptcy.

Osborne believed that the current state of affairs was linked to the rise of a business oligarchy which, unchecked by President Wilson and his Republican successors, had resulted in hot-house growth, overproduction, boom and bust, and the abandonment of higher ideals for crude materialism. But more important than overproduction or economic slump was the decline of America's racial elite, which he defined as the underlying cause of its crisis.

> There is no American race. ... The melting pot long ago ceased to function. The Anglo-Saxon race is stationary. The negro race is rapidly increasing. There are undigested and apparently indigestible local aggregations of every variety of European, Asiatic and Africa stock. ... History offers little guidance to an opinion on the racial development of the country.

The United States, he explained, had had the opportunity of 'grafting a new branch of civilisation onto the old European stock' in a new land with magnificent resources, and it had abjectly failed.

> The excuse of youth is generally advanced by the American Anglo-Saxon, and is probably inspired by a subconscious but repressed realisation that America is no longer an Anglo-Saxon country, i.e. by a consciousness of failure to preserve the hegemony and ideals of the Anglo-Saxon race. And it is undeniable that the Anglo-Saxon race in America, the original ruling class, is losing control,

is being outbred by more prolific, but less developed, racial elements, and is going to the wall.[232]

Osborne's belief that America's Anglo-Saxon governing élite had tolerated too many immigrants of inferior race and had lost its nerve was a long-held view in Britain as well as France and the United States itself.[233] This perhaps explains why senior Foreign Office colleagues praised his report and the foreign secretary instructed that it should be circulated to all the principal missions abroad. None of the officials, however, betrayed more than a hint of *Schadenfreude* at America's plight. Nor did they lose hope that under more vigorous leadership the United States would eventually regain order and prosperity. But aside from MacDonald, Keynes, Churchill and a handful of others, British observers in 1932 saw little to hope for from across the Atlantic. America's crisis left them feeling that, for now at least, they had no alternative but to fall back on their kith and kin within the Empire.

The Imperial Economic Conference opened in Ottawa on 21 July and lasted a month, but to British delegates it doubtless seemed like a lifetime. They had agreed beforehand to extend imperial preferences by means of tariff reductions among participating countries, to avoid quantitative trade controls so far as possible and to avoid the subject of an Empire monetary policy. But as they feared, the Dominions and Indian delegates arrived with other ideas. None of them had any intention of permitting British exports unrestricted access to their markets, fearing that this would destroy their industrial base. Accordingly, they offered free entry only for a limited range of British goods, and for the most part they granted concessions only by increasing duties on goods from third countries. In return, they demanded a guaranteed share of the British market, expecting Britain to introduce quota arrangements favourable to them, which would reduce if not completely exclude imports from Soviet Russia, Argentina, Denmark and other foreign competitors. India, Australia, New Zealand and Canada also vigorously demanded closer monetary cooperation.[234]

Dominions' demands almost immediately threw the conference into crisis. The Canadians were especially insistent that Britain should drastically curtail cereal and timber imports from Soviet Russia. This annoyed the British delegation not only because of the modest concessions Canada was prepared to offer Britain in return,[235] but also because they had belatedly learned that trade with Soviet Russia provided employment for at least 20,000 in Britain.[236] What had seemed a modest concession to Canada a few months earlier was thus regarded with grave misgivings even in Conservative parliamentary circles.[237] R. B. Bennett, the Canadian prime minister, however, was extremely exigent, alternately wheedling, bullying and threatening to turn to the United States for markets if Britain did not curb Russian imports. Reluctantly the British delegation gave way. Similarly with Australia and New Zealand, their demands for a secure market for meat exports were scarcely matched by comparable concessions on British manufactured exports. The British delegation, knowing how unpopular a tax on foreign meat would be at home, held out. But when the Dominions delegations spoke of abandoning the conference, they gave way and agreed to a quota scheme for regulating meat imports which favoured the Dominions.[238] Socially regressive and politically unpopular, the scheme was also protective and went against Board of Trade policy of discouraging quantitative trade controls.[239]

Monetary policy proved rather less controversial than seemed possible at the start of the conference. Sir George Schuster, financial secretary to the Indian government, assisted by Sir Henry Strakosch, repeatedly called for coordinated price reflation through open market operations.[240] This received support from the industrial and labour representatives attending the conference at the invitation of the British government.[241] But they and the Dominions delegates betrayed uncertainty as to appropriate monetary action, and Chamberlain, Britain's chief negotiator at the conference, persuaded them to accept an anodyne statement affirming the need for international – not merely imperial – measures to raise prices, while warning of the dangers of inflation through 'rash experiments in currency policy'.[242]

The British delegation returned to London on 26 August in a thoroughly chastened mood.[243] In face of intense criticism from Snowden and Samuel, leaders of the free trade group in the Cabinet, they defended the outcome of the conference as essential to save the Empire from certain disintegration. Chamberlain acknowledged that he was

> Struck ... how thin the bonds of Empire had worn, and the growth of nationalism in the Dominions. He did not think the bonds could have survived but for this Conference, which had strengthened the sense of belonging to a great Commonwealth and of the advantages to be derived therefrom.[244]

Baldwin, who publicly claimed that the conference had been a success on economic grounds,[245] privately made the issue of Empire unity his main line of argument when he appealed unsuccessfully to the free traders to remain in the government:

> [The British delegation] believed ... that they had removed the imminent danger of the absorption of Canada into the economic orbit of the United States of America, with all the serious consequences entailed thereby, such as the closing of Canada to British trade and ultimately to British immigrants. Instead, preferential advantages to our traders had been gained in the Canadian market, which, until recently, had been regarded as an impossibility. This was a great advantage to the United Kingdom. He believed also that the fiscal co-operation of the Empire had been achieved at the last moment at which this was possible. Had the Conference failed, the various units of the Empire would have drifted apart and it would have been too late to re-assemble them.[246]

In view of the trend towards greater Dominions and Indian independence, ministers had every reason to feel a sense of urgency. Nevertheless, they were aware that Ottawa scarcely contributed to economic recovery. Besides Canada, India had conceded preferences on British goods for the first time, but it had made no concessions on cotton textiles, by far the largest item of British export. For the most part, the concessions negotiated at Ottawa had been on foodstuffs and raw materials, which traded at world prices, and were therefore of little value to the Dominions and none to Britain. They promised merely to divert trade from foreign countries rather than stimulating additional trade, and since they were generally accompanied by higher external duties, the aggregate effect was almost certainly to reduce world trade.

The international ramifications were scarcely reassuring. British officials did not worry greatly about retaliation from foreign countries adversely affected by the Ottawa agreements, since most countries still relied heavily upon access to the British market.[247] But they anticipated that one or another of them would take Britain to the International Court for breaching its commitment to the principle of most-favoured-nation treatment,[248] and Sir William Malkin, the Foreign Office legal adviser, feared that if this happened, Britain would almost certainly lose.[249] Whether challenged or not, Foreign Office advisers accepted that many foreign countries would resent the loss of trade to Britain.[250] The United States, they estimated, would be the largest loser in absolute terms with losses of $100 million in annual trade,[251] and reports strongly indicated that Washington would not simply acquiesce in this treatment.[252] The decision to introduce a meat quota was another source of embarrassment, since it would require Britain to denounce the international Prohibitions Convention outlawing quantitative trade controls, which it had been chiefly responsible for promoting only two years earlier.[253] British leaders still hoped they could renegotiate trade relations with major trading partners. But with the Ottawa agreements in place for five years, they had few concessions to make.[254] Indeed, by now the only possible result of third country negotiations would be to reduce trade to narrowly bilateral channels, thus further undermining multilateralism.

Gone was the dream of Britain, having demonstrated it could promote freer trade within the Empire, providing a new lead in a globalized world. In its place was the grim reality that the price of Empire was Britain's further isolation from Europe and the rest of the world, as well as antagonism with the United States and encouragement to Japan, Germany, Italy and other powers to form their own economic blocs.

7.4.4 The Stresa conference

The final French effort to stave off German domination of Eastern Europe came in September 1932, when the government convened a conference at Stresa to organize economic assistance to the beleaguered countries in the region. Georges Bonnet, minister of public works in Herriot's government, now took over the lead from Tardieu and Flandin. He shared their fears that unless the Danube countries were helped to dispose of their cereal surpluses, Germany would be sure to exploit the resulting crisis. He also accepted that the London four-power conference demonstrated the impracticability of organizing the countries into a regional group based upon a customs union or trade preferences. Accordingly,

he devised a programme comprising four elements: first, bilateral trade preferences for cereals from the Danube, granted unilaterally (without counterpart)
by European cereal importing countries; second, a price-stabilization fund of
75 million French francs (£0.9 million) to enable the Danube countries to avoid
the need to sell their surpluses at distress prices; third, a monetary stabilization
fund to enable them to remain on the gold standard; and fourth, the agreement
of the Danube countries to reduce or remove various tariff and non-tariff barriers
to trade.[255]

Bonnet also shared Tardieu's and Flandin's optimism that Britain would feel
bound to support assistance to the region because of its financial commitments
there. The deputy-governor of the Bank of England had recently told him that
these amounted to over £120 million, a huge sum even for the City of London.[256]
In his capacity as chairman of the CEUE therefore he convened a conference at
the Swiss town of Stresa for Monday 5 September, to which he invited the eight
cereal surplus countries that had recently met at Warsaw – Poland, Roumania,
Czechoslovakia, Hungary, Yugoslavia, Bulgaria, Estonia and Latvia – as well as
Austria and Greece along with Belgium, Britain, France, Germany, Italy, the
Netherlands and Switzerland on whom he counted to provide markets or financial help or both. The date was chosen to allow time for recommendations from
the conference to be examined by the CEUE and passed to the League Assembly
in late September. Stresa was selected as the venue to avoid the impression that
the conference was a French affair and to appeal to nearby Italy. Like Tardieu in
the spring, Bonnet sought an invitation to London to coordinate strategy with his
British colleagues.[257] MacDonald discouraged him from crossing the Channel.[258]
Bonnet, however, still assumed that Britain shared France's anxiety to avoid the
collapse of the region, and disconcerted to hear that Britain might be represented
at the conference only by a civil servant rather than a government minister, he
insisted upon visiting MacDonald in London.[259] The visit, on 27 August, passed
off smoothly enough. Bonnet could not know that MacDonald had only reluctantly agreed that Britain should be represented at the Stresa conference even
by a middle-level diplomat let alone a government minister,[260] and had recently
written in his diary:

> I do my best to have confidence in [the] French, but am always defeated.
> They seem to be incapable of disinterested diplomacy. I suspect that what is
> really prompting them now is to get something done in the Danubian area to
> strengthen their protégés and get a chance of withdrawing their money given
> in [the] form of military equipment & goods mainly & not pure credit. The
> diplomacy of France is an ever active influence for evil in Europe.[261]

The Stresa conference, attended by 16 countries, marked the last occasion when
Europe's economic problems were addressed by all the major powers before Hitler's
seizure of power ushered in the era of the dictators. For three days in plenary session, delegates set out their views of what should or could be done to aid the
Danube region. Joseph Addison, the minister in Prague who represented Britain,

remained silent, and the German and Italian delegates seemed unwilling to agree on a common approach. Nonetheless, at the end of the third day, Bonnet vigorously promoted his four-part programme, and eventually persuaded the reluctant Italian and German delegates to cooperate, the first on the basis of unilateral trade preferences and a reduced contribution to the common funds, the second on the basis of unilateral preferences and no contribution to the funds. He also obtained the provisional agreement of the Dutch, Belgians and Swiss to support the funds. But he counted on Britain to make at least some contribution to the funds, and was dismayed to learn on 13 September that it opposed the financial components of his programme.[262] He appealed to Addison not to acknowledge this openly, fearing that an open division between Britain and France would cause Italy and Germany to pull away.[263] Addison, who indicated to Bonnet his personal support for French policy, persuaded the Foreign Office to play along.[264] This enabled Bonnet to secure agreement in principle to his programme, which was forwarded to the CEUE.

Briefly, Bonnet believed that Stresa had been a success.[265] At the meeting of the CEUE, however, Anthony Eden, the British representative, followed Treasury instructions and dug in his heels against the financial provisions of the conference recommendations. When the German and Italian representatives joined in, it became evident that none of the recommendations had sufficient support to be implemented.[266] In the short run, the consequences were not as dire as French statesmen feared. None of the Danube countries actually collapsed, and in the summer of 1934, Italy intervened when Hitler threatened the independence of Austria. But there was now no hope of collective action to address the region's problems, especially as France was sinking ever deeper into economic depression. Germany, with its large import requirements, was left to exploit the crisis. Its revisionist agenda was well known, and it could be merely a matter of time before it absorbed Austria, isolated Czechoslovakia and extended its domination over the whole region. When this did eventually happen, British statesmen faced up to the fact, so clear to their French counterparts since 1918 and indeed long before, that Eastern Europe formed a vital component of the European balance of power and that no coherent framework of international security could be constructed without it. But by then, of course, it was too late.

7.5 The climax of American isolationism

7.5.1 From Hoover to Roosevelt

Hoover, who had hoped to keep the world crisis at bay with his debt moratorium in June 1931, was soon disappointed. On 19 September, speculative pressure spread from sterling to the dollar, and between then and 31 October, US gold reserves declined by $727 million (£150 million): in the words of the New York Fed, 'the most rapid outflow of gold ever experienced by this country and probably by any country.'[267] The Federal Reserve had entered the crisis in September with over $5 billion in gold reserves, and should have had enough resources to meet any exigency. However, under existing rules most of the gold was earmarked as reserves for the currency note issue, leaving only a small fraction as 'free reserves', which now dwindled, forcing the Fed to abandon its policy of cheap money.[268] Hoover had already turned to regional bankers, forming in September a federal advisory council on national credit with thirteen members including Eugene Meyer, chairman of the Federal Reserve Board, but not a single New York representative.[269] With the slump intensifying, he approached leading New York bankers, who in October formed a National Credit Corporation, which offered mutual assistance to commercial banks prepared to pool some of their resources. But once again, voluntary action was not enough. Without a Federal contribution, the Corporation's scope was modest, and in any case it did nothing to shore up the Fed's reserves. Hoover, therefore, with the greatest reluctance, used his message to Congress in December to request help.[270]

Congress soon approved the Reconstruction Finance Corporation, modelled on the War Finance Corporation and introduced in January 1932 with patriotic rhetoric as a means of defending the country against foreign financial attack. It made $2 billion available to lend to railways, banks and other financial institutions facing a temporary cash flow crisis.[271] The following month, Congress also approved the Glass-Steagall Bank Credit Bill, which released gold reserves to meet demand from sellers of dollars by permitting the Federal Reserve to substitute government securities for commercial paper as legal backing for the currency note issue, and increased resources to the member banks by broadening the range of securities eligible for rediscounting.[272] The Act was timely, for in January the run on Federal reserves resumed and continued until mid-June 1932, reducing them by a further $549 million (£113 million).[273] It did not, as Hoover claimed, save the dollar from being driven off the gold standard by foreign speculators, since the Federal Reserve could have, and no doubt would have, exercised its existing power to release gold committed to currency reserves to meet a continuing demand from sellers of dollars. But it did save the country from a sharp intensification of deflation and an even deeper slump.[274]

In January 1932, the United States had entered its third year of economic depression with no sign of recovery. Unemployment stood at 12 million and would soon rise to 15 million, with perhaps as many as 2 million men wandering the country in search of work. In June, unemployed war veterans marched on the capital to demand that Congress make advance payment of their promised bonus. Congress, worried by the budget deficit, refused, and in July violence erupted when soldiers drove the veterans who remained in Washington out of their makeshift camp on the edge of town. Meanwhile tax revenues dwindled, driving the federal budget ever deeper into deficit, from an estimated $1 billion in September 1931 to $2 billion at the New Year, and to $3 billion in June 1932. By then, barely a quarter of federal spending was covered by revenue.[275] Hoover, trapped by his own isolationism and liberal free-market ideology, saw no way of escaping. He called for increased taxes and economies to balance the budget.[276] Meanwhile, as in his message to Congress in December 1931, he vented his frustration upon Europe and financial excesses in America itself – Wall Street, in short – which he blamed for the economic slump.

Hoover, who believed that the New York bankers had engaged in profligate foreign lending in the 1920s, believed they were now financing bear speculation on the stock market and against the dollar. Indeed, he appears to have shared Henry Ford's belief in an elaborate conspiracy of the European powers and the Wall Street bankers, organized by the Jewish financier, Bernard Baruch, and directed against him, aimed at forcing him to abandon American claims for war debts.[277] In January 1932 therefore he launched an assault on Wall Street, singling out Richard Whitney, president of the New York Stock Exchange, for supposedly covering up the role of short sellers.[278] On 19 February, he publicly called upon the Stock Exchange to curb the operations of the bear traders, and requested Congress to launch an investigation.[279] Thus encouraged, the Senate Sub-Committee on Banking and Currency accused the New York banks of negligence for selling worthless bonds to the public in the 1920s. In April it began its enquiry into stock exchange manipulation, calling as its first witness the same Richard Whitney.[280] In the words of one historian, 'The great bear hunt had officially begun. [M]ore ... than at any time in its history, Wall Street now became the target of fear and loathing.'[281] Hoover himself was deluged with letters from individual citizens condemning the bankers for their unpatriotic behaviour.[282]

Hoover believed the European powers had created allies of the international bankers by threatening to block repayment of their commercial loans if Washington did not abandon its war debt claims. He was greatly relieved to hear that the Federal Reserve believed the American banking system could withstand the consequences of a large-scale repudiation of overseas loans.[283] It infuriated him nonetheless that the international bankers favoured writing down, if not completely writing off, the war debts. So strong was his hostility that in April 1932 Thomas Lamont of the bankers J.P. Morgan had to ask Stimson if he would not be embarrassed to travel on the same ship as him to Europe.[284] Stimson distanced himself from Hoover's attack on New York bankers and the European powers. In turn, he found himself cold shouldered by the White House and contemplated resignation when Hoover angrily rejected his advice to compromise on war debts.[285] Shortly afterwards, Lamont experienced Hoover's anger at second hand when he sent a colleague to Washington to urge American support for the reparation-war debt agreement reached at the Lausanne conference. His colleague reported that he had never seen Hoover so emotional about an issue.[286]

Hoover's other target was 'old Europe' and in particular France. The rundown of the Federal gold reserves since September 1931 was due to many factors, including the repatriation of balances that had fled London before the suspension of sterling from the gold standard and the rise in hoarding within the United States as well as the Bank of France's decision to dispose of its remaining foreign exchange balances after incurring severe losses on sterling. The Federal Reserve estimated that domestic hoarding might have reached $700 million (£145 million) before foreign withdrawals even began, and it continued on a large scale for the next 18 months.[287] Hoover nevertheless reserved his criticism for France, which he chose to believe was deliberately attacking the dollar to force him to concede America's right to war debts. According to William Castle,

> He [Hoover] has the feeling that through manipulation of gold, used for political purposes, France is responsible for a great deal that has happened. She first tried to ruin Germany, then turned on England which supported Germany, and finally made a campaign against the United States which has failed with the withdrawal of the larger part of the French gold here.[288]

This view, it seems, was widely shared in Congress. While not prepared to cancel war debts, Hoover was aware of the danger that the European countries might default on their debts if Washington made no effort to cooperate. Accordingly, in December 1931 he agreed that Stimson should request Congress to reconstitute the World War Foreign Debt Commission to determine which debtors, if any, should receive temporary relief.[289] Congress, still more isolationist than Hoover, refused Stimson's request and initially refused even to approve the one-year moratorium on inter-governmental debts that Hoover had initiated the previous summer.[290] During debate, Hiram Johnson, a leading Progressive from California, blamed America's international bankers for the pressure to abandon war debt claims, and urged colleagues to initiate an investigation into the bankers' foreign lending activity as well as the State Department for allegedly encouraging it.[291]

Among other targets of Congressional attack, France once more stood out, but Britain did not escape unscathed. Benjamin Anderson, chief economist of the Chase National Bank, America's largest bank, had recently claimed that Britain had deliberately abandoned the gold standard to gain an exchange advantage over the United States and other competitors, a claim reprinted in newspapers across the country.[292] David Reed of Pennsylvania, the senior Republican member of the Senate banking and currency subcommittee and a close friend of Hoover, questioned how Britain could justify its demand for relief on war debts when it still possessed a far-flung empire and museums bulging with art treasures.[293]

Introducing his emergency bank credit bill in the Senate, Glass referred to reports that French gold purchases were politically motivated. While not prepared to confirm or deny the reports, he declared: 'The real purpose of this section of the bill is to put foreign nations upon notice that if they, in conjunction with their businessmen, want to raid the gold supply over here, we have this method of meeting the situation.'[294] Alan Goldsborough, a leading member of the House of Representatives banking committee, put it more bluntly: 'France can take her money and go to hell with it.'[295] So isolationist had Congress become that it approved the Glass-Steagall Bank Credit Bill without a formal vote, believing it was needed to protect America from 'old Europe'. It soon threatened to go further and force Hoover's hand on foreign economic policy. Several resolutions were introduced calling for still higher tariffs on foreign imports and for surcharges on goods from Britain and other countries that had abandoned the gold standard and allowed their currencies to depreciate.[296] More than fifty bills advocating currency expansion were also introduced in Congress in Hoover's last two years of office.[297] One of them, tabled by Goldsborough, was supported by the Stable Money Association and debated for several weeks in Congress in the spring of 1932.[298]

For the time being conservatives in the Senate blocked the inflationary proposals, but Hoover, thoroughly orthodox on money and banking, became increasingly anxious about the mounting pressure. Accordingly, despite his isolationism, he grasped the proposal for an international monetary conference mooted by Winston Churchill in the Commons budget debate in May 1932, and swiftly let it be known that America was prepared to participate in any such conference.[299] British statesmen, scanning the horizon for signs that America would return to international affairs, welcomed Hoover's offer. They appreciated that his exclusion of reparations, war debts, tariffs and the gold standard from the agenda and his insistence upon including silver made it unlikely that anything practical could emerge from an international conference.[300] Nonetheless, they hoped to begin a constructive dialogue that might eventually produce results.[301] Herriot in Paris also indicated support. Like most French statesmen, he was sceptical of what he called the British mania for international conferences, but he was not prepared to offend MacDonald or Hoover by refusing to attend.[302]

From the summer of 1932, the presidential election dominated public life in America. Hoover, re-nominated at the Republican convention in Chicago on 15 June, defended his record of protecting 'the American system' and promised to continue his narrowly nationalist policies in a second term of office.[303] Europe, he repeated over the following months, was responsible for America's depression and delaying its recovery. Europe had dislocated the world economy by going to war in 1914, squandered its wealth on weapons of war, raised its tariffs before the United States had done so and had recently withdrawn no less than $2.4 billion from America's banking system. 'The American people did not originate the age-old controversies of Europe. We did not inaugurate the Great War or the panics in Europe.'[304] To safeguard American jobs, he indicated he would further increase the tariff, perhaps especially against countries that had recently abandoned the gold standard and allowed their currencies to depreciate, and tighten further America's already draconian immigration controls.[305] Absurdly, he maintained that American protectionism – unlike foreign protectionism – was actually good for international trade. America's debtors supposedly could earn dollars so long as the American economy was protected from destructive competition. In any case, they could help themselves by reducing their heavy spending on weapons of war.[306]

Hoover's Democratic opponent was Franklin D. Roosevelt, the governor of New York. Born into a wealthy East Coast family, Roosevelt had attended Groton, an exclusive prep school, and Harvard, and worked for a prominent Wall Street law firm before turning to politics in 1910. That year he gained election to the New York legislature, and in 1917 he joined Woodrow Wilson's wartime Administration as assistant secretary of the navy. Regarded by foreign observers as a liberal internationalist, and an opponent of the eighteenth amendment prohibiting the manufacture and sale of alcoholic beverages, as the Democratic candidate in 1932 he seemed to possess many of the handicaps that had doomed his predecessor, Al Smith, in the 1928 election. But in fact voters regarded him very differently. For one thing, his name associated him with his uncle, T. R. Roosevelt, the bellicose imperialist and reforming president of prewar days. For another, his reputation was that of an opponent of Tammany Hall, the corrupt party machine in New York, and the defender of the common man against big business. Significantly, he secured the nomination at the Democratic convention in Chicago on 2 July on the strength of votes not from the commercial East Coast but from the agrarian South and West.[307]

In his acceptance speech, Roosevelt spoke of 'a new deal for the American people', and thereafter he mounted a campaign against the 'new despotism', the 'industrial dictatorship', the rule of the 'economic royalists' and the profligacy of 'the international bankers'.[308] Mere phrases, they were nonetheless strongly redolent of the midwest Progressive tradition and its onslaught against the East Coast money power. This and his refusal to be precise about his commitment to the gold standard prompted Hoover to present him as a dangerous radical in the final weeks of the campaign. America had been only a fortnight from being forced off gold earlier in the year, Hoover claimed. A victory for Roosevelt would again jeopardize the currency, threatening German-style inflation and 'moral and social chaos, with years of conflict and derangement [*sic*]'.[309] In his last major address of the campaign, before an overflow crowd in Madison Square Gardens in New York on 31 October, Hoover again warned that Roosevelt, if elected, would strip away the protection he had given to producers, jettison the gold dollar and 'destroy the very foundations of our American system.' '[G]rass will grow in the streets of a hundred cities and a thousand towns, and weeds will overrun the fields of millions of farms, if [existing] protection be taken away.'[310] The odd thing was that Roosevelt, despite his privileged East Coast background, his time on Wall Street and his friendship with prominent Wall Street bankers and financiers, actually shared the Progressives' dislike of international bankers and believed that their insistence upon a strong currency enriched them at the expense of the rest of the country. As he wrote privately to Colonel House, Woodrow Wilson's confidant:

> The real truth ... is, as you and I know, that a financial element in the larger centers has owned the Government ever since the days of Andrew Jackson – and I am not wholly excepting the administration of W.W. [Woodrow Wilson]. The country is going through a repetition of Jackson's fight with the Bank of the United States – only on a far bigger and broader basis.[311]

He also believed that after three years of unprecedented economic depression, the electorate was impatient for change rather than more of the same. On this he could not have been more correct, as the 8 November polls showed.

The outcome of the 1932 presidential election was as one-sided as the election of 1928. Whereas Hoover had won 40 of 48 states including 6 in the South and 58.2 per cent of the popular vote, this time he won only 8 states, all of them in the North-East (Maine, Vermont, New Hampshire, Rhode Island, Connecticut,

New Jersey, Delaware and Pennsylvania), while Roosevelt won 40 states, including every one in the South, the Midwest and West and 57.4 per cent of the popular vote. The Democrats also emerged with massive majorities in the House of Representatives (312 to 123), and in the Senate (59 to 37).[312]

Countries that owed war debts to America, having held back during the election campaign, immediately approached Hoover for relief on their 15 December instalment.[313] Hoover again attempted to reconstitute the World War Foreign Debt Commission, and called on Roosevelt to join him in appointing its members.[314] Through various go-betweens, Roosevelt had indicated that he favoured debt cancellation, and encouraged the British government to count on his cooperation.[315] Through Norman Davis, he assured MacDonald that 'Anglo-Saxon cooperation should be made foundation of world work.'[316] But it seems only now to have occurred to him that in the current isolationist climate in America he would lose valuable political capital by making concessions to Europe on war debts. Besides, notwithstanding his superficially friendly attitude towards Britain and France, he shared Hoover's isolationist hostility towards Wall Street bankers and 'old Europe', for he suspected that the international bankers were behind the drive for cancellation and that the European countries could pay with little difficulty.[317] Indeed, improbable as this now seems, he shared the suspicions of many Democrats that Hoover was in league with the international bankers and had secretly promised concessions to Britain and France.[318] Roosevelt therefore informed Hoover that this was 'not my baby', leaving him to do as he wished.[319] Wall Street displayed open frustration at Roosevelt's non-cooperation. But as Ray Moley, Roosevelt's closest adviser, observed, this was no bad thing, since outside New York his supporters would be reassured to see him at odds with Wall Street.[320]

With no further concessions on offer, Britain faced the demand for another war debt payment of $95,550,000 (£28.4 million) on 15 December. Chamberlain, the minister responsible, had persuaded himself that the reparation-war debt tangle must be removed if Europe was ever to emerge from its slump. It was also a personal matter, for he was determined to uphold 'his' Lausanne settlement, and for some months he had refused even to contemplate a further payment.[321] Roosevelt's inaction briefly hardened his opposition. But as the December deadline approached, he yielded to the imprecations of MacDonald and Montagu Norman. MacDonald, as ever, sought to avoid a clash with the United States. Norman, as Chamberlain reported to Cabinet, feared that if Britain deliberately defaulted on its obligations, its own debtors might do so as well. It might also influence Britain's working classes, with incalculable consequences for the existing social order. Baldwin emphatically agreed:

> Whatever name we gave to a refusal to pay, in fact it would amount to repudiation. That was an ugly word. He thought that repudiation might bring the world within sight of the end of Capitalism. Our word was unique in the world. If we broke it we should give an example to the Argentine, Germany, Australia: and the effect on public and private debts throughout the world would be very serious. Moreover it would be a tremendous shock to the vast majority

of the working classes of this country if they realised that we were able to pay and did not pay. ... By instinct and reason he supported the line taken by the Chancellor of the Exchequer.[322]

Accordingly, when Washington demanded payment, Britain acquiesced. Nonetheless, it left Chamberlain intensely hostile towards the United States.[323]

France was placed in an even more acute predicament. There the sense of injustice over war debts had mounted sharply after Hoover, without consultation, introduced his moratorium which halted German reparation payments. Herriot along with his ministerial colleagues and senior advisers nonetheless remained convinced that France must not default on war debts. Liberals to a man, they placed a high value on the sanctity of contracts. They also believed that, with Germany in the hands of extremists, France must continue payments to keep in with both the Anglo-Saxon powers and ensure continued access to the US capital market 'in the event of an ever possible European conflict.'[324] But now that Germany was relieved of reparation payments, opposition in Parliament to any further war debt payment left Herriot helpless to affect the outcome. During an all-night sitting of the Chamber of Deputies he made a lengthy, impassioned plea for one further payment in the interests of national security. To no avail. Despite the modest amount owing – a mere 481 million francs (£4.5 million) – France defaulted on 15 December.[325]

In retrospect, it is clear that all the European powers made too much of war debts or reparations as a burden on their economy, as a transfer problem or as a source of revenue. Britain and France could have maintained payments without substantial effect upon their domestic economic performance or external stability throughout the slump. For Britain, debt payments in 1932 and 1933 required 6d on income tax and thereafter 1/- a year, or an additional 4.3–4.9 per cent in total government expenditure.[326] For France the burden would have been a mere 2 per cent of its national budget. Nor did either power face serious difficulty in transferring payments across the exchanges. The real importance of war debts was rather as a symbol of their frustration over the perceived injustices of the peace settlement. The main consequences of the *dispute* over war debts were also political in that it embittered relations among the creditor powers as well playing into Hitler's hands in Germany.

Several more times in the winter of 1932, Roosevelt refused Hoover's request for cooperation. Hoover sought to bring forward the date for the World Economic Conference and called on Roosevelt to share responsibility for appointing American representatives to the preparatory committee.[327] Roosevelt, however, was put off by the agenda of the conference, which threatened to commit him to the gold standard and other international constraints. Privately he affirmed that 'no entanglements should stand in the way of the domestic recovery programme.'[328] Rumours circulated that he was preparing to abandon the gold standard, which unsettled the foreign exchange markets and led Hoover to request him to issue a firm denial. Roosevelt's refusal increased the flight from the dollar.[329]

The crisis intensified when John Nance Garner, Roosevelt's incumbent vice-president, called on the Administration to publish the names of banks that had received loans from the Reconstruction Finance Corporation.[330] Garner hoped to embarrass Hoover by exposing a link between the Republicans and the distribution of federal largesse. But the practical effect was to arouse suspicions about the financial solvency of the banks in question. Hoarding increased and on 4 February 1933, the governor of Louisiana was forced to declare a temporary closure of state banks, known euphemistically as a bank holiday, to forestall a general collapse. Ten days later the contagion spread to Michigan, Maryland, Ohio, Pennsylvania, Arkansas and Indiana, then to the big city banks when the regional correspondent banks withdrew balances to meet the withdrawal of deposits.[331] On 3 March, Herbert Lehman, the governor of New York, appealed to Hoover to use his power under the Trading with the Enemy Act to declare a national bank holiday. But since his term of office ended that day, Hoover was prepared to act only with Roosevelt's agreement, and once more Roosevelt refused his cooperation.[332] Therefore, at 3.30 a.m. on 4 March, as queues formed outside banks in Manhattan, Brooklyn and elsewhere, Lehman declared a state moratorium.[333] By then the National City Bank, the country's largest bank, had lost over a third of its deposits and survived on credits from the New York Fed, whose own gold reserves had fallen below the legal minimum.[334] The great financial centres, Chicago and New York, were now shut down, and nearly every state in the Union had imposed a bank holiday or restrictions on deposit withdrawals.[335] Hoover thus ended his presidency with the 'American system' at a standstill.

7.5.2   Roosevelt, radical nationalist

On the morning of 4 March, Roosevelt was sworn in as the thirty-second president, and promised in his inaugural address to put 'first things first' by giving priority to 'the establishment of a sound national economy' over international action.[336] As historians have pointed out, his statements during the recent election campaign and four-month interregnum had revealed oddly inconsistent notions of policy.[337] He was, it seemed, in favour of balancing the budget through economies and also in favour of greater public spending. He endorsed monetary orthodoxy and mocked Hoover's 'new economics', while in almost the same breath calling for an end to old economic shibboleths. His advisers, too, were a remarkably disparate group. Some such as James Warburg, Lew Douglas, Dean Acheson and William Woodin favoured the conventional liberal options of unilateral domestic action (deflation) and international cooperation (to defend the gold standard and reduce trade barriers). Others including Raymond Moley, Rexford Tugwell, Henry Morgenthau Jr and Henry Wallace were economic nationalists who favoured a combination of unilateral domestic action (reflation) and unilateral external action (active currency depreciation). Roosevelt listened to both camps, but it was evident from the outset that he leaned to the nationalists' side. Moreover, he seemed convinced that the first requisite was to remove the influence of Wall Street over monetary and financial policy and consolidate control in the hands of the federal authorities in Washington. This was the main theme of his inaugural address:

> our distress comes from no failure of substance. We are stricken by no plague of locusts. ... Nature still offers her bounty and human efforts have multiplied it. Plenty is at our doorstep, but a generous use of it languishes in the very sight of the supply. Primarily this is because rulers of the exchange of mankind's goods have failed through their own stubbornness and their own incompetence, have admitted their failure, and have abdicated. Practices of the unscrupulous money changers stand indicted in the court of public opinion, rejected by the hearts and minds of men. ... The money changers have fled from their high seats in the temple of our civilization. We may now restore that temple to the ancient truths. The measure of the restoration lies in the extent to which we apply social values more noble than mere monetary profit. ... Finally, in our progress toward a resumption of work we require two safeguards against a return of the evils of the old order: there must be a strict supervision of all banking and credits: and investments, so that there will be an end to speculation with other people's money; and there must be provision for an adequate but sound currency.[338]

For fully four months after the inauguration, Roosevelt seemed unsure how to proceed. At 1 a.m. on Monday, 6 March, before the financial markets reopened, he appeared to turn his back on liberal internationalism by declaring a national bank holiday accompanied by an embargo on gold exports, and prohibited banks from dealing in foreign exchange.[339] William Woodin, his secretary of the Treasury, nevertheless reassured the public that the United States had not left the gold standard.[340] And when the domestic banking crisis ended on 15 March, Woodin authorized the export of gold already earmarked for foreign governments, central banks and the BIS. That same day, Roosevelt invited Warburg to see if Britain and France were prepared to participate in a tripartite stabilization fund to contain the problem of hot money movements. Warburg understood him to mean that the broader aim was to facilitate Britain's return to the gold standard and enable the three great creditor powers to operate on a reformed gold standard.[341] On this assumption, he began informal negotiations with British experts on 28 March, under the guise of consultations on the World Economic Conference.[342] On 6 April, Roosevelt invited MacDonald, the British prime minister, to Washington for informal talks on the forthcoming conference, and over the next few days, he issued similar invitations to France, Germany, Italy, Argentina, Brazil and five other countries.[343] Meanwhile, he introduced legislation to balance the federal budget, including substantial reductions in the veterans' bonus and the salaries of federal employees including members of Congress.[344] All this suggested that Roosevelt would rely upon the orthodox liberal combination of unilateral domestic action and international cooperation to address the crisis. Yet he maintained the ban on commercial transactions in gold, and on 18 April, just as MacDonald reached New York, he informed his Cabinet of his decision to abandon the gold standard and allow the dollar to find its own level.[345]

Roosevelt nevertheless continued to issue contradictory signals. In conversation with MacDonald, Herriot and other foreign visitors, he explained that his hand had been forced by agrarian interests in Congress who threatened to impose their dangerously inflationary proposal for the unlimited monetization of silver if he did not demonstrate his willingness to act, and he offered to cooperate closely with them on economic issues. Their joint press statements affirmed his commitment to a multilateral approach to problems rather than resort to unilateral external action.[346] As he explained in his second 'fireside chat', broadcast nationally on 7 May, his conversations with foreign statesmen had four objectives:

> First, a general reduction of armaments ... and, at the same time, a reduction in armament costs, in order to help in the balancing of government budgets and the reduction of taxation. Secondly, a cutting down of the trade barriers, in order to re-start the flow of exchange of crops and goods between nations. Third, the setting up of a stabilization of currencies, in order that trade can make contracts ahead. Fourth, the reestablishment of friendly relations and greater confidence between all nations.
>
> Our foreign visitors these past three weeks have responded to these purposes in a very helpful way. All of the Nations have suffered alike in this great depression. They have all reached the conclusion that each can best be helped by the common action of all. It is in this spirit that our visitors have met with us and discussed our common problems. The international conference that lies before us must succeed. The future of the world demands it and we have each of us pledged ourselves to the best joint efforts to this end.[347]

These were reassuring words, and as yet British and French leaders were puzzled but not deeply disturbed by Roosevelt's actions. Since 5 April, when Americans were ordered to turn in all privately held gold, the dollar had declined by over 15 per cent against the franc (see Table 7.1). But French observers, ignoring the increased overvaluation of the franc, chose to regard the inflow of flight capital from New York and other centres as an endorsement of their conservative monetary policy. Their situation improved in the ten days after Roosevelt's 'fireside chat', when the dollar recovered more than half its depreciation against the franc. They assumed that Roosevelt's monetary action was directed chiefly at Britain, and that the effect on the franc was merely collateral damage, which would be removed once Britain agreed to stabilize the pound. Since they regarded Britain's refusal to restore the gold standard as a major obstacle to world economic recovery, they directed their impatience at Britain and became increasingly annoyed when British authorities resisted pressure to stabilize the pound.[348]

Yet Roosevelt was remarkably casual in selecting the American delegation at the World Economic Conference, eventually assembling an odd assortment of internationalists and nationalists who could scarcely be expected to work together.[349] His offhandedness continued when, after the Conference opened on 12 June, he allowed Warburg to resume negotiations with British and French Treasury and central bank officials on a temporary currency stabilization agreement, only to reject

Table 7.1 Exchange rates and currency depreciation on selected days

Date	£/$ rate	Sterling depreciation against the dollar	£/franc rate	Sterling depreciation against the franc	$/franc rate	Dollar depreciation against the franc
	$	%	francs	%	francs	%
Gold parity	4.86¾	0	124.21	0	3.9179	0
1933						
2 Jan.	3.39¼	30	85½	31	3.92¼	0
1 Apr.	3.42¼	30	87⅛	30	3.93	0
15 Apr.	3.48	29	86 15/16	30	3.95⅛	1
19 Apr.	3.71½	24	86¾	30	4.26½	8
1 May	3.89	20	86	31	4.68½	16
10 Jun.	4.15¾	15	85 15/16	31	4.82¼	19
1 Jul.	4.34	11	86⅛	31	5.02	22
3 Jul.	4.47½	8	86⅛	31	5.19¼	25
5 Jul.	4.49¾	8	85 3/16	31	5.28¼	26
18 Jul.	4.85	0	85 5/32	31	5.70½	31
31 Jul.	4.48½	8	85 3/32	31	5.28	26
22 Aug.	4.50⅞	7	84 9/32	32	5.34	27
2 Oct.	4.78¾	2	78 23/32	37	6.08½	36
23 Oct.	4.62⅛	5	79 1/32	36	5.58	30
16 Nov.	5.52*	-13	82 13/32	34	6.71½*	42
1934						
31 Jan.	5.03 ½	-3	79 13/32	36	6.42	39
1935						
1 Jan.	4.94¼	-2	74 23/32	40	6.61⅞	41
1936						
2 Jan.	4.93	-1	74 29/32	40	6.61⅝	41
25 Sep.	5.01⅞	-3	76 19/32	38	6.58⅜	40
26 Sep.	4.97	-2	#	15	5.14~	24
28 Sep.	4.94½	-2	#		5.27	26
2 Oct.	4.93¼	-1	105 23/32		4.66¼	16

Note: Sterling/dollar and dollar/franc rates in New York; sterling/franc rates in London. All are closing rates with the exception of those marked *, indicating the daily high. The symbol # indicates not traded; ~ indicates nominal rate only.

their agreed plan of action. With wholesale commodity prices at last recovering, he refused to jeopardize this stimulus to the American economy by a *de facto* return to the gold standard. Indeed, he became convinced that the only beneficiaries of currency stabilization would be the international bankers, who, he believed, always favoured currency stability over economic growth.[350] Accordingly, he ignored the advice of Warburg, Woodin and Sprague, his banking and Treasury advisers, as well as the urgings of Britain and France. Twice more, his representatives in London helped to draft statements promising cooperation among the main creditor powers to contain the hot money movements and end the violent fluctuations in gold and currency prices. But every time reports circulated that the Western powers were moving towards an agreement on exchange rates, commodity prices fell back and Roosevelt dissociated himself from their work.

On 17 June, Roosevelt boarded a private yacht for a holiday off the Maine coast, and for a time was isolated by fog. He was thus unavailable when his advisers forwarded to him their second proposal for currency stabilization on 29 June. The long wait for his reply added to the uncertainty and intensified speculative activity in the foreign exchange markets. Georges Bonnet, head of the French delegation, became increasingly anxious when the Dutch florin, one of the few remaining gold standard currencies, faced a massive flight of capital and threatened to collapse. Britain, he believed, controlled the fate not only of the Conference but also of the gold countries themselves.[351] He therefore warned MacDonald and Chamberlain that if they joined the United States in currency depreciation, several of the gold countries would undergo 'irremediable catastrophes' and Europe itself would face 'monetary anarchy', which could scarcely fail to produce the most severe political, social and economic consequences.[352]

Chamberlain and his Treasury advisers were unwilling to stabilize sterling on a gold basis while wholesale price levels remained far below pre-slump levels and especially while American monetary policy remained obscure. But on 28 June, he cautiously agreed to take note of a declaration by the gold countries that 'the ultimate objective of monetary policy should be to restore, under proper conditions, an international standard based on gold', while adding that the timing of their return and the rate of exchange would be 'determined largely by the level of prices required to restore their internal equilibrium.'[353] On Saturday, 1 July, Bonnet, on the urging of his Dutch and Belgian colleagues, called representatives of the gold standard countries – Belgium, Italy, the Netherlands, Poland, Switzerland and France – to the suite of Professor Charles Rist at the Savoy Hotel, to consider means of coordinating the defence of their currencies. The following day they met again and agreed to form a Gold Bloc, sharing resources for intervention on the exchanges. Bonnet forwarded their proposal to Paris for approval.[354]

Roosevelt's long-awaited reply to the latest currency stabilization proposal was released in London on the morning of Monday, 3 July.[355] His 'bombshell message', as it immediately became known,[356] flatly rejected currency stabilization, which it described as a diversion from the important issues on the Conference agenda. The effect on the currency markets was immediate. From $4.36 = £1 at the opening, the dollar fell 13 cents or nearly 3 per cent against the pound before the end of the day and continued falling for the next six days, reaching a low of $4.85 on Monday, 10 July: a decline of over 11 per cent in a single week. The French franc was even worse affected (see Table 7.1). Between March and the opening of the Conference, the dollar had declined approximately 16 per cent against the franc. It fell further amidst the confusion over stabilization plans, and fell again after the bombshell message, reaching a discount of over 31 per cent by mid-July.

British and French leaders feared that Roosevelt's deliberate abandonment of gold and efforts to talk down the dollar would force the remaining countries off gold, with incalculable consequences for the whole world. His hectoring manner which accompanied his disruptive action added to their fury. They had come to the Conference prepared to support liberal international action. But in the absence of a currency agreement, they saw no prospect of progress on trade liberalization or other issues on the Conference agenda. Delegates from the gold standard countries demanded the immediate suspension of the Conference and sought to draw Britain to their side.[357] MacDonald, who had accepted the presidency of the Conference on the assumption that he could secure the cooperation of the Americans, felt so humiliated that he briefly sided with the gold country delegates.[358] Chamberlain was even more annoyed.[359] But while sympathizing with the plight of the gold countries and fearing the consequences if they were driven off the gold standard, he was not prepared to line up with them. Nor would he yield to pressure from the Dominions and India to side with the United States in a policy of active reflation.[360] Late on the same day as the 'bombshell message', delegates from the gold standard countries met again at the Savoy Hotel where they drafted a declaration confirming the formation of a 'Gold Bloc' for collective defence.[361] Evidence of their commitment to the gold standard reassured the markets, which had briefly threatened to get out of hand. Cordell Hull, the secretary of state and head of the American delegation, managed with difficulty to gain enough support to keep the Conference going.[362] But it merely limped along in a semi-moribund state and finally closed on 27 July in total discredit.[363]

Roosevelt had briefly given hope to the American farm, forestry and mining industries by encouraging inflationary expectations. But since his policies had done nothing to stimulate demand, indeed had discouraged new investment and dislocated international trade, the recovery in commodity prices threatened to be short-lived.[364] Among East Coast bankers, businessmen and liberal economists, opposition to Roosevelt's economic nationalism sharply increased.[365] Roosevelt, however, was delighted with the reaction to his 'bombshell message' in America's isolationist hinterland and dismissed his critics, whom he suspected of being in the pocket of Wall Street bankers.[366] Since it seemed to him that raising commodity prices was essential to recovery, he also brushed aside advice from his liberal aides and turned to two obscure economists, George Warren and James Harvey Rogers, who claimed that by bidding up the price of gold, the dollar could be further devalued and commodity prices raised.[367] Roosevelt signalled his intention to lower the price of the dollar in August. At his instigation, the Reconstruction Finance Corporation, an agency of the US Treasury, began on 25 October to buy new gold reaching the American market.

Roosevelt eventually became renowned as a statesman with a global vision and the ability to work effectively with foreign powers. Yet in 1933, his outlook was still that of a typical American isolationist. Warned that his deliberate depreciation of the dollar threatened to drive the French franc off the gold standard and create chaos, his response was one of complete indifference. To him, France was the exemplar of 'old Europe': an imperialist power that had gorged itself on the world's gold and deserved taking down a peg or two.[368] As for Britain, he appreciated its culture and political institutions, but he shared the isolationists' belief that it was dominated by the bankers of the City. In his view, they were an aggressive, manipulative, imperialist clique who had created the Exchange Equalization Account in 1932 artificially to reduce the value of sterling and undercut American goods in world markets. By this reasoning, the massive increase in the Account's resources in 1933 constituted an assault on America rather than a means of cushioning sterling against violent short-term financial movements, the official rationale for its introduction. Roosevelt thus believed he had turned the tables on Britain by taking the dollar off the gold standard. Having done so, he did not intend to return to gold or stabilize the dollar unless Britain stabilized the pound at the same time. Otherwise, he suspected, the British authorities would hang back and gain a new exchange advantage at the expense of America's exporters.[369]

To test his hypothesis, Roosevelt requested Governor Harrison of the New York Fed in late November to propose a joint stabilization scheme to Norman. Chamberlain, his Treasury advisers and Norman himself were anxious for a currency arrangement of some sort, but they remembered the 1925 when Britain had returned to the gold standard only to find itself struggling to adjust to declining wholesale price levels and an overvalued exchange rate. They therefore refused to consider stabilization without an American commitment to price stability and time to assess the impact of recent monetary experiments.[370] Roosevelt seized on Norman's rejection of Harrison's offer as proof of the City's predatory character.[371] He resumed his unilateral gold-buying policy, to drive down the dollar and drive up world commodity prices.[372]

On 31 January 1934, Roosevelt signed the Gold Reserve Act, formally re-establishing a fixed gold/dollar rate of $35 = 1 oz of gold. But this fell far short of returning to the gold standard. In the first place, private purchases of gold were not permitted; second, the Federal Reserve's gold was henceforth to be used only for foreign payments. The link between the central bank's gold reserves and domestic credit thus remained severed. Before stabilizing the dollar, moreover, Roosevelt appointed Henry Morgenthau Jr secretary of the Treasury in place of Woodin, whose health had given way. Morgenthau, a friend of Roosevelt's and neighbour from upstate New York, was closer to the economic nationalists within the president's 'brains trust', and his appointment confirmed the shift in the locus of central bank policy-making from New York to Washington. Roosevelt also secured Congressional approval to create an exchange equalization fund, modelled on the British fund and using $2 billion gained from the devaluation of the dollar, as a protection against international pressures.[373]

Roosevelt's deliberate depreciation of the dollar probably contributed to the recovery of the American economy which began in 1933 and continued at nearly 10 per cent a year until the recession of 1937. The recovery, however, started from a very low base and remained incomplete, largely because the currency manipulation of 1933 damaged confidence among American wealth-holders as well as further dislocating international monetary and economic relations. To many well-to-do Americans who feared the loss of their savings and investments as well as bankers and economists still wedded to liberal economics, Roosevelt's actions had been those of a revolutionary or madman. Walter Stewart, the economist with the New York Fed, as well as James Warburg, the banker, described him as mentally ill and too dangerous to be trusted.[374] The prevalence of this attitude contributed to low levels of investment in America for the balance of the decade and high liquidity among deposit banks.[375] Abroad, Roosevelt's actions placed acute strain upon monetary relations in every direction. Predictions of currency chaos and total economic collapse proved to be excessive. But the consequences were serious enough.

British bankers and Treasury experts sympathized with Roosevelt's objective of raising price levels. But they deplored his unilateral currency manipulation which threatened to drive the last remaining countries off the gold standard and leave international monetary relations in chaos. They therefore held back from any commitments on exchange rates, while minimizing the impact of the dollar's gyrations on the British economy by leaving the pound to float.[376] But even then the pound rose well above the old gold parity of $4.86 ¾. Treasury experts estimated that at $5.03, where the pound stood after Roosevelt halted his gold-buying experiment, it was at least 14 per cent above the equilibrium rate of exchange.[377] They also found themselves confronting acute problems in their currency relations with other countries. India, Canada and other British Dominions, whose economies depended upon commodity exports, were anxious to devalue their currencies as far and as fast as the US dollar.[378] This did not appeal to the British Treasury or City bankers because of the adverse effect upon investments denominated in sterling and the reputation of the City as well as the threat it posed to the stability of the countries still on gold. Norman, Chamberlain and his Treasury advisers were thus left deeply frustrated by Roosevelt's policy, which endangered the unity of the British Empire and undermined international monetary relations. In Leith-Ross's words, it was 'a policy financial[ly] speaking of murder and suicide, in which we could scarcely be asked to co-operate.'[379]

However, if Roosevelt's deliberate depreciation of the dollar discomfited Britain, the predicament it created for France was much more serious (see Table 7.1). In November 1933, Roosevelt's actions drove the dollar nearly 42 per cent below its former parity with the franc. On 31 January 1934, the day after the adoption of the Gold Reserve Act, which formally devalued the dollar, the discount was still 39 per cent. In view of the fact that the United States enjoyed a substantial current account surplus – indeed the surplus in 1933 was considerably greater than in 1932 or 1931[380] – whereas France's current account was already in deficit and rapidly worsening,[381] this was a grotesque and unsustainable situation.

7.6   France: Depressed, disarmed, demoralized, 1932–4

7.6.1   Conflicts with the Anglo-Saxon powers over gold and debts

As late as 1931, French statesmen remained hopeful that the world economic slump, if it did not strengthen their hand in international affairs, would at least not weaken it. By their lights, France had not made the mistake of the Anglo-Saxon powers since the war of lending profligately to Germany or elsewhere. Nor had the French domestic economy, unlike that of Britain or Germany, been excessively industrialized, but remained soundly balanced between industry and agriculture, making it largely invulnerable to world market forces. Equally important, the franc was on a firm footing, backed by gold almost equal to the currency in circulation and seemingly beyond challenge. On 2 January 1932, the Bank of France's gold reserves stood at $2695 million or £805.5 million at the current exchange rate, up from $2118 million or £632 million a year before: 32.4 per cent of the total reserves of the world's eleven leading central banks; and in addition to gold, the Bank also held large foreign exchange reserves.[382] The massive reserves sustained confidence in the franc. This was reflected in the price of government bonds or *rentes*, which, having slumped to 44 in the 1926 financial crisis, stood at nearly 90 in 1932.[383]

From the autumn of 1931, however, the comfortable assumption that France was an *île heureuse*, insulated from the economic storm lashing the rest of the world, was undermined by sharply declining price levels, economic activity and public revenues, and by soaring unemployment. At another time, France might have reduced the burden of adjustment by devaluing the franc or like Britain abandoning a fixed exchange rate altogether and allowing the franc to find its own equilibrium rate. But in 1931, these options were not available to France's political leadership.[384] Barely five years earlier, the experience of inflation, currency depreciation and devaluation had caused so much frustration as to threaten serious civil unrest. The middle classes felt cheated by the erosion of their savings. The working classes felt similarly ill-treated since their wages seemed never to keep up with rising prices. Now, with the economy in decline and hoarding on the increase, the same political divisions were reappearing. If this was not deterrent enough, the growing menace of Germany made a strong, stable currency seem an essential underpinning for national security. A succession of governments therefore chose to cling on to the gold standard. As revenues diminished and the budget deficit increased, they raised consumption taxes and reduced spending on welfare and defence. But this merely aggravated unemployment and increased social tensions, which contributed to the rise of hoarding. Meanwhile the overvalued exchange rate damaged trade, worsening the already serious current account deficit. Despite their general preference for liberal international economic policies, French governments saw no alternative but greater protectionism. This in turn brought protests and eventually retaliation from Britain. France's cautious monetary and financial policy, so far from strengthening national security, thus proved an economic straightjacket and damaged relations with friends and foe alike.

French political leaders had hoped that their credits to the Bank of England and the British government during the run on the pound in the summer of 1931 would earn them some gratitude in London and strengthen the *Entente*. In the event, they received only grudging thanks and no compensation when exchange losses on their sterling credits threatened to bankrupt the Bank of France. While the politicians refrained from comment, the conservative press in Paris angrily criticized British behaviour.[385] French frustration over this episode was nothing, however, compared to feelings aroused by the inter-governmental debt issue. President Hoover's call for a moratorium on inter-governmental debt payments struck French observers as a narrowly self-serving initiative taken to save American investors who had unwisely lent huge amounts to Germany. The danger, as they correctly anticipated, was that once Germany was relieved of its contractual obligation to pay reparations, it would refuse to resume payments when the moratorium ended and tempt them towards further Treaty revision. France accepted the moratorium in the interests of solidarity with the Anglo-Saxon powers. And in October 1931, Laval obtained, or believed he obtained, Hoover's assurance of cooperation if Europe took the initiative in settling the inter-governmental debt problem. But in January 1932, Bruening declared that Germany would not resume reparation payments when the moratorium ended in June.

French statesmen were further annoyed when Hoover sought to make disarmament a condition of any American concession on war debts. To be asked to compromise national security in return for concessions that French leaders believed America already owed the international community seemed grossly unreasonable. All the same, France attended the Lausanne conference in the summer of 1932 where MacDonald once again dangled before Herriot the hope of a strengthened *Entente* in the form of a bilateral *accord de confiance* and a common approach to Washington for a final settlement of the war debt issue. Herriot, encouraged to think that both the Anglo-Saxon powers were prepared to write off war debts, agreed to abandon reparations except for one final payment from Germany. Barely a week after the conference, Britain signalled a retreat when Simon denied in Parliament that the *accord* in any way committed Britain to a common policy with France on war debts to the United States. Yet until a fortnight after the US presidential election in November 1932, French leaders continued to hope that if Britain spoke for all the debtors, Washington might suspend the 15 December payment demand in anticipation of a final settlement.[386]

Reports that Hoover and Roosevelt had met on 22 November, but failed to agree on suspending war debts, put Herriot in a quandary.[387] On the one hand, his advisers were emphatic that France must continue debt payments, since the amount was small – a mere $19,261,437 (481 million francs), one-fifth the amount ($95,950,000) Britain owed on the same date[388] – and failure to pay would jeopardize access to the American capital market, which would be vitally important in the event of another war.[389] It might also trigger a flight of US capital from Europe, bringing the Continent to its knees.[390] On the other hand, French political opinion overwhelmingly opposed any further payment to the United States. Lord Tyrrell, the British ambassador, doubted that Herriot would obtain 15 votes from the over 600 deputies in the Chamber, unless he could assure them that this was absolutely the last payment.[391] 'There is a strong feeling in the Chamber that France has been tricked; that America having led Europe on to believe that if reparations and European war debts were first settled she would do her part in a general clean-up, has now backed out.'[392]

Tyrrell, who met Herriot on 1 December, found him 'profoundly discouraged by the American response to his own advance at Lausanne where he did his utmost to give effect to American advice.'[393] Given the mood in France, Herriot could see no way forward. Yet he was more suspicious of Germany than ever. Since his first premiership six years earlier, nothing had altered his belief that France's fate rested with the Franco-British *Entente* and US friendship. Now that General Schleicher occupied the chancellor's office while Hitler hovered just outside, Herriot was desperate to keep in with the Anglo-Saxon powers.[394] On Thursday, 5 December, therefore, he appealed to London to take no decision on payment before they could discuss options together.[395] Meanwhile he made one further appeal to Washington.

Writing to Stimson, Herriot reminded him of France's efforts at cooperation. It was the United States that had linked war debts with reparations by requesting them both to be suspended under the Hoover moratorium. France had accepted the moratorium and taken Hoover at his word when he assured Laval during his visit to Washington in October 1931 that if Europe took the lead on debt revision by tackling reparations, America would do the right thing on war debts. This was exactly what he, Herriot, had done at Lausanne. Herriot also reminded Stimson of the warning from the international bankers at Bâle, including a prominent American, that large financial transfers unaccompanied by counterpart trade or investment were bound to be destabilizing. This was surely the case with war debt payments, and especially so since the United States still enjoyed a large current account surplus with Europe. Since the Lausanne conference, signs had appeared of a recovery in the world economy, which were bound to be stifled if America did not contribute to the settlement of the inter-governmental debt problem. Surely Washington was not indifferent to the consequences of intensifying the crisis? Herriot also reminded Stimson that America relied upon France to maintain order in Europe. France had done so since American institutions began pulling their money out of Europe in 1930, by lending to Germany, Austria, Hungary and other countries. It was also trying to keep Germany in check. Could Stimson not see that American disregard for France's efforts would undermine its commitment?[396]

Washington showed no appreciation of Herriot's argument, but London's response encouraged him. As de Fleuriau, the ambassador in London, warned they would do, the British Cabinet on 6 December decided to make a further war debt payment on 15 December.[397] MacDonald and Simon preferred simply to go ahead without regard for France, claiming that Britain was not committed to consultation but merely 'keeping in touch and exchanging views.'[398] Chamberlain, however, was extremely anxious to avoid the unravelling of the Lausanne settlement, fearing this would mean confrontation with Germany and a potentially uncontrollable financial crisis.[399] He therefore insisted they should assue Herriot that, despite making a further payment to the United States, Britain would not reopen the Lausanne settlement by demanding the resumption of French war debt payments.[400] He and MacDonald also promised to visit Paris on Saturday, 8 December.

At the Cabinet meeting on Friday, Herriot found his colleagues disturbed by Britain's decision to resume payments to America, which seemed contrary to the *accord de confiance*, and strongly opposed to a further French payment. With difficulty he parried their complaints. Britain, in its recent diplomatic exchanges, he pointed out, had never sought special treatment from the United States and had behaved with complete loyalty to France. Eventually he persuaded them to leave the decision on a further payment until after his conversation with British ministers.[401]

As expected, MacDonald and Chamberlain, who did most of the talking when they met the following morning at the British embassy, encouraged Herriot to hope that if only they could remain united on 15 December, the *Entente* would be restored.[402] Herriot expressed his frustration with American behaviour.

> France [he said] would not take lessons in morality from a people like the United States, which abandoned their obligations such as Versailles, which they had signed. ... If [France] revolted against America, it was because Mr. Hoover, who had tried to make France accept a moratorium in three days, now treated her like this. Mr. Hoover sheltered himself behind the Monroe Doctrine; and when he wanted something from Europe he treated Europe as though she were a colony, and as though the Europeans were negroes. ... [But] it would be a disaster for civilisation and humanity if America succeeded, in what was a question of money, in dissociating the two countries [Britain and France].[403]

Such was his relief at finding Britain keen to cooperate that he determined upon payment.

News that British ministers were coming to Paris had attracted great interest in France. From the tone of the French press and soundings in political circles, Tyrrell was hopeful that evidence of Franco-British solidarity would enable Herriot to secure Parliamentary acceptance of his policy.[404] But once it became known that Britain intended to pay America, Herriot could not persuade the Parliamentary Finance and Foreign Affairs Commissions to approve a further payment without stating that it was conditional upon negotiations for a final settlement.[405] With his own Cabinet colleagues taking the same view, Herriot had no choice but to accept the principle of 'payment under reserves'.[406] Unfortunately for him, the British note of 11 December requesting an assurance that the United States would participate in a final settlement evoked a stern warning from Washington that it would accept no payment if any conditions were attached. Until then, observers believed that Herriot had a reasonable chance of getting his way in Parliament. News of the American reply markedly hardened French opinion against further payment.[407]

At 3 p.m. on Wednesday 12 December, Herriot opened the debate in the Chamber on war debts by urging deputies to recognize the implications for French security of the 15 December payment. Non-payment would isolate France from Britain and the United States, and encourage the revisionists in Germany.

Payment on the other hand would encourage the Anglo-Saxon powers to share in the containment of Germany. 'Respect for signature given was the French defence against Germany. It was the French hope of peace. The honour of France was to defend the laws of political morality.'[408] But by the evening of 13 December, when the debate resumed, the American reply to the British note had become public knowledge. British and American statesmen, certain that France would default unless they acted, hastily sent assurances to Herriot that they remained interested in a final settlement.[409] This however was not the firm commitment demanded by the French Parliamentary Commissions. Right-wing deputies charged Britain with betraying France by agreeing to make payment to the United States, and accused Herriot of 'following in the wake of England.'[410] Meanwhile outside the Chamber of Deputies at the Palais Bourbon, police detachments were barely able to control the demonstrators comprising largely of members of the war veterans associations and the extreme right-wing *Action Française* and its student supporters. Herriot wound up the debate at 5 a.m. on the 14th with a powerful and moving speech in which he stressed and re-stressed the security implications of payment. But whereas Léon Blum, leader of the Socialist Party, and Paul Reynaud, a leading centre-right deputy, were prepared to endorse payment on security grounds, Herriot failed to carry even his own ministers. The government motion was defeated by a margin of 402 to 187 with 17 abstentions.[411]

Herriot, frustrated at the outcome and furious with colleagues for refusing to support his call for payment, immediately resigned. Joseph Paul-Boncour, a Radical colleague, agreed to form a new government. Equally worried at the security implications of France's default, Paul-Boncour took the unprecedented step of calling at the US embassy even before obtaining parliamentary approval for his government, to appeal for help in securing parliamentary approval for a further debt payment.[412] Along with Herriot, Blum, Reynaud and all the government advisers who favoured payment, he had good reason to be disturbed at France's predicament. On 15 December, the day Britain paid its war debt instalment and France defaulted, the foreign exchanges turned decisively against the franc and for the first time since 1926 the Bank of France lost gold. Other gold currencies, notably the Swiss franc, also betrayed uncommon weakness.[413] Hitler was now just six weeks away from becoming chancellor of Germany. Although Paul-Boncour left the American embassy empty-handed, French statesmen were not prepared to acquiesce in their country's isolation.

Over the next three years, France's relations with the Anglo-Saxon powers declined further, reaching an interwar nadir in 1934. But in the spring of 1933, a sort of false dawn occurred when it seemed that Britain and France might be able to work constructively with the new Democratic administration in Washington. Already in January, Chamberlain seemed again prepared to take drastic action to uphold the Lausanne settlement, including opposition to any further war debt payment to the United States and postponing the World Economic Conference until a final settlement was reached.[414] In a speech directed at the United States that month, he bluntly warned Americans – 'without using threats' – that further debt payments would only hurt their own trade by obliging European debtors to depreciate their currencies, export more to America or increase import restrictions. Any debt settlement, he added, must be final and modest enough to avoid the need for renewed claims on Germany.[415] A few weeks later, Roosevelt went out of his way to assure Ambassador Claudel that he wanted closer relations with France and Britain when he became president. In an obvious allusion to Japan and Germany, he observed that the world was now divided between 'the forces of greed and destruction' and the forces of 'conciliation and stabilisation', led by the three great democratic powers. To reconcile the differences that had arisen between the latter powers, he promised to seek an early settlement of the war debt problem. The Hoover administration had been too 'hasty' in its treatment of France, he declared; 'in his opinion, there had been no default on [France's] part, only delay.'[416]

Shortly after taking office in March, Roosevelt followed up his commitment by inviting a leading French statesman to visit Washington for talks on war debts, the forthcoming World Economic Conference and other subjects; and when Daladier, the new premier, was unable to go, Roosevelt welcomed the choice of Herriot who had demonstrated his good will on the debt issue.[417] Visiting Paris on 10 March, MacDonald assured Daladier that he could trust Britain to work on France's behalf in negotiations with Washington on a debt settlement.[418] Speaking with Bonnet the following week, Chamberlain disputed his prediction that Roosevelt would soon float the dollar and swept aside his proposal of a large tripartite fund to assist currency stabilization. Yet he did not dissent when Bonnet affirmed that the key to economic recovery was 'the need of confidence and the monetary problems, including the gold standard.' Indeed, he appeared to endorse this view by agreeing to ask Norman to initiate conversations with Moret of the Bank of France on the technical arrangements for 'the new gold standard'.[419]

The implication that Britain was prepared to return to the gold standard hugely encouraged Bonnet and his colleagues.[420] Since Britain had left gold in 1931, over forty other countries had followed in its wake, leaving the French franc increasingly overvalued. Moreover, much of the grassroots pressure on Roosevelt to take the dollar off the gold standard arose from the conviction that Britain was gaining an unfair advantage in trade by depreciating sterling. If, as French statesmen thought likely, Roosevelt yielded to the pressure, the franc and with it French commerce would be gravely affected. When, therefore, Roosevelt abandoned the gold standard and allowed the dollar to float on 18 April, they were dismayed and angry. By their lights this was a dangerously irresponsible act with no economic justification, which however might be the prelude to Britain returning to the gold standard.

Herriot, who arrived in America days later, was disappointed to find Roosevelt unwilling to approach Congress for a settlement of the war debt issue unless France first paid at least part of the 'deferred' December obligation, which Herriot knew to be unacceptable to the Chamber of Deputies.[421] On the currency question, however, the Americans encouraged him to believe that the United States had only temporarily abandoned the gold standard, to persuade Britain to return to it. Roosevelt expressed a wish to have tripartite conversations on currency stabilization, although not in New York or with a representative of the New York Federal Reserve Bank.[422] Herriot, more concerned with France's security than monetary or financial issues, was even more pleased to find Roosevelt interested in European affairs and friendly towards France. Roosevelt made no commitment, of course. In the words of Pertinax, pen name of the conservative journalist, André Giraud, who accompanied Herriot to Washington, Roosevelt offered merely 'atmospheric security'. All the same, as Sir Ronald Lindsay suggested, Herriot's visit 'may have done something to counter-act the anti-French prejudice which has been latent for so long in this country.'[423]

French statesmen, inured to the professionalism of European great power diplomacy, signally failed to grasp that Roosevelt, preoccupied with domestic politics, would wilfully encourage irresponsible initiatives or leave economic internationalists and nationalists in his entourage to fight it out for influence within the first New Deal. Since Woodin, the secretary of the Treasury, Hull, the secretary of state, and the president himself seemed to support currency stabilization talks, French statesmen expected to secure at least a temporary agreement. On 12 June, the World Economic Conference began in London, three days before the deadline for payment of another instalment of war debts. Despite French appeals to unite against further payment, Chamberlain again backed down when Roosevelt agreed to accept a token $10 million (£2.4 million) payment.[424] That same day experts in London initialled a tripartite agreement on stabilizing currencies for the duration of the conference, and sent it to Washington for Roosevelt's approval.[425] When he rejected it on the 22nd, Bonnet, head of the French delegation, impatiently requested Chamberlain to come off the fence and side with the countries still clinging to gold, by confirming Britain's commitment to a fixed exchange rate regime.[426]

Over the following ten days, Roosevelt's inscrutable behaviour and Britain's ambiguous posture contributed to a speculative run on the florin and pressure on all the gold currencies. This led to angry comments in the Paris press. Marcel Pays in *Excelsior* urged Bonnet to persuade his British colleagues to abjure the chimera of inflation and join the countries that 'do not seek to commit suicide'. Pertinax in *l'Echo de Paris* similarly complained of Britain's support for inflation, presenting it as a deliberate attack on France: 'At Geneva they are trying to disarm us; at London they are trying to take away our financial power.' In almost identical language, Albert Julien in *Le Petit Parisien*, Lucien Romier in *Paris Soir* and the special correspondent of the *Journal des Débats*, a paper now controlled by de Wendel, the steel magnate, asserted that the fate of the conference and the future of international monetary stability itself rested in Britain's hands. On 30 June, *Figaro*'s correspondent in London gloomily warned readers to expect nothing from MacDonald: 'For him, fear of Uncle Sam is the beginning of wisdom.' Emile Buré in *l'Ordre* expressed equal cynicism: 'What can we expect from a government led by Ramsay MacDonald, vague, nebulous, in the service of the *Wilhelmstrasse?*'[427]

Roosevelt's 'bombshell' message, denouncing the very idea of currency stabilization, further hardened opposition to the policy of the Anglo-Saxon powers. Tardieu, the former premier, warned in *La Liberté*: 'If Europe, led by England, which does not know how to say no to America, allows itself to yield, it will succumb to the greatest dislocation (*ébranlement*) it has ever known.'[428] Reynaud, who had recently broken ranks to urge that France should join the Anglo-Saxon powers in a policy of devaluation and price reflation, wrote in *La Liberté* deploring 'the opening of the monetary war' that 'divided the world into two camps.'[429] Some journals called on Bonnet to leave the conference immediately and return to Paris. They were relieved to report the meeting of delegates from the gold countries at the Savoy Hotel and their declaration on the formation of the Gold Bloc.[430] Temporarily, speculation against their currencies ceased and short-term interest rates eased slightly in Paris. But as the foreign exchange dealers in London and elsewhere appreciated, Gold Bloc central bankers had no weapon against the serious overvaluation of their currencies. They could raise interest rates and restrict credit, and their governments could take unilateral domestic action (retrenchment) or unilateral external action (tariff increases, quantitative trade controls, embargoes on foreign lending). But with the dollar trading at a discount of 22 per cent against the franc on 1 July and 31 per cent before the end of the month, and sterling declining alongside it, the gold currencies were almost bound to remain overvalued, no matter how rigorous their unilateral action.[431] Sooner or later they would be forced to devalue. Meanwhile their deflationary measures would inflict upon them a 'slow suicide', as Reynaud warned, undermining their domestic political and social stability and further weakening their national security.[432]

For five years after Poincaré's return to office in 1926, French governments had enjoyed the fruits of national prosperity, with each year's budget ending in surplus and the Treasury accumulating 19 billion francs (£153 million) by 1930. By the autumn of 1931, however, the prevailing winds had decisively shifted. Nominally the budget remained balanced. But extra expenditure for defence and social provision had been levied against the Treasury surplus, which all but disappeared, and the national accounts faced a 5 billion franc deficit in the absence of government action.[433] Conventional economic wisdom throughout the capitalist world assumed that markets instantly cleared and that budget deficits inevitably meant inflation, the loss of international competitiveness and ultimately the destruction of the currency. Accordingly, the Laval government, in an initiative the *Economist* described as 'heroic', undertook to reduce spending by 3 billion francs (£24.6 million) and to raise new income through import duties and other taxes.[434] But as in Germany in 1930 and Britain in 1931, the deflationary effect of France's commitment to a balanced budget increased unemployment and reduced tax revenue. This in turn aggravated divisions within society, which threatened to undermine democratic government. To make matters worse, the increased trade protectionism and reductions in defence spending had the doubly subversive effect of antagonizing friends and encouraging enemies.

Herriot, who formed the first government after the May 1932 election, reduced expenditure by a further 2 billion francs of which 1485 million francs (£16.2 million) came from defence. A large loan conversion operation in September reduced debt service costs by 1407 million francs and briefly eased the fiscal pressure. But government bonds had already lost four-fifths of their value in the wartime and postwar inflation, and the middle classes were angered by the loss of revenue.[435] Moreover, the fiscal deficit had re-emerged to dog the government before it fell in December 1932.[436] Herriot's successor and fellow Radical, Paul-Boncour, shared his fears of Germany, especially with Hitler on the verge of taking power, and sought to resume war debt payments to maintain solidarity with the Anglo-Saxon powers. Despite his fears and despite resisting Anglo-Saxon pressure for concessions to Germany on disarmament, however, he could not ignore the deficit, now estimated at 10,541 million francs (£124 million) or fully 20 per cent of planned expenditure. He sought to address it by means of 5241 million francs in higher income tax and import duties, and 5300 million francs in economies, including 638 million francs (£7.5 million) from defence: a 5 per cent reduction in defence spending on top of the 5 per cent across-the-board reduction in departmental allocations and the special reduction of 1485 million francs (11 per cent) inflicted by Herriot in respect to the 1933 budget.[437] But the Radicals did not command a majority in Parliament, and whereas the Socialists opposed reductions in public sector wages while urging greater reductions in defence, nationalists on the right of the Chamber loudly opposed tax increases. Attacked from both sides, the government was defeated at 6 a.m. on 28 January 1933, after a furious 24-hour debate.[438]

That same day a group calling itself the Committee for the Defence of Taxpayers convened a well-attended meeting at the Magic City dance-hall in Paris, and on 30 January another group, the Committee for Economic Salvation, convened an even larger gathering at the *Salle Wagram*. In each case the purpose was to demonstrate the fear and anger of the middle classes at the spectre of runaway budget deficits, inflation and the destruction of savings. Speakers denounced politicians and Parliament, and called on supporters to demonstrate outside the *Palais Bourbon* where the cry went up: '*Plus d'impôts, plus un sou; plus de parlement; plus de députés; dictature; dissolution.*'[439]

Daladier, who formed a government on 31 January, faced an acute budget crisis the day he took office. To address it, he made minor concessions to the Socialists while retaining the tax increases and most of the defence cuts. Since this still did not balance the Treasury's books, he conjured away the problem by adopting more optimistic assumptions about revenue in the coming year. The Chamber eventually approved the new finance bill on 1 March, but at the cost of rifts within the Socialist and the Radical parties as well as tensions between the Chamber and the more conservative Senate.[440] In April, the government negotiated a three-month £30 million credit from a consortium of British banks led by Lazard Brothers, with an option to renew for another three months.[441] But any hopes that this would stem the outflow of gold from France, which had begun in December, were dashed by the depreciation of the dollar and the turmoil over currency stabilization. Between 1 January and 31 March 1933, the Bank of France lost 2.5 billion francs (£29.4 million at £1/85 francs) in gold reserves. With the United States' departure from gold, the Bank suffered further losses to London, but gained an equivalent amount from Holland and Switzerland which now experienced severe exchange crises. In the first week of July, the French franc came under renewed pressure.[442] Meanwhile private hoarding sharply increased, and *rentes*, having reached a high of 90 in June, slid to 63 by February 1934. For almost everyone in France, the second half of 1933 was a time of mounting desperation.

Since June 1932, Radical governments had succeeded in reducing public expenditure by 7 billion francs (£80 million) or fully 15 per cent, which was greater than the reductions imposed by Britain's National government in the financial crisis of 1931. But as the slump worsened, so the French deficit continued to grow. Conservative critics in the Chamber and the press constantly attacked the Radicals for the collapse of the franc in 1926: proof, they claimed, that the Radicals could not be trusted to govern now. Daladier asserted his commitment to fiscal orthodoxy at the party conference at Vichy in October 1933, when he promised to eliminate the deficit. But the Socialists, whom the Radicals counted on to support their finance bill, rejected the proposed 6 per cent reduction in public sector wages. On 24 October, with the *Palais Bourbon* surrounded by angry demonstrators and 'virtually in a state of seige', the Daladier government fell after a tumultuous, ill-tempered debate.[443]

Camille Chautemps, another Radical, soon formed a government, and in December he secured parliamentary approval of a finance bill that in theory removed the deficit.[444] But this was a short-lived success, for the slump worsened, gold hoarding increased, the reserves of the Bank of France declined and the market for *rentes* – the clearest measure of unease among the middle classes – remained severely depressed. Between 1 September and 1 December 1933, the Bank lost 4905 million francs in gold. It lost a further 414 million francs in December and 2756 million francs in the first two months of 1934: a total of 8075 million francs (£97 million) in six months. By now *rentes* had fallen to the point where the government could not hope to issue a long-term loan, and commercial banks in Paris and London were reluctant to purchase the *bons de défense* and treasury bills the Ministry of Finance issued each month to cover the shortfall in its revenue.[445] French journalists aggravated the crisis by claiming that Britain was deliberately bearing the franc.[446] Hoarding increased, and in the midst of the financial crisis, the Stavisky affair, a political-financial scandal of extraordinary proportions, disrupted parliamentary government and further damaged business confidence.

Serge Stavisky, a naturalized Russian-born Jew, had issued several series of commercial bonds on a false prospectus in the 1920s which had passed unnoticed while the French economy was booming. But from 1930, he had found it impossible to cover redemptions with new loans and was charged with fraud. His success in securing no less than nineteen delays in his trial date, along with photos depicting him in the company of certain Radical politicians, fed rumours that he was being protected by men in high office. On the run, the police located him at his villa in Chamonix where on 8 January 1934 he allegedly took his own life before he could be arrested. This immediately gave rise to further rumours that the police had shot him to cover up for the politicians.[447] At other times, unsupported allegations of this sort might not have mattered. But in the already tense atmosphere in the winter of 1933 conservative observers seized upon them as proof that the Radicals were not merely incompetent but corrupt and leading the country to ruin. Joseph Garat, a Radical deputy and mayor of Bayonne, had been complicit in Stavisky's fraud. Albert Dalimier, the minister of colonies, was known to have recommended Stavisky's bonds to investors, and Georges Pressard, head of the Paris Parquet, which had delayed Stavisky's prosecution, was Camille Chautemps' brother-in-law. Philippe Henriot, a member of Louis Marin's right-wing parliamentary group, on 18 January 1934 also accused Georges Bonnet, minister of finance, of an association with Stavisky. Lord Tyrrell seemed more than half persuaded. As he reported to London:

> M. Bonnet rose at once to defend himself amid scenes of great excitement. He admitted somewhat lamely that it was possible that he had seen Stavisky at Stresa, but he declared that [Stavisky] had not had any relation with the French delegation. ... M. Bonnet's defence was extremely weak and unconvincing, whilst the implication of so many other Ministers in previous affairs made a deep impression. ... The worst feature of the situation is the general popular belief that all parties and almost all Ministers are equally compromised by this and previous financial scandals.[448]

The Stavisky affair coincided with an equally ominous development in America. This was the passage through Congress of a bill sponsored by the isolationist California senator, Hiram Johnson, to punish France and other war debt defaulters by excluding them from borrowing or raising capital in American financial markets. In December 1933, as yet another debt payment date passed, Lindsay reported from Washington that the US Administration was not publicizing their continued default, but nonetheless maintained its 'steady but relentless pressure' for a settlement. His French and Belgian colleagues were 'extremely uncomfortable' and longed for some means of resolving the dispute.[449] Their discomfort increased in the New Year when the Administration, having hitherto remained silent on the Johnson bill, indicated its cautious support.[450] The bill, with minor amendments proposed by the State Department, received Senate approval on 1 February 1934. Lindsay protested against the bill, which appeared to rule out further token payments.[451]

In London, government ministers, their advisers and much of the business community betrayed deep resentment at Roosevelt, whom they had counted on to adopt an internationalist stand and who instead had embarked upon a reckless monetary experiment, acquiesced in the Johnson bill, and now turned his back on the debt problem.[452] When the US attorney general confirmed that another token payment would put Britain in default, they therefore determined at once to cease payments.[453] Chamberlain still worried about the effect upon British credit. But his deeply orthodox sensibility was so affronted by Roosevelt's off-handed approach to policy that he yielded to the advice of Treasury officials and colleagues.[454] Despite Lindsay's repeated appeals to continue war debts for the sake of American friendship, they seemed unconcerned by the consequences of defaulting.[455] Britain owed $85.7 million (£18 million) on 15 June and its outstanding debt to the United States stood at $4.8 billion, $500 million more than it had originally borrowed to pay for the war.[456] But since they did not anticipate another war in the foreseeable future, they did not regret losing access to American financial markets. 'My hope is that it [the Johnson bill] will become law – & with any luck, even in a still more foolish form', Sir Warren Fisher, the permanent secretary of the Treasury, commented to Leith-Ross.[457] Vansittart at the Foreign Office seemed equally unconcerned. 'Senator Johnson may, for the first and last time in his life, prove a blessing in disguise', he scornfully commented in April 1934.[458] With Hitler in power in Germany and practically all opposition suppressed, some of Vansittart's colleagues betrayed a flickering of concern, but they made no protest against default.[459]

It was a different story in Paris. There, expectations of another war made access to American markets a much more acute issue. Since 1932, Claudel, the ambassador in Washington, had urged ministers to follow Britain's example and make token payments. Herriot, Paul-Boncour and other Radical leaders agreed in principle, and when Herriot joined the Doumergue government of national concentration in the aftermath of the Stavisky affair in February 1934, he evidently made it a condition that the government should attempt to remove the charge of default, through a token payment or other means.[460] In May, with the Cabinet still divided, rumours circulated that France would resume war debt payments to the United States. The leading ex-servicemen's association immediately placarded Paris with posters denouncing this 'surrender'.[461] Facing certain trouble in Parliament and on the streets over any concession, ministers were relieved to learn in June that Britain would cease war debt payments altogether. This at least realigned Britain and France on the debt issue.[462] But it meant that they were both further estranged from the United States. Meanwhile, other differences between Britain and France ruled out any revival of the *Entente*.

7.6.2 Conflicts with Britain over trade and commerce

Not once since the end of the war had French political leaders ever lost sight of the importance of retaining Britain's friendship in the interests of national security. But with the onset of the world slump, economic disputes with Britain multiplied. Solutions became hard to find because ministers in both countries became intensely preoccupied with domestic affairs. They were also handicapped by the structure of government, which in both countries had been shaped by the long ascendancy of liberal doctrine. Thus, economic issues remained the preserve of economic ministries whose remit was essentially to hold the ring for private investment and consumption, and which resisted the subordination of economic policy to the broader concept of national interest advanced by the foreign ministries. Britain bore responsibility for some of the disputes that arose, France for others. But because British political leaders placed far less value on Franco-British friendship than their French counterparts, they were prepared to intensify the disputes until the French felt obliged to yield.

Until the summer of 1931, Franco-British commercial relations remained stable, though viewed very differently from opposite sides of the Channel. Britain was France's largest customer, absorbing £55.1 million or nearly 18 per cent of its exports in 1930 as well as providing approximately £30 million per annum in invisible exports mainly from tourism.[463] The secretary of the British Chamber of Commerce in Paris claimed that Britain offered France 'virtually an open door for her goods', for which it deserved special treatment. 'If we are to continue to keep it open, why not have something for it?'[464] France, in contrast, imported only £29.7 million of British goods and £14.5 million of British re-exports or 9.2 per cent of British export trade.[465] Moreover, France levied duties on the bulk of goods from Britain. British businessmen and Board of Trade officials thus regarded it as a one-sided relationship in which protectionist France took advantage of Britain's liberal commercial regime. This view was reinforced in May 1931 when France resorted once again to import quotas to make up for its inability to raise import duties, some 72 per cent of which had been fixed in commercial treaties with other countries.[466]

French businessmen and politicians saw the relationship differently. While it was true that bilateral trade left France with a surplus, this was not the case if one included the British Empire as a whole. Moreover, Britain, the supposedly liberal power, raised nearly three times as much in revenue on imports from France as France raised on imports from Britain. Retreating from free trade in the 1920s, Britain had introduced stiff protectionist duties on a number of goods that figured prominently among French exports, notably woollens, lace, silk and artificial silk (rayon). It also increased excise duties on important items of French export such as wines and spirits, sugar and dried fruit. British officials vigorously denied that excise duties were protectionist, since 'equivalent' duties were levied on similar goods produced in Britain. But, as the French were painfully aware, Britain scarcely produced any of the dutiable goods, the 'equivalent' duties were not actually equal, Empire producers received substantial preferences, and all such duties discouraged consumption. Thus in 1929, France collected 270 million francs in duties or an average duty of 4.6 per cent on 5828 million francs of imports from Britain, whereas Britain collected £6 million (730 million francs) or an average duty of 9.6 per cent on 7573 million francs of goods imported from France.[467]

Board of Trade officials rejected these statistics as misleading. For one thing, fully two-thirds of British exports to France were raw materials, the largest being coal, which the French did not tax on account of their essential importance, whereas the great majority of French exports to Britain were manufactured goods. For another, France levied a 2 per cent import tax to offset a business turnover tax on domestic producers, which substantially increased its total tax levy. The Board estimated that French duties on imports from Britain averaged 6.6 per cent if the supplementary tax was included, and nearly 11 per cent on British imports minus raw materials. Third, France earned a large surplus on invisible exports to Britain mainly through tourism.[468] Both countries put the most favourable gloss on their record. But while French business and politicians understood the protective element of French taxes, their British counterparts deluded themselves in imagining that Britain was still uniquely liberal in its commercial relations.

The British use of veterinary and phytopathological (plant disease) restrictions added considerably to the misperception. Encouraged by the country's island location, the Ministry of Agriculture and Fisheries had applied embargoes or restrictions on numerous imports in the 1920s to protect domestic production from infectious disease or infestation. French politicians and officials did not dispute their right to do so, but suspected that, in the absence of other means of protection under free trade, Ministry officials regularly yielded to pressure from the National Farmers' Union (NFU) to apply veterinary and phytopathological restrictions more severely than was scientifically justified. Britain repeatedly rejected French requests to negotiate an international convention on the application of these restrictions or for expert bilateral negotiations.[469] Its invariable reply was that issues affecting British health and safety were non-negotiable.[470] French dissatisfaction increased when Britain sought to shore up sterling in September 1931 by introducing emergency duties on luxury imports, which fell with particular force upon France since over 50 per cent of its exports to Britain were defined as luxuries.[471] Then on 1 October 1931, the British Ministry of Agriculture announced a massive increase in restrictions on French potato and other vegetable imports to stop the Colorado beetle from reaching England.[472]

The beetle, a voracious invertebrate which thrives on potato, aubergine and tomato plants, had almost certainly been carried to France with supplies for the American army during the Great War, for it was discovered in 1922 in the region around Bordeaux, the army's chief port of disembarkation.[473] Britain had imposed a 200-km embargo around infested areas the following year, then relented under French protests and reduced it to 40 km.[474] But in May 1931, after infestations were reported further north, it increased the zones to 75 km, and in October 1931, when the beetle was found in a few places north of the Loire, Britain signalled its intention to increase the exclusion zones again to a radius of 200 km. This constituted a sevenfold increase in the embargo, which included the whole of Brittany, a region of small-holders heavily dependent upon the British market and as yet wholly free of the insect. Moreover, as an extra precaution, the embargo was to include an expanded range of agricultural products from within the restricted zone.[475] Britain was France's largest export market and its second largest market for agricultural products (after Belgium and Luxembourg together), taking 1558 million francs (£12.8 million) in farm goods in 1928.[476] French peasants and landowners, however, were in no mood to yield on what they saw as disguised protection aimed at them. Having made huge sacrifices during the war, they had fared poorly during the 1920s, with price levels declining and manufacturing interests receiving greater support from the state. Depressed and frustrated, they expected a vigorous reaction to the British action, especially as Tardieu was now minister of agriculture.[477]

The Vicomte de Halgouet, commercial attaché at the London embassy, at once led a delegation of experts from the French Ministries of Commerce and Agriculture to see Sir John Gilmour, the British minister of agriculture and fisheries, to request the withdrawal of the expanded restrictions. In their new form, the French complained, they amounted to a virtual embargo upon French potato exports as well as including other produce that could not possibly carry the beetle. The restrictions only applied to perhaps £1.5 million or 3 per cent of total French exports to Britain. Nevertheless, they would severely affect the livelihood of tens of thousands of peasant families, and in France, where nearly 50 per cent of the population lived on the land, the rural vote was crucially important to a majority of parliamentarians. French officials were prepared to accept a range of measures, including the presence of British inspectors in French ports and restricting exports to washed and treated consignments. But they grew annoyed and 'protested indignantly and volubly' when Gilmour dismissed their proposals while refusing to offer any good reason for the drastic increase in the restrictions. They alleged that the restrictions were based on 'economic and not on scientific grounds'. Gilmour's confirmation that he intended to announce the order in Parliament without the opportunity for bilateral negotiations was the last straw. Du Halgouet ended the two days of exchanges by entering 'the strongest possible protest on behalf of the two Ministries; it would be for the French Government to take what steps they may think necessary in the matter.'[478]

The French experts had good reason for doubting the rationale of the British restrictions. British experts knew the beetle could easily reach England on vehicles returning from France or even by flying the Channel unaided, and that administrative barriers, however stringent, could do little to hinder its movement. British farm interests led by the NFU, however, had mounted intense pressure on Gilmour and the Ministry for import restrictions and the maximum use of sanitary restrictions.[479] In the circumstances, neither Gilmour nor his officials wished to be held responsible for an invasion of the beetle, if this were to occur. As the French suspected, the large increase in restrictions was thus motivated chiefly by politics and economics rather than scientific logic. But it was consistent with Britain's liberal traditions of government that the minister of agriculture should be left to his own area of responsibility, and consistent with the mood in Britain where, amidst an unprecedented financial crisis, the demand for protection was strong. Although the Foreign Office was uneasy about disregarding French appeals for a compromise settlement, none of Gilmour's Cabinet colleagues questioned his decision to announce the new order on 6 October.[480]

French statesmen, angered by what they regarded as Britain's sharp practices and driven on by a wave of resentment in rural areas, warned that retaliation was certain if the British banning order was not soon rescinded. Dining at the British embassy in Paris on 7 October, Louis Rollin, the minister of commerce, spoke to Lord Reading of the 'very unpleasant impression' created in France by the British restrictions, of the 'very great agitation' in Brittany and the strong protests he was receiving from deputies in regions affected.[481] The following day, de Fleuriau called at the Foreign Office to complain of the restrictions and the shabby treatment meted out to du Halgouet's delegation. He warned that 'the order would certainly provoke reprisals on the French side.'[482] That same evening, M. Guernier, the minister for posts, who represented western Brittany in the Chamber, called on Robert Cahill, the commercial counsellor at the British embassy, to appeal for concessions.

> He said it would mean ruin for a large proportion of the agricultural popu-
> lation of the Departments of the Ille-et-Vilaine and Côtes-du-Nord.... [T]he
> greater part of Brittany, especially the ports such as St. Malo and Roscoff, were
> deeply concerned in the trade... it would spell ruin for these districts.[483]

France, Guernier affirmed, would consider almost any inspections or regulations Britain requested, but it would not tolerate the ruin of a whole province due
to arbitrary restrictions. If Britain refused to modify the beetle order, 'he and his
political friends' would insist upon retaliatory action. Tardieu was absent from
Paris for a few days, Guernier added, but he was 'entirely in sympathy with his
attitude, and would take action on his return.' Tardieu appeared to corroborate
Guernier's claim when, at a press conference on Friday 13 November, he warned
of 'an agricultural battle like the long extensive battle of the great war. The weapons, he insisted, include tariffs, bonuses for home producers, orders regarding
hygiene, obligatory use of domestic produce, and Customs reprisals'.[484]

The very next day, France introduced a 15 per cent surcharge on imports from
Britain and 14 other countries that had recently abandoned the gold standard and
allowed their currencies to depreciate. As in the case of Britain's Colorado beetle
order, this too appears to have been the initiative of a single minister, Rollin,
acting with the support of Tardieu and perhaps a few other colleagues.[485] Rollin
was aware of the severe decline in French exports and the prospect that France
would face a deficit on its trade balance for the first time since the mid-1920s. He
also knew that the deficit would be aggravated by the British anti-dumping duties
due to come into effect within a few days. Under relentless pressure from manufacturers and agricultural interests for greater protection, he seized upon the surcharge as a means of addressing his predicament. Since it applied to all countries
with recently depreciated currencies, he evidently hoped it would not fall foul of
France's most-favoured-nation commitments.[486] If so, he gravely underestimated
the Board of Trade's hostility to trade discrimination in any form. For nearly a
century under Free Trade, the Board had had nothing with which to bargain for
trade concessions and therefore relied upon the most-favoured-nation principle
to ensure equitable treatment for British commerce. Despite Britain's turn towards
protectionism, the Board remained intensely opposed to discrimination.[487] So
too did Walter Runciman, the president of the Board and a life-long free trader,
who received loud complaints about the French surtax from British coal exporters
as well as numerous questions in Parliament, and threatened retaliation if it was
not quickly removed.[488]

The emerging spectre of a trade war startled politicians on both sides of the
Channel. Laval wrote to MacDonald to assure him that he was doing everything
to resolve the dispute. With Germany more threatening than ever and economic
relations in Europe breaking down, 'a tariff war between the two countries' was
the last thing he wanted. 'He would consider this a world calamity especially

at the present time when big problems are awaiting solution rendering Anglo-French co-operation essential."[489] He and Briand pressured Rollin to give ground, and by early December Laval was able to report that his government was prepared to exempt British coal exports from the surcharge.[490] This was an important concession both because coal constituted by far the largest item of British exports to France, in value as well as volume, and because it meant opposing the French mining industry which was in deep depression and had sought extra protection from import competition. To be politically acceptable, however, Laval needed some counter-concession from Britain, such as the relaxation of the Colorado beetle order and if possible other restrictions on French agricultural exports.[491]

In London, Foreign Office and Treasury officials were similarly disturbed by the trade dispute and hoped to see it quickly ended. By their lights, the commercial stakes were small compared with the problem of reparations, which kept Germany in turmoil and threatened to bring the international political and financial systems down on their heads. The Foreign Office, being equally concerned for the fate of the forthcoming disarmament conference, persuaded Simon to intervene with his Cabinet colleagues. At his request, MacDonald responded to Laval with a vague appeal for economic cooperation and Franco-British solidarity.[492] But the very next week Parliament enacted the government's Horticultural Products (Emergency Customs Duties) Act, which struck another blow at French trade by defining all early fruit, vegetables and flowers as luxuries and subject to swingeing duties.[493] Since neither Runciman nor Gilmour was prepared to give way on import restrictions, the French 15 per cent surtax also stayed.[494]

Through 1932 and 1933, Franco-British commercial relations went from bad to worse. In late January 1932, France (also Poland) reduced its quota on imported coal to 64 per cent of the 1928–30 average volume of imports, which British industry spokesmen estimated would cost 16,000 miners' jobs.[495] In February, the British government approved retaliatory duties on a wide range of goods from countries that discriminated against British trade.[496] Subsequently, France extended the range of imports subject to quotas. National quotas were distributed in proportion to average imports over the previous three years, though considerably reduced overall. The French Ministry of Commerce regarded quotas as the only means of escaping the straightjacket of consolidated import duties. The British Board of Trade, however, regarded them as scarcely legitimate since they tended to fix trade into rigid bilateral paths, blocked trade expansion and by disregarding changes in international competitiveness led inevitably to *de facto* discrimination. Moreover, the Board was not equipped to manage the allocation of the British quota, which it left to the Federation of British Industries and the Association of British Chambers of Commerce to distribute.[497] Even so, the Board flatly refused France's repeated requests to negotiate a new commercial treaty.

In February 1932, Chamberlain encouraged the French to believe that Britain was prepared to negotiate on quotas, the surtax and other outstanding commercial issues.[498] This led Laval to affirm the French decision to exempt British coal from the surtax, which Runciman immediately announced in London. But shortly afterwards, the Board of Trade ruled out trade negotiations until after the

Ottawa conference in August, while demanding nonetheless that France remove its surtax from all British goods.[499] The misunderstanding was evidently unintentional, and arose from Chamberlain's impatience to end the trade dispute in the interests of a reparation settlement. But to Rollin and his colleagues it seemed like another instance of sharp practice.[500] As George Mounsey of the Foreign Office put it, 'We shall be "perfide Albion" over again as a result of all this.'[501]

Britain struck a new blow on 9 May 1932, when Chamberlain included in his budget sharply higher duties on important French exports, in particular silk and artificial silk (rayon). Raw silk imports now attracted a duty of nearly 22 per cent and silk products a duty of 43 per cent, which on top of the 25 per cent depreciation of the pound sterling against the franc practically excluded them from the British market. De Fleuriau pointed to the remarkable conjuncture of British restrictions on products such as potatoes, early vegetables, cherries, silk and luxury apparel, all of which acutely affected the Lyon region. During the winter, deputies from Lyon and the Paris sewing trades had helped secure the lifting of the surtax on British coal, and had also appealed to the French government to resist the retaliation demanded by other industries when the first British anti-dumping duties were announced, even though they constituted an extra 50 per cent hurdle for silk and *haute-couture* exports to the British market.[502] But so furious were they at Chamberlain's increased silk duties in the spring of 1932 that they agreed to join other industries in protest. British concessions were essential if the two countries were not to be drawn into tit-for-tat action, de Fleuriau warned. They were all the more important since Herriot was likely to be the next premier, and as mayor of Lyon he would find it hard to cooperate with Britain if something were not done to appease local interests.[503]

Chamberlain, no more than Runciman or Gilmour, was prepared to yield, and Franco-British trade precipitously declined. In the first ten months of 1932, French imports from Britain had declined 40 per cent in gold francs. This was closely similar to the decline in French imports from all countries (39 per cent) as well as French exports to all countries (37 per cent.) French exports to Britain, however, declined by an extraordinary 58 per cent.[504] Of all items France exported to Britain, silk was one of the worst affected. In 1929, France shipped 1152 million francs of raw silk and silk products to Britain. By 1932, French silk exports had declined to 355 million francs, down almost 70 per cent, and by 1934 they were down 80 per cent, despite the partial recovery of the British economy.[505]

Franco-British trade relations worsened in the summer of 1932 after France created a new form of trade discrimination. To raise revenue, Rollin increased the French domestic business turnover tax, while removing the advantage this gave to foreign competition by raising the compensatory duty on semi-manufactured imports from 2 to 4 per cent and on fully manufactured imports from 4 to 6 per cent. Britain could scarcely object to these actions until an element of discrimination was introduced, which occurred when Rollin received concessions from Belgium and Italy and thereupon rescinded the compensation taxes on their exports while maintaining them on goods from Britain.[506] With this, British manufacturers and merchants complained as loudly as their French counterparts did over British restrictions.[507] Official protests followed,[508] and in March 1933, Paul-Boncour, the foreign minister, was obliged to warn colleagues that the issue was causing *'un veritable malaise'* in economic relations with Britain.[509] When Bonnet, the minister of finance, approached the British government for a loan in April, Chamberlain indicated that France must first remove all discriminatory measures from British trade.[510] Daladier promised to introduce the necessary legislation.[511] But after the loan was arranged, the French government withdrew only the compensatory tax and not the surtax, because French industry and agriculture, urged on by Tardieu, mounted a vigorous campaign against concessions until Britain agreed to reduce agricultural sanitary restrictions or duties on silk and wine.[512] British protests rose to new heights.[513] So shrill were they and so embarrassing was the French government's refusal to honour its promise that Jacques Rueff, the French financial attaché in London, approached Bonnet in Paris to say that he was not prepared to return to London until the surtax issue was settled.[514]

With the franc increasingly overvalued, protectionism elsewhere on the rise and France's current account rapidly worsening, the Daladier government decided upon a more aggressive policy of reciprocal trade. On 1 September, it announced that from 1 January 1934, 75 per cent of all French import quotas would be withheld until recipient countries granted satisfactory concessions. French officials acknowledged that the new policy was directed mainly at Nazi Germany, which enjoyed the one-sided benefits of their 1927 commercial treaty and was taking unfair advantage of France's commitment to the most-favoured-nation principle on quotas.[515] They planned to exclude Britain from the reciprocal requirement, but changed their minds after receiving another curt refusal to reconsider the sanitary restriction orders on French agricultural exports.[516] This infuriated Runciman who obtained Cabinet approval to apply penal duties on French imports if, after one more warning, France failed to remove both the surtax and turnover compensation taxes from British goods.[517] Laurent-Eynac, the minister of commerce, appealed for a delay to secure parliamentary approval for the removal of the offending duties, and just before the end of the year he was able to confirm their suppression.[518] The new reciprocal policy on import quotas, however, went ahead in the New Year, despite a strong British protest against these 'ruthless restrictions'. British trade faced a provisional 75 per cent reduction in its share of the French market.[519]

On 10 January 1934, after learning that Belgium and the United States had regained 100 per cent of their quotas in return for concessions, Runciman once more accused France of discrimination and threatened immediate retaliation on goods of a commensurate value. Before the end of the day he received the promise of a restoration of quotas on most goods.[520] But when, ten days later, he learned that only 90 per cent of the quotas would be restored and that the coal quota in particular would be 10 per cent lower than before, he threatened retaliation on silk, clothing and other French exports, if the quotas were not fully restored by 7 February.[521] French officials appealed for some understanding. Britain, they pointed out, had used its ham and bacon quotas similarly as a bargaining instrument; and France had restored nearly 97 per cent of quotas on British goods without any reciprocal concessions, as a gesture of goodwill. But France's current account deficit made it essential for them to introduce a reciprocal trade policy. If Britain carried out its threat of retaliation, France would be obliged to denounce the 1882 convention governing Franco-British commercial relations and insist upon negotiating a new agreement.[522] At this point, MacDonald and Simon became uneasy and urged Runciman to find a way out of the impasse.[523] Runciman threatened to resign rather than back down, however, and it was not until Tuesday, 6 February, a fateful day for France, that he agreed to take a step back.[524]

Since the start of the year France faced growing turmoil on account of the Stavisky affair. On 9 January, following news of Stavisky's death, Charles Maurras's *Action Française*, Pierre Taittinger's *Jeunesses Patriotes* and Colonel de la Rocque's *Croix de Feu* organized a noisy demonstration in Paris, and for the rest of the month demonstrations took place daily near the *Palais Bourbon*. When the Chautemps government fell on 27 January, Daladier sought to form a new government. But right-wing critics charged that it was the same old gang, and on 6 February, when Daladier was expected to present his new government for parliamentary approval, the *Union Nationale des Combattants*, *Solidarité Française* and the *Fédération des Contribuables,* along with *Action Française*, *Jeunesses Patriotes*, the *Camelots du Roi*, the *Croix de Feu* and other *ligues* prepared to march on the parliament building. With Hitler firmly in control in Berlin and Kurt von Schuschnigg in Vienna at this very moment employing the Austrian army to crush the remnants of Socialist opposition to his clerico-fascist government, French Socialist and Communist party leaders feared a similar outcome in Paris and independently urged supporters to mobilize. At 2:40 p.m. on the 6th, Ronald Campbell, the chargé at the Paris embassy, standing in for the absent Tyrrell, telephoned the Foreign Office to hold off the trade sanctions.

> Internal situation is increasingly menacing. There may well be bloodshed tonight and chaos tomorrow. It is impossible at present to discuss quota question with anybody. We have hitherto advised that firm attitude on commercial questions would not affect our general relations but I could not maintain this opinion if Order were published in the middle of this crisis. I am sending in ... a letter to Monsieur Daladier emphasising the very grave view which His Majesty's Government take and asking him to receive me as soon as it is possible for him to do so. I would earnestly ask you to reconsider the decision to make announcement tomorrow and to give French Government forty-eight hours final notice in accordance with your original intention.[525]

British observers, including those who should have had an informed and balanced view, were agreed: France was a decadent country, its political class riddled with corruption, its policies short-sighted, foolish and destructive in the extreme. Campbell, the chargé, wished London to know that the rioters in Paris were 'wholehearted republicans and democrats and only determined to put a stop to the corrupt activities of the old gang of politicians'.[526] Chamberlain, who had dined the previous week with Lord Derby, the former ambassador to France, accepted his fanciful assertion that there were 'over 160 Deputies in Stavisky's pay and were paid through Chautemps; Bonnet took no money himself but Mme. Bonnet accepted jewels which she converted into cash!'[527] MacDonald grimly recorded that 'the Stavisky affair if probed to the bottom will reveal rottenness in all kinds of quarters.' Daladier he rather liked. 'His cherub & sparkling young eyes were not French & he had real courage in action & not only in words.' But the others were thoroughly corrupt and 'an increasing menace to European democracy [sic].'[528] Having driven Germany into the arms of Hitler, they were still obstructing the disarmament process, which made MacDonald more than once question if Britain should not denounce the Locarno treaty and turn its back on Europe. Now, on top of this, they had provoked a commercial conflict with Britain that was completely their fault, and were threatening to embark upon a trade war.[529] Chamberlain was scarcely less annoyed: 'I don't think we have handled the affair very skilfully but the French have behaved like madmen. If they are going to quarrel with their best friends they will deserve what they will get.'[530] Ministers therefore agreed that Runciman need accept only a three-day delay in implementing the trade sanctions, and that in Runciman's words, 'barricades or no barricades' he could publish the order on Saturday, 10 February.[531]

Lord Tyrrell, who returned to Paris on 8 February, immediately warned of the folly of launching a trade war in current circumstances. The march of the *ligues* on the evening of the 6th had led to a violent confrontation with police outside the Palais Bourbon, resulting in 15 people killed and nearly 1500 injured.[532] The riot spread through the centre of Paris causing widespread damage and further bloodshed, and continued sporadically for three more days. Inside the *Palais Bourbon*, Daladier had been shouted down by right-wing deputies when he attempted to speak. On the 7th he resigned, making way for Gaston Doumergue, a former president of France, to form a government of national concentration. However, since it was not yet in place and Paris remained in turmoil, Tyrrell feared that British trade sanctions would seem like hitting a man while he was down and infuriate French leaders.

I find on my return the country confronted by one of the most serious crises it has had to face since the foundation of the Republic. The street demonstrations which are largely attributed to parties of the Right had led to the downfall of the government of the day which was based on a parliamentary majority. M. Doumergue has consented to form a national ministry. He may succeed but he will be confronted by a very determined Socialist opposition and I am not at all sure that demonstrations engineered by the Right will not provoke counter demonstrations from Socialist quarters. I am confirmed in this impression by announcement of a general strike for next Monday. In any event I foresee a period of very grave internal disquiet the scope of which cannot be exaggerated. It is bound to have its repercussions on foreign affairs. It is under the latter aspect that I venture to submit to you whether our economic dispute with the French Government should be allowed to override the political consequences of a tariff war which I consider we should avoid so long as there remains any possibility of doing so.[533]

Tyrrell had his way and a truce was arranged to enable negotiations to take place on outstanding trade differences.[534] The negotiations were difficult and protracted, but on 16 June, a comprehensive agreement was initialled.[535] French statesmen continued to believe their duties and quotas had been reasonable in the circumstances. But once again, they chose to put national security first. Since the British negotiators were prepared to resume the conflict in the absence of agreement, the French gave way all along the line. Orme Sargent of the Foreign Office commented:

> I take my hat off to the way the Board of Trade have put this over the French. They seem to have achieved everything they set out to obtain at the cost of some minor concessions. ... The French have been compelled to give up their policy of using their quotas for purposes of trade bargaining. They have failed to obtain any relief as regards the measures of protection which we have given to the British silk industry against French competition. We have obtained an undertaking that the French will not reduce the import of our coal, as well as satisfactory guarantees as regards our imports of fish and cotton goods. And lastly, we have maintained our embargo on French potatoes and forced the French to give up theirs on our seed potatoes. My only fear is that the French negotiators, when they get back to Paris, may be disowned by their own Government.[536]

Although the agreement was ratified, Sargent had reason to be worried. In official British circles it tended to reinforce the view that the French were opportunistic, unprincipled and understood only superior power. On the French side it left ministers frustrated and demoralized. Equally important, bilateral trade remained severely depressed, since Britain had not relaxed its import duties or restrictions and France returned to propping up the franc through non-discriminatory reductions in import quotas. The agreement, so far from bringing the powers closer together, thus further undermined the international economic and political systems.

7.7   Conclusion

The conventional narrative of diplomatic historians for the period between 1931 and 1934 gives prominence to the Manchurian crisis, disarmament, negotiations over reparations and war debts, the advent of Hitler and his first feints towards Poland and Austria. Economic historians generally emphasize the adverse effects of inappropriate policy choices by the leading capitalist powers, notably their attempts to remain on the gold standard which constrained them to pursue deflationary monetary, financial and fiscal policies as well as trade protection. Literally incoherent, these separate approaches possess all too little explanatory power.

The foregoing chapter indicates how the politico-diplomatic and the economic aspects of the period can be combined in a single narrative which is capable of explaining the extraordinary destructiveness of the dual crisis. Its features may be summarized as follows.

With the onset of the crisis, the Anglo-Saxon powers retreated behind protectionist trade barriers, in Britain's case with the further provocation of discriminatory concessions to its Empire partners at the expense of other countries. This however did not alter their insistence upon respect for liberal principles in their political and economic dealings with the rest of the world. Hence they professed to rely upon the League of Nations to restrain Japanese aggression, even though there was never the slightest chance that the international community would unite behind League sanctions. Meanwhile they engaged in increasingly futile arguments with France, the third major democratic power, over disarmament. Yet at the same time they refused to contemplate a security framework to maintain order in Europe and continued to agitate for the removal of restraints upon Germany, including the disarmament and reparation obligations fixed by the Treaty of Versailles. They thus encouraged Japanese, Italian and German revisionism, which found expression in increasingly aggressive words and action, and further damaged business confidence. They also opposed second-best solutions to the world economic slump which departed from liberal principles. The Anglo-Saxon powers thus retreated from liberalism so far as their own economic policies were concerned, but dogmatically insisted that they should continue to apply in the rest of the world: behaviour that contributed to the wholesale rejection of economic liberalism for the next 17 years.

The resilience of the world economy was demonstrated in the winter of 1930 when, despite the deflationary bias of the international gold standard, world production and trade practically ceased to decline and signs appeared of incipient recovery. International confidence, however, was shattered by the Austro-German customs union scheme, which led in quick succession to the run on the Austrian schilling, the Reichsmark and the pound sterling, the freezing of bank credits in Central Europe, Britain's retreat towards Imperial protectionism, a massive run on the US dollar's gold reserves, and widespread hoarding in France and elsewhere. Meanwhile France, the Benelux countries, the Northern countries and the Danube countries all sponsored initiatives for reopening markets among an open-ended coalition of the willing. Potentially, any one of these initiatives might have contributed to reversing the slump, especially if Britain, the world's largest trading nation, had been willing to participate. But none of them could be implemented, for not only did Britain refuse to participate, but in each case they also involved some departure from the most-favoured-nation principle, the mainstay of liberal trade relations, on which neither Britain nor the United States was prepared to yield.

In the third quarter of 1932, signs again appeared that the worst of the slump might be over. American industrial activity was up, companies reported improved results and foreign trade also showed signs of recovery.[537] Referring to the United States, the *Economist* reported on 10 December, 'The improvement in the past three months was more than seasonal, and while here and there the decline also seems to have exceeded the pace of this time of year, no branch of industry has yet sunk back to the summer low levels.'[538] Germany experienced a similar upturn. In its third-quarter report, the *Institut für Konjunkturforschung* spoke of the four-year economic decline as virtually at an end.[539] Unemployment had fallen steadily from February onwards, and for the first time since 1927, the total was lower at the end of the year than at the start.[540] Chancellor Papen's reflationary policy was probably the main cause of the upturn in Germany, but Britain had contributed by supporting the standstill on short-term bank credits in Germany and promoting the reparations settlement reached at the Lausanne conference in July. Yet, hardly had this been accomplished when Britain shook international confidence by entering into protectionist and discriminatory arrangements with its Dominions partners at Ottawa. Confidence was further damaged by France's war debt default in December 1932, Hitler's accession to power in January 1933, which portended intensified German revisionism, and in May 1933 by the start of Roosevelt's monetary experiments. The uncertainty added to the seasonal effect upon unemployment not least in Germany where it climbed back almost to the same height reached in the winter of 1932, before Hitler gave priority to its reduction.[541] Political and economic factors thus interacted in a continuous and almost continually destructive way.

As the recurrent signs of recovery indicate, there was probably nothing inherently wrong with the world economy, and the slump need not have been so deep and prolonged. But globalization ensured that practically all countries were thoroughly exposed to the slump, and the slump drove the three great liberal powers even further apart. Individually each was vitally interested in world stability and together they could have provided effective leadership, but disunited they allowed the world economic and political systems to break down. During the long era of globalization that ended with the slump, countries had been expected to rely upon unilateral domestic adjustments of monetary and fiscal policy to remain competitive. In the new era that now opened, countries abandoned hope of collective international action and refused any longer to bear the burden of adjustment through unilateral domestic adjustments. The United States cautiously turned back towards economic internationalism after 1934, when it promoted trade liberalization through reciprocal tariff reductions. In September 1936, it joined Britain and France in facilitating the devaluation of the franc. But far more than this was necessary to repair the damage caused by its earlier economic actions and continued inaction on the security front. Even now, Roosevelt and Hull, his secretary of state, identified British economic 'imperialism' as the principal source of world tensions.[542]

Elsewhere countries continued to rely upon unilateral external adjustment: beggar-your-neighbour policies such as currency devaluation, exchange controls, bargaining tariffs and quantitative trade controls including import quotas and licensing and bilateral clearing offices. As in economic relations so too in political relations, narrow nationalism and aggressive imperialism became the feature of the next 15 years. In this grim Hobbesian state of each against all, few dreamed of returning to a globalized world. The aim instead was to realize the world glimpsed in the 1920s, of a constellation of self-contained politico-economic blocs on a scale comparable to the United States. With Conservatives in power in London, Stalin in Moscow, Mussolini in Rome, Hitler in Berlin and a coalition of civilian and military imperialists in Tokyo, this was the dream that shaped world affairs until 1945 and beyond.

8

Conclusion: From the Great Interwar Crisis to the Present

8.1 Towards a new history of the interwar period

The usual periodization of twentieth-century history treats 1914 as a major turning point, marking the end of the second great era of globalization and the start of an era of upheaval that lasted until 1945. The title of E. H. Carr's famous study, *The Twenty Years' Crisis*, refers to the period 1918–39, but its underlying assumption is that the crisis was bracketed by the two world wars which together formed an uninterrupted period of conflict. This account presents a different way of seeing this epoch and indeed the twentieth century itself. As explained here, the outbreak of war in 1914 brought a collapse of the international states system but only a hiatus in global economic relations. In economic terms the 1920s bore a much closer resemblance to the prewar period than is commonly assumed. Following the war, the three main victor powers broadly agreed on the desirability of restoring a globalized economic system, and largely through their efforts or those of the international sectors of their business communities, states retreated from their wartime directing role, the major currencies were re-linked to one another through the gold standard and markets were reopened. Thus by the second half of the 1920s, world trade and financial flows were greater than before the war and increasing at twice the rate of national growth. The Great War also brought important changes to the international states system, most notably the eclipse of Russia, the expanded role of the United States and constraints upon Germany's sovereignty from 1918; but for the most part the changes proved to be short-lived. By the mid-1920s, Soviet Russia had practically regained its place as a great power, while the United States had retreated to its prewar status as merely a potential great power. As for Germany, it had largely regained its sovereignty and was already the chief threat to the states system, just as it had been before the Great War. The decisive turning point occurred not in 1914 but in 1927, when the great interwar crisis began, bringing the collapse of both the global economic and political systems. The importance of this periodization is threefold.

In the first place, it casts the events of the 1920s in a radically new light. Economic historians commonly represent the decade as one in which most countries and regions enjoyed economic growth, albeit modest in Britain and uneven in Germany and generally constrained by a substantial increase in protectionism. While this is true enough, the most remarkable feature of the decade was arguably the progress made in re-establishing a globalized economy and the pace of expansion of international trade and investment after the settlement of the Ruhr crisis in 1924. For their part, diplomatic historians commonly treat every effort by Britain, the United States and international bankers to modify the Versailles settlement to accommodate Germany within the international states system as a step towards peace. In fact, it is more accurate to represent Britain and America as opponents of France's commitment to the postwar settlement who stripped away key components of the global security framework. The combined effect of these developments was to recreate a globalized world which was remarkably prosperous but also exceptionally vulnerable to systemic crisis. For whereas the three victor powers agreed upon liberalizing international trade and payments, they did not agree upon managing the global system. No less than five countries, Bulgaria, Hungary, Italy, Soviet Russia and Germany, remained unreconciled to the existing states system. Yet, the victor powers failed to agree upon rules for operating the international gold standard or addressing chronic international imbalances; they failed to establish international institutions capable of containing market failure; and so far from establishing a robust framework of international security, the Anglo-Saxon powers systematically undermined the framework adopted in 1919 at Versailles. Thus, while the world was relatively peaceful and prosperous in the 1920s, the essential conditions of stability actually diminished rather than increased.

The second value of this periodization follows from the first, in clarifying the nature and dynamics of the world economic slump. Economic historians have never succeeded in providing a fully adequate explanation of it, while diplomatic historians merely mention it without including it in their analysis, and deal instead only with fragments such as war debts, reparations and foreign lending or with its political consequences. The key to understanding the slump is to recognize its dual character and the fact that the causal connection between economic and political factors ran in both directions from start to finish. This poses a challenge to those who would reduce history to either its economic or its political constituents. Inevitably it makes for more complicated, not to say confusing, history. But it also brings us much closer to the past.

With the possible exception of Germany and the other revisionist powers, at least until 1936 or thereabouts, politics and international relations in the interwar period had more to do with the day-to-day challenge of earning a living at home and abroad than with matters of high diplomacy. This was particularly so during the great interwar crisis starting in 1927. With trade and investment collapsing, unemployment soaring, currencies undermined and banking systems endangered, the very survival of countries depended upon their economic relations with other countries. The crisis was one of the greatest calamities in modern world history, which devastated the lives of a whole generation of people and deserves a prominent place in any general history of the period. As the present account illustrates, it also radically reshaped international relations. Among the great powers, those with large empires or extensive territories – Britain, France, the United States, the Soviet Union – were driven to organize them more effectively, while other powers without empires – Germany, Italy, Japan – sought to acquire them through aggression, and all of them resorted to beggar-your-neighbour policies, even for a time the United States. Before the international economic and political systems collapsed, however, some powers also promoted constructive responses to the crisis. Every one of these initiatives deserves to be included in a serious account of interwar history since, as contemporaries appreciated, their implementation might well have alleviated the crisis sufficient to divert the world from the path to war. The present account therefore offers a corrective to the conventional narrative by demonstrating the dynamic interaction of forces that led to the great interwar crisis, efforts to address the crisis, its culmination in the simultaneous collapse of the international economic and political systems and the end of the second great era of globalization.

The third contribution of this periodization is to expose more clearly the influence of ideas upon the shaping of international affairs in the first half of the twentieth century. So long as diplomatic historians treat only the political consequences of the crisis rather than the crisis itself, they are almost bound to dwell upon the rise of the dictators and the cautious reactions of the democratic powers. Practically every one of their accounts identifies fascism, Nazism, militarism and Communism as the destructive political doctrines of the age, while presenting liberalism as benign, albeit ineffectual. But as the foregoing account demonstrates, by treating economic and political affairs as two sides of the same coin, the political ideas of the period appear in a very different light. With the victory of the major democratic powers in the Great War, the dominant political doctrine or 'ideology' was not Communism or fascism but liberalism and specifically its extreme Anglo-Saxon version. In the economic sphere, liberalism found expression in the return to convertible currencies and open markets or more generally globalization. In the political sphere it was manifested in the rejection of the 'old diplomacy' of alliances, secret agreements and the concept of balance of power in favour of a new internationalism symbolized by the League of Nations, multilateral initiatives and summit diplomacy bringing representatives of the 'people' into direct contact with one another.

Until 1927, liberalism remained in the ascendant and dominated global economic and political relations. But the chief proponents of liberalism pursued a high-risk, not to say foolhardy, strategy, since they favoured globalization and stood to gain the most from it, yet they proved unable or unwilling to introduce the measures required to deal with global imbalances, market failure or renewed threats to the international states system. Thus they largely restored open markets, exposing most of the world to the risk of contagion, without implementing the essential framework of agreed rules, institutions and security. As early as 1927, signs appeared that major countries did not agree upon the rules and would not address their adjustment problems in mutually compatible ways, while other countries, Germany in particular, remained intent upon disrupting the states system. From 1927, support for globalization itself diminished and the great interwar crisis began. By 1933–4, the crisis had brought to a violent close the world's second great era of globalization.

This was in a very real sense the failure of liberalism. Not surprisingly therefore, the dominant feature of the 1930s was support for socialist or radical-nationalist movements whose common ground was hostility to liberalism. Yet remarkably, while our library shelves groan under the weight of studies devoted to socialism, Communism, anarchism, militarism, fascism or Nazism, the decisive importance of liberalism and the role of the liberal powers in fostering the conditions for these extreme doctrines to thrive are almost wholly overlooked. Much more research is needed to establish liberalism's precise role in shaping the behaviour of individual states as well as the international system. But the present account will have served some purpose by highlighting this extraordinary lacuna in our treatment of interwar history.

Along with liberalism, the present account also argues for a new understanding of the influence of racism in interwar international relations. It is now a commonplace to assume that in great power relations, race prejudice was the monopoly of the aggressor powers and played little if any part in the policy-making of the liberal democratic powers. While their individual statesmen no doubt harboured prejudices, the conventional narrative encourages the impression that their failures were due to imperfect information and occasionally poor judgement, not irrational likes and dislikes. As the present account demonstrates, this is a comforting but far from accurate view of the past. It hardly needs saying that race prejudice led the aggressor powers to appalling acts of repression and organized murder. Nevertheless, they had no monopoly on racism, nor were they alone in allowing it to affect their international behaviour.

Race prejudice, albeit present, appears to have had little effect upon the shaping of French external policy between the wars, since however the German threat was defined the French response was likely to have been similar. French anti-Americanism, informed by notions of an aggressive, uncultured Americanized Anglo-Saxon race, existed in intellectual circles among the extreme Left and especially the ultra-nationalist Right, where it sharply intensified after the onset of the dual crisis.[1] But it had little if any effect upon official policy until December 1932 and the vote against resuming war debt payments. As for French Anglophobia, British historians commonly assert that this was as virulent as Francophobia in Britain. But by and large it emerged only in the 1930s after Britain began actively to appease Hitler, and was limited to an extreme Right-wing fringe. Henri Béraud's *Faut-il réduire l'Angleterre en esclavage?* is almost invariably cited as illustration of French prejudice, for want of other substantial evidence.[2] In fact, far from displaying Anglophobia, leading French politicians, diplomats and officials throughout the 1930s generally displayed something closer to its opposite, namely optimism that the good sense of Britain must eventually revive the *Entente cordiale*. Only with the *débâcle* of the Battle of France, including Britain's pell-mell retreat from Dunkirk, in June 1940, the Royal Navy attack on the French squadron at Mers el-Kébir the following month and subsequent incidents did Anglophobia become evident among a significant minority of French conservatives and especially career officers in the army and navy.

The American case differs somewhat, since the return to isolationism after the Armistice in 1918 appears to have been influenced by a variety of factors including long-standing suspicions of 'old Europe'. Many Americans still felt an affinity for Britons, whom they regarded as their Anglo-Saxon cousins, and most included Germans within this category.[3] But the war also strengthened fears of contaminating Anglo-Saxon or WASP America with the blood of inferior races from Slavic and Latin Europe as well as Asia.[4] This led to the first general restrictions on immigration. It also contributed to the bifurcation in outlook between 'nationalist' Washington and 'cosmopolitan' New York and to America's dangerously incoherent external policy in the 1920s and early 1930s. Whereas economically the country enjoyed a large competitive advantage over other countries, and its international banks were prepared to meet the huge demand for dollars in Europe and the rest of the world, Washington, reflecting the fears of small-town America, resisted an increase in the country's global exposure. It therefore refused to coordinate external economic policy with the requirements of large-scale industry and banking centred on New York, to accept the authority of the Federal Reserve Bank of New York over monetary policy or to provide American backing for the international institutions and regulatory agencies required to forestall market failure in a globalized world. In short, race prejudice contributed to America's isolationism and its weak and potentially destructive role in international affairs at precisely the moment when American interests demanded that it assume a responsible, indeed leading, role. Granted, racial prejudice was only one of many factors that contributed to this failure. But so massive were the consequences for America and the whole world that even as a secondary factor its influence should not be overlooked.

The British case is different again. By 1914, Britain was a strongly liberal country, the concepts of the rule of law, limited government and respect for individual freedom as well as a liberal approach to economics including free trade and the discipline of the gold standard having become accepted by most of the political community stretching from the main body of the Labour Party to the Liberal Party and all but a right-wing fringe of the Conservative Party. But it was also a commonplace of liberal thought to associate Britain's liberal freedoms with its Anglo-Saxon heritage, which in turn encouraged a sense of affinity with other supposedly Anglo-Saxon peoples including the dominant element in the United States, the 'white' Dominions and Germany. Not all British observers shared this view, and some of those who did so spoke only of a cultural rather than a racial affinity. But as often as not, their references bore a racist cast, revealing a view of humankind comprised of races which stamped their members with distinctive and largely immutable personalities. This, as the foregoing account explains, profoundly influenced the mood in which Britain entered the First World War, the way it greeted the abdication of the German Kaiser and collapse of the German high command in November 1918, its approach to the subsequent peace-making and its support for treaty revision in the 1920s. It also helps explain Britain's ambivalence towards the United States, its disdain for the Slav countries, its suspicion and dislike of France and its curious blindness to evidence of German rearmament and territorial ambitions. More generally, it helps explain Britain's opposition to a Continental commitment or support for a multilateral security framework.

The eruption of aggression in 1939–41 by powers influenced by, and in the case of Germany and Japan driven by, racial ambition led to a reaction against racism in the principal forms that it took during the conflict, namely anti-Semitism and colour prejudice. But it also had the unfortunate effect of narrowing historical perceptions of racism largely to these forms. Thus the massive output of publications on the interwar period almost completely obscures the fact that for many if not most people in the developed world racism applied not just to one or a few categories of people but to *all* people and formed an element in their calculations of friend or foe in the world beyond their shores. What is more, this appears to have been as true of liberals in the Anglo-Saxon countries as those of a conservative, authoritarian, reactionary or fascist cast of mind in the countries that turned to aggression. While the form their racism took was different, the consequences of the liberal powers' racism were as terrible, since it was an essential constituent of the great interwar crisis, and without the crisis the Second World War and the Holocaust would scarcely have occurred.

The conventional narrative of interwar history presents the Anglo-Saxon powers' commitment to appeasement in the 1920s as a rational and constructive policy, even if, according to some accounts, it was pursued longer in the 1930s than was appropriate. As the present account explains, this is a serious misreading of both decades. Neither at the Paris peace conference in 1919 nor afterwards were the Anglo-Saxon powers necessarily wrong to appease Germany or other revisionist powers. But they were extremely unwise to encourage hope that all contentious aspects of the peace settlement were amenable to revision, including Germany's eastern frontiers with Czechoslovakia, Lithuania and above all Poland, since this played into the hands of nationalist agitators in all the countries directly concerned while threatening the security of France and the stability of Europe and the world. Above all, the Anglo-Saxon powers were unwise to encourage revision without creating an effective framework of security. This was the essential precondition of a managed revision of the peace settlement that would address some grievances of the defeated powers without increasing insecurity elsewhere. In the circumstances, it was scarcely surprising that France should drag its heels on treaty revision. This made France the target of criticism by the Anglo-Saxon powers. The fact remained nonetheless that the main obstacle to the maintenance of the original security framework or the construction of a new one was not France but the two Anglo-Saxon powers, Britain and the United States.

The present account points to a similar conclusion for the 1930s. The conventional narrative acknowledges the contribution of the economic slump to conditions favouring the rise of militarist and fascist challenges to the international order, but so far as the liberal powers are concerned, it does little more than pose the question whether their shift from appeasement to a deterrence policy came too late in view of the mounting evidence of aggressive intentions on the part of

Japan, Germany and Italy, or whether they had any practical alternative before this time. But, as we have seen in the present account, the liberal powers, at least the Anglo-Saxon powers, actually helped to provoke and then to prolong the slump by their individual or collective action. The United States bears a heavy responsibility on account of its withdrawal from the security framework agreed at Versailles, its efforts to promote disarmament without regard for the broader security implications, its indifference to the global imbalances which posed massive adjustment problems for all concerned, its decision in 1922 and again in 1929 to make swingeing increases in its protective tariff, its refusal to participate in or even endorse collective action once the slump began, beyond the belated one-year suspension of its war debt demands in 1931, its frighteningly inconsistent signals on the future of the dollar from March to July 1933 and its unilateral manipulation of the exchange rate later that year.

Britain's responsibility was of a similar order. In the first place, it began its retreat from economic liberalism in 1927, just when the need for international leadership was becoming greater than ever. It then turned decisively towards protectionism just when the decision to let the pound sterling float in September 1931 largely removed the justification for further unilateral external adjustment, and it extended Imperial preferences even though it was clear that this would merely divert trade from existing channels and increase aggregate levels of protection. Second, it failed to contribute to the international security framework. Indeed, it actively subverted the Versailles settlement in the 1920s, and even as Japan, Italy and Germany brought down the global political order in the 1930s, it stripped away the last remnants of the framework constructed at Versailles, thus aggravating the general insecurity. While the effect cannot be measured with any precision, the insecurity engendered by this attack on the security framework almost certainly intensified and prolonged the economic slump.

There is a further irony. In the early stages of the slump, the Anglo-Saxon powers retreated from liberal policies. Yet they presented a righteously liberal face to the rest of the world by insisting that other countries abide by liberal rules of behaviour. Thus they demanded respect for lenders' rights, priority for private contracts, non-discrimination in the allocation of foreign exchange, and above all, adherence to the principle of most-favoured-nation treatment in trade relations. This may have had disastrous consequences, for instead of assisting France, the Northern countries or the Benelux countries in their efforts to create areas of freer trade open to all countries to join on the same terms, they systematically discouraged them. One cannot be certain that any of these second-best regional responses to the collapse of trade would have alleviated the slump. But it seems entirely possible that any one of them could have turned a vicious circle of increasing beggar-your-neighbour policies into a virtuous one of improving trade relations. In that case, the whole course of subsequent events might have been altered.

That is not all. Attaching central importance to commerce and finance, the liberal powers became preoccupied by the slump and blamed one another for it. The

British and French pointed an accusing finger at American protectionism; the British and Americans in turn pointed to France's gold hoarding, insistence upon reparations and financial 'blackmail' of Austria and Germany. The Americans and French resented the competitive advantage Britain allegedly obtained from its Exchange Equalization Account; the British protested at France's arbitrary trade restrictions which seemed directed mainly at them; the Americans deplored Britain's Ottawa agreements, whose discriminatory character seemed calculated to cut them out of trade with Empire countries; and the French regretted that Britain and the United States opposed all their efforts to organize Continental trade relations in such a way as to prop up their Eastern allies and avoid German domination. The slump itself reached its nadir in 1932, but relations among the liberal capitalist powers reached their low point in 1934, with the French still annoyed at the United States for demanding that Germany should be relieved of reparation payments to safeguard American commercial credits in Europe, the British threatening to launch an all-out tariff war with France, the British and French furious at the United States for its reckless monetary experiments and – as they saw it – forcing them to default on their war debt obligations, Americans convinced of Britain's 'economic aggression', and Americans and British furious at France for refusing to appease Germany with further disarmament, as if this would contribute to international stability. Thereafter relations among the liberal powers gradually improved, but the lingering frustrations, humiliation and resentment formed a barrier to effective cooperation.

Meanwhile, the liberal world economy gave way not to narrow nationalism and atomized economic units as most accounts claim, but to a general struggle for large economic blocs. Economic liberals as well as conservatives, as we have seen, widely anticipated this outcome in the 1920s, but the struggle was far more brutal than anyone had imagined. In the East, Japan unsheathed its sword to force Manchuria, China and eventually the whole of Southeast Asia to join its Asian Co-Prosperity Sphere. In the West, Mussolini sought to carve out an empire around the Mediterranean, while Hitler aggressively extended the Third Reich eastwards towards the Urals. British leaders, having sought at Ottawa to emulate the United States and Soviet Russia by promoting the unity of their Empire, were discomfited by these developments but reluctant to oppose them. To their frustration they found French leaders prepared to resist Hitler's imperialist activity, American leaders opposed to Japan extending its sphere, and the British public hostile to Mussolini's African empire-building. British efforts to appease the expansionist powers merely earned their scorn while annoying France and the United States and creating embarrassment at home. By the late 1930s, keen-eyed observers could see that the transformation of the world of liberal national economies to that of large blocs was bound to end in world war.

Despite the widely held view in the Anglo-Saxon countries between the wars that France was more bureaucratic, authoritarian and protectionist and less democratic than themselves, in general France was their equal as a liberal state: certainly its statesmen believed it to be, which in some respects is equally significant. Yet by comparison, France's interwar record, whether in economics, social harmony or international affairs, seems to have been dismal. From 1918, its leaders bore responsibility for the failure to enforce the Versailles Treaty, a financial situation that briefly threatened to end in hyper-inflation, the devaluation of the franc by four-fifths of its prewar value, and after 1930 an economic slump that lasted nearly five years longer than in any other major power. With France mired in depression when other powers were well on the way to recovery, its leaders failed to prepare the country adequately to withstand German military aggression or to rebuild a security framework comprising reliable allies. As a result, in 1940 France was overrun in barely seven weeks and forced to accept humiliating terms from Germany and Italy. The country thus seemed to have experienced a sort of decadence or collapse from within, and if politically it was more divided than ever, the Left and Right could at least agree upon the need for national renewal. This view was generally accepted in the Anglo-Saxon countries, and even now, despite their more circumspect view of France's military defeat in 1940, historians have little to say in favour of its prewar régime.

Yet as the present account has shown, there are grounds for claiming that France's interwar leaders were as competent as their own predecessors or their contemporaries in Britain and the United States. For one thing, they were almost invariably more clear-sighted about the danger posed by Germany to European and world peace. While prepared to support Treaty revision and even economic integration with Germany, their policy was constantly informed by the primary requirement of security and a realistic appreciation of the risks they faced. For another, with few exceptions they did not lose sight of the importance of Eastern Europe as an integral part of the European balance of power. Having sought to isolate and destroy the fledgling Bolshevik régime after the Great War, they turned to Poland and the Little Entente as substitutes until the mid-1930s when they turned cautiously back to Soviet Russia to forestall Nazi Germany's domination first of the East, then the whole of Europe. The efforts of French politicians to address the fundamental issue of European security were completely vindicated by events and distinguished them from their British and American contemporaries, who displayed no such clarity of vision.

French leaders also held to liberal principles of economic policy. Almost without exception, they favoured the discipline of fixed exchange rates provided by the gold standard, accepted the need to balance the national budget and supported efforts to keep markets open. In the 1920s their record was mixed: while they allowed inflation to wipe out the bulk of public and private debt, creating a brief but acute financial, monetary and political crisis, industry benefited from this non-policy, and in terms of output and employment the French economy performed better than practically any other economy in the 1920s. It was a different story in 1930s. Reluctant to repeat the inflationary experience or to discard the sacrifices involved in the stabilization of the franc in 1926–8 and the apparent contribution of a stable, gold-backed currency to national security, French leaders clung to the gold standard longer than their counterparts elsewhere. With revenue dwindling, they retrenched more rigorously than their liberal counterparts in Britain and the United States. When even this proved insufficient, they defended the gold standard by retreating into protectionism before belatedly devaluing the franc in September 1936. By then, however, the prolonged slump had not only damaged industry and provoked political extremism but also weakened France's international standing. While French governments began to rearm in 1936, they found themselves almost as preoccupied with domestic strife as with the threat of German and Italian aggression.

Two features of the French experience should be evident from the foregoing account. The first is the intimate link between France's economic policy and its security needs. From the 1920s until the Lausanne conference in 1932, French insistence upon German reparation payments was driven by several motives, one of which was the conviction that reparations were necessary to reduce the fiscal advantage enjoyed by German industry, which would otherwise extend its domination over Europe. As we have seen, France's decision to return to the gold standard in 1928 at a defendable exchange rate similarly reflected its determination to regain national independence and the means to reassert its influence in Eastern Europe and elsewhere. The revival of Paris as a financial market and France's granting of loans and credits to Austria, Germany, Hungary, Britain, Poland and other countries before and during the slump were also intimately linked to national security. This was equally the case with France's promotion of European federation between 1929 and 1931, which included the long-term goal of economic union, and its support for an economic association of Danubian states based upon mutual tariff preferences. So too was its decision to remain on the gold standard long after Germany, Britain, the United States and most of the world departed from it.

The second feature of the French experience was the way in which France fell victim to the interwar crisis. The onset of the slump triggered a vicious circle in which economic distress fuelled German nationalism and competition between Germany and France for influence over Austria and Eastern Europe, beginning in earnest with the Austro-German customs union project. The practical effect of this political confrontation was to shake confidence in business circles, which smothered signs of recovery in the spring of 1931 and brought a resumption of the downward economic slide. The ensuing financial crisis drew the three liberal powers into collective action to stave off a German collapse. But it also exposed differences in their international outlook and aggravated relations among them. French statesmen hoped that constructive application of their new-found economic strength would facilitate a rapprochement with the Anglo-Saxon powers. In the event, it did the opposite. The Anglo-Saxon powers or their leading bankers, even while retreating from economic liberalism, intensified their efforts to relieve Germany of its reparation burden while opposing French efforts to assist East European countries, which formed an essential part of the existing security framework. When France began to feel the full force of the economic slump in the winter of 1931, its principal response was the liberal one of active deflation, thus further weakening its military capacity, but it also reduced its foreign exchange balances and increased trade restrictions, which further aggravated relations with the Anglo-Saxon powers.

Relations between the Anglo-Saxon powers and France remained little changed over the next nine years. British political leaders had been suspicious of the Kaiser and his Prussian circle before 1914, but reluctant to believe that Britain and Germany could ever come to blows. From 1933, British political leaders became suspicious of Hitler and his Nazi circle, but continued to imagine that Britain could negotiate a 'general settlement' with Germany. This, historians commonly suggest, was at least partly attributable to the deep political divisions that emerged in the 1930s, which made conservatives more fearful of Soviet-backed Communism and correspondingly less wary of extreme anti-Communist regimes such as Hitler's and Mussolini's. But it was not just conservative politicians who allowed themselves to be so misled. As late as April 1938, when Edouard Daladier, the French premier, warned that Hitler's ambitions exceeded those of Napoleon, Sir Alexander Cadogan, the permanent head of the Foreign Office, dismissed Daladier's warning as 'awful rubbish'.[5] Moreover, it was of a piece with British attitudes towards Germans – as well as French – since long before the rise of Hitler. In 1936, Sir Horace Rumbold, the former ambassador to Berlin, complained to the editor of the *Times*:

> I have rather come to the conclusion that the average Englishman – whilst full of common-sense as regards internal affairs – is often muddleheaded, sloppy and gullible when he considers foreign affairs. One often hears such phrases as 'the Germans are so like us'. Nothing is more untrue. I could quote many points of difference. For one thing Germans have a streak of brutality which is quite absent in the ordinary Englishman. And Germans like or put up with things that are repugnant to the average man of this country.[6]

However, more remarkable than the confusion of certain conservatives and the 'average Englishman' was the readiness of prominent liberals to visit Germany or attend functions at the German embassy in London until the very eve of the war.[7] Many, it seems, still assumed that the threat Germany posed was due to an alien Prussian minority, whose aggressiveness and brutality Hitler somehow embodied, and that the vast majority of Germans, including Goering and other Nazis, being 'so like us', would not permit Hitler to resort to war in the West.[8] At the same time, they were not opposed to Germany's control over all German-speaking lands or its expansion into the Slavic lands of the East. On the contrary, they believed it was 'natural and normal' for Germany to dominate Central and Eastern Europe, as Lord Halifax, the foreign secretary, wrote in November 1938, since Germans were racially superior to the Slavs and needed space to expand.[9] The danger arose not from German expansion but from French efforts to obstruct Germany's expansion by encouraging the Slav countries to resist, for if France became involved in the conflict Britain would find it hard to keep out. Britain's challenge therefore was not to contain Germany, but to discourage France from maintaining or honouring its commitments in the East. British leaders therefore resumed their tactics of the 1920s, using the carrot of staff conversations and the stick of threats that Britain would not come to France's help if it provoked a war over Czechoslovakia or Poland.

This was the core of Chamberlain's appeasement policy from May 1937, when he became prime minister. He was dismayed by reports of Nazi brutality and occasionally referred to Germans as 'bullies' and Hitler as a 'lunatic' and 'half mad'.[10] Yet if Hitler was excitable and impatient, he was also 'a man who could be relied upon when he had given his word', and who would place the same importance upon economic stability as Chamberlain himself. In contrast, Chamberlain paid almost no heed to Hitler's intended victims in the East. He likened Germany's ambitions to those of the Uitlanders in the Transvaal who sought control of Togoland and the Kamerouns. It would be difficult to smooth the path, but

> I don't see why we shouldn't say to Germany, give us satisfactory assurances that you won't use force to deal with the Austrians and Czecho-Slovakians and we will give you similar assurances that we won't use force to prevent the changes you want if you can get them by peaceful means.[11]

Britain's temporizing enabled Hitler to occupy the Rhineland and absorb Austria without challenge. Hitler's decision to seize the Sudetenland, the German-speaking fringe around the western half of Czechoslovakia, was more problematical. British historians can point to half a dozen reasons why, on the basis of balance-of-power calculations, appeasing Germany was preferable to confrontation over the Sudetenland in 1938: Britain's current account weakness, the incomplete state of its rearmament, its lack of reliable, robust or enthusiastic allies, including the Soviet Union, France, the United States and the British Dominions, and the presence of not one but three dangerous enemies in Japan, Italy and Germany. But what is far from evident is that the two men who dominated British policy-making, Chamberlain and Halifax, based their decisions upon such balance-of-power calculations. Weak as it might have been, Chamberlain and Halifax probably regarded France, their one firm ally, as strong, not weak, indeed possibly too strong for its own good.[12] Nor did either man weigh up the implications of sacrificing Czechoslovakia, whose military and industrial capacity were far from insignificant, for it was only after they had taken the decision to appease Germany that Halifax learned that stripping Czechoslovakia of the Sudetenland would undermine its ability to defend itself.[13] More relevant than *post hoc Realpolitik* rationalizations are the reports of Sir Nevile Henderson, ambassador in Berlin, which both Chamberlain and Halifax avidly read. Henderson's advice was clear: 'The German is certainly more civilized than the Slav', and hence 'it is not fair to prevent Germany from completing her unity or from being prepared for war against the Slav.'[14]

> We neither could nor should try to hamper Germany's legitimate economic freedom of action in Central or Eastern Europe....The French dog-in-the-manger attitude in this respect is not only futile but silly....I admit that personally I am only too glad to wish that she [Germany] should look eastwards instead of westwards.[15]

As late as 1938, Henderson appears to have imagined it possible to establish an informal alliance of the three great Anglo-Saxon powers, Britain, Germany and the United States, as Joseph Chamberlain had done in the heyday of imperialism at the turn of the century.[16]

The Cabinet sought to forestall conflict by sending Lord Runciman, a National Liberal peer and former minister, to 'mediate' between the Czechoslovak government and the Sudeten Germans: in fact, to outline Czech territory for transfer to Germany. British statesmen scarcely doubted the legitimacy of this action. 'It is morally unjust to compel this solid Teuton minority [in the Sudetenland] to remain subjected to a Slav central Government at Prague', Henderson assured Halifax.[17] Runciman agreed. 'I have much sympathy ... with the Sudeten case. It is a hard thing to be ruled by an alien race.'[18] More obliquely, Chamberlain made the same point to Parliament on 27 September 1938, just before the Munich conference. The British Empire embraced peoples in places as distant as Bloemfontein, Bulawayo, Belmopan, Bangalore and Singapore. Yet, in Parliament Chamberlain affirmed that the people of Czechoslovakia were too remote to warrant Britain's support. 'How horrible, fantastic, incredible it is that we should be digging trenches and trying on gas masks here because of a quarrel in a far-away country between people of whom we know nothing.'[19]

Chamberlain persuaded reluctant French leaders to accept the immediate transfer of the Sudetenland to Germany, and at the Munich conference, without informing the French, he approached Hitler to propose a 'general settlement'. Subsequently, however, Hitler embarrassed the British government by belligerent speeches, loosing Nazi stormtroopers on Jewish shops and synagogues throughout Germany on *Kristallnacht*, 9 November, and on 15 March 1939 seizing the rest of Czechoslovakia. Poland, Hitler's next target, threatened to be a harder nut to crack, and to demonstrate its disapproval of Hitler's methods Chamberlain found himself obliged to exchange commitments with Poland, guarantee Roumania and Greece, and seek a defensive agreement with Soviet Russia. By now, practically no one in Britain could doubt that Hitler was a highly dangerous man, whose ambitions threatened to end in war. Yet, Chamberlain, supported by Halifax and other members of the Cabinet, continued to pursue a 'general settlement' with Germany, opening new channels of communication to Berlin as late as August 1939.[20]

In an uncanny repetition of its misleading actions in 1914, Britain's obvious reluctance to extend practical help to Poland or associate with the Soviet Union, together with its ambiguity over military cooperation with France and continued pursuit of a settlement with Germany, persuaded Hitler that Britain would not oppose his expansionist ambitions in the East. Only on the eve of invading Poland did he learn to his dismay that London intended to honour its commitment to Warsaw. Determined to proceed, he manufactured a *casus belli* to justify going to war on 1 September. With the exception of Bonnet, the foreign minister, French statesmen were never under any illusion about Germany and had been resigned to war since 1938. They were just emerging from the slump, their rearmament was still incomplete, they had lost Belgium, Czechoslovakia and the Soviet Union as allies, right-wing extremists were confusing the public by making scapegoats of the Jews for France's plight, and Communists, who exercised influence over half the urban working class, threatened to oppose war once the Soviet Union became Germany's *de facto* ally in August 1939. But after Germany invaded Poland, the French government scarcely hesitated before declaring war.

Even now the Anglo-Saxon powers moved with agonizing slowness towards backing Europe's beleaguered democracies. President Roosevelt accepted that the United States could not risk being left alone with Germany, Japan and Italy, and should therefore support their European opponents, but he would not make the mistake of Wilson, his mentor, in 1918, who imagined that he could lead his reluctant, isolationist electorate into foreign commitments without regard for Congress. Since 1933, Americans had been shocked by Nazi displays of anti-Semitism, and as in 1914 they now broadly sympathized with Britain's plight. But isolationism had been intensified by the slump, and in 1939 the country had still not fully recovered from it. Moreover, many Americans still accepted the 'two Germany' thesis, which increased their reluctance to become involved. As Archibald MacLeish, the Librarian of Congress and senior advisor on propaganda, wrote in 1942.

> The policy of distinction between the Nazis and the rest of the [German] population was the only policy that the American government could pursue; it would never be possible to secure support for a racial war against the German people simply because they were German by 'race'.[21]

Until Pearl Harbor freed his hands, Roosevelt therefore restricted his efforts to re-supplying Britain and France, to enable them to contain the aggressor powers. This proved sufficient to keep Britain but not France in the war.

Despite declaring war in 1939, British leaders still hankered for a settlement with Germany. They did not put the British economy on a full war footing, nor did they antagonize Germany by military operations in the West. Like the Americans, they also based their propaganda on the 'two Germany' thesis, to the annoyance of the French.[22] Briefly, to stave off a French collapse, the Foreign Office encouraged the BBC and British press to support permanently closer Franco-British relations.[23] But even in June 1940, as the remnants of Britain's expeditionary force were being collected from the beaches at Dunkirk, the majority of the War Cabinet still favoured one more attempt at a 'general settlement' with Germany. It was of course sad to see Poland overrun and France defeated, but they believed the Slav and Latin powers had been foolish to antagonize Germany while it was down. This may well have been the subtext of King George VI's comment, 'Personally, I feel happier now that we have no allies to be polite to and to pamper.'[24] Only with Winston Churchill in charge, the Battle of Britain under way and the government keen to persuade the United States and the Dominions to underwrite Britain's survival, did talk of appeasing Germany cease. But so too did talk of a permanent alliance with France. Once again, Britain turned from Europe and instead looked to America and the Empire for its security.[25]

8.2   Since the great interwar crisis

The dual politico-economic crisis that began in 1927 and culminated in 1933–4 gave way to a more general crisis comprising imperialism, autarky, industrialized warfare and genocide, which lasted for more than a decade. The usual periodization of the twentieth century is to present the two world wars as the key demarcation points, with the 1914–45 period as one unit of history and the 1945–91 period, when the Soviet-American confrontation created a bipolar world, as another. But just as it makes better sense to recognize that the First World War constituted only a hiatus in the great era of globalization that began in 1815 and continued until 1927, so it makes better sense to see the years from 1927 to 1947 as a single generalized crisis, since only in 1947 did this grimmest of periods end and a new era of (partial) globalization get properly under way. Thus, we might say that the long nineteenth century was even longer than is generally assumed: from 1815 to 1927. Similarly, the term 20-years-crisis, which E. H. Carr used to describe the interwar period, is better applied to the years 1927–47, which experienced the calamitous effects of the collapse of globalization.

The date 1947 perhaps needs further explanation. Before the Second World War ended, the developed countries of the West had begun to apply some lessons from their recent experience. They created new international institutions, including the International Monetary Fund (IMF), the International Bank for Reconstruction and Development, which became the central component of today's World Bank, and the General Agreement on Tariffs and Trade (GATT), to help regulate the world economy. Through the IMF they agreed upon new rules on international payments adjustment to avoid a return to the beggar-your-neighbour policies that characterized the 1930s. Member countries agreed to return to fixed exchange rates and to pursue balance of payments equilibrium through unilateral domestic adjustments of fiscal as well as monetary policy. But the IMF provided additional liquidity to address temporary shortages, and where countries faced an ill-defined 'fundamental disequilibrium' in their international payments, they could seek approval for unilateral currency devaluation. This formalized the procedure introduced in 1936 when Britain and the United States endorsed and assisted the devaluation of the French franc. It constituted a major advance, since it established agreed rules for monetary and exchange rate policy, including recognition that the burden of adjustment of international payments should be shared by the surplus as well as the deficit countries.

Nonetheless, in the capitalist West the immediate postwar period was marked by two contradictory developments. On the one hand, most developed countries reacted to the great interwar crisis by adopting versions of economic planning and limiting the exposure of their economies to the vagaries of market forces. Most of them also leaned towards policies of full employment at the expense of inflation. (If paradoxically West Germany and Italy held back, it was because after the experience of war and shattering defeat the desire to regain the virtues of liberalism outweighed fear of its consequences.) By and large, the middle classes in the developed world hoped to see government intervention in economic affairs rolled back and taxes reduced to 'normal' prewar levels, as had generally happened after the First World War. But in 1945, this went largely unrealized, since aside from the United States the domestic balance of political power had shifted leftwards, and having experienced the shortcomings of liberalism, supporters of progressive parties sought greater expenditure on health, education and social care in what came to be known as a welfare state.[26]

On the other hand, the United States, picking up where Britain left off in 1927, promoted the stabilization of currencies, the removal of exchange controls and the reopening of commercial markets, in short the return to globalization, while at the same time refusing to accept the need to underwrite a robust security framework for Europe. Together, the Anglo-Saxon powers again instituted a global forum, the United Nations, to deliberate upon international conflicts, but no more than with the League of Nations were they prepared to invest it with real power. Once again, they persisted in the 'two Germany' thesis, this time treating the Nazis rather than the Prussians as the corrupting element who had hijacked the state and drawn Germany into war and crimes against humanity.[27] With the Nazis removed from power and the German majority 're-educated', they impatiently sought to restore Germany to the international states system and re-establish it as the economic powerhouse of Europe. Once again, this put them on a collision course with France, which was not prepared to see Germany regain its economic power let alone military power, in the absence of an effective security framework. As in 1918, France desperately hoped the Anglo-Saxon powers would underpin such a framework. But this time it did not hesitate to approach the Soviet Union in search of countervailing power, and once again it reluctantly promoted European integration when neither the Anglo-Saxon powers nor the Soviet Union appeared willing to contribute to European security.

To their credit, a few authorities within the Anglo-Saxon powers appreciated the shortcomings of their strategy. John Foster Dulles, foreign policy adviser to the Republican party, called for recognition that Germany's recovery must be accompanied by a commitment to Europe's long-term security, including active support for European integration.[28] George Kennan, the American diplomat, was equally clear sighted.

> The great mistake of the statesmen at Versailles in 1919 had been to reconstitute Germany as a national entity, to give no wider horizon than the national one to the aspirations of the German people, and at the same time to set up nothing else in Europe that could rival Germany in physical strength. Now we were faced with this problem once again. What were we to do this time? The idea of partition – of breaking up the country once again into a multiplicity of small sovereign states, no longer seemed to me realistic. ... But if Germany could not be broken up – if the problem of German nationalism could not be solved by thrusting Germany further into the past – then the only thing to do was to thrust both Germany and Europe farther into the future; to create, that is, some sort of united federal Europe into which the united Germany could be imbedded, and in this way to widen that horizon of aspiration and loyalty

which, at its purely linguistic and national limits, had proved too narrow for the safety of Europe, too narrow for the safety of Germany herself. ... When I returned from Germany, in 1942, I tried to win understanding for this idea in the Department of State; but the effort was fruitless. ... Instead, [we] staggered into the post-hostilities period with a set of concepts which envisaged nothing more than an interim period of four-power collaboration in the occupation and military government of a defeated Germany, after which that country was to be restored once more, and launched again onto the sea of international life, as a sovereign entity among others, overshadowing once again all of its neighbors in potential physical strength, and with no higher focus for the collective ideals and aspirations of its people than the framework of German nationalism itself. Whatever elements of insecurity this might involve from the standpoint of the peace of the continent were apparently supposed to be contained and counteracted by the authority of the United Nations, supported by a continued collaboration among the great powers, including Russia and China. To my own deep despair, this utterly unrealistic concept continued – despite the growing evidence of the unsubstantiability of its assumption – to inspire American policy down to 1948.[29]

Uncommon as Kennan's view was in postwar Washington, it was even less common in London. Winston Churchill, Harold Macmillan and Anthony Eden now favoured a unified Europe, but not including Britain. Leaders of the Labour government did not even favour that and ordered party members to stay away from the Hague congress in May 1948, which marked the rebirth of the European movement. Neither they nor their Foreign Office advisers believed that Europe deserved Britain's commitment or was solid enough to be trusted in a closer relationship. Until 1947, therefore, American and British assistance to Continental Europe was limited almost exclusively to *ad hoc* economic aid. But while more extensive than aid after 1918, it could not remove the insecurity that threatened to undermine Europe's stability. Only with the onset of the Cold War did the Anglo-Saxon powers join in a framework of security for Western Europe. The first step came with the announcement of the Truman doctrine in March 1947, affirming America's support to countries threatened by Soviet-encouraged subversion, followed in June of that year by the announcement of the European Recovery or Marshall Plan, confirming America's support for Western Europe's recovery. In contrast to its interwar and postwar position, Washington now took direct responsibility for Europe's economic stability by a four-year programme of economic gifts totalling $13 billion, effectively reducing trade imbalances and international payments adjustments. As late as 1945, Washington had insisted upon the end of Imperial preferences as a condition of its loan to Britain. But in a remarkable reversal of policy, it accepted, indeed insisted upon, intra-European trade preferences as part of the Marshall Plan. In 1948 came the American decision to confront the challenge of the Soviet Union's blockade of Berlin, and after the presidential election in November formal negotiations with Canada, Britain and West European countries for a North Atlantic Alliance. The American security guarantee, which required a British commitment as well, removed the threat overhanging Western Europe's recovery. With the Anglo-Saxon powers also committed to the international economic institutions as weapons in their struggle against the Communist bloc, other developed countries set aside the option of planning, and the new era of globalization in the 'first' and 'third' worlds continued for the next 50 years. When the Communist bloc collapsed in 1989 and the Soviet Union vanished two years later, globalization spread to the 'second' world as well.

The third great era of globalization that began in 1947 brought enormous prosperity to most parts of the world. Numerous regional conflicts occurred, in East Asia, the Middle East, Africa, the Balkans and the southern Caucasus, yet the superpowers avoided major war and since the demise of the Soviet Union most of the world has enjoyed peace. The recent financial crisis thus seemed to come out of the blue, encouraging commentators to focus almost exclusively upon the shortcomings of the financial markets while largely ignoring the political framework within which the markets operated, or to use current academic jargon, to fix upon the endogenous rather than the exogenous causal factors. One feature of the crisis evident to all was the huge increase in leverage – of debt to equity – of the major US and British commercial banks at the centre of the global financial system. Since the end of the era of Keynesian economics in the late 1960s, they had remained dangerously undercapitalized, operating on a debt to equity ratio of at least 30:1.[30] Another feature was the practice of the same banks as well as many of their main clients, the private equity firms and hedge funds, systematically to misprice risk. This prompted most experts to attempt to explain why the financial intermediaries allowed themselves, or were allowed, to become so vulnerable to systemic crisis. Some singled out the banks' over-reliance upon mathematical models for estimating risk and their suspension of traditional, common-sense rules of caution.[31] Others pointed to the vast increase in exotic debt instruments such as securitized sub-prime mortgages, collateralized debt obligations, credit default swaps and other securities and derivatives. Their value has proven so difficult to establish that they have undermined trust in the banks that borrowed against them.[32] Still others emphasized the distortions of the reward system whereby bankers were allegedly induced by the promise of large financial bonuses to take excessive risks with their banks' or clients' funds; changes in accounting rules, which practically guaranteed a cascading decline in financial asset values in the event of a market setback; or the conflict of interest that led credit rating agencies to overstate the quality of debt instruments issued by their banking clients.[33] But just like the onset of the great interwar crisis, which also began in conditions of peace and increasing prosperity, the present crisis cannot be understood without regard to its exogenous causes, or to use the non-technical language of the present account, without regard to weaknesses in the political framework surrounding the markets.

One element of the political framework is the international institutions created at the end of the Second World War to help member countries address short-term payments imbalances, coordinate economic policies, facilitate international payments adjustment and help keep global markets open. The importance of these institutions grew in line with the increase in globalization, yet largely because of the Cold War they remained dominated by the United States and its Western allies, and shaped by Anglo-Saxon thinking, and they have thus declined in representativeness, international respect and influence. This is equally true of the World Bank, the International Monetary Fund (IMF), the World Trade Organization (WTO), the Group of Seven leading industrial nations (G7), and the United Nations (UN). In the case of the UN, the problem has arisen because the United States has continued to project its enormous power into practically all quarters of the world with little regard for international opinion, while using its veto on the Security Council to block opposition. In the case of the WTO, Western dominance has been aggravated by the reluctance of certain Western countries to heed the Organization's injunctions to remove subsidies which distort trade, prompting many non-Western countries to react in kind. The Doha round of negotiations on trade liberalization, begun in 2001, reached stalemate once again in July 2007, with the developing countries accusing the United States and EU of maintaining unacceptable subsidies to farm exports and the Western powers accusing the developing countries of protecting their own small farmers by invoking the 'special safeguard mechanism'. The long-running stalemate has accelerated the trend away from multilateralism and towards bilateral trading agreements.[34]

The IMF's inadequacies are of a similar order. The United States dominates the Fund by controlling 17 per cent of voting rights within it, since the Fund's decisions require a majority of 85 per cent. Together, the United States and its European Union allies control approximately 50 per cent of voting rights, while China's share is only 3.5 per cent, Russia's is 2.7 per cent and India's a mere 2 per cent.[35] The IMF's credibility has been further undermined by the decision of the Western powers to create the Financial Stability Forum, largely bypassing the IMF, after the Asian financial crisis in 1997–8; and by the Western powers' recent insistence that the IMF should focus its attention upon global exchange rate misalignments, an implicit assault on Chinese economic policy.[36] But above all, its reputation has been damaged by the impression, created most vividly in the aftermath of the Asian financial crisis, that non-Western countries must respect strict market discipline as laid out in the rigorous conditions – known with unintended irony as the 'Washington [policy] consensus' – which the IMF usually demands when its help is requested, whereas Western countries have no such obligations. As Kishore Mahbubani, dean of the University of Singapore's Lee Kuan Yew School of Public Policy, wrote shortly after Western banks were bailed out by their governments in October 2008,

> In many ways, US and European policy-makers are doing the opposite of what they advised Asian policymakers to do in 1997–98: do not rescue failing banks, raise interest rates, balance your budget. Millions of Indonesians and Thais would have been better off if their governments had been permitted to do

what western governments are doing now. An apology from the west to Asia would not be inappropriate.[37]

One consequence of the IMF's declining legitimacy has been a tendency of developing countries to seek help elsewhere, from China, Venezuela or the sovereign wealth funds of one or another of the Gulf states, although here too loans come with strings.[38] Another has been a decline in the Fund's lending resources. Thus, by the start of the present crisis, the Fund's capital base was wholly inadequate to meet problems created by the huge increase in global capital flows. With a total lending capacity of merely $250 billion, the Fund has been prepared to help Iceland, Pakistan and Ukraine, but is in no position to address short-term crises in any of the larger member countries.

In the 1990s, the World Bank under its president James Wolfensohn substantially reformed its own operations, if not its structure. Its weakness is that, as another Washington-based institution, it has chosen not to challenge the IMF when the latter intervenes abroad.[39] The G7, even with the addition of Russia making it the G8, has no specific remit, but has been handicapped in its efforts to promote international cooperation by its narrow membership. The decision of President George W. Bush to convene an *ad hoc* meeting of the 20 largest industrial countries – the G20 – in November 2008 marked a belated recognition of the problem.[40] But much more will be required to repair the damage done to international cooperation by the West's, and above all America's, neglect of international institutions.

Problems with the two other essential elements of the global political framework, namely agreed rules of economic behaviour and international security, may be taken together. The Western powers, led by the United States and Britain, regularly insisted upon extreme liberal solutions whenever countries approached the IMF for assistance. But at the same time, as the Anglo-Saxon powers deregulated their own financial markets, they resisted efforts by their European allies to increase the transparency of the financial markets, extend control over offshore tax havens and tighten regulation of financial intermediaries.[41] Developing countries, in contrast, reacted to the stiff medicine they had been obliged to take in previous crises by ensuring that they would never again be beholden to Western institutions. Among other things, they introduced greater fiscal discipline, tougher regulation of their banks, in many cases reduced their reliance upon capital imports, and assisted 'national champion' firms to gain access to foreign markets. As the result, many of the largest developing countries generated strong current account surpluses and built up enormous foreign exchange reserves.[42] By August 2007, the total foreign currency reserves of the developing countries reached a total of $5500 billion. This is partly explained by the greater risks that accompanied the liberalization of capital markets.[43] But there seems little doubt that it also reflects a political determination on the part of the individual countries to reduce their vulnerability to foreign, that is to say Western, interference: security in other words.[44] Whether it can produce security, however, is another matter, since the global imbalances require the surplus countries to continue lending to the debtor countries, which must ultimately become unsustainable.

The largest of the developing countries, China, also adopted the most determinedly independent policy, which strengthened its economy while also paradoxically drawing it into steadily closer interdependence with the Western powers. Emerging from self-imposed isolation in the 1980s, it drew on foreign direct investment from the West to develop its export-oriented manufacturing industries. From 1994, it also held down the exchange rate of its currency, the renminbi, by pegging it to the dollar, thereby gaining an exchange advantage and accelerating the penetration of the US, EU and other foreign markets. Most importantly, it ensured an abundant supply of well-educated, low-paid workers for its rapidly expanding manufacturing sector.[45] China's share of world exports rose from an average of 1.4 per cent in 1980–90 to 2.5 per cent in 1990–2000, to approximately 6 per cent in 2004 and to an estimated 8 per cent in 2007.[46] More disturbing, however, was its increasing trade surplus with Europe and the United States. Since 1985, when its surplus with the United States stood at $10 billion, the total has rapidly risen to $124 billion in 2003, and to $256 billion in 2007, or one-third of America's overall trade deficit.[47]

This enabled the Chinese central bank to accumulate foreign currency reserves of approximately $2000 billion by 2008, most of it probably held in US government securities, and this in turn enabled Washington to concede tax concessions to high income earners and prosecute its wars in Iraq and Afghanistan without running up against America's huge federal budget and current account deficits.[48] Meanwhile, the massive inflow of cheap Chinese goods restrained US wage and price inflation, and enabled the Federal Reserve Board to bring down interest rates to historically low levels. This in turn encouraged America's deregulated banks and mortgage lenders to increase their borrowing, since with a 1 per cent base rate (from 2003) the opportunities for profitable lending or investment seemed almost unlimited. American (and British) firms added to their own precariousness by taking on greater borrowings and increasing returns on capital, not through investment, but by disposing of 'surplus' capital and buying back their own issued shares.[49] The sharp rise in the price of oil and other imported commodities, driven skywards by demand from the developing countries, adversely affected personal savings rates and increased household debt, a trend aggravated by the stagnation of working-class and even middle-class incomes while upper-class incomes soared. By 2006, the distribution of income in the United States had become as skewed towards the very rich as in 1928, with the top 10 per cent of Americans taking 49.6 per cent of national income, more than at any time since 1917.[50] US public, corporate and household debt meanwhile rose from 163 per cent of gross domestic product in 1980 to 346 per cent in 2007, and the US current account deficit also soared to over 6 per cent of gross domestic product in 2006 and just below 6 per cent in 2007 (more than double the Chinese current account surplus).[51] The United States, which had been the world's greatest debtor before the First World War and the world's greatest creditor in the following 80 years, was once again the world's greatest debtor. In 2006 alone, it borrowed $900 billion from the rest of the world.[52]

By 2005, the Chinese authorities recognized that the huge global imbalances were unsustainable, and entered into a dialogue with the United States while allowing their currency to rise part way towards its equilibrium rate.[53] Between July 2005 and October 2008, the real effective rate of the renminbi rose 21.8 per cent, and with the euro, the yen and other currencies of the developing Asian economies also rising against the dollar, the US current account deficit modestly narrowed.[54] But by then, as one Chinese official put it, 'America [had] drowned itself in Asian liquidity.'[55] The United States and Britain, which adopted closely similar policies, had allowed their loosely regulated markets to generate what a leading economist has described as 'the largest leveraged asset bubble and credit bubble in history.'[56] Sooner or later it was bound to burst, with severe consequences for their banking systems and the world economy as a whole.

To be sure, 2007–9 is not 1927–9. Among the more obvious differences, the great interwar crisis began at a time of deflation whereas the present crisis began at a time of accelerating inflation. It should be stressed that the deflation of the second half of the 1920s was price deflation as opposed to monetary contraction, and may not have been an insuperable obstacle to world growth and stability. But it does seem to have added to Britain's payments adjustment problems, pressures on the Bank of England and a decline in support for free trade especially in manufacturing centres and rural areas. The United States and other countries faced similar political consequences, and after the Wall Street crash, when the decline in general price level accelerated, they had little choice but to defend their currencies by the more pernicious form of deflation, monetary contraction, which acutely aggravated their economic and political problems. Before the recent crisis, levels of inflation were tolerable for most countries, although the scale of the credit bubble in 2007–8 was considerably greater than in 1927–9.

A second difference is the greatly enlarged role of the state in practically every country since the Second World War. Commonly triple the size of prewar times as a fraction of the national economy, the state is by far the largest employer, and with no obligation to turn a profit it exercises a stabilizing influence on the private sector of the economy. Linked to this is a third difference, namely the broader geographical distribution of economic activity, beyond Europe and the United States where it was overwhelmingly concentrated in the 1920s, to South and East Asia, South America and elsewhere today. Developing countries cannot hope to 'decouple' from the banking crisis in the West, and they may be vulnerable to greater fluctuations in economic activity than the developed countries, since their service sector is relatively smaller. Nevertheless, their potential for growth remains enormous, and with consumer spending in China alone exceeding that of the United States, the developing countries can accelerate the world's recovery from an economic slump.[57]

A fourth difference is the impressive advance of economic knowledge since 1927–9. While economists still differ on many issues, they are broadly agreed on the unwisdom of relying exclusively upon unilateral domestic adjustments, such as deflationary fiscal and monetary policies, the prescription of nearly all their counterparts in the first stages of the interwar crisis, to restore international payments equilibrium. Nor do they favour fixed exchange rates, whether defined in gold or paper currencies, although like their predecessors they also generally oppose unilateral external adjustments, such as trade protection or foreign lending controls. The general shift of academic thought away from Keynesianism towards a neoclassical paradigm in the 1960s and 1970s has almost certainly contributed to the liberalization of capital markets, the acceleration of globalization and latterly global instability.[58] Arguably the popularity of mathematical modelling among economists has also tended to simplify and therefore distort their grasp of relationships in the real world. Nevertheless, there is no gainsaying the great advances in the analytical techniques of contemporary economics and its capacity to contribute to solutions to the current crisis.

The fifth and probably the most important difference of all is the contrasting behaviour of the world's powers in the two crises. In 1927–9, as we have seen, the leading powers proved wholly unwilling or unable to cooperate on commercial, financial or monetary policy. In fact, they were already pulling apart two years before the Wall Street crash, behaviour which contributed to the fragility of the global economic system at the moment when the contemporary asset bubble broke. The contrast with the behaviour of leading powers in the present crisis – so far – could scarcely be greater. The United States, despite President George W. Bush's first-term preference for unilateralism, which was all too reminiscent of Hoover's isolationism, has strongly affirmed its commitment to multilateral action. The European Union, despite initial signs that individual countries would pull apart, has not only remained united but also continued to look outwards. The Franco-German axis, now a constructive partnership, has contributed to European unity, and the existence of a single currency and the European Central Bank has reduced the risk of individual countries succumbing to speculative attack, as was the case in the great interwar crisis. Britain, too, has joined in European efforts to address the financial crisis, having hitherto disdained cooperation with its European partners.[59]

Beyond the West, China has also demonstrated its willingness to contribute to multilateral action. Despite its narrowly nationalist pursuit of foreign markets since the 1980s, which was all too reminiscent of US behaviour in the 1920s, it joined Western central banks in October, evidently without consultation, in reducing interest rates, and further demonstrated its solidarity by continuing to purchase US Treasury bills. It also signalled its intention to offset the calamitous slump in world export demand by bringing forward plans to stimulate domestic consumption through fiscal reforms and a massive expansion of public spending on infrastructure and health care.[60] Even Russia, while maintaining an aggressively nationalist defence posture, has indicated its wish to cooperate with the European Union and the United States in overcoming the crisis.[61] It phrased its renewed demand for reform of international institutions including the IMF in aggressive language, but this can be seen as evidence that Russia seeks to remain inside the global political framework rather than undermining it.[62] In contrast to the great interwar crisis, therefore, the framework has not disintegrated. Despite its weaknesses, which contributed to the onset of the crisis, the powers appear to be alive to just how close the world came in the autumn of 2008 to total financial collapse, and to their common interest in rebuilding the political framework.

The future nevertheless remains obscure. Although capitalism has nowhere been radically challenged, the Anglo-Saxon model of deregulated markets has been severely discredited and the institutions created at the start of the postwar era of globalization have taken a heavy knock. Particularly in the West, frustration is also building up at the impact of globalization. In the United States, trade unions and representatives of states that have lost manufacturing jobs to Asian competitors are increasingly vocal in demanding a more aggressive 'fair trade' policy. President Obama encouraged the protectionists during his election campaign when he endorsed calls to renegotiate the North America Free Trade Agreement, complained of business 'shipping out American jobs' and accused China of 'currency manipulation'.[63] In the White House, Obama is likely to be more cautious, but isolation remains strong in America. In a recent survey of opinion, 36 per cent of respondents agreed that the United States should 'stay out of world affairs', 6 per cent up from 2006 and higher than at any time since the question was first asked in 1947. More importantly, the number of Americans who believe that globalization is 'mostly bad' for the United States has grown steadily from 31 per cent in 2004, to 35 per cent in 2006 and to 42 per cent in September 2008.[64] Similar grassroots pressure to retreat from globalization has also emerged in Germany, France and throughout the West, and a prolonged recession can be expected to drive up support.[65] Given that this is a very real possibility, the spectre has reappeared of a general resort to protectionism and regionalism, as occurred in the great interwar crisis, and along with a steep decline in commodity prices the return of price deflation with its attendant pressures on social and political stability.[66]

However, even if the present crisis is surmounted without systemic damage, the rapid growth of the developing countries is certain to bring intensified competition for non-renewable resources and markets. With the West facing the prospect of a deep recession of shorter or longer duration, the shift in power towards the East seems certain to accelerate. And with the leading developing countries, Brazil, Russia, India and China – the BRIC countries – widely expected to equal the combined gross domestic product of the original G7 industrial countries by 2040 and exceed it by 40 per cent by 2050, even assuming a slowing of Russian and Chinese growth rates, international tensions seem inescapable.[67] According to one leading analyst,

> Since this century is seeing a huge shift in the balance of economic and so political and military power, conflicts over the nature of the international order and over more mundane matters – particularly access to resources and markets – are certain. They will become more probable and more dangerous the more restrained access to resources and markets becomes.[68]

The future is as open-ended as ever. But since the past provides the only means of gaining perspective on the present, the interwar period holds a special importance for us. In 1927, the great interwar crisis began, ending the second era of globalization begun over a century before and only temporarily interrupted by the Great War, and ushering in the worst 20 years of economic and political strife the world has ever experienced. The situation today, 60 years after the return to globalization and 16 years after the end of the Cold War, is of course not the same. Yet, understanding the history of the interwar crisis may be essential if this reduces the risk of repeating the mistakes that led to the end of the previous era of globalization and the calamities that ensued.

Notes

Abbreviations

AA	Auswärtiges Amt
AC	Austen Chamberlain papers
ADAP	Germany, Auswärtiges Amt, *Akten zur deutschen auswärtigen Politik 1918–1945*
BdF DCG	Banque de France, Sécretariat du Conseil Général, Archives Centrales, Délibérations du Conseil Général
BCC	Boyce, *British Capitalism at the Crossroads*
BDFA	Bourne and Cameron Watt (eds), *British Documents on Foreign Affairs*
BEAMA	British Electrical and Allied Manufacturers' Association
BoE	Bank of England papers
BB	Baring Brothers and Company archives
BT	United Kingdom Board of Trade
CAB	United Kingdom Cabinet
DBFP	United Kingdom, *Documents on British Foreign Policy*
DCF	Link (ed.), *Deliberations of the Council of Four*
DDF	France, *Documents Diplomatiques Françaises*
FBI	Federation of British Industries
FO	United Kingdom Foreign Office
FRBNY	Federal Reserve Bank of New York
FRUS	United States State Department, *Foreign Relations of the United States*
GV	Papers of George V, Royal Archives
HHCP	Herbert Hoover Commerce papers
HHPP	Herbert Hoover Presidential papers
HO	United Kingdom Home Office
IPCH	Seymour (ed.), *The Intimate Papers of Colonel House*
JO	France, *Journal Officiel*
JRM	James Ramsay MacDonald papers
LG	Lloyd George papers
LN	League of Nations
MA	France, Ministère de l'Agriculture
MAE PA-AP	France, Ministère des Affaires Etrangères, Papiers Privés – Agents Particuliers
MAE RC B-IE	France, Ministère des Affaires Etrangères, Relations Commerciales, B-Informations économiques
MAE RC B-NC	France, Ministère des Affaires Etrangères, Relations Commerciales, B-négociations commerciales
MAE Europe 1918–40, GB	France, Ministère des Affaires Etrangères, Europe 1918–40, Grande-Bretagne
MAE, SdN SG	France, Ministère des Affaires Etrangères, Société des Nations, Secrétariat Général
MAE, SdN IJ-QEF	France, Ministère des Affaires Etrangères, Société des Nations, Questions Economiques et Financières
MAE, SdN, UE	France, Ministère des Affaires Etrangères, Société des Nations, Union Européenne

MAF	United Kingdom Ministry of Agriculture and Fisheries
MF	France, Ministère des Finances
MGC	Morgan Grenville & Company papers
MPC	Lloyd George, *Memoirs of the Peace Conference*
NAC	National Archives of Canada
NC	Neville Chamberlain papers
Quesnay	France, AN, 374 AP 6, Papiers de Pierre Quesnay
POST	British Post Office archives
PP	United Kingdom, *Parliamentary Papers*
PWW	Link (ed.), *The Papers of Woodrow Wilson*
RIIA	Royal Institute of International Affairs
TY	United Kingdom Treasury
TWL	Thomas W. Lamont papers
256 H.C. Deb 5s, col. 100	United Kingdom Parliamentary Debates, House of Commons, 5th series, vol. 256, column 100
USBC	US Bureau of the Census, *Historical Statistics of the United States*
USDC	US Department of Commerce, *The United States and the World Economy*
US DS	United States National Archives, Department of State
US RG80	US National Archives, General Records of the Department of the Navy, Office of the Secretary of the Navy

Introduction

1. FO371/12900, C2116/652/18, minute by Tyrrell, 20 Mar. 1928.
2. JRM 30/69/2/12, Stimson to MacDonald, 27 Jan. 1932.
3. Wrench, *Geoffrey Dawson*, p. 334.
4. Steiner, *The Lights That Failed: European International History, 1919–1933*, the first of two volumes on the interwar period, is at the time of writing the latest and the longest synthesis of the standard narrative. See also Cohrs, *The Unfinished Peace after World War I* and Johnson (ed.), *Locarno Revisited*.
5. Estimates vary, but according to one recent study the First World War cost the lives of 8.6 million combatants, perhaps 7 million civilians or 29 million if the victims of the influenza epidemic of 1918–19 are included, and approximately three times the 1914 gross economic product of the world. The same study estimates that the Second World War cost the lives of 17.1 million soldiers and 20 – 27 million civilians. The physical cost of the Second World War is almost impossible to quantify, but was far greater than the First World War, since it left a vastly broader swath of destruction. Bairoch, *Victoires et débcires*, iii, pp. 17–19, 34–5, 108–10 and passim.
6. Thus in France, which relied more than most Western countries upon the state for administration and services, the public sector provided 3.9 per cent of total employment in 1913, 5.5 per cent in 1921 and 7.2 per cent in 1936, but 14.0 per cent in 1962 and 24.7 per cent in 2000: Dormois, *The French Economy in the Twentieth Century*, p. 45, table 4.1.
7. The dynamism of the world economy in the 1920s is often overlooked because the declines of the wartime or immediate postwar period are included in the statistical averages. Thus one widely used economics textbook affirms that world trade grew at 'a modest … 1 per cent per annum', and capital movements played a very small role during the interwar period. Södersten, *International Economics*, pp. 100, 104. But see LN, *The Course and Phases of the World Economic Depression*, p. 19; Kenwood and Lougheed, *The Growth of the International Economy*, p. 211.
8. Maddison, *Monitoring the World Economy*, table 1–4, p. 239.
9. James, *End of Globalization*, is one of the very few accounts that argues for a similar chronology.

10. LN, *World Production and Prices, 1936/37*, table 2, p. 41.

11. Maddison, *Monitoring the World Economy*, table 1–4, p. 239; LN, *Monthly Bulletin of Statistics*, vol. 15, no. 12 (Dec. 1934), table 1, p. 537.

12. Arndt, *The Economic Lessons of the Nineteen Thirties*, p. 33; Ziebura, *World Economy and World Politics*, table 8, p. 63; Kindleberger, *The World in Depression*, table, p. 172 and p. 86.

13. Bairoch, *Victoires et déboires*, iii, table XXIV.4, p. 59. German unemployment reached a peak of 6,128,400 or 44.3 per cent of the industrial workforce in February 1932. *Wirtschaft und Statistik*, 2nd heft, Aug. 1932, p. 489.

14. 'Deutsche Wirtschaftszahlen', *Wirtschaft und Statistik*, 2nd heft, Dec. 1929, p. 977; *ibid.*, 28 Feb. 1933, p. 101; *ibid.*, 30 May 1933, p. 289.

15. Ziebura, *World Economy and World Politics*, table 19, p. 131.

16. Immigrant numbers reached an interwar peak of 2,715,000 in 1931, then declined to 2,198,000 in 1936 before rising again to 2,700,000 in 1939: Sauvy, *Histoire économique*, ii, p. 43, table II, pp. 554–5; Kemp, *The French Economy*, pp. 109–14. Most affected were the immigrants from southern Europe employed in agriculture; practically none of the Polish immigrants, who worked mainly in mining and industry, returned home: MAE, Europe 1944–60, Pologne 85, Direction des Renseignements Généraux, 6e Section, 'Le repatriement des émigrés polonais du Nord et du Pas-de-Calais', 5 Mar. 1946.

17. Dormois, *The French Economy in the Twentieth Century*, p. 97. Unemployment among the industrial workforce remained above 400,000 or 10 per cent as late as March 1937: Sauvy, *Histoire économique*, ii, table II, pp. 554–5; Bairoch, *Victoires et déboires*, iii, table XXIV.7, p. 80.

18. Cashman, *America Ascendant*, p. 259.

19. Urquhart and Buckley (eds), *Historical Statistics of Canada*, Series A221, p. 22.

20. Mussolini, *Opera Omnia*, xxv, p. 148. Historians disagree on the question of a turning point in Mussolini's foreign policy, but see Bosworth, *Mussolini*, pp. 264–5; Knox, *Common Destiny*, pp. 96, 138; Milza, *Mussolini*, pp. 613, 665; Di Nolfo, *Mussolini e la politica estera italiana*, p. 306.

21. While Britain made a start in 1934 to address shortfalls in its existing procurement policy, rearmament only began in March 1936: Gibbs, *Grand Strategy*, i, p. 266.

22. Such a comparison may seem implausible today, but it did not seem so at the time. For example, the *Economist*, 9 Jan. 1932, p. 56, affirmed in its opening leader of 1932 that the current crisis 'can only be compared with the disturbance created by the Great War itself'.

23. Mouré, *The Gold Standard Illusion*, p. 162.

24. Two recent examples are Hall and Ferguson, *The Great Depression*, and Smiley, *Rethinking the Great Depression*. The latter presents Germany's economic downturn as a discrete event and the Smoot-Hawley tariff as a consequence rather than a cause of the American downturn. The present account offers a different treatment of these events.

25. Kenwood and Lougheed, *The Growth of the International Economy*, p. 232. For a similar acknowledgement in a standard American text, see Walton and Rockoff, *History of the American Economy*, pp. 452, 460–9.

26. The argument is developed in Boyce, 'Economics'.

27. Cf. the pioneering work of Karl Polanyi, *The Great Transformation*, also Heilbroner, *Between Capitalism and Socialism*. The cyclical pattern of regulation in the American context is nicely summarized in Wilkins, 'Cosmopolitan Finance in the 1920s', pp. 284–5. We are witnessing a repeat of the same pattern today.

28. For an excellent description of the informal framework that held the globalized world together before the First World War, see Frieden, *Global Capitalism*, ch. 2.

29. The phrase 'dual crisis' is not completely original. Knipping employs the term 'Doppelkrise', in *Deutschland, Frankreich und das Ende der Locarno-Ära*, p. 226. Wurm, *Business, Politics and International Relations*, refers to 'the dual crisis of the years 1929–1933', p. 289. Best, Hanhimaki, Maiolo and Schulze, *An International History of the*

Twentieth Century employ it following a conversation with the present author. But neither there nor anywhere else has it been used as an analytical construct.

30. Thus, the following works of international history centred on Germany: Knipping, *Deutschland, Frankreich und das Ende der Locarno-Ära*; Ziebura, *World Economy and World Politics*; Becker and Hildebrand (eds), *Internationale Beziehungen in der Weltwirtschaftskrise*.

31. LN, *Industrialisation and Foreign Trade* (1945), table, p. 13; Kenwood and Lougheed, *The Growth of the International Economy*, table 25, p. 220.

32. LN, *Monthly Bulletin of Trade Statistics*, vol. xi, no. 11 (Nov. 1930), table, p. 446.

33. Klein, *Frontiers of Trade*, p. 262.

34. Britain and the United States alone provided over 85 per cent of capital issues for foreign account and nearly all the foreign direct investment during this period: United Nations Department of Economic Affairs, *International Capital Movements during the Interwar Period*, table 4, p. 26 and pp. 25, 28. See also *The Problem of International Investment*, pp. 221–2.

35. Strakosch, 'Gold and the Price Level', Annex B, p. 10, *Economist*, Supplement, 5 Jul. 1930.

36. Kahler and Link, *Europe and America*; also works by Braeman, Burner, Cohen, Costigliola, Gardner, Hogan, Hunt, Leffler, McCormick, Rhodes, Smith, VanMeter Jr and most recently Cohrs. This largely mythical view has been accepted by certain European scholars; see for instance, Artaud, 'L'impérialisme américain en Europe', *Relations internationales*, 1976, no. 8, pp. 323–41; Link, *Die amerikanische Stabilisierungspolitik in Deutschland*.

37. The term is from two influential books by Wilson, *American Business and Foreign Policy*, pp. xvi, 9, and *Herbert Hoover*, p. 168.

38. Carr, *The Twenty Years Crisis*, encourages the impression that idealism was a hallmark of statesmen everywhere in the interwar period, although virtually all his illustrations are drawn from Britain and the United States.

39. Boyce, 'Wall Street', pp. 19–31.

40. The one exception was heavy chemicals, where Germany maintained its lead.

41. *USDC*, pp. 27–35, 89–92, 151–5 and passim.

42. *BCC*, pp. 8–31.

43. Kindleberger, *The World in Depression*, pp. 291–2.

44. See for instance, the essays in McKercher and Moss (eds), *Shadow and Substance in British Foreign Policy* and Dockrill and McKercher (eds), *Diplomacy and World Power*; Johnson (ed.), *The Foreign Office and British Diplomacy*; also Watt, *Personalities and Policies* and *How War Came*.

45. *BCC*, ch. 1.

46. Marquand, *Ramsay MacDonald*, pp. 517–5.

47. Kennedy, *The Realities Behind Diplomacy*, p. 236.

48. Gibbs, *Grand Strategy*, i, p. 799.

49. Bond, *British Military Policy between the Two World Wars*, pp. 36, 338–9. Bond convincingly explains Britain's need for a continental commitment, but unaccountably asserts that Britain's strategic interests lay solely in Western Europe, despite adducing evidence that in 1939, as in 1914, Europe's balance of power depended crucially upon Eastern Europe and denying Germany control over it.

50. Sharp and Jeffrey, ' "Après la Guerre finit, Soldat anglais partit..." ', pp. 123, 124, 132, 135.

51. Tombs and Tombs, *That Sweet Enemy*, pp. 526–7.

52. Cassels, 'Repairing the *Entente Cordiale*', p. 134, refers to France's 'craving for security'; Turner, *The Cost of War*, p. 19, writes of its 'obsessive preoccupation with national security'. See also Adamthwaite, *Grandeur and Misery*; Kent, *The Spoils of War*; Schuker, *The End of French Predominance in Europe*; Dockrill, *British Establishment Perspectives on France*.

53. Typically of British historians, Roberts, *'The Holy Fox'*, pp. 94–5, writes of 'the glaring deficiencies of The Third Republic, with its interminable political crises, short-lived ministries, dodgy politicians, labour unrest and far-Left Popular Front'. He also claims that 'British and French policy-makers drew the erroneous conclusions that it had been the encirclement policy towards Germany of 1904–7, the "destabilizing" alliance system, the armaments race, faulty communications, secret diplomacy, staff talks and strategic plans which had caused the [first world] war' (p. 48). This, as will be seen, fairly sums up opinion in interwar Britain, but constituted only a minority view in France.

54. Bonin, *Histoire économique de la France*, pp. 50, 77; Lévy-Leboyer and Casanova, *Entre l'état et le marché*, p. 263.

55. MAE, PA-AP 261-Seydoux 37, Seydoux to Herbette, 7 Aug. 1925; MAE, PA-AP 166-Tardieu 527, Briand to Flandin and François-Poncet, 12 Apr. 1930; MAE., RC, B-NC 2, 'Projet de circulaire', 1 Dec. 1929. The Ministry of Colonies, with a total of 129 employees in 1935, was also remarkably under-resourced: Marseille, *Empire colonial et capitalisme français*, pp. 304–5.

56. Boyce, 'Business as usual'.

57. Marguerat, 'Banque de France et politique de puissance dans l'entre-deux-guerres', pp. 475–85.

58. See for instance, Johnston et al., *The Living Races of Mankind*, 1, frontispiece map. This view remained common well after the Second World War. Thirty years later, the most popular school atlas, prepared by faculty of the LSE, still divided the 'peoples' of Europe along these lines: *The Faber Atlas*, p. 69.

59. Gelber, *The Rise of Anglo-American Friendship*, p. 70. Ramsden, *Don't Mention the Germans*, surveys this affinity.

60. Roberts, *'The Holy Fox'*, p. 68.

61. See, for instance, the work of the prominent ethnologist Brinton, *Races and Peoples*; and the sociologist Ripley, *The Races of Europe*. Ripley cautions against explaining national behaviour solely by race, but notes the profound difference in behaviour of Celts and Teutons (*sic*) in the limited space of Britain: p. 332. Brinton's survey, which makes no such reservations, is replete with racial stereotypes.

62. Horsman, *Race and Manifest Destiny*, pp. 9–24.

63. Perkins, *The Great Rapprochement*, pp. 8–11, 74–88; Anderson, *Race and Rapprochement*, ch. 1; Adams, *Brothers across the Ocean*, p. 12; Hunt, *The American Ascendancy*, pp. 34–6.

64. See for instance, Grant, *The Passing of the Great Race*, pp. 84–94; Ross, *The Old World in the New*, p. 282; Ross, *The Social Trend*, p. 17; Ross, *Standing Room Only?*, ch. 28–29; Gordon, *Assimilation in American Life*, p. 136. Horne, 'Race from Power', p. 442, notes President Theodore Roosevelt's acquaintance with Madison Grant and shared forebodings but misleadingly presents it as colour racism. For a useful introduction to the subject, see Brookhiser, 'Others, and the WASP world they aspired to', pp. 360–7.

65. Jacobson, *Barbarian Virtues*, pp. 155–7; Parrillo, *Strangers to These Shores*, ch. 6.

66. Nor did it vanish with the rise of Nazism and the Second World War. Anglo-Saxonism continued to play a prominent part in Southern politics into the 1960s: see Smith, *Managing White Supremacy*, p. 12; Bartley, *The Rise of Massive Resistance*, p. 105. George Kennan, the distinguished American diplomat, proudly affirmed, 'You can comb the family records for three centuries back and you won't find a person who wasn't of straight Anglo-Saxon origin.' Mayers, *George Kennan*, p. 16.

67. Maurras yielded to this view in the 1930s when he warned against Hitler while favouring the establishment of a Latin league including Italy: Weber, *Action Française*, pp. 284, 287.

68. Sauvy, *Histoire économique*, ii, p. 22; more generally, Roger, *The American Enemy*, ch. 5.

69. Prochasson and Rasmussen, *Au nom de la patrie*, pp. 131–40; Digeon, *La Crise allemande de la pensée française*, pp. 433, 443; Richard, 'Aspects des relations

intellectuelles', pp. 112–13, 115; Temime, 'Races, nationalités et régionalisme', p. 274; Fleury, 'L'image de l'Allemagne dans le journal *La Croix* (1918–1940)', p. 183; Nolan, *The Inverted Mirror*, pp. 24–5, 110–11 who acknowledges the racism but makes little of the Prussian issue. On French contact with Germans in the Rhineland after the war: Cabanes, *La victoire endeuillée*, ch. 3.

70. Johannet, *Le principe des nationalités*, pp. 220–1; Le Fur, *Races, nationalités, états*, ch. 2; Paligot, *La République raciale*, p. 173; 'The Real France', *Manchester Guardian*, 26 Oct. 1932, p. 11.
71. Maurras, *Mes idées politiques*, pp. 286, 303 and passim.
72. Notably Siegfried, *Tableau des partis en France*, which contrasts Latin France with Anglo-Saxon England; Decugis, *Le destin des races blanches*, for which Siegfried wrote the preface; and Martial, *La race française*, which acknowledges that the doctrine of race, while broadly popular among the French public, was unfashionable among intellectuals, pp. 7–8, 286–7.
73. Birnbaum, *'La France aux Français'*, p. 120; Weber, *Action Française*, p. 197; Grosser, *Une vie de Français*, pp. 62–4.
74. 'Women of Latin Race and the Vote', *Manchester Guardian*, 23 Jun. 1927, p. 11. Racist assumptions about Latin women were (and are) common in the Anglo-Saxon world. According to the managing director of a British clothing firm, 'The Latin race will always dress women in the way which will please her. The Anglo-Saxon will never be able to render her this service.' 'Why Paris Leads in Fashions', *ibid.*, 21 Aug. 1929, p. 12.
75. Noiriel, *Les origines républicaines de Vichy*, p. 133.
76. This argument is nicely summarized in Overy, *The Origins of the Second World War*, ch. 3.
77. Clarke, *Anglo-American Economic Collaboration in War and Peace*, pp. 139–45; Marseille, *Empire colonial et capitalisme français*, pp. 351–2.

1   The Liberal Powers, Peace-Making and International Security, 1914–19

1. The French title for this office at this time was *président du conseil*.
2. Saint-Aulaire, *Confession*, p. 538; *MPC*, i, p. 110. Wilson's reception in England was also 'noticeably cooler than that in France': Bailey, *Woodrow Wilson and the Lost Peace*, p. 112.
3. Beloff, *Imperial Sunset*, i, ch. 3.
4. Steiner and Nielson, *Britain and the Origins of the First World War*, pp. 149, 206–25.
5. Gooch and Temperley (eds), *British Documents on the Origins of the War*, iii, App. A, 'Memorandum on the Present State of British Relations with France and Germany', pp. 250–5.
6. Lowe and Dockrill, *The Mirage of Power*, iii, pp. 443–4.
7. Bell, *France and Britain*, pp. 45–8.
8. Barnett, *The Swordbearers*, pp. 72–4.
9. Duroselle, *Clemenceau*, p. 696.
10. Howard, *War and the Liberal Conscience*, ch. 3.
11. See the useful discussion in Kirshner, *Appeasing Bankers*, ch. 1.
12. Jenkins, *Asquith*, pp. 242–5; David (ed.), *Inside Asquith's Cabinet*, pp. 107–8; Steiner, *The Foreign Office and Foreign Policy*, pp. 87–8; Bell, *France and Britain*, pp. 39–40, 46; Coogan and Coogan, 'The British Cabinet and the Anglo-French Staff Talks, 1905–1914', pp. 110–31.
13. MacDougall, *Racial Myth in English History*, pp. 91, 98, 99, 91–2. The same British historians exercised a comparable influence in the United States: Anderson, *Race and Rapprochement*, ch. 2.
14. Ramsden, *Don't Mention the Germans*, ch. 2.

15. German nationalists accused Britain of cynically encouraging France and Russia to hem in Germany and thus exclude it from commercial opportunities in Africa, Asia and elsewhere. This was true not least of Kaiser Wilhelm II himself, who, ignoring the evidence of his diplomats, insisted that Britain was responsible for the coalition of powers 'surrounding' Germany: Kantorowicz, *The Spirit of British Policy*, pp. 111–13, 297, 395–6, 438–46 and passim. Despite the myth of encirclement, Germans nevertheless displayed a 'curious love-hate ... of Britain': Geiss, *German Foreign Policy*, p. 125. Sir Evelyn Wrench, a frequent visitor to Germany before the war, found that middle-class Germans remained convinced: 'The British will never join hands with those Slav barbarians the Russians. We Germans and British belong to a superior racial order.' Wrench, *Struggle*, p. 78. A recent study of university students confirms the strength of Anglophilia among the German educated classes on the eve of the war: Weber, *Our Friend 'The Enemy'*, ch. 2. Thus, despite prior indications that Britain would side with France in the event of a German attack, its decision to declare war on Germany came as a shock and even betrayal: 'German Public and the War', *Times*, 10 Aug. 1914, p. 5; Verhey, *The Spirit of 1914*, pp. 118, 122; Kohn, *The Mind of Germany*, p. 298. The influence of racial categories upon German political assumptions in this period remains largely unexamined, although it is touched on in Kennedy, *The Rise of Anglo-German Antagonism*, ch. 19, and Kennedy and Nicholls (eds), *Nationalist and Racialist Movements in Britain and Germany before 1914*.
16. 'An Appeal to Scholars', *Manchester Guardian*, 1 Aug. 1914, p. 9.
17. *Ibid.*, 3 Aug. 1914, p. 9.
18. 'Cambridge University' and 'The Movement for British Neutrality', *Daily Chronicle*, 3 Aug. 1914, p. 4; 'Cambridge Support' and 'Balance of Power', *Daily News and Leader*, 3 Aug. 1914, p. 7; 'The Text of the Manifesto' and 'Cambridge Scholars' Manifesto', *Manchester Guardian*, 3 Aug. 1914, p. 10; 'England Should Not Go to War', *Daily Herald*, 3 Aug. 1914, p. 2.
19. Hynes, *A War Imagined*, p. 68.
20. Skidelsky, *John Maynard Keynes*, i, pp. 317–21. As a student at Eton at the turn of the century, Keynes had written that Jews 'can no more be assimilated to European civilisation than cats can be made to love dogs'; and he concluded that racial characteristics 'are unchanged by lapse of time and by revolution'. But by 1918 his judgement was affected not by the place of Jews but of Germans with whom he sympathized and the French and Russians whom he despised: *ibid.*, pp. 92 93, 296, 367.
21. Beveridge, *Power and Influence*, p. 133.
22. Webb, *The Diary of Beatrice Webb*, 3, pp. 212–13, also pp. 263, 273, 290.
23. Barker et al., *Why We Are at War*.
24. The money was then diverted into additional Rhodes scholarships for Dominions candidates. In July 1929, however, Stanley Baldwin, enthusiastically supported by the Prince of Wales, announced the creation of new German Rhodes scholarships. 'Rhodes Scholarships for Germans', *Economist*, 13 Jul. 1929, p. 63.
25. Attitudes of enlisted men were not greatly different. The men cited in Brown, *The Imperial War Museum Book of the Somme*, almost invariably refer to the Hun, but not one speaks ill of the Germans and several acknowledge sympathy and respect. Similarly, British troops entering Germany after the Armistice did so in a mood of 'curiosity and compassion'. Williamson, *The British in Germany*, p. 17. See also Holmes, *Tommy*, pp. 535–6, 541.
26. Trevelyan, *Grey of Fallodon*, p. 271, also pp. 314, 333, 334. Speaking at a public meeting in Berwick he repeated, 'It is against German militarism we must fight ... for it is not the German people, but Prussian militarism that had driven Germany and Europe into this war': 'Sir E. Grey on German Militarism', *Times*, 5 Sept. 1914, p. 9. Confusingly, in his memoirs written ten years later he suggested that this was not his view in 1914 when he wrote, 'A section [in Parliament and in the country] identified Germany with Prussian militarism, and identified Prussian militarism with all that was evil and hostile to Britain. It was a concentrated and active section, but it did not express the prevailing feeling in the country.' Viscount Grey of Fallodon, *Twenty-Five Years*, pp. 324–5.

27. Asquith, *Speeches by the Earl of Oxford and Asquith*, p. 224.

28. Wells, 'The Sword of Peace', *Daily Chronicle*, 7 Aug. 1914, p. 4.

29. Henderson, *Failure of a Mission*, pp. 4–5, 23.

30. Ramsden, *Don't Mention the War*, p. 105, 121–6,' The Scales of War', *Observer*, 16 Aug. 1914, p. 4; 'The Objects of the War', *Manchester Guardian*, 20 Aug. 1914, p. 4; 'The Two Germanies', *ibid.*, 24 Aug. 1914, p. 4; Wallace, *War and the Image of Germany*, p. 31.

31. Barker et al., *Why We Are At War*, p. 114, argued that Germany's acceptance of the principle of *raison d'état* was largely due to the corrupt influence of the historian Treitschke, the soldier Bernhardi and certain others, but they added, 'Let us only remember, in justice to a great people, that it is not really the doctrine of Germany, but rather the doctrine of Prussia (though Treitschke will tell us that Germany is "just merely an extended Prussia").' The war was thus a contest between Prussianism and Anglo-Saxonism: 'England has drawn her sword. How could she have done otherwise, with those traditions of law so deep in all Anglo-Saxon blood – traditions as real and vital to Anglo-Saxon America as to Anglo-Saxon England; traditions which are the fundamental basis of Anglo-Saxon public life all the world over?' p. 116.

32. Rowland, *Lloyd George*, pp. 251, 287–8, 384, 428; Davies, *Europe*, p. 892.

33. Haldane, *Before the War*, pp. 83–4, 184–5.

34. 'Mr. Churchill on the British Case', *Times*, 31 Aug. 1914, p. 5. See also 'Why England is Fighting', *Observer*, 16 Aug. 1914, p. 7, Sir Frederick Pollock's statement for the Council of the Atlantic Union, explaining Britain's decision for war.

35. Gwynn (ed.), *The Letters and Friendships of Sir Cecil Spring Rice*, ii, p. 434.

36. McDonough, *The Conservative Party and Anglo-German Relations*, pp. 110–11.

37. 'First Steps to the Real Settlement', *Observer*, 18 May 1919, p. 10; also 'How to Mend it', *ibid.*, 25 May 1919, p. 10; 'Second Thoughts at Paris', *ibid.*, 15 Jun. 1919, p. 10.

38. Despite later claims to the contrary, both Grey and Asquith justified their decision for war in Parliament by stressing Britain's moral obligation to France and especially Belgium, and the Commons debate on 3 and 6 August 1914 was almost wholly given over to this moral obligation, not the balance of power or national security: 65 H.C. Deb 5s, cols 1809–27, 2079–80; Trevelyan, *Grey of Fallodon*, pp. 257, 265.

39. Wickham Steed, 'What is Right?', p. 201.

40. Beckett, 'The British Army', table 6.5, p. 111.

41. *DCF*, i, p. 65.

42. Wickham Steed, 'What is Right?', pp. 207–8.

43. In the words of A. J. P. Taylor, 'Lloyd George was the nearest thing England has known to Napoleon', *English History*, p. 109.

44. *MPC*, i, p. 171; Busch, *Hardinge of Penshurst*, pp. 286–7; Nicolson, *Peacemaking*, pp. 109–10.

45. Hughes, *To the Maginot Line*, table 1, p. 11; Doise and Vaïsse, *Diplomatie et outil militaire*, p. 324; statistics on widows and orphans from Faron, *Les enfants du deuil*, tableau 6, p. 310.

46. Magraw, *France*, pp. 227–9; Godfrey, *Capitalism at War*, discusses the shortcomings in the administration of production while ignoring its successes.

47. See for instance LG/FLS/4/11, diary 14 Mar. 1919.

48. Poincaré exposed his own pettiness and vanity in this rant against Clemenceau after the Armistice:

    étourdi, violent, vaniteux, ferrailleur, gouailleur, effroyablement léger, sourde physiquement, intellectuellement incapable de raisonner, de réfléchir, de suivre une discussion. [...] C'est ce fou dont le pays a fait un dieu. [...] Il a sauvé la France à la fin de 1917. [...] Il n'a fait cette besogne qu'aidé et poussé par moi.

    Poincaré, *Au Service de la France*, xi, pp. 321–3, quoted in Duroselle, *Clemenceau*, p. 750.

49. Watson, 'Les contacts de Clemenceau avec l'Angleterre', p. 55, describes him as the most Anglophile French leader of the past two centuries.
50. On Keynes's 'antipathy to the French', see Skidelsky, *John Maynard Keynes*, i, pp. 367, 359 and passim.
51. Jeannesson, *Poincaré, la France et la Ruhr*, p. 30.
52. Grosser, *Une vie de Français*, pp. 62–4.
53. Clemenceau, *Discours de Paix*, pp. 4–29.
54. Carroll and Carroll, *George Washington*, vii, p. 406.
55. Brogan, *The Penguin History of the USA*, p. 252.
56. Pratt, De Santis and Siracusa, *A History of United States Foreign Policy*, p. 168.
57. *Ibid.*, p. 169.
58. See the excellent discussion of American isolationism in Dulles, *America's Rise to World Power*, ch. 1.
59. According to one account, Washington was gripped by 'mass hysteria' at the time Wilson presented his war resolution to Congress, but the rest of the country was by no means so excited: Millis, *Road to War*, p. 441. The Senate voted 82 to 6 in favour of the resolution, and the House of Representatives 373 to 50.
60. Bailey, *Woodrow Wilson and the Lost Peace*, pp. 15, 20–2 and passim.
61. The Fourteen Points are reprinted in Baker, *Woodrow Wilson and World Settlement*, iii, doc. 3, pp. 42–5; and White, *Woodrow Wilson*, Appendix B, pp. 501–3.
62. *PWW*, 53, pp. 314–15.
63. Link, *Woodrow Wilson*, p. 2. According to Link, Wilson was better qualified to manage foreign relations than any President since John Quincy Adams.
64. Levin, Jr, *Woodrow Wilson and World Politics*; also Parrini, *Heir to Empire*; Wells, Jr, 'New Perspectives on Wilsonian Diplomacy', 387–419. This view receives qualified endorsement from Wilson's biographer: Link, *The Higher Realism of Woodrow Wilson*, pp. 78–9. Recent accounts are scarcely more effective in locating Wilson within the American tradition: see the useful review by D. Steigerwald, 'The Reclamation of Woodrow Wilson?', pp. 79–99.
65. Fraser, *Wall Street*, p. 284.
66. McAdoo, *Crowded Years*, pp. 218, 238–9.
67. Warburg, *The Federal Reserve System*, i, pp. 17–18; Chandler, *Benjamin Strong*, pp. 255–6; Cherny, *A Righteous Cause*, pp. 131–3; also Livingston, *Origins of the Federal Reserve System*.
68. Geisst, *Visionary Capitalism*, p. 112; Cleveland and Huertas, *Citibank*, pp. 61, 66; Duroselle, *Clemenceau*, p. 735.
69. Wilson's biographer nevertheless denies that this reflected a suspicious, solitary nature or reluctance to delegate work: Link, *Woodrow Wilson*, pp. 14–15.
70. *Ibid.*, pp. 104–5; Brogan, *The Penguin History of the USA*, pp. 482–3.
71. *PWW*, 53, p. 351; Nicolson, *Peacemaking*, p. 199; Bailey, *Woodrow Wilson and the Lost Peace*, p. 109.
72. Clemenceau, *Discours de Paix*, pp. 4, 5.
73. MAE, PA-AP 72-Fleuriau 1, 'Note' by Foch, 28 Nov. 1918; *MPC*, i, pp. 78–9; reprinted in J. Autin, *Foch ou le triomphe de la volonté*, pp. 295–300.
74. CAB28/5, IC 97-102, minutes of the Imperial War Cabinet, 1 – 3 Dec. 1918; Callwell, *Field-Marshal Sir Henry Wilson*, ii, p. 153; *MPC*, i, pp. 78–80.
75. Roskill, *Hankey*, ii, pp. 28–9; Stevenson, *French War Aims against Germany*, pp. 145–6; MacMillan, 'Clemenceau and Lloyd George', pp. 82–3.
76. *MPC*, i, p. 78.
77. Watson, 'The Making of the Treaty of Versailles', p. 71; Watson, *Clemenceau*, pp. 353, 337, concludes that Clemenceau was simply raising the stakes in the hope of British concessions. Nelson, *Land and Power*, pp. 13, 204, 207, havers within the same account, advancing the view at one point that Clemenceau agreed with Foch on the need for a radical and permanent change on the Rhine, but later affirming that it was probably

nothing more than a bargaining ploy. Duroselle, *Clemenceau*, p. 727, speculates that Clemenceau had not yet been convinced by Foch of the feasibility for his Rhineland policy. But Soutou, *L'Or et le sang*, p. 788, is in no doubt that Clemenceau was fully behind Foch.

78. Clemenceau, *Grandeurs et misère d'une victoire*, pp. 175–6; also Lloyd George, *Memoirs*, i, pp. 253–4.
79. Bariéty, *Les relations franco-allemandes après la première guerre mondiale*, pp. 35–6.
80. Tardieu, *La Paix*, p. 164.
81. Mordacq, *Le Ministère Clemenceau*, iv, p. 72.
82. Butler, *Lord Lothian*, pp. 74–5.
83. Gilbert (ed.), *Winston S. Churchill*, iv, Companion Pt. I, p. 192; Self (ed.), *The Austen Chamberlain Diary Letters*, p. 109.
84. Taylor, *English History*, pp. 191–2.
85. 'The Three Flags', *Morning Post*, 11 Nov. 1918, p. 4; also 'The New Germany: Reality of Make-Believe?', *ibid.*, 13 Nov. 1918, p. 3; 'The Purge of Pride', *Pall Mall Gazette*, 9 Nov. 1918, p. 4; 'Deliverance', *ibid.*, 11 Nov. 1918, p. 4; 'The Armistice Terms', *ibid.*, 12 Nov. 1918, p. 4. *Daily Mail* and *Daily Express*, while regularly referring to Germans as the Hun during the war and insisting that nearly all of them had supported the war, nonetheless emphasized the special responsibility of the Kaiser along with 'Hindenburg and the Junker fire-eaters'. See for instance, 'The Fallen Giant', *Daily Express*, leader 9 Nov. 1918, p. 2; 'Trial of the Kaiser the Duty of the Allies', *ibid.*, 13 Nov. 1918, p. 1; 'France is Free! The Barbarian Expelled', *Daily Mail*, 11 Nov. 1918, p. 2; 'The Arch-Criminal', *ibid.*, 11 Nov. 1918, p. 2; 'The Huns Must Pay', *ibid.*, 13 Nov. 1918, p. 2. The *Yorkshire Post* used slightly different language to make the same point: see untitled leaders, 11 Nov. 1918, p. 4, 12 Nov. 1918, p. 4 and 23 Nov. 1918, p. 6.
86. 'End of the Hohenzollerns', *Daily Telegraph*, 11 Nov. 1918, p. 6.
87. Wrench, *Struggle*, p. 346.
88. 'Banquet Speeches at Guildhall', *Times*, 11 Nov. 1918, p. 4. Lloyd George's speech is reported in full in 'Premier's Great Speech', *Daily Chronicle*, 11 Nov. 1918, p. 2. See also 'Mr. Asquith & the War', *Manchester Guardian*, 2 Nov. 1918, p. 8.
89. 'The Dawn', *Daily News*, 11 Nov. 1918, p. 4. See also 'The Kaiser's Downfall', *Daily Chronicle*, 11 Nov. 1918, p. 4; 'The Great Day', *Manchester Guardian*, 12 Nov. 1918, p. 4. 'War's Aftermath', *ibid.*, 24 Nov. 1918, p. 7, an unsigned leader which presented a cautious, realistic survey of postwar German attitudes, remained an anomaly.
90. See for instance, H. N. Brailsford, 'He Can Have Peace', *Herald*, 12 Oct. 1918, p. 5; '"The Unspeakable Hun"', *ibid.*, 2 Nov. 1918, p. 2 'Is it a New Germany?', *ibid.*, 9 Nov. 1918, p. 6.
91. Petrie, *The Life and Letters of the Right Hon. Sir Austen Chamberlain*, ii, pp. 128–9.
92. Riddell, *Intimate Diary of the Peace Conference*, p. 188. Though Riddell wrote this in 1920, it evidently applied to the whole post-Armistice period.
93. 'France on Her Guard. Watching the Hun "Democrats"', *Daily Mail*, 12 Nov. 1918, p. 5; 'Sceptical Paris: No Belief in German Repentence', *Morning Post*, 14 Nov. 1918, p. 5.
94. LG/FLS/4/11, diary 14 Mar. 1919.
95. Beloff, *Britain's Liberal Empire*, i, p. 268.
96. *PWW*, 53, pp. 557–8.
97. Field Marshal Sir Henry Wilson, diary, 23 Mar. 1919.
98. Clemenceau, *Grandeurs et misère d'une victoire*, p. 166, quoted in Duroselle, *Clemenceau*, p. 728. See also Curzon papers, EUR MSS, F112/196, Hardinge to Curzon, enclosing minute of interview with 'Pertinax', 27 Nov. 1919.
99. Watson, *Clemenceau*, p. 344.
100. Bourgeois, *Pour la Société des Nations*.
101. Quoted in Boorstin, *America and the Image of Europe*, p. 21.
102. Kennan, *American Diplomacy*, p. 95.
103. *PWW*, 56, pp. 80, 82.

104. *PWW*, 55, p. 271.
105. Nor was it the first time he alluded to this claim for the League: see for instance, Link, *Woodrow Wilson*, pp. 75, 114.
106. Wilson was not alone in favouring a reference to the Monroe doctrine in the covenant. Leo Amery, the under-secretary of state at the Colonial Office, looked forward to a postwar world divided into vast imperial blocs and sought a league that recognized the right of each one to its own Monroe doctrine. Amery, *My Political Life*, ii, p. 163.
107. Link, *Woodrow Wilson*, pp. 115–16.
108. *PWW*, 55, p. 74.
109. *Ibid.*, pp. 76, 78–9.
110. *Ibid.*, pp. 79–80.
111. As Boorstin put it in *America and the Image of Europe*, p. 22:
    Beneath all lay the arrogant expectation that through a League of Nations the peoples of France, Germany, Italy, and of many lesser nations would seize the opportunity to deal with each other in the manner of Massachusetts, New York, and California. Wilson's program was not merely an embodied idealism, it was a projection of the American image onto Europe.
    For a more recent instance of the isolationist impulse behind US support for an international institution, see Kaplan, *The United States and NATO*, pp. 88–9.
112. *PWW*, 55, p. 78.
113. *Ibid.*, p. 80.
114. *Ibid.*, p. 118.
115. *FRUS* PPC, 1919, iii, pp. 490–1, 582–3, 589–93, 623–42, 647–68; *PWW*, 54, pp. 182–4; Hankey, *Supreme Control*, pp. 51–4.
116. Duroselle, *Clemenceau*, p. 805.
117. Gilbert (ed.), *Winston S. Churchill*, iv, Companion Pt. I, ch. 13.
118. Hankey, *Supreme Control*, pp. 68–9.
119. *Ibid.*, pp. 69–70.
120. LG/F/89/2/24, Lloyd George to Kerr, 19 Feb. 1919; Gilbert (ed.), *Winston S. Churchill*, iv, *Companion Volume*, Pt. I, pp. 538–9.
121. Gilbert (ed.), *Winston S. Churchill*, iv, *Companion Volume*, Pt. I, pp. 549–50.
122. Callwell, *Field-Marshal Sir Henry Wilson*, ii, p. 170.
123. *PWW*, 56, p. 51; Hankey, *Supreme Control*, p. 73.
124. Headlam-Morley, *A Memoir of the Peace Conference*, pp. 169–71; *FRUS* PPC, 1919, iv, meeting of the Council of Ten, 19 Mar. 1919, pp. 413–19.
125. *FRUS* PPC, 1919, iv, meeting of the Council of Ten, 22 Mar. 1919, pp. 449, 452–4. On the Polish frontier dispute, see Wandycz, *France and Her Eastern Allies*, pp. 39–40.
126. *DCF*, i, pp. 44–9.
127. FO371/3787, doc. 42059, minute by George Saunders, 27 Mar. 1919.
128. *BDFA*, Pt. II, ser. 1, vol. 8, no. 83, H.J. Paton memorandum, 27 Feb. 1919. On Paton see *DBFP*, ser. 1, xvi, doc. 13 annex, memorandum by Headlam-Morley, 6 Apr. 1921.
129. Wilson (ed.), *The Political Diaries of C. P. Scott*, p. 387; also Riddell, *Intimate Diary of the Peace Conference*, pp. 40, 191, 227; McEwen (ed.), *The Riddell Diaries*, p. 313.
130. Cecil papers, Add. Ms. 51078, Cecil to Austen Chamberlain, 11 Feb. 1926.
131. Self (ed.), *The Austen Chamberlain Diary Letters*, p. 116; also MacMillan, *Paris, 1919*, p. 220.
132. Wilson (ed.), *The Political Diaries of C. P. Scott*, p. 329; Taylor (ed.), *Lloyd George*, pp. 176–7; Wrench, *Struggle*, p. 418.
133. Riddell, *Intimate Diary of the Peace Conference*, p. 230.
134. Hankey papers 8/10, Hankey to Lloyd George, 19 Mar. 1919; Hankey papers 1/5, diary, 20 Jul. 1920.
135. D'Abernon, *Ambassador of Peace*, iii, pp. 41–2. See also Scrutator in the *Empire Review*, 'Georgians v. Jews: The Real Split in Moscow', pp. 223–9. Hitler

similarly credited 'the Germanic element in a race of inferior worth' with building up the Russian state, and the Jewish Bolsheviks for tearing it down. *Mein Kampf*, p. 533.

136. This was a prominent theme of his Fontainebleau memorandum of 25 Mar. 1919; see Baker, *Woodrow Wilson and World Settlement*, iii, doc. 65, pp. 452–4.
137. *PWW*, 55, p. 319. See *PWW*, 54, pp. 102–3, 245; *DCF*, i, p. 47.
138. *PWW*, 54, p. 22; *MPC*, i, pp. 207–8, 218; Beloff, *Britain's Liberal Empire*, I, p. 325.
139. *DCF*, i, p. 49.
140. *PWW*, 54, p. 155.
141. *MPC*, i, p. 222. Max Beloff asserts that at the time of the peace conference British statesmen were more worried about the Bolshevik threat than the German threat: *Britain's Liberal Empire*, i, p. 275. This may be true, but only if it is also clear that British statesmen were little worried about the German threat.
142. Gilbert (ed.), *Winston S. Churchill*, iv, *Companion Volume*, Pt. I, Lloyd George to Churchill, 16 Feb. 1919, p. 539.
143. *Ibid.*; LG/F/89/2/24, Lloyd George to Kerr, 19 Feb. 1919; *PWW*, 55, p. 233.
144. Two million Poles under German rule, one million Germans under Polish rule: Cienciala, *Poland and the Western Powers*, p. 2.
145. After the war, Germans claimed that their country had been 'mutilated' by the settlement, with the loss of approximately 13 per cent of its territory and 10 – 13 per cent of its population (in Europe). British and American contemporaries, who generally sympathized with Germany, uncritically accepted this claim, and even today the same statistics are commonly quoted in English-language accounts. See, for instance, Benns, *Europe since 1914 In Its World Setting*, 8th ed., p. 126; Gilbert, *First World War Atlas*, p. 144; Richie, *Faust's Metropolis*, pp. 315–16; MacMillan, *Paris, 1919*, p. 465; Ferguson, *The Pity of War*, p. 409; Marks, *The Ebbing of European Ascendancy*, p. 94; Stevenson, *Cataclysm*, p. 422. The truth is somewhat different.
146. Balfour papers, Add. Ms. 49749, Balfour minute, 18 Mar. 1919; copy in LG/F/3/4/19.
147. *PWW*, 54, pp. 156–7.
148. The document is reprinted in Tardieu, *La Paix*, pp. 163–4.
149. Liddell Hart, *Foch*, pp. 413–14.
150. The document is reprinted in Tardieu, *La Paix*, pp. 165–87, and Bourgeois, *Le Traité de Paix de Versailles*, 2nd ed., App. I, pp. 271–99.
151. Foch presented it orally to Lord Robert Cecil: LG/F/3/4/2, Cecil to Lloyd George, 8 Jan. 1919.
152. Tardieu, *La Paix*, p. 165.
153. *Ibid.*, p. 177.
154. *PWW*, 53, p. 610.
155. Seymour, *Letters from the Peace Conference*, p. 157. Seymour, a member of Wilson's wartime Inquiry, was chief of the Austro-Hungarian division of the American Commission to Negotiate Peace.
156. *PWW*, 54, pp. 558, 477.
157. *Ibid.*, p. 178.
158. *Ibid.*, 55, p. 3.
159. *Ibid.*, 55, p. 153.
160. Cairns, 'A Nation of Shopkeepers in Search of a Suitable France', pp. 710–43, offers a wealth of illustrations of unreasoning British hostility towards Latin France and solidarity with Anglo-Saxon Germany, from the political left as well as the right. As he suggests (p. 719, f. 32), what is equally remarkable is the readiness of Anglophone historians even 75 years later to echo these prejudices.
161. Thus the deeply ambivalent comment of Harold Nicolson, a young Foreign Office official, a month after arriving in Paris: 'The French are behaving far better than I imagined, and are sufficiently intelligent to see that the only possible line to go on is that of honesty and reason.' *Peacemaking*, 1919, p. 270.

162. As Haig revealingly complained in April 1918, 'Henry Wilson did not help us at all in our negotiations with Foch. His sympathies always seem to be with the French.' Blake (ed.), *The Private Papers of Douglas Haig*, p. 302.

163. *Ibid.*, pp. 305, 303, 313–14 and passim.

164. *Ibid.*, pp. 346–7.

165. Clemenceau, *Grandeurs et misère d'une victoire*, p. 93. Clemenceau repeated the claim to the American journalist Frank Simonds: Wickham Steed papers, Add. Ms. 74126, Simonds to Steed, [c. 1] May 1925.

166. Hancock and Van Der Poel (eds), *Selections from the Smuts Papers*, iv, p. 13 and passim. Smuts never shed his Francophobia. In October 1942 he claimed that 'the almost total loss of the entire Allied possessions in the Far East and in South-East Asia was due to the fall of France', and that the Vichy government in French Indo-China 'opened the door' for the Japanese to Singapore, Siam, Malaya and Burma. Mansergh, *Survey of British Commonwealth Affairs*, p. 190.

167. Lentin, *Lloyd George and the Lost Peace*, p. 64.

168. Curzon papers, MSS EUR, F112/242, memorandum, 28 Dec. 1921. Crowe's biographers confirm that he was the author of this document circulated in Curzon's name to the Cabinet: Crowe and Corp, *Our Ablest Public Servant*, p. 415. His biographers deny that Crowe was either a Francophile or a Germanophobe: 'he sometimes passed judgments on French policy, both after and before the formation of the Anglo-French Entente, as severe as those he passed on German policy.' p. 129.

169. Hardinge, *Old Diplomacy*, pp. 255, 264.

170. Busch, *Hardinge of Penshurst*, p. 305, also pp. 298–9.

171. In the words of the diplomat, Lord D'Abernon, the French displayed

    a characteristic which has done much to diminish French popularity among friendly nations, viz. a curious unwillingness to recognise service rendered or to express normal feelings of gratitude for assistance. You may search the histories of the Great War which have been written in France [for] mention of the British Army

    Ambassador of Peace, ii, p. 18. Woodrow Wilson's attitude towards France was informed by the same assumptions. As he told the other heads of delegation, the United States entered the war solely 'out of a commitment to liberty and justice'. *PWW*, 54, p. 266.

172. Barnett, *The Collapse of British Power* and Lentin, *Lloyd George and the Lost Peace*, pp. 76–9, 85, ascribe the appeasement policies and pro-German, anti-French bias of postwar British governments to a moralistic view of the world order inculcated by the English public schools, Oxbridge and the Church of England. There is perhaps something in this, but it does not easily square with their ready resort to force within the Empire and insistence upon the primacy of the Royal Navy, even to the extent of contemplating conflict with the United States.

173. Laroche, *Au Quai d'Orsay*, p. 59. In a remarkably generous tribute to Tardieu, House later wrote,

    No man worked with more tireless energy and none had a better grasp of the delicate and complex problems brought before the Congress [i.e. Peace Conference]. He was not only invaluable to France, but to his associates from other countries as well. He was in all truth the one nearly indispensable man at the Conference.

    IPCH, p. 408.

174. *PWW*, 55, p. 387; Tardieu, *La Paix*, pp. 191–3.

175. *IPCH*, pp. 316–17; *MPC*, i, p. 265; Watson, *Clemenceau*, p. 345.

176. *Times*, 24 Feb. 1919.

177. Tardieu, *La Paix*, pp. 195–6; Loucheur, *Carnets Secrets*, pp. 71–2. Lloyd George draws a discreet veil over this episode in his *Memoirs of the Peace Conference*.

178. *PWW*, 56, pp. 11–14, 201–2.

179. Tardieu, *La Paix*, pp. 290–6; *DCF*, i, pp. 54–66, 204–6; *IPCH*, pp. 411–12; *PWW*, 56, pp. 351–2.

180. *DCF*, i, pp. 86–8. See also Recouly, *Marshal Foch*, ch. 27; Autin, *Foch*, pp. 308–11.

181. *DCF*, i, p. 181 f. 4. See also Callwell, *Field-Marshal Sir Henry Wilson*, diary, 2 Apr. 1919, p. 180; Tardieu, *La Paix*, p. 300.

182. Tardieu, *La Paix*, pp. 297–305; *DCF*, i, pp. 214–17.

183. Clemenceau, *Grandeurs et misère d'une victoire*, p. 176; *DCF*, i, p. 87.

184. *PWW*, 56, pp. 11–14; copy in Tardieu, *La Paix*, pp. 197–200; *DCF*, i, pp. 86–7, 141.

185. Tardieu, *La Paix*, pp. 201–4; Duroselle, *Clemenceau*, p. 753; Liddell Hart, *Foch*, p. 416; *IPCH*, pp. 422–3.

186. *PWW*, 56, pp. 11–14; copy in Tardieu, *La Paix*, pp. 197–200; Mordacq, *Le Ministère Clemenceau*, iii, p. 206.

187. Loucheur, *Carnets Secrets*, pp. 71–2; Tardieu, *La Paix*, p. 196; Duroselle, *Clemenceau*, p. 753.

188. Hardinge, *Old Diplomacy*, p. 241; Lentin, 'The Treaty That Never Was', pp. 117–18 and f. 10. He did not inform the dominions prime ministers until 5 May: Lentin, *Lloyd George and the Lost Peace*, p. 53, f. 28.

189. War Cabinet minutes, 28 Feb. 1919, Gilbert (ed.), *Winston S. Churchill*, iv, *Companion Volume*, Pt. 1, p. 557.

190. Lentin, 'The Treaty that Never Was', p. 123. The idea of making Britain's commitment conditional upon the American commitment probably came from Louis Botha, the South African prime minister: Hancock and Van Der Poel (eds), *Selections from the Smuts Papers*, iv, p. 150. Lentin, who provides the most careful analysis of Lloyd George's negotiation of the guarantee, describes it as a vanishing act, although he sees merit in basing British and European postwar security on a deception: *Lloyd George and the Lost Peace*, pp. 18–19.

191. Curzon papers, MSS EUR, F112/211, Curzon to Grey, 22 Nov. 1919.

192. Nelson, *Land and Power*, p. 234.

193. *PWW*, 56, pp. 81–2. Colonel House was of the same view: 'It is practically promising only what we promise to do in the League of Nations, but since Clemenceau does not believe in the League of Nations it may be necessary to give him a treaty on the outside.' *IPCH*, p. 409.

194. *PWW*, 56, pp. 178, 164–5, 179, 181.

195. Bailey, *Woodrow Wilson and the Lost Peace*, p. 240.

196. Butler, *Lord Lothian*, pp. 72–3; Tardieu, *La Paix*, p. 315.

197. Nicolson, *Peacemaking*, 1919, p. 21. Lloyd George later denied any attempt to raise false hopes: 'The only reference I made to reparations during the election campaign was a few days before the poll in a speech I delivered at Bristol and it was intended to depress exalted hopes.' *MPC*, i, p. 306.

198. Skidelsky, *John Maynard Keynes*, i, p. 356.

199. 'Guillaume II doit payer', *Le Matin*, 12 Nov. 1918, p. 1.

200. Petrie, *The Life and Letters of the Right Hon. Sir Austen Chamberlain*, ii, pp. 132–6.

201. Cunliffe, something of a Francophobe, was also strongly anti-German by the end of the war. Asked how he had arrived at the sum of £25 billion, he answered, 'Because it's twice as much as they've got.' Kynaston, *The City of London*, iii, p. 57. This is a memorable comment, but it should not be allowed to obscure the evidence that Cunliffe and Sumner were convinced of Germany's ability to pay a very large sum and Britain's need for large-scale compensation. See Lentin, 'Lord Cunliffe, Lloyd George, Reparations and Reputations at the Paris Peace Conference', pp. 72–3; Lentin, *Lloyd George and the Lost Peace*, p. 29; Lentin, *Lloyd George, Woodrow Wilson and the Guilt of Germany*, pp. 20–1.

202. Tardieu, *La Paix*, p. 321; Carls, *Louis Loucheur and the Shaping of Modern France*, pp. 154–5.

203. Baker, *Woodrow Wilson and World Settlement*, iii, doc. 54, pp. 376–9.

204. *DCF*, i, p. 5, f. 2.

205. Baker, *Woodrow Wilson and World Settlement*, viii, doc. 56, pp. 383–96.

206. *PWW*, 56, p. 208.

207. *DCF*, i, 26 Mar. 1919; Carls, *Louis Loucheur and the Shaping of Modern France*, pp. 156–7.
208. LG/F/213/5/21, Smuts 'Note on Reparation', 31 Mar. 1919.
209. *PWW*, 56, pp. 498–9, 501; *IPCH*, pp. 412–13; Link, *Woodrow Wilson*, p. 91.
210. Baker, *Woodrow Wilson and World Settlement*, iii, doc. 49, p. 345.
211. *PWW*, 56, pp. 179, 181. He had collapsed and confined to his bed the day Lloyd George secured his concession.
212. *DCF*, i, 5 Apr. 1919, p. 149; Baker, *Woodrow Wilson and World Settlement*, ii, pp. 380–1; Skidelsky, *John Maynard Keynes*, i, p. 366.
213. The reparations commission made one attempt to raise war debts on 1 March 1919, but this was abandoned after a strong protest from the US Treasury experts in Paris: Baker, *Woodrow Wilson and World Settlement*, ii, p. 374.
214. Soutou, *L'Or et le sang*, pp. 767–8, 776, 832–4.
215. *Ibid.*, pp. 841–2.
216. *Ibid.*, pp. 835–6.
217. Pruessen, *John Foster Dulles*, p. 34.
218. Baker, *Woodrow Wilson and World Settlement*, iii, doc. 47, p. 331.
219. *Ibid.*, pp. 332–4.
220. *Ibid.*, doc. 48, pp. 336–43. On Keynes's motives, see Skidelsky, *John Maynard Keynes*, i, pp. 368–9.
221. Baker, *Woodrow Wilson and World Settlement*, iii, doc. 53, p. 374.
222. *Ibid.*, doc. 50, pp. 347–51; *ibid.*, doc. 51, pp. 352–62.
223. Callwell, *Field-Marshal Sir Henry Wilson*, pp. 188–9; Gilbert (ed.), *Winston S. Churchill*, iv, *Companion Volume*, Pt. I, p. 670.
224. LG/F/45/9/33, Smuts to Lloyd George, 5 May 1919; LG/F/45/9/34, Smuts to Lloyd George, 14 May 1919; LG/F/45/9/35, Smuts to Lloyd George, 22 May 1919; LG/F/45/9/39, Smuts to Lloyd George, 2 Jun. 1919.
225. Lloyd George, *Memoirs*, i, pp. 462–81.
226. Lentin, an authority on the peace, describes the memorandum as 'wise and far-sighted', although he accepts that it was also 'a deliberate attack on French policy': *Lloyd George and the Lost Peace*, pp. 5, 18. Nelson, *Land and Power*, pp. 224–5, describes it as 'a mixture of commonsense and impractical idealism'. Morgan, *Lloyd George*, pp. 133–4.
227. Gilbert, *Lloyd George*, pp. 63–4. The memorandum is also reprinted in Baker, *Woodrow Wilson and World Settlement*, iii, doc. 65, p. 454.
228. *Ibid.*, pp. 464–5.
229. *Ibid.*, p. 462.
230. See, for instance, LG/F/89/2/23, Lloyd George to Kerr, 18 Feb. 1919; LG/F/30/3/40, Lloyd George to Bonar Law, 30 Mar. 1919; Taylor (ed.), *Lloyd George*, p. 176; Riddell, *Intimate Diary of the Peace Conference*, pp. 40, 61, 247; CAB29/92, I.C.P.182, Notes of an Allied Conference at 10 Downing Street, 9 Mar. 1921 at 6 p.m.: 'There was a real horror in this country of creating another Alsace-Lorraine. Alsace-Lorraine had cost Europe so much; we had had to pay for it.'
231. As one writer put it, 'the more nimble quicker-witted French, as against the stolid Teuton': 'The Marching Capacity of Germans', *Observer*, 16 Aug. 1914, p. 6.
232. Wandycz, *France and Her Eastern Allies*, pp. 43–5.
233. Ludlow, 'The unwinding of appeasement', pp. 9–48; Ludlow, 'Britain and the Third Reich', pp. 141–62.
234. 118 H.C. Deb 5s, cols 1115–28.
235. Young, *Power and Pleasure*, pp. 156–7; Ziebura, 'Léon Blum et la conception de la sécurité collective', p. 18; Duroselle, *Clemenceau*, pp. 769–73; Watson, *Clemenceau*, p. 361. Although the Senate unanimously ratified the treaty, its reservations about the security aspects are clearly set out by Léon Bourgeois, rapporteur of the foreign relations commission, in *Le Traité de Paix de Versailles*, pp. 179, 237–40 .

236. Lodge, in private at least, harboured less suspicion than Wilson of Britain and shared many of France's specific security aims. Widenor, *Henry Cabot Lodge*, pp. 292–5, 325–6, 328–32 and passim.

237. Lodge, *The Senate and the League of Nations*, App. iv, pp. 351–8.

238. *Ibid.*, pp. 399, 405, 407, 409. On the reception of this speech, see Garraty, *Henry Cabot Lodge*, p. 370.

239. Chambers II, *The Tyranny of Change*, pp. 270–1; Murray, *Red Scare*, pp. 192–3; Heale, *American Anti-Communism*, ch. 4.

240. Lodge, *The Senate and the League of Nations*, p. 159; Widenor, *Henry Cabot Lodge*, pp. 370–1.

241. Link, *Woodrow Wilson*, pp. 125–6. Seeking to explain why Wilson did not accommodate Lodge's reservations 'when the two sides were so close together', Link stresses the effect of Wilson's illness and plays down his pride and stubbornness, *ibid.*, p. 122.

242. Stevenson, *The First World War and International Politics*, pp. 314–5.

243. *The Economic Consequences of the Peace*. Before publication, Keynes omitted the scathing portrait of Lloyd George, which had it been included might have gone some way to reduce the anti-French balance: Skidelsky, *John Maynard Keynes*, i, p. 383. Dr George Adamkiewicz of the Polish ministry of foreign affairs protested, 'Mr. Keynes, who is so full of pity for the present unhappy state of Germany and Austria, has no word of compassion or even of understanding for the treatment Poland has experienced during the war at the hands of the representatives of the above-mentioned two states.' 'Treaty Revision: A Polish Reply to Mr Keynes', *Times*, 8 Mar. 1920, p. 20.

244. Graves, *Goodbye to All That*, p. 240.

245. Fussell, *The Great War and Modern Memory*, pp. 204–20.

246. Gedye, *The Revolver Republic*, pp. 32–3, 18–20 and passim.

247. Parker, *Chamberlain and Appeasement*, p. 64.

248. 'Oxford Union and the Treaty', *Times*, 27 Feb. 1920, p. 11; 'Oxford Union and Germany', *ibid.*, 28 May 1920, p. 9.

249. 'Reconciliation. Oxford Letter to German Intellectuals', *Times*, 18 Oct. 1920, p. 8.

250. 'Cambridge and the German Professors', *Times*, 10 Nov. 1920, p. 9.

251. 'Cambridge Union and France', *Times*, 9 Feb. 1921, p. 7; 'Oxford and the Entente', *ibid.*, 6 May 1921, p. 7.

252. 'Mr. Lloyd George at Oxford', *Times*, 23 Jun. 1923, p. 14; Kantorowicz, *The Spirit of British Policy*, pp. 166–7.

253. 'Oxford Union Debate', *Times*, 11 Feb. 1933, p. 8. According to Hollis, *The Oxford Union*, p. 191, there is no evidence that the debaters had Germany in mind. This is more than a little surprising, given that the debate took place less than a fortnight after Hitler took power and public demonstrations were taking place against him in London, New York and elsewhere. A year later, the Union voted 125 to 25 for the motion, 'That the acceptance of the German claim to arms equality is essential to the preservation of European peace.' *Ibid.*, p. 194.

254. Ferguson, *The Pity of War*, p. 397; Cassels, 'Repairing the Entente Cordiale and the New Diplomacy', p. 137; Mowat, *Britain between the Wars*, p. 422.

255. Blunden, *Undertones of War*, pp. 204–5; Webb, *Edmund Blunden*, p. 171.

256. Roberts, *Siegfried Sassoon*, p. 274.

257. MacDougall, whose excellent *Racial Myth in English History* ends in 1914, affirms that 'Not much was heard of Teutonic excellence after World War I.' p. 129. See also Boussabha-Bravard, 'Ici Londres'.

258. Barker, *National Character*, p. 25. This is consistent with Lord Bryce's observation during the war that race consciousness, having 'run underground ... during so many centuries, suddenly emerged to become a tremendous force in international relations'. Bryce, *Race Sentiment as a Factor in History*, p. 29.

259. Barker, *National Character*, p. 46.

260. CAB21/171, 'Channel Tunnel: Summary of the Views Held by the Different Departments and Ministers on the More Important Aspects of the Case', n.d.; *ibid.*, CID 98-A, 'Two Memoranda by the Chief of the Imperial General Staff', 23 Dec. 1919; 'The Channel Tunnel: Recent Parliamentary History', by the Channel Tunnel Company, Feb. 1920; Report of the House of Commons Channel Tunnel Committee, 7 Jul. 1919; Report of meeting of MPs on 5 Jul. 1920 and deputation to the Prime Minister on 12 Nov. 1920.

261. CAB21/171, CID 4, Hankey memorandum, 28 Jan. 1920; CAB21/171, CID4., Hankey to Sir Auckland Geddes, 5 Feb. 1920; CAB21/171, CID4, Hankey to Addison, 3 Mar. 1920; CAB21/171, CID4, Hankey to E. Shortt (Home Office), 27 Jan. 1920; FO371/3765, 18704, Hankey memorandum, 23 Oct. 1920; Hankey papers 1/5, diary 19 November, 19 Dec. 1919; Wilson, *Channel Tunnel Visions*, ch. 6.

262. FO371/3765, 18704, memorandum by Balfour, 5 Feb. 1920.

263. CAB21/171, 101-A, Curzon memorandum, 1 May 1920 (copy in Curzon papers, MSS EUR, F112/233).

264. Hardinge, *Old Diplomacy*, p. 264; Wilson, *Channel Tunnel Visions*, p. 150.

265. CAB21/171, Churchill memorandum, 9 Feb. 1920 (copies of all relevant CID papers in Curzon papers, MSS EUR, F112/233).

266. CAB21/171, CID99-A, Austen Chamberlain memorandum, 26 Feb. 1920; CID100-A, Addison memorandum, 4 Mar. 1920; CID94-A, A.C. Geddes memorandum, 17 Mar. 1930.

267. Wilson, *Channel Tunnel Visions*, p. 191. See also Grayson, 'The British Government and the Channel Tunnel', pp. 127–9.

268. *Morning Post*, 13 Mar. 1919, quoted in Wilson, *Channel Tunnel Visions*, p. 109. Repington's reference to tunnels in the plural refers to the contemporary plan for a rail tunnel comprising two separate tubes 18 feet in diameter.

2   The Emasculation of International Security after the Great War

1. 'Mr. Harding's Message: Desire for Peace', *Times*, 5 Mar. 1921, p. 10.

2. 'Mr. Harding's Speech: America's Place in the World', Times, 5 Mar. 1921, p. 9. For this and other inaugural speeches: http://www.yale.edu/lawweb/avalon

3. Inter-university Consortium for Political and Social Research, 'United States Historical Census Browser', http://fisher.lib.virginia.edu/census

4. See for instance, Glaab, 'Metropolis and Suburb: The Changing American City', p. 399; also Ostrander, 'The Revolution in Morals', *ibid.*, p. 323; Dumenil, 'Re-Shifting the Perspectives on the 1920s', p. 63.

5. Gayer and Schmidt, *American Economic Foreign Policy*, p. 29.

6. Whereas the book value of all foreign direct investment rose by a third, the book value of foreign direct investment in manufacturing rose by two-thirds, from $478 million to $795 million: Wilkins, *The Maturing of Multinational Enterprise*, table 1.3 p. 31.

7. Lewis, *America's Stake in International Investments*, p. 119.

8. Geisst, *Wall Street*, p. 157.

9. Chernow, *The House of Morgan*, p. 303.

10. Soule, *Prosperity Decade*, pp. 228–9.

11. *USDC*, pp. 122–3; Moulton and Pasvolsky, *World War Debt Settlements*, table, p. 97.

12. *USBC*, Series U 1 – 25, p. 867.

13. *USBC*, Series U 317 – 334, p. 903; *USBC*, Series U 335 – 352, p. 906.

14. *USBC*, Series U 1 – 25, p. 867.

15. *USDC*, p. 31.

16. This is the implication of Burk, *Britain, America and the Sinews of War*.

17. 'United States Historical Census Browser', http://fisher.lib.virginia.edu/census

18. Wilson, *American Business and Foreign Policy*, p. 24.
19. Parrish, *Anxious Decades*, pp. 94–5.
20. Hofstader, *Anti-Intellectualism in American Life*, p. 123.
21. Nye, *Midwestern Progressive Politics*, pp. 106–7.
22. Cherny, *A Righteous Cause*, p. 60.
23. Geisst, *Wall Street*, p. 112; also Clements, *William Jennings Bryan*, p. 24.
24. More generally see Boyce, 'Wall Street', pp. 19–31.
25. Downes, *The Rise of Warren Gamaliel Harding*, p. 87.
26. *Ibid.*, pp. 57, 62–5, 66–73 and passim.
27. *Ibid.*, p. 255.
28. Murray, *The Harding Era*, pp. 16–17.
29. Quoted in Adler, *The Isolationist Impulse*, p. 97.
30. Downes, *The Rise of Warren Gamaliel Harding*, pp. 614–15.
31. Murray, *The Harding Era*, p. 206.
32. *USBC*, Series U 207 – 212, p. 888. The percentages are the ratio of duties to total imports (free and dutiable) for the five-year averages, 1915–19 and 1924–28. See also Link and Catton, *American Epoch*, ii, pp. 67–8. Schuker, 'American Foreign Policy', p. 78, a strongly pro-Republican or at least pro-American account, claims that 'the overall level of protection rose only a few percentage points'. On the Republicans' own statistics, the rise in duties on dutiable imports was 62 per cent (from 21.9 per cent during the 92 months of the Underwood Tariff to 35.4 per cent during the first 39 months of the Fordney-McCumber Tariff), and the rise in duties on total imports was 95 per cent (from 7.4 per cent to 14.5 per cent during the same periods): HHCP 208, Chalmers to Hoover, 29 Dec. 1925. The rise in industrial duties was 11.5 percentage points (from 27 per cent to 38.5 per cent) or nearly 43 per cent: Murray, *The Harding Era*, p. 279. But of course the main point is that by 1922 the USA had *even less justification* for a policy of protection, let alone one of *intensifying* protection: see 'The New American Tariff', *Observer*, 27 Aug. 1922, p. 6.
33. Leffler, *The Elusive Quest*, p. 32.
34. Ferrell, *The Presidency of Calvin Coolidge*, p. 113; Hicks, *Republican Ascendancy*, pp. 131–2. Hicks entitles the relevant chapter, 'The Diplomacy of Isolation'. See also Ross, *Standing Room Only?*, p. 338; 'U.S. Immigration Bill Signed', *Times*, 27 May 1924, p. 16.
35. Gayer and Schmidt, *American Economic Foreign Policy*, p. 126; Leffler, *The Elusive Quest*, p. 59; Link, *Die amerikanische Stabilisierungspolitik in Deutschland*, pp. 123–4; Artaud, 'L'impérialisme américain en Europe', pp. 331–3; also Hogan, 'Revival and Reform', pp. 288–90, who makes the extraordinary claim that Harding, Coolidge and Hoover's foreign policy was governed by the same motives that led the United States to offer the Marshall Plan for the reconstruction of Europe after the Second World War: after both world wars, 'American leaders tried to project their vision of a corporative political economy on the European and world systems, to build, in other words, an economically ordered and organically integrated community of states.'
36. The phrase comes from two books by Wilson, *Herbert Hoover* and *American Business and Foreign Policy*, but see also the panglossian studies of American foreign policy in the 1920s such as Leffler, 'The Origins of Republican War Debt Policy', pp. 585–601; and Costigliola, 'Anglo-American Financial Rivalry in the 1920s', pp. 911–34. So completely has the view that isolationism does not apply to the United States in the 1920s come to prevail in the American historical profession that any dissent seems to verge on apostasy: see the triumphalist assertions in Kahler and Link, *Europe and America*, Introduction; also Cohen, 'America and the World in the 1920s', pp. 233, 241–2; Gardner, *Economic Aspects of New Deal Diplomacy*, pp. 7–9; Hunt, *The American Ascendancy*, pp. 96, 113–14; and the otherwise excellent Girault and Frank, *Turbulente Europe*, pp. 99–101, 143.
37. *FRUS*, 1922, i, Young to Dearing, 1 Feb. 1922, pp. 556–7; *FRUS*, 1922, i, State Department press release, 3 Mar. 1922, pp. 557–8.

38. On several occasions postwar Administrations indicated the criteria they would like to see applied to overseas loans, but drew back from fear of assuming responsibility for the loans, which such interference threatened to create. See Viner, 'Political Aspects of International Finance, II', pp. 359–63; Dulles, 'Our Foreign Loan Policy', pp. 33–48; Feis, *The Diplomacy of the Dollar*, pp. 684–701; Rosenberg, *Financial Missionaries to the World*, pp. 105–7.

39. Ferrell, *The Presidency of Calvin Coolidge*, p. 16; on his origins, Coolidge, *Biography*, ch. 1; on his sudden prominence in 1919, Shannon, *Between the Wars*, p. 27; Cashman, *America Ascendant*, p. 178.

40. Murray, *The Harding Era*, pp. 99–100.

41. The same criticism levelled at William Appleman Williams 30 years ago applies almost equally to more recent historians: see Thompson, 'William Appleman Williams and the "American Empire"', pp. 91–104, and the useful critique of Maddox, 'Another Look at the Legend of Isolationism in the 1920s', pp. 35–43.

42. *BCC*, pp. 31–4.

43. *Ibid.*, pp. 18–31.

44. The main exception were the chairmen of the deposit banks, several of which lent large amounts to domestic industry for their reconversion at the end of the war and remained sensitive to their fate. But as lenders of other people's money, they were assumed to be biased towards inflation and excluded from representation on the Court of the Bank of England until the 1930s.

45. *BCC*, pp. 22–4.

46. The Committee comprised Sir John Bradbury, the secretary of the Treasury, Alfred Pigou, professor of political economy at Cambridge, and eleven bankers. T185/1, Report, 1918, p. 81.

47. T185/2, FBI memorandum, 19 Jul. 1918.

48. UK, Parliamentary Papers, *Committee on Currency and Foreign Exchanges after the War, First Interim Report*, 1919, Cmd. 9182, p. 5. On the hidden division, see Boyce, 'Creating the Myth of Consensus'.

49. CAB27/58, G-237, Conference on Unemployment and the State of Trade, minutes, 24 Feb. 1919.

50. *Ibid.*, Report, 14 Mar. 1919. Mar. 1920; ibid., nos 347-52

51. Howson, *Domestic Monetary Management in Britain*, p. 11.

52. Mallet and George, *British Budgets, Second Series*, pp. 181–7 and 368; Armitage, *The Politics of Decontrol of Industry*, pp. 13–15; Johnson, *Land Fit for Heroes*, pp. 375, 394–402.

53. Howson, *Domestic Monetary Management in Britain*, p. 15.

54. Mallet and George, *British Budgets, Second Series*, p. 233.

55. *BCC*, pp. 36–8, 45–6, 48–9, 51–2; 'Traders and Deflation: Plea for Revision of Policy', *Times*, 25 Oct. 1923, p. 14.

56. Dunning and Thomas, *British Industry*, p. 19. Between 1922 and 1929 French industrial production rose by 60 per cent (exceeding prewar levels by 44 per cent). During the same period German industrial production rose by 48 per cent, while US manufacturing (*sic*) production rose fully 88 per cent, but British industrial production rose by barely a third. Sauvy, *Histoire économique*, i, annexe vi, p. 464; *USDC*, p. 150; Potter, *The American Economy between the World Wars*, table, p. 15; Mitchell, *International Historical Statistics: Europe*, table D1, pp. 423–4.

57. Booth and Glyn, 'Unemployment in the Interwar period', p. 619 table 5; Garside, *British Unemployment*, pp. 9–10 and table 4.

58. Annual surpluses on the current balance averaged £114 million between 1920–29, compared with more than twice this amount in the prewar decade, according to the estimates in 'The balance of payments in the interwar period: further details', pp. 47–52.

59. Gibbs, *Grand Strategy*, i, p. 3.

60. *Ibid.*, pp. 3–4.

61. CAB23/15, 606-A, War Cabinet minutes 5 Aug. 1919.

62. Doise and Vaïsse, *Politique étrangère de la France*, p. 328.
63. CAB2/3, CID, 163rd meeting, 2 Aug. 1922; Gibbs, *Grand Strategy*, i, p. 47; Howard, *The Continental Commitment*, pp. 82–3.
64. Nicolson, *Curzon: The Last Phase*, pp. 194–5.
65. Saint-Aulaire, *Confession*, pp. 536, 547.
66. Bernard and Dubief, *The Decline of the Third Republic*, p. 144.
67. Kuisel, *Capitalism and the State in Modern France*, pp. 34–6: Bonin, *Histoire économique de la France*, p. 50.
68. The name was retained despite the decision at the party congress in Strasbourg in February 1920 to break with the Second International.
69. Bernard and Dubief, *The Decline of the Third Republic*, pp. 161–2.
70. Artaud, *La question des dettes interalliées*, i, p. 63, f. 156.
71. *Ibid.*, pp. 63–4, table p. 63 bis, 124–5; Kent, *The Spoils of War*, p. 26 table I; Turner, *The Cost of War*, p. 4.
72. Tardieu, *La Paix*, pp. 441–2. Lloyd George quoted closely similar statistics in CAB29/91, I.C.P.172, Notes of an Allied conference, St. James's Palace, 3 Mar. 1921.
73. These statistics differ from the ones used in the Introduction, since estimates of the total victims exceed the number who received compensation. On the emotional cost to those who survived the fighting, see Sirinelli, 'La génération du feu', pp. 298–311.
74. Frank, *Le Prix de réarmement français*, p. 38.
75. Thus in May 1929, registered unemployment in Britain was 1,177,000, while in France it was under 1,000. 'Statistical Abstract for the United Kingdom', Cmd. 3991, 1932; *Economist*, 18 May 1929, p. 1108.
76. FO371/10728, C3531/459/18, Lord Crewe to Chamberlain, enclosure, record by Mr Phipps of a conversation with Marshal Foch, 11 Mar. 1925. Phipps reported that Foch's views 'are so well known it is not necessary for me to deal with them at length.'
77. Tardieu, *La Paix*, pp. 479–81; Bardoux, *L'Île et l'Europe*, p. 181.
78. Curzon papers, MSS EUR, F112/240, Curzon to Derby, no. 1121, 1 Apr. 1920; Curzon papers, MSS EUR, F112/240, Curzon to Derby, no. 1178, 8 Apr. 1920; Curzon papers, MSS EUR, F112/240, Curzon to Derby, no. 1185, 10 Apr. 1920; MAE, PA-AP 42-Paul Cambon 60, Cambon to Millerand, no. 361, 1 Apr. 1920; MAE, PA-AP 42-Paul Cambon 60, Cambon to Millerand no. 370, 5 Apr. 1920; MAE, Europe 1918–40, GB 44, Cambon to Millerand, no. 387, 8 Apr. 1920.
79. MAE, PA-AP 42-Paul Cambon 60, Cambon to Millerand, nos 255-6, 19 Mar. 1920; *ibid.*, nos 271-2, 23 Mar. 1920; *ibid.*, nos 278-9, 21 Mar. 1920; *ibid.*, nos 287-8, 22 Mar. 1920; *ibid.*, nos 347-52, 31 Mar. 1920.
80. Curzon papers, MSS EUR, F112/240, Curzon to Derby, no. 1178, 8 Apr. 1920; Nicolson, *Curzon*, p. 200. In this case Bonar Law administered the dressing down: Roskill, *Hankey*, ii, p. 152.
81. MAE, PA-AP 42-Paul Cambon 60, Cambon to Millerand, nos 398-9, 10 Apr. 1920. On secret intelligence, MAE, Europe 1918–40, GB 44, 'Politique de la France et de l'Angleterre: Divergences de vues. Note pour le Ministre', 24 Mar. 1920.
82. Farrar, *Principled Pragmatist*, p. 244.
83. Hankey papers 1.5, diary 20 Apr. 1920.
84. Curzon papers, MSS EUR, F112/244 Curzon memorandum to Cabinet, 161315, 31 Dec. 1919.
85. Curzon papers, MSS EUR, F112/197, Derby to Curzon, 19, 29 Feb., 5 Mar. 1920; Curzon papers, MSS EUR, F112/198A, Derby to Curzon, 7 Jun. 1920; MAE, PA-AP 118-Millerand 1, Vienot to Millerand, 10 Apr. 1920.
86. FO 371/3765/187041, Curzon memorandum, 'The Channel Tunnel', 1 May 1920.
87. CAB29/87, I.C.P.109A, Notes of a conversation between Lloyd George and Millerand at Belcaire, Lympne, Kent, 15 May 1920.
88. MAE, PA-AP 118-Millerand 44, Notes of meeting at Boulogne in the Villa Belle, 21 Jun. 1921; CAB29/87, I.C.P.110, Notes of a meeting at the Villa Belle, 21 Jun. 1920; Artaud, *La question des dettes interalliées*, i, pp. 277–8, 291; Farrar, *Principled Pragmatist*, pp. 252–3.
89. Laroche, *Au Quai d'Orsay*, p. 122.

90. MAE, PA-AP 72-de Fleuriau 1, note on Brussels and Spa conferences, n.d.; CAB29/88, I.C.P.133, Notes of an Inter-Allied Conference held at the Villa Fréneuse, Spa, 12 Jul. 1920, pp. 570–1; CAB29/88, I.C.P.134, 14 Jul. 1920.
91. CAB29/89, I.C.P.143, Notes of a conversation at the Villa Haslihorn, Lucerne, 22 Aug. 1920; CAB29/88, I.C.P.128, Notes of a meeting at the Villa Neubois, Spa, 9 Jul. 1920; Callwell, *Field-Marshal Sir Henry Wilson*, ii, pp. 257–8.
92. CAB29/89, I.C.P.142E, Notes of an Anglo-French conference, Lympne, 8 Aug. 1920.
93. CAB29/88, I.C.P.128A, Notes of a conversation held at the Villa Fraineuse, Spa, 10 Jul. 1920.
94. And a young army staff officer, Captain Charles de Gaulle.
95. Davies, 'Sir Maurice Hankey and the Inter-Allied Mission to Poland', pp. 557, 559–61.
96. Davies, 'Lloyd George and Poland', p. 146.
97. Curzon papers, MSS EUR, F112.198A, Derby to Curzon, 9 Jun., 15 Aug. 1920; CAB29/89, I.C.P.142F, Notes of a meeting held at Lympne, 9 Aug. 1920; Callwell, *Field-Marshal Sir Henry Wilson*, ii, p. 258; Farrar, *Principled Pragmatist*, pp. 273–4.
98. Curzon papers, MSS EUR, F112/198A, Derby to Curzon, 13, 14, 16, 20, 21, 27 Aug. 1920.
99. *Ibid.*, 19 Aug. 1920; Curzon papers, MSS EUR., F112/199, Hardinge to Curzon, 19 Aug. 1920.
100. CAB29/89, I.C.P.144C, Notes of a conversation between Lloyd George and Take Jonescu, 20 Oct. 1920.
101. François-Poncet, *De Versailles à Potsdam*, p. 65. Clemenceau had been remarkably optimistic about Franco-American cooperation before the peace settlement as well: see *FRUS PPC*, 1919, i, House to Wilson, 9 Nov. 1918, p. 344.
102. Curzon papers, MSS EUR, F112.198A, Derby to Curzon, 17 Aug. 1920; Artaud, *La question des dettes interalliées*, i, pp. 271, 281–2; Farrar, *Principled Pragmatist*, pp. 222, 224–5.
103. Farrar, *Principled Pragmatist*, pp. 258, 260, 261–6; Turner, *The Cost of War*, pp. 27, 39, 42, 46.
104. CAB29/87, I.C.P.109G, Notes of a conference at Lympne, 20 Jun. 1920.
105. Artaud, *La question des dettes interalliées*, i, pp. 281–3.
106. *Ibid.*, i, pp. 224–7; Turner, *The Cost of War*, p. 31.
107. Artaud, *La question des dettes interalliées*, i, pp. 317–8.
108. Murray, *The Harding Era*, p. 361; Schrecker, *The Hired Money*, pp. 57–68, 95–128; Turner, *The Cost of War*, pp. 28–32.
109. Schrecker, *The Hired Money*, pp. 103–4; Orde, *British Policy and European Reconstruction*, p. 154.
110. Orde, *British Policy and European Reconstruction*, pp. 156–8.
111. CAB29/94, I.C.P.209, Notes of a meeting between Lloyd George and Briand, 19 Dec. 1921.
112. Saint-Aulaire, *Confession*, p. 534; Laroche, *Au Quai d'Orsay*, p. 133.
113. Saint-Aulaire, *Confession*, p. 536.
114. *Ibid.*, pp. 553, 582. Others regarded Briand as lazy, but disagreed on his effectiveness: Riddell, *Intimate Diary of the Peace Conference*, p. 277; Hardinge, *Old Diplomacy*, p. 254; Flandin, *Politique française*, p. 41.
115. Saint-Aulaire, *Confession*, p. 538.
116. On the assumptions informing Briand's approach to economics and politics, see Boyce, 'Aristide Briand'.
117. Taylor (ed.), *Lloyd George*, pp. 209, 214. One seasoned British observer wrote of Lloyd George and Briand, 'The two men are so alike in so many ways. Of Breton or Celtic blood, physically they resemble each other. Both are eloquent; but Briand has infinitely more knowledge and he plays with Lloyd George.' Esher (ed.), *Journals and Letters of Reginald, Viscount Esher*, 4, pp. 49–50. For a comparison of the two men, contrasting Lloyd George's opportunism with Briand's integrity and clarity of purpose, see Suarez, *Briand*, v, pp. 118–20.

118. Jeannesson, 'Jacques Seydoux', p. 19.

119. Briand, *Aristide Briand*, p. 46.

120. MAE, Europe 1918–40, GB 48, Préfet de Police to Briand, 26 Nov. 1921. The cabaret acts are described in Sisley Huddleston, 'Great Britain According to the French Stage: A Word of Advice to Our French Citizens', *The Illustrated London News*, 10 Dec. 1921.

121. CAB29/90, I.C.P.149, Notes of an Allied Conference, Quai d'Orsay, Paris, 11 a.m., 24 Jan. 1921.

122. CAB29/90, I.C.P.150, Notes of an Allied Conference, Quai d'Orsay, Paris, 4 p.m., 24 Jan. 1921.

123. *Ibid.*

124. *Ibid.*, I.C.P.153, Notes of an Allied Conference, Quai d'Orsay, Paris, 11 a.m., 26 Jan. 1921.

125. *Ibid.*, I.C.P.154A, Notes of an Allied Conference, Quai d'Orsay, Paris, 6 p.m., 26 Jan. 1921.

126. MAE, PA-AP 261-Seydoux 20, Note no. 53-L, 'Réunion de 23 janvier chez le Président de la République', 24 Jan. 1921. It may also be that Briand, who did not get along with Doumer, preferred to have the latter's ambitious reparations demand denounced by the British as a way of deflating his pretensions to control French reparations policy. On their relations, see Suarez, *Briand*, v, pp. 103–4; Saint-Aulaire, *Confession*, p. 554.

127. As he wrote to Curzon on 12 Nov. 1921, 'With Latin races it is essential to stand up to them, the only thing that really matters being the question of form.' Busch, *Hardinge of Penshurst*, p. 305.

128. *Ibid.*, p. 299. Confusingly, Hardinge's biographer affirms that he favoured the maintenance of an alliance with France, while accepting that he firmly opposed a military guarantee – or indeed any commitment – to France (pp. 279, 298–9). Evidently Hardinge, like most other Foreign Office officials at this time, favoured a loose *Entente* as a means of restraining France rather than bolstering its security.

129. Hardinge, *Old Diplomacy*, p. 256.

130. CAB29/90, I.C.P.156, Notes of an Allied Conference, Quai d'Orsay, Paris, 11 a.m., 29 Jan. 1921, Appendix 1; Suarez, *Briand*, v, pp. 135–6.

131. The vote was 387 to 125: Suarez, *Briand*, v, pp. 149–54.

132. Curzon papers, MSS EUR, F112/242, memorandum by Crowe, 12 Feb. 1921.

133. Crowe and Corp, *Our Ablest Public Servant*, p. 410.

134. FO371/6038, C22661/2740/18, Hardinge to Curzon, 1 Dec. 1921, no. 917; also FO371/7000, W13355/12716/17, Curzon memorandum, 28 Dec. 1921; statement by Baldwin, 292 H.C. Deb 5s, col. 2339, 30 Jul. 1934.

135. CAB29/91, I.C.P.171, Notes of an Allied Conference at 10 Downing Street, 5 p.m., 2 Mar. 1921.

136. CAB29/91, I.C.P.178, Notes of an Allied Conference at St James's Palace, London, 4.30 p.m., 7 Mar. 1921.

137. Suarez, *Briand*, v, pp. 178, 180.

138. CAB29/92, I.C.P.182, Notes of an Allied Conference at 10 Downing Street, London, 6 p.m., 9 Mar. 1921.

139. CAB29/93, I.C.P.197, Appendix 2, 3 May 1921.

140. MAE, PA-AP 118-Millerand 17, Saint-Aulaire telg. (for Berthelot) no. 309-16, 25 Apr. 1921; Suarez, *Briand*, v, pp. 185–6.

141. CAB29/93, I.C.P.200A, Notes of an interview between the prime minister and the German ambassador, 11 a.m. Thursday, 5 May 1921.

142. The results for all the voting districts are set out in *ibid.*, no. 96, Appendix 96, annex I, pp. 682–3; the economic character of the voting pattern is set out in *ibid.*, annex II, pp. 683–8; Laroche, *Au Quai d'Orsay*, pp. 139–43; Martin, *France and the Après Guerre*, pp. 78–80.

143. FO371/5892, C6032/92/18, Curzon to Percival, no.-, 22 Mar. 1921.

144. CAB29/93, I.C.P.202, Notes of an Allied Conference at the Quai d'Orsay, 11 a.m., 9 Aug. 1921.
145. FO371/5899, C9758/92/18, Curzon telg. to Hardinge, no. 244, 13 May 1921.
146. FO371/5900, C9873/92/18, Hardinge to Curzon, no. 270, 13 May 1921; FO371/5902, C10444/92/18, Briand to Lloyd George, 14 May 1921; MAE, Europe 1918–40, GB 46, Saint Aulaire to Ministry, nos 404-07, 14 May 1921.
147. 141 H.C. Deb 5s, cols 2380–8.
148. FO371/5904, C10700/92/18, Hardinge to Curzon, no. 314, 24 May 1921.
149. MAE, Europe 1918–40, GB 46, Saint-Aulaire, no. 399, 14 May 1921; *ibid.*, Saint-Aulaire, no. 258, 21 May 1921; 'The Silesian Danger: Statement by Mr. Lloyd George', *Times*, 19 May 1921, p. 10.
150. FO371/5901, C10322/92/18, Curzon to Cheetham, no. 1388, 18 May 1921; FO371/5904, C10645/92/18, Curzon to Saint-Aulaire, 24 May 1921.
151. Busch, *Hardinge of Penshurst*, p. 305.
152. FO371/5906, C11032/92/18, Curzon to Hardinge, no. 1488, 26 May 1921; also FO371/5900, C9874/92/18, Curzon to Cheetham, no. 250, 16 May 1921.
153. FO371/5910, C12012/92/18, Hardinge to Curzon, no. 368, 9 Jun. 1921; FO371/5911, C12331/92/18, Curzon to Hardinge, no. 1634, 13 Jun. 1921; FO371/5916, C14772/92/18, Saint-Aulaire to Curzon, 16 Jul. 1921.
154. FO371/5916, C14770/92/18, Stuart to Curzon, no. 267, 19 Jul. 1921; FO371/5916, C14774/92/18, Stuart to Curzon, no. 268, 19 Jul. 1921.
155. FO371/5917, C14810/92/18, Curzon to Cheetham, no. 413, 22 Jul. 1921; FO371/5917, C14810/92/18, Curzon to Cheetham, no. 414, 22 Jul. 1921.
156. FO371/5918, C15085/92/18, Curzon to Cheetham, no. 418, 24 Jul. 1921; FO371/5918, C15319/92/18, Curzon to Cheetham, no. 2075, 27 Jul. 1921.
157. CAB29/93, I.C.P.205B, Notes of a meeting at Rambouillet, 11 Aug. 1921.
158. CAB29/93, I.C.P.205E, Notes of a conversation between the British and French prime ministers, Hôtel Crillon, Paris, 12 Aug. 1921. Hankey, who shared Lloyd George's viewpoint, reported that the prime minister was a paragon of moderation: Balfour papers, Add. Ms. 49,704, Hankey to Balfour, 12 Aug. 1921.
159. Hardinge, *Old Diplomacy*, pp. 259–60.
160. CAB29/93, I.C.P.205E, Notes of a conversation between the British and French prime ministers, Hôtel Crillon, Paris, 12 Aug. 1921.
161. FO371/5927, C19546/92/18, Cheetham to Curzon, no. 737, 11 Oct. 1921; FO371/5928, C19904/92/18, Muller to Curzon, no. 412, 16 Oct. 1921.
162. Saint-Aulaire, *Confession*, pp. 464, 465.
163. FO371/5909, C11751/92/18, Crowe conversation with Saint-Aulaire, 1 June 1921; FO371/6519, E7154/143/44, Notes of an Allied meeting, Paris, 18–19 Jun. 1921.
164. FO371/6519, E7154/143/44, Notes of an Allied meeting, Paris, 18–19 Jun. 1921.
165. *Ibid.*
166. Busch, *Hardinge of Penshurst*, p. 305; Saint-Aulaire, *Confession*, p. 564.
167. FO371/6514, E6263/143/44, Crowe memorandum, 30 May 1921.
168. FO371/5909, C11751/92/18, Crowe conversation with Saint-Aulaire, 1 Jun. 1921.
169. FO371/6995, W6618/6298/17, Hardinge to Curzon, no. 1671, 3 Jun. 1921.
170. Curzon papers, MSS EUR, F112/242, Robertson to Curzon, no. 73R, 2 Jun. 1921.
171. FO371/6995, W6618/6298/17, Hardinge to Curzon, no. 1671, 3 Jun. 1921.
172. FO371/5995, C11894/416/18, Hardinge to Curzon, no. 1709, 8 Jun. 1921; FO371/6995, W6298/6298/17, Crowe minute, 14 Jun. 1921.
173. On Derby see MAE, Europe 1918–40, GB 71, Saint-Aulaire to Poincaré, no. 196, 8 Apr. 1922.
174. MAE, Europe 1918–40, GB 46, Saint-Aulaire to Briand, no. 315, 7 Jun. 1921.
175. MAE, Europe 1918–40, GB 47, Saint-Aulaire to Briand, no. 963-6, 4 Nov. 1921; Saint-Aulaire, *Confession*, p. 565. The treaty is printed in *British and Foreign State Papers*, cxiv, pp. 771–3.

176. See for instance, 'Ça craque!', *Le Matin*, 23 Sept. 1921, p. 1; 'L'Accord Franco-Turc', *ibid.*, 9 Nov. 1921, p. 1; 'A propos d'un traité secret anglo-turc', *ibid.*, 10 Nov. 1921, p. 1; 'Constantinople Captive. Le terrorisme anglais règne encore dans la capitale turque', *ibid.*, 15 Nov. 1921, p. 1.

177. Loucheur papers, MF1/reel 4, agreement signed by Loucheur and Rathenau, 6 Oct. 1921; Loucheur, *Carnets Secrets*, pp. 92–3; Carls, *Louis Loucheur*, pp. 228–31. Copy in UK, *PP*, Cmd. 1547 (1921).

178. FO371/5922, C16527/92/18, D'Abernon to Curzon, no. 418, 13 Nov. 1921. As D'Abernon reported, Sir John Bradbury, the British representative on the Reparations Commission, also favoured acceptance on the same terms.

179. 'German Reparations', *Times*, 22 Nov. 1921, p. 11; France, MAE PA-AP 261-Seydoux 32, Note, 25 Feb. 1925; Bariéty, *Les relations franco-allemandes après la première guerre mondiale*, pp. 134–44. This account is summarized in Bariéty, 'France and the Politics of Steel'. See also, Jeannesson, *Poincaré, la France et la Ruhr*, p. 24.

180. Bariéty, *Les relations franco-allemandes après la première guerre mondiale*, p. 88; Carls, *Louis Loucheur*, pp. 232–3; 'German Reparations', *Times*, 24 Nov. 1921, p. 11.

181. See for instance, Saint-Aulaire, *Confession*, pp. 555–6; Suarez, *Briand*, v, pp. 129–31, 183.

182. FO371/6040, C24173/2740/18, D'Abernon to Curzon, enclosure, no. 1439, 24 Dec. 1921.

183. *Ibid.*

184. See for instance, Ferguson, *The Pity of War*, p. 407.

185. FO371/6039, C22814/2740/18, memorandum by Waterlow, 30 Nov. 1921.

186. FO371/5881, C8778/58/18, Seeds to Curzon, no. 1012, 11 Oct. 1920, p. 533; FO371/588, C8401/58/18, Curzon to Seeds, no. 327, 15 Oct. 1920; FO371/588, C9803/58/18, Crowe to de Fleuriau, 29 Oct. 1920. On German capital exports, see the highly stimulating analysis in Schuker, *American 'Reparations' to Germany*, pp. 110–16.

187. FO371/5881, C9802/58/18, Derby to Curzon, no. 1247, 27 Oct. 1920; FO371/5881, C9919/58/18, Derby to Curzon, no. 3261, 28 Oct. 1920; FO371/5881, C10073/58/18, Curzon to Derby, no. 3557, 29 Oct. 1920; France MAE, PA-AP 261-Seydoux, 19, Seydoux to Millerand, 10 Nov. 1920, enclosing copy of de Fleuriau telegram, 27 Oct. 1920.

188. France MAE, PA-AP 261-Seydoux, 19, Seydoux to Millerand, 10 Nov. 1920, enclosing copy of de Fleuriau telegram, 27 Oct. 1920.

189. CAB2/3, CID minutes of 146th Meeting, 21 Oct. 1921; *ibid.*, minutes of 147th Meeting, 31 Oct. 1921.

190. Gibbs, *Grand Strategy*, I, p. 47; 275 H.C. Deb 5s, cols 1795, 1367; Butler, *Lord Lothian*, p. 197; Mackay, *Balfour*, p. 335; Howard, *The Continental Commitment*, pp. 81–5.

191. CAB16/47, N.D. 31, General Staff Note on French Air Situation, May 1923.

192. Immediately after the war, two-thirds of French squadrons were dissolved, and the aircraft industry, which employed 200,000 in 1919, was reduced to 10,000 employees by 1920: Doise and Vaïsse, *Politique étrangère de la France*, p. 360. Nonetheless, the irrational fear that the French bomber will always get through remained common among British ministers. In 1925 Sir Samuel Hoare, secretary of state for air, warned Cabinet colleagues: 'France continues to maintain an air strength more predominant than was ever her military strength under Napoleon or Louis XIV.' CAB24/175, C.P.421(25), Hoare memorandum, Oct. 1925.

193. CAB8/63, Committee of Imperial Defence, Sub-Committee on National and Imperial Defence, minutes of the 10th meeting, 16 May 1923.

194. 165 H.C. Deb 5s, col. 2142.

195. FO371/6039, C22814/2740/18, Crowe minute, 30 Nov. 1921.

196. Nish, *Alliance in Decline*, pp. 289–90, 325, 328–9, 345, 351, 372, 396–7 and passim; Maurer, 'Arms Control and the Washington Conference', pp. 282–3.

197. Suarez, *Briand*, vi, pp. 256–7; Blatt, 'The Parity That Meant Superiority', p. 235.

198. Suarez, *Briand*, v, pp. 267–79; Elisha (ed.), *Briand*, pp. 113–23; Briand, *Aristide Briand*, pp. 113–23.

199. Oudin, *Aristide Briand: La Paix?*, pp. 421–2.
200. MAE, PA-AP 118-Millerand 19, Montille to Ministry, nos 1102-03, 8 Dec. 1921; Loucheur, *Carnets Secrets*, pp. 92–3; Suarez, *Briand*, v, p. 347.
201. Curzon papers, MSS EUR, F112/242, Curzon to Hardinge, no. 3223, 5 Dec. 1921.
202. Artaud, *La question des dettes interalliées*, i, p. 382 f. 51 bis accepts that Millerand was probably behind it. But according to Jules Laroche, director of the political and economic section of the Quai d'Orsay, it was Briand himself who initiated the proposal, in face of sustained criticism from Poincaré that he had accomplished nothing at Washington or in securing reparations: Laroche, *Au Quai d'Orsay*, pp. 146–7.
203. Saint-Aulaire, *Confession*, p. 584.
204. CAB23/71, 36th meeting of the Financial Committee, minutes, 1 Dec. 1921.
205. Curzon papers, MSS EUR, F112/242, I.C.211A, Notes of a conversation between Lloyd George and Briand, 21 Dec. 1921 (copy in CAB29/94, I.C.P.211).
206. *Ibid.* (copy in CAB29/94, I.C.P.211A).
207. MAE, Europe 1918–40, GB 69, Saint-Aulaire to Briand, no. -, 14 Dec. 1921.
208. CAB29/94, I.C.P.211A, Notes of a meeting between Lloyd George and Briand, 10 Downing Street, 21 Dec. 1921.
209. Curzon papers, MSS EUR, F112/242, I.C.211A, Notes of a conversation between Lloyd George and Briand, 21 Dec. 1921 (copy in CAB29/94, I.C.P.211).
210. Curzon papers, MSS EUR, F112/200, Hardinge to Curzon, 18, 25 Nov., 2, 26, 27 Dec. 1921, 3 Jan. 1922.
211. MAE, Europe 1918–40, GB 69, minutes of meeting at Villa Valetta, Cannes, between Briand, Loucheur and Lloyd George, 4 Jan. 1922; Curzon papers, MSS EUR, F112/242, I.C.220A, Notes of a conversation between Lloyd George and Briand, 4 Jan. 1922.
212. MAE, PA-AP 118-Millerand 58, de Fleuriau despatch with enclosure to Briand, no. 674, 28 Dec. 1921; MAE, Europe 1918–1940, GB 69, Saint-Aulaire to Briand, no. 1178, 31 Dec. 1921; MAE, Europe 1918–1940, GB 48, Saint-Aulaire to Briand, no. 9, 4 Jan. 1922; MAE, Europe 1918–1940 GB 69, Draft treaty between the Governments of the British Empire and the French Republic, Secret, A.J.320, revised, Cannes, 11 Jan. 1922; Laroche, *Au Quai d'Orsay*, pp. 149–51; Saint-Aulaire, *Confession*, p. 585.
213. MAE, Europe 1918–40, GB 69, minutes of meeting at Villa Valetta, Cannes, between Briand and Lloyd George, 8 Jan. 1922.
214. CAB23/29, conclusion 1(22), 10 Jan. 1922. Italics added.
215. *Ibid.*
216. *Ibid.*
217. On the scepticism of the French press, see articles by J. Sauerwein in *Le Matin*, 9 Jan. 1922; P. Millet in *Le Petit Parisien*, 9 Jan. 1922; 'Pertinax' in *Echo de Paris*, 9 and 11 Jan. 1922; J. Bainville in *Action Française*, 10 and 12 Jan. 1922; E. Buré in *L'Éclair*, 11 Jan. 1922; A. Tardieu in *Echo National*, 11 and 13 Jan. 1922; L. Lazarus, *Le Figaro*, 12 Jan. 1922.
218. L. Lazarus, *Le Figaro*, 12 Jan. 1922, Millerand to Briand, 11 Jan. 1922; S. Lauzanne, 'Retour brusqué de M. Briand', *Le Matin*, 12 Jan. 1922.
219. 'Le Ministère Briand est démissionaire', *Le Matin*, 13 Jan. 1922; Briand, *Aristide Briand*, pp. 130–40; Laroche, *Au Quai d'Orsay*, pp. 154–5; Saint-Aulaire, *Confession*, pp. 588–92; Suarez, *Briand*, v, pp. 352–410; Oudin, *Aristide Briand*, pp. 436–8.
220. MAE Europe 1918–40, GB 47. In the month of June 1921 alone Poincaré contributed articles addressing Franco-British relations to the *Revue des Deux Mondes* (1 and 15 June), *Revue de Paris* (1 and 15 June), *Correspondant* (10 and 25 June), and *l'Europe Nouvelle*. His most frequent outlet at this time was however *Le Matin*, see 'Lendemain d'ultimatum', *Le* Matin, 4 Oct. 1921, p. 1; 'Le Débiteur Prodigue', *ibid.*, 21 Nov. 1921, p. 1; 'Heures de malaise', *ibid.*, 5 Dec. 1921, p. 1.

221. 'Le Ministère Poincaré Un Cabinet d'Union Sacrée', *Le Matin*, 16 Jan. 1922; Roth, *Raymond Poincaré*, pp. 402–3; Keiger, 'Raymond Poincaré and the Ruhr Crisis', pp. 49–53.
222. MAE, Europe 1918–40, GB 69, minutes of meeting between Lloyd George and Poincaré at British embassy, 14 Jan. 1922; MAE, Europe 1918–40, GB 70, Poincaré no. 185 to Saint-Aulaire, 23 Jan. 1922; Curzon papers, MSS EUR, F112/242, C.P.3612, Note of conversation at British Embassy, 14 Jan. 1922; Hardinge, *Old Diplomacy*, p. 267; Suarez, *Briand*, v, p. 418.
223. S. Lauzanne, 'M. Poincaré chez M. Lloyd George', *Le Matin*, 14 Jan. 1922.
224. Riddell, *Intimate Diary of the Peace Conference*, p. 349.
225. MAE, Europe 1918–40, GB 70, Saint-Aulaire note, 'Rensignement venant de très bonne source', 20 Jan. 1921.
226. MAE, Europe 1918–40, GB 69, de la Panousse to Chief of the Army General Staff, Paris, 17 Jan. 1922; MAE, Europe 1918–40, Grande-Bretagne 70, de la Panousse to the Chief of the Army General Staff, 7 Mar. 1922.
227. MAE, Europe 1918–40, GB 70, Poincaré to Saint-Aulaire, no. 185, 23 Jan. 1922; Curzon papers, MSS EUR, F112/242, French draft of proposed Anglo-French Treaty, 26 Jan. 1922.
228. MAE, Europe 1918–40, GB 70, Saint-Aulaire to Poincaré, nos 79-81, 27 Jan. 1922; Curzon papers, MSS EUR, F112/242, Curzon to Hardinge, no. 289, 28 Jan. 1922.
229. MAE, Europe 1918–40, GB 70, Poincaré to Saint-Aulaire, no.-, 30 Jan. 1922.
230. MAE, Europe 1918–1940 GB 70., Saint-Aulaire to Poincaré, nos 79-81, 27 Jan. 1922; MAE, Europe 1918–1940 GB 70, Saint-Aulaire to Poincaré, nos 110-15, 1 Feb. 1922; MAE, Europe 1918–1940 GB 70, Saint-Aulaire telg. to Poincaré, no. 155, 9 Feb. 1922; MAE, Europe 1918–1940 GB 70, Saint-Aulaire to Poincaré, no. 180, 15 Feb. 1922; Curzon Papers, MSS EUR, F112/240, Saint-Aulaire to Poincaré, nos 190-91, 17 Feb. 1922; Curzon papers, MSS EUR, F112/240, Curzon to Hardinge, no. 405, 9 Feb. 1922; Curzon Papers, MSS EUR, F112/240, no. 528, 21 Feb. 1922; *ibid.*, Balfour to Hardinge, no. 2125, 4 Jul. 1922.
231. *Ibid.*, I.C.P.236, Notes of meeting at Boulogne, 25 Feb. 1933; MAE, PA-AP 261-Seydoux 24, minutes of conversation between Poincaré and Lloyd George, 1 Mar. 1922; *ibid.*, Europe 1918–40, GB 70, Poincaré to Saint-Aulaire, no.-, 2 Mar. 1922; Riddell, *Intimate Diary of the Peace Conference*, p. 359–60.
232. Laroche, *Au Quai d'Orsay*, p. 407.
233. MAE, Europe 1918–40, GB 70, Note de M. Laroche: Alliance franco-britannique. Arrangements entre Etats-Majors', 21 Feb. 1922.
234. MAE, Europe 1918–40, GB 71, 'Copie d'une lettre d'un informateur sûr', 17 Mar. 1922.
235. Poincaré's original demands are summarized in MAE, Europe 1918–40, GB 70, Memorandum concernant les modifications à apporter au projet britannique du traité entre la France et la Grande-Bretagne', 31 Jan. 1922. His later modifications are contained in *ibid.*, GB 71, Poincaré to Saint-Aulaire, no. 929, 2 May 1922.
236. MAE, Europe 1918–40, GB 71, Saint-Aulaire to Poincaré, no. 480, 16 May 1922; *ibid.*, Saint-Aulaire to Poincaré, nos 490-91, 21 May 1922; *ibid.*, Saint-Aulaire to Poincaré, nos 519-20, 31 May 1922; *ibid.*, Poincaré to Saint-Aulaire, no. 1432, 28 Jun. 1922; *ibid.*, Saint-Aulaire to Poincaré, no. 334, 5 Jul. 1922.
237. *Le Matin*, 3 Feb. 1922.
238. MAE, Europe 1918–40, GB 70, Saint-Aulaire to Poincaré, no. 130, 3 Feb. 1922.
239. *Ibid.*, 48, Bardoux report to Poincaré, 7 Mar. 1922.
240. *Ibid.*
241. Hardinge, *Old Diplomacy*, p. 269.
242. Young, *Power and Pleasure*, pp. 170–2.
243. MAE, Europe 1918–40, GB 71, Poincaré to Saint-Aulaire, no. 929, 2 May 1922.
244. *Ibid.*, Saint-Aulaire to Poincaré, no. 480, 16 May 1922.
245. Roth, *Raymond Poincaré*, p. 414.
246. Quoted in Ferris, *Men, Money, and Diplomacy*, p. 109. British statesmen should have recognized that it was largely their own refusal to engage in European affairs that was

leading France to fend for itself against a potentially much stronger Germany. Ferris erroneously claims that

> Virtually every [British] decision maker had wanted an alignment with one or another power to guarantee British security. Circumstances, not intent, had driven them into Imperial isolation. Since no ally or collective security arrangements offered it strategic support, Britain would have to deal with any dangers through its own strength alone. Although Britain did not perceive imminent threats, it did fear that France and to a lesser extent, Japan, might endanger British interests.

247. MAE, Europe 1918–40, GB 48, Waterlow to Seydoux, 6 Dec. 1921.
248. *Ibid.*, Seydoux personal to Waterlow, 20 Dec. 1921.
249. Mackay, *Balfour*, p. 336.
250. CAB23/30, conclusions, 16 Jun. 1922.
251. *Ibid.*, conclusions, 25 Jul. 1922; Balfour papers, Add. Ms. 49,749, Balfour note to France, 1 Aug. 1922.
252. Glad, *Charles Evans Hughes*, p. 219. A copy of the Note is in *FRUS*, 1922, i, Harvey to Hughes, no. 1550, 4 Aug. 1922, pp. 406–9.
253. Artaud, *La question des dettes interalliées*, i, pp. 438–9.
254. *Ibid.*, i, p. 436, CAB29/97, I.C.P.252, Notes of a Conversation at 10 Downing Street, 14 Aug. 1922 at 11 a.m.
255. Roth, *Raymond Poincaré*, p. 418.
256. Amery, *My Political Life*, ii, p. 235.
257. Gilbert, *Churchill a Life*, p. 453.
258. MAE, Europe 1918–40, GB 50, Saint-Aulaire to Poincaré, nos 988-89, 20 Oct. 1922; *ibid.*, Poincaré telegramme to Saint-Aulaire, nos 2196-2201, 23 Oct. 1922; *ibid.*, Poincaré to Saint-Aulaire, nos 2351-53, 11 Nov. 1922.
259. The consequences became apparent at the next Imperial conference, which met in London in 1923: Barnett, *The Collapse of British Power*, p. 195.
260. MAE, Europe 1918–40, GB 39, de Montille to Ministry, nos 808-09, received 9 Sept. 1922.
261. Curzon papers, MSS EUR, F112/242, Hardinge (for Curzon to Cabinet), no.- 20 Sept. 1922; *ibid.*, Hardinge (for Curzon), no. 472, 22 Sept. 1922; Busch, *Hardinge of Penshurst*, p. 307; MAE, Europe 1918–40, GB 50, Poincaré to Saint-Aulaire, nos 2180-81, 21 Oct. 1922; *ibid.*, Poincaré to Saint-Aulaire, nos 2196-2201, 23 Oct. 1922.
262. *Ibid.*, Saint-Aulaire to Poincaré, no. 973, 17 Oct. 1922.
263. *Ibid.*, GB 39, Saint-Aulaire to Poincaré, no. 457, 14 Oct. 1922.
264. *Times*, 7 Oct. 1922, p. 11.
265. MAE, Europe 1918–40, GB 50, Saint-Aulaire to Poincaré, 'extrême urgence' no.-, 6 Oct. 1922; *ibid.*, Saint-Aulaire to Poincaré, no. 471, 9 Oct. 1922; *ibid.*, Saint-Aulaire to Poincaré, 21 Oct. 1922 enclosing Steed to Saint-Aulaire, 20 Oct., and Saint-Aulaire to Steed, 21 Oct. 1922 (copy in MAE, PA-AP 118-Millerand 23).
266. *Ibid.*
267. MAE, PA-AP 118-Millerand 23, Dubois to Millerand, 10 Oct. 1922; MAE, PA-AP 261-Seydoux 26, Seydoux note for Millerand, P.33, 12 Oct. 1922.
268. MAE, PA-AP 118-Millerand 23, minutes of meeting at premier's office, 13 Oct. 1922.
269. *Ibid.*, Europe 1918–40, GB 50, Saint-Aulaire to Poincaré, nos 1021-22, 1 Nov. 1922; *ibid.*, PA-AP 118-Millerand 23, Seydoux note for Millerand, 8 Nov. 1922; *ibid.*, Dupuis to Millerand, 13 Nov. 1922.
270. MAE, PA-AP 118-Millerand 23, Laurent to Poincaré, nos 1622-23, 28 Oct. 1922; *ibid.*, PA-AP 261-Seydoux 26, note no. 37 for the premier, 21 Nov. 1922; *ibid.*, minutes of meeting at the office of the premier, 23 Nov. 1922; Roth, *Raymond Poincaré*, pp. 419–21; Laroche, *Au Quai d'Orsay*, p. 170.
271. MAE PA-AP 118-Millerand 24, minute of meeting in prime minister's office, 3 Dec. 1922; *ibid.*, Europe 1918–40, GB 50, Saint-Aulaire to Poincaré, nos 1171-77, 24 Dec. 1922; *ibid.*, Millerand 23, Poincaré circular telg. to London, etc., no. 2681,

26 Dec. 1922; *ibid.*, Millerand 25, Barrère to Poincaré, nos 270-71, 5 Jan. 1923; *ibid.*, Barthou and Delacroix, Reparations Commission, to French government, 9 Jan. 1923; *ibid.*, PA-AP 261-Seydoux 8, Seydoux note, 4 Jun. 1924.

272. MAE, PA-AP 26- Seydoux 26, Réunion chez le President du Conseil. 23 Nov. 1922.

273. Jeannesson, *Poincaré, la France et la Ruhr*, pp. 76, 84, 142 and passim.

274. MAE, PA-AP 261-Seydoux 26, reunion, 23 Nov. 1922.

275. Curzon papers, MSS EUR, F112/240, FO memorandum, 3 Nov. 1923; F112/241, Curzon to Kilmarnock, no. 1107, 3 Dec. 1923; Jeannesson, *Poincaré, la France et la Ruhr*, ch. XI.

276. Artaud, *La question des dettes interalliées*, i, p. 236. This is also a central claim in accounts by Costigliola, Link and others.

277. See for instance, *FRUS*, 1922, ii, Hughes to Herrick, no. 321, 17 Oct. 1922, pp. 168–70; *ibid.*, Houghton to Hughes, 23 Oct. 1922, pp. 171–5; *ibid.*, Herrick to Hughes, no. 423, 23 Oct. 1922.

278. Dawes, *A Journal of Reparations*, Appendix I. Another copy is reprinted in *FRUS*, 1922, ii, Phillips to Herrick, 29 Dec. 1922, p. 202.

279. *FRUS*, 1923, ii, Hughes to Whitehouse, no. 393, 24 Oct. 1923.

280. *Ibid.*, Chilton to Hughes, 13 Oct. 1922, pp. 68–70.

281. *Ibid.*, Hughes memorandum of conversation with de Laboulaye, 26 Oct. 1922, p. 84; *ibid.*, Whitehouse to Hughes, no. 428, 26 Oct. 1922, p. 85.

282. Case and Case, *Owen D. Young and American Enterprise*, p. 277.

283. Roth, *Raymond Poincaré*, pp. 460–4.

284. JRM 1/123, quoted in Marquand, *Ramsay MacDonald*, p. 430.

285. As he said to Austen Chamberlain on 7 March 1925, 'I tell you I look forward with terror at her making war upon us again in ten years.' Petrie, *The Life and Letters of the Right Hon. Sir Austen Chamberlain*, ii, p. 263.

286. Cassels, 'Repairing the Entente Cordiale and the New Diplomacy', pp. 133–53.

287. TWL 176-10, Grenfell to J. P. Morgan, 6 June 1929; *ibid.*, 176-12, Lamont and Grenfell to Morgan and Morrow, 10 Jul. 1929; *ibid.*, 176-24, Lamont to J. P. Morgan and Company, 11 Aug. 1924.

288. Herriot, *Jadis*, ii, pp. 150, 183.

289. Bariéty, *Les relations franco-allemandes après la première guerre mondiale*, pp. 42 f. 42, 374–9; Schuker, *The End of French Predominance in Europe*, pp. 292–300; A. Adamthwaite, *Grandeur and Misery*, pp. 102–5; Cassels, 'Repairing the *Entente Cordiale*', pp. 144–6.

290. See the acute and sympathetic treatment in Berstein, *Edouard Herriot*, p. 119; also Beau de Loménie, *Les responsabilités des dynasties bourgeoises*, iv, pp. 13–14; Frank, *La hantise du déclin*, p. 158. Significantly, Jules Laroche, a senior diplomat, wrote that the Quai d'Orsay regretted Herriot's departure. Although 'less fussy [pointilleux] and less the slave of his dossiers, he took as much care reading them, annotating them, and drafting in his own hand the essential notes and instructions, not without taking the advice of his collaborators, whose goodwill facilitated his task.' Laroche, *Au Quai d'Orsay*, p. 208.

291. 175 H.C. Deb 5s, MacDonald's statements, 26 Jun. and 7 Jul. 1924.

292. Herriot, *Jadis*, ii, pp. 169–71. Jackson, 'France and the Problems of Security and International Disarmament after the First World War', p. 276, describes endorsement of the Protocol as 'the culmination of a revolution in French security policy', although the underlying aim of interwar French policy, namely drawing Britain into a Continental commitment, remained unchanged.

293. Marquand, *Ramsay MacDonald*, p. 356.

294. MAE Europe 1918–40, GB 57, Saint-Aulaire no. 589 to Briand, 17 Oct. 1924.

295. CAB2/4, CID 513-B, Note from Herriot to MacDonald, 11 Aug. 1924; *ibid.*, minutes of 192nd meeting of CID, 16 Dec. 1924.

296. CAB4/11, CID 516-B, 'French Security': Memorandum by the General Staff, 29 Sept. 1924.

297. CAB4/12, CID 545-B, 'Belgian and French Security', Memorandum by the Naval Staff, 8 Dec. 1924.
298. CAB4/11, CID 518-B, 'French Security', Preliminary Note by the Air Staff, 1 Oct. 1924.
299. CAB4/12, CID 560-B, 'French and Belgian Security', Memorandum by the Air Staff, 4 Jan. 1925.
300. CAB4/12, C.P.116(25), 'French Security', Memorandum by the Secretary of State for War, enclosing a Note by the General Staff, 26 Feb. 1925. Italics in original.
301. CAB24/172, C.P.106(25), 'British Policy Considered in Relation to the European Situation', 20 Feb. 1925; *ibid.*, C.P.122(25), 'British Foreign Policy and the Problem of Security', 26 Feb. 1925.
302. FO 371/11064, Chamberlain minute, 4 Jan. 1925.
303. CAB23/49, conclusions 2–4 Mar. 1925; Dutton, *Austen Chamberlain*, p. 243.
304. Petrie, *Life and Letters of the Right Hon. Sir Austen Chamberlain*, p. 263.
305. Self (ed.), *The Austen Chamberlain Diary Letters*, pp. 267–8.
306. *Ibid.*, p. 356; MAE, PA-AP 89-Herriot 19, de Fleuriau to Herriot, no. 158, 16 Mar. 1925; Barnes and Nicholson (eds), *The Leo Amery Diaries*, i, p. 384 and f.
307. Gibbs, *Grand Strategy*, i, p. 43. In a nice irony, Churchill, who had taken a leading role in resisting a military commitment to France in 1925, while supporting Locarno because it involved no military obligations, wrote of Britain's Locarno commitment in *The Second World War*, i, p. 27: 'This far-reaching military commitment was accepted by Parliament and endorsed warmly by the nation. The histories may be searched in vain for a parallel to such an undertaking.'
308. As N. H. Gibbs writes,
   > It might have been supposed that Locarno, and the strategic appreciations that preceded it, would draw attention to Britain's military deficiencies and underline the need for her Government to think once more in terms of an expeditionary force which would enable the frontier guarantees to be backed, if necessary, by force. But this was not so.

   Nor did the Chiefs of Staff argue for it in their Annual Review of 1926 or thereafter: *Grand Strategy*, i, p. 53. See also Ferris, *Men, Money, and Diplomacy*, p. 152.
309. MAE Europe 1918–40, GB 73, de Fleuriau to Herriot, no. 108, 25 Feb. 1925; *ibid.*, 89, memorandum for Briand, n.d.; *ibid.*, note by Massigli, 6 Mar. 1925; *ibid.*, 76, Massigli letter to [Berthelot] 7 Jun. 1925; *ibid.*, 78, Briand to de Fleuriau, no. 1343, 27 Jun. 1925.
310. The standard English-language account of the Locarno negotiations presents the Rhineland Pact as a welcome development, while acknowledging that it weakened the security of both Eastern and Western Europe: Jacobson, *Locarno Diplomacy*, pp. 3–4, 31, 35 and passim.
311. Grayson, *Austen Chamberlain*, p. 138.
312. FO371/11065, W2070/9/98, memorandum, 10 Mar. 1925; reprinted in Headlam-Morley, *Studies in Diplomatic History*, pp. 184–5.
313. *Ibid.*, p. 184.
314. FO371/10747, C15928/459/18, Addison to A. Chamberlain, no. 671, 10 Dec. 1925.
315. *Ibid.*
316. FO371/10702, C8/2/18, Chamberlain to D'Abernon, no. 3, 2 Jan. 1925, enclosing draft Allied note of 27 Dec. 1924. See also FO371/10708, C2853/21/18, summary of final report of inter-allied military commission, 15 Feb. 1925.
317. Barnett, *The Collapse of British Power*, p. 21.
318. *Ibid.*, pp. 323–4.
319. FO371/10719, C15323/117/18, FO memorandum, 3 Dec. 1925; FO371/10719, C15576/117/18, Knatchbull-Hugesson to Lampson, with enclosure, 3 Dec. 1925. Predictably, the German authorities did nothing further to meet their disarmament obligations: see FO371/10710, C12381/21/18, War Office to FO, 29 Sept. 1925, containing report by General Wauchope, 19 Sept. 1925.

320. FO371/11880, W3903/78/98, annex, Beckett memorandum, memorandum by Beckett, annex to memorandum by Hurst, 7 May 1926.
321. Jacobson, *Locarno Diplomacy*, pp. 124, 135.
322. *Ibid.*
323. MAE, PA-AP, 261-Seydoux, 35, Seydoux note, nos 21-26, 25 Feb. 1926; *ibid.*, Seydoux, 3 bis, Seydoux note nos 57-26, 23 Jun. 1926.
324. Headlam-Morley, *A Memoir of the Peace Conference*, pp. 52, 163. Antony Lentin singles out Headlam-Morley along with Keynes as members of the British delegation with exaggerated sympathy for Germany: *Lloyd George and the Lost Peace*, p. 81.
325. Headlam-Morley, *A Memoir of the Peace Conference*, p. 161.
326. As Kennan, in the midst of the Cold War, put it, *American Diplomacy*, p. 95: 'I see the most serious failing of our past policy formulation to lie in something that I might call the legalistic-moralistic approach to international problems. This approach runs like a red skein through our foreign policy of the last fifty years.'
327. Ferris, *Men, Money, and Diplomacy*, p. 180.
328. Balfour papers, Add. Ms. 51078, Cecil to Austen Chamberlain, 11 Feb. 1926.
329. FO800/257, Chamberlain to D'Abernon, 2 Apr. 1925. One of the few historical accounts to address the issue of British interest in Eastern Europe is Goldstein, 'The Evolution of British Diplomatic Strategy for the Locarno Pact', pp. 81, 126 and passim.
330. FO800/257, minute by Tyrrell, 21 Dec. 1925.
331. FO371/11247, C797/1/18, FO memorandum respecting the Locarno Treaties, by Bennett, 10 Jan. 1926, p. 4.
332. FO371/11324, C5436/5139/18, Lampson to Phipps, 6 May 1926, p. 732. Italics in the original.
333. *Ibid.*, C5503/5139/18, Phipps to Lampson, 8 May 1926, p. 738.
334. FO371/11247, C797/1/18, Bennett memorandum, 10 Jan. 1926, p. 6. One historian, struck by the tendency of Foreign Office officials to caricature Germans in racial terms, presents them as chronically anti-German. But throughout the interwar period their racial prejudice was directed mainly against France: Jacobson, *Locarno Diplomacy*, p. 212.
335. See for instance, McKercher, '"The Deep and Latent Mistrust"', p. 218, who describes France as 'paranoid'; Turner, *The Cost of War*, p. 19, who writes of 'an obsessive pre-occupation with national security'; and Cassels, 'Repairing the Entente Cordiale and the New Diplomacy', p. 134, who refers to 'France's craving for security'.
336. On antisemitic practices in the French higher civil service, see Birnbaum, *The Jews of the Republic*, pp. 376–7 and passim.
337. 'Entente in Culture', *Times*, 28 Feb. 1921, p. 11; Tiemann, 'Zweigstelle Paris des DAAD und Institut français de Berlin', p. 288.
338. See for instance, Schuker, *The End of French Predominance in Europe*, pp. 241–2; Trachtenberg, *Reparation in World Politics*, pp. 329, 334; Adamthwaite, *Grandeur and Misery*, ch. 6.

3 The Limits of Globalization

1. 'New York-Paris Flight', *Times*, 23 May 1927, p. 14; Berg, *Lindbergh*, ch. 6; Lardner, 'The Lindbergh Legends', pp. 200–1.
2. Berg accepts the story that this was due to the quick thinking of the French pilots, a version similar to the account in 'Alone Across the Atlantic', *Manchester Guardian*, 23 May 1927; but see also Root, *The Paris Edition*, p. 32.
3. Castle papers, France, Jun.–Dec. 1927, Box 5, Herrick to Castle, 10 Jun. 1927.
4. BdF, 1397199401/120 (Crédit de Stabilisation, 1926–1928), Quesnay to Siepmann, 19 Oct. 1926.
5. Berg, *Lindbergh*, p. 165; Chernow, *The House of Morgan*, p. 291.
6. LN, *The World Economic Conference*, May 1927, Final Report, p. 29.
7. Platt, *British Investment Overseas on the Eve of the First World War*, estimates British direct and indirect overseas investment in 1913 at £3.1 billion, and foreign-owned

investments acquired through London at another 15 per cent: pp. 36 and 60 table 2.3; on French foreign investment, pp. 131–4.

8. Pollard, *Development of the British Economy*, p. 19; 'The Balance of Payments in the Interwar Period: Further Details', table B, p. 49. The contemporary Treasury estimate was that Britain had annually invested £200 million abroad before the war, but had at most an annual £100 million to invest abroad in the mid-1920s: T176/17, Pt. 2, First Draft Overseas Loan Sub-Committee Report, 2 Oct. 1925.

9. Moulton and Pasvolsky, *World War Debt Settlements*, pp. 25–7.

10. Sayers, *The Bank of England*, i, pp. 8–9; Mouré, *The Gold Standard Illusion*, p. 147.

11. *BCC*, pp. 22–4; Williams, *A Pattern of Rulers*, p. 196; Jones, *Georgian Afternoon*, pp. 122, 125; Boyle, *Montagu Norman*, p. 198 and passim.

12. Sir Charles Addis papers, MS.14/454, diary 28 Sept. 1926, 23 Feb. 1927, 24 and 31 May 1928, 18 Oct. 1928, 7 and 13 Oct. 1931; FRBNY, Strong papers, 1000.9, Strong to Stewart, 8 Jul. 1928.

13. The only other currencies fully restored to their prewar parities were those of Denmark, the Netherlands, Sweden and eventually Japan; the American dollar remained on gold: LN, *The Course and Control of Inflation*, pp. 92–3.

14. Cottrell, 'Norman, the Bank of England and Europe during the 1920s', p. 79.

15. Boyce, 'Economics', p. 19. Only briefly during the 1931 financial crisis was this practice suspended, see FO371/16380, W20/20/50, Waley to A. Leeper, 31 Dec. 1931.

16. Clay, *Lord Norman*, pp. 286–7, 289; FO371/13705, C520/47/92, Bateman minute to Wellesley and Wellesley minute, 18 Jan. 1929. Norman reluctantly visited the Foreign Office in March 1929, to explain why City lending should not be tied to industrial orders or subject to public controls: *ibid.*, T175/34, Lindsay memorandum to Hopkins, 11 Apr. 1929.

17. The Bank of England was not alone in eschewing public attention: investment banks as well as central banks elsewhere acted similarly: Beyen, *Money in a Maelstrom*, pp. 114–15.

18. *Daily Herald*, 1 Jan. 1925, p. 9; 'Mr. Montague', *Daily Mail*, 24 Aug. 1931, p. 3; FO371/15882, A6014/6014/45, Osborne to Simon, no. 1322, 1 Sept. 1932. Sir Robert Vansittart, permanent under-secretary of the Foreign Office, was led to comment: 'Mr. Norman makes a monkey of himself with these antics. I will see that this opinion reaches him – but I fear the false nose habit has long been growing on him.' *Ibid.*, minute, 22 Sept. 1932. See also Hargrave, *Professor Skinner, alias Montagu Norman*.

19. *BCC*, pp. 25, 60–1, 294, p. 381, f. 81.

20. Quesnay, 374 AP 6, Politique monétaire 1926–1927, Compte rendu de mission à Londres (lundi 11 – samedi 16 octobre1926).

21. Hoover, *Memoirs*, ii, p. 178; Murray, *The Harding Era*, pp. 363–4. Several American historians, echoing Hoover, have stressed the generosity of the terms extended to Britain and other countries, without however assessing the burden on the debtors or the implications for the international economy. See for instance, Rhodes, 'Reassessing "Uncle Shylock"', pp. 787–803; Leffler, 'The Origins of Republican War Debt Policy', pp. 585–601; Wilson, *Herbert Hoover*, p. 183.

22. See for instance, Hogan, 'Revival and Reform', pp. 291–2; Costigliola, 'Anglo-American Financial Rivalry in the 1920s', pp. 911–34. Norman's former firm, Brown, Shipley and Company, had been created to help finance the British purchase of American cotton, and retained close ties with its American associate, Brown Brothers Harriman.

23. Boyce, 'Creating the Myth of consensus', ch. 7.

24. Strong, in an unfortunate choice of words, later claimed that

> in 1923 he had voluntarily adopted, in the interests of the London market, a veritable policy of inflation in maintaining a very low discount rate precisely in order to force England to return as soon as possible to the gold standard.

Quesnay, 374 AP 6, file VII, 'Aide mémoire des conversations du 29 au 30 juin entre M. Rist, M. Strong et M. Harrison', 1 Jul. 1927. Strong was in no position to force the issue, which ultimately was a matter for decision by the British government, not the Bank of England. But the claim has found its way into a number of accounts, including one which asserts without supporting evidence that the United States was 'exerting pressure on Whitehall [*sic*] to return to gold': Dayer, 'Anglo-American Monetary Policy and Rivalry in Europe and the Far East', p. 171.

25. FRBNY, BoE cables, 1925, Norman to Deputy-Governor (Lubbock), no. 15 and 16, 6 Jan. 1925; *ibid.*, Bank of England Revolving Credit, C261.1, Strong minute, 11 Jan. 1925; TWL 103-13, Leffingwell to Lamont, 8 Mar. 1929.

26. Cottrell, 'Norman, the Bank of England and Europe during the 1920s', pp. 38–9.

27. *Bankers' Magazine*, Mar. 1925, pp. 445–6, 460–6; FRBNY, BoE cables, Lubbock to Norman, no. 54, 9 Jan. 1931; *ibid.*, Strong papers, 1116.5, Norman to Strong, 24 Jan. 1925; Addis diary, 21 Jan. 1925. Churchill also found Sir William Goodenough of Barclays cautious about returning: T172/1499B, Churchill minute, 6 Feb. 1925.

28. T175/9, Norman memorandum, 2 Feb. 1925.

29. Grigg, *Prejudice and Judgment*, pp. 182–4.

30. H.C. Deb 5s, vol. 183, cols 57–8.

31. See, for instance, Moggridge, *British Monetary Policy*. L. S. Pressnell, however, described it was 'a major historic error': '1925', p. 67.

32. T188/95, Hawtrey, 'The French Memorandum on the English Crisis', 27 Nov. 1931.

33. Church, *Herbert Austin*, p. 105.

34. T172/1499B, Niemeyer to Churchill, 21 Apr. 1925.

35. T176/13, Pt.2, Niemeyer to Norman, 21 Jul. 1925; Addis diary, 28 Jul. 1925; TWL 111-16, Grenfell to Lamont, 29 Jul. 1925; FRBNY, Strong papers, 1000.6, Strong to Case, 1 Aug. 1925. Churchill's annoyance with Norman for his duff advice was still evident seven years later when he unfavourably compared 'the venerable and chilling orthodoxy of Mr. Montagu Norman' with the reflationary policy of President Roosevelt: 'Mr. Churchill and Two Paths in Finance', *Sunday Times*, 13 Aug. 1933.

36. BoE, ADM 34/14, Norman diary, 3 Dec. 1925; Clay, *Lord Norman*, p. 292; Grigg, *Prejudice and Judgment*, p. 193.

37. 'The Midland Bank Limited: Annual Meeting', *Empire Review*, Mar. 1927, pp. 267–84; 'Episodes of the Month', *National Review*, Mar. 1927, pp. 36–7, 148–56; *World Power*, Apr. 1927 p. 167; J. Strachey, 'The Need for an Enquiry into Our Banking System', *The Socialist Review* (Apr. 1927), p. 1; *British Industries, Economic Supplement*, 30 Apr. 1927, p. i; H.C. Deb 5s, vol. 208, col. 99.

38. T172/1500B, Mond-Turner memorandum, 'Gold Reserve and Its Relations with Industry', 12 Apr. 1928; letter from Sir Alfred Mond, *Times*, 25 Apr. 1928, p. 12; T160/384, F9780/1, Sir A. Geddes, Lord Denbigh, F. Farrell and others to the prime minister, 25 Apr. 1928; T175/1500B, Corcoran (NUM) to Churchill, 21 May 1928; *British Industries*, 15 Jun. 1928; BEAMA, *Trade Survey*, Jun. 1928, p. 2.

39. *BCC*, pp. 150–1.

40. Amery diary, i, 7 May, 4, 9, 10, 11, 23 Jul., 2, 5 Aug. 1928; CAB23/58, conclusion 37(28)3, 11 Jul. 1928; *ibid.*, 43(28)2, 2 Aug. 1928; Gilbert (ed.), *Winston S. Churchill, Companion Volume* v, p. 1316.

41. T176/16, Hawtrey to Hopkins, 12 Jul. 1928; FRBNY, Bank of England general, C261, Lubbock to Harrison, 3 Aug. 1928.

42. Sayers, *The Bank of England*, iii, Appendix 17.

43. *Ibid.*, Appendix 30; Atkin, 'Official Regulation of British Overseas Investment', p. 331.

44. Kuisel, *Capitalism and the State in Modern France*, ch. 3–4, dwells upon innovating and dissenting attitudes in interwar France, but acknowledges the practical emphasis upon liberal principles.

45. Sauvy, *Histoire économique*, i, annexe ii, p. 445.

46. Debeir, 'La crise du franc de 1924: Un exemple de spéculation internationale', p. 43.

47. This is Schuker's argument in *The End of French Predominance in Europe*. But see the author's review in the *Historical Journal*, vol. 21, no. 3 (1978), pp. 757–9.

48. MAE PA-AP, 261-Seydoux 29, Poincaré to Barthou, 2 Nov. 1923; also statement by Seydoux, 5 Nov. 1923, quoted in McDougall, *France's Rhineland Diplomacy*, p. 345.
49. Debeir, 'La crise du franc de 1924', p. 48; Jeanneney, 'De la spéculation financière comme arme diplomatique', pp. 22–5; Roth, *Raymond Poincaré*, p. 454.
50. Berstein, *Histoire du Parti Radical*, ii, table 5, pp. 261–3.
51. Berstein, *Edouard Herriot*, pp. 131–2, 136–8; Soulié, *La vie politique d'Edouard Herriot*, pp. 215–17, 226.
52. Soulié, *La vie politique d'Edouard Herriot*, pp. 218–22.
53. Herriot, *Jadis*, ii, pp. 201, 254–5. Among others, Kuisel, *Capitalism and the State in Modern France*, pp. 71–4, presents it as a problem of budget deficits.
54. Herriot, *Jadis*, ii, pp. 199, 255.
55. *Ibid.*, p. 203.
56. Debeir, 'La crise du franc de 1924', p. 32. While some industrialists, including Andé Citroen and Théodore Laurent, may have welcomed inflation, they were extremely loath to admit it in public: Weiss, *Mémoires d'une Européenne*, ii, p. 194.
57. *Ibid.*, p. 237; BdF, DCG, draft statement for annual meeting of the Bank, 26 Jan. 1926.
58. BdF, DCG, 20 Apr., 11, 15, 20, 21 May, 2, 7 Jun. 1926.
59. Soulié, *La vie politique d'Edouard Herriot*, pp. 268–70.
60. Herriot, *Jadis*, ii, p. 250.
61. Soucy, *French Fascism*, p. 217.
62. *Ibid.*, pp. 27, 174.
63. Soulié, *La vie politique d'Edouard Herriot*, p. 271.
64. TWL 113-5, Jay to Whigham, 15 June 1926; FRBNY, French Situation C261.1, Strong to Harrison, 21 Jul. 1926, and Strong to Mellon, 1 Aug. 1926.
65. 'Au Vérités de la Palisse', *Le Petit Journal*, 23 Jul. 1926, p. 1.
66. MAE PA-AP 261-Seydoux 38, Seydoux to de Fleuriau, 29 Mar. 1926; *ibid.*, Seydoux 39, Seydoux to de Fleuriau, 8 May and 7 Jun. 1926; FRBNY, French situation, C261.1, Strong to Harrison, 21 Jul. 1926.
67. Soulié, *La vie politique d'Edouard Herriot*, p. 271; Neurrisse, *Histoire du franc*, p. 61.
68. 'Les manifestations d'hier soir', *Le Petit Journal*, 22 Jul. 1926, p. 8; Becker and Berstein, *Victoire et frustrations*, pp. 274–5.
69. Roth, *Raymond Poincaré*, pp. 484–7.
70. 'La livre au dessous de 200', *Le Petit Journal*, 26 Jul. 1926, p. 1; *ibid.*, various issues; MF, F[30], B12606, Pouyanne to Poincaré, no. 45,752, 25 Oct. 1926; Wolfe, *The French Franc between the Wars*, pp. 43–7.
71. Moreau, *Souvenirs*', pp. 74, 96; Roth, *Raymond Poincaré*, pp. 494–6; Sabouret, *MM.Lazard Frères et Cie*, pp. 78–9; MAE PA-AP 261-Seydoux 38, de Fleuriau private letter to Seydoux, 18 Sept. 1926. As Moreau recorded on 3 Sept. 1926, 'Les intérêts des petits rentiers semblent seuls préoccuper le président du Conseil. Il n'accorde pour le moment aucune attention aux intérêts de l'industrie et du commerce, ni à la balance des comptes, ni aux charges fiscales.' Moreau, *Souvenirs*, p. 94.
72. *Ibid.*, pp. 61, 66, 74.
73. Rueff, *De l'aube au crépuscule*, p. 59. Mouré minimizes Jouhaux's influence: *The Gold Standard Illusion*, p. 113.
74. *Ibid.* Rueff submitted his report at the end of November, recommending a rate of 120 – 145Ff = £.
75. Moreau, *Souvenirs*, pp. 94, 140, 147, 162, 163, 164, 177, 179; BdF, DCG, Poincaré to Moreau, 28 Oct. 1926.
76. *Ibid.*, 18 and 25 Nov. 1926; Quesnay, 374, AP 6, Poincaré to Moreau, 18 and 23 Nov. 1926.
77. Moreau, *Souvenirs*, p. 183.
78. As Norman told Lionel and Anthony Rothschild, 'No French loans are welcome here – State, Railway or Municipal of any kind.' BoE, ADM 34/16, Norman diary, 8 Mar. 1927;

see also *ibid.*, 3 Jan. 1927. The only exception seems to have been the £15 million in private credits for the French Treasury arranged before the Ruhr crisis: see MF, F^{30}, B12679, Pouyanne note, 19 Sept. 1924; *ibid.*, Pouyanne note, 1 Nov. 1924; Moreau, *Souvenirs*, p. 251.

79. MAE PA-AP 6-Papiers Avenol 11, Avenol to Léon Bourgeois, 26 Nov. 1924, enclosure; *ibid.*, PA-AP 89-Herriot 19, note 'Très confidentiel', 3 Dec. 1924.

80. Herriot, *Jadis*, ii, p. 187.

81. MAE Série Y 289, Daeschner telg. nos 140-41, 'sans date, sans heure', received 2 Apr. 1925, 5.10 p.m.

82. MAE PA-AP 261-Seydoux, 33, note, nos 67-25, 24 Jun. 1925.

83. This was the main gist of repeated warnings from the Bank of France to the government: BdF, DCG, 6 Jul. 1922, enclosing letter from Robineau to de Lasteyrie, 5 Jul. 1922; *ibid.*, 30 Jun. 1925, enclosing letter from Robineau to Caillaux, 8 Jun. 1925; *ibid.*, 30 Jun. 1926, discussion of forthcoming meeting with Painlevé.

84. Cottrell, 'Austria between diplomats and bankers', pp. 18–19.

85. BdF, DCG, 5 Jul. 1923. According to Burk, 'The House of Morgan in Financial Diplomacy', p. 145, the partners of J. P. Morgan and Company 'force[d] the French government to coerce the French bankers' into subscribing, by threatening to withhold support for a $100 million long-term loan. In fact, the French government scarcely required encouragement to participate in the Dawes loan, since by its own calculations it stood to gain £20 million in reparations from the £3 million investment. Hence, when the commercial banks held back, the Bank of France took it up. See BdF, DCG, 8 Oct. 1923, containing Clémentel to Robineau, 7 Oct. 1924.

86. Clay, *Lord Norman*, pp. 183–4; MAE PA-AP 261-Seydoux 32, note: 'Autriche: attitude de M.Norman', 31 Mar. 1925.

87. BoE, ADM 34/13, Norman diary, 11 Jan., 24 Jan., 31 Mar. 1924; FRBNY, BoE cables, 1925, Norman to Strong, no. 49, 24 Jan. 1924; Clay, *Lord Norman*, pp. 190–1. On Norman and Czech currency stabilization, FRBNY, Strong papers, 1116.4, Norman to Strong, 15 Nov. 1924.

88. MAE PA-AP 261-Seydoux 1, note, 27 Feb. 1925; *ibid.*, Seydoux 34, note, 4 Aug. 1925; *ibid.*, Seydoux 38, Seydoux to de Fleuriau, 29 Mar. 1926. Schacht revealed the extremism of his political views in a book published in 1927: Quesnay 374 AP 7, file XI, Sargent to Moreau, 24 Feb. 1927; *ibid.*, note by de Margerie, 25 Feb. 1927.

89. MAE PA-AP 261-Seydoux 40, Seydoux to Poliakoff, 14 Apr. 1924; *ibid.*, Seydoux 41, Beaumarais to Seydoux, 21 Jul. 1926; *ibid.*, Seydoux to Beaumarais, 30 Jul. 1926; *ibid.*, Seydoux to Herbette, 27 May 1926; *ibid.*, Seydoux to de Margerie, 3 Jun. 1926; *ibid.*, Europe 1918–40, GB 89, note by Seydoux, 15 Jun. 1926.

90. The total debt comprised $6,847,674,104 to the United States and £653,127,900 to Britain, and for the first ten years repayments totalled $464 million and £103 million. Artaud, *La question des dettes interalliées*, ii, annexes, table p. 794, table p. 795.

91. Artaud, 'L'impérialisme américain en Europe', p. 334.

92. Quesnay, 374 AP8, Notes remises au Ministère des Finances, 'Note sur l'urgence de la retour monétaire', n.d.; MGC, Belgian government loan 1926/2 file, Lamont telegram to New York, 21 May 1926 (hereafter MGC, Belgian etc.); Moreau, *Souvenirs*, pp. viii, 245; FRBNY, French Situation C261.1, Moreau to Strong, 5 Jul. 1927.

93. A fundamental review of the Bank's role and operations prepared shortly after Moreau's appointment asserted that 'The Banque de France must regain its role of arbiter among the economic interests of the nation; to return as soon as possible to its normal mission which is to dispense credit to business, to assure the control of the capital market and that of the national note issue.' BdF, 29.7.1994, 202, Notes historiques et techniques. Direction des études, XXIX 2-5-2-4, memorandum, n.d. but *c.* Jul. 1926.

94. MAE PA-AP 261-Seydoux 39, de Fleuriau to Seydoux, 18 Sept. 1926; *ADAP*, Ser.B, Band 1, 2 no. 159, Stresemann Runderlass, 26 Oct. 1926.

95. MAE PA-AP 261-Seydoux 38, Seydoux to de Fleuriau, 31 May 1926; *ibid.*, Europe 1918–40, GB 93, note by Seydoux, 23 Jun. 1926.
96. Moreau, *Souvenirs*, pp. 48–9.
97. MAE PA-AP 261-Seydoux 41, Seydoux to de Margerie, 3 Jun. 1926.
98. BdF, DCG, Moreau to Poincaré, 14 Oct. 1926; also diary, 24 Feb. 1927 in Moreau, 'Le relèvement financière et monétaire de France (1926–1928), Part I', pp. 53–62.
99. Moreau, *Souvenirs*, p. 306 puts the total at £100 million, a figure used in most accounts including Chandler, *Benjamin Strong*, p. 371. But see Moreau, *Souvenirs*, pp. 223, 288, 298; and Blancheton, *Le Pape et l'Empereur*, pp. 410–11 and graphique 6-5.
100. BdF, DCG, Poincaré to Moreau, 17 Feb. 1927; *ibid.*, 14 Apr. 1927; Moreau, 'Le relèvement financier et monétaire de la France (1926–1928), Part I', diary entries of 24 and 26 Mar. 1927; FRBNY, Benjamin Strong papers, 1116.7, Norman to Strong, 17 Apr. 1927; 'City Notes', *Times*, 22 Apr. 1927.
101. See for instance, *Paris-Midi*, 29 Mar. 1927, *Le Messager de Paris*, 29 Mar. 1929; *L'Homme Libre*, 29 Mar. 1927; *Le Matin*, 29 Mar. and 1 Apr. 1927; *Le Petit Journal*, 31 Mar. 1927; *Petit Bleu*, 3/4 Apr. 1927; *L'Agence Economique et Financière*, 2 and 8 Apr. 1927; *Aux Écoutes*, 10 Apr. 1927. In fact, the gold had been sold to Britain in 1916, and interest had been paid only on the actual loan of £48 million: MF, F^{30}/B12639, Pouyanne note, 4 Apr. 1927; *ibid.*, B12607, Pouyanne to Paris, no. 47148, 6 Apr. 1927.
102. 'City Notes', *Times*, 22 Apr. 1927.
103. BdF, 1397199403/161, Change, Achats d'or, Moreau to Norman, 16 May 1927.
104. Moreau, 'Le Relèvement financier et monétaire de la France (1926–1928)', Part II, p. 315.
105. Moreau explained his motives in Quesnay, 374 AP6, file VIII, Moreau to Poincaré, 21 Jun. 1927. He insisted that he was pursuing the policy 'avec une extrême modération'. See also BoE, G1/34, Quesnay to Siepmann, 17 May 1927; *ibid.*, Siepmann to Quesnay, 18 May 1927; *ibid.*, Siepmann to Norman, 20 May 1927; Moreau, *Souvenirs*, pp. 308, 315.
106. MF, F^{30}/B12607, Pouyanne to Poincaré, no. 47,491, 21 May 1927, no. 47,503, 24 May 1927, no. 47,542, 27 May 1927, no. 47,544, 28 May 1927, no. 47,597, 7 Jun. 1927, no. 47,625, 11 Jun. 1927.
107. FRBNY, Strong papers, 1116.7, Norman to Strong, 22 May 1927; BoE G1/34, Norman to Strong, no. 38, 24 May 1927; FRBNY, Bank of England General, C261, Norman to Strong, no. 40, 25 May 1927.
108. Quesnay, 374 AP 6, de Fleuriau to Briand, no. 227, 3 Jun. 1926 (copy in Fonds Flandin, 60); *ibid.*, Berthelot to Poincaré, no. 1685, 17 Jun. 1927.
109. FRBNY, French Situation, C261.1, Quesnay, minutes of May 27, 1927; BoE G1/34, 'Procès-verbal', 27 May 1927; *ibid.*, Siepmann, note of conversation, 27 May, 1927; Quesnay, 374, file VIII, memorandum for Norman's visit, 27 May 1927; Moreau, *Souvenirs*, pp. 324–35.
110. *Ibid.*
111. Clarke, *Central Bank Cooperation*, p. 117; FRBNY, Harrison papers, Bank of France cables, Strong to Moreau, no. 15, 26 May, no. 19, 1 Jun. 1927.
112. Fonds Flandin, 60, Moreau to Poincaré, 21 Jun. 1927; FRBNY, Bank of England General, C261, Moreau to Strong, no. 23, 8 Jun. 1927.
113. Moreau, *Souvenirs*, p. 192.
114. FRBNY, BoE cables, Norman to Harrison, 21 Dec. 1927; Clay, *Lord Norman*, pp. 258–60. These operations are summarized in Orde, *British Policy and European Reconstruction*, pp. 300–10.
115. Moreau, *Souvenirs*, pp. 488, 505; BoE, ADM 34/18, Norman diary, 26 Jan. 1928; FRBNY, Strong papers, 1117.1, Lubbock to Strong, 28 Feb. 1928.
116. Sayers, *The Bank of England*, iii, Appendix 18, pp. 101–7; Moreau, *Souvenirs*, p. 544.
117. FRBNY, Harrison papers, Bank of France cables, Strong to Moreau, no. 46, 24 Feb. 1928; *ibid.*, Moreau to Strong, no. 12, 27 Feb. 1928; *BCC*, pp. 142–6; Mouré, *The Gold*

Standard Illusion, pp. 167–70; Marguerat, 'Banque de France et politique de puisssance dans l'entre-deux-guerres', pp. 475–85.

118. BdF, 1069199810/35 (Intervention de la banque sur le marché libre, 1938), Quesnay, 'Note sur l'établissement d'un important marché hors banque à Paris', Aug. 1928; *ibid.*, DCG, 23 Aug. 1928, 28 Nov. 1929; Frédéric Jenny, 'L'Avenir de notre Marché Monétaire', *Le Temps*, 9 Jul. 1928; 'La Banque de France et la Réforme Monétaire', *L'Economiste Français*, 14 Jul. 1928; R. Théry, 'Questions du Jour: Organisons le marché monétaire de Paris', *L'Economiste Européen*, 28 Dec. 1928; C. Rist, 'Le marché de Paris se doit de jouer un rôle international', *L'Europe Nouvelle*, 11 Jan. 1930, pp. 38–9; J. Caillaux (transl. from *The Banker*), 'Paris centre financier international', *L'Information financière*, 14 Jan. 1930; J. Schaeffer, 'Le marché des acceptances', *La France Economique et Financière*, 12 Apr. 1930.

119. MAE RC 1918–40, B-Informations économiques 55, H. Cambon to Briand, no. 25, 19 Mar. 1929; *ibid.*, Dard to Briand, no. 121, 10 Jun. 1929; *ibid.*, Clauzel to Briand, no. 189, 3 Aug. 1929.

120. Girault, 'L'Europe centrale et orientale dans la stratégie des hommes d'affaires et des diplomats français', p. 127.

121. François. *Raymond Poincaré*, pp. 534, 499; Moreau, *Souvenirs*, p. 94; Weber, *The Hollow Years*, pp. 29, 49–50.

122. Hereafter the key rates were 125.21Ff = £1, and 25.53 francs = $1. Formally, of course, the franc was defined in terms of gold, with one franc worth 65.5 mg of gold 900/1000 fine: Neurrisse, *Histoire du franc*, p. 66.

123. BdF, DCG, Séance extraordinaire, 23 Jun. 1928. National security was also the central theme of the last entry in Moreau's diary: Moreau, *Souvenirs*, Thursday 28 Jun. 1928, p. 603:

> But our task is not complete. We must still remove the effects of the war and post-war on our financial market and restore the Bank of France and France their prewar strength and prestige in the financial order, strength and prestige which contributed so considerably to the balance of victory in 1918. To defend the gains made against the short-sightedness and demagoguery of the politicians, to reorganize the Paris market to make it one of the premier markets of the world, to coordinate and extend the activities of French banks abroad, these will be the essential tasks after stabilisation.

124. *JO*, Chambre des Députés, 21 Jun. 1928, p. 1016.

125. Boyce, 'Business as Usual'. Soutou, 'L'impérialisme du pauvre', pp. 219–39, stresses the efforts of French governments to suborn French banks and industrial firms in support of their East European ambitions, but acknowledges that the results were meagre with the sole exception perhaps of Czechoslovakia, which was always economically more attractive to commercial lenders and investors.

126. *FRUS*, 1927, i, Houghton to Kellogg, no. 157, 8 Jul. 1927, p. 84; *ibid.*, Kellogg to Coolidge, 22 Jul. 1927, pp. 124–7; *ibid.*, Coolidge to Kellogg, 27 Jul. 1927, pp. 133–4; *ibid.*, Kellogg to Gibson, no. 71, 29 Jul. 1927, pp. 139–40; *ibid.*, Kellogg to Coolidge, 4 Aug. 1927, pp. 155–6; *ibid.*, 10 Aug. 1927, pp. 157–9; also Rhodes, 'The Image of Britain in the United States', ch. 6.

127. *FRUS*, 1928, i, Kellogg to Fletcher, no. 105, 22 Sept. 1928, pp. 281–2; Carlton, 'The Anglo-French Compromise on Arms Limitation', p. 143; McKercher, 'Of Horns and Teeth', p. 179.

128. The subsidies evidently continued until Mar. 1929, then were revived in Apr. 1930 by Curtius, Stresemann's successor. Baechler, 'L'Alsace-Lorraine dans les relations franco-allemandes', pp. 85–95.

129. Quoted in Ferencuhová, 'L'accueil du Plan Briand dans les milieux politiques tchèques et slovaques', p. 203.

130. Doise and Vaïsse, *Diplomatie et outil militaire*, p. 345; Young, 'Preparations for Defeat', p. 10.

131. The elements of non-compliance were set out in MAE, PA-AP 261-Seydoux 7, Foch to president of the Conference of Ambassadors, 1 Mar. 1925 enclosing the 'Avis du Comité Militaire Allié de Versailles', 28 Feb. 1925.

132. MAE, PA-AP 261-Seydoux 7, note, 16 Nov. 1926.

133. MAE, PA-AP 006-Avenol 11, Avenol to Bourgeois, 26 Nov. 1924.

134. Suarez, *Briand*, vi, pp. 268–74; Unger, *Briand*, pp. 534–6; Oudin, *Aristide Briand*, pp. 510–11.

135. Prochasson and Rasmussen, *Au nom de la patrie*, pp. 130–40, 188–9, 204–7, 282–3, 256–63.

136. L'Huillier, *Dialogues franco-allemands*, ch. 1 and annex viii; Auffray, *Pierre de Margerie*, pp. 480–95; Kessler, *The Diaries of a Cosmopolitan*, pp. 299–300, 302–3, 343, 393; Papen, *Memoirs*, pp. 127–8; Stern-Rubarth, *Three Men Tried*, p. 137; Schor, *L'Opinion française*, p. 149; US DS, RG59, M560, Roll 31, 851.000 P.R./69, Armour to Stimson, no. 9712, 23 Jul. 1929; Richard, 'Aspects des relations intellectuelles', pp. 120–1; Schroeder-Gudehus, 'La science ignore-t-elle vraiment les frontiers?', p. 394.

137. Schor, *L'Opinion française*, p. 148; Blattmann, 'Frankreich, 'Geist', Heil', p. 136; FO371/14365, C1358/230/18, Rumbold letter to Sargent, 13 Feb. 1930. According to the British ambassador in Berlin, the French mission, led by François Marsal and Vladimir D'Ormesson, included deputies, priests, writers 'and even ladies'. See also *ibid.*, C1963/230/18, Tyrrell to Sargent, 10 Mar. 1930.

138. FO371/14366, C3561/230/18, R. Campbell to Vansittart, no.-, 6 May 1930.

139. Tiemann, 'Zweigestelle Paris des DAAD und Institut français de Berlin', pp. 287–8, 291.

140. Schroeder-Gudehus, 'La science ignore-t-elle vraiment les frontiers?', p. 394.

141. Bouvier et al., *Histoire économique et sociale de la France*, iv, pp. 742, 736; Milward, 'Les placements français à l'étranger et les deux guerres mondiales', pp. 301–2, accepts the loss of foreign investments to be approximately 30 billion gold francs and the official figure for domestic war damage of 136.5 billion gold francs, and concludes that the financial losses were 'negligible'. It is difficult to accept this description, when the loss was equal to 80 per cent of annual national revenue in 1910–13: see Lévy-Leboyer, 'La balance des paiements et l'exportation des capitaux français', p. 125.

142. Sauvy, *Histoire économique*, iv, pp. 12–18.

143. Bouvier et al., *Histoire économique et sociale de la France*, iv, 2, pp. 743–4. Sauvy, *Histoire économique*, iv, p. ii, accepts Nogaro's estimate that the French tariff provided overall protection of 8.77 per cent in 1913. He estimates that the comparable figure after the signing of the Franco-German commercial treaty in August 1927 was approximately 15 per cent, although after subsequent negotiations with Belgium and Switzerland this figure was reduced to approximately 12 per cent. However, a contemporary analysis based on revenue from import duties placed French protection at 8.81 per cent in 1913 and only 3.30 per cent in 1925: see LN, *International Economic Conference. Tariff Level Indices*, annex ii. The editor of the *Economist*, Walter Layton, commented in 1927, 'One could imagine what would have happened had French commercial policy been as imperialistic as French political policy during recent years. It is only fair to recognize that it had been relatively liberal since the end of the war.' *International Affairs*, Nov. 1927, p. 362.

144. Bouvier et al., *Histoire économique et sociale de la France*, iv, Pt. 2, table, p. 731 and pp. 733–4; Lévy-Leboyer, 'La balance des paiements et l'exportation des capitaux français', table XIV, p. 135. René Girault typically describes French political and business leaders of the time as thoroughly 'protectionist'; *ibid.*, pp. 737–8. See also Guillen, 'La politique douanière de la France dans les années vingt', p. 315; Haight, *A History of French Commercial Policies*, p. 104. It should be said that in face of exceptional import demand for reconstruction and the absence of any foreign aid, protectionism was probably unavoidable.

145. MAE PA-AP 261-Seydoux 32, Note, 25 Feb. 1925.

146. FO 371/14378, C6268/6268/18, Cahill memorandum, 4 Feb. 1929.

147. See the description of the spillover effects in BEAMA, *Trade Survey*, 1928, pp. 17–24.
148. MAE SdN, SG, 1194, Massigli (Geneva) to Briand, no. 1416, 29 Aug. 1925.
149. French Sûreté officers allowed Stresemann to enter without his passport: Weiss, *Mémoires d'une Européenne*, ii, pp. 271–2.
150. *ADAP*, Serie B, Band 1, 2, no. 159, Runderlass Stresemann, 26 Oct. 1926; *ibid*., no. 174, Aufzeichnung Stresemann, 1 Nov. 1926; Stresemann, *His Diaries, Letters and Papers*, iii, pp. 17–26; Wright, *Gustav Stresemann*, pp. 373–81; Baechler, *Gustave Stresemann*, pp. 687–95; Suarez, *Briand*, vi, pp. 215–17; US DS, RG59, M569, Roll 3, 751.62/80, Poole to Secretary of State, no. 1638, 29 Oct. 1926; Jacobson, *Locarno Diplomacy*, pp. 87–90.
151. MAE PA-AP 261-Seydoux 1, 'Note: Situation de l'industrie allemande. Visite de M.Mayrisch, Paris 27 février 1925'.
152. Keeton, *Briand's Locarno Policy*. pp. 47–8.
153. *Ibid*. See also Seydoux 32, 'Note: Danger de la concurrence industrielle allemande', 4 Mar. 1925; and *ibid*.-Seydoux 36, 'Note', 15 Jun. 1926; Seydoux, *De Versailles au Plan Young*, p. 30. Seydoux's minute of 15 Jun. 1926 is reproduced in L'Huillier, *Dialogues franco-allemands*, pp. 35–6.
154. For an excellent introduction to this issue, see Bariéty, 'France and the Politics of Steel'.
155. MAE PA-AP 261-Seydoux 37, Note: visite de M.Thyssen, nos 70-26, 5 Aug. 1926; *ibid*., Note by Seydoux to Berthelot, n.d. (*c*.6 Aug. 1926).
156. The German interests of François de Wendel, president of the Comité des Forges, are described in MAE PA-AP 261-Seydoux 32, Seydoux note, 25 Feb. 1925.
157. The full list is appended to MAE PA-AP 261-Seydoux 36, Appendix to Note, 15 Jun. 1926. See also François-Poncet, *De Versailles à Potsdam*, p. 138; L'Huillier, *Dialogues franco-allemands*, pp. 143–4 and annexe iii; Auffray, *Pierre de Margerie*, pp. 496–7.
158. Liefmann, *Cartels, Concerns and Trusts*, pp. 149–58.
159. Becker and Berstein, *Victoire et frustrations*, p. 285.
160. MAE RC B-IE 30, de Saintquentin to Seydoux, 12 Apr. 1926; Badel, *Un milieu liberal*, pp. 178–80.
161. Stern-Rubarth, *Three Men Tried*, p. 37; Badel, *Un milieu libéral*, p. 136.
162. MAE RC B-IE 30, Elbel to de Saintquentin, 9 Apr. 1926; *ibid*., de Saintquentin to Elbel, 15 Apr. 1926; *ibid*., de Saintquentin to Seydoux, 12 Apr. 1926; *ibid*., de Margerie to Briand, no. 784, 17 Jun. 1926.
163. *Ibid*., Briand to Le Troquer, 6 May 1927.
164. *Ibid*.; M. Aulard, 'Il faut, pour établir la paix, créer les Etats-Unis d'Europe', *Le Quotidien*, 14 Mar. 1926; L. Coquet, 'Où va l'Europe', *L'Europe Nouvelle*, 14 Mar. 1926; Coquet, 'Etats-Unis d'Europe', *Revue d'Alsace et de Lorraine*, Jun. 1926.
165. MAE PA-AP 261-Seydoux 43, Seydoux to Léger, 2 May 1928. See also Loucheur papers, MF1/reel 2, Loucheur to Marcel Ray, 31 Jan. 1928; MAE PA-AP 261-Seydoux 42, Berthelot to Seydoux, 5 Apr. 1928.
166. Morinosuke, de Launay, Pons and Zurcher, *Coudenhove-Kalergi*, pp. 15, 102.
167. Badel, *Un milieu liberal*, p. 163; Loucheur, *Carnets Secrets*, p. 165; Carls, *Louis Loucheur*, p. 271.
168. Carls, *Louis Loucheur*, p. 264.
169. MAE SdN IJ-QEF 1195, minutes, 26 Feb. 1926; Loucheur, *Carnets Secrets*, pp. 158–63, 167; 'Mr. Loucheur on Europe's Needs', *Manchester Guardian Commercial*, 29 Oct. 1925, p. 459; Greenwood, 'International Agreement in Trade and Industry', p. 43; Zurcher, *The Struggle to Unite Europe*, p. 5; Bussière, 'Premiers schémas européens et économie internationale', pp. 57–61.
170. MAE SdN IJ-QEF, 1196, 'Conference Internationale Economique', 6 May 1926.
171. MAE Y Internationale 1918–40, 629, de Laboulaye to Briand, no. 1355, 9 Nov. 1925.
172. MAE SdN SG 1195, 'Compte-rendu de la réunion inter-ministerielle du 26 février 1926'.

173. MAE SdN IJ-QEF 1195, Direction des Affaires Politiques et commerciales, Service Française de la SdN, 'Complementary questions for study by the Preparatory Committee of the WEC', 15 Apr. 1926.
174. Salter, *The United States of Europe*, pp. 33–43; Bussière, 'L'Organisation économique de la SDN', pp. 305–6.
175. 'Europe's Trade Shackles – A Plea for Freedom', *Economist*, 23 Oct. 1926, pp. 659–60, 'A Plea for the Removal of Restrictions upon European Trade', *ibid.*, 668–70; 'The Bankers' Manifesto', *Morning Post*, 20 Oct. 1926, pp. 10, 12; 'Propaganda for the Proper Goose' and 'A Backhander at Imperial Conference', *National Review*, Nov. 1926, pp. 319–21; 'The Bankers' Dilemma', *ibid.*, Dec. 1926, pp. 543–54.
176. MAE SdN IJ-QEF 1195, Briand to Serruys, 20 Apr. 1926; *ibid.*, SDN IJ-QEF 1196, 'Conférence Internationale Economique', 6 May 1926; *ibid.*, Y 629, Berthelot to Clauzel, nos 46-51, 20 Sept. 1926; *ibid.*, Clauzel to Berthelot, no. 3, 16 Nov. 1926; Carls, *Louis Loucheur*, p. 265.
177. LN, *Report and Proceedings of the World Economic Conference Held at Geneva*, i, p. 5; FO371/12659, W4247/53/98, Bentinck to Chamberlain, no. 59 LNCC, 7 May 1927.
178. LN, *Report and Proceedings of the World Economic Conference Held at Geneva*, i, p. 48.
179. LN, *Commercial Policy in the Interwar Period*, pp. 23, 47; Loveday, 'World Economic Conditions', pp. 13–14.
180. LN, *The World Economic Conference*, Geneva, May 1927, Final Report.
181. 'The Work of the Economic Conference', *Economist*, 28 May 1927, pp. 1107–9; Economic Tendencies in Europe', *Times*, 30 May 1927, p. 15.
182. LN, *Commercial Policy in the Interwar Period*, p. 42.
183. Sauvy, *Histoire économique*, iv, pp. 23–4; Haight, *A History of French Commercial Policies*, p. 136; Schirmer, 'La dénonciation du traité du commerce franco-allemand d'août 1927', p. 164.
184. The other less important exception was Spain, which accepted the most-favoured-nation principle in 1928.
185. Haight, *A History of French Commercial Policies*, p. 138; 'The Franco-German Commercial Treaty', *Economist*, 24 Sept. 1927, pp. 505–6.
186. LN, *Commercial Policy in the Interwar Period*, pp. 42–3; Hill, *The Economic and Financial Organization of the League of Nations*, pp. 39–45.
187. LN, Report of the Economic Consultative Committee on its First Session. Held in Geneva from May 14th to 19th, 1928, 19 May 1928.
188. Statement by Salter in 'The World Economic Conference', *International Affairs*, Nov. 1927, p. 355.
189. LN, 'Application of the Recommendations of the International Economic Conference. Report on the Period May 1928 to May 1929. Prepared for the Second Meeting of the Consultative Committee (May 6th, 1929). Statement for the Period Ending Mar. 15th, 1929', 1 Apr. 1929.
190. *Economist*, Supplement, 23 Jan. 1932, p. 36.
191. Aldcroft, *Studies in the Interwar European Economy*, p. 39.
192. Falkus, 'United States Economic Policy and the "Dollar Gap" of the 1920s', pp. 599–623.
193. 'Annual Payments of America's Debtors', *Economist*, 3 Aug. 1929, table p. 215.
194. Murray, The Harding Era, p. 278; Gayer and Schmidt, American Economic Foreign Policy, pp. 65–8.
195. *USBC*, Series U324, p. 903, U342, p. 906.
196. *Ibid.*, Series U253, U254, U249, p. 895.
197. Between 1925 and 1929, US exports of finished manufactures to all countries rose by 37 per cent, and from 38 per cent of total exports to 50 per cent: *ibid.*, Series U218, U213, p. 889.
198. De Grazia, *Irresistible Empire*, ch. 6.
199. 'The Film Industry', *European Finance*, 24 Aug. 1928, p. 38.

200. Wilkins, *The Maturing of Multinational Enterprise*, pp. 52–3.
201. *Ibid.*, table III.1, p. 55.
202. NAC, RG3, vol. 1001, f. 21-5-7, Stuart to Gaboury, 28 Mar. 1928; Headrick, *The Invisible Weapon*, pp. 140–1.
203. British Post Office archives, POST 33/1063, M8232/1923, file: bottom (hereafter POST 33/1063, etc.), Cable Landing Rights Committee, Use of German Cables, Further Report, 17 Aug. 1916.
204. RG80, M1493, Roll 17, Statement by Commander S. C. Hooper to Hearings of the General Board on Foreign Radio Policy of the Navy, 31 May 1923; *ibid.*, Box 50, G.B.419 (no. 1571), memorandum by Hooper to Chief of Naval Operations, 26 Mar. 1932; Clark, *International Communications*, p. 243; Hogan, *Informal Entente*, pp. 133–7.
205. *FRUS*, 1919, iv, minutes of Supreme War Council, 6 Mar. 1919, pp. 226–7; *ibid.*, 24 Mar. 1919, pp. 463–9; *ibid.*, meeting of Council of Ten, 1 May 1919, pp. 486–7; *ibid.*, 2 May 1919, pp. 494–5.
206. Link (ed.), *Deliberations of the Council of Four*, i, pp. 275, 438, 462, 465; POST 33/1064, M8232/1923, f. flvii, Brown memorandum, 31 Dec. 1921; US Government Printing Office, *Treaty Series*, no. 664, 1922, 'Treaty between the United States and Japan regarding rights of the two Governments and their respective nationals in former German islands in the Pacific Ocean north of the equator and in particular the Island of Yap', signed Washington, 11 Feb. 1922; Clark, *International Communications*, p. 165; Headrick, *The Invisible Weapon*, pp. 174–7.
207. POST 33/1091, M8538/1923, f. xv, Geddes to Curzon, telg. no. 571, 2 Aug. 1920; *Morning Post*, 'Mr. Wilson's Dramatic Attitude', 6 Aug. 1920; US DS, RG59, Box 5226, 811.731/834, Barnes to Doggett, Jul. 1937; POST 33/1092, M8539/1923, f. xxxvi, J. Denison-Pender to Sperling, 10 Feb. 1922.
208. POST 33/1063, M8232/1923, f. xx, Sir A. Geddes to Curzon, no. 751, 4 Nov. 1920; *ibid.*, f. v, vol. 1289, f. 126, Geddes to Curzon, no. 806, 29 Nov. 1920; *ibid.*, Geddes to Curzon, no. 811, 30 Nov. 1920; *ibid.*, f. viii, Report of the British Delegation, Dec. 1920.
209. *Ibid.*, 33/973, M4059, f. vii, Wheeler note to Balfour, 24 Jul. 1922; *ibid.*, f. x, Wheeler to Curzon, 21 Dec. 1922.
210. POST 33/1063, M8232/1923. F. II, extracts of meeting of Imperial Communications Committee, 23 Jan. 1920; US Senate, 66th Congress, 3rd Session, Committee on Interstate Commerce, Cable-landing licenses: Hearings on S. 4301, a bill to prevent the unauthorized landing of submarine cables in the United States, December 15, 1920 – January 11, 1921, memorandum by Root, p. 87; *ibid.*, statement by Clarence Mackay, Dec. 1920; POST 33/973, M4059/1923, f. v, Curzon to Carnegie, no. 22, 22 Mar. 1922; *ibid.*, Carnegie to Curzon, no. 105, 25 Mar. 1922; *ibid.*, Seymour (for Earl Balfour) to Carnegie, no. 234, 30 Jun. 1922.
211. *Ibid.*, f. xix, Phillips memorandum, 20 Nov. 1923.
212. *Ibid.*, 33/1063, M8232/1923, f. viii, Report of the British Delegation, Dec. 1920; also Hogan, *Informal Entente*, pp. 107, 109.
213. *Ibid.*, 33/973, M4059/1923, f. vii, Tyrrell to Harvey, 18 Aug. 1922; *ibid.*, 33/1065, M8232/19232, f. li, F. J. Brown to Sir E. Crowe, 5 Sept. 1922; Boyce, 'The Origins of Cable and Wireless Limited'.
214. Hogan, *Informal Entente*, p. 107.
215. POST 33/1065, M8232/19232, f. lii, Chilton to Curzon, no. 968, 16 Aug. 1922; *ibid.*, no. 968, 18 Aug. 1922. Hogan, *Informal Entente*, ch. 6, perpetuates the one-sided view by omitting from his account any discussion of the discriminatory and predatory character of American communication firms.
216. *Ibid.*, 33/973, M4059/1923, f. i, Extract from evidence given by Mr. Willever, Vice-President, Western Union Telegraph Co., 7 Jul. 1920; *ibid.*, 33/1091, M8539/1923, f. xv, Phillips memorandum, 6 Aug. 1920; *ibid.*, 33/973, M4059/1923, f. i, memorandum, 'Inland Facilities for Cablegrams', Oct. 1920; *ibid.*, 33/1091, M8539/1923, f. xxvi, Brown to Sperling, 20 May 1921.

217. Wilkins, *The Maturing of Multinational Enterprise*, p. 129f.
218. Sobell, *ITT*, pp. 36–7; Southard, *American Industry in Europe*, pp. 43–53.
219. Wilkins, *The Maturing of Multinational Enterprise*, p. 70.
220. Southard, *American Industry in Europe*, p. 43; Wilkins, *The Maturing of Multinational Enterprise*, pp. 71, 130.
221. Sobell, *ITT*, pp. 52–3, 63–4.
222. Boyce, 'The Origins of Cable and Wireless Limited'.
223. Wilkins, *The Maturing of Multinational Enterprise*, pp. 117–19.
224. *Ibid.*, pp. 84–8.
225. Lewis, *America's Stake in International Investments*, table p. 230.
226. Wilkins, *The Maturing of Multinational Enterprise*, pp. 87–8.
227. See HHCP 210, Roberts to Jones, enclosing Bank newsletter, 18 Oct. 1926; also 'Mr Hoover's Anger about Rubber', *Daily Mail*, 30 Dec. 1925, which reproduces criticism of Hoover in *New York Times*, and 'Sir Robert Horne Assails Agitation over Rubber Here', *New York Times*, 3 Jan. 1926.
228. HHCP 211, Hoover to Capper, 6 Mar. 1924; *ibid.*, 208, 'Foreign Combinations to Control Prices of Raw Materials: Statements by Herbert Hoover, Secretary of Commerce and other Officers of the Department of Commerce', 6 Jan. 1926; CAB24/174, C.P. 364(25), memorandum by A. Chamberlain, 22 Jul. 1925; Castle papers, box 3, Blair to Castle, 6 Jan. 1926; 'Mr. Hoover Complains', *Morning Post*, 16 Dec. 1925; 'Mr Hoover's Anger about Rubber', *Daily Mail*, 30 Dec. 1925; 'Sir Robert Horne Assails Agitation over Rubber Here', *New York Times*, 3 Jan. 1926; 'Rubber Supplies', *Times*, 9 Jan. 1926; 'Rubber Restrictions', *Manchester Guardian*, 12 Jan. 1926.
229. 'British Rubber Industry' and 'City Notes', *Times*, 1 Nov. 1928, pp. 14, 19.
230. Hogan, *Informal Entente*, pp. 191–207; Wilkins, *The Maturing of Multinational Enterprise*, pp. 98–102.
231. Wilkins, *The Maturing of Multinational Enterprise*, p. 10; also p. 254 on successful efforts to block Japanese access to this strategic resource. On American Smelting and Refining's further expansion, 'Mining Trust Ltd', *Economist*, 26 Jul. 1930, p. 190.
232. Wilkins, *The Maturing of Multinational Enterprise*, p. 26.
233. *Ibid.*, pp. 112–13, 107.
234. *Ibid.*, pp. 12, 102, 109, 111.
235. *Ibid.*, p. 113.
236. 'Nickel Shares', *European Finance*, 4 Jan. 1929, p. 9.
237. Boyce, *British Capitalism at the Crossroads*, p. 178.
238. 'The City', *New Statesman*, 22 Jun. 1929, p. 354; 'The City', *Daily Telegraph*, 27 Jun. 1929, p. 2; 'Lautaro Nitrate and American Control', *Economist*, 31 Aug. 1929, p. 403.
239. 'U.S. Interests in Rhodesian Copper', *Times*, 29 Jan. 1929, p. 20; 'Americans and Rhodesian Copper', *ibid.*, 6 Feb. 1929, p. 21; 'Stock Exchange', *The Times Annual Financial and Commercial Review*, 5 Feb. 1929, p. vi; 'N'Changa Copper Mines', *Economist*, 2 Feb. 1929, p. 232; *ibid.*, 9 Feb. 1929, p. 298; A. E. Davies, 'The City', *New Statesman*, 9 Feb. 1929, p. 582.
240. Wilkins, *The Maturing of Multinational Enterprise*, p. 88.
241. 'Is Copper Too Dear?', *Manchester Guardian Commercial*, 3 Jan. 1929, p. 16; 'The Ramp in Copper', *ibid.*, 7 Feb. 1929, p. 156; 'Check to Copper Cartel', *ibid.*, 28 Mar. 1929, p. 364; 'Will London Again Control Copper?', *Statist*, 2 Feb. 1929, p. 188; A. E. Davies, 'The City', *New Statesman*, 23 Mar. 1929, p. 776; 'Copper Producers' Position', *Economist*, 22 Jun. 1929, p. 1394.
242. Southard, *American Industry in Europe*, pp. 166–70.
243. FO371/12018, A1458/351/35, Hervey to Sir A. Chamberlain, no. 10, 24 Jan. 1927; *ibid.*, 13459, A1914/52/2, Robertson to Wellesley, 13 Feb. 1929; *ibid.*, 13460, A2531/52/2, Robertson to FO, no. 16, 9 Apr. 1929; *ibid.*, A2578/52/2, Robertson to Craigie, 14 Mar. 1929; 214 H.C. Deb 5s, col. 624, statement by Sir R. J. Thomas, 1 Mar. 1928; *ibid.*, col. 1939, statement by Barclay-Harvey, 14 Mar. 1928.

244. CAB23/57, conclusions 14(28)5, 13 Mar. 1928.
245. CAB24/194, C.P.-145(28), 'Electrical Development and American Capital', 30 Apr. 1928; CAB23/57, conclusions 27(28)1, 4 May 1928.
246. In 1928 alone, US investors acquired control of the Chile Telephone Company, the Pernambuco Tramways Company, the United River Plate Telephone Company and the City of Santos Improvement Company: 'Stock Exchange', *The Times Annual Financial and Commercial Review*, 5 Feb. 1929, p. vi.
247. Wilkins, *The Maturing of Multinational Enterprise*, pp. 131–14.
248. Southard, *American Industry in Europe*, p. 38.
249. 'British Electricity and U.S. Capital', *Manchester Guardian Commercial*, 21 Feb. 1929, p. 226; A. E. Davies, 'The City', *New Statesman*, 23 Feb. 1929, p. 648; *ibid.*, 11 May 1929, p. 164; 'Onlooker', letter to editor, *Economist*, 18 May 1929, pp. 111–12; Southard, *American Industry in Europe*, pp. 37–8.
250. 'Germany: G.E.C. and A.E.G.', *Manchester Guardian Commercial*, 15 Aug. 1929, p. 181; Schröter, 'Europe in the Strategies of Germany's Electrical Engineering and Chemicals Trusts', pp. 42–3.
251. Southard, *American Industry in Europe*, p. 27.
252. FRBNY, Bank of England General C261, Harrison to Norman, no. 83/29, 12 Mar. 1929; 'City Notes. General Electric Controversy', *Times*, 13 Mar. 1929, p. 22; 'American Finance and British Industry. The Principle Involved – Is Control Sought by New York?', *European Finance*, 15 Mar. 1929, pp. 173, 177; A. E. Davies, 'The City', *New Statesman*, 16 Mar. 1929, p. 744; *ibid.*, 23 Mar. 1929, p. 776; 'The General Electric Affair', *Manchester Guardian Commercial*, 21 Mar. 1929, p. 342; 'City Notes', *Times*, 30 Mar. 1929, p. 18.
253. 'Stocks and Shares', *European Finance*, 1 Mar. 1929, p. 140; 'City Notes', *Times*, 12 Mar. 1929, p. 22; 'American Finance and British Industry', *European Finance*, 15 Mar. 1929, p. 173; 'The Free Movement of Capital', *Manchester Guardian Commercial*, 16 May 1929, p. 578; 'The City', *Daily Telegraph*, 22 Jun. 1929, p. 2; 'Company Meetings: General Electric Company Limited', *ibid.*, 5 Jul. 1929, p. 4; 'General Electric "British Share" Issue', *Economist*, 16 Mar. 1929, p. 583; 'British Control – the G.E.C. Affair', *ibid.*, 23 Mar. 1929, pp. 636–7; 'General Electric Issue Abandoned', *ibid.*, 27 Apr. 1929, p. 934; 'American Buying of British Securities – I', *ibid.*, 8 Jun. 1929, p. 1292; 'American Buying of British Securities – II', *ibid.*, 15 Jun. 1929, p. 1350; 'America Capital in Britain', *ibid.*, 22 Jun. 1929, pp. 1386–8. The reference to 'financial Bolshevism' is quoted in Denny, *America Conquers Britain*, p. 142. Beaverbrook the financier contradicted Beaverbrook the imperialist in condemning Hirst's actions as a danger to cosmopolitan capital: 'British Shares and Foreign Money', *Daily Express*, 11 Mar. 1929, p. 1; 'Sir Hugo's Withdrawal', *Daily Express*, 18 Mar. 1929, p. 1.
254. BoE, G1/326, minute of interview with Szarvasy, 3 Apr. 1929.
255. *Ibid.*, Satterthwaite, Stock Exchange, circular, n.d.; *ibid.*, Szarvasy memorandum on General Electric Company Limited, 10 Jun. 1929.
256. Henri, 'Comptes, mécomptes et redressement d'une gestion industrielle', p. 43; Wilkins and Hill, *American Business Abroad*, p. 89.
257. Wilkins, *The Maturing of Multinational Enterprise*, p. 74.
258. Vauxhall, with output of 1,700 units a year in 1925, was Britain's fourth largest vehicle manufacturing firm: Wilkins and Hill, *American Business Abroad*, p. 145; Farber, *Sloan Rules*, pp. 135–6.
259. Dingli, *Louis Renault*, p. 158.
260. 'General Motors and Opel Co. Suggested Absorption', *Times*, 13 Mar. 1929, p. 15; 'Germany – Opel', *Manchester Guardian Commercial*, 28 Mar. 1929, p. 369; A. E. Davies, 'The City', *New Statesman*, 13 Apr. 1929, p. 28; Wilkins and Hill. *American Business Abroad*, p. 204.
261. In 1928 some 90 per cent of British motor vehicle exports went to Empire markets. Yet British manufacturers held barely 10 per cent of these markets, with virtually all

the rest in American hands: Society of Motor Manufacturers and Traders, Ltd., *The Motor Industry of Great Britain, 1929* (London, 1929), table LXII, p. 104; 'British Motor Number', *Times*, 20 Mar. 1928, pp. xv, xvii; J. P. Castley, 'The Empire's Foreign Cars', *Empire Review*, no. 341 (Jun. 1929), pp. 371–6.

262. *The Motor Industry of Great Britain, 1929*, table LXIII and LXIV, p. 105; 'The World's Motor Industry', *Manchester Guardian Commercial*, 13 Jun. 1929, p. 701; 'American Motor Exports Increasing', *ibid.*, 21 Nov. 1929, p. 629; 'European Motor Car Imports', *ibid.*, 28 Nov. 1929, p. 660; 'The Motor Export Trade', *Economist*, 16 Nov. 1929, pp. 903–4; Overy, *Viscount Nuffield*, p. 205.

263. US SD, RG59, M560, Roll 27, 851.00/1022, Dawson to Stimson, no. 757, 23 Oct. 1929; 'U.S. Motor-Car Interest in Germany', *Manchester Guardian Commercial*, 28 Nov. 1929, p. 660; 'France', *European Finance*, 7 Feb. 1930, pp. 88–9; Southard, *American Industry in Europe*, p. 74.

264. 'The New Ford Company', *Times*, 14 Nov. 1928, p. 13; *New Statesman*, 17 Nov. 1928, pp. 178–9. Construction of the plant began the following spring: 'New Ford Motor Works', *Daily Telegraph*, 17 May 1929, p. 10; Wilkins and Hill, *American Business Abroad*, pp. 543–7.

265. FO371/13460, A2578/52/2, Chalkley memorandum of 13 Mar. 1929 enclosed in Robertson to Craigie, 14 Mar. 1929; *ibid.*, Wellelsey and Chamberlain minutes, 19 Apr. 1929.

266. Fridenson, 'Ford as a Model for French Car Makers, 1911 – 1939', pp. 130–3.

267. 'The American Invasion of Europe', *Economist*, 20 Apr. 1929, p. 848; 'America's Economic Imperialism', *Daily Telegraph*, 11 Jun. 1929, p. 9; Jones Jr, *Tariff Retaliation*, pp. 71–2, 115.

268. Jones, *Tariff Retaliation*, pp. 70–5, 115–21.

269. Schuker, *American 'Reparations' to Germany*, p. 97.

270. 'Sir Alfred Mond's Outburst', *National Review*, 13 Oct. 1926, p. 12; 'The £43,000,000 Combine', *ibid.*, 22 Oct. 1926, p. 12; 'Episodes of the Month', *ibid.*, Jan. 1927, p. 671; Haber, *The Chemical Industry*, pp. 296–9; Sir A. Mond, 'A United Economic Empire', *Spectator*, 30 Oct. 1926, p. 729; 'International Cartels', pp. 265–77.

271. Mond, *Industry and Politics*, p. 277.

272. *Ibid.*, p. 275.

273. *Ibid.*, p. 278.

274. *National Review*, Dec. 1927, p. 507; 'Lord Melchett Testifies', *Morning Post*, 30 Nov. 1928, p. 10; Melchett Committee, 'Interim Report on Unemployment'; 'Reorganisation of Industry. The Melchett Report', *Times*, 13 Mar. 1929, p. 10; 'Economic Unity of the Empire', *Times*, 15 Nov. 1929, p. 11.

275. Petter, *The Disease of Unemployment and the Cure*, pp. 49–52; Petter, 'Industry's Rights and Wrongs', *19th Century and After*, Jan. 1926, pp. 57–67; Petter, 'Missing the Tide', *National Review*, Mar. 1929, pp. 64–79; 'Empire Industries Club', *Times*, 17 Dec. 1927, p. 17; 'The British Iron and Steel Industry and the Future', *Iron and Coal Trades Review*, 27 Apr. 1928, pp. 607–8; 'Steel and Safeguarding', *ibid.*, 18 May 1928, p. 762; 'Safeguarding and Procedure', *ibid.*, 15 Jun. 1928, p. 912.

276. 'Trade Conditions in the United States', *Times*, 31 Oct. 1925, p. 7; 'A Tourist's Impressions', *National Review*, Dec. 1925, pp. 490–2; 'The *Daily Mail*'s Mission to the United States', *ibid.*, Mar. 1926, pp. 27–8; 'The *Daily Mail* Mission', *ibid.*, May 1926, pp. 349–52; 'Master Printers' Visit to America', *Times*, 13 Oct. 1927, p. 11; CAB23/53, conclusion 4(26)3, 16 Jun. 1926; also *Report of the Proceedings of the 59th Annual Trades Union Congress, 1927*, statement by E. Bevin, p. 392; 213 H.C. Deb 5s, cols 469–72, 479, 491, statements by Col. Applin, Morgan Jones, H. Snell, 10 Feb. 1928; 217 H.C. Deb 5s, col. 2187, statement by Commander Kenworthy, 24 May 1928; 'A Visit to Mr. Ford and his Works', *United Empire*, Jun. 1928, pp. 375–9; 222 H.C. Deb 5s, col. 306, 1301, statements by R. G. Ellis, O. Mosley, 8 Nov. 1928.

277. As W. Layton of the *Economist* wrote in the foreword to the book, 'No European can visit America without realising that across the Atlantic changes are occurring which

amount to an economic revolution.' If Britain did not learn the appropriate lessons, it would 'sink into the respectable but unexciting status of a comparatively poor relation'. See also 'The New Industrial Gospel', *Spectator*, 13 Feb. 1926, p. 260; *ibid.*, 27 Mar. 1926, p. 573.

278. See also Molteno, 'The Causes and Extent of American Prosperity', pp. 176–84.
279. *National Review*, Jan. 1927, pp. 702–8.
280. For a list of publications, see 'Selected Bibliography on the International Economic Position of the United States', *International Affairs*, Jan. 1931, pp. 234–41.
281. *Daily Express*, 21 Mar. 1928, 14 Nov. 1928.
282. 'Europe at the Crossroads', *Round Table*, Jun. 1926, pp. 476–501; also 'Anglo-American Relations', *Round Table*, Dec. 1926, pp. 1–17; 'The Economic Future of Great Britain', *Round Table*, Jun. 1927, pp. 528–45.
283. 'The Forthcoming Conference', *International Affairs*, 8 Feb. 1927, pp. 70–83.
284. 'The Empire's Resources', *Morning Post*, 18 Nov. 1925, p. 12; 'Forward or Backward', *National Review*, Aug. 1926, pp. 818–20; Amery, *The Empire in the New Era*.
285. CAB24/192, C.P.46(28), Amery memorandum, 13 Feb. 1928.
286. CAB24/196, C.P.210(28), Amery memorandum, 2 Jul. 1928.
287. Barnes and Nicholson (eds), *The Leo Amery Diaries*, i, 2 Aug. 1928; Middlemas and Barnes, *Baldwin*, pp. 472–3.
288. The inroads on free trade are summarized in BT 55/58.S.O.I/9, Memorandum, 4 Mar. 1930; Royal Institute of International Affairs, *Interim Report on Measures taken…in Mar., 1932*.
289. The Board of Trade estimates were the Netherlands £1.81, Belgium £3.17, France £3.25, Denmark £3.99, Germany £4.49, Sweden £9.01, Britain £8.73 and Italy £11.07: BT 11/35, CRT2107/28, Shackle memorandum, 13 Jun. 1927.
290. Barnes and Nicholson (eds), *The Leo Amery Diaries*, i, 24 Sept. 1928.
291. CAB23/58, conclusion 43(28)2, 2 Aug. 1928.
292. NC2/22, diary 30 Jun., 21 Jul. 1927; Baldwin papers, 28, Amery to Baldwin, 10 Apr. 1927; *ibid.*, 30, Amery to Baldwin, 11 Jul., 24 Sept., 1 Oct., 13 Dec. 1928, 11 Feb. 1929; Barnes and Nicholson (eds), *The Leo Amery Diaries*, i, 7 May, 4, 9, 11 Jul. 1928.
293. NC2/22, diary 1 Jul. 1927; BT55/58, S.O.I./12, memorandum, 2 Jul. 1929.
294. Balfour papers, Add. Mss. 49,704, Hankey to Balfour, 29 Jun. 1927.
295. CAB24/189, C.P.292(27), FO, 'Memorandum Respecting the Future of Anglo-American Relations', 17 Nov. 1927.
296. CAB24/198 C.P.344(28), Craigie memorandum in Cushendon note to Cabinet, 14 Nov. 1928; *BCC*, pp. 181–2.
297. *Free Trader*, Aug.–Sept. 1927, p. 166; H.C. Deb 5s, vol. 208, col. 1827; *ibid.*, vol. 209, cols 519, 521; 'The World Economic Conference', *International Affairs*, Nov. 1927, p. 358.
298. Sir S. Chapman, unpublished autobiography (British Library of Political and Economic Science), pp. 236–8; MAF 40/5, SS12620, minutes by Thomson, 30 Aug., 3, 10 Oct. 1927; *ibid.*, Fountain to Howell Thomas, 25 Oct. 1927, Howell Thomas minute, 27 Oct. 1927, Guinness to Cunliffe-Lister, 27 Oct. 1927, Hamilton to Chapman, n.d.; *ibid.*, 'Report of the British Delegation to the International Conference for the Abolition of Import and Export Prohibitions held in Geneva in Oct. and Nov. 1927'; FO371/17661, C1964/873/22, Thomas to Under-Secretary of State, 9 Feb. 1928; MAF 40/6, TAY 13783, Franklin to Pinsent, 29 Aug. 1928.
299. Boyce, 'Insects and International Relations', pp. 1–27.
300. FO371/14094, W1846/1846/50, Chamberlain memorandum, 16 Feb. 1929; *ibid.*, 13510, A1397/12/45, Wellesley minute, 19 Feb. 1929, Chamberlain minute, 23 Feb. 1929, Cunliffe-Lister minute, 1 Mar. 1929; *ibid.*, 13459, A2578/52/2, Chamberlain minute, 19 Apr. 1929.
301. FO371/13460, A2713/52/2, Cunliffe-Lister to Churchill, 19 Mar. 1929, Churchill to Cunliffe-Lister, 26 Mar. 1929.
302. BoE, G1/326, Norman to Harrison, no. 70/29, 15 Mar. 1929.
303. *BCC*, pp. 173–4.

304. Jones, *Whitehall Diary*, ii, p. 177; *BCC*, p. 419 f. 240.
305. BoE, G1/326, Norman to Lawrence, 4 Mar. 1929.
306. BB, DPP, 2.4.4, Revelstoke to Peacock, 8 Mar. 1929; *ibid.*, Revelstoke diary, 9 Mar. 1929.
307. BoE, G3/195, Norman to Fisher, 13 Sept. 1929.
308. BoE, ADM 34/18, Norman diary 15 May 1929, 3.45 p.m.; *ibid.*, G1/326, minutes, 15 May 1929.
309. 'City Notes', *Times*, 10 May 1929, p. 24; *ibid.*, 21 Jun. 1929, p. 20; *ibid.*, 22 Jun. 1929, p. 18; *ibid.*, 4 Jul. 1929, p. 22; 'Argentine Railways', 'American Buying of British Securities – II', *Economist*, 15 Jun. 1929, pp. 1350–1; 'Free Movement of Capital', *Manchester Guardian Commercial*, 16 May 1929, p. 578, and 'The International Cartel', *ibid.*, 30 May 1929, p. 632; *Daily Telegraph*, 22 Jun. 1929, p. 2; 'British Capital in Argentina', *Times*, 2 Aug. 1929, p. 11.
310. Amery diaries, 1, 4, 13 Jul. 1929; AC5/1/478, Austen to Hilda Chamberlain, 3 Jul. 1929; H.C. Deb 5s, 299, cols 116, 125–6, 737–42; *BCC*, pp. 200–1, 230.
311. Krüger, 'European Ideology and European Reality', pp. 87–8.
312. Wright, *Gustav Stresemann*, pp. 283–4.
313. MAE RC B-IE 30, French Consul at Stuttgart to Briand, no. 113, 11 Dec. 1928; Feldmann, 'Foreign Penetration of German enterprises after the First World War', pp. 101–7; L'Huillier, *Dialogues Franco-Allemands*, pp. 47–8; 'Foreign Capital in German Industry', *Economist*, 10 Aug. 1929, p. 268; Freymond, *Le IIIe Reich et la réorganisation économique de l'Europe*, pp. 19, 21–2, 31.
314. Southard, *American Industry in Europe*, pp. 121–2.
315. MAE. Serie Y Internationale, 1918–40, vol. 630, de Margerie to Briand, no. 561, 13 Jul. 1929; Schröter, 'Europe in the Strategies of Germany's Electrical Engineering and Chemicals Trusts, 1919–1939', pp. 41, 49–50; Hayes, *Industry and Ideology*, pp. 32–8.
316. LN, *Memorandum sur le commerce international et sur les balances des paiements 1912–1926*, i, pp. 53–4; *ibid.*, vol. i (1930), pp. 80–1.
317. Quoted in Freymond, 'Gustav Stresemann et l'idée d'une "Europe économique"', p. 348. Original in Stresemann, *Les papiers de Stresemann*, iii, pp. 213–14, 218, 219.
318. Stresemann, *His Diaries, Letters, and Papers*, iii, p. 504.
319. Valentin, *Stresemann*, pp. 295–6; 'The Poor Relations', *Economist*, 29 Jun. 1929, pp. 1439–40; Freymond, *Le IIIe Reich et la réorganisation économique de l'Europe*, p. 31; MAE SdN UE, 1, 'Copie d'un rapport du Ministre plénipotentiaire Frank, Berlin, 1er août, 1929. Z1.213/Poland, à Monsieur le Chancelier du Bund, Objet: Initiative de Briand en vue de la réunion d'une Conférence des Etats Européens' (obtained by the Army 2eme Bureau, sent 'Très confidentiel' to Fouques Duparq, Seydoux, Massigli, Corbin, 27 Nov. 1929.
320. D'Abernon, *Ambassador of Peace*, iii, p. 219.
321. *Ibid.*
322. Herf, *Reactionary Modernism*, pp. 18–19, 35 and passim.
323. On the burgeoning literature on the American challenge, see *ibid.*, p. 163; Beck, *Germany Rediscovers America*.
324. Murphy, *The Heroic Earth*, pp. 195, 246–7 and passim.
325. *Ibid.*, pp. 225–6; Schulz, *Deutschland, der Völkerbund und die Frage der europäischen Wirtschaftsordnung*, pp. 64, 67–8; Krüger, 'European Ideology and European Reality', pp. 94–5.
326. Weinberg (ed.), *Hitler's Second Book*, p. 107. For a slightly different translation, see Hitler, *The Second Book*, p. 98.
327. Hitler, *Reden, Schriften, Anordnungen*, Band II A, p. 84.
328. Even then, he added, the union could not long endure because it would mean a mixing of the races and the decline of the unifying power. The United States could afford the mixing of races because it had received the healthiest stock from Europe and a critically important 'Nordic admixture'. Hitler, *The Second Book.*, pp. 103–8; Weinberg (ed.), *Hitler's Second Book*, pp. 114–17.

329. Baynes, *The Speeches of Adolf Hitler*, pp. 777–829.
330. Turner, *German Big Business and the Rise of Hitler*, pp. 191, 197, 203; but see also Boyce, 'Economics', pp. 258–60.
331. *FRUS*, 1927, ii, Gordon to Kellogg, no. 331, 3 Sept. 1927, pp. 670–1; *ibid.*, no. 341, 8 Sept. 1927, p. 671; *ibid.*, Kellogg to Claudel, 14 Sept. 1927, pp. 672–3; *ibid.*, Castle to Claudel, 19 Sept. 1927, pp. 677–8; *ibid.*, Carr to Whitehouse, no. 282, 19 Sept. 1927, pp. 678–81; *ibid.*, Kellogg to Whitehouse, no. 315, 8 Oct. 1927, pp. 691–3; *ibid.*, Castle to Claudel, 18 Oct. 1927, pp. 695–6; *ibid.*, Kellogg to Whitehouse, no. 330, 22 Oct. 1927, pp. 696–8; *ibid.*, no. 346, 7 Nov. 1927, pp. 701–2; MAE Europe 1919–40, GB 109, British aide-mémoire, 'Importation of Coal into France', n.d.; *ibid.*, Briand to Minister of Public Works, 14 Jun. 1927; *ibid.*, British aide-mémoire, 2 Mar. 1928, forwarded by Briand to Ministers of Public Works (Mines), Commerce, and the Premier, 7 Mar. 1928; *ibid.*, de Fleuriau to Briand, no. 166, 15 Mar. 1928.
332. Liepmann, *Tariff Levels and the Economic Unity of Europe*, p. 246. For the year 1929, French exports to Britain were worth 7.6 billion francs and incurred duties of 729 million francs or 9.6 per cent, whereas British exports to France were worth 5.8 billion francs and incurred duties of 270 million francs or 4.6 per cent. However, a much higher fraction of French exports were manufactures. Taking only the British manufactured exports, the duties incurred were slightly over 12 per cent: FO371/15643, W14713/137/17, memorandum from Berthelot to Tyrrell, 24 Dec. 1931; FO371/16360, W60/16/17, Tyrrell to Simon, no. 4(C), 3 Jan. 1932.
333. Guillen, 'La politique douanière de la France dans les années vingt', p. 324, claims that France made no concessions to Britain, particularly as the Ministry of Public Works, which had the final say on coal imports, refused to give way. But according to the British records, French officials gave way on both the most-favoured-nation principle and on coal duties: CAB24/195, C.P.-157(28), memorandum by Cunliffe-Lister, 17 May 1928. See FO371/13341, W138/138/17, Chamberlain to Crewe, no. 59, 9 Jan. 1928; FO371/13342, W2762/138/17, Chamberlain to Crewe, no. 659, 20 Mar. 1928; *ibid.*, W3300/138/17, Phipps to Chamberlain, no. 605C, 29 Mar. 1928; CAB24/193, C.P.-89(28), memorandum by Cunliffe-Lister, Mar. 1928.
334. Seventy-five years later, rhetoric about the Open Door is still repeated uncritically by American historians. Thus according to one account, the postwar Republican administrations were committed to 'multilateral free trade', and sought 'to convince the world to adopt policies leading to an international economy characterized by free trade, convertible currencies and open markets, and along with that…to convince countries to disarm. All American administrations from 1919 to 1939 would have agreed with these policy imperatives.' Burk, 'The Lineaments of Foreign Policy: The United States and a "New World Order"', pp. 384, 377, also p. 386. Burk's account draws heavily on the publications of M. Leffler and F. Costigliola, which have been influential in perpetuating this myth.
335. Guillen, 'La politique douanière de la France dans les années vingt', p. 324, Leffler, *The Elusive Quest*, p. 169.
336. Duranton-Crabol, 'De l'anti-américanisme en France vers 1930', p. 120; Bonin, *Histoire économique de la France*, p. 97. Strauss, *Menace in the West*, especially ch. 4 and Weber, *The Hollow Years*, pp. 94–9 discuss only the extremist literature.
337. Laroche, *Au Quai d'Orsay*, p. 101f.
338. Bariéty, 'Aristide Briand', p. 8. See also Keeton, *Briand's Locarno Policy*, p. 126.
339. Bonnefous, *Histoire politique de la Troisième République*, iv, pp. 71–2.
340. Bonin, *Histoire économique de la France*, p. 75.
341. Southard, *American Industry in Europe*, pp. 121–2.
342. MAE Serie Y Internationale 1918–40, vol. 630, Gueyraud (for Serruys) telg. no. 3, 8 Jul. 1928; US Department of State, RG59, M560, Roll 30, 851.00PR/57, Armour to Stimson, 27 Apr. 1929; *ibid.*, 851.00PR/60, Armour to Stimson, 18 May 1929; *ibid.*, 851.00PR/61, Armour to Stimson, 25 May 1929; *ibid.*, 851.00PR/62, Armour to Stimson, 1 Jun.

1929; *ibid.*, 851.00PR/63, Armour to Stimson, 8 Jun. 1929; *ibid.*, Roll 31, 851.00PR/68, Armour to Stimson, 19 Jul. 1929.

343. Bonnefous, *Histoire politique de la Troisième République*, iv, pp. 135, 154–5.
344. MAE PA-AP 261-Seydoux 3 bis, Seydoux note no. 21, 17 Aug. 1928.
345. Statement by the French Socialist Party in 'The Franco-American Debt', *Economist*, 8 Jun. 1929, p. 1279; statement by the Association of French Chambers of Commerce in 'American Protection and European Defence', *ibid.*, 22 Jun. 1929, p. 1393.
346. *Gustav Stresemann*, iii, pp. 387, 388–9; Wright, *Gustav Stresemann*, pp. 430–1; Jacobson, *Locarno Diplomacy*, p. 194.
347. *ADAP* ser.B, Band XII, no. 43, René to AA, 24 Jun. 1929. A German intelligence report, which fell into French hands, portrayed Poincaré as the driving force behind this policy:

> I learned a few days ago from an absolutely reliable source that the French Government and in particular Poincaré are very seriously committed to an economic union of the European states. While their ideas are still vague, they go so far as a customs union with Germany and other states. In Poincaré's thinking, this economic concentration of Europe is mainly directed against America, but also necessarily against England and Russia.

MAE SdN UE 1, copy of report by minister Frank, Berlin, 1 Aug. 1929, obtained by the Army 2ème Bureau.
348. Bussière, 'L'Organisation économique de la SDN', pp. 307–8.
349. Chapman, unpublished autobiography, p. 253.

4   The Crisis Begins, 1927–9

1. 'New Freemen of London', *Times*, 20 Dec. 1929, p. 16.
2. *Ibid.*, p. 16.
3. 'When Mr. Ramsay MacDonald was a City Clerk', *Daily Mail*, 20 Dec. 1929, p. 7; 'When Premier was a Clerk', *Daily Telegraph*, 20 Dec. 1929, p. 15; 'Prime Minister and Chancellor', *Yorkshire Post*, 20 Dec. 1929, p. 10; 'From Poverty to Premiership', *Daily Herald*, 20 Dec. 1929, p. 2. The ILP journal *Forward* and the left-wing *New Leader* maintained a discreet silence on the event. Only the *Daily Express* seemed mildly shocked that socialists should be thus honoured, though it assured readers that MacDonald and Snowden deserved favourable treatment: 'The New Freemen', 20 Dec. 1929, p. 3.
4. See below, pp. 278–9.
5. TWL 113-14, Morrow to Lamont, 5 Sept. 1925.
6. BoE, G1/414, Norman to Schacht, 28 Dec. 1926. Two weeks earlier, Norman privately recorded his frustration at the City of London's 'subservience' to the New York market. He had discussed it with Hilton Young, the financial journalist, but they had agreed it should be kept out of the newspapers: *ibid.*, ADM 34/15, Norman diary, 13 Dec. 1926.
7. *Ibid.*, G1/414, Schacht to Norman, 31 Dec. 1926.
8. FRBNY, Strong papers, 1116.7, Norman to Strong, 22 May 1927; BoE G1/34, Norman to Strong, no. 38, 24 May 1927; FRBNY, Bank of England General, C261, Norman to Strong, no. 40, 25 May 1927.
9. FRBNY, George Harrison papers, Bank of France cables, Moreau to Strong, no. 16, 31 May 1927. Within a few months Strong was able to dispose of all his sterling balances at a profit: *ibid.*, Bank of England General, C261, Strong to W. P. G. Harding, 5 Oct. 1927.
10. *Ibid.*, Moreau to Strong, no. 23, 8 Jun. 1927.
11. BdF, DCG, Séance extraordinaire, 23 Jun. 1928.
12. Blancheton, *Le Pape et l'Empereur*, p. 410, Graphique 6-5.
13. BdF, 1397199403/181, minutes of conversations on 29–30 Jun., 1 Jul. 1927.
14. *Ibid.*

15. FRBNY, French Situation, C261.1, R. B. Warren minutes of conversations with Rist on 25 Aug. and Quesnay on 26 Aug. 1926.
16. On the French position at the time of the Long Island conference, see O. Feiertag, 'La Banque de France, la monnaie et l'Europe au XXe siècle', i, ch. 5.
17. Quesnay 374 AP 6, file VII, minutes of conversations, 1–7 Jul. 1927.
18. *BCC*, pp. 60–1, 68.
19. Quesnay 374 AP 6, file VII, minutes of conversations, 1–7 Jul. 1927.
20. Grigg, *Prejudice and Judgment*, p. 193; Gilbert (ed.),, *Winston S. Churchill, Companion Volume*, v, Part 1, pp. 685, 1306–7; Boyle, *Montagu Norman*, p. 230.
21. Boyce, 'Government-City of London Relations under the Gold Standard'.
22. Fisher, *Stabilised Money*, pp. 104–7.
23. *Ibid.*
24. HHPP 151, J. G. Strong to Hoover, 26 Jul. 1929.
25. FRBNY, Strong papers, 1012.3, Strong to Pierre Jay, 4 Aug. 1927.
26. James, *The Reichsbank and Public Finance in Germany*, p. 40.
27. 'Commercial History and Review of 1928', *Economist*, 9 Feb. 1929, p. 11.
28. Borchardt, *Perspectives on Modern German Economic History and Policy*, pp. 146, 172. German registered unemployment stood at 19.4 per cent in January 1929. This was partly due to strikes, but the trend towards higher unemployment was already established. Thus, for instance, unemployment stood at 6.3 per cent in June 1927, 6.2 per cent in June 1928, but 8.5 per cent in June 1929. *Wirtschaft und Statistik*, 1st heft, Jan. 1928, p. 1; *ibid.*, 2nd heft, Aug. 1929, p. 645, etc.
28. Moreau, *Souvenirs*, p. 431.
29. BoE, G1/368, Salter to Norman, 2 Jun. 1927.
30. *Ibid.*, G3/191, Norman to J. P. Morgan, 16 Jun. 1927; *ibid.*, OV9/257, Norman to Lubbock, 19 Jul. 1927; *ibid.*, Strong to Young, 21 Jul. 1927; *ibid.*, Niemeyer to Salter, 29 Jul. 1927.
31. *Ibid.*, G3/191, Norman to J. P. Morgan, 16 Jun. 1927.
32. BdF, DCG, 9 Jun. 1927; Clay, *Lord Norman*, pp. 259–60; Chandler, *Benjamin Strong*, pp. 381–422.
33. FRBNY, Bank of England General, C261, Norman to Strong, no. 246, 29 Dec. 1927; BoE, ADM 34/17, Norman diary, 26 Jan. 1928; *ibid.*, OV9/331, minutes of 31 Jan., 7, 10 Feb. 1928; Moreau, *Souvenirs*, pp. 488–9, 505–9, 511; FRBNY, Harrison papers, Bank of France cables, Strong to Moreau, no. 46, 24 Feb. 1928; *ibid.*, Moreau to Strong, no. 12, 27 Feb. 1928; *ibid.*, Strong papers, 1117.1, Lubbock to Strong, 28 Feb. 1928; Sayers, *The Bank of England*, iii, Appendix 18, pp. 101–7; Clay, *Lord Norman*, p. 265.
34. FRBNY, French Situation, C261.1, Moreau to Strong, 5 Jul. 1927: 'The experience of these last few months has shown how fragile was the return of the pound sterling to parity on an insufficient gold basis.' To the President of France, Gaston Doumergue, who worried that France would lose prestige if Italy stabilized at a higher rate relative to its prewar parity, Moreau replied that they must not make Britain's mistake of sacrificing their economy for the sake of prestige: Moreau, *Souvenirs*, 30 Nov. 1927, p. 438.
35. Moreau, *Souvenirs*, p. 431.
36. BoE, G1/29, Siepmann memorandum, 'The Gold Exchange Standard: Note of Conversation in Paris on Saturday November 19th 1927'.
37. 'Monetary Stability and the Gold Standard', *Economist* Supplement, 10 Nov. 1928, p. 7. An early draft, dated London, Apr. 1928, is in BoE, G1/29. Strakosch had been alerted to the problem by the Swedish economist, Gustav Cassel, and Joseph Kitchin, the economist employed by Strakosch's own firm, the Union Corporation: UK, Cd. 7238, *Royal Commission in Indian Currency and Finance*, 1914, Vol. III, Appendices.
38. BoE, ADM 34/16, Norman diary, 24 Jun. 1927.
39. At virtually the same time as Strakosch approached Norman, Keynes published 'The Question of the Price Level' in *The Nation & Athenaeum*, 18 Jun. 1927, p. 358. On Hawtrey's views at this time, see Sir Ralph Hawtrey papers, T176/16, Hawtrey memorandum, 12 Jul. 1928.

40. FRBNY, Strong papers 1000.9, Strong to Harrison, 27 Jul. 1928. Norman later acknowledged to Lord Revelstoke of Brothers that he would have preferred to veto the Gold Delegation proposal, but 'Niemeyer's position made it difficult for us.' See BB, D.P.P., 2.4.4, minute, 9 Mar. 1929.

41. BoE, G1/29, note by Siepmann on conversation between Norman and Louis Franck (Belgian National Bank) on 28 Nov. 1927; *ibid.*, memorandum by Siepmann of conversation with Bachmann (Swiss National Bank), 8 Dec. 1927; *ibid.*, minute by Niemeyer on conversation with Pospisil (Czech National Bank), 12 Dec. 1927; *ibid.*, Siepmann letter to Strakosch, 7 Feb. 1928 on conversation with Schober (National Bank of Austria).

42. *Ibid.*, minute by Niemeyer, 13 Dec. 1927.

43. BoE, ADM 34/16, Norman diary, 25 Nov. 1927.

44. FRBNY, Strong papers, 1116.7, Norman to Strong, 28 Nov. 1927.

45. BoE, G1/422, Strong to Norman, 27 Mar. 1928. See also FRBNY, Strong papers, 1116.8, C252, memorandum by Strong for Harrison, 24 Dec. 1927.

46. FRBNY, *14th Annual Report*, 1928, p. 7.

47. HHPP 151, Strong to Hoover, 26 Jul. 1929.

48. Chandler, *American Monetary Policy*, pp. 38–9.

49. See, for example, *ibid.*, pp. 47, 89; Chandler, *Benjamin Strong*, p. 465; Meyer, *The Fed*, p. 154.

50. Wigmore, *The Crash and Its Aftermath*, p. 94.

51. Chandler, *American Monetary Policy*, p. 39.

52. Malkiel, *A Random Walk Down Wall Street*, p. 46.

53. BoE G1/453, Harrison to Norman, no. 181/29, 10 Jun. 1929.

54. The loan statistics include short- and long-term portfolio lending but exclude direct investment: *USBC*, Series U20, U21, p. 867.

55. Clarke, *Central Bank Cooperation*, p. 148.

56. FRBNY, Bank of England General, C261, Norman to Strong, 29 Dec. 1927; BoE, OV9/331, minutes of 31 Jan., 7 and 10 Feb. 1928.

57. *BCC*, p. 42.

58. BoE, OV9/262, Strakosch to Salter, 9 May 1928.

59. *Ibid.*, OV9/257, Niemeyer to M. Wallenberg, 26 May 1928; *ibid.*, 13 Jun. 1926; 'World Trade: Report of Geneva Conference', *Times*, 22 May 1928, p. 15; LN, *Report of the Financial Committee*, 4 Jun. 1928; BoE G1/29, LN, Council resolution, 8 Jun. 1928.

60. FRBNY, Strong papers, 1000.9, memorandum, 25 May 1928; copy in BoE, OV9/262.

61. FRBNY, Strong papers, 1000.9, Strong to Young, 11 Jun. 1928; *ibid.*, Strong to Harrison, 6 Jul. 1928; *ibid.*, Strong to Harrison, 7 Jul. 1928; BoE, OV9/262, memorandum by Salter, 25 Jun. 1928; Moreau, *Souvenirs*, 25 Jun. 1928, p. 600, 26 Jun. 1928, p. 601; BLPES, Per Jacobsson diary, 7 Jul. 1928; BoE G1/29, Siepmann minute, 31 Jul. 1928.

62. 'Annual Report of the Bank of France, 1928', *Federal Reserve Bulletin*, Mar. 1929, p. 206. According to a recent account, the Bank held balances of over £170 million and over $700 million, which is substantially more than was officially reported: Blancheton, *Le Pape et l'Empereur*, p. 410.

63. BoE, G1/29, memorandum by Siepmann, 20 Jan. 1928.

64. BoE, G1/453, Siepmann minute, 'Gold', 26 Nov. 1928.

65. BoE, OV9/263, Siepmann minute, 26 Nov. 1928.

66. BoE, G1/29, Niemeyer to Norman, 9 Dec. 1928; *ibid.*, Norman to Schacht, 13 Dec. 1928; *ibid.*, 'Extract of a note of Mr. Siepmann's conversation with Dr. Bachmann and Monsieur Weber in Zurich, on Thursday, 20th December 1928'. "Report of the Financial Committee of the Work of its Thirty-third Session', League of Nations, Official Journal, vol. 10, no. 1 January 1929, pp. 176-82; 'Fifty-third Session of the Council, 5th Meeting, 14 December 1928, ibid., pp. 47–8.'

67. BoE, OV9/262, Salter to Strakosch (copy to Niemeyer), 23 Nov. 1928.

68. BoE, OV9/263, minute by Siepmann, 26 Nov. 1928.

69. BoE, G1/29, Moreau to Norman, 28 Dec. 1928.

70. BoE, OV9/263, Norman to Moreau, 8 Jan. 1929.
71. Before the Financial Committee's decision to proceed, Norman had appealed to Strakosch: 'Please go slow & don't break up our C[entral] Bk party.' BoE, ADM 34/17, Norman diary, 27 Nov. 1928. See also FRBNY, Bank of England General, C261, Norman to Lubbock, no. 33/29, 2 Feb. 1929.
72. BoE G1/453, Norman to Schacht, 11 Dec. 1928.
73. *Ibid.*, Norman to Vissering, 7 Dec. 1928.
74. BoE, ADM 34/17, Norman diary, 17 Dec. 1928.
75. BoE G1/29, Norman to Lubbock, 2 Feb. 1929; LN, *Report of the Financial Committee*, Mar. 1929; *ibid.*, Jun. 1929; BoE, OV9/263, 'HS' (Strakosch) to Niemeyer, 10 Jun. 1929.
76. Bouvier, 'A propos de la stratégie d'encaisse (or et devises) de la Banque de France', p. 353. During 1928 alone, the Bank of France purchased £13.6 million (Ff 1,680,260,000) gold, which it held on earmark in London and New York, and between 23 June 1928 and 2 May 1929 it purchased £61 million gold: BdF, DCG, statement by Governor, 10 Jan. 1929; *ibid.*, 2 May 1929.
77. J. Henry Schroder & Co., *Quarterly Review*, Jul. 1930, pp. 1–11.
78. Pressnell, '1925', pp. 81–3.
79. Quesnay 374 AP 7, file XI, Bachmann to Moreau, 25 Aug. 1928. The London discount houses agreed to increase the three-month bill rate on 8 Aug.: *The Banker*, Sept. 1928, p. 204. Before the end of the month, the Bank of England started selling dollars to prop up the pound sterling: FRBNY, Strong papers, 1117.1, Lubbock to Strong, 31 Aug. 1928.
80. 'Commercial History and Review of 1928', *Economist*, 9 Feb. 1929, p. 11.
81. BoE, G1/453, Lubbock to Harrison, 3 Aug. 1928.
82. BoE, G1/453, Norman to Harrison, no. 166/28, 6 Sept. 1928.
83. BoE G1/29, Norman cable from FRBNY to Lubbock, 2 Feb. 1929.
84. *BCC*, pp. 172–3.
85. 225 H.C. Deb 5s, col. 547, 14 Feb. 1929.
86. Norman explained the constraints to J. P. Morgan: TWL 178-18, J. P. Morgan to New York, 11 Mar. 1929.
87. 'Mr. Norman's Visit to New York', *Times*, 31 Jan. 1929, p. 11.
88. Federal Reserve Governors in 1929 blamed Strong for reducing interest rates for the sake of Europe back in 1927. This was not just the view of regional bankers: while holding that most Board members were 'pleasant incompetents', Russell Leffingwell of J.P. Morgan now held that 'Norman and Strong are responsible for the mess we are in today'. See TWL 103-13, Leffingwell to Lamont, 8 Mar. 1929.
89. *Ibid.*, also 178-19, Leffingwell to J. P. Morgan, 12 Mar. 1929.
90. As Norman wrote to the deputy governor back in London, he was still hoping the American authorities would raise rates to break the bubble, but his visit to Washington was 'so disappointing and unhelpful that no one can prophesy [if or when they would act].' FRBNY, Bank of England General, C261, Norman to Lubbock, telg. no. 41/29, 7 Feb. 1929.
91. 'English Bankers and U.S. Credit', *Times*, 11 Feb. 1929, p. 11; 'U.S. Credits and the Bank of England', *ibid.*, 20 Feb. 1929, p. 16.
92. BoE G1/453, Norman to Harrison, no. 47/29, 18 Feb. 1929; *ibid.*, no. 62/29, 12 Mar. 1929; *ibid.*, no. 67/29, 14 Mar. 1929; MGC, bundle 'B.G. loan 5', Grenfell to Leffingwell, 6 Mar. 1929; FRBNY, Bank of England General, C261, Norman to Harrison, telg. no. 108/29, 10 May 1929.
93. BB, D.P.P. 2.4.4, Revelstoke diary, 10 Mar. 1929; TWL 173-1, Lamont diary, 10 Mar. 1929; *ibid.*, 178-18, J. P. Morgan to New York, 11 Mar. 1929; MGC, Bundle 'B.G. Loan 5', Norman to Harrison, 12 Mar. 1929.
94. BoE, G1/506, Norman to Addis, 10 May 1929; *ibid.*, G1/453, minute, unsigned, n.d. (*c.*14 May 1929).
95. T176/13 Part 2, minute by Hopkins, n.d.

96. Clay, *Lord Norman*, pp. 251, 252. See also MGC, bundle 'Gold', Morgan to Leffingwell, 13 Aug. 1929; FRBNY, Bank of England General, C261, Norman to Harrison, no. 205/29, 13 Aug. 1929.
97. TWL 103-12, Leffingwell to Lamont, 12 Jul. 1927.
98. FRBNY, Strong papers, Strong to Jay, no. 1012, 21 Jul. 1927.
99. BoE, G1/412, Gilbert memorandum for German government, 20 Oct. 1927.
100. BoE, G1/413, Gilbert memorandum for the Reparation Commission, 22 Feb. 1928. On the background, Kent, *The Spoils of War*, pp. 272–3.
101. CAB24/197, C.P.281(28), Churchill memorandum, 28 Sept. 1928; Grayson, *Austen Chamberlain*, p. 131, f. 110.
102. MF, F³⁰/B12652, Poincaré and de Lasteyrie to Briand, no. 10/50, 29 Sept. 1929; FO371/12887, C3919/193/18, Chamberlain to Crewe, no. 1215, 30 May 1928; FO371/12896, C4154/394/18, Chamberlain to Crewe, no. 43, 1 Jun. 1928; FO371/12902, C4747/969/18, Chamberlain to Henderson, no. 1541, 6 Jul. 1928; FO371/12903, C6444/969/18, Selby minute, 22 Aug. 1928.
103. Whaley, *Covert German Rearmament*.
104. Jacobson, *Locarno Diplomacy*, pp. 145, 155, 182.
105. Keeton, *Briand's Locarno Policy*, p. 306; also Jacobson, *Locarno Diplomacy*, pp. 152–3, 155–6; Beau de Loménie, *Les responsabilités des dynasties bourgeoises*, iv, pp. 358–9.
106. Artaud, *La question des dettes interalliées*, ii, p. 897. Briand was evidently sceptical of the practical value of the proposed commission: *ADAP*, Ser.B, Band XII, no. 29, Hoesch to AA, 14 Jun. 1929.
107. BB, D.P.P., 2.4.4., Lord Revelstoke's Private Diary, 14 Feb. 1929 and passim; *ibid.*, 2.4.5, Note of discussion between Stamp, Moreau and Schacht respectively, 18 Feb. 1929; *ibid.*, Revelstoke to Peacock, 16 Mar. 1929; O. D. Young papers, Stuart Crocker diary, 12 Feb., 18 Mar. 1929.
108. James, *The Reichsbank and Public Finance in Germany*, p. 77; Clay, *Lord Norman*, p. 250.
109. MF, F³⁰/B42173, Farnier, Directeur du Mouvement Général des Fonds, to Chéron, 19 Apr. 1929; *ibid.*, note by Moret, 24 Apr. 1929; *ibid.*, Farnier note to minister, no. 271/50, 25 Apr. 1929; *ibid.*, B42181, de Fleuriau to Briand, no. 178, 28 Apr. 1929; *ibid.*, Farnier note to Chéron, 26 Apr. 1929; *ibid.*, note by Moret, 26 Apr. 1929; *ibid.*, Chéron to Poincaré, 26 Apr. 1929; TWL 178-22, Lamont cable to New York of conversation with Quesnay, 27 Apr. 1929.
110. *ADAP*, Ser.B, Band XII, no. 19, Schmidt Aufzeichnung, 11 Jun. 1929.
111. O. D. Young papers, Crocker diary, 26 Apr., 4 May, 6 May 1929; Link, *Die amerikanische Stabilisierungspolitik in Deutschland*, pp. 466–7; Eyck, *A History of the Weimar Republic*, ii, pp. 187–90; J. Jacobson, *Locarno Diplomacy*, pp. 262–3; Schacht, *The End of Reparations*, pp. 77–80.
112. O. D. Young papers, Crocker diary, 24 Apr. 1929.
113. *Ibid.*, 12 Apr. 1929. Recent accounts, seeking to discredit claims of American isolationism in the 1920s, generally credit Young with masterminding the plan that bears his name. There is no question that Young played a central part in the negotiations. Young himself was critical of Stamp because of his strongly expressed doubts as to how much Germany could pay. By the same token, the Crocker papers confirm that Stamp was the most active participant in the plenary sessions and subcommittee meetings, the principal drafter of memoranda and the expert for whom Young had the greatest respect. See *ibid.*, 13, 22 Feb. 1929; also Addis papers, Charles to Eba Addis, 24, 25 Apr. 1929; Case and Case, *Owen D. Young and American Enterprise*, p. 552.
114. Britain, Parliamentary Papers, Report of the Committee of Experts on Reparations, Cmd. 3343, Jun. 1929. Carlton, *MacDonald versus Henderson*, ch. 2, accepts the deprecatory claims of Churchill and Snowden, trumpeted as part of the 1929 general election campaign, and overlooks most of the creative features of the scheme.

115. In 1930, the first year of the Young plan, Britain received £19.4 million in reparations and £17.7 million in war debts or £37.1 million in all. After war debt payments of £33.0 million to the United States, it enjoyed a surplus of £4.1 million: 273 H.C. Deb 5s, cols 45–6. The calculations of loss are from T160/388, F11300/3, Hopkins memorandum, 'German Reparations. Experts' Report. Principal Questions for Consideration', 19 Jun. 1929.

116. PREM 1/83, Stamp memorandum, 4 Jul. 1929. The schedule of payments is set out in 'Germany's Payments under the Young Plan', *Economist*, 3 Aug. 1929, table, p. 214.

117. FO371/14378, C6268/6268/18, Cahill memorandum, 4 Feb. 1929.

118. T160/209, F7800/4, Walter Preston, M.P., to prime minister on competition for British shipbuilders, 23 Jan. 1929; *ibid.*, director, Federation of British Industries, to Leith-Ross, 6 Feb. 1929; *ibid.*, R. B. Dunwoody, Secretary, Association of British Chambers of Commerce, to Permanent Secretary, Board of Trade, 14 Mar. 1929.

119. T160/268, F11150/02/1, Fryer memorandum, 27 Mar. 1929; *ibid.*, CAB24/195, C.P.157(28), memorandum by Cunliffe-Lister, 17 May 1928; *ibid.*, C.P.194(28), memorandum by Cunliffe-Lister, 19 Jun. 1928; *ibid.*, CAB29/116, British Delegation, Financial Note No. 7A, British Coal Trade and the Young Plan, n.d.; BB, D.P.P. 2.4.3, 'The Effect of Deliveries of Reparation upon the British Coal Trade', no. 14, n.d.

120. MAE, PA-AP 261-Seydoux 32, note, 25 Feb. 1925; *ibid.*, PA-AP 217-Massigli 7, Seydoux, note, no. 83–26, 23 Nov. 1926; Artaud, *La question des dettes interalliées*, p. 893.

121. UK *PP*, Cmd. 3343, 'Report of the Committee of Experts on Reparations', Jun. 1929. The Young plan is summarized in 'Reparations', *Times*, 8 Jun. 1929, p. 14.

122. HHPP 1006, Stimson to Paris Embassy, telg. no. 102, 'Double Priority. No distribution', 8 Apr. 1929; Stimson diary, 28 Aug. 1930. Case and Case, *Owen D. Young and American Enterprise*, p. 444.

123. Stamp papers, memorandum on first four weeks of experts' deliberations, n.d. (*c.* Mar. 1929).

124. Castle papers 18, Armour to Stimson, 11 Apr. 1929, no. 145; HHPP 1006, Castle telg. no. 112 to US Embassy Paris, 15 Apr. 1929; *ibid.*, Young telg. via Everett Case Genetic New York, 13 Apr. 1929; *ibid.*, Mellon to Young, 16 Apr. 1929; Castle diary, 14 Apr. 1929; Case and Case, *Owen D. Young*, pp. 446–9.

125. CAB24/205, C.P.203(29), Snowden memorandum, 17 Jul. 1929; CAB29/109, minutes of third meeting, 27 Aug. 1929. The Hague conference is described in *BCC*, pp. 207–12.

126. Beatrice Webb diary, pp. 43, 74, 87–8, entry 18 Aug. 1929.

127. Kent, *The Spoils of War*, pp. 302, 386.

128. Leopold, *Alfred Hugenberg*, pp. 55–60; A. Bullock, *Hitler*, pp. 143–50; Heiden, *The History of National Socialism*, pp. 111–12.

129. BB, D.P.P., 2.4.4, Lord Revelstoke's Private Diary, 21, 22 Feb. 1929; *ibid.*, 2.4.5, Summary of eighth meeting of British members of Experts Committee, 4 Mar. 1929; *ibid.*, Revelstoke to Hopkins, 13 Mar. 1929; O. D. Young papers, Crocker diary, 22 Feb. 1929; *ibid.*, R35, Young to Kellogg, 2 Mar. 1929.

130. Schacht set out his views fully in BB, D.P.P., 2.4.5, Committee of Experts on Reparations, 19th Meeting, 11 a.m., 11 Mar. 1929.

131. O. D. Young papers, Crocker diary, *c.* 25 Feb. 5 Mar. 1929; R31, 'Young Plan and B.I.S. in the Making', n.d.; Costigliola, 'The Other Side of Isolationism', p. 606, represents the creation of the Bank as the outcome of a struggle between British and American bankers, which could hardly be further from the truth, and presents the episode as an illustration of Washington's skilful use of financial power in pursuit of international goals, largely passing over the fact that Washington was actually opposed to US banking participation.

132. Fisher, *Stabilised Money*, pp. 78–81, 139. On Stamp's interest in the BIS, see the obviously inspired articles, 'Reparations. The Proposed Bank', *Times*, 11 Mar. 1929, and 'Reparation Payments. The Proposed Bank', *ibid.*, 13 Mar. 1929; 'Reparations', *ibid.*, 16 May 1929.

133. O. D. Young papers, R34, Record of meeting no. 14, 11 Mar. 1929 and passim.
134. T160/388, Report of the Young Committee on Reparations, Part 6: Bank for International Settlements, 8 Jun. 1929.
135. HHPP 1006, Hoover to Coolidge, 8 Apr. 1929.
136. *Ibid.*, Stimson to Paris Embassy, telg. no. 102, 'Double Priority. No distribution', 8 Apr. 1929; O. D. Young papers, Crocker diary, 9 Apr. 1929; Castle papers 18, Armour telg. to Stimson, 17 May 1929, no. 264; *ibid.*, Stimson telg to Armour, 17 May 1929, no. 164; FRBNY, Harrison papers, 2013.1, Harrison memorandum, 23 May 1929, noting that the Under-Secretary of the Treasury, Ogden Mills would not even let Harrison see the BIS proposal, claiming he did not have a copy.
137. O. D. Young papers, green box, minute of meeting between Root, Young, Gilbert and Lamont, 9 Apr. 1929; MF, F^{30}/B42181, Lacour-Gayet (New York) to Chéron, no. 6301, 20 May 1929.
138. T160/388, F11300/3A, Leith-Ross minute, 24 Jun. 1929. See also Baring Brothers and Company archives, D.P.P., 2.4.4, Lord Revelstoke's Private Diary, 24, 26 Feb. 1929.
139. Clay, *Lord Norman*, p. 297.
140. *Ibid.*, pp. 364–5.
141. Feiertag, 'Les banques d'émission et la BRI face à la dislocation de l'étalon-or', pp. 715–36.
142. Dulles, *The Bank for International Settlements at Work*, p. 38; Clarke, *Central Bank Cooperation*, p. 147.
143. Knipping, *Deutschland, Frankreich und das Ende der Locarno-Ära*, pp. 32–3.
144. The first two terms are those of Wilson, *Herbert Hoover*; the latter description is from Leffler, 'Herbert Hoover, The "New Era," and American Foreign Policy', p. 151. See also Lloyd, *Aggressive Introvert*.
145. See the correspondence and clippings in HHPP 1011, including Holt to Taylor, memorandum, 'British 1920 Plan for 335 Billion Dollar International Loan', 7 Jan. 1932.
146. Leffler, 'Herbert Hoover', p. 151.
147. The history of postwar deliberations on regulating foreign lending is summarized in HHCP 221, Jones memorandum, 'The Foreign Loan Policy of the United States', to R. P. Lamont, Secretary of Commerce, 13 Jul. 1929. On State Department unease at Hoover's position, see Castle diary, 16 Apr., 10 May 1927. Leffler, 'Herbert Hoover', p. 162, encourages the impression that Hoover sought 'informal cooperation with private bankers' and worked in friendly fashion with them. Nothing could be further from the truth. HHCP 261, Christian Herter, 'Memorandum', 22 Apr. 1922.
148. An edited version of Hoover's speeches and the public response are published in 'The Cancellation Controversy', *Congressional Digest*, vol. II, no. 3, Dec. 1922, pp. 77–8.
149. See press cuttings in HHCP 216, including, 'Philip Drunk vs. Philip Sober', *Journal of Commerce*, 18 Oct. 1922; 'Mr. Hoover on the Debts', *New York World*, 18 Oct. 1922; E. R. A. Seligman, 'The Allied Debts: A Constructive Criticism of Secretary Hoover's Views', *New York Times* on 7 Nov. 1922; B. M. Anderson, Chase National Bank, to the Arizona Bankers' Assoc., 11 Nov. 1922; J. H. Hollander, 'Towering Allied Debts Restraint Against War', *New York Times*, 26 Nov. 1922, p. 3; HHCP 216, B. C. Forbes to Hoover, 8 Mar. 1923.
150. 18 Oct. 1922.
151. HHCP 216, Hoover to Irving T. Bush, 21 Oct. 1922.
152. HHCP 211, Hoover to Capper, 6 Mar. 1924; *ibid.*, box 208, 'Statement by Secretary Hoover Regarding Foreign Monopolies', 4 Jan. 1926; *ibid.*, 'Foreign Combinations to Control Prices of Raw Materials: Statements by Herbert Hoover, Secretary of Commerce and other Officers of the Department of Commerce', 6 Jan. 1926; *ibid.*, Hoover to Kellogg, 13 Nov. 1925; *ibid.*, box 210, Roberts to Jones, 18 Oct. 1926; 'Mr Hoover's Helpfulness', *Wall Street Journal*, 1 Jan. 1926; 'Mr. Hoover's Reply', *ibid.*, 8 Jan. 1926. The controversy is summarized in Brandes, 'Product Diplomacy', pp. 185–216.
153. Castle papers 5, Castle to Mrs P. Maddux, 10 Feb. 1928. Morgan became even more disaffected after the election, when his efforts to devise a new reparation scheme

with Owen Young in the spring of 1929 were repudiated by Stimson and Mellon, and Hoover refused to lift a finger in their defence. As Young's biographers write, 'In the whole entourage of Republicans, from his wife to J. P. Morgan (and company), any mention of Hoover now aroused nothing but resentment and disgust.' Case and Case, *Owen D. Young*, pp. 448–9.

154. Parrish, *Anxious Decades*, p. 211; Burner, *Herbert Hoover*, pp. 200–7; McCoy, 'To the White House', pp. 38–41; Fausold, *The Presidency of Herbert C. Hoover*, pp. 26–31.
155. Carter, *America in the 1920s*, p. 75. As Harold Faulkner put it, he 'may not have had the stigma of Wall Street, but to many a farmer he was a clever city politician who could not be trusted.' *From Versailles to the New Deal*, p. 315. This is also the view of Goldberg, *Discontented America*, p. 181, and Hicks, *Republican Ascendancy*, pp. 204–9.
156. Religion entered the campaign when a member of the Republican National Committee sent a letter to women voters warning, 'We must save the United States from being Romanized and rum-ridden.' Hoover immediately repudiated the letter, and he later claimed that it was Smith who raised the religious issue: *Memoirs*, ii, p. 208. Other Republicans, however, sustained the campaign, deploying a statement by Hoover made some time before the election that 'the Roman Catholic Church is in no way suited to this country [because] its thought is Latin and entirely at variance with the dominant thought of our country.' 'U.S. Presidency', *Times*, 1 Oct. 1928, p. 14.
157. 'The Peace Pact' and 'U.S. Presidential Election', *Times*, 8 Oct. 1928, p. 16.
158. 'U.S. Election Issues', *Times*, 15 Oct. 1928, p. 16.
159. 'Smith Pledges a Tariff to Protect All Classes; Acclaimed in Louisville', *New York Times*, 13 Oct. 1928, p. 1.
160. 'Hoover Promises to Call Congress to Act on Farm Aid If Dec. Session Fails', *New York Times*, 28 Oct. 1928, p. 1.
161. 'Hoover Citizenship Never Changed, Says State Department', *New York Times*, 18 Oct. 1928, p. 1, 'U.S. Election Methods', *Times*, 19 Oct. 1928, p. 16. The writer is presumably *Times* Washington correspondent, Willis J. Abbot.
162. 'Text of Hoover's Speech on Relation of Government to Industry', *New York Times*, 23 Oct. 1928, p. 2; 'Hoover Presses Farm Board Plan before Big St. Louis Audience', *ibid.*, 3 Nov. 1928, p. 1.
163. 'Hoover Wins All But Eight States, Thanks Nation', *New York Times*, 8 Nov. 1928, p. 1.
164. 'Mr. Hoover's Triumph', *Times*, 8 Nov. 1928, p. 16.
165. Hoover, *Memoirs*, ii, pp. 210–15; Burner, *Herbert Hoover*, pp. 285–6.
166. US DS, RG59, M560, Roll 30, Armour to State Department, 25 Dec. 1928.
167. HHPP 279, statement of 7 Mar. 1929.
168. Hoover, *Memoirs*, ii, pp. 291–5; Wilson, *American Business and Foreign Policy*, p. 96; Burner, *Herbert Hoover*, pp. 297–8; Fausold, *The Presidency of Herbert C. Hoover*, pp. 53–4, 94–7; 'Introduction', Fausold and Mazuzan (eds), *The Hoover Presidency: A Reappraisal*, p. 21.
169. 'Mr. Hoover and Congress', *Times*, 28 Dec. 1928, p. 12.
170. HHPP 279, Auchinbaugh to Ritchie, 2 Jul. 1929; 'U.S. Tariff Bill', *Times*, 9 Jul. 1929, p. 15; 'New U.S. Tariff', *ibid.*, 6 May 1930, p. 15; 'New U.S. Tariff', *ibid.*, 21 Jun. 1930, p. 11; FO371/14280, A4769/41/45, Lindsay to Henderson, no. 1066, 3 Jul. 1930.
171. HHPP 279, Fisher to Hoover, 14 Mar. 1929.
172. CAB23/61, conclusion 27(29)5, 17 Jul. 1929; 'U.S. Tariff Walls', *Manchester Guardian*, 13 Jun. 1929, p. 6; 'New US Tariff. Protests by 40 Nations. Hints of Retaliation', *Daily Telegraph*, 11 Jul. 1929, p. 11; 'World Trade Threats to United States', *Daily Mail*, 11 Jul. 1929, p. 11; 'Putting It Gently', *Manchester Guardian Commercial*, 18 Jul. 1929, p. 64; 'The American Tariff', *New Statesman and Nation*, 20 Jul. 1929, pp. 462–3.
173. HHPP 279, Auchinbaugh to Ritchie, 2 Jul. 1929.
174. 'The United States Tariff', *The Statist*, 6 Jul. 1929, p. 21.
175. Jones, *Tariff Retaliation*, ch. 2–4.

176. H.C. Deb 2nd ser., vol. 235, cols 210–11, 11 Feb. 1930; statement by Schmidt, in LN, *Proceedings of the Preliminary Conference with a View to Concerted Economic Action, 17 Feb.–24 Mar. 1930*, 18 Feb. 1930; 'Association of British Chambers of Commerce Annual Meeting', *Chamber of Commerce Journal*, 18 Apr. 1930, p. 444.

177. Beard and Beard, *The American Leviathan*, p. 456; Jones, *Tariff Retaliation*, pp. 19–23.

178. Temin, *Lessons from the Great Depression*, p. 46.

179. Dornbusch and Fischer, 'The Open Economy', p. 469. More generally, Hall and Ferguson, *The Great Depression*, pp. 71–3.

180. Eckes, 'Revisiting Smoot-Hawley', p. 299. The claim that the United States continued to adhere to the most-favoured-nation principle also rang hollow, since it granted tariff preferences to Cuba. FO371/11991, A6218/849/14, J. J. Wills to Craigie, 21 Oct. 1927; *ibid.*, 12759, A755/5/14, Craigie to Board of Trade, 1 Mar. 1928; *ibid.*, A2869/5/14, Fountain to FO, 28 Apr. 1928.

181. *Ibid.*, table 1, p. 298.

182. Wigmore, *The Crash and Its Aftermath*, p. 95.

183. *Ibid.*, p. 27.

184. Galbraith, *The Great Crash*, p. 75.

185. Wyckoff, *Wall Street and the Stock Markets*, pp. 68–9; R. Sobel, *The Big Board*, table 13.8, p. 283.

186. Wyckoff, *Wall Street and the Stock Markets*, table 2, pp. 178–9.

187. Sobel, *The Big Board*, pp. 268–9; Cleveland and Huertas. *Citibank*, pp. 132–3.

188. Cleveland and Huertas, *Citibank*, p. 157.

189. HHPP 151, Akerson to Herter, 2 Apr. 1929.

190. Wigmore, *The Crash and Its Aftermath*, p. 29. It was by no means only the none-too-respectable retail brokers who betrayed deep ambivalence about the current height of the stock market. In 1929 J. P. Morgan and Company, the most prestigious financial house on Wall Street, continued to solicit hundreds of millions of dollars for new trusts, which invested in the market. Yet as early as December 1927, Lamont, the senior partner, was privately advising insider clients to minimize their exposure to the market: TWL 125-12, Lamont to Dr William S. Rainsford, 19 Dec. 1927.

191. McGrattan and Prescott, 'The 1929 Stock Market: Irving Fisher Was Right'.

192. Sobel, *The Big Board*, table 13.8, p. 283; Wigmore, *The Crash and Its Aftermath*, pp. 3–4.

193. Miscellaneous undated documents in TWL 131-26. Chernow, *The House of Morgan*, pp. 315–16; Allen, *Only Yesterday*, p. 453.

194. Wyckoff, *Wall Street and the Stock Markets*, p. 69.

195. Wigmore, *The Crash and Its Aftermath*, p. 25.

196. Since Coolidge's re-election in 1926, the markets have declined 10 out of 20 times in the first year of a president's term and 8 out of 20 times in the second year, but only 2 out of 20 times in the third year and 3 out of 20 times in the fourth year. The average rise in the four years is respectively – 1.0 per cent, 5.3 per cent, 23.4 per cent and 16.5 per cent. Fisher, *The Only Three Questions That Count*, table 2.3, p. 73.

197. Chandler, *American Monetary Policy*, p. 77, table 7–12 p. 107; *USBC*, i, Series F163, p. 235, Series U27, p. 869; Denny, *America Conquers Britain*, pp. 127–8.

198. Thus Fréderic Jenny, the financial correspondent of *Le Temps* and a frequent mouthpiece of the governor of the Bank of France, welcomed the crash as a release from the problems caused by the boom: see Beau de Loménie, *Les responsabilités des dynasties bourgeoises*, iv, p. 440.

199. E. H. H. Simmons, 'The Principal Causes of the Stock Market Crisis of Nineteen Twenty Nine', Address to the Transportation Club, The Pennsylvania Railroad, Philadelphia, Pennsylvania, 25 Jan. 1930; HHPP 151, Meyer to Hoover, 5 Feb. 1930; 'The Last of Its Shareholdings', *Journal of Commerce*, 27 Feb. 1930, in TWL 131-28.

200. This was Keynes's view: see 'The Wall Street Collapse', *The Nation & Athenaeum*, 2 Nov. 1929, pp. 162–3.

201. Statement to Press, 29 Oct. 1929, J. P. Morgan and Company, in TWL 131-27.
202. Friedman and Schwartz. *A Monetary History of the United States, 1867–1960*, pp. 340–1.
203. TWL 131-27, Lamont to Harrison, 24 Oct. 1929.
204. Quoted in Chernow, *The House of Morgan*, p. 322; see also Hoover, *Memoirs*, ii, p. 30.
205. Hicks, *Republican Ascendancy*, p. 235.
206. Galbraith, *The Great Crash*, pp. 157, 162.
207. The British Treasury estimated that wholesale prices declined by fully 42 per cent from January 1925 to September 1931: T188/95, Hawtrey, 'The French Memorandum on the English Crisis', 27 Nov. 1931.
208. The market recovery between November 1929 and April 1930 is commonly assumed to be a classic bear market rally, or 'suckers' rally', as if only fools should have been taken in by it. But this is being wise after the event. Chancellor, *Devil Take the Hindmost*, p. 219.
209. Wyckoff, *Wall Street and the Stock Markets*, table 2, p. 178.
210. Sobel, *The Big Board*, p. 282; Chandler, *American Monetary Policy*, table 7–8, p. 100; Parrish, *Anxious Decades*, p. 228; Romasco, *The Poverty of Abundance*, p. 70.

5 The Crisis, September 1929–April 1931

1. Masur, *Imperial Berlin*, p. 137.
2. Coudenhove-Kalergi, *An Idea Conquers the World*, pp. ix, 162–4; Morinosuke et al., *Coudenhove-Kalergi*, p. 102.
3. MAE, Papiers 1940-Léger 3, de Margerie to Briand, nos 444-9, 19 May 1930; Pegg, *Evolution of the European Idea*, p. 144; Morinosuke et al., *Coudenhove-Kalergi*, p. 16.
4. Amery diary, 18 May 1930; FO371/14981, W5336/451/98, Rumbold to Henderson, no. 408, 20 May 1930.
5. 'France to Quit Rhineland', *New York Times*, 18 May 1930, p. 27.
6. 'Briand Plan Based on Monroe Doctrine', *New York Times*, 18 May 1930, p. 1. An English version of the memorandum is in UK, *PP*, 1930, Cmd. 3595, 'Dispatch to His Majesty's Ambassador in Paris enclosing the Memorandum of the French Government on the Organisation of a System of European Federal Union, 28 May 1930'; the original French version is in Keller et al. (eds), *Le Plan Briand d'Union fédérale européenne*, pp. 37–49.
7. L'Huillier, *Dialogues franco-allemands*, p. 98.
8. Mussolini, *Opera Omnia*, xxiv, pp. 235–6; 'Fascist Italy', *Times*, 19 May 1930, p. 14.
9. LN, *The Course and Phases of the World Economic Depression*, p. 128. It is still commonly assumed that the slump began later in France as well as reaching crisis much later, but see Bouvier, 'A propos du déclenchement de deux "grandes crises"du XXe siècle', *L'historien sur son métier*, pp. 125–53.
10. According to one acute British observer, the gravity of the crisis was not appreciated in London until the autumn of 1930. Einzig, *The World Economic Crisis*, p. 5. If British observers were slow to recognize the crisis elsewhere, it was probably because they had long regarded Britain itself as in crisis, and hence the 1920s had never seemed normal to them.
11. *ADAP*, Serie B, Band XII, no. 19, Schmidt Aufzeichnung, 11 Jun. 1929.
12. *Ibid.*, no. 44, René to AA, 24 Jun. 1929.
13. *Ibid.*, Serie B, Band xii, no. 21, Punder Fortsetzung von Nr.15, 12 Jun. 1929; Stresemann, *His Diaries, Letters, and Papers*, iii, p. 451; also Suarez, *Briand*, vi, p. 294.
14. *ADAP*, Serie B, Band XII, no. 138, Schubert Aufzeichnung, 1 Aug. 1929.
15. *Ibid.*, no. 153, Bülow Aufzeichnung, 7 Aug. 1929. Similarly Bülow's successor, see Hill (ed.), *Die Weizsäcker-Papiere*, pp. 407, 663f43.
16. US State Department, RG59, M560, Roll 30, Armour to Stimson, no. 9606, 8 Jun. 1929.

17. MAE, Papiers 1940-Léger 3, Claudel telg. nos 346-51 to Briand, 10 Jul. 1929; E. Raymond Streat, 'Results of the Chambers of Commerce Congress', *Manchester Guardian Commercial*, p. 69.
18. *ADAP*, Serie B, Band XII, no. 138, Dufour-Feronce to Köpke, 30 Aug. 1929.
19. US SD, RG59, M560, Roll 31, Armour to Stimson, no. 9749, 6 Aug. 1929; 'America and Europe', *Economist*, 13 Jul. 1929, p. 64; 'European Customs Union', *ibid.*, 27 Jul. 1929, pp. 163–4.
20. M. Ray, 'Vers un Locarno Européen', *Le Petit Journal*, 12 Jul. 1929, p. 1; J. Sauerwein, 'La Fédération Européenne', *Le Matin*, 12 Jul. 1929, p. 1. On the interview, *ADAP*, Ser.B, Band XII, no. 87, Hoesch to AA, 12 Jul. 1929.
21. For a contemporary description of Briand's address, see Dumoulin, 'La Belgique et le Plan Briand', pp. 94–5.
22. LN, *Official Journal*, Records of the Tenth Assembly, Plenary Meetings, 1929, pp. 51–2. The speech is reproduced *in extenso* in Herriot, *Europe*, pp. 47–9.
23. *Ibid.*
24. LN, Work of the Economic Committee during its Twenty-Eighth Session, 8–12 Apr. 1929, presented to the 55th Session of the Council, 14 Jun. 1929, and adopted (reprinted in LN, *Official Journal*, 1929, pp. 1228–9); LN, *Commercial Policy in the Interwar Period*, p. 47.
25. LN, Recommandations du Comité Economic concernant la politique commerciale, 18 Jun. 1929; Chapman, unpublished autobiography, pp. 253–4.
26. MAE, SdN IJ-QEF 1172, Flandin to Briand, J805/B, 8 Aug. 1930.
27. MF, F^{30}/B12657, Note by Rueff, 17 Dec. 1929, reproduced in Rueff, *De l'Aube au crépuscule*, Annexe I: 'Note sur un projet de "Pacte économique", décembre 1928 – mars 1929', pp. 287–93.
28. MAE, SdN SG 859, Note de Massigli, The Hague, 19 Aug. 1929; Vanlangenhove, *L'élaboration de la politique étrangère de la Belgique entre les deux guerres mondiales*, pp. 87–8; Bussière, *La France, la Belgique*, p. 330.
29. LN, *Official Journal*, Records of the Tenth Assembly, 1929, Plenary Meetings, pp. 79–81.
30. MAE, SdN IJ-QEF 1428, Elbel to Loucheur, 11 Sept. 1929; MAE, Serie Y Internationale 1918–40, 630, Massigli report, no. 91, 13 Sept. 1929, 20.45 p.m.
31. MAE, SdN IJ-QEF 1398, Massigli to Serruys, 5 Apr. 1929.
32. MAE, Serie Y Internationale 1918–40, 630, Massigli to Briand, no. 91, 13 Sept. 1929.
33. *Ibid.*, Massigli to Briand, no. 99, 14 Sept. 1929.
34. Badel, 'Trêve douanière, libéralisme et conjoncture', pp. 144–5; Bussière, 'Premiers schémas européens et économie internationale', pp. 64–6.
35. MAE, SdN IJ-QEF 1428, note to minister, 18 Oct. 1929.
36. MAE, SdN, IJ-QEF 1172, compte-rendu, 15 Nov. 1929.
37. *Ibid.*, Serie Y Internationale 1918–40, 630, Tripier report no. 428, 29 Nov. 1929, 11.20 a.m.; *ibid.*, Berthelot no. 632 to Warsaw and 963 to Berlin, 9 déc. 1929, 22.30 p.m.; *ibid.*, Laroche no. 467, 10 déc. 1929, 20.27 p.m.; *ibid.*, Corbin to Seguin, nos 362-66, 15 déc. 1929, 2 p.m.; *ibid.*, Corbin to Laroche, nos 641-44, 15 déc. 1929, 3.30 p.m.; *ibid.*, Seguin report no. 326, 17 déc. 1929, 1.50 p.m.; *ibid.*, Charles Roux no. 334, 20 déc. 1929, 11.30 p.m.; *ibid.*, Laroche report no. 480, 17 déc. 1929, 8.40 p.m.
38. MAE, SdN, IJ-QEF 1430, compte-rendu, 1 Feb. 1930.
38. *Ibid.*, Flandin to Briand, no. 3, 17 Feb. 1930.
40. *Ibid.*, Y International 1918–1940, 631, Flandin no. 36, 11 Mar. 1930; Fonds Flandin 43, contains an unsigned, undated memorandum, 'Analyse du Memorandum sur l'Organisation d'un Régime d'Union Fédérale Européenne', which affirms that 'the economic problem should be subordinated to the political problem'.
41. 'The Poor Relations', *Economist*, 29 Jun. 1929, pp. 1439–40.
42. Barré, *Le Seigneur-Chat*, p. 407.
43. MAE, IJ-QEF 1429, minister in Copenhagen to Quai d'Orsay, 5 Dec. 1929; *ibid.*, ambassador in Berlin to Quai d'Orsay, 13 and 14 Dec. 1929; *ibid.*, note for Massigli, 20 Dec. 1929.

44. *Ibid.*, 1428, Hennessy letter to Briand, 14 Oct. 1929; *ibid.*, 1172, compte-rendu, 18 Oct. 1929.
45. Beau de Loménie, *Les responsabilités des dynasties bourgeoises*, iv, p. 446.
46. *Ibid.*, IJ-QEF 1428, F. Seydoux note for Massigli, 21 Oct. 1929; *ibid.*, Elbel note for Massigli, 21 Oct. 1929; *ibid.*, Seydoux note for Briand, 23 Nov. 1929; *ibid.*, IJ-QEF 1429, petition from Chamber of Agriculture of the Meurthe-et-Moselle, 20 Dec. 1929; *ibid.*, F. Seydoux, compte-rendu, 21 Dec. 1929; *ibid.*, Papiers 1940-Léger 3, Massigli note for Briand, 23 Nov. 1929; *ibid.*, RC, B-NC 2, Rapport, Chambre d'Agriculture de la Gironde, Dec. 1929; *ibid.*, Série Y Internationale 1918-40, 630, Sen. Bachelot on behalf of the Fédération des sociétés agricoles du nord de la France, to Briand, 10 Dec. 1929.
47. MAE, IJ-QEF 1429, F. Seydoux, compte-rendu, 21 Dec. 1929.
48. *Ibid.*, Serie Y Internationale 1918–40, 630, Puaux to Briand no. 426, 25 Jan. 1930; *ibid.*, PA-AP 166-Tardieu 527, de Laboulaye for Briand to Tardieu and François-Poncet, 12 Apr. 1930.
49. *Ibid.*, IJ-QEF 1430, Henri Gueyraud to Léger, 15 Feb. 1930.
50. *Ibid.*, IJ-QEF 1429, Gueyraud to Massigli, 15 Feb. 1930. Lawrence Badel, 'Trêve douanière, libéralisme et conjoncture', p. 157, argues that Serruys, chief French delegate to the tariff truce conference, opposed the truce because, as a zealous economic liberal, he did not wish present levels of tariff protection endorsed by an international agreement.
51. MAE, Papiers 1940-Léger 3, Minister in Prague to Briand, no.-, 13 Sept. 1929.
52. Ferencuhová, 'L'accueil du Plan Briand dans les milieux politiques tchèques et slovaques', pp. 191, 200.
53. MAE, Papiers 1940-Léger 3, Claudel to Briand, nos 346-51, 10 Jul. 1929; *ibid.*, no. 424, 13 Sept. 1929.
54. MAE, SdN IJ-QEF 1430, Massigli to Gueyraud, 10 Feb. 1930.
55. FO 371/14980, W5193/451/98, Bentinck to Howard Smith, 6 May 1930.
56. MAE, Papiers 1940, Papiers Léger 3, first three drafts and a printed 12pp. copy of the 'Memorandum sur l'organisation d'un régime d'Union Federale Européenne'.
57. Italics added. Keller et al. (eds), *Le Plan Briand d'Union fédérale européenne: documents*, pp. 37–49.
58. FO371/14366, C5529/230/18, Tyrrell to Henderson, no. 784, 8 Jul. 1930; FO 371/14366, C6393/230/18, R. H. Campbell to Henderson, no. 930, 13 Aug. 1930; Graml, *Zwischen Stresemann und Hitler*, pp. 48–50; Auffray, *Pierre de Margerie*, pp. 471–2; Beau de Loménie, *Les responsabilités des dynasties bourgeoises*, iv, p. 465.
59. 'Frontier Affray in East Prussia', *Times*, 27 May 1930, p. 15; 'East Prussian Frontier Affray', *ibid.*, 28 May 1930, p. 15; 'East Prussian Frontier Incident', *ibid.*, 29 May 1930, p. 15; 'German-Polish Dispute', *ibid.*, 9 Jun. 1930, p. 9; 'The German-Polish Frontier: Another Incident', *ibid.*, 21 Jun. 1930, p. 11; 'East Prussian Frontier', *ibid.*, 4 Jul. 1930, p. 16.
60. Graml, *Zwischen Stresemann und Hitler*, p. 47.
61. 'German Relations with Poland', *Times*, 16 Aug. 1930, p. 9; 'The German Frontiers', *ibid.*, 12 Aug. 1930, p. 10; 'German-Polish Frontier: "Right" of Revision: "What every German thinks"', *ibid.*, 13 Aug. 1930, p. 10; 'German-Polish Frontier', *ibid.*, 14 Aug. 1930, p. 9; FO371/14370, C5484/680/18, Rumbold to Henderson, no. 548, 3 Jul. 1930; *ibid.*, C6384/680/18, Rumbold to Henderson, no. 662, 12 Aug. 1930; *ibid.*, C6462/680/18, Rumbold to Henderson, no. 674, 15 Aug. 1930; *ibid.*, C6555/680/18, Rumbold to Henderson, no. 681, 18 Aug. 1930.
62. Boyle, *Montagu Norman*, p. 250.
63. *BCC*, pp. 226–9.
64. *Ibid.*, pp. 214–15.
65. BoE, G3/195, Norman to Hopkins, 30 Sept. 1929; Clay, *Lord Norman*, p. 363.
66. Labour Party, *Report of the 29th Annual Conference*, 30 Sept.–4 Oct. 1929, pp. 227–30; 'Mr. Snowden's Speech', *Times*, 4 Oct. 1929, p. 15; 'The Brighton Conference', *The Economist*, 5 Oct. 1929, pp. 603–4; 'Mr. Snowden and the Banks', *ibid.*, pp. 610–11.

67. The standard work on the second Labour government's economic policy, Skidelsky, *Politicians and the Slump*, wrongly suggests that the central issue was fiscal innovation and the introduction of a proto-Keynesian policy of public works. This was never more than marginal to political deliberations.

68. That year Britain's imports totalled £1220.8 million, its domestic exports £729.3 million, and its re-exports £109.7 million. Imports minus domestic exports left a deficit of £491 million. Mitchell and Deane, *Abstract of British Historical Statistics*, table p. 284.

69. 'A Time for Thinking', *Times*, 6 Dec. 1928, p. 17; 'Anglo-American Relations', *ibid.*, 1 Dec. 1928, p. 13.

70. MAE, Europe 1919–40, GB 42, de Fleuriau to Briand, no. 283, 17 Jun. 1929.

71. Marquand, *Ramsay MacDonald*, pp. 501–9.

72. HHPP 984, Stimson to Cotton, telg. no. 195, 2 Apr. 1930.

73. *Ibid.*, Gordon to Stimson, no. 478, 16 Oct. 1929; *ibid.*, Stimson to Cotton, no. 161, 25 Mar. 1930; *DBFP*, ser. 2, i, no. 123, memorandum from de Fleuriau, 20 Dec. 1929, pp. 173–7.

74. MAE, SdN, Secrétariat Général 859, Note (by Massigli?) for Briand, 30 Aug. 1929; *ibid.*, PA-AP 006-Avenol 13, Avenol to Massigli, 14 Dec. 1929, enclosing memorandum, 13 Dec. 1929.

75. HHPP 984, Stimson to Cotton, no. 126, 10 Mar. 1930.

76. *Ibid.*, Stimson to Cotton, no. 156, 23 Mar. 1930.

77. Hoover, *Memoirs*, ii, p. 348. Hoover recalled with bitterness that East coast internationalists immediately accused the Administration of wrecking the conference, 'and our usual New York associations on foreign policies joined in the howl.'

78. HHPP 984, Stimson to Cotton, telg. no. 156, 23 Mar. 1930; Stimson diary 1930 (reel 2), minute by DWM (Morrow), 21 Mar. 1930.

79. Stimson diary, 22 Mar. 1930 (reel 2).

80. JRM 30/69/1753, diary, 12, 14 Feb. 1930.

81. *Ibid.*, 16 Feb. 1930.

82. Stimson diary, 22 Mar. 1930 (reel 2), minute, 'The Secretary and Mrs Stimson at Stanmore'.

83. Speaking in Canada the previous year, Churchill had warned of the danger in trying to impose disarmament upon France. He pointed out that every country had different security requirements. France lived next door to a country with twice the potential manpower, which had twice invaded it in a single lifetime. Would Britain and the United States act differently in these circumstances, he asked. *Montreal Gazette*, 14 Aug. 1929. On British reactions to the London conference, Gilbert (ed.), *Winston S. Churchill*, v. *Companion Volume*, 2, pp. 156–7; 238 H.C. Deb 5s, cols 2085–2205.

84. Ferris, *Men, Money, and Diplomacy*, p. 181,
    MacDonald's second government made Britain's single gravest strategic error of the interwar years. At the London naval conference of 1930, for no compelling reason, it destroyed the navy's ability to match the Imperial Japanese Navy and any European power. It forced the navy to scrap many warships, its actions precluded any major naval rearmament until 1937, and it again cancelled the Singapore base.

85. *BCC*, pp. 201–2.

86. Statements by Graham in LN, *Proceedings of the Preliminary Conference with a iew to Concerted Economic Action*, plenary session, 18 Feb. 1930, 14, 24 Mar. 1930.

87. *Ibid.*, 21 Feb. 1930; T172/1713, memorandum by British delegation, Feb. 1930.

88. RIIA, *British Tariff Policy*, p. 10 and table I, page 43.

89. On debate inside the German government over its reply to the plan, see Schulz, *Deutschland, der Völkerbund und die Frage der europäischen Wirtschaftsordnung*, pp. 320–39.

90. Badel, *Un milieu liberal*, pp. 118–19, 163–9, 178–81 and passim.

91. Boyce, 'Economics', pp. 9–41.

92. Grayson, *Austen Chamberlain*, p. 34, where it is called the 'Franco-German steel cartel'; Bussière, 'L'Organisation économique de la SDN', pp. 301–13.
93. FO371/14134, W7294/6739/98, memorandum, 24 Jul. 1929.
94. *Ibid.*
95. FO371/14366, C3439/230/18, minute by A. Leeper, 8 May 1930.
96. FO371/14350, C3358/3358/62, Vansittart memorandum, 1 May 1930; also in CAB24/225, C.P. 317(31), 10 Dec. 1931; and reprinted in *DBFP*, ser. 1A, vii, Appendix, pp. 834–52.
97. J. Seydoux, 'France and Germany. A Necessary Entente', *Times*, 15 Mar. 1928, p. 15.
98. FO371/12900, C2116/652/18, minute by Sargent, 20 Mar. 1928.
99. FO371/14134, W6932/6739/98, enclosure by Wigram for Tyrrell, 16 Jul. 1929.
100. *Ibid.*, W6739/6739/98, minute by Sargent, 18 Oct. 1929.
101. FO371/14365, C230/230/18, minute by Howard Smith, 9 Jan. 1930; *ibid.*, C1002/230/18, Sargent to Grigg, 3 Feb. 1930; *ibid.*, Vansittart to Tyrrell, 3 Feb. 1930.
102. FO371/14980, W5111/451/98, minute by Leeper, 21 May 1930.
103. FO371/14134, W9966/6739/98, minute by Gaselee, 17 Oct. 1929.
104. *Ibid.*, minute by Thompson, 18 Oct. 1929. Emphasis in the original.
105. *Ibid.*, minute by Snow, 18 Oct. 1929. Italics in original.
106. FO371/14365, C1570/230/18, minute by Leeper, 24 Feb. 1930; *ibid.*, minute by Howard Smith, 25 Feb. 1930; FO371/14366, C3439/230/18, minute by Leeper, 8 May 1930.
107. FO371/14981, W5585/451/98, memorandum by A.W.A. Leeper, 30 May 1930.
108. FO800/281, memorandum by Salter, 20 May 1930.
109. *Ibid.*, memorandum by Noel-Baker, n.d., copy in FO371/14981, W5585/451/98, 26 May 1930. The League of Nations Union offered Henderson similar advice, see FO800/281, Henderson to Gilbert Murray, 27 Jun. 1930.
110. *Ibid.*, memorandum by Cecil, 1 Jun. 1930.
111. FO371/14982, W5805/451/98, minute by Howard Smith, 5 Jun. 1930; Boyce, 'Britain's first "No" to Europe'.
112. FO371/14982, W5919/451/98, minute by Mallet, 10 Jun. 1930.
113. See for instance, *ADAP*, Ser.B, Band XV, no. 52, Aufzeichnung Schubert, 28 May 1931, and *ibid.*, f. 3, Aufzeichnung Curtius, 30 Apr. 1931; FO371/14982, W6386/451/98, minute by Vansittart, 30 Jun. 1930.
114. FO371/14917, W6464/6464/17, Tyrrell to Henderson, 25 Jun. 1930.
115. FO800/281, Henderson to Tyrrell, 26 Jun. 1930.
116. *Ibid.*, Tyrrell to Henderson, 28 Jun. 1930.
117. See for instance, FO371/14365, C1753/230/18, Tyrrell to Sargent, 10 Mar. 1930; FO800/281, Tyrrell to Henderson, 5 Jul. 1930.
118. FO371/14365, C2841/230/18, Tyrrell to Henderson, no. 411, 11 Apr. 1930. See also, FO371/14365, C1753/230/18, Tyrrell to Sargent, 10 Mar. 1930; FO371/14982, W6050/451/98, Tyrrell to Henderson, no. 638, 11 Jun. 1930; FO800/281, Tyrrell to Henderson, 5 Jul. 1930.
119. CAB27/424, memorandum by Henderson, 3 Jul. 1930; CAB24/213, C.P. 243(30), 'M. Briand's Memorandum for a Federated Union of Europe', 14 Jul. 1930.
120. 'Rapport du gouvernement français sur les résultats de l'enquête instituée au sujet de l'organisation d'un régime d'Union fédérale européenne', n.d., in Fleury and Jílek (eds), *Le Plan Briand d'Union fédérale européenne*, annexe II, pp. 582–602. An English version is contained in LN, A.46.1930.VII, Memorandum on the Organisation of a System of Federal Union, 15 Sept. 1930.
121. MF, F^{30}/B12612, de Chalendar to Directeur du Mouvement des Fonds, no. 53,778, 3 Oct. 1929; *ibid.*, B25452, de Chalendar to Minister of Finance, no.- , 3 Oct. 1929; *ibid.*, B25452, de J. de la Taille to Minister of Finance, nos 54,247, 27 Dec. 1929.
122. 'Lombard Street', *Financial News*, 25 Jul. 1929, p. 6; *ibid.*, 30 Jul. 1929, p. 6; *ibid.*, 6 Aug. 1929, p. 4; *ibid.*, 7 Aug. 1929, p. 4; 'City Notes', *Times*, 31 Jul. 1929, p. 20; City Editor, 'More Gold to Go', *Daily Express*, 31 Jul. 1929, p. 1; 'Further Large Gold Sales to France', *ibid.*, 19 Aug. 1929, p. 10; 'Markets Firm Despite £1,700,000 Gold Sale', *ibid.*, 20 Aug.

1929, p. 10; 'The Money Market', *Statist*, 10 Aug. 1929, p. 204; A. E. Davies, 'The City', *New Statesman and Nation*, 27 Jul. 1929, p. 510; *ibid.*, 21 Sept. 1929, p. 724; 'The Gold Efflux', *Manchester Guardian Commercial*, 3 Oct. 1929, p. 383; George Glasgow, 'Foreign Affairs', *Contemporary Review*, Nov. 1929, p. 659; *ibid.*, Dec. 1929, p. 779.

123. BdF, DCG, 28 Nov. 1929, 30 Jan. 1930, 1 May 1930; Charles Rist, 'Le Mar.é de Paris se doit de jouer un rôle international', *L'Europe Nouvelle*, 11 Jan. 1930, pp. 38–9; Julien Schaeffer, 'Le Mar.é des acceptances', *La France Economique et Financière*, 12 Apr. 1930.

124. T160/430, F12317/1, note of conversations, 2–3 Jan. 1931.

125. BdF, 4oN384H, Direction des Etudes. Correspondance, liasse 20(4), 1931, Lacour-Gayet to Serruys, 17 Jan. 1931.

126. 'Gold and the Price Level', *The Economist*, Supplement, 5 Jul. 1930, Annex B, p. 10; 'Bank of England', 'Bank of France', *The Economist*, 10 Jan. 1931, pp. 85, 86; *Financial Times*, Banking Supplement, 30 Mar. 1931, p. 3.

127. See for instance, 'France Drains Gold from England: Political Motives Suspected', *Daily Herald*, 20 May 1930, p. 7; G. Glasgow, 'French Raid on the World's Gold', *Observer*, 20 Jul. 1930, p. 2; 'The Golden River', *Daily Mail*, 16 Aug. 1930, p. 8.

128. MF, F³⁰/B12613, Rueff to Directeur du Mouvement des Fonds, nos 56,743, 29 Jul. 1930.

129 James, *The Reichsbank*, pp. 124, 129.

130. France, Ministère des Finances, F³⁰/B12625, nos 59,020, Farnier note to Germain Martin, n.d. (c. 2 Jan. 1931); FO 371/15641, W629/56/17, Leith-Ross to Howard Smith, 16 Jan. 1931.

131. LN, Interim Report of the Gold Delegation of the Financial Committee, Sept. 1930.

132. BoE, OV9/257, Strakosch to Niemeyer, 15 Jun. 1930.

133. BoE, OV9/264, Niemeyer to Strakosch, 29 Jul. 1930; OV9/258, Niemeyer to Strakosch, 25 Oct. 1930.

134. *Ibid.*, Strakosch to Niemeyer, 1 Sept. 1930.

135. BoE, ADM 34/19, Norman diary, 28 Aug. 1930; *ibid.*, G1/30, unsigned minute, copy to Addis, 1 Sept. 1930.

136. See Ch. 4.

137. According to one well-placed source, the City put up two-thirds of the Conservative's election funds in 1929: JRM 30/69/1753, diary, 30 Apr. 1929; also James, *Memoirs of a Conservative*, p. 289. On Norman's apprehension, see Clay, *Lord Norman*, pp. 325, 335, 358.

138. MF, F³⁰/1411, Farnier to Moreau, 24 Sept. 1930.

139. MF, F³⁰/B12625, Escallier 'Note pour le Ministre', n.d. (c. 1 Jan. 1931); T188/22, note on conversations, 2–3 Jan. 1931; MF, F³⁰, B12614, Rueff to Escallier, no. 57,840, 17 Feb. 1931; T160/430, F12317/1, Tyrrell to Henderson, 28 Jan. 1931.

140. MF, F³⁰/1411, Laboulaye to Escallier, no. 3149, 23 Dec. 1930.

141. T160/430, F12317/1, Leith-Ross to Hopkins, 17 Nov. 1930; FO371/14919, W12605/12605/17, Vansittart minute, 24 Nov. 1930.

142. T160/430, F12317/1, Leith-Ross to Hopkins and Pethwick-Lawrence, 2 Dec. 1930; FO371/15640, W56/56/17, Leith-Ross to Vansittart, 2 Dec. 1930.

143. BdF, DCG, statements by the governor, 13, 20, 27 Nov., 4, 11 Dec. 1930; FRBNY, Bank of England General, C261, Sproul note of Carriguel-Harrison conversation, Paris, 19 Nov. 1930.

144. BdF, DCG, statement by the governor, 27 Nov. 1930; *ibid.*, Banques d'emission des Etats-Unis, no. 14: 1926–1932; Moret to Harrison, 10 Dec. 1930; FRBNY, Bank of England General, C261, Norman to Harrison, no. 263/30, 12 Dec. 1930; *ibid.*, Harrison papers, 3117.1, Harrison minute, 2 Jan. 1931.

145. Briand confirmed to Tyrrell, the British ambassador in Paris, that 'it was on his initiative that the bank rate had been lowered in Paris to please us and that he had impressed upon the Ministry of Finance that they must look upon us as friends and associates in the task of rebuilding Europe.' T160/430, F12317/1, Tyrrell to 'Victor'

[Wellesley], 7 Jan. 1931. The British press offered grudging thanks: see for instance, 'French Bank Rate Lowered', *Times*, 3 Jan. 1931.

146. BdF, Banques d'émission des Etats-Unis, no. 14: 1926–1932, compte-rendu, 28 Aug. 1931; also BdF, DCG, statements by the governor, 2 Jan. 1931 and 3 Sept. 1931, where Moret elaborated on his decisions.

147. FRBNY, C261 Bank of England General, Sproul memorandum, conversation with Harrison, 19 Nov. 1930.

148. *Banker*, XVII/61, Feb. 1931, p. 129.

147. T160/430, F12317/1, Leith-Ross to Hopkins and Snowden, n.d. (*c.* 15 May 1930).

149. T188/22, Leith-Ross minute of conversations, 2–3 Jan. 1931; *ibid.*, note by Leith-Ross, 16 Jan. 1931. On the progress of the international loans, BdF, Banques d'Emission des Etats-Unis, no. 14, 1926–1932, Moret to Harrison, no. 15, 14 Jan. 1931.

150. T160/430, F12317/2, Leith-Ross to Bizot, 23 Jan. 1931; Bizot to Leith-Ross, 2 Feb. 1931.

151. FO371/15641, W1485/56/17, Leith-Ross to Howard Smith, 6 Feb. 1931.

152. T188/22, Leith-Ross to Sargent, 24 Feb. 1931.

153. T188/22, Leith-Ross note of conversations on 20–21 Feb. 1931; *ibid.*, Leith-Ross minute to Hopkins and Snowden, 23 Feb. 1931.

154. FO371/15712, W645/102/98, Leith-Ross to Niemeyer, 16 Jan. 1931.

155. LN, 'Second Interim Report of the Gold Delegation of the Financial Committee', Jan. 1931.

156. BdF, Banques d'emission des Etats-Unis, number 14: 1926–1932, compte-rendu, 17–22 Nov. 1930, topic C, relations between the Paris and London markets.

157. *Ibid.*, Moret to Harrison, 10 Dec. 1930; FRBNY, Bank of England General, C261, Norman to Harrison, no. 263/30, 12 Dec. 1930.

158. T160/430, F12317/1, Leith-Ross note of interview with M. Pouyanne, 16 Dec. 1930. Norman made no mention of the loan in his report of the meeting to Harrison on 12 Dec. 1930.

159. FO371/15640, W278/56/17, Tyrrell telg. no. 14, 5 Jan. 1931; Bennett, *Germany and the Diplomacy of the Financial Crisis*, pp. 83–4.

160. T160/430, F12317/1, Howard Smith to Leith-Ross, 13 Jan. 1931.

161. *Ibid.*, Leith-Ross to Howard Smith, 14 Jan. 1931.

162. FRBNY, C261, Bank of England General, Record of Sprague-Harrison conversation, London, 5 Dec. 1930. On Courtney Mill's discouragement of hopes for an international solution, see 'City Notes', *Times*, 4, 7 Oct., 8 Dec. 1930.

163. T160/430, F12317/2, Waley minute, 30 Jan. 1931.

164. Clay, *Lord Norman*, p. 370.

165. FRBNY, Harrison-Norman correspondence, Harrison to Stimson, 21 Apr. 1931.

166. CAB58/2, E.A.C./9th Meeting, 7 Nov. 1930; CAB24/219, C.P.3(31), Snowden memorandum, 7 Jan. 1931.

167. *Ibid.*

168. Skidelsky, *Politicians and the Slump*, pp. 335–6.

169. See below, pp. 314–5, 318.

170. BdF, Banques d'émission des Etats-Unis, no. 14: 1926–1932, Harrison to Moreau, telg. no. 86, 31 Jul. 1930.

171. *Ibid.*, compte-rendu, 17–22 Nov. 1930, topic B, foreign loans.

172. FRBNY, Bank of England General, C261, Crane to Roy Young, 20 Mar. 1931.

173. BdF, Banques d'émission des Etats-Unis, no. 14: 1926–1932, compte-rendu, 17–22 Nov. 1930, topic B, foreign loans.

174. *Ibid.*, Crane to Lacour-Gayet, 11 Mar. 1930.

175. FRBNY, Bank of England General, C798, Crane to Norman, 210/30, 4 Sept. 1930; C798, Young to Norman, 211/30, 4 Sept. 1930; C261, Burgess, to Sprague, 16 Sept. 1930.

176. BdF DCG, statement by governor, 6 Nov. 1930.

177. 'France', *Economist*, 24 Jan. 1931, p. 168.

178. BdF, Banques d'émission des Etats-Unis, no. 14: 1926–1932, compte-rendu, 17–22 Nov. 1930, topic G, economic situation in France; BdF, Banques d'émission des Etats-Unis, no. 14: 1926–1932, Moret to Harrison, 10 Dec. 1930.

179. FO371/15641, W629/56/17, Leith-Ross to Howard Smith, 16 Jan. 1931. On the prospect of German repudiation, FO371/15213, C402/11/18, Rumbold (Berlin) to Henderson, no. 47, 16 Jan. 1931; FO371/15213, C402/11/18, Sargent to Leith-Ross, 9 Feb. 1931; FO371/15213, C945/11/18, Leith-Ross to Sargent, 10 Feb. 1931.

180. T160/404, F557/011, Leith-Ross to Hopkins and Snowden, 2 Feb. 1931; Hopkins to Fisher, 3 Feb. 1931.

181. *Ibid.*, Fisher to Snowden, 7 Feb. 1931, Snowden minute, n.d.

182. FO371/15213, C402/11/18, Rumbold to Henderson, no. 47, 16 Jan. 1931.

183. T160/404, F557/011, Fisher to Snowden, 7 Feb. 1931.

184. Childers, 'The Social Bases of the National Socialist Vote', p. 26.

185. *Ibid.*, p. 29.

186. *Wirtschaft und Statistik*, 1 Jan.-Heft 1928, p. 1; *ibid.*, 1 Apr.-Heft 1928, p. 229; *ibid.*, 2 Aug.-Heft 1929, p. 645; *ibid.*, 2 Aug.-Heft 1930, p. 653.

187. Some historians, recognizing signs that support for the NSDAP had stopped declining and was beginning to increase before the 1928 election, conclude that Hitler's rise to power was not driven by economic conditions. See for instance, Peukert, *The Weimar Republic*, pp. 157, 233. While of course one cannot prove that other factors would not have brought about his victory, the evidence is scarcely compelling. Moreover it seems very odd to overlook the ways in which Hitler exploited the economic crisis for his own ends.

188. Hamilton, *Who Voted for Hitler?*, pp. 83, 90–1, 121, 198, 202, 206, 211.

189. *Wirtschaft und Statistik*, 2 Apr.-Heft 1931, p. 309.

190. Borchardt, *Perspectives*, p. 146.

191. *Wirtschaft und Statistik*, 2. Heft Aug. 1931, p. 589; also BdF, 1069199005/33 (L'Allemagne. Crise Monétaire et Financière. Press. mars 1930 au 30 juin 1931), Ambassade de France à Berlin, l'Attaché Financier, no. 83, Revue de presse du 10 avril 1931; *ibid.*, 1069199005/35, no. 291, Revue de presse du 9 décembre 1931.

192. Keynes, 'Proposals for a Revenue Tariff', *New Statesman and Nation*, 7 Mar. 1931, pp. 53–4.

193. London Chamber of Commerce, Ms.16650/1, Seely to Leigh, secretary, LCC, 28 Jan. 1931; also FRBNY, Harrison-Norman correspondence, Harrison to Stimson, 21 Apr. 1931.

194. *BCC*, pp. 257–68.

195. MacDonald's biographer makes light of his interest in a national government: Marquand, *Ramsay MacDonald*, pp. 576–81. But see *BCC*, pp. 260, 265, 274–5, 278–9.

196. 'Le franc au secours de la livre', *Les Nouvelles Economiques et Financières*, 6 Mar. 1931, p. 1, which affirmed that sterling 'est rongé par le chancre du socialisme', and objected to British demands that France should pay the cost 'de leur vanité et de leur ignorance'; 'Doutes sur l'efficacité de la nouvelle mesure de la Banque de France', *Agence Economique et Financière*, 14 Jan. 1931, p. 1; also BdF, carton 1069199521/44 'Grande Bretagne', 'Note sur la politique industrielle de la Banque d'Angleterre', by H. Pouyanne, 29 Jul. 1930; CAB27/435, T.P.C.(30) 1st Meeting, Cabinet Committee on Trade Policy, 1 Dec. 1930, statement by Snowden; R. H. Brand papers, 31, Keynes to Brand, 7 Mar. 1931; MF, F^{30}/807, 'Rapport sur la Situation Financière de l'Angleterre en 1930', by J. Rueff, 15 Apr. 1931.

197. MF, F^{30}/B12613, Rueff to Flandin and Moret, 29 Jul. 1930; MGC., bundle 'Morgan & Cie., Misc.13', Michael Herbert memorandum on visit to Paris, 10 Dec. 1930; FRBNY, Harrison-Norman correspondence, Harrison to Stimson, 21 Apr. 1931; also BoE, ADM 34/19, Norman diary, 5 Feb. 1931, where Norman recorded his efforts to dissuade Lord Bearsted from transferring his sterling balances into dollars.

198. *Documents Diplomatiques Belges*, ii, doc. 221, Vanlangenhove-Colijn conversation, 21 Nov. 1930; van Roon, *Small States in Years of Depression*, p. 73. The Convention was published in *L'Europe Nouvelle*, 24 Jan. 1931, pp. 121–3.

199. 'The Choice before Europe', *Economist*, 24 Jan. 1931, p. 156.

200. FO371/15688, W218/1/98, Johnstone to Henderson, no. 344, 22 Dec. 1930; FO371/14954, W13832/17/98, Hohler to Henderson, no. 416, 29 Dec. 1930; Noel-Baker papers, 4/221, Chapman to Andvord, 30 Jan. 1931; *ibid.*, Andvord to Chapman, 14 Feb. 1931; *ibid.*, Andvord to Noel-Baker, 17 Apr. 1931; Munch, *La Politique du Danemark dans la Société des Nations*, pp. 36–42; Vanlangenhove, *L'élaboration de la politique étrangère de la Belgique entre les deux guerres mondiales*, pp. 115–16; van Roon, *Small States*, pp. 11–12.

201. FO371/14936, W7680/7399/50, Erskine to Henderson, no. 373, 23 Jul. 1930; *ibid.*, W9119/7399/50, Broadmead to Henderson, no. 438, 2 Sept. 1930.

202. *Ibid.*, W10320/7399/50, Erskine to Henderson, no. 471, 30 Sept. 1930, and minute by A. Leeper, 7 Oct. 1930; W11292/7399/50, Palairet to Henderson, no. 343, 21 Oct. 1930; W12816/7399/50, Erskine to Henderson, no. 538, 24 Nov. 1930; MAE, SdN IJ-QEF 1433, Puaux to Briand, no. 445, 19 Oct. 1930; Charles Roux to Briand, no. 315, 23 Oct. 1930; 1434, Gautier to Briand, no. 3 C.E., 19 Nov. 1930.

203. MAE, Série Y Internationale 1918–40, 632, Gautier to Briand for Flandin and Sérot, no. 4 C.E., 20 Nov. 1930; no. 5 C.E., 20 Nov. 1930; no. 6 C.E. 21 Nov. 1930.

204. 'The United States of Europe', *European Finance*, 23 May 1930, p. 175; Loucheur, 'Economic Federation of Europe', *ibid.*, 27 Jun. 1930, p. 291; MAE, SdN Union Européenne 5, Loucheur to Briand, no. 8359B, 20 Dec. 1930.

205. MAE, SdN UE 5, 'Note du rôle de l'Allemagne en Europe Centrale', by Léger, 1 Dec. 1930; F. Seydoux (Geneva) note for Coulondre, 26 Dec. 1930; F. Seydoux note for Massigli, 29 Dec. 1930; Fouques Duparq note, 30 Dec. 1930; Dard to Briand, no. 309, 26 Dec. 1930; SdN UE 14, François Seydoux 'Note pour M. Arnal', 31 Dec. 1930; 'Note sur le Problème des Etats Agricoles' (unsigned, undated,? F. Seydoux, *c.* 12 Jan. 1931).

206. MAE, PA-AP 166-Tardieu 523, Pernot to Tardieu, 6 Aug. 1930

207. MAE, SdN UE 5, de Margerie to Briand, nos 148-53, 10 Feb. 1931.

208. *Ibid.*

209. *Ibid.*, Avenol note to Briand and de Laboulaye, 21 Jan. 1931.

210. MAE, SdN UE 14, Briand to Tardieu, no. 202, 31 Jan. 1931; *ibid.*, note by F. Seydoux, 14 Feb. 1931.

211. *Ibid.*, Tardieu to Briand, 17 Feb. 1931.

212. *Ibid.*, Manceron to Briand, nos 49-50, 25 Feb. 1931; Ponsot to Briand, telegram no. 235, 28 Feb. 1931.

213. *Ibid.*, Massigli circular despatch to all principal missions, 9 Mar. 1931; *ibid.*, F. Seydoux, de Laboulaye memorandum, 'Le Ministre des Affaires Etrangères', 6 Mar. 1931.

215. *Ibid.*, Briand to François-Poncet, no. 199, 15 Apr. 1931; François-Poncet to Briand, 8 Apr. 1931.

216. LN, Commission of Enquiry for European Union, 'Economic Depression', 14 May 1931; the index of industrial production (1913 = 100) stood at 144 in January 1930 and 133 in January 1931, Sauvy, *Histoire économique*, i, annexe vi, p. 464; 'France', *Economist*, 21 Mar. 1931, p. 614; *ibid.*, 11 Apr. 1931, p. 783; *ibid.*, 18 Apr. 1931, p. 840.

217. *Industrial Review*, vol. v, no. 4 (Apr. 1931), p. 11. The same journal estimated that if French unemployment were calculated on the same basis as in Britain, 'the actual figure would be well over 1,000,000.' *Ibid.*, vol. v, no. 11 (Nov. 1931), p. 4. The figures took no account of foreign workers who had lost their employment and left the country.

218. *Banker*, vol. XVIII, no. 63 (Apr. 1931), p. 6. The Bank of England lost approximately £13 million of bullion in Dec. 1930 and £15 million in Jan. 1931, but barely £5 million in the 5 1/2 months between 2 Feb. and 13 Jul. 1931: *Samuel Montagu & Co. Weekly Bullion Letter*, various issues 1931.

219. *Ibid.*, 14 Mar. 1931, p. 128.

220. Link and Catton. *American Epoch*, ii, p. 120.
221. 'The State of Trade', *Manchester Guardian Commercial*, 8 Jan. 1931, p. 23; *ibid.*, 2 Apr. 1931, p. 319.
222. 'The Week in the City', *New Statesman and Nation*, 28 Feb. 1931, p. 40; 'Europe', *Economist Monthly Supplement*, 25 Apr. 1931, p. 27; *Wirtschaft und Statistik*, 2nd heft, Aug. 1931, p. 589, etc.; Borchardt, *Perspectives*, p. 146.
223. 'The Open Question', *Economist*, 7 Mar. 1931, p. 483.
224. *Financial Times Banking Supplement*, 30 Mar. 1931, p. 17.
225. FO371/15162, Rumbold to Henderson, no. 337, 6 May 1931; Graml, *Zwischen Stresemann und Hitler*, pp. 90–1.
226. BdF, 1069199005/33, Attaché financier, Berlin, revue de presse, 21, 24, 31 Mar. 1931.
227. *DBFP*, 2nd ser, ii, doc. 1, de Fleuriau to Henderson, 20 Mar. 1931; *ibid.*, doc. 3, Henderson to Rumbold, 25 Mar. 1931, enclosing de Fleuriau to Henderson, 23 Mar. 1931; FO371/15159, C2347/673/3, memorandum of conversation with Léger by Wigram, 27 Mar. 1931.
228. Suval, *The Anschluss Question in the Weimar Era*, p. 151; *DBFP*, 2nd ser, ii, doc. 3, Henderson to Rumbold, no. 286, 25 Mar. 1931, enclosing de Fleuriau to Henderson, 23 Mar. 1931; *ibid.*, doc. 5, Tyrrell to Rumbold and Phipps, no. 1, 25 Mar. 1931; *ibid.*, doc. 15, Henderson to Rumbold, no. 322, 31 Mar. 1931.
229. FO371/15159, C2349/673/3, Tyrrell to Henderson, no. 72, 9 Apr. 1931; FO371/15160, C2631/673/3, R. Campbell to Vansittart, 19 Apr. 1931.
230. 'Germany and Austria', *Times*, 24 Mar. 1931, p. 17; 'A Sensible Suggestion', *Times*, 26 Mar. 1931, p. 15; 'Germany and Austria', *Economist*, 28 Mar. 1931, pp. 659–60; 'The Austro-German Convention', *Statist*, 28 Mar. 1931, p. 499; 'Comments', *New Statesman and Nation*, 28 Mar. 1931, p. 169; E. F. Wise, M.P. 'The Austro-German Union', *New Leader*, 3 Apr. 1931, p. 9.
231. Stimson diary, 8 Apr. 1931.
232. FO371/15159, C2270/673/3, Rumbold to Henderson, no. 237, 1 Apr. 1931; *ibid.*, C2273/673/3, Rumbold to Henderson, no. 253, 3 Apr. 1931, with enclosure by Thelwall, 2 Apr. 1931; C2274/673/3, Rumbold to Henderson, no. 254, 3 Apr. 1931; FO371/15160, C2706/673/3, Rumbold to Henderson, no. 292, 17 Apr. 1931, with enclosure by Thelwall, 16 Apr. 1931.
233. *ADAP*, Serie B, Band XVII, no. 41, Neurath to AA, 25 Mar. 1931; FO371/15160, C2274/673/3, minute by Sargent, 9 Apr., minute by Vansittart, 11 Apr. 1931; *ibid.*, C2462/673/3, memorandum by Sargent, 14 Apr. 1931.
234. FO371/15160, C2701/673/3, memorandum by Noel Baker, 18 Apr. 1931; also FO371/15159, C2502/673/3, minute by Noel Baker, 16 Apr. 1931.
235. FO371/15160, C2703/673/3, memorandum by Sargent, 22 Apr. 1931.
236. MAE, RC C-Autriche 31, Briand to Charles Roux, nos 649-64, 28 Apr. 1931.
237. MF, F^{30}/1384, 'Mémoire sur l'Anschluss économique', by François-Poncet, n.d., received at Ministry of Finance, 15 Apr. 1931.
238. *Ibid.*, 'Memorandum Flandin', 16 Apr. 1931.
239. FO371/15160, C2703/673/3, memorandum by Sargent, 22 Apr. 1931.
240. FO371/15160, C2790/673/3, minutes of inter-departmental meeting at FO, 23 Apr. 1931; FO371/15689, W4918/1/98, minute by Noel Baker, 24 Apr. 1931, minutes by Sargent and Vansittart, 30 Apr. 1931.
241. FO371/15159, C2349/673/3, minute by Sargent, 11 Apr. 1931; FO371/115160, C2470/673/3, Phipps to Henderson, no. 22, 14 Apr. 1931; C2538/673/3, Rumbold to Henderson, no. 271, 13 Apr. 1931; FO, Phipps papers, 2/9, Phipps to Sargent, 30 Apr. 1931.
242. FO371/15161, C2966/673/3, 'Memorandum communicated by French Ambassador', 4 May 1931. The proposals were first submitted to the Treasury: T188/19, note by Leith-Ross, 2 May 1931.

243. FO371/15161, C3142/673/3, note by Leith-Ross, 7 May 1931; MF, F³⁰/12614, Rueff to Flandin and Cariguel, no. 58,318, 7 May 1931.
244. CAB23/67, conclusion 27(31)2, 6 May 1931; CAB24/221, C.P.115(31), 'Agreement between the German and Austrian Governments to Conclude a Customs Union', memorandum by Henderson, 5 May 1931.
245. FO371/15161, C2854/673/3, Rumbold to Henderson, no. 312, 24 Apr. 1931. Rumbold sought to involve the King in protecting Bruening: GV, PS/PSO/GV/C/P/586/147, Rumbold to George V, 3 Apr. 1931.
246. FO371/15161, C2981/673/3, Phipps to Henderson, no. 157, 29 Apr. 1931.
247. *Ibid.*, C2927/673/3, memorandum by Pinsent to FO, 27 Apr. 1931; *ibid.*, Drummond to Cadogan, 30 Apr. 1931.
248. *Ibid.*, C2982/673/3, minute by Sargent, 30 Apr. 1931.
249. FO371/15689, W5150/1/98, BT memorandum to Henderson, 2 May 1931. See also the appeal from M. Beerlaerts, the Dutch foreign minister, for a British lead, in FO371/15162, C3376/673/3, Russell to Henderson, no. 167, 12 May 1931.
250. See particularly the remarks of François-Poncet in FO371/15161, C2927/673/3, memorandum by Pinsent to FO, 27 Apr. 1931; also C3180/673/3, Tyrrell to Henderson, no. 534, 7 May 1931.
251. PREM 1/106, memorandum by Sargent, 11 May 1931.
252. PREM 1/105, MacDonald to Vansittart, 15 May 1931.
253. PREM 1/105, Thomas to Duff for Prime Minister, 16 May 1931; PREM 1/106, 'Van' (Vansittart) to 'My dear P.M.', 20 May 1931.
254. FO371/15730, W5383/4884/98, FO to Henderson, no. 36, 18 May 1931.
255. LN, *Official Journal*, minutes of 63rd session of the Council, 18 May 1931, pp. 1068, 1073–4; FO371/15162, C3425/673/3, Patteson to FO, no. 39 L.N., 18 May 1931.
256. FO800/284, Henderson to Tyrrell, 16 May 1931.
257. FO371/15695, W6356/7/98, provisional minutes of CEUE, 6th meeting, 3rd session, 20 May 1931; W6359/7/98, provisional minutes of CEUE, 7th meeting, 3rd session, 21 May 1931; *ibid.*, W6357/7/98, Leith-Ross to Vansittart letter and memorandum, 27 May 1931.
258. 'Annual Report of the Bank of France', *Federal Reserve Bulletin*, vol. 17, no. 3 (Mar. 1931), p. 146; J. M. Keynes, 'A Gold Conference', *New Statesman and Nation*, 12 Sept. 1931, pp. 300–1.
259. T160/398, F12377, memorandum by Kindersley, 2 Feb. 1931.
260. T160/430, F12317/2, memorandum by Leith-Ross, 17 Feb. 1931.
261. MF, F³⁰/B12657, 'Echanges de vues avec les représentants de la Trésorerie Britannique au cours des travaux de la Sous-Commission Européenne', unsigned (? Jean-Jacques Bizot), 24 Apr. 1931.
262. T160/398, minute by Leith-Ross to Fergusson and Waley, 16 Apr. 1931.
263. FRBNY, Harrison-Norman correspondence, Harrison to Stimson, 21 Apr. 1931.
264. FO371/15127, A1786/41/45, Lindsay to Henderson, no. 411, 5 Mar. 1931, and *United States Daily*, 16 Feb. 1931.
265. *FRUS*, 1931, i, Stimson to Dawes, no. 38, 16 Feb. 1931, pp. 608–9.
266. *Ibid.*, Dawes to Stimson, no. 49, 20 Feb. 1931, pp. 609–10; *ibid.*, no. 158, 21 May 1931, p. 617; T175/53, minute by Leith-Ross to Hopkins and Snowden, 6 Feb. 1931; Thomas to Snowden, 16 Feb. 1931; Snowden to Thomas, 17 Feb. 1931; Wedgwood Benn to MacDonald, 12 Feb. 1931; FO371/15487, F2205/672/10, to Henderson, no. 642, 8 Apr. 1931; F3566/672/10, Lindsay to Henderson, no. 937, 8 Jun. 1931; FRBNY, Harrison-Norman correspondence, Harrison to Stimson, 21 Apr. 1931.
267. TWL 173-3, diary, 8 May 1931.
268. FO371/14350, C3358/3358/62, memorandum by Vansittart, 1 May 1930. Copy in *DBFP*, ser 1A, vii, Appendix, pp. 834–52.
269. CAB24/221, C.P.125 (31), memorandum by Vansittart, 14 May 1931.
270. CAB23/67, conclusion 29(31)10, 20 May 1931.

6 In the Eye of the Storm, May 1931–February 1932

1. 'League Assembly Opens', *Times*, 8 Sept. 1931, p. 12.
2. 'Disarmament and Economics', *Times*, 14 Sept. 1931, p. 11.
3. LN, *Official Journal*. Records of the Twelfth Ordinary Session of the Assembly. 9th Plenary Meeting, 12 Sept. 1931, p. 89; 'Another Session at Geneva', *Times*, 8 Sept. 1931, p. 13.
4. Fonds Flandin 51, Briand to Laval, 19 June 1931, claimed that British banks had 1 billion schillings (£30 million) tied up in the Credit Anstalt. But see also Clarke, *Central Bank Cooperation*, p. 182; Cottrell, 'Austria between Diplomats and Bankers', pp. 293–311. A useful chronology is provided in Brown, *The International Gold Standard Reinterpreted*, ii, pp. 1040–6.
5. BdF, DCG, statement by Governor, 21 May 1931.
6. Stimson diary, 26 Mar. 1931.
7. BdF, DCG, 15 May 1931.
8. FO371/15226, C2251/2018/18, de Fleuriau to Henderson, 4 Apr. 1931.
9. FO800/284, Henderson to Tyrrell, 1 Jun. 1931.
10. MAE, SDN IJ-QEF 1237, Berthelot to de Fleuriau and Clauzel, 'urgent', 29 May 1931; *ibid.*, de Fleuriau to Briand. no. 303, 30 May 1931; *ibid.*, de Laboulaye to Clauzel, no. 980 'extrême urgence', 30 May 1931; *ibid.*, de Fleuriau to Briand, nos 309-10, 3 Jun. 1931; MF, F30/B12657, Rueff to Flandin, 4 Jun. 1931.
11. MAE, SDN IJ-QEF 1237, Quai d'Orsay to Clauzel, nos 948-51, 28 May 1931.
12. *Ibid.*, Clauzel to Briand, nos 344-45, 3 Jun. 1931.
13. *Ibid.*, de Fleuriau to Briand, nos 309-10, 3 Jun. 1931; MF, F30/B12657, Rueff to Flandin, 4 Jun. 1931; MF, F30/B31728, Rueff to J. J. Bizot, 12 Jun. 1931.
14. *FRUS*, 1931, i, Atherton to Stimson, no. 175, 8 Jun. 1931; *ibid.*, MacDonald to Stimson, no. 177, 9 Jun. 1931.
15. 'Finances of Germany', *Times*, 6 Jun. 1931, p. 12; 'German Emergency Decree', 'German Cabinet's Manifesto', *Times*, 8 Jun. 1931, p. 14.
16. FO371/15226, C3960/2018/18, Leith-Ross to Vansittart, 7 Jun. 1931; *ibid.*, C4041/2018/18, no. 627, Henderson to Yencken, 13 Jun. 1931, enclosure; *ibid.*, FO800/284, Henderson to Graham, 9 Jun. 1931; FRBNY, Harrison papers, 3115.2, Harrison minute, 8 Jun. 1931.
17. MF, F30/B31728, Rueff to Bizot, 12 Jun. 1931; *ibid.*, MAE, PA-AP, 217-Massigli 91, Avenol to Massigli, 22 Jun. 1931, copy of letter to François-Poncet of 21 Jun. 1931.
18. FRBNY, Harrison papers, 3115.2, Harrison minutes, 15 and 18 Jun. 1931; Fonds Flandin 51, Briand to Laval, 19 Jun. 1931; BoE, OV28/69, memorandum by Francis Rennell Rodd, 20 Jun. 1931.
19. BoE, OV28/69, memorandum by Rennell Rodd, 20 Jun. 1931; MAE, SDN IJ-QEF 1238, Berthelot circular telg. (to Vienna nos 1057-60), 18 Jun. 1931, 18 Jun. 1931; *ibid.*, MF, F30/B31728, Berthelot to de Fleuriau, no. 70,501, 20 Jun. 1931.
20. CAB23/67, conclusion 34(31)1, 17 Jun. 1931; *FRUS*, 1931, i, Atherton to Stimson, no. 191, 17 Jun. 1931; *ibid.*, Atherton to Stimson for Mellon, no. 196, 18 Jun. 1931.
21. BoE, OV28/69, memorandum by Rennell Rodd, 20 Jun. 1931.
22. JRM 30/69/8/1, diary, 17 Jun. 1931.
23. Fonds Flandin 51, Briand to Laval, 19 Jun. 1931.
24. PREM 1/95, memorandum by Leith-Ross to Snowden, 20 Jun. 1931; MF, F30/B31728, Berthelot to de Fleuriau, no. 70,501, 20 Jun. 1931.
25. Feiertag, *Wilfrid Baumgartner*, p. 105.
26. BdF, BRI 25, Crédit Hongrois, 1930–33, Note sur la situation en Hongrie, 13 Aug. 1931.
27. Feiertag, *Wilfrid Baumgartner*, table 2, p. 108.
28. Stimson diary, 8 Apr. 1931.
29. *FRUS*, 1931, i, Atherton to Stimson, no. 175, 8 Jun. 1931. See also his comments to City bankers in BoE, ADM 34/20, Norman diary, 10 Jun. 1931.
30. *ADAP* Serie B, Band XVII, Aufzeichnung Curtius, 10 Jun. 1931.

31. FRBNY, Harrison papers, 3115.2, Harrison minutes, 15 and 18 Jun. 1931; BoE, ADM 34/20, Norman diary, 18 Jun. 1931; *ibid.*, ATM 14/10, Norman to Harrison, 19 Jun. 1931.
32. *FRUS*, 1931, i, Atherton to Stimson, no. 175, 8 Jun. 1931.
33. James, *The Reichsbank and Public Finance in Germany*, p. 190.
34. *FRUS*, 1931, i, memorandum of Trans-Atlantic telephone conversation, 19 Jun. 1931.
35. JRM 30/69/8/1, diary, 14, 21 Jun. 1931.
36. HHPP 985, Stimson to Hoover, 17 Feb. 1931; *ibid.*, President's Diary of Developments 1931, 6 May–22 Jun.
37. The phrase is Hoover's, see HHPP 1009, 'Telephone conversation with Secretary Stimson – 7.00 pm', 18 Jul. 1931.
38. Ferrell, *American Foreign Policy in the Great Depression*, pp. 12–13; Warren, *Herbert Hoover and the Great Depression*, pp. 128, 155.
39. HHPP, President's Diary of Developments 1931, 6 May – 22 Jun.
40. HHPP 1006, paraphrase of telg. no. 67 from Gordon, 2 Jun. 1931; Stimson diary, 5, 6, 8, 9 Jun. 1931.
41. HHPP 1009, 'Telephone conversation with Secretary Stimson – 7.00 pm', 18 Jul. 1931.
42. FO371/15183, C4599/172/62, Hoover's statement to the press, 20 Jun. 1931.
43. PREM 1/95, Fergusson to Miss Rosenberg, 30 Jun. 1931.
44. JRM 30/69/8/1, diary, 21 Jun. 1931.
45. Stimson diary, 8 Jun. 1931.
46. Stimson diary 12 Jun. 1931; HHPP 1006, memorandum by Mills to the President, 18 Jun. 1931.
47. FO371/15181, C4009/172/62, Dudley to R. Leeper, no. 1567, 28 May 1931.
48. 'Text of Mr. Hoover's Address', *New York Times*, 5 May 1931; HHPP 1015, Hoover conversation with Sackett, 6 May 1931.
49. MAE, PA-AP 217-Massigli 91, Avenol to Massigli, 22 Jun. 1931, copy of letter to François-Poncet of 21 Jun. 1931; Edge, *A Jerseyman's Journal*, pp. 192–4; FO371/15182, C4340/172/62, Tyrrell to Henderson, no.- , 22 Jun. 1931; *ibid.*, C4391/172/62, minute by Vansittart, 22 Jun. 1931; *ibid.*, C4452/172/62, minute by Cahill, 24 Jun. 1931; *ibid.*, C4393/172/62, Tyrrell to Henderson, no. 129, 24 Jun. 1931; *FRUS*, 1931, i, French Embassy to Department of State, 24 Jun. 1931.
50. *ADAP* Serie B, Band XVII, no. 187, Hoesch to AA, 17 Jun. 1931.
51. HHPP 984, Edge to Stimson, no. 342, 23 Jun. 1931; *ibid.*, Edge to Stimson, no. 361, 27 Jun. 1931; Fonds Flandin 53, French reply prepared by Flandin and 'modified by Tardieu', 3 Jul. 1931.
52. FO800/283, Tyrrell to Henderson, 30 Jun. 1931.
53. JRM 30/69/8/1, diary, 25 June, 5 and 11 Jul. 1931.
54. Stimson diary, 25 Jun. 1931.
55. Castle diary, 27 Jun. 1931.
56. Eichengreen, *Golden Fetters*, p. 277.
57. FRBNY, Harrison papers, 3125.2, Harrison minutes, 23, 24, 25 Jun. 1931; BdF, DCG, 24 Jun. 1931.
58. FO371/15185, C4851/172/62, Tyrrell to Henderson, no.-, 7 Jul. 1931; BoE, G1/451, 'The Franco-American Agreement about the Hoover Plan [sic]', 7 Jul. 1931.
59. BoE G1/438, Harrison to Norman, no. 225.31, 8 Jul. 1931.
60. BoE G1/438, Harrison-Norman conversation, 9 Jul. 1931.
61. *ADAP*, ser. B, Band xviii, no. 6, Neurath to AA, 2 Jul. 1931.
62. PREM 1/95, minute by Vansittart, 15 Jul. 1931. Vansittart had received general corroboration of de Fleuriau's claim, nevertheless dismissed it as preposterous.
63. FRBNY, Harrison papers, 3013.1, Harrison minutes, 14, 21 Jul. 1931; *ibid.*, 3013.2, Harrison minute, 14 Jul. 1931; BdF, DCG, statement by Governor, 13 Jul. 1931.
64. FO371/15182, C4386/172/62, Vansittart to Henderson and minute by Selby, 25 June, draft telegram no. 442, 25 Jun. 1931.

65. HHPP 1008, Castle to Sackett, no. 98, 2 p.m., 30 Jun. 1931; FO371/15184, C4722/172/62, Lindsay to Henderson, no. 387, 1 Jul. 1931.
66. FO371/15185, C4853/172/62, Lindsay to Henderson, no. 407, 7 Jul. 1931; *ibid.*, C4860/172/62, Henderson to Tyrrell, no. 178, 7 Jul. 1931.
67. *ADAP*, ser.B, band xviii, no. 69, Aufzeichnung Curtius, 22 Jul. 1931.
68. Fonds Flandin 51, 'Note pour Monsieur le Président du Conseil', n.d. (*c.*15 Jul. 1931); FO371/15187, C5286/172/62, Tyrrell to Henderson, no. 171, 16 Jul. 1931.
69. Fonds Flandin 51, 'Les Dépenses Militaires de l'Allemagne d'après le Budget de 1931'.
70. Warner, *Pierre Laval and the Eclipse of France*, p. 23.
71. Laval told Stimson that the Corridor was the greatest bone of contention, but if it could be solved, there would be 'no other difficulty of importance with the Germans.' HHPP 1010, Stimson no. 266, 24 Jul. 1931. See also the observations of Pierre Quesnay, who remained with Laval at the Matignon during Bruening's visit to Paris, in BoE G1/451, Siepmann minute, 20 Jul. 1931.
72. FO371/15938, C83/83/18, Rumbold to Simon, no. 1, 1 Jan. 1932; François-Poncet, *The Fateful Years*, p. 8.
73. *ADAP*, ser.B, band xviii, no. 98, Hoesch to AA, 31 Jul. 1931; MAE RC B-IE 47, press release, 28 Sept. 1931; *ibid.*, Papiers 1940-Léger 6, François-Poncet despatch to Briand, no. 14, 5 Oct. 1931. Not without justice, Laval declared Franco-German rapprochement to be 'la base de la stabilité du monde.' See *ibid.*, RC, C-Allemagne 71, Réunion préliminaire de la Commission d'Entente Economique Franco-Allemande, Paris 15 Oct. 1931.
74. FO371/15187, C5249/172/62, Tyrrell to MacDonald, no. 166, 15 Jul. 1931; statements by Flandin and Laval in *ibid.*, 15188, C5366/172/62, Tyrrell to Vansittart, no. 780, enclosure, 17 Jul. 1931; HHPP 1009, Edge for Stimson to Castle, no. 451, 17 Jul. 1931; *ibid.*, statement by Stimson, 'Conversation between the President and Mr. Stimson at 4 p.m.', 20 Jul. 1931.
75. *ADAP*, ser.B, band xviii, no. 16, Hoesch to AA, 8 Jul. 1931; *ibid.*, no. 25, Aufzeichnung Saurma, 10 Jul. 1931; FO371/15189, C5610/172/62, FO memorandum, Appendix, Tyrrell to Henderson, no. 187, 19 Jul. 1931; *ibid.*, 15191, C5800/172/62, minute by Sargent of conversation with Cambon, 24 Jul. 1931; HHPP 1010, Dawes to Hoover, no. 277, 30 Jul. 1931; Knipping, 'Die deutsch-französischen Beziehungen und die Weltwirtschaftskrise', p. 48.
76. JRM 30/69/8/1, diary, 16 Jul. 1931.
77. HHPP 1009, 'Conversation between Stimson & President, Sunday morning at 9', 19 Jul. 1931; *FRUS*, 1931, i, Castle to Atherton, no. 219, 19 Jul. 1931.
78. Hoover used the term trick or trickery four times with reference to France in HHPP 1008, telephone conversation with Mr Mellon in Paris, 6 Jul. 1931.
79. Castle diary, 19 Jul. 1931.
80. HHPP 1009, Edge to State Department, no. 452, 18 Jul. 1931.
81. Stimson diary, 17 Jul. 1931.
82. HHPP 1009, 'Telephone conversation with Secretary Stimson – 7.00 pm', 18 Jul. 1931.
83. *Ibid.*, 'Telephone conversation with Secretary Stimson [in Paris]', 17 Jul. 1931.
84. *Ibid.*, 'Telephone conversation with Secretary Stimson – 7.00 pm', 18 Jul. 1931.
85. *Ibid.*, Castle to Atherton, no. 212, 15 Jul. 1931.
86. FO371/15188, C5433/172/62, minute by Leith-Ross of conversation with Rueff, 20 Jul. 1931; HHPP 1010, Dawes to Hoover, no. 277, 30 Jul. 1931.
87. CAB29/136, London conference, second meeting, 21 Jul. 1931.
88. *FRUS*, 1931, i, memorandum of a conversation at the residence of the American ambassador, Paris, 16 Jul. 1931; HHPP 1009, 'Conversation between the President and Mr. Stimson at 4 p.m.', 20 Jul. 1931.
89. Fonds Flandin 51, minute by Moret, 'Evaluation des credits d'acceptations sur l'Allemagne', n.d. (*c.*15 Jun. 1931); CAB29/136, London conference, committee of finance ministers, first meeting, 21 Jul. 1931.
90. *Ibid.*, committee of finance ministers, third meeting, 22 Jul. 1931.

91. Borchardt, *Perspectives*, pp. 149–50.
92. JRM 30/69/8/1, diary, 22 Jul. 1931.
93. Hawtrey, *The Gold Standard in Theory and Practice*, p. 115.
94. MF, F^{30}/12639, Rueff to Farnier, no. 56,743, 'Note sur la politique industrielle de la Banque d'Angleterre', 29 Jul. 1930; copy in BdF, carton 1069199521/44 'Grande-Bretagne'.
95. 'The French Gold Shipments', *Economist*, 24 May 1930, p. 1160; 'The Monetary Half-Year', *ibid.*, 5 Jul. 1930, p. 7.
96. BoE OV9/264, Strakosch to Niemeyer, 1 Sept. 1930.
97. Clay, *Lord Norman*, pp. 370–1.
98. CAB23/66, Conclusions, 13(31), 11 Feb. 1931; *BCC*, pp. 299–300.
99. 'Banking Supplement', *Economist*, 9 May 1931, p. 9.
100. CAB58/18, E.A.C.(E.I.) 3, 'Provisional Board of Trade Estimate of Changes in the Balance of Trade', 3 Sept. 1931; CAB27/462, F.S.C.(31) 7, Committee on the Financial Situation, 'Changes in the balance of trade', 16 Sept. 1931; T172/1746, H. D. Henderson, 'The Balance of Payments', 18 Sept. 1931.
101. Moggridge, 'The 1931 Financial Crisis – a New View', pp. 832–9, argues that the balance of payments deficit rather than financial movements was chiefly responsible for bringing down the gold standard and the Labour government. In fact, the Treasury became steadily more concerned about the payments deficit even as the crisis occurred. But it remains the case that the Bank of England had no difficulty defending sterling so long as London served as a haven for flight capital.
102. Clay, *Lord Norman*, p. 384.
103. BoE, G1/438, Harrison to Norman, no. 231/31, 15 Jul. 1931; *ibid.*, Norman to Harrison, no. 223/31, 16 Jul. 1931.
104. 'Finance and Industry', *Daily Herald*, 13 Jul. 1931; also W. N. Ewer, 'France's Menace is – France', *Daily Herald*, 21 Jul. 1931; 'City and Finance', *Daily Herald*, 21 and 22 Jul. 1931.
105. 'City Notes', *Daily Mail*, 13 Jul. 1931, p. 3; also 'New French Gold Raid', *Daily Mail*, 11 Jul. 1931, p. 9.
106. 'Money Market Notes', *Financial Times*, 13 Jul. 1931. The same allegation was made on 12, 14 15 and 16 Jul. 1931. See also, 'Lombard Street', *Financial News*, 14 Jul. 1931; 'City Notes', *Times*, 16 Jul. 1931, p. 17, and 25 Jul. 1931, p. 18.
107. 'City Notes: France Taking Gold', *Evening Standard*, 14 Jul. 1931.
108. Glascow, 'Foreign Affairs', *Contemporary Review*, Sept. 1931, p. 381. According to G.E.R. Gedye, 'France Astride Middle-Europe', *The Contemporary Review*, Oct. 1931, p. 448, French financial imperialism was accepted as a fact throughout Europe.
109. GV PS/PSO/GV/C/M/2329/10, Wigram to Rumbold, 3 Aug. 1931.
110. FO371/15187, C5298/172/62, Tyrrell to Vansittart, no. 174, 16 Jul. 1931.
111. Dalton diary, 27 Aug. 1931.
112. Johnston, *Financiers and the Nation*, pp. 197–8; Johnston, *Memories*, p. 109.
113. The evidence is fragmentary, but see BoE, G1/456, Siepmann, 'Note of conversations with Monsieur Moret on Friday, 7 Aug. 1931', 10 Aug. 1931; Dalton diary, 20 Aug. 1931; MGC, bundle 'Gold Standard 1931', Lamont telegram to Grenfell, no. 2413, 31 Aug. 1931; JRM 30/69/1/260, Rowe Swann & Co., Stockbrokers, circular letter to clients, 3 Sept. 1931; *ibid.*, 30/69/5/180, MacDonald to George V, 14 Sept. 1931; GV PS/PSO/GV/C/K/2330(2)/76, Peacock to Wigram, 11 Sept. 1931; MF, F^{30}/930, Rueff to Flandin, no. 59,056, 20 Sept. 1931; 'The National Crisis', *Banker's Magazine*, Oct. 1931, p. 492; 'Review of the Year', *Times*, 1 Jan. 1932, p. ii.
114. BoE, ATM 14/10, Thompson-McCausland memorandum, p. 11; BdF, Délibérations du Conseil Général, statement by Moret, 27 Jul. 1931.
115. BoE, G1/456, 'Meeting of Members of Committee of Treasury held at 11 a.m. on the 27th July, 1931'.
116. Fonds Flandin 60, Farnier to Flandin, 'Les Avoirs de la Banque de France en Angleterre et aux Etats-Unis', n.d. (*c.* 1 Dec. 1931). Feiertag, *Wilfrid Baumgartner*, p. 103 table 5 and

p. 104, confirms that the French Treasury switched an 'important' part of its sterling balances into dollars shortly before sterling was driven off the gold standard. But it is difficult to be sure of the motive for this operation. In any case, the sum involved appears to have been much smaller than the additional sterling liabilities the Treasury took on that summer and smaller still than the combined additional Treasury-Bank of France liabilities. See MGC, bundle 55, M. Pesson-Didier to J. P. Morgan, New York, 14 Jul. 1931; MF, F^{30}/B897, French Treasury balances in London, various dates; BdF, DCG, 23 Jul. 1931.

117. On the French government's role behind the scenes, see Moret to regents, BdF, DCG, 22 Sept. 1931.

118. BdF, carton 1069199521/18, Grande-Bretagne, 1931–1938, R. Lacour-Gayet, 'Note sur l'émission d'un emprunt anglais à long term', 24 Jul. 1931; T188/21, Leith-Ross, 'Note of a Discussion with French Treasury Experts, 11th Aug. 1931'; T160/431, F12414/01/1, Layton to Snowden, 11 Aug. 1931.

119. BdF, DCG, 27 Jul. 1931; J. Bouvier, 'A propos de la stratégie d'encaisse (or et devises) de la Banque de France de juin à l'été 1932', in Bouvier, *L'historien sur son métier*, pp. 364–5.

120. *FRUS*, 1931, i, Stimson to Hoover, 15 Jul. 1931, pp. 315–16.

121. MAE, Europe 1918–40, GB 288, de Fleuriau despatch to Briand, no. 307, 30 Jul. 1931. In Vansittart's words, 'the anti-French virus is widespread and almost unreasoning – not only in the Cabinet, but in all parts of the House of Commons, in the City and in the Press.' Dalton diary, 19 Jul. 1931.

122. FO371/15194, C6353/172/62, Tyrrell to Henderson, no. 888, 14 Aug. 1931. Among the critical commentaries in the Paris press: F. de Brinon, 'Les suites du plan Hoover et l'opinion britannique', *L'Information Financière*, 26 Jul. 1931; J. Bainville, 'Le sort de la livre sterling', *La Liberté*, 26 Jul. 1931; 'Un ennemi de la France, M. Montagu Norman', *Les Nouvelles Economiques et Financières*, 28 Jul. 1931; 'Le problème de la coopération financière franco-britannique', *Le Petit Journal*, 29 Jul. 1931; 'Les négociations franco-britanniques', *Le Figaro*, 29 Jul. 1931; 'Inflations de crédits', *Aux Ecoutes*, 1 Aug. 1931; 'La Cité peut-elle se passer de l'aide de la France?', *Aux Ecoutes*, 1 Aug. 1931; E. Lautier, 'La verité sur les fluctuations récentes de la livre sterling', *L'Homme Libre*, 7 Aug. 1931; 'L'Ingratitude de la Banque d'Angleterre', *Aux Ecoutes de la Finance*, 8 Aug. 1931; 'L'Homme funeste de l'Angleterre: La disparition de M. Montagu Norman', *Les Nouvelles Economiques et Financières*, 11 Sept. 1931.

123. UK, *PP*, Cmd. 3897, 'Committee on Finance and Industry, Report, June 1931', p. 112.

124. UK, *Reports from Commissioners, Inspectors, and Others*, vii, Cmd. 3920, Committee on National Expenditure Report, Jul. 1931.

125. Mallet and George, *British Budgets*, table III, pp. 558–9.

126. T175/51, Hopkins minute to Snowden, n.d. (C. 23 Jul. 1931).

127. BdF, DCG, 6 Aug. 1931; JRM 30/69/1/260, Harvey to Snowden and MacDonald, 6 Aug. 1931.

128. 'Finance and Industry', *Daily Herald*, 6 Aug. 1931, p. 4; J. C. Rea Price, 'The City Editor's Diary', *News Chronicle*, 6 Aug. 1931; 'Lombard Street', *Financial News*, 5 Aug. 1931; 'Sharp Fluctuations in Sterling', *ibid.*, 6 Aug. 1931; A. S. Wade, 'City Notes', *Evening Standard*, 8 Aug. 1931. As usual, the Foreign Office was left in the dark: FO371/15192, C5995/172/62, Sargent minute, 7 Aug. 1931; *ibid.*, C5997/172/62, Nichols minute, 7 Aug., Vansittart minute, 10 Aug. 1931. 'Money Market Notes', *Financial Times*, 6 Aug. 1931, almost alone produced an accurate account of the events, though without divining the motives behind them.

129. Fonds Flandin 60, Jehan Martin, 'Note pour le Ministre', 5 Aug. 1931; BdF, Banque d'Emission, Banque d'Angleterre, 1397199403/137, 'Note sur les mouvements de la livre sterling', 5 Aug. 1931.

130. BoE, ATM 14/10, Thompson-McCausland memorandum, Harvey to Snowden, 6 Aug. 1931; *ibid.*, visit of Snowden and MacDonald to the Bank of England, 11 Aug. 1931; Swinton papers, 174/2/1, N. Chamberlain to Cunliffe-Lister, 15 Aug. 1931.

131. Samuel papers, A/78.2, Joint Committee to Prime Minister and Chancellor of the Exchequer, 6 Aug. 1931 (copy in JRM 30/69/1/260.)
132. JRM 30/69/1/260, Keynes to MacDonald, 5 Aug. 1931.
133. Addis diary, 17, 18 Jul. 1931; Sabouret, *MM.Lazard Frères et Cie*, pp. 87–8.
134. Kynaston, *The City of London*, iii, pp. 228–9. Bickham Sweet-Escott papers, 'Gallant Failure', p. 56; FO371/15190, C5667/172/62, Cahill to Selby, 20 Jul. 1931; T188/21, Leith-Ross minute, 13 Aug. 1931.
135. FRBNY, Harrison papers, 3125.2, Harrison minute, 8 Aug. 1931.
136. BdF, DCG, 13 Aug. 1931.
137. T175/51, Hopkins minute to Snowden, n.d. (*C.* 23 Jul. 1931)
138. JRM 30/69/1/260, Joint Committee of the British Bankers' Association and the Accepting Houses Committee to Norman, 27 Jul. 1931; *ibid.*, Harvey to Snowden and MacDonald, 6 Aug. 1931; JRM 30/69/8/1, diary 11 Aug. 1931; CAB58/12, EAC(H)145, Sir A. Balfour, 'The Economic Situation', 7 Aug. 1931; 'The Lesson for Britain', *Times*, 27 Jul. 1931, p. 11; 'A Courageous Report', *Daily Mail*, 1 Aug. 1931, p. 8.
139. JRM 30/69/8/1, diary, 17 Aug. 1931; CAB23/67, 41(31), conclusions, 19 Aug. 1931 and Appendix, C.P.302(31); Malament, 'Philip Snowden and the Cabinet Deliberations of Aug. 1931', p. 31.
140. *Ibid.*
141. NC 1/26/446, Neville to Mrs Chamberlain, 20 Aug. 1931; *ibid.*, 2/22, diary, 22 Aug. 1931; BoE, Thompson-MacCausland memorandum, p. 29; Clay, *Lord Norman*, pp. 389–90.
142. CAB23/67, conclusion 45(31), 22 Aug. 1931.
143. The myth of the bankers' ramp originated in the *Daily Herald*, 24 Aug. 1931. See Clay, *Lord Norman*, p. 397; also Labour Party-TUC manifesto, 27 Aug. 1931.
144. NC 2/22, diary, 22 Aug. 1931; MGC, bundle 'Gold Standard 1931', diary of events, 22 Aug. 1931.
145. FRBNY, Harrison papers, 3115.2, Harrison memorandum, 24 Aug. 1931; Reports of Norman's intervention soon reached Paris: MAE Europe 1918–40, GB 323, de Fleuriau despatch to Briand, no. 372, 1 Sept. 1931.
146. *Ibid.*
147. BoE, ATM 14/10, Thompson-McCausland memorandum, 23 Aug. 1931.
148. MGC, bundle 'Gold Standard 1931', diary of events, 23 Aug. 1931; BoE, ATM 14/10 Thompson-McCausland memorandum, 23 Aug. 1931.
149. CAB23/67, conclusion 46(31)1, 23 Aug. 1931.
150. MGC, bundle 'Gold Standard 1931', diary of events, 23–4 Aug. 1931.
151. 256 H.C. Deb 5s, cols 297–313.
152. The Bank's reserve position was reported daily to the prime minister, see PREM 1/97 various dates.
153. MGC, bundle 233, J. P. Morgan & Co. to Morgan Grenfell & Co., telg. no. 31/2450, 17 Sept. 1931.
154. CAB27/462, F.S.C.(31) 2nd meeting, 17 Sept. 1931.
155. CAB27/462, F.S.C.(31) 1st meeting, 14 Sept. 1931; FO800/226, Reading to Snowden, 15 Sept. 1931; F.S.C.(31) 2nd meeting, 17 Sept. 1931; CAB23/68, 59(31), conclusions, 17 Sept. 1931; T172/1746, H. D. Henderson, 'The Balance of Payments', 18 Sept. 1931; T188/286, Leith-Ross minute, 18 Sept. 1931.
156. BdF, DCG, 22 Sept. 1931.
157. FO371/15681, W11075/10755/50, Campbell to Reading, no. 1024, 22 Sept. 1931.
158. *Ibid.*, Osborne to Reading, no. 1495, 25 Sept. 1931.
159. JRM 30/69/1/260, Keynes to MacDonald, 12 Aug. 1931; Keynes's role on the Macmillan Committee is summarized in *BCC*, pp. 282–3.
160. CAB58/2, EAC/12th Meeting, 12 Mar. 1931.
161. CAB58/12, EAC(H)144, Keynes memorandum, 16 Jul. 1931.
162. J. M. Keynes, 'The Budget', *New Statesman and Nation*, 19 Sept. 1931, p. 329.
163. See for instance, Keynes, *Essays in Persuasion*, p. 289; 'What Going Off the Gold Standard Means', *New Statesman and Nation*, 26 Sept. 1931, pp. 365–6; Dalton, *Memoirs*, i,

pp. 290–1; T188/235, Keynes memorandum, F.Q.1, 'Notes on the Currency Question', 16 Nov. 1931.

164. *Times*, 29 Sept. 1931, p. 15, reprinted in *Liberal Magazine*, Oct. 1931, p. 465, and *Essays in Persuasion*, p. 294.

165. Passfield papers, Section IV, Item 26, A. Henderson, 'Labour and the Crisis', 25 Sept. 1931; CAB24/223, C.P.243(31), 'The Present Situation. Memorandum by the Home Secretary', 24 Sept. 1931 (copy in Samuel papers, A/81.3); Samuel papers, A/81.5, 'Note by the Prime Minister of a General Election', 26 Sept. 1931; 'City Notes', *Times*, 22 Sept. 1931, p. 20; 'The World and Its Gold', *Financial Times*, 24 Sept. 1931; 'The Suspension of the Gold Standard', *Statist*, 26 Sept. 1931, pp. 423–4; 'The End of an Epoch', *Economist*, 26 Sept. 1931, p. 548; 'What Going Off the Gold Standard Means', *New Statesman and Nation*, 26 Sept. 1931, pp. 365–6; 'Labour's Constructive Proposals', *Labour Magazine*, Oct. 1931, pp. 262–3; 'England's Crisis and Its Effects Abroad', *Industrial Review*, Oct. 1931, p. 15; 'Finance and Trade', *Empire Review*, Oct. 1931, pp. 291–2.

166. T160/431, F12414/01/2, Leith-Ross to Rowe-Dutton, 28 Sept. 1931; NC 8/12/1, Fergusson to Chamberlain with enclosures from Treasury and Bank of England, 5 Oct. 1931; T188/235, Leith-Ross minute on Keynes's memorandum of 16 Nov. 1931, n.d.; *ibid.*, T175/58, Hopkins minute on Keynes's memorandum, 15 Dec. 1931; H. Clay, 'Finance and the International Market', *Banker*, Oct. 1931, pp. 28–34; 'The National Crisis', *The Bankers' Magazine*, Oct. 1931, pp. 489–98; 'Consequences', *Financial News*, 22 Sept. 1931; 'United the Nation Stands', *Financial Times*, 22 Sept. 1931; 'The Suspension of the Gold Standard', *Statist*, 26 Sept. 1931, pp. 423–4; 'The End of an Epoch' and 'Carry On', *Economist*, 26 Sept. 1931, pp. 547–8, 552–3; 'The Suspension of the Gold Standard', *Lloyds Bank Limited Monthly Review*, Oct. 1931, pp. 386–90; statement by Mr F. C. Goodenough, *Barclays Bank Monthly Review*, Oct. 1931, pp. 2–4; Clay, *Lord Norman*, p. 401.

167. 'The Suspension of the Gold Standard', *Banker*, Oct. 1931, pp. 6–10.

168. T175/56, Niemeyer minute, 26 Sept. 1931.

169. *Ibid.*, Siepmann memorandum to Leith-Ross, 25 Sept. 1931; *ibid.*, T188/28, Leith-Ross letter to H. D. Henderson, 25 Sept. 1931; *ibid.*, T188/20, Leith-Ross memorandum to Hopkins, Philips, Siepmann and Waley, n.d. (*c.* 24 Sept. 1931); *ibid.*, T160/431, F12414/01.2, Leith-Ross to Rowe-Dutton, 28 Sept. 1931.

170. FO800/226, Leith-Ross to Reading, 5 Oct. 1931. See also *ibid.*, T160/431, F12414/01/3, Leith-Ross letter to H. D. Henderson, 30 Sept. 1931.

171. T175/56, 'Secret. The Exchange Position', 8 Dec. 1931; *ibid.*, Hopkins memorandum to Fergusson, 15 Dec. 1931; FO371/15199, C8852/172/62, N. Law to Sargent, 29 Nov. 1931; FO371/15682, W14120/10755/50, FO minute, 10 Dec. 1931.

172. CAB24/223, C.P.243(31), 'The Present Situation. Memorandum by the Home Secretary', 24 Sept. 1931; *ibid.*, CAB63/44, M.O.(31)7, 'Note of Events during the Week ended Saturday, Oct. 3rd, 1931'; *ibid.*, CAB23/68, Conclusions, 69(31)4, 2 Oct. 1931; JRM 30/69/8/1, diary, 25 Sept. 1931; NC 18/1/756, Neville to Hilda Chamberlain, 26 Sept. 1931 and 'postscript', 27 Sept. 1931; *ibid.*, 2/22, diary entry, 29 Sept. 1931; *ibid.*, 18/1/757, Neville to Ida Chamberlain, 4 Oct. 1931.

173. CAB23/68, Conclusion 70(31)1, 5 Oct. 1931; JRM 30/69/8/1, diary, 5 Oct. 1931.

174. CAB27/463, E.B.C.(31)4, 'Manifesto', issued by Baldwin to members of the Conservative and Unionist Party, 9 Oct. 1931.

175. CAB27/463, E.B.C.(31)5, 'Labour's Call to Action', 9 Oct. 1931; Labour Party and TUC, 'Why It Happened' (Oct. 1931).

176. Baldwin papers, 45, Gower to Baldwin, 15 Oct. 1931. As Baldwin's campaign speeches indicated, he needed no prompting to emphasize the risk of catastrophe: 'Conservative Policy', *Times*, 10 Oct., p. 14, 'Mr. Baldwin's Broadcast', *Times*, 14 Oct. 1931, p. 7.

177. 'Sir John Simon', *Times*, 13 Oct. 1931, p. 8; 'Stability or Ruin', *ibid.*, 13 Oct. 1931, p. 8; Jones, *Georgian Afternoon*, pp. 128–9; Kennet papers, 80/13-15, campaign addresses, 13, 17, 20 Oct. 1931.

178. 'Mr. MacDonald at Seaham', *Times*, 13 Oct. 1931, p. 8. See also J. R. MacDonald, 'My Final Word', *Daily Mail*, 26 Oct. 1931, in which he refers to the 'old twenty thousand German mark notes, paid as wages [which] were not worth 10d. in purchasing power', which he displayed throughout the election campaign.

179. 'Mr. Snowden and the Red Light', *Times*, 19 Oct. 1931, p. 18; *New Statesman and Nation*, 24 Oct. 1931, p. 504, referred sarcastically to 'Snowdenism Run Mad'.

180. 'A Final Word', *Times*, 27 Oct. 1931, p. 11.

181. 'The Victory Complete', *Times*, 29 Oct. 1931, p. 12; 'The Voters' Verdict', *Economist*, 31 Oct. 1931, p. 795.

182. NC 18/1/756, Neville to Hilda Chamberlain, 26 Sept. 1931; *ibid.*, 18/1/757, Neville to Ida Chamberlain, 4 Oct. 1931; *ibid.*, 18/1/765, Neville to Ida Chamberlain, 12 Dec. 1931.

183. Chamberlain, *The Struggle for Peace*, p. 11; 260 H.C. Deb 5s, cols 2108–14, 10 Dec. 1931. Amery later observed of Chamberlain that 'the Treasury and City influences were too strong for a Chancellor of the Exchequer who...never really understood monetary problems.' *My Political Life*, iii, p. 81.

184. NC 18/1/764, Neville to Hilda Chamberlain, 6 Dec. 1931; Feiling, *The Life of Neville Chamberlain*, p. 201.

185. CAB23/69, conclusion 73(31)3, 3 Nov. 1931; *ibid.*, conclusion 75(31)4, 11 Nov. 1931; *ibid.*, conclusion 79(31)16, 18 Nov. 1931.

186. *Ibid.*, conclusion 77(31)3, 13 Nov. 1931; *ibid.*, conclusion 79(31)13, 18 Nov. 1931.

187. *Ibid.*, conclusion 81(31)5, Nov. 1931.

188. *Ibid.*, conclusion 84(31)2, 2 Dec. 1931.

189. NC 18/1/763, Neville to Ida Chamberlain, 29 Nov. 1931.

190. *Ibid.*, 18/1/764, letter to Ida, *c.* 6 Dec. 1931; CAB58/2, E.A.C./14th Meeting, 15 Jan. 1932.

191. FO371/15707, W12764/47/98, minutes by Howard Smith, 24, 25 Nov. 1931; *ibid.*, T160/646, F10685/6, Fergusson to Leith-Ross, n.d. (*c.* 10 Dec. 1931); *ibid.*, CAB23/69, conclusion 91(31)2, 15 Dec. 1931.

192. CAB27/467, B.T.(31)5th Mtg, 18 Jan. 1932.

193. Runciman papers 245, Runciman to MacDonald, 21 Dec. 1931; NC 7/11/25/41, letter to Snowden, 15 Jan. 1932; *ibid.*, 7/11/25/42, Snowden to Chamberlain, 16 Jan. 1932; CAB27/467, C.P.25(32), 'Memorandum of Dissent from the Committee's Report by the Lord Privy Seal', 18 Jan. 1932; *ibid.*, C.P.32(32), 'Memorandum by the Home Secretary', 19 Jan. 1932; Samuel papers A/87.1, 'Course or Political Events – Jan. 18th – 23rd 1932'; *ibid.*, A/87.2, press statement, 25 Jan. 1932; CAB23/70, conclusion 5(32) Appendix, 21 Jan. 1932; *ibid.*, conclusion 7(32)1–3, 22 Jan. 1932; JRM 30/69/8/1, diary, 22 Jan. 1932; Amery, *My Political Life*, iii, p. 76; Snowden, *An Autobiography*, ii, pp. 1007–10.

194. NC 18/1/763, Neville to Ida Chamberlain, 29 Nov. 1931; *ibid.*, Bridgeman to Chamberlain, 29 Dec. 1931.

195. 261 H.C. Deb 5s, col. 284; Feiling, *The Life of Neville Chamberlain*, pp. 204–5.

196. 'The Weakness of Sterling', *Economist*, 5 Dec. 1931, p. 1060.

197. As Chamberlain put it on 9 May 1932, 'the provision of cheap and abundant supplies of money.' 265 H.C. Deb 5s, col. 1673.

198. Ordinary expenditure for 1932–3 was estimated at £733,510,000, of which £276,000,000 was required for interest and management of the national debt; the saving from the 1932 conversion was £27,750,000: 'Government Returns, &c', *Economist*, 5 Nov. 1932, p. 853; '£1,850,000,000', *Statist*, 20 Aug. 1932, p. 245. On the effect of later conversions, Aldcroft, *The Interwar Economy*, p. 335.

199. Toreador, 'The Week in the City', *New Statesman and Nation*, 28 Nov. 1931, p. 688.

200. German note cover stood at 31.2 per cent on 2 October, at 30.1 per cent on 9 October and at 28.6 per cent on 17 October: 'A Diary of the Crisis', *Economist*, 10 Oct. 1931, p. 647, 17 Oct. 1931, p. 698, 24 Oct. 1931, p. 749.

201. FO371/15196, C7321/172/62, Rumbold to Sargent, 25 Sept. 1931.
202. Warner, *Pierre Laval*, p. 42.
203. MAE, Papiers 1940-Léger 6, François-Poncet to Briand, annex 4, no. 14, 5 Oct. 1931; *ibid.*, 'Note remise par le chargé d'affaires d'Allemagne le 21 septembre 1931'.
204. FO371/15938, C727/8/18, Rumbold to Simon, no. 43, 19 Jan. 1932.
205. MAE, RC 1930–40, C-Allemagne 71, Réunions de la Commission d'Entente Economique Franco-Allemande, 13 Nov. 1931, etc.; *ibid.*, PA-AP 166-Tardieu 523, Commission Economic Franco-Allemand, Secretariat General. Report on the Organisation and Activity of the Commission, 25 Feb. 1932; François-Poncet, *De Versailles à Potsdam*, pp. 179–80.
206. FO800/285, Selby minute to Vansittart, 2 Oct. 1931.
207. A.-L. Jeune, 'La livre blessée', *Paris-Midi*, 21 Sept. 1931; A. Albert-Petit, 'Une heure critique', *Les Débats*, 22 Sept. 1931; 'La crise monétaire anglaise', *Journée Industrielle*, 22 Sept. 1931. Some of the French press commentary is summarized in FO371/15680, W10993/10755/50, 'Press Comments on the Financial and Political Situation in England', Tyrrell to Reading, no. 223, 24 Sept. 1931; FO371/15681, W11170/10755/50, Tyrrell to Reading, no. 1030, 26 Sept. 1931.
208. T208/152, 'Note sur les causes et les enseignements de la crise financière anglaise', 1 Oct. 1931; C. Rist, 'A French View of the Pound', *Economist*, 3 Oct. 1931, p. 600.
209. The French criminal police service, the Sûreté, sent agents to monitor operations on the Bourse: France, Préfecture de Police de Paris, Cabinet du Préfet, Archives de la Sûreté, Côte B^A 1649 'Crise financière anglaise août 1931', 'Informations de Bourse', n.d. (21 Sept. 1931, etc.).
210. FO371/15680, W10764/107555/50, Campbell to FO, no. 215, 21 Sept. 1931; *ibid.*, W10767/10755/50, Campbell to FO, no. 216, 21 Sept. 1931.
211. FO800/226, Tyrrell to Reading, 25 Sept. 1931.
212. MF, F^30/B12625, Le Norcy to Flandin, no. 59,080, 24 Sept. 1931; FO371/15655, W11360/11360/17, Reading to Tyrrell, no. -, 28 Sept. 1931.
213. The statistics are from J. Chastenet and E. Mireaux letter, *Morning Post*, 5 Apr. 1932. On the official origins of their letter, see FO371/16362, W2868/67/17, 5 Apr. 1932.
214. FO371/15680, W11062/10755/50, Tyrrell to Reading, no. 225, 23 Sept. 1931; *ibid.*, W11065/10755/50, Reading to Campbell, no. 2378, 24 Sept. 1931; FO371/15196, C7599/172/62, Rumbold to Sargent, 5 Oct. 1931.
215. FO371/15197, C7717/172/62, Reading, record of conversations in Paris, 7 and 8 Oct. 1931; BdF, DCG, statement by Moret to Regents, 8 Oct. 1931.
216. This was the scale of the losses on 7 October 1931. By December 1931, they had risen to 3.15 billion francs (£25.4 million), and by 24 June 1932 to 35.5 billion francs (£28.6 million): see BdF 1928–1936, carton 1069199810/24, Convention du 7 décembre 1931, 'Etat répondant à question numero 22'.
217. 'The Dilemma of the Bank of France', *Financial News*, 30 Nov. 1931, p. 1.
218. FO371/15656, W11784/11671/17, copy of letter from Moret to Flandin, 6 Oct. 1931.
219. T160/403, F12666, Leith-Ross to Norman, Snowden and Hopkins, 'Note of an Interview with Monsieur Moret at the Banque de France on the 7th October, 1931'.
220. *Ibid.*, Leith-Ross note of interview with French Treasury, 8 Oct. 1931.
221. FO371/15684, W11768/11768/50, Note of interview with Laval, 7 Oct. 1931.
222. BdF, carton 1069199521/18, Grande-Bretagne, 1931–1938, Harvey to Moret, 22 Oct. 1931; *ibid.*, Moret to Harvey, 22 Oct. 1931.
223. MF, F^30/B12615, Rueff to Bizot, no. 59,425, 12 Nov. 1931, confirming that most of the French Treasury balances in London had been renewed. Between 1 Jul. and 4 Dec. 1931, the Bank of France reduced its London balances from 9.1 billion francs (£73.9 million) to 7.6 billion francs (£61.4 million): see BdF 1928–1936, carton 1069199810/24, Convention du 7 décembre 1931, Moret to Minister of Finance (Flandin), 12 Dec. 1931, 'Etat répondant à la question numero 2'.
224. T188/95, Leith-Ross memorandum, 'Germany and Reparations', 8 Oct. 1931.

225. 'United States', *Economist*, 19 Sept. 1931, p. 516.
226. M. Coste, 'Movements of Capital in France from 1929 to 1933', BIS Monetary and Economic Department, C.B.76 (May 1934).
227. Chandler, *America's Greatest Depression*, p. 104.
228. FRBNY, *Monthly Bulletin*, Oct. 1931, pp. 73–5; *ibid.*, Nov. 1931, pp. 84–5; FRBNY, *Seventeenth Annual Report For the Year Ended December 31, 1931*, p. 13; Chandler, *American Monetary Policy*, pp. 167–70; Clarke, *Central Bank Cooperation*, pp. 218–19.
229. 'United States', *Economist*, 7 Nov. 1931, p. 857.
230. Including the *New York Times* and the *New York American*: FO371/15129, A6303/81/45, British embassy to American department, 16 Oct. 1931.
231. BdF, Banques d'émission des Etats-Unis, no. 14: 1926–1932, 'Memorandum d'une conversation entre M. Moret et M. Burgess, de 11.45 à midi [9 Oct. 1931]'.
232. Fonds Fandin, 60, 'Note sur l'article de Garret', 23 Dec. 1931.
233. HHPP 157, Edge to Hoover, no. 671, 19 Oct. 1931.
234. FO371/15676, W12289/4633/50, Note on Goodenough interview with Hoover on 16 October, Osborne to Reading, no. 1625, 16 Oct. 1931.
235. Edge, *A Jerseyman's Journal*, p. 207; also Hooker (ed.), *Moffat Papers*, p. 47.
236. T160/477, F12505/8, Osborne to FO, 20 Sept. 1931.
237. HHPP 984, Edge to Stimson, 18 Sept. 1931; *ibid.*, Stimson to Embassy, no. 455, 19 Sept. 1931; *ibid.*, 1010, Edge personal to Stimson, 18 Sept. 1931; *ibid.*, Edge to Stimson, no. 591, 25 Sept. 1931; FO800/226, Tyrrell to Reading, 25 Sept. 1931.
238. FO371/15684, W11768/11768/50, note on interview with Laval, 7 Oct. 1931; HHPP 984, Boal to Newton, 22 Sept. 1931, copy of interview of Laval by Bickel, 22 Sept. 1931; *ibid.*, 985, Edge to Stimson, no. 641, 2 Oct. 1931.
239. HHPP 984, Castle letter to Hoover, 31 Jul. 1931 enclosing memorandum of conversation with French Ambassador on 30 Jul. 1931.
240. HHPP 157, T. W. Lamont, 'Memorandum for the President, Re Laval Visit', 20 Oct. 1931.
241. HHPP 1010, S. Morgan memorandum, 'Outline Project for Realizing on the Debts', 30 Sept. 1931.
242. *Ibid.*, Wilson Memorandum, 19 Oct. 1931.
243. Stimson diary, 'memorandum of conference with Laval', 23 Oct. 1931.
244. HHPP 152, Harrison memorandum to Meyer, 8 Dec. 1931.
245. FO371/15196, C7591/172/62, Osborne to Reading, no. 625, 8 Oct. 1931; *ibid.*, FO371/15197, C7717/172/62, Osborne to Reading, no. 1570, 8 Oct. 1931; T160/404, F557/012, Osborne to Reading, no. 1609, 16 Oct. 1931; *ibid.*, FO371/15681, W11767/10755/50, Wilberforce to Willert, no. 375-C, 2 Oct. 1931.
246. FO371/15197, C7967/172/62, Lindsay to Reading, no. 661, 26 Oct. 1931; HHPP 985, 'A Joint Statement by the President of the United States and the President of the Council of Ministers of France, 25 Oct. [1931]'.
247. FO371/15198, C8252/172/62, Tyrrell to Reading, 4 Nov. 1931; *ibid.*, C8227/172/62, Tyrrell to FO, 5 Nov. 1931; *ibid.*, C8385/172/62, Leith-Ross minute of conversation with Rueff, 6 Nov. 1931; 'The Feeling in France: Disappointment and Relief', *Times*, 26 Oct. 1931.
248. HHPP 1011, memorandum of conversation between Stimson and P. Claudel, 3 Dec. 1931.
249. *FRUS*, 1931, i, Castle memorandum of a conversation with von Prittwitz, 20 Oct. 1931; FO371/15197, C8002/172/62, Leith-Ross to Vansittart, 27 Oct. 1931.
250. Castle diary, 24 Oct. 1931; FO371/15198, C8095/172/62, Lindsay to Reading, no. 1668, 24 Oct. 1931; Ferrell, *American Foreign Policy in the Great Depression*, p. 202.
251. FO371/15127, A5930/41/45, Osborne to Reading, no. 1529, 1 Oct. 1931.
252. FO371/15197, C7906/172/62, Lindsay to Reading, no. 659, 23 Oct. 1931.
253. To which Stimson added, 'I, myself, am very much discouraged with the tightness with which Laval is tied up to his people's military ideas.' Stimson diary, 24 Oct. 1931.

254. *FRUS*, 1931, i, Hoover message to Congress, 8 Dec. 1931, p. xiii.
255. Hoover, *Memoirs*, iii, p. 171.
256. FO371/15198, C8359/172/62, Lindsay to Reading, no. 1688, 28 Oct. 1931.
257. FO371/15655, W13372/10611/17, minute of conversation between Simon and Flandin, 18 Nov. 1931.
258. FO371/15652, W13770/4580/17, minute of discussions with Flandin, 29 Nov. 1931.
259. 'Germany', *Economist*, 5 Dec. 1931, p. 1067; 'City Notes', *Times*, 28 Nov. 1931, p. 16.
260. FO371/15652, W13770/4580/17, minute of Discussions with Flandin, 29 Nov. 1931; Bond, *British Military Policy between the Two World Wars*, p. 4.
261. 'France', *Economist*, 21 Nov. 1931, pp. 955–6.
262. FO371/15199, C8833/172/62, Tyrrell to Simon, no. 1281, 27 Nov. 1931; FO371/15200, C9063/172/62, French memorandum on reparations, 4 Dec. 1931.
263. Estimates of British commitments were always very approximate. In the autumn of 1931, the Standstill agreement put British short-term credits in Germany at £55 million, but as the Treasury noted, this did not include credits to industrial firms, £20 million in German municipal bills and certain credits that had not been reported to the Standstill committee: T160/438, F12681/02, Leith-Ross to Rowe-Dutton, 28 Nov. 1931. One City banker believed the Standstill covered only half the City's liabilities in Germany, which included £18 million in municipal bills, £3.5 million in cash advances and £33 million to industry. Hence the total was nearer £110 million: FO371/15199, C8852/172/62, Law to Sargent, 29 Nov. 1931. R. H. Brand of Lazard Brothers offered a similar estimate: *ibid*., C8695/172/62, minute by Simon, 30 Nov. 1931. See also T188/50, minute of meeting between Ball (Bank of England), Leith-Ross and Phillips, 20 Oct. 1931; CAB24/224, C.P.281(31), 'German Reparations: The Standstill Agreement. Note by the Chancellor of the Exchequer', 16 Nov. 1931; T160/438, F12681/02, Norman to Leith-Ross, 28 Nov. 1931; CAB24/225, C.P.306(31), Letter from the chairmen of the British Bankers' Association and the Accepting Houses Committee to Norman, 30 Nov. 1931.
264. T160/F12630/03/1, Leith-Ross note to Chamberlain for talk with Flandin, 27 Nov. 1931.
265. FO371/15197, C8029/172/62, Leith-Ross to Sargent, copy of letter to Norman, 28 Oct. 1931.
266. FO371/15200, C9039/172/62, Wallace (the *Economist*) to Secretary of State, 4 Dec. 1931.
267. FO371/15208, C9443/8480/62, Cowan memorandum of meeting at Treasury on 17 Nov. 1931; *ibid*., C9223/8480/62, Leith-Ross memorandum, 5 Dec. 1931; T160/437, F12630/03/1, Leith-Ross to Norman, 9 Dec. 1931; BoE G1/451, Norman to Leith-Ross, 14 Dec. 1931.
268. T188/95, 'Impression left by the discussion with Monsieur Flandin', 29 Nov. 1931; FO371/15652, W13770/4580/17, 'Record of Discussions with M. Flandin on November 29 [1931]'; FO371/15201, C9511/172/62, Tyrrell to Simon, 8 Dec. 1931.
269. See Ch. 7.
270. Senatus, 'Oeil pour oeil', *L'Avenir*, 17 Sept. 1931, p. 1; 'La réaction de l'opinion française', *La Journée Industrielle*, 19 Sept. 1931, p. 1; 'France', *Economist*, 19 Sept. 1931, p. 517; FO371/15647, W14843/907/17, Cahill to Wellesley, 23 Dec. 1931.
271. 'France', *Economist*, 28 Nov. 1931, p. 1006.
272. MAE, Europe 1918–40, GB 288, De Fleuriau to Briand, no. 655, 17 Dec. 1931.
273. *Ibid*., Ministère de l'Intérieur, direction de la Sûreté Générale, au Ministère des Affaires Etrangères, no. 2030, 1 Dec. 1931.
274. FO371/15655, W13014/10611/17, Simon to Tyrrell, no. 2746, 13 Nov. 1931.
275. FO371/15643, W14099/137/17, Tyrrell to Simon, no. 24, 11 Dec. 1931.
276. T160/437, F12630/03/1, 'Note given to the Chancellor for his talk with Flandin. F.W.L.R.', 27 Nov. 1931.
277. NC 18/1/764, letter to Hilda, 6 Dec. 1931.

278. MAE, Europe 1918–40, GB 288, De Fleuriau to Briand, no. 581, 18 Nov. 1931.
279. FO, Phipps papers, I, 2/21, Mendl to Phipps (Vienna), 20 Nov. 1931.
280. FO371/15201, C9284/172/62, Sargent minute, 7 Dec. 1931.
281. Sauvy, *Histoire économique*, ii, p. 22.
282. 'La bataille du sterling', *La France Économique et Financière*, 19 Sept. 1931; Pertinax in *L'Echo de la Bourse*, 21 Sept. 1931; E. Lautier, 'Le jeu du mauvais cheval', *L'Homme Libre*, 22 Sept. 1931; A. Albert-Petit, 'Une heure critique', *Les Débats*, 22 Sept. 1931; F. de Brignon, 'La Crise Anglaise', *L'Information*, 22 Sept. 1931; J. Lescure in *Le Capital*, 1 Oct. 1931; 'L'Avenir de la Livre', *Radio*, 2 Oct. 1931; F. F. Legueu in *L'Avenir*, 2 Oct. 1931; 'Finis Britanniae', *Les Nouvelles Économiques et Financières*, 2 Oct. 1931; A. Liesse in *L'Economiste Français*, 3 Oct. 1931. Reports clearly warning that France would not escape the consequences included 'La crise anglaise', *Le Temps*, 22 Sept. 1931; 'L'abondon de l'étalon d'or en Angleterre', *La Vie Financière*, 22 Sept. 1931; C. Aymard in *La Liberté*, 22 Sept. 1931.
283. MAE, PA-AP 166-Tardieu, 522, 'Politique économique de la France (1930)', note from Briand to Tardieu, 24 Nov. 1930.
284. 'France', *Economist*, 24 Oct. 1931, p. 756; Lévy-Leboyer, 'Les contraintes du marché', p. 191.
285. 'France', *Economist*, 19 Sept. 1931, p. 517; Germain-Martin, *Le problème financier*, pp. 107–8.
286. 'The Effects Abroad', *Economist*, 26 Sept. 1931, p. 550.
287. Fonds Flandin 60, 'BNF, 14 novembre 1933'; 'French Bank's Affairs', *Times*, 28 Sept. 1931, p. 12; Einzig, *France's Crisis*, pp. 44–5; Bonin, *La Banque nationale de credit*, pp. 159–80; Beau de Loménie, *Les responsabilités des dynasties bourgeoises*, iv, pp. 471, 485.
288. Bonin, *La Banque de l'Union Parisienne*, pp. 371–3.
289. 'A Diary of the Crisis', *Economist*, 10 Oct. 1931, p. 647; *ibid.*, 7 Nov. 1931, p. 851; *ibid.*, 5 Dec. 1931, p. 1066.
290. FO371/15903, C243/18/62, Law to Sargent, 8 Jan. 1932; FO371/16365, W1263/189/17, Cahill to Sargent, no. B.043, 23 Jan. 1932.
291. FO371/15682, W13972/10755/50, Law to Sargent, 7 Dec. 1931.
292. 'French Treasury Loans', *Times*, 24 Nov. 1931, p. 13; 'The French Line: Increased Assistance from the State', *ibid.*, 17 Dec. 1931, p. 11.
293. 'France', *Economist*, 19 Dec. 1931, p. 1176; 'Bank of France: Loss on Sterling Holdings', *Times*, 16 Dec. 1931, p. 12.
294. 'Annual Report of the Bank of France', *Federal Reserve Bulletin*, Mar. 1933, p. 151; Coste, 'Movements of Capital in France', p. 21.
295. Coste, 'Movements of Capital in France', p. 21.
296. CAB24/221, 'An Aspect of International Relations', 14 May 1931.
297. FO800/285, Sargent to Simon, 9 Dec. 1931. See also FO371/15196, C7563/172/62, Sargent minute, 12 Oct. 1931; FO371/15197, C7932/172/62, Sargent minute, 27 Oct. 1931; FO371/15652, W13770/4580/17, Wellesley minute, 1 Dec. 1931; FO371/15200, C8945/172/62, Sargent minute, 3 Dec. 1931; *ibid.*, Eden to Simon, 8 Dec. 1931; FO371/15201, C9284/172/62, Sargent minute, 7 Dec. 1931; FO800/285, Selby to Simon, 14 Dec. 1931.
298. FO371/15201, C9216/172/62, Sargent minute, 11 Dec. 1931.
299. CAB24/225, C.P.301(31), 'Changing Conditions in British Foreign Policy, with reference to the Disarmament Conference, a possible Reparations Conference and other contingent Problems', 26 Nov. 1931.
300. *Ibid.*
301. 'The International Crisis', *Round Table*, Mar. 1932, pp. 227–45, acknowledging the duality of the crisis and calling for Britain to adopt an 'all-in' approach was probably inspired by R. H. Brand of the City merchant bank Lazard Brothers.
302. T160/646, F10685/6, Leith-Ross to Fergusson, 10 Dec. 1931, Leith-Ross to Fergusson, n.d. cf. Watt, *Personalities and Policies*, pp. 5, 101, who, writing before the opening of

the official papers, dismissed Selby's claim that the Treasury sought to suppress any Foreign Office paper.
303. FO800/285, memorandum by Selby, 14 Nov. 1931.
304. CAB23/69, conclusion 91(31)2, 15 Dec. 1931.

7   The Collapse of the Postwar Order, 1932–4

1. 'M. Briand. The Lying-in-State', *Times*, 11 Mar. 1932, p. 11.
2. 'Tributes at Geneva', *Times*, 8 Mar. 1932, p. 16.
3. 'M. Briand's Funeral', *Times*, 14 Mar. 1932, p. 13.
4. Briand's biographers also pass over the speech: Suarez, *Briand*, vi, p. 373; Oudin, *Aristide Briand*, pp. 553–4; Siebert, *Aristide Briand*, pp. 634–5.
5. 'The German Election', *Times*, 15 Mar. 1932, p. 14.
6. LN, *World Production and Prices, 1925–1934*, table 8, p. 23.
7. Mitchell, *International Historical Statistics: Europe*, series B2, pp. 167–8; *The Industrial Review*, vol. VI, no. 1 (Jan. 1932), p. 4; *USDC*, series D1 – 10, p. 126; *Wirtschaft und Statistik*, 2. Apr.-Heft, p. 225.
8. LN, *Review of World Trade, 1938*, p. 8. The comparison is in price in terms of gold.
9. FO371/15220, C2531/136/18, Henderson to Rumbold, no. 425, 23 Apr. 1931.
10. MAE, SdN II-Désarmement 849, Massigli 'Note', 21 May 1928.
11. MAE, PA-AP 006-Avenol 11, Clauzel to Avenol, 20 Nov. 1925; *ibid.*, 37th Session of League of Nations Council, Secret Sessions, 8 Dec. 1925; *ibid.*, SdN SG 835, Clauzel to Briand, nos 21-3, 23 May 1925; *ibid.*, SdN II-Désarmement 860, Massigli 'Note pour le Président du Conseil', 10 Apr. 1930.
12. FO371/15705, W8237/47/98, Tyrrell to Henderson, no. 762, 15 Jul. 1931, enclosure from Briand.
13. British estimates were similar. Between 1924 and 1928 the Reichswehr budget rose from 490 million marks to 827 million marks, and while it declined slightly in money terms during the slump – to 766 million marks in 1932, the year the disarmament conference opened – in real terms it probably remained constant: Wheeler-Bennett, The Nemesis of Power, p. 187 f. 2.
14. FO371/15221, C5293/136/18, Tyrrell to Henderson, no. 765, 17 Jul. 1931, enclosing note from French Ministry for Foreign Affairs.
15. Stimson diary, 24 Oct. 1930, 2 and 3 Mar., 9 Jul. 1931; MAE, SdN IJ-QEF 1106, Resumé of meetings between Briand, Dumont, Henderson and Alexander, 1 Mar. 1931; Castle papers 5, Edge to Hoover, 9 Jun. 1931; FO371/15704, W4975/47/98, note by Drummond of conversation with Grandi, 19 Apr. 1931; HHPP 984, Edge to Stimson, no. 575, 11 Sept. 1931; ibid., Wilson to Stimson, no. 146, 20 Sept. 1931.
16. MAE RC 1930–1940, C-Autriche 31, note by Massigli, 6 Jan. 1932; ibid., SdN UE 24, 'Note pour Berthelot', nos 268-9, 5 Mar. 1932; ibid., PA-AP 217-Massigli 15, Aide-mémoire from Russo to Massigli, 7 Mar. 1932; Knox, Common Destiny, p. 132.
17. FO371/15708, W13899/47/98, Rumbold to Simon, no. 991, 4 Dec. 1931; Herriot, Jadis, ii, pp. 276-7. Evidence exists that Tardieu, a government minister hostile to the peace movement, assisted the protesters. Machefer, 'Tardieu et La Rocque', pp. 11–21.
18. FO371/15938, C1696/211/18, War Office memorandum to FO, 1 Mar. 1932.
19. FO371/15706, memorandum by Cadogan of conversation with Frohwein, 23 Sept. 1931, in Cecil to Reading, no. 107, 28 Sept. 1931.
20. FO371/15938, C1696/211/18, War Office memorandum to FO, 1 Mar. 1932.
21. CAB24/227, C.P.4(32), 'The British Position in Relation to European Policy', 1 Jan. 1932; ibid., C.P.5(32), 'Disarmament Conference. Note by the Secretary of State for Foreign Affairs on the Report of the Cabinet Committee', 11 Jan. 1932.
22. MacDonald diary, 7 Apr. 1932.
23. FO371/16438, W10506/47/98, Cecil to Reading, no. 63, 11 Sept. 1931; CAB23/70, conclusion 2(32)3, 13 Jan. 1932.

24. CAB23/70, conclusion 2(32)3, 13 Jan. 1932.
25. Richardson and Kitching, 'Britain and the World Disarmament Conference', p. 41 are probably right to claim that '[t]he decision effectively sounded the death knell of the conference even before it had started', although the decision by default of the United States also to refuse a Continental commitment and Japanese aggression in East Asia deserve equal consideration.
26. CAB23/70, conclusion 4(32)3, 20 Jan. 1932.
27. Castle diary, 7 Jan. 1931.
28. Stimson diary, 18 Nov. 1931, 5 Jan. 1932.
29. Vaïsse, *Sécurité d'abord*, p. 202.
30. FO371/16369, W2271/300/17, Tyrrell to Simon, no. 247, 23 Feb. 1932.
31. CAB24/228, C.P.98(32), Simon memorandum on conversation with Tardieu, 12 Mar. 1932; *ibid.*, no. 236, memorandum by Simon, 12 Mar. 1932.
32. FO371/16460, W3074/1466/98, Simon to Rumbold, no. 331, 30 Mar. 1932.
33. Hooker (ed.), *Moffat Papers*, p. 59
34. MAE, PA-AP 217-Massigli 8, compte-rendu of Bülow-Massili conversation, 25 Apr. 1932.
35. As MacDonald explained to the Americans, his Cabinet had decided unanimously against 'additional commitments involving military or naval responsibilities in the event of a Continental war.' FO371/16462, W7141/1466/98, minutes of meeting of UK and US delegations, Geneva, 18 June 1932; Stimson diary, 20 April 1932; Ferrell, *American Diplomacy in the Great Depression*, pp. 208–9.
36. MacDonald diary, 1 May 1932.
37. Stimson diary, 19 Jun. 1932; HHPP 1012, memorandum of Hoover conversation with Gibson and Davis, 10.20 a.m. 19 Jun. 1932; Leffler, *The Elusive Quest*, p. 282.
38. Stimson diary, 24 May 1932.
39. Davies, 'France and the World Disarmament Conference of 1932–34', pp. 772–3, argues that Britain, not France, was the chief opponent of the Hoover plan. This was not how Washington saw it: see Castle papers 18, Gibson to Stimson, no. 260, 20 Jun. 1932; *ibid.*, Gibson to Stimson, no. 329, 14 Jul. 1932, memorandum of conversation between Davis and Simon.
40. FO371/16369, W5439/300/17, Tyrrell to FO, no. 654, 11 May 1932. The French political scene is more fully described in *ibid.*, 16370, W8940/300/17, Tyrrell to FO, no. 1074, 5 Aug. 1932.
41. Flandin, *Politique française*, p. 75; Debû-Bridel, L'Agonie de la Troisième République, p. 170.
42. Ziebura, 'Léon Blum et la conception de la sécurité collective', p. 21.
43. FO371/16370, W6320/300/17, Campbell for Tyrrell to FO, no. 763, 1 Jun. 1932; Ziebura, 'Léon Blum et la conception de la sécurité collective', p. 21; France, *Rapport fait au nom de la Commission chargée d'enquêter sur les événements survenus en France de 1933 à 1945*, annexes, i, p. 244.
44. HHPP 985, Gibson to Stimson, no. 355, 20 Jul. 1932.
45. 'Mr. Hoover's Plan', *Times*, 24 Jun. 1932, p. 12.
46. Berstein, *Edouard Herriot*, p. 188.
47. FO371/16482, W11793/11650/98, Nadolny declaration to Disarmament Conference, 22 Jul. 1932.
48. Vaïsse, *Sécurité d'abord*, pp. 316–7.
49. France, *DDF*, 1er sér, i, doc. 6, Massigli to Herriot, 17 Nov. 1932.
50. FO371/16470, W13651/1466/98, 'Declaration', in Simon to Vansittart, 13 Dec. 1932, pp. 377–8.
51. 'Hitler and His Creed', *Manchester Guardian*, 16 May 1933, p. 15.
52. 'Herr Hitler's First Year, Part III – Revolution and Reaction', *Times*, 1 Feb. 1934, p. 15. A year later, the *Times* published a long two-part article by Lord Lothian, the leading liberal, who on his return from visiting Hitler assured readers of Germany's pacific

intentions. 'One thing...about it is not generally understood. It is not imperialist in the old sense of the word.... Its very devotion to race precludes it from trying to annex other nationalities.' 'Germany and France', *Times*, 1 Feb. 1935, p. 15.

53. MAE, Europe 1918–40, GB 270, de Fleuriau to Herriot, no. 718, 12 Nov. 1932 and no. 737, 24 Nov. 1932; *ibid.*, GB 250, de Fleuriau to Paul-Boncour, no.-, 15 Mar. 1933; Petrie, *Life and Letters of the Right Hon. Sir Austen Chamberlain*, pp. 392, 394–5.

54. MAE, PA-AP 6-Avenol 36, Hoden to Avenol, 18 Mar. 1933; *ibid.*, PA-AP 217-Massigli 8, Massigli notes, 2 May, 8 Jun., 1 Jul. 1933.

55. MAE, PA-AP 217-Massigli 9, séance de la commission spéciale du 14 avril 1934; *ibid.*, séance...du 17 avril 1934; Ulrich-Pier, 'René Massigli', i, pp. 230–4.

56. Young, *Power and Pleasure*, p. 216.

57. £600 million was the German official estimate: CAB24/225, C.P.306(31), Joint Committee of the British Bankers Association and the Accepting Houses Committee to Norman, 30 Nov. 1931, circulated to the Cabinet by Chamberlain, 4 Dec. 1931 (copy in T188/150, Norman to Leith-Ross, 1 Dec. 1931). The estimate of £150 million in short-term credits was given by Leith-Ross in T160/443, F12800/020, 'Notes of a Meeting held at the Hôtel Beau Rivage on Thursday, June 30, 1932, at 2.30 p.m.'

58. CAB24/224, C.P.281(31), 'German Reparations: The Standstill Agreement. Note by the Chancellor of the Exchequer', 16 Nov. 1931; PREM 1/117, Salter to MacDonald, 18 Nov. 1931; T188/150, 'Note of a Discussion with the Bankers Committee, 20 November, 1931', by Leith-Ross; FO800/286, Leith-Ross to Simon, 1 Jan. 1932; FO371/15903, C243/18/62, Law to Sargent, 8 Jan. 1932; *ibid.*, C995/18/62, Law to Sargent, 22 Jan. 1932.

59. T188/96, Leith-Ross to Stewart, 26 Jan. 1932.

60. T160/436, F12630/2, Leith-Ross memorandum, 11 Apr. 1932.

61. See below, pp. 422–3.

62. United Kingdom, *PP*, 1932, Cmd. 3995, 'Report of the Special Advisory Committee convened under the Agreement with Germany concluded at The Hague on Jan. 20, 1930', Basle, 21 Dec. 1931, pp. 3, 10–11.

63. FO800/286, Simon to MacDonald, 1 Jan. 1932; *ADAP* Serie B, Band XIX, no. 161, Aufzeichnung Neurath, 6 Jan. 1932; Graml, *Zwischen Stresemann und Hitler*, pp. 188–9. Nigel Law, reporting City opinion, similarly stressed the need to bring the French to heel: FO371/15903, C243/18/62, Law to Sargent, 8 Jan. 1932.

64. *ADAP* Serie B, Band XIX, no. 167, Aufzeichnung Pünder, 8 Jan. 1932; T188/286, Rumbold to Simon, no. 2, 8 Jan. 1932. The German ambassador's presence is confirmed in CAB23/70, conclusion 1(32)1, 11 Jan. 1932.

65. CAB27/466, R.W.D.(31) 3rd Conclusions, 12 Jan. 1932. Leith-Ross, the Treasury official responsible for reparation policy, acknowledged that Britain had encouraged Bruening to speak out: T188/96, Leith-Ross to Chamberlain, 22 Jan. 1932.

66. T160/436, F12630/1, FO memorandum, 11 Jan. 1932.

67. HHPP 1011, paraphrase of telg. no. 81 from Edge, 2 Feb. 1932.

68. T188/96, note of conversation between Leith-Ross and Flandin, 8 and 9 Jan. 1932.

69. T160/437, F12630/03/1, Simon to Tyrrell, 11 Jan. 1932.

70. T188/96, note of conversation between Leith-Ross and Flandin, 8 and 9 Jan. 1932; Warner, *Pierre Laval*, p. 53.

71. T188/96, note of conversation between Leith-Ross and Flandin, 8 and 9 Jan. 1932.

72. . *Ibid.*, Wigram minute, 9 Jan. 1932.

73. FO371/16360, W970/16/17, Tyrrell to FO, no. 27 Saving, 27 Jan. 1932; *ibid.*, 16365, W2439/189/17, Tyrrell to FO, no. 151, 2 Feb. 1932; *ibid.*, W1798/189/17, Tyrrell to FO, no. 206(C), 12 Feb. 1932.

74. The negotiations are summarized in T172/1781, memorandum, 15 Feb. 1932.

75. 'The French Cabinet' and 'M. Laval Resigns', *Times*, 13 Jan. 1932, pp. 12, 13.

76. T160/436, F12630/2, H.M. Consul at Geneva to FO, no.-, 12 Feb. 1932.

77. BdF DCG, 29 Feb. 1932.

78. T188/96, Tyrrell to Simon, no. 21, 15 Jan. 1932; PREM 1/117, Tyrrell to FO, no. 7, 17 Jan. 1932.

79. 'Trade with France, Part II', *Times*, 6 Jan. 1932, p. 9.
80. 'A Challenge of France', *New Statesman and Nation*, 2 Jan. 1932, p. 4.
81. T188/96, memorandum, 'Germany's Competitive Power', n.d.; *ibid.*, Leith-Ross to Sargent, 20 Jan. 1932.
82. CAB24/227, C.P.13(32), Simon memorandum, 'Reparations and Debts – A Bird's-Eye View', 9 Jan. 1932.
83. The statistics are quoted in FO371/16362, W2868/67/17, copy of letter from Jacques Chastenet and Emile Mireaux to *Morning Post*, 5 Apr. 1932.
84. FBI/EA/Glenday/9, 'Reparations', memorandum by R. Glenday, 4 Feb. 1932; *ibid.*, minutes of meeting of the British national committee of the International Chamber of Commerce committee on reparations, 9 Feb. 1932; T160/729, F12829/1, minute on FBI deputation, 17 Feb. 1932. See also T172/1787, Waley minute on Churchill's criticism of Lausanne settlement, 12 Jul. 1932.
85. T188/96, Wigram letters to Leith-Ross, 21 and 23 Jan. 1932.
86. FO800/286, Selby note to Simon, 29 May 1932.
87. FO371/15874, A251/251/45, Lindsay to FO, no. 1, 'Annual Report, 1931', 2 Jan. 1932. See also FO371/15874, W4461/20/50, Washington Chancery to FO, 8 Apr. 1932.
88. See for instance, CAB24/227, C.P.(32), 'The British Position in Relation to European Policy', 11 Jan. 1932, wherein he complains of France's 'hegemony, if not dictatorship, political and financial', in Europe.
89. MacDonald diary, 18 Jan. 1932.
90. MacDonald papers, 30/69/2/12, MacDonald to Stimson, 8 Jan. 1932.
91. *Ibid.*, Stimson to MacDonald, 27 Jan. 1932.
92. FO800/286, note by Simon on reparations policy, 31 May 1932.
93. NA. T188/184, Leith-Ross to Fergusson and Hopkins, 23 Apr. 1932; T172/1788, Leith-Ross to Chamberlain, 27 May 1932; T188/184, Leith-Ross to Brown, 17 May 1932; T188/184, Leith-Ross to Chamberlain, n.d (*c.* 25 May 1932); *ibid.*, Leith-Ross to Butler, 25 May 1932.
94. T188/184, Leith-Ross to Hankey, 9 Jun. 1932.
95. CAB27/488, R.C.(32)6, memorandum by Runciman, 23 May 1932; T188/219, Fergusson to Leith-Ross, 31 May 1932.
96. T188/219, Waley to Leith-Ross, 3 Jun. 1932.
97. FO800/287, Chamberlain to Fergusson telephone message, 1 Jun. 1932.
98. NC18/1/785, Neville to Ida Chamberlain, 5 Jun. 1932; *ibid.*, 18/1/781, Neville to Hilda Chamberlain, 15 May 1932. See also his reference to 'the folly and selfishness of Congress' in Baldwin papers 167, Chamberlain to Baldwin, 30 May 1932.
99. T188/219, Fergusson memorandum, 'The Chancellor's views', 1 Jun. 1932; NC18/1/786, Neville to Hilda Chamberlain, 11 Jun. 1932.
100. T160/436, F12630/2, minute of meeting at the Beau-Rivage Hotel, 29 Apr. 1932; T188/219, Fergusson to Leith-Ross, 31 May 1932.
101. FO800/287, Simon to MacDonald, 2 Jun. 1932.
102. *Ibid.*, MacDonald to Simon, 3 Jun. 1932.
103. *Ibid.*, Simon to MacDonald, 3 Jun. 1932.
104. T172/1815, Lindsay to FO, no. 235, 26 May 1932; FO371/16383, W6278/20/50, minute of meeting of Mellon, Atherton and Simon, 30 May 1932; *FRUS*, 1932, i, Stimson to Mellon, no. 164, 1 Jun. 1932.
105. FO371/16383, W6278/20/50, minute of Mellon-Simon conversation, 25 May 1931; *ibid.*, Lindsay to FO, no. 251, 3 Jun. 1932.
106. T160/477, F12505/10, Lindsay to FO, 1 Jun. 1932.
107. FO371/16370, W7447/300/17, Tyrrell to FO, no. 889, 28 Jun. 1932.
108. Herriot, *Jadis*, ii, p. 308; Germain-Martin, *Le problème financier*, pp. 112–14; Soulié, *La vie politique d'Edouard Herriot*, pp. 401–2. Typical of English-speaking historians, P. J. Larmour writes scornfully of Herriot's notorious 'financial incompetence', but does not explain what options a competent politician in those circumstances might have chosen: *The French Radical Party in the 1930's*, p. 71.

109. Herriot, *Jadis*, ii, pp. 56–7, 293.
110. FO371/16370, W6446/300/17, Tyrrell to Simon, no. 780, 5 Jun. 1932; FO371/16362, W13486/16/17, Campbell for Tyrrell to Simon, no. 1614(C), 5 Dec. 1932; Germain-Martin, *Le problème financier*, pp. 7–8, 38–40, 104; Reynaud, *Mémoires*, i, p. 341; Edouard Berstein, *Edouard Herriot*, p. 187.
111. Herriot, *Jadis*, t2, p. 331; CAB21/357, L.(G.B.F.) 1st Mtg., 'Notes of a Conversation held in the Prime Minister's Room at the Hotel Beau-Rivage, Lausanne, on Monday, June 20th, 1932, at 10 a.m.'
112. FO371/16370, W6482/300/17, Tyrrell to FO, no. 66(R), 6 Jun. 1932; also FO800/287, Tyrrell to Vansittart, 8 Jun. 1932.
113. MAE PA-AP 089-Herriot, 26, Journal, vol. 1, 11–12 Jun. 1932; FO800/287, note of Franco-British conversation, Paris, 6.30 p.m., 11 Jun. 1932; *ibid.*, note of Franco-British conversation, Paris, 10 a.m., 12 Jun. 1932.
114. T172/1787, 'Declaration of June 16th, 1932'.
115. T160/443, F12800/022, note of discussion between MacDonald and Chamberlain, 16 Jun. 1932; CAB63/45, M.O.(32)7, Hankey to Baldwin, 19 Jun. 1932.
116. CAB21/357, L.(G.B.F.) 1st Mtg., note of a conversation, 10 a.m., 20 Jun. 1932.
117. *Ibid.*
118. The phrase is Runciman's, in CAB21/357, L.(G.B.F.) 2nd Mtg., note of a conversation, 10 a.m., 21 Jun. 1932.
119. T188/184, Leith-Ross to Hopkins, 24 Jun. 1932; Baldwin papers, 119, MacDonald to Baldwin, 24 Jun. 1932. Chamberlain used almost the same phrase as Leith-Ross: *ibid.*, Chamberlain to Baldwin, 24 Jun. 1932.
120. Baldwin papers, 119, Runciman to Baldwin, n.d. (*c.* 25 Jun. 1932).
121. MAE PA-AP 089-Herriot, 26, Journal, vol. 1, 18, 29 Jun. 1932; *ADAP* Serie B, Band XX, no. 174, Aufzeichnung Papen, 29 Jun. 1932; CAB21/355, summary of Franco-German meeting, 4:30 – 8:30 p.m., 27 Jun. 1932; T160/443, F12800/021, note of conversation, 12 noon, 28 Jun. 1932; Papen, *Memoirs*, pp. 175–6; Herriot, *Jadis*, ii, p. 322.
122. FO371/15933, C8072/4928/62, minutes of MacDonald-Herriot conversation, 27 Jun. 1932.
123. *Ibid.*, minutes of MacDonald-Herriot conversation, 27 Jun. 1932; Papen, *Memoirs*, pp. 180–5.
124. T160/443, F12800/024, note of first session, 6:15 p.m., 29 Jun. 1932; *ibid.*, note of second session, 9 p.m., 29 Jun. 1932.
125. *ADAP* Serie B, Band XX, no. 193, MacDonald to Papen, 3 Jul. 1932; T172/1787, 'Note of conversation between MacDonald, Runciman and Bonnet, 12.30 p.m., 1 July 1932'; *ibid.*, Leith-Ross to Hopkins, 3 Jul. 1932; T160/443, F12800/020, note of meeting, 6 p.m., 4 Jul. 1932; T172/1787, extracts of minutes of meeting, 5 Jul. 1932, 5 p.m.
126. CAB21/355, British delegation to Baldwin, no. 46, 4 Jul. 1932; *ADAP* Serie B, Band XX, no. 195, Papen to AA, 5 Jul. 1932.
127. FO371/ 16370, W7635/300/17, Tyrrell to FO, no. 96S, 4 Jul. 1932.
128. T172/1787, extracts of minutes of meeting, 6 Jul. (morning and afternoon) 1932; *ibid.*, 'Discussions on Draft Resolutions with the French Delegation, 6th July 1932'; Soulié, *Herriot*, p. 366.
129. United Kingdom, *PP*, 1932, Cmd. 4126, 'Final Act of the Lausanne Conference. Lausanne, July 9, 1932'; *ibid.*, Cmd. 4129, 'Further Documents Relating to the Settlement Reached at the Lausanne Conference'.
130. CAB23/72, conclusion 44(32)6, 12 Jul. 1932; FO800/287, FO memorandum, 'Anglo-French Agreement for Mutual Consultation in regard to German demands for revision of the Versailles Treaty', 14 Jul. 1932; published as United Kingdom, Parliamentary Papers, 1932 (Cmd. 4131), 'Declaration issued by His Majesty's Government in the United Kingdom and the French Government regarding Future European Co-operation', 13 Jul. 1932. The French version is in MAE, PA-AP 89-Herriot 28, 'Accord de confiance', 12 Jul. 1932.

131. Runciman papers 254, Runciman to Chamberlain, n.d.
132. *Ibid.*, Chamberlain to Runciman, 10 Jul. 1932.
133. NC2/16, diary, 19 Jun. 1932.
134. NC18/1/789, Neville to Hilda Chamberlain, 26 Jun. 1932.
135. FO371/15912, C5803/29/62, Lindsay to FO, no. 295(R), 10 Jul. 1932.
136. 'Debts to U.S.', *Times*, 11 Jul. 1932, p. 12; 'Congress and the War Debts', *ibid.*, 13 Jul. 1932, p. 14.
137. Hoover, *Memoirs*, iii, p. 173; Stimson, *On Active Service*, p. 213; Feis, *1933*, p. 19.
138. Myers (ed.), *State Papers of Herbert Hoover*, p. 235.
139. T160/441, F12800/08, extract of despatch, 16 Jul. 1932.
140. *DDF* 1er sér, i, doc. 16, Herriot to Tyrrell, 13 Jul. 1932.
141. 'France and the New Pact', *Manchester Guardian*, 15 Jul. 1932, p. 1.
142. *DDF* 1er sér, i, doc. 10, Claudel to Herriot, nos 474-9, 12 Jul. 1932. Always the optimist, Claudel encouraged hope that notwithstanding the generally unfavourable reception, enlightened American opinion was pleased with France's work at Lausanne: MAE, SdN UE 9, Claudel to Briand, nos 496-501, 16 Jul. 1932. Subsequent reports from Washington displayed no such optimism.
143. *DDF* 1er sér, i, doc. 104, Henry to Herriot, no. 249, 15 Aug. 1932.
144. FO371/15912, C5895/29/62, Lindsay to FO, no. 298(R), 12 Jul. 1932.
145. T160/441, F12800/08, Lindsay to FO, no. 299(R), 13 Jul. 1932. But as the British consul-general in New York wrote, 'Things have not gone well of course…': T160/441, F12800/08, Fletcher to Willert, 15 Jul. 1932.
146. *DDF* 1er sér, *i*, doc. 11, François-Poncet to Herriot, 12 Jul. 1932. The British ambassador reported in similar terms: FO371/15912, C6161/29/62, Rumbold to FO, no. 532, 13 Jul. 1932.
147. *DDF* 1er sér, *i*, doc. 19, de Fleuriau to Herriot, no. 454, 14 Jul. 1932.
148. MAE, SdN UE 9, Massigli to Quai d'Orsay, no. 735, 15 Jul. 1932; *ibid.*, Claudel to Briand, nos 496-501, 16 Jul. 1932; FO800/287, Simon to Davis, 14 Jul. 1932; 'The Franco-British Agreement' and 'Franco-British Declaration', *Manchester Guardian*, 14 Jul. 1932; 'Europe and America', *ibid.*, 15 Jul. 1932.
149. As Jacques Bariéty and Charles Bloch point out, French efforts to assist the Danube were in essence a continuation of the Briand plan and the French 'plan constructif' of April 1931: 'Une tentative de réconciliation franco-allemande et son échec', p. 438.
150. MF, F^{30}/B32307, 'Note sur l'abandon de la politique tendant à maintenir au régime de l'étalon d'or les pays de l'Europe centrale et orientale', 15 Feb. 1932.
151. MAE, RC 1930-40, C-Autriche 43, Coulondre note, 11 Feb. 1932.
152. *Ibid.*, and MF, F^{30}/B32302, Bizot to Monick, 12 Mar. 1932.
153. MAE, SdN IJ-QEF 1240, Rist to Loveday, 2 Feb. 1932; MAE, RC 1930-40, C-Autriche 31, Clauzel to Laval, nos 103-09, 16 Feb. 1932.
154. MAE, SdN IJ-QEF 1240, Massigli to Quai d'Orsay, no. 167, 17 Feb. 1932.
155. MAE, RC 1930-40, C-Autriche 43, Coulondre note, 11 Feb. 1932; *ibid.*, SdN IJ-QEF 1240, Massigli to Quai d'Orsay, no. 167, 17 Feb. 1932; MF, F^{30}/B32302, Bizot minute of conversation with Coulondre, 16 Feb. 1932; MAE, PA-AP 217-Massigli 15, Berthelot to Massigli, 22 Feb. 1932; *ibid.*, Massigli to Berthelot, 27 Feb. 1932.
156. MAE, SdN IJ-QEF 1240, Massigli to Quai d'Orsay, no. 167, 17 Feb. 1932; MF, F^{30}/B32302, Coulondre to Bizot, no. 879, 11 Mar. 1932.
157. MAE, SdN UE 24, 'Projet d'union douanière des pays danubiens', 4 Mar. 1932.
158. MF, F^{30}/B32302, Bizot minute, 7 Mar. 1932.
159. MAE, RC 1930-40, C-Autriche 43, Note Coulondre, 'Situation financière et économique de l'Europe Centrale', 11 Feb. 1932; MF, F^{30}/B32302, Tardieu to François-Poncet, no. 361, 17 Mar. 1932.
160. MAE, SdN IJ-QEF 1240, François-Poncet to Tardieu, nos 504-07, 4 Mar. 1932; *ibid.*, Clauzel to Tardieu, nos 138-42, 4 Mar. 1932.
161. MAE, PA-AP 217-Massigli 15, Berthelot to Massigli, 22 Feb. 1932.

162. MAE, RC 1930-40, C-Autriche 43, Massigli note, 6 Jan. 1932; MAE, SdN, IJ-QEF 1240, Berthelot (for Bizot) to Massigli, nos 214-18, 16 Feb. 1932.

163. MAE, SdN UE 24, Aide Mémoire Italien, Rome, 7 Mar. 1932; *ibid.*, Massigli to Quai d'Orsay, no. 292, 8 Mar. 1932; *ibid.*, Massigli to Quai d'Orsay, nos 306-10, 9 Mar. 1932.

164. MAE, RC 1930-40, C-Autriche 31, Clauzel to Briand, no. 4, 6 Jan. 1932.

165. MAE, SdN IJ-QEF 1240, Massigli to Quai d'Orsay, no. 167, 17 Feb. 1932.

166. MAE, RC 1930-40, C-Autriche 31, Clauzel to Laval, no. 478, 12 Feb. 1932.

167. MAE, SdN IJ-QEF 1240, Massigli to Quai d'Orsay, no. 167, 17 Feb. 1932.

168. CAB23/70, conclusion 18(32)1, 16 Mar. 1932; MF, F[30]/B32302, Simon to Tardieu, 22 Mar. 1932.

169. FO371/16369, W2271/300/17, Tyrrell to Simon, no. 247, 23 Feb. 1932; *ibid.*, 16362, W2772/67/17, Vansittart minute, 7 Mar. 1932; *ibid.*, W2868/67/17, Wigram (for Tyrrell) to FO, no. 307, 9 Mar. 1932; 'Franco-British Relations', *Times*, 10 Mar. 1932, p. 11.

170. 'Pioneer Work at Ottawa', *Times*, 16 Apr. 1932, p. 14.

171. FO371/16363, W1588/109/17, Home Office to FO, 8 Mar. 1932; *ibid.*, W3232/109/17, Note of conversation between Simon and de Fleuriau, 17 Mar. 1932; *ibid.*, 16361, W3541/16/17, Tyrrell to FO, no. 50, 30 Mar. 1932; *ibid.*, FO to Tyrrell, nos 75-6, 30 Mar. 1932; *ibid.*, W4528/16/17, Paris Embassy to FO, no. 529(C), 19 Apr. 1932. The conflict is analysed in Boyce, 'Insects and International Relations', pp. 1–30.

172. FO371/16365, W2542/189/17, Tyrrell to FO, no. 267(C), 29 Feb. 1932; T175/46, BT memorandum, 'Quota Restrictions', 31 Mar. 1932; MAE, PA-AP 166-Tardieu, 528, Rueff to Flandin, no. 60,234, 31 Mar. 1932; FO371/16361, W4437/16/17, Jenkins to Cahill, 11 Apr. 1932; BT 11/82, CRT3623(32), memorandum for Runciman, 'Import Restrictions and Quotas', 11 Jun. 1932.

173. CAB24/224, C.P.290(31), Simon to Tyrrell, 20 Nov. 1931; CAB23/69, conclusion 80(31)3, 20 Nov. 1931; *ibid.*, 86(31)3, 9 Dec. 1931; *ibid.*, 88(31)3, 11 Dec. 1931; FO371/15643, W14219/1137/17, Brown to Selby, 15 Dec. 1931; *ibid.*, W14752/137/17, Fountain to Howard Smith, 29 Dec. 1931.

174. FO371/16360, W1094/16/17, minute by Mallet, 12 Jan. 1932; *ibid.*, FO telg. to Tyrrell, no. 33, 26 Jan. 1932; *ibid.*, W970/16/17, minute by Vansittart, 28 Jan. 1932; *ibid.*, Simon to Runciman, 3 Feb. 1932; *ibid.*, W2043/16/17, Runciman to Tyrrell, 15 Feb. 1932; FO371/16361, W2058/16/17, Tyrrell to FO, no. 39(R), 19 Feb. 1932.

175. CAB23/70, conclusion 18(32)1, 16 Mar. 1932.

176. MAE, PA-AP 166-Tardieu 528, Flandin to Chalendar, 10 Mar. 1932; MF, F[30]/B32307, Bizot to Flandin, 18 Mar. 1932.

177. MF, F[30]/B32302, Rueff to Ministry of Finance, Direction du Mouvement des Fonds, 17 Feb. 1932.

178. MAE, PA-AP 166-Tardieu 528, note by Avenol, 1 Apr. 1932.

179. MAE, SdN UE 9, Massigli 'très confidentielle' to Quai d'Orsay, 1 Apr. 1932.

180. FO800/286, note of MacDonald-Tardieu conversation, 3 Apr. 1932.

181. CAB29/138, A.F.C.(32)2, note of Anglo-French conversation, 2.30 p.m., 4 Apr. 1932.

182. CAB29/138, A.F.C.(32)1, note of Anglo-French conversation, 10 a.m., 4 Apr. 1932.

183. The estimates are from BT 11/223, CRT 2897(32), memorandum by Vansittart in Simon to Tyrrell, 21 Apr. 1932.

184. MF, F[30]/B32302, copy of 'Situation in the Danubian States', FO draft print, n.d.

185. T172/1780, Waley minute to Hopkins and Chamberlain, 30 Mar. 1932.

186. CAB29/138, A.F.C.(32)1, note of Anglo-French conversations, 2:30 p.m., 4 Apr. 1932.

187. MF, F[30]/B32307, 'Note sur l'abandon de la politique tendant à maintenir au régime de l'étalon d'or les pays de l'Europe centrale et orientale', 15 Feb. 1932.

188. CAB29/138, D.S.C. (32) 1st Mtg., stenographic notes of first session of conference, 2:30 p.m., 6 Apr. 1932; *ibid.*, D.S.C.(H)32 1st Mtg., stenographic notes of first meeting of heads of delegation, 11 a.m., 7 Apr. 1932; *ibid.*, D.S.C.(H)32 2nd Mtg., stenographic

notes of second meeting, 2:30 p.m., 7 Apr. 1932; *ibid.*, D.S.C.(32) 2nd Mtg., steno-graphic notes of second session of conference, 10 a.m., 7 Apr. 1932.

189. T172/1788, 'Report of the Financial Experts Appointed by the London Conference of Apr. 1932'; MF, F^{30}/B32303, 'Note pour le Président du Conseil', n.d. (*c.* 20 May 1932).

190. CAB21/356, minute by Shackle, 4 Jul. 1932; T172/1787, Leith-Ross minute, 'The French Proposals as Regards Central Europe', 6 Jul. 1932; *ibid.*, Chamberlain minute, n.d.

191. BT11/223, CRT 2317(32), Leith-Ross memorandum to Runciman, 14 Apr. 1932.

192. *Ibid.*, Runciman minute and O'Malley note to Jenkins, 20 Apr. 1932; *ibid.*, CRT2897(32), copy of Simon to Tyrrell, 21 Apr. 1932, enclosing Vansittart memorandum.

193. Vanlangenhove, *L'Elaboration de la politique étrangère de la Belgique entre les deux guerres mondiales*, p. 123.

194. T160/486, F13017/1, Wingfield to Simon, no. 169, 28 Jun. 1932; MAE, SdN UE 18, Corbin to Quai d'Orsay, 23 Jun. 1932; Van Roon, *Small States in Years of Depression*, pp. 37–40.

195. T160/447, F13017/09/1, D.P.C. Paper 8, 16 Sept. 1932; Van Roon, *Small States*, p. 40.

196. W. Layton, 'Notes of the Day', *News Chronicle*, 22 Jun. 1932; Van Roon, *Small States*, p. 44.

197. 'Free Trade Policy', *Economist*, 5 Dec. 1931, pp. 1059–60; 'Scandinavian Trade Policy', *ibid.*, 9 Jan. 1932, p. 64; 'Two Wise Speeches', *News Chronicle*, 8 Dec. 1931; 'Central Europe and Lausanne', *Manchester Guardian*, 25 May 1932; 'Wanted – Leadership', *ibid.*, 26 May 1932; 'General Reduction of Tariffs', *ibid.*, 19 Jun. 1932.

198. 'The Best News Yet', *News Chronicle*, 21 Jun. 1932; also *Manchester Guardian*, 'Wanted – Leadership', 26 May 1932; *Manchester Guardian*, 'General Reduction of Tariffs', *Manchester Guardian* 19 Jun. 1932; 'Freer Trade' and 'Move Towards Ending Trade Restrictions', *Manchester Guardian* 21 Jun. 1932; 'The Dutch-Belgian Tariff Convention' and 'League of Nations', *Economist*, 25 Jun. 1932, pp. 1400, 1404; 'Belgian-Dutch Tariff Agreement', *Statist*, 25 Jun. 1932, p. 1056, which described it as 'one of the few hopeful developments of the week.'

199. 'Mr Lloyd George and Hoover Plan', *Manchester Guardian*, 27 Jun. 1932.

200. BT11/87, CRT4697(32), Nugent (FBI) to Brown, 20 Jul. 1932.

201. *Ibid.*, p. 45.

202. National trade statistics from Mitchell, *Monitoring the World Economy*, table E1, pp. 576–80; world total from LN, *Monthly Bulletin of Statistics*, vol. XI, no. 11 (Nov. 1930), table p. 446.

203. MAE, SdN UE 18, Massigli to Quai d'Orsay, 30 Jul. 1932.

204. 'The Direction of British Overseas Trade', *Economist*, 21 Nov. 1931, pp. 948–9. The totals exclude re-exports.

205. T160/447, F13017/09/1, D.P.C. Paper 7, 13 Sept. 1932, Part VI: Dutch-Belgian Proposed Commercial Convention.

206. 'Lower Tariff Pact Signed', *Manchester Guardian*, 19 Jul. 1932.

207. T160/447, F13017/09/1, D.P.C. Paper 8, 16 Sept. 1932, containing copy of A. Leeper to Baron de Cartier de Marienne, 8 Sept. 1932; statement by Runciman in *ibid.*, minute of FBI delegation to Board of Trade, 10 Nov. 1932; MAE, RC 1930-40, B-IE 47, Le Trocquer to Chautemps, 24 Nov. 1937.

208. T160/487, F13017/2, Roberts to Simon, no. 389, 6 Dec. 1932.

209. Feiling, *The Life of Neville Chamberlain*, pp. 201–2; Amery, *My Political Life*, iii, p. 76.

210. MacDonald diary, 22 Jan. 1932; Samuel papers, A/87.7, minute, 'Course of Political Events – Jan. 18th – 23rd 1932', 25 Jan. 1932.

211. Feiling, *The Life of Neville Chamberlain*, p. 203.

212. 261 H.C. Deb 5s, col. 284.

213. CAB21/364, joint report of three industrial advisers to UK delegates to Imperial conference, 1 Oct., Appendix 3, record of interview with Bank of England representatives, 8 Jun. 1932; Boyle, *Norman*, p. 284.

214. 'Mr. F. C. Goodenough's Address', *Barclays Bank Monthly Review*, Feb. 1932, pp. 2–3.

215. FO371/15903, A6064/18/62, Law to Sargent, 15 Jul. 1932.

216. 'Uniform Empire Currency', *Times*, 14 Jan. 1932, p. 7.
217. 'A Policy to Help Industry', *Times*, 15 Jan. 1932, p. 7. The appeal was repeated with equal emphasis in 'Way to Revival', a joint statement of the FBI and the TUC, *Times*, 8 Jul. 1932, p. 9.
218. Blackett participated actively on FBI's monetary policy committee: see FBI/C/65, minutes of meetings, 28 Sept., 17 Nov. 1931; also FBI/EA/Glenday/20, Nugent to Blackett, 1 Mar. 1932.
219. 'Management of Sterling: Sir B. Blackett's Views', *Times*, 23 Jan. 1932, p. 12; also 'Sir B. Blackett and Ottawa', *Times*, 5 May 1932, p. 9.
220. R. McKenna, 'The Gold Standard and Monetary Management: The Inescapable Choice', Midland Bank Monthly Review, Jan.–Feb. 1932, p. 4. McKenna followed shortly with statements affirming his support for development of a wide sterling area. See 'The Monetary Outlook and Britain's Opportunity', ibid., Feb.–Mar. 1932, pp. 1, 4; 'Errors and Omissions: Can Half a Policy Pay?', ibid., Apr.–May 1932, pp. 1–3.
221. Toreador, 'The Week in the City', *New Statesman and Nation*, 6 Feb. 1932, p. 180; Sir W. Dampier, 'Introduction', *Lloyd's Bank Monthly Review*, Supplementary Number, Mar. 1932, p. 9; Sir E. Grigg, 'The Vindication of Joseph Chamberlain', *National Review*, Mar. 1932, pp. 325–6; 'Mr. Amery and the Ottawa Conference', *Times*, 11 Mar. 1932, p. 16; 'Remonetarisation of Silver: Sir R. Horne's Plan', *Times*, 15 Mar. 1932, p. 11; 'The Financial Problem: Sir Robert Horne on "Raising Prices"', *Times*, 8 Apr. 1932, p. 11; 'Amery letter', *Times*, 14 Mar. 1932, p. 15; Beaverbrook papers, House of Lords Library, BBK C/47, Boothby to Beaverbrook, 28 Apr. 1932; Sir J. Stamp in 'Arresting the Rise in Prices', *Times*, 24 May 1932, p. 9; See also statements by Amery, Boothby and Cripps in 264 H.C. Deb 5s, col. 1539, 1742 and 1756, 20 Apr. 1932; statement by Horne in 265 H.C. Deb 5s, cols 1578–9, 9 May 1932; statement by Amery in vol. 266, col. 441, 25 May 1932; letter from Col. Sir A. Weston Jarvis, chairman of the council, the Royal Empire Society, to *Times*, 14 May 1932, p. 11; E. H. Davenport, 'A New Currency: I. Goodbye to Gold', *New Statesman and Nation*, 28 May 1932, pp. 697–8; 'A New Currency: II. A Paper Pound and Foreign Trade', *ibid.*, 4 Jun. 1932, pp. 725–6.
222. 'Topics of the Month', *Chamber of Commerce Journal*, May 1932, p. 441.
223. 'Another Problem for Ottawa', *Times*, 2 Mar. 1932, p. 13; letter from Norman Crump, *Times*, 16 Apr. 1932, p. 8; 'A Policy for Sterling', *Times*, 21 Jun. 1932, p. 15; Clay, *Lord Norman*, pp. 411–12.
224. 'Empire Preference and the Home Producer', *The N.F.U. Record*, Feb. 1932, p. 102; *The C.L.A.* [Central Landowners' Association] *Journal*, Jun. 1932, p. 76; *ibid.*, Sept. 1932, p. 204.
225. NC18/1/786, Neville to Hilda Chamberlain, 11 Jun. 1932; CAB27/473, O.C.(31)10th Cons., 10th meeting of industrial advisors to British delegation to Imperial Economic Conference, 13 Jun. 1932.
226. 265 H.C. Deb 5s, cols 1672–4, 9 May 1932.
227. T160/480, F12600/011/2, Waley to Howard Smith, 26 Feb. 1932; T175/58, memorandum by Hopkins, n.d. (*c.* 5 Mar. 1932); T177/8, memorandum by Phillips, n.d. (*c.* 1 Jul. 1932); Sayers, *The Bank of England*, ii, p. 448.
228. NC1/20/1/157, Neville to Mary Chamberlain, 19 Mar. 1932. On his way to Ottawa he wrote, 'I must confess to you that I am very anxious about Ottawa', on account of the Dominions' excessive demands and the unrealistic expectations built up: *ibid.*, 1/20/1/159, Neville to Mary Chamberlain, 13 Jul. 1932.
229. NC18/1/763, Neville to Ida Chamberlain, 29 Nov. 1931.
230. NC18/1/722, Neville to Hilda Chamberlain, 27 Feb. 1932.
231. T160/463, F7768/02/8, Lindsay to FO, 27 Apr. 1932. City bankers also anticipated trouble: see FO371/15903, C3385/18/62, Law to Sargent, 22 Apr. 1932; *ibid.*, C7499/18/62, Jessel to Sargent, 1 Sept. 1932.
232. FO371/15875, A4028/268/45, Osborne memorandum, Jun. 1932.

233. See for instance, the remarks of Lord Riddell, Lloyd George's close colleague, to the American Luncheon Club at the Savoy Hotel, in 'America and the Old World', *Times*, 28 Jan. 1922, p. 5. On French racial interpretations, see Roger, *The American Enemy*, ch. 6, 7. American warnings of 'race suicide' came from, among others, the prominent sociologist, E. A. Ross in *The Old World in the New*, p. 282; Ross, *The Social Trend*, p. 17; Ross, *Standing Room Only?*, ch. 28–29.

234. CAB24/232, C.P.277(32), memorandum by the Lord Chancellor, 'The Ottawa Conference', 3 Aug. 1932.

235. CAB21/363, 'The Canadian Tariff Proposals, Note by the United Kingdom Delegation', 8 Aug. 1932.

236. CAB24/230, C.P.169(32), 'Committee on Trade with Russia, Third Report', 30 May 1932; *ibid.*, C.P.190(32), memorandum by the President of the Board of Trade, 'Trade with Russia', 6 Jun. 1932; *ibid.*, CAB23/71, conclusion 32(32)5 and 33(32)1, 8 Jun. 1932.

237. CAB24/232, C.P.267(32), Memorandum by Minister of Labour, 'Trade with Russia', 28 Jul. 1932.

238. CAB21/363, Note by the Secretary to the British Delegation, 'The Australian and New Zealand Negotiations and a Duty on Meat', 15 Aug. 1932; MacDonald papers, 30/69/1/594, Thomas to MacDonald, 15 Aug. 1932; *ibid.*, Thomas to Harding and MacDonald, 16 Aug. 1932.

239. CAB23/72, conclusion 55(32)6, 26 Oct. 1932; BT11/190, CRT 2187(33), memorandum by Shackle, 24 Mar. 1933; 278 H.C. Deb 5s, col. 1084.

240. CAB32/101, 0.(U.K.)(32)21st Mtg, conclusions of the 21st meeting of the UK delegation, 29 Jul. 1932; *ibid.*, conclusions of the 22nd meeting, 29 Jul. 1932; *ibid.*, conclusions of the 23rd meeting, 30 Jul. 1932.

241. CAB21/364, 'Memorandum by Industrial Advisers Representing the British Trades Union Congress', 8 Aug. 1932; *ibid.*, 'Joint Report to United Kingdom Delegates by Three Industrial Advisers, 1 October 1932: Appendix 1, "Price Levels", 9 Aug. 1932'.

242. CAB32/114, I.E.C.(32)162(CD)(4), 'Report of the Committee on Monetary and Financial Questions', 11 Aug. 1932. Chamberlain's statement is in FO371/16408, W9281/1167/50, Gwatkin to Wellesley, no. 4, 29 Jul. 1932.

243. Jones, *A Diary with Letters*, pp. 49–50; Runciman papers, 254, Runciman to MacDonald, 2 Sept. 1932.

244. CAB23/72, conclusion 46(32)1, 27 Aug. 1932.

245. 'The Ottawa Agreements', *Listener*, 31 Aug. 1932.

246. CAB23/72, conclusion 47(32)1, 28 Sept. 1932.

247. CAB27/475, O.C.(31)86, FO memorandum, 'United Kingdom and British Empire Tariffs in Relation to Foreign Countries', 30 Jun. 1932.

248. FO371/16390, W6574/63/50, minute by Howard Smith, 10 Jun. 1932.

249. FO371/16406, W3498/1167/50, minutes of inter-departmental committee on inter-imperial relations, 17 Mar. 1932.

250. FO371/16409, W9649/1167/50, Ashton Gwatkin to Wellesley, 19 Aug. 1932.

251. HHPP 1016, Chapin to Richey, 28 Aug. 1932, enclosure, Chalmers to Chapin, 22 Aug. 1932.

252. FO371/16387, W2208/63/50, Lindsay to FO, no. 259, enclosing memorandum by Chalkley, 11 Feb. 1932; *ibid.*, 16388, W2743/63/50, UK delegation to LN, no. 75, 4 Mar. 1932.

253. CAB24/233, C.P.316(32), memorandum by the Foreign Secretary, 'The Regulation of Meat Imports in Relation to the International Obligations of the United Kingdom', 26 Sept. 1932; *ibid.*, C.P.342(32), joint memorandum by the Foreign Secretary and the President of the Board of Trade, 'The Regulation of Meat Imports in Relation to the International Obligations of the United Kingdom', 10 Oct. 1932; FO371/16392, W9983/63/50, minute by Beckett, 20 Sept. 1932, letter from Vansittart to Fountain, 26 Sept. 1932.

254. Samuel papers, A/89.1, Snowden to Samuel, 23 Aug. 1932.
255. MAE, SdN UE 31, Coulondre to Quai d'Orsay, no. 5, 7 Sept. 1932.
256. Bonnet cited the figure £120 million in MAE, SdN UE 31, Bonnet to Herriot, nos 22-31, 15 Sept. 1932.
257. MacDonald papers, 30/69/1/302, Bonnet to MacDonald, 29 Jul. 1932; FO371/15923, C6803/58/62, Wigram letter to Sargent, 1 Aug. 1932; *ibid.*, Butler to Selby, 2 Aug. 1932.
258. MacDonald papers, 30/69/1/302, MacDonald to Bonnet, 4 Aug. 1932.
259. *Ibid.*, Bonnet to MacDonald, 10 Aug. 1932, Wellesley to MacDonald, 17 Aug. 1932, MacDonald to Bonnet, 20 and 24 Aug. 1932.
260. MF, F^{30}/1412, Rueff to Ministère des Finances (Mouvement Général des Fonds), no. 60,767, 16 Jul. 1932; FO371/15923, C6524/58/62, O'Malley minute, 28 Jul. 1932; *ibid.*, C6759/58/62, Simon minute, 3 Aug. 1933.
261. MacDonald diary, 7 Apr. 1932.
262. MAE, SdN UE 31, Coulondre to Quai d'Orsay, telg. nos 9-13, 7 Sept. 1932, no. 17, 13 Sept. 1932; *ibid.* Léger to de Fleuriau, nos 990-95, 13 Sept. 1932.
263. FO371/15924, C7721/56/62, Addison to O'Malley, 13 Sept. 1932.
264. *Ibid.*, Bonnet to Herriot, nos 22-31, 15 Sept. 1932.
265. *Ibid.*, 'Exposé relatif à la Conférence de Stresa', unsigned, n.d. (*c.*18 Sept. 1932).
266. T177/10, Waley (for Leith-Ross) to Chamberlain, 30 Sept. 1932; FO371/15925, C8278/58/62, Waley to Perowne, 30 Sept. 1932; *ibid.*, C8292/58/62, Patteson (for Eden) to Simon, no. 83, 2 Oct. 1932.
267. FRBNY, *Seventeenth Annual Report for the Year Ended December 1931*, p. 13.
268. FO371/15869, A1410/187/45, Lindsay to FO, no. 345, 25 Feb. 1932.
269. HHPP 152, minute, 'Federal Advisory Council', 14 Sept. 1931.
270. HHPP 157, minute by Hoover, n.d.; *FRUS*, 1931, i, statement, 8 Dec. 1931, pp. x – xxv.
271. Hicks, *Republican Ascendancy*, pp. 271–2.
272. Chandler, *America's Greatest Depression*, p. 90.
273. FRBNY, *Monthly Bulletin*, Oct. 1931, p. 74, Nov. 1931, pp. 81, 84, Dec. 1931, p. 91, Jan. 1932, p. 4, Mar. 1932, p. 21, Jul. 1932, p. 52; Chandler, *American Monetary Policy*, pp. 104, 167; Clarke, *Central Bank Cooperation*, pp. 218–19.
274. B. M. Anderson, 'Our Gold Standard Has Not Been in Danger for Thirty-Six Years', *The Chase Economic Bulletin*, 10 Nov. 1932, pp. 3–16; HHPP 157 [mis-filed], Anderson to Wiggin, 5 Oct. 1932.
275. 'United States', *Economist*, 19 Sept. 1931, p. 516; *ibid.*, 5 Dec. 1931, p. 1065; *ibid.*, 28 May 1932, p. 172.
276. 'Washington and the Budget', *Economist*, 11 Jun. 1932, p. 1230; 'United States Finances', *ibid.*, p. 1284.
277. Belief in a conspiracy involving the bankers, the British, the French or all of them was widespread in Republican circles at this time: Castle papers 5, Castle to General Dawes, 6 Oct. 1931; HHPP 157: Edge to Hoover, no. 671, 19 Oct. 1931; Geisst, *Wall Street*, pp. 207–08; Sobel, *The Big Board*, p. 286.
278. Chernow, *The House of Morgan*, p. 352.
279. HHPP 159A, Press conference report, 19 Feb. 1932.
280. Cleveland and Huertas, *Citibank*, pp. 177–9.
281. Geisst, *Wall Street*, p. 208.
282. HHPP 152: Hoover minute to George L. Harrison, 26 Apr. 1932.
283. HHPP 1011, Sackett telg. no. 26, 'Confidential for the Secretary and the President', 8 Feb. 1932; Hoover minute, n.d.; Stimson diary, 3, 7 Jun. 1932.
284. Stimson diary, 5 Apr. 1932.
285. *Ibid.*, 11, 12, 14 Jul. 1932. Stimson contemplated resignation over war debts a second time in January 1933: Morison, *Turmoil and Tradition*, p. 44.
286. Chernow, *The House of Morgan*, p. 351.
287. HHPP 152, Meyer to Richey, 14 Sept. 1931; *ibid.*, memorandum by Goldenweiser to Meyer, 14 Sept. 1931.

288. Castle diary, 9 Aug. 1932.

289. Stimson diary, 16 Dec. 1931.

290. Hoover, *Memoirs*, iii, p. 171; FO371/15202, C9782/172/62, Lindsay to Simon, no. 1947, 18 Dec. 1931; *ibid.*, Lindsay to FO, no. 749, 18 Dec. 1931; *ibid.*, C9542/172/62, Lindsay to FO, no.-, 20 Dec. 1931; *FRUS*, 1931, i, Public Resolution No. 5, 23 Dec. 1931.

291. FO371/15202, C9514/172/62, Lindsay to FO, no. 1920, 11 Dec. 1931; Stimson diary, 9, 16 Jan. 1932.

292. B. N. Anderson, 'The Gold Standard and the American Tradition', *Chase Economic Bulletin*, 20 Nov. 1931; also HHPP 157, Anderson to Wiggin, 5 Oct. 1932; FO371/15647, W14633/10755/50, Dudley to Fletcher, no. 375C, 11 Dec. 1931.

293. 'War Debts. Bitter Feeling in Congress', *Times*, 17 Dec. 1931, p. 12.

294. FO371/15869, A1267/187/45, Lindsay to FO, no. 302, 18 Feb. 1932.

295. FO371/15869, A1578/187/45, Lindsay to FO, no. 386, 4 Mar. 1932, minute by Caccia, 19 Mar. 1932; also statement by Rep. Dyer reported in *ibid.*, 15870, A2486/87/45, Lindsay to FO, no. 631, 14 Apr. 1932.

296. FO371/15860, A2365/53/45, Lindsay to FO, no. 604(C85), 8 Apr. 1932; *ibid.*, A2488/53/45, Lindsay to FO, no. 637, 14 Apr. 1932.

297. Crawford, Monetary Management under the New Deal, pp. 17–18; Studenski and Krooss. Financial History of the United States, p. 369.

298. HHPP 562, Fisher to Sen. Frederic C. Walcott, 5 May 1932.

299. FO371/15860, A3086/53/45, Lindsay to FO, no. 794(C85), 12 May 1932.

300. Sir Ronald Lindsay, the British ambassador in Washington reported that Hoover's aim was to draw together the countries still clinging to the gold standard and thus 'to defeat advocates of inflation and other unsound financial nostrums.' FO371/16383, W6314/20/50, Lindsay to FO, no. 245, 1 Jun. 1932.

301. FO371/16382, W5517/20/50, minutes by Mounsey and Wellesley, 18 May 1932; *ibid.*, W5999/20/50, minutes by Vansittart, 23 May and Simon, 24 May 1932; FO371/16383, W6427/20/50, minutes by Craigie, Smith and Mounsey, 6 Jun., and Vansittart 7 Jun. 1932.

302. MAE, PA-AP 089-Herriot 26, minute, n.d. (*c*. 2 Jun. 1932); also MAE, RC, Crise économique mondiale 33, de Fleuriau to Tardieu, no. 343 'très confidentielle', 1 Jun. 1933; *ibid.*, Claudel to Quai d'Orsay, nos 330-36, 1 Jun. 1933, Coulondre minute, 1 June 1933.

303. *New York Tribune*, 16 Jun. 1932, in FO371/15875, A3933/268/45, Lindsay to FO, no. 986, 17 Jun. 1932.

304. Hoover, *The State Papers and Other Publics Writings of Herbert Hoover*, ii, p. 344, also pp. 248, 298, 299–300, 437; FO371/15871, A6015/187/45, Osborne to FO, no. 1323, 1 Sept. 1932; 'U.S. Election: Mr. Hoover in the West', *Times*, 5 Oct. 1932, p. 13; 'U.S. Election', *Times*, 11 Oct. 1932, p. 20.

305. 'U.S. Presidency', *Times*, 24 Oct. 1932, p. 14; 'U.S. Election Campaign', *Times*, 27 Oct. 1932, p. 12.

306. FO371/15912, C7199/29/62, Osborne to Sargent, 12 Aug. 1932.

307. 'The American Presidency', *Times*, 4 Jul. 1932, p. 13.

308. *The Public Papers and Addresses of Franklin D. Roosevelt*, i, p. 659; Nye, *Midwestern Progressive Politics*, p. 323; Feis, *The Diplomacy of the Dollar*, p. 14 and f.; *The Public Papers and Addresses of Franklin D. Roosevelt*, i, pp. 679–80, 683, 717, 749–54.

309. Hoover, *State Papers and Other Publics Writings*, ii, p. 302; 'U.S. Election: Mr. Hoover in the West', *Times*, 5 Oct. 1932, p. 13; Hoover, *Memoirs*, iii, pp. 197, 383–4.

310. 'U.S. Election: Mr. Hoover and Low Taxes', *Times*, 2 Nov. 1932, p. 12.

311. Roosevelt to House, quoted in Leuchtenburg, *Franklin D. Roosevelt and the New Deal*, p. 80.

312. The American Presidency Project, http://www.presidency.ucsb.edu/elections.php

313. *FRUS*, 1932, i, Lindsay to Stimson, no. 354, 10 Nov. 1932; *ibid.*, memorandum from Claudel to Stimson, 10 Nov. 1932.

314. Hoover, *Memoirs*, iii, p. 198.
315. Runciman papers, 259, A. J. Cummings, *News Chronicle*, to Runciman, 9 Sept. 1932.
316. MacDonald diary, 11 Oct. 1932.
317. Moley, *After Seven Years*, pp. 69–72; Tugwell, *Roosevelt's Revolution*, p. 256.
318. Hoover was attacked by Sen. Thomas Gore of Oklahoma for allegedly giving way on the debts, see 'Debts to U.S.', *Times*, 11 Jul. 1932, p. 12. Hoover later claimed he had lost in California because the Democrats alleged that he had entered into a secret deal with the Europeans to reduce or cancel the debts: see Feis, *1933*, p. 34; Moley, *After Seven Years*, pp. 70–2.
319. Hoover, *Memoirs*, iii, p. 183.
320. Moley, *After Seven Years*, p. 78; Moley, *The First New Deal*, p. 35.
321. NC18/1/807, Neville to Hilda Chamberlain, 26 Nov. 1932; Feiling, *The Life of Neville Chamberlain*, p. 219; MacDonald diary, 27, 29 Nov. 1932.
322. CAB23/73, conclusion 63(32) Appendix, 28 Nov. 1932; Clay, *Lord Norman*, p. 447.
323. NC18/1/807, Neville to Hilda Chamberlain, 26 Nov. 1932; *ibid.*, NC18/1/809, Neville to Hilda Chamberlain, 10 Dec. 1932; *ibid.*, Neville to Ida Chamberlain, 17 Dec. 1932; *ibid.*, 18/1/815, Neville to Hilda Chamberlain, 4 Feb. 1933.
324. *DDF*, 1ᵉʳ sér, i, 'Note de la Direction du Mouvement Général des Fonds', doc. 284, 28 Oct. 1932; also *ibid.*, doc. 245, Germain-Martin to Herriot, doc. 687, 15 Oct. 1932; Herriot, *Jadis*, ii, p. 357; Soulié, *Herriot*, pp. 408–15; Reynaud, *Mémoires*, i, pp. 347–8; *FRUS*, 1932, i, Edge to Stimson, no. 717, 14 Dec. 1932; FO371/15916, C10416/29/62, Tyrrell to FO, no. 139, 14 Dec. 1932; *ibid.*, 15917, C10452/29/62, Tyrrell to FO, no. 167, 14 Dec. 1932.
325. See section 7 below. As well as Britain, Czechoslovakia, Finland, Italy and Lithuania made payment on 15 December; Belgium, Poland, Hungary, Esthonia and Yugoslavia lined up with France in refusing further payment: Hodson, *Slump and Recovery*, p. 142.
326. FO371/15913, C8442/29/62, Leith-Ross to Vansittart, 6 Oct. 1932. The British debt to the United States in 1932 was $161,100,000 (£33.1 million), and estimated government expenditure was £766 million; in 1933 the comparable figures were $183,900,000 (£37.8 million) and £779.9 million: 'Annual Payments of America's Debtors', *Economist War Debts Supplement*, 12 Nov. 1932, table p. 15; 'The Budget', *The Statist*, 23 Apr. 1932, p. 633; *ibid.*, 29 Apr. 1933, pp. 646–7.
327. Hoover, *State Papers and Other Publics Writings*, ii, p. 555; Hoover, *Memoirs*, iii, p. 185.
328. Moley, *The First New Deal*, pp. 39–40; Tugwell, *Roosevelt's Revolution*, p. 261; Myers, *State Papers*, pp. 556–7.
329. Myers, *State Papers*, pp. 589; Hoover, *Memoirs*, iii, pp. 202–3.
330. Cleveland and Huertas, *Citibank*, p. 72.
331. Chandler, *America's Greatest Depression*, pp. 119–20.
332. Hoover, *Memoirs*, iii, pp. 213–14, 358.
333. Feis, *1933*, pp. 84–6.
334. Cleveland and Huertas, *Citibank*, p. 189.
335. Friedman and Schwartz, *A Monetary History of the United States*, pp. 326–7; Eichengreen, *Golden Fetters*, p. 325.
336. *The Public Papers and Addresses of Franklin D. Roosevelt*, ii, *1933*, p. 11.
337. See for instance, Badger, *The New Deal*, p. 65; Burns, *Roosevelt*, p. 144; also Hooker (ed.), *Moffat Papers*, p. 77.
338. *The Public Papers and Addresses of Franklin D. Roosevelt*, ii, p. 11.
339. FRBNY, *Monthly Bulletin*, May 1933, p. 35.
340. Feis, *1933*, p. 110.
341. *Ibid.*, pp. 121–2.
342. T188/150, 'Note of meeting with James Warburg', 31 Mar. 1933; FO371/17304, W4009/5/50, Lindsay to Simon, no. 499, 30 Mar. 1933; *ibid.*, 16604, A2836/54/45, Rowe-Dutton to FO, 31 Mar. 1933; *ibid.*, 17304, W3607/5/50, Lindsay to Simon,

no. 191, 31 Mar. 1933; *ibid.*, W3669/5/50, Lindsay to Simon, no. 192, 3 Apr. 1933; *ibid.*, W3763/5/50, Lindsay to Simon, no. 196, 4 Apr. 1933; *ibid.*, W3769/5/50, Lindsay to Simon, nos 198 and 199, 5 Apr. 1933 (copy in T160/487, F13017/3).

343. Hull, *The Memoirs of Cordell Hull*, pp. 246–7.

344. Leuchtenburg, *Franklin Roosevelt and the New Deal*, pp. 43–5, 47–8; Royal Institute of International Affairs, *Survey of International Affairs, 1933*, p. 30.

345. Ickes, *The Secret Diary*, i, p. 23; Feis, *1933*, pp. 125–7; Moley, *After Seven Years*, pp. 159–60; Lindley, *The Roosevelt Revolution*, pp. 120–1.

346. FO371/17305, W4442/5/50, Lindsay to Simon, no. 245, 24 Apr. 1933; *ibid.*, W4443/5/50, Lindsay to Simon, no. 246, 25 Apr. 1933; *FRUS, 1933*, i, joint statement by Roosevelt and Herriot, 28 Apr. 1933.

347. FDR's Second Fireside Chat, Sunday, 7 May 1933, 'Outlining the New Deal Programme', in http://www.fdrlibrary.marist.edu/050733.html

348. MF, F^{30}/1415, Bizot memorandum, 'Stabilisation des monnaies', 12 May 1933; *ibid.*, de la Baume to Ministère des Finances (Direction du Mouvement des Fonds), no. 1730, 23 Jun. 1933; *DDF*, 1er sér, iii, no. 274, Paul-Boncour to Laboulaye, nos 516-20, 14 May 1932; *ibid.*, no. 417, Coulondre to Paul-Boncour, no. 31, 22 Jun. 1933.

349. Remarkably, he did not even consult Hull, his secretary of state, on the appointment of the delegation: Hull, *Memoirs*, p. 254.

350. Warburg, *The Money Muddle*, p. 113; Nixon (ed.), *Franklin D. Roosevelt and Foreign Affairs*, i, pp. 240–1; T188/279.2, 'Note of a Joint Meeting between Treasuries and Central Banks held at the Treasury at 12 noon on June 16th, 1933'; *ibid.*, minute from Phillips to Fergusson 17 Jun. 1933; *ibid.*, Leith-Ross minute, n.d. (*c.* 17 June 1933); *FRUS, 1933*, i, Phillips for Roosevelt to Hull, no. 48, 20 Jun. 1933.

351. France, F^{30}/1415, Bonnet to Daladier and Cabinet, unnumbered, 26 and 28 Jun. 1933; *ibid.*, Foreign Ministry (de la Baume) to Directeur du Mouvement des Fonds (Bizot), no. 1834, 30 June 1933; *ibid.*, memorandum, 'Conditions dans lesquelles la délégation française a pris position à Londres sur les questions monétaires', 30 Sept. 1933; Bonnet, *Vingt ans de vie politique*, pp. 174–5; NC7/11/26/5, Bonnet to Chamberlain, 28 Jun. 1933; *ibid.*, 2/22, diary, 29 Jun. 1933.

352. *DDF*, 1er sér, iii, no. 426, Bonnet to Paul-Boncour, nos 46-51, 27–8 Jun. 1933; FO371/17307, W8346/5/50, H. D. Henderson conference diary, 28–30 Jun. 1933.

353. *DDF*, 1er sér, iii, doc. 438, Coulondre to Paul-Boncour, nos 56-60, 30 Jun. 1933; T172/1811, M.E. Conv.18, Note of conversation in Prime Minister's room, June 28, 1933, at 3:15 P.M., Appendix C; FO371/17307, W8346/5/50, H. D. Henderson conference diary, 29–30 Jun. 1933.

354. MF, F^{30}/1415, de la Baume to Bizot, no. 1845, 4 Jul. 1933; *ibid.*, Bonnet to Farnier, no. 469/50, 22 Jul. 1933; *ibid.*, memorandum, 'Conditions...à Londres ...', 30 Sept. 1933; FO371/17307, W8071/5/50, Tyrrell to Simon, no. 165(S), 9 Jul. 1933; Bonnet, *Vingt ans de vie politique*, pp. 174–5.

355. CAB29/142, M.E.(U.K.)17, statement by Roosevelt, 3 Jul. 1933; *FRUS, 1933*, i, Roosevelt to Phillips, no. 19, 2 Jul. 1933; copy in Nixon (ed.), *Franklin D. Roosevelt and Foreign Affairs*, i, 269–70.

356. Chamberlain was using the term 'bombshell' within 24 hours of the message reaching London: T172/1810A, M.E.(U.K.) 19th Mtg., conclusions, 3 Jul. 1933.

357. FO371/17307, W7746/5/50, Tyrrell to Simon, no. 153(S), 29 Jun. 1933; *ibid.*, W7889/5/50, Tyrrell to Simon, no. 160S, 4 Jul. 1933, T172/1813, draft speech by Chamberlain (not given), 3 Jul. 1933; T172/1811, M.E.Conv.28A, Note of conversation between MacDonald, Cox and Warburg with Hankey present, 3 Jul. 1933; T172/1810A, M.E.(U.K.) 19th Mtg., conclusions, 3 Jul. 1933; T172/1811, M.E.Conv.31, Note of meeting of conference president and vice-presidents, 5 Jul. 1933; FO371/17307, W7871/5/50, Ashton-Gwatkin minute, 1 Jul. 1933; *ibid.*, W8385/5/50, 15 Jul. 1933.

358. Feis, *1933*, pp. 235, 245; Warburg, *The Money Muddle*, p. 121; Hull, *Memoirs*, pp. 262–5; Moley, *After Seven Years*, pp. 263–4; Nixon (ed.), *Franklin D. Roosevelt and Foreign Affairs*, i, p. 307.

359. NC2/22, diary, 4, 6 Jul. 1933; *ibid.*, 2/23A, diary, 24 Jul. 1933; *ibid.*, 18/1/835, Neville to Hilda Chamberlain, 10 Jul. 1933; *ibid.*, 18/1/837, Neville to Hilda Chamberlain, 23 Jul. 1933; *ibid.*, 18/1/843, Neville to Hilda Chamberlain, 24 Sept. 1933; *ibid.*, 18/1/848, Neville to Ida Chamberlain, 28 Oct. 1933.

360. T172/1811, M.E.Conv.23, Note of conversation in MacDonald's room, 30 Jun. 1933; *ibid.*, M.E.Conv.26, draft conclusions, 2 Jul. 1933; *ibid.*, M.E.Conv.27, Note of conversation in Treasury Board Room, 2 July 1933, 5:45 p.m.; CAB21/375, M.E.Conv.28, Note of conversation, 2 July, 1933, 6:15 p.m., Appendix I; NA FO371/17307, W8346/5/50, H. D. Henderson conference diary, 30 June, 4 Jul. 1933; FO371/17307, W8071/5/50, Tyrrell to FO, no. 165(S), 9 Jul. 1933.

361. MacDonald papers, 30/69/1/596, communiqué, 3 Jul. 1933; MF, F30/1415, Bonnet to Farnier, no. 469/50, 22 Jul. 1933.

362. *FRUS*, 1933, i, Hull to Phillips, no. 99, 4 Jul. 1933; Nixon (ed.), *Franklin D. Roosevelt and Foreign Affairs*, i, pp. 289–91; T172/1811, Note of a Meeting of Presidents and Vice-Presidents, 5 Jul. 1933, 10:30 a.m.; Hull, *Memoirs*, pp. 263–7; Feis, *1933*, pp. 241–2; Moley, *After Seven Years*, pp. 264–5.

363. 'Conference Verdict', *Sunday Times*, 23 Jul. 1933, p. 14; 'Barren Harvest', *Economist*, 29 Jul. 1933, pp. 215–16; 'After the Conference', *Statist*, 29 Jul. 1933, p. 159; 'Stalemate and Recovery', *New Statesman and Nation*, 5 Aug. 1933, p. 152; 'A Policy for the Pound', *Round Table*, Sept. 1933, p. 722, began, 'Let us weep no futile tears beside the deserted grave of the World Economic Conference in the cemetery of vain hopes'.

364. T175/84, Part I, Phillips, 'Note on the American Position at end of July', 28 Jul. 1933; FRBNY, *Monthly Bulletin*, Jul. – Oct. 1933.

365. Ickes, *Secret Diary*, i, pp. 99–100; Nixon (ed.), *Franklin D. Roosevelt and Foreign Affairs*, i, pp. 413–4, 483–4, 497f.; T175/79, Leith-Ross record of conversation with Warburg, to Hopkins, 5 Oct. 1933; T188/250, Leith-Ross to Fisher, no. 561, 18 Oct. 1933; *ibid.*, Leith-Ross to Lindsay, 14 Nov. 1933; T208/170, Chamber of Commerce press release, 18 Nov. 1933; *ibid.*, Bewley to Waley, 23 Nov. 1933; FO371/16610, A8770/60/45, Washington Chancery to American Department, 23 Nov. 1933; FO371/16609, A8948/54/45, Lindsay to FO, no. 1545, 30 Nov. 1933; Pasvolsky, *Current Monetary Issues*, pp. 213–23; Blum, *From the Morgenthau Diaries*, i, p. 121; Warburg, *The Money Muddle*, pp. 155–7.

366. Moley, *After Seven Years*, pp. 270–1.

367. Warburg, *Money Muddle*, pp. 134–40; Blum, *From the Morgenthau Diaries*, i, pp. 65–8; Samuel papers, A96.5, note of interview with Roosevelt, 26 Sept. 1933; Nixon (ed.), *Franklin D. Roosevelt and Foreign Affairs*, i, Roosevelt to Woodin, 30 Sept. 1933, p. 416; T175/79, Leith-Ross report to Hopkins of conversation with Warburg, 5 Oct. 1933; *ibid.*, Leith-Ross note conversation with Acheson, 23 Oct. 1933; FO371/16607, A7668/54/45, Lindsay (for Leith-Ross) to Fisher, no. 568, 23 Oct. 1933.

368. T188/250, Leith-Ross note of conversation with Warburg, 9 Nov. 1933; *FRUS*, 1933, i, Roosevelt to Phillips, no. 15, 28 Jun. 1933.

369. Feis, *1933*, pp. 146, 232–3; Nixon (ed.), *Franklin D. Roosevelt and Foreign Affairs*, i, pp. 265–6, 522–3.

370. T188/279.3, Leith-Ross to Norman, 4 Dec. 1933; *ibid.*, Leith-Ross minute to Hopkins and Chamberlain, 4 Dec. 1933; FO371/17566, A22/15/45, Bewley to FO, no. 1602, 18 Dec. 1933.

371. T188/279.3, Norman to Leith-Ross with enclosure, 2 Dec. 1933; Nixon (ed.), *Franklin D. Roosevelt and Foreign Affairs*, i, pp. 522–3; Gardner, *Economic Aspects of New Deal Diplomacy*, pp. 273–4.

372. Nixon (ed.), *Franklin D. Roosevelt and Foreign Affairs*, i, memorandum by Roosevelt, pp. 537–8.

373. FO371/16609, A8780/54/45, Lindsay to FO, no. 1514, 21 Nov. 1933; Friedman and Schwartz, *A Monetary History of the United States*, p. 470; Johnson, *The Treasury and Monetary Policy*, pp. 99–100.
374. T175/79, Leith-Ross note of conversation with Stewart, 13 Oct. 1933; T188/250, Leith-Ross note of conversation with Stewart on 7 and 13 Nov. 1933; *ibid.*, Leith-Ross note of conversation with Warburg on 9 Nov. 1933.
375. Cleveland and Huertas, *Citibank*, p. 199.
376. T188/250, Fisher for Chamberlain to Leith-Ross, 10 Oct. 1933; T175/82, Phillips to Leith-Ross, 13 Oct. 1933; T175/79, Leith-Ross note of conversation with Harrison, 16 Oct. 1933; T175/84, Pt.1, Phillips minute, 30 Dec. 1933.
377. T175/71, Phillips memorandum, 'Future Exchange Problems', 15 Feb. 1934; T188/279.4, Hopkins memorandum to Fisher and Chamberlain, 16 Feb. 1934.
378. T172/1811, M.E.Conv.23, Note of conversation in President's Room, 30 June 1933 at 12.30 p.m.; T172/1810A, M.E.(U.K.)21st Mtg., Conclusions, 5 Jul. 1933, at 10.30 a.m.; T172/1810C, 'Memorandum for Consideration of the British Commonwealth Delegations', by J. C. Smuts, 13 Jul. 1933; *ibid.*, M.E.(U.K.)28, Treasury minute on Smuts memorandum, 17 Jul. 1933; FO371/16608, A8353/54/445, India Office to FO, 20 Nov. 1933; T175/84 Part I, Phillips minute to Fergusson and Hopkins on Indian rupee, 20 Nov. 1933; *ibid.*, Phillips memorandum, 27 Nov. 1933.
379. T175/79, Leith-Ross to Fisher, 1 Nov. 1933; T188/250, Fisher to Lindsay (for Leith-Ross), nos 419-20, 10 Oct. 1933.
380. 'Balance of Payments of the United States, 1933', FRBNY, *Monthly Bulletin*, Apr. 1934, pp. 29–30.
381. Lévy-Leboyer, 'Les contraintes du marché', pp. 191–5.
382. 'The Year's Gold Movements', *Economist*, 16 Jan. 1932, p. 105.
383. T208/179, Rowe-Dutton memorandum, 'The French Budget for 1935', 2 Jan. 1935.
384. FO371/17296, W11224/106/17, Tyrrell to FO, no. 1401, 3 Oct. 1933.
385. See above, pp. 317, 331-3.
386. *DDF*, 1ᵉʳ sér, i, doc. 245, Germain-Martin to Herriot, no. 867, 15 Oct. 1932; *ibid.*, doc. 292, Herriot to de Fleuriau, nos 1103-09, 3 Nov. 1932; *ibid.*, doc. 296, Herriot to de Fleuriau, nos 1114-16, 4 Nov. 1932; *ibid.*, doc. 313, Claudel to Herriot, nos 794-6, 9 Nov. 1932.
387. Edge, *A Jerseyman's Journal*, p. 223; 'War Debts to Be Paid: The President's Statement. No Help from Mr. Roosevelt', *Times*, 24 Nov. 1932, p. 12; 'Meeting of French Cabinet Today', *ibid.*, 26 Nov. 1932, p. 10.
388. T188/248, Payments due by US Debtors, 15 Dec. 1932; Soulié, *Herriot*, p. 408.
389. *DDF* 1ᵉʳ sér, i, doc. 245, Germain-Martin to Herriot, no. 867, 15 Oct. 1932; *ibid.*, doc. 278, Monick to Paris, no.-, 27 Oct. 1932; *ibid.*, doc. 284, Bizot note, 28 Oct. 1932; Soulié, *La vie politique d'Edouard Herriot*, p. 381.
390. *DDF* 1ᵉʳ sér, i, doc. 729, Claudel minute of conversation with Stimson, 11 Nov. 1932.
391. T188/183, copy of Tyrrell to Simon, no. 168, 14 Dec. 1932.
392. T188/248, copy of Tyrrell to Simon, no. 162, 6 Dec. 1932.
393. FO371/15915, C9973/29/62, Tyrrell to FO, no. 127, 1 Dec. 1932.
394. *DDF* 1ᵉʳ sér, i, doc. 132, Herriot to Chargé d'affaires in Washington, nos 518-24, 31 Aug. 1932; FO371/16370, W11512/300/17, Tyrrell to FO, no. 142, 19 Oct. 1932.
395. FO371/15916, C10125/29/62, Patteson to FO, no. 433, 5 Dec. 1932.
396. *FRUS*, 1932, i, Note from the French Government to Secretary of State, 1 Dec. 1932.
397. *DDF* 1ᵉʳ sér, ii, doc. 18, de Fleuriau to Herriot, no. 755, 21 Nov. 1932; *ibid.*, doc. 70, de Fleuriau to Herriot, no. 786, 6 Dec. 1932; CAB23/73, conclusion 65(32)1, 7 Dec. 1932.
398. FO371/15914, C9682/29/62, Vansittart to Fisher, 10 Nov. 1932.
399. T160/417, F6677/06/1, Note of meeting in FO, 21 Nov. 1932, to discuss Lindsay's telegrams nos 461 and 463; ibid., Fisher to Vansittart, 22 Nov. 1932; T188/248, Note

of meeting at Treasury, 23 Nov. 1932; ibid., Leith-Ross memorandum, 25 Nov. 1932; T188/183, Leith-Ross to Tyrrell, 5 Dec. 1932.

400. FO371/15916, C10125/29/62, Vansittart (for Chamberlain) to MacDonald, 6 Dec. 1932.
401. *Ibid.*, C10433/29/62, British Embassy, Paris, minute of interview with A. Sarraut, 7 Dec. 1932.
402. NC18/1/809, Neville to Hilda Chamberlain, 10 Dec. 1932.
403. CAB24/235, C.P.425(32), copy of Tyrrell to Simon, no. 1623, 8 Dec. 1932; FO371/15916, C10255/29/62, Tyrrell to FO, no. 164, 8 Dec. 1932.
404. T188/183, copy of Tyrrell to FO, nos 130, 131, 9 Dec. 1932.
405. FO371/15916, C10312/29/62, Tyrrell to Simon, no. 132, 10 Dec. 1932; FO371/16663, C49/1/62, Campbell to FO, no. 1717, 29 Dec. 1932; Soulié, *Herriot*, pp. 408–10.
406. T188/248, copy of Tyrrell to FO, no. 135, 11 Dec. 1932.
407. T188/183, copy of Tyrrell to FO, no. 138, 13 Dec. 1932; *ibid.*, no. 168, 14 Dec. 1932; CAB23/73, conclusion 66(32)2, 13 Dec. 1932; FO371/16664, C285/1/62, Craigie minute, 16 Jan. 1933.
408. T188/183, copy of Tyrrell to FO, no. 136, 12 Dec. 1932; for another account of the debate, see FO371/15917, C10935/29/62, Campbell to FO, no. 1690, 23 Dec. 1932.
409. FO371/15916, C10312/29/62, Tyrrell to FO, no. 132, 10 Dec. 1932; FO371/15916, C10312/29/62, de Fleuriau to Vansittart, 10 Dec., Vansittart minute, 10 Dec., Nichols minute, 12 Dec. 1932; FO371/15916, C10391/29/62, Tyrrell to Vansittart (by telephone), 12 Dec., minute by Fisher, 12 Dec. 1932; CAB23/73, conclusion 66(32)2, 13 Dec. 1932; *FRUS*, 1932, i, Mills to Stimson, 14 Dec. 1932.
410. Similar accusations were made by S. de Givet, 'Comment la "solidarité" franco-britannique se manifeste', *L'Ordre*, 12 Dec. 1932, p. 1.
411. FO371/15916, C10416.29/62, Tyrrell to FO, no. 139, 14 Dec. 1932; *ibid.*, 15917, C10452/29/62, Tyrrell to FO, no. 167, 14 Dec. 1932; T188/183, copy of Tyrrell to Simon, no. 168, 14 Dec. 1932; Reynaud, *Mémoires*, i, pp. 347–8; *FRUS*, 1932, i, doc. 763, Edge to Stimson, no. 717, 14 Dec. 1932; Soulié, *Herriot*, pp. 412–15; Bonnefous, *Histoire politique de la Troisième République*, v, p. 132.
412. *FRUS*, 1932, i, Edge to Stimson, no. 745, 23 Dec. 1932; Edge, *A Jerseyman's Journal*, pp. 225–6; FO371/16370, W13897/300/17, Tyrrell to Simon, no. 170(S), 19 Dec. 1932; 'France', *Economist*, 7 Jan. 1933, p. 21; *ibid.*, 14 Jan. 1933, p. 173.
413. M.Coste, 'Movements of Capital in France', p. 21; 'Annual Report of the Bank of France (1932)', *Federal Reserve Bulletin*, Mar. 1933, p. 149; 'Money Market', *Times*, 14 Dec. 1932, p. 18; 'Foreign Exchanges in 1932', *Economist*, 14 Jan. 1933, p. 59.
414. T188/249, Chamberlain to MacDonald, 4 Jan. 1933; T188/193, Leith-Ross to Vansittart, 20 Mar. 1933.
415. 'British War Debts. Mr. Chamberlain's Statement', *Times*, 25 Jan. 1933, p. 12; NC18/1/814, Neville to Ida Chamberlain, 29 Jan., 12 Feb. 1933.
416. FO371/17323, W2597/685/50, de Fleuriau minute to Simon, 24 Feb. 1933.
417. *DDF*, 1er sér, iii, doc. 86, Claudel to Paul-Boncour, nos 337-9, 5 Apr. 1933; T160/487, F13017/3, copy of Tyrrell to Simon, no. 62, 9 Apr. 1933.
418. T160/487, F13017/3, 'Minutes of meeting at French Ministry of War, 10 Mar. 1933, 10:30 a.m.'
419. *DDF*, 1er sér, iii, doc. 1, compte rendu, 17 Mar. 1933; T188/99, Notes of meeting in Treasury Board Room, 17 Mar. 1933, 3.30 p.m.
420. T188/275, Tyrrell to Leith-Ross, 23 Mar. 1933; Bonnet, *Vingt ans de vie politique*, p. 162.
421. *DDF*, 1er sér, iii, doc. 58, Paul-Boncour to Claudel, nos 242-7, 28 Mar. 1933.
422. MF, F^{30}/1415, 'Conditions dans lesquelles la délégation française a pris position à Londres sur les questions monétaires, I. Conversations Roosevelt-Herriot à Washington', 30 Sept. 1933.
423. T160/487, F13017/4, copy of Lindsay to Simon, no. 666, 4 May 1933.

424. CAB23/76, conclusion 39(33), Appendix II, 9 Jun. 1933; *ibid.*, conclusion 41(33)1, 13 Jun. 1933; MacDonald diary, 11 Jun. 1933.
425. MacDonald papers, 30/69/1/596, 'Agreement between Central Banks', 15 Jun. 1933; *ibid.*, Fergusson to Vincent, 20 Jun. 1933; T188/279.2, Phillips memorandum, 'Temporary Exchange Stabilisation for Period of Conference', 17 Jun. 1933.
426. MF, F^{30}/1415, 'Conditions...à Londres...questions monétaires, III', 30 Sept. 1933; NC7/11/26/5, Bonnet to Chamberlain, 28 Jun. 1933.
427. T160/489, F13017/023/1, 2, 3 and 4, Review of the French Press, 19, 21, 28, 29, 30 Jun., 3 Jul. 1933.
428. *Ibid.*, 4 Jul. 1933.
429. *Ibid.*, 7 Jul. 1933.
430. *Ibid.*, 6 Jul. 1933; MF, F^{30}/1415, de la Baume to Bizot, no. 1845, 4 Jul. 1933.
431. FRBNY, *Monthly Bulletin*, Aug. 1933, p. 60.
432. FO371/17650, C7340/14/17, memorandum by Rowe-Dutton, in R. H. Campbell to FO, no. 1683, 2 Nov. 1934.
433. 'France', *Economist*, 10 Oct. 1931, p. 658; *ibid.*, 24 Oct. 1931, pp. 755–6; *ibid.*, 21 Nov. 1931, p. 955; *ibid.*, 28 May 1932, p. 1183.
434. 'France', *Economist*, 10 Oct. 1931, p. 658.
435. FO371/16365, W10369/189/17, Tyrrell to Simon, no. 1247, 17 Sept. 1932; Germain-Martin, *Le problème financier*, pp. 168–78.
436. FO371/16370, W13035/300/17, Tyrrell to Simon, no. 153(S), 25 Nov. 1932; FO371/16365, W13120/189/17, Tyrrell to Simon, no. 1561(C), 29 Nov. 1932.
437. FO371/17295, W320/106/17, Tyrrell to Simon, no. 2(S), 10 Jan. 1933; *ibid.*, no. 8(S), 18 Jan. 1933; *ibid.*, W891/106/17, Tyrrell to Simon, no. 16(S), 26 Jan. 1933; 'France', *Economist*, 21 Jan. 1933, p. 119; *ibid.*, 28 Jan. 1933, p. 177.
438. FO371/17295, W927/106/17, Tyrrell to Simon, no. 5, 28 Jan. 1933; 'France', *Economist*, 4 Feb. 1933, p. 238; Reynaud, *Mémoires*, i, pp. 364–5; Bonnet, *Vingt ans*, pp. 154–5; Bonnefous, *Histoire politique de la Troisième République*, v, pp. 133–42.
439. Beau de Loménie, *Les responsabilités des dynasties bourgeoises*, iv, pp. 541–4.
440. FO371/17295, W1481/106/17, Tyrrell to Simon, no. 189, 9 Feb. 1933; *ibid.*, W1648/106/17, Tyrrell to Simon, no. 24(S), 14 Feb. 1933; *ibid.*, W1887/106/17, Tyrrell to Simon, no. 28(S), 20 Feb. 1933; *ibid.*, W2283/106/17, Tyrrell to Simon, no. 9, 1 Mar. 1933; Bonnet, *Vingt ans*, pp. 155–60; France, Assemblée Nationale, *Rapport fait au nom de la Commission chargée d'enquêter sur les événements survenus en France de 1933 à 1945*, Annexes (Dépositions), i, pp. 9–10; 'The French Budget', *Times*, 8 Feb. 1933, p. 12; 'The French Budget', *ibid.*, 4 Mar. 1933, p. 11; 'Budgeting in France', *ibid.*, 10 Mar. 1933, p. 11; 'France', *Economist*, 4 Feb. 1933, p. 238; *ibid.*, 11 Feb. 1933, pp. 298–9; *ibid.*, 18 Feb. 1933, pp. 351–2; *ibid.*, 4 Mar. 1933, p. 463; *ibid.*, 11 Mar. 1933, pp. 524, 526; *ibid.*, 18 Mar. 1933, p. 581; *ibid.*, 22 Apr. 1933, p. 861.
441. 'City Notes', *Times*, 29 Apr. 1933, p. 20; FO371/16604, A3248/54/45, Treasury to Leith-Ross, no. 229, 29 Apr. 1933; FO371/17296, W4611/106/17, Hopkins to Vansittart, no. 6, 29 Apr. 1933.
442. 'Annual Report of the Bank of France (1933)', *Federal Reserve Bulletin*, Mar. 1934, p. 162.
443. FO371/17296, W12135/106/17, Tyrrell to Simon, no. 1510, 24 Oct. 1933; 'France', *Economist*, 21 Oct. 1933, pp. 765–6; *ibid.*, 28 Oct. 1933, pp. 807, 812; 'The French Budget', *Times*, 23 Oct. 1933, p. 13; 'French Crisis', *Times*, 24 Oct. 1933, p. 14; 'The Fall of Mr. Daladier', *Times*, 26 Oct. 1933, p. 13.
444. 'France', *Economist*, 30 Dec. 1933, pp. 1281–2.
445. L. Romier, 'Avec des finances solides la France ne risque rien. Avec des finances en ruines elle risque tout, y compris la guerre', *Le Petit Parisien*, 15 Nov. 1933; 'French Gold Losses', *Economist*, 25 Nov. 1933, p. 1012; FO371/17296, W13712/106/17, Law to Sargent, 28 Nov. 1933; BdF, DCG, 30 Nov. 1933.
446. For instance, 'L'attaque contre le franc', *Commentaires*, 26 Nov. 1933.

447. Berstein, *Le 6 février*, p. 90; also Weber, *The Hollow Years*, pp. 133–4.
448. FO/371/17655, C473/125/17, Tyrrell to Simon, no. 116, 19 Jan. 1934.
449. FO371/17585, A500/383/45, Lindsay to FO, no. 1636, 27 Dec. 1933.
450. Nixon (ed.), *Franklin D. Roosevelt and Foreign Affairs*, ii, pp. 26–7f.
451. FO371/17567, W1061/15/45, Lindsay to FO, no. 54, 5 Feb. 1934.
452. CAB16/109, DRC12, note by Fisher, 29 Jan. 1934; FO371/17516, A1473/29/14, Chancery to American Department, 5 Feb. 1934, minutes by Kelly, Craigie, Wellesley, Vansittart, 27 Feb. – 2 Mar. 1934; FO371/17593, A785/785/45, minute by Vansittart, 5 Feb. 1934; FO371/17568, A2573/15/45, minutes by Gore-Booth, Craigie, Wellesley, Vansittart, Stanhope, 4 – 26 Apr. 1934; T188/251, Leith-Ross to Lindsay, 7 May 1934; MacDonald papers, 30/69/2/14, Glyn to MacDonald, 14 May 1934; *ibid.*, 30/69/8/1, diary, 3 Jun. 1934.
453. CAB23/79, conclusion 22(34)3, 30 May 1934; T188/251, copy of FO to Lindsay, 140, 141, 30 May 1934; UK *PP*, 1934 Cmd. 4609, 'Papers Relating to the British War Debt', 15 Jun. 1934.
454. NC18/1/848, Neville to Ida Chamberlain, 28 Oct. 1933; Leith-Ross, *Money Talks*, p. 179.
455. T188/251, Lindsay to Leith-Ross, 26 Apr. 1934; FO371/17585, A3280/383/454, Lindsay to FO, 26 Apr. 1934; *ibid.*, A3513/383/45, Lindsay to FO, no. 139, 3 May 1934; *ibid.*, 17586, A4602/383/45, Lindsay to Leith-Ross, 23 May 1934; Runciman papers, 272, A. Asquith to Runciman, 13 Jun. 1934.
456. T188/251, memorandum, 'United States Dept – Situation as at 15 June 1934', 23 May 1934.
457. T188/251, Fisher to Leith-Ross, 26 Feb. 1934.
458. FO371/17585, A3099/383/45, Vansittart minute, 22 Apr. 1934.
459. FO371/17567, A1015/15/45, minutes by Craigie, Wellesley and Selby, 5 – 8 Feb. 1934. As Sir Victor Wellesley, the assistant under-secretary, put it, 'Default or no default, America is not going to be paid and the world will still go around.' *Ibid.*, 17568, A2429/15/45, Wellesley minute, 26 Mar. 1934.
460. FO371/17586, A3923/383/45, Clerk to Vansittart, 11 May 1934.
461. T188/251, Leith-Ross to Chamberlain, 17 May 1934.
462. FO371/17586, A4512/383/45, Clerk to FO, no. 152, 6 Jun. 1934.
463. FO371/16388, W3491/63/50, 'United Kingdom Tariffs and Foreign Countries. Memorandum II', 24 Mar. 1932; *ibid.*, 'Memorandum III. France', 1 Apr. 1932.
464. Letter from J. Butler, *Times Trade Supplement*, 18 Jul. 1931.
465. FO371/16388, W3491/63/50, 'United Kingdom Tariffs and Foreign Countries. Memorandum II', 24 Mar. 1932.
466. Haight, *A History of French Commercial Policies*, pp. 9–13; Gordon, *Barriers to World Trade*, pp. 245–7; p. 13; FO371/16365, W2542/189/17, Tyrrell to FO, no. 267C, 29 Feb. 1932.
467. FO371/15643, W14713/137/17, Berthelot to Tyrrell, 24 Dec. 1931.
468. FO371/16360, W60/16/17, memorandum by Cahill in Tyrrell to FO, no. 4C, 3 Jan. 1932.
469. FO371/7661, C1964/873/22, Thompson to FO, 9 Feb. 1922; *ibid.*, MAF 40/5, S.S.12620, minute by Thompson, 30 Aug. 1927; *ibid.*, Guinness to Cunliffe-Lister, 27 Oct. 1927; *ibid.*, minutes by Jackson, Thomas, Guinness, 20–25 Jan. 1928; *ibid.*, MAF 40/6, TAY13783, Franklin to Treasury, 29 Aug. 1928; *ibid.*, MAF 40/9, SG5904A, 'Proposed Anglo-European Tariff Negotiations', copy of BT memorandum to FO, 21 Apr. 1931.
470. MAF 40/5, SS12620, minute by Jackson, 27 Oct. 1927; *ibid.*, MAF 43/12, HH5155, Cahill (Board of Trade) to Taylor, 11 May 1929; *ibid.*, HH5172, Dale (MAF) minute, 30 Jan. 1930; *ibid.*, HH5178, copy of Tyrrell to Henderson, no. 576, 19 May 1931; *ibid.*, Tyrrell to Vansittart, 19 May 1932; *ibid.*, Vandepeer to A. Leeper, 26 May 1931; *ibid.*, Dale to FO, 17 Mar. 1932; France, F12/8802, memorandum, 26 Aug. 1930; FO371/16363, W5220/109/17, Ministry of Agriculture to FO, 6 May 1932. The issue is surveyed in Boyce, 'Insects and International Relations', pp. 1–30.

471. See above, p. 327.

472. CAB24/223, C.P.256(31), MAF memorandum, 'Colorado Beetle. Prohibition of Imports of Potatoes etc. from France', 30 Sept. 1931.

473. MA, F10/2177, Departments affected by Colorado beetle, 1922–36, n.d.; FO371/8268, W6893/2579/17, Bryan (MAF) to FO, 16 Aug. 1922; HO445/15186, 569.731/16, memorandum by Ministry of Agriculture, 'Colorado Beetle', 21 Oct. 1931.

474. FO371/8268, W10498/2579/17, MAF to FO, n.d.; *ibid.*, MAF 43/13, HH245, Floud to Treasury, 3 Aug. 1923; *ibid.*, HH5154, Fryer minute, Oct. 1923.

475. This decision was eventually questioned by FO and Treasury officials, but defended by the Ministry of Agriculture on the grounds that they were commonly produced near potato fields and might carry the insect: T160/728, F12743/1, Vansittart to Hopkins, 1 Aug. 1933; *ibid.*, Vansittart to Howell Thomas, 1 Aug. 1933; *ibid.*, Waley to Hopkins, 2 Aug. 1933; F12743/2, Howell Thomas to Vansittart, 25 Aug. 1933.

476. MA, F12/8802, memorandum, 26 Aug. 1930; *ibid.*, 2179, 'Doryphore. Reglementation Britannique', n.d. (*c.* 1932).

477. Augé-Laribé, *La Politique agricole de la France*, pp. 371, 381, 384–5, 391; Faure, *Les Paysans dans la société française*, pp. 43, 46 and passim.

478. HO45/15186.569.731/12, copy of MAF, 'Notes of Meetings with French Representatives, 5th and 6th October 1931'.

479. *N.F.U. Record*, Jan. 1931, p. 85; MAF 43/13, HH245, J. B. Guild (Secretary, NFU) to Taylor, 27 Mar. 1931; *ibid.*, HH5161, press cuttings from the *Daily Telegraph*, 12 Sept. 1931, *Times*, 14 Sept. 1931, *Fruit Grower*, 24 Sept. 1931, *Yorkshire Post*, 7 Oct. 1931, *Morning Post*, 8 Oct. 1931; 'The Colorado Beetle in Potatoes', *Times*, 7 Oct. 1931, p. 14; *NFU Yearbook*. 1932, p. 388.

480. FO371/15646, W11703/689/17, minutes by Vansittart, Mallet, Mounsey, 8 – 9 Oct. 1931; CAB23/68, conclusion 68(31)1, 1 Oct. 1931; FO800/226, minute by Howard Smith, 15 Oct. 1931; MAF, 43/13, HH5161, Keeble to Gilmour, 15 Oct. 1931 enclosing Vansittart to Gilmour, 16 Oct. 1931.

481. FO371/15684, W11768/11768/50, Note of conversation with Rollin, British embassy, Paris, 7 Oct. 1931; HO45/15186, 569.731/16, Howard Smith to MAF, 15 Oct. 1931.

482. FO371/15646, W11703/687/17, minute by Vansittart, 8 Oct. 1931.

483. HO45/15186, 569.731/16, minute by Cahill, 9 Oct. 1931.

484. 'Trade Gloom Over Tariff War', *Daily Herald*, 14 Nov. 1931, p. 14.

485. FO371/ 15643, W13408/137/17, Tyrrell to FO, no. 1269(C), 25 Nov. 1931; 15903, C18/18/62, Law to Sargent, 29 Dec. 1931.

486. MAE, SdN UE 16, Rollin to Briand, 26 Oct. 1931; *ibid.*, RC, B-Négociations commerciales 2, Briand to Rollin, 6 Nov. 1931; FO371/15655, W13372/10611/17, 'Record of Conversation between Sir John Simon and Monsieur Flandin', 18 Nov. 1931; *ibid.*, 15643, W13408/137/17, Tyrrell to FO, no. 1269(C), 25 Nov. 1931; 'The British Tariffs: Uneasiness in France', *Times*, 7 Dec. 1931, p. 12.

487. FO371/15642, W12994/137/17, minute by Howard Smith, 16, 17 Nov. 1931; CAB24/224, C.P.290(31), Simon to Tyrrell, no. 2788, 20 Nov. 1931; 260 H.C. Deb 5s, cols 1473–6; Runciman papers, 269, memorandum by Fountain, 'Most-Favoured-Nation Treatment', 9 May 1933; BT 11/234, memorandum by Hill, 'Most-Favoured-Nation Treatment', 1 Dec. 1933.

488. FO371/15643, W13324/137/17, Fountain to Howard Smith, 19 Nov. 1931; *ibid.*, W13421/137/17, Tyrrell to FO, no. 1256C, 23 Nov. 1931; *ibid.*, W14051/137/17, Simon to Tyrrell with enclosure, no. 2939, 9 Dec. 1931; CAB23/69, conclusion 80(31)3, 20 Nov. 1931; FO800/285, Runciman to Simon, 10 Dec. 1931; CAB24/227, C.P.50(32), memorandum by Runciman, 'Discrimination against United Kingdom Exports', 27 Jan. 1932.

489. FO371/15643, W14266/137/17, Tyrrell to Simon, no.-, 11 Dec. 1931.

490. FO371/15643, W13323/137/17, Simon to Runciman, no. 22, 24 Nov. 1931; FO800/285, Tyrrell to Simon, 10 Dec. 1931; FO371/15643, W14266/137/17, Tyrrell to Simon, no.-, 11 Dec. 1931.

491. FO371/15643, W14099/137/17, Tyrrell to Simon, no. 24, 11 Dec. 1931.
492. FO800/285, Simon to MacDonald, 16 Dec. 1931; *ibid.*, MacDonald to Laval, 16 Dec. 1931.
493. International Institute of Agriculture, *The Agricultural Situation in 1931–32*, pp. 162–3.
494. CAB23/69, conclusion 86(31)3, 9 Dec. 1931; *ibid.*, conclusion 87(31)8, 10 Dec. 1931; FO371/15643, W14713/137/17, Berthelot to Tyrrell, 24 Dec. 1931; FO371/16360, W600/16/17, Tyrrell to FO, 17 Jan. 1932; *ibid.*, W1907/16/17, MAF to FO, 16 Feb. 1932; MAF 43/13, HH5161, MAF to FO, 16 Feb. 1932, 21 Mar. 1932.
495. FO371/16360, W1106/16/17, report in *Daily Telegraph*, 29 Jan. 1932; *ibid.*, W1561/16/17, Forsyth to Mallet, 5 Feb. 1932.
496. CAB23/70, conclusion 11(32)4, 3 Feb. 1932.
497. FO371/16361, W4888/16/17, Fountain to Cahill, 16 and 28 Apr. 1932.
498. FO371/16360, W1662/16/17, Tyrrell to Vansittart, 9 Feb. 1932.
499. FO371/16360, W2043/16/17, Tyrrell to Runciman, 10 Feb. 1932, Runciman to Tyrrell, 15 Feb. 1932; *ibid.*, W1744/16/17, Leith-Ross to Howard Smith, 11 Feb. 1932; *ibid.*, Tyrrell to FO, no. 36, 11 Feb. 1932.
500. FO371/16361, W2057/16/17, Tyrrell to FO, no. 38, 19 Feb. 1932.
501. *Ibid.*, W1907/16/17, minute by Mounsey, 19 Feb. 1932.
502. 'France', *Economist*, 28 Nov. 1931, p. 1006.
503. FO371/16389, W5538/63/50, note from de Fleuriau, 17 May 1932; also *ibid.*, WW5537/63/50, minute by Howard Smith, 9 May 1932.
504. FO371/16371, W13535/656/17, statistics on French trade compiled by Ashton Gwatkin, 3 Dec. 1932.
505. T160/728, F12743/4, minutes of Franco-British commercial negotiations, 30 May 1934.
506. FO371/16365, W8593/189/17, Wigram to FO, 25 Jul. 1932.
507. FO371/16362, W12279/16/17, Wills to FO, 7 Nov. 1932; T160/814, F12659/09/3, copy of Tyrrell to Simon, no. 93C, 19 Jan. 1933.
508. T188/275, Leith-Ross minute to Fountain, 9 Mar. 1933; T188/99, Leith-Ross minute of Chamberlain-Bonnet conversation, 17 Mar. 1933; *ibid.*, 'Anglo-French Conversations at the Board of Trade, Mar. 18 [1933], at 11 a.m.'; T188/275, Leith-Ross to Tyrrell, 20 Mar. 1933.
509. MF, F³⁰/B1412, Foreign Minister to Minister of the Budget, no. 35, 23 Mar. 1933.
510. T160/497/F13413, minute by Phillips of Chamberlain-Rueff meeting, 22 Apr. 1933.
511. *Ibid.*, memorandum by Phillips, 23 Apr. 1933; FO371/17296, W4451/106/17, Wellesley minute, 24 Apr. 1933; T160/728, F12743/1, Phillips to Rueff, 25 Apr. 1933.
512. *Ibid.*, Waley note to Phillips, 12 May 1933; *ibid.*, Phillips minute to Hopkins and Fergusson, 13 May 1933; Leith-Ross minute to Hopkins and Chamberlain, 24 May 1933; *ibid.*, Hopkins to Under-Secretary, FO, 21 Jun. 1933.
513. *Ibid.*, Leith-Ross minute, 18 May 1933; *ibid.*, excerpt from minutes of UK Delegation (WEC), 22nd meeting, 5 Jul. 1933; *ibid.*, Chamberlain minute, 11 Jul. 1933; *ibid.*, Hopkins letter to Under-Secretary, FO, 17 Jul. 1933.
514. T160/728, F12743/2, Leith-Ross minute to Hamilton, 22 Sept. 1933. See also *ibid.*, Leith-Ross to Chamberlain, 4 Sept. 1933; *ibid.*, minute by Chamberlain, 5 Sept. 1933; *ibid.*, copy of Vansittart to Corbin, 7 Sept. 1933.
515. Schirmer, 'La dénonciation du traité de commerce franco-allemand d'août 1927', p. 164; T160/572, F14473/1, Campbell to Simon, no. 1289, 7 Sept. 1933.
516. T160/572, F13373/1, Overton to FO, 23 Oct. 1933.
517. CAB24/243, C.P.248(33), Runciman memorandum, 'French Discriminatory Measures against British Trade', 30 Oct. 1933; CAB23/77, conclusion 59(33)10, 2 Nov. 1933; *ibid.*, conclusion 64(33)6, 22 Nov. 1933; *ibid.*, conclusion 66(33)3, 29 Nov. 1933.
518. T160/728, F12743/3, Waley to Phillips, 21 Nov. 1933; *ibid.*, copy of Tyrrell to Simon, no. 1775, 28 Dec. 1933.

519. FO371/17636, C102/10/17, copy of BT memorandum, 'The New French Quotas', 4 Jan. 1934.
520. FO371/17636, C205/10/17, FO to Tyrrell to FO, no. 7, 10 Feb. 1934.
521. T160/572, F13373/2, copy of Tyrrell to FO, no. 17, 20 Jan. 1934; *ibid.*, copy of Fountain to FO, 25 Jan. 1934; MacDonald papers, 30/69/1/429, copy of FO to Campbell, no. 25R, 25 Jan. 1934.
522. *Ibid.*, Campbell to FO, no. 23, 1 Feb. 1934.
523. *Ibid.*, Ronald to Brown, 2 Feb. 1934; *ibid.*, note by Butler, 3 Feb. 1934.
524. *Ibid.*, Brown to Butler, 3 Feb. 1934; *ibid.*, Brown to Ronald, 5 Feb. 1934.
525. *Ibid.*, copy of Campbell to Simon, no. 31, 6 Feb. 1934.
526. FO371/17655, C932/125/17, Campbell to FO, no. 40, 7 Feb. 1934.
527. NC2/23A, diary, 3 Feb. 1934. Evidence of wrongdoing existed for at most half a dozen politicians at this time: Berstein, *Le 6 février*, p. 93.
528. MacDonald diary, 4, 8 Feb. 1934.
529. *Ibid.*, 10 Feb. 1934.
530. NC18/1/868, Neville to Ida Chamberlain, 10 Feb. 1934.
531. FO371/17637, C865/10/17, minute by Sargent, 7 Feb. 1934.
532. Berstein, *Le 6 février*, p. 168.
533. MacDonald papers, 30/69/1/429, copy of Tyrrell to Simon, no. 43, 8 Feb. 1934.
534. FO371/17638, C1033/10/17, Tyrrell to FO, no. 49, 12 Feb. 1934; T160/728, F12743/4, copy of Simon to Corbin, 15 Feb. 1934; T160/572, F13373/2, copy of Overton to FO, 15 Feb. 1934; FO371/17638, C1201/10/17, Simon to Tyrrell, no. 309, 21 Feb. 1934.
535. FO371/17639, C1739/10/17, memorandum by Wigram, 15 Mar. 1934; T175/84 Part II, Leith-Ross to Fergusson, 17 Mar. 1934; FO371/17640, C2011/10/17, memorandum by Wigram, 21 Mar. 1934; FO371/17641, C2541/10/17, minute by Sargent, 28 Apr. 1934; FO371/17644, C3919/10/17, memorandum by Wigram, 4 Jun. 1934; *ibid.*, C3898/10/17, draft agreement, 16 Jun. 1934. The final agreement is in UK, *PP*, Cmd. 4632, 'France No. 1 (1934) Agreement between His Majesty's Government and French Government relating to Trade and Commerce, with Protocols', 27 Jun. 1934.
536. *Ibid.*, minute by Sargent, 22 Jun. 1934.
537. 'United States', *Economist*, 29 Oct. 1932, p. 778.
538. *Ibid.*, 10 Dec. 1932, p. 1080.
539. 'Germany', *ibid.*, 10 Dec. 1932, p. 1083; more generally, Borchardt, *Perspectives*, p. 148.
540. Registered unemployment in Germany stood at 16.5 per cent in January 1927 and 12.9 per cent in December. The Jan./Dec. percentages in the following years were 1928: 11.2/16.7 per cent; 1929: 19.4/20.1 per cent; 1930: 22.0/31.7 per cent; 1931: 34.2/42.4 per cent; 1932: 43.8/42.1 per cent. *Wirtschaft und Statistik*, 1 Apr.-Heft 1927, pp. 305, 1 Jan.-Heft 1928, p. 1, and selected issues.
541. *Ibid.*, 2 Aug.-Heft 1933, p. 485, 2 Aug.-Heft 1934, p. 517.
542. Hearden, *Roosevelt Confronts Hitler*, pp. 85–7; MacDonald, *United States, Britain and Appeasement*, pp. 12–14, 28.

Conclusion

1. Roger, *The American Enemy*, p. 302 and passim.
2. Guiffan, 'Les survivances de l'anglophobie', pp. 108–9; Cornick, 'Faut-il réduire l'Angleterre en esclavage? French Anglophobia in 1935', pp. 3–17; Bunard, 'Français-Anglais: 100 ans de "mésentente cordiale"?', http://www.europeplusnet.info/article92.html; Bell, *France and Britain*, pp. 165, 202; the otherwise excellent Tombs and Tombs, *That Sweet Enemy*, p. 512; and more generally Sharp and Jeffrey, ' "Après la Guerre finit, Soldat anglais partit ..." ', p. 123.

3. This diminished after the Nazi regime took power. For example, Robert A. Millikan, president of California Institute of Technology and winner of the Nobel Prize for physics, included a statement in the Westinghouse time capsule in 1938 which referred to the struggle of 'the Anglo-Saxon, French, and Scandinavian countries' against 'despotism', implicitly including Britain and the United States but excluding Germany. http://www.openlibrary.org/details/timecapsulecups00westrich

4. On Asia, see Dower, *War without Mercy: Race and Power in the Pacific War.*

5. Dilks (ed.), *Diaries of Sir Alexander Cadogan*, p. 73

6. Wrench, *Geoffrey Dawson*, p. 334. A public opinion poll at this time confirmed that 55 per cent of respondents preferred to associate with Germans, compared with only 25 per cent with the French. Carswell, 'Britain Could Not Ask for a Better Ally', p. 27.

7. On liberal appeasers, Marwick, *Clifford Allen*, pp. 159–60, 176–8; Rouse, *All Souls and Appeasement*, pp. 38, 43–8, 116–17. Of course, not all liberals were misled. Sir Edward Grigg, a loyal follower of Lloyd George, loudly warned of the threat posed by Germany. Another liberal anti-appeaser was Lionel Robbins. See Grigg, *Britain Looks at Germany*, and Robbins, *Autobiography.*

8. This, as MacDonogh, *Prussia*, p. 350, points out, was a travesty of the truth.

9. *DBFP*, 3rd ser. vol. iii, Appendix ii, no. 285, Halifax to Phipps, 1 Nov. 1938.

10. Self (ed.), *The Neville Chamberlain Diary Letters*, iv, pp. 363, 324, 325, 344, 348.

11. Parker, *Chamberlain and Appeasement*, pp. 100–1.

12. The almost universal assumption that France was strong became evident in June 1940 when Roosevelt, Churchill, Stalin and even Hitler betrayed their complete surprise at France's collapse: Boyce, 'Introduction', pp. 2–4.

13. Murray, 'Britain', p. 121.

14. Roberts, '*The Holy Fox*', pp. 68–9.

15. FO371/21743, C11049/1941/18, Henderson to Halifax, 3 May 1938.

16. Roberts, '*The Holy Fox*', p. 68.

17. FO371/21743, C11049/1941/18, Henderson to Halifax, 17 Apr. 1938.

18. FO371/21741, C10677/1941/18, Runciman to Benes, 21 Sept. 1938.

19. 339 H.C. Deb 5s, col. 361.

20. Lamb, *The Drift to War*, pp. 318–24.

21. Moore, 'American Interpretations of National Socialism', p. 5.

22. Colville, *The Fringes of Power*, vol. 1, p. 27.

23. Wheeler-Bennett, *King George VI*, p. 460. On others in the Establishment who shared this view, see Carswell, 'Britain Could Not Ask for a Better Ally', p. 214

24. Reynolds, '1940', pp. 330–1; Dockrill, *British Establishment Perspectives on France*, p. 159. Bonnery, 'La France de la B.B.C.', ch. 1.

25. Dockrill, *British Establishment Perspectives on France*, p. 163; Reynolds, '1940', pp. 332–3.

26. See the useful discussion in Judt, *Postwar*, ch. 3.

27. Though de Gaulle and Churchill still remained anxious about Prussianism. See Merrill (ed). *Documentary History of the Truman Presidency*, vol. 2, p. 21; Grosser, *Une vie de Français*, p. ?64

28. Pruessen, *John Foster Dulles*, pp. 309–12.

29. Kennan, *Memoirs*, pp. 416–18.

30. Martin Wolfe, 'Why Agreeing a New Bretton Woods Is Vital and So Hard', *Financial Times*, 5 Nov. 2008, p. 13.

31. John Kay, 'Banks Got Burned by Their "Innocent Fraud"', *ibid.*, 15 Oct. 2008, p. 17.

32. Jagdish Bagwati, 'We Need to Guard against Destructive Creation', *ibid.*, 17 Oct. 2008, p. 15; Shiller, 'Has Financial Innovation Been Discredited?' Mar. 2008; Rogoff, 'The Hedge Fund Hegemon', Mar. 2007.

33. Rogoff, 'The End of Financial Triumphalism?' Aug. 2008; Sean O'Grady, 'Economist Stiglitz Blames Crunch on Flawed City Bonus System', *Independent*, 24 Mar. 2008.

34. Alan Beattie, 'The Saga That Became a Never-Ending Story', *FT World Economy 2008 Special Report*, 10 Oct. 2008, p. 10.

35. Eswar Prasad, 'No More Tinkering at the IMF', *Financial Times*, 3 Nov. 2008, p. 20; Martin Wolfe, 'Why Agreeing a New Bretton Woods Is Vital and So Hard', *ibid.*, 5 Nov. 2008, p. 13.
36. Alan Beattie, 'The IMF Needs to Make Some Facebook Friends', *ibid.*, 17 Oct. 2008, p. 5.
37. Kishore Mahbubani, 'Why Asia Stays Calm in the Storm', *ibid.*, 29 Oct. 2008, p. 15. See also Stiglitz, 'The Overselling of Globalization', pp. 238–41; David Pilling and Geoff Dyer, 'Asia Ponders Its Troubled Relationship with the IMF', *Financial Times*, 10 Nov. 2008, p. 5.
38. David Rothkopf, 'The Fund Faces Up to Competition', *ibid.*, 22 Oct. 2008, p. 15.
39. Stiglitz, 'Democratizing the International Monetary Fund and the World Bank', pp. 121–3 and passim.
40. Philip Stephens, 'Globalisation and the New Nationalism Collide', *Financial Times*, 24 Oct. 2008, p. 13.
41. Gideon Rachman, 'Conservatism Overshoots Its Limits', *ibid.*, 7 Oct. 2008, p. 15; George Parker, 'Europe to Press US for Reforms of World Finance', *ibid.*, 10 Nov. 2008, p. 5.
42. Rodrik, 'How to Save Globalization from Its Cheerleaders' (revised), Sept. 2007; Delury, 'Will America's Pain Be China's Gain?' Oct. 2008; Philip Stevens, 'The Financial Crisis Marks Out a New Geopolitical Order', *Financial Times*, 10 Oct. 2008, p. 13.
43. Obstfeld, Shambaugh and Taylor, 'Reserve Accumulation and Financial Stability', 18 Oct. 2008.
44. Martin Wolfe, 'Asia's Revenge', *Financial Times*, 9 Oct. 2008, p. 13.
45. Lardy, 'China: The Great New Economic Challenge?', ch. 4.
46. '*World Development Indicators*, 2008, Country Statistical Information, China', *World Bank*.
47. 'Table 1: US-China Trade Statistics and China's World Trade Statistics', *US-China Business Council*.
48. 'Key Indicators: China', *World Bank*.
49. John Kay, 'Surplus Capital Is Not for Wimps After All', *Financial Times*, 22 Oct. 2008, p. 15.
50. Saez, 'Striking It Richer'.
51. Martin Wolfe, 'Why Paulson's Plan Was Not a True Solution to the Crisis', *Financial Times*, 24 Sept. 2008, p. 19; Wolfe, 'Asia's Revenge', *ibid.*, 9 Oct. 2008, p. 13.
52. Blanchard, review of Brender and Pisani, 'Preface to Global Imbalances', 20 Feb. 2007.
53. 'Statement by the Hon. Yi Gang', *International Monetary Fund*, 13 Oct. 2008.
54. Paulson, 'The Benefits of US-China Strategic Economic Dialogue'; OECD StatExtracts, Balance of Payments, USA.
55. Philip Stevens, 'The Financial Crisis Marks Out a New Geopolitical Order', *Financial Times*, 10 Oct. 2008, p. 13.
56. Martin Wolfe, 'The World Wakes from the Wish-Dream of Decoupling', *ibid.*, 22 Oct. 2008, p. 15.
57. John Plender, 'The Unkind Reality about Emerging Economies', *ibid.*, 12 Nov. 2008, p. 40.
58. Davidson, 'Reforming the World's International Money', 14 Nov. 2008.
59. 'Whatever It Took', *ibid.*, 15 Oct. 2008, p. 15.
60. 'China's 4 Trillion Yuan Stimulus to Boost Economy, Domestic Demand', *Window of China*, 9 Nov. 2008.
61. 'Russia Finds It Is in Same Sinking Boat', *Financial Times*, 8 Oct. 2008, p. 16.
62. 'Russia's Finance Minister to Talk IMF Quota Reform in U.S.', *Novosti*, 7 Apr. 2008; 'Russia Wants Further IMF Reform: Pankin', *Financial Express*, 14 May 2008; 'Medvedev Calls for Reform of World Financial System', *Russia Today*, 3 Nov. 2008.
63. James Politi, 'Mixed Messages Leave Stance on Trade Unclear', *Financial Times*, 6 Nov. 2008, p. 8; David Pilling, 'The President-Elect Must Ease Asian Anxieties', *ibid.*, p. 17.
64. 'Global Views 2008', *Chicago Council on Global Affairs*.

65. 'World Publics Welcome Global Trade – but Not Immigration', *Pew Global Attitudes Project*, 10 Apr. 2007.
66. Summers, 'The Global Consensus on Trade Is Unravelling', 26 Aug. 2008; Dominique Moïsi, 'A Global Downturn in the Power of the West', *Financial Times*, 6 Oct. 2008, p. 15; Martin Wolfe, 'Preventing a Global Slump Should Be the Priority', *ibid.*, 29 Oct. 2008, p. 15.
67. Quentin Peel, 'Crunch Time for the Old World Order', *Financial Times Global Agenda*, 7 Nov. 2008, p. 2.
68. Martin Wolfe, 'Big Questions in a Fast Changing World', *ibid.*, p. 1.

Bibliography

For reasons of space, this bibliography is restricted to sources and published works cited in the footnotes.

Primary Sources

Unpublished

Addis, Sir Charles, papers. School of Oriental and African Studies, University of London.
American Presidency Project, http://www.presidency.ucsb.edu/elections.php, accessed 17 Sept. 2008.
Amery, Leopold S., papers. Private hands, London.
Baldwin, Stanley, 1st Earl, papers. Cambridge University Library.
Balfour, Sir Arthur James, papers. British Library.
Bank of England, papers, London.
Banque de France, papers, Paris.
Canada, Postmaster Generals', papers. National Archives, Ottawa.
Castle, William, papers. Herbert Hoover Presidential Library, West Branch, Iowa.
Cecil of Chelwood, Robert Viscount, papers. British Library.
Chamberlain, Austin and Neville, papers. University of Birmingham Library.
Chapman, Sir Sydney, unpublished autobiography. British Library of Political and Economic Science, London.
Cunliffe-Lister, Philip, 1st Earl of Swinton, papers. Churchill College Archives.
Curzon, George Nathaniel, 1st Earl of Kedleston, papers. British Library.
D'Abernon, Edgar Vincent, 1st Viscount, papers. British Library.
Dalton, Hugh, diary. British Library of Political and Economic Science, London.
Federal Reserve Bank of New York, papers. New York.
Federation of British Industry, papers. Modern Record Centre, University of Warwick.
Flandin, Pierre Etienne, papers. Archives Nationales, Paris.
France, Ministère des Affaires Etrangères, Ministère des Finances, Ministère du Commerce, Ministère de l'Agriculture, papers. Paris.
George, David Lloyd, papers. House of Lords Records Office, London.
George V, papers. Royal Archives, Windsor.
Hankey, Maurice, 1st Baron, papers. Churchill College Archives.
Harmsworth, Alfred, Lord Northcliffe, papers. British Library.
Hoover, Herbert, papers. Herbert Hoover Presidential Library, West Branch, Iowa.
Jacobsson, Per, diary. British Library of Political and Economic Science, London.
Lamont, Thomas W., Collection. Baker Library Historical Collections, Harvard Business School.
Leeper, Alexander W. A., papers. Churchill College Archives.
Loucheur, Louis, papers. Institut Pierre Renouvin, Université de Paris IV-Sorbonne.
Morgan Grenfell, papers. London.
Noel-Baker, Philip John, Baron, papers. Churchill College Archives.
Passfield papers, Beatrice Webb diary. British Library of Political and Economic Science, London.
Phipps, Sir Eric, papers. Churchill College Archives.
Poincaré, Raymond, papers. Archives Nationales, Paris.
Quesnay, Pierre, papers. Archives Nationales, Paris.

Revelstoke, 2nd Baron, papers. Baring Brothers and Company archives, London
http://www.fdrlibrary.marist.edu/050733.html, accessed 17 Sept. 2008.
Runciman, Walter, 1st Viscount of Doxford, papers. University of Newcastle Library.
Samuel, Herbert, 1st Viscount, papers. House of Lords Record Office.
Spender, J. A., papers. British Library.
Stamp, Josiah, 1st Baron of Shortlands, papers. Private hands, London.
Stimson, Henry Lewis, papers. Manuscripts and Archives, Yale University Library.
Sweet-Escott, Bickham, papers. British Library of Political and Economic Science, London.
United Kingdom Board of Trade, Cabinet, Foreign Office, Prime Ministers Office and
    Treasury, papers. National Archives, Kew.
United States, Department of State, papers. Washington.
Wickham Steed, Henry, papers. British Library.
Wilson, Field Marshal Sir Henry, papers. Imperial War Museum.
Wrench, Evelyn, papers. British Library.
Young, Owen D., papers. Cooperstown, New York.

Published

The Agricultural Situation in 1931–32 (Rome: International Institute of Agriculture, 1933).
Amery, Leopold S. *The Empire in the New Era: Speeches Delivered during an Empire Tour, 1927–
    1928* (London: Arnold, 1928).
Amery, Leopold S. *My Political Life*, Vol. 2, *War and Peace, 1914–1929* (London: Hutchinson
    & Co., 1953).
Asquith, Herbert Henry. *Speeches by the Earl of Oxford and Asquith, K. G.* (London: Hutchinson
    & Co., 1927).
Barker, Ernest, H. W. C. Davis, C. R. L. Fletecher, Arthur Hassall, L. G. Wickham Legg and
    F. Morgan, *Why We Are at War by Members of the Oxford Faculty of Modern History*, 3rd ed.
    rev. (Oxford: Clarendon Press, 1914).
Barnes, John and David Nicholson (eds), *The Leo Amery Diaries*, 2 Vols (London: Hutchinson,
    1980).
Baynes, Norman H. *The Speeches of Adolf Hitler*, April 1922–August 1939 (London and New
    York: Oxford University Press, 1942).
Belgium, *Documents diplomatiques belges*, eds, Vol. II 1920–1940: 1a politique de sēcuritē.
Béraud, Henri. *Faut-il réduire l'Angleterre à l'esclavage?* (Paris: Editions de France, 1935).
Beveridge, Lord. *Power and Influence* (London: Hodder and Stoughton, 1953).
Beyen, J. W. *Money in a Maelstrom* (London: Macmillan, 1951).
Blake, Robert (ed.), *The Private Papers of Douglas Haig, 1914–1919* (London: Eyre &
    Spottiswoode, 1952).
Blum, John M. *From the Morgenthau Diaries*, Vol. 1 (Boston MA: Houghton Mifflin, 1959).
Blunden, Edmund. *Undertones of War*, rev. ed. (London: Cobden-Sanderson, 1930).
Bonnet, Georges Etienne. *Vingt ans de vie politique 1918–1938: de Clemenceau à Daladier*
    (Paris: Fayard, 1969).
Bourgeois, Léon. *Pour la Société des Nations* (Paris: Bibliothèque Charpentier, 1910).
Bourgeois, Léon. *Le Traité de Paix de Versailles*, 2nd ed. (Paris: Librairie Félix Alcan, 1919).
Bourne, Kenneth and D. Cameron Watt (eds), *British Documents on Foreign Affairs: Reports
    and Papers from the Foreign Office Confidential Print*, Part I, Series F and Part II, Series 1
    (Washington DC: University Publications of America, 1990, 1991).
Briand, Aristide. *Aristide Briand. Discours et écrits de politique étrangère*, ed., Achille Elisha
    (Paris: Librairie Plon, 1965).
Brinton, Daniel G. *Races and Peoples: Lectures on the Science of Ethnography* (Philadelphia
    PA: David McKay, Publisher, 1901, eds, Charles de Visscher and Fernand Vanlangenhove
    (Bruccellis: Acadēmie Royale de Belgique, 1964).
Bryce, James Viscount. *Race Sentiment as a Factor in History. A Lecture Delivered before
    the University of London on February 22, 1915* (London: University of London Press,
    1915).

Case, Josephine Young and Everett Needham Case. *Owen D. Young and American Enterprise* (Boston MA: David R. Godine, 1982).

Chamberlain, Neville. *The Struggle for Peace* (London: Hutchinson & Co., 1939).

Clarke, Sir Richard. *Anglo-American Economic Collaboration in War and Peace, 1942–1949*, ed., Sir Alec Cairncross (Oxford: Clarendon Press, 1982).

Clemenceau, Georges. *Discours de Paix* (Paris: Librairie Plon, 1938).

Clemenceau, Georges. *Grandeurs et Misère d'une victoire* (Paris: Librairie Plon, 1930).

Colville, John. *The Fringes of Power: Downing Street Diaries, 1939–1955, vol. i: September 1939–September 1941* (London: Hodder and Stoughton, 1985).

Coolidge, Calvin. *The Biography of Calvin Coolidge* (London: Chatto & Windus, 1929).

Coste, M. 'Movements of Capital in France from 1929 to 1933', BIS Monetary and Economic Department, C.B.76 (May 1934).

Coudenhove-Kalergi, Richard Count. *An Idea Conquers the World* (London: Hutchinson, 1953).

D'Abernon, Viscount. *Ambassador of Peace. Lord D'Abernon's Diary*, Vols II, III (London: Hodder and Stoughton, 1929, 1930).

Dalton, Hugh. *Memoirs*, Vol. I, *Call Back Yesterday, 1887–1931* (London: Frederick Muller, 1953).

Dawes, Charles G. *A Journal of Reparations* (London: Macmillan, 1939).

Decugis, Henri. *Le destin des races blanches*, préface de l'André Siegfried, 2nd ed. (Paris: Librairie de France, 1936).

Dilks, David (ed.), *The Diaries of Sir Alexander Cadogan 193–1945* (London: Cassel, 1971).

Edge, Walter Evans. *A Jerseyman's Journal: Fifty Years of American Business and Politics* (Princeton NJ: Princeton University Press, 1948).

Einzig, Paul. *France's Crisis* (London: Macmillan, 1934).

Esher, Oliver Viscount (ed.), *Journals and Letters of Reginald, Viscount Esher*, Vol. 4, *1916–1930* (London: Ivor Nicholson & Watson, 1938).

Feis, Herbert. *1933: Characters in Crisis* (Boston MA: Little, Brown & Co., 1966).

Fisher, Irving. *Stabilised Money: A History of the Movement* (London: Allen & Unwin, 1935).

Flandin, Pierre-Etienne. *Politique française 1919–1940* (Paris: Les Éditions Nouvelles, 1947).

France, *Documents Diplomatiques Françaises*, 1er série (Paris: Imprimerie Nationale, 1964).

France, Assemblée Nationale. Commission chargée d'enquêter sur les événements survenus en France de 1933 à 1945, *Rapport*, Annexes (Dépositions), i (Paris: Imprimerie Nationale, 1951).

François-Poncet, André. *The Fateful Years. Memoirs of a French Ambassador in Berlin, 1931–1938*, transl. by Jacques Leclercq (New York: Howard Fertig, 1949).

François-Poncet, André. *De Versailles à Potsdam: la France et le problème allemand contemporain 1919–1945* (Paris: Flammarion, 1948).

Gedye, G. E. R. *The Revolver Republic: France's Bid for the Rhine* (London: Arrowsmith, 1930).

George, David Lloyd. *Memoirs of the Peace Conference*, Vol. 1 (New Haven CN: Yale University Press, 1939).

Germain-Martin, Henry. *Le problème financier 1932–1936* (Paris: Les Éditions Domat-Montchrestien, F. Loviton & cie, 1936).

Germany, *Akten zur deutschen auswärtigen Politik 1918–1945*, Serie B: 1925–1933, Bands I/II – XX (Göttingen: Vandenhoeck & Ruprecht, 1968–83).

Germany, Reichsamt für Statistik, *Statisches Jahrbuch für das Deutsches Reich, 1920, 1921*, etc.

Germany, Reichsamt für Statistik, *Wirtschaft und Statistik*, 1919, 1920, etc.

Gilbert, Martin (ed.), Winston S. Churchill, Vol. IV, Companion Part I, Documents, January 1917–June 1919 (London: Heinemann, 1977).

Gooch, G. P. and Howard Temperley. (eds), *British Documents on the Origins of the War, 1898–1914*, Vol. III (London: HMSO, 1928).

Grant, Madison. *The Passing of the Great Race, or The Racial Basis of European History*, 2nd ed. (New York: C. Scribner's Sons, 1918).

Graves, Robert. *Goodbye to All That* (London: Penguin Books, 2000).

Grey of Fallodon, Edward Grey. *Twenty-Five Years, 1892–1916* (London: Hodder & Stoughton, 1928).

Grigg, Sir Edward. *Britain Looks at Germany* (London: Nicholson and Watson, 1938).

Grigg, Percy James. *Prejudice and Judgment* (London: Cape, 1948).

Grosser, Alfred. *Une vie de Français: mémoires* (Paris: Flammarion, 1997).

Gwynn, Stephen (ed.), *The Letters and Friendships of Sir Cecil Spring Rice: A Record*, Vol. II (London: Constable & Co., 1929).

Haldane, Viscount. *Before the War* (London: Cassell and Company, 1920).

Hancock, W. Keith and Jean Van Der Poel (eds), *Selections from the Smuts Papers*, Vol. IV, *November 1918–August 1919* (Cambridge: Cambridge University Press, 1966).

Hankey, Maurice Lord. *The Supreme Control at the Paris Peace Conference, 1919* (London: Allen and Unwin, 1963).

Hardinge, Charles. *Old Diplomacy: The Reminiscences of Lord Hardinge of Penshurst* (London: John Murray, 1947).

Hawtrey, R. G. *The Gold Standard in Theory and Practice*, 2nd ed. (London: Longmans, 1931).

Headlam-Morley, James. *A Memoir of the Peace Conference, 1919*, eds, Agnes Headlam-Morley, Russell Bryant and Anna Cienciala (London: Methuen & Co. Ltd., 1972).

Headlam-Morley, James. *Studies in Diplomatic History* (London: Methuen, 1930).

Henderson, Nevile. *Failure of a Mission: Berlin, 1937–1939*, 2nd ed. (Toronto: Musson Book Company, 1940).

Herriot, Edouard. *Europe* (Paris: Les Editions Rieder, 1930).

Herriot, Edouard. *Jadis*, t. 2, *D'une guerre à l'autre 1914–1936* (Paris: Flammarion, 1952).

Hill, Leonidas E. (ed.), *Die Weizsäcker-Papiere 1900–1932* (Berlin: Verlag Ullstein, 1982).

Hitler, Adolf. *Mein Kampf*, transl. by Richard Murphy (London: Hurst & Blackett, 1939).

Hitler, Adolf. *Reden, Schriften, Anordnungen, Februar 1925 bis Januar 1933*, Band II A, *Aussenpolitische Standortbestimmung nach der Reichstagswahl Juni–Juli 1928*, eingeleitet von Gerhard Weinberg (München: K. G. Saur, 1995).

Hitler, Adolf. *The Second Book*, transl. by Salvator Attanasio (New York: Grove Books, 1961).

Hooker, Nancy Harvison (ed.), *Moffat Papers: Selections from the Diplomatic Papers of J. Pierrepont Moffat, 1919–1943* (Cambridge MA: Harvard University Press, 1956).

Hoover, Herbert. *The Memoirs of Herbert Hoover*, Vol. II, *The Cabinet and the Presidency, 1920–1933* (New York, Macmillan, 1952).

Hoover, Herbert. *The State Papers and Other Publics Writings of Herbert Hoover*, Vol. II, ed., William Starr Myers (Garden City NY: Doubleday, Doran & Co., 1934).

Hull, Cordell. *The Memoirs of Cordell Hull* (London: Hodder and Stoughton, 1948).

Ickes, Harold L. *The Secret Diary*, Vol. 1, *The First Thousand Days, 1933–36* (London: Weidenfeld & Nicolson, 1955).

International Institute of Agriculture. *The Agricultural Situation in 1931–32* (Rome, 1933).

James, Robert Rhodes (ed.) *Memoirs of a Conservative: J. C. C. Davidson's Memoirs and Papers, 1910–37* (London: Weidenfeld & Nicolson, 1969).

Johnston, Sir Harry Hamilton, Henry Neville Hutchinson, Augustus Henry Keane, Arnold Henry Savage Landor, Joseph Henry Longford, Richard Lyddeker and Robert Wilson Shufeldt *The Living Races of Mankind*, 2 Vols (London: Hutchinson, n.d. (*c.* 1905).

Johnston, Tom. *Financiers and the Nation* (London: Methuen & Co., 1934).

Johnston, Tom. *Memories* (London: Collins, 1952).

Jones, Lawrence Evelyn. *Georgian Afternoon* (London: Rupert Hart-Davis, 1958).

Jones, Thomas. *Whitehall Diary*, Vol. II, *1926–30*, ed., Keith Middlemas (London: Oxford University Press, 1969).

Kennan, George F. *Memoirs, 1925–1950* **(London: Hutchinson, 1969).**

Kessler, Harry. *The Diaries of a Cosmopolitan*, ed. and transl. by Charles Kessler (London: Weidenfeld and Nicolson, 1971).

Keynes, John Maynard. *The Economic Consequences of the Peace* (London: Macmillan, 1919).

Keynes, John Maynard. *Essays in Persuasion* (London: Macmillan, 1931).

Laroche, Jules. *Au Quai d'Orsay avec Briand et Poincaré 1913–1926* (Paris: Hachette, 1957).

League of Nations, 'Application of the Recommendations of the International Economic Conference. Report on the Period May 1928 to May 1929. Prepared for the Second Meeting of the Consultative Committee (May 6th, 1929). Statement for the Period Ending March 15th, 1929', C.130.M.45.1929.II, 1 April 1929.

League of Nations, *Commercial Policy in the Interwar Period: International Proposals and National Policies*, L.N.II.1942.II.A.6 (Geneva: League of Nations, 1943).

League of Nations, *Council Resolution*, 8 June 1928.

League of Nations, *The Course and Control of Inflation: A Review of Monetary Experience in Europe after World War* I, L.N.II.A.6 (Princeton NJ: Princeton University Press, 1946).

League of Nations, *The Course and Phases of the World Economic Depression*, by Bertil Ohlin, rev. ed., Off. no. A.22.1931.IIA (Geneva: League of Nations, 1931).

League of Nations, *Industrialisation and Foreign Trade* (1945).

League of Nations, *International Economic Conference. Tariff Level Indices* (1927) .

League of Nations, *Memorandum sur le commerce international et sur les balances des paiements 1912–1926*, Vol. I (1927).

League of Nations, *Monthly Bulletin of Statistics*, 1934, 1935, etc.

League of Nations, *Monthly Bulletin of Trade Statistics*, 1930, 1931, etc.

League of Nations, *Official Journal*, 1921, 1922, etc.

League of Nations, *Proceedings of the Preliminary Conference with a View to Concerted Economic Action, 17 February–24 March 1930*, C.222.M.109.1930.

League of Nations, Report of the Economic Consultative Committee on Its First Session. Held in Geneva from May 14th to 19th, 1928, C.217.M.73.1928.II., 19 May 1928.

League of Nations, *Report of the Financial Committee*, L.N.C.281.1928.II, 4 June 1928.

League of Nations, *Report and Proceedings of the World Economic Conference Held at Geneva, May 4th to 23rd, 1927*, 2 Vols.

League of Nations, *Review of World Trade*, 1931–32, etc.

League of Nations, *World Production and Prices, 1925–34, 1936/37, etc.*

Le Fur, Louis Erasmé. *Races, nationalités, états* (Paris: Félix Alcan, 1922).

Leith-Ross, Sir Frederick W. *Money Talks: Fifty Years of International Finance* (London: Hutchinson, 1968).

Link, Arthur S. (ed.), *The Deliberations of the Council of Four (March 24–June 28, 1919), Notes of the Official Interpreter Paul Mantoux*, Vol. 1 (Princeton NJ: Princeton University Press, 1992).

Link, Arthur S. (ed.), *The Papers of Woodrow Wilson*, Vols 53–56 (Princeton NJ: Princeton University Press, 1986).

Lodge, Henry Cabot. *The Senate and the League of Nations* (New York: Charles Scribners Sons, 1925).

Loucheur, Louis. *Carnets Secrets 1908–1932*, ed., Jacques de Launay (Brussels and Paris: Brepols, 1962).

Lowe, C. J. and M. L. Dockrill, *The Mirage of Power: British Foreign Policy, 1902–22*, Vol. 3: *Documents* (London: Routledge and Kegan Paul, 1972).

Mackenzie, Norman and Jean (eds), *The Diary of Beatrice Webb*, Vol. 3, *1905–1924: The Power to Alter Things* (London: Virago, 1984).

McAdoo, William. *Crowded Years* (Boston MA and New York: Houghton Mifflin Company, 1931).

McEwen, J. M. (ed.), *The Riddell Diaries, 1908–1923* (London: Athlone Press, 1986).

Moley, Raymond. *After Seven Years*, 4th ed. (New York: Harper, 1939).

Moley, Raymond. *The First New Deal* (New York: Harcourt Brace, 1966).

Mond, Sir Alfred. *Industry and Politics* (London, Macmillan, 1927).

Mordacq, J. J. Henri. *Le Ministère Clemenceau, Journal d'un témoin*, Vol. 4 (Paris: Librairie Plon, 1930).

Moreau, Emile. 'Le relèvement financière et monétaire de France', Parts I and II, *Revue des Deux Mondes*, 1 March 1937, pp. 53–62, 15 March 1937, pp. 299–319.

Moreau, Emile. *Souvenirs d'un Gouverneur de la Banque de France: Histoire de la Stabilisation du Franc (1926–1928)* (Paris: Editions M.-Th. Génin, 1954).

Munch, Peter. *La Politique du Danemark dans la Société des Nations* (Geneva: Kundig, 1931).

Mussolini, Benito. *Opera Omnia*, Vol. XXV, *dal dodicesimo Anniversario dalla Fondazione dei Fasci al Patto a Quattro* (24 marzo 1931–giugno 1993), a cura di Edoardo e Duilio Susmel (Florence: La Fenice, 1958).

Nicholson, David and John Barnes (eds), *The Leo Amery Diaries*, Vol. 1, *1896–1929* (London: Hutchinson, 1980).

Nicolson, Harold. *Peacemaking, 1919* (London: Constable & Co. Ltd., 1934).

Nixon, Edgar B. (ed.), *Franklin D. Roosevelt and Foreign Affairs*, Vol. 1 (Cambridge MA: Belknap Press of Harvard University Press, 1969).

Papen, Franz von. *Memoirs*, transl. by Brian Connell (London: André Deutsch, 1952).

Petter, Sir Ernest. *The Disease of Unemployment and the Cure* (London: Hutchinson, 1925).

Poincaré, Raymond. *Au Service de la France. Neuf années de souvenirs. Tome XI, A la recherche de la paix 1919* (Paris, Librairie Plon, 1974).

Recouly, Raymond. *Marshal Foch: His Own Words on Many Subjects*, transl. by Joyce Davis (London: Thornton Butterworth, 1929).

Reynaud, Paul. *Mémoires*, t. 1 (Paris: Flammarion, 1960).

Riddell, Lord. *Lord Riddell's Intimate Diary of the Peace Conference and After, 1918–1923* (London: Victor Gollancz Ltd., 1933).

Ripley, William Z. *The Races of Europe: A Sociological Study* (London: Kegan Paul, Trench, Trübner & Co., 1900).

Roosevelt, Franklin D. *The Public Papers and Addresses of Franklin D. Roosevelt*, Vols 1 and 2 (New York: Random House, 1938).

Root, Waverley. *The Paris Edition: The Autobiography of Waverley Root, 1927–1934* (San Francisco CA: North Point Press, 1987).

Ross, Edward Alsworth. *The Old World in the New: The Significance of Past and Present Immigration to the American People* (New York: The Century Company, 1914).

Ross, Edward Alsworth. *The Social Trend* (New York: The Century Company, 1922).

Ross, Edward Alsworth. *Standing Room Only?* (London: Chapman & Hall, 1928).

Rouse, A. L. *All Souls and Appeasement: A Contribution to Contemporary History* (London: Macmillan, 1961).

Royal Institute of International Affairs, *British Tariff Policy. Interim Report on Measures Taken by the British Government to Promote Exports and Protect the Home Market in Force in March 1932* (London: Oxford University, 1932).

Royal Institute of International Affairs, *Interim Report on Measures taken by the British Government to Promote Exports and Protect the Home Market in Force in March, 1932* (London: RIIA, 1932).

Royal Institute of International Affairs, *The Problem of International Investment. A Report by a Study Group of Members of the Royal Institute of International Affairs* (London: Oxford University Press, 1937).

Royal Institute of International Affairs, *Survey of International Affairs, 1933*, ed., Arnold Toynbee (London: Oxford University Press, 1934).

Rueff, Jacques. *De l'aube au crépuscule –Autobiographie* (Paris: Plon, 1977).

Saint-Aulaire, Comte de (Auguste Félix Charles de Beaupoil). *Confession d'un vieux diplomate* (Paris, Flammarion, 1953).

Salter, Sir Arthur. *The United States of Europe and Other Papers* (London: Allen & Unwin, 1933).

Salter, Sir Arthur (ed.), *The Economic Consequences of the League: The World Economic Conference* (London: Europa Publishing, 1927).

Self, Robert C. *The Austen Chamberlain Diary Letters, Vol. 5: The Correspondence of Sir Austen Chamberlain with His Sisters Hilda and Ida, 1916–1937* (Cambridge: Cambridge University Press, 1995).

Self, Robert C. (ed.), *The Neville Chamberlain Diary Letters, Vol. 4: The Downing Street Years, 1934–1940* (Aldershot: Ashgate, 2005).

Schacht, Hjalmar. *The End of Reparations*, transl. by Lewis Gannett (New York: Jonathan Cape & Harrison Smith, 1931).

Seydoux, Jacques. *De Versailles au Plan Young: réparations, dettes interalliés, reconstruction européenne* (Paris: Jacques Arnavon et E. de Felcourt, 1932).

Seymour, Charles. *Letters from the Peace Conference* (New Haven CN: Yale University Press, 1965).

Seymour, Charles. (ed.), *The Intimate Papers of Colonel House*, Vol. IV: *The Ending of the War, June 1918–November 1919* (London: Ernest Benn Limited, 1928).

Siegfried, André. *England's Crisis*, transl. by H. H. and D. Hemming (London: Jonathan Cape, 1931).

Siegfried, André. *Tableau des partis en France* (Paris: Bernard Grasset, 1930).

Snowden, Philip Viscount. *An Autobiography*, Vol. 2, *1919–1934* (London: Ivor Nicholson and Watson, 1934).

Stresemann, Gustav. *His Diaries, Letters, and Papers*, ed. and transl. by Eric Sutton, 3 Vols. (London: Macmillan, 1940).

Stresemann, Gustav. *Les papiers de Stresemann. Six années de politique allemande*, éd. par Henry Bernhard avec la collaboration de Wolfgang Goetz et Paul Wiegen (Paris: Plon, 1932–33).

Tardieu, André. *La Paix* (Paris: Payot, 1921).

Taylor, A. J. P. (ed.), *Lloyd George: A Diary by Frances Stevenson* (London: Hutchinson & Co., 1971).

Trades Union Congress, *Report of the Proceedings of the 59th Annual Trades Union Congress, 1927, 1928,* etc.

Tugwell, Rexford G. *Roosevelt's Revolution. The First Year: A Personal Perspective* (New York: Macmillan, 1977).

United Kingdom, *Documents on British Foreign Policy*, 1st, 1A, 2nd and 3rd series.

United Kingdom, House of Commons Parliamentary Debates, 5th series.

United Kingdom, Norman H. Gibbs, *History of the Second World War: Grand Strategy*, Vol. 1, *Rearmament Policy* (London: HMSO, 1976).

United Kingdom, *Parliamentary Papers*, 1919, Cmd. 9182. 'Committee on Currency and Foreign Exchanges after the War, First Interim Report'.

United Kingdom, *Parliamentary Papers*, 1921, Cmd. 1547. 'Papers Relating to the Agreement between the French and German Governments concerning the Application of Part VIII of the Treaty of Versailles Regarding Deliveries in Kind'.

United Kingdom, *Parliamentary Papers*, 1930, Cmd. 3595. 'Dispatch to His Majesty's Ambassador in Paris Enclosing the Memorandum of the French Government of the Organisation of a System of European Federal Union, 28 May 1930'.

United Kingdom, *Parliamentary Papers*, 1931, Cmd. 3897. 'Committee on Finance and Industry, Report, June 1931'.

United Kingdom, *Parliamentary Papers*, 1932, Cmd. 3991. 'Statistical Abstract for the United Kingdom'.

United Kingdom, *Parliamentary Papers*, 1932, Cmd. 3995, 'Report of the Special Advisory Committee Convened under the Agreement with Germany Concluded at The Hague on January 20, 1930', Basle, 21 December 1931'.

United Kingdom, *Parliamentary Papers*, 1932, Cmd. 4131, 'Declaration Issued by His Majesty's Government in the United Kingdom and the French Government Regarding Future European Co-operation', 13 July 1932.

United Kingdom, *Parliamentary Papers*, 1934, Cmd. 4609, 'Papers Relating to the British War Debt', June 1934.

United Kingdom, *Parliamentary Papers*, 1934, Cmd. 4632, 'France No. 1 (1934) Agreement between His Majesty's Government and French Government Relating to Trade and Commerce, with Protocols, 27 June 1934'.

United Kingdom, Post Office papers, BT archives, London.

United Kingdom, *Reports from Commissioners, Inspectors, and Others*, Vol. VII, 1931, Cmd. 3920, 'Committee on National Expenditure Report, July 1931'.

United Kingdom, Royal Commission in Indian Currency and Finance, 1914, Cd. 7238, 'Report'.

United Nations Department of Economic Affairs, *International Capital Movements during the Interwar Period*, U.N.II.D.1949.2 (October 1949).

United States Bureau of the Census. *Historical Statistics of the United States: Colonial Times to 1970* (Washington DC: US Government Printing Office, 1975).

United States, Department of Commerce, *Historical Statistics of the United States: Colonial Times to 1970* (Washington DC: US Government Publishing Office, 1975).

United States, Department of Commerce, *The United States and the World Economy. The International Transactions of the United States during the Interwar Period*, by Hal B. Lary (Washington DC: US Government Printing Office, 1943).

United States, Department of State, *Papers Relating to the Foreign Relations of the United States: The Paris Peace Conference, 1919*, Vols III–IV (Washington DC: US Government Printing Office, 1943).

'United States Historical Census Browser'. Inter-university Consortium for Political and Social Research, http://fisher.lib.virginia.edu/census, accessed 4 Dec. 2008.

United States, National Archives, General Records of the Department of the Navy.

United States, Presidential Inaugural Speeches. Avalon Project at Yale Law School, http://www.yale.edu/lawweb/avalon, accessed 17 Sept. 2008.

Valentin, Antonina. *Stresemann*, transl. by Eric Sutton (London: Constable, 1931).

Vanlangenhove, Fernand. L'élaboration de la politique étrangère de la Belgique entre les deux guerres mondiales (Bruxelles: Palais des Académies, 1979).

Warburg, James P. *The Money Muddle* (New York: Alfred A. Knopf, 1934).

Webb, Beatrice. *The Diary of Beatrice Webb*, Vol. 3. *1905–1924: The Power to Alter Things*, ed. Norman and Jeanne MacKenzie (London: Virago in conjunction with the London School of Economics, 1984).

Weinberg, Gerhard L. (ed.), *Hitler's Second Book: The Unpublished Sequel to Mein Kampf*, transl. by Krista Smith (New York: Enigma Books, 2003).

Weiss, Louise. *Mémoires d'une Européenne*, t. 3, *Combats pour l'Europe 1919–1934* (Paris: Albin Michel, 1979).

Wilson, Trevor (ed.), *The Political Diaries of C. P. Scott, 1911–1928* (London: Collins, 1970).

Newspapers and Journals

France

Action Française.
L'Agence Economique et Financière.
l'Avenir.
Correspondant.
Les Débats.
Echo de la Bourse.
Echo de Paris.
Echo National.
L'Éclair.
L'Economiste Européen.

L'Economiste Français.
Aux Écoutes.
l'Europe Nouvelle.
Le Figaro.
La France Economique et Financière.
L'Homme Libre.
L'Information financière.
Journée Industrielle.
Le Matin.
Le Messager de Paris.
Les Nouvelles Economiques et Financières.
Paris Midi.
Petit Bleu.
Le Petit Journal.
Le Petit Parisien.
Revue de Paris.
Revue des Deux Mondes.
Le Temps.

United Kingdom

The Banker.
The Bankers' Magazine.
Barclays Bank Monthly Review.
British Industries.
Contemporary Review.
Daily Chronicle.
Daily Express.
Daily Herald.
Daily Mail.
Daily News and Leader.
Economist.
Empire Review.
European Finance.
Evening Standard.
Financial News.
Financial Times.
Forward.
The Free Trader.
The Industrial Review.
International Affairs.
The Iron and Coal Trades Review.
J. Henry Schroder & Co. Quarterly Review.
Labour Magazine.
The Liberal Magazine.
The Listener.
Manchester Guardian.
Manchester Guardian Commercial.
Midland Bank Monthly Review.
Morning Post.
The Motor Industry of Great Britain, 1929, 1930, etc.
The Nation & Athenaeum.
New Leader.
The New Statesman and Nation.

News Chronicle.
Observer.
Pall Mall Gazette.
The Round Table.
Samuel Montagu & Co., Weekly Bullion Letter.
The Socialist Review.
The Spectator.
The Statist.
Sunday Times.
Times.
The Times Annual Financial and Commercial Review.
Trade Survey (Journal of the Electrical and Associated Manufacturing Industries).
United Empire.
World Power.
Yorkshire Post.

United States

Chase Economic Bulletin.
Federal Reserve Bank of New York Monthly Bulletin.
Federal Reserve Bulletin.
Journal of Commerce.
New York Stock Exchange Bulletin.
New York Times.

Secondary Sources

Books

Adams, Iestyn. *Brothers Across the Ocean: British Foreign Policy and the Origins of the Anglo-American 'Special Relationship', 1900–1915* (London and New York: Taurus, 2005).

Adamthwaite, Anthony. *Grandeur and Misery: France's Bid for Power in Europe, 1914–1940* (London: Hodder Headline, 1995).

Adler, Selig. *The Isolationist Impulse: Its Twentieth Century Reaction* (New York: Abelard-Schuman, 1957).

Aldcroft, Derek H. *The Interwar Economy: Britain, 1919–1939* (London: B. Batsford, 1970).

Aldcroft, Derek H. *Studies in the Interwar European Economy* (Aldershot Hants: Ashgate, 1997).

Allen, Frederick Lewis. *Only Yesterday: An Informal History of the Nineteen-Twenties in America* (Harmondsworth Middlesex: Penguin, 1931).

Anderson, Stuart, *Race and Rapprochement: Anglo-Saxonism and Anglo-American Relations, 1895–1904* (Rutherford NJ: Fairleigh-Dickinson University Press, 1981).

Armitage, Susan. *The Politics of Decontrol of Industry: Britain and the United States* (London: Weidenfeld & Nicolson, 1969).

Arndt, H. W. *The Economic Lessons of the Nineteen Thirties* (London: Oxford University Press for the Royal Institute of International Relations, 1944).

Artaud, Denise. *La question des dettes interalliées et la reconstruction de l'Europe (1917–1929)*, t. 1 (Lille: Atelier Reproduction des Theses, Université de Lille III, 1978).

Auffray, Pierre. *Pierre de Margerie (1861–1942) et la vie diplomatique de son temps* (Paris: Librairie C. Klincksieck, 1976).

Augé-Laribé, Michel. *La politique agricole de la France, de 1880 à 1940* (Paris: Presses Universitaires de France, 1950).

Autin, Jean. *Foch ou le triomphe de la volonté* (Paris: Perrin, 1987).

Badel, Laurence. *Un milieu liberal et européen: le grand commerce français 1925–1948* (Paris: Ministère de l'économie, des finances et de l'industrie, Comité pour l'histoire économique et financière de la France, 1999).

Badger, Anthony J. *The New Deal: The Depression Years, 1933–1940* (Houndmills, Basingstoke: Macmillan, 1989).

Baechler, Christian. *Gustave Stresemann (1878–1929): De l'impérialisme à la sécurité collective* (Strasbourg: Presses universitaires de Strasbourg, 1996).

Bailey, Thomas A. *Woodrow Wilson and the Lost Peace* (New York: Macmillan, 1944).

Bairoch, Paul. *Victoirēs et déboires in Bairoch, Poul*, Vol. III, *Victoires et déboires* (Paris: Galimard, 1997).

Baker, Ray Stannard. *Woodrow Wilson and World Settlement*, 3 Vols (Garden City NY: Doubleday, Page & Company, 1922).

Bardoux, Jacques. *L'Île et l'Europe: La Politique anglaise (1930–1932)* (Paris: Librairie Delagrave, 1933).

Bariéty, Jacques. *Les relations franco-allemandes après la première guerre mondiale, 10 novembre 1918–10 janvier 1925, de l'Exécution à la Négociation* (Paris: Pedone, 1977).

Bariéty, Jacques, Alfred Guth and Jean-Marie Valentin (eds), *La France et l'Allemagne entre les deux guerres mondiales. Actes du colloque tenu en Sorbonne (Paris IV) 15–16–17 janvier 1987* (Nancy: Presses universitaires de Nancy, 1987).

Barker, Ernest. *National Character and the Factors in Its Formation* (London: Methuen & Co., 1927).

Barnett, Corelli. *The Collapse of British Power* (London: Eyre Methuen, 1972).

Barnett, Corelli. *The Swordbearers: Studies in Supreme Command in the First World War* (Harmondsworth Middlesex: Penguin, 1966).

Barré, Jean-Luc. *Le Seigneur-Chat: Philippe Berthelot 1866–1934* (Paris: Plon, 1988).

Bartley, Numan V. *The Rise of Massive Resistance: Race and Politics in the South during the 1950s* (Baton Rouge LA: Louisiana State University Press, 1969).

Beard, Charles Austin and William Beard. *The American Leviathan: The Republic in the Machine Age* (London: Cape, 1930).

Beau de Loménie, Emmanuel. *Les responsabilités des dynasties bourgeoises*, t. IV, *du Cartel à Hitler 1924–1933* (Paris: Éditions Denoël, 1963).

Beck, Earl R. *Germany Rediscovers America* (Tallahassee, FL: University of Florida Press, 1968).

Becker, Jean-Jacques and Serge Berstein. *Victoire et frustrations 1914–1929* (Paris: Seuil, 1990).

Becker, Joseph and Klaus Hildebrand (eds), *Internationale Beziehungen in der Weltwirtschaftskrise 1929–1933: Referate und Diskussionsbeiträge eines Augsburger Symposions 29 März bis 1 April 1979* (Munich: Vögel, 1980).

Bell, P. M. H. *France and Britain, 1900–1940: Entente and Estrangement* (Harlow: Longman, 1996).

Beloff, Max. *Imperial Sunset*, Vol. 1, *Britain's Liberal Empire, 1897–1921* (London: Methuen & Co. Ltd., 1969).

Bennett, Edward W. *Germany and the Diplomacy of the Financial Crisis, 1931* (Cambridge MA: Harvard University Press, 1962).

Benns, F. Lee. *Europe since 1914 in Its World Setting*, 8th ed. (New York: F. S. Crofts & Co., 1955).

Berber, Fritz. (ed.), *Das Diktat von Versailles: Entstehung – Inhalt – Zerfall. Eine Darstellung in Dokumenten* (Essen: Essener Verlagsantalt GmbH, 1939).

Berg, A. Scott. *Lindbergh* (London: Macmillan, 1998).

Bernard, Philippe and Henri Dubief. *The Decline of the Third Republic, 1914–1938*, transl. by Anthony Forster (Cambridge: Cambridge University Press, 1988).

Berstein, Serge. *Edouard Herriot ou la République en personne* (Paris: Presses de la Fondation Nationale des Sciences Politiques, 1985).

Berstein, Serge. *Histoire du Parti Radical*, 2 t. (Paris: Presses de la Fondation des Sciences Politiques, 1980, 1981).

Berstein, Serge. *Le 6 février* (Paris: Gallimard/Julliard, 1975).

Best, Antony, Jussi Hanhimäki, Joseph A. Maiolo and Kirsten E. Schulze. *An International History of the Twentieth Century* (London: Routledge, 2004).

Birnbaum, Pierre. *'La France aux Français': Histoire des haines nationalistes* (Paris: Seuil, 1993).

Birnbaum, Pierre. *The Jews of the Republic: A Political History of State Jews in France from Gambetta to Vichy*, transl. by Jane Marie Todd (Stanford CA: Stanford University Press).

Blancheton, Bertrand. *Le Pape et l'Empereur: La Banque de France, la direction du Trésor et la politique monétaire de la France (1914–1928)* (Paris: Albin Michel, 2001).

Bond, Brian. *British Military Policy between the Two World Wars* (Oxford: Clarendon Press, 1980).

Bonin, Hubert. *La Banque de l'Union Parisienne (1874/1904–1974): Histoire de la deuxième grande banque d'affaires française* (Paris: Editions Plage, 2001).

Bonin, Hubert. *La Banque nationale de credit (1913–1932): Histoire de la quatrième banque de dépôt française en 1913–1932* (Paris: Editions Plage, 2002).

Bonin, Hubert. *Histoire économique de la France depuis 1880* (Paris: Masson, 1988).

Bonin, Hubert, Yannick Lung and Steven Tolliday (eds), *Ford, 1903–2003: The European History*, Vol. 1 (Paris: Editions Plage, 2003).

Bonnefous, Edgar and George. *Histoire politique de la Troisième République*, t. IV, *Cartel des gauches et Union nationale* (Paris: Presses Universitaires de France, 1960).

Boorstin, Daniel J. *America and the Image of Europe: Reflections on American Thought* (New York: Meridian Books, 1960).

Borchardt, Knut, *Perspectives on Modern German Economic History and Policy*, transl. by Peter Lambert (Cambridge: Cambridge University Press, 1991).

Bosworth, R. J. B. *Mussolini* (London: Arnold, 2002).

Bouvier, Jean, André Armengaud, Pierre Barral , *Histoire économique et sociale de la France*, t. IV, Vol. 2, *Le temps des Guerres mondiales et de la Grande crise (1914–vers 1950)* (Paris: Presses Universitaires de France, 1980).

Boyce, Robert W. D. *British Capitalism at the Crossroads: A Study in Politics, Economics and International Relations* (Cambridge: Cambridge University Press, 1987).

Boyce, Robert (ed.), *French Foreign and Defence Policy, 1918–1940: The Decline and Fall of a Great Power* (London: Routledge, 1998).

Boyce, Robert and Joseph Maiolo (eds), *The Origins of World War Two* (Basingstoke: Palgrave Macmillan, 2003).

Boyle, Andrew. *Montagu Norman* (London: Cassell, 1967).

Braeman, John, Robert H. Bremner and David Brody (eds), *Change and Continuity in Twentieth-Century America: The 1920's* (Columbus OH: Ohio State University Press, 1968).

Brodziak, Sylvie and Michel Drouon (eds), *Clemenceau et le monde anglo-saxon* (La Crèche: Geste Editions, 2005).

Brogan, Hugh. *The Penguin History of the USA*, 2nd ed. (Harmondsworth Middlesex: Penguin, 2001).

Brown, Malcolm. *The Imperial War Museum Book of the Somme* (London: Sidgewick and Jackson, 1996).

Brown, W. A. *The International Gold Standard Reinterpreted*, Vol. II (New York: National Bureau of Economic Research, 1940).

Bullock, Alan. *Hitler, a Study in Tyranny*, rev. ed. (London and New York: Hamlyn, 1973).

Burk, Kathleen. *Britain, America and the Sinews of War, 1914–1918* (London: Allen & Unwin, 1985).

Burner, David. *Herbert Hoover, A Public Life* (New York: Alfred A. Knopf, 1979).

Burns, James M. *Roosevelt: The Lion and the Fox* (London: Secker and Warburg, 1956).

Busch, Briton Cooper. *Hardinge of Penshurst. A Study in the Old Diplomacy* (South Bend: Archon Books, 1980).

Bussière, Eric. *La France, La Belgique et l'organisation économique de l'Europe (1918–1935)* (Paris: Comité pour l'histoire économique et financière, 1992).

Butler, J. R. M. *Lord Lothian (Philip Kerr), 1882–1940* (London: Macmillan, 1960).

Cabanes, Bruno. *La victoire endeuillée: la sortie de guerre des soldats français (1918–1920)* (Paris: Seuil, 2004).

Callwell, Sir C. E. *Field-Marshal Sir Henry Wilson: His Life and Diaries*, Vol. II (London: Cassell and Company, Ltd., 1927).

Cannadine, David. *Mellon: An American Life* (London: Allen Lane, 2006).

Carls, Stephen D. *Louis Loucheur and the Shaping of Modern France, 1916–1931* (Baton Rouge LA: Louisiana State University Press, 1993).

Carlton, David. *MacDonald versus Henderson: The Foreign Policy of the Second Labour Government* (London: Macmillan, 1970).

Carr, Edward Hallet. *The Twenty Years Crisis, 1919–1939: An Introduction to the Study of International Relations*, 2nd ed. rev. (Basingstoke: Macmillan, 1995).

Carroll, John Alexander and Mary Wells Carroll, *George Washington*, Vol. 7, *First in Peace* (New York: Charles Scribner's Sons, 1957).

Carter, Paul A. *America in the 1920s* (London: Routledge and Kegan Paul, 1969).

Cashman, Sean Dennis. *America Ascendant: From Theodore Roosevelt to FDR in the Century of American Power, 1901–1945* (New York and London: New York University Press, 1998).

Chambers II, John Whiteclay. *The Tyranny of Change: America in the Progressive Era, 1890–1920* (New Brunswick NJ: Rutgers University Press, 2000).

Chancellor, Edward. *Devil Take the Hindmost: A History of Financial Speculation* (London: Macmillan, 1999).

Chandler, Lester V. *American Monetary Policy, 1928–1941* (New York: Harper and Row, 1971).

Chandler, Lester V. *America's Greatest Depression, 1929–1941* (New York: Harper and Row, 1970).

Chandler, Lester V. *Benjamin Strong, Central Banker* (Washington DC: The Brookings Institution, 1958).

Chernow, Ron. *The House of Morgan* (London: Simon & Schuster, 1990).

Cherny, Robert W. *A Righteous Cause: The Life of William Jennings Bryan* (Boston MA and Toronto: Little, Brown and Co., 1985).

Church, Roy A. *Herbert Austin: The British Motor Car Industry to 1941* (London: Europa, 1979).

Churchill, Winston S. The Second World War, Vol. 1, The Gathering Storm (London: Cassel & Co., 1950).

Cienciala, Anna Maria. *Poland and the Western Powers 1938–1939 a Study in the Interdependence of Eastern and Western Europe* (London: Routledge and Kegan Paul, 1968).

Clark, Keith. *International Communications: The American Attitude* (New York: Columbia University Press, 1931).

Clarke, Stephen V. O. *Central Bank Cooperation, 1924–1931* (New York: Federal Reserve Bank of New York, 1967).

Clay, Sir Henry. *Lord Norman* (London: Macmillan, 1957).

Clements, Kendrick A. *William Jennings Bryan: Missionary Isolationist* (Knoxville: University of Tennessee Press, 1982).

Cleveland, Harold van B. and Thomas F. Huertas, *Citibank, 1812–1970* (Cambridge MA and London: Harvard University Press, 1985).

Cohrs, Patrick O. *The Unfinished Peace after World War I: America, Britain and the Stabilisation of Europe, 1919–1932* (Cambridge MA: Harvard University Press, 2008).

Crawford, Arthur W. *Monetary Management under the New Deal: The Evolution of a Managed Currency System – Its Problems and Results* (Washington DC: American Council on Public Affairs, 1940).

Crowe, Sybil and Edward Corp. *Our Ablest Public Servant: Sir Eyre Crowe, 1864–1925* (Braunton Devon: Merlin Books, 1993).

David, Edward (ed.), *Inside Asquith's Cabinet: From the Diaries of Charles Hobhouse* (London: John Murray, 1977).

Davies, Norman. *Europe, a History* (London: Pimlico, 1997).

Dawson, William Harbutt. *Germany under the Treaty* (London: Allen & Unwin, 1933).

De Grazia, Victoria. *Irresistible Empire: America's Advance through Twentieth-Century Europe* (Cambridge MA: Belknap Press of Harvard University Press, 2005).

Debû-Bridel, Jacques. *L'Agonie de la Troisième République 1929–1939* (Paris: Editions du Bateau Ivre, 1948).

Denny, Ludwell. *America Conquers Britain: A Record of Economic War* (New York: Alfred A. Knopf, 1930).

Di Nolfo, Ennio. *Mussolini e la politica estera italiana (1919–1933)* (Padua: CEDAM, 1960).

Dingli, Laurent. *Louis Renault* (Paris: Flammarion, 2000).

Dockrill, Michael. *British Establishment Perspectives on France, 1936–40* (Basingstoke: Macmillan, 1999).

Dockrill, Michael and Brian McKercher (eds), *Diplomacy and World Power: Studies in British Foreign Policy, 1890–1950* (Cambridge: Cambridge University Press, 1996).Doise, Jean and Maurice Vaïsse, *Diplomatie et outil militaire 1871–1991*, 2nd ed. (Paris: Editions du Seuil, 1992).

Donald, Sir Robert. *The Polish Corridor and the Consequences* (London: Thornton Butterworth, 1929).

Dormois, Jean-Pierre. *The French Economy in the Twentieth Century* (Cambridge: Cambridge University Press, 2004).

Dower, John. *War without Mercy: Race and Power in the Pacific War*, rev. ed. (New York: Pantheon, 1993).

Downes, Randolph C. *The Rise of Warren Gamaliel Harding, 1865–1920* (Ohio, Ohio State University Press, 1970).

Dulles, Eleanor Lansing. *The Bank for International Settlements at Work* (New York: Macmillan, 1932).

Dulles, Foster Rhea. *America's Rise to World Power, 1898–1954* (London: Hamilton, 1955).

Dunning, J. H. and C. J. Thomas, *British Industry. Change and Development in the Twentieth Century* (London: Hutchinson, 1961).

Duroselle, Jean-Baptiste. *Clemenceau* (Paris: Arthème Fayard, 1988).

Dutton, David. *Austen Chamberlain: Gentleman in Politics* (Egerton: Ross Anderson, 1985).

Eichengreen, Barry. *Golden Fetters: The Gold Standard and the Great Depression, 1919–1939* (Oxford: Oxford University Press, 1992).

Einzig, Paul. *The World Economic Crisis, 1929–1931* (London: Macmillan, 1931).

Eyck, Erich. *A History of the Weimar Republic*, Vol. 2 (Cambridge MA: Harvard University Press, 1964).

Farber, David R. *Sloan Rules: Alfred P. Sloan and the Triumph of General Motors* (Chicago IL: University of Chicago Press, 2002).

Faron, Olivier. *Les enfants du deuil: orphelins et pupilles de la nation de la première guerre mondiale 1914–1941* (Paris: La Découverte, 2002).

Farrar, Margorie Milbank. *Principled Pragmatist: The Political Career of Alexandre Millerand* (New York and Oxford: Berg, 1991).

Faulkner, Harold. *From Versailles to the New Deal: A Chronicle of the Harding-Coolidge-Hoover Era* (New Haven CN and London: Yale University Press, 1951).

Faure, Marcel. *Les Paysans dans la société française* (Paris: Librairie Armand Colin, 1966).

Fausold, Martin L. *The Presidency of Herbert C. Hoover* (Lawrence KS: University of Kansas Press, 1985).

Fausold, Martin L. and George T. Mazuzan (eds), *The Hoover Presidency: A Reappraisal* (Albany NY: State University of New York Press, 1974).

Feiertag, Olivier. *Wilfrid Baumgartner: Un grand commis des finances à la croisée des pouvoirs (1902–1978)* (Paris: Ministre de l'Économie, des Finances et de l'Industrie, 2006).

Feiling, Sir Keith G. *The Life of Neville Chamberlain* (London: Macmillan, 1946).

Feis, Herbert. *The Diplomacy of the Dollar: First Era, 1919–1932* (Baltimore MD: Johns Hopkins University Press, 1950).

Ferguson, Niall. *The Pity of War* (London: Penguin, 1999).

Ferrell, Robert H. *American Diplomacy in the Great Depression: Hoover-Stimson Foreign Policy, 1929–1933* (New Haven CN: Yale University Press, 1957).

Ferrell, Robert H. *The Presidency of Calvin Coolidge* (Lawrence KS: University Press of Kansas, 1998).

Ferris, John Robert. *Men, Money, and Diplomacy: The Evolution of British Strategic Policy, 1919–1926* (Ithaca NY: Cornell University Press, 1989).

Fisher, Ken. *The Only Three Questions that Count* (New York: John Wiley and Sons, 2007).

Fleury, Antoine and Lubor Jílek (eds), *Le Plan Briand d'Union fédérale européenne* (Bern: Peter Lang, 1998).

Frank, Robert. *La hantise du déclin: le rang de la France en Europe, 1920–1960: finances, défense et identité nationale* (Paris: Belin, 1994).

Frank(enstein), Robert. *Le Prix de réarmement français 1935–1939* (Paris: Publications de la Sorbonne, 1980).

Fraser, Steve. *Wall Street: A Cultural History* (London: Faber and Faber, 2005).

Freymond, Jean. *Le IIIe Reich et la réorganisation économique de l'Europe, 1940–1942: origines et projets* (Genève: Université de Genève, Institut universitaire de hautes études internationales, 1974).

Frieden, Jeffrey A. *Global Capitalism: Its Fall and Rise in the Twentieth Century* (New York: W. W. Norton & Co., 2006).

Friedman, Milton and Anna J. Schwartz. *A Monetary History of the United States, 1867–1960* (Princeton NJ: Princeton University Press, 1963).

Fussell, Paul. *The Great War and Modern Memory* (Oxford: Oxford University Press, 2000).

Galbraith, John Kenneth. *The Great Crash, 1929* (Harmondsworth Middlesex: Penguin, 1961).

Gardner, Lloyd C. *Economic Aspects of New Deal Diplomacy* (Madison WI: University of Wisconsin Press, 1964).

Garraty, John A. *Henry Cabot Lodge, a Biography* (New York: Alfred Knopf, 1953).

Garside, W. R. *British Unemployment, 1919–1939: A Study in Public Policy* (Cambridge: Cambridge University Press, 1990).

Gayer, Arthur D. and Carl T. Schmidt. *American Economic Foreign Policy: Postwar History, Analysis, and Interpretation. A Report to the Twelfth International Studies Conference, Bergen, August 27–September 1939* (New York: American Coordinating Committee for International Studies, 1939).

Geiss, Imanuel. *German Foreign Policy, 1871–1914* (London: Routledge, 1976).

Geisst, Charles R. *Visionary Capitalism: Financial Markets and the American Dream in the Twentieth Century* (New York and Westport CN: Praeger, 1990).

Geisst, Charles R. *Wall Street: A History* (New York and Oxford: Oxford University Press, 1997).

Gelber, Lionel M. *The Rise of Anglo-American Friendship: A Study in World Politics, 1898–1906* (London: Oxford University Press, 1938).

Gilbert, Martin. *Churchill, a Life* (London: Heinemann, 1991).

Gilbert, Martin. *First World War Atlas* (London: Weidenfeld and Nicolson, 1970).

Gilbert, Martin. *Winston S. Churchill, Vol. IV, 1916–1922* (London: Heinemann, 1975).

Gilbert, Martin. (ed.), *Lloyd George* (Englewood Hills NJ: Prentice-Hall Inc. 1968).

Girault, René and Gilbert Ziebura (eds), *Léon Blum, socialiste européen* (Bruxelles: Editions Complexe, 1995).

Girault, René and Robert Frank. *Turbulente Europe et nouveaux mondes, 1914–1941*, 2nd ed. (Paris: Aramand Colin, 1998).

Glad, Betty. *Charles Evans Hughes and the Illusions of Innocence: A Study in American Diplomacy* (Urbana IL: University of Illinois Press, 1966).

Godfrey, John F. *Capitalism at War: Industrial Policy and Bureaucracy in France, 1914–1918* (Leamington Spa: Berg, 1987).

Goldberg, David J. *Discontented America: The United States in the 1920s* (Baltimore MD and London: The Johns Hopkins University Press, 1999).

Gordon, Margaret S. *Barriers to World Trade: A Study of Recent Commercial Policy* (New York: Macmillan, 1941).

Gordon, Milton M. *Assimilation in American Life* (New York: Oxford University Press, 1964).

Graml, Hermann. *Zwischen Stresemann und Hitler: Die Aussenpolitik der Präsidialkabinette Brüning, Papen und Schleicher* (Munich: R. Oldenbourg Verlag, 2001).

Grayson, Richard S. *Austen Chamberlain and the Commitment to Europe: British Foreign Policy, 1924–29* (London: Frank Cass, 1997).

Haber, L. F. *The Chemical Industry, 1900–1930* (Oxford: Oxford University Press, 1971).

Haight, Frank Arnold. *A History of French Commercial Policies* (New York: Macmillan , 1941).

Hall, Thomas E. and J. David Ferguson. *The Great Depression: An International Disaster of Perverse Economic Policies* (Ann Arbor MI: The University of Michigan Press, 1998).

Hamilton, Richard. *Who Voted for Hitler?* (Princeton NJ: Princeton University Press, 1982).

Hardach, Gerd. *Weltmarktorientierung und Relative Stagnation: Währungpolitik in Deutschand 1924–1931* (Berlin: Duncker und Humbolt, 1976).

Hargrave, John. *Professor Skinner, alias Montagu Norman* (London: Wells Gardner, Darton & Co., 1939).

Hayes, Peter. *Industry and Ideology: IG Farben in the Nazi Era* (Cambridge: Cambridge University Press, 1987).

Haynes, John Earl (ed.), *Calvin Coolidge and the Coolidge Era: Essays on the History of the 1920s* (Washington DC: Library of Congress, 1998).

Headrick, Daniel R. *The Invisible Weapon: Telecommunications and International Politics, 1851–1945* (New York: Oxford University Press, 1991).

Heale, M. J. *American Anti-Communism: Combating the Enemy within, 1830–1970* (Baltimore MD: Johns Hopkins University Press, 1990).

Hearden, Patrick J. *Roosevelt Confronts Hitler: America's Entry into World War II* (DeKalb IL: North Illinois University Press, 1987).

Heiden, Konrad. *The History of National Socialism* (London: Methuen, 1934).

Heilbroner, Robert. *Between Capitalism and Socialism: Essays in Political Economics* (New York: Vintage, 1970).

Herf, Jeffrey. *Reactionary Modernism: Technology, Culture and Politics in Weimar and the Third Reich* (Cambridge: Cambridge University Press, 1984).

Hicks, John D. *Republican Ascendancy, 1921–1933* (London: Hamish Hamilton, 1960).

Hill, Martin. *The Economic and Financial Organization of the League of Nations: A Survey of Twenty-Five Years' Experience* (Washington DC: Carnegie Endowment for International Peace, 1946).

Hodson, Henry V. *Slump and Recovery, 1929–1937: A Survey of World Economic Affairs* (London: Oxford University Press for the Royal Institute of International Affairs, 1938).

Hofstader, Richard. *Anti-Intellectualism in American Life* (London: Jonathan Cape, 1964).

Hogan, Michael. *Informal Entente: The Private Structure of Cooperation in Anglo-American Diplomacy, 1918–1928* (Columbia MO: University of Missouri Press, 1977).

Hollis, Maurice Christopher. *The Oxford Union* (London: Evans, 1965).

Holmes, Richard. *Tommy: The British Soldier on the Western Front, 1914–18* (London: HarperCollins, 2004).

Horsman, Reginald. *Race and Manifest Destiny: The Origins of American Racial Anglo-Saxonism* (Cambridge MA: Harvard University Press, 1981).

Howard, Michael. *The Continental Commitment* (Harmondsworth Middlesex: Penguin, 1972).

Howard, Michael. *War and the Liberal Conscience: The George Macaulay Trevelyan Lectures in the University of Cambridge, 1977* (New Brunswick NJ: Rutgers University Press, 1989).

Howson, Susan. *Domestic Monetary Management in Britain, 1918–38* (Cambridge: Cambridge University Press, 1975).

Hughes, Judith M. *To the Maginot Line: Politics of Military Preparation in the 1920s* (Cambridge MA: Harvard University Press, 1971).

Hunt, Michael H. *The American Ascendancy: How the United States Gained and Wielded Global Dominance* (Chapel Hill NC: University of North Carolina Press, 2007).

Hynes, Samuel. *A War Imagined: The First World War and English Culture* (New York: Collier Books, 1990).

Jacobson, Jon. *Locarno Diplomacy: Germany and the West, 1925–1929* (Princeton NJ: Princeton University Press, 1972).

Jacobson, Matthew Frye. *Barbarian Virtues: The United States Encounters Foreign Peoples at Home and Abroad, 1876–1917* (New York: Hill and Wang, 2000).

James, Harold. *The End of Globalization: Lessons from the Great Depression* (Cambridge MA: Harvard University Press, 2001).

James, Harold. *The Reichsbank and Public Finance in Germany, 1924–1933: A Study of the Politics of Economics during the Great Depression* (Frankfurt: Fritz Knapp Verlag, 1985).

Jeannesson, Stanislas. *Poincaré, la France et la Ruhr 1922–1924: Histoire d'une occupation* (Strasbourg: Presses Universitaires de Strasbourg, 1998).

Jenkins, Roy. *Asquith* (London: Collins, 1964).

Johannet, René. *Le principe des nationalités* (Paris: Nouvelle Librairie Nationale, 1918).

Johnson, Gaynor (ed.), *The Foreign Office and British Diplomacy in the Twentieth Century* (London: Routledge, 2004).

Johnson, Gaynor (ed.), *Locarno Revisited: European Diplomacy, 1920–1929* (London: Frank Cass, 2004).

Johnson, Gove G. *The Treasury and Monetary Policy* (Cambridge MA: Harvard University Press, 1939).

Johnson, H. Clark. *Gold, France, and the Great Depression, 1919–1932* (New Haven CN: Yale University Press, 1997).

Johnson, Paul Barton. *Land Fit for Heroes: The Planning of British Reconstruction, 1916–1919* (Chicago IL: University of Chicago Press, 1968).

Jones, Joseph M. Jr *Tariff Retaliation: Repercussions of the Smoot-Hawley Bill* (Philadelphia PA: University of Pennsylvania Press, 1943).

Judt, Tony. *Postwar: A History of Europe since 1945* (London: Penguin, 2006).

Kahler, Miles and Werner Link. *Europe and America: A Return to History* (New York: Council on Foreign Relations Press, 1996).

Kantorowicz, Hermann. *The Spirit of British Policy and the Myth of the Encirclement of Germany*, transl. by W. H. Johnston (London: Allen & Unwin, 1931).

Kaplan, L. S. *The United States and NATO: The Formative Years* (Lexington KY: University of Kentucky Press, 1984).

Keeton, Edward David. *Briand's Locarno Policy: French Economics, Politics, and Diplomacy, 1925–1929* (New York: Garland, 1987).

Kemp, Tom. *The French Economy, 1913–1939: The History of a Decline* (London: Longmans, 1972).

Kennan, George F. *American Diplomacy, 1900–1950* (Chicago IL: University of Chicago Press, 1951).

Kennedy, Paul M. *The Realities behind Diplomacy: Background Influences on British External Policy, 1865–1980* (London: Fontana, 1981).

Kennedy, Paul M. *The Rise of Anglo-German Antagonism, 1860–1914* (London: The Ashfield Press, 1980).

Kennedy, Paul M. and Anthony Nicholls (eds), *Nationalist and Racialist Movements in Britain and Germany before 1914* (London: Macmillan, 1981).

Kent, Bruce. *The Spoils of War: The Politics, Economics, and Diplomacy of Reparations, 1918–1932* (Oxford: Clarendon Press, 1989).

Kenwood A. G. and A. L. Lougheed, *The Growth of the International Economy, 1820–2000*, 4th ed. (London: Routledge, 1999).

Kindleberger, Charles P. *The World in Depression, 1929–1939* (London: Allen Lane The Penguin Press, 1973).

Kirshner, Jonathan. *Appeasing Bankers: Financial Caution on the Road to War* (Princeton NJ: Princeton University Press, 2007).

Klein, Julius. *Frontiers of Trade* (New York: Century, 1929).

Knipping, Franz. *Deutschland, Frankreich und das Ende der Locarno-Ära 1928–1931: Studien zur internationalen Politik in der Anfangsphase der Weltwirtschaftskrise* (Munchen: R. Oldenbourg Verlag, 1987).

Knox, MacGregor. *Common Destiny: Dictatorship, Foreign Policy, and War in Fascist Italy and Nazi Germany* (Cambridge: Cambridge University Press, 2000).

Kohn, Hans. *The Mind of Germany: The Education of a Nation* (New York: Charles Scribner's Sons, 1930).

Kuisel, Richard F. *Capitalism and the State in Modern France: Renovation & Economic Management in the Twentieth Century* (Cambridge: Cambridge University Press, 1983).

Kynaston, David. *The City of London*, Vol. III, *Illusions of Gold 1914–1945* (London: Chatto & Windus, 1999).

Lamb, Richard. *The Drift to War, 1922–1939* (London: Bloomsbury, 1991).

Larmour, Peter. *The French Radical Party in the 1930's* (Stanford CA: Stanford University Press, 1964).

Leffler, Melvyn P. *The Elusive Quest: America's Pursuit of European Stability and French Security, 1919–1933* (Chapel Hill NC: University of North Carolina Press, 1979).

Lentin, Antony. *Lloyd George and the Lost Peace: From Versailles to Hitler, 1919–1940* (London: Palgrave, 2001).

Lentin, Antony. *Lloyd George, Woodrow Wilson and the Guilt of Germany: An Essay in the Pre-history of Appeasement* (Leicester: Leicester University Press, 1984).

Leopold, John A. *Alfred Hugenberg: The Radical National Campaign against the Weimar Republic* (New Haven CN and London: Yale University Press, 1977).

Leuchtenburg, William E. *Franklin D. Roosevelt and the New Deal, 1932–1940* (New York: Harper & Row, 1963).

Levin, N. Gordon Jr. *Woodrow Wilson and World Politics: America's Response to War and Revolution* (New York, Oxford University Press, 1968).

Lévy-Leboyer, Maurice and Jean-Claude Casanova. *Entre l'état et le marché: l'économie française des années 1880 à nos jours* (Paris: Gallimard, 1991).

Lévy-Leboyer, Maurice (dir.), *La position internationale de la France: Aspects économiques et financiers XIXe – XXe siècles* (Paris: Editions de l'École des Hautes Études en Sciences Sociales, 1977).

Lewis, Cleona. *America's Stake in International Investments* (Washington DC: The Brookings Institution, 1938).

L'Huillier, Fernand. *Dialogues franco-allemands (1925–1933)* (Gap: Presses de l'Université de Strasbourg, 1971).

Liddell Hart, Basil H. *Foch, The Man of Orleans* (London: Eyre and Spottiswoode, 1931).

Liefmann, Robert. *Cartels, Concerns and Trusts*, transl. by D. H. MacGregor (London: Methuen, 1932).

Liepmann, Heinrich. *Tariff Levels and the Economic Unity of Europe*, transl. by H. Stenning (London: Allen & Unwin, 1938).

Lindley, Ernest K. *The Roosevelt Revolution: First Phase* (London: Gollancz, 1934).

Link, Arthur S. *The Higher Realism of Woodrow Wilson and Other Essays* (Nashville TN: Vanderbilt University Press, 1971).

Link, Arthur S. *Woodrow Wilson: Revolution, War, and Peace* (Arlington Heights, IL: AHM Publishing Corporation, 1979).

Link, Arthur S. and William B. Catton. *American Epoch, a History of the United States since 1900*, Vol. II: *The Age of Franklin D. Roosevelt, 1921–1945*, 4th ed. (New York: Alfred A. Knopf, 1973).

Link, Werner. *Die amerikanische Stabilisierungspolitik in Deutschland 1921–32* (Düsseldorf: Drost Verlag, 1970).

Livingston, James. *Origins of the Federal Reserve System: Money, Class, and Corporate Capitalism, 1890–1913* (Ithaca NY: Cornell University Press, 1986).

Lloyd, Craig. *Aggressive Introvert: A Study of Herbert Hoover and Public Relations Management, 1912–1932* (Columbus OH: Ohio State University Press, 1972).

MacDonald, C. A. *United States, Britain and Appeasement, 1936–1939* (London: Macmillan, 1981).

MacDonogh, Giles. *Prussia. The Perversion of an Idea* (London: Sinclair-Stevenson, 1994).

MacDougall, Hugh A. *Racial Myth in English History: Trojans, Teutons, and Anglo-Saxons* (Montreal: Harvest House and Hanover and London: University Press of New England, 1982).

Mackay, Ruddock F. *Balfour: Intellectual Statesman* (Oxford: Oxford University Press, 1985).

MacMillan, Margaret. *Paris, 1919: Six Months that Changed the World* (New York, Random House, 2002).

Maddison, Angus. *Monitoring the World Economy, 1820–1992* (Paris: OECD, 1995).

Magraw, Roger. *France, 1815–1914: The Bourgeois Century* (London: Fontana, 1983).

Maier, Charles S. *Recasting Bourgeois Europe: Stabilization in France, Germany, and Italy in the Decade after World War I* (Princeton NJ: Princeton University Press, 1975).

Malkiel, Burton G. *A Random Walk Down Wall Street*, rev. ed. (New York: W. W. Norton & Co., 1996).

Mallet, Sir Bernard and C. Oswald George, *British Budgets, Third Series, 1921–22 to 1932–33* (London: Macmillan, 1933).

Mansergh, Nicholas. *Survey of British Commonwealth Affairs*, Vol. 4, *Problems of Wartime and Post-War Change, 1939–1952* (London: Oxford University Press, 1958).

Marks, Sally. *The Ebbing of European Ascendancy: An International History of the World, 1914–1945* (London: Arnold, 2002).

Marquand, David. *Ramsay MacDonald* (London: Jonathan Cape, 1977).

Marseille, Jacques. *Empire colonial et capitalisme français: histoire d'un divorce* (Paris: Albin Michel, 1984).

Martial, René. *La race française* (Paris: Mercure de France, 1934).

Martin, Benjamin F. *France and the Après Guerre, 1918–1924: Illusions and Disillusionment* (Baton Rouge LA: Louisiana State University Press, 1999).

Marwick, Arthur. *Clifford Allen: The Open Conspirator* (Edinburgh: Oliver and Boyd, 1964).

Masur, Gerhard. *Imperial Berlin* (New York: Dorset Press, 1989).

Maurras, Charles. *Mes idées politiques* (Paris: Editions Abatros, 1986).

Mayers, David. *George Kennan and the Dilemmas of U.S. Foreign Policy* (New York: Oxford University Press, 1988).

McDonough, Frank. *The Conservative Party and Anglo-German Relations, 1905–1914* (Houndmills, Basingstoke: Palgrave, 2007).

McDougall, Walter A. *France's Rhineland Diplomacy, 1914–1924: The Last Bid for a Balance of Power in Europe* (Princeton NJ: Princeton University Press, 1978).

McKercher, B. J. C. and D. J. Moss (eds), *Shadow and Substance in British Foreign Policy, 1895–1939: Memorial Essays Honouring C. J. Lowe* (Edmonton: University of Alberta Press, 1984).

Meyer, Martin. *The Fed: The Inside Story of How the World's Most Powerful Financial Institution Drives the Markets* (New York: Free Press, 2001).

Middlemas, Keith and John Barnes, *Baldwin: A Biography* (London: Weidenfeld and Nicolson, 1969).

Millis, Walter. *Road to War: America, 1914–1917* (Boston MA and New York: Houghton Mifflin, 1935).

Milza, Pierre. *Mussolini* (Paris: Fayard, 1999).

Mitchell, B. R. *International Historical Statistics: Europe, 1750–2000* (Basingstoke: Palgrave Macmillan, 2003).

Mitchell, B. R. and Phyllis Deane, *Abstract of British Historical Statistics* (Cambridge: Cambridge University Press, 1962).

Mitchie, Ranald and Philip Williamson (eds), *The British Government and the City of London in the Twentieth Century* (Cambridge: Cambridge University Press, 2004).

Moggridge, D. E. *British Monetary Policy, 1924–1931: The Norman Conquest of $4.86* (Cambridge: Cambridge University Press, 1972).

Morgan, Kenneth O. *Lloyd George* (London: Weidenfeld and Nicolson, 1974).

Morinosuke, Kajima, Jacques de Launay, Vittorio Pons and Arnold Zurcher, *Coudenhove-Kalergi, le pionnier de l'Europe unie* (Lausanne: Université de Lausanne, 1971).

Morrison, Elting. *Turmoil and Tradition: A Study of the Life and Times of Henry L. Stimson* (Boston MA: Houghton Mifflin, 1960).

Morrow, Ian F. D. with L. M. Sieveking, *The Peace Settlement in the German-Polish Borderlands: A Study of Conditions To-day in the Prewar Prussian Provinces of East and West Prussia*, for the Royal Institute of International Affairs (London: Oxford University Press, 1936).

Moulton, H. G. and Leo Pasvolsky, *World War Debt Settlements* (New York: Brookings Institution, 1926).

Mouré, Kenneth. *The Gold Standard Illusion: France, the Bank of France, and the International Gold Standard, 1914–1939* (Oxford: Oxford University Press, 2002).

Mowat, Charles Loch. *Britain between the Wars, 1918–1940* (London: Methuen, 1978).

Murphy, David T. *The Heroic Earth: Geopolitical Thought in Weimar Germany, 1918–1933* (Kent OH: Kent State University Press, 1997).

Murray, Robert K. *The Harding Era: Warren G. Harding and His Administration* (Minneapolis MN, University of Minnesota Press, 1969).

Murray, Robert K. *Red Scare: A Study in National Hysteria, 1919–1920* (Minneapolis MN: University of Minnesota Press, 1955).

Nelson, Harold I. *Land and Power. British and Allied Policy on Germany's Frontiers, 1916–19* (Newton Abbot: David & Charles, 1971).

Neurrisse, André. *Histoire du franc*, 2nd ed. (Paris: Presses Universitaires de France, 1967).

Nicolson, Harold. *Curzon: The Last Phase, 1919–1925: A Study in Postwar Diplomacy* (London: Constable, 1934).

Nish, Ian. *Alliance in Decline: A Study in Anglo-Japanese Relations, 1908–23* (London: Athlone Press, 1972).

Noiriel, Gérard. *Les origines républicaines de Vichy* (Paris: Hachette, 1999).

Nolan, Michael E. *The Inverted Mirror: Mythologizing the Enemy in France and Germany, 1898–1914* (New York and Oxford: Berghahn Books, 2005).

Nye, Russel B. *Midwestern Progressive Politics: A Historical Study of Its Origins and Development, 1870–1958* (East Lansing MI: Michigan State University Press, 1959).

Orde, Anne. *British Policy and European Reconstruction after the First World War* (Cambridge: Cambridge University Press, 1990).

Oudin, Bernard. *Aristide Briand* (Paris: Perrin, 2004).

Overy, Richard J. *The Origins of the Second World War*, 2nd ed. (Harlow: Longman, 1998).

Overy, Richard J. *Viscount Nuffield* (London: Europa, 1976).

Paligot, Carole Reynaud. *La République raciale: Paradigme raciale et idéologie républicaine 1860–1930* (Paris: Presses Universitaires de France, 2006).

Parker, R. A. C. *Chamberlain and Appeasement: British Policy and the Coming of the Second World War* (Basingstoke: Macmillan, 1993).

Parrillo, Vincent N. *Strangers to These Shores: Race and Ethnic Relations in the United States*, 2nd ed. (New York: John Wiley and Sons, 1985).

Parrini, Carl. Heir to Empire: United States Economic Diplomacy, 1916–1923 (Pittsburgh PA: Pittsburgh University Press, 1969).

Parrish, Michael E. *Anxious Decades: America in Prosperity and Depression, 1920–1944* (New York and London: Norton, 1992).

Pasvolsky, Leo. *Current Monetary Issues* (Washington DC: Institute of Economics, 1933).

Pegg, Carl H. *Evolution of the European Idea, 1914–1932* (Chapel Hill NC: University of North Carolina Press, 1983).

Perkins, Bradford. *The Great Rapprochement: England and the United States, 1895–1914* (New York: Atheneum, 1968).

Petrie, Sir Charles. *The Life and Letters of the Right Hon. Sir Austen Chamberlain*, Vol. II (London: Cassell and Company Ltd., 1940).

Peukert, Detlef J. K. *The Weimar Republic: The Crisis of Classical Modernity*, transl. by Richard Deveson (London: Allen Lane, 1991).

Platt, D. C. M. *British Investment Overseas on the Eve of the First World War: The Use and Abuse of Numbers* (Basingstoke: Macmillan, 1986).

Pollard, Sidney. *Development of the British Economy, 1914–1950* (London: Edward Arnold, 1962).

Polanyi, Karl. *The Great Transformation* (Boston MA: Gower Beacon Press, 1957).

Potter, Jim. *The American Economy between the World Wars* (London: Macmillan, 1974).

Pratt, Julius W., Vincent P. De Santis and Joseph M. Siracusa, *A History of United States Foreign Policy*, 4th ed. (Englewood Cliffs NJ: Prentice-Hall, 1980).

Prochasson, Christophe and Anne Rasmussen, *Au nom de la patrie: les intellectuels et la première guerre mondiale 1910–1919* (Paris: Editions la Découverte, 1996).

Pruessen, Ronald W. *John Foster Dulles: The Road to Power* (New York: Free Press, 1982).

Ramsden, John. *Don't Mention the Germans: The British and the Germans since 1890* (London: Little Brown, 2006).

Richie, Alexandra. *Faust's Metropolis: A History of Berlin* (New York: Carol & Graf, 1998).

Roberts, Andrew. *'The Holy Fox': A Biography of Lord Halifax* (London: Weidenfeld and Nicolson, 1991).

Roberts, John Stuart, *Siegfried Sassoon, 1886–1967* (London: Richard Cohen, 1999).

Roediger, David R. *Working towards Whiteness: How America's Immigrants Became White* (New York: Basic Books, 2006).

Roger, Philippe. *The American Enemy: A Story of French Anti-Americanism*, transl. by Sharon Bowman (Chicago IL: University of Chicago Press, 2005).

Romasco, Albert U. *The Poverty of Abundance: Hoover, Nation, the Depression* (New York: Oxford University Press, 1965).

Rosenberg, Emily S. *Financial Missionaries to the World: The Politics and Culture of Dollar Diplomacy, 1900–1930* (Cambridge MA and London: Harvard University Press, 1999).

Roskill, Stephen. *Hankey, Man of Secrets*, Vol. II, *1919–1931* (London: Collins, 1972).

Roth, François. *Raymond Poincaré* (Paris: Fayard, 2000).

Rowland, Peter. *Lloyd George* (London: Barrie & Jenkins, 1975).

Sabouret, Anne. *MM. Lazard Frères et Cie. Une saga d'une fortune* (Paris: Editions Olivier Orban, 1987).

Sauvy, Alfred. *Histoire économique de la France entre les deux guerres*, t. I – IV (Paris: Fayard, 1965–75).

Sayers, Richard S. *The Bank of England, 1891–1944*, 3 Vols (Cambridge: Cambridge University Press, 1976).

Schor, Ralph. *L'Opinion française et les étrangers 1919–1939* (Paris: Publications de la Sorbonne, 1985).

Schrecker, Ellen. *The Hired Money: The French Debt to the United States, 1917–1929* (New York: Arno Press, 1979).

Schuker, Stephen A. *American 'Reparations' to Germany, 1919–33: Implications for the Third-World Debt Crisis*. Princeton Studies in International Finance No. 61 (Princeton NJ: Princeton University Press, 1988).

Schuker, Stephen A. *The End of French Predominance in Europe. The Financial Crisis of 1924 and the Adoption of the Dawes Plan* (Chapel Hill NC: University of North Carolina Press, 1976).

Schulz, Matthias. *Deutschland, der Völkerbund und die Frage der europäischen Wirtschaftsordnung 1925–1933* (Hamburg: Verlag Dr. R. Kramer, 1997).

Self, Robert C. (ed.), *The Austen Chamberlain Diary Letters* (Cambridge: Cambridge University Press, 1995).

Shannon, David A. *Between the Wars: America, 1919–1941* (Boston MA: Houghton Mifflin Co., 1965).

Siebert, Ferdinand. *Aristide Briand 1862–1932. Ein Staatsmann zwischen Frankreich und Europa* (Erlenbach-Zürich und Stuttgart, 1973).

Skidelsky, Robert. *John Maynard Keynes*, Vol. 1: *Hopes Betrayed, 1883–1920* (London: Macmillan, 1983).

Skidelsky, Robert. *Politicians and the Slump: The Labour Government of 1929–1931* (Harmondsworth Middlesex: Penguin, 1970).

Smiley, Gene. *Rethinking the Great Depression* (Chicago IL: Ivan R. Dee, 2002).

Smith, J. D. *Managing White Supremacy: Race, Politics and Citizenship in Jim Crow Virginia* (Chapel Hill NC: University of North Carolina Press, 2002).

Sobel, Robert. *The Big Board: A History of the New York Stock Market* (New York: The Free Press, 1965).

Sobel, Robert. *ITT. The Management of Opportunity* (London: Sidgwick & Jackson, 1982).

Södersten, Bo. *International Economics*, 2nd ed. (London: Macmillan, 1984).

Soucy, Robert. *French Fascism: The First Wave, 1924–1933* (New Haven CN: Yale University Press, 1986).

Soule, George. *Prosperity Decade: From War to Depression, 1917–1929* (New York: Rhinehart, 1964).

Soulié, Michel. *La vie politique d'Edouard Herriot* (Paris: Librairie Armand Colin, 1962).

Southard, Frank A. *American Industry in Europe* (Boston MA and New York: Houghton Mifflin Co., 1931).

Soutou, Georges-Henri. *L'Or et le sang. Les buts de guerre économiques de la Première Guerre mondiale* (Paris: Librairie Arthème Fayard, 1989).

Steiner, Zara S. *The Foreign Office and Foreign Policy, 1898–1914* (Cambridge: Cambridge University Press, 1969).

Steiner, Zara S. *The Lights That Failed: European International History, 1919–1933* (Oxford: Oxford University Press, 2005).

Steiner, Zara S. and Keith Nielson, *Britain and the Origins of the First World War*, 2nd ed. (Basingstoke: Palgrave, 2003).

Stern-Rubarth, Edgar. *Three Men Tried: Austen Chamberlain, Stresemann, Briand and Their Fight for a New Europe: A Personal Memoir* (London: Duckworth, 1939).

Stevenson, David. *Cataclysm: The First World War as Political Tragedy* (New York: Basic Books, 2004).

Stevenson, David. *The First World War and International Politics* (Oxford: Oxford University Press, 1988).

Stevenson, David. *French War Aims against Germany, 1914–1919* (Oxford: Clarendon Press, 1982).

Strauss, David. *Menace in the West: The Rise of French Anti-Americanism in Modern Times* (Westport CN: Greenwood Press, 1978).

Studenski, Paul and Herman E. Krooss. *Financial History of the United States*, 2nd ed. (New York: McGraw Hill, 1963).

Suarez, Georges. *Briand, sa vie – son oeuvre avec son journal et de nombreux documents inédits*, t. V–VI, *L'artisan de la paix 1918–1923* (Paris: Plon, 1941, 1952).

Suval, Stanley. *The Anschluss Question in the Weimar Era: A Study of Nationalism in Germany and Austria, 1918–1932* (Baltimore MD: Johns Hopkins University Press, 1974).

Taylor, A. J. P. *English History, 1914–1945* (Harmondsworth Middlesex: Penguin, 1976).

Temin, Peter. *Lessons from the Great Depression* (Cambridge MA: MIT Press, 1989).

Temperley, H. W. V. (ed.), *A History of the Peace Conference of Paris*, Vol. II, *The Settlement with Germany* (London: Hodder and Stoughton, 1920).

Tombs, Robert and Isabelle Tombs. *That Sweet Enemy* (London: William Heinemann, 2006).

Trachtenberg, Marc. *Reparation in World Politics: France and European Economic Diplomacy, 1916–1923* (New York: Columbia, 1980).

Trevelyan, George M. *Grey of Fallodon* (London: Longmans, Green & Co., 1940).

Turner, Arthur. *The Cost of War: British Policy on French War Debts, 1918–1932* (Brighton: Sussex Academic Press, 1999).

Turner, Henry Ashby. *German Big Business and the Rise of Hitler* (New York: Oxford University Press, 1985).

Unger, Gérard. *Briand* (Paris: Fayard, 2005).

Urquhart M. C. and K. A. H. Buckley (eds), *Historical Statistics of Canada* (Cambridge: Cambridge University Press, 1965).

Vaïsse, Maurice. *Sécurité d'abord: La politique française en matière de désarmement, 9 décember 1930–17 avril 1934* (Paris: Presses Universitaires de France, 1981).

Van Roon, Ger. *Small States in Years of Depression: The Oslo Alliance, 1930–1940* (Assen, Netherlands: Van Gorcum, 1989).

Vanlangenhove, Fernand. *L'élaboration de la politique étrangère de la Belgique entre les deux guerres mondiales* (Bruxelles: Palais des Académies, 1979).

Verhey, Geoffrey. *The Spirit of 1914: Militarism, Myth and Mobilization in Germany* (Cambridge: Cambridge University Press, 2000).

Wallace, Stuart. *War and the Image of Germany: British Academics, 1914–1918* (Edinburgh: John Donald Publishers, 1988).

Walton, Garry M. and Hugh Rockoff, *History of the American Economy*, 10th ed. (Mason OH: South-Western, 2005).

Wandycz, Piotr S. *France and Her Eastern Allies, 1919–1925: French-Czechoslovak-Polish Relations from the Paris Peace Conference to Locarno* (Minneapolis MN: The University of Minnesota Press, 1962).

Warburg, Paul M. *The Federal Reserve System, Its Origin and Growth: Reflections and Recollections*, Vol. 1 (New York: Macmillan, 1930).

Warner, Geoffrey. *Pierre Laval and the Eclipse of France* (London: Eyre & Spottiswoode, 1968).

Warren, Harris Gaylord. *Herbert Hoover and the Great Depression* (Westport CN: Greenwood Press, 1980).

Watson, David Robin. *Georges Clemenceau: A Political Biography* (London: Eyre Methuen Ltd., 1974).

Watt, Donald Cameron. *Personalities and Policies: Studies in the Formation of British Foreign Policy in the Twentieth Century* (London: Longman, 1965).

Watt, Donald Cameron. *How War Came: The Immediate Origins of the Second World War, 1938–1939* (London: Heinemann, 1989).

Webb, Barry. *Edmund Blunden: A Biography* (New Haven CN: Yale University Press, 1990).

Weber, Eugen. *Action Française: Royalism and Reaction in Twentieth-Century France* (Stanford CA: Stanford University Press, 1962).

Weber, Eugen. *The Hollow Years: France in the 1930s* (New York: W. W. Norton, 1994).

Weber, Thomas. *Our Friend 'The Enemy': Elite Education in Britain and Germany before World War I* (Stanford CA: Stanford University Press, 2008).

Whaley, Barton. *Covert German Rearmament, 1919–1939* (Frederick MD: University Publications of America, 1984).

Wheeler-Bennett, John W. *King George VI: His Life and Reign* (London: Macmillan, 1958).

Wheeler-Bennett, John W. *The Nemesis of Power. The German Army in Politics, 1918–1945* (London: Macmillan, 1953).

White, William Allen. *Woodrow Wilson: The Man, His Times and His Tasks* (Boston MA: Houghton, 1924).

Widenor, William C. *Henry Cabot Lodge and the Search for American Foreign Policy* (Berkeley CA: University of California Press, 1980).

Wigmore, Barrie A. *The Crash and Its Aftermath: A History of Securities Markets in the United States, 1929–1933* (Westport CT: Greenwood Press, 1985).

Wilkins, Mira. *The Maturing of Multinational Enterprise: American Business Abroad from 1914 to 1970* (Cambridge MA: Harvard University Press.

Wilkins, Mira and Frank Ernest Hill, *American Business Abroad: Ford on Six Continents* (Detroit: Wayne State University Press, 1964).

Williams, Francis. *A Pattern of Rulers* (London: Longmans, 1965).

Williamson, David G. *The British in Germany, 1918–1930: The Reluctant Occupiers* (New York and Oxford: Berg, 1991).

Wilson, Joan Hoff. *American Business and Foreign Policy, 1920–1933* (Lexington KY: The University Press of Kentucky, 1971).

Wilson, Joan Hoff. *Herbert Hoover: Forgotten Progressive* (Boston MA: Little Brown, 1975).
Wilson, Keith M. *Channel Tunnel Visions, 1850–1945: Dreams and Nightmares* (London: Hambledon, 1995).
Wolfe, Martin. *The French Franc between the Wars* (New York: Columbia University Press, 1951).
Wrench, John Evelyn. *Geoffrey Dawson and Our Times* (London: Hutchinson, 1955).
Wrench, John Evelyn. *Struggle, 1914–1920* (London: Ivor Nicholson & Watson, 1935).
Wright, Jonathan. *Gustav Stresemann, Weimar's Greatest Statesman* (Oxford: Oxford University Press, 2002).
Wurm, Clemens. *Business, Politics and International Relations: Steel, Cotton and International Cartels in British Politics, 1924–39*, transl. by Patrick Salmon (Cambridge: Cambridge University Press, 1993).
Wyckhoff, Peter. *Wall Street and the Stock Markets: A Chronology (1644–1971)* (Philadelphia PA, New York and London: Chilton Book Company, 1972).
Young, Robert J. *Power and Pleasure: Louis Barthou and the Third French Republic* (Montreal: McGill-Queen's University Press, 1991).
Ziebura, Gilbert. *World Economy and World Politics, 1924–1931: From Reconstruction to Collapse*, transl. by Bruce Little (Oxford and New York: Berg, 1990).
Zurcher, Arnold. *The Struggle to Unite Europe, 1940–1958: An Historical Account of the Development of the Contemporary European Movement from Its Origin in the Pan-European Union to the Drafting of the Treaties for Euratom and the European Common Market* (Westport CN: Greenwood Press, 1975).

Articles and Contributions to Collective Works

Artaud, Denise. 'L'impérialisme américain en Europe, au lendemain de la première guerre mondiale', *Relations internationales*, 1976, no. 8, pp. 323–41.
Atkin, John. 'Official Regulation of British Overseas Investment, 1914–1931', *Economic History Review*, 2nd ser. 23/2 (August 1970), pp. 324–35.
Badel, Lawrence. 'Trêve douanière, libéralisme et conjoncture (septembre 1929–mars 1930)', *Relations internationales*, no. 82 (été 1995), pp. 141–61.
Baechler, Christian. 'L'Alsace-Lorraine dans les relations franco-allemandes de 1918 à 1933', in Bariéty, Guth and Valentin (eds), *La France et l'Allemagne entre les deux guerres mondiales*, pp. 85–95.
'The Balance of Payments in the Interwar Period: Further Details', *Bank of England Quarterly Review*, vol. 14, no. 1 (March 1974), pp. 47–52.
Bariéty, Jacques. 'Aristide Briand: les raisons d'un oubli', in Antoine Fleury and Lubor Jílek (eds), *Le Plan Briand d'Union fédérale européenne* (Bern: Peter Lang, 1998), pp. 1–13.
Bariéty, Jacques. 'France and the Politics of Steel, from the Versailles Treaty to the International Steel Entente, 1919–1926', in Robert Boyce (ed.), *French Foreign and Defence Policy, 1918–1940: The Decline and Fall of a Great Power* (London: Routledge, 1998), ch. 2.
Bariéty, Jacques and Charles Bloch. 'Une tentative de réconciliation franco-allemande et son échec (1932–1933)', *Revue d'histoire moderne et contemporaine*, no 15 (juillet–septembre 1968), pp. 433–65.
Beckett, Ian. 'The British Army, 1914–18: The Illusion of Change', in John Turner (ed.), *Britain and the First World War* (London: Unwin Hyman, 1988), pp. 99–116.
Berstein, Serge. 'Les conceptions du parti radical en matière de politique économique extérieure', *Relations internationales*, vol. 13 (1978), pp. 71–89.
Blanchard, Olivier. Review of Brender and Pisani, 'Preface to Global Imbalances. Is the World Economy Really at Risk?' 20 February 2007, http://blogs.ft.com/wolfforum, last accessed 10 November 2008.
Blatt, Joel. 'The Parity That Meant Superiority: French Naval Policy towards Italy at the Washington Conference, 1921–22 and Interwar French Foreign Policy', *French Historical Studies*, vol. 12, no. 2 (Autumn 1981), pp. 223–48.

Blattmann, Ekkehard. 'Frankreich, "Geist", Heil. Über einige Züge von Heinrichs Manns Frankreichverehrung', in Bariéty, Guth and Jean-Marie Vallentin (eds), *La France et l'Allemagne entre les deux guerres mondiales*, pp. 125–46.

Booth, Alan E. and Sean Glyn. 'Unemployment in the Interwar period: A Multiple Problem', *Journal of Contemporary History*, vol. 10, no. 4 (Oct. 1975), pp. 611–36.

Bouvier, Jean. 'A propos de la stratégie d'encaisse (or et devises) de la Banque de France de juin 1928 à l'été 1932', in Bouvier, *L'Historien sur son métier: Etudes économiques XIXe – XX e siècles* (Paris: Editions des archives contemporaines, 1989), pp. 347–67.

Bouvier, Jean. 'A propos du déclenchement de deux "grandes crises" du XXe siècle', in Bouvier, *L'Historien sur son métier: Etudes économiques XIXe – XX e siècles* (Paris: Editions des archives contemporaines, 1989), pp. 125–33.

Boyce, Robert. 'Business as Usual: The Limits of French Economic Diplomacy, 1926–1933', in R. Boyce (ed.), *French Foreign and Defence Policy, 1918–1940: The Decline and Fall of a Great Power* (London: Routledge, 1998), ch. 6.

Boyce, Robert. 'Creating the Myth of Consensus: Public Opinion and Britain's Return to the Gold Standard in 1925', in P. L. Cottrell and D. E. Moggridge (eds), *Money and Power: Essays in Honour of L. S. Pressnell* (London: Macmillan, 1987), ch. 7.

Boyce, Robert. 'Economics', in R. Boyce and J. Maiolo (eds), *The Origins of World War Two: The Debate Continues* (Houndmills Basingstoke: Palgrave, 2003), pp. 249–72.

Boyce, Robert. 'Economics and the Crisis of British Foreign Policy Management, 1914–45', in Dick Richardson and Glyn Stone (eds), *Decisions and Diplomacy: Essays in Twentieth-Century International History* (London: Routledge, 1995), ch. 1.

Boyce, Robert. 'The Government, the City of London and the Subversive Impact of the Gold Standard, 1925–1931', in Ranald Michie and Phillip Williamson (eds), *The Power to Influence: The British Government and the City of London* (Cambridge: Cambridge University Press, 2004), pp. 215–35.

Boyce, Robert. 'Insects and International Relations: Canada, France, and British Agricultural "Sanitary" Restrictions between the Wars', *International History Review*, 9/1 (February 1987), pp. 1–30.

Boyce, Robert. 'Introduction: 1940 as End and Beginning in French Inter-War History and Historiography', *French Foreign and Defence Policy, 1918–1940: The Decline and Fall of a Great Power* (London: Routledge, 1998), pp. 1–9.

Boyce, Robert. 'The Origins of Cable and Wireless Limited, 1918–1939: Capitalism, Imperialism and Technical Change', in Bernard Finn and Daqing Yang (eds), *Communications Under the Seas: A Twice-Rejuvenated 19th-Century Technology and Its Social Implications* (Cambridge MA: MIT Press, forthcoming).

Boyce, Robert. 'Wall Street and the Spectre of the "Money Power" in Small-Town America before and after the Crash of 1929', in Antoine Capet, Philippe Romanski and Aïssatou Sy-Wonyu (eds), *Etats de New York* (Rouen: Publications de l'Université de Rouen, 2000), pp. 19–31.

Brandes, Joseph. 'Product Diplomacy: Herbert Hoover's Anti-Monopoly Campaign at Home and Abroad', in Hawley (ed.), *Herbert Hoover as Secretary of Commerce*, pp. 185–216.

Brookhiser, Richard. 'Others, and the WASP World They Aspired To', in Richard Delgado and Jean Stefancic (eds), *Critical White Studies: Looking Behind the Mirror* (Philadelphia PA: Temple University Press, 1997), pp. 360–67.

Bunard, Stephan. 'Français-Anglais: 100 ans de "mésentente cordiale"?: Entretien avec Fabrice Serodes', http://www.europeplusnet.info/article92.html, last accessed 17 Sept. 2008.

Burk, Kathleen. 'The House of Morgan in Financial Diplomacy, 1920–1930', in McKercher (ed.), *Anglo-American Relations in the 1920s*, pp. 125–57.

Burk, Kathleen. 'The Lineaments of Foreign Policy: The United States and a "New World Order", 1919–1939', *Journal of American Studies*, vol. 26, no. 3 (1992), pp. 377–91.

Bussière, Eric. 'L'Organisation économique de la SDN et la naissance du régionalisme économique en Europe', *Relations internationales*, no. 75 (automne 1993), pp. 301–13.

Bussière, Eric. 'Premiers schémas européens et économie internationale durant l'entre-deux-guerres', *Relations internationales*, no. 123 (automne 2005), pp. 51–68.

Cairns, John C. 'A Nation of Shopkeepers in Search of a Suitable France, 1919–40', *American Historical Review*, vol. 79, no. 3 (June 1974), pp. 710–43.

'The Cancellation Controversy', *Congressional Digest*, vol. II, no. 3 (December 1922), pp. 77–8.

Carlton, David. 'The Anglo-French Compromise on Arms Limitation, 1928', *Journal of British Studies*, vol. 8, no. 2 (May 1969), pp. 141–62.

Cassels, Alan. 'Repairing the Entente Cordiale and the New Diplomacy', *Historical Journal*, vol. 23, no. 1 (Mar. 1980), pp. 133–53.

Castley, J. P. 'The Empire's Foreign Cars', *Empire Review*, no. 341 (June 1929), pp. 371–6.

Childers, Thomas. 'The Social Bases of the National Socialist Vote', *Journal of Contemporary History*, vol. 11, no. 4 (October 1976), pp. 17–42.

'China's 4 Trillion Yuan Stimulus to Boost Economy, Domestic Demand', Window of China, 9 November 2008, http://news.xinhuanet.com/english/2008-11/09/content_10331324.htm, last accessed 10 November 2008.

Coogan J. W. and P. F. 'The British Cabinet and the Anglo-French Staff Talks, 1905–1914: Who Knew What and When Did They Know It?', *Journal of British Studies*, 24/1, 1985, pp. 110–31.

Cornick, Martyn. 'Faut-il réduire l'Angleterre en esclavage? French Anglophobia in 1935', *Franco-British Studies*, special number (January 1993), pp. 3–17.

Costigliola, Frank. 'Anglo-American Financial Rivalry in the 1920s', *Journal of Economic History*, vol. 37, no. 4 (December 1977), pp. 911–34.

Costigliola, Frank. 'The Other Side of Isolationism: The Establishment of the First World Bank', *Journal of American History*, vol. 59, no. 3 (December 1972), pp. 602–20.

Cottrell, Philip L. 'Austria between Diplomats and Bankers, 1919–1931', in Gustav Schmidt (ed.), *Konstellationen International Politik 1924–1932: Politische und wirtschaftliche Faktoren in den Beziehungen zwischen Westeuropa und den Vereinigten Staaten* (Bochum: Studienverlag Dr. N. Brockmeyer, 1983), pp. 293–311.

Cottrell, P. L. 'Norman, the Bank of England and Europe during the 1920s: Case Studies of Belgian and Italian Stabilisation', Eric Bussière and Michel Dumoulin (eds), *Milieux économiques et intégration européenne en Europe occidentale au XXe Siècle* (Arras: Artois Presses Université, 1998), pp. 37–84.

Daieff, Guillaume 'Paul Claudel: pour une Europe formée des pays complémentaires', *Revue d'histoire diplomatique*, no. 106 (1992), pp. 63–76.

Davidson, Paul. 'Reforming the World's International Money', 14 November 2008, http://econ.bus.utk.edu/november%20newsschool.pdf, last accessed 4 December 2008.

Davies, Norman. 'Lloyd George and Poland, 1919–1920', *Journal of Contemporary History*, vol. 6, no. 3 (1971), pp. 132–54.

Davies, Norman. 'Sir Maurice Hankey and the Inter-Allied Mission to Poland, July–August 1920', *The Historical Journal*, vol. 15, no. 3 (September 1972), pp. 553–61.

Davies, Thomas R. 'France and the World Disarmament Conference of 1932–34', *Diplomacy & Statecraft*, vol. 15, no. 4 (2004), pp. 132–54.

Dayer, Roberta Allbert. 'Anglo-American Monetary Policy and Rivalry in Europe and the Far East, 1919–1931', in McKercher (ed.), *Anglo-American Relations in the 1920s*, pp. 158–86.

Debeir, Jean-Claude. 'La crise du franc de 1924: Un exemple de spéculation internationale', *Relations internationales*, no. 13 (1978), pp. 29–49.

Delury, John. 'Will America's Pain be China's Gain?' http://www.project-syndicate.org/commentary/delury2, last accessed 10 November 2008.

Dornbusch, Rudiger and Stanley Fischer. 'The Open Economy: Implications for Monetary and Fiscal Policy', in Robert J. Gordon (ed.), *The American Business Cycle: Continuity and Change* (Chicago IL: University of Chicago Press, 1986), pp. 459–516.

Dulles, John Foster. 'Our Foreign Loan Policy', *Foreign Affairs*, vol. 5 (1926–27), pp. 33–48.

Dumenil, Lynn. 'Reshifting the Perspectives on the 1920s: Recent Trends in Social and Cultural History', in John Earl Haynes, ed. *Calven Coolidge Era: Essays on the History of the 1920s* (Washington, DC: Library of Congress, 1998), pp. 63–96.

Dumoulin, Michel. 'La Belgique et le Plan Briand: l'annonce de réformes de structure au plan européen', in Antoine Fleury and Lubor Jilek (eds), *Le Plan Briand d'union fédérale européenne – Actes du colloque de Genève, septembre 1991* (Berne: Peter Lang, 1998), pp. 93–102.

Duranton-Crabol, Anne-Marie. 'De l'anti-américanisme en France vers 1930: la réception des Scènes de la vie future', *Revue d'histoire moderne et contemporaine*, vol. 48, no. 1 (janvier–mars 2001), pp. 120–37.

Eckes, Alfred E. Jr 'Revisiting Smoot-Hawley', *Journal of Policy History*, vol. 7, no. 3 (1995), pp. 295–310.

Falkus, M. E. 'United States Economic Policy and the "Dollar Gap" of the 1920s', *Economic History Review*, 2nd ser., vol. 24 (November 1971), pp. 599–623.

Feiertag, Olivier. 'Les banques d'émission et la BRI face à la dislocation de l'étalon-or (1931–1933): l'entrée dans l'âge de la coopération monétaire internationale', *Histoire, Économie et Société*, 18e année, 4e trimestre 1999, no. 4, pp. 715–36.

Ferencuhová, Bohumila. 'L'accueil du Plan Briand dans les milieux politiques tchèques et slovaques', in Antoine Fleury and Lubor Jilek (eds), *Le Plan Briand d'union fédérale européenne – Actes du colloque de Genève, septembre 1991* (Berne: Peter Lang, 1998), pp. 183–207.

Fleury, Alain. 'L'image de l'Allemagne dans le journal La Croix (1918–1940)', in Bariéty, Guth and Valentin (eds), *La France et l'Allemagne entre les deux guerres mondiales*, pp. 177–92.

Freymond, Jean F. 'Gustav Stresemann et l'idée d'une "Europe économique" (1925–1927)', *Relations internationales*, no. 8 (1976), pp. 343–60.

Girault, René. 'L'Europe centrale et orientale dans la stratégie des hommes d'affaires et des diplomats français', in Centre d'Etudes Européenes, *Relations financières internationales, facteurs de solidarités ou rivalités?* (Bruxelles: Bruylant, 1979), pp. 119–32.

'Global Views 2008', Chicago Council on Global Affairs, http://www.thechicagocouncil. org/UserFiles/Files/POS, last accessed 11 November 2008.

Goldstein, Erik. 'The Evolution of British Diplomatic Strategy for the Locarno Pact, 1924–1925', in Dockrill and McKercher (eds), *Diplomacy and World Power: Studies in British Foreign Policy, 1890–1950*, pp. 115–35.

Grayson, Richard S. 'The British Government and the Channel Tunnel, 1919–39', *Journal of Contemporary History*, vol. 31, no. 1 (Jan. 1996), pp. 125–44.

Greenwood, H. Powys. 'International Agreement in Trade and Industry', *Contemporary Review*, no. 733 (January 1927), pp. 41–5.

Guiffan, Jean. 'Les survivances de l'anglophobie dans la press française depuis la signature de l'Entente Cordiale (1904–2004)', in Diana Cooper-Richet and Michel Rapoport (eds), *L'Entente cordiale: cent ans de relations culturelles franco-britanniques (1904–2004)* (Paris: CREAPHIS, 2006), pp. 105–15.

Guillen, Pierre Guillen, 'La politique douanière de la France dans les années vingt', *Relations internationales*, vol. 16 (1978), pp. 315–31.

Henri, Daniel. 'Comptes, mécomptes et redressement d'une gestion industrielle: les Automobiles Peugeot de 1918 à 1930', *Revue d'Histoire Moderne et Contemporaine*, 32 (janvier–mars 1985), pp. 30–74.

Hogan, Michael. 'Revival and Reform: America's Twentieth-Century Search for a New Economic Order Abroad', *Diplomatic History*, vol. 8, no. 4 (Fall, 1984), pp. 287–310.

Horne, Gerald. 'Race from Power: U.S. Foreign Policy and the General Crisis of "White Supremacy"', *Diplomatic History*, 23/3 (Summer 1999), pp. 437–61.

Horsman, Reginald. 'Race and Manifest Destiny: The Origins of American Racial Anglo-Saxonism', in R. Delgado and J. Stefancic (eds), *Critical White Studies: Looking Behind the Mirror* (Philadelphia PA: Temple University Press, 1997), pp. 139–44.

'International Cartels', *International Affairs*, VI/5 (September 1927), pp. 265–77.

Jackson, Peter. 'France and the Problems of Security and International Disarmament after the First World War', *Journal of Strategic Studies*, 29/2 (April 2006), pp. 247–80.

Jeanneney, Jean-Noël. 'De la spéculation financière comme arme diplomatique: A propos de la première "bataille du franc" (november 1923–mars 1924)', *Relations internationales*, vol. 13 (1978), pp. 5–27.

Jeannesson, Stanislas. 'Jacques Seydoux et la diplomatie économique dans la France de l'après-guerre', *Revue d'histoire diplomatique*, no. 121 (printemps 2005), pp. 9–24.

Keiger, John F. V. 'Raymond Poincaré and the Ruhr Crisis', in Robert Boyce (ed.), *French Foreign and Defence Policy, 1918–1940: The Decline and Fall of a Great Power* (London: Routledge, 1998), ch. 3.

'Key Indicators: China', World Bank, http://siteresources.world.bank.org/INTEAPHALFYEARLYUPDATE/Resources, last accessed 10 November 2008.

Knipping, Franz. 'Die deutsche-französischen Beziehungen und die Weltwirtschaftskrise', in Bariéty, Guth and Valentin (eds), *La France et l'Allemagne entre les deux guerres mondiales*, pp. 48–57.

Krüger, Peter. 'European Ideology and European Reality: European Unity and German Foreign Policy in the 1920s', in Peter M. R. Stirk (ed.), *European Unity in Context: The Interwar Period* (London and New York: Pinter Publishers, 1989), pp. 84–98.

Lardner, John. 'The Lindbergh Legends', in Isabel Leighton (ed.), *The Aspirin Age, 1919–41* (Harmondsworth Middlesex: Penguin, 1964), pp. 200–23.

Lardy, Nicholas R. 'China: The Great New Economic Challenge?' in C. Fred Bergsten (ed.), *The United States and the World Economy: Foreign Economic Policy for the Next Decade* (Washington DC: Economic Policy Institute, 2004), ch. 4.

Leffler, Melvin P. 'The Origins of Republican War Debt Policy, 1921–1923: A Case Study in the Applicability of the Open Door Interpretation', *Journal of American History*, vol. 59, no. 3 (December 1972), pp. 585–601.

Leffler, Melvyn P. 'Herbert Hoover, The "New Era," and American Foreign Policy, 1921–29', in Ellis W. Hawley (ed.), *Herbert Hoover as Secretary of Commerce: Studies in New Era Thought and Practice* (Iowa City IA: University of Iowa Press, 1981), pp. 148–82

Léger, Yannick. 'Vers une démocratie européenne? Le concept de démocratie libérale dans la politique extérieure d'Aristide Briand dans les années 1920', *Revue d'histoire diplomatique*, no. 2 (2007), pp. 153–67.

Lentin, Antony. 'Lord Cunliffe, Lloyd George, Reparations and Reputations at the Paris Peace Conference, 1919', *Diplomacy & Statecraft*, vol. 10, no. 1 (March 1999), pp. 50–86.

Lentin, Antony. 'The Treaty That Never Was: Lloyd George and the Abortive Anglo-French Alliance of 1919', in Judith Loades (ed.), *The Life and Times of David Lloyd George* (Bangor: Headstart History, 1991), pp. 115–28.

Le Rider, Jacques. 'La Revue d'Allemagne: les germanistes francis, témoins et interprètes de la crise de la République de Weimar et du nazisme', in Hans-Manfred Bock, Reinhart Meyer-Kalkus and M. Trebitsch (eds), *Entre Locarno et Vichy: Les relations culturelles franco-allemandes dans les années 30 – Actes du colloque de Paris, 6 – 8 décembre 1990*, t. 1 (Paris, 1993), pp. 363–74.

Lévy-Leboyer, Maurice. 'La balance des paiements et l'exportation des capitaux français', in Lévy-Leboyer (dir.), *La position internationale de la France*, pp. 75–142.

Lévy-Leboyer, Maurice. 'Les contraintes du marché, les années 1880–1940: Introduction', in Lévy-Leboyer and Casanova (dirs), *Entre l'état et le marché*, pp. 189–98.

Ludlow, Peter. 'Britain and the Third Reich', in Hedley Bull (ed.), *The Challenge of the Third Reich: The Adam von Trott Lectures* (Oxford: Clarendon Press, 1986), pp. 141–62.

Ludlow, Peter. 'The Unwinding of Appeasement', in Lothar Kettenacker (ed.), *Das 'Andere Deutschland' im Zweiten Weltkrieg: Emigration und Widerstand in internationaler Perspektive* (Stuttgart: Ernst Klett Verlag, 1977), pp. 9–48.

Machefer, Philippe. 'Tardieu et La Rocque', *Bulletin de la Société d'Histoire Moderne*, 72/5 (1973), pp. 11–21.

MacMillan, Margaret. 'Clemenceau and Lloyd George: Friends or Something Else?', in Brodziak and Drouin (eds), *George Clemenceau et le monde anglo-saxon*, pp. 73–89.

Maddox, Robert James. 'Another Look at the Legend of Isolationism in the 1920s', *Mid-America*, vol. 53, no. 1 (January 1971), pp. 35–43.

Malament, Barbara C. 'Philip Snowden and the Cabinet Deliberations of August 1931', *Society for the Study of Labour History Bulletin*, 41 (autumn 1980), pp. 31–3.

Marguerat, Philippe. 'Banque de France et politique de puissance dans l'entre-deux-guerres: le problème des stabilisations monétaires en Europe orientale, 1927–1931', *Relations internationales*, no. 56, hiver 1988, pp. 475–85.

Maurer, John. 'Arms Control and the Washington Conference', in Eric Goldstein and John H. Maurer (eds), *The Washington Conference, 1921–22: Naval Rivalry, East Asian Stability and the Road to Pearl Harbor* (Ilford: Frank Cass, 1994), pp. 267–93.

McCoy, Donald R. 'To the White House: Herbert Hoover, August 1927–March 1929', in Martin Fausold and George T. Mazuzan (eds), *The Hoover Presidency: A Reappraisal* (Albany NY: State University of New York Press, 1974), pp. 29–49.

McGrattan, Ellen R. and Edward C. Prescott, 'The 1929 Stock Market: Irving Fisher Was Right', *Federal Reserve Bank of Minneapolis Research Department Staff Report*, No. 294, Revised December 2003.

McKercher, B. J. C. '"The Deep and Latent Mistrust": The British Official Mind and the United States', in McKercher (ed.), *Anglo-American Relations in the 1920s: The Struggle for Supremacy* (London: Macmillan, 1987), pp. 208–38.

McKercher, B. J. C. 'Of Horns and Teeth: The Preparatory Commission and the World Disarmament Conference, 1926–1934', in McKercher (ed.), *Arms Limitation and Disarmament: Restraints on War, 1899–1999* (Westport CN: Praeger, 1992), pp. 173–201.

'Medvedev Calls for Reform of World Financial System', 3 November 2008, Russia Today, http://www.russiatoday.com/business/news/32808, last accessed 12 November 2008.

Merrill, Dennis (ed.), *The Documentary History of the United States*, vol. 2 (Bethesda MD: University Publications of America, 1997)

Milward, A. S. 'Les placements français à l'étranger et les deux guerres mondiales', in Maurice Lévy-Leboyer (dir.), *La position internationale de la France: Aspects économiques et financiers XIXe – XXe siècles* (Paris: Editions de l'École des Hautes Études en Sciences Sociales, 1977), pp. 299–311.

Moggridge, D. E. 'The 1931 Financial Crisis – a New View', *The Banker* (August 1970), pp. 832–39.

Molteno, P. A. 'The Causes and Extent of American Prosperity', *Contemporary Review* (August 1927), pp. 176–84.

Moore, Michaela Hönicke. 'American Interpretations of National Socialism, 1933–1945', in Alan E. Steinweis and Daniel E. Rogers (eds), *The Impact of Nazism: New Perspectives on the Third Reich and Its Legacy* (Lincoln NE: University of Nebraska Press, 2003), pp. 1–18.

Murray, Williamson, 'Britain', in Robert Boyce and Joseph A. Maiolo (eds), *The Origins of World War II: The Debate Continues* (Basingstoke: Palgrave Macmillan, 2003), pp. 111–33.

Obstfeld, Maurice, Jay C. Shambaugh and Alan M. Taylor, 'Reserve Accumulation and Financial Stability', 18 October 2008, http://blogs.ft.com/wolfforum, last accessed 10 November 2008.

Organization for European Cooperation and Development. 'OECD StatExtracts, Balance of Payments, USA', http://stats.oecd.org/wbos/Index.aspx?datasetcode=MEI_BOP, last accessed 10 November 2008.

Paulson, Henry M. 'The Benefits of US-China Strategic Economic Dialogue', http://www.project-syndicate.org/commentary/paulson1, last accessed 10 November 2008.

Petter, Sir Ernest. 'Industry's Rights and Wrongs', *19th Century and After* (January 1926), pp. 57–67.

Pew Global Attitudes Project, 'World Publics Welcome Global Trade – But Not Immigration', 10 April 2007, http://pewglobal.org/reports/display.php?ReportID=258, last accessed 11 November 2008.

Pressnell, L. S. '1925: The Burden of Sterling', *Economic History Review*, 2nd ser., vol. 31, no. 1 (February 1978), pp. 67–88.

Reynolds, David. '1940: Fulcrum of the Twentieth Century?', *International Affairs*, vol. 66, no. 2 (April. 1990), 325–50.

Rhodes, Benjamin D. 'The Image of Britain in the United States, 1919–1929: A Contentious Relative and Rival', in B. J. C. McKercher (ed.), *Anglo-American Relations in the 1920s: The Struggle for Supremacy* (London: Macmillan, 1991), ch. 6.

Rhodes, Benjamin Rhodes, 'Reassessing "Uncle Shylock": The United States and the French War Debt, 1917–1929', *Journal of American History*, vol. 55 (March 1969), pp. 787–803.

Richard, Lionel. 'Aspects des relations intellectuelles et universitaires entre la France et l'Allemagne dans les années vingt', in Bariéty, Guth and Valentin (eds), *La France et l'Allemagne entre les deux guerres mondiales*, pp. 111–24.

Richardson, Dick and Carolyn Kitching, 'Britain and the World Disarmament Conference', in Peter Catterall with C. J. Morris (eds), *Britain and the Threat to Stability in Europe, 1918–45* (London: Leicester University Press, 1993), ch. 3.

Rodrik, Dani, 'How to Save Globalization from Its Cheerleaders' (revised), September 2007, http://www.project-syndicate.org/series/27/description, last accessed 10 November 2008.

Rogoff, Kenneth. 'The End of Financial Triumphalism?', http://www.project-syndicate.org/commentary/rogoff45, last accessed 10 November 2008.

Rogoff, Kenneth. 'The Hedge Fund Hegemon', http://www.project-syndicate.org/commentary/rogoff28, last accessed 10 November 2008.

'Russia Wants Further IMF Reform: Pankin', 14 May 2008, Financial Express, http://www.financialexpress.com/news/russia-wants-further-imf-reform-pankin/309541/, last accessed 1 September 2008.

'Russia's Finance Minister to Talk IMF Quota Reform in U.S.', Novosti, 7 April 2008, http://en.rian.ru/russia/20080407/103937944.html, last accessed 1 September 2008.

Saez, Emmanuel. 'Striking It Richer: The Evolution of Top Incomes in the United States (Update using 2006 preliminary estimates)', http://elsa.berkeley.edu/~saez/saez-UStopincomes-2006prel.pdf, last accessed 10 November 2008.

Schirmer, Sylvain. 'La dénonciation du traité de commerce franco-allemand d'août 1927: étapes et enjeux', *Relations internationales*, no. 82 (été 1995), pp. 163–73.

Schroeder-Gudehus, Brigitte. 'La science ignore-t-elle vraiment les frontiers? Les relations franco-allemandes dans le domaine des sciences', in Hans-Manfred Bock, Reinhart Meyer-Kalkus and M. Trebitsch (eds), *Entre Locarno et Vichy: Les relations culturelles franco-allemandes dans les années 30 – Actes du colloque de Paris, 6–8 décembre 1990*, t. 1 (Paris, 1993), pp. 393–403.

Schröter, Harm G. 'Europe in the Strategies of Germany's Electrical Engineering and Chemicals Trusts, 1919–1939', in Volker R. Berghahn (ed.), *Quest for Economic Empire: European Strategies of German Big Business in the Twentieth Century* (Oxford: Berghahn Books, 1996), pp. 35–54.

Scrutator, 'Georgians v. Jews: The Real Split in Moscow', *Empire Review*, vol. xlvii, no. 327 (April 1928), pp. 223–29.

Sharp, Alan and Keith Jeffrey, ' "Après la Guerre finit, Soldat anglais partit ...": Anglo-French Relations, 1918–25', *Diplomacy & Statecraft*, vol. 14, no. 2 (2003), pp. 119–38.

Shiller, Robert J., 'Has Financial Innovation Been Discredited?', http://www.project-syndicate.org/series/27/description, last accessed 10 November 2008.

Sirinelli, Jean-François. 'La génération du feu', in Antoine Prost (ed.), *14–18: Mourir pour la patrie* (Paris: Éditions du Seuil, 1992), pp. 298–311.

Soutou, Georges-Henri. 'L'alliance Franco-polonaise (1925–1933) ou comment s'en débarrasser?', *Revue d'Histoire Politique*, 2–4 (1981), pp. 295–347.

Soutou, Georges-Henri. 'De l'échec de Locarno à la naissance de la République Fédérale 1928–1948', *Revue d'histoire diplomatique*, no. 104 (1990), pp. 203–17.

Soutou, Georges-Henri. 'L'impérialisme du pauvre: la politique économique du gouvernment français en Europe Centrale et Orientale de 1918 à 1929', *Relations internationales*, no. 7 (1976), pp. 219–39.

'Statement by the Hon. Yi Gang, Governor of the Fund for the People's Republic of China at the Joint Annual Discussion', International Monetary Fund, 13 October 2008, www.imf.org/external/am/2008/speeches/pr16e.pdf, last accessed 31 October 2008.

Steigerwald, David. 'The Reclamation of Woodrow Wilson?', *Diplomatic History*, vol. 23, no. 1 (Winter 1999), pp. 79–99.

Stiglitz, Joseph E., 'Democratizing the International Monetary Fund and the World Bank: Governance and Accountability', *Governance, an International Journal of Public Policy, Administration and Institutions*, 16/1 (January 2003), pp. 111–39.

Stiglitz, Joseph E., 'The Overselling of Globalization', in Michael M. Weinstein (ed.), *Globalization: What's New?* (New York: Columbia University Press, 2005), pp. 228–61.

Strakosch, Sir Henry. 'Gold and the Price Level: A Memorandum on the Economic Consequences of Changes in the Value of Gold', *Economist* Supplement, 5 July 1930.

Summers, Lawrence. 'The Global Consensus on Trade Is Unravelling', 26 August 2008, http://blogs.ft.com/wolfforum, last accessed 11 November 2008.

'Table 1: US-China Trade Statistics and China's World Trade Statistics', US-China Business Council, http://www.uschina.org/statistics/tradetable.html, last accessed 10 November 2008.

Taussig, Frank W. 'The Tariff Act of 1930', *Quarterly Journal of Economics*, vol. 45, no. 1 (November 1930), pp. 1–21.

Temime, Émile. 'Races, nationalités et régionalisme', in Pierre Guiral and Émile Temime (dirs), *L'Idée de race dans la pensée politique française contemporaine* (Paris: Éditions du CNRS, 1977), pp. 270–9.

Thompson, J. A. 'William Appleman Williams and the "American Empire"', *Journal of American Studies*, vol. 7, no. 1 (1973), pp. 91–104.

Tiemann, Dieter. 'Zweigestelle Paris des DAAD und Institut français de Berlin: Zwei Einrichtungen der auswärtigen Kulturpolitik mit jugendpolitischer Orientierung', in Hans-Manfred Bock, Reinhart Meyer-Kalkus and M. Trebitsch (eds), *Entre Locarno et Vichy: Les relations culturelles franco-allemandes dans les années 30 – Actes du colloque de Paris, 6–8 décembre 1990*, t. 1 (Paris, 1993), pp. 287–300.

Viner, Jacob. 'Political Aspects of International Finance, II', *Journal of Business*, vol. 1 (1928), pp. 359–63.

Watson, David Robin. 'Les contacts de Clemenceau avec l'Angleterre 1865–1920', in Brodziak and Drouin (eds), *Clemenceau et le monde anglo-saxon*, ch. 10.

Watson, David Robin. 'The Making of the Treaty of Versailles', in Neville Waites (ed.), *Troubled Neighbours: Franco-British Relations in the Twentieth Century* (London: Weidenfeld and Nicolson, 1971), pp. 67–99.

Wells, Samuel F. Jr, 'New Perspectives on Wilsonian Diplomacy: The Secular Evangelism of American Political Economy', *Perspectives in American History*, vol. 6 (1972), pp. 387–419.

Wickham Steed, Henry. 'What Is Right?', in Francis Younghusband (ed.), *For the Right: Essays & Addresses by Members of the 'Fight for Right Movement'* (London: T Fisher Unwin, 1916), pp. 193–211.

Wilkins, Myra. 'Cosmopolitan Finance in the 1920s: New York's Emergence as an International Financial Centre', in Richard Sylla, Richard Tilly and Gabriel Tortella (eds), *The State, the Financial System and Economic Modernization* (Cambridge: Cambridge University Press, 1999), pp. 271–91.

'World Development Indicators', 2008, Country Statistical Information, China', World Bank, http://web.worldbank.org/WBSITE/EXTERNAL/DATASTATISTICS, last accessed 10 November 2008.

Young, Robert J. 'Preparations for Defeat: French War Doctrine in the Interwar Period', in Young (ed.), *An Uncertain Idea of France: Essays and Reminiscence on the Third Republic* (New York: Peter Lang, 2005), pp. 17–29.

Ziebura, Gilbert. 'Léon Blum et la conception de la sécurité collective', in René Girault and Gilbert Ziebura (eds), *Léon Blum, socialiste européen* (Bruxelles: Editions Complexe, 1995), pp. 17–27.

Unpublished theses and papers

Badel, Laurence. 'L'État à la conquête des marchés extérieurs au 20e siècle: Aux sources de la diplomatie économique de la France', dossier d'habilitation, Université de Paris-I Panthéon-Sorbonne, 2007.

Bonnery, Audrey. 'La France de la B.B.C., 1938–1944', Thèse de Docteur de l'Université de Bourgogne, 2005.

Boussabha-Bravard, Myriam. 'Ici Londres, des Européens parlent de l'Europe, 1904–1914: Emil Reich, J. Ellis Barker et les "races" européennes dans les grandes revues édouardiennes', unpublished conference paper, 2006.

Boyce, Robert. 'Aristide Briand: défendre la République par des accommodements économiques', paper presented at the conference on Aristide Briand, the League of Nations and Europe, Institut d'Etudes Politiques, Paris, 2002.

Carswell, Richard J. '"Britain Could Not Hope for a Better Ally": The British Press and France, 1939–40'. Reading Ph.D., 2008.

Cottrell, P. L. 'Austria between Diplomats and Bankers, 1919–1931', unpublished paper presented at Clare College Cambridge, 1982.

Feiertag, Olivier. 'La Banque de France, la monnaie et l'Europe au XXe siècle', dossier d'habilitation, Université de Paris X-Nanterre, 2003, t. 1, ch. 5.

Ulrich-Pier, Raphaële. 'René Massigli (1888–1988): Une vie de diplomate', t. 1, Thèse de Docteur de l'Université de Paris I, 2003.

Index

Secret of High Wages, The, 191
Seeley, J. R., 26
Seipel, Mgr Ignaz, 174, 368
Selby, Sir Walford, 344, 358
Seligmans, 319
Senate, 45–6, 61, 70, 71, 80, 82, 98, 410
  Senate Foreign Relations Committee, 158, 336, 364
  Sub-Committee on Banking and Currency, 386
Serbia, 27, 32
Serruys, Daniel, 250, 253
Sèvres, Treaty of, 96
Seydoux, Jacques, 1, 101, 123, 170–1, 173
  and Franco-British relations, 267
  and 'Norman system', 161
Seymour, Charles, 57
Sforza, Count, 174
Shanghai Municipal Council, 186
Shaw, George Bernard, 114, 174, 302
Shone, William, 313
Siegfried, André, 172, 191, 200, 283
Siemens & Halske, 186
Siepmann, Harry, 163, 216, 319, 325
silk duties, 199, 417
Simon, Sir John, 337, 344, 349, 350, 355, 358, 365, 368–9, 370, 372, 401, 419
Simons, Walter, 97, 104
Simson, Ernst von, 172
Sinclair, Sir Archibald, 328
Singapore, 437
Singer Sewing Machine, 187
Skinner, E. H. D., 147
Slavs, 19, 26, 27, 28, 50–1, 69, 138, 429, 435–8
  countries, 31, 34, 72, 73, 368
Smith, Al, 232
Smith, Charles Howard, 268
Smith, Goldwyn, 26
Smuts, Field-Marshal Jan Christiaan, 32, 45
  prejudices, 51, 58
  and reparations, 64
Smyrna, 124
Snow, T. M., 268
Snowden, Philip, 248, 276, 279, 294, 303, 304, 314, 327, 328, 381
  and BIS, 230
  budget crisis (1931), 320–1
  defends free trade, 260, 283
  deflects criticism from Bank of England, 259
  hysterical address, 326
  influence of Norman, 281
  receives freedom of the City, 205–6

resists tariff, 375–6
retains revenue duties, 263–4
revisionism, 313
Young plan, 227
Social Darwinism, 19
Socialist Party *(SFIO)*, 91, 101, 155, 166, 348, 351, *404*, 408–9, 419
Socialist Party (SPD), 286
  Reichsbanner, 282
Société Commerciale des Potasses, 185
Société Générale, 341
Society of Motor Manufacturers and Traders, 191
Solidarité Française, 419
Somme, battle of, 89
Sommer, Oskar, 197
Sonnino, Sidney Baron, 49
Sorel, Albert, 123
South Africa, 24, 32, 184, 185, 214, 231, 236
South America, 34, 180, 197, 446
Soviet Union, *see* Russia, Soviet
Spa conference (1920), 96–7, 102
Spain, 4, 11, 25, 236, 252
  war with the United States (1898), 82
Sprague, Oliver M. W., 274–5, 396
Spring Rice, Sir Cecil, 29
Stable Money Association, 211, 212, 217, 229
Stahlhelm, 257
Stalin, Joseph, 424
Stamp, Sir Josiah, 377
  and BIS, 229–30
  devises Dawes plan, 129
  and gold standard, 151
  Stable Money Association, 211
  Young plan, 225–6
Standard Oil of New Jersey, 183, 238, 242
Standstill, 329
Stanford University, 231
Statist, 373
Stavisky, Serge, 409–11, 419–20
steel, 96, 170
  cartel, 173
Stephenson, Rome C., 286
Stern-Rubarth, Edgar, 173
Stevenson rubber scheme, 183–4
Stewart, Walter, 399
Stimson, Henry L., 227, 287, 304, 305, 306, 323, 350, 351, 360, 386, 402
  and France, 311–12, 317
  at London naval disarmament conference, 262–3
Stoppani, Pietro, 292

Strakosch, Sir Henry, 145, 381
  promotes gold standard reform, 214–16,
    218, 274–5, 281, 293
Strauss, Emil Georg von, 172
Stresa conference, 382–4
Stresemann, Gustav, 127, 169, 195–6,
    202, 206
  dies, 254–5
  and European movement, 174, 250
  funds Alsace separatists, 166
  meets Briand at Thoiry, 170
  and occupation zones, 137
  and Rhineland Pact, 134
Strong, Benjamin, 99, 150, 163, 212,
    223, 244
  dies, 219
  convenes central bankers' conference,
    209–11
  favours gold bullion standard, 164
  resists gold standard reform, 215–17, 218
Strong, James, 212, 217
Strong, T. B., 27
Stubbs, William, 26
Stucki, Walter, 252–3, 285, 292
Stuttgart, 247
Submarine cables, *see* telecommunications
Sudbury, 184
Sudetenland, 436–7
Suez Canal, 172
Sumner, Lord, and reparations, 63, 64
Supreme Economic Council, 64, 129
Supreme War Council, 58
Sweden, 252
Switzerland, 178, 236, 252, 289, 334, 383
Syria, 109

Taittinger, Pierre, 418
Tangier, 117
Tardieu, André, 41, 119, 157, 248, 255, 263,
    367, 382, 406–7, 415, 418
  agrees to ending Rhineland
    occupation, 248
  appeals to Britain, 350
  on Briand, 345–6
  and Briand plan, 271
  Danube plan, 370, 383
  disappointed in Britain, hopeful of the
    United States, 98
  disarmament proposal, 350–1, 352, 353
  and postwar security, 55–7, 59, 60
Tariff, Underwood (1913), 82, 233 237
  Fordney-McCumber (1922), 83, 178, 236
  Reform (1905), 85, 86
  Smoot-Hawley, 236–7, 242

tariff truce proposal, 252–3, 255, 283
  first conference, 264, 270
  second conference, 283
Teagle, Walter, 183
telecommunications, 143, 180
Tennessee, 233
Ten-Year Rule, 89, 90, 352
Teutons, 19, 26, 27
Thoiry, 170
Thomas, J. H., 258–9, 276, 291–2
Thompson, G. H., 268
Thomson-Houston Company, 186
Thyssen, Fritz, 172
Times, 29, 59, 75, 125, 148, 215, 267, 279,
    299, 316, 317, 324, 325, 326, 352,
    356–7, 435
Tirard, Paul, 41
Titulescu, Nicolae, 298
Togoland, 436
Tokyo, 424
Tower, Sir Ronald, 98
trade
  international, 1, 3, 4
  and quantitative controls, 3, 18, 168, 176,
    194, 254, 365, 369, 382, 423
  and treaties, 8, 177, 178
trade unions, 6
Trades Union Congress (TUC), National
    Executive, oppose Franco-British pact,
    121
  call for monetary enquiry, 259
  and free trade, 282
Transvaal, 436
Treasury, 11, 21, 27, 88, 140, 145, 162,
    194–5, 211, 265, 314, 332–3, 338, 378,
    398, 399, 416
  and City opinion, 354
  conversations on monetary policy with
    French, 277–8
  and Danube, 372
  obstructs Foreign Office, 344
  and reparations, 63–4, 111, 223
  view of French, 340
  and war debts, 98, 410
Treaty of Trianon, 368
Trenchard, Air Marshal Sir Hugh, 112
Trendelenberg, Ernst, 175
Trevelyan, G. M., 27
Treveranus, Gottfried, 257
Triple Alliance, 19
Trocadero, 348
Troquer, Yves Le, 173
Trotsky, Leon, 116
Truman doctrine, 441